LATIN
AMERICAN
WRITERS

LATIN AMERICAN WRITERS

Carlos A. Solé

EDITOR IN CHIEF

Maria Isabel Abreu

ASSOCIATE EDITOR

VOLUME II

CHARLES SCRIBNER'S SONS • NEW YORK

José Enrique Rodó

(1871–1917)

Peter G. Earle

In a brief lifetime (1871–1917) José Enrique Rodó acquired fame throughout Hispanic America because of one short book. Of course he wrote much more than that, but *Ariel* (*Ariel*, 1900) set forth the theme of all that was to follow: the intellectual and spiritual renovation of Latin American culture. Soon after 1900 the efforts of others to spread the independent spirit of his timely essay became known as *arielismo* (spiritualism). Rodó had three professions: writing, teaching, and politics, which he undertook in that order and which are repeatedly evident in the singularly functional nature of his style. Teaching could be called his basic vocation, for though he left his literary professorship for politics in 1902, an appropriate subtitle for most of what he wrote could have been "My Advice to the Youth of Latin America."

The Uruguayan writer Mario Benedetti remarks on a photograph, reproduced in Emir Rodríguez Monegal's 1954 edition of Rodo's *Obras completas* (Complete Works),* of José Enrique at the age of a year-and-a-half that he strikes "a comically serious pose." The picture is an appropriate introduction to a

*Except where noted, excerpts reproduced in this article have been taken from the 1954 edition of Rodó's *Obras completas*, hereafter referred to as OC. Translations are the work of the author.

person who in childhood, adolescence, and maturity was relentlessly austere. Nothing in subsequent photos of him, in his writings, or in his biography—so scarce in intimate detail—contradicts that image. He was neither playful nor sociable. He never married. His few friendships were intellectual. The only semblance of a smile comes to us within the metaphorical opulence of his prose—in his most evident joy at transforming quite vague ideals into ornate imagery.

That seriousness enhanced his precocity; tutored by an older sister, he learned to read at four. At eleven he was cofounder with a classmate of a student newspaper, for which he wrote an essay on Benjamin Franklin and, on the occasion of Simón Bolívar's centenary in 1883, another in which he calls on Latin Americans "to sever the shackles that continue to hold several American nations still enslaved by a foreign power."

Rodó was born in Montevideo on 15 July 1871, the seventh and youngest child of José Rodó Janer, a prosperous Catalonian businessman, and Rosario Piñeiro y Llamas, daughter of an upperclass Uruguayan family. In 1883 Rodó Janer's business suffered serious losses and José Enrique was transferred from the Escuela Elbio Fernández, a model of superior instruction in that era, to a tuition-free public school. Thenceforth his scholastic performance was erratic in everything except literature and history. His father died in 1885, and the boy, now fourteen, had to take a part-time job as a clerk.

Little is known of his activities before 1895, when his literary career formally began, aside from a brief courtship in 1890 of Luisa Gurméndez, which apparently got no further than the letter-writing stage. Photographs reveal his homeliness and suggest timidity; one tends to accept his contemporaries' impression that he held no attraction for women. Many years later an acquaintance of his drew from memory the following portrait, circa 1890:

> An elongated, skinny, faded thing; a body pushing upward through his collar, as if drawn by the energy that condensed his entire cross-eyed, sniffle-faced image in the gleam of his spectacles. Leading the way, a protruding, disproportionate nose; the face was cold and pale; one shoulder rose well above the other, and suspended from it was an arm that adhered to his side.
>
> (Arturo Giménez Pastor, *Figuras a la distancia*, Buenos Aires, 1940)

In 1895 the young writer published his first adult pieces in the periodical *Montevideo noticioso*: a short poem entitled "La prensa" (The Press) and a long book review. Also in 1895, together with his future biographer Víctor Pérez Petit and Carlos and Daniel Martínez Vigil, he founded an important journal, *Revista nacional de literatura y ciencias naturales*. In the *Revista* he published, in 1896, the first of his essays to attract critical attention, *El que vendrá* (Our Redeemer); here he foresees the imminent arrival of a brilliant cultural prophet from whom his young generation may or may not be able to benefit: "We wait, but without knowing for whom. A voice calls from a dark and distant mansion. We too have raised in our hearts a temple to the unknown god" (OC, p. 154). A few months later, in *La novela nueva* (The New Novel), he criticized Carlos Reyles' negative view of the contemporary Spanish novel in Reyles' prologue to his own *Academias* (1896).

El que vendrá and *La novela nueva* together make up the first of three monographs (Rodó called them *opúsculos*, or pamphlets) to be published under the title *La vida nueva* (New Life, 1897). The second, *Rubén Darío* (1899), and the third, *Ariel*, received continental acclaim. In these two essays the author added a spiritual dimension to the Spanish American *modernista* movement, which—until the publication of Darío's *Prosas profanas* (Secular Songs) in 1896—had been dominated by the more decadent symbolism of Darío's poetry and of the work of two other important poets, the Cuban Julián del Casal and the Colombian José Asunción Silva. Although the cults of decadence (art as pleasure and pleasure as art) and of beauty for its own sake would live on in the prose of Manuel Díaz Rodríguez (Venezuela) and Enrique Gómez Carrillo (Guatemala), Rodó's exhaustive scrutiny of *Prosas profanas* became a strong influence for Darío's spiritual enrichment, evident in what he wrote after 1900. The central theme of the first and best-known poem in *Cantos de vida y esperanza* (Songs of Life and Hope, 1905) and his dedication of the first section of the volume to Rodó are an eloquent recognition of that influence.

In 1894 Rodó quit school before graduating, having been interested only in literature and history. But his brilliant beginning as essayist and critic earned him an adjunct professorship in literature at the University of Montevideo in May 1898, less than a month after the Spanish-American War had begun. The three years he held this position were the most important for his development as a writer, both historically and literarily. It was then that he developed his perception of the United States not only as Spain's imperialist successor in the New World but also as a detrimental utilitarian influence on Latin American culture, and it was in this period of teaching that he developed the basic ideas for his two best-known books, *Ariel* and *Motivos de Proteo* (*The Motives of Proteus*, 1909). The apprehensions about North America expressed in *Ariel* had appeared previously in more militant tones in other Latin American works: "Nuestra América" (Our America, 1892) and several other short essays by the Cuban activist José Martí; the Brazilian Eduardo Prado's *A Ilusão Americana* (The Yankee Illusion, 1895), and the Venezuelan César Zumeta's *El continente enfermo* (The Sick Continent, 1899). Later, the Argentine Manuel Ugarte, in *El porvenir de la América Latina* (The Future of Latin America, 1911) and *El destino de un continente* (Destiny of a Continent, 1923), and the Mexican José Vasconcelos, in *La raza cósmica* (The Cosmic Race, 1925), would offer new rationales, and generally less esoteric ones, for Hispanic American solidarity as the basic response to the United States' burgeoning hegemony. The most complete revision of *Ariel* would come much later with the Cuban Roberto Fernández Retamar's *Calibán* (1971).

Rodó had a much less skeptical view of the world than any of the writers just mentioned, but his crusade for American cultural harmony within a uniquely progressive Greco-Judeo-Christian tradition was just as energetic in its way as their more aggressive exhortations. He also proved to be an energetic politician. Joining the more liberal and cosmopolitan of Uruguay's two main parties in 1901 (the Colorado Party), he was elected to the House of Representatives the following year and resigned his professorship. In his long introduction to Rodó's *Obras completas*, Rodríguez Monegal writes that the young legislator "scrupulously avoided indulging in petty politics; he always strove to present a broad, strictly legalistic view of national life, placing the interests of State above those of his own party; he gave special support to cultural projects" (*OC*, p. 33). But civil war broke out in early 1904, and on 20 March Rodó wrote to Miguel de Unamuno in Spain of his disillusionment:

> Nothing new or worthwhile to tell you about my country. There's nothing noteworthy about civil war in countries where it takes on the appearance of a national spectacle or sport. . . . I have no Ivory Tower aspirations: I like literature, which, in its way, is a militancy, but only when it's a question of fighting for great ideas, of education, of redemption. All in all I'm fed up with what's going on here; and maybe, maybe if I can set my affairs in order, in less than a year I'll be able to aerate my soul with a long stay in Europe.
>
> (*OC*, p. 1393)

But Rodó would not get to Europe—where he would die within eight months of his arrival—until August of 1916. Although he was reelected for a second three-year term, he resigned from the House of Representatives on 8 February 1905. Possibly overwrought by the intensity of his political and literary work as well as by financial setbacks in the preceding two or three years, he seems to have experienced emotional problems in late 1905 and early 1906. In diary notes dated 3 May 1906 he refers to "this terrible past year that hasn't allowed me one day of peace, freedom, or tranquillity . . . that has seen me shed, probably, more tears than in all the other years of my life" (*OC*, p. 37).

His distraught state notwithstanding, between 1904 and 1907 Rodó was able to complete the 158 predominantly optimistic chapters of *The Motives of Proteus*, a work as replete with inspirational didacticism as *Ariel*. In 1907 he began writing for *La Nación* of Buenos Aires, which was then and still is today Latin America's most prestigious daily newspaper. These contributions to *La Nación* would be collected and published with other pieces—some revised—that had previously appeared in other periodicals. The collection was entitled *El mirador de Próspero* (Prospero's Balcony, 1913). This is the collection in which the author excels as literary critic, as, for example, in "Rumbos nuevos" (New Directions), an essay-review of Carlos Arturo Torres' *Idola fori* (Idols of the Forum, 1910). Torres' work complements Rodó's *Ariel* and *Motives* in the sense that it too calls for prudent idealism that can bring about future harmony in Latin American intellectual and political life. In "Rumbos nuevos," Rodó asserts that European positivism (which he had partially assimilated from Ernest Renan, Hippolyte Taine, Herbert Spencer, and Auguste Comte) "is the keystone of our intellectual formation, but no longer the cupola that crowns it." In "Rumbos nuevos" he also reflects on his continual struggle in trying to conciliate two of his three vocations: refined literature and rough-and-tumble politics. He speaks of "the torture of adaptation" experienced by one "whose soul is on a slightly higher level" than the common run of souls, "the repugnance one feels in forced contact with vulgarity, awkwardness, and servility" (*OC*, p. 522). This persistent incompatibility was at the heart of his most important writings; accordingly, he constantly tried to purify aristocratic thought of its selfish, discriminatory elements, and democratic thought of its susceptibility to the vulgar and the mediocre.

Of the three Latin American literary leaders of the *modernista* era (José Martí, Rubén Darío, and Rodó), Rodó was the most eclectic, attempting always to follow the best features of various traditions: the Greek concept of creative leisure, the evolutionary and positivist ideal of progressive perfectibility, the symbolist cult of beauty, a philosophy based on hope ("faith in the future") and disinterestedness. He was aware that freethinking entailed problems as well as joy. In 1906 he wrote "Liberalismo y jacobinismo" (Liberalism and Radicalism), in which he objected to the removal by order of the Commission for Public Welfare in Montevideo of crucifixes from all hospital rooms, not because Rodó was a fervent Christian but because Jesus Christ was for him (as he had been for Renan in *Vie de Jésus*, 1863) a creative historical *hero,* the paladin of charity. The removal was decreed in the name of "freedom of thought," to which Rodó replied: "I find in our Latin freethinking a tendency to forensic declamation, always the enemy of an austere sensibility, and a lack of delicacy and intuitive insight" (OC, p. 297).

Ariel, as the title suggests, is based in part on William Shakespeare's *The Tempest* (Ariel is the sprite, symbolic of the free imagination, who serves the philosopher and magician Prospero) and Renan's *Caliban* (1878). In both Shakespeare's and Renan's plays, Caliban symbolizes man's primitive urges; for both Renan and Rodó these urges amounted to gross, anti-aesthetic materialism.

Ariel begins with a brief exordium and ends with a brief farewell from Próspero, the venerable professor who in the essay's six chapters offers his students their final lecture of the school year (the work as a whole is dedicated to the "Youth of America"). The first chapter deals with the young generation's potential for intellectual development. Chapter 2 stresses the need for individual integrity and a unity of spiritual purpose: even under material slavery, "inner freedom" is possible. Chapter 3 attempts to demonstrate that justice and moral conviction are best served by "an educated sense of the beautiful." In chapter 4 Rodó develops the thesis that democracy, the best of all political systems, must be tempered by a constant sense of "active moral authority" and an equally active "disdain for mediocrity." The United States, "utilitarianism incarnate," is the main topic of chapter 5. The South American admires North Americans for their great energy but thinks that their materialism is excessive and basically incompatible with Latin American spirituality. He praises North American *systems,* especially public education, but finds serious flaws in North American culture:

The descendent of the austere Puritans is unenthused by the ideal of beauty. The ideal of truth doesn't enthuse him either. He disdains all enterprises of the mind that lack an immediate purpose as vain and sterile. A disinterested desire for truth is not what leads him to science.

(OC, p. 238)

In chapter 6, Rodó articulates a futuristic philosophy ("In the life of human societies the future is the supreme agent for idealistic thought").

Fourteen years later, in the brief essay "El nuevo Ariel" (The New Ariel; published, appropriately enough, in the first issue of a journal called *Ariel*), Rodó offered a succinct résumé of his famous work:

The meaning of the name *Ariel,* in the evolution of the ideas that underlie the current orientation of Hispanic American thought, is in the expression of an idealist sense of life, as against the limitations of utilitarian positivism; in the spirit of quality and selectivity, as against the egalitarianism of false democracy; and in the revindication of the sentiment of our race, our Latin historical heritage as the indispensable strength to save and maintain these nations against the triumphal expansion of others.

(OC, p. 1197)

Every essay is a mirror and echo, as partial as it may be, of its era. The era of *Ariel* was one of utilitarian confidence but also of political fear. The crisis of 1898, called "The Disaster" in Spain, was a major stimulus in the writing of *Ariel.* The easy defeat of Spain was not interpreted by most Latin Americans as the end of a colonial period so much as the ominous consequence of more than half a century of North American Manifest Destiny. Distrust and fear of the United States's expansionism has been a factor of Latin American intellectual life ever since. But *Ariel* is also the mirror and echo of Spanish American *modernismo:* youth, beauty, and aesthetic self-discipline are its values. Rodó, like Martí and Darío, was the advocate and prophet of cultural independence. Rodó did not think in terms of changing systems but of purifying and strengthening thought. The parable of the Hospitable King in chapter 2 of *Ariel* is an allegory of the mind; the palace is open to all visitors (that is, ideas), but its inner sanctum is reserved only for the King (that is, the self).

"A foolish consistency is the hobgoblin of little minds," Ralph Waldo Emerson had said in "Self-Reliance" (1841). "To change is to live" is the opening sentence of chapter 1 of *The Motives of Proteus.* For both writers a better culture, a better society, a better spiritual life were matters of individual education and motivated self-development. *The Motives of Proteus* is an open-ended spiritual autobiography, that is, the history of a soul in continuous transformation. Proteus, according to Greek mythology, could change into any form he pleased, and if somehow he could be caught and held—despite his willful metamorphoses—he would foretell the future. In a note to his editors before submitting the manuscript, Rodó writes that he'll never give "a specific architecture" to the book, which, though vast and unified in its central theme of the developing personality, is also fragmentary in its alternation of teaching, epiphany, confession, parable, allegory, and exhortations to the young. In the same note he concludes that *Motives* is a "book in a perpetual state of 'becoming,' an open book on an undefined perspective" (OC, p. 309). Although he meant nothing analogous to what André Breton would say years later about "automatic writing" in the surrealist tradition, Rodó did seem to be seeking out his own secret voices, and in chapter 17 he spoke of "the mysterious superiority of what is dreamed over what is certain and tangible." Among his unpublished notes, Rodó left the following summary of *Motives:*

"The Conscious and Guided Transformation of Personality" (1–14)

"The Subconscious Element of Personality" (15–39)

"Vocation and Genius" (40–79)

"Proteism in the 'Fashioned' Souls of the Delirious, the Dilettantish, and the Histrionic" (80–85) (The suggestion here of humor is deceptive.)

"The Formative Value of Travels" (86–97)

"Simple and Unchangeable Souls and Souls in Which Several Vocations Coexist" (98–110)

"The Soul Is Governed by *Conviction* (Faith, Love)" (111–147)

"Will and Hope (Hope as Light; Will as Power)" (148–158)

The trajectory of these subtitles, with its emphasis on vocation, personal development, and conviction, reveals an important complementary concept in *Motives* and in other significant essays of Rodó's (for example, "Garibaldi," "Bolívar," and "Montalvo" in *El mirador de Próspero*): the cult of the hero. In passing it should be noted that the author of *The Motives of Proteus* attentively read and frequently mentioned Thomas Carlyle, Emerson, and Friedrich Wilhelm Nietzsche, each of whom created his own hero cult.

In 1908 Rodó returned to politics and was again elected to the House of Representatives. His speeches and legislative activity during this and his final term in office (he was reelected in 1911) were consistently moderate. His fundamental principle, as he summarized it in a parliamentary debate on 13 June 1912, was "the absolute right" of the constitutionally free individual to examine and evaluate every reform, idea, or initiative—whether it was centuries old or the latest innovation. In 1914 he chose not to run for reelection; the Colorado Party, of which he had become the legislative leader in 1911, was rife with factionalism, and Rodó found himself in an increasingly cool relationship with José Batlle y Ordóñez, the reform-minded president of Uruguay then serving his second term of office.

Since 1907, meanwhile, Rodó's skill as a journalist had steadily grown and he could comfortably write about an increasing range of subjects: literary, political, historical. Like Martí and Darío and, before them, Domingo Faustino Sarmiento—not to mention Alejo Carpentier, Carlos Fuentes, Gabriel García Márquez, and many other fiction writers of our own time—he was living proof that newspaper writing (reviews, essays, polemics, travel literature) was quite compatible with the most original kinds of Hispanic American creative writing.

The outbreak of World War I in August 1914 resulted in his immediate support of France and her allies, which he identified with "the cause of humanity." That year he published twelve articles in *El Telégrafo* of Montevideo under the general title "La guerra a la ligera" (Glimpses of War). In one of these, "La voz de la estadística" (Statistics Talk, 14 September 1914), he reflects on Gustave Le Bon's notorious opinion that "mixed" races are inevitably inferior to "pure" ones and, in consequence, relentlessly warlike. Rodó ironically concludes,

> From this day forward we should modestly decline the honor that those like Gustave Le Bon bestow upon us, attributing our incapacity for peace to the proportion of indigenous barbarism that contaminates our blood, by recognizing our illustrious European ancestry as the true source of the itch to fight.
>
> (OC, p. 1227)

In other words, the widespread assumption until 1914 that the planet could be divided between a peacefully civilized, Eurocentric Old World and a motley array of aggressive, undereducated peoples of other races was being scornfully discredited by a Latin American humanist steeped in the best qualities of Old World tradition.

In 1916 Rodó finally began his long-awaited tour of Europe, not suspecting that his return trip would be delayed until three years after his death. His scheduled itinerary, after the voyage from Montevideo to Lisbon via Rio de Janeiro, Bahía, and Recife, was to include Spain, southern France, a prolonged stay in Italy, and Switzerland. After that, he intended to "take up residence" in Paris. A national Commission of Honor in collaboration with a university student committee paid him an elaborate homage on 13 July, including a banquet at the Jockey Club in Montevideo that featured on its menu "Parfait Ariel" and "Gateau Motivos de Proteo." The next morning he embarked on the English steamer *Amazon*.

From the moment he set foot on European soil, the solitary traveler experienced disillusionment, financial hardship, and illness. Second-guessers would probably be unanimous in saying that his basic mistake was his decision not to accept the offer of another professorship in literature at the University of Montevideo. But he himself, in chapters 94 through 96 of *The Motives of Proteus*, had elaborated on the inspirational advantages of travel for artists and writers, and Italy was his cultural Mecca.

His arrival in Portugal began with a friendly interview for the Argentine popular magazine *Caras y caretas*, his first assignment as correspondent for that publication. The interview was with Bernardino Machado, who had been elected president of Portugal the year before. A day or two later he was in Madrid. No preparations had been made to receive him, probably because his trip through Spain was a virtual secret; he met only with the poet Juan Ramón Jiménez for a brief visit. After a few days in Barcelona, birthplace of his ancestors, he went on to Italy, stopping briefly in Marseilles. When he decided to make the long journey, Rodó reportedly was depending on a certain amount of income from his family (which over the years had recuperated some of the wealth lost in the 1880's) and the modest compensation he would receive from *Caras y caretas*. According to one account (Juan José Soiza Reilly) quoted by Rodríguez Monegal in his introduction to the *Obras completas* (p. 64), *Caras y caretas* failed to send his first paycheck on time, and Rodó was not allowed to leave his hotel in Genoa until he received enough money to pay the bill. His illness appears to have begun with bronchitis while he was in Genoa, or possibly before, and to have worsened gradually over the fall of 1916 and the winter of 1917. The cause of his death on 1 May 1917 in Palermo was diagnosed as a combination of abdominal typhus and nephritis.

Despite all the pain and hardship, Rodó basically carried out the first phase of his travel-and-writing plan; he spent a month in Florence, two months in Rome, and then visited several other Italian cities on his way south to Palermo, the unpremeditated end of his odyssey. His very first impressions, written on board the *Amazon* on a day when the Brazilian coastline was still visible behind him—"Cielo y agua" (Sea and Sky)—has Homeric premonitions of possible adventures and reminiscences of unfulfilled hopes, traced in a sensitive symbolism of waves:

> My sea and my waves. It's a pleasurable pastime to watch them come to life, pass away, and come to life again, and in sweet abandon to feel that all immensity invades our soul and our spirit, and not to know, in the end, whether the object of contemplation is in the infinite water or in the depth of our soul. Delightful then to relate each wave to a thought, a memory, a fiction, and say: this one surging strong is the faith that sustains me, the aspiration

on which I ride; those whitecaps in the distance are memories of those who love me; this other little one, fading into froth, is a promise I left unfulfilled, a dream of mine that disappeared with childhood, a longing for something I'll never achieve.

(OC, p. 1245)

Mario Benedetti appropriately reminds us that the essay in the grand style is not Rodó's only style (Benedetti, 1966, p. 118). To be sure, it predominates in both *Ariel* and *The Motives of Proteus*, often with pompous overtones. But many other passages throughout those two works, in the literary criticism and historical evaluations of *El mirador de Próspero*— for example, "Rumbos nuevos," "Mirando al mar" (Marine Meditations), "Iberoamérica," "La España niña" (Spain the Younger), "Los que callan" (Silent Spirits), and in the impressions and misgivings collected posthumously in *El camino de Paros* (Journey to Paros, 1918)—show us in much the same way as "Cielo y agua" how in the later years his writing improved. The improvement can be attributed to an increased sensitivity to nature, a propensity to nostalgia (Rodó aged prematurely in his sentiments), and, together with growing intimations of death, the conviction that solitude is the first prerequisite of creativity. The mystic appeal of nature, nostalgia, and the various captivations of potential death (as reflected, for example, in the symbolism of the swan) were standard features of the Hispanic American modernist aesthetic.

For many critics and literary historians those features constituted an evasion. But like many other tendencies within the canon of "pure art"—including even Arthur Symons' contention that the artist or poet should be exempt from the social, ethical, and political obligations of "normal" people (see *The Symbolist Movement in Literature*, 1899)—evasion is more important as a sign of something else than as a phenomenon in itself. As Nelson Osorio suggests in a forthcoming article, "Para una caracterización histórica del modernismo crepuscular" (A Historical View of Crepuscular *Modernismo*), for *Revista Iberoamericana*, the word "evasion" should be read "as the sign of an implicit rejection of a degraded reality." That rejection, then, is really a statement of ethical principle, a consciousness of paradise lost, a clear recognition that things ought to be better, a longing

for Utopia. That is the context in which Rodó's works—all his works, but especially those published after *The Motives of Proteus*—can best be read.

In his late years Rodó gravitated toward an autumnal view of the world that was also a harmonious balance of nature, history, and personal existence. He repeatedly tells us, from *Ariel* to *El camino de Paros*, that the best of all possible lives consists in working diligently toward the realization of that balance.

Reconstructing Charles Darwin's theory of natural selection and Spencer's principle of "persistence of force" as the primary agent of change and development, he adapted the theory of each to his own idealistic system. He wrote as an advocate, first, of spiritual evolution and secondarily of artistic perfection. Thus his own doctrine of perfectibility was a philosophical transformation of Darwin's biological and Spencer's sociological principles, which he attempted to apply to the young, developing Latin American mind. His frequently serene, Apollonian settings and sometimes overelaborate mythological allusions create the impression in many readers that he is more concerned about art for art's sake than about character fulfillment. For many readers, also, his definition in *Ariel* of morality as "an aesthetic of behavior" is misleading; it is not intended to strengthen aesthetics at the expense of good morals but, on the contrary, to use beauty both as a secondary ideal and as a primary instrument. Beauty is a secondary ideal in the sense that it is the highest metaphorical goal we can perceive. And it is a primary instrument in the sense that our clear perception of that sign, that Protean metaphor of universal perfection, is our best possible means of attaining spiritual plenitude.

A certain rigidity of form, probably a result of his obsession with harmony and balance and analogous in a way to the legendary seriousness of his everyday existence, is less prevalent in what he wrote in the final decade of his life. But rigidity is part of his reputation and has not favored his status in literary history. Critics, academics, and students have tended to overlook the spiritual substance of his essays, in large measure because of the meticulousness of his presentation.

With Rodó himself, of course, must rest the

ultimate responsibility for his readers' reception of his works. John A. Crow, in his essay "Ariel and Caliban," criticizes his failure to recognize

> the existence of a powerful and creative culture in the United States. Unfortunately this error was magnified by many of Rodó's less well-informed readers, and it became the fashion in Latin America to remember only the writer's premise: Ariel and Caliban. This was the starting point, not the end of Rodó's thinking.
>
> (Crow, 1980, p. 696)

Justifiably, Crow points out a deplorable gap in Rodó's reading of then current and recently past North American literature. Arturo Torres Ríoseco mentions a flawed prophecy: the hopes expressed in *Ariel* were altruistic beyond reason; "it would be a mockery [in 1963] to speak of aesthetic ideals, of *otium,* among illiterate and oppressed peoples" (Torres Ríoseco, 1963, p. 50). Years before, in 1941, Alberto Zum Felde underscored what he considered to be the author's lack of real-life substance: "Arielism, as a norm for meaning and culture, was never more than words; beautiful words, if you will, that falsely encouraged Latin American intellectuals and which, logically enough—given their tone— lacked force as a true element of independent culture" (Zum Felde, 1941, p. 243). A similarly negative view of Rodó's idealism was expressed by Luis Alberto Sánchez in *Balance y liquidación del 900,* his study of the Generation of 1900 (1941).

In conclusion, and in fairness to Rodó—always the stately stylist in an intellectual environment that was not quite prepared for him—it should be emphasized that on a one-to-one basis, author to private reader, he has genuine enlightenment to offer. Literary historians are not likely ever to discover how many have taken full advantage of his Word.

SELECTED BIBLIOGRAPHY

First Editions

La vida nueva 1: *El que vendrá* and *La novela nueva.* 2: *Rubén Darío.* 3: *Ariel.* Montevideo, 1897–1900.
Liberalismo y jacobinismo. Montevideo, 1906.
Motivos de Proteo. Montevideo, 1909.
El mirador de Próspero. Montevideo, 1913.
El camino de Paros. Valencia, Spain, 1918.
Epistolario. With two preliminary notes by Hugo D. Barbagelata. Paris, 1921.
Los últimos motivos de Proteo. Montevideo, 1932.

Modern Editions

Ariel; Calibán. Edited and with a prologue by Abelardo Villegas. Mexico City, 1982.
Ariel; Motivos de Proteo. Edited by Ángel Rama. With two prologues by Carlos Real de Azúa. Caracas, 1976.
Rodó: Su americanismo. Edited and with a prologue by Arturo Ardao. Montevideo, 1970.

Collected Works

Obras completas. 7 vols. Valencia and Barcelona, 1917–1927.
_____. 4 vols. Edited by José Pedro Segundo and Juan Antonio Zubillaga. Montevideo, 1945–.
_____. 1 vol. Edited by Alberto José Vaccaro. Buenos Aires, 1948.
_____. 1 vol. Edited and with an introduction by Emir Rodríguez Monegal. Madrid, 1954. Rev. ed. Madrid, 1967. An accurate and the closest-to-complete edition of Rodó's works. With an extensive biographical and critical introduction, critical bibliography, and index.

Translations

Ariel. Translated by Margaret Sayers Peden. With a prologue by Carlos Fuentes. Austin, Tex., 1988.
The Motives of Proteus. Translated by Ángel Flores. With an introduction by Havelock Ellis. London, 1929.

Biographical and Critical Studies

Alas, Leopoldo. Review of *Ariel. El Imparcial* (Madrid), 23 April 1900. Reproduced as prologue for 2nd edition of *Ariel* (1901).
Albarrán Puente, Glicerio. *El pensamiento de José Enrique Rodó.* Madrid, 1953.
Barbagelata, Hugo D., ed. *Rodó y sus críticos.* Paris, 1920.
Beltrán Guerrero, Luis. "Rodó y Venezuela." In his *Modernismo y modernistas.* Caracas, 1978. Pp. 73–109.
Benedetti, Mario. *Genio y figura de José Enrique Rodó.* Buenos Aires, 1966.
Crow, John A. "Ariel and Caliban." In *The Epic of Latin*

America. 3rd ed. Berkeley, Calif., 1980. Pp. 675–697.

Darío, Rubén. "José Enrique Rodó." *Mundial,* January 1912. Reproduced in *Rodó y sus críticos,* edited by Hugo D. Barbagelata. Pp. 105–107.

Earle, Peter G., and Robert G. Mead, Jr. "José Enrique Rodó (1871–1917)." In *Historia del ensayo hispanoamericano.* Mexico City, 1973. Pp. 61–64.

Henríquez Ureña, Pedro. "Marginalia: José Enrique Rodó" and "La obra de José Enrique Rodó." In *La utopía de América,* edited by Rafael Gutiérrez Girardot. Caracas, 1978.

Homenaje a José Enrique Rodó. Montevideo, 1920. Special issue, published in book form, of the journal *Ariel* (Montevideo) 1/8–9.

Ibáñez, Roberto. "Americanismo y modernismo." *Cuadernos americanos* 37:230–252 (1948).

Lauxar (pseud. of Osvaldo Crispo Acosta). *Rubén Darío y José Enrique Rodó.* Montevideo, 1924.

Nosotros: A José Enrique Rodó. Buenos Aires, 1917. Special issue on Rodó.

Pérez Petit, Víctor. *Rodó. Su vida. Su obra.* 2nd ed. Montevideo, 1937.

Sánchez, Luis Alberto. *Balance y liquidación del novecientos.* Santiago, Chile, 1941.

Torres Ríoseco, Arturo. "José Enrique Rodó and His Idealistic Philosophy." In his *Aspects of Spanish-American Literature.* Seattle, 1963. Pp. 31–50.

Vitier, Medardo. "El mensaje de Rodó." In his *Del ensayo americano.* Mexico City, 1945. Pp. 117–136.

Zum Felde, Alberto. "José Enrique Rodó." In his *Proceso intelectual del Uruguay y crítica de su literatura.* Montevideo, 1941. Pp. 223–250.

Mariano Azuela

(1873–1952)

Luis Leal

The Mexican Revolution of 1910 produced not only social reforms, but also a new art and a new literature. In painting, Diego Rivera, José Clemente Orozco, and Álfaro Siqueiros created world-famous murals; and in literature, Mariano Azuela, Rafael Muñoz, Martín Luis Guzmán, Gregorio López y Fuentes, and others produced what is known as the novel of the Mexican Revolution. Both painters and novelists broke away completely from the aesthetics of the previous generation, that of the *modernistas*, who were interested mainly in the formal aspects of their works and in the creation of exotic worlds, while they ignored the problems of a society living under a dictatorship; Porfirio Díaz had ruled the nation with a strong hand for more than thirty years, until his regime was overturned by the followers of the idealist Francisco Madero.

The subject matter of the novelists of the Revolution came from what they observed directly during the campaigns and on the field of battle. Azuela established this trend in 1911 with his first novel about the Revolution, *Andrés Pérez, maderista* (Andrés Pérez, the Maderista). He had by then published three novels and several short stories, all of them in the naturalist mode and concerned with life in Mexico under Don Porfirio. His criticism of the regime, although guarded, was already present in

these early works. After 1911 he continued criticizing the revolutionary government, for he was convinced that the Revolution had been betrayed; he was, perhaps, the earliest critic of revolutionary Mexico. But his voice was not heard until 1924, when his novel *Los de abajo* (*The Underdogs*), published in 1915, was discovered by the critics and a large readership.

Born in Lagos de Moreno, in the state of Jalisco in central Mexico, on 1 January 1873, Mariano Azuela was the product of Don Porfirio's world. His father, Evaristo Azuela, and his mother, Paulina González, were members of the middle class. Don Evaristo had to borrow a few hundred pesos from an uncle to open a grocery, a business in which he did so well that he soon paid off his debt, built his own store, and bought a small ranch nearby. It was in this small-town and rural environment that Mariano grew up and where he learned the typical speech of the ranchers of the highlands of Jalisco. He tells us that at his father's ranch he learned more than he did at the elementary school at Lagos and the Liceo de Varones del Estado (State Lyceum for Boys), where he studied Latin, grammar, and sciences.

Early in life, Azuela became interested in literature, especially the novel: "Inside the soap boxes, my father used to hide prohibited books, among them

457

some novels like *The Count of Monte Cristo*. . . . When my father dozed in his easy chair, I used to sneak to the attic and there enjoy the forbidden book" (*Obras completas* 3, p. 1126). When he told a school friend what he was reading, the boy was astonished: "Alexander Dumas! . . . My father says that it is a sin to read his books." For the rest of his life, Azuela was to break that strict moral code.

It was customary in Mexico at that time for one son in each family to enter the priesthood; young Mariano was sent to Guadalajara in 1887 to study at the seminary. But his mother's wish was not to be fulfilled. "The priesthood never attracted me, and my passage through this institution was incidental" (*Obras* 3, p. 1127). After leaving the seminary in 1889, he registered in the Liceo de Varones del Estado. During that year, he wrote what can be considered his first prose work, a collection of sketches about daily life in Guadalajara, later to be published under the title "Registro" (Registry).

While still in the Liceo Varones Azuela discovered other novelists, among them the Spaniard Benito Pérez Galdós, the Frenchman Alain-René Lesage, and the Colombian Jorge Isaacs. In 1891 he completed his preparatory studies, and the following year he registered in the School of Medicine at the University of Guadalajara, from which he received his medical degree in 1899. While still a medical student, he published his first collection of short stories, appropriately called *Impresiones de un estudiante* (1896). Not daring to use his own name, he employed the pseudonym "Beleño." The stories reveal the direct influence of Émile Zola. One of them, about the life of a prostitute very much like Zola's Nana, was to be enlarged into a novel and published in his hometown in 1907 under the title *María Luisa*.

After receiving his degree, Azuela went back to Lagos de Moreno to practice medicine. Having lived twelve years in Guadalajara, he was unable to adjust to life in a provincial town. He renewed his earlier courtship of Carmen Rivera, whom he married in 1900. He was later to dedicate a biography, published in 1942, to his father-in-law, the local philosopher Agustín Rivera.

Azuela's first years as a small-town doctor were not happy ones. He had to spend long hours reading medical treatises, learning what medical school had not taught him. As a form of relief from the study of medical cases, he wrote fiction. His first full-length novel, *Los fracasados* (The Failures), appeared in 1908. It is a realistic novel about life in a provincial Mexican town, where clashes between liberals and conservatives are frequent. The implied author sympathizes with the liberals, who are unable to predominate over the alliance between the clergy and the *hacendados* (landowners). The novel was hardly noticed, but Azuela received encouraging words from several writers. That fact made him decide to become a novelist. "The medical doctor had the absolute sensation of having something amputated, and he had to resign himself. The parasite was hard to dislodge from his flesh. *Los fracasados* has been followed by twenty-six blood sisters and four natural ones. Finally, the parasite devoured the medical doctor" (*Obras*, 3, p. 1054).

The action of his next novel, *Mala yerba*, published in Guadalajara in 1909 and translated into English in 1932 with the title *Marcela* (the name of the protagonist), takes place in a rural area of Jalisco. The dramatic conflict is between the well-to-do *hacendados* and the enslaved peons. This novel contains a compelling portrayal of life in an hacienda during the regime of Don Porfirio. The description of the injustices committed against the peons helps the reader to understand the factors that brought about the revolution of 1910. In writing this work, Azuela employed the narrative techniques and devices of the French novelists then in vogue. Like them, he observed life with the eye of a social scientist or a clinical doctor. "The characters were transplanted from a nearby region. . . . I found them during my house calls as a small town and often rural doctor. I had the occasion to observe them in the privacy of their own homes" (*Obras* 3, p. 1059).

Marcela is the best of Azuela's naturalist novels. Translated into English, it was very well received in the United States, where novels of similar subject matter were being written during the years of the Great Depression.

It was not until the middle 1920's, when literary critics in Mexico City began to debate the decadence of Mexican literature, that Professor Francisco Monterde discovered *The Underdogs* and presented it as proof that Mexican writers were producing works of great dramatic strength, on topics that could not be said to be decadent. This event was of great importance to Azuela, for by this time he was very much discouraged; although he had published several novels, he was still unknown in the literary circles of Mexico City. After the discovery of *The Underdogs*, he became Mexico's foremost novelist and remained in that position until his death on 1 March 1952. Today *The Underdogs* is still a best-seller, although its subject matter is a historical event of seventy-five years ago.

Why this novel is so popular is a difficult question to answer. Azuela said that he received a letter from a butcher in London telling him that he read *The Underdogs* once a year, for he considered it the best novel in the world. That interest is not confined to the working class but extends to academic circles. Literary critics have praised the work for its dynamic style, which reflects the nature of the Revolution; for its unique structure, admirably adapted to the nature of the subject matter; and for its descriptions of the landscape, always integrated with the other elements of the book, whether the action, the characters, or the vivid descriptions of battles and skirmishes. Novelists like Carlos Fuentes have valued it for having introduced ambiguity in characterization into the Latin-American novel. In the works of Azuela and other novelists of the Revolution, Fuentes observed in his book *La nueva novela hispanoamericana* (The New Latin American Novel, 1969), "Heroes can be villains, and villains can be heroes. . . . In the literature of the Mexican Revolution there is this narrative seed: heroic assuredness can turn into critical ambiguity, natural fatality into contradictory action, and romantic idealism into ironic dialectic" (p. 15). Historians quote from *The Underdogs* to illustrate the factors that brought about the Revolution, and linguists use its text to illustrate the speech of the Mexican *campesino*.

Azuela had personally observed the action he describes in the novel; he had joined the revolutionary movement when it began. When Madero was assassinated in 1913 and Francisco (Pancho) Villa took up arms against Victoriano Huerta's government, Azuela, who was a *maderista*, became a *villista*. He accompanied Villa's armies until they were defeated by the rival revolutionary leader, Álvaro Obregón. With some of the remnants of Villa's armies, Azuela took refuge in El Paso, Texas, where he completed *The Underdogs* and published it, first late in 1915 in the literary pages of the newspaper *El Paso del Norte*, and then in book form. In payment he received copies of the book, most of which he left in El Paso when he returned to Mexico early in 1916. Today, the first edition has become very rare.

The Underdogs, Azuela's masterpiece and one of the great Mexican novels, appeared precisely a hundred years after the first novel published in Mexico, *El Periquillo Sarniento* (*The Itching Parrot*, translated into English in 1942) by José Joaquín Fernández de Lizardi. Lizardi's work revived a lost genre, the picaresque novel; Azuela's initiated another, the novel of the Mexican Revolution.

The Underdogs is Azuela's most carefully planned novel. Divided into three parts (of twenty-one, fourteen, and seven chapters), the novel opens with a scene in the Cañón de Juchipila, where a group of *campesinos* under the leadership of the peon Demetrio Macías defeats the federal troops. From there until the end of the second part, the action increases progressively, both in violence and in dramatic intensity. For the rebels fighting with Demetrio, the results are easy victories and rich spoils. The third part opens with a letter written from El Paso, Texas, by the deserter Luis Cervantes, which serves—because of its humorous tone—as an interlude in the grim drama of the Revolution. In the third part the luck of Demetrio and his men changes, and nothing turns out right for them. The novel ends with Demetrio's death in the same Cañón de Juchipila where he had so soundly beaten the enemy in the opening scenes.

The underdogs return to the position, both physical and social, from which they had started. This closed structure is similar to a *bola* (ball); in Mexico, a revolution is also called a *bola*. Azuela structured the novel to reflect the theme; in *The Underdogs*, the reader finds an internal, organic order in which there are no loose scenes, no actions without a proper function in the apparently dissonant whole. As an organism, the novel is characterized by its dynamic essence, not only in the plot, but also in the style, in the painting of nature, and in the violent quality of the scenes, not dissimilar from those painted by Azuela's contemporary, the muralist Orozco.

The structure of *The Underdogs* is an innovation in Spanish-American narrative. Azuela consciously created a new novelistic form that reflects the nature of the New World. For the first time a Latin American novelist disregarded European forms and wrote a work in which the theme and the structure complement each other.

In Mexico City in 1916, Azuela practiced medicine among the indigent in one of the city's poorest neighborhoods. At the same time, he continued writing novels about the Revolution. Three appeared in 1918: *Las moscas* (*The Flies*), *Domitilo quiere ser diputado* (*Domitilo Wants To Be a Congressman*), and *Las tribulaciones de una familia decente* (*The Trials of a Respectable Family*). In none of them did he surpass his achievements in *The Underdogs*, although the three novels are of interest: he describes aspects of the Revolution and continues to criticize the direction it was taking under Obregón and the leaders who came later.

These three novels, and the earlier ones, continued to be ignored by the critics as well as the public. Very few reviews appeared before Azuela was discovered in 1924. By that time, he had already published his first experimental novel, *La Malhora* (*The Evil One*, 1923), followed by *El desquite* (*Revenge*, 1925) and *La luciérnaga* (*The Firefly*, 1932). About the change in style and technique reflected in these three novels, Azuela gave this explanation: "Around 1921 or 1922, tired of being an unknown writer, although I had already published nine novels— . . . which are now the ones that sell the most—the reading public did not even recognize my name. I made up my mind to stop writing novels if after another try I was to fail again" (*Obras* 3, p. 1112).

To get the attention of the reading public and the critics, Azuela decided to try the latest narrative techniques. He said ironically, "I studied this technique carefully and discovered that it consists in making concepts and expressions unintelligible in order to give the appearance of modernity" (*Obras* 3, p. 1113). The products of this effort were his experimental novels, which attracted the attention of some vanguard critics, who found more in them than the desire to make their reading unintelligible.

In *La Malhora* Azuela makes use of narrative devices that were to be employed by later novelists, such as the superimposing of narrative time periods, the unexpected changing of thematic elements, the distorting of the plot, the use of internal flashbacks, the abrupt ending of scenes, and the use of unfinished characterization. The most striking aspect of this novella's structure is the nonchronological development of the plot. The story opens with the murder of La Malhora's father, but it is only at the end of the novella that the reader finds out that the murderer is the man who raped her when she was a child. The four parts of the work take place in four environments of Mexico City connected only by the presence of La Malhora. The first part takes place in Tepito, Mexico City's most famous slum area; the second, in the office of a deranged doctor, the narrator; the third, in the home of two very religious sisters, where La Malhora works as a servant; and the last, in the home of a follower of the late Don Porfirio.

Azuela had either misunderstood the critics or his technique was too far advanced for the period, for his novel was rejected by the jury in a narrative contest he had entered under a pseudonym. When he found out about the rejection, he made a bonfire of all his literary manuscripts. "And when my doubt about my ability as a novelist was at its highest, success knocked on my door" (*Obras* 3, p. 1117).

In 1924, Monterde brought *The Underdogs* to the attention of critics and the reading public. Encouraged by the fame that the discovery of the book brought him, Azuela continued to write novels, and in 1932 he published *The Firefly*, the last of the experimental novels. In it he reveals a mastery of the new technique. The theme of *The Firefly* had been treated in an earlier novel, *The Trials of a Respectable Family*: the problems encountered in Mexico City by a family from a provincial town. In *The Firefly*, Azuela deals not with the external forces that ruin the family but with internal struggles in the souls of the characters. The world is seen from the point of view of the protagonists, Dionisio and Conchita. The slender narrative thread deals with the physical and spiritual decay of Dionisio, the provincial, honest man who settles in Mexico City with his family. Unlike the Vázquez Prados of *The Trials*, Dionisio's family was not driven from the provinces by the

Revolution; they went voluntarily to Mexico City, like thousands of others, attracted by the promise of a richer life. Soon after arriving, Dionisio and the members of his family discover that they have been deceived. Life in the big city is corrupt; the inhabitants live a daily life of trickery, mutual mistrust, and general restlessness. Dionisio's inheritance soon dwindles, and he ends up driving a city bus. The value of *The Firefly*, one of Azuela's best novels, is to be found in the memorable characterization of the protagonists and the masterful descriptions of Mexico City's slums, descriptions that have not been equaled by any other novelist, including Fuentes in his famous novel *La región más transparente* (*Where the Air Is Clear*, 1958), considered one of the best about life in the great metropolis.

Disillusioned with the corrupt public life in Mexico City, Azuela turned his back on politics and took refuge in the writing of historical novels (*Pedro Moreno, el insurgente* [Pedro Moreno, the Rebel, 1933–1934]; *Precursores* [Forerunners, 1935]). But this interlude was to be short-lived. It was difficult for Azuela to close his eyes to political events, and in 1937 he published *El camarada Pantoja* (Comrade Pantoja), the first of a new series of novels dealing with political problems. This book marks a return to the straightforward manner of presentation. Perhaps the change was dictated by Azuela's desire to reach a wider reading public, for in it and those that soon followed (*San Gabriel de Valdivias*, 1938; *Regina Landa*, 1939; *Avanzada*, 1940), he unveils the many injustices committed by the new rulers. In these novels, the artist in Azuela yields to the man of wrath who exposes the evils of the body politic.

Azuela's outstanding novel of this period is *Nueva burguesía* (The New Bourgeoisie, 1941), in which he skillfully traces the rise of a new social class in Mexican society, a class composed of revolutionaries who took advantage of the turmoil to attain power, abandoning the reforms promised to the people by previous governments. Throughout the novel, there is criticism of the methods used by the political party to elect the new president. This theme, however, is not at the core of the work. Much more important is the description of the new social classes that have appeared, as the author observes them in a tenement house in the neighborhood of Nonoalco, later made

famous by Luis Buñuel in his film *Los olvidados*. Azuela knew the neighborhood and its inhabitants well, since he himself lived not far from there. An endless procession of characters makes the novel a true human comedy. Azuela's technique is cinematic; he rapidly passes from scene to scene, giving close-ups of his characters without worrying too much about transitions. No single action is important, except perhaps the killing of the linotypist Benavides, but all of the scenes taken together carry an impact superior to that of many novels structured around a single action. No less important is the nature of the dialogue, always interesting and reflecting the social status of the speakers. Azuela knew tenement life in Mexico City and depicted it better than a trained sociologist in this short novel, perhaps his best of this period.

He did not achieve the same success with his next two novels, *La marchanta* (The Vendor, 1944) and *La mujer domada* (The Tamed Woman, 1946), both set in Mexico City. The last novel published during his lifetime, *Sendas perdidas* (Lost Paths, 1949), was first written as a movie script but was never produced. The plot, which deals with a man-devouring woman, is not very original; Azuela himself had used it in an undeveloped form in *La marchanta*. Nor is there anything new in technique. *Sendas perdidas* is a departure from his other works in that he dramatizes events of the past. One year after he published the novel, he made this observation: "*Sendas perdidas* was composed with characters and events of more than fifty years ago, when I first began to practice my profession" (*Obras* 3, p. 1044). Was this novel written, or perhaps outlined, in 1900? The naturalistic attitude of the narrator supports that hypothesis.

Azuela did not publish any novels during the last three years of his life. He did, however, write at least two that were published posthumously: *La maldición* (The Curse, 1955) and *Esa sangre* (Blood Tells, 1956). In the first, he repeats his favorite theme: the destruction of a rural family that migrates to the capital. Upon the death of the head of the family, the farmer Basilio Montelongo, who had been divested of his land by the government, his wife and two sons decide to go to Mexico City. On the way they stop at Celaya to say good-bye to an uncle, who tells them: "Here in Celaya you could live modestly working like honest people. . . . But no, what you are looking for is something else. I do not know if you can become rich in Mexico City, but what I can tell you is that the happiness and tranquillity you have left in your souls will be lost there" (*Obras* 2, p. 468). In the capital, the curse is fulfilled. Although he was severely criticized for condemning life in the large cities, Azuela continued through his writing to defend the maintenance of family life in the small towns.

Esa sangre is a continuation of the earlier novel *Marcela*. Here Azuela returns to the theme of the struggle between the *hacendados* and the peons, although his interest has shifted from the description of the physical struggle to the psychological problems faced by the characters, especially the protagonist, the *hacendado*'s son Julián, now a poor, feeble old man. For the reader unacquainted with the earlier novel, a summary of the plot has been worked into the first part of *Esa sangre*. Although Azuela was not able to improve upon the vivid scenes of *Marcela*, in the psychological analysis of the protagonist he surpassed his earlier effort.

Besides his novels, Azuela published several short stories, three plays (dramatizations of his novels), four biographies, and a short autobiography. His short stories seem to be prose fragments not used in his novels. For this reason they are often not well rounded. His technique is that of a novelist and not of a short-story writer, and he was seldom successful with the short narrative.

Azuela was officially recognized as a major novelist as early as 1940 when he received the Prize in Letters offered by the Ateneo Nacional de Ciencias y Artes (Nacional Society for the Arts and Sciences). The gold medal that he received in a ceremony held in March 1941 was the first official recognition he had accepted from the government, which he continued to criticize. In May of the following year, he was invited by the secretary of education to become a member of the Seminario de Cultura Mexicana. His tongue-in-cheek comment regarding this appointment, which he accepted, was: "I accepted the membership in this society with pleasure because I have run out of bad things to say about our government" (*Obras* 3, p. 1176). In August of the same year he was invited to become a member of the exclusive and traditional Academia Mexicana de la Lengua, an

honor reserved for a very limited number of writers. Azuela, showing his independence, did not accept, in spite of the pressure put upon him by family and friends. In the tradition of the great poet Rubén Darío, he could very well have exclaimed: "De las academias, líbranos, Señor!" (Oh Lord, deliver us from academies!)

In April 1943, Azuela received one of the highest honors that the Mexican government can bestow upon a writer. He was appointed by President Manuel Ávila Camacho to take part in the foundation of the Colegio Nacional and to become one of its twenty members. As in the case of the Academia Mexicana de la Lengua, Azuela's first reaction upon receiving the invitation was to reject it. Friends and members of the family, however, were able this time to prevail upon him to accept the invitation. That same year he gave a series of lectures at the academy on the development of the Mexican novel. These lectures, published as *Cien años de novela mexicana* (A Century of the Mexican Novel) in 1947, dealt with the novels of the most important Mexican fiction writers, beginning with Lizardi, the author of the first Mexican novel, *The Itching Parrot*, and ending with an analysis of the works of the naturalist Federico Gamboa, the author of the well-known novel *Santa*.

As a critic, Azuela's judgment of novels was based on a simple principle in which he firmly believed. According to him, the novel is a genre to be read by a large number of people. This principle—that the novel is written for the masses—does not mean that it should be a form of propaganda: "Paul Bourget and Émile Zola lost all their strength as novelists when they turned into social reformers" (*Obras* 3, p. 611). He also insisted on making it clear that the novel should not be a didactic instrument, that it should not be written with the purpose of teaching anything. The value of a novel, he often repeated, depends greatly on its literary content, and therefore its characters should be alive, it should have a solid structure, it should present a credible story, and its theme should have human interest. "When the novels of the most famous stylists lack human value, they become a mere bibliographical curiosity. On the other hand, we continue to read the novels of Cervantes, Prévost, Stendhal, Balzac, etc." (*Obras* 3, p. 623).

mately twenty volumes printed in Spanish by the Parisian firm of Garnier were directed. His name appeared in much of the peninsular press, most frequently in *El Liberal,* one of the two Madrid dailies with the largest circulations. He became Paris correspondent for *El Liberal* in 1898, later assumed the editorship for a brief period, and contributed to its pages, sometimes daily, until 1920. Between 1919 and 1921, he edited in Madrid a monthly literary magazine that he had founded and that, in light of the heavily French slant of its contents, he aptly named *Cosmópolis.* At the same time, he dispatched chronicles to the press in Latin America, for example, to *El Mercurio* in Santiago, Chile, *El Universal* in Mexico City, and particularly *La Nación* and *La Prensa* in Buenos Aires, the American center with which he established the closest ties. He also contributed to all the modernist magazines. On the other hand, he introduced Spanish and Latin American writers and events to his French public in a column in the *Mercure de France,* and he founded a modernist review, *El nuevo mercurio,* in the French capital in 1907, in addition to contributing to Darío's *Mundial Magazine.* One commentator fittingly referred to Gómez Carrillo as the most French of Spaniards and the most Spanish of Americans. A latter-day Hermes, always on the move, Gómez Carrillo sent the message of the reigning cultural gods from one land to another, with an impulse that was truly literary and cosmopolitan rather than national and political.

French writers and the modernists began to exert influence on the young Guatemalan in 1890, and his first book, a pamphlet of portraits of contemporary writers, mostly French, published in Madrid in 1892, bore the French title *Esquisses* (Sketches). This slim volume also reflects Gómez Carrillo's conversion to the French style of impressionistic criticism that was to mark his writings from that point on. His last published work was in the same vein: *La nueva literatura francesa* (The New French Literature), which appeared in the year of his death. It closed a career that was a continuous campaign on behalf of the latest in French literature and whose most immediate fruit was an awakened consciousness on the part of his readers. He was, in this regard, a pioneer. His final book confirms that Gómez Carrillo seldom

wavered in his preference for newcomers to the scene over consecrated figures: the latest trend always fanned his enthusiasm and moved him to its defense.

By his own confession, Gómez Carrillo preferred legend to analysis and the writer to the work, and he emphasized human interest over interpretive criticism. Proof of the inclination to play to his public rests in volumes like *El alma encantadora de París* (The Enchanting Spirit of Paris, 1902), *Literatura extranjera* (Foreign Literature, 1894), and *El modernismo* (Modernism, 1905). But if he aimed to please with his anecdotal slant and with the cadences of his prose, he also instructed. Many are the names of the French authors whom he brought to the attention of Hispanic readers, some for the first time. He took a strong role as a relentless propagandist for symbolism in the Hispanic world. He surveyed the movement's techniques and postures, and sang the special praises of its most bohemian practitioner, Paul Verlaine. Against considerable resistance in an environment that he considered stodgy at best and retrograde at worst, he paraded a modern sensitivity in art well before it found ready acceptance in Spain. The fact that Gómez Carrillo was a journalist catering to popular tastes rather than a critic addressing himself exclusively to an intellectual minority allowed him to exert considerable influence.

If on the one hand Gómez Carrillo deserves recognition as the purveyor of the grandeur, vitality, and feverish rhythm of life and literature in Paris, on the other hand the stylistic polish of his chronicles served as an incentive as robust as Darío's in spurring expressive renovation. No less than his novels, his chronicles exhibit a rich vocabulary nuanced with adjectives; a highly conscious style with balanced sentences, reiterative series, and unexpected images and juxtapositions; insinuating synesthesia; and provocative ambiguities. It is a prose designed to seduce with its rhythms, its suggestiveness, and its surprises, yet a prose whose agility and lucidity permit ready communication. While the Hispanic literary scene was still struggling to rid itself of the burden of the nineteenth-century rhetorical mode, Gómez Carrillo aligned himself with the modernists on both sides of the Atlantic to participate actively in their efforts to purify and revitalize the language. Some writers devoted themselves to the renovation of verse forms;

he joined the campaign to cleanse Spanish prose of its academic encumbrances. He belonged to that group of modernists who believed that language, beyond its function as a vehicle of communication, had an artistic end in itself. His position echoes the formalist precepts of the French Parnassian poets of the 1860's and the subjective stance of the later symbolists, as well as the Flaubertian faith in the word's power to project pure meaning.

Modernismo, the literary movement with which he is commonly associated, was not a restrictively Spanish-American phenomenon for Gómez Carrillo. Rather, he viewed it as the broadly based artistic practice and expression of a worldview that critics have recently come to recognize. He regarded it correctly as a movement linked to the artistic ferment universally evident at the century's turn, in Gustave Flaubert, Gabriele D'Annunzio, and Algernon Swinburne, as much as in the Hispanic writers. And he certainly partook of that ferment.

Gómez Carrillo was a man of his time who wrote for his time. There is little evidence in his production of the writer's sense of his transcendence. He was a dilettante and not a seeker of inner states, philosophical heights, or ultimate truths. His style of impressionistic criticism has gone out of fashion, and his chronicles have met the inevitable fate that their ephemeral nature had reserved for them. He merchandised salable wares that he knew how to make enticingly piquant, and so he gained a following that, as he must have realized, was as circumstantial as it was intense. His novels, exemplars of modernist prose, have taken on for contemporary readers the parodic tinge that time can impose on a fashion that has lapsed. Gómez Carrillo's value as a writer, consequently, may seem in a certain sense archaeological and therefore diminished.

He is, nevertheless, a figure to be reckoned with in the annals of Hispanic literature. His chronicles and books were in the limelight for over a quarter-century. Literary figures as well as the general public reacted to him. His role as a propagator of modern French literary currents among his Hispanic readers was decisive and far-reaching. He was a gifted writer who had a substantial impact through his flair for language, his titillating chronicles, and his literary criticism, which he turned into literature. Both the writer and the man incarnate the spirit of the time: a dynamic, effervescent moment in cultural history that was turning its back on the answers, the practices, and the monistic comforts of the past, in preparation for the burst of radical experimentation that was to explode all tradition.

SELECTED BIBLIOGRAPHY

First Editions

Fiction

Del amor, del dolor y del vicio. Paris, 1898.
Bohemia sentimental. Guatemala City, 1899.
Maravillas. Madrid, 1899.
Flores de penitencia. Paris, 1913.
El evangelio del amor. Madrid, 1922.

Travel Accounts

Sensaciones de Rusia. Barcelona, 1905.
El alma japonesa. Paris, 1906.
De Marsella a Tokío: Sensaciones de Egipto, la India, la China y el Japón. Paris, 1906.
La Rusia actual. Paris, 1906.
Desfile de visiones. Valencia, 1906.
Cómo se pasa la vida. Paris, 1907.
Grecia. Madrid, 1908.
El Japón heroico y galante. Madrid, 1912.
Romerías. Paris, 1912.
La sonrisa de la Esfinge. Madrid, 1913.
Jerusalén y la Tierra Santa. Paris, 1914.
El encanto de Buenos Aires. Madrid, 1914.
Ciudades de ensueño: Constantinopla, Jerusalén, Atenas, Damasco, Nikko. Madrid, 1920.
Fez, la andaluza. Madrid, 1926.

War Chronicles

Campos de batalla y campos de ruinas. Madrid, 1915.
Crónica de la guerra. Madrid, 1915.
Reflejos de la tragedia. Madrid, 1915.
En el corazón de la tragedia. Madrid, 1916.
En las trincheras. Madrid, 1916.
El alma de los sacerdotes soldados. Barcelona, 1918.
La gesta de la legión (Los voluntarios españoles e hispanoamericanos en la guerra). Madrid, 1918.
Tierras mártires. Madrid, 1918.

ENRIQUE GÓMEZ CARRILLO

Essays

Esquisses: Siluetas de escritores y artistas. Madrid, 1892.
Sensaciones de arte. Paris, 1893.
Literatura extranjera: Estudios cosmopolitas. Paris, 1894.
Almas y cerebros. Paris, 1898.
Sensaciones de París y de Madrid. Paris, 1900.
El alma encantadora de París. Barcelona, 1902.
Bailarinas. Madrid, 1902.
Entre encajes. Barcelona, 1905.
El modernismo. Madrid, 1905.
Psicología de la moda femenina. Madrid, 1907.
El teatro de Pierrot. Paris, 1909.
Vanidad de vanidades. Paris, 1909.
Cultos profanos. Paris, 1910.
Pequeñas cuestiones palpitantes. Madrid, 1910.
Nostalgias. Valencia, 1911.
Raquel Meller. Madrid, 1919.
Safo, Friné y otras seductoras. Madrid, 1921.
El misterio de la vida y de la muerte de Mata Hari. Madrid, 1922.
En el reino de la frivolidad. Madrid, 1923.
Las cien obras maestras de la literatura universal. Madrid, 1925.
La nueva literatura francesa. Madrid, 1927.

Memoirs

Treinta años de mi vida 1: El despertar del alma. Madrid, 1918. 2: *En plena bohemia.* Madrid, 1919. 3: *La miseria de Madrid.* Madrid, 1921.

Collected Works

Obras completas. 27 vols. Madrid, 1919–1923. Some of these volumes include chronicles not collected earlier.
Páginas escogidas. Edited by Edelberto Torres. 3 vols. Guatemala City, 1954.

Translations

Among the Ruins. Translated by Florence Simmonds. London, 1915. War chronicles.
In the Heart of the Tragedy. New York and London, 1917. War chronicles.

Biographical and Critical Studies

Abreu Gómez, Ermilo. "Prólogo." In *Whitman y otras crónicas,* by Enrique Gómez Carrillo. Washington, D.C., 1950. Pp. 11–17.

Barrientos, Alfonso E. *Enrique Gómez Carrillo, treinta años después.* Barcelona, 1959. 2nd ed. Guatemala City, 1973.
Bastos, María L. "La crónica modernista de Enrique Gómez Carrillo o la función de la trivialidad." *Sur* 350–351: 65–88 (1982).
Blanco-Fombona, Rufino. "Gómez Carrillo." In *Letras y letrados de Hispano-América.* Paris, 1908. Pp. 91–101.
Cáceres, [Zoila] Aurora. *Mi vida con Enrique Gómez Carrillo.* Madrid, 1929.
Demetriou, Sophia. "La decadencia y el escritor modernista: Enrique Gómez Carrillo." In *Estudios críticos sobre la prosa modernista hispanoamericana,* edited by José Olivio Jiménez. New York, 1975. Pp. 223–236.
González-Ruano, César. *E. Gómez Carrillo: El escritor y el hombre.* Madrid, 1928.
Horwinski, Linda J. "Enrique Gómez Carrillo, Connoisseur of *La Belle Époque:* His Prose Works, 1892–1927." Ph.D. diss., University of California, 1981.
Kronik, John W. "Enrique Gómez Carrillo, Francophile Propagandist." *Symposium* 21:50–60 (1967).
Meyer-Minnemann, Klaus. "Enrique Gómez Carrillo, *Del amor, del dolor y del vicio:* Anotaciones en torno a una novela del modernismo hispanoamericano." *Nueva revista de filología hispánica* 22:62–77 (1973).
Mendoza, Juan M. *Enrique Gómez Carrillo: Estudio crítico-biográfico.* 2 vols. Guatemala City, 1940. 2nd ed., 1946.
Pavlovic, Liliana S. "Enrique Gómez Carrillo, redactor de 'Lettres espagnoles' en el *Mercure de France* (1903–1907)." *Revista iberoamericana* 33:71–84 (1967).
Phillips, Allen W. "Nueva luz sobre Clarín y Gómez Carrillo." *Revista de archivos, bibliotecas y museos* 81: 757–779 (1978).
———. "Sobre Rubén Darío y Gómez Carrillo: Sus relaciones literarias y amistosas." In *Homenaje a Luis Alberto Sánchez,* edited by Robert G. Mead. Madrid, 1983. Pp. 407–441.
Sánchez, Luis Alberto. "Enrique Gómez Carrillo y el modernismo." *Atenea* 299:185–205 (1950).
Torres, Edelberto. *Enrique Gómez Carrillo, el cronista errante.* Guatemala City, 1956.
Ulner, Arnold R. "Enrique Gómez Carrillo en el modernismo: 1889–1896." Ph.D. diss., University of Missouri, 1972.
Zuleta, Ignacio M. "*El nuevo mercurio* (1907)." *Revista interamericana de bibliografía* 31:385–403 (1981).

Enrique Larreta

(1873–1961)

Adelia Lupi

In the late nineteenth and early twentieth centuries, political and economic maturity was reached by Spanish America, after its long colonial subordination to Spain. In a corresponding movement in art and literature, the winds of change brought about by *modernismo* represented cultural maturity and independence as well. The sovereign pontiff of modernist poetry is generally considered to be the great aesthete Rubén Darío. The apex of modernist Latin American prose was reached in 1908 by Enrique Larreta with his first novel and masterpiece, *La gloria de Don Ramiro* (*The Glory of Don Ramiro*).

Larreta, born in Buenos Aires on 4 March 1873 (he died there on 6 July 1961), belonged to a rich family of aristocratic landowners of distant Basque origin. His studies in law and the social sciences prepared him for a diplomatic career in later life. Larreta showed early signs of literary leanings by taking part in the activities of the cultural groups in the capital. He became known in 1896 with "Artemis," a refined short story set in classical Greece, which Paul Groussac published in his famous literary review *La biblioteca*. Those were the years of great cultural activity in Buenos Aires (the capital since 1880), a city that more than any other had maintained a living contact with Europe and that had been open to French influence from the beginning of the nineteenth century, that is, from the time of the revolutionary romantic movement, with its appeal for national independence. After almost a century of hostile feeling toward Spain, which reached its extreme point with Domingo F. Sarmiento's *Facundo* (1845), a new and more productive relationship with the former mother country was launched at the end of the century. Spain is present in many aspects of modernism, both as a source of inspiration and as the necessary destination in a journey, almost a pilgrimage, to the cultural roots.

When, in 1902, Larreta arrived in Spain for the first time, the enthusiasm and emotion he felt for Ávila during his trip through old Castile inspired the theme of his historical novel: *The Glory of Don Ramiro* was to evoke the Spain of the Golden Age. Its action was set within the impressive and suggestive walls of "the Ávila of the saints and knights"—a city that symbolized proud feudal destinies, which began to decline with the leveling, "modern" politics of the Hapsburgs.

During his stay in Madrid, Larreta had stimulating contacts with modernist literary circles and with writers from the Generation of '98, as well as a firm friendship, based on similar interests, with Maurice Barrès, the decadent French writer who had elected Toledo as his ideal city because it symbolized the past grandeur of Spain. After six years of work, study, perfecting, and revising, *The Glory of Don Ramiro* was published in 1908 and had an immediate, international success, with good opinions from the highest authorities and many reissuings and translations, especially in French. In this intense evocation of Philip II's Spain, Larreta embodied the aesthetic preferences that so animated the climate of the European *fin de siècle*, rich in the converging and diverging artistic drives that might be defined as decadence.

Elitist, modernist, and decadent writers in Europe and Latin America were dissatisfied with contemporary thought that focused exclusively on material progress, positivistic sciences, and industrial techniques and that wanted to use art for progress or for morality. These artists chose exotic lands and remote, idealized eras so that their artistic expression could be independent and pure, and exist for its own sake. Brought into focus in literature by the Parnassians and the French symbolists, these preferences had animated other artistic fields as well: figurative art beginning with the Pre-Raphaelites, the philosophies of Arthur Schopenhauer and Friedrich Nietzsche, and Richard Wagner's music. Already by the mid-nineteenth century Gustave Flaubert had shown with *Salammbô* (1862) that the reconstruction, archaeologically perfect, of the remote and exotic past was not only possible but even preferable, especially if the stories and settings contained omens of imminent dissolution.

For *The Glory of Don Ramiro*, subtitled *Una vida en tiempos de Felipe II* (*A Life in the Times of Philip II*), Larreta chose a moment in history that was distant but one with which he felt sympathetic, because of his nostalgic, aristocratic, and traditional cultural attachments. The story is presented with all its internal ferment and collective forces (for example, the revolts of Moorish and Spanish nobles). It recreates a widely varying series of locations: the palaces of the nobility, Arab quarters, monks' cells, and the court itself. We are taken down a gallery populated by a diversity of characters: *hidalgos* from the refined portraits of Velázquez, Titian, and El Greco; sinister anchorites from Francisco de Zurbarán; demons from Johann Heinrich Füssli; bewitching charmers from Gustave Moreau and J. K. Huys-

mans; theologians from the English Gothic tales of terror; *pícaros* (rogues) and *celestinas* (bawds) in action; soldiers of fortune; conquerors of the Indies; miraculous mystics; brotherhoods and the Inquisition; maids of honor and young men in precious conversation while the melancholic *Romancero* melodies are played. In this enormous fresco, the spirit of the age takes on life in an exact documentation, pursued with a precision and a passion that are witness to Larreta's ability as a historian as well as to his great culture.

Don Ramiro de Alcántara, the only descendant of a noble and ruined family of Ávila, lives an unhappy childhood, spent in isolation and daydreaming. He is unaware that he is the illegitimate child of an Arab, an ignominious fact within the context of the ideal of purity of the Catholic Castilian race. He is proud and bold; his lust for life and his great imagination cause him to seek "the glory" that he dreams of achieving, first through brave deeds and then through a life pledged to asceticism and saintliness. Generous and possessed of many noble qualities, he is also slothful and spineless, capable of submitting to the bad influences of various companions. He is especially swayed by his tutor, the theologian Vargas Orozco, an overwhelming person who is masterfully described by Larreta (the portrayal of Orozco won the enthusiastic admiration of Miguel de Unamuno). Repeatedly torn in two by internal mental strife with those close to him, and always justifying himself when he takes contradictory decisions, Ramiro tries to gain the love of Aixa, a *femme fatale* and, at the same time, a mystic Moorish odalisque; but he accuses her and she is burned at the stake by the Inquisition. Ramiro also loves Beatriz, the daughter of a rich merchant of Ávila, but he kills her along with his rival. Fleeing from his Ávila, ancient, malignant soil, "city-prison, where sloth softened even the noblest spirits, . . . and where only those with wings strong enough to fly constantly in the direction of God could free themselves from delusion and tedium" (part 2, ch. 6), Ramiro crosses Spain and boards ship for the Indies, where he hopes to finally reach his longed-for glory as a conqueror or outlaw. In the end, glory does smile upon him in death when, after redeeming him, the maiden Santa Rosa de Lima places a rose on his corpse.

Like so many characters of the decadent period, Ramiro alternates between a fading languidness and an ardent pride, between moments of depression and moments of violence and cruelty. In this failed Nietzschean superman, the critic Amado Alonso sees the conflict of two dualisms. The first one, dramatic and powerful, pits the freedom of the individual against the conditioning of society. The second conflict is even more dramatic, because it is more personal: "Lacking the will to act and the temperament for struggle, he shelters himself in his dreams, and imagines the deeds done and the obstacles overcome" (*Ensayo* . . . , pp. 176–177). With this great care for complex detail, Larreta distinguishes Ramiro from other decadent heroes. And so it is with the entire work, which emerges from the brush strokes of modernism, taking on a new dimension and authenticity precisely because it is deeply rooted in the spiritual territory of Spanishness presented in the fullness of its universal values. It is a Spanishness with deep contrasts, as reflected in Ramiro: mysticism and knightly enterprises, the sword and the cross, body and soul, East (Muslim Spain) and West (Catholic Spain); but these contrasts are a long way from the superficial, false, moralistic interpretations of the clichés of the *leyenda negra*, the critical view of Spain as the bastion of religious intolerance both at home and abroad, typical of the historical novels of European romanticism. In *The Glory of Don Ramiro*, the contrasts form a unique historic whole, seen from a nostalgic distance, as in an aquarium, and in a light that is described as in infinite and continual change. And the light itself plays a leading part, even if only as an incorporeal presence, wrapping itself around everything and changing it to such an extent that it often seems that the characters and the objects are the materials necessary for the play of light. Added to these strong visual images are impressions of other sensations, including smells and sounds: perfumes, rustles, tones of voice, echoes, and so on.

Almost twenty years passed between *The Glory of Don Ramiro* and Larreta's second novel, *Zogoibi* (1926). In that time, the writer had an intense political as well as cultural life. From 1910 to 1916, he was the Argentine ambassador in Paris. He was thus able to live in the intellectual exaltation of the artistic and social whirl that typified Parisian life,

sharpening his already keen perception while viewing the final days of the *belle époque*. Later, in *Tiempos iluminados* (Illuminating Times, 1939), a collection of autobiographical memories, Larreta recalled those years as the fullest in his life, because of the friends who linked him to the Parisian artistic scene: Anatole France, Edmond Rostand, Henri de Régnier, and Remy de Gourmont, as well as the Basque painter Ignacio Zuloaga, who had painted him, in a famous picture, in front of his beloved Ávila.

In the novel *Zogoibi*, Larreta created a dynamic portrayal of *gaucho* life on the Argentine pampas. The novel's protagonist, Federico de Ahumada, likes to call himself Zogoibi, after the last unhappy king of Granada. He is, like Ramiro, a character with no will, constantly struggling between opposing passions, then inevitably defeated because he is unable to face up to reality. Against *gauchesco* settings, the story is of Federico's unfortunate loves, for the pure Lucía, a creature of the pampas, and for the sensual European adventuress Zita, the cause of the final tragedy. Beyond the conventionalism of the plot, the novel is a demonstration of the evolution of modernism toward a major reevaluation of native and American themes.

The reawakening of interest by literature in the *gaucho* and the pampas, a literary genre that began in the early 1800's and culminated in José Hernández' *Martín Fierro* (1872), was part of the maturing of the Argentine national identity. This renewed, nostalgic interest in native topics and the *gaucho*, at the time when the *gaucho* was disappearing from the pampas, became focused on *Don Segundo Sombra* of Richard Güiraldes, which also came out in 1926. Güiraldes' book unfortunately and unjustly eclipsed *Zogoibi*. The two approaches to the topic differed. Güiraldes, through a series of poetic and suggestive images, put a seal on the end of the *gauchos* and their world, already archaic and remote, even though he continued to be fascinated by them. His Don Segundo is the last hero of a mythical world, on its way to inevitable extinction. Like the Argentine novelist Benito Lynch, Larreta in *Zogoibi* defends the indigenous values of his own land against false imitations that come from without and that can bring only unhappiness and ruin. In opposition to the illusionary attraction that the Creole oligarchy felt toward

European civilization in all its glamour, Larreta indicates, in the attachment to the traditions of the past and to the soil of the fatherland, the salvation and the way to achieve a true, authentic Argentina. There is nostalgia for the past, but the life on the land is presented from the point of view of the rich *estanciero* (rancher) who also appreciates the new dynamism that is sweeping the pampas. Where the previous writers of the *gaucho* genre had described the excitement or the sadness of the life of the loyal and strong *gauchos*, with the pampas as only the background to their existence, the pampas of Larreta are in the forefront, always there: wild, pure nature, desolate and deadly, a vastness that fascinates with the uniformity of its horizon. It becomes, for the first time, an emotional attraction of transcending value, a metaphysical symbol that inexorably attracts man and nullifies him in its primordial reality.

Thus the Argentine hero of Larreta's last novel, *El Gerardo* (1956), a bitter character, indecisive and with no illusions, after living in Spain, in Granada, responds to the nostalgic call of his land and returns there. Fleeing from the company of men after a life of failure, longing to remain in distant solitude, Gerardo is finally alone with his "I," pure and simple, and settles himself in the pampas to look for a definitive peace. He does not kill himself, but in his refuge, which is also a return to the source that generates and nullifies, he abandons himself. He gives himself up completely, becomes one with himself: "Calcified bones . . . discolored by the sun . . . and the wind and the dew. His mineral self, his indestructible, definitive 'I'" (part 2, ch. 50).

The extreme pantheistic existentialism of this later Larreta was already there, though only hinted at, in his novel *Orillas del Ebro* (The Banks of the Ebro, 1949), located in the Rioja region of Spain, in the 1920's. Larreta contrasts the decadent, idle life that characterizes the court of Alfonso XIII with the quality of life lived close to the values of the land, described as a harmonious union between tradition and progress. The hero, Máximo, finds serenity and the solution to his problems by dedicating himself to work on his land. Once again the ancient lands of Castile, though seen in the present, are the symbol of the true Spain. In this constructive return to his own land, in the pride of the Spanish race in its own

traditions, and in the cult of the past and the nobility of labor, Larreta, like the other writers in the Generation of '98, makes way for the possible rebirth of a Spain that has been disoriented and humiliated by the loss of its colonial empire.

In contrast to the themes treated in Larreta's highly precious, modernist depiction of the distant world of *The Glory of Don Ramiro*, the didactic and ethical messages of his later novels can sometimes seem a bit outdated. Nonetheless, it is above all for the wide range of his stylistic expression that Larreta is the most notable representative of the linguistic phenomenon of Spanish-American prose in the first half of the twentieth century.

At the beginning of the century, together with Rubén Darío, Larreta had contributed to the rejuvenation and enrichment of the Spanish and Spanish-American languages. As a true purist of the language, throughout his life he was dedicated with noble passion to his literary vocation, purifying, setting, styling, and perfecting his means of expression. Larreta also worked for a perfection of expression through the conciseness required for his dramatic works; through the perfect and contained structure of the sonnets in *La calle de la vida y de la muerte* (The Narrow Street of Life and Death, 1941), a series of images of various characters and of the countryside; and through the thoughts, monologues, and considerations on art, philosophy, and life contained in *La naranja* (The Orange, 1947).

In his works for the theater, Larreta developed, although more superficially, themes that he treated with greater insight and subtlety in his novels. They are tenuous, sentimental dramas of the *belle époque* of the moneyed classes: *La lampe d'argile* (The Lamp of Clay, 1915); his version of the same play in Spanish, *Pasión de Roma* (Passion of Rome, 1937); and dramas set in Argentina: *Tenía que suceder* (It Had to Happen, 1943) and the *gaucho* drama *El linyera* (The Vagabond, 1932). Even though most of these works seem dated, the historical play *Santa María del Buen Aire* (1935) continues to be of interest. It is a reconstruction of the tragic expedition of Don Pedro de Mendoza, in 1536, to the river Plate. Once again, the best in Larreta comes out when, on the basis of research and documentation from archives, he shows how he can write with singular art and skill of the history of the Spanish conquests, made from "extraordinary illusions and bitter destiny" and that "sacred Spanish madness, creator of nations."

This historical period had already been remembered by Larreta in *Las dos fundaciones de Buenos Aires* (The Two Foundations of Buenos Aires, 1933), a short work that is something between a history and a monologue, and that passes from the past to the present and back again to the past. The same knowledgeability in use of language and free flow of thought are found in *La naranja*, written in imitation of Montaigne and witness to the wisdom and existentialist serenity achieved by Larreta in his old age.

The charming lane of *La calle de la vida y de la muerte* can be found at one side of the majestic Cathedral of Ávila, a temple and a fortress at the same time; it is the unforgettable point about which revolve the contrasting lives in *The Glory of Don Ramiro*. Today it is to that world that the fame of Larreta is tied. Nevertheless, he was also a great interpreter and narrator of his own land and of Argentine civilization. With a metaphorical bridge he unites two shores of the Atlantic, and he knew how to exalt the common values that continue to inspire both the Spanish and Spanish-American civilizations.

SELECTED BIBLIOGRAPHY

First Editions

Prose Narratives and Novels

Artemis. Buenos Aires, 1896.
La gloria de Don Ramiro. Madrid, 1908.
Zogoibi. Buenos Aires, 1926.
Orillas del Ebro. Madrid, 1949.
El Gerardo; o la torre de las damas. Buenos Aires and Madrid, 1953.
En la pampa. Buenos Aires and Madrid, 1955.
El Gerardo. Madrid, 1956.

Poetry

La calle de la vida y de la muerte. Buenos Aires, 1941.

Plays

La lampe d'argile. Paris, 1915.
El linyera. Buenos Aires, 1932.
Santa María del Buen Aire. Madrid, 1935.
Pasión de Roma. Buenos Aires, 1937.
La que buscaba Don Juan. Buenos Aires, 1938.
Tenía que suceder. Buenos Aires, 1943.
Clamor. Buenos Aires, 1959.

Essays

Las dos fundaciones de Buenos Aires. Buenos Aires, 1933.
Tiempos iluminados. Buenos Aires, 1939.
La naranja. Buenos Aires, 1947.

Collected Works

Obras completas. Madrid, 1948.
_____. Buenos Aires, 1959.

Translations

The Glory of Don Ramiro. Translated by L. B. Walton. London and Toronto, 1924.

Biographical and Critical Studies

Alonso, Amado. *Ensayo sobre la novela histórica: El modernismo en "La gloria de don Ramiro."* Buenos Aires, 1942.
Berenguer Carisomo, Arturo. *Los valores eternos en la obra de Enrique Larreta.* Buenos Aires, 1946.
Berenguer Carisomo, Arturo. *Las dos últimas novelas de Enrique Larreta. Cuadernos hispanoamericanos* 75/327–340 (1956).
Giménez Caballero, Ernesto. "La gloria de don Ramiro en la novela hispanoamericana." *Cuadernos hispanoamericanos* 8:319–329 (1949).
Giusti, Roberto. "Dos novelas del campo argentino." In *Crítica y polémica.* Buenos Aires, 1927. Pp. 147–160.
"La gloria de don Ramiro" en veinticinco años de crítica: Homenaje a don Enrique Larreta 1908–1933. Buenos Aires, 1934.
Jansen, André. *Enrique Larreta, novelista hispanoargentino.* Madrid, 1967. A complete biography and bibliography.
Lida, Raimundo. "La técnica del relato en *La gloria de don*

Ramiro." In *Cursos y conferencias* 9. Buenos Aires, 1936. Pp. 225–247.

Lupi, Adelia. "Historia y modernismo en *La gloria de don Ramiro* de Enrique Larreta." In *Actas del VIII Congreso de la Asociación Internacional de Hispanistas.* Madrid, 1986. Pp. 195–203.

Unamuno, Miguel de. *Temas argentinos.* Buenos Aires, 1943.

_____. *Por tierras de Portugal y de España.* Madrid, 1941.

Zaldumbide, Gonzalo. "Enrique Larreta: De Ávila a la Pampa." *Cuadernos hispanoamericanos.* 13:25–48 (1950).

Guillermo Valencia

(1873–1943)

Sonja P. Karsen

Colombia has produced many outstanding literary figures. In colonial times, writers of both poetry and prose were influenced by the prevailing literary tendencies of Spain. This trend did not change until the early nineteenth century, when Bogotá became known for its literary circles. The *cenáculos*, as they were called, also played an important political role, as they were instrumental in formulating the ideological basis for the country's emancipation from Spanish rule. In Colombia, as in other parts of the continent, the period following the wars of independence (which for Colombia ended with Simón Bolívar's victory in the Battle of Boyacá in 1819) and the establishment of a constitutional government was marked by political unrest. Out of this turmoil emerged a new literary movement, romanticism, which produced poets such as José Eusebio Caro, Rafael Pombo, Julio Arboleda, and Jorge Isaacs (the latter perhaps best known for his romantic novel *María* [1867]), whose fame quickly spread beyond Colombia's borders.

Toward the turn of the century, Spanish-American poets experimented with new forms of literary expression. The rather formal type of poetry favored by Colombian romantic poets came to be discarded in favor of a more musical verse, characterized by the selection of words according to their musical quality and the enhancement of the music through the use of novel rhyme schemes and unusual imagery.

The birth of Guillermo Valencia on 20 October 1873 in Popayán, capital of the department of Cauca, occurred during a period of great political ferment and intellectual change in Colombia. The poet's father was the lawyer and politician Joaquín Valencia Quijano, and his mother was Adelaida Castillo Caicedo. Valencia belonged to an aristocratic family directly descended from distinguished Colombians of the colonial period. The poet was brought up in an atmosphere of books. His parents were avid readers who often read aloud and favored literary discussions in their home.

It was his mother's influence that awakened Valencia's interest in poetry. After being taught at home by his mother, he entered the Seminario Conciliar in Popayán, a school run by French priests of the order of Saint Vincent de Paul. Many of the poet's ideas on literature and his later approach to political and social problems were formed during the five years he spent with these French teachers. Upon graduation, he entered the University of Cauca in Popayán to study law. Valencia never took his law degree, entering politics before he was twenty.

In 1896, Valencia was elected to the Colombian house of representatives. He was two years too young to hold such office, but the oratorical ability he displayed won him a waiver of the legal age requirement. This fact was discussed in the newspapers at the time and immediately gave the twenty-three-year-old Valencia national renown. Valencia's political career was temporarily suspended when in 1899 he was appointed first secretary of the Colombian legation in France, Switzerland, and Germany under the legation's minister, General Rafael Reyes. During his stay in Europe, civil strife erupted again in Colombia. The War of the Thousand Days lasted from 1899 to 1902, the longest and cruelest period of turmoil Colombia had experienced since the country's emancipation from Spanish rule.

Valencia returned to his political career in 1903, when he was again elected as a representative to congress. Five years later he was elected senator, and he remained a member of congress throughout his lifetime. During that period, he ran twice for the presidency, once in 1918 as a candidate of the progressive coalition and again in 1930 on the conservative ticket. Both times he was unsuccessful. At the time of his death, on 8 July 1943, he had been reelected senator. Valencia had participated in the political life of Colombia for half a century and, as a consequence, helped to determine the policies of both conservative and liberal administrations. Politics was as much a part of Valencia's life as was poetry.

Valencia had appeared on the literary scene when modernism had begun to capture the imagination of writers in Spanish America. The movement's tenets were in opposition to prevailing literary practices. French literature during the nineteenth century had greatly influenced Spanish-American writers. However, the poets of Valencia's generation looked to other literatures for inspiration as well. The work of these poets assimilated the influences of the romantic, the Parnassian, and the symbolist schools, which in France had succeeded and reacted against each other. In addition to the strong French influence, there emerged for the first time in the literatures of the Hispanic world a curiosity regarding authors of other European countries and of North America. Many of the new techniques were adapted and found their way into modernist style, which was highly original in its themes and versification. The modernist movement blended opposing tendencies and aesthetic notions into a harmonious whole, creating an eclectic and completely new and original form of poetry.

The poet who introduced modernism in Colombia was José Asunción Silva, who made use of the new verse forms, choosing rhyme schemes and words for their musical qualities alone. Silva's work was such a complete renewal of poetry that one might almost say the genre was revolutionized. When Valencia came to Bogotá in 1895, he already knew and admired Silva's poetry, especially the poem "Nocturno" (Nocturne), which was recited everywhere. Through Silva Valencia became acquainted with the contemporary literary movements and their leaders, and Valencia soon became a habitué of the literary circles of Bogotá. Most of the poems that appear in *Ritos* (Rites, 1899) were written in the capital between 1896 and 1897. The same year *Ritos* was published, Valencia went to Paris, where he met Rubén Darío, Oscar Wilde, Enrique Gómez Carrillo, Evaristo Rivas Groot, Ernest La Jeunesse, Jean Moréas, and José María de Heredia. Upon his return to Colombia in 1901, he was received enthusiastically in the *cenáculos* of Bogotá. Many of the younger poets were influenced by Valencia's success with the new type of poetry, and modernism as a movement gradually took hold in his native land.

In the period between the first edition and the second edition (1914) of *Ritos*, Valencia, although very much involved in politics, found time to write some of his most famous poems. "Las dos cabezas" (The Two Heads) was greatly praised when it appeared in 1901. "A Popayán" (To Popayán), the most acclaimed of all his compositions, was written in 1906. The second, expanded edition of *Ritos* made Valencia's poetry famous in both Spanish America and Spain. Over the next thirty years, he wrote an enormous amount of poetry. He translated German, English, French, Italian, and Portuguese authors. *Catay* (Cathay), a volume of Chinese poems Valencia had rendered into Spanish, appeared in 1929; because he did not know Chinese, he relied on Franz Toussaint's French prose version in making Chinese poetry available to Colombians.

A theme that occurs again and again in Valencia's poetry is the haunting one of the poet who feels misunderstood by his fellow men. As a consequence, he avoids contact with the world of men and retreats into his own fantasy world. The sentiment of a world unsympathetic to the artist is expressed in poems such as "Los camellos" (The Camels):

> ¡Oh artistas! ¡Oh camellos de la Llanura vasta,
> que vais llevando el sacro Monolito!
> . . . .
> ¡Sólo calmáis vosotros la sed de lo infinito!
> *(Ritos,* 1899, p. 18)

> Oh artists! Camels of the vast plain
> who are carrying the holy Monolith!
> . . . .
> Only you are able to soothe the thirst of the infinite!

The theme of love, although not prominent in Valencia's poetry, appears in "Motivos" (Motives), a work that glorifies pure love. The composition is divided into two parts: "A la manera antigua" (In the Traditional Way) presents the theme of love in a "traditional" manner, in simple and direct images, whereas "A la manera moderna" (In the Modern Way) interprets the theme according to the symbolist school. The influence of love, how it can change a person's behavior, is the subject of "Palemón el estilita" (Palemón Perched on a Column). Palemón, a saintly man, preaches to travelers and traders in the desert on how to avoid sin, until his attention is drawn to a beautiful young woman who is listening to him and he is unable to continue with his sermon:

> Y el buen monje
> la miraba,
> la miraba,
> la miraba,
>   y queriendo hablar, no hablaba,
> y sentía su alma esclava
> de la bella pecadora de mirada tentadora,
> y un ardor nunca sentido
> sus arterias encendía,
> y un temblor desconocido
> su figura,
> larga
> y flaca
> y amarilla,
> sacudía:
> ¡era amor! . . .
> *(Ritos,* 1899, p. 97)

> And the good monk
> watched her,
> watched her,
> watched her,
>   and wanting to speak, did not speak,
> and felt his soul becoming enslaved
> by the beautiful sinner with the enticing gaze,
> and a never felt ardor
> burned his arteries
> and an unknown tremor
> shook
> his long,
> thin
> and yellow
> face:
> It was love! . . .

In Palemón's inner battle between deeply felt religious convictions and love, he chooses the latter.

Another theme of concern to the poet is the drama of life and death and how they interlock. Valencia sees life as an eternal cycle that links past, present, and future in rapid succession. The most important element in life becomes time: the poet emphasizes the brevity of every moment we live, each one bringing us closer to our ultimate destiny, death, which is within us from the moment we are born. He expresses the evanescent quality of life in "La parábola del foso" (The Parable of the Trench).

Valencia composed many poems of a religious nature. For some, his sources were the stories of the Bible, and for others he used the accounts of the church fathers. Among his best known is "San Antonio y el Centauro" (Saint Anthony and the Centaur), in which he contrasts the aesthetic beauty of the pagan world—including its deities and its ideals of force, grace, liberty, and love—with the simplicity and ethical greatness of Christ:

> El Centauro
> Y soy la Fuerza alegre; mi brazo poderoso
> sabe peiner la ninfa y estrangular el oso;
> San Antonio
> Yo soy Antonio, un siervo del Señor tu enemigo,
> que atempera sus pasos a la celeste norma de Jesús . . .
> *(Ritos,* 1899, pp. 131–132)

> The Centaur
> I represent joyful Strength; my powerful arm

is able to comb a nymph's hair and strangle a bear;
Saint Anthony
I am Anthony, a servant of the Lord your enemy,
who adjusts his steps to the celestial norm of Jesus . . .

Valencia evokes in masterly fashion the supplanting of one philosophy by another concept and another way of seeing and interpreting life.

One of Valencia's most original poems, "Anarkos" ("Anarchs"), deals with the plight of the dispossessed. Written in 1899, the work attests to a growing awareness among Latin America's intellectuals of the social and political responsibilities of the continent, a tendency typical of modernism in its evolution from escapism to greater realism. "Anarchs" is the poet's most forceful poem, and because of its social theme was useful in furthering Valencia's political campaigns. (He quoted the poem during his presidential campaign in 1917.)

Some of Valencia's most famous compositions were dedicated to Colombia. In "A Popayán," he sings the glories of his native city, describing its history, which in many ways is also the history of Colombia. In 1938, the poet was asked to compose a poem to commemorate the four-hundredth anniversary of the founding of Bogotá. "Himno a la raza" (Hymn to the Race) expresses the hopes and dreams America represents to people of other lands, especially to those who have suffered from oppression:

> . . . ¡Tierra!
> Tierra buena que acoges al hombre,
> mata el odio, cultiva el amor;
> sólo así vivirás tu destino:
> ¡una sangre, una Patria y un Dios!
> (Obras poéticas completas,
> 1952, p. 443)

> . . . Land!
> Good land that welcomes man,
> puts an end to hatred and cultivates love;
> only in this way will you fulfill your destiny:
> Of one blood, one Country and one God!

The modernists were highly selective in their use of words, and Valencia followed this precept, choosing words for their musicality. The symbolists taught Valencia the transcendent truth that words are symbols and that language developed because man is able to transform reality into poetic symbols. Both the Parnassians and the symbolists influenced Valencia in the use of color, which also plays an important role in his poetry. The former taught him the use of strong colors; from the latter he learned the importance of shading or nuance, expressed so well in Paul Verlaine's poem "Art Poétique" (Poetic Art, ca. 1874).

Like Victor Hugo, Valencia had a visual sense that was more highly developed than his auditory or olfactory senses, and the images most prevalent in his poetry are visual ones. Frequent too is the use of synesthesia. These images of mixed sensation reflect the precepts expressed in Charles Baudelaire's poem "Correspondances" ("Correspondences," first published in Les fleurs du mal, 1857), wherein the French poet suggests that "Like long echoes which mingle far away / in a shadowy and profound unity / so perfumes, colors and sounds respond to one another." This was the important model from which the symbolist school of Verlaine and Stéphane Mallarmé had emerged; to Baudelaire the symbolists owed their disdain for eloquence and their love for complex and subtle harmonies. Valencia, in his turn, was likewise strongly influenced by this attempt at forging the "complete" work of art, a concept that found its equivalent in the German word Gesamtkunstwerk, which had been coined to characterize Richard Wagner's revolutionary synthesis of the visual, the auditory, and the dramatic in his operas.

The modernists considered versification to be one of the most important elements of style, and Valencia was no exception. In "Leyendo a Silva" (Reading for Silva), he stresses his desire for perfection in versification: "sacrificar un mundo para pulir un verso" (to sacrifice a world in order to polish a verse). Valencia used traditional verse forms together with the innovations in strophe, meter, and rhyme schemes introduced by modernism, which changed Spanish prosody forever.

Valencia was not only a great poet but also an accomplished translator, rendering in Spanish poetry from different schools and different periods. The poet had a special liking for the work of Verlaine, Mallarmé, A. V. Samain, Hugo von Hofmannsthal, Stefan George, Gabriele D'Annunzio, and Eugênio de Castro, major figures of the symbolist movement. Romantic and Parnassian poets are also represented in his translations from the poetry of J. W. von Goethe, Heinrich Heine, Hugo, Théophile Gautier, Heredia, C. M. Leconte de Lisle, Baudelaire, John Keats, Oscar Wilde, J. M. Machado de Assis, and Olavo Bilac. The themes of Valencia's translations are as varied as his original poems. The poets he translated have one thing in common: all strove for perfection in their choice of vocabulary and form, and like the Colombian poet, all exhibited a universality of spirit.

Valencia was not only one of Colombia's major poets but also one of the leading orators of his time. Of the hundreds of speeches he delivered during his lifetime, only a fraction had been published until in 1973 and 1974 a three-volume edition of his *Discursos* (Speeches) appeared. The speeches fall into two groups: historical or patriotic orations and political speeches. The latter he delivered as a senator and a candidate for the presidency in 1917 and 1918 and in 1929 and 1930. Valencia recorded Colombia's history as he spoke of the accomplishments of the conquistador Sebastián de Belalcázar; the heroic figures of the struggle for independence Simón Bolívar, Camilo Torres, Francisco José de Caldas, Francisco de Paula Santander, and Antonio Ricaurte; and the politicians and statesmen of the republic Julio Arboleda, Carlos Albán, Manuel Casabianca, Miguel Antonio Caro, Rafael Uribe Uribe, and Pedro Nel Ospina. His speeches show that the poet was an outstanding historian and that he possessed an unusually varied prose vocabulary. His speeches draw on a wealth of imagery reminiscent of his poetic compositions; more than oratory, they are poetry-in-prose, and for that reason they form an integral part of his artistic oeuvre.

Influences of the literary trends from the romantic to the symbolist movements can be found in Valencia's poetry. The poet absorbed and incorporated into his work many of the ideas and innovations introduced by these schools, a practice common among the modernist poets. What makes his style unique is that he was able to blend these diverse elements into a harmonious whole, thus creating a style entirely his own. This highly personal integration can be seen in various aspects of his poetry. Foremost in his work is the classical element, as in "A Popayán," in which he used the Homeric hexameter. While allusions to the classics and antiquity can be found in his themes and vocabulary, the most notable classical characteristic in his work is the plasticity of his poetic language, which gives his images an almost three-dimensional effect. What is most remarkable about his poetry can be explained largely by this characteristic, allied with an ever-present deeper symbolic meaning. Contrary to the work of Darío, which corresponds to three clearly defined periods, Valencia's poetry did not evolve beyond, and remains linked to, the early stage of modernism. Many of the themes Valencia uses had appeared before, but he was able to endow them with new life. Whatever theme the poet chooses, whether it be taken from antiquity or the present day, it has only one purpose: to make us see by analogy and through the use of symbolic language the deeper meaning of man's emotions.

The extraordinary cultural wealth of Valencia's background is reflected in the themes and the highly original imagery displayed in his poetry and discourses, and to these may be added his rare gifts as a translator. He stands out among the poets of his time in both Colombia and the rest of Spanish America, in having such a universal outlook while at the same time identifying so intimately with the life of a single locale: his native Popayán.

SELECTED BIBLIOGRAPHY

Editions

Individual Works

Ritos. Bogotá, 1899.
A Popayán. Popayán, 1906.
Poesías. Bogotá, 1912.
Ritos. 2nd ed., expanded. With an introduction by Baldomero Sanín Cano. London, 1914.
Oraciones panegíricas. Bogotá, 1915.
Alma Mater. Popayán, 1916.
Poemas selectos. With an introduction by M. Toussaint. Mexico City, 1917.
Poemas. Buenos Aires, 1918.
Sus mejores poemas. Madrid, 1919. 2nd ed. 1926.
Polémica sobre la pena de muerte. Bogotá, 1925.
Job. Bogotá, 1927.
Catay. Bogotá, 1929.

A San Antonio de Padua en el séptimo centenario de su muerte. Popayán, 1931.

Panegíricos, discursos, artículos. Edited by A. Villa Ramírez and G. Marín. Armenia, Colombia, 1933.

Discursos. Bogotá, 1935.

El vengador de Wilde. Popayán, 1936.

Himno a la raza. Popayán, 1938.

Anarkos. Bogotá, 1941.

Collected Works

Discursos. 3 vols. With an introduction by José M. Rivas Sacconi. Bogotá, 1973–1974.

Obras poéticas completas. With an introduction by Baldomero Sanín Cano. Madrid, 1948. 2nd ed. 1952. 3rd ed. 1955.

Poemas. Selected by Josefina Valencia de Hubach. Bogotá, 1973.

Poesías y discursos. Selected and with an introduction and notes by Carlos García Prada. Madrid, 1959.

Translations

Anarkos. Translated by Cecil Miles. Medellín, Colombia, 1945.

"From Anarchs." Translated by Muna Lee. *Poetry* 26:125–126 (1925).

"Turris Eburnea." Translated by T. Walsh. *Pan American Magazine* 27:208–209 (1918).

"Two Beheadings." Translated by T. Walsh. *Pan American Magazine* 26:332–335 (1918).

"White Storks." Translated by A. S. Blackwell. *Poet Lore* 37:616–622 (1926).

Biographical and Critical Studies

Acosta Polo, Benigno. *La poesía de Guillermo Valencia.* Barranquilla, Colombia, 1965.

Arías Trujillo, Bernardo. *Balada de la cárcel de Reading.* Manizales, Colombia, 1936.

Blanco Fombona, Rufino. "Guillermo Valencia." In *El modernismo y los poetas modernistas.* Madrid, 1929. Pp. 221–235.

Castillo, Eduardo. "Guillermo Valencia íntimo." *Repertorio americano* (San José, Costa Rica) 9:13–14 (1924).

Craig, G. D. *The Modernist Trend in Spanish American Poetry.* Berkeley, Calif. 1934. Pp. 112–125; 297–300.

Cruz Santos, Camilo. "La influencia del medio ambiente en la carrera literaria de Guillermo Valencia." *Repertorio americano* (San José, Costa Rica) 17:209–211 (1928).

Duarte French, Alberto. *Guillermo Valencia.* Bogotá, 1941.

García Prada, Carlos. "El paisaje en la poesía de Guillermo Valencia." *Anuario de la Academia Colombiana* (Bogotá) 9:126–147 (1941–1942).

——. "Guillermo Valencia." In his *Poetas modernistas hispanoamericanos.* Madrid, 1956. Pp. 241–263.

Gerdes, Dick, and Tamara Holzapfel. " 'Las dos cabezas': Lo erótico y lo exótico en función de lo ético." *Hispania* 68:49–54 (1985).

Glickman, Robert J. "Guillermo Valencia and the Poetic World of *Ritos.*" Ph.D. diss., University of California, Los Angeles, 1963.

——. "Guillermo Valencia: A Psycho-Philosophical Evaluation." *Revista de Letras* (Mayagüez, P.R.) 6/21:62–73 (1974).

Holguín, Andrés. "Traducciones poéticas de Guillermo Valencia." *Revista de las Indias* (Bogotá) 54:436–446 (1943).

Karsen, Sonja. *Guillermo Valencia: Colombian Poet (1873–1943).* New York, 1951.

——. "Guillermo Valencia: Poeta modernista." *Thesaurus: Boletín del Instituto Caro y Cuervo* 35:1–8 (1980).

——. "Guillermo Valencia: El poeta como traductor." *Thesaurus: Boletín del Instituto Caro y Cuervo* 40:349–361 (1985).

Lleras Camargo, Felipe. *Un grande hombre de Colombia y América. Apuntes para una biografía.* Madrid, 1974.

Maya, Rafael. "Guillermo Valencia." In *Alabanzas del hombre y de la tierra.* Bogotá, 1934. Pp. 67–87.

——. "Sobre Guillermo Valencia." *Revista de América* (Bogotá) 2/4:56–68 (1945).

——. "Guillermo Valencia." In *Estampas de ayer y retratos de hoy.* Bogota, 1954. Pp. 233–257.

Sanín Cano, Baldomero. "Guillermo Valencia y el espíritu." In *Ensayos.* Bogotá, 1942. Pp. 57–60.

——. "Guillermo Valencia o el modernismo." *Boletín de la Comisión Chilena de Cooperación Intelectual* (Santiago) 5/34:6–16 (1943).

——. "Guillermo Valencia." In *Letras colombianas.* Mexico City, 1944. Pp. 188–192.

——. "Guillermo Valencia: La amistad y el genio." In *De mi vida y de otras vidas.* Bogotá, 1949. Pp. 57–61.

Serrano Blanco, Manuel. *Valencia.* Bucaramanga, Colombia, 1945.

Torres, Hernán, ed. *Estudios: Edición en homenaje a Guillermo Valencia 1873–1943.* Cali, Colombia, 1976.

Uribe Ferrer, René. "Guillermo Valencia." *Revista de la Universidad de Antioquia* 48:369–382 (1973).

Valencia, Gerardo. "La creación poética en *Catay.*" *Noticias culturales.* Instituto Caro y Cuervo 153:41–48 (1973).

Macedonio Fernández

(1874–1952)

Naomi Lindstrom

Macedonio Fernández has come to be recognized as a significant figure in the twentieth-century development of new forms of the novel. He is an important source of the ideas behind the Latin American "new novel" that won worldwide fame in the 1960's. Macedonio, as he is commonly known, at one time had a tenuous fame as a literary legend of Buenos Aires. Jorge Luis Borges, the most renowned contemporary Spanish-language writer, claimed him as his mentor. Numerous other Argentine literary figures, including the country's most esteemed novelist, Julio Cortázar, recognized a debt to him. Yet by 1964 the only Macedonio work in print was the 1961 anthology enthusiastically compiled by Borges. The story of this reformer of literature, whose works have become widely accessible in new editions only since 1966, is a classic case of an innovator ahead of his time, as well as of a creator reluctant to make public his innovations.

Macedonio's life and career reflected his great love of privacy and solitude. Born 1 June 1874 into a wealthy family, Macedonio was not required to work for a living, but his family sent him to the Law School of the University of Buenos Aires. During his law-school years, he established a reputation as a brilliant, self-taught student of philosophy and political theory, favoring a systematically irrationalistic view.

While it was fashionable to read such philosophers as Friedrich Nietzsche and Arthur Schopenhauer for their pessimistic outlook, Macedonio found hope in their devaluation of humankind's powers of reason. In addition, he read more traditionally logical philosophers to see how their ideas might be adapted to an intuitively based system. In 1896, he published three philosophical articles in El Tiempo.

In 1897, Macedonio completed a doctor of jurisprudence degree. He joined an expedition to found a utopian community in Paraguay, but since the settlers had given more thought to philosophical principles than to the logistics of rural life, they soon returned to the city. In 1901, Macedonio married Elena de Obieta, who died in 1920. One of their sons, Adolfo de Obieta, would later undertake to order and edit Macedonio's vast, chaotic literary estate. Macedonio neglected the legal profession, devoting himself to the reading of aesthetics and metaphysics. He began a correspondence with William James and another with the Spanish experimental writer Ramón Gómez de la Serna. The latter proved a strong source of support as Macedonio began to move from the formulation of ideas to their application in his literary texts. The two innovators drew closer through a lengthy correspondence, preserved at the University of Pittsburgh. When Gómez de la Serna joined the

Buenos Aires literary scene, first as a visiting lecturer and then as an exile, he vigorously promoted Macedonio's ideal of making readers do much of the work of creating a literary text.

In 1921, Borges became Macedonio's literary heir. Macedonio was a friend of the Borges family and was waiting to greet Borges when the latter returned to Buenos Aires. Borges had spent his teenage years in Europe and had become motivated to start an avant-garde movement of the type he had observed. He quickly recognized that Macedonio, generally considered a charming eccentric, was developing an aesthetic program parallel to the best principles of the avant-gardists. Consequently, when Borges began to organize an avant-garde group in Buenos Aires, he was eager to involve Macedonio in its activities so as to give the would-be experimentalists an example of how a radical aesthetic could be developed. Borges became the most outstanding of the writers who felt Macedonio's direct influence. Borges has said of his early mentor: "I felt Macedonio *was* metaphysics, *was* literature. I copied him to the point of transcription, of devout and passionate plagiarism. Not to imitate such a paragon would have been unthinkable." These remarks, which preface his 1961 anthology *Macedonio Fernández,* are typical of his efforts to have Macedonio's importance recognized.

During the 1920's, Macedonio was lionized by the youthful band of avant-gardists Borges had succeeded in forming in Buenos Aires. Still, he managed to retain some of his hermitlike ways. Though a featured speaker at banquets, he often failed to appear, instead sending a text to be read. This practice became a source of humor, as his speeches would allude to the fact that the speaker was elsewhere. Macedonio found the avant-gardists stimulating but also burdensome company, and he increasingly avoided contact as the 1920's wore on. He finally preferred telephone contact and letters to face-to-face encounters.

It is impressive how willing the avant-gardists and other admirers were to involve Macedonio in literary life, given his rejection of its customs. Macedonio balked at putting his writings in any sequence and, indeed, would gladly have left them strewn about here and there. He disparaged the correction of proofs, saying that errors were more original than the products of human invention. Consider, then, that

Borges made Macedonio coeditor of the magazine *Proa* (Prow) in 1922 and that other editors sought his collaboration. All Macedonio's books resulted from the efforts of friends and admirers, who coaxed his work from him and attended to all the editorial matters normally deemed the responsibility of authors. When Macedonio died on 10 February 1952, the effects of his unusual notion of literary life became clear. He left a huge miscellany of writings in great disorder and a few out-of-print books.

Macedonio's publishing history is an extraordinary one, reflecting both his eccentric ways and the changing reading public of this century. His colleagues and friends were disturbed to find that Macedonio not only neglected to publish his writings but made little effort to preserve what he had written. Visitors found Macedonio's living quarters crammed with pieces of paper to which the author had committed fragments of novels, fiction, and poetry, essays, political theory, and other notations. Papers were stuffed into furniture or clothing. Macedonio never established a home after the death of his wife, and he often left his writings behind when moving between boardinghouses or the homes of friends.

When Macedonio became the friend and "tribal elder" of the avant-gardists, they urged him to change his habits enough to permit his work to be read. Leopoldo Marechal and Raúl Scalabrini Ortiz obtained the manuscript of Macedonio's philosophical treatise written in literary form, *No toda es vigilia la de los ojos abiertos* (Eyes Open Isn't Always Awake), which Manuel Gleizer published in 1928. The following year, *Proa,* Borges' avant-garde publishing concern, produced Macedonio's literary miscellany *Papeles de recienvenido* (A Newcomer's Notes).

The publication of these two works in close succession reflects Macedonio's appeal among the avant-gardists. His subsequent publishing history gives perhaps a truer picture of the small audience that existed for Macedonio's writings. The avant-garde dissolved at the end of the 1920's, and no work by Macedonio appeared during the next decade, though vast amounts of unpublished writings were known to exist. In 1941, the Peruvian poet Alberto Hidalgo, who had participated in the Buenos Aires avant-garde, obtained Macedonio's *Una novela que comienza* (A Novel Underway) and published it with Ercilla in

Santiago, Chile, the first mainstream press to print his work. The next year Marcos Fingerit produced a small edition of Macedonio's poetry, *Muerte es beldad* (Death is Beauty).

By 1943, Macedonio's sons were grown and made an attempt to reinvolve their father in literary life. They were motivated by a loyalty to his literary achievement but also hoped to establish contact with their distant father. The magazine the three founded, *Papeles de Buenos Aires* (Buenos Aires Letters), was principally significant in reminding literary Buenos Aires of the presence of this withdrawn cultural radical. In 1944, Losada brought out an expanded edition of *Papeles de recienvenido* with a praise-filled preface by Gómez de la Serna.

As Macedonio withdrew still further, his work lapsed back into obscurity. Over the next twenty years, there appeared nothing but a posthumous volume of his poetry published in 1953 by Editorial Guaranía and edited by a devoted cousin and friend, Gabriel del Mazo; Borges' 1961 anthology; and a little-noted compilation by Adolfo de Obieta, the author's son, *Papeles de Macedonio Fernández* (Macedonio Fernández' Notes, 1965).

Up to this point, the vigorous exertions of Macedonio's enthusiasts had failed to establish him beyond the confines of a small cult of readers. The impasse was broken by the great success in the 1960's of the Latin American new novel. To appreciate the new novel, readers had to master the skills needed to approach Macedonio's work. They learned to construe meanings for fragmented texts, to accept characters who were not meant to be lifelike, and to follow narrative leaps in time and space. Starting in 1966, the publisher Centro Editor de América Latina, strongly associated with the new novelists and the cultural radicalism of the 1960's, had spectacular success in launching reissues and previously unpublished work by Macedonio, scoring unexpected best sellers. Obieta now threw himself into arranging the Macedonian oeuvre in publishable form. Because the new novel had currency all across Latin America, Macedonio's work could be grasped by readers far from Buenos Aires. The Havana publisher Casa de las Américas had success with an anthology, the 1969 *Papeles de recienvenido*, aimed at readers who knew nothing of Macedonio but understood radically ex-

perimental writing. In 1974, the centennial of Macedonio's birth, the Buenos Aires publisher Corregidor undertook to print his complete works. Though it remains incomplete, this project has brought to light such works as the novel *Adriana Buenos Aires* (1974).

Of the material to surface during the Macedonio "boom" of the late 1960's, two works are especially important. The 1966 edition of *Papeles de recienvenido* expands on the 1944 version by adding miscellaneous material selected by the author's son. The aphorisms, short texts, reflective jottings, and letters give a picture of Macedonio's rejection of realism and advocacy of new, discontinuous, irrationalistic, and antirealistic writing. *Papeles de recienvenido* is the essential Macedonio anthology, covering the range of his interests. *Museo de la novela de la Eterna* (Museum of the Novel of the Eternal Woman, 1967) is equally important but more specialized; its purpose is to convey Macedonio's vision of how readers of novels should learn to cooperate in the creative process.

The other works that appeared during this period are mostly interesting to specialists; an example is *Adriana Buenos Aires*, dedicated to satirizing at length the realist novel. The 1967 reprint of Macedonio's philosophical work of 1928, *No toda es vigilia la de los ojos abiertos*, is essentially a period or museum piece. In its literary character as a work of expository prose and in its use of highly artistic rhetoric to set forth Macedonio's mix of anarchist social philosophy and antilogical metaphysics, it illustrates the irrationalistic, intuitive concept of philosophy that was much vaunted early in the century but has since been supplanted by new breakthroughs in analytic philosophy. The other works to emerge during the Macedonio revival are even more narrowly of interest to specialized researchers or "fans"; they include letters, notebooks, and the author's rambling theoretical writings.

As Macedonio's publication history indicates, he has rapidly become a more accessible figure than the highly influential but little-read source he long had remained. The subsequent writings of "new novelists" directly or indirectly affected by Macedonio and the widespread discussion of his work during the Macedonio revival of the late 1960's and 1970's have created a readership able to follow his convoluted texts. However, it should not be thought that readers have now seen everything that Macedonio wrote. As of this writing, there are still a number of unpublished Macedonio texts, such as a rumored novel based on his whimsical campaign for the Argentine presidency.

Macedonio's poetry is the aspect of his work that has drawn the least response from critics and readers. Macedonio's prose is obviously unusual: fragmented, discontinuous, lacking conclusions. His poetry is more traditional. The author had come under the influence of Edgar Allan Poe when he needed a literary form to treat questions of death and grief. The theme of the death of a beloved woman, along with expressions of hope for an afterlife or eternal region beyond death, became the basic elements of Macedonio's poetic production. The poetry constitutes an interesting sidelight for students of Macedonio's work, but it is fair to say that if its author were not otherwise distinguished, this body of writing would not have enduring interest. These poems, relatively traditional in form, may be found in the 1966 augmented edition of *Papeles de recienvenido*.

Macedonio is widely regarded as a great influence on other writers. He has had a profound effect; but until well after his death few understood what Macedonio meant by "making readers into authors" through incomplete, sketchy writings.

The avant-gardists were so eager to proclaim Macedonio their mentor and predecessor that some failed to make the effort to understand his program of aesthetic ideas. Years later, when Germán Leopoldo García collected contemporaries' reminiscences of Macedonio, it became evident that most knew him only as an appealingly odd person. He had gone beyond them in his vigorous efforts to rethink the basis of literary communication, and they could not see the overall design that held together his many proposals for literary experimentation.

Borges is undeniably Macedonio's prime heir, but his statements about his mentor's influence also present some problems. Every reader has a unique understanding of Macedonio, and Borges is no exception. He situated Macedonio firmly on the playful side of literature. Borges followed Macedonio's lead in treating philosophical problems as the starting point for literary game-playing. Borges' "fictions" are texts that question the worth of philosophy in deter-

mining truth. A fondness for "putting on" readers and bewildering them with nonsensical intricacies are further Macedonian traits in Borges.

Borges' success in extending this line of Macedonio's thought should not obscure the fact that Macedonio also belongs on the serious side of literature. He developed his irrationalistic philosophical system not only to provoke skepticism but also to discover truth. His method of exposition was indeed fantastic and eccentric, yet he trusted it to lead him toward realities that logic would only distort. While Borges set out to deconstruct the supporting beliefs of metaphysics, Macedonio was eager to keep metaphysics alive and evolving.

Macedonio had other heirs who considered him a serious social philosopher and metaphysician. The most important of these was Raúl Scalabrini Ortiz, the much-imitated journalist who developed a style of intuitive social commentary. In his 1931 book *El hombre que está solo y espera* (The Man Who Is Alone and Waits), considered to have had a great impact on Argentine social critics and journalists, Scalabrini urges his readers to study and emulate Macedonio, "the first metaphysician of Buenos Aires," and acknowledges a great debt to his mentor's irrationalistic approach to the discussion of issues. This disciple was able to spread Macedonio's influence outside literary circles to the world of journalism.

The influence of Macedonio on a second generation of writers is illustrated by Julio Cortázar, Argentina's foremost novelist. Born too late to join the avant-garde, Cortázar shared its enthusiasms and brought them into the current era. In his acclaimed novel *Rayuela* (*Hopscotch*, 1963) Cortázar paid a perceptive tribute to Macedonio. A fictional literary theorist in this work, Morelli, is evidently modeled after Macedonio. Even though his proposals for reforming the novel and human thought sound bizarre and extreme, they are not so dissimilar from the principles that serve to organize the text of *Hopscotch* itself. As a result, Cortázar makes the implied overall statement that one can marvel at the eccentricity of Macedonio's literary and philosophical ideas and yet utilize them to some extent in the elaboration of texts meant to be aesthetically satisfying and to deal with human and philosophical ideas.

The post-Cortázar generation of Argentine writers

has also been quick to pay homage to Macedonio's ideas for fragmenting the novel and making novel writing a game between author and reader. The "novelists of language" of the 1970's, who were also influenced by such experimentalists as William Burroughs of the United States, named their journal *Macedonio* and acknowledged a debt to him for his pioneering use of fragmented and truncated textual fragments and "silent" writing (that is, literature that does not explicitly signal its meaning or purpose).

Outside the Argentine literary scene where the debt to Macedonio is most evident, the Latin American new novel embodies many of the author's proposed measures for making the novel more discontinuous and less realistic. English-language readers familiar with the writings of the Colombian Gabriel García Márquez or the Mexican Carlos Fuentes, to name two outstanding practitioners, already have a start on mastering Macedonio's sometimes convoluted and inaccessible texts. These writers did not have enough contact with Macedonio or his work to count as direct recipients of his influence. Yet it is widely recognized that Macedonio did much to set in motion the process of change that resulted in the new novel.

Non-Argentine new novelists did not grow up hearing the legends of and tributes to Macedonio that are part of Buenos Aires literary life. They cannot be considered direct heirs as can Borges and Cortázar. Yet they came of age in a period when novels were becoming less continuous, their characters less lifelike, and their meanings less clearly established. These are the very reforms that Macedonio proposed.

However impressive Macedonio may be as a precursor of later developments, it is important to recognize him as an original thinker and creator in his own right. His life work has an independent status as an example of what one individual can accomplish with a universal plan to reconceptualize and remake literature. Macedonio should be deemed both a great influence and a major twentieth-century innovator comparable to such quintessentially modern figures as Ezra Pound or André Breton.

The critic Noé Jitrik proved extremely helpful to the new readers who approached Macedonio's work during its revival. He encouraged these modern readers to use what they knew about twentieth-century experimental writing to make sense of Macedonio's work. In "La novela futura de Macedonio Fernández," (The Future Novel of Macedonio Fernández), Jitrik sees the innovator's writings as a call for the realist novel of his time to move forward—and well beyond—what today is considered the modern novel. With hindsight, readers can see that Macedonio was struggling to replace such traditional novelistic features as linear plot, lifelike characters, and the observance of everyday logic.

While recommending the reading of Macedonio's work as a summons to the making of the new novel, Jitrik warns against examining a page of Macedonian writing as if it were a page from a treatise on the novel. Macedonio preferred a tangled form of exposition that illustrated his ideal of irrationalistic, discontinuous writing. As a result, he may seem to propound incompatible notions.

Good general advice to Macedonio's readers would be not to guide themselves by any of his statements in isolation. Rather, the best method is to consider the overall tendency that emerges from the many statements he puts forward. The pattern to be found in his assertions about literature should then be checked against his actual literary practice. When Macedonio repeatedly urges a given reform of writing and then implements this innovation in his own work, it can be counted as one of his basic tenets.

All of Macedonio's texts should be understood as performing two functions. First, they constitute a call for the invention of a new form of expression, one in which readers will be much more active in the development of the work's meaning and in which verisimilitude will be abandoned. Second, they give readers an exercise in comprehending sample passages of this "future novel." His own writings do not constitute the utopian "good literature," but they foreshadow it and provide a transition toward it. Because the true future novel has not yet been produced, and because readers do not yet know how to read it, Macedonio casts himself in the role of the incautious experimenter who is willing to make mistakes and fall into ridiculous inconsistencies in his efforts to move toward this ideal.

The two texts most essential to seeing how these ideas work are *Papeles de recienvenido* in the expanded edition of 1966, and, somewhat more difficult to approach, *Museo de la novela de la Eterna.* The first of these is an especially good starting point because it contains an abundance of Macedonio's bons mots, or *ocurrencias.* These are sentences containing a memorable violation of everyday logic. Macedonio's mots often go against commonly held notions of space, time, and causality; they may quantify, evaluate, and compare entities that are either absolute or nonexistent. Another category derives humor from exposing the arbitrariness of standard fictional conventions. Here is a sampling from *Papeles de recienvenido:*

So many people didn't come that if one more had shown up, there would have been no room for him (p. 153).

He was so stubborn and boorish that up to the instant before he died, he was living (p. 153).

The autobiography of such a stranger it's not even known whether he's the one (p. 131).

Hurry up; we won't have time to miss the train (p. 330).

I've booked passage to an undiscovered country (p. 151).

He was so ugly that even people uglier than he was weren't that ugly (p. 153).

When the *ocurrencias* happen in Macedonio's philosophical writings and fiction works, they often bring the argument or plot being developed to a halt, after which it is not resumed.

A serious reader of Macedonio aspires to go beyond these elegant jokes to envision his overall program. *Papeles de recienvenido* begins with Macedonio's toasts, letters, and other occasional pieces testifying to his involvement in the avant-garde of the 1920's. The newcomer in question is Macedonio himself, startled that after years of solitary literary labor he should suddenly be thrust into the effervescent high life of the Buenos Aires literary scene. The newcomer's eccentric concept of literature prevents him from complying with the code of literary life, and he is perpetually "out of step." A typical format is the toast that somehow deviates from its supposed function. In many cases, Macedonio planned not to attend the literary banquets for which the toasts were written, and instead composed elaborate jokes around the

oddity of a speaker toasting an admired friend by proxy.

"Artículo diferente" (Different Article), a brief note from this original section, illustrates the newcomer's role as literary deviant: Macedonio has been engaged to write an article for an avant-garde literary review but finds the specifications too conventional. The article must be "fenced in, come with a solution ready at hand, and it all has to go in just one space." One should recall that for Macedonio, "good" writing could appear in fragmentary form in many places; he thought of dispersing a novel in pieces throughout Buenos Aires and requiring readers to find these shreds and assemble from them a literary work. In "Artículo diferente," despite misgivings, he agrees to commit his text to one specified space, but in other respects he is incorrigibly deviant. For example, the main point of the article is to explain why Macedonio finds it so difficult to adapt to the standards of literary publishing. However, other thematically diverse material intrudes among the statements of Macedonio's "difference." To further provoke the reader to a stimulating state of confusion, Macedonio does not specify the alternatives he envisions to what he calls "written out" and "bounded" literature. This information must be constructed by readers from hints and suggestions scattered here and there throughout the newcomer's writings.

The persona of the literary newcomer also allows Macedonio to applaud those avant-garde projects that move away from the conventions deplored in "Artículo diferente" and its companion piece, "Un articulo que no colabora" (An Article That Doesn't Collaborate). Chief among these is Alberto Hidalgo's *Revista oral (Oral Magazine).* This venture requires collaborators to speak all the items that would normally appear in a magazine, from the information on the masthead titles and bylines to the content of editorials and stories. This project fit Macedonio's aesthetic ideal. Listening to what was routinely read made the magazine format seem unfamiliar and roused an awareness of the arbitrariness of journalistic conventions. Moreover, reading aloud and following oral discourse absorbed more of the audience's attention than the relatively passive act of reading a magazine. Macedonio's praise for this enterprise is high but, as usual, convoluted and indirect; in his material written for this magazine, he calls it the best one "never read" and suggests it will reveal reading and writing to be defective human activities. In the same spirit, Macedonio applauds such unusual formats as a wall magazine that avant-gardists plastered upon walls and sides of buildings. In other words, the more the avant-garde exerts itself to undo the standard procedures and expectations of literary activity, the more praise it draws; but the reasons for the praise are hidden in a tangle of intricately witty, conceitful language.

The rest of the expanded *Papeles de recienvenido* is composed of writings from many periods of Macedonio's life and reflects his love of digression and fragmentation. These texts are helpful in gaining an idea of Macedonio's chief strategies for disrupting the reader's tendency to read without giving thought to the way narratives are organized or contributing an effort of imagination. Some texts terminate abruptly, with instructions to the reader to develop a suitable ending. In other cases, the segments of the text lack continuity with one another; the subject matter may change, or the narration of an anecdote may suddenly give way to notebook-style jottings on art, language, and philosophy. Macedonio suggests projects for novels to be undertaken in the future, when readers are better prepared to take upon themselves the major burden of elaboration. These include a novel composed of rumors or hints, which the reader must act upon as he sees fit; an already existing or already planned set of actions that constitutes a novel (perhaps illustrated in real life by Macedonio's absurdist campaign for the presidency); a perfect novel developed in thought by a group of author-readers but never translated into text; and various plans for making an abstraction the hero of a novel.

Reading the many proposals in *Papeles de recienvenido* for a new novel is a good preparation for approaching *Museo de la novela de la Eterna*. This work, which consists primarily of prefaces and afterwords, has as its main purpose to undo the working rules of realist fiction. To prevent the reader from identifying with the characters or becoming involved in their destinies, none of the protagonists is assigned a stable, recognizable set of traits or made to pursue a course of action. There is a good deal less reference to the characters and their attributes than to the novel

itself and how it is meant to work. Macedonio believed that no novel had the right to hide from the reader the processes by which it was constructed and those by which it gave meaning to characters and events. In *Museo*, the mockery of the mechanisms of narrative is carried to an extreme. One finds lengthy passages explicating the rationale behind the work and the decisions the author had to make to arrive at the work as it stands; alternative possibilities are considered as well. The result may be compared to a sculpture that is displayed at various stages in its progress, together with the sculptor's notes, sketches, and discussion of his creative decisions; however, the work is never seen in a completed form.

However proficient readers become at understanding Macedonio's writings, they should remember that the author gave less importance to what he had written than to what he had refrained from writing, his "silence." By his cultivation of silence, he did not mean literal cessation of literary activity and expression. Instead, this concept embraced both the sketchiness and insubstantiality of certain literary texts, which would force readers to invent their own connective material, and the development of plans for an unwritten novel.

In the first category—silence within written texts—Macedonio included many literary strategies that would assign the reader more responsibility for developing meaning out of the words on the page. A typical plan was to omit the contextualizing clues that hint to readers how a text is to be understood. In the expanded *Papeles de recienvenido* of 1966, for instance, one finds such peculiar stories as that of "El zapallo que se hizo cosmos" (The Squash That Became the Cosmos) and "Autobiografía por correo" (Autobiography by Mail). The events described appear ludicrous; for example, the two texts respectively tell of the unstoppable growth of a vegetable and the arrival in the mail of a startled individual's autobiography, written, without his participation, by a stranger. The abrupt start and unfinished termination of these narratives require the reader to judge what they contain of slapstick, allegory, and aesthetic experimentation.

Following the second notion of silence, Macedonio urges readers and friends to undertake what would today be called happenings or performance art. Macedonio was eager to launch an elaborate happening in which readers trained in creative reading-as-authorship would become characters. During the period this novel was being elaborated through the characters' actions, the city in which the event occurred would be not only a real-world metropolis, but also a fictional setting; the time that passed would be real time but also its novelistic representation. This and other novels remain to be read, and authored, by readers even bolder and more imaginative than those who learned to construe their own meanings from the fragments offered in Macedonio's written work. The "future novel" as Macedonio envisioned it extends well beyond current-day literary practice into a utopian future of readers ready to take responsibility for the form of the literary text.

Macedonio's contribution to literature includes his influence on particular individuals, especially his disciple Borges; his more general influence on the climate of literary opinion, which he helped to turn against realism; and the works he wrote. As a source of ideas utilized by other writers, Macedonio is becoming more widely recognized. In addition to his direct effect on such luminaries as Borges and Cortázar, Macedonio's more general pioneering of the ideas of the "new novel" has won wide attention. This innovator's literary production has become easier to appreciate with the new editions of his work. Most difficult to assess is the accuracy of Macedonio's vision of the literary future. The Latin American new novel certainly fulfills many of Macedonio's precepts for the utopian future novel but is still too "written out" to qualify as the perfect novel with its strong element of "silence." Such art forms as the happening live up to other of Macedonio's ideals, but such typically Macedonian notions as the novel without a text have not yet been attempted. It remains for future observers to see how close readers and writers come to the ideal conditions of silence, reader participation, and spontaneous invention that Macedonio urged as essential to a new literary age.

SELECTED BIBLIOGRAPHY

First Editions

No toda es vigilia la de los ojos abiertos: Arreglo de papeles que dejó un personaje de novela creado por el arte, Deunamor

el No Existente Caballero, el estudioso de su esperanza. Buenos Aires, 1928.

Papeles de recienvenido. Buenos Aires, 1929.

Una novela que comienza. Santiago, Chile, 1941.

Muerte es beldad. La Plata, Argentina, 1942.

Poemas. Mexico City, 1953.

Macedonio Fernández. Edited by Jorge Luis Borges. Buenos Aires, 1961.

Papeles de Macedonio Fernández. Edited by Adolfo de Obieta. Buenos Aires, 1965.

Museo de la novela de la Eterna. Buenos Aires, 1967.

Cuadernos de todo y nada. Buenos Aires, 1972.

Teorías. Buenos Aires, 1974.

Adriana Buenos Aires: Ultima novela mala. Buenos Aires, 1974.

Manera de una psique sin cuerpo. Edited by Tomás Guido Lavalle. Barcelona, 1973.

Later Editions

Papeles de recienvenido: Continuación de la nada. Buenos Aires, 1944.

Papeles de recienvenido. Poemas. Relatos, cuentos, miscelánea. Edited by Adolfo de Obieta. Buenos Aires, 1966.

No toda es vigilia la de los ojos abiertos y otros escritos. Buenos Aires, 1967.

Papeles de recienvenido. Havana, 1969. (A selection of Macedonio's writings not corresponding to other editions under this title.)

Museo de la novela de la Eterna. Buenos Aires, 1975.

Epistolario. Edited by Alicia Borinsky. Buenos Aires, 1976.

Translations

Macedonio: Selected Writings in Translation. Edited by Jo Anne Engelbert. Fort Worth, Tex., 1984. This anthology is the work of several translators.

Biographical and Critical Studies

Barrenechea, Ana María. "Macedonio Fernández y su humorismo de la nada." In *La literatura fantástica en Argentina.* Mexico City, 1957. Pp. 37–53.

Borinsky, Alicia. "Macedonio: Su proyecto novelístico." *Hispamérica* 1/1:31–48 (1972).

Engelbert, Jo Anne. *Macedonio Fernández and the Spanish American New Novel.* New York, 1978.

Jitrik, Noé. *La novela futura de Macedonio Fernández.* Caracas, 1973.

Lindstrom, Naomi. *Macedonio Fernández.* Lincoln, Nebr., 1981.

Murchison, John C. "The Visible Work of Macedonio Fernández." In *The Cardinal Points of Borges,* edited by Lowell Dunham and Ivar Ivask. Norman, Okla., 1971. Pp. 55–62.

Rodríguez Monegal, Emir. "Macedonio Fernández, Borges y el ultraísmo." *Número* 19:171–183 (1952).

Leopoldo Lugones

(1874–1938)

Merlin H. Forster

One of the major figures in turn-of-the-century Spanish American modernism, Leopoldo Lugones was younger than some of the other principals, notably José Martí and Rubén Darío. Lugones' first literary contributions came in the late 1890s, and he was a presence to be reckoned with in Argentina and Spanish America well into the fourth decade of the twentieth century. He was widely esteemed as a creative writer, journalist, and public speaker, and his more than thirty-five published volumes include poetry, prose fiction, political commentary, historical and educational treatises, and literary and cultural studies. A person of strongly held but not always consistent opinions (he defended socialism as a young man and just as energetically supported fascism in his later years), Lugones enjoyed a good fight and was never distant from controversy in defending his literary, cultural, and political views.

Leopoldo Lugones y Argüello was born on 13 June 1874 in Villa de Santa María del Río Seco, a small community in the province of Córdoba. His early years were spent in that rural area, and at the age of nine he moved with his family to the provincial capital, Córdoba. There he completed his formal education (secondary school and brief attendance at the Colegio Nacional) and began, still as a very young man, a lifelong commitment to the profession of letters, including public speaking and journalism.

In 1896 he took up residence in Buenos Aires, where a modest position in the postal service allowed him to continue his literary and journalistic activities. Later the same year he married Juana González, daughter of a prominent Córdoban family; she was his companion throughout his life and the inspiration for some of his poetic works. In the national capital he was soon in touch with a number of young writers and poets, including Rubén Darío. Within a few months Lugones had also allied himself with the socialist cause, writing for such militant journals as *La vanguardia* (The Avant-garde) and *La montaña* (The Mountain, which he himself helped to found) and speaking in many public meetings. Darío received the younger poet with a laudatory article entitled "Leopoldo Lugones: A Socialist Poet," in which he made this rather prophetic observation: "Time will teach you many things. Among them the fact that ideas evolve and colors change. I have noticed today quite by chance that the red streamers which were left in the streets at carnival time are now completely white (*El Tiempo*, 12 May 1896).

Lugones' first major book, an audacious collection of poetry he called *Las montañas del oro* (Mountains of Gold), appeared in Buenos Aires in 1897, the first in a steady stream of books and monographs published in the Argentine capital (only one of his major works, a 1912 collection of poems done in Paris, was printed elsewhere). In 1901 he was named visiting official in the National Department of Secondary and Normal Education, and in 1904 Inspector General of Education. He traveled widely within the country and also held special commissions during these years; several historical studies and publications on Argentine secondary education resulted from these experiences. Lugones was a born educator, a man of energy and strong views who was nonetheless able to achieve only a portion of the educational reforms he had envisioned.

Lugones had several periods of residence abroad, which gave him an international view and a firsthand involvement in many of the events that shaped his world. In 1906 he traveled to Europe for the first time with an assignment from the Argentine government to study educational systems in France and Switzerland. He and his family spent most of the period from 1911 through 1914 in Paris and London, which enabled him to establish closer relations with European writers and also with Latin American writers abroad. He continued his association with Darío, now also a resident in Europe, and carried forward his own voluminous literary and journalistic endeavors. In 1914 he founded in Paris the ambitious literary and cultural journal *Revue sud-américaine*, from the pages of which he could express a unique Latin American point of view. In its first number (only nine numbers appeared), he envisioned a significant role to be played by American politics and culture in the onrushing events that threatened to engulf the whole world: "We are clearly on the eve of a new conflict, analogous to that of the Holy Alliance against liberal Europe; we [the American republics] can represent, for civilization as it becomes progressively more democratic, what we were for the equilibrium of the Old World." In 1919 and 1924 Lugones was once again in Europe; on the first occasion he visited war zones at the invitation of the French government and on the second he was a member of a League of Nations commission.

During the same years Lugones carried on an active program of literary and political activities in Argentina. In 1907 he resigned from his position in the

Ministry of Education and as an independent journalist launched a noisy campaign against President Figueroa Alcorta. He took an important part in the 1910 centenary of independence, which also marks a turn toward national concerns in his own work. Four of his books appeared in that year, foremost among them *Odas seculares* (Secular Odes), which included "Oda a los ganados y las mieses," (Ode to Livestock and Harvests) written especially for the occasion. In 1911 he prepared and published, at the specific request of the National Council of Education, his *Historia de Sarmiento* (History of Sarmiento); in 1915 he was appointed librarian for the same council, a post he was to hold until his death. In 1913 Lugones presented a series of brilliant lectures on José Hernández' gaucho epic *Martín Fierro*, which were then published in 1916 as *El payador* (The Singer). And, as Darío had earlier intuited, Lugones turned away from his passionate advocacy of socialism and during the war years declared himself in support of the Anglo-Franco European democracies. He engaged in a typically energetic campaign in favor of Argentine intervention in the conflict, speaking often and writing voluminously in support of his ideas. These were gathered together in *Mi beligerancia* (My Belligerence, 1917) and *La torre de Casandra* (Cassandra's Tower, 1919).

By the early 1920's Lugones had begun yet another series of literary and political encounters. His own creative work, particularly in such poetry collections as the 1924 *Romancero* (Ballads) and the 1928 *Poemas solariegos* (Poems of the Old Homestead), showed ever more clearly an increasing commitment to simplicity of form and to traditional Argentine values. He came into sharp conflict, however, with younger writers, especially those grouped around the journal *Martín Fierro*, who boldly suggested that a revolutionary process of innovation was once again in order, and for whom Lugones was the prototypical outmoded figure of the immediate past.

Lugones' political ideas took still another turn, this time toward the reactionary right, a change that he defended with his usual vehemence and dogmatism. He became more and more discouraged with postwar developments both in Argentina and in the European democracies he had defended, and in a series of public speeches delivered in the Teatro Coliseo in

Appears like a perfect isosceles triangle, alongside the
  obese mother-in-law,
Who takes on her salamander role
With a gross
Diving-suit inflation,
While like the comings and goings of a poorly-handled
  sloop
The solid citizens of this family enjoy their fireworks.

The next four collections, all less polemical and
experimental, make up a second period in the development of Lugones' poetry. *Odas seculares* was published in 1910 as one of the poet's contributions to
the first centenary of Argentine independence and
represents a turning point in his development toward
Argentine themes and imagery. The collection includes ten individual compositions, all of them in
solid hendecasyllabic strophes, written to praise heroic places and people: the River Plate, the Andes,
Buenos Aires, the gaucho, the founders of the nation. The best-known text here is the 1,500-line
long "A los ganados y las mieses" which celebrates
the fertile expanses of the Argentine pampa and the
men and animals who move across its surface:

> Piérdese el tren por los desiertos campos,
> Al paso que en vedijas perezosas
> Se deshacen sus blancas balas de humo
> Por las cañadas húmedas de sombra.
> En vasta dispersión pace el rebaño
> Que entre el profuso pastizal engorda,
> Asegurando al semental pujante
> Su plantel de lucientes vaquillonas.

The train disappears into the empty countryside,
While in lazy tangles
Its white balls of smoke are dissipated
In the dark and humid stream courses.
The herd grazes in wide dispersion
And becomes fat in the lush pasture land,
Assuring the powerful breeding male
His school of resplendent heifers.

El libro fiel (Book of Fidelity), published in Paris in
1912, is a book of delicate love poems that Lugones
dedicated to his wife. One of the best poems in the
collection is "La Blanca soledad" (White Solitude),
in which, with assonant rhyme and irregular line
lengths, the poet is aware only of the absence of his

beloved amidst the spectral forms of the night. *El libro
de los paisajes* (Book of Landscapes, 1917), and *Las
horas doradas* (The Golden Hours, 1922) are contemplative in tone and make use of simple poetic forms
and limpid images in the presentation of the beauties
of the poet's rural world: trees, birds, flowers, butterflies, animals, as well as the cyclic natural forces that
affect them. Perhaps the best poem from these
collections, and certainly the most frequently anthologized, is "Salmo pluvial" (Pluvial Psalm), from *El
libro de los paisajes*. In four titled and progressively
shorter segments, the poet communicates in an
impressive fashion the visual, auditory, and olfactory
impressions of an onrushing summer thunderstorm.
The last two segments describe the returning calm
after the storm has passed:

> CALMA
> Delicia de los árboles que abrevó el aguacero.
> Delicia de los gárrulos raudales en desliz.
> Cristalina delicia del trino del jilguero.
> Delicia serenísima de la tarde feliz.

> PLENITUD
> El cerro azul estaba fragrante de romero,
> Y en los profundos campos silbaba la perdiz.

> CALM
> The delight of the trees which the storm has watered.
> The delight of the noisy torrents as they flow downward.
> The crystalline delight of the linnet bird's song.
> The most serene delight of a happy afternoon.

> FULLNESS
> The blue hills smelled of rosemary
> And in the deep fields the partridge was calling.

A third period in the development of Lugones'
poetry is made up of his last three collections, which
together represent the poet's increasing interest in
the heroic past and the epic poetic forms capable of
expressing that past. *Romancero* (Ballads), published
in 1924, makes use of certain established poetic and
musical patterns, such as the ballad, the lied, and the
romanza, in expressing the theme of romantic love.
Poemas solariegos, from 1928, and the posthumous
Romances del Río Seco, show the same interest in the
epic form of the ballad and other recognized forms but
tie that interest much more strongly to an Argentine

setting than was the case in *Romancero*. These stanzas from "El reo" (The Criminal), from *Romances del Río Seco*, give a sense of both the strong story line of many of these poems, as well as the traditional tone and form of the Spanish ballad:

> Apenas la villa ocupa
> La vanguardia federal,
> Pone en la plaza el banquillo
> De la pena capital.
>
> Así entonces lo estilaban
> Los ejércitos, señores,
> Para terror de enemigos
> Y escarmiento de traidores.
> . . . .
> No bien raya el nuevo día,
> Todo el pueblo acude a ver.
> Si no se ha quedado un hombre,
> Menos falta una mujer.
>
> Había corrido la voz
> Que el reo era un lindo mozo,
> Medio de mala cabeza,
> Pero de muy buen carozo.

As soon as the town is occupied
By the federal vanguard
They put in the central plaza
The capital punishment platform.

Back then, sirs
That's the way the army did things
In order to scare enemies
And give an example to traitors.
. . . .
No sooner does the new day break
Than the whole town comes out to see.
If no man has remained at home
Then much less any woman.

The rumor had gotten around
that the criminal was a handsome kid,
A little crazy maybe
But really good at heart.

Prose Fiction

An important dimension of turn-of-the-century modernism in Spanish America is the development of an "artistic" fictional prose, and Lugones published two works in the first decade of the century that place him alongside Martí, Darío, and others in that development. The first, and one of Lugones' most unusual works, is *La guerra gaucha* (The Gaucho War), which appeared in 1905, had many subsequent editions, and was made into a motion picture. More a historical epic than a totally fictional novel, *La Guerra Gaucha* is a series of twenty-three interrelated episodes dealing with the life and exploits of Martín Güemes, a *gaucho* hero in the nineteenth-century struggle for independence in the Argentine Northeast. As Allen Phillips points out in his excellent study (*La Torre* 5/17 [1957]), the work has two principal dimensions: a naturalistic concentration on violent action and compelling individual figures, which also allows Lugones to make use of his encyclopedic knowledge of rural and gaucho life, and an alternating lyrical depiction of the countryside, in which the author displays his command of the chromatic subtleties of modernist literary language. In addition, the book is written in a complex and almost overworked style—Jorge Luis Borges calls it baroque—which makes it very tough going even for an Argentine reader. (Lugones' son added lengthy notes and a glossary to the 1948 edition.) These qualities can be seen in this passage from "A muerte" (To the Death), in which a member of the rebel troop is dying amidst the beauties of a late afternoon:

> A young guerrilla fighter lay under the trees, on his back and opening and closing his mouth in a death rattle. On his dark cheeks was the beginning of a blondish beard. His chiripa of blue merino wool and his short black jacket both gave evidence of luxurious quality. . . . The sweat stood out on his eyebrows and upper lip; a shadow was cast across his eyelids and his lips were brought together in agony.
>
> The afternoon gathered its shimmering fabric in the western sky. In the distance, against a field of dull gold, dark stands of trees could be seen. Touched with gold in spots or dipped in vermillion, the clouds unrolled themselves, spinning and carding their threads and balls of yarn, like great cats stretching. They were pushed toward the horizon by the waves of a large cloud, from whose layers blood seemed to ooze. The tops of some hills showed a green cast while below they were still a smoky blue. The smell of thyme and pennyroyal hung heavy in the air.

In 1906 Lugones published a collection of short stories, entitled *Las fuerzas extrañas* (Strange Forces), which is poles apart from *La guerra gaucha* and represents a significant contribution to the development of fantastic fiction. The twelve tales of the collection (plus a curious essay on cosmogony) have nothing to do with the intense Argentinism nor the involved style of the preceding work. Rather, they make clear Lugones' fascination with the occult and with scientific experimentation, as well as a debt to such writers as Edgar Allan Poe. Lugones' originality is very much in evidence in this collection, especially in such tales as "La lluvia de fuego" (The Firestorm), "Los caballos de Abdera" (Abdera's Horses), and "Yzur" (Yzur), and yet another facet of his immense creativity as a writer is developed. "Yzur" is one of Lugones' masterpieces. The persona of the story, never identified by name, acquires a chimpanzee, Yzur, and attempts to train him to speak, using the theory that the lack of speech in simians comes from conscious abstention and not from incapacity. The narrator works over a number of years, using the best theories of speech and training (and even beating the animal in a fit of temper), but to no avail. Yzur sickens and with his dying breath apparently confirms the narrator's initial idea:

> The monkey, with his eyes wide open, was definitely dying this time, and his expression was so human that it filled me with horror. But his hand and his eyes motioned me toward him with such eloquence that I had to bend over near his face; then, with his last breath, which crowned and destroyed my hopes at the same time, came—I am certain—came in a sigh (how can I explain the tone of a voice that has not spoken for ten thousand centuries?) these words, whose humanity brought our two species together:—*Master, water. I love, my master . . .*

Lugones continued his involvement with the fantastic in *Cuentos fatales* (Fatal Stories), which was published in 1924. The five stories included in this work, of which the best is probably "El puñal" (The Dagger), are longer, slower moving, and in general not up to the standard set by the best of the previous collection. Lugones' only attempt at a full-length novel, which he published in 1926 under the title *El ángel de la sombra* (The Angel of Shadow), was even less successful and deserves no further commentary.

Essays

As we have already observed, Lugones was a prolific journalist, essayist, and public speaker, and he published during his lifetime some twenty volumes of prose writings that contain his views on a multitude of literary, cultural, and political topics. There is obviously not enough space here to deal at length with this dimension of Lugones' work, but a brief characterization of major groupings is in order.

The largest single segment of Lugones' prose is made of educational, historical, and biographical studies. His early involvement with educational assessment and reform motivated *La reforma educacional* (Educational Reform), an acerbic 1903 denunciation of the minister of education and his policies, and *Didáctica* (Didactics), an extensive educational commentary that appeared in the centenary year of 1910. *El imperio jesuítico* (The Jesuit Empire) was an erudite 1904 historical essay on the Jesuit colonies established in the province of Misiones and in Paraguay, based on extensive firsthand travel through those areas. Lugones developed over the years an interest in Greek civilization, in particular its interconnections with Argentine culture, and works such as *Prometeo* (Prometheus)—another of the books published at the occasion of the 1910 celebration—and the 1919 semianthropological essay *Las industrias de Atenas* (Athenian Industries) are substantial expressions of that interest. Finally, Lugones was an accomplished if not always evenhanded biographer. His best work in this field is the 1911 *Historia de Sarmiento*, which provides a vivid portrait of the major nineteenth-century figure, without excessive adulation. *Elogio de Ameghino* (In Honor of Ameghino, 1915) was devoted to the life and work of the Argentine paleontologist Carlos Ameghino and, as already mentioned, a biography on the nineteenth-century Argentine statesman Julio Roca was left incomplete by Lugones at the time of his death.

Lugones' political works represent the next largest segment of his prose writings. These generally came late in his career, and were often the compilation of the very frequent political speeches for which Lugones was famous. Examples are *Mi beligerancia* and *La torre de Casandra*, which represent his interventionist position in World War I, *La organización de la paz* (The Organization for Peace), a 1925 commentary on postwar developments, and *La patria fuerte, La grande Argentina* (Heroic Argentina), and *Política revolucionaria* (In Defense of Revolution), all of which were published in 1930 and 1931 in support of Lugones' promilitary position.

A final segment of Lugones' prose writings has to do with his literary and cultural interests. For example, he continued his studies on Greek culture and literature with *Estudios helénicos* (Hellenic Studies, 1924) and *Nuevos estudios helénicos* (New Hellenic Studies, 1928). The materials in these collections are based on lectures given in Buenos Aires and include both comments on Homer's epic poems and translations from the original Greek into Spanish. Lugones' best work as a literary critic, however, is *El payador*, which centers on José Hernández' *Martín Fierro*. Based in large part on a highly successful series of public lectures presented in Buenos Aires in 1913, *El payador* is the introductory portion, published in 1916 as *El hijo de la pampa* (Son of the Pampa), of a projected three-volume study and annotated edition of Hernández' poem. The other two volumes were never completed, but in this initial volume we have a major exposition of Lugones' ideas on epic poetry and the place that the Argentine poem should have in this genre. The work has ten chapters, proceeding from a general epic vision to a much more specific reading and commentary on the text itself. As might be expected, the expository style makes evident the initial oral presentation, and as readers we find once again in Lugones' prose vividness of image, command of expressive language, and compelling handling of often controversial concepts. In the following passage, taken from "La poesia gaucha" (Gaucho Poetry), Lugones makes a connection between Martín Fierro and the ancient wandering troubadours:

The bucolic themes of those ancients were love, the secrets of nature, interpretations of fate: exactly the same things that happen in the singing duel between Martín Fierro and the black man, which can be taken as a prime example in this area.

In this respect, I have seen scenes in the La Rioja carnival celebrations that are completely Greek in character; the most typical among them is that of the costumed groups which move through the streets, made up of eight or ten individuals mounted on donkeys, with faces whitened with flour and crowns made of vines, going from house to house singing *vidalitas* (little folk poems). Generally an old man sings the verses, and the whole group, as a chorus, sings the endings.

Leopoldo Lugones was a major literary and cultural figure, who, as his modernist associate Rubén Darío early predicted, was destined to undergo almost constant change in his life and writings. As a poet he moved from noisy socialist verse to an obviously modernist verse to a studied classical simplicity, through a number of different styles, without staying with any pattern for too long. As a novelist and short story writer he delved deep into both Argentine life and into the realm of the fantastic; as a historian and literary critic he worked toward an enhanced appreciation of the heroic values of both the ancient Greeks and popular Argentine literature and culture. As a journalist and political commentator he moved from the position of a committed socialist in his early years to unquestioning support for fascism and the military in the latter part of his life. Allen Phillips asserts that it is impossible to encompass Lugones and his work within any single term or literary school and suggests that the constants of this complex and always controversial writer are his insistent search for aesthetic beauty and his passionate devotion to his Argentine homeland. Now somewhat removed from his time, we might perhaps frequently disagree with Lugones' ideas, or find some of his works to be less convincing that we would like. There can be no doubt, however, that he was one of a handful of literary figures from the first decades of the twentieth century who helped shape Latin American literature as it is today.

SELECTED BIBLIOGRAPHY

First Editions

Poetry

Las montañas del oro. Buenos Aires, 1897.
Los crepúsculos del jardín. Buenos Aires, 1905.
Lunario sentimental. Buenos Aires, 1909.
Odas seculares. Buenos Aires, 1910.

El libro fiel. Paris, 1912.

El libro de los paisajes. Buenos Aires, 1917.

Las horas doradas. Buenos Aires, 1922.

Romancero. Buenos Aires, 1924.

Poemas solariegos. Buenos Aires, 1928.

Romances del Río Seco. Buenos Aires, 1938.

Fiction

La guerra gaucha. Buenos Aires, 1905.

Las fuerzas extrañas. Buenos Aires, 1906.

Cuentos. Buenos Aires, 1916.

Cuentos fatales. Buenos Aires, 1924.

El ángel de la sombra. Buenos Aires, 1926.

Essays

La reforma educacional, un ministro y doce académicos. Buenos Aires, 1903.

El imperio jesuítico; Ensayo histórico. Buenos Aires, 1904.

Didáctica. Buenos Aires, 1910.

Las limaduras de Hephaestos. 1: *Piedras liminares* 2: *Prometeo.* Buenos Aires, 1910.

Historia de Sarmiento. Buenos Aires, 1911.

Elogio de Ameghino. Buenos Aires, 1915.

El payador. 1: *Hijo de la pampa.* Buenos Aires, 1916.

Mi beligerancia. Buenos Aires, 1917.

La torre de Casandra. Buenos Aires, 1919.

Las industrias de Atenas. Buenos Aires, 1919.

Estudios helénicos. Buenos Aires, 1923–1924.

Filosofícula. Buenos Aires, 1924.

La organización de la paz. Buenos Aires, 1925.

Nuevos estudios helénicos. Buenos Aires, 1928.

La patria fuerte. Buenos Aires, 1930.

La grande Argentina. Buenos Aires, 1930.

Política revolucionaria. Buenos Aires, 1931.

El estado equitativo (Ensayo sobre la realidad argentina). Buenos Aires, 1932.

Roca. Buenos Aires, 1938.

Collected Works

Antología poética. Selected and with a prologue by Carlos Obligado. Buenos Aires, 1941.

Antología poética. Selected and with an introduction by Jorge Luis Borges. Madrid, 1982.

Antología de la prosa. Selected and with commentary by Leopoldo Lugones, hijo. Buenos Aires, 1949.

Los caballos de Abdera; cuentos escogidos. Mexico City, 1919.

Los cien mejores poemas de Leopoldo Lugones. Selected and with a prologue and with notes by Antonio Castro Leal. Mexico City, 1971.

Excerpta. Selección de verso y prosa de Leopoldo Lugones. With an introductory study and vocabulary by Leopoldo Lugones, hijo. Buenos Aires, 1971.

Obras en prosa. Selected and with a prologue by Leopoldo Lugones, hijo. Madrid, Mexico City, and Buenos Aires, 1962.

Obras poéticas completas. With a prologue by Pedro Miguel Obligado. Madrid, 1948.

El payador y antología de poesía y prosa. With a prologue by Jorge Luis Borges. Selection, notes, and chronology by Guillermo Ara. Caracas, 1979.

Poesías. With an introduction by Antonio Castro Leal. Mexico City, 1917.

Las primeras letras de Leopoldo Lugones. With notes and an introductory guide by Leopoldo Lugones, hijo. Buenos Aires, 1963.

Selección de poesía y prosa. With a prologue by Leopoldo Lugones, hijo. Buenos Aires, 1962.

Selección (poesías). With a prologue by Rubén Darío. Montevideo, 1919.

La voz contra la roca. San José, Costa Rica, 1912.

Biographical and Critical Studies

Ara, Guillermo. *Leopoldo Lugones.* Buenos Aires, 1958.

_____. *Leopoldo Lugones, uno y múltiple.* Buenos Aires, 1967.

Becco, Horacio Jorge. *Leopoldo Lugones; Bibliografía en su centenario (1874–1974).* Buenos Aires, 1978.

Borges, Jorge Luis, in collaboration with Betina Edelberg. *Leopoldo Lugones.* Buenos Aires, 1955.

Cambours Ocampo, Arturo. *Lugones: El escritor y su lenguaje.* Buenos Aires, 1957.

Canedo, Alfredo. *Aspectos del pensamiento político de Leopoldo Lugones.* Buenos Aires, 1974.

Capdevila, Arturo. *Lugones.* Buenos Aires, 1973.

Ghiano, Juan Carlos. *Lugones escritor: Notas para un análisis estilístico.* Buenos Aires, 1955.

Hernández, Juan José. "Leopoldo Lugones: La Luna Doncella en su poesía erótica." *Cuadernos hispanoamericanos* 371:266–280 (1981).

"Homenaje a Leopoldo Lugones (1874–1938)." *Revista iberoamericana* 30/57:93–187 (1964).

Homenaje a Leopoldo Lugones (1874–1974). Buenos Aires, 1975.

Irazusta, Julio. *Genio y figura de Leopoldo Lugones.* Buenos Aires, 1968.

Kirkpatrick, Melinda Gwen. "The Early Poetry of Leopoldo Lugones (1893–1909): From Monumentalism to

Dislocation." Ph.D. diss., Princeton University, 1979.

Lermón, Miguel. *Contribución a la bibliografía de Leopoldo Lugones.* Buenos Aires, 1969.

Lugones, Leopoldo, hijo. *Mi padre.* Buenos Aires, 1949.

Magis, Carlos Horacio. *La poesía de Leopoldo Lugones.* Mexico City, 1960.

Martínez Estrada, Ezequiel. *Leopoldo Lugones: Retrato sin retocar.* Buenos Aires, 1968.

Más y Pí, Juan. *Leopoldo Lugones y su obra.* Buenos Aires, 1911.

Moreau, Pierina Lidia. *Leopoldo Lugones y el simbolismo.* Buenos Aires, 1973.

Nosotros: A Leopoldo Lugones 7/26–28 (May–July 1938). Special issue.

Omil, Alba. *Leopoldo Lugones; Poesía y prosa.* Buenos Aires, 1968.

Phillips, Allen W. "La prosa artística de Leopoldo Lugones en *La guerra gaucha.*" *La Torre* 5/17:161–198 (1957).

Pio del Corro, Gaspar. *El mundo fantástico de Leopoldo Lugones.* Córdoba, Argentina, 1971.

Pultura, Raúl, Jr. *Lugones: Elementos cardinales destinados a determinar una biografía.* Buenos Aires, 1956.

Rebaudi Basavilbaso, Oscar. *Leopoldo Lugones: Ensayo sobre su obra literaria.* Buenos Aires, 1974.

Roggiano, Alfredo A. "Bibliografía de y sobre Leopoldo Lugones." *Revista iberoamericana* 28:155–213 (1962).

————. "Qué y qué no del *Lunario sentimental.*" *Revista iberoamericana* 42:71–77 (1976).

Scari, Robert M. "El lenguaje de *La guerra gaucha.*" *Nueva revista de filología hispánica* 20:389–398 (1971).

————. "Algunos procedimientos técnicos y temáticos del *Lunario sentimental,* de Leopoldo Lugones." *Cuadernos hispanoamericanos* 263–264:369–397 (1972).

————. "La formación literaria de Lugones." *Revista de letras (Puerto Rico)* 7/25–26:7–17 (1975).

Scroggins, Daniel. "Leopoldo Lugones' Defense of the Monroe Doctrine in the *Revue sud-américaine.*" *Revista interamericana de bibliografía* 28/2:169–175 (1978).

Tello, Belisario. *El poeta solariego: La síntesis poético-política de Leopoldo Lugones.* Buenos Aires, 1971.

Rufino Blanco Fombona

(1874–1944)

Guillermo Servando Pérez

In Spanish-American literature of the first three decades of the twentieth century, few writers attained an international outlook comparable with that of Rufino Blanco Fombona. He made his first steps toward becoming a writer by contributing, at a very young age, to the two most important Venezuelan literary magazines current at the end of the century, *El cojo illustrado* (The Illustrated Cripple, published 1892–1915) and *Cosmópolis* (published 1894–1895).

Modernism inevitably influenced Blanco Fombona, but he in turn left his mark on modernism. He absorbed many elements of the spirit of his time: postromanticism, realism, and, in particular, naturalism. He was also influenced by positivism and evolutionism, by Arthur Schopenhauer's pessimism, Thomas Carlyle's historic individualism, and Friedrich Nietzsche's vitalism.

He was born in Caracas, Venezuela, on 17 June 1874 into a family related to one of the country's founding fathers and also to remote conquerors and colonizers. At the age of eighteen, when he was a student at the military academy, he took part in a revolution that opposed President Raimundo Andueza Palacio's intention to stay in office for a second term. When the revolution succeeded, he was appointed consul in Philadelphia in spite of his very

young age (nineteen) and in 1896 was attaché at the legation in Holland.

When Blanco Fombona went back to Venezuela in 1897, his hostile declarations to President Ignacio Andrade caused an incident between him and one of the president's aides-de-camp, as a result of which he was put in jail for several weeks. When, in 1899, another revolution succeeded, General Cipriano Castro became the country's dictator. Castro was licentious, megalomaniac, theatrical, and passionately nationalistic, but Blanco Fombona's situation changed for the better under Castro's presidency.

When Blanco Fombona was twenty-five, he published his first book, *Trovadores y trovas* (Poets and Poems, 1899), which consists of poetic prose and poems. In the poems of this book and those of the next, *Pequeña opera lírica* (Small Lyric Opera, 1904)—with a preface by Rubén Darío—the reader will observe, together with the conventional postromantic and modernist theme, a feature that is characteristic of all his works: the exaggerated projection of "I," clothed in vitalism and sensuality. "I feel"—he writes in one of those first poems—"like drinking milk, taming a colt, fording a river." In these books, two aspects of expression draw attention: first, the poet's attempts to revitalize the metrics, using new and old forms—very much within the modernist style—and second, the oscillation between the spontaneity that the writer wished to achieve and the use of artificiality, which was difficult to avoid. Some unfavorable features include a tendency toward prosaism and a degree of carelessness in maintaining the internal coherence of the poems.

The same tension between spontaneity and artificiality characterizes Blanco Fombona's first short stories: Cuentos de poeta (Stories of a Poet, 1900) and Cuentos americanos (American Short Stories, 1904). In these stories three movements coincide: realism, late nineteenth-century naturalism, and modernism of the creole type, passionately defended by Blanco Fombona in later writings of literary criticism. The predominant features of the short stories are thematic pessimism and expressive condensation, that is, reducing the story and writing to the essential. As far as the thematic pessimism is concerned, we find in the first of these short stories what will be, developed and harmonized, the implicit thesis of his novels and one of the central points of his thought. According to this point of view, which has evident Darwinist roots, the life of man consists of struggle. As in the world of the inferior species, the fittest succeed, and these, in certain societies, are precisely the vilest. Two important considerations color this radical pessimism. The first is that man is not an inferior animal. He has intelligence and a free will, and consequently he can foresee and act freely. The second consideration is that whether a man's actions are good or bad, they do not depend on the motive that drives him.

Blanco Fombona's appointment as consul in Amsterdam took him abroad again (1901–1904). From the capital of Holland he traveled frequently to Paris, where he associated with many Spanish-American writers, like Rubén Darío and Enrique Gómez Carrillo, who lived there, fascinated by French civilization. In those days he published Más allá de los horizontes (Beyond the Horizons, 1903), a book of miscellaneous content, as were many of his later works, consisting principally of memories and lyric impressions of his travels through Europe and the United States.

In 1905 he was called back from the consulate in Amsterdam to become governor of the Amazon Territory. This was a highly dangerous post in the middle of the jungle, from which few people came out alive because the smugglers of rubber and tonka beans opposed any interference with their trade. Upon his arrival, Blanco Fombona decided to put an end to the smugglers' abuses. But his enemies surrounded his residence, the Government House, intending to kill him. Although the attempt failed, Blanco Fombona was made a virtual prisoner. This experience was surely the most memorable of his life. The sections in his diary that describe this period read like an adventure novel and have been compared with the adventure tales of Robert Louis Stevenson.

During his confinement he wrote, in only a few weeks, his first novel: El hombre de hierro (The Man of Iron, 1907), one of his most enduring books, according to the North American critic Isaac Goldberg. This novel tells the story of Crispín Luz, who, because of his weakness and his lack of what Blanco Fombona calls "the elements of combat necessary in the society in which he lives," succumbs to those who are fitter, in spite of his obvious moral nobleness. That is to say, the strongest and the vilest prevail. Evidently the story is not about a "man of iron," and the title is cruelly ironic. The novel contains a number of scenes that, without the conventional descriptions that were then common, give us a picture of Caracas society at the beginning of the century, as seen from the author's satirical point of view.

His narrative technique complies with the rules of realism and nineteenth-century naturalism. Max Nordau, one of his first commentators, described this technique as Balzac-inspired. As is characteristic of Blanco Fombona's style, the technique sometimes gives the impression of naturalness or spontaneity, duly achieved. But at other times it produces an effect of artificiality, the result of the writer's feverish search for the particular feature that he wished to attain.

The publication of El hombre de hierro was followed by the first compilation of "articles, observations, fragmentary notes, some of them excessively fragmentary," which had appeared in magazines in Caracas, Paris, and Madrid. This quote is from the introduction to Letras y letrados de Hispanoamérica (Literature and Writers of Spanish America, 1908), which is heterogeneous in content, like Más allá de los horizontes and many other writings of Blanco Fombona, but is also dedicated predominantly to literary reviews of a markedly Spanish-American orientation, as its title suggests.

Special importance should be attached to one of the essays in this book, "La americanisación del mundo" (The Americanization of the World, 1902). It was a reply to *The Americanization of the World; or, The Trend of the Twentieth Century,* (1902) by the English journalist W. T. Stead, who advocated the alliance of Great Britain and the United States for the purpose of imposing on the world the hegemony of the latter. In those first years of the century it was fashionable to talk about the decline of the Latin nations and the supremacy of the Anglo-Saxons and Germanics. Concrete historical events—such as North American intervention in Spanish America, Spain's defeat in its war with the United States, Venezuela's dispute with Great Britain about marking the boundaries with Guiana, and the blockade of the Venezuelan coast by European warships—had contributed to the creation of an atmosphere favorable for the stimulation of Spanish-Americanism (or Pan-Hispanism, a term coined by Blanco Fombona) to counterbalance official Pan-Americanism, which, for many, carried imperialistic connotations.

Blanco Fombona had moved farther and farther away from Cipriano Castro's autocratic and corrupt regime. When, at the end of 1908, the seriously ill dictator sailed to Europe, Blanco Fombona was among those who ardently cried out for his overthrow and induced the acting president, General Juan Vicente Gómez, to assume control. He did not know then that Gómez would be the master of Venezuela for the next twenty-seven years and that he would keep Blanco Fombona in exile for nearly as many years as the dictatorship would last.

Blanco Fombona, who had been nominated secretary of the Chamber of Deputies, asked for an inquiry into the presence of American warships—solicited by the government itself—in Venezuelan waters at the time of Castro's downfall. Such a request implied a doubt about the new dictator's nationalism. Neither a proffered overseas diplomatic post nor the imprisonment to which he was eventually subjected undermined the writer's firmness.

Since his plans to gain the support of Blanco Fombona did not succeed, the dictator ordered that he be sent into exile, an exile that was to last for more than twenty-five years (1910–1936) and that would end only with the demise of General Gómez in December 1935. (Although he did not return to Venezuela until the following February, Blanco Fombona considered his exile over with the despot's death.)

First Blanco Fombona lived in Paris, where he worked intensely as a writer and editor. His exile deepened his hatred for Gómez. Shortly after he had settled in Europe, he published his third book of poems, *Cantos de la prisión y del destierro* (Songs of Prison and Exile, 1911), with a prologue that is a passionate outcry against the tyrant. Blanco Fombona described the poems of this book as the "human screams of a man who suffered," "written with blood, tears, and bitterness." In this volume he paid little attention to form and made no effort to avoid prosaism.

After Gómez took power, he unleashed a campaign to discredit his opponents, including the exiled Blanco Fombona. The vileness of the attacks against Blanco Fombona impelled him to retort, and thus was born *Judas capitolino* (Judas in the Capitol, 1912), written in order to give Gómez, according to the writer, "the celebrity he deserves, the celebrity of disgrace."

In 1911 Blanco Fombona published in Madrid *La evolución política y social de Hispanoamérica* (The Political and Social Evolution of Spanish America), a work of historical and sociological interpretation, very much influenced by positivism. He studied colonial times, independence, the organization of the new nations, and the republic; this brought him to the conclusion that the people of Spanish America have "a common mentality and a common soul," that this identity is revealed in their literature, and that one of the major dangers that threatens this unity is the hegemony of some countries over others, caused by the uneven distribution of population and foreign capital in the continent. "Expansion and imperialism," he writes in the conclusion to *La evolución política y social* "are natural phenomena that should not surprise us. They are, translated into the language of sociology, the Darwinian survival of the fittest and the strongest. But we, human beings, are not inferior animals. We have intelligence and a will. We are able to foresee and act freely." With this book Blanco Fombona initiated his important work of interpreting Spanish-American history. His principal subjects would be Simon Bolívar as the Liberator of Spanish America and the Spanish conquistadors of the sixteenth century.

The key to understanding Blanco Fombona's interpretation of Bolívar is contained in his view that Bolívar was not at the lower level, where the fittest and the strongest are the vilest, but at a higher level, where the fittest and the strongest are what they are because they use their intelligence and their will to foresee and act.

Although Blanco Fombona's admiration for Bolívar was deeply rooted in this ethical concept and in the fact that Bolívar was Venezuelan, it is probably justified to say that two circumstances enhanced this admiration: Blanco Fombona's banishment from his homeland and the chronological parallelism between this exile, which started in 1910, and the course of events one hundred years earlier (1810–1830), when Bolívar performed his historical work. In 1913 Blanco Fombona started in Paris the editing of the *Cartas de Bolívar* (Letters of Bolívar), prefaced by José Enrique Rodó, that he continued, some years later, in Madrid with the publication of a second and third volume. The next year he published, also in Paris, the *Discursos y proclamas* (The Speeches and Proclamations) of Bolívar and the *Biografía de José Félix Ribas* (Biography of José Félix Ribas), written by Juan Vicente González, a representative work of romantic Venezuelan historiography. The importance of these editions lies in their prologues and notes. The notes attached to *Cartas de Bolívar* represent a synthesized biography of the Liberator. The prologue of *Discursos y proclamas* is a study of "Bolívar, escritor" (Bolívar, The Writer) and that of the *Biographía de José Félix Ribas* an interpretation of Bolívar's "Guerra a muerte" (War to the Death) of 1813.

Another expression of Blanco Fombona's Spanish-Americanism is his support of *criollismo* (literature inspired by native themes), which he considered to be the literary and intellectual component of the process of independence that Bolívar had started politically a century earlier. He made his strongest contribution to *criollismo* with his first novel and his first two books of short stories.

In 1913 he made another important contribution, a revised and enlarged edition of *Cuentos americanos*. He said that the short stories were made with the elements of the Venezuelan way of life. He dedicated the book to the Venezuelan *criollo* writers, who, for the last few decades, had made a sustained effort to develop an American trend of thought, free from European influence.

When World War I broke out in 1914 and France was invaded by Germany, Blanco Fombona moved to Madrid, where he established the publishing house Editorial América. He continued and intensified his Spanish-Americanist work and published within a few years a great number of important historical and literary writings.

Blanco-Fombona's Spanish-Americanism developed in three directions. The first led to a better understanding of Spain's intervention in America, and one of Blanco Fombona's basic works belongs to this period. *El conquistador español del siglo XVI* (The Spanish Conquistador of the Sixteenth Century, 1921) is "an essay of interpretation" of a historical, sociological, and psychological nature, in which the influence of positivism is persistent.

The book is divided into two parts. The first—"Caracteres de España" (Characters of Spain)—examines the psychology of the conquistadors. The second part—"Los conquistadores" (The Conquistadors)—analyzes their social background and the time in which they lived. Blanco Fombona repudiated the aspects of the conquistadors that he considered negative, principally their cruelty and greed. But he felt that these characteristics were no worse than those of contemporary colonizers of other countries and could, to a certain extent, be explained by the dangers to which they had to expose themselves. On the other hand, he praised other qualities that he considered positive, in particular their courage and the social, political, and civilizing work that they performed unintentionally.

The second direction in which Blanco Fombona's Spanish-Americanism developed was his study of Bolívar as a person of historical value. He thus rescued Bolívar from becoming a mysticized personality, a tendency that had been in progress in the last decades of the nineteenth century.

In 1918 he published a new edition of the already

famous *Vida del libertador Simón Bolívar* (The Life of the Liberator Simón Bolívar), by the Venezuelan writer Felipe Larrazábal, one of the promotors of the so-called Bolívar cult. As happened in the editions of *Cartas de Bolívar*, the *Discursos y proclamas*, and the *Biographía de José Félix Ribas*, by González, the most important parts of the edition are the prologue and the notes. Along with a very personal interpretation as editor, Blanco Fombona provided important corrections to the text. In 1921 he edited the second volume of the *Cartas de Bolívar* and, in 1922, the third, with detailed notes.

Blanco Fombona's Spanish-Americanism followed, finally, a third road that led to the assertion of Spanish-American independence at a political and cultural, or, more precisely, literary level. This road would, he hoped, also lead to a better knowledge of Spanish America in Spain, Europe, and the United States, and to better mutual understanding. In particular, his essays of literary criticism represent a fervent approach that paid more attention to psychological and social aspects than to strictly literary ones and fiercely defended *criollismo*, which the author described in the introduction to *Letras y letrados de Hispanoamérica* as an "art sprung from the soil, native, continental, American, ours, like our rivers, like our mountains, like our plains."

Grandes escritores de América (Great Writers of America, 1917), is a compilation of essays on Andrés Bello, Domingo Faustino Sarmiento, Eugenio María de Hostos, Don Juan Montalvo, and Manuel González Prada, considered to be representative because they were "men with free minds." This book was meant to refute the belief that America had only natural resources and revolutionary leaders, and to prove that, in the nineteenth century, it had thinkers and artists who lived and fought for high ideals. In 1929 he published *El modernismo y los poetas modernistas* (Modernism and the Modernist Poets). Basing his criticism on a differentiation between modernism and "Rubendarismo," Blanco Fombona considered the former a revolution of liberation that gave Spanish-American literature the creole character that it had never had before.

Other books of miscellaneous content are *La lámpara de Aladino* (Aladdin's Lamp, 1915), *La Espada del samuray* (The Samurai's Sword, 1924),

and *Motivos y letras de España* (Motives and Letters from Spain, 1930), which contain articles and essays of great interest on Spanish-American themes, principally of a literary nature.

In 1915 Blanco Fombona published his second novel, *El hombre de oro* (The Man of Gold). It is, according to his own definition, the "biography" of another common man, Camilo Irurtia, a crude, greedy man, without moral rectitude, but with a strong egotism. With this egotism, selfishly stimulated by some of the wretched people who surround him, he manages not only to satisfy his insatiable lust for money but also to become, through a meteoric career, minister of finance. Where Crispín Luz, the main character of *El hombre de hierro*, succumbs, Irurtia succeeds because of his strong will. The strong ones, though they are bad, succeed, while the good but weak ones fail. The implicit thesis of the novel confirms the one found in *El hombre de hierro*. In accordance with Darwin's teachings, the fittest succeed. But in a corrupt society as existed in Caracas in the days of General Cipriano Castro, the fittest are precisely the vilest.

The Man of Gold contains two main characters, Irurtia and Olga Emmerich. Although she does not belong to the same social class as Irurtia—she is an impoverished aristocrat—Olga has in common with him both a moral vileness and the energy to reach her goals irrespective of the means. The title of the novel, identifying the main character as a man of wealth, is meant ironically, as in *El hombre de hierro*, since "a man of gold" is, in Spanish, a laudatory expression indicating a person with qualities of moral nobility.

In 1918 Blanco Fombona published his fourth poetic book, *Cancionero del amor infeliz* (Lyrical Poems About Unhappy Love), which consists partly of new poems and partly of poems that he took from previous books. All of them refer to "the unhappy love" that existed between the writer and his Venezuelan girlfriend, who was much younger than he. This relationship had started when the girl was still a child and came to a stop when he went into exile. Later, she traveled to Madrid, where they married in 1916. However, her later discovery that Blanco Fombona had maintained a stable relationship with another woman caused her so much grief that she committed suicide.

His hatred toward the dictator Juan Vicente Gómez is constant in Blanco Fombona's work. In 1911 he had expressed himself in *Cantos de la prisión y del destierro* and, in 1912, in the satire *Judas capitolino.* In 1923 he came back to the same theme in *La máscara heroica* (The Heroic Mask). Although the publisher presented it as a novel, it is, as its subtitle suggests, more like a collection of "Scenes from a Barbarocracy," (a word, invented by Blanco Fombona, meaning a government under the control of barbarians). This satire, whose central figure is General Gómez, mentioned with his full name, shows the writer's unrestrained hatred. This extreme portrait does not spare anything in either the tyrant's public or private life, or, for that matter, in the lives of those who surrounded him, with the exception of the general's favorite daughter, who accompanies him and looks after him and who, in significant contrast, is presented as "the flower on the dunghill."

The thesis of the triumph of the worst appears implicitly again in the next two novels. *La mitra en la mano* (The Mitre in Hand, 1927) is the "biography" of Father Blandín, a hypocritical, ambitious, lewd, and crafty priest. His lewdness very nearly leads him into disaster, but his cunning enables him to climb to a high position in the hierarchy of the church by taking advantage of his sacrilegious relations with Marta, a weak sinner, whom he had obliged to become his submissive lover. Some of the characters of this novel, principally Marta, appear again in the next, *La Bella y la Fiera* (The Beauty and the Beast, 1931).

Between the publication of these novels, two attempted revolts against General Gómez occurred. In 1928 there was a student protest of little direct effect but with a far-reaching echo throughout the country. A year later a small expedition failed in its intent to land in Venezuela. It had been organized by a group of prominent exiles, among them Blanco Fombona, and formed part of a political project that included the invasion of Venezuela, the overthrow of the dictator, and the restoration of democracy. The repression that General Gómez unleashed as a result of these incidents rekindled the writer's hatred and helped him create the atmosphere of terror that

pervades *La Bella y la Fiera.* This time the triumph of the worst is personified by the daughter of Marta, Griselda, who is the Beauty of the title. But where Marta (weak like Crispín Luz) surrenders, the "victim of her temperament and her sex," her daughter is strong (like Irurtia, Olga Emmerich, and Blandín) and "is in control because of her sex."

Griselda goes to beg "the general," who is the Beast—a veiled reference to the hated dictator—to release two imprisoned young revolutionaries, one of whom is her own and the other her mother's lover. The Beast tries to seduce the Beauty, who first turns him down but eventually accepts him. She becomes his official concubine, allowing her egotism to take precedence over her sentiments in order to satisfy her ambitions of power, wealth, and social position. Although she does not forget the two young men altogether, she is in no hurry to intercede again in their favor because she knows the Beast well by now and is aware of the danger the young men, and, above all, she herself, would face. When more on her mother's insistence than on her own initiative, she asks again for the release of the young men, she sparks a disaster.

Two books of Blanco Fombona's short stories, *Dramas mínimos* (Minute Dramas, 1920) and *Tragedias grotescas* (Grotesque Tragedies, 1928), are characterized, as were the previous ones, by his *criollismo,* an intensely bitter pessimism and irony, and a tendency toward expressive spontaneity and condensation.

Blanco Fombona had kept a diary from the time he was very young. This diary is a very important component of his work. His dedication to it seemed to stem from his strong egocentricity, a feature that also explains the autobiographic inclination of all his writings. He had published some parts in *Más allá de los horizontes* and *La lámpara de Aladin.* In 1926, in *Por los caminos del mundo* (Along the Pathways of the World), he had published writings of autobiographic interest together with episodes from his youth. But it was not until 1929, when he was fifty-five years old, that he started the formal publication of his *Diario de mi vida* (The Diary of My Life). The first installment, *La Novela de dos años* (The Novel of Two Years), covers the period 1904–1905 and includes his journey to the Upper Orinoco as governor of the Amazon Territories. The second installment, published in

1933 under the title *Camino de imperfección* (The Road of Imperfection), is a continuation of the first.

When World War I came to an end, Blanco Fombona could have gone back to Paris, but he stayed in Madrid to manage the successful Editorial América. As a liberal and a freemason, he celebrated the end of dictatorial rule in Spain and, shortly thereafter, the dethronement of the king and the proclamation of the republic (1931).

By virtue of the rights that the new republican constitution afforded Spanish-American residents, Blanco Fombona was appointed civil governor of Almería (September–October 1933) and of Navarre (December 1933–May 1934). In 1933 he published what would be his last novel, *El secreto de la felicidad* (The Secret of Happiness). Although twenty-six years had passed since the publication of his first novel, he kept pounding the same theme, the triumph of the worst, without introducing major changes in his style.

Luis Carmona, the main character of this novel, is a journalist and politician who fights for his ideals. He seems to be fitted for success and, at a certain moment in his life, it looks as if it is within his grasp. But it eludes him because he lacks the necessary intelligence to foresee and the necessary will to act. Although he does not belong to the category of the worst, he commits the error of giving in to certain "weaknesses" that do not bring him any personal advantage and are bad enough to bring his rising career to a dead stop. With this work Blanco Fombona adds a new element to his well-known thesis: Although success in life belongs to the worst, happiness does not belong to anybody; nobody possesses its secret; it is nobody's domain; nobody has a lien on his happiness.

In February 1936, shortly after General Gómez died, Blanco Fombona went back to Venezuela, where democracy was gradually being restored. On his return he was received with honors, which included important political and diplomatic appointments and even membership in the National Academy of History. However, his return was accompanied by bitterness caused by maladjustment and incomprehension, and was exacerbated by the Spanish Civil War, World War II, and his declining health. He published a new book of miscellaneous content, *El espejo de tres faces* (The Mirror with Three Faces, 1937) with commentaries on disparate subjects and, again, special emphasis on Spanish-Americanism.

The return to his native country seems to have revived his interest in Bolívar, on whom he wrote five works in succession. In 1939 he delivered a speech, on the occasion of his admission to the National Academy of History, entitled *La inteligencia en Bolívar* (Bolivar's Intelligence). In 1942 he published *Mocedades de Bolívar* (Bolívar's Youth), a study of "the hero before he became a hero," as the subtitle explains; *El pensamiento vivo de Bolívar* (Bolívar's Living Thoughts), an introduction to a selection of the Liberator's writings; and *Bolívar y la guerra a muerte* (Bolívar and the War to the Death), an analysis of the most bloody and decisive period of the War of Independence. In 1943, Blanco Fombona completed *El espíritu de Bolívar* (The Spirit of Bolívar), an "essay of psychological interpretation," incorporating thoughts from his 1939 speech at the National Academy of History.

In 1942 he added a third installment to the diary of his life, under the title *Dos años y medio de inquietud* (Two and a Half Years of Anxiety), which covers the years 1928–1930. There is a great gap between 1914, when the second installment ends, and 1928, when the third begins. This unfilled space corresponds to a part of the diary that, according to Blanco Fombona, was stolen by agents of General Gómez from his home in Madrid.

Mazorcas de oro (Golden Corncobs, 1943) was his fifth and last book of poems, of which approximately half are new and the rest selected from previous books. It contains various themes and metrics, but it does not offer a high level of quality nor any important innovation.

Mazorcas de oro and *El espíritu de Bolívar* were the last books Blanco Fombona would publish. While on a trip through the south of the continent, he died on 17 October 1944 in Buenos Aires.

Blanco Fombona left behind a very extensive oeuvre—novels, short stories, poems, essays (mainly of historical interpretation and literary criticism), diaries, travel books, and political satires—characterized by the subordination of aesthetic qualities to psychological, social, and political values. His work has a markedly egotistic and passionately autobiographic undercurrent, together with a sustained Spanish-Americanism in all its varieties: Pan-Hispanism, Bolívarism, *criollismo,* and anti-imperialism. He was convinced that in corrupt societies—and he considered the society of Caracas in the days of Castro and Gómez as such—the worst and the vilest will succeed. However, he softened this conviction by making allowances for intelligence and willpower, and by admitting that good or evil in human deeds is unrelated to the motives behind such deeds. And finally, he consciously kept his style very personal and free from tradition, trends, fashion, and academicism. His diary beyond 1930 apparently was left unedited. His work *Bolívar el hombre* (The Man Bolívar) was published posthumously, in 1984, but many of his articles that appeared in Spanish and Venezuelan newspapers remain uncollected. It appears that some of his manuscripts are lost, among them those of his diary covering the period from 1915–1927.

Translated from the Spanish by George Veltman

SELECTED BIBLIOGRAPHY

First Editions

Poetry

Trovadores y trovas. Caracas, 1899.
Pequeña opera lírica. Madrid, 1904.
Cantos de la prisión y del destierro. Paris, 1911.
Cancionero del amor infeliz. Madrid, 1918.
Mazorcas de oro. Caracas, 1943.

Tales

Cuentos de poeta. Maracaibo, Venezuela, 1900.
Cuentos americanos. Madrid, 1904.
Cuentos americanos. Paris, 1913. Revised and enlarged edition.
Dramas mínimos. Madrid, 1920.
Tragedias grotescas. Madrid, 1928.

Novels

El hombre de hierro. Caracas, 1907.
El hombre de oro. Madrid, 1915.

La mitra en la mano. Madrid, 1927.
La Bella y la Fiera. Madrid, 1931.
El secreto de la felicidad. Madrid, 1933.

Voyages and Journals

Más allá de los horizontes. Madrid, 1903.
Por los caminos del mundo. Madrid, 1926.
Diario de mi vida. La novela de dos años. 1904–1905. Madrid, 1929.
Camino de imperfección. Diario de mi vida. 1906–1913. Madrid, 1933.
Dos años y medio de inquietud. 1928–1930. Caracas, 1942.

Critical Studies

Grandes escritores de América. Madrid, 1917.
El modernismo y los poetas modernistas. Madrid, 1929.

Miscellaneous Writings

Letras y letrados de Hispanoamérica. Paris, 1908.
La lámpara de Aladino. Madrid, 1915.
La espada del samuray. Madrid, 1924.
Motivos y letras de España. Madrid and Buenos Aires, 1930.
El espejo de tres faces. Santiago, Chile, 1937.

History

La evolución política y social de Hispanoamérica. Madrid, 1911.
El conquistador español del siglo XVI. Madrid, 1921.
Mocedades de Bolívar: El héroe antes del heroísmo. Buenos Aires, 1942.
Bolívar y la guerra a muerte: Epoca de Boves. 1813–1814. Caracas, 1942.
El espíritu de Bolívar. Caracas, 1943.

Political Writings

Una página de historia: Ignacio Andrade y su gobierno. Caracas, 1900.
De cuerpo entero. El negro Benjamín Ruiz. Amsterdam, 1900.
La americanisación del mundo. Amsterdam, 1902.
Judas capitolino. Chartres, 1912.
La máscara heroica. Madrid, 1923.

Later Editions

El Hombre de oro. Edited and with an introduction, exercises, notes, and vocabulary by Virgil A. Warren. New York, 1948.

El conquistador español del siglo XVI. Caracas and Madrid, 1956.

Obras selectas. Edited and with a prologue and biliographical study by E. Gabaldón Márquez. Madrid and Caracas, 1958.

Cartas de Blanco Fombona a Unamuno. Prologue by M. Falcón Briceño. Caracas, 1968.

El hombre de hierro. Caracas, 1972.

El hombre de oro. Caracas, 1972.

Rufino Blanco Fombona intimo. Edited and with a prologue by A. Rama. Caracas, 1975.

Rufino Blanco Fombona. Edited and with a prologue by N. Galasso. Caracas, 1977.

Ensayos históricos. Prologue by J. Sanoja Hernández. Edited and with a chronology by R. R. Castellanos. Caracas, 1981.

Bolívar. 3 vols. With a prologue by R. R. Castellanos. 1: *Mocedades de Bolívar. El espíritu de Bolívar.* 2: *Bolívar el hombre* (posthumously published). *La inteligencia de Bolívar. Bolívar pintado por sí mismo.* 3: *Bolívar y la guerra a muerte. Pensamiento vivo de Bolívar.* Caracas, 1984.

Translations

The Man of Gold. Translated and with an introduction by Isaac Goldberg. New York, 1920, 1977.

Biographical and Critical Studies

Carmona Nenclares, F., et al. *R. Blanco Fombona: Su vida y su obra.* Caracas, 1944.

Castellanos, R. R. *Rufino Blanco Fombona: Ensayo biobibliográfico.* Caracas, 1975.

Fogelquist, D. F. "Rufino Blanco Fombona." In *Españoles de América y americanos de España.* Madrid, 1968. Pp. 319–325.

Goldberg, Isaac. "Rufino Blanco Fombona." In *Studies in Spanish-American Literature.* New York, 1920.

Granell, M. "Blanco Fombona y la vida." In *Del pensar venezolano.* Caracas, 1967. Pp. 107–153.

Lovera de Sola, R. J. "Bio-bibliografía de Rufino Blanco Fombona." *Imagen* (Caracas) 101–102:154–162 (1975).

Rama, A. *Rufino Blanco Fombona y el egotismo latinoamericano.* Valencia, Venezuela, 1975.

Ratcliff, Dillwyn F. "Rufino Blanco Fombona." In *Venezuelan Prose Fiction.* New York, 1933. Pp. 145–172.

Rivas, R. A. *Fuentes documentales para el estudio de Rufino Blanco Fombona.* Caracas, 1979.

Sánchez, Luis Alberto. "Rufino Blanco Fombona." In *Escritores representativos de América*, 3rd series, 1. Madrid, 1976. Pp. 112–126.

Stegmann, W. *Rufino Blanco Fombona und sein episches Werk.* Hamburg, 1959.

José María Eguren

(1874–1942)

Peter Elmore

José María Eguren was born 7 July 1874 in Lima, the capital of Peru. He died in the same city on 19 April 1942. One could say, then, that Eguren lived between modernism and vanguardism. His poetry developed within the parameters of both, and it is in fact the critical consensus that Eguren is the most notable Peruvian representative of postmodernism.

Although his poetic production was not small, José María Eguren published only three books during his lifetime. The first, *Simbólicas* (Symbolics, 1911), is not an immature work but rather the result of a long apprenticeship. The symbolist poetics and fantastic imagery of that first collection of poems are continued in *La canción de las figuras* (The Song of the Figures, 1916). Those two volumes were followed by a period of editorial silence, which was interrupted by *Poesías* (Poems, 1929). *Poesías* is a sort of personal anthology that draws upon texts from his earlier books, as well as from two other collections of poems, *Sombra* (Shadow) and *Rondinelas*, parts of which appeared in several magazines after 1916. Around 1930 Eguren began to write brief prose notes, which he called *motivos* (motifs); they were published posthumously as *Motivos estéticos* (Aesthetic Motifs, 1959). Those writings, although they do not claim theoretical rigor, reveal the intimacy and aestheticism of his worldview.

Eguren's life was not eventful. Because of his delicate health, he was unable to finish his secondary studies at the Jesuit school and was to spend long periods of solitude in haciendas near Lima. After the death of his parents, Eguren, a timid and sedentary person, lived with two of his sisters who, like him, were unmarried. For more than thirty years, the three remained in the resort of Barranco, near Lima. Eguren wrote most of his works there and only left the resort when, in the early 1930's, the family income dissipated. At that time Eguren moved to Lima, where he had to accept a low-paying job as a librarian. Accustomed to the life-style of a small landowner, Eguren faced financial pressures during the last fifteen years of his life. To assist him, some of his friends gave him small amounts of money each month, claiming that the funds were generated through foreign sales of Eguren's watercolors and other articles.

A versatile artist, Eguren also dedicated himself to painting and photography. His watercolors reveal the influence of the French impressionists and the English Pre-Raphaelites and may be seen as visual illustrations of the dreamlike, diffuse universe to which he gives being in his poetry. It is worth noting that Eguren's photographs, curious miniatures of artistic intent, were taken with a camera that Eguren himself made. The craftsmanlike attention to detail and the lack of documentary concern revealed by Eguren in his photographs are also traits of his literary work.

Although he was not a musician, music was a central point of cultural reference for Eguren. Following the line of the French symbolists, he wrote that "music is the most metaphysical, the least burdened of the arts; it dwells in a sweet chamber and in winged landscapes, in fantasy and in the soul." Eguren mentions musical instruments throughout his work: cymbals, drums, violins, pianos, ocarinas, accordions, and flutes, among others. Several of his poems are titled "Lied," in an allusion to Robert Schumann, and both *La canción de las figuras* and *Rondinelas*, beginning with their very titles, draw upon Eguren's obsession with music. His favorite composers are mentioned frequently, and their creations, symptomatically, serve to define and suggest emotional states. In "Rêverie," a poem from *Simbólicas*, the lyrical voice, evoking two mysterious ladies, says:

Así, su memoria me traía
las baladas de Mendelssohn claras;
pero ni Beethoven poseía
la tristísima luz de esas caras.

Thus, their memory brought back to me
the clear ballads of Mendelssohn;
but not even Beethoven possessed
the very sad light of those faces.

It is no coincidence that Eguren preferred romantic music, to which one would have to add the music of Maurice Ravel and Claude Debussy. Romanticism underlies the symbolism of Eguren, contributing, for example, the exaltation of intuition and the disdain for reason that flow in the idealist poetry of the author of *Rondinelas*. This context explains why music was for Eguren the paradigm of the arts; in music, communication occurs without rational meaning. The supposed "obscurity" of Eguren's poetry stems from his desire to emphasize the connotation of discourse more than its denotation. The reader cannot identify definite reference points linked to daily experience. On the contrary, the poet offers a vast array of suggestions in his texts. But rather than simply transmitting ideas or describing objects, Eguren aspires to create a psychological environment characterized by mystery and ambiguity.

Thus, Eguren constructs his poems on the basis of Baudelairian *correspondences*. Verbal signs transport the reader to another world, different from the real one, and therefore are strongly charged with mysticism and allegory. Often, the poem is presented as a vision of that Platonic, spiritual world in which forms are stripped of their material nature. One of the most famous and representative poems of Eguren, "Los reyes rojos" (The Red Kings), which forms part of *Simbólicas*, is a good example of this. The first strophe informs us that

Desde la aurora
combaten dos reyes rojos
con lanza de oro

Since dawn
two red kings have been fighting
with lances of gold.

The unidentified "red kings" are carrying on an endless struggle that at the end of the poem is revealed to be mythic and infinite:

Viene la noche
y firmes combaten fuscos
los reyes rojos.

The night comes
and with dark resolve
the red kings struggle.

To a large degree, the aesthetic effect of "Los reyes rojos" is based on its cosmic and fantastic setting, and on the mystery that surrounds the combatants. The poetic self sees the invisible and reveals it in plastic images (the contrast between red and gold, for example). In those images, the function of color is emblematic rather than decorative. Estuardo Núñez has established the allegorical significance of certain colors in Eguren's poetry. Blue, the favorite color of Rubén Darío and the modernists, represents profundity and creation. Red symbolizes strength, and yellow, death. White is applied to sadness and happiness alike.

A yearning for the next world, toward the ideal sphere in which only essences exist, takes on the appearance of a spiritual journey in Eguren's works. The meaning of that journey is strictly artistic, rather than religious. Better still, Eguren conceives of art as a religion, in agreement with the modern aesthetic tradition. The use of poetry to surpass the material order is seen in "La niña de la lámpara azul" ("The Girl with the Blue Lamp"), which by no coincidence begins *La canción de las figuras*. The vaporous and spiritual character attracts the poet with a coquetry that veils her eroticism without denying it completely. The "girl with the blue lamp" is an emissary from beyond, from the utopic realm of poetry. Her human and sensual aspects are transfigured in her supernatural character. When he describes her, the poet says:

> Agil y risueña se insinúa,
> y su llama seductora brilla,
> tiembla en su cabello la garúa
> de la playa de la maravilla.

Nimble and smiling, she hints of her affection,
her seductive flame shining,
and on her hair trembles the drizzle
of the beach of wonder.

The end of the poem emphasizes the function of the girl with the blue lamp as an intermediary between the world of the senses and the aesthetic ideal, imagined as "un mágico y celeste camino" (a magical and heavenly road). In Eguren's works, female characters express an eroticism that is sexually silent. The circumspect poet considers sexual intercourse degrading. He proffers an association typical of English romanticism, repeatedly linking eroticism to death. The phantomlike girl with the blue lamp is related to this topic, which has its most stylized and gallant representation in "La dama I" (Lady I) in *Simbólicas*, and its most explicit version in "La muerta de marfil" (The Dead Woman of Ivory) in *Sombra*. In fact, the subtle but identifiable necrophilia of José María Eguren's poetry reminds one of Edgar Allan Poe, whom Eguren read attentively and with whose ideas about poetic tension and effect he appears to have identified.

In "La niña de la lámpara azul," the messenger from the spiritual world appears in a completely positive light. However, emissaries of mystery can provoke uneasiness and even horror. This is obviously the case in "El andarín de la noche" (The Night Wanderer) in *Sombra*. The traveler from beyond the grave will be forgotten after prophesying a devastating war. The "deceased captain" of "Viñeta obscura" (Dark Vignette) plays a similar role in *Rondinelas*. In this poem, the ghostly apparition announces disaster:

> Siempre llega la víspera nefasta,
> siempre enlutado
> de su muerte.

> The evening of rest always arrives,
> he, always dressed in mourning
> for his own death.

Thus, in the poetry of Eguren the supernatural is perceived as more powerful and authentic than reality, but not necessarily more pleasant. In fact, the tenebrous and ghostly is more persistent in Eguren's poetry than the angelical. For this reason some critics described Eguren as a "Gothic" poet. The Gothic ornamentation, of romantic origin, that appears repeatedly throughout Eguren's work is only one of the nonrealistic elements the poet employs.

Beginning with the first productions of Darío, Spanish-American modernism utilized a profusion of aristocratic or exotic scenes. Eguren is, in a way, a tributary of this literary custom. In his case, however, environments far removed from daily life do not usually connote aristocratic luxury. In some poems, which uncreatively repeat modernist clichés, we find Japanese, Hispanic, or French landscapes. But what distinguishes Eguren's imaginary geography is its Germanic or Nordic ambience, usually loosely set in an idealized medieval period. Eguren also makes use of the Norse Eddas and the old Teutonic legends. Eguren is more interested in tragic resonances and mystery than in promoting a minoritarian ideal of elegance. "El dios cansado" (The Tired God) in *La canción de las figuras* is the mortal divinity of Germanic mythology. In the same book, the poem "El caballo" (The Horse) draws on the same legendary background. In turn, the towers, castles, abbeys, and ships that appear in Eguren's work also point to Germanic imagery, infused with romantic gloominess. It is no coincidence that in most of these poems Eguren employs chiaroscuro or haziness to depict landscapes, accentuating their strange, startling effect. "La ronda de espadas"

(The Round of Swords), in *Sombra*, is a good example of this type of composition:

> *Por las avenidas,*
> *de miedo cercadas,*
> *brilla en noche de azules oscuros,*
> *la ronda de espadas.*

> Along the avenues
> Walled with fear
> Shines in the night of dark blues
> The round of swords.

The fearsome "round of swords" challenges the deep darkness of the night with its brilliance, in a powerful chromatic counterpoint. The poet's intention was not to offer a lifelike picture, but rather to emphasize the fleshless, almost abstract nature of the world he evoked.

Eguren's production is lyrical and intimate. In spite of this, the poetic self is generally not at the center of the poem, speaking of itself. Eguren's subjectivity is recognized in the visions he presents, among them a gallery of imaginary characters based on legends or fairy tales. From this comes the mistake of considering Eguren, who was a hermetic poet, an "infantile" or ingenuous creator. Among the figures that circulate in his poetry are the already-mentioned girl with the blue lamp and night wanderer, as well as Steel Peter from "Pedro de acero," Juan Volatín from the poem of the same name, and Duke Nut from "El duque" in *Simbólicas*. One of the most interesting members of this family of living dolls is Peregrín, figure hunter, from "Peregrín, cazador de figuras" (in *La cancion de las figuras*), who seems to be a magical alter ego of Eguren.

Eguren subverts the puerile appearance of his characters and frequently introduces a tragic element into their actions. In a veiled manner, violence and a certain perversity impregnate situations that at first glance are pleasant, even playful. In fact, Eguren cultivates an attenuated form of the grotesque in part of his poetry. In his animated toys there is something misshapen that is at once comical and disturbing. The best expression of this is found in "Las bodas vienesas" (The Viennese Weddings) and in "El pelele" (The Scarecrow), two poems from *Simbólicas*.

In order to describe his poetic universe, Eguren resorts to a language far removed from the colloquial norm. His lexicon rejects words from daily life, which he considers contaminated with vulgarity. This is, without a doubt, one of the central contrasts between Eguren and César Vallejo, the central figure of contemporary Peruvian lyric poetry. But Eguren's elusive vocabulary is also quite different from that of José Santos Chocano, who is mainly interested in the brilliant, sonorous effects of a poetry that is, above all, accessible and declamatory.

Parts of Eguren's work show a debt to the language of Rubén Darío. However, in the most important section of his work he devises an unmistakably personal dialect. The cultured roots of Eguren's lexicon and his baroque syntax make him opaque and foreign to the average reader. That is in fact the poet's intention, to draw attention to the very verbal fabric of his poems. Eguren's poetics insists on the autonomous nature of works of art, and to a great degree Eguren's unusual poetic language is an embodiment of that concept. In 1928 the Peruvian historian Jorge Basadre evaluated the sociological significance of Eguren's hermeticism:

> It is Eguren who initiates the radical separation among the public. The intellectual bourgeoisie begins to feel something about which nothing had been written, the uneasiness of not understanding, and from that point on, it learns to mock and lament because things are written in a "difficult language."
>
> (In Silva-Santisteban, p. 96.)

Archaisms, foreign words (usually of French origin), and neologisms abound in Eguren's poetry. He only draws upon Peruvian Spanish when it is impossible to locate a cultured, original synonym. Eguren's verbal creativity, which distances him from ordinary communication, bears the mark of his cosmopolitanism and his elitist vocation.

Although he never traveled outside Peru, Eguren was always attentive to modern European literature. His reading in French, English, and Italian familiarized him with the works of Charles-Pierre Baudelaire, Paul Verlaine, John Ruskin, and Gabriele D'Annunzio, and also exposed him to rhythms and cadences unlike those of Spanish poetry. Along with the modernists, Eguren favored an intensive renovation of Spanish verse. His poetry, which uses syllabic and accentual principles at the same time, represents a vast catalog of versification. However, *verso menor* (minor verse) and binary rhythms predominate in his work as a whole, relegating his alexandrines and twelve-syllable verse to a secondary plane.

Eguren was not successful during his lifetime. The poet laureate of his time was José Santos Chocano, who claimed to be "the Walt Whitman of the South." The generation to which Eguren belonged tended to underestimate him, considering him too abstract and unusual. It is revealing that in 1938, when Ventura García Calderón edited the series titled Library of Peruvian Culture, he did not dedicate a single volume to the poetry of Eguren. Other conservative intellectuals, such as José de la Riva Agüero and Clemente Palma, were also skeptical of the value of his work.

Eguren found readers among the younger writers. The latter-day modernists of the magazine *Colónida*, founded in 1916 and headed by Abraham Valdelomar, praised him with fervor. Those poets saw in Eguren and in Manuel González Prada—a Parnassian and an anarchist thinker—two alternatives to the cultural establishment of the time. Several years later, the vanguardist poets Emilio Adolfo Westphalen, Carlos Oquendo de Amat, Martín Adán, and Xavier Abril recognized Eguren as a legitimate precursor of the new tendencies. The most eloquent proof of this support is the February 1929 issue of the magazine *Amauta*, tribune of the artistic vanguard and socialist ideas in Peru, which was dedicated to Eguren. Almost involuntarily, Eguren was proclaimed by his colleagues and by the critics of the day as the founder of contemporary Peruvian poetry, alongside César Vallejo. The passing years have demonstrated the durability and influence of this judgment.

Translated from the Spanish by Philip Donley

SELECTED BIBLIOGRAPHY

Editions

Poetry

Simbólicas. Lima, 1911.
La canción de las figuras. Lima, 1916.
Poesías. Lima, 1929.

Prose

Motivos estéticos. Edited by Estuardo Núñez. Lima, 1959.

Collected Works

Obras completas. Edited by Ricardo Silva-Santisteban. Lima, 1974.
Obra poética completa. Edited by Carlos Milla Batres. With a prologue by Luis Alberto Sánchez. Lima, 1974.
Poesías completas. Edited by Estuardo Núñez. Lima, 1961.

Biographical and Critical Studies

Abril, Xavier. "Traducción estética de Eguren." *Amauta* 21:12–15 (1929).
_____. "José María Eguren, poeta simbolista." *Le lingue straniere* (Rome) 15/1:3–23 (1966).
_____. *Eguren, el obscuro: El simbolismo en América.* Córdoba, Argentina, 1970.
Adán, Martín (pseudonym of Rafael de la Fuente Benavides). "Eguren." *Mercurio peruano* 182:246–260 (1942).
Basadre, Jorge. "José María Eguren y la nueva poesía." *Amauta* 3:7–8 (1926).
_____. "Elogio y elegía de José María Eguren." *Amauta* 21:21–31 (1929). Reprinted in Silva-Santisteban, below, with the title "Elogio de José María Eguren." Pp. 95–110.
Blanco López, Desiderio, and Raúl Bueno Chávez. "'La niña de la lámpara azul': Fundamentos de una lectura plural." *Hispamérica* 7/20:25–44 (1978).
Bustamente y Ballivián, Enrique. "Hacia la belleza y la armonía, 1." *Balnearios* 54/2 and 56/1 (1911 and 1913). Reprinted in Silva-Santisteban, below. Pp. 45–53.
Carrillo, Enrique A. "Ensayo sobre José María Eguren." *Colónida* 1/2:5–12 (1916). Reprinted in Silva-Santisteban, below. Pp. 85–94.
Cisneros, Luis Jaime. "Lengua y creación en José María Eguren." *Revista hispánica moderna* 34:330–332 (1967).
Corvalán, Octavio. In *Modernismo y vanguardia*. New York, 1967. Pp. 26–32.
Debarbieri Casagrande, César. *Los personajes en la poética de José María Eguren.* Lima, 1975.
Díaz Herrera, Jorge. "Contra el Eguren que no es." *Revista de crítica literaria latinoamericana* 7/13:83–91 (1981).
Eielson, Jorge, Sebastián Salazar Bondy, and Javier Solo-

guren. *La poesía contemporánea del Perú*. Lima, 1946. Pp. 7–34.

Ferrari, Américo. "La función del símbolo: Notas sobre José María Eguren." *Insula* 4:332–333 (1974). Reprinted in Silva-Santisteban, below. Pp. 127–134.

Goldberg, Isaac. "José María Eguren." In his *Studies in Spanish-American Literature*. New York, 1920. Pp. 292–306.

Higgins, James. "The Rupture Between Poet and Society in the Work of José María Eguren." *Kentucky Romance Quarterly* 20:59–74 (1973).

———. In *The Poet in Peru*. Liverpool, 1982. Pp. 1–23, 91–108.

Mariátegui, José Carlos. "Eguren." In his *Siete ensayos de interpretación de la realidad peruana*. Lima, 1928. Pp. 218–226. 3rd ed. Lima, 1959. Pp. 312–323.

———. "Contribución a la crítica de Eguren." *Amauta* 21:35–40 (1929).

Monguió, Luis. In *La poesía postmodernista peruana*. Mexico City, 1954. Pp. 17–21, 150–152.

Núñez, Estuardo. *José María Eguren: Vida y obra, antología, bibliografía*. New York, 1961.

———. *José María Eguren: Vida y obra*. Lima, 1964.

Ortega, Julio. In *Figuración de la persona*. Barcelona, 1971. Pp. 89–116.

Paoli, Roberto. "Eguren, tenor de las brumas." *Revista de crítica literaria latinoamericana* 2/3:25–53 (1976).

Rodríguez-Peralta, Phyllis White "The Modernism of José María Eguren." *Hispania* 56:222–229 (1973).

———. In *Tres poetas cumbres en la poesía peruana: Chocano, Eguren, Vallejo*. Madrid, 1983. Pp. 61–95.

Sánchez, Luis Alberto. "José María Eguren." In his *La literatura peruana*. 4. Asunción, 1951. Pp. 329–337.

———. In *Escritores representativos de América* 2. Madrid, 1957. Pp. 209–218.

Silva-Santisteban, Ricardo, ed. *José María Eguren, aproximaciones y perspectivas*. Lima, 1977.

Westphalen, Emilio Adolfo. "Eguren y Vallejo: Dos casos ejemplares." *Diálogos* 5/84:3–7 (1978).

Zulen, Pedro. "El neo-simbolismo poético." *Ilustración peruana* 112:1482–1483 (1911). Reprinted in Silva-Santisteban, above. Pp. 54–60.

Bibliography

Freudenthal, Juan R. and Patricia M. Freudenthal, eds. *Index to Anthologies of Latin American Literature in Translation*. Boston, 1977. P. 54. Cites five translations of Eguren poems.

Julio Herrera y Reissig

(1875–1910)

Hugo Achugar

According to one account, Julio Herrera y Reissig died—in his hometown, Montevideo, on 18 March 1910—reciting poetry while his wife, Julieta de la Fuente, played Chopin and Schumann at the piano. This story, as well as the one concerning Herrera's addiction to drugs, is presumably not true but suitable to the poet's life and personality.

The son of a patrician banker and the nephew of Julio Herrera y Obes, president of Uruguay (1890–1894), Herrera was born on 9 January 1875 into an elegant and wealthy family that soon after 1882 experienced financial difficulties. Educated according to his social status, Herrera attended different schools, most of them Catholic, though his real education was not systematic; the family library and certain relatives were more important than school. His self-education was typical for the "Generación del 900" (Generation of 1900), when writers like Florencio Sánchez, Horacio Quiroga, and Carlos Reyles did not attend the university. At the age of fifteen, following his uncle's accession to the presidency of the republic, Herrera got his first job as a clerk at the General Customs Office. As many of his biographers say, he was an overprotected boy because of his heart condition (which led to his premature death when he was thirty-five). This arrhythmia set a pace to his life; two years after starting his job, he

underwent a new health crisis and left the position. He went for a while to the countryside in Salto which, according to some critics, inspired most of the descriptions of nature and rural work in the sonnet collection *Los éxtasis de la montaña* (*The Ecstasies of the Mountain*, 1909) and other poems.

Because of his poor health and also probably because of the impassioned nature of his personality, he never worked for uninterrupted periods of time and for most of his life was financially dependent on his parents and later his brothers. In 1895, Herrera's family, economically ruined but still politically powerful, arranged for him a position within the state's bureaucracy; he worked as an assistant to the general inspector of the National Board of Elementary Schools. Due to changes in the political situation and boredom with his job, he resigned two years later. At this time, he met a schoolteacher with whom he later had a daughter, Soledad Luna (Solitude Moon), a name that reveals his poetic temperament. He legally recognized her when she was two years old, in 1904.

From 1897 on Herrera's life was devoted almost completely to his poetic work. In 1898 "La dictadura" (The Dictatorship) and "Miraje" (Mirage) were his first poems to be published. The latter received recognition from literary critics and, as he himself put it, the publication of the "craggy [verses of] 'Miraje' made me an instantaneous celebrity."

The following year Herrera published *La revista* (The Review), a literary journal concerned with art and science. At this time he was introduced to the most recent trends in poetry, both in France and Latin America. Until then he had been an epigonal romantic poet or, as Angel Rama put it, "the pedestrian verisifier," and from 1898 on [he collected] . . . all that which in the extinction of the nineteenth century represented the literary dross" (1973). In 1899, while publishing *La revista,* he met Toribio Vidal Belo and Roberto de las Carreras. The former, a minor poet who soon turned to politics, is considered to have acquainted Herrera with the new poetic forms, while de las Carreras, a more important influence, introduced him to a radically bohemian way of life. During the short period, not even a year, that *La revista* was published, Herrera was initiated into *modernismo,* the major cultural movement of the Hispanic world at the turn of the century. (Spanish American *modernismo* is different from Anglo-Saxon or Brazilian modernism; the latter two are close to what avant-garde was in Spanish America.)

Modernismo, as Federico de Onís has pointed out, was a major transformation in the last decades of the nineteenth century, involving not only literature and art but also philosophy, religion, and politics. It was, to a certain extent, the cultural answer that the Hispanic world gave when the first wave of industrialization reached that region and dramatically transformed society. In sociocultural language, *modernismo* has been described as the cultural phenomena accompanying modernization. Literary *modernismo* involved the blending of romanticism, Parnassianism, and symbolism as well as a profound attempt to change style and the concept of art and the artist.

Herrera's initiation to *modernismo* included his discovery of new rhymes, meters, and metaphors, and also his adoption of a set of values in which *écriture artistique* and spiritualized art constitute a statement against a rising bourgeoisie, whose values were devalued by the fetishization of merchandise. Herrera and the *modernistas* in general reacted against accumulation of wealth, scientific materialism, and the security of positivism and stressed the ideals of Beauty and Harmony. This does not mean that they did not

appreciate a luxurious or easy life; their attitude was more a neoromantic stance toward the new, emerging society. It is not surprising that they flirted with socialist and anarchist ideas. Herrera's short story "Eppur si muove . . ." (written in Buenos Aires and first published in *Prosas* [Prose, 1918]) shows this tendency, although he never dedicated any notable amount of writing to such inclinations. Herrera, as did many *modernistas,* heard the "music" of his era and much of the time he did not like it. Herrera's description of Montevideo's harbor construction in *Epílogo wagneriano a la "política de fusión"* (Wagnerian Epilogue to the "Politics of Fusion," 1902), is characteristic of his general attitude toward society: "I also hear, day and night, the thundering hammers—they don't let me sleep—the infernal humming of people involved in the works of the harbor . . . and nothing interests me."*

Whatever interest Herrera did have in sociopolitical issues was undoubtedly related to his family background and to the social function artists had during the nineteenth century. Since the beginning, with his first poem, "La dictadura," Herrera demonstrated a social and political sensibility that is best exemplified in his involvement with the political debate of 1899. That year Herrera was involved in the dispute among factions of the Partido Colorado, the ruling party. His participation in the question at hand—the desirability of engaging in the politics of alliance—was mostly ideological and propagandistic. In 1902 he published *Epílogo wagneriano a la "política de fusión,"* a major sociopolitical essay concerning this issue. Of the many essays the poet wrote on subjects other than literature, this is practically the only one that was published. Here he studied the characteristics of Uruguayan society and stated his most poignant opinions on the local middle class.

To the Uruguayans' minds the one who changes his opinions is a *miserable turncoat,* a shameless traitor; or they say about the heretic, "he has become crazy." They do not see in change the conquest of an idea not present

* Julio Herrera y Reissig, *Poesiás completas y páginas en prosa,* edited by Roberto Bula Piriz (Madrid, 1961). All quotations are from this edition, which hereafter will be referred to as RBP, followed by a page number. All translations from Herrera's work are those of this essay's author.

before, the dazzling ray of the way to Damascus, the long journey toward Truth on the steppes of reflection . . . the abandonment of the heavy harness full of conventional dust by the modernista peplum that opens its superb folds to the wind of persuasion.

(RBP, p. 779)

Even more eloquent is the passage in which Herrera comments on the Uruguayan family and on the general social condition. The following quotation shows the other side of the refined poet Herrera was generally considered to be.

> What other reason than the narrowness of a regimented life, the fear of unendowed daughters, the subdivision of a scarce income, the aristocratic perspective of pauperization, will lead the mother not to have more than one child? The selfish pleasure, the secret surgery, the galant obstetrician, and the most refined filters of Aphrodite thus become the accomplices to a deadly sterility that will be able to prepare the way for the victory of their adversaries.
>
> And then consider the Latin migration, the strikes, the terrorist attempts, the sonorous rages of the proletarian roaring, the unprecedented epilepses of the social organism, and you will find in those movements, just prior to the hemorrhage, a conspiration of hunger howling everywhere.

(RBP, pp. 788–789)

This *Epílogo* is also, in a sense, his farewell to Uruguayan politics. Herrera became disenchanted and decided not to pursue a political career. He was breaking not only with politics and with his family tradition, but also with the civic function artists traditionally had had within society. Like other *modernistas*, Herrera retreated to the world of art. Although not entirely lacking in social awareness, his poetic work from this point on was not notably "political." His poems, sophisticated and sometimes obscure, became a conscious and elaborated creation of a world torn by competing emotions: social, aesthetic, traditional, modern. This struggle has prompted some of his critics to speak of a typically *modernista* baroque writing or a baroque cultural universe.

As we have noted, Herrera's friendship with Roberto de las Carreras was of great importance. The role of the poet or the artist had changed since romanticism and de las Carreras and Herrera exem-

plified that change. The former's own work was of some consideration, but his really important "work" was his personal life. An illegitimate child of a wealthy and well-known lady (a matter of pride for de las Carreras), he became a major scandal in the sleepy and provincial Montevideo the moment he arrived from Paris. Not only his attire but also his *boutades* made him, in the eyes of local bourgeoisie, a dreadful dandy. Herrera and he "terrorized" the city with their outrageous behavior and dress. They published poems and letters in newspapers and journals and behaved as the *poètes maudits* they had read about or, in the case of de las Carreras, had seen in Paris. They referred to Montevideo as "Tontovideo" (Sillyvideo), and this came to typify their literary attitude at the time.

The social image that de las Carreras and Herrera cultivated was a far cry from the civic and bard image that romantic writers had developed during the preceding century. In fact, with the great social and economic transformations, poets no longer had a place in society. They were not considered "productive." With their undervalued skills—writing and speaking—they had to resort to journalism or teaching. In this sense, Herrera and de las Carreras were enacting a noisy protest against a society that relegated artists to a decorative or devalued function. That is precisely the meaning of Rubén Darío's well-known short story "El rey burgués" (The Bourgeois King, 1888), as well as much of Herrera's and other modernists' writings. Though the friendship with de las Carreras ended abruptly (in 1906)—because of a dispute over the authorship of some lines of poetry—Herrera had, by that time, gained a social and literary experience that became the watershed of his later work.

Herrera's major transformation occurred during the years between 1900 and 1902. In February 1900 he suffered his worst heart attack. He described this tremendous experience in rather sarcastic terms: "paroxysmal, arrhythmic, I arrived riding with my three legs to the peristyle of the funeral mansion," but the crisis affected both his life and his writing. This confrontation with death permeates his long poem "La vida" (The Life), written in 1900 and published in 1906. The poem attests to a dramatic change in Herrera's poetic and private life, his philosophy, and his aesthetics. *La vida* is a pseudo-philosophical reflection on the meaning of life, mainly through footnoted symbols. The poet, as often in *modernista* poems and novels, appears as the protagonist. He sees a seductive and incredible Amazon riding a mythical horse, and he pursues her in a symbolic journey through strange regions to the kingdom of Death. There this beloved one transforms herself into a dreadful knight, who in the philosophical consideration of the poem represents a symbol of life and the Poet's fate. The poem shows Herrera's early interest in technical words and unusual or difficult rhymes. It also shows his modernist belief in beauty and harmony as supreme values.

"La vida" was the major poem that showed a change in Herrera's poetry, though other poems have been mentioned as examples of his new poetic writing; perhaps the most quoted one is the sonnet "Holocausto" (Holocaust, 1899–1901), which is mainly important as the poet's first attempt to write a modernist poem. But since it belongs to an earlier period, when Herrera had not yet gone through his encounter with "his friend Death" (as he put it), it is not considered to be central to the change in his poetry. "Las pascuas del tiempo" (The Easter of Time, 1901) and "Ciles alucinada" (Ciles Hallucinated, 1903) are other first attempts in the new direction of Herrera's poetry. Written in 1902, "Ciles alucinada" is a transitional poem that deals with the subject of a hallucinated girl who lays down in the fields "covered by dream, moon and mystery." Many of the images in this poem were recovered by the poet later on; the important things about this poem are not only its stylistic elements but the interest Herrera starts showing in a world where imagination and irrealism are fundamental. In "Las pascuas del tiempo," a grotesque masquerade and parody along with metaphysics appear to be Herrera's attempt to widen his poetic world. At any rate, neither "Ciles alucinada" nor "Las pascuas del tiempo" have the poetic or philosophical importance of his long poem "La vida," and most surely they do not represent Herrera's major turning point.

In 1903 Herrera's family moved again, and the poet installed himself in a sort of attic of a house that became legendary. This attic room was baptized "La Torre de los Panoramas" (the Panoramas Tower), referring not only to the panoramic view but also to the openness of the place and its inhabitants. The tower became a meeting place for the local bohemians, where Herrera and many friends read poems, discussed literary questions, and proclaimed Herrera's "terrorist" opinions on local matters. In those days Herrera dubbed himself "Emperador Julio" (Julius the Emperor), and also was photographed by his friend Soiza Reilly in the legendary picture in which he is supposedly injecting himself with morphine. Horacio Quiroga, Vidal Belo, de las Carreras, Leopoldo Lugones, and others visited the Panoramas Tower, a place people still associate with the poetic transformation of *modernismo* and Herrera's extravaganzas.

Idea Vilariño said that the really important part of Herrera's poetic work consists of the poems he wrote from 1903 until his death in 1910. During this period he composed, almost without pause, his major poems; he traveled to Buenos Aires; his father and mother died; and he married Julieta de la Fuente. His trip to Buenos Aires in 1904 has been linked to the ongoing civil war in Uruguay. Although Herrera made some comments on the war, it seems that this trip was more motivated by personal and financial reasons. In Buenos Aires, in need of income, he worked with the census, the kind of work he typically disliked, but he did not stop writing. Many of the sonnets of *Los éxtasis de la montaña* were written at this time.

Back in Montevideo in 1905, he worked as a journalist, and in 1907 he published a new magazine, *La nueva atlántida* (The New Atlantis), which ended its circulation after the second issue. That year his father died, and the family, still financially insecure, moved again. While visiting his fiancée, Herrera suffered another heart attack and, because of his poor health, installed himself in Julieta de la Fuente's house; on 22 July 1908 he married Julieta, and soon after that his mother died. Herrera's economic situation was by that time quite precarious; journalism did not pay well enough so he tried to become a businessman. His attempt to run a liquor store ended in failure, as did his venture with the insurance field in 1909. So once again he turned to the state bureaucracy. It was during these sad and unfortunate years that Herrera wrote his most perfect and imaginative poems. He also experienced some public recognition, though not necessarily to the extent that he deserved or expected.

Herrera's poetry of this period is impressive for its variety and excellence. The variety, ambiguity, and, from time to time, obscureness of these works, reveal the assimilation of the hegemonic poetics of the aestheticist *modernismo* into his own style. The peculiar emphasis of his work has been analyzed from the point of view of style and has inspired some critics to characterize his poetry as an anticipation of the avant-garde. Other critics called Herrera a typical *modernista*, or a cubist *avant la lettre*. These characterizations focus on one of his main stylistic elements: his peculiar use of the metaphorical, which imbued his metaphors with new referents and new levels of meaning.

Luxurious and vertiginous, Herrera's poetry also revealed elements of incisiveness, imagination, irony, mockery, and parody—elements that did not follow an evolution but rather were simultaneous. His posthumous book of poems, *Los peregrinos de piedra* (The Stone Pilgrims; the title page is dated 1909, but the book appeared in mid 1910) is a holistic sample of his poetic register, a register that implies ways of imagination or "looping the loop," as the critic Carlos Roxlo called it in 1916. These ways include the bucolic, the nostalgic, and the metaphysical. Aestheticism is present in all of them, even in the celebratory "El laurel rosa" (The Rosebay), which opens the book. Subtitled "Apoteosis" (Apotheosis), this poem is dedicated to the French poet Sully Prudhomme, with all the mythological arsenal of Western tradition. But it is the image of the poet himself that is celebrated here and not just this particular French author. The celebration is mythological and serves as the foundation for the universe of the entire book. Space in "El laurel rosa," as well as in the whole collection, belongs to art and those who are invoked are the

> Almas amigas y bellos
> gimnastas, liras a sones
> de la orquesta de Pitágoras,
> venusinos Sacerdotes
> de la hembra Arquitectura
> y taumaturgos del bloque,
> príncipes doctos del Cromos,

> panidas trasnochadores,
> bajo la vinosa lámpara
> del sátiro Anacreonte,
> navegantes espectrales
> del Océano Aristóteles:
> en los imperios acústicos
> rueda el soberbio desorden . . .
> (RBP, p. 106)

> Friendly souls and beautiful
> gymnasts, assonant lyres
> from Pythagoras' orchestra
> Venusian Priests
> of female Architecture
> and thaumaturges from the block,
> wise princes from Chromes,
> Pan's nighthawks
> under satyr Anacreon's
> winy lamp,
> spectral navigators
> of Ocean Aristotle:
> in the acoustic Empires
> rolls the superb disorder . . .

These lines describe a harmonic society close to the speaker: an exclusive society, mostly Hellenic, that is able to enjoy the refinement and sophistication of the sonority of the lines. Poet and poetry are centers and saviors of "acoustic empires" and music and imagination have hegemony over ideology. This preference of the euphonic over any other reality does not mean an escape from reality but rather implies an imaginary way to construct and to destroy dialectic universes totally tied to the social process.

The following and best-known section of *Los peregrinos de piedra, Los éxtasis de la montaña*, reflects the bucolic temperament of the poet. The ecstasy seems to come from the mountain or is being experienced by the mountain itself, and is tied to mythology. Presumably the mountain could be Melanus, Pan's homeland and the location of mythical Arcadia. In this sense, the poems are literarily filiated and the mythical universe is a literary one: a universe in which ritualization, idyllic peace, pure communion, dream, and Chimera are united in order to initiate a process of mythification and irreality. An arcadic vision is described in "La vuelta de los campos" (The Return from the Fields):

Eapatos claveteados y báculos y chales . . .
Dos mozas con sus cántaros se deslizan apenas.
Huye el vuelo sonámbulo de las horas serenas.
Un suspiro de Arcadia peina los matorrales . . .
(RBP, p. 112)

Shoes garnished with nails and walking sticks and
shawls . . .
With their pitchers two maids slide by with difficulty.
The somnambulist flight of the serene hours glides
away.
An Arcadic sigh combs the bushes . . .

"An arcadic sigh," along with the "pillow of roses on which the orchard dreams," is the apotheosis of Nature. It is the universe free from the worldly noise where dream and the Chimera pervade everything, and Arcadia is identified with poetry and poetic sensibility. This world is inhabited by characters that come from a synthesis of Greek, Jewish, pagan, and Christian traditions: the idyllic shepherds and "the cassock / of the priest (who) seriously promenades himself in the orchard," are joined by a modern "Arcadia"—an elementary school, a drugstore, and a wealthy bourgeois. The parody is destroyed while being constructed, in a double movement of enthronement and dethronement, which blurs the arcadic character of the bucolic universe. That is what happens in the last tercet of "El guardabosque" (The Woodsman):

Los domingos visita la cocina del noble,
y al entrar, en la puerta deja el palo de roble.
De jamón y pan duro y de lástimas toscas

cuelga al hombro un surtido y echa a andar taciturno;
del cual comen, durante la semana, por turno:
él, los gatos y el perro, la consorte y las moscas . . .
(RBP, pp. 126–127.)

On Sundays he visits the noble's kitchen,
and when he enters, puts down his oak stick.
Ham and hard bread and coarse pity

hang packed from his shoulder, then he leaves
taciturn;
and during the week, by turns he will eat from the pack,
then the cats and the dog, his wife and the flies . . .

The ironic last line reveals that this Arcadia is neither very heavenly nor so Golden–Age–like. It is inhabited with farmers rather than shepherds, and their duplicity or duality is discovered with the ironic attack on the notions of progress, plutocratic materialism, and positivistic science. An aesthetic Arcadia is only possible in the poetic space:

Jardín de rosa angélico, la tierra guipuzcoana!
Edén que un Fra Doménico soñara en acuarelas . . .
Los hombres tienen rostros vírgines de manzana,
y son las frescas mozas óleos de antiguas telas.
("La misa cándida," in RBP, p. 124)

Angelic rose garden, the guipuzcoan land!
An Eden dreamed in watercolor by a Fra
Doménico . . .
Men have virginal faces of apples,
and the oil paintings of old canvasses are fresh girls.
(Candid Mass)

In *Los éxtasis de la montaña*, the only way to Arcadia is by the redemptive dream or art. Thus, it is through Chimera, made of art and dream, that it is possible to reach peace, the true and only peace of Arcadia. The ecstasy of the mountain is only possible in the poetic dream. This is not really escape from reality, though many readers have interpreted it this way. A more satisfying reading of these poems is to understand them as the creation of an image of a plutocratic reality that precludes any possibility for the poet's existence outside the realms of dream and irony. Herrera's Arcadia is a Januslike divinity that parodies, at the same time it celebrates, itself—it is both literary motive and the bourgeois modernity that encourages greed and vain science and tries to deconstruct the dream. If in "Los éxtasis de la montaña" reality tends to disappear through poetic dreams, in "Tertulia lunática" (Lunatic Party), the following section, the deconstruction of that reality is exacerbated through an intensification of the metaphor and the crazy loops of the "airplane of imagination," as Roxlo described it. In a certain way, "Tertulia lunática" and "Las Clepsidras" (The Clepsydras)—a beautiful and strange group of poems that do not form part of *Los peregrinos de piedra*—constitute a deliberate attempt to abolish the referential function of language and to free imagination, which is made possible by presenting the euphonic music of the line and free association of images as the only valid elements in poetry. This metaphorical excess is not divorced from other forms of excess, mainly grotesque, or from the shining appeal of metaphysics. In this sense, Emir Rodríguez Monegal has said that "Herrera's Pythagoreanism is not philosophical but poetic." On the other hand, Oscar Hahn has characterized "The Tower of the Sphinxes" (the main title of the "Tertulia lunática") as "an unintelligible Tower of Babel whose hermetism originates in the pulverization of the signified, as a consequence of the scandalous proliferation of the signifiers, the rhythmomania, and the lexical paranoia."

"Tertulia lunática" represents a rejection or a mistrust of reality. Reality, in this case, means a measurable object that can be reached and that is sovereign. The rejection of reality by use of a hyperbolic apparatus of rhymes and images works as an ironic decoder of the referential function of language. At the same time, an inner kingdom is established as an entity truer than the exterior one.

> Del insonoro interior
> de mis oscuros naufragios,
> zumba, viva de presagios,
> la Babilonia interior . . .

> From the soundless interior
> of my obscure failures,
> hums, alive in omens,
> the interior Babylon.

Herrera thus emphasizes subjectivity and interiorization. A "spectral reality" is produced by the fact that

> Las cosas se hacen facsímiles
> de mis alucinaciones
> y son como asociaciones
> simbólicas de facsímiles . . .
> (RBP, p. 137)

> Things become facsimiles
> of my hallucinations,
> and are like symbolic
> associations of facsimiles.

Here mimesis works not in relation to an empirical referent but in relation to hallucinations. Reality is

mediated by a mythifying idealism; or, as the poet says

> Fuegos fatuos de exorcismo
> ilustran mi doble vista,
> como una malabrista
> rutilación de exorcismo . . .
> (RBP, p. 134)

> Fatuous fires of exorcism
> illustrate my double vision,
> like a juggler's
> scintillation of exorcism.

This fire illuminates the discourse through irony—the double vision—and through discourse it also illuminates the disenchanted world, the pampered universe of the bourgeois, and the modernist paraphernalia. Herrera's poetry is, in consequence, a translation of the world and not just a mere reflection—a translation and also an unavoidable treason.

> Tal como en una capilla
> ardiente de hiperestesia,
> entre grillos de anestesia,
> tiembla la noche en capilla . . .
> Un gato negro a la orilla
> del cenador de bambú
> telegrafía una cu
> a Orión que le signa un guiño
> y al fin estrangula un niño
> impromptu hereje en miaú!

> La luna de plafon chino
> prestidigita en su riesgo,
> la testa truncada en sesgo . . .
> de algún Quasimodo chino . . .
> ("Officium tenebrarum,"
> in RBP, p. 143)

As in a chapel
burning with hyperesthesia,
between the irons of anesthesia,
shudders the night in the chapel . . .
A black cat on the edge
of the bamboo gazebo
telegraphs a *q*
to Orion that signals him a wink,
and at the end strangles a child
heretic impromptu in meeow!

The moon of Chinese soffit
prestidigitates at its own risk
the aslant truncated head
of some Chinese Quasimodo . . .

Translation in this case is practically impossible; it entails a major interpretation of the lines, and the intended ambiguity of the original is completely lost. It is precisely this difficulty of Herrera's well-known poem that has both alienated and fascinated readers. As with symbolism, allusions and euphony seem more important than meaning. Yet, one cannot escape the irony and the humor that permeate the poem and, above all, the rhythmomania that carries the lyric speaker to a total cut with the referent. This cut can also be found in such poems as "Solo verde-amarillo para flauta. Llave de U" (Yellow-Green Solo for Flute. In the Key of U), where all the rhyme is based on the *u* sound, reminiscent of certain poems by Edgar Allan Poe. With this poem music and, in Herrera's words, a "sixth sense" dominate, and the poet "dreams and says mass." The ironic, grotesque, and playful dream allows him to say in his essay "Psicologia literaria" that "in the empire of Chimera, to be a visionary is to be real, is to see the bottom" (Vilariño, 1978, pp. 343–351). This dream, though, costs him much suffering, because it implies a way to understand the world, the otherworld, and all that is opposite to the established world.

The section titled "Los parques abandonados" (The Forsaken Parks) is representative of Herrera's love poetry. Unlike the alexandrine sonnets of "Los éxtasis de la montaña," these endecasyllabic sonnets are melodramatic and ritualized versions of the operatic genre. As is the case of limit situations, everything seems to be final, ultimate, consecratory, superlative, without equal. There has been some critical discussion about whether these poems are *cursi* (kitsch). It seems impossible that a sophisticated poet such as Herrera could have written some of these poems without making fun of himself or a certain kind of love poetry. In any case, these sonnets go beyond the decadent posture, fashionable in those days, which displayed a morbid pleasure in many peculiar images. And they are quite different from Lugones' sonnets. Herrera was accused of plagiarism and fervently defended. It appears that he heard a primitive recording of Lugones' *Los crepúsculos del*

jardín (Garden Sunsets, 1905) and was "inspired" by some of them. (Fortunately, the Lugones/Herrera polemic over the authorship of many images and lines is finally finished.) Herrera's sonnets tend to be more parodical than Lugones'. They parody the rhetoric and universe of romanticism by hyperbolizing the modernist code and thus become, at the same time, a parody of the modernist code itself. It is in this context that we are inclined to understand the proliferation of images of the addressee—soul or beloved—as chalice, executioner, empress. In "Decoración heráldica" (Heraldic Decoration), for instance, there is a morbid conjunction of images like "dark velvet," "purest ivory," "satanic inclemency," "perjured love," and even a "sweet love" that is compared to a "sad little blind lamb," or the final image of the masochist "slave's heart" being offered as "a carpet" to the "satin of your executioner foot." Is this a parody? Is the poet mocking? Is it just kitsch? Or is it, along with the mansions, violet circles under the eyes, gazebos, and the rest of the paraphernalia, as Carlos Real de Azúa has suggested, a reconstruction of a closed universe? The sonnets are a reconstruction of a lost paradise, but at the same time they are the derision of that closed universe.

Errando en la heredad yerma y desnuda,
donde añoramos horas tan distintas,
bajo el ciprés, nos remordió una aguda
crisis de cosas para siempre extintas . . .

Vistió la tarde soñadoras tintas,
a modo de romántica viuda;
¡y al grito de un piano entre las quintas,
rompimos a llorar, ebrios de duda!

Llorábamos los íntimos y aciagos
muertos, que han sido nuestros sueños vagos . . .
Por fin, a trueque de glacial reproche,

sembramos de ilusión aquel retiro;
¡y graves, con el último suspiro,
salimos de la noche, hacia la noche! . . .
("Expiación," in RBP, p. 159)

Wandering in the nude and barren inheritance,
where we waxed nostalgic upon such distinctive hours,
under the cypress, an acute crisis
of things forever extinct, stung us with remorse . . .

The afternoon dressed in dreamy hues,
in the way of a romantic widow;
and at a cry of a piano among the villas,
we started weeping, drunk with doubt!

We wept for the intimate and unfortunate
dead, who have been our vague dreams . . .
Finally, in exchange for a glacial reproach,

we sowed with illusion that retreat;
and grave then, with our last sigh,
we left the night into night! . . .

Thanks to the image of "the romantic widow," the lost paradise is compared to the romantic universe. The evoking or mediating sensibility is that of morbid decadentism, but here it is hyperbolized and functions as ritual and sterile. Hyperbole, the exaggeration of affectivity, allows the rhetorical final line. Nevertheless, it is the evocation and the ritualization that announces the presence of a strong illusion— parodical illusion but illusion indeed. Illusion, Chimera, dream, artistic imagination, refinement, and, as before, "double vision," fascinate both the poem's speaker and its reader. Language for Herrera is an intellectual joy but not a romantic identification— with phrases like "the minimal sheepfold of your fingers" or the "determinative aneurysm," or, more obviously, with the last tercet of the sonnet "La sombra dolorosa" (The Painful Shadow):

> manchó la soñadora transparencia
> de la tarde infinita el tren lejano,
> aullando de dolor hacia la ausencia.
> (RBP, p. 150)

stained the dreaming transparence
of the infinite afternoon, the distant train,
painfully howling toward absence.

The final howl sounds like a derision, like an hyperesthetic questioning of opposed values and disarrangements, a little more complex than just a closed sentimental universe. Imagination, music, and excess are forms of construction and destruction of artistic universes hurt by "satanic inclemency," by disenchantment, and by the inescapable irony of a nostalgic double vision. Herrera imaginatively expresses his experience of the agonizing and the decadent, obtaining, nevertheless, seraphic and crystalline spaces.

The last section of *Los peregrinos de piedra* defines a transparent though complacently tragic world. Titled "Las campanas solariegas" (The Manorial Bells), it contains the long poem "La muerte del pastor" (The Shepherd's Death). As Bernard Gicovate has said, "The poem is unique among Herrera's work for its simplicity and serene beauty. Built around a symbolic 'carreta' [cart] that appears several times, it is a moving elegy on the death of a shepherd." Undoubtedly a stylized elegy, "La muerte del pastor" appears to be the final chord that restores to the parodic universe of *Los peregrinos de piedra* the harmony announced in "El laurel rosa." The pictorial impressionism of the octosyllables that constitutes the elegy displays a rich gamut, going from the opal to the yellow, and serves as a background to the "violet path" and "the lilac tears." In a way, the poem recalls the settings and soft colors of Pierre Puvis de Chavannes' paintings (many of which were of Greek or Roman inspiration, although his technique was not academicist or neoclassical but impressionist). Herrera's elegy, however, is a restoration of a classical universe; yet he mixes opal illusions and "the soul of the mountain" with tambourine and bacon to make that universe less sculptural and more in the realm of the everyday. "La muerte del pastor" is an idealistic and aesthetic affirmation, an affirmation related to poetry. The poetic system seemed close to breaking point, and this poem attempts to save it or, at least, tries to save the poetic language. And this is precisely Herrera's major poetic bet. The irony of the book's title—those pilgrims made out of stone dialectically still and traveling—serves to overshadow the everlasting elegiacal simplicity of "La muerte del pastor" as a final statement.

Herrera's poetry, during the productive years 1903 to 1910, does not reduce itself to *Los peregrinos de piedra*. This frenetical period of Herrera's poetic life coincides with the literary splendor of Uruguayan culture. He wrote many other poems, some essays, short stories, and even a couple of plays. He translated several poems by French authors like Émile Zola, Charles Baudelaire, and his admired Albert Victor Samain. After Herrera's death, his editor, Orsini Bertani, published his *Complete Works* in five volumes (1909–1913); included were *Los peregrinos de piedra*, *El teatro de los humildes* (The Theater of the Humble), *Las lunas de oro* (The Golden Moons), *Las pascuas del tiempo*, and *La vida y otros poemas* (Life and Other Poems). Besides the *Epílogo wagneriano*, Herrera wrote a number of prosaical pieces that were later collected in *Prosas* and an essay *El renacimiento en España* (The Renaissance in Spain, 1919). Of all his work, the late "Sonetos vascos" (Basque Sonnets), "Las Clepsidras," and "Berceuse Blanca" (White Berceuse) are probably the most important of the poems not collected in *Las peregrinos de piedra*. Written in the last two years of Herrera's life, the "Sonetos vascos" are similar to the poems of *Los éxtasis de la montaña*—though more vivid and depicting basque characters, tradition, and culture. "Las Clepsidras," generally subtitled "Cromos exóticos" (Exotic Chromes), is a group of eight sonnets. While rich in images and exquisite rhymes, these poems are best known for Herrera's mastery of rhythm and erotic subject matter. The exotic setting of "Las Clepsidras" and their obvious erotic allusions were part of the modernist posture. "Berceuse Blanca," dedicated to his wife, Julieta, was written between 1909 and 1910; it is considered to be Herrera's last work. The poem is rhythmically prodigious and is essentially constructed like a nursery rhyme—although this nursery rhyme concerns death. The simplicity of the first lines is not sustained; as the poem progresses, symbolism and hermetism complicate the image of the addressee: the beloved, poetry, soul, the universal and eternal woman. Which is it? There is no clear answer. The speaker promises love beyond death, and as in the other poems by Herrera a morbid atmosphere pervades the lines.

Herrera was totally conscious of his passion for art and his aesthetic view of the world. "Great Art is the art that evokes, the emotional art that works through suggestion, the one that needs a harmonious reader to be an instrumental soul and a clavecin to be a man to be felt," he said in "Psicologia literaria." Joining the modernist writers, he requires a consonant reader: a reader not very common in his day. His poetry requires a sister soul able to understand his poetic illusions as well as his mockery; both illusion and mockery were Herrera's proposal to a society that had forsaken the central values of art, spirituality, and

beauty. As with many other modernists, Herrera's work has been misread, acclaimed, and derided. Today Herrera's poetry stands as a cornerstone of Latin America's literary heritage: Latin American and Spanish poets from Jorge Luis Borges to César Vallejo and from Vicente Huidobro to Pablo Neruda have either recognized or been directly influenced by his work. Undoubtedly, Herrera y Reissig has gained a permanent place in literary history.

SELECTED BIBLIOGRAPHY

First Editions

Poetry

Los peregrinos de piedra. Montevideo, 1909. (The book actually appeared in 1910.)

Ciles alucinada. With a prologue by Roberto Brenes Mesén. San José, 1916.

Ópalos (poemas en prosa). Buenos Aires, 1919.

Los parques abandonados. Buenos Aires, 1919.

Las pascuas del tiempo. Madrid, 1920.

Las lunas de oro. Buenos Aires, 1924.

Los éxtasis de la montaña. La Plata, Argentina, 1943. This edition is a reprint of *Los peregrinos de piedra*.

Prose

Epílogo wagneriano a la "política de fusión." Montevideo, 1902.

Prosas. Críticas, cuentos, commentarios. With a prologue by Vicente A. Salaverri. Montevideo and Valencia, 1918.

El renacimiento en España. Montevideo, 1919.

Later Editions

Collected Works

Although some of the following titles are called "complete works," none of them are really complete. No such edition yet exists.

Herrera y Reissig: Antologia, estudio crítico y notas. With a prologue by Roger Mirza. Montevideo, 1975.

Obras completas. 5 vols. Montevideo, 1909–1913. 1: *Los peregrinos de piedra*. 2: *El teatro de los humildes*. 3: *Las lunas de oro*. 4: *Las pascuas del tiempo*. 5: *La vida y otros poemas*. Herrera prepared and titled only the first volume. This was the first edition of the collected works.

Obras poéticas. With a prologue by Alfredo Zum Felde. Montevideo, 1966.

Páginas escogidas. With a prologue by Juan Más y Pí. Barcelona, 1914.

Poesía completa y prosa selecta. With a prologue by Idea Vileriño. Caracas, 1978.

Poesías. With a prologue by Mario J. Alvarez. Montevideo, 1975.

Poesías. Edited and with an introduction by Ana Victoria Mondada. Mexico City, 1977.

Poesías completas. With a preliminary essay by Guillermo de Torre. Buenos Aires, 1942.

Poesías completas. Edited by Roberto Bula Píriz. Madrid, 1951.

Poesías completas y páginas en prosa. Edited by Roberto Bula Píriz. Madrid, 1961. The most useful edition to date.

Selected Unpublished Work

Herrera's manuscripts are held in the Biblioteca Nacional in Montevideo. In 1951 Roberto Bula Píriz provided a (still incomplete) list of unpublished works.

"Cosas de aldea" [Town Matters], 1897. Prose.

"Mi capital" [My Assets], 1898–1901. Prose.

"Discurso ante la tumba de Federico Ferrando" [Speech Before the Grave of Federico Fernando], 1902. Prose.

"La sombra" [The Shadow], 1905. Play.

"Manuel Medina Betancourt," 1906. Literary criticism.

"Relaciones del hombre con el suelo" [Relationships of Man with the Land], n.d. Prose essay.

"El payador" [The Minstrel], 1908. Prose.

Translations

Most of Herrera's work is still untranslated. Additional translations of poems are listed in Juan R. and Patricia M. Freudenthal, *Index to Anthologies of Latin American Literature in English Translation.* Boston, 1977. P. 82.

"Berceuse Blanca." Translated by Thomas Walsh. *Poetry Lore* 33:601–607 (1922).

"Los carros." Translated by Thomas Walsh. In *Hispanic Anthology,* edited by Thomas Walsh. New York, 1920.

"La cena." Translated by G. Dundas Craig. In Arturo Torres-Ríoseco, *The Epic of Latin American Literature.* New York, 1942. Pp. 112–113.

"El Cura." Translated by Thomas Walsh. In his *Hispanic Anthology.* New York, 1920.

"La iglesia." Translated by Thomas Walsh. In his *Hispanic Anthology.* New York, 1920.

"Otoño." Partial translation by H. R. Hays. In *12 Spanish American Poets.* New Haven, Conn., 1943, P. 8.

"La siesta." Translated by H. R. Hays. In *12 Spanish American Poets.* New Haven, Conn., 1943. P. 9.

Biographical and Critical Studies

Anido, Nayode. "Le modernisme dans la poésie de Julio Herrera y Reissig." In *Aspects du XIXème siècle ibérique et ibero-américain. Actes du XIIème congres de la Sociéte des hispanistes français de l'enseignement supérieur.* Lille, France, 1977.

Ardao, Arturo. *Etapas de la inteligencia uruguaya.* Montevideo, 1971. P. 438.

Blanco Fombona, Rufino. *El modernismo y los poetas modernistas.* Madrid, 1929. Pp. 191–219.

_____. "El poeta uruguayo Julio Herrera y Reissig." *Sol,* 6 June 1923.

Blengio, Brito Raúl. *Approximación la poesía de Herrera.* Montevideo, 1967.

_____. *Herrera y Ressig: Del modernismo a la vanguardia.* Montevideo, 1978.

Borges, Jorge Luis. "Julio Herrera y Reissig." In *Inquisiciones.* Buenos Aires, 1925. Pp. 139–145.

Bula Píriz, Roberto. *Herrera y Reissig (1875–1910). Vida y obra, bibliografía, antología.* New York, 1952.

_____. "Estudio preliminar." Prologue to Julio Herrera y Reissig. *Poesías completas y páginas en prosa.* Madrid, 1961.

Caballo verde para la poesía 5 (Madrid) (1937, ?). Special issue devoted to Herrera; includes essays by Rubén Darío and Gómez de la Serna, and poems by Pablo Neruda and others.

Cernuda, Luis. "Julio Herrera y Reissig." *Cultura moderna,* November 1945.

Colquhoun, Elizabeth. "Notes on French Influences in the Work of Julio Herrera y Reissig." *Bulletin of Spanish Studies* 21:145–158 (1944).

Crispo Acosta, Osvaldo (published under the pseudonym Lauxar). *Motivos de crítica 2.* Montevideo, 1965. Pp. 55–113.

La cruz del sur 5/28 (1930). This issue dedicated to Julio Herrera y Reissig includes essays by E. Mario Barreda, Jorge Luis Borges, R. Cansinos-Asséns, and others.

Daireaux, Max. *Panorama de la littérature hispano-américaine.* Paris, 1930. Pp. 108–112.

Flores, Ángel, ed. *The Literature of Spanish America 3,* part 1. New York, 1968. Pp. 493–505.

Gicovate, Bernard. *Julio Herrera y Reissig and the Symbolists.* Berkeley, Calif., and Los Angeles, 1957.

Hahn, Oscar. "Herrera y Reissig o el indiscreto de lo cursi." *Texto crítico* 5/12:261–266 (1979).

Herrera y Reissig, Herminia. *Julio Herrera y Reissig: Grandeza en el infortunio*. Montevideo, 1949.

Herrera y Reissig, Teodoro. "Algunos aspectos ignoradas de la vida y la obra de Julio Herrera y Reissig." *Hiperión* 87:2–14 (1943).

Huidobro, Vicente. "Al fin se descubre mi maestro." *Atenea* 2/7:217–244 (1925).

Onís, Federico de. *Antología de la poesía española e hispano-americano (1882–1932)*. Madrid, 1934. Pp. 469–488.

Oribe, Emilio. *Poética y plástica*. Montevideo, 1930. Pp. 214–299.

———. "La voz de la Universidad y de la Academia Nacional de Letras." *Revista nacional* 6/63:352–355 (1943).

Pereira Rodríguez, José. "El caso Lugones-Herrera y Reissig: Examen retrospectivo de la cuestión." *Repertorio americano* 11:10–11 (1925).

Pérez Pintos, Diego et al. *Homenaje a Julio Herrera y Reissig*. Montevideo, 1963.

Phillips, Allen W. "La metáfora en la obra de Julio Herrera y Reissig." *Revista iberoamericana* 16/31:31–48 (1950).

Pino Saavedra, Yolando. *La poesia de Julio Herrera y Reissig. Sus temas y su estilo*. Santiago, Chile, 1932.

Quiroga, Horacio. "El caso Lugones-Herrera y Reissig." *El Hogar*, 17 July 1925.

Rama, Ángel. "La estética de Julio Herrera y Reissig: El travestido de la muerte" *Revista Río piedras 2* (1973).

———. *Las máscaras democráticas del modernismo*. Montevideo, 1985.

Rodríguez Monegal, Emir. "La poesía modernista y la crítica." Paper at Gainesville (Florida) Conference of the Instituto Internacional de Literatura Iberoamericana, 1977.

Seluja, Antonio. *Julio Herrera y Reissig, vida y obre*. Montevideo, 1984.

Sucre, Guillermo. *La máscara, la transparencia*. Caracas, 1976.

Vilariño, Idea. "Julio Herrera y Reissig. Seis años de su poesías." *Número* 2/6–8:118–161 (1950).

———. "*La torre de las esfinges* como tarea." *Número* 2/10–11:601–609 (1950).

———. *Julio Herrera y Reissig*. Montevideo, 1978.

Villavicencio, Laura N. "La distorsión de las imágenes en la poesía." de Julio Herrera y Reissig." *Cuadernos Hispanoamericanos* 309:389–402 (1976).

Visca, Arturo Sergio. *Antología de poetas modernistas menores*. Montevideo, 1971.

Walsh, Thomas. "Julio Herrera y Reissig. A Disciple of Edgar Allan Poe." *Poet Lore* 33:601–607 (1922).

Yurkievich, Saúl. *Celebración del modernismo*. Barcelona, 1976. Pp. 75–98.

Florencio Sánchez

(1875–1910)

Georgette M. Dorn

Playwright and social reformer Florencio Sánchez was born on 17 January 1875 in Montevideo, Uruguay, the oldest of eleven children of Olegario Sánchez and Jovita Musante. The family moved north to Treinta y Tres when Sánchez was an infant and to the town of Minas when he was seven. Here he attended grade school. He enrolled in a private secondary school in Montevideo but left after one year. With the help of an uncle he secured a position in the municipal government of Minas in 1890. While working as a clerk, he began writing articles for *La Voz del Pueblo*, the Minas newspaper. His often caustic and trenchant pieces of social and political commentary were signed with the pseudonym Jack the Ripper, signifying his intention when he was still in his teens of "ripping apart" society's complacency.

From an early age Sánchez' true vocation seemed to be the theater. Always shielded by a pseudonym, he wrote mock farces in the form of short plays poking fun at local personalities in the guise of dramatic figures. He excelled at writing idiomatic, humorous, and pungent dialogue. He also acted in amateur theatricals, becoming somewhat of a local celebrity. Friends called him *el charrúa* (the *Charrúas* were the fierce native inhabitants of Uruguay at the time of the Spaniards' arrival in the sixteenth century), partly because of his thick black hair and large hooded eyes and partly because of his combativeness. Since he seemed to be devoting more time to journalism and theater than to his job, he was asked to leave.

In 1893 Sánchez crossed the River Plate, the broad estuary separating Uruguay and Argentina, and found a job with the government of Buenos Aires province in the capital city of La Plata working for the Office of Demography and Statistics. He began reading voraciously books and articles on criminal sociology, particularly the works of Jean Charcot and César Lombroso, whose theories on psychiatry and criminology were very influential in Argentina. When his department closed down a year later owing to budget cutbacks, Sánchez returned to Montevideo and wrote articles for *La Razón* (Reason) and *El Siglo* (Century), gaining valuable experience and meeting influential Uruguayan journalists and writers. He taught himself to read French and occasionally was asked to translate bulletins from *Le Figaro* of Paris for *La Razón*. He also wrote theater reviews.

The Sánchez family belonged to the *blanco* (white) party, the more conservative of Uruguay's two main political parties, with deep rural roots and a tradition of being led by *caudillos* (strong, personalistic leaders). Sánchez joined *caudillo* Aparicio Saraiva's forces in a civil war against what was perceived as the corrupt government of President Juan B. Idiarte Borda. He fought with a unit that invaded Rio Grande do Sul in Brazil. There he met the Brazilian *caudillo* João Francisco, who was helping Saraiva. The conflict was settled after the *colorados* (reds, or more liberal party) granted minority representation to the *blancos* in congress. Saraiva, one of the last of the nineteenth-century *caudillos*, was not defeated completely until 1904.

Carnage and bloodshed on the battlefield led Sánchez to reflect on *caudillo* rule and to perceive that it was always personalistic, cruel, demagogic, exploitative, and opposed to progress. Taking as an example the ruling *caudillo* João Francisco, he wrote *El caudillaje criminal en Sud América* (Criminal *Caudillo* Rule in South America, 1914), which first appeared as a monograph in 1903 in the series entitled "Archivos de Psicología y Criminología" (Archives of Psychology and Criminology), edited by the well-known Argentine sociologist José Ingenieros. Another monograph, *Estudio sobre João Francisco* (Study on João Francisco), was published in the same series. These studies were also serialized in several newspapers, among them *El Sol* of Montevideo and *La República* of Rosario, Argentina. Sánchez saw the *caudillo*-dominated *blancos* clinging to a vanishing past, fighting against the more progressive *colorados* in a losing battle. He forsook his family's allegiance to the *blanco* party and joined the even more progressive forces in the anarchist movement, which was experiencing a resurgence in the River Plate region at the turn of the century. Sánchez summed up his disillusionment with traditional politics and his newfound faith in the anarchist movement in *Cartas de un flojo* (Letters from a Lazybones, 1914), portions of which he read in public at the International Center of Social Studies of Montevideo where anarchists dominated. The essay was also serialized in newspapers. He began making short trips to Buenos Aires, where he wrote occasional pieces for such anarchist newspapers as *La Protesta Humana* and *La Questione Soziale*.

In 1898 Sánchez moved to Rosario, Argentina, invited by Lisandro de la Torre, a rising political figure in progressive movements, to work on the staff of *La República*. He resigned after a few months, disliking the routine of working during the day and preferring to work late into the night. He chose to free-lance for several Rosario newspapers, chiefly *La Época*, while working in political causes and helping to organize labor unions. He also contributed essays to the sporadically published anarchist newspaper *Demoliamo* (We Shall Demolish), which took pride in not accepting subscriptions. When the Italian anarchist and journalist Luigi Barzini visited Rosario, it was Sánchez who showed him around. Not having steady employment, not eating regularly, and living in rooming houses gave Sánchez an opportunity to observe the plight of the poor firsthand and convinced him that anarchism could solve society's ills. He took part in demonstrations, once participating in a sit-in against his old employer *La República*, and was briefly jailed.

In addition to newspaper articles, Sánchez wrote theater reviews for *La Época* and worked in amateur theater. From time to time he visited Buenos Aires to familiarize himself with theater in the Argentine capital. Buenos Aires had become transformed during the previous two decades from a sprawling, muddy village into a glittering metropolis. In the capital, Sánchez became a steady customer of the cafés Los Inmortales (The Immortals) and Polo Bamba, favorite watering-places of artists, newspapermen, writers, and bohemians, who met to discuss politics or art, often until dawn. Lacking a steady income, borrowing from friends, keeping irregular hours, smoking and drinking began to take their toll, and Sánchez' health deteriorated.

The first public presentation of one of his plays in a professional theater would have been *Gente pobre* (Poor Folk) on 26 June 1902, in Rosario. However, at the last minute the city police banned the performance. The play contained thinly veiled satirical portrayals of Rosario citizens. During the ensuing melée Sánchez was clubbed by a policeman. Having found his vocation as a playwright, Sánchez realized that his anarchist tendencies collided with the prevailing traditionalist views of the city's establishment. He finally succeeded in opening his first play in Rosario, the musical *Canillita* (The Newspaperboy), on 2 October 1902, to enormous popular acclaim and excellent reviews. Based on a character in an earlier play, *Ladrones* (Thieves), which he had presented with amateurs in 1900 in Montevideo at the International Center for Social Studies, the protagonist of *Canillita* was modeled after the ragged adolescents who hawked *La República* on the streets of Rosario. They wore threadbare stovepipe trousers in real life, inspiring Sánchez to coin the word *canillita* (little stovepipe) to describe them. The word immediately became part of the River Plate lexicon. The play presents the plight of a newspaper vendor, a youth who supports his invalid brother and tries to shield his mother from an irresponsible stepfather. The stark realism tempered with humor, the music, and the irrepressible central character captured the public's fancy and catapulted Sánchez to local fame.

Exhausted after the success of *Canillita* and on the verge of a nervous breakdown, Sánchez accepted a friend's invitation to take a long vacation at the latter's *estancia* (country estate) in Colonia Aldao in Santa Fe province. Sánchez had been told by a physician that he had weak lungs, suffered from depression, and needed rest and regular meals. During his vacation in the lush Santa Fe countryside, he once again was struck by the beauty and simplicity of the rural Argentina of the *gaucho* (South American cowboy) and the *criollo* (originating in the Americas, also used to refer to authentic Argentines). He perceived how rapidly the ways of the city and the arrival of waves of foreign immigrants had been altering traditional rural values and producing culture clashes and strife between natives and foreigners. It was here that he conceived the topic of *La gringa* (The Immigrant Girl, premiered in 1904), his most successful play. It deals not so much with the protagonist as with Cantalicio, who symbolizes the vanishing *gaucho*, whose way of life was becoming obsolete in an age of technological change.

Upon his return to Rosario, Sánchez realized that he would have to move to Buenos Aires to gain a national reputation. His ambition was fueled by his desire to marry Catalina Raventos, a girl he had met in 1897 during one of his trips to Buenos Aires. She came from an educated, middle-class family, and her parents were not eager for her to marry a man whose way of life and politics they distrusted. Although Sánchez worked hard on new plays, articles, and essays for the magazine *Caras y caretas* (Faces and Masks), he also continued his life of nonchalance,

spending his nights at Los Inmortales or Polo Bamba, where he met such writers and journalists as Leopoldo Lugones, Joaquín de Vedia, Roberto J. Payró, and Martín Doello Jurado, who became a lifelong friend.

Theater in Buenos Aires was vigorous and boasted a long tradition dating from colonial days. At the turn of the century, two genres—*gaucho* pantomime playlets and the circus—united, and these hybrid productions were popular throughout the country. *Gaucho* pantomime developed into *sainetes* (musical farces) and into drawing-room dramas. Sánchez worked feverishly on such a drama during the cold Southern Hemisphere winter of Buenos Aires and finished *M'hijo el dotor* (My Son the Lawyer) in about six days, working almost around the clock. Joaquín de Vedia pronounced it "the best dramatic piece produced in Buenos Aires to date" and convinced Gerónimo Podestá to stage it. The Podestá family of actors, directors, and producers, who dominated the theater scene in the capital, produced and acted in many of Sánchez' most acclaimed plays. *M'hijo el dotor* opened on 13 August 1903 to rave reviews and great popular acclaim. It brought overnight fame to its author.

Set in the countryside, *M'hijo el dotor* belongs to Sánchez' group of "rural plays" and focuses on the rapidly vanishing traditional and rural way of life and *criollo* values. The lovable old *criollo* Olegario (which was Sánchez' father's name) has a selfish and deceitful son, Julio, who is steeped in modern book-learning and revolutionary theories. Julio seduces Jesusa, a sweet girl and Olegario's protégée, but then refuses to marry the girl because he loves a city girl. Jesusa is perhaps the most fully realized of Sánchez' female characters. The play deals with generational conflict and the antagonism between traditional values and modern, pragmatic ways. It reminds the reader of works by Hermann Sudermann, Ivan Turgenev, and Eugène Brieux. Julio claims freedom from moral responsibility, while Olegario resents his son's rejection of the old values of honoring one's commitments and adherence to high personal ethics. In the end, Julio agrees to marry Jesusa, forsaking his city girlfriend. The Uruguayan critic Emilio Frugoni said that *M'hijo* was the first truly artistic national drama in the River Plate and Sánchez the originator of first-class theater in the region.

The money received from the play allowed the playwright to marry Catalina Raventos. The wedding took place at a Catholic church on 25 September 1903, despite Sánchez' agnosticism. Sánchez remained devoted to his wife throughout his short life. The couple rented a flat in the center of Buenos Aires and a few years later a suburban house and garden in Banfield, where Sánchez kept a pet heron. Owing to his weak lungs and bouts of depression, Sánchez also took occasional vacations in the country.

In 1904 *Canillita* was staged in Buenos Aires and took the capital by storm. Sánchez opened three new successful plays that same year. *Cédulas de San Juan* (Midsummer Day Parents) made its debut in August; it deals with country folk celebrating the feast of St. John the Baptist, the patron saint of Juan, the father in the play. Adela has two suitors—Juan's son, Fortunato, and Hilario. The rival suitors fight a knife duel over Adela in time-honored *gaucho* fashion. As Hilario is brought in fatally wounded, the fickle Adela confesses her love for him. The play's theme is familiar, the *gaucho* drama centering on a fight to defend one's honor. The next play, *Gente pobre* (Poor Folk), opened a few months later. Unlike the sunny rural setting of *Cédulas*, this drama takes place in a wretched tenement house. The central character is a seamstress married to a man unable to support the family. They suffer a series of mishaps. Frugoni compared the realism and social depth in *Gente pobre* to the best in Émile Zola.

The third play staged by Sánchez in 1904 was *La gringa*, and it remains his best-known piece. *Gringo* was a word Argentines used for European immigrants; at the turn of the century in the River Plate area these immigrants were mostly Italians. The play portrays the social and economic impact of the industrious immigrants on the native Argentines' indolent way of life. Cantalicio, one of Sánchez' most memorable characters, is an old *criollo* who loses his ranch to the industrious Italian Nicola. The *gringa* is Victoria, Nicola's daughter. She falls in love with Próspero, Cantalicio's son, who is then fired by Nicola. The Italian, although fond of the young man, disapproves of the native Argentines' leisurely ways. Cantalicio and his family move away. On a return visit, he is knocked down by an automobile; the old *gaucho* succumbs to a machine. Cantalicio is nursed

by Victoria, and she confesses her love for Próspero to the old man. Finally, both fathers give their blessings to the young couple, a happy ending that according to Argentine critic Ricardo Rojas symbolizes the union of the *gringo* and *criollo* lineages. One of the characters states, "From this union will evolve the strong race of the future."

La gringa highlights racial antagonism between Argentines and immigrants. The natives feel threatened by the enterprising immigrants, while the immigrants despise what they perceive as the Argentines' indolence. Yet the Italians in their own country also tend toward indolence and prize love of nature; it is only when they emigrate that they become such strivers. Victoria inherits some of the old atavistic Italian traits and is thus more like an Argentine.

The first of the four Sánchez plays that opened in 1905, *Barranca abajo* (Down the Gully), is considered with *La gringa* to be the best of his production. *Barranca abajo* is a somber *gaucho* drama that vividly depicts customs in the Argentine countryside. The protagonist is the lovable old *criollo* Zoilo, husband of Dolores and father of three daughters. Owing to depressed circumstances he has to sell his ranch and move away. The family faces grim poverty, and Zoilo's attempted suicide is thwarted by his friend Aniceto. Sánchez portrays passion, jealousy, and above all the anguish and uncertainty suffered by the poor. *Barranca* is the most forceful of his plays, a masterful depiction of the struggle between the old order and the new. It is also the play of Sánchez' most analyzed by social historians.

The playwright called his next play, *Mano Santa* (Healing Hand), a social satire. Staged by the Podestás in 1905, it is set in a tenement where Carlos and his wife, Luisa, fight constantly over Luisa's visits to a quack healer. *En familia* (Family Circle), which opened in October of the same year, is carefully executed and delineated. Jorge, the father, represents a negligent and decadent *gaucho*, lacking in integrity and loyalty. Two of his sons are lazy and his daughters vain, but Damián, the third son, becomes a success in the city. Upon returning, he tries to redeem the family and change its fortunes. In the figure of Damián, the helpful son, Sánchez creates "the reformer," a complex character.

Los muertos (The Dead) followed on 23 October

1905. It featured a middle-class family in an urban environment. Lisandro, masterfully played by José Podestá, is Amelia's estranged husband. Amelia is raising the couple's little son, also named Lisandro. Her love interest is Julián. During the climax, the drunken husband kills Julián. It is Lisandro who declaims the central point of the drama: "Of course I am dead, like so many people around here. A man whose character is dead is a dead man who moves about." Alberto Zum Felde considered this drama of bloodshed and orgy a masterpiece. Frugoni praised its irresistible tragic force and deemed it a milestone in Sánchez' theater.

Struggling with bouts of depression and incipient tuberculosis, Sánchez took almost eight months to finish a new play. *El conventillo* (The Tenement) was produced by a Spanish company in June 1906. In July he opened *El desalojo* (The Eviction), a one-act drama also set in a tenement and focusing on the eviction of a poor woman with small children, while her husband is in the hospital. The play features inquisitive, cruel neighbors as well as a kind friend who tries to help. The message concerns the dissolution of the family against the background of a society that does not seem to care.

El pasado de una vida (One's Past), produced in 1906, is a three-act play in which Ernesto, the protagonist, is forced to break his engagement to Carmen, owing to her mother's staunch opposition. Struggling to find the real reason for this opposition, the young man extracts the truth from his own mother, namely that she had had an affair with Carmen's father many years ago and thus the betrothed may be siblings. *Pasado* is not considered one of his best plays.

Los curdas (The Drunkards), which opened at the beginning of January 1907, is also one of Sánchez' weaker works. It portrays character types rather than clear-cut individuals, presenting low-life men and women of Buenos Aires. *La Tigra* (The Tigress) opened on 2 January 1907, the same night as *Los curdas*, but at a different theater. The woman protagonist, Tigra, starts out as a nightclub singer and ends up a prostitute, but she retains an abiding love for her mother. *Tigra* was harshly criticized; many thought it extolled immorality.

Six days later *Moneda Falsa* (Phony Money) opened to universal praise and critical acclaim. Set in Buenos Aires, *Moneda Falsa* features thieves, pimps, and counterfeiters—many of them Italian. However, the racial antagonism found in some of his other plays is absent here. Antonio, the protagonist, is nicknamed "Moneda Falsa" at the age of nine and has no incentive to reform. Carmen, his mistress, hides counterfeit bills in Antonio's clothes at her husband's bidding. The husband then alerts police, and Antonio is caught. He assumes responsibility for a crime not his own to protect the woman he loves, who betrayed him. *Moneda Falsa* contains excellent characterizations and lively street scenes.

Sánchez opened yet another play in January 1907, a light *gaucho* operetta, *El cacique de Pichuela* (The Cacique of Pichuela). In addition to *Moneda Falsa*, the other acclaimed play in 1907 was *Nuestros hijos* (Our Children), which opened in May. The drama, set in Montevideo, features Señor Díaz, his wife, and their two daughters and son. Daughter Mecha becomes pregnant by Enrique, scion of a prominent family, who plans a swift escape to Europe. However, Alberto, Mecha's brother, challenges Enrique to a duel. The latter then agrees to marry the girl. Mecha discovers she no longer loves Enrique, decides to remain single, and is backed by her father. Díaz had been compiling statistics on illegitimate children for years; when the situation occurs in his own family, he faces it squarely. The play is a ringing defense of motherhood—"It is never a crime," in Díaz' words. The play also indicts bourgeois society's hypocrisy. Díaz is a solitary figure, reminiscent of Henrik Ibsen's title character from *John Gabriel Borkman* (1896). Critics hailed *Nuestros hijos* as a masterpiece and one of the most successful dramas to be produced in the River Plate region.

Sánchez' last successful drama, *Los derechos de la salud* (The Rights of Health) opened on 20 December 1907. In this gripping drama, Roberto, the husband of tubercular Luisa, is in love with Renata, Luisa's sister. Luisa survives an attempted suicide and is quite ill. Early one morning, Luisa comes out of her room to find Renata asleep with her head on Roberto's shoulder, both exhausted from caring for Luisa. The sick wife faints as the play ends. *Los derechos* was loosely based on Roberto Bracco's *Il diritto di vivere* (The Right to Live, 1900) and on Hermann Sudermann's *Der Wunsch* (The Wish, 1886). It deals with alienation of affection and the right to love, as it is pitted against previous commitments. Frugoni considered *Derechos* Sánchez' best play; he said it was "perfectly constructed; nothing is missing and nothing is in excess. . . . [It] is one of the most serious and transcendental dramas of ideas that has been written in the Spanish language in the last few years."

Plagued by worsening health, Sánchez finished only one play in 1908, *Marta Gruni* (Marta Gruni), a drama that opened in Montevideo in July of that year and in Buenos Aires in November. The protagonist, Marta Gruni, is a lively and popular girl who lives in a tenement with her family, who continually harass her. Marta's alcoholic brother, Marcos, wants Marta to marry his friend Stefano, another drunkard. Marta, however, loves a man from the middle class and meets him clandestinely. Fidela, a rival for Stefano's love, informs on Marta to Marcos. During a party to celebrate Marcos' birthday, Marta and her lover plan to elope. Having heard of the plan from Fidela, Marcos kills Marta's lover during the party. Music relieves the intense and grim realism of the play. Although a lesser work, *Marta Gruni* possesses charm and a firm structure and presents well-defined characters. It is one of Sánchez' few plays featuring a well-defined female protagonist. He had been more successful with male characters, perhaps because he spent most of his life in such male environments as newspaper offices and bars, and among political organizers. Although happily married, his life with Catita (his nickname for Catalina) seemed a thing apart.

Sánchez' last play staged was *Un buen negocio* (A Good Deal), an unconvincing one-act play that opened in 1908. It features Marcelina, a middle-class mother of four children who discovers upon her husband's death that his business partner had embezzled most of their money. Rogelio, the business partner, offers to help out, if Ana María, one of the daughters, will agree to marry him. Ana María asks her boyfriend to take her away from her dreadful family, but she returns out of loyalty and agrees to her mother's demands. Seeing her daughter's magnanimity, Marcelina refuses to allow her to make such a sacrifice. In a rare happy ending for a Sánchez play, Rogelio discovers new feelings of generosity and offers to ease the family's financial woes without expecting a reward—it is their money after all.

Toward the end of 1908 and in 1909 Sánchez returned to political activities and wrote for *La Protesta Humana*. Anarchists were facing persecution, and foreigners could be deported under a law excluding subversive aliens. Sánchez took part in a demonstration against the police in Buenos Aires on 1 May 1909, which ended in a bloody confrontation with several dead and many wounded. During trips to Montevideo he worked toward fulfilling an old dream—taking a trip to Europe in order to publicize his plays and present them in Italy. Members of parliament and leading intellectuals such as José Enrique Rodó and Julio Herrera y Reissig supported his plan. On 22 September 1909 Sánchez was commissioned by President Claudio Williman to represent Uruguay at the International Arts Exposition in Rome. The playwright sailed for Europe three days later, after attending several farewell parties given by his many friends and associates. He arrived in Genoa on 13 October, considerably weakened from the rough sea voyage.

Sánchez' health continued to deteriorate and he traveled to Nice early in 1910 searching for a better climate. In February 1910 he met former and future Uruguayan president José Batlle y Ordoñez and spent about two weeks with him in Milan. Batlle and the progressives were avid followers of Sánchez' work, and Batlle had found compelling the realistic depictions of social ills in the playwright's plays and newspaper articles. He listened carefully as Sánchez described the dismal social conditions in Uruguay. Years later, Batlle incorporated many social welfare measures into the Uruguayan constitution of 1919.

After the first few months in Italy, Sánchez ran out of money and desperately sought government grants to survive abroad, in order to make contact with the theater circles in Rome and Milan. His mood altered between optimistic struggle and dark despair as tuberculosis rapidly crippled his left lung. On 2 November 1910, Sánchez was taken to the Fate bene Fratelli Hospital in Milan, with his heart weakened considerably and his lung ailment in a terminal stage. He died on 7 November at the age of thirty-five, and was buried in a cemetery in Milan. His remains were exhumed at the request of the Uruguayan government, taken to Montevideo, and reinterred with national honors in January of 1921. A statue of Florencio Sánchez was erected in Buenos Aires in 1927 and transferred to the theater street of Corrientes a few years later. Augustín Riganelli's statue bears a haunting resemblance to the gaunt and dreamy figure of the playwright in real life.

Sánchez is considered one of the most important playwrights of Latin America. Writing in the heyday of realism and naturalism, he concentrated on objectively portraying squalor and poverty. His personal experience convinced him that wretched social conditions broke down self-esteem and led to alcoholism and to a peculiar psychology of fatalistic resignation. A desire to ameliorate social injustice prompted Sánchez to write muckraking articles in newspapers on both sides of the River Plate and to work with groups trying to establish trade unions. His articles were collected in book form and appeared in 1914 in *El caudillaje criminal en Sud América. Cartas de un flojo. Orientales y basta. No creo en ustedes* . . . [Criminal Caudillo Rule in South America. Letters from a Lazybones. Uruguayans, Enough! I Don't Believe in You . . .]

Sánchez also explored the human psyche, which together with his interest in people and ear for dialogue led him to the theater. He had an exceptional talent for reproducing the various speech patterns of the inhabitants of the River Plate. His remarkable skill at portraying psychological despair prompted critics to compare him to Eugene O'Neill. Sánchez' masterful and artistic portrayal of the dispossesed and the underworld captivated the imagination of the critics and the public for over half a century.

One of Sánchez' greatest contributions to Latin American literature was the depiction of racial antagonism between the native *criollos* and the immigrants. A *criollo* himself, he had grown up in intimate contact with country life and rued the deterioration of homespun *criollo* virtues. Sánchez felt that the *criollos*, being a mixture of *chulo* fathers (Spaniards who live by their wits) and *charrúa* mothers, inherited more from the fun-loving Spanish side than from the brave determination of the Indians. Sánchez' mastery lay in presenting in his plays the pungent and lusty language of the *gaucho*, as well as the underworld

dweller's argot and the immigrants' idiosyncratic idiom. His theater was thoroughly modern and spare; he always used props or scenery to save words, which made his plays strikingly effective.

A first-rate dramatist whose work was produced in France, Spain, and Italy during the 1920's and 1930's, he also wove psychology and social problems into his plots. Sánchez left a lasting impact on Uruguayan, Argentine, and Latin American literature and thought.

SELECTED BIBLIOGRAPHY

Editions

Nuestros hijos: Comedia en tres actos. Montevideo, 1909.

Barranca abajo. La gringa. Marta Gruni. Buenos Aires, 1910.

Un buen negocio. Buenos Aires, 1910.

La gringa. Los derechos de la salud. Buenos Aires, 1910.

Marta Gruni: Sainete en un acto y tres cuadros. Buenos Aires, 1910.

El teatro del uruguayo Florencio Sánchez. 3 vols. Barcelona, 1911–1926.

El caudillaje criminal en Sud América. Cartas de un flojo. Orientales y basta. No creo en ustedes. Ídolos gauchos. Diálogos de actualidad. Pedro y Juna. El nuevo affiche. Montevideo, 1914. A collection of his newspaper articles.

Canillita: Sainete en un acto. Buenos Aires, 1915.

El teatro del uruguayo Florencio Sánchez. 3 vols. Barcelona, 1917–1920.

Canillita y Cédulas de San Juan: Sainete y comedia dramática. Buenos Aires, 1921.

Barranca abajo. La gringa. El desalojo. With a prologue by Vicente Salvarrerr. Barcelona, 1926.

Teatro: La gringa, Barranca abajo, Marta Gruni. Montevideo, 1936.

Barranca abajo; Los muertos. Complete text with an introduction by Vicente Cuitiño. Buenos Aires, 1939.

M'hijo el dotor, Los derechos de la salud, En familia, Moneda Falsa, El desalojo. Buenos Aires, 1939.

Teatro de Florencio Sánchez. 2 vols. Buenos Aires, 1939.

Teatro completo de Florencio Sánchez. Compiled and annotated by Dardo Cúneo. Buenos Aires, 1941.

La gringa [comedia]. En familia [comedia]. Barranca abajo [tragedia]. With a prologue and notes by José María Monner Sans. Buenos Aires, 1946.

Teatro completo. With a prologue by Vicente Martínez Cuitiño. Buenos Aires, 1951.

Teatro. Havana, 1963.

M'hijo el dotor; La gringa. Buenos Aires, 1965.

El caudillaje criminal en Sud América y otras páginas. Selected and with notes by E. M. S. Danero. Buenos Aires, 1966.

Teatro. 2 vols. Selected, with a prologue and notes, by Walter Rela. Montevideo, 1967.

Obras completas. 3 vols. Compiled, with an introduction and notes, by Jorge Lafforgue. Buenos Aires, 1968–1969.

Teatro completo de Florencio Sánchez. With an introduction and notes by Fernando García Esteban. Montevideo, 1975.

Translations

Plays of the Southern Americas. By the Stanford University Dramatists' Alliance. Stanford, Calif., 1942.

Representative Plays. Translated by Willis Knapp Jones. With an introduction by Ruth Richardson. Washington, 1961.

Biographical and Critical Studies

Corti, Dora. *Florencio Sánchez.* Buenos Aires, 1937.

Cruz, Jorge. *Genio y figura de Florencio Sánchez.* Buenos Aires, 1966.

Dibarboure, José Alberto. *Proceso del teatro uruguayo, 1808–1938.* Montevideo, 1940.

Echagüe, Juan Pablo. *Seis figuras del Plata.* Buenos Aires, 1938.

Florencio Sánchez: Centenario de su nacimiento, 1875–1975. Montevideo, 1975.

Frugoni, Emilio. *La sensibilidad americana.* Montevideo, 1920.

García Esteban, Fernando. *Vida de Florencio Sánchez, con cartas inéditas del insigne dramaturgo.* Santiago, Chile, 1939.

Giordano, Enrique. *La teatralización de la obra dramática de Florencio Sánchez a Roberto Arlt.* Buenos Aires, 1982.

Giusti, Roberto Fernando. *Florencio Sánchez: Su vida y su obra.* Buenos Aires, 1920.

Gómez Brown, Juan Carlos. *Barranca abajo de Florencio Sánchez.* Montevideo, 1968.

González, Juan Antonio. *Dos figuras cumbres del Uruguay: Florencio Sánchez en el teatro; Julio Herrera y Reissig en la poesía.* Colonia, Uruguay, 1944.

Imbert, Julio A. *Florencio Sánchez: Vida y creación.* Buenos Aires, 1954.

Jiménez, Wilfredo. *Pasión de Florencio Sánchez; biografía dramaizada en tres actos.* Buenos Aires, 1955.

Lafforgue, Jorge Paul. *Florencio Sánchez.* Buenos Aires, 1967.

Martínez, Miguel Víctor. *Florencio Sánchez: Episodios de su vida.* Montevideo, 1918.

Muñoz, Vladimiro. *Florencio Sánchez: A Chronology.* Translated by Scott Jacobsen. New York, 1980.

Ordaz, Luis. *Florencio Sánchez.* Buenos Aires, 1972.

Pignataro, Jorge. *Florencio Sánchez.* Buenos Aires, 1979.

Rela, Walter. *Florencio Sánchez: Persona y teatro.* Montevideo, 1967.

———. *Repertorio bibliográfico anotado sobre Florencio Sánchez.* Buenos Aires, 1973.

Richardson, Ruth. *Florencio Sánchez and the Argentine Theatre.* New York, 1933.

Riva, Hugo. *Valoración de Florencio Sánchez en el teatro latinoamericano.* Montevideo, 1976.

Rosell, Avenir. *El lenguaje en Florencio Sánchez.* With a prologue by Arturo Sergio Visca. Montevideo, 1975.

Shedd, Karl Eastman. *Florencio Sánchez's Debt to Eugène Brieux.* Baltimore, Md., 1936.

Sorenson, Thora. *Florencio Sánchez.* Mexico City, 1948.

Vázquez Cey, Arturo. *Florencio Sánchez y el teatro argentino.* Buenos Aires, 1929.

Zum Felde, Alberto. *Crítica de la literatura uruguaya.* Montevideo, 1921.

Juan Ramón Molina

(1875–1908)

Ramón L. Acevedo

P oet, journalist, and short story writer, the Honduran Juan Ramón Molina is considered his country's national poet and one of the best writers within Spanish America's *modernismo*, a literary movement that marked the coming of age of the region's literature. He was born in Comayagüela, Honduras, on 17 April 1875. His father was a Spaniard established in Honduras; his mother was Honduran. During his childhood, Molina lived in his native country, but, in 1888, when he was still very young, he was sent to Guatemala to study law. During these early years, he revealed an exceptional interest in literature, motivated by his skepticism and his search for truth. Among his readings we find works of William Shakespeare, Friedrich Wilhelm Nietzsche, the Bible, Greek classic authors, Edgar Allan Poe, Karl Marx, Johann Wolfgang von Goethe, Gérard de Nerval, Charles Darwin, Giovanni Boccaccio, and Molière, plus Spanish and Spanish-American writers such as Francisco Gómez de Quevedo, Benito Pérez Galdós, José Batres Montúfar, and José Asunción Silva. In Guatemala, Molina met Rubén Darío in 1891. The Nicaraguan poet, *modernismo*'s principal leader, would soon become the most important living poet in the Hispanic world. Molina's first writings date from these early years.

In 1893 Molina established himself in Quetzalte-nango, Guatemala, where he was the editor of the newspaper *El Bien Público* (The Public Good). Three years later, he returned to the capital city, where he wrote for the most prestigious newspapers: *La Ilustración Guatemalteca* (The Guatemalan Enlightenment) and *Diario de Centro América* (Central American Daily News). He identified himself as a man of liberal ideas and a supporter of President Justo Rufino Barrios' political, social, and economic reforms. This was one of the most productive periods of his short life. When he returned to Honduras in 1897, after Barrios' death, he had already earned a growing reputation as poet and journalist. Under Dr. Policarpo Bonilla's presidency, he was designated as subsecretary of the Department of Economic Development and Public Works.

In Tegucigalpa, Molina published *El Cronista*, (The Chronicler), a short-lived newspaper, and later became chief editor of an important national newspaper, *Diario de Honduras*. He resigned his government post to have more freedom as a journalist and in 1900 was jailed because of his persistent criticism of General Terencio Sierra's government. Three years later, he participated in a successful revolution under Manuel Bonilla's leadership. During this period, he published another newspaper, *El Día* (The Day), and married Dolores Hinestroza. He was elected to Honduras' National Congress, although soon afterward the president eliminated the legislative branch of government. His marriage was also brief, since his wife died in 1905.

Molina was at the peak of his career as a writer, and the government designated him as Honduran delegate to the Pan-American Conference to be held in Rio de Janeiro in 1906. This conference was, among other things, a very important cultural event. Many of the most significant literary figures from all over Latin America met in Rio, including Darío from Nicaragua, Guillermo Valencia from Colombia, and Manuel María Machado de Assís from Brazil. His trip to Brazil and his return to Honduras, after visiting Spain, Portugal, France, and the United States, was one of the happiest and most productive experiences of his life. But a revolution, backed by Nicaragua, toppled Bonilla's government, and Molina went into exile in El Salvador. There he became editor of *Ritos*, a literary journal, and wrote some of his best and most deeply felt poems. Molina died in El Salvador on 2 November 1908. He felt defeated and forgotten, and was destroyed by alcohol and morphine. Three years after his death, his friend Froylán Turcios, a prominent writer, published most of his literary production in a small volume entitled *Tierras, mares, y cielos* (Lands, Seas, and Skies).

Molina can be considered the best Central American modernist poet after Darío. *Modernismo* was a general Spanish-American literary movement that had Darío as its main leader and that profoundly modernized the region's literary expression. Inspired by French symbolism and French poetry in general, plus many other European and North American writers, the modernists created a new type of poetry, one that reflected their longing for a modern Latin American cultural expression and a modern Latin America that could achieve the socioeconomic and cultural level of the most developed countries in the world. In political and economic terms, these decades (from 1880 to 1920) marked the definite incorporation of Latin America into expanding international capitalism. The affirmation of individuality, aestheticism, and artistic freedom characterized *modernismo*, which gave Spanish America some of its most prominent literary figures—José Martí, Darío, Silva, Leopoldo Lugones, Julio Herrera y

Reissig—and deeply transformed all literature written in Spanish.

Molina reflects in his life and writings the tensions and contradictions of life and literature in Central America during this period. The Honduran novelist and literary critic Julio Escoto, in a penetrating essay, analyzes the contradiction between Molina's image as a successful, respected, and feared politician, journalist, and poet, and his intimate metaphysical and existential anguish. As a result of his many readings, motivated by the spiritual crisis of his time, Molina came face to face with doubt, disbelief, and metaphysical emptiness. Such confrontations are clearly expressed in some of his best autobiographical poems, such as "Madre melancolía" (Mother Melancholy), "Río grande" (Great River), and "Autobiografía." In this last poem, he writes:

> Al mirarme al espejo ¡cuán cambiado
> estoy! No me conozco ni yo mismo;
> tengo en los ojos, de mirar cansado,
> algo del miedo del que ve un abismo.

When I look at myself in the mirror, how changed I am! Not even I know myself: I have in my eyes, tired of seeing, some of the fear of one who sees an abyss.

The poet struggles against his skepticism and looks for firm spiritual values, but he ends by recognizing his defeat. Because of this inner conflict, he defines himself as a contradictory being.

This intimate conflict has undoubted social dimensions. As did many other modernist writers, the Honduran poet felt out of place within the provincial world that fate had reserved for him. He felt the obligation to live within a social, political, and cultural context that he both loved and hated with passion, and he attacked it because of his ideals and his love for his country. His strong articles against clericalism and religion, against the shortsighted politics of his country and the empty romanticism that predominated in literature, alternated with his defense of new ideas and modernist aesthetics. He was also conscious of the growing influence of the United States in Central American affairs and adopted an anti-imperialist position. He fought aggressively and with arrogance, but privately recognized his impotence against these circumstances.

Even his death can be seen as ambivalent; it was caused by an overdose of morphine that may or may not have been intentional.

As a modernist poet, Molina was moderate, spiritually close to the first generation of modernist writers, and little inclined to the formal experiments or artificially brilliant verbosity that Darío's many followers later transformed into a stereotyped style. He admired Darío but also Silva and Julián del Casal. In fact, he is closer to the mature Darío, who, after writing the bright, sensuous, and aristocratic poetry that made him famous, turned toward a more intimate, profound, and direct style in *Cantos de vida y esperanza* (Songs of Life and Hope, 1905).

Much of Molina's best poetry is an anguished expression of deeply felt existential and philosophical themes. As a frequent background and sometimes as a main theme, Honduran and Central American elements are present, not as picturesque local color but as part of the poet's authentic reality. His tone is generally strong and dramatic, but it can also be tender and delicate. Molina was not a great formal innovator like Darío, although he managed old and new forms with ease. He wrote excellent sonnets, some traditional in form but most adopting French meters, which were very popular with modernist poets.

Some of these poems, like "Autobiografía," "Rio grande," "Anhelo nocturno" (Night Yearning), and "Los cuatro bueyes" (The Four Oxen), are outstanding for their rich sonority and their deeply human dimensions. Others, like "Salutación á los poetas brasileros" (A Salute to the Brazilian Poets) and "Aguilas y cóndores" (Eagles and Condors), imply a more collective type of expression in which the poet acts as a spokesman and interpreter of Latin American dreams and fears. Still others, such as "Metempsicosis" and "El fakir," (The Fakir), are lyrical renderings of philosophical and somewhat mystical and esoteric themes. A note of lightness and tenderness is also present in a few poems like "Letrilla eglógica" (Pastoral Song) and "Tréboles de navidad" (Christmas Clover), in which the poet nostalgically remembers the simple religious feelings of his childhood.

Almost half of Molina's poetry is written in sonnets. "Pesca de sirenas" (Fishing Mermaids) is an expression of pagan eroticism. "La muerte del león" (The Death of the Lion) is a poem of tragic beauty. Descriptive sonnets such as "Selva americana" (American Jungle), "Pernambuco," and "Bahía de Río de Janeiro" (Rio de Janeiro Bay) are poems in which Molina demonstrates a rare ability for painting Latin American landscapes with impressionist pictorial techniques.

Molina could also write very good prose, although he tended to waste his talent in ephemeral journalism. "En el Golfo de Fonseca" (In the Gulf of Fonseca), for example, is a brief descriptive poem in prose in which Molina begins by describing immediate scenery, only to expand his scope until he ascends to a cosmic vision of the world. Other outstanding brief texts in prose are "La niña de la patata" (The Girl with the Potato), "El grillo de la muerte" (The Cricket of Death), and "Copo de espuma" (Flake of Foam). In these texts, Molina achieves a perfect balance between description, lyricism, and exposition. Some of his other articles—"Cartas" (Letters), "Por qué se mató Domínguez" (Why Domínguez Killed Himself), "La Siguanaba" (The Siguanaba)—are also interesting as personal interpretations of his Honduran, Central American world. All of these texts belong to his production as a journalist, but in them Molina goes beyond the transient nature of journalism because of the quality of his artistic prose, his personal approach, and the permanent nature of his themes. Molina tried to outdo Darío as a lyric poet, but it is in his best prose writings that he sometimes surpasses him. His prose has a density and force generally absent in Darío's brief texts.

Molina also wrote a handful of short stories—"Mr. Black," "El Chele" (The Chele), "La intrusa" (The Intruder), "Un entierro" (A Funeral)—and can be considered one of the first short-story writers in Honduras. Most of Molina's literary production was published in one small volume, *Tierras, mares, y cielos*, in 1911. This book has been reprinted, with some additions and omissions, in Mexico, Honduras, Guatemala, and Costa Rica. Although he is well known in Central America, Molina has not yet attained the international recognition he deserves as a *modernista* writer. Although critical literature on his life and works has also been rather scarce, there are some fundamental essays and studies. William Chaney published the first systematic panorama of Molina's life and writings in 1921. Nobel Prize winner Miguel Ángel Asturias wrote an interesting essay in which he compares Molina's poetry with Darío's. One of the most recent and most valuable studies is the previously mentioned one written by Escoto, a penetrating interpretation of Molina's life, personality, and literary production with special emphasis on the poet's relation to his sociopolitical context.

SELECTED BIBLIOGRAPHY

First Edition

Poetry and Prose

Tierras, mares, y cielos. Edited by Froylán Turcios. Tegucigalpa, Honduras, 1911. Posthumous.

Later Editions

Antología: Verso y prosa. Prologue by Miguel Ángel Asturias. San Salvador, 1959.

Tierras, mares, y cielos. With a preface by Enrique González Martínez and bibliography by Rafael Heliodoro Valle. Tegucigalpa, Honduras, 1937.

————. With a prologue by Argentina Díaz Lozano and bibliography by Rafael Heliodoro Valle. Guatemala City, 1947.

————. Edited and with an introduction and notes by Julio Escoto. San José, Costa Rica, 1977.

Biographical and Critical Studies

Asturias, Miguel Ángel. "Juan Ramón Molina: Poeta gemelo de Rubén." In *Antología: Verso y prosa,* by Juan Ramón Molina. San Salvador, 1959. Pp. 9–32.

Carías Reyes, Marcos. *Juan Ramón Molina.* Tegucigalpa, Honduras, 1943.

Chaney, William. *Juan Ramón Molina.* Colorado College Language Series 2/35:473–515 (1921).

Escoto, Julio. "Juan Ramón Molina: Poeta del modernismo centroamericano." In *Tierras, mares, y cielos,* by Juan Ramón Molina. San José, Costa Rica, 1977. Pp. 7–48.

Rivera y Morillo, Humberto. *Juan Ramón Molina.* 2 vols. San Pedro Sula, Honduras. 1966.

José Santos Chocano

(1875–1934)

Augusto Tamayo y Vargas

José Santos Chocano was born in Lima on 14 May 1875. In 1894 his youthful attacks against the dictator General Andrés A. Cáceres in *La Tunda* (The Whipping), a satirical newspaper, led to his imprisonment in Los Aljibes y Casas Matas del Callao, where he wrote some of the verses for his first book. The influences of Luis Benjamín Cisneros, Manuel José Quintana, and Ramón de Campoamor, whom Chocano considered his master, are visible in *Iras santas* (Holy Wrath, 1895); of particular note is the influence of Victor Hugo, who, because of his struggle against Napoleon, became the young Chocano's example for poetic action.

Chocano's persisting romanticism can be appreciated in *En la aldea* (In the Village, 1895), in *Azahares* (Orange Blossoms, 1896), and in *Selva virgen* (Virgin Jungle, 1898—with poems different from those in his 1893 work of the same title). In these works his intention is to design a program of poetic action modeled after Hugo, who, according to Chocano, "strangled paralytic classicism with a Herculean hand." His romanticism is imbued with Hugo's humanism, which he also was to find in his readings of Peruvian poets like Cisneros, Arnaldo Márquez, and Germán Amézaga.

"Before being a poet . . . one must be a man!" Chocano would say in *Los cantos del Pacífico* (Songs of the Pacific, 1904), selections from his earlier books of poetry; he would continue, "of he who proclaims to the new world / not artifice, but human art." He maintained that his was not "art for art's sake," but rather that he was singing "to humanity," with an accent drawn from human potential and with the expression of the New World.

In his verses he defended noble causes: "My soul is a cloak for all orphans / and a strong shield for all breasts." He exalted the values of patriotism, as in these lines from "Proclama" (Proclamation), in *Los canto del Pacífico:*

> Cuando invoco a las musas inmortales,
> vuelvo los ojos a la patria mía.

> When I invoke the immortal muses
> I turn my eyes to my country.

With Dionysian enthusiasm, in the "triumphal hymns" of Tirteus and the "elegies" of Simonides, Chocano exclaims:

> Canto, para dar gloria al heroísmo;
> canto, para dar vida al moribundo;
> canto, porque a la voz de mi lirismo,
> le arrancaré su lauro al combatiente

que quiera ensangrentar el nuevo mundo,
y en ese lauro envolveré mi frente!

I sing to glorify heroism;
I sing to give life to the dying;
I sing, so that the voice of my lyricism
will seize the laurel from the combatant
who would bloody the new world
and I'll place that laurel on my forehead!

But at the same time he followed romanticism in its strong and penetrating sense of Nature. Chocano discovered this vast road and in the 1898 *Selva virgen* began to show his animating sense of landscape, giving it tonalities of light and color in a richly sensuous fantasy.

Chocano's work appeared in the pages of *El Perú ilustrado* and *La neblina* (The Mist); he would found *La gran revista* and later *Siglo XX*. Of great importance in his decision to become a poet and in his appreciation of nature was his journey to the region of Chanchamayo, from which he returned to publish the 1898 *Selva virgen,* in which there is only one poem actually about the jungle. In those restless years he wrote a play of little literary value, *Sin nombre* (Without a Name, premiered in 1906), and his epic poem, *La epopeya del Morro* (The Epic of the Hill, 1899). Even amid the monotony and imperfection of this work, Chocano's poetic language shows through in aggressive metaphor, pictorial sentiment, and his orchestration of phrases seeking to echo Nature itself.

Chocano's *El canto del siglo* (Song of the Century, 1901), is a new example of the humanism of Hugo and Cisneros, but his poetry is infiltrated by Rubén Darío, to whom he had already dedicated "El sermón de la montaña" (Sermon on the Mount) in *Iras santas:*

Mustio y enflaquecido por la fiebre,
Cristo va con su caña de viajero
y sus vagos ensueños de pesebre.

Dejected and emaciated by fever
Christ walks with his traveler's staff
and his vague dreams of the manger.

Chocano takes up Darío's Christian message and his poetic manner but gives them the grandiloquence of his own poetic style. At the same time, he continues with his dreams of greatness, his fantastic descriptions, and his belief in the triumph of future generations of humanity.

In 1901, at the height of his local success, he was sent by the government of Peru to Central America; he visited countries on the way until he arrived in Guatemala City, where he published *El fin de Satán* (The End of Satan, 1901) and an anthology, the already mentioned *Los cantos del Pacífico,* which was a collection of his earlier poems accompanied by his "Proclama a compañeras de letras, de Guatemale," his first poetic "profession of faith." During this trip he began to become a political influence as well as a prominent poet. As secretary of the Peruvian legation in Bogotá, Chocano enjoyed resounding prestige. There the poet Soto-Borda said of him: "Hail poet, hail to you of the aeolic harp / in whose magical strings vibrates the Soul of America," demonstrating that in 1904 Chocano had already finished the book that would later be published with the name *Alma América* (American Soul, 1906). En route to Spain as a diplomat, his presence in Chile caused a commotion when the Chilean Workers' Union honored him as a "socialist" poet. After visiting Buenos Aires and Montevideo, he moved on to Spain, where he lived for more than four years.

During this time Chocano definitively aligned himself with modernism, rebelling against romantic forms but also remaining distant from naturalistic prose and poetic expressionism. Chocano, who had published so many collections of poems combining intense emotion and plastic description, culminated his poetic journey in Spain with the publication of *Alma América* in 1906, the heroic three-act verse drama *Los conquistadores* (The Conquerors), which premiered in the same year, and *¡Fiat lux!* (Latin: "Let There Be Light") in 1908.

Alma América is the fundamental work of Chocano's poetry. Subtitled *Poemas indo-españoles* (Indo-Spanish Poems), in many verses it bears the stamp of several motifs of Latin American history and geography, based on a conscientious reading of tradition, but with a view to the future. In *Alma América* there are condors and vicuñas, but also Pizarro and the Limean of Spanish stock; there are folkloric motifs and a profusion of panoramas of Lima, of the Andes, and of the jungles. *Alma América* exalts Incas and viceroys, swamps and waterfalls; it sings with Spanish tambourines and sinks into the fiction of Indian melancholy, then raises its voice to call "the nation of the Amazon" the "center of the world." Chocano professes faith in his poetic creed—"with Incan majesty and Spanish pride"—and proves that his poetry burns in the furnace where strong words are forged: "I will seek out another Muse to amaze the Universe." Chocano also expresses a *mestizo* (of mixed European and Indian ancestry) sentiment in his poetry: "How many times have I been born! How many times incarnate! / I am twice American and twice a Spaniard . . ." Also, in "Blasón" (Blazon) from *Alma América*:

> *Cuando me siento Inca, le rindo vasallaje*
> *al Sol, que me da el cetro de su poder real;*
> *cuando me siento hispano y evoco el Coloniaje,*
> *parecen mis estrofas trompetas de cristal.*

When I feel Incan, I render homage
to the Sun, which gives me the scepter of its royal
   power;
when I feel Hispanic and I evoke the Colony,
my verses appear like crystal trumpets.

On the other hand, Chocano at that time considered that he had surpassed his first phase as a humanist poet and was now a poet first and man second. He had come full circle. Abandoning the humanism of the romantic period, in "Profesión de fe" (Profession of Faith) from *Los cantos del Pacífico*, he joins the ranks of those select spirits, essentially aristocratic and decadent, engendered by modernism:

> *Seamos los artistas fuertes como el misterio;*
> *y tengamos al Arte por un cruel imperio*
> *donde se hace una noche para hacer una estrella.*

Artists, let us be strong as mystery;
and let us make of Art a cruel Empire
where night is brought down in order to create a star.

Chocano speaks of a third aspect of his work, his goal of creating a new poetry that would contain many of the new lyric currents, but that would be defined by the search for the American landscape and spirit. Nothing demonstrates this poetic attitude

better than the sonnet "Troquel" (a die or stamp for coins and medals):

> *No beberé en las linfas de la castalia fuente,*
> *ni cruzaré los bosques floridos del Parnaso,*
> *ni tras las nueve hermanas dirigiré mi paso;*
> *pero, al cantar mis himnos, levantaré la frente.*

I will not drink of the waters of the Castalian fount
nor will I pass through the flowered forests of
   Parnassus,
nor will I follow the path of the nine sisters;
but I will lift up my face as I sing my hymns.

In *Alma América* he launches a torrent of jungle poetry, utilizing the classical meter of the quaternary trimeter, that is, feet of four syllables, with the accent falling on the third:

> *Soy el alma primitiva de los Andes y las selvas;*
> *soy el ruido de las hojas en la noche,*
> *que parece que en mis versos ensayaran una orquesta;*
> *soy el canto de turpiales y sinsontes, cuando el alba*
> *ruboriza la blancura de la nieve de las crestas;*
> *soy el himno de las aguas y los vientos.*

I am the primitive soul of the Andes and the jungles;
I am the sound of the leaves in the night,
an orchestra rehearsing in my verses;
I am the song of troupials and mockingbirds, when the
   dawn
blushes the white snow of the summits;
I am the hymn of the waters and the winds.

In this poem, the foot "so-iel-al-ma" unfolds into multiples of eight, sixteen, twenty-four, giving the sensation of the unfurled strength of nature. So it was in other poems: Chocano was the poet of the Andes and of the fine landscape of the valleys, but also of the Inca Tupec Yupanquí, the conqueror Hernando de Soto, the Prince of Esquilache, and finally of Peru itself, the "divine and sacred." He said in *Alma América*: "My poetry is objective, and in that sense I wish to be the Poet of America." He felt called to this role by destiny, and he glorified the importance of his verse, comparing it to the fire given to humanity by Prometheus. The world itself hardly provided adequate space for his poetry, and so he crowned himself with the laurels of glory. The idea of the superman came to his philosophy from the writings of Friedrich

Nietzsche; and thus, beyond good and evil, Chocano also called himself "artist"—shepherd of the masses, poet above the peaks of the Andes, violating customs in order to generate new laws. Thus Chocano's work is characterized by magnificence and individualism. "Singer of America" and of himself, Chocano approached poetry with a multitude of images, each one a bolt of lightning, yielding a message full of rhetoric, yet fresh in its effects.

In a letter of 4 May 1903, José Enrique Rodó wrote to him, after reading his poem "El derrumbe" (The Precipice): "I recognized you, that is, the poet who combines in a rare and impressive partnership the proud audacity of inspiration with the firm sculpture of form, and who in my opinion will be the American poet of the near future." ("*El derrumbe*," originally published in 1899, was later retitled "El derrumbe-miento" in *Alma América*.)

Luis Alberto Sánchez documents, after the recognition of *Alma América* and the many praises accorded the poet by Spaniards as well as Spanish Americans, the "sad night" that befell Chocano in Spain. First he suffered financial problems, which he resolved hastily but which deprived him of his diplomatic charge; next he was involved in the Bank of Spain affair, in which a swindler led him into the most serious and dramatic complication of his life. In the midst of all this, he published *¡Fiat lux!* in which he alludes to his "enemies" with insolent pride; at the same time, he amended other earlier poems with meticulous sensitivity, changing them and often correcting them lyrically.

In the years following 1910, his work, collected under the name *Primicias de oro de Indias* (First Gold of the Indies) in 1934, gradually became more diluted and its impact lessened. His travels in Mexico are of anecdotal value and full of romantic color, as he gave full rein to his adventurous spirit and gave his moral support to the Mexican people in revolution. In "Sinfonía heroíca" (Heroic Symphony), he poetically mourned the murders of Francisco Madero and José María Pino Suárez and praised Venustiano Carranza. When the dictatorship of Victoriano Huerta expelled him, he went to Puerto Rico, where he enjoyed another period of triumph and Iberoamerican affirmation, and where he said, "My art is made of History and Nature." But at the same time he

declared, "I believe that America is for Americans; but by the same token, Spanish America is for Spanish Americans." His stay in Puerto Rico was a happy moment in Chocano's difficult life, and he again felt himself to be a conductor and guide in literature and politics. Returning to Mexico, he traveled with Carranza and Francisco (Pancho) Villa, witnessed the capture of Chihuahua, and sang in the bivouacs. Later, distanced from both men, he went to Guatemala, where he received the support of the dictator Manuel Estrada Cabrera. When the dictatorship fell to an impassioned revolution, Chocano was sentenced to be shot, and he spent several months in prison. Spanish and American intellectuals intervened on his behalf.

He was first democratic and anti-imperialist, as in "La epopeya del Pacífico" (The Epic of the Pacific), in *Alma América*:

> Los Estados Unidos, como argolla de bronce,
> contra un clavo torturan de la América un pie;
> y la América debe, ya que aspira a ser libre,
> imitarles primero e igualarles después.

> The United States, like a bronze shackle,
> torture America's foot with a spike;
> and as it aspires to be free, America should
> first imitate them and then equal them.

In this sentiment also, he followed the example of his generation. Darío, for example, had composed the beautiful "A Roosevelt" (To Roosevelt) against North American imperialism. But they both gave in somewhat on this point. Darío sang to the "North American Eagle," and Chocano became personalistic and arrogant; he spoke of the "petulant mob" and advanced his theory of "organized dictatorship," definitively separating himself from "the masses."

As a result of his advocacy of such ideas, a violent controversy arose with the young writer Edwin Elmere, who was killed in a personal quarrel with Chocano before the entranceway to the offices of the newspaper *El Comercio*. Chocano was sentenced to four years in prison for the killing, despite his claim of self-defense. In Chile, where he lived after being freed from prison, he published *Primicias de oro de Indias* and *Poemas del amor doliente* (Poems of Sorrowful Love, which appeared posthumously in 1937), in which only a few signs of his poetic brilliance can be discerned. Chocano was killed on 13 December 1934 on a tram in Santiago by the mentally ill Martín Bruce Badilla, with whom he had made plans to search for hidden treasure.

If indeed Chocano began as a late-blooming romanticist, he came to figure among the modernists, bringing together the resonance of Walt Whitman, the musicality and the fluidity of José Asunción Silva, and, from Darío's renovating lyricism, the expressions of the French symbolists and Parnassians.

Like Silva, Chocano mixed the basic twelve-syllable verse with lines of four, eight, and sixteen syllables. One example is his musical "Elegía del órgano" (Elegy of the Organ), from *Alma América*:

Suena el órgano,
suena el órgano en la iglesia solitaria,
suena el órgano en el fondo de la noche;
y hay un chorro de sonidos melodiosos en sus flautas,
que comienzan blandamente . . . , blandamente . . . ,
como pasos en alfombras, como dedos que acarician, como
    sedas que se arrastran,
y, de súbito, se encrespan
y se hinchan y rebraman,
a manera de ancho río que sepulta
en un lecho rocalloso la solemne pesadumbre de sus
    aguas . . .

The organ is playing
the organ is playing in the solitary church,
the organ is playing in the deep of night;
and there is a stream of melodious sounds in its flutes,
that begin softly . . . , softly . . . ,
like footsteps on carpet, like caressing fingers, like
    creeping silks,
and, suddenly, they spring up
and swell and bellow,
like a wide river hiding
the solemn weight of its waters in a rocky bed . . .

Despite these similarities, Chocano differs from Silva in his boisterous zeal, in the exuberance of his adjectives, in the open, public nature of his poetry, declaimed in the plaza. Chocano wrote to extract the jungle's very sap, not the vague perfume of orchids placed at the foot of the balcony in the final sleepless night of the neurotic poet.

Chocano's vocabulary augments the language with American expressions, and he emphasizes words that to him are particularly euphonious, such as *follaje* (foliage), *ánfora* (amphora), *selva* (jungle), *cofre* (coffer), *balcón* (balcony), and, curiously and constantly, the word *copa* (goblet): "and like goblets overfilled with sadness"; "one is the goblet in which flesh sleeps"; "like an abyss the emptiness of a goblet"; "the banquet goblet that my hand raises"; "the dry goblet, the inanimate body"; "as if in a chiseled goblet"; "and anger overflowing the goblet"; "a boiling goblet is filled with pleasure"; "goblets of honey"; and "the whole goblet." This word enlarges on the amphora motif, also very much used, which fills the whole of Chocano's work with "concave sonority." In Chocano's poetry, the use of numbers is also important.

Chocano is hyperbolic but also measured in the composition of his contrasting figures. And he feeds feverishly on life—death appearing only rarely in the scintillating comparisons built from his rich lexicon, and never with the agonizing consciousness of its eternal vigilance. Hence his distance from Silva; hence his separation from Darío's second stage. And he is much closer to Salvador Díaz Mirón than to the Uruguayan Julio Herrera y Reissig, creator of landscapes and words and literary figures from his permanent watchtower of solitude. Initially he sought the external perfection of his verses but then let himself be carried away by the sound of the words, as in "La musa fuerte" (The Hardy Muse) from *Alma América*:

Confieso que, yo amo las pompas coloniales,
a las más finas cuerdas prefiero los metales:
tal doy con mis clarines imperativas diarias;
y, entonces, sacrifico mis bellas baratijas,
como los viejos nobles que echaban sus sortijas
al bronce destinado para fundir campañas.

I confess that I love colonial pomp,
to the finest strings I prefer metals:
giving daily clarion commands;
and then sacrificing my beautiful trinkets,
as the old nobles threw their rings
into the bronze destined to found bells.

Like the image in one of his poems in which a tiger, hanging from a horse's back, goes at a fantastic gallop through the jungle, so Chocano's poetry, having lost logical control, guided by instinct, becomes submerged in a grandiose thicket, above which "some red crescent moon" shows its profile like an enormous knife raised against life itself, running into the sunset. One might accuse the irregularity of the Pindaric ode, but the Doric poet knew the regularities of its irregularity and managed them deftly, not losing in the undergrowth anything substantial or fundamental. In the epic Chocano, there is a continuous torrent that does not stop even when it reaches the pool. For him, images are reality itself, and his imagination is strong and extremely sensitive. His poetic imagination manifests itself in two forms, the comparison or simile and the actual metaphor. In each of Chocano's compositions we can find examples of both. His appreciation of nature inspires such similes as the following in "Los pantanos" (The Swamps) from *Alma América*:

> El río es como un ímpetu salvaje;
> el lago es como un fondo de tristeza;
> el pantano cubierto de maleza,
> es como un vicio entre el pudor de un traje.

> The river is like a wild impetus;
> the lake is like a fund of sadness;
> the swamp covered with weeds
> is like vice hidden by a modest suit.

We can find equally plain examples of metaphor throughout Chocano's poetry, such as in "Los ríos" (The Rivers) from *Alma América*:

> Lloran las cumbres lágrimas de hielo,
> que corren por las trágicas pendientes
> y van formando en su camino fuentes,
> enamoradas del azul del cielo.

> The summits weep tears of ice
> that run down the tragic slopes
> and on their way form fountains
> in love with the blue of the sky.

But his character as a man of the Peruvian coast is there, constant, in his particularly Limean vision of reality; and if we wish to find an Indian spirit in his poetry we would have to refer to his "¡Quién sabe!" (Who Knows!), his "Ahí, no más" (Just Over There), his "Otra vez será" (It Will Be Again) (all

from *Oro de Indias*, vol. 3). Pedro Henríquez Ureña considered that the first of these was the first voice in indigenist poetry:

> Indio que asomas a la puerta
> de ésta tu rústica mansión,
> ¿Para mi sed no tienes agua?
> ¿Para mi frío, cobertor?
> ¿Parco maíz para mi hambre?
> ¿Para mi sueño, mal rincón?
> ¿Breve quietud para mi andanza?

> Indian who comes to the door
> of this your rustic mansion,
> For my thirst have you no water?
> For my cold, a blanket?
> A little corn for my hunger?
> For my fatigue, some corner?
> Brief respite from my fortunes?

Chocano lacks meditation and intellectual transcendence, but undoubtably he is one of this century's most effective poets in the Spanish language. He lived in search of sonorous oratorical effects, but he also gave free rein to a fantastic imagination and was always on the lookout for a particular note in poetry: the very transcription of nature, both Peruvian and American in the widest sense.

Translated from the Spanish by Jane A. Johnson

SELECTED BIBLIOGRAPHY

Editions

Poetry

La selva virgen. Lima, 1893.
En la aldea. Lima, 1895.
Iras santas. Lima, 1895.
Azahares. Lima, 1896.
La selva virgen. Lima, 1898.
La epopeya del Morro. Iquique, Chile, and Lima, 1899.
El canto del siglo. Lima, 1901.
El fin de Satán y otros poemas. Guatemala City, 1901.
Poesías completas. Barcelona, 1902.
Los cantos del Pacífico. Mexico City and Paris, 1904.
Alma América. Madrid and Paris, 1906.
¡Fiat lux! Madrid and Paris, 1908.
Poemas del amor doliente. Santiago, Chile, 1937.

Primicias de oro de Indias. Santiago, Chile, 1934.

Oro de Indias. 4 vols. Santiago, Chile, 1939–1941.

Plays

Sin nombre. Madrid, 1906.

Los conquistadores. Madrid, 1906.

Collected Works

José Santos Chocano: Sus mejores versos. Edited and with a tribute by Eduardo Carranza. Bogotá, 1941.

Obras completas. Edited by Luis Alberto Sánchez. 4 vols. Mexico City, 1954.

Obras completas de José Santos Chocano. Edited and with notes and introduction by Luis Alberto Sánchez. Mexico City, 1964.

Obras escogidas. Edited and with notes and introduction by Luis Alberto Sánchez. Lima, 1988.

Poemas escogidos de José Santos Chocano. Edited and with a foreword by Ventura García Calderón. Paris, 1938.

Poesías completas. 2 vols. Barcelona, 1902.

Poesías de J. S. Chocano. Edited and with an introduction by Luis Favio Xammar. Buenos Aires, 1945.

Poesías selectas. Edited by Manuel Beltroy. Lima, 1922.

Biographical and Critical Studies

Sánchez, Luis Alberto. *Aladino; o, Vida y obras de José Santos Chocano.* Mexico City, 1960.

Henríquez Ureña, Pedro. *Historia de la cultura de la America Hispanico.* Mexico City, 1947.

Tamayo Vargas, Augusto. *Literatura peruana.* 2 vols. Lima, 1954. 4th ed. 1977.

Tauro, Alberto. *Elementos de literatura peruana.* Lima, 1946.

Horacio Quiroga

(1878–1937)

George D. Schade

The short story has attained the stature of a major genre in Spanish-American literature, and its first undisputed master was Horacio Quiroga, who began writing his tales about 1900 and continued to do so for more than thirty years. Several illustrious short story writers in Spanish America preceded him: Esteban Echeverría with his lone but impressive contribution, *El matadero* (The Slaughterhouse, 1870–1874); Ricardo Palma with his *Tradiciones peruanas* (Peruvian Traditions, 1883–1896), sprightly fictions larded with history and legend; and Rubén Darío with his elaborately lacquered modernist tales. But with Quiroga the short story genre truly came of age in Latin America.

Quiroga was a pioneer on several significant frontiers. Though his earliest stories were composed in an artificial modernist mode, he soon cast aside this mannered style and began to write tales in a realistic vein, many of them set in the Misiones jungle of far northeastern Argentina. At the same time, he was one of the first in the River Plate region, along with his friend Leopoldo Lugones, to write stories with the fantastic as an important element. The use of the fantastic has flourished to an astonishing degree throughout Latin America from the 1940's on with Jorge Luis Borges, Julio Cortázar, and other gifted writers. But aside from these compelling historical considerations, what today seems most important is the enduring vitality and artistry of Quiroga's narratives. Though some of his stories are clearly dated, his best work lives on with undeniable universal appeal. The critics rightly regard him as a classic.

For a full appreciation and understanding of Quiroga's work, a knowledge of his life must enter. His life—filled with adventure, tragedy, and violence—furnished him with an enormous amount of material for his stories. In many of them the protagonist resembles Quiroga, revealing the author's character and temperament. And certain thematic designs run through both his life and his stories. He was born on 31 December 1878 in Salto, a border town in Uruguay, of an Uruguayan mother, Juana Petrona Forteza, and an Argentine father, Prudencio Quiroga. The latter was related to Juan Facundo Quiroga, a notorious despot of the pampas, immortalized in Domingo Faustino Sarmiento's famous treatise on Argentine life *Facundo* (1845). When Horacio was three months old, his father was killed in a hunting accident. According to several of his biographers, this violent death traumatized Quiroga, who later suffered neurasthenia. Shortly after this accident, Quiroga's mother moved with her four children to Córdoba, Argentina, the origin of her husband's family. In 1883 they returned to Salto, where Quiroga attended his first school. In 1891 the family moved to the capital city of Montevideo, and that year Quiroga's mother remarried. Five years later tragedy struck again when his stepfather, despondent and incapacitated from the effects of a stroke, committed suicide by shooting himself. In 1902, at age twenty-three, Quiroga accidentally shot and killed one of his best friends with a handgun; though exonerated, he was shaken by this terrible event and fled from Montevideo to Buenos Aires to take refuge with his sister who was living there. Surely the most horrifying tragedy occurred in 1915. Quiroga's first wife, who couldn't stand the harsh life in the wilderness where they were living, swallowed a dose of poison, which killed her after several days of agony, leaving Quiroga with two small children. This extraordinary amount of violence cannot be emphasized too much, for it explains Quiroga's obsession with violent death that is so pervasive in his writings.

The intensity of Quiroga's life informs and characterizes most of his work. Early on he displayed a creative imagination and superior intelligence, but as a schoolboy he was often fractious and willful, shunning the company of others and finding pleasure in reading, especially travel books. As a youth he displayed many interests: photography, ceramics, chemical experiments, bicycling, and the manual arts, particularly carpentry and ironwork. For a short while he attended the University of Montevideo, and in 1899 he founded a little magazine, Revista del Salto, with the subtitle "A Literary and Social Science Weekly," which ran for twenty numbers and included imitations of Edgar Allen Poe and such topics as sadomasochism. Narcotics apparently fascinated Quiroga, too; he took chloroform for his asthma and experimented with hashish.

Quiroga's love affairs and two marriages were turbulent and ended badly. At age nineteen he fell desperately in love with María Ester, a girl he had met in Salto, but her mother objected to him as a suitor. This frustrated romance served as the material for what some critics have called a short Dostoyevskian novel, Historia de un amor turbio (An Ill-Fated Love, 1908). In 1909 he married Ana María Cirés, a former student, after three years of arduous courtship and wearing down her parents to get their grudging permission. Two decades later he married one of his

daughter's classmates who was nearly thirty years his junior. Both marriages were full of discord. In his stories and short novels, Quiroga portrays the relationship between the sexes as being fraught with love and hate, contention and tension, and the woman is frequently much younger than the man.

In 1900 Quiroga realized the dream of most young Latin American writers of visiting Paris, where he met Darío, leader of the modernist movement in Spanish America. Unable to succumb to the charm of the French capital, Quiroga stayed only a few months. He soon ran out of funds, went hungry, and assessed his visit as "a succession of unexpected disasters." Returning to Montevideo, he and some of his friends founded the first Uruguayan modernist literary circle. The following year he published his first book, Los arrecifes de coral (Coral Reefs, 1901), a mixture of poetry and prose in the mannered style of the modernists. This publication was not enthusiastically received; the poems showed little talent, and the stories were not much better. Wisely, Quiroga abandoned verse and soon began writing stories in a realistic mode, although they frequently contained unusual or monstrous elements.

Quiroga's relish for adventure and his attraction to the tropical Misiones province of northern Argentina are other biographical factors that are relevant to his work. His first trip there was in 1903, accompanying his friend and fellow writer Lugones as photographer on an expedition to study the Jesuit ruins. In 1904 he was drawn to the northwestern Chaco Territory, where he spent his paternal inheritance on some land that he thought would make his fortune. He planted cotton, built his own hut, and embarked on his first pioneering venture. Though his cotton plantation failed and he lost the money he had invested, Quiroga was undeterred; in 1906 he bought another tract of virgin jungle to clear and settle, this time in San Ignacio, Misiones. From then on he divided his time between his beloved wilderness and Buenos Aires.

From various accounts, it would appear that Quiroga was enthralled with what he found in Misiones: the broad expanse of the Paraná River, the tropical forest, the exotic animals (including deadly serpents). He became an integral part of this land and its people, its mighty rivers and treacherous jungle. A skilled craftsman, he constructed his own bungalow, which is depicted in many of his stories, as well as his own furniture and canoes. Fascinated by technology, he spent much time on inventions: he devised a machine to kill ants and a furnace for making charcoal. He also experimented with distilling an orange liqueur from the fruit in his grove. While all these experimental endeavors were financial failures, they provided him with excellent material for his collection of short stories.

In the midst of all his feverish physical activity in Misiones, Quiroga continued to write stories. In 1904 his second book, *El crimen del otro* (Another's Crime) appeared, and in 1905 he published *Los perseguidos* (The Pursued), a longish story which may well be one of the most modern and ambiguous pieces he wrote, elaborating on the theme of madness. This same year he started contributing regularly to several prominent Buenos Aires magazines, especially the lavishly illustrated *Caras y caretas* (Faces and Masks), which had a rather large readership for the times. Among the ten stories he published in this journal in 1907 was "El almohadón de plumas" ("The Feather Pillow"), a fine example of his treatment of the Gothic tale. Elements of horror, and perversity, reminiscent of Poe, pervade the atmosphere throughout the story, and Quiroga skillfully prepares the terrain, so that we are perhaps ready for the sensational revelation at the end: a servant discovers a swollen vampire bat in the feather pillow of the ailing protagonist, Alicia; the bat had been sucking her blood. But the simple anecdote assumes more meaning and sophistication when we realize that it is charged with symbolism: Alicia is suffering from hallucinations caused specifically by her husband's coldness, because he is the real monster.

From 1906 until 1911, Quiroga took a teaching job in a Normal School, where his future bride was one of his students. Though teaching was never his forte, he did it for several years to help make ends meet. After their marriage, he and Ana María went to his ranch in remote San Ignacio with his firm intention to stay there permanently. In January 1911 Quiroga's daughter, Eglé, was born without the aid of a physician—Quiroga thought that childbirth should be entrusted to nature alone—and his wife almost died. For the birth of their second child, a son Darío in 1912, Ana

María returned to Buenos Aires. Economic crises continued to plague Quiroga. Though he and his wife loved each other, they quarreled constantly. She was excitable and he was stubborn and bad tempered. She was particularly irritated by his ideas on rearing children—which later appear in such well-known stories as "El desierto" ("The Wilderness") and "El hijo" ("The Son")—for he wanted to raise them as young animals in what he thought was nature's way. In one of her moments of despair Ana María took poison and died a lingering death in December 1915. Quiroga, at first enraged that she would do this, then incredulous, became utterly despondent. Life had to go on though without her, and he struggled with the household. A year later he gave up the battle and returned to Buenos Aires, leaving his small children in the care of his mother-in-law.

The next ten years were the most productive of his writing career, wherein he published his best books. Two story collections frame this period as high points: *Cuentos de amor, de locura y de muerte* (Stories of Love, Madness, and Death, 1917) and *Los desterrados* (The Exiles, 1926). The splendid title of the former sets forth his major themes and could properly be the heading for his entire work. Quiroga also achieved great popularity with his *Cuentos de la selva* (South American Jungle Tales, 1918), a volume for children of all ages, permeated with tenderness, humor, and whimsy.

In 1917 Quiroga secured a position in the Uruguayan consulate in Buenos Aires, which helped to relieve the strain on his finances. For almost eight years he lived in the Argentine capital, where he was revered as a great short story writer. He continued writing stories and in 1922 inaugurated in the literary magazine *Atlántida* a section of criticism on the cinema, a medium which fascinated him. Since Quiroga could not tolerate a routine post, he obtained a leave of absence from the consulate in 1925 and returned to his old place in Misiones. There he fell madly in love with Ana María Palacio, a young girl of seventeen whom he had known some years before. She responded to his love, but her parents put an end to the affair by sending her away. Thwarted, Quiroga also abandoned Misiones and returned to Buenos Aires. Several years later he dramatized this frustrated love in his second novel, *Pasado amor*

(Bygone Love, 1929), which is mainly of interest as a personal confessional.

Quiroga moved into a house in Buenos Aires with his children, his menagerie of tame and wild animals, and his souvenirs of the jungle, mainly the skins of animals he had slain. He took up with his literary friends again, indulged in his favorite diversion, the cinema, and enjoyed his fame, including an homage payed to his work in 1926 by an Argentine publishing house that dedicated a special issue of its journal *Babel* to him. His photo appeared on the periodical's cover with the statement: "Horacio Quiroga, the finest short story writer in the Spanish language." One of his best works—some critics say *the* best—*Los desterrados* was also published in 1926. This collection, as Emir Rodríguez Monegal has observed, contains an interior unity that gives it maturity. At the emotional center of the stories in this book, though often on the margin as a spectator, one finds Quiroga, for this is his world. He, too, is one of the exiles.

Quiroga fell in love with María Elena Bravo, a young woman of twenty, whom he married in 1927. Differences soon arose between them; he was jealous and not easy to live with, and she seems to have married him mainly because of his fame. The birth of their daughter the next year did not help much. Again weary of city life, Quiroga managed to get his consul post transfered to San Ignacio. Early in 1932 he left with his wife, three children, his tools and Ford automobile for his outpost home in Misiones, happy to return to his old way of life in the rather primitive wilderness. But his wife hated the setting, and domestic strife escalated. Another serious blow occurred two years later when the Uruguayan government abruptly closed its San Ignacio consulate, leaving him without salary. Quiroga's economic situation became precarious. During these gloomy days his last book, with the rather foreboding title *Más allá* (The Great Beyond, 1935), appeared. In general, the stories in this collection are a letdown after those in *Los desterrados.*

Plagued off and on with such serious ailments as asthma and neurasthenia, Quiroga now began to suffer from a prostate problem. In 1935, through the interception of old friends, he was appointed an honorary consul, but almost a year elapsed before he received any salary. Shortly after this, his wife and their small daughter abandoned Misiones and him for good. As his illness grew progressively worse, Quiroga decided reluctantly that he must leave Misiones in order to seek adequate medical attention. He sailed down the Paraná River for the last time in September 1936 and was admitted to a hospital in Buenos Aires. After some months of treatment there, his illness was finally diagnosed as cancer. Quiroga took his own life by ingesting a dose of cyanide on 18 February 1937, and was found lifeless the next day. He died penniless and was buried at the expense of friends in his native Salto.

During more than three decades Quiroga published over two hundred stories, many of them of impressive quality. If we examine the very best of them—two dozen or so—we will find passages full of penetration about mankind. The impact of many of his tales is felt after the ending, a kind of afterimage that imprints the story on the reader's consciousness. Quiroga clearly sees man's problems, not only those brought on by nature (treacherous floods and murderous heat, snakes and wild beasts of the forest) but also those involving relationships between people. His characters are often greedy and filled with driving ambition, but they are held in check by circumstances they cannot control. The reader grasps man's despair, but also his diversity. Sometimes he is heroic, other times abject. Though Quiroga never glosses over man's defects, he also stresses such noble virtues as bravery, generosity, and compassion.

In his best moments Quiroga shapes all this rich and multifarious human material into excellent stories. He is quite conscious of the problems involved in the art of the short story. Like another expert of the genre, his self-acclaimed master, Poe, Quiroga wrote about narrative construction. His "Decálogo del perfecto cuentista" (Decalogue of the Perfect Short Story Writer) is succinct and filled with cogent advice. He stresses the importance of economy of expression and, following Poe's dictum, the necessity of careful advance planning: "Don't start to write without knowing from the first word where you are going. In a story that comes off well, the first three lines are as important as the last three."

Quiroga practiced such skillful planning and economy. This brevity excludes anything redundant but nothing that is really meaningful, as in his powerful, stark tale "A la deriva" ("Drifting"). The initial scene, in which the main character is bitten by a poisonous snake, is the source of all that follows. Quiroga uses taut language and straightforward action to propel his story along. We watch as the protagonist's foot, then leg, swell up in an angry purple mass of flesh; we see him rush to his canoe and push off into the Paraná River, desperate and urgently trying to find someone to save his life. The entire action moves from start to finish "like an arrow to its target," to use Quiroga's own phrase referring to narrative art in the short story ("Ante el tribunal," *El Hogar*, 11 September 1930). The title is especially symbolic, for just as the dying man literally drifts downriver seeking aid, he is helplessly adrift on the river of life from the very beginning when the snake bites him.

The tenth commandment in Quiroga's decalogue may be the most suggestive and has prompted admiration from the noted contemporary writer Cortázar: "Don't think about your friends when you write or the impression your story will make. Tell the tale as if the story's only interest lay in the small surroundings of your characters, of which you might have been one. In no other way is *life* achieved in the short story." Quiroga perspicaciously emphasizes the word "life," because he is well aware that his stories are infused with this quality.

These technical aspects of Quiroga's art undeniably manifest some of Poe's authority, for Quiroga himself cites them. However, Poe's thematic sway over the Uruguayan seems even more pronounced, especially during his early period up to 1917. Echoing Poe, Quiroga exhibits a fondness for the extraordinary and the monstrous in his early stories. His first book, *Los arrecifes de coral*, includes "El tonel de Amontillado" (The Cask of Amontillado), whose theme and title come straight from the North American. Quiroga later acknowledged that during those early years, "Poe was the only author I read. That cursed madman had come to dominate me completely. On my reading table there wasn't a single book which wasn't by him" (Franco, introduction to *Cuentos escogidos*, 1968, p. 4).

Quiroga's first major collection, *Cuentos de amor, de locura y de muerte*, includes many tales that bear the stamp of Poe. Probably the best known of these,

in addition to "The Feather Pillow," is the often anthologized "La gallina degollada" ("The Decapitated Chicken"), which was first published in 1909. With this cruelly tragic tale, we have Quiroga at his lurid best. Mazzini and Berta, a young Buenos Aires couple, have the misfortune to produce four baby boys, one after another, who become violently ill when a year old and turn into complete idiots. Finally, a beautiful and healthy daughter is born. The parents lavish all their love and attention on her, neglecting their idiot sons, who spend their days sitting open-mouthed and speechless in the patio, their heads lolling in the glaring sun. At the end the idiot brothers kill their little sister, imitating the cook they watched beheading a chicken in the kitchen. This horrible story is quite effective, though perhaps too violent for many tastes. It is related in a straightforward fashion, creating a mood of anxiety and uneasy tension. Mazzini and Berta are well delineated, and the representation of the idiots with their bestial characteristics is masterful.

In a letter dated 8 June 1917 to José María Delgado, Quiroga confessed that this type of story written for effect no longer interested him so much: "One fine day I realized that it is much more difficult to wind up a story with an end that the reader has already guessed at." From Poe, and especially from Guy de Maupassant, he had learned the art of preparing surprise endings to his stories. But in his more mature fiction, most set in Misiones, the reader knows more or less what to expect; the surprise lies not in the solution but in the way Quiroga reaches it. Many good writers have transferred the interest of what happened to how it happened, and in his maturity Quiroga learned this essential lesson. He also learned that he could create extreme situations without relying on the supernatural. So he no longer used Poe's technique of the supernatural as an effective way for showing the human personality under stress. As the critic Jean Franco observed in her introduction to *Cuentos escogidos* (1968): "Quiroga turned from his early imitations of Poe to draw increasingly on his own real experiences, which, in any case, were often as bizarre as Poe's fantasies."

In addition to Poe and Maupassant, writers such as Charles Baudelaire, Gustave Flaubert, and Fyodor Dostoyevsky (in *Historia de un amor turbia*) influenced

Quiroga's early work. Another influence often cited is Rudyard Kipling's *The Jungle Book* (1894), although this influence has been overly exaggerated by critics. Both Kipling and Quiroga admired the jungle and were fond of animal stories. For Kipling, though, the jungle was primarily a literary theme and not something with which he identified. While he had grown up in India, Kipling viewed his Indian jungle and its inhabitants from the perspective of a colonialist. Quiroga, on the other hand, almost always chooses to stress the tragic daily existence of his jungle denizens, of which he was one himself.

In addition to the popular *Cuentos de la selva* of 1918 often associated with Kipling, Quiroga published another volume with animals as characters, *Anaconda* (1921). The title story, one of his longest, is about a world of serpents and how they fight with one another and with man, their enemy. Though Quiroga's animal characterization lacks the subtlety of some of his shorter pieces, such as "La insolación" ("The Sunstroke"), in this tale he is inventive and makes interesting things happen. The tight-knit, tense structure of "Drifting" is lacking here, but Quiroga compensates for this by giving us a story rich in imagination and irony, satirizing man's behavior. Like *Cuentos de la selva*, "Anaconda" will have a special appeal for youngsters, although it was written with an adult audience in mind.

Sentimentality plays no part in Quiroga's animal tales. Though he endows animals with speech like such fable writers as Aesop, he does not usually point up a moral or use animals to express human attitudes. Quite the contrary, he prefers animals whose natures remain unchanged by human contact, like the boa constrictor Anaconda or the bull in "El alambre de púa" (The Barbed Wire Fence). In the latter, an unusual and compelling tale with humorous touches, Quiroga tells how a bull meets his tragic death when he fails to recognize man's right to fence in his own land. Two horses that escape from their field to roam the area are the narrators. In their wanderings they meet a herd of cows and the mighty bull that tears down fences. Man tries to control nature, and the bull dies from the effects of charging against the barbed wire. In some way, the story suggests a sort of bullfight, a South American version of the bullring where the arrogant beast winds up being a mountain

of sacrificed flesh. In the last ironic scene we witness one of the narrating horses hauling off two kilos of the bull's meat for his owner's table. "El alambre de púa" presents multiple points of view: the horses', the fascinated cows', the bull's and his owner's, and the farmer's whose crops are trampled and eaten by the foraging beasts. This story, published in 1912, shows elements of a more mature writer making manifest the play of irreconcilable perspectives.

Another excellent story with multiple points of view is "Los mensú" ("The Contract Laborers"), which first appeared in 1914. Here Quiroga describes in vivid detail the life and the exploitation of Misiones lumberjacks. Here the author does not seem to have a social ax to grind, but this story and others like it, such as "Una bofetada" ("A Slap in the Face"), contain some of the most trenchant social criticism in Spanish-American prose of that time. Such stories are precursors of a whole movement of fiction stressing problems of social significance, like José Eustasio Rivera's *La vorágine* (*The Vortex*, 1924). In "The Contract Laborers" no preaching is involved; though Quiroga is clearly on the side of the oppressed, he does not express their thoughts exclusively. Consequently, the reader feels the social impact all the more. With admirable powers of synthesis, Quiroga graphically traces some moments in the lives of the lumberjacks. We see how they live and work, what they eat, how they speak. The story begins with a group of workers disembarking at a small river town, where they exuberantly spend all their hard-earned pay on wine, women, and gambling. The last part of the story concentrates on two of them who are friends and their attempted escape from the vicious cycle they are caught up in. They do manage to escape from camp, but one meets death on the river and the other will have his bondage renewed when the boat that rescues him carries him back upriver to the same old place of exploitation. Only death will liberate these slaves, the story implies.

Quiroga plays on a life/death tension in many fine stories, such as "Drifting," "The Son," and "El hombre muerto" ("The Dead Man"). While the agonies of death slowly reduce the protagonist in the very short "The Dead Man," nature and the environment surrounding him throb with life—the ordinary day-to-day details the protagonist is accustomed to—so much so that he cannot accept the fact that he is actually dying. Few writers have plumbed the feelings and the reactions of a dying man with such economy and truth. Here as elsewhere Quiroga treats death matter-of-factly, without sentimentality, but there is no naturalistic wallowing in repulsive clinical details either.

In Quiroga's best work there is abundant suggestion and implication rather than outright telling, characteristics much admired today. In this respect, Quiroga's reputation has taken an upward swing: the author who for so long was chiefly admired for his violent themes, tales of horror, and tragic jungle tales has in the last two decades received more critical attention and acclaim for his narrative art. While "The Dead Man" is frequently cited as probably the most skillful instance of this technique of implication, other examples abound.

In addition to narrative art, setting has a critical importance for Quiroga, especially the wilderness, the jungle and plantations of the Chaco and Misiones, and the Paraná River with its cliffs and rapids. But this indispensable landscape is never described for its own sake; it always has a function in the stories, sometimes serving as a way of evaluating men or as a metaphor for their state of mind. Most often, Quiroga stresses the ominous character of nature in the wilderness, the physical obstacles against which man struggles. The jungle hovers at the edge of the plantations, threatening to invade and conquer man. Nature is a powerful force against which man can do battle, but he will never win. The jungle setting also became inseparable from the real and everyday experience for Quiroga. Misiones province is not just a setting for his tales but an integral part of them and, like Quiroga himself, bursting with vitality and violent drama.

Recognition for his supremacy as a short story writer came to Quiroga early, and he continued to enjoy renown throughout most of his life; but toward the end a certain neglect set in. New writers in Argentina such as Borges with more philosophical and metaphysical aims took up the short story, looking askance at the work of Quiroga or ignoring it completely. This attitude has been tempered in recent years, and in the Spanish-speaking world Quiroga is popular today, admired by critics and reading public alike, though his favorite theme of pitting man against nature is no longer in vogue.

Among his staunchest admirers was Cortázar, a master himself in the short story genre. Cortázar has set forth some of Quiroga's best and most enduring qualities: he knew his métier extremely well and was universal in appeal; he gave his themes a literary form and dramatic cast, communicating to the reader all their values and ferment; he wrote in a taut fashion and described with intensity so that a story would have an impact on the reader and stay fixed in his memory. One can only concur in this perspicacious appraisal and add slightly to this list of positive attributes. In Quiroga's finest work action is perfectly illustrative, for his stories not only have brisk movement but also considerable depth. The spareness even allows for a greater complexity and suggestion. Quiroga not only transcribes life, but he dramatizes it, and the reader is caught up in this drama.

SELECTED BIBLIOGRAPHY

First Editions

Short Story Collections

Los arrecifes de coral. Montevideo, 1901.
El crimen del otro. Buenos Aires, 1904.
Los perseguidos. Buenos Aires, 1905.
Cuentos de amor, de locura y de muerte. Buenos Aires, 1917.
Cuentos de la selva para los niños. Buenos Aires, 1918.
Las sacrificadas. (Cuento escénico en cuatro actos). Buenos Aires, 1920.
El salvaje. Buenos Aires, 1920.
Anaconda. Buenos Aires, 1921.
El desierto. Buenos Aires, 1924.
Los desterrados. Buenos Aires, 1926.
Más allá. Buenos Aires, 1935.

Novels

Historia de un amor turbio. Buenos Aires, 1908.
Pasado amor. Buenos Aires, 1929.

Travel Books

Diario de viaje a París. With an introduction and notes by Emir Rodríguez Monegal. Montevideo, 1949.

Letters

Cartas inéditas. 2 vols. Montevideo, 1959.

Later Editions

Short Story Collections

Cuentos. Edited with an introduction by Raimundo Lazo. Mexico City, 1968.
Cuentos escogidos. Edited with a prologue by Guillermo de Torre. Madrid, 1950.
Cuentos escogidos. Edited with an introduction by Jean Franco. London and New York, 1968.
Horacio Quiroga. Cuentos. Prologue by Emir Rodríguez Monegal. Caracas, 1981.
Horacio Quiroga. Sus mejores cuentos. Edited with an introduction by John A. Crow. Mexico City, 1943.
Sus mejores cuentos. Edited with a prologue by Mario Rodríguez. Santiago, Chile, 1971.

Collected Works

Cuentos. 13 vols. Montevideo, 1937–1945.
Cuentos completos/Horacio Quiroga. 2 vols. Montevideo, 1978.
Novelas completas. Horacio Quiroga. Montevideo, 1979.
Obras inéditas y desconocidas de Horacio Quiroga. 6 vols. Edited by Ángel Rama. Montevideo, 1967–1969.

Translations

The Decapitated Chicken and Other Stories. Translated by Margaret Sayers Peden. With an introduction by George D. Schade. Austin, Tex., and London, 1976.
The Exiles and Other Stores. Selected, translated, and with an introduction by J. David Danielson. Austin, Tex., 1987.
South American Jungle Tales. Translated by Arthur Livingston, New York, 1941.

Biographical and Critical Studies

Alazraki, Jaime. "Relectura de Horacio Quiroga." In *El cuento hispanoamericano ante la crítica.* Edited by Enrique Pupo-Walker. Madrid, 1973.
Boule-Christauflour, Annie. "Los animales en los cuentos de Horacio Quiroga." *Boletín cultural de la embajada argentina* (Madrid) 1–2 (1963).
_____. "Una historia de locos. *Los perseguidos* de Horacio Quiroga." *Mundo Nuevo* (Paris) 8:51–57 (1967).
_____. "Science et fiction dans les contes de Horacio Quiroga." *Bulletin hispanique* (Bordeaux) 72/3–4:360–366 (1970).
Bratosevich, Nicolás. *El estilo de Horacio Quiroga en sus cuentos.* Madrid, 1973.
Chapman, Arnold. "Between Fire and Ice: A Theme in Jack London and Horacio Quiroga." *Symposium* 24:17–26 (1970).
Delgado, José María, and Alberto J. Brignole. *Vida y obra de Horacio Quiroga.* Montevideo, 1939.
Englekirk, John E. *Edgar Allan Poe in Hispanic Literature.* New York, 1934. Pp. 340–368.
Etcheverry, José Enrique. "Horacio Quiroga y la creación artística." *Revista iberoamericana de literatura* (Montevideo) 1/1:35–44 (1959).
Flores, Ángel, ed. *Aproximaciones a Horacio Quiroga.* Caracas, 1976.
Glanz, Margo. "Poe en Quiroga." In *Aproximaciones a Horacio Quiroga.* Caracas, 1976. Pp. 93–118.
Jitrik, Noé. *Una obra de experiencia y riesgo.* Buenos Aires, 1959.
Martínez Estrada, Ezequiel. *El hermano Quiroga.* Montevideo, 1957.
Montenegro, Ernesto. "Horacio Quiroga, Literary Kin of Kipling and Jack London." *New York Times Book Review,* 25 October 1925.
Rodríguez Monegal, Emir. *Las raíces de Horacio Quiroga.* Montevideo, 1961.
_____. *Genio y figura de Horacio Quiroga.* Buenos Aires, 1967.
_____. *El desterrado: Vida y obra de Horacio Quiroga.* Buenos Aires, 1968.
Spell, Jefferson Rea. "Renowned Short Story Writer, Horacio Quiroga." In *Contemporary Spanish-American Fiction.* Chapel Hill, N.C., 1944. Pp. 153–178.
Speratti Piñero, Emma Susanna. "Hacia la cronología de Horacio Quiroga." *Nueva revista de filología hispánica* 9/4:367–382 (1955).
_____. "Realismo e imaginación en la obra de Horacio Quiroga." In Emma Susanna Speratti Piñero and Ana María Barrenechea, *La literatura fantástica en la argentina.* Mexico City, 1957. Pp. 17–36.
Yurkievich, Saúl. "Quiroga: Su técnica narrativa." *Revista iberoamericana de literatura* (Montevideo) 2–3:91–99 (1960–1961).

Benito Lynch

(1880–1951)

David William Foster

Benito Lynch is a figure of enigma and controversy. He was born in Buenos Aires on 25 July 1880—the date is disputed—to an Uruguayan mother and a father of Irish descent. When he was a child, the family moved to a cattle ranch in the province of Buenos Aires; his early life there left such a deep and indelible impression on him that years later, in his *De los campos porteños* (On Buenos Aires Countryside, 1931), he relived some of his experiences through his autobiographical protagonist, Mario.

At the age of ten, Lynch returned to Buenos Aires and there completed his formal education. He began a career as a journalist and published in *El día* a series of narrative sketches entitled *Cuadritos domésticos* (Domestic Sketches). His first novel, *Plata dorada* (Golden Silver), appeared in 1909; eight novels and scores of short stories followed.

Lynch's adult life was characterized by an attitude of isolation and withdrawal, an idiosyncrasy that intensified after 1923 when he challenged a presumed slanderer to a duel; the affair was resolved peaceably. In 1938, he declined an honorary degree from the National University of La Plata. He would not attend the openings of theatrical versions of his works. After authorizing translations of his work, he refused royalty payments so as to avoid associating with the Socidad Argentina de Autores (Argentine Society of Writers), from whose list he demanded his name be dropped. After the death of his mother in 1938, he lived alone in the family house.

Apparently feeling rootless, Lynch chose a life of isolation while clinging stubbornly to the memory of the countryside of his childhood, of which traces recur repeatedly throughout almost all of his writing. His narrative production took place between 1909 and 1933. After long years of not publishing and of refusing to allow his work to be reissued, because of acute misanthropy and increasing reclusiveness, he died of cancer on 24 December 1951.

Lynch belongs to a rather nebulous sector of Latin American literature: writers who lack the secure position assigned to the founders of Latin American letters and who have not aroused the immense interest generated by certain contemporary authors both in Latin America and abroad. The result is that such authors tend to be forgotten, editions of their works disappear from bookstores, and critics cease to concern themselves with their writing. While this neglect may be the case with all literary traditions, it is particularly characteristic of the Latin American tradition, in which academic and intellectual concentration is devoted almost exclusively to founding figures or to prominent contemporary authors. Concerted efforts are being made toward revisionist literary history, but Lynch's books do not accord with the current interest in ethnic minorities, countercultural issues, or women's writing.

Yet Lynch occupies an undeniably authoritative place in Argentine letters—and in Latin American letters, insofar as Argentine writers have always provided influential models for all of Latin America. It has been customary to group Lynch's works under the heading of creolism, a powerful current of early twentieth-century Latin American writing. The creolist writers saw themselves as witnesses of regional, national, and local values and life-styles. Reacting against the tendency to promote a culture of uniform models and styles for all of Latin America, the creolist writers sought to address themselves to a more localized community of readers who would discover a detailed image of themselves in the literature. Moreover, since the emphasis in late-nineteenth-century Latin American writing—the so-called modernist aesthetic—had been on imitating French and English authors in an attempt to create a sophisticated and cosmopolitan Latin American society, the creolists set out to explore those sectors of society that remained on the margin of the Europeanized social and cultural elite.

The interests of the creolists did not mean that they eschewed foreign models or styles. Recognizing the need to create specifically national literatures in countries with fragmentary and discontinuous literary traditions, they attempted to augment folkloric and autochthonous modes with the methods suggested by foreign examples. While the cosmopolitan writer was interested in writing *like*, say, Émile Zola or Oscar Wilde, the creolist concerned himself with the possibility of *applying* the foreign mode to unique Latin American realities.

Thus, in the case of Lynch's fiction, we find the patient and cumulative depiction, in nine novels and approximately one hundred short stories, of a very restricted range of human situations and experiences: the representation of life on the estancias (large cattle ranches) of the province of Buenos Aires in the area of the Salado River during the closing years of the nineteenth century and the first decades of the twentieth. During this period, there was enormous interest in the literary representation of Buenos Aires, a city that was undergoing rapid transformation from a large village into one of Latin America's major megalopolises, dominating virtually every aspect of Argentine life. The emphasis of a writer like Lynch, however, was on the traditional aspects of Argentine rural existence, which had already developed a national myth of an agrarian society. This myth is frequently portrayed in utopian or Arcadian terms as an abiding constant of Argentine literature, particularly during the creolist period (for example, in Ricardo Güiraldes' famous gaucho novel *Don Segundo Sombra* [1926]).

Nevertheless, although his writing provides a concentrated representation of this one segment of society, Lynch's interest goes far beyond the simple, lyrical evocation of an idealized, Edenic life-style free of urban corruption. For within creolism there is another tendency, wherein a respectful attitude toward a mythified rural existence is attenuated and tempered by an unflinchingly critical stance toward the dynamics of that existence. Lynch's earliest novels are more directly descriptive of rural existence, as the author works to construct the parameters of the world that all of his fiction will depict. In these as in later works, however, one notes the increasing presence of a critical realism or naturalism, in the Zolaresque tradition, in which the hardships, interpersonal conflicts, and disruptive pressures of particular traditional modes of existence provide the basis for narrative exposition. Even in Lynch's first novel, *Plata dorada*, life is viewed as the brutal collision of individuals guided by blind instinct, while in a mature work like *Los caranchos de La Florida* (The Vultures of La Florida, 1916), relatively urbane men, a father and son, are locked in homicidal conflict, moved by base human passions.

Cosmopolitan Latin American authors in the mainstream of naturalism tended to adopt a condescending, ironic, and often disdainful narrative attitude toward primitive types, who, in their opinion, lamentably continued to inhabit the outback and were becoming legion in the cities. But Lynch, despite the influence of naturalism, was always able to maintain a sympathetic attitude toward his material. This attitude, while somewhat tinged with the indulgent paternalism that we today identify with so much of the creolist writing of the period, made his novels appeal to a wider audience of readers than did the grim accounts of the more doctrinaire naturalists.

One may identify an ethical ambiguity in Lynch's fictional world. This ambiguity, rather than indicating any presumed inability of the author to decide on a unified point of view, may be seen as providing a denser or more comprehensive vision of human experience within the confines of the society and experiences addressed. While it is true that many of his characters evince the obedience to blind instinct, primitive life forces, and deterministic behavior prescribed by canonical naturalism, he created other individuals who are capable of self-reflection and of a conduct based on the adherence to "natural" values belied or repudiated by naturalism, like friendship, the maternal instinct, or a spiritual attachment to the land. To be sure, a romanticized or sentimentalized naturalism is often to be found in Latin American writing of the period. Whether this demonstrates the inability of Latin American writers to assimilate fully their foreign models or their success in freeing themselves from slavish imitation is a matter of controversy. Lynch's work is a significant locus of this issue in Latin American literary history.

Lynch's best-known novel is *El inglés de los güesos* (The Englishman of the Bones). Originally published in Spain in 1924 (the only one of Lynch's novels not to appear as an Argentine first edition), *El inglés* is the story of the tragic encounter between an English archaeologist, Mr. James Gray, and the young daughter of a family in the area of Gray's diggings. The initial point of departure of the narrative is the curiosity provoked by Gray's presence, which is so obviously foreign, English, and alien. Not only is Gray different from the locals, but his activity, the excavation of fossils, is patently ridiculous to them, since the bones he so diligently seeks and collects are for them only an annoying accident of the countryside. Initially, Gray is an object of ridicule and humiliation; because of his primitive Spanish, he is often unaware of the remarks about him, and he appears not to understand when he is victimized.

But Gray emerges as far more than merely a caricature of the many Englishmen who "invaded" Argentine society in the period from 1880 to 1930, men who were either invited by the government to provide services for the country (for example, the

vast network of railroads) or drawn by socioeconomic conditions that permitted easy exploitation of Argentine natural resources. The early chapters of the novel dwell on humorous details associated with Gray's presence in the community and the many cultural conflicts involved. The carefree Balbina is particularly amused by Gray, and her consciousness (although she is hardly able to verbalize her feelings) is an important sustaining element in the novel, as one record of the conflict between the traditional beliefs and values of people like her family and the rush of alien ideas in a society undergoing profound transformations. Indeed, Argentine literature of this period is particularly rich in versions of this conflict, and *El inglés* is of some interest for the characteristics of this encounter.

The novel assumes tragic dimensions, however, and the issues of cultural conflict range far beyond differences of language and behavior, when Balbina falls desperately in love with Gray. Gray is aware of what he considers simply the infatuation of a naive and high-spirited young woman. Although he is not indifferent to her affections and indeed at one point considers giving up his work for her, in the final analysis the scientist's commitment to his research wins out, and, at the conclusion of his fieldwork, Gray returns to England to pursue his career. Balbina commits suicide.

Balbina's disastrous love for Gray provides the novel with several axes of cultural conflict. The principal motivating disjunction lies between the "natural" feelings of the inhabitants toward the Argentine countryside, which forms the foreground of the novel without being idealized, and the self-serving egotism of Gray, who is willing to sacrifice everything in the pursuit of his scientific objectives. Variants of this disjunction concern the Argentine rural life-style versus the cosmopolitan values of the archaeologist and the primitive world of the countryside versus the "civilized" realm of scientific investigation (the disjunction between barbarism and civilization is one of the recurrent motifs of Argentine culture). By extension, science is contrasted with feelings or emotions, reason against the heart: that is, there is a fundamental opposition, to use an anthropological concept, between culture and nature. Balbina knows only the latter; Gray knows both but sacrifices the latter in favor of his determined pursuit of scientific knowledge. Certainly, there are elements of a conflict between the simplicity of tradition and the complexity of modernity: Balbina's "simple" and direct expressions of love meet the resistance of Gray's identification with a complex worldview in which momentary feelings must be balanced against the demands of career and the future.

Nevertheless, the novel allows no interpretive ambiguity. *El inglés*, Lynch's masterpiece, may be seen as a somberly eulogistic representation of the traditional values of the Argentine countryside. There can be no question that our sympathies must lie with Balbina, who is driven to suicide because of rejection, and Lynch's "eulogy" is for the life-style represented by Balbina. Two irreconcilable points of view are at work in the novel, and Lynch leaves no doubt that there is a tragic dimension to the fact that one will prevail over the other.

The language of the novel functions ironically to confirm this narrative posture. As with most of Lynch's fiction, *El inglés* contains an abundant number of words and constructions of rural speech. As is often the case with creolist writing, the speech of the characters is represented in a modified orthography designed to give the flavor of their rural pronunciation and phrasings. The very title of the novel contains such an example: *güesos* is a deviation from the standard word for "bones," *huesos*. Such attempts at vernacular, reminiscent of the American novelists Joel Chandler Harris and Mark Twain, seem not to have been done with any degree of consistency. Some readers (typically, Argentines) often delight in such a practice because of the "charm" attributed to the attempt to reflect styles routinely excluded from academic standard, while other readers find these attempts distracting, if not linguistically naive. Lynch was committed to representing honestly the speech patterns of the world evoked in his fiction, and he succeeds quite well on the levels of phonology (despite occasional inconsistencies), vocabulary, and syntax.

Yet there is another dimension to the linguistic aspect of *El inglés*, having to do with Gray's attempts at Spanish. To be sure, Gray does not have much to say, and as the stereotype of the Englishman lost on the pampa and patronizingly oblivious to its features,

he misses most of the flow of language around him. From the point of view of a novel of customs and types, *El inglés* would have some entertainment value for the Argentine reader in the fact that Gray, despite his presumed intelligence as a scientist, is unable to handle the Spanish language with any degree of accuracy.

Gray's lack of ability with Spanish echoes the ultimately tragic vision of the novel in his repeated comment in Spanish, which would be, in English, something like saying "Me no understand." Gray's incomprehension is clearly more than simply linguistic when viewed in terms of the cultural conflict that Lynch explores. It is the archaeologist's ignorance of the human dimensions of the society that hosts his research that triggers the tragic denouement. Throughout the novel, the leitmotiv of "Me no understand" acquires greater and greater resonance as a correlative of this ignorance. Gray may not have been completely deaf and blind to Balbina's growing emotional involvement with him, but his fundamental inability to accept and to understand her world, despite his scientific interest in one aspect of it, is the basis of his final, overriding ignorance, with all of its tragic implications for Balbina.

Although modern readers may find Lynch's novel quaint and dated, as is the case with so much of creolist writing, the fundamental issues of cultural conflict with which it deals are still very pertinent today for Argentina and Latin America, in terms of the inability and unwillingness of other countries to understand what they view as insignificant, marginal societies.

SELECTED BIBLIOGRAPHY

First Editions

Plata dorada. Buenos Aires, 1909.
Los caranchos de La Florida. Buenos Aires, 1916.
Raquela. Buenos Aires, 1918.
La evasión. Buenos Aires, 1918.
Las mal calladas. Buenos Aires, 1923.
El inglés de los güesos. Madrid, 1924.
El antojo de la patrona y palo verde. Buenos Aires, 1925.
De los campos porteños. Buenos Aires, 1931.
El romance de un gaucho. Buenos Aires, 1933.

Biographical and Critical Studies

Anderson Imbert, Enrique. "Benito Lynch: Voice of the New Gaucho." *Américas* 4/6:9–11, 31 (1952).

Caillet-Bois, Julio. *La novela rural de Benito Lynch.* La Plata, Argentina, 1960.

Cócaro, Nicolás. *Benito Lynch.* Buenos Aires, 1954.

Davis, Jack Emory. "The *americanismos* in *El inglés de los güesos.*" *Hispania* 33/4:333–337 (1950).

García, Germán. *Benito Lynch y su mundo campero.* Bahía Blanca, Argentina, 1954.

Gates, Eunice Joiner. "Charles Darwin and Benito Lynch's *El inglés de los güesos. Hispania* 44/2:250–253 (1961).

Ghiano, Juan Carlos. "Benito Lynch: Una versión del realismo." In *Relecturas argentinas.* Buenos Aires, 1978. Pp. 103–112.

Giusti, Roberto Fernando. "Benito Lynch [*El inglés de los güesos*]." In his *Crítica y polémica, tercera serie.* Buenos Aires, 1927. Pp. 24–40.

González, Juan B. "El novelista Benito Lynch." In his *En torno al estilo.* Buenos Aires, 1930. Pp. 173–194.

Head, Gerald Louis. "El estanciero: Héroe secreto de Benito Lynch." *Et caetera* 19:37–54 (1971).

_____. "El extranjero en las obras de Benito Lynch." *Hispania* 54/1:91–97 (1971).

Leslie, John-Kenneth. "Símiles campestres en la obra de Benito Lynch." *Revista iberoamericana* 17/34:331–338 (1952).

Magis Otón, Carlos Horacio. "Trayectoria del realismo en la Argentina y una novela rural [*El romance de un gaucho*]." *Cuadernos hispanoamericanos* 137:103–125 (1961).

Nason, Marshall R. "Benito Lynch: ¿Otro Hudson?" *Revista iberoamericana* 23/45:65–82 (1958).

_____. "En torno al estilo de Benito Lynch." *Revista de la Universidad de La Plata* 13:141–157 (1961).

Owre, J. Riis. "Los animales en las obras de Benito Lynch." *Revista iberoamericana* 3/6:357–369 (1941).

Petit de Murat, Ulises. *Genio y figura de Benito Lynch.* Buenos Aires, 1968.

Romano, Eduardo. *Fábula y relato en un cuento de Benito Lynch.* Buenos Aires, 1966.

Salama, Roberto. *Benito Lynch.* Buenos Aires, 1959.

Settgast, Edward E. "Some Aspects of the Rural Argentine Dialect in *El inglés de los güesos.*" *Hispania* 52/3:393–400 (1969).

Torres de Peralta, Elba. "Actitud frente a la vida de los personajes en *El inglés de los güesos* de Benito Lynch." *Explicación de textos literarios* 5:13–22 (1976).

Torres-Ríoseco, Arturo. "Benito Lynch." In his *Novelistas contemporáneos de América.* Santiago, Chile, 1939. Pp. 151–210. Also in his *Grandes novelistas de la América hispana* 1. 2nd ed. Berkeley, Calif., 1949. Pp 111–171.

Viñas, David. "Benito Lynch: La realización del Facundo." *Contorno* 5–6:16–21 (1955).

_____. "Benito Lynch y la pampa cercada." *Cultura universitaria* 46:40–53 (1954).

Wapnir, Salomón. "Benito Lynch." In his *Imágenes y letras.* Buenos Aires, 1955. Pp. 31–61.

Afonso Henriques de Lima Barreto

(1881–1922)

Francisco de Assis Barbosa

Afonso Henriques de Lima Barreto was born in Rio de Janeiro on 13 May 1881 and died in the same city on 1 November 1922. "I was born without money, a mulatto and a free man," he stated in the magazine *ABC* on 12 May 1917. He was taught to read and write by his mother, who died when he was seven years old. His godfather and protector, the Viscount of Ouro Preto, a minister of the empire, financed his schooling at the Liceu Popular Niteroiense and the Ginásio Nacional (the present-day Colégio Pedro II) and then at the Polytechnic School, which he joined in 1897 with the intention of becoming a civil engineer. In 1902 Lima Barreto had to give up his studies to take care of his family; his father had gone mad and was forced to give up his post as administrator of an insane asylum on the Ilha do Governador. In the same year Lima Barreto made his debut in the student press.

The family moved to a suburb of Rio de Janeiro, and the future writer obtained a position at the Ministry of War. Lima Barreto moved to a modest house in another suburb, supporting his family with his meager income. In 1904 he started the first version of his novel *Clara dos Anjos* (Clara of the Angels, 1948; published in English as *Clara dos Anjos*). A year later he started writing his novel *Recordações do Escrivão Isaías Caminha* (Memoirs of

Isaias Caminha, Notary Public), which was published in Lisbon in 1909. He also published a series of newspaper reports for the *Correio da Manhã* (Morning Post). In 1906 he started writing his novel *Vida e Morte de M. J. Gonzaga de Sá* (The Life and Death of M. J. Gonzaga de Sá), which was not published until 1919.

Lima Barreto contributed to the magazine *Fon-Fon* and at the end of 1907 launched with some friends the magazine *Floreal*. Although the latter lasted only four issues, it came to the attention of the literary critic José Veríssimo. During that same period, Lima Barreto started reading the great works of world literature at the Biblioteca Nacional. His selection included the contemporary realistic European writers, and he was one of the few Brazilian writers to acknowledge and read the Russian novelists. In 1910 he served as a member of the jury in the trial of participants in the Primavera de Sangue (Bloody Springtime) episode, condemning the military police for the death of a student. As a consequence, from that moment on he was passed over for promotion at the Ministry of War. In 1911, in only three months, he wrote his novel *Triste Fim de Policarpo Quaresma* (The Sad End of Policarpo Quaresma, 1915), which was serialized in the newspaper *Jornal do Comércio*. Lima Barreto contributed as well to the *Gazeta da*

Tarde (Afternoon Gazette). In 1912 he published the two installments of *Aventuras do Dr. Bogóloff* (Adventures of Dr. Bogoloff), along with two other small humorous works, one of them in the magazine *Riso* (Laugh). It was at that time that Lima Barreto's alcoholism started showing its effects, although it did not prevent him from continuing to contribute to the press.

Starting in 1914 Lima Barreto produced a series of daily chronicles in the *Correio da Manhã*. In 1915 the newspaper *A Noite* (The Evening) published in installments his novel *Numa e a Ninfa* (Numa and the Nymph). At the same time, he started a long association with the magazine *Careta* (Grimace), writing political articles on various subjects. At the beginning of 1915, *The Sad End of Policarpo Quaresma* was published in one volume, along with some short stories, such as "A Nova California" (The New California) and "O Homem Que Sabia Javanês" (The Man Who Spoke Javanese). The book was well received by the critics, who saw in Lima Barreto the rightful heir of Joaquim Maria Machado de Assis. The author began to write for the political weekly magazine *ABC*, and in July 1917 Lima Barreto turned over to his publisher, Jacinto Ribeiro dos Santos, his satirical work *Os Bruzundangas* (The Bruzandangas, 1922) which was not published until a month after the author's death.

Lima Barreto sought election to the Brazilian Academy of Letters, but his application was not even acknowledged. In 1917 he published the second, revised and augmented edition of *Isaías Caminha*, as well as the novel *Numa e a Ninfa* in one volume. He started publishing articles and chronicles in such literary periodicals as *O Debate, Voz Cosmopolita, ABC*, and *Braz Cubas*. It was *Braz Cubas* that printed the article in which he stated his sympathy with the Russian revolutionary cause. After being diagnosed as suffering from toxic epilepsy, Lima Barreto retired from the Ministry of War with a pension in December 1918. He moved to another street in Rio de Janeiro, where he remained until his death. At the start of 1919, he ended his collaboration with the weekly *ABC* because the magazine printed an article attacking Negroes.

That same year Lima Barreto decided to sell his novel *The Life and Death of M. J. Gonzaga de Sá*,

which he revised himself and which was typed by order of the editor, Monteiro Lobato. This was one of his few works that received such care before publication, was supported by strong promotional publicity, and was successful not only financially but critically. The book won applause from both old and new literary critics, such as João Ribeiro and Alceu Amoroso Lima. Lima Barreto then tried for the second time for election to the Brazilian Academy of Letters. This time his application was accepted, but he nonetheless failed to be elected.

In March 1919, under the title "As Mágoas e os Sonhos do Povo" (The Woes and Dreams of the People), Lima Barreto started publishing weekly, in *Hoje* (Today), chronicles of urban folklore. He also revived his association with *Careta*, which he maintained until his death. From December 1919 through January 1920, the author was committed to a hospital because of a serious nervous crisis. From that experience came some notes for the first chapters of *Cemitério dos Vivos* (The Cemetery of the Living), memoirs that were not published in book form until 1953, in the volume *Diário Íntimo* (Intimate Diary).

In December 1920 Lima Barreto competed for the Brazilian Academy of Letters literary prize for best book of 1919 with *The Life and Death of M. J. Gonzaga de Sá*, receiving an honorable mention. Also in December, his publisher started selling his volume of short stories, *Histórias e Sonhos* (Stories and Dreams), while he finished *Marginália* (Marginalia), which was not published until 1953. In January 1921, he published in the magazine *Souza Cruz*, under the title "As Origens" (The Origins), part of his incomplete, handwritten *Cemitério dos Vivos*.

In April 1921 Lima Barreto went to the small city of Mirassol in the state of São Paulo. There Ranulfo Prata, a doctor, writer, and friend of the author's, tried in vain to treat his alcoholism. Lima Barreto returned to Rio and because of his shattered health lived in partial seclusion in his house, where his sister Evangelina took care of him. His friends visited him at home, and whenever his health permitted Lima Barreto continued to roam through the city he loved. In July 1921, he competed for the third time for the Brazilian Academy of Letters, but withdrew unexpectedly from the competition for "reasons totally private and intimate." He delivered to his publisher a collection of articles entitled *Bagatelas* (Trifles), in which he considered, with rare vision and lucidity, postwar Brazilian and world problems. *Bagatelas*, however, was not published until the year after his death.

In October/November 1921, Lima Barreto published in *Souza Cruz* his lecture "O Destino da Literatura" (The Fate of Literature), which he never delivered. In December he started the second version of his novel *Clara dos Anjos*, which he finished in January. *Feiras e Mafuás* (Fairs and Amusement Parks) was submitted for publication in 1920, but was not printed until 1953. In May 1922 the magazine *Mundo Literário* (Literary World) printed the first chapter of *Clara dos Anjos*, "O Carteiro" (The Postman). Lima Barreto's health was deteriorating monthly, aggravated by rheumatism, his continued drinking, and other problems. He died of a stroke in November of that year.

In 1953 some of Lima Barreto's original works were first published. In 1956, under the direction of the present writer, with the collaboration of Antonio Houaiss and Manuel Cavalcanti Proença, his complete works were brought out in seventeen volumes. In addition to those already mentioned, titles not published during the author's lifetime include *Impressões de Leitura* (Impressions of Reading), *Vida Urbana* (Urban Life), *Coisas do Reino de Jambon* (Peculiarities of the Kingdom of Jambon), and two other volumes containing all of his correspondence. Since his death, Lima Barreto has been the subject of studies not only in Brazil but abroad. His novels and short stories have been translated into English, French, Russian, Spanish, Czech, Japanese, and German. Congresses and conferences were held throughout Brazil during the centennial of his birth in 1981; they resulted in several essays, bibliographies, and studies about the author and his work.

Lima Barreto left three definitive novels: *Recordações do Escrivão Isaías Caminha*, *The Sad End of Policarpo Quaresma*, and *The Life and Death of M. J. Gonzaga de Sá*. His short stories are numerous, and most are of the highest literary quality; examples are "Nova California," "O Homem Que Sabia Javanês," and Graciliano Ramos' favorite, "Sua Excelência" (His Excellency). But Lima Barreto's work is not limited to novels and short stories. His memoirs,

Diário Íntimo and *Cemitério dos Vivos*, are of great human interest and contain some of the author's best writing. A large selection of articles originally published in magazines and in both popular and semi-clandestine newspapers were gathered together in the *Bagatelas*, *Vida Urbana*, *Marginália*, and *Impressões de Leitura*. *Os Bruzundangas* and *Coisas do Reino de Jambon* fall into the category of social satire, although Lima Barreto's fiction almost always reflects a consistent inclination to denounce the injustices and blemishes of the political system and of the organization of society.

Lima Barreto's novels and newspaper articles constitute a large canvas that unfolds in a succession of pictures of Brazil during the First Republic. His subjects include the revolt against Floriano Peixoto, the reurbanization of Rio de Janeiro, the campaign against yellow fever, the Barão do Rio Branco's (Baron of Rio Branco's) action at Itamaraty, the coffee evaluation policy, the small military flare-up during Marshall Hermes Rodrigues da Fonseca's government, Brazil's participation in World War I, the first manifestations of feminism, the workers' strikes of 1917 and 1918, the Versailles Conference, and Brazilian Modern Art Week. In addition, he warned against Brazilian complaisance in response to the threats of a new economic imperialism that arose in the aftermath of the war from the weakness of the peace treaty and the League of Nations itself. He also covered lighter topics, such as the carnival, soccer, and the lottery. While revealing the country's miseries, he never forgot its greatness and the sweetness of its people.

Lima Barreto's work as a novelist and journalist is broad in scope. He provides an impressive documentary of the social and political changes in Brazil in its transition from a liberal society that incorporated slavery to a false democratic system. He describes the emergence of an oligarchy that was paradoxically much more aristocratic in character than the ruling classes in the days of imperial parliamentarism. Plutocracy is the name he gave the curious form of government of plantation owners, capitalists, and lawyers, many of whom worked for these privileged groups. This assessment may be slightly exaggerated, but it is not totally without merit. Lima Barreto is a clear if generally severe observer. His crushing criticism is aimed at the politicians and decision-makers, the craze for ostentation, the intellectual emptiness, the corruption, and the incompetence of the relative democracy of the First Republic.

Lima Barreto saw the rotten core of Brazilian society and had none of the falsity characteristic of most of his contemporaries. He showed many politicians and writers as they really were: caricatures of leaders and writers. Without retouching or distorting his characters, he revealed the mentality of the middle class, with its weaknesses and alienation.

Published one year after Machado de Assis' death, *Recordações do Escrivão Isaías Caminha* tells the story of a young man of humble origin who struggles to better his position in society and is almost crushed in the process. It is a moving and real book that reveals a great deal about Lima Barreto's own personal drama. However, the protagonist is different from his creator. Isaías Caminha ends up compromising himself in an uneven clash against everything and everybody. At the price of great concessions and his dignity, Isaías Caminha is granted a bitter and painful half-victory. Racial prejudice is ever present in this story about an anguished and helpless antihero. Caminha is an office boy in one of the most prestigious newspapers in the country, a citadel of support for liberal democratic principles and respect for the constitution, its laws, and the assurance of human rights. At the end of his memoirs, Caminha acknowledges that he was defeated for not having taken out of his experience "something big and strong." The conclusion of the novel is moralistic in tone: "The general ill will, the excommunication of others, had frightened me, intimidated me, and put to sleep my pride, with its show of greatness and force."

The Sad End of Policarpo Quaresma is also a novel about a failure. The protagonist is an antihero, too, but he does not abase himself and give up fighting. He is finally stopped, though, when he is arrested as a traitor and a bandit, and is branded as an enemy of republican institutions. Policarpo started out as a pure and naive patriot who ardently craved to save the country from the clutches of corrupt politicians. He wanted Brazil to return to its authentic origins, even proposing at the Brazilian National Congress the adoption of Tupi-Guarani as the official national language, instead of Portuguese. He took up other similar causes, such as the rehabilitation of the traditional guitar, the study of folklore, and the advocacy of agricultural reform. He supported the conversion of land into small diversified holdings that would replace the large estates and the coffee monopoly, chronic evils of the Brazilian economy. *The Sad End of Policarpo Quaresma* is probably the most perfect of all of Lima Barreto's novels in its architecture and polishing touches. It is surely one of the more felicitous humorous creations by the author, although the humor is not devoid of pathos. In the remarkably delineated character of Quaresma, the great historian Manuel de Oliveira Lima saw something similar to a Brazilian Don Quixote.

In *Numa e a Ninfa* Lima Barreto was inspired by the political plot that took Marshall Hermes Rodrigues da Fonseca to the presidency of the republic. The writer painted a tragicomic gallery of military and civilian bigwigs, all eager for power and money. Among them appears the prototype of "the good guy" and the happy son-in-law: Numa Pompílio de Castro, a member of the Chamber of Representatives, is a mixture of imbecility and cynicism. The array of characters in the novel is extensive. Primary among them are the ward boss Lucrécio Barba de Bode (Lucrécio Goatbeard), a characteristic type from the First Republic, and the charming adventurer Doctor Bogóloff. Also known as Gregori Petrovich Bogóloff, the Russian-born graduate in Oriental languages at the University of Kazan becomes an important member of the bureaucracy as director of the Brazilian Ministry of Agriculture. Bogóloff takes advantage of his university title, reaching a preeminent position as an administrator. A blond, a doctor, and a foreigner, he meets all the requirements for gaining the admiration and respect of the ruling class. Senator Sofonias and Minister Xandu are so impressed by Doctor Bogóloff's amazing knowledge that they decide to grant him one of the highest positions at the Ministry of Agriculture. Bogóloff presents a program to increase the country's livestock through the administration of a special treatment that would render the hogs the size of oxen and the oxen larger than elephants.

Lima Barreto's satire has not been fully studied. The comedy in his work is reminiscent of Mateo Aleman's *Guzmán de Alfarache* (1599, 1604; translated as *The Spanish Rogue*), *Lazarillo de Tormes* (1554), of indeterminate authorship, and Alain-René Lesage's *Histoire de Gil Blas* (1715–1735; translated as *The Adventures of Gil Blas of Santillane*). All three books were his favorites at a certain time. Lima Barreto's comic approach appears not only in *Numa e a Ninfa* but also in *Os Bruzundangas*. The latter is a volume that contains a series of caricatures about a nonexistent country very similar to the Brazil of Lima Barreto's time. "Bruzundanga" is a word derived from "burundanga," meaning a confused jumble of words, a mixture of sounds, anything confused, a dirty or repugnant stew, or a rigmarole. The author's creation is a rigmarole country or, as he describes it, "a country of complications." A reader of Jonathan Swift, who is frequently evoked in these caricatures, Lima Barreto conceived a strange republic that—although copied from Brobdingnag, the country of the giants—is more similar to the lands of the Houyhnhnms and Lilliputians.

Small chronicles without polish, but full of humor and scorn, constitute the material not only for *Os Bruzundangas* but also for *Coisas do Reino de Jambon*. The theme of the caricature is always Brazil, specifically the First Republic. The political classes and the people in the Kingdom of Jambon, as in *Os Bruzundangas*, find themselves at opposite poles. According to the preface,

> There is not an influential man who hasn't at least thirty relatives employed by the state. There is not an influential politician who doesn't consider his the right to leave to his children, grandchildren, nephews, and cousins fat annuities paid by the national treasury. However, the land lives in poverty; the landed estates abandoned and undivided. . . . The rural population lives shorn, starved, in tatters, haggard, yellowish, so a hundred idiots, in the capital city, with high-sounding degrees, doctors of this and that, can enjoy allowances, subsidies, duplicated or triplicated (apart from profits derived from any other origin), using big words as though they were going to perform miracles.

Very different is the satire in *The Life and Death of M. J. Gonzaga de Sá*, a novel in which the Brazilian Foreign Office and the Barão do Rio Branco appear veiled in irony. It tells the story of two public clerks of opposite character: the venerable Gonzaga de Sá

and the mediocre Xisto Beldroegas. The first one loves his city and is an understanding and quiet man, fearless when faced with the powerful. Hence he feels an aversion to the Barão do Rio Branco, who was considered a national glory during his lifetime, but whom he considers an autocrat who placed his will above the constitution and the law. Beldroegas is the other side of the coin: a submissive and crawling toady, a man who has no pity for the humble and the helpless and who cares only about the subtleties of the bureaucracy, with its orders, warnings, and decrees.

However, the circumstantial does not prevail in *The Life and Death of M. J. Gonzaga de Sá*, which is a beautiful poem written in prose. Lima Barreto describes Rio de Janeiro's urban and suburban life, and defends its original character. One could even say he defends the ecology of the city, which was erected between the sea and the mountains and has been threatened ever since by bad administration, the greed of real estate developers, and the incompetence of its mayors. Lima Barreto once said of this work, "It was the only novel that I ever started and finished." In relation to his city, for which he had absolute empathy, he added: "I live in it and it lives in me."

Lima Barreto's two last novels were *Clara dos Anjos* and *Cemitério dos Vivos*. In the first, he took the theme of racial prejudice from *Recordações do Escrivão Isaías Caminha* and transferred it to the story of a postman's daughter, who is deluded, seduced, and finally jilted by a young man from a higher social class. Unfortunately the book's plot is poor, and it is almost devoid of fictional character. In his youth Lima Barreto had wanted to write a great novel about slavery and had written a few chapters, but he was unable to continue the project at the end of his life. His decadent way of life had drained him of the vigor of his youth, and the drive one finds in the roaring pages of *Isaías Caminha* is totally lacking in *Clara dos Anjos*. The same cannot be said about *Cemitério dos Vivos*, which he started writing later in life when his health was destroyed by alcohol and when he was already disenchanted with existence, parading in his pain through the streets of Rio like a ragged bum. However, the two chapters he left us, which are almost complete, are fragments from a work that shows great scope, and that may have become the masterpiece of the author, if one can speculate about literary works that were never finished.

In memorializing Lima Barreto, one should not focus simply on his obsessive self-analysis of his personal problems, his anguish, and his frustration. Instead greater emphasis should be placed on his nobler feelings, especially his revolt against mediocrity, imposture, and injustice. He became the spokesman of the woes and dreams of a tattered and marginalized sector of the Brazilian population. Lima Barreto is the main character of his novels, disguised in the masks of Isaías Caminha, Policarpo Quaresma, Gonzaga de Sá, Leonardo Flores (in *Clara dos Anjos*), and Vicente Mascarenhas (in *Cemitério dos Vivos*). Of them all only Isaías Caminha fails morally. However, the intention of the author was precisely to show "a case of 'demoralization,' of individual enfeeblement at the hands of society, of fear in the face of society's prejudices." In a letter to a friend in 1911, he would be even more precise:

> What I aimed for was to make clear that a young man like Isaías, with all good will, could fail not because of his inner qualities but because he was beaten, crushed, pressed by prejudice with its retinue, which is, I believe, an entity in itself. . . . If I wrote about some characters and about the newspaper it was because I wanted to shock and call attention to my work. I don't know if it was a moral thing to do, but it was the only way I had to fight against the indifference and the ill will of our literary mandarins.

Lima Barreto was condemned to loneliness beginning in his youth, practically since the founding of *Floreal*. In literature, as in his private life, he was always alone. He was a bachelor, and there is no evidence in his forty-one years of existence of a single love affair that lasted. His contact with women was essentially limited to his unmarried sister and his occasional meetings with prostitutes. He was a great loner, like his characters, who ranged from the restless youth Isaías Caminha to the hieratic, fifty-ish Gonzaga de Sá. In the preface of the second edition of *Isaías Caminha*, the author stated that after the end of the novel the protagonist would end up a widower without children and a candidate for the Chamber of Representatives. Among Lima Barreto's feminine characters, Clara dos Anjos would be rejected and condemned to solitude, on her way perhaps to prostitution, after an unhappy love affair.

The inferior status of women in Brazilian society was a constant theme in Lima Barreto's work for the press. He warned against the systematic tolerance with which juries absolved husbands and lovers who killed their mates. However, he was critical of women's renunciation of old values. He did not support the naming of the first woman to an administrative post in the public service. He condemned the feminist movement, and attacked the public parade promoted by Leolinda Daltro during Fonseca's government and later the foundation of the Brazilian Women's Legion in 1920.

In a chronicle in 1911 Lima Barreto comments about Madame Louise d'Épinay's *Mémoires* (1818), concluding that in the Brazil of his time there could not exist "the blooming of superior women as occurred in the extraordinary French eighteenth century." And he even argues against the existence of women who could exert a strong influence over men, especially in either politics or literature. According to the testimony of his sister Evangelina, it would have been very hard for Lima Barreto to find someone of his own kind who could understand him. Most likely the illiterate suburban mulatto girls with whom he came in contact were like his character Clara dos Anjos and were incapable of appreciating his intelligence or literary gifts.

The writer Carmen Dolores was an exception in Lima Barreto's life. She died very young and in his *Diário Íntimo* he wrote an almost amorous record of her:

> She is a young, svelte girl, not more than twenty-five years old, self-contained, always very discreetly dressed, who almost never is seen in those places where we parade ourselves. Her great round eyes are peopled with intimate dreams, and all of her, with that slender body and spiritualized profile, seems wrapped up in art, hearing the music from the spheres and the harmonies of the archangels. Very young, she is not fascinated by the triviality of elegance, something that does not occupy her thoughts. She despises dresses, expensive fabrics, laces, fashions, and hats. She seldom goes to parties or salons, for she finds no attraction of any order in them; she finds them futile, devoid of the intellectual atmosphere favorable to the life of her spirit and her soul.

She might have been for him the archetype of the ideal woman.

However, neither Carmen Dolores nor any other woman was the love of Lima Barreto's life. As Antônio Cândido very wisely observed, this humble and hurt man's entire capacity for love was concentrated on literature. And Lima Barreto himself took care to announce his marriage to literature, not without some pride, because literature offered the best prospect of influencing humanity.

Alcoholism, however, rendered Lima Barreto's marriage to literature turbulent and dramatic. Until the publication of *Isaías Caminha*, although he was not entirely sober, he was not yet dominated by alcohol, which ended up devouring all his vital energies and damaging his creativity. At first he dedicated himself to drinking as a posture, but later it became a vice that ruled him completely. "The bourgeois drink champagne; the heroes drink aquavitae" was one of his aphorisms. In a photograph taken when he was twenty-five years old, he appears as a handsome young man who is decently dressed. Not long after, he began his descent into the abyss.

It might have been loneliness, or the lack of love that was the catalyst for Lima Barreto's drinking. He was, in his own words, an "orphan of love and of women's caresses," having lost his mother when he was seven, and having lived his life without the affection of a lover or a wife. His father had become hopelessly sick just at the moment when the author (barely emerged from adolescence) needed him most. He speaks of love in this pathetic soliloquy, from his *Diário Íntimo*, written during the period of his second sojourn at the hospital:

> I have to attribute my mental crisis to this problem with alcohol, which afflicts me, for I have drunk a lot, along with everybody else. Yet I know well it is not the main factor. I wonder why the doctors have not found the reason in love, from its lowest and most carnal form up to its most elevated expression, when it becomes true mysticism, a deification of the loved object. So, I ask myself, is not that a contributing factor to madness, too?
>
> (p. 29)

And in another part of the same confession, a true examination of conscience occurs, in which Lima Barreto takes up the question again, no longer in a theoretical sense, but dealing with his own personal case: "I ask myself if by any chance it is not love that erodes me. But I see clearly it is not. I have passed the age of having it, by running away from it, so it would not make me suffer and would not damage my ambition for glory." It is literary glory that he is referring to in this passage. In his youth he had thought he could compensate for his craving for affection by exchanging it for a broader feeling aimed at all those who were miserable and were suffering. Eager for intimacy and tenderness, Lima Barreto needed something that would make him forget his pain and that would transport him to another world, one whose form he could not define, one perhaps made up of dreams.

Hence Lima Barreto felt despair beginning at the age of thirty, as he went from one extreme of existence to another. He would either go on a series of drinking binges or dedicate himself completely to his intellectual work. When he was working he would lock himself up for weeks on end in the front parlor of his suburban house, a room that served him as bedroom and library. Through alcohol he tried to annihilate himself completely, in an effort to be forgotten, to disappear. Through his literary creations, on the contrary, he tried to affirm himself, to be somebody, in short, to leave his mark on this earth. At the same time that he struggled to free himself from drinking, he clung to literature as if to the remains of a shipwreck. He had very strong feelings about literature, feelings almost religious in nature, that enabled him and even compelled him to write. If Lima Barreto believed in anything, it was in literature as the only force that could make all men reach an understanding, creating a country held together by aesthetics. As he said: "Man, through art, is not dependent upon the prejudices and the precepts of his time, his birth, his country, his race; he goes beyond these, as far as he can, to reach the total life of the Universe and to incorporate into his own life that of the whole world."

In his last years, Lima Barreto wore ragged clothing, reeked of alcohol, and made a point of flaunting his appearance by showing up in the affluent section of town, where the dandies and the flappers paraded the latest fashions. He had already included himself in the outlaw part of the population, trying with this posture to embody a protest against the rules of society. "I feel," he once said, "a great voluptuousness in comparing the refinement of perfection in dressing with . . . my absolute slackness." In that masochistic exhibitionism there was something very similar to Charlie Chaplin's genial tramp. However, it was not only because of his appearance that Alceu Amoroso Lima called Lima Barreto the Brazilian Charlie Chaplin: "The work and not the life of Lima Barreto is what makes him like Charles Chaplin. Both raised their voices against the bourgeoisie, conformism, false joy of living, triumphal mundane living, against all the false values of modern pharisaism. One did it through images, the other did it with words."

SELECTED BIBLIOGRAPHY

First Editions

Novels

Recordações do Escrivão Isaías Caminha. Lisbon, 1909.
Triste Fim de Polycarpo Quaresma. Rio de Janeiro, 1915.
Numa e a Ninfa. Rio de Janeiro, 1915.
Vida e Morte de M. J. Gonzaga de Sá. São Paulo, 1919.
Clara dos Anjos. Rio de Janeiro, 1948. Also in later edition of *Diário Íntimo.* São Paulo, 1956.

Short Stories

Histórias e Sonhos. Rio de Janeiro, 1920.

Humor and Satire

Aventuras do Dr. Bogóloff. Rio de Janeiro, 1912.
Os Bruzundangas. Rio de Janeiro, 1922.
Coisas do Reino de Jambon. In *Bruzundangas.* Rio de Janeiro, 1952.

Chronicles

Bagatelas. Rio de Janeiro, 1923.
Feiras e Mafuás. Rio de Janeiro, 1953.
Marginália. Rio de Janeiro, 1953.
Vida Urbana. São Paulo, 1956.

Criticism

Impressões de Leitura. São Paulo, 1956.

Memoirs

Diário Íntimo. Rio de Janeiro, 1953. Contains *O Cemitério dos Vivos.*

Correspondence

Correspondência 1: With preface by Antônio Noronha Santos. *2:* With preface by B. Quadros. São Paulo, 1956.

Modern Editions

Os Bruzundangas incluindo Outras Histórias dos Bruzundangas. São Paulo, 1985.
Cemitério dos Vivos. São Paulo, 1956. Contains *Diário do Hospício.*
Clara dos Anjos. 10th ed. São Paulo, 1983.
Histórias e Sonhos. Rio de Janeiro, 1951.
O Homen Que Sabia Javanês. São Paulo, 1965.
Marginália. With preface by Agripino Grieco. São Paulo, 1956. Contains *Casa de Poetas* and *Os Negros.*
A Nova Califórnia. 3rd ed. São Paulo, 1982.
Numa e a Ninfa. With preface by João Ribeiro. São Paulo, 1956.
Recordações do Escrivão Isaías Caminha. With preface by Francisco de Assis Barbosa. 9th ed. São Paulo, 1983.
Triste Fim de Policarpo Quaresma. With preface by M. de Oliveira Lima. 18th ed. São Paulo, 1977.
Vida e Morte de M. J. Gonzaga de Sá. São Paulo, 1943.

Translations

Clara dos Anjos. Translated by Earl Fitz. In *Lima Barreto: Bibliography and Translations,* edited by Maria Luisa Nunes. Boston, 1979.
The Life and Death of M. J. Gonzaga de Sá. Translated by Rosa Veloso Dwyer and John P. Dwyer. In *Lima Barreto: Bibliography and Translations,* edited by Maria Luísa Nunes. Boston, 1979.
The Patriot. Translated by Robert Scott-Buccleuch. London and Rio de Janeiro, 1978.
The Sad End of Policarpo Quaresma. Translated by Gregory Rabassa. In *The Borzoi Anthology of Latin American Literature,* edited by E. Rodríguez Monegal and Thomas Colchie. New York, 1977.

Biographical and Critical Studies

Antônio, João. *Calvário e Porres do Pingente Afonso Henriques de Lima Barreto.* Rio de Janeiro, 1977.
Atanásio, Enéias. *O Mulato de "Todos os Santos."* Piraquara, Brazil, 1982.

Barbosa, Francisco de Assis. *Aldebarã ou A Vida de Lima Barreto (1881–1922)*. 4th ed. Rio de Janeiro, 1967.

_____. "Lima Barreto, Precursor do Romance Social." In *Achados do Vento*. Rio de Janeiro, 1958. Pp. 95–116.

_____. "Prefácio." In *Recordações do Escrivão Isaías Caminha*, by Lima Barreto. São Paulo, 1956. Pp. 9–27.

Beiguelman, Paula. *Por quê Lima Barreto*. São Paulo, 1981.

Belo, José Maria. *À Margem dos Livros*. Rio de Janeiro, 1923. Pp. 154–156.

Bosi, Alfredo. "Lima Barreto e Graça Aranha." In *O Pré-modernismo*. São Paulo, 1967. Pp. 93–104.

_____. "O Romance Social: Lima Barreto." In *História Concisa da Literatura Brasileira*. São Paulo, 1970. Pp. 355–365.

Brayner, Sônia. "Lima Barreto: Mostrar ou Significar?" In *Labirinto do Espaço Romanesco*. Rio de Janeiro, 1979. Pp. 145–176.

Broca, José Brito. *A Vida Literária no Brasil—1900*. 2nd, rev. ed. Rio de Janeiro, 1960. Pp. 156–157.

Buarque de Hollanda, Sérgio. "Em Torno de Lima Barreto." In *Cobra de Vidro*. 2nd ed. São Paulo, 1978. Pp. 131–146.

Coutinho, Carlos Nelson. "O Significado de Lima Barreto na Literatura Brasileira." In *Realismo e Anti-realismo na Literatura Brasileira*. Rio de Janeiro, 1974. Pp. 1–56.

Cury, Maria Zilda Ferreira. *Um Mulato no Reino de Jambom (As Classes Sociais na Obra de Lima Barreto)*. São Paulo, 1981.

Dimmick, Ralph E. "Social Satire in the Novels of Lima Barreto." In *International Colloquium on Luso-Brazilian Studies*. Washington, D.C., 1950. Pp. 155–156.

Duggan, Vincent Paul. *Social Themes and Political Satire in the Short Stories of Lima Barreto*. Ann Arbor, Mich., 1977.

Fantinati, Carlos Erivany. *O Profeta e o Escrivão: Estudo sobre Lima Barreto*. São Paulo, 1978.

Freyre, Gilberto. "O Diário Íntimo de Lima Barreto." In *Vida, Forma e Cor*. Rio de Janeiro, 1962. Pp. 330–336.

Gicovate, Moisés. *Lima Barreto: Uma Vida Atormentada*. São Paulo, 1953.

Gomes, Eugênio. "Lima Barreto." In *Aspectos do Romance Brasileiro*. Salvador, Brazil, 1958. Pp. 155–173.

Grieco, Agripino. *Memórias 2*. Rio de Janeiro, 1972. Pp. 93–105.

Herron, Robert D. *The Individual, Society and Nature in the Novels of Lima Barreto*. Ann Arbor, Mich., 1971.

Houaiss, Antônio. "Prefácio." In *Vida Urbana*, by Lima Barreto. São Paulo, 1956. Pp. 9–41.

Hulet, Claude L. "Afonso Henriques de Lima Barreto (1881–1922)." In *Brazilian Literature 1880–1920 2*. Washington, D.C., 1974–1975. Pp. 258–260, 267–269.

Lima, Alceu Amoroso. "Um Discípulo de Machado." In *Estudos Literários 1*. Rio de Janeiro, 1966. Pp. 63–65.

_____. "Prefácio." In *Vida e Morte de M. J. Gonzaga de Sá*, by Lima Barreto. São Paulo, 1956. Pp. 9–16.

Lins, Osman. *Lima Barreto e o Espaço Romanesco*. São Paulo, 1976.

Martins, Luís. "O Suburbano Lima Barreto." In *Homens e Livros*. São Paulo, 1962. Pp. 23–26.

Montello, Josué. "O Conto Brasileiro de Machado de Assis a Monteiro Lobato." In *Curso de Conto*. Rio de Janeiro, 1958. Pp. 133–168.

Morais, Régis de. *Lima Barreto*. São Paulo, 1983.

Peixoto, Afrânio. "Afonso Henriques de Lima Barreto." In *Humour*. 2nd ed. São Paulo, 1946. Pp. 196–200.

Pereira, Astrojildo. "Confissões de Lima Barreto." In *Interpretações*. Rio de Janeiro, 1944. Pp. 114–132.

Pereira, Lúcia Miguel. "Introdução." In *Clara dos Anjos*, by Lima Barreto. Rio de Janeiro, 1948. Pp. 13–21.

_____. "Prefácio." In *Histórias e Sonhos*, by Lima Barreto. São Paulo, 1956. Pp. 9–16.

Picchio, Luciana Stegagno. "Da Lima Barreto ad Adelino Magalhães: Romanzo Sociale ed Escercizi nella Penombra." In *La Letteratura Brasiliana*. Florence and Milan, 1972. Pp. 440–444.

Proença, Manuel Cavalcanti. "Impressões de Leitura." In *Estudos Literários*. Rio de Janeiro, 1974. Pp. 316–346.

Rabassa, Gregory. *The Negro in Brazilian Fiction Since 1888 . . .* New York, 1954. Pp. 363–401.

Serpa, Focion. *Lima Barreto*. Rio de Janeiro, 1943.

Silva, Hélcio Pereira da. *Lima Barreto: Escritor Maldito*. Rio de Janeiro, 1976.

Veríssimo, José. "O Modernismo." In *História da Literatura Brasileira*. 5th ed. Rio de Janeiro, 1969. Pp. 228–236.

José Vasconcelos

(1882–1959)

Gabriella de Beer

José Vasconcelos is a name that is well known in Latin America. Not only was he the author of a number of important works, but he was a politician, educator, journalist, and longtime public figure whose career held the interest of his compatriots as well as of students of literature and Mexican history. Writing was but one aspect of Vasconcelos' personality. In this regard he resembled the early writers of Latin America, often soldiers or missionaries, who wrote to tell of their exploits, to protest existing conditions, or to ask for support or recognition from the authorities. He is also closely linked to those Latin American writers generally classified as essayists.

The *ensayo* (essay) as a genre has had a long tradition in Latin America. It was particularly suited to those writers and thinkers who wished to express themselves on the fundamental questions in their cultural development. As the writer's attempt at self-understanding and historical consciousness, the essay can deal with many topics as seen and interpreted by him. The essay's most salient trait is its subjective nature, for the essayist is an integral part of his writing and his personality is ever present. Its aesthetic or literary quality lies in its style. Almost all of Vasconcelos' works are basically essays. They reflect his opinions and interpretations of everything

with which he came into contact. His topics include Mexico from the conquest to his time, society and its populations, educational systems, and international relations. These themes pervade even those works classified as novels, short stories, or drama.

José Vasconcelos was a person completely molded by his environment and moment in history. He had a compulsive need to be heard, to participate in the events of his time, and to react to his environment. Thus Vasconcelos is a complex figure—educator, writer, politician, journalist, historian. His life spanned the end of the nineteenth century until well into the twentieth; he lived through the long dictatorship of Porfirio Díaz, the revolution of 1910, its aftermath of civil strife, and subsequent consolidation into a republican form of government based on a constitutional succession to the presidency. He was both participant in and witness to these events, as his voluminous writings indicate. As a man of quick and strong opinions, Vasconcelos inspired followers and detractors. Both admirers and critics point out his ability to change his mind and to fervently support positions completely opposed to those held previously. However, it is agreed that, as a writer and thinker, Vasconcelos was a central figure in Mexico and Latin America. The republication of his works and the continuous flow of scholarship about him and his writings attest to the interest he holds for readers and scholars.

The life of Vasconcelos is that of an exciting personality during the important period of history that gave rise to modern Mexico. In addition, his life is significant for the reader of Latin American prose because he wrote a vast autobiography that dramatically presents this panorama to the reader as no book of history can. This is so much the case that his *Ulises criollo: La vida del autor escrita por él mismo* (*A Mexican Ulysses: An Autobiography*, 1935), the first volume of his autobiography, is often included among the novels of the Mexican Revolution. Also, many of his other writings deal with his travels, experiences, and the positions he held in his country and elsewhere. We have access to a large amount of detail about his life and the Mexico of his time, because he made of it the stuff of his writings.

Vasconcelos was born on 28 February 1882 to Ignacio Vasconcelos and Carmen Calderón in Oaxaca, Mexico. Both parents exercised important roles in their son's life. His mother, strict, strong-willed, and devout, was very attached to her son, and he in turn was dependent on her. From his earliest years, they read and discussed literary works. His honest and hardworking father, although not as well read as his wife, held a position as customs inspector, which caused the family to move from place to place frequently. However, these moves provided Vasconcelos the opportunity to be near the North American border, attend school in the United States, and master English—an ability that was to serve him well in later years. He studied law and graduated from the Escuela Nacional de Jurisprudencia (National School of Jurisprudence) in 1905. Vasconcelos married Serafina Miranda in 1909 and Esperanza Cruz in 1942, having become a widower in the interim. Two children were born of the first marriage—José Ignacio and Carmen—and one—Hector—of the second.

Shortly before the outbreak of the revolution of 1910 Vasconcelos became active and known in the intellectual circles of Mexico. In the National School of Jurisprudence he had befriended many of those who were to found with him the Ateneo de la Juventud (Athenaeum of Youth) in 1909. Although not a political group, most of its members sympathized with the Revolution. Their main purpose was the revival and dissemination of culture, free of the shackles that the official policy of positivism (a philosophy that controlled the education and thinking of the time) had imposed on Mexico. The members of this group were drawn together by common interests and intellectual curiosity. First in informal circles and later in public forums, they read and discussed different philosophers, and European, American, and Mexican literature, and opened themselves up to all schools of knowledge. The members, a heterogeneous group that included Antonio Caso, Isidro Fabela, Carlos González Peña, Pedro Henríquez Ureña, Roberto Montenegro, Alfonso Reyes, Martín Luis Guzmán, and Diego Rivera, to mention only a few, were united in their seriousness of purpose, their belief in the acquisition of knowledge as a professional activity, their interest in their own culture, and their desire to study different philosophies and literatures. In addition to private gatherings and public lectures, they left their mark on the educational system of Mexico. Although the Athenaeum of Youth as a formal body existed only from 1909 to 1914, its effects were long-lasting. This spirit, which was to dominate Mexican culture for several decades, preceded and coexisted with the revolution of 1910.

Vasconcelos was one of the figures who dominated the Mexican scene as a writer of the Revolution and a vociferous proponent of Mexican culture and education. His *A Mexican Ulysses* is often included among that amorphous classification of the "novel of the Mexican Revolution," a broad category that refers to the novels inspired by the revolution of 1910 in all its manifestations. They are most often episodic narrations of events, memoirs, and newspaper reporting—direct observations of reality captured in narrative form. The novels differ in intent and intensity, but they are cast as epics showing the Mexican people in a struggle for a better way of life. Much of the variation among the novels is the result of each individual writer's temperament, point of view, and degree of participation in the Revolution. Among other writers who contributed to the Mexican novel are Mariano Azuela, Martín Luis Guzmán, Nellie Campobello, Rafael F. Muñoz, and José Rubén Romero.

With the rise of Francisco I. Madero in the first

decade of the twentieth century, a new era in the life of Vasconcelos began. For the next twenty years he was absorbed by his activities as a revolutionary and politician. Madero and his followers desired the end of the long dictatorship of Díaz through a nonviolent change in the government, by means of the free exercise of the vote. As a supporter of Madero, Vasconcelos organized political clubs, edited and wrote newspaper articles against the Díaz regime, and held an official post in the Partido Constitucional Progresista (Progressive Constitutional Party). His outspoken attacks on the Díaz government resulted in his first short exile to the United States. During this period Vasconcelos was appointed by Madero as his official representative in Washington, D.C., and, with the triumph of the Madero Revolution in 1911, he returned to Mexico and his private law practice. Unfortunately, the government of Madero was short-lived, and in February 1913 he and his vice-president, José María Pino Suárez, were betrayed and killed.

For the next seven years Vasconcelos' life was as unsettled as was Mexico during this period of civil strife among the factions vying for power. He was imprisoned for a short time by General Victoriano Huerta, who had assumed control upon Madero's death, and when released made his way to the United States. At this time Vasconcelos offered his services to Venustiano Carranza, who had taken for himself the title Primer Jefe del Ejército Constitucionalista (First Chief of the Constitutionalist Army), and named him to several official posts in Europe and the United States. However, during this period Vasconcelos became increasingly disenchanted with Carranza and returned to Mexico. He went to the city of Aguascalientes in October 1914 to assist in drawing up a brief proclaiming that the only legal authority in Mexico was La Convención Militar de Aguascalientes and that the nation's provisional president was Eulalio Gutiérrez and not Carranza. Gutiérrez appointed Vasconcelos minister of public education, but opposition to both of them caused Vasconcelos to leave for New York, where he became one of Carranza's bitterest enemies. Carranza had a great deal of support and with the title First Chief of the Constitutionalist Army functioned as provisional president until elected president in March 1917. Vasconcelos

disliked Carranza with a passion, considering him vain, unintelligent, vacillating, and suspect because of his former position as senator in the Díaz government. Therefore, from the end of 1915 until the assassination of Carranza in May 1920 Vasconcelos chose to lead a peripatetic life that took him to Peru and various parts of the United States. During this time he dedicated himself to several business ventures and to his writing. Upon the death of Carranza, Vasconcelos returned to Mexico.

During the interim government of Adolfo de la Huerta, Vasconcelos was named *rector* of the Universidad Nacional (president of the National University), a post from which he worked for the reestablishment of the Ministry of Public Education, which he headed from 1920 until 1924. This was a vast undertaking and one that is generally regarded as Vasconcelos' greatest contribution to Mexico. The ministry, with branches throughout the country, consisted of three departments—schools, libraries, and fine arts. The scope of each department was broad, encompassing elementary through adult education. There were auxiliary departments for the education of the indigenous populations as well as for adult literacy. New school buildings were constructed, printing presses ran off thousands of classic works and textbooks, free breakfasts were distributed to needy children, and vocational training was made available to men and women. Educators from other countries were invited to participate and work as missionaries among the indigenous and rural populations. Two journals aimed at teachers and librarians were published. It was during this period that the painting of murals as an expression of popular art was promoted. Vasconcelos' accomplishments were recognized beyond the borders of Mexico; student groups in several Latin American countries named him "Maestro de la Juventud" (Teacher of Youth).

In 1924 Vasconcelos resigned as minister of public education and ran for the governorship of the state of Oaxaca. When he lost the election, he alleged fraud. This defeat marked the beginning of another period of travel, work, and residency outside Mexico. In 1925 he left for Europe; his travels took him to Spain, Portugal, Italy, Greece, Turkey, Hungary, Austria, and France. He delivered lectures and wrote a weekly article for the Mexican newspaper *El Universal*. Vasconcelos accepted offers to teach at the University of Puerto Rico, the University of Chicago, Stanford University, and the University of California at Berkeley. Between semesters he traveled in Europe and the Middle East, lecturing and writing all the time. However, the events that took place in Mexico continued to determine his plans and actions.

Álvaro Obregón, who had been elected president of Mexico for the second time, after an intervening term of Plutarco Elías Calles, was assassinated in 1928 before taking office. This made it necessary to call a special election. Vasconcelos, having assured himself that there was considerable support for his candidacy, became in 1929 a presidential candidate opposing Pascual Ortiz Rubio of the Partido Nacional Revolucionario (National Revolutionary Party). Vasconcelos attracted many supporters and sympathizers, especially among intellectual circles and the young. When the election results were announced and Ortiz Rubio declared the winner, Vasconcelos announced that the election was a fraud. Modeling himself on Madero, he retired across the border into the United States and waited in vain for a rebellion of his supporters. He then went to El Paso, Texas, declaring himself as the only legal Mexican head of state. Because of this declaration, Vasconcelos was forbidden reentry into Mexico, and he returned to California. This was another of the turning points in his life.

With this defeat at the polls, Vasconcelos began to wander again, and for ten years he lived and worked outside Mexico. He gave lectures in Panama, Costa Rica, Colombia, Honduras, and El Salvador. However, he preferred to go to France and Spain and work on the publication of *La Antorcha* (The Torch), a journal that expressed his opposition to the government of Mexico and to dictatorships in general. Vasconcelos lived and wrote in Spain, but his conservative views on Spain and his harsh attacks on Calles, who was considered the power controlling Mexico even after leaving the presidency in 1928, served to alienate him from the Spanish government. He went to Argentina, where he lectured and worked for a newspaper until 1935. He then returned to the United States and made several unsuccessful attempts to rekindle the spirit of the old *vasconcelismo* among different groups and even to achieve a reconciliation

with his archenemy Calles. When his residency permit in the United States expired, Vasconcelos ended his exile and entered Mexico via the state of Sonora in September 1938 and Mexico City in August 1939.

For the next twenty years Vasconcelos actively participated in the intellectual life of Mexico and other countries. He held the positions of director of the National Library and the Library of Mexico; he was a founding member of El Colegio de México; he wrote regularly for a number of newspapers and magazines; he lectured at universities in the United States and Latin America. Vasconcelos died on 30 June 1959.

José Vasconcelos wrote numerous books and articles. Much of what he wrote first appeared in newspapers and journals and later was published in book form. His subjects are many and range from his own life to the conquest of Mexico, the revolution of 1910 and its leading figures, the educational system, theories on race, international relations, travel notes, and many more topics. Vasconcelos wrote a number of philosophical works on ethics, aesthetics, and logic that are of particular interest to students of philosophy. To give order to the works of Vasconcelos, it is helpful to consider them as belonging to one of five broadly defined categories.

Autobiography. Probably the best known of Vasconcelos' works is the first volume of his autobiography, *A Mexican Ulysses.* Written during the writer's exile following his unsuccessful bid for the presidency, the book deals with approximately the first thirty years of his life, which correspond to the period leading up to the revolution of 1910 and its short triumph and temporary defeat with the death of Madero. It is a vivid personal account of those turbulent years, coupled with the details of the author's family background, schooling, and his relationship to the Revolution and its protagonists. Of the autobiographical works of Vasconcelos, this one is the most interesting. Its style shows Vasconcelos at his best—dynamic, witty, and always absorbing. Although by its very nature personal in approach, *A Mexican Ulysses* gives one an insight into those turbulent years and an understanding of the period that it would be difficult for a book of history to provide. Vasconcelos' descriptions are graphic, some of the details intimate, but the overall effect is gripping. This volume was followed by three more during the writer's lifetime and one published posthumously. Each one combines the life of the author with the events of the years he is writing about. Consequently, each volume is a personal history of the time written by one who both observed and participated. However, the tone of each succeeding volume is different. Often Vasconcelos seems angry or bitter or unduly harsh in his criticism. And none of the subsequent volumes, despite numerous editions and reprintings, ever achieved the popularity and critical acclaim of the first. In 1936 *La tormenta: Segunda parte de Ulises criollo* (The Storm: Second Part of a Mexican Ulysses) was published. It encompasses the turbulent years following the death of Madero in 1913 to 1920 when Carranza was assassinated. As a personal view of the civil strife of those years, it allows the reader an inside look at the factionalism that divided the country. The changing allegiances to the principal revolutionary leaders—Carranza, Gutiérrez, Francisco Villa, Emiliano Zapata—and the different directions that the Revolution was taking become graphic and palpable through Vasconcelos' rendition. *El desastre: Tercera parte de Ulises criollo* (The Disaster: Third Part of a Mexican Ulysses) followed in 1938. This volume continues where the previous one ended and covers in great detail the presidencies of Obregón from 1920 to 1924 and Calles from 1924 to 1928. Of particular interest in this book is the author's account of his work, often considered the high point of his career, in the Ministry of Public Education. It is a story told by a Vasconcelos who was idealistic, energetic, and enthusiastic about his position and its responsibilities. One is caught up by the momentum of the many activities Vasconcelos initiated and directed and by his commonsense approach to the problems of education. The fourth volume of the autobiography, *El proconsulado: Cuarta parte de Ulises criollo* (The Proconsulate: Fourth Part of a Mexican Ulysses, 1939) deals mainly with Vasconcelos' election campaign and its aftermath. Until the writer's death in 1959 these four volumes were considered to make up his autobiography. However, the posthumous publication that same year of *La flama: Los de arriba en la Revolución; Historia y tragedia* (The Flame: Those at the Top in the Revolution; History and Tragedy) can

be said to bring his autobiography up to 1938, the year of his reentry into Mexico from exile. Originally published in serial form, the book is a collection of much that had been written previously about his presidential campaign, stories about some Mexican martyrs, and autobiographical material that completes Vasconcelos' personal history up to his final return to Mexico.

History and Biography. This category is made up of works that are concerned with the history of Mexico and figures of Mexican history. Generally, these books were inspired by the strong feelings and passions of an essayist rather than the carefully documented studies of a historian. Although Vasconcelos was well read and knowledgeable, he was not a meticulous scholar and many of these works aroused negative criticism because of their subjective nature. *La caída de Carranza: De la dictadura a la libertad* (The Fall of Carranza: From Dictatorship to Freedom, 1920) documents the fall of Carranza, president of Mexico from 1917 to 1920, through a collection of documents, speeches, articles, and letters. In 1924 Vasconcelos published a slim textbook, *Los últimos cincuenta años* (The Last Fifty Years) intended for use in the classroom. It reviews the main events and figures of the preceding fifty years of Mexican history. *Mexico* (1928), written in English with J. Fred Rippy and Guy Stevens, was the result of a series of lectures given at universities in the United States. It is a sober and sensitive treatment of Mexican and North American relations. In 1937 Vasconcelos undertook an ambitious work, *Breve historia de México* (A Brief History of Mexico), a book that has enjoyed numerous editions and later revisions and has provoked much adverse criticism. In this far from brief and ultimately very controversial volume, Vasconcelos relates the history of Mexico from the time of the conquest through the presidency of Manuel Ávila Camacho. It is Vasconcelos' personal interpretation of that history, based in large measure on his experiences and observations. Uneven in his treatment of different periods of Mexico's past, Vasconcelos wrote subjectively with an impassioned tone. A biography of Hernán Cortés, of whom Vasconcelos was a great admirer, followed in 1941. The conquest of Mexico and the role of Cortés are described in full detail in *Hernán Cortés: Creador de la nacionalidad* (Hernán

Cortés: Creator of the Mexican Nation). *Apuntes para la historia de México: Desde la conquista hasta la Revolución de 1910* (Notes on the History of Mexico: From the Conquest to the Revolution of 1910) published in 1943, is a short history of Mexico from before the conquest to the time of Carranza. In 1958 Vasconcelos published *Don Evaristo Madero: Biografía de un patricio* (Don Evaristo Madero: Biography of a Patrician), a biography of Francisco I. Madero's grandfather. Written with true affection, the work is a tribute to the memory of the younger Madero, whom Vasconcelos revered.

Sociology and Education. Next to *A Mexican Ulysses*, the writer's most popular book in Mexico and Latin America is *La raza cósmica: Misión de la raza iberoamericana; Notas de un viaje a la América del Sur* (*The Cosmic Race*) of 1925. In this, as well as in sections of two publications of 1926, *Indología: Una interpretación de la cultura ibero-americana* (The Indian Heritage in an Interpretation of Iberoamerican Culture) and *Aspects of Mexican Civilization* (a series of lectures originally delivered at the University of Chicago), Vasconcelos proposes the evolution of a new race in Latin America that would combine all the existing races and produce a superior one. He was convinced at the time that his theory was intellectually sound, morally right, and biologically feasible. Vasconcelos felt that Latin America, where there had been a long history of racial admixture, would be the natural place for the evolution of the cosmic race that would be the definitive synthesis of all the existing races. He hypothesized that people would procreate, governed by emotions and aesthetics, with the aim of producing superior offspring. The human species itself would aspire to gradual perfection by a process of self-elimination wherein those who were best suited would engage in reproduction and those who were physically or mentally inferior would choose not to mate. Consequently, unfavorable traits would gradually become extinct and a single universal race composed of favorable and superior traits would evolve. Although some twenty years later Vasconcelos repudiated his theory, at the time of its publication it was well received. Despite the fact that it was scientifically untenable, it was an appealing theory that favored a society without racial barriers, one in which friendships and marriages would be based on those forces that drew people together irrespective of race.

Two volumes published in 1934, *Bolivarismo y monroísmo: Temas iberoamericanos* (Bolivarism and Monroism: Iberoamerican Themes) and *Hispano-américa frente a los nacionalismos agresivos de Europa y Norteamérica* (Spanish America vis-à-vis the Aggressive Nationalism of Europe and North America), consist mainly of lectures delivered at the University of La Plata in Argentina. Their tone and substance reflect Vasconcelos' anti–United States sentiment of that period. *De Robinsón a Odiseo: Pedagogía estructurativa* (From Robinson Crusoe to Odysseus: The Structure of Pedagogy, 1935) is a volume in which the author expounds on his theory of education. He contrasted his ideas with the theories and practices then current in the educational system of the United States.

Collections of Essays, Short Stories, Speeches, and Letters. This is a category that encompasses numerous volumes difficult to classify because of their diverse nature. *Divagaciones literarias* (Literary Ramblings, 1919) and *Artículos* (Articles, 1920) are similar in content and contain the same two short stories and the same essays on various themes. Of note in these early works is the short story "Una cacería trágica" (A Tragic Hunting Party, 1916), which contains elements of the social novel and has been much read and very popular. *Ideario de acción* (Ideology of Action, 1924), *Pesimismo alegre* (Cheerful Pessimism, 1931), and *La sonata mágica* (The Magic Sonata, 1933) are small collections of speeches, letters, and short stories, most of which had appeared in newspapers, magazines, or other compilations. *Qué es el comunismo* (What is Communism, 1936) is a series of essays on the left-wing element of the Spanish republic. They reflect Vasconcelos' sharp turn to the political right at that time; he interpreted the political situations in Spain and in Mexico to be the result of Communist infiltration. In 1937 Vasconcelos published another collection of essays and newspaper articles entitled *Qué es la revolución* (What is Revolution), which were for the most part political in nature. Two volumes—*La cita* (The Appointment), a collection of short stories, and *El viento de Bagdad* (The Wind of Bagdad), short stories, essays, and philosophical pieces, all of which had been published previously—came out in 1945. *Discursos: 1920–1950* (Speeches: 1920–1950), published in 1950, is a compilation of Vasconcelos' public addresses of the previous thirty years.

During Vasconcelos' final years he published two books of essays for the most part new and light in tone. In *Temas contemporáneos* (Contemporary Themes, 1956) the author recounts his visits to North and South American universities, his receptions there, and his impressions of these institutions and their scholars. The other, *En el ocaso de mi vida* (In the Sunset of My Life, 1957), contains a number of delightful essays on a variety of topics of contemporary interest. In 1959, the year of Vasconcelos' death, he collaborated extensively in magazines and prepared three books that were published posthumously. In addition to *La flama,* he edited his *Cartas políticas* (Political Letters), letters to his friend Alfonso Taracena written during the ten-year exile following his defeat in the presidential election of 1929. Also, in 1959, his son José Ignacio published *Letanías del atardecer* (Litanies of Dusk), short poetic pieces expressing Vasconcelos' renewed religious fervor.

Drama. Although drama is not really a genre to which Vasconcelos dedicated himself, he did write several small dramatic pieces. *Prometeo vencedor* (Prometheus the Conqueror, 1916) is about man's struggle for immortality; *Simón Bolívar* (1939) is a script written for the cinema; *Los robachicos* (The Kidnappers, 1946) is a play that denounces the practice of kidnapping and maiming children and then forcing them to become beggars.

Vasconcelos is well known for his opinions—opinions on everything and everyone he came in contact with. The writer's impulsive nature together with his need to express himself resulted in a vast amount of published material. However, he did not always abide by his own judgments and exercised the privilege of changing his mind completely and with great frequency. Thus, unless one is familiar with everything Vasconcelos wrote, it is difficult to say whether he was for or against someone or something. As a result, one is faced either with Vasconcelos' reactions of a particular moment or a mass of opinions that evolved over a period of time. For example, although he was clearly opposed to Porfirio Díaz and

his long dictatorship and was active in supporting his overthrow and the exercise of free elections, Vasconcelos' writings show an attitude that ranges from dislike and disgust to tolerance and mild admiration. Vasconcelos' recollections from his youth tell of his own experiences as a participant in ceremonies applauding the dictator, which were reported by the controlled press as spontaneous public acclamations. However, he realized that despite certain areas of progress that had been made in Mexico during the Díaz regime, it was time for a complete change. Later, to Vasconcelos' mind, Díaz assumed a certain dignity and integrity because, although he condoned dishonesty in others, he did not permit it in himself. And what made Díaz almost respectable was his conciliatory attitude toward the religious question in not enforcing some of the anticlerical legislation contained in the Mexican constitution.

Álvaro Obregón, during whose presidency Vasconcelos served as Minister of Public Education, was also the subject of a cycle of opinion. At first Vasconcelos viewed him with suspicion for having been a supporter of Díaz and for having joined the backers of Madero only after the dictator's fall. Distrust of Obregón increased when the convention held at Aquascalientes in 1914 named Gutiérrez provisional president and Obregón threw his support to Carranza, who had established himself as provisional president in Veracruz. Vasconcelos was critical of this action because Obregón had been one of the signers of the agreement drawn up at Aguascalientes. However, in time Vasconcelos bowed to Obregón's increasing popularity and joined his administration. Toward the end of Obregón's presidential term, Vasconcelos broke with him because of his decision to impose his own successor, Calles, and to pursue a foreign policy designed to obtain official recognition of Mexico by the United States. In addition, Obregón's ambition to assume the presidency again, after an intervening term of Calles, was for Vasconcelos a betrayal of the principle of "no reelection" that had been fought for during the Revolution.

A topic that traditionally has been of interest to the essayists of Latin America—the United States—is one that runs through much of Vasconcelos' writings. In reflecting on the United States and its role vis-à-vis Mexico and the Americas, Vasconcelos spoke knowledgeably because of his many associations with Mexico's northern neighbor. As one might expect, he was not consistent in his opinions about the United States no matter how strongly he expressed them. On the one hand, he liked North Americans and admired their institutions; on the other, he disliked, sometimes to the point of hatred, the United States as a political entity. Even within this broad range of feeling there were exceptions and contradictions. As a young boy Vasconcelos attended public school in Texas, and from this experience stems his favorable impressions of the United States. He spoke glowingly of the instruction he received there and of the high caliber of the teachers. After having spent his first exile in New York City, he returned to Mexico deeply impressed by the opportunities afforded him, the free public libraries, and well-administered museums. This was the United States he admired and with which he was associated during different periods of his life.

However, there was another United States—the one represented by its diplomats and politicians—that was the target of his harsh criticism. For example, ambassadors Henry Lane Wilson and Dwight Morrow were both subjects of attack because of their interference in the internal affairs of Mexico, the former during the short-lived presidency of Madero and the latter during the administration of Calles. President Woodrow Wilson, who took office a month after Madero's death, relieved Ambassador Wilson of his duties, thus gaining Vasconcelos' admiration. However, President Wilson's official recognition of Carranza as president of Mexico earned him the writer's severe criticism. Yet Vasconcelos praised President Wilson for the unsuccessful expedition into Mexico, led by General John J. Pershing, to capture Francisco Villa. During the years following Vasconcelos' defeat at the polls and subsequent exile, his views on the United States tended to be negative. He dwelled upon his idea that the United States had been plotting for over one hundred years to uproot Spanish and Mexican civilization and to absorb the country physically and culturally. To substantiate the existence of this plot, he pointed to, among other things, the Monroe Doctrine, the colonization and loss of Texas, the support given Benito Juárez, the satisfaction with the regime of Díaz, the Bucareli

Treaties, and the influence of Ambassador Morrow on President Calles, who enforced the anticlerical legislation. Vasconcelos' own return in later life to the religion of his youth caused him to view North Americans as anti-Catholic Protestants who wished to curtail the spiritual power of the church.

Despite the fact that so much of Vasconcelos' writing is devoted to criticizing the United States, a substantial part of it expresses his admiration and approval. He spoke with respect of President Franklin D. Roosevelt and his Good Neighbor policy, and considered the United States as an ally of Latin America in pursuit of a common destiny. His most positive opinions are those of the North American people and their institutions. He found North Americans kind, hospitable, hardworking, and efficient; he considered their schools, universities, libraries, and other public and private cultural facilities outstanding.

José Vasconcelos, Mexican essayist, politician, and educator, was a sensitive and complex individual. A man of noble spirit and worldly outlook, he could be stubborn and unreasonable. When he renewed his relationship with the church, he allowed his ultra-conservative feelings to attribute the world's ills to a war on Catholicism; he reevaluated the history and heritage of Mexico and the roles played by its heroes and statesmen. Although he could be inconsistent and irrational, he was very often sensible, liberal, and modern for his time. His love of country was deep and personal; the proximity of the United States posed a constant threat and served as a reminder that Mexico had been reduced to a fraction of its original size. The Mexico he loved did not share his later denunciation of the Indian and his acclamation of the Spanish heritage. Many Mexicans disagreed with his opinions on the history of Mexico and the leading figures of the revolution of 1910. However, Vasconcelos believed, more than half a century ago, that the leadership of a truly democratic government must be entrusted to an intellectual and not to a military chieftain; he realized that Latin America's most pressing problem was its soaring birthrate; he advocated the equality of the races and their inalienable right to equal opportunities; he maintained that every individual was obligated to contribute his talents to the betterment of society. Vasconcelos will be remembered as a thinker of his time, a modern educator, and as a writer who made the period of the Mexican revolution of 1910 a vivid event for his readers, thus contributing in large measure to the literature of Latin America.

SELECTED BIBLIOGRAPHY

First Editions

Autobiography

Ulises criollo: La vida del autor escrita por él mismo. Mexico City, 1935.

La tormenta: Segunda parte de Ulises criollo. Mexico City, 1936.

El desastre: Tercera parte de Ulises criollo. Mexico City, 1938.

El proconsulado: Cuarta parte de Ulises criollo. Mexico City, 1939.

La flama: Los de arriba en la Revolución; historia y tragedia. Mexico City, 1959.

History and Biography

La caída de Carranza: De la dictadura a la libertad. Mexico City, 1920.

Los últimos cincuenta años. Mexico City, 1924.

Mexico. In collaboration with J. Fred Rippy and Guy Stevens. Chicago, 1928.

Breve historia de México. Mexico City, 1937.

Hernán Cortés: Creador de la nacionalidad. Mexico City, 1941.

Apuntes para la historia de México: Desde la conquista hasta la Revolución de 1910. Mexico City, 1943.

Don Evaristo Madero: Biografía de un patricio. Mexico City, 1958.

Sociology and Education

La raza cósmica: Misión de la raza iberoamericana; Notas de un viaje a la América del Sur. Barcelona, 1925. Subsequent editions were retitled . . . *notas de viajes . . . .*

Indología: Una interpretación de la cultura ibero-americana. Paris and Barcelona, 1926.

Aspects of Mexican Civilization. Chicago, 1926.

Bolivarismo y monroísmo: Temas iberoamericanos. Santiago, Chile, 1934.

Hispanoamérica frente a los nacionalismos agresivos de Europa y Norteamérica. La Plata, Argentina, 1934.

De Robinsón a Odiseo: Pedagogía estructurativa. Madrid, 1935.

Essays, Short Stories, Speeches, Letters

Divagaciones literarias. Mexico City, 1919.

Artículos. San José, 1920.

Ideario de acción. Lima, 1924.

Pesimismo alegre. Madrid, 1931.

La sonata mágica: Cuentos y relatos. Madrid, 1933.

Qué es el comunismo. Mexico City, 1936.

Qué es la revolución. Mexico City, 1937.

La cita. Mexico City, 1945.

El viento de Bagdad: Cuentos y ensayos. Mexico City, 1945.

Discursos: 1920–1950. Mexico City, 1950.

Temas contemporáneos. Mexico City, 1956.

En el ocaso de mi vida. Mexico City, 1957.

Cartas políticas. Mexico City, 1959.

Letanías del atardecer. Mexico City, 1959.

Plays

Prometeo vencedor: Tragedia moderna en un prólogo y tres actos. Madrid, 1916.

Simón Bolívar. Mexico City, 1939.

Los robachicos. Mexico City, 1946.

Collected Works

Obras completas. 4 vols. Mexico City, 1957–1961. This edition does not contain the complete works of the author. It does include a number of his philosophical works in addition to his autobiography, some of his historical and sociological works, essays, and short stories.

Páginas escogidas. Edited and with a prologue by Antonio Castro Leal. Mexico City, 1940.

Vasconcelos. Edited and with a prologue by Genaro Fernández MacGregor. Mexico City, 1942. A selected anthology.

Modern Editions

Individual Works

Breve historia de México. Mexico City, 1979.

El desastre: Tercera parte de Ulises criollo. Mexico City, 1958.

Hernán Cortés: Creador de la nacionalidad. Mexico City, 1975.

El proconsulado: Cuarta parte de Ulises criollo. Mexico City, 1968.

La raza cósmica: Misión de la raza iberoamericana. Buenos Aires, 1977.

La sonata mágica: Cuentos y relatos. Buenos Aires, 1950.

La tormenta: Segunda parte de Ulises criollo. Mexico City, 1964.

Ulises criollo: La vida del autor escrita por él mismo. Mexico City, 1978.

Collected Works

Antología de José Vasconcelos. Edited and with an introduction by Genaro Fernández MacGregor. Mexico City, 1980.

Memorias. 2 vols. Mexico City, 1982. Contains the four parts of Ulises criollo.

Translations

A Mexican Ulysses: An Autobiography. Translated and abridged by W. Rex Crawford. Bloomington, Ind., 1963. Reprinted, Westport, Conn., 1972.

La raza cósmica. The Cosmic Race. A bilingual edition with an introduction and notes by Didier T. Jaén. Los Angeles, 1979.

Biographical and Critical Studies

Ahumada, Herminio. José Vasconcelos: Una vida que iguala con la acción el pensamiento. Mexico City, 1937.

Alessio Robles, Vito. Mis andanzas con nuestro Ulises. Mexico City, 1938.

Azuela, Salvador. La aventura vasconcelista, 1929. Mexico City, 1980.

Blanco, José Joaquín. Se llamaba Vasconcelos: Una evocación crítica. Mexico City, 1977.

Bravo Ugarte, José. "Historia y odisea vasconceliana." Historia mexicana 10/4:533–556 (1961).

Camp, Roderic A. "La campaña presidencial de 1929 y el liderazgo político en México." Historia mexicana 27/2:231–259 (1977).

Carballo, Emmanuel. "José Vasconcelos." In Protagonistas de la literatura mexicana. Mexico City, 1986. Pp. 19–26.

Cárdenas Noriega, Joaquín. José Vasconcelos, 1882–1982: Educador, político y profeta. Mexico City, 1982.

Cotto-Thorner, Guillermo. "Germen novelístico en Vasconcelos." La nueva democracia 36/1:32–35 (1956).

Crawford, W. Rex. "José Vasconcelos." In A Century of Latin American Thought. Rev. ed. New York, 1961. Pp. 260–276.

de Beer, Gabriella. José Vasconcelos and His Social Thought. New York, 1966.

———. "José Vasconcelos vis-à-vis the United States." Inter-American Review of Bibliography 17/4:414–430 (1967).

———. "La raza cósmica: An Ethical and Scientific Consideration." Inter-American Review of Bibliography 25/1:35–40 (1975).

Foster, David William. "A Checklist of Criticism on José Vasconcelos." Los ensayistas 14–15:177–212 (1983).

Giordano, Jaime A. "Notas sobre Vasconcelos y el ensayo hispanoamericano del siglo veinte." Hispanic Review 41:541–554 (1973).

Haddox, John H. Vasconcelos of Mexico, Philosopher and Prophet. Austin, Tex., 1967.

Hilton, Ronald. "José Vasconcelos." The Americas 7/4:395–412 (1951).

Jaén, Didier T. "La raza cósmica de Vasconcelos: Una re-evaluación." Texto crítico 1:14–21 (1975).

Langhorst, Rick. "Los Estados Unidos vistos por José Vasconcelos." Los ensayistas 10–11:117–122 (1981).

Magdaleno, Mauricio. Las palabras perdidas. Mexico City, 1956.

Martínez, José Luis. "La obra literaria de José Vasconcelos." In Literatura mexicana siglo veinte 1. Mexico City, 1949. Pp. 265–279.

Morton, F. Rand. "José Vasconcelos." In Los novelistas de la Revolución mexicana. Mexico City, 1949. Pp. 184–192.

Pineda, Hugo. José Vasconcelos: Político mexicano, 1928–1929. Mexico City, 1975.

Reinhardt, Kurt F. "Facets of Mexican Thought: José Vasconcelos." The Americas 2/3:322–334 (1946).

Robb, James Willis. "José Vasconcelos y Alfonso Reyes: Anverso y reverso de una medalla." Los ensayistas 16–17:55–65 (1984).

Salazar Parr, Carmen. "José Vasconcelos: Thought and Ideology in the Chicano Literary Arts." Denver Quarterly 16/3:52–60 (1981).

Silva Herzog, Jesús. "Vasconcelos." Nivel. Gaceta de cultura 8:1–2 (1959).

Skirius, John. José Vasconcelos y la cruzada de 1929. Mexico City, 1978.

Taracena, Alfonso. José Vasconcelos. Mexico City, 1982.

Young, Howard T. "José Vasconcelos." Hispania 42/4:570–572 (1959).

Manuel Gálvez

(1882–1962)

Myron I. Lichtblau

Manuel Gálvez is a traditional, realistic writer who portrayed the whole fabric of Argentine life. Inheriting his craft of fiction from such European masters as Gustave Flaubert, Honoré de Balzac, and Fyodor Dostoyevski, Gálvez depicted the gamut of Argentine society, from bustling Buenos Aires to the tranquil provinces, from the liberal politician to the reactionary zealot of Córdoba, from the prostitute and tough of the city slums to the affluent businessman. Gálvez' brand of realism is objective and photographic, with a minimum of literary artifice and verbal glitter. His goal as a novelist was not to present intellectually challenging works but rather to depict with a most direct, straightforward technique and style the lives and customs of Argentines in a wide variety of settings.

Born 18 July 1882 in the provincial city of Paraná, Gálvez boasts celebrated Spanish forebears, among them Juan de Garay, who founded the city of Santa Fe in 1573, and Gabriel de Quiroga, high-ranking official of the inquisition. With the advantages of family position, Gálvez was able to spend a comfortable youth in varied cultural pursuits. He received his law degree in 1904 but never practiced his profession. The subject of his dissertation, white slavery, revealed an early interest in social problems that led him to write such novels as *El mal metafísico* (The

Metaphysical Ill, 1916) and *Nacha Regules* (*Nacha Regules*, 1919). Gálvez was an important member of the literary generation of 1910–1920 and one of the founders of *Ideas*, a short-lived magazine of literature and the arts. This formative period in his career is carefully recounted in the first volume of his memoirs, entitled *Amigos y maestros de mi juventud* (Friends and Teachers of My Youth, 1944). Gálvez was also very much interested in promoting the cause of Argentine literature and divulging that literature to the outside world. To that end he founded the Cooperativa Editorial Buenos Aires in 1917 and was the editor until its demise in 1926. In 1919 Gálvez also founded Editorial Pax, which lasted just four years. In 1930 he established the Argentine P.E.N. Club, and in 1931 his proposal for the founding of an Argentine Academy of Letters became a reality. Gálvez was Latin America's candidate for the Nobel Prize three times, in 1932, 1933, and 1951; his best chance for winning came in 1932 when he had recently published the last volume of his widely acclaimed trilogy on the Paraguayan War. Gálvez died on 14 November 1962.

Gálvez is probably Hispanic America's best example of a Catholic writer. Oddly, his youthful spirit of rebellion brought about his renunciation of Catholicism in 1905, but he returned to his faith two years later with rekindled ardor and dedication. In subsequent novels, Gálvez became a fervent defender of Catholicism, a stern moralist who not only rewarded those characters who led a devout life, but who felt that fulfillment and happiness were more readily achieved through spiritual devotion. In such works as *Miércoles santo* (*Holy Wednesday*, 1930), and *La noche toca a su fin* (*The Spiritual Hymn*, 1935), his religious faith hovers inescapably over the destiny of his characters. In *Holy Wednesday*, the protagonist is Father Eudosio Solanas, an austere and ascetic priest with a rare understanding of the human heart, who doubts, however, that he is without carnal desire. The novel centers on the problems of those who seek his counsel and on the inner conflicts of the priest himself. What is most important is the ironic parallelism between the anguish of Father Solanas and the weaknesses and vices of the parishioners he comforts. And when his personal torment and the suffering of a penitent he is confessing become interrelated, the irony becomes emotionally charged and highly dramatic. Another important religious novel, *Perdido en su noche* (*Lost in His Darkness*, 1958), concerns a young Jesuit who abandons the order shortly after taking his final vows. Gálvez handles this delicate theme of apostasy with great sensitivity, particularly the conflict between religious devotion and the dictates of conscience.

Gálvez is at his best as a novelist when he focuses on a particular Argentine environment and peoples it with characters who for better or for worse are caught in that milieu. Buenos Aires and the interior provinces represented for Gálvez two opposing elements that he portrayed with all their virtues and imperfections. Gálvez' first novel, *La maestra normal* (*The Normal-school Teacher*, 1914), is perhaps his best and most representative of that group of "novels of environment." *La maestra normal* is a masterly portrayal of provincial life in La Rioja at the turn of the century—the lethargic town; the apathetic inhabitants; the pretentious, petty officials; the Normal School and its rival, the Colegio Nacional (National College); the cafés; the holiday festivals. The story revolves around the seduction of a young, ingenuous teacher, Raselda, by the more sophisticated and selfish Solís, who has come to La Rioja to recuperate his health after a life of dissipation in the capital. In

its deepest social significance, the novel is an open attack on the weaknesses of normal-school education, government bureaucracy, and parochialism. Far more significant than the simple plot of *La maestra normal* is the wealth of environmental detail and character depiction. The three local settings in La Rioja, all an integral part of Solís' life—the *pensión*, the pharmacy shop, and the *confitería*, or café—enable Gálvez to display his gift for descriptive narrative and provide some of the most interesting material of the novel.

The cosmopolitan, dynamic Buenos Aires is the scene of Gálvez' second novel, *El mal metafísico*, but the principal focus is limited to the literary world. The story of Gálvez' generation, *El mal metafísico* concerns a young writer's inadaptability to the crass materialism of the capital, the daily struggle of a romantic dreamer against the indifference and smugness of a big city. Gálvez juxtaposes the most earthly realism and the most exalted idealism as he decries the debasement of cultural values in modern society. The protagonist, Carlos Riga, becomes a victim of poverty, disease, and alcoholism, and finally succumbs. He is the quintessential *abúlico* so common in Hispanic-American literature, the one who lacks the will and the determination to achieve, to rise above his adverse environment.

In his third novel, *La sombra del convento* (*The Shadow of the Convent*, 1917), Gálvez returned to the provinces, to the "learned" city of Córdoba, the seat of Jesuit influence and Catholic dogmatism. The intent of the novel is to attack the religious authoritarianism and narrow-mindedness that stifle intellectual vitality and impede progress. Not incompatible with Gálvez' deeply religious feeling, his rebuke of the Catholic church's intolerance and austerity is fundamentally a censure of outmoded colonial attitudes. What is portrayed so effectively in *La sombra del convento* is Córdoba caught in the grip of powerful reactionary segments of society, in particular the struggle of José Alberto Flores against these forces to win the girl he loves.

In 1919, Gálvez published his most popular and commercially successful work, *Nacha Regules*, the story of a prostitute. No doubt influenced by Émile Zola's *Nana*, it is a thesis novel whose propagandistic qualities weaken its literary merit. Containing many elements of the naturalistic novel, *Nacha Regules* shows how the relentless forces of heredity and environment bear down on Nacha and eventually crush her. Redemption through love is the theme; that is, Nacha's moral regeneration through the love and care of Fernando Monsalvat. Despite the pervasive determinism of the novel, Gálvez is more the idealistic social reformer than the exponent of scientific naturalism. Encouraged by *Nacha Regules*, Gálvez wrote an even more explicitly sordid naturalistic novel, *Historia de arrabal* (Story of a Slum Neighborhood, 1922), a work that suffers from poor narrative development within the social context. The story relates how El Chino forces an innocent girl into prostitution and controls her life. The ills of an industrialized society are symbolized in the meatpacking plant, where workers represent the oppressed masses with whom Gálvez so ardently sympathizes.

Gálvez wrote several novels of deep psychological penetration, among them *La tragedia de un hombre fuerte* (The Tragedy of a Strong-willed Man, 1922), in which the lives of five women who have loved Victor Urgel are analyzed with unusual understanding of the feminine heart. Urgel's varied emotional response to each of these women also probes the male psyche to a degree rarely found in Hispanic-American writers of the 1920's. Congressman Urgel, representing the spirit of social unrest that presses for renovation, is unhappily married to Asunción, whose parochial views on life clash with his. The story and ultimate failure of each of Victor's affairs constitutes an independent and complete narrative unit. Victor's feeling of emotional isolation and inner solitude is a theme that Gálvez broaches in this novel, anticipating by some fifteen years writers like Eduardo Mallea, who used it within the literary movement of existentialism. The theme of emotional solitude, peripheral in *La tragedia de un hombre fuerte*, becomes the predominant one in *Hombres en soledad* (Men in Solitude, 1938), one of Gálvez' richest novels in social content but a work flawed by a disorderly narrative structure. This novel is notable for its portrayal of the upper class in Buenos Aires in the 1920's. The prototype of Gálvez' man of solitude is Gervasio Claraval, a lawyer by training who is more interested in the arts than in the law. Surrounding Claraval is a group of malcontents who, like him, are

all fleeing from the banal reality of their existences, finding escape in politics, illicit love, frivolities, and extended trips to Europe.

An important part of Gálvez' fiction is the historical novel. The trilogy on the Paraguayan War (1865–1870) ranks among his best work and brought him international recognition as a sensitive interpreter of that contest between Paraguay on one side and Argentina, Brazil, and Uruguay on the other. The three novels form a well-defined thematic and artistic unit, although each one is independent of the other in plot and characters. Gálvez is the omnipresent narrator of the events, but his vantage point is different in each novel. In *Los caminos de la muerte* (The Roads of Death, 1928), the conflict is seen mostly from the Argentine battlefield in and around the province of Corrientes. In *Humaitá* (Humaitá, 1929), the focus is the heroism of the Brazilians, while in *Jornadas de agonía* (Marches of Agony, 1929) the enfeebled Paraguayan troops are cast in the central position.

A more ambitious series of historical novels, but one of inferior literary quality, is *Escenas de la época de Rosas* (Scenes from the Rosas Era), a seven-volume reconstruction of the iron rule of Juan Manuel de Rosas, the dictator who governed Argentina from 1835 to 1852. The first novel of the series, *El gaucho de Los Cerrillos* (The Gaucho of the Cerrillos, 1931), is a minute account of Rosas' early years in Buenos Aires as an aggressive political figure. The last novel, *Y así cayó Don Juan Manuel* (The Fall of Don Juan Manuel, 1954), continues to reveal Gálvez' overwhelming sympathies for the dictator. Gálvez also wrote an isolated historical novel called *La muerte en las calles* (Death in the Streets, 1949), which deals with the English invasions of Argentina in 1806–1807. In this novel Gálvez suggests that these British attacks played a significant role in Argentina's independence from Spain, for the victory gave Argentines the confidence and resoluteness to overthrow the mother country a few years later. One of the novel's notable features is the depiction of the social and political climate in Buenos Aires in the late-colonial period.

At the age of seventy-four Gálvez published the controversial *Tránsito Guzmán* (Tránsito Guzmán, 1956), a novel about the turbulent Perón dictatorship he supported or at least tolerated during most of the regime. But when Perón attacked the church, Gálvez openly broke with the dictator, unable to reconcile this brazen act with his own devotion to Catholicism. The historical events depicted in *Tránsito Guzmán* revolve around the fateful night of 16 June 1955, when scores of temples, parsonages, and other church properties in Buenos Aires were burned and sacked by government partisans in retaliation for the bombing of the Casa Rosada (the Argentine presidential mansion) at the hands of revolutionaries. The fictional element in the novel centers on Tránsito, a deeply religious woman strongly opposed to the regime, who tries to reconcile her devotion to God with her love for a police officer in Perón's special corps.

Gálvez' interest in Argentine history did not stop with the historical novel but led him to write the biographies of several national leaders. Biography for Gálvez was a natural extension of his fiction. In 1933 he published his first work in that genre, *Vida de Fray Mamerto Esquiú* (Life of Fray Mamerto Esquiú), but it received a rather tepid response from the public. From 1938 to 1948 Gálvez wrote no fiction, being totally absorbed in biography. Of the nine biographies Gálvez published, seven are on Argentine subjects—Mamerto Esquiú, Hipólito Yrigoyen, Juan Manuel de Rosas, Domingo Faustino Sarmiento, Aparicio Saravia, José Hernández, and Ceferino Namuncura. One biography deals with the Colombian Francisco de Miranda; another, with the Ecuadorian Gabriel García Moreno. The Rosas biography raised a storm of controversy because it defended the dictator and tried to vindicate his repressive regime by arguing that it helped preserve the political and economic sovereignty of Argentina. In the Sarmiento biography, Gálvez again took an unpopular stand, this time attacking one of his country's most distinguished statesmen and educators. The biography is an imposing work of investigation and documentation, but its intent, unfortunately, is to stain the image of the "schoolmaster president."

Any assessment of Gálvez as a writer must include his biographies, for they form a significant part of his literary production. Gálvez' biographical works reveal him to be a fervent nationalist who respects law and order above individual freedom, who seeks to preserve at any cost a rigid and narrow concept of national sovereignty. His most important biographies were written to expound his nationalistic views: the basic role of the Catholic church in maintaining the essence of the Argentine spirit; the seeking of Argentina's cultural heritage not only in the colonial world, but also in Spain itself; mild distrust of Anglo-Saxon civilizations; and grave doubts about the value of a totally democratic government.

Gálvez' place in the development of the Argentine novel is secure and well defined. And his position in the larger story of Hispanic-American fiction is no less important. With rich environmental detail and perceptive character portrayal, Gálvez faithfully depicted the Argentine scene in over thirty novels and three volumes of short stories. Few writers in Hispanic America had a more intense literary vocation; indeed he lived his life through his literature. His best fiction adds a notable dimension to the Argentine novel in its uncompromising realism and psychological study of character. It is unjust to label Gálvez, as some critics have done, the last of the nineteenth-century realists. He is a better and far more interesting novelist than most of those who represented realism and naturalism from 1860 to 1900. His narrative technique is surer, his character studies more incisive, and his descriptions more colorful, exact, and forceful. Indeed, Gálvez is Argentina's first complete novelist.

SELECTED BIBLIOGRAPHY

Editions

Prose Narratives

La maestra normal. Buenos Aires, 1914.
El mal metafísico. Buenos Aires, 1916.
La sombra del convento. Buenos Aires, 1917.
Nacha Regules. Buenos Aires, 1919.
Luna de miel y otras narraciones. Buenos Aires, 1920.
La tragedia de un hombre fuerte. Buenos Aires, 1922.
Historia de arrabal. Buenos Aires, 1922.
El cántico espiritual. Buenos Aires, 1923.
Los caminos de la muerte. Buenos Aires, 1928.
Humaitá. Buenos Aires, 1929.
Jornadas de agonía. Buenos Aires, 1929.
Miércoles santo. Buenos Aires, 1930.
El gaucho de Los Cerrillos. Buenos Aires, 1931.

La noche toca a su fin. Buenos Aires, 1935.
Hombres en soledad. Buenos Aires, 1938.
La muerte en las calles. Buenos Aires, 1949.
Y así cayó Don Juan Manuel. Buenos Aires, 1954.
Las dos vidas del pobre Napoleón. Buenos Aires, 1954.
Tránsito Guzmán. Buenos Aires, 1956.
Perdido en su noche. Buenos Aires, 1958.

Poetry

El enigma interior. Buenos Aires, 1907.
El sendero de humildad. Buenos Aires, 1909.

Play

Calibán. Buenos Aires, 1943.

Biographies

Vida de Fray Mamerto Esquiú. Buenos Aires, 1933.
Vida de Hipólito Yrigoyen. Buenos Aires, 1939.
Vida de Don Juan Manuel de Rosas. Buenos Aires, 1940.
Vida de Aparicio Saravia. Buenos Aires, 1942.
Vida de Don Gabriel García Moreno. Buenos Aires, 1942.
Vida de Sarmiento. Buenos Aires, 1945.
José Hernández. Buenos Aires, 1945.
Don Francisco de Miranda. Buenos Aires, 1947.

Essays

El diario de Gabriel Quiroga. Buenos Aires, 1910.
El solar de la raza. Buenos Aires, 1913.
Este pueblo necesita. Buenos Aires, 1934.

Memoirs

Recuerdos de la vida literaria. 4 vols. Buenos Aires, 1944–1965.

Collected Works

Biografías completas. 2 vols. Buenos Aires, 1962.
Obras escogidas. Madrid, 1949.

Translations

Nacha Regules. Translated by Leo Ongley. New York, 1922.
Holy Wednesday. Translated by Warre B. Wells. New York and London, 1934.

Biographical and Critical Studies

Anzoátegui, Ignacio B. *Manuel Gálvez.* Buenos Aires, 1961.
Brown, Donald F. "The Catholic Naturalism of Manuel Gálvez." *Modern Language Quarterly* 9:165–176 (1948).
Carrero del Mármol, Elena. "Gálvez y Mallea: Imágenes de la Argentina." *Duquesne Hispanic Review* 2:167–178 (1963).
Chapman, Arnold. "Manuel Gálvez y Eduardo Mallea." *Revista iberoamericana* 49:71–78 (1953).
Crawford, William R. "Manuel Gálvez." In *A Century of Latin-American Thought.* Rev. ed. Cambridge, Mass., 1961. Pp. 149–164.
Desinano, Norma. *La novelística de Manuel Gálvez.* Santa Fe, Argentina, 1965.
Foster, David W. "Ideological Ruptures in Manuel Gálvez's *Historia de arrabal:* Linguistic Conventions." *Hispanic Journal* 4/2:21–27 (1983).
———. Discussion of Galvez in *Currents in the Contemporary Argentine Novel.* Columbia, Mo., 1975. Pp. 10–12.
Ghiano, Juan Carlos. "Vigencia de la obra literaria de Gálvez." *Boletín de la Academia Argentina de Letras* 47:215–227 (1982).
Jaimes Freyre, Mireya. "Gálvez y su laberinto." *Revista iberoamericana* 18:315–337 (1953).
Jitrik, Noé. "Los desplazamientos de la culpa en las obras 'sociales' de Manuel Gálvez." *Duquesne Hispanic Review* 1:143–166 (1963).
Kobzina, Norma. "An Argentine *Nana:* Gálvez and Zola." *Revista de estudios hispánicos* 10:163–179 (1976).
Lafforgue, Jorge, and Jorge B. Rivera. "Realismo tradicional: Narrative urbana." In *Capítulo: Historia de la literatura argentina.* Buenos Aires, 1924.
Lichtblau, Myron I. *Manuel Gálvez.* New York, 1972.
Minc, Rose S. "De *La maestra normal* a *Perdido en su noche:* arquetipos en progresión retrogresiva." *Symposium* 36/4:345–351 (1983).
Olivari, Nicolás, and Lorenzo Stanchina. *Manuel Gálvez: Ensayo sobre su obra.* Buenos Aires, 1924.
Schwartz, Kessell. "Two Faces of Feminism in the 1920's." *Revista de estudios hispánicos* 13:461–471 (1979).
Spell, Jefferson R. "City Life in the Argentine As Seen by Manuel Gálvez." In *Contemporary Spanish-American Fiction.* Chapel Hill, N. C., 1944. Pp. 15–63.
Symposium 36/4 (1983). Special issue on Manuel Gálvez.
Torres-Ríoseco, Arturo. "Manuel Gálvez." In his *Grandes novelistas de la América Hispana* 2. Berkeley, Calif., 1943. Pp. 137–160.
Walker, John. "Gálvez, Barrios, and the Metaphysical Malaise." *Symposium* 36/4:352–358 (1983).
Zum Felde, Alberto. "Manuel Gálvez." In *Indice crítico de la literatura hispanoamericana: La narrativa.* Mexico City, 1959. Pp. 217–225.

Ricardo Rojas

(1882–1957)

Antonio Pagés Larraya

A humanist of profound intellectual influence in Argentina during the first half of the twentieth century, Ricardo Rojas belonged to a family deeply rooted in the Northwest since colonial times. He was born in Tucumán on 16 September 1882, but from early childhood he lived in the neighboring province of Santiago del Estero, where his father, Don Absalón, was governor and where he is remembered, to this day, with great fondness. The writer used to say that he came from the last province of the Incan Empire, with which he felt racially linked. A typical Hispanic American, he took pride in his mixed racial background. In his active political years, he was always moved to hear himself cheered as "the Indian Rojas."

Rojas' sensibility of his mixed blood projects itself into his work in a positive way. He openly contradicts the pessimism with which Domingo F. Sarmiento passed judgment on the American synthesis of Indians and Spaniards in *Conflictos y armonías de las razas en América* (Conflict and Harmonies of the Races in America, 1883), and he counters the pessimism that became noticeable in the positivistic sociologists, from Carlos Octavio Bunge to José Ingenieros. Rojas vindicates Argentina's indigenous cultural inheritance and exalts Spain's contribution to the genesis of a new, original culture. In *Eurindia* (Eurindia, 1924), he takes his ideas on cultural crossbreeding onto a theoretical plane, with a certain Utopian tension. On the aesthetic level, the tales of *El país de la selva* (The Jungle Country, 1907) and his tragedy *Ollantay* (Ollantay, premiered in 1939) constitute the most valuable creative testimonies of his oeuvre. Both *El país de la selva* and *Ollantay* exalt the pre-Hispanic tradition, seeking to promote Hispanic American subjects emphasizing national spiritual identity.

This new, enthusiastic appreciation of Indian America and of colonial culture stands in marked contrast to the increasing contempt shown by modern Argentina toward transculturation. It forms the emotional center that inspires Rojas' message, from his essays in *Cosmópolis* (Cosmopolis, 1908) and *La restauración nacionalista* (Nationalist Restoration, 1909)—a truly pedagogical program founded on the humanities, fundamentally on history—to books like *Blasón de plata* (Silver Blazon, 1912) and *La argentinidad* (Argentinehood, 1916), which point out the historical and political dimensions of the country as an ethnic entity with full consciousness of its national life-style. Rojas was no xenophobe toward the waves of immigrants that changed the physiognomy of the country from the turn of the nineteenth century on, but he censured cosmopolitanism, which he defined as exoticism, opposing it to Indianism. His manual *Silabario de la decoración americana* (Syllabary of

American Decoration, 1930) argues for the aesthetic possibilities of the Inca tradition, and an early book, *El alma española* (The Spanish Soul, 1908), marks the beginning of an approving attitude toward Spanish culture, elaborated later in his drama *La casa colonial* (The Colonial House, 1932) and in a lively, vigorous chronicle of pre–Civil War Spain, *Retablo español* (Spanish Altarpiece, 1938).

Rojas' political ideals find expression in *El radicalismo de mañana* (Tomorrow's Radicalism, 1932), in which he expounds on the theoretical foundations of his adherence to a popular movement that he identifies with the ideals of continental independence. Another important contribution to Argentine sociohistorical literature is *Archipiélago* (Archipelago, 1942), written during his exile in Usuhaia, and first published in *La Nación* from August 1941 to January 1942. He was exiled to Usuhaia, the southernmost point in Argentina, by a decree of President Agustin P. Justo, as a punishment for a policy championed by Rojas recommending "intransigence" and "ballot abstention" in view of cheating. This profusely documented work puts forth a new political orientation that exalts with prophetic passion the future role of the Argentine southern provinces. His well-known biographies of José Francisco de San Martín and Sarmiento, *El santo de la espada* (Knight of the Andes, 1933) and *El profeta de la pampa* (Prophet of the Pampa, 1945), respectively, extol exemplary, heroic values as a means of changing the collective ethos, which Rojas thought was deviating from the ideals of the founding fathers. Covering various genres, expressed in a vibrant, rhythmical, often oratorical style (he was a great political orator and teacher), his work is marked by a romantic stamp that does not vanish even in the modernist prose of *El país de la selva*. His creative productions share a common aim, the revival of those values of the past that will sustain a strong independent nation in the face of cultural and economic colonialism, materialism, and depersonalization.

The four original volumes of *La literatura argentina* (Argentine Literature, 1917–1922) occupy a place of prominence in Rojas' vast corpus, maintaining their high value despite the passage of time. It is an immense body of work, covering all the genres: poetry, drama, biography, essay, history. His poetic works oscillate between postromanticism and modernism. They include *La victoria del hombre* (Man's Victory, 1903), *Las lises del blasón* (The Blazon's Fleur-de-lis, 1911), "La sangre del sol" (The Sun's Blood, 1915), and *Canciones* (Songs, 1920). Besides *Ollantay*, his most important theatrical composition, he contributed to the enrichment of a drama of native American inspiration with three other pieces: *Elelín* (premiered in 1929), *La casa colonial*, and *La salamanca* (The Salamander, premiered in 1943). With a sensitivity to the Argentine past and Argentine soil, his theater pieces recreate decisive moments of national history.

Rojas' *El Cristo invisible* (The Invisible Christ, 1927), a dialogue about Christ's iconography evidencing Rojas' mysticism and religious knowledge, provoked polemical discussions at the time of its publication. It constitutes an expression of faith related to the Christian existential experience described by Miguel de Unamuno. Among the many writers who dealt with Rojas' works and whose testimonies were compiled in *La obra de Rojas: Veinticinco años de labor literaria* (Rojas's Oeuvre: Twenty-five Years of Literary Production, 1928), Unamuno wrote about the Argentine author with the best understanding of his idealistic message, as well as with vibrant intellectual sympathy. They were twin souls, as their intense spiritual interchange shows.

Upon completion of his secondary education in Santiago del Estero, Rojas traveled to Buenos Aires, where he studied law. He soon gave up his formal studies, declaring himself a "perpetual unenrolled student," and devoted himself to journalism. The provincial man's sensibility clashed with the capital city of the turn of the century, a center of intense social and literary life, swept by new ideas and marked by splendor and vitalistic optimism. At the same time, urban life awakened the young man's critical spirit, which embarked upon an examination of national identity with a sense of mission.

The University of Buenos Aires recognized Rojas' merits and awarded him an honorary doctorate in 1927. Many other Argentine and foreign universities also conferred this honor on him on the recommendations of students and professorial colleagues. Rojas served as president of the University of Buenos Aires and dean of the School of Philosophy and Letters, and held the chairs of Spanish literature and of Argentine literature, the latter his own creation. His teaching career did not present an obstacle to his active participation in life: he always faced the problems of his country and the world with rectitude and courage, even in times of peril and passion. His political participation, far from earning him any reward, brought him imprisonment and banishment; despite his constant militancy, he never occupied any public position. This adversity contributed to his retirement in 1946 and left him with an overwhelming sense of moral ostracism from his own land in the last years of his life. His was an inner banishment ("banished here, in my own country," as he put it), an isolation marked by a deep religious feeling, akin to that of the Spanish mystics, whom he greatly admired. He felt that Argentina was becoming estranged from the ideals of the period of Independence and of the early Republic, particularly under Peron. He died on 29 July 1957, impoverished but the object of the respect of the Argentine people, especially the young.

Rojas left to his country his Andalusian-Indian-style house, which he loved so much, as well as his books and all his possessions. With the passage of time, somewhat mysteriously, as no effort was made by anyone, Rojas' memory has been reawakened in the consciousness of the Argentine people. Today streets, schools, parks, libraries, and political centers are named in his honor. Now that many of the tensions in the midst of which he lived have spent themselves, Rojas emerges as an exemplary teacher, as a writer with a sense of duty, and as an archetypal citizen.

Rojas sought to continue in contemporary Argentina the tradition of the great writers of the nineteenth century—fundamentally Sarmiento and Juan María Gutiérrez—who had striven to delve deeply into the national identity. When analyzing or passing judgment on their work he often betrayed an essential identification with them. He resembles them in his Americanist passion, in his belief in teaching as a forger of nationality, in the often pathetic search for the solid foundations of a nation threatened by despotism and demagogy. Like those archetypal figures whose work he studied with love, Rojas was an incorruptible interpreter of Argentine reality.

The fate of any successful original creation is

probably to enter the incessant stream of its culture without being alien to its own times. When examining Rojas' work after the passage of time, one can pass over the anecdotal elements and concentrate on what remains, on the profound truth of his work: his engaged vision. In a style often surprising for its fluctuation between a Hegelian objectivity and a Nietzschean fervor, Rojas' discourse is marked by esotericism and mythical projection. However, most characteristic of him is his search for original features in Argentine culture. Hostile to foreign models, he makes an effort to give voice to a culture that has been stifled and condemned to imitation and historical mutism. Rojas' texts, however, do not present a simplified vision of Argentina by means of dogmatic reductionism: he does not apply to concrete problems images of false, pacifying clarity, nor does he champion a concept of negative isolationism. Despite his nationalistic fervor, Rojas does not resort to retrospective complacency.

Rojas' characters are animated by an intense yearning for survival, as well as by actions that reveal the Argentine national identity. Without parting with the ecumenical rootedness of new cultures, his communion with his country and with Hispanic America asserts, together with a temporal link, a kind of Faustian alliance. The auguries that close and, more often, open his books (such as that of Onaisín in *Archipiélago*) and his attraction to myths and cosmogonies betoken a writing anxiously in search of a revelation of the imperishable. The most profound conflicts of nationality besiege the reader.

In his look backward, Rojas found in Argentine romanticism the fundamental points of departure for an original reflection about the New World and specifically about Argentina. His reading of Johann Gottfried von Herder encouraged him to search for the defining features of national culture in folkloric roots and in the Argentine temperament. Through Hippolyte Adolphe Taine, he confirmed his faith in aesthetic values as the sustenance of an original culture, despite his realization of the limitations imposed by Taine's determinism. Between 1912 and 1917, Rojas read G. W. F. Hegel with close attention, incorporating into his thought many ideas of the German philosopher, particularly those having to do with language and aesthetics. Spanish literature, especially epic and mystical poetry and theology, weighed heavily on him. As a historian and critic, he felt the fundamental influence of the work and counsel of Ramón Menéndez Pidal, with whom he maintained friendly correspondence from the beginning of the twentieth century.

To the diverse universal influences exerted over Rojas' work must be added those of his Argentine teachers, especially Gutiérrez and Sarmiento. In the portrait of Gutiérrez drawn in the third volume of *La literatura argentina, Los proscriptos* (The Outlaws, 1919), one senses the throbbing of deep affinities. Some of the features that point to Rojas as an intellectual heir of Gutiérrez are their shared nationalistic fervor, their study of universal culture, their pedagogical involvement, their love for indigenous and *gaucho* (cowboy) traditions, their need to throw light on the spiritual legacy of colonialism, their shared faith in the social promise implied in humanistic teachings, and their quiet abandonment of poetry in favor of research and teaching. Rojas confronted Sarmiento incessantly, arguing against his ideas, yet they share a passion for popular education, a deep feeling for America, and an eager search for guiding truths. These two self-taught men from the provinces hold strong opinions about race, and they are passionate interpreters of native reality, and counselors and admonishers of their country's destiny.

Regardless of the genre in which he wrote, Rojas always attributed reason and inspiration to the New World, particularly to Peru, Latin America's heart, which he monitored with care. "He gives breath to his America, and draws life from it," Rubén Darío said of him ("Ricardo Rojas," *Mundial* [Paris], January 1913). It was by virtue of his Americanist perspective that Rojas was able to widen the universal spaces of Argentine cultural expression. In his studies of and peregrinations to other cultures, he never forgot his native soil. His familiarity with abstruse philosophical treatises, his inexhaustible intellectual curiosity, and his self-criticism run undisclosed through his polemical texts. It is not possible to cover in a brief summary the rich, diverse oeuvre of this humanist of the New World. The fact that the cultural mélange assembled by Rojas contains subtle contradictions resulting from its diverse sources does not threaten its coherence or dissipate its dramatic features.

If it is true that in his work *La restauración nacionalista* Rojas conceived of history as the center of an Argentine *paideia*, with the passing of time and particularly after his intense research in Argentine literature he derived more confidence from the live message of contemporary writers as the nucleus of the Argentine renaissance that he proclaimed. He recognized that literature is not a cultural ornament but a signal of a profound critical displacement toward man. Argentina stopped being the land of cattle and corn, a peripheral geography marked by isolation and imitation, to become the soil from which the original word could sprout, from which a prophetic voice could speak.

Rojas' work in its totality, despite the many challenges and reservations it caused, represents one of the most intense contributions to an understanding of Argentina. Any Argentine who searches for the roots of his historic personality will find inspiration in it. Whether with singular dialectical vigor or with quivering lyrical mysticism, with erudite analyses or original dramatizations, Rojas' obsessive theme is always his country. Rojas' permanence, however, is founded not only in his books but also in what we may term his ethical genius. Together with his efforts and devotion as writer and teacher, poet and erudite, his Americanist idealism plunged him into action, far from the cultural bureaucracies. His was constantly the heroic solitude of the intellectual pitted against the powers of the world. The glory of this formidable humanist of the New World has streaks of passion and pain, wisdom and beauty. Even the least dramatic of his writings discloses the burning bush. His words do not need phantasmal resurrections, linked as they are to the richest, most valuable expressions of the Argentine spirit. His life and work constitute an idealistic incentive, an outstanding example.

Translated from the Spanish by Rolando Costa Picazo

SELECTED BIBLIOGRAPHY

Editions

Poetry

La victoria del hombre. Buenos Aires, 1903.
Las lises del blasón. Buenos Aires, 1911.

Canciones. Buenos Aires, 1920.
Oda latina. Buenos Aires, 1954.

Plays

Elelín. Buenos Aires, 1929.
La casa colonial. Buenos Aires, 1938.
Ollantay. Buenos Aires, 1939.
La salamanca. Buenos Aires, 1943.

Short Stories

El país de la selva. Paris, 1907.

Essays and Biographical and Critical Studies

El alma española. Valencia, 1908.
Cartas de Europa. Barcelona, 1908.
Cosmópolis. Paris, 1908.
La restauración nacionalista. Buenos Aires, 1909.
Blasón de plata. Buenos Aires, 1912.
La argentinidad. Buenos Aires, 1916.
La literatura argentina. 4 vols. Buenos Aires, 1917–1922.
Los arquetipos. Buenos Aires, 1922.
Eurindia. Buenos Aires, 1924.
El Cristo invisible. Buenos Aires, 1927.
Las provincias. Buenos Aires, 1927.
Silabario de la decoración americana. Buenos Aires, 1930.
El radicalismo de mañana. Buenos Aires, 1932.
El santo de la espada: Vida de San Martín. Buenos Aires, 1933.
Cervantes. Buenos Aires, 1935.
Retablo español. Buenos Aires, 1938.
Archipiélago: Tierra del Fuego. Buenos Aires, 1942.
El profeta de la pampa: Vida de Sarmiento. Buenos Aires, 1945.
Un titan de los Andes. Buenos Aires, 1949.
Ensayo de crítica histórica sobre episodios de la vida internacional argentina. Buenos Aires, 1951.

Collected Works

Obras de Ricardo Rojas. 29 vols. Buenos Aires, 1923–1930.
Obras completas de Ricardo Rojas. 30 vols. Buenos Aires, 1947–1953.

Translations

"The Incubus." Translated by Harriet de Onís. In *The Golden Land.* New York, 1948. Pp. 205–209.
The Invisible Christ. Translated by Webster E. Browning. New York, 1931.
Latin Ode. Translated by Bernardo Frichard. Buenos Aires, 1953.
San Martín, Knight of the Andes. Translated by Herschel Brickell and Carlos Videla. New York, 1945.

Biographical and Critical Studies

Díaz, Exequiel. *Ricardo Rojas, el escritor argentino.* Tucumán, Argentina, 1980.
Glauert, Earl T. "Ricardo Rojas and the Emergence of Argentine Cultural Nationalism." *The Hispanic American Historical Review* 43/1:1–13 (1963).
Guardia, Alfredo de la. *Ricardo Rojas.* Buenos Aires, 1967.
"Homenaje a Ricardo Rojas." *Revista iberoamericana* 23/46:221–448 (1958).
Homenaje a Ricardo Rojas. Revista de la Universidad de Buenos Aires 3/3 (1958).
Moya, Ismael. *Ricardo Rojas.* Buenos Aires, 1961.
La obra de Rojas: Veinticinco años de labor literaria. Buenos Aires, 1928.
Pagés Larraya, Antonio. *Ricardo Rojas y su valoración de la cultura argentina.* Córdoba, Argentina, 1966.
———. "Ricardo Rojas: Literatura y espíritu nacional." *Boletín de la Academia Argentina de Letras* 185–186:165–210 (1982).
Payá, Carlos, and Fernando Cárdenas. *El primer nacionalismo argentino en Manuel Gálvez y Ricardo Rojas.* Buenos Aires, 1978.
Pickenhayn, Jorge Oscar. *La obra literaria de Ricardo Rojas.* Buenos Aires, 1982.
Stabb, Martin S. *In Quest of Identity.* Chapel Hill, N.C., 1967. Pp. 61–74, 147–151.
Testimonios sobre Ricardo Rojas. Buenos Aires, 1984.

Bibliographies

Becco, Jorge Eduardo. "Bibliografía de Ricardo Rojas." *Revista iberoamericana* 23/46:335–350 (1958).
Salvador, Nélida. "Ensayo de bibliografía de Ricardo Rojas." *Revista de la Universidad de Buenos Aires* 3/3:479–490 (1958).

Pedro Henríquez Ureña

(1884–1946)

Enrique Anderson Imbert

Pedro Henríquez Ureña is one of the greatest humanists of Spanish America. Although he cultivated almost all literary genres with elegance, his position in the history of the culture is not that of an artist but of an educator. He was born in Santo Domingo, Dominican Republic, on 29 June 1884. His father, Francisco Henríquez y Carvajal, was a doctor and a writer, and became president of the republic. His mother, Salomé Ureña, a poet, founded the Instituto de Señoritas. Henríquez Ureña was already writing poems and essays when in 1901 he graduated from high school in Santo Domingo. The following year he continued his studies at New York's Columbia University.

In 1904 Henríquez Ureña moved to Cuba, where he published studies about Rubén Darío, Eugenio Maríade Hostos, Gabriele D'Annunzio, George Bernard Shaw, and Oscar Wilde, works that he gathered together in his first book, *Ensayos críticos* (Critical Essays, 1905). When in 1906 he established himself in Mexico, his thinking was still positivist, in the line of Auguste Comte, but soon he converted to idealism, influenced by his readings of Immanuel Kant. His studies from his years in Mexico deal with the Renaissance in Spain, for example, "El maestro Hernán Pérez de Oliva" (Hernán Pérez de Oliva, the Teacher) and his psychological and moral interpreta-

tion of Don Juan Ruiz de Alarcón. With the publication of the essay "El verso endecasílabo" (The Hendecasyllabic Verse), he began his lifelong study of Spanish versification.

In 1914, having obtained his law degree in Mexico, Henríquez Ureña passed through Cuba en route to the United States, where he remained until 1921. These were very busy years: he contributed literary articles, in both Spanish and English, to newspapers of several countries; he published the definitive version of *El nacimiento de Dionisos: Ensayo de tragedia antigua* (The Birth of Dionysus: Essay of Ancient Tragedy, 1916); he taught at the University of Minnesota (1916); from the same university he received the degrees of master of arts (1917) and doctor of philosophy (1918). He interrupted this second stay in the United States twice to visit Spain, in 1917 and 1919. He made contacts during these visits with the philological group of the Centro de Estudios Históricos, directed by Ramón Menéndez Pidal.

In 1920 Menéndez Pidal wrote the prologue to Henríquez Ureña's doctoral dissertation at Minnesota: "The Irregular Stanza in the Spanish Poetry of the Sixteenth and Seventeenth Centuries." Henríquez Ureña expanded his dissertation in a reissue and continued to refine it; in the posthumous edi-

597

tion of *Estudios de versificación española* (Studies of Spanish Versification, 1961) it was included along with other works about meter and with the article "En busca del verso puro" (In Search of Pure Verse, 1926–1928), in which he proposes a basic definition of verse. The example of Menéndez Pidal and his disciples stimulated him to work with a scientific method. His "Observaciones sobre el español en América" (Observations about Spanish in America), published in the *Revista de filología española* in 1921, 1930, and 1931, outlined a map of Hispanic-American linguistic regions. (See in the bibliography his other works about Hispanic-American linguistics and dialectology.)

In 1921 Henríquez Ureña resigned his teaching position at Minnesota and accepted an appointment as a professor at the University of Mexico. When he visited Buenos Aires the following year, he already had completed *En la orilla: Mi España* (On the Shore: My Spain, 1922), a compilation of his essays about Spanish literature. He returned to Mexico, and in 1923 he discovered his calling as a storyteller: first he wrote stories for children—*Cuentos de la Nana Lupe* (Stories of Nanny Lupe, 1966)—and later, between 1924 and 1946, he wrote four stories for adult readers. He married in 1923, and the next year he made a permanent move to Argentina. He lived in La Plata until 1930, and after that in Buenos Aires.

In this Argentine period, Henríquez Ureña was in his prime. In La Plata, as a professor at the Colegio Nacional, he and Alejandro Korn, a philosopher and director of the magazine *Valoraciones* (Evaluations), contributed to the transformation of the city into an important cultural center. Upon moving to Buenos Aires, he devoted himself to such a variety of activities that it is not possible to follow him step by step. Even his long list of publications does not give an idea of the many things that he did: classes at the Colegio Nacional, at the universities of La Plata and Buenos Aires, at the Instituto del Profesorado, and at other private institutions, such as the Colegio Libre de Estudios Superiores; contributions in newspapers all over the continent, especially in the *Revista de filología hispánica,* directed by Amado Alonso; the editing of anthologies and of the series "Cien obras maestras de la literatura y del pensamiento universal" (One Hundred Master Works of Literature and Uni-

versal Thought); the direction of doctoral dissertations, lectures, and participation in literary gatherings, where he was always a master because of the Socratic quality of his dialogue; and the publication of several books.

Two trips interrupted his stay in Argentina: one to the Dominican Republic from December 1931 to June 1933 to hold the position of general superintendent of education; and the other to the United States in 1940–1941, where he had been invited by Harvard University to occupy the Charles Eliot Norton chair. At Harvard he delivered the eight lectures that constitute one of his principal works: *Literary Currents in Hispanic America* (1945). The subject of this book is the unity of Spanish America, a unity with different gradations of color. Most importantly, he analyzes the differences with Europe and English-speaking America, as well as the differences between the Portuguese and Spanish populations in America. Within the Spanish portion, he describes the personality of each country. Aesthetic trends are not treated as empty abstractions. Henríquez Ureña is attentive to the contradictory features of each aesthetic period without neglecting the personality of each writer. Literary aspects appear in the foreground but are not separated from the other manifestations of American life. When Henríquez Ureña describes the evolution of artistic ideals, he skillfully alludes to the social context. Although the main merit of the book lies in his vision of the whole, his brief characterizations of some writers, such as José Martí, are also excellent. Discussions of music, the plastic arts, philosophy, and science also contribute to an admirable balance. Behind this work—indeed, behind all that he wrote and did—lies his conception of the world.

The first philosophical system that Henríquez Ureña became acquainted with was the positivism of Comte, Ernst Haeckel, and Herbert Spencer. He discovered it in his own home, since his parents had been collaborators of Eugenio María de Hostos, a Puerto Rican who was the most talented representative of positivism in Hispanic America. In all the studies that Henríquez Ureña dedicated to Hostos or in those in which he spoke about him, he always emphasized the importance that Hostos assigned to morality:

. . . his moral preoccupation was never absent. Every-thing has an ethical meaning for this thinker. . . . And his ethic is rational: he believes that the knowledge of good leads to the practice of good; evil is error. . . . Since reason is the cornerstone of his moral code, he will spread the cult of reason and its product in modern times: natural sciences.

("Ciudadano de América," *La Nación* [Buenos Aires], 28 April 1935)

Apparently Hostos did not see any conflict between Truth and Good. For him, as for his teachers Comte and Christian F. Krause, those values were harmonious. However, Henríquez Ureña came to feel that Hostos' theory of knowledge weakened the affirmative tone of his theory of values. If we are not able to know the Truth, how can we know what Good is? This doubt assailed him when he continued his readings in Mexico between 1906 and 1914. His thinking matured with disquieting questions, and thanks to his new readings, above all of the works of Kant, he renounced positivism. "Positivism," he wrote in 1909 to his brother Max, "is already dead and buried. Now it's a matter of resolving what value knowledge has. Modern philosophy since Kant has arrived at the conclusion that we cannot know the essence of things." As evidenced by this quote, Henríquez Ureña had become a skeptic. But there are many types of skepticism. Which kind of skeptic was he? The key is found in his essay about Enrique José Varona that, with the title "El maestro de Cuba" (The Teacher of Cuba), he published in *La Nación* of Buenos Aires on 15 March 1936:

> . . . from the time his thinking reaches its period of maturity, Varona separates himself step by step from all positivism. The public began to regard him as a skeptic. . . . He confessed intellectual *skepticism* in the area of pure reason, but he declared that he espoused practical reason. Skepticism is not divorced from action.

Note the deliberate and emphatic opposition of the next-to-last sentence, "pure reason" versus "practical reason," with which Henríquez Ureña alludes to the two *Critiques* of Kant. Kant passed from the *Critique of Pure Reason* (1781), where he denied metaphysical knowledge, to the *Critique of Practical Reason* (1788), which based morality on a metaphysical "good will." Henríquez Ureña, on the other hand, passes from

skepticism to action without reference to metaphysics; man's animal nature is enough for him. And, in fact, in that same essay about Varona he writes: "Years later another thinker of Hispanic origin, George Santayana, adopts a similar position: he takes skepticism to its profound roots, but later on he resorts to practical faith in the existence of the universe, to 'animal faith'."

Here Henríquez Ureña refers to *Scepticism and Animal Faith* (1923), in which Santayana—after showing that idealistic skepticism challenges the existence, not only of the external world, but also of the "I" of all men—diverts his skeptical philosophy toward a positivist position: the "animal faith" in a world of things and happenings impossible to prove, but one that is the source of a vital wisdom. Henríquez Ureña had pointed out the importance of *Scepticism and Animal Faith* as early as 1927. He said then that Santayana's work "contained the seeds of the philosophical conception that would be defined as characteristic of the twentieth century: critical realism."

The philosophical position of Henríquez Ureña is between "critical realism" and "critical idealism." For him there is a reality independent of consciousness, although we are aware of it through consciousness. Consciousness constructs its own world but is part of nature, and consequently there must be some correspondence between the qualities that we perceive and the nature of things, there must be some foundation between the form of our understanding and sensory matter. For Henríquez Ureña, such a correspondence is natural, not metaphysical. He never explained his theory of knowledge in a systematic fashion and as a result, we cannot know at what point in his skeptical philosophy originate the aesthetic and ethical values that he recommended as true ones. He probably believed that the Gordian knot of problems is cut with the blade of action, and for this reason he devoted himself to the history of culture, which in reality is a history of actions. He did not formulate norms of art or of morality, but they are implied in his judgments of the creations and conduct of man.

In aesthetics Henríquez Ureña practiced a criticism that was mindful of the most prominent expressive values in each artist, in every period, in every tendency, in every culture. He cultivated all the arts, celebrating in their respective mediums—word, sound, color, movement, solid material—the same desire for beauty. His attitude was anthological, and in fact, he planned, published, and disseminated several anthologies of poetry and prose. His principles originated at the point of convergence, discussed earlier, of "critical realism" and "critical idealism." In other words, as Wilhelm Humboldt declared, "language is not a product but a producing"; genres and schools are not normative institutions but historical concepts; literature is not imitation, but creation. Progress is achieved, not with exterior conquests in the field of art, but from within the soul, when the artist passes from spiritual tension to expressive achievement. Surprise or amazement in the presence of change is certainly an aesthetic emotion, but so is the capacity to be amazed by the great styles of the past. The most important aspect is individual originality, but since man lives in society, even his innovations carry traditions within them. A profound work surges from the author's total vision of the world, and if that vision fills itself with images that enter from the pursuit of philosophy, morality, mysticism, or politics, the work gains in universal meaning without losing its aesthetic value.

Perhaps the page that best allows us to glimpse Henríquez Ureña's attitude toward literature is the one that, with the title of "El ansia de perfección" (The Longing for Perfection), makes up "El descontento y la promesa" (Discontent and the Promise), one of the *Seis ensayos en busca de nuestra expresión* (Six Essays in Search of Our Expression, 1928). For Henríquez Ureña, such a longing for perfection is not that of aesthetics, which considers art to be superior to life, but is rather that of an ethical norm: we should strive to attain an expression that reveals not only intimate personal experiences, but also the universal meaning of life.

"I am not contemplative," he wrote to Alfonso Reyes in 1925. "Perhaps I am not even a writer in the pure sense of the word; I feel the need to influence people with my activity, even on a small scale." Henríquez Ureña tended to throw himself into action, pedagogical action; however, this action, because of his profound moral commitment, encouraged his students to militate in favor of a liberal, parliamentary, secular, anti-imperialistic, and socialist democracy. His skepticism did not allow him to defend an objective axiology. Nevertheless, he placed himself at the service of a lived morality as if it were not subjective and relative. He was aristocratic in his tastes. He corrected ignorance, denounced barbarism, pitied mediocrity, and hated demagoguery. He wanted the intelligent, cultured, just minorities to raise up the masses. He was in favor of change—not just any kind of change, but change dictated by the intellect. He was in favor of a change in the economic structure to eliminate the inequality of the classes; a change in the political regime to install an enlightened democracy; a change in the pedagogical system in order to foster a secular morality, personal interpretation, scientific education, and the complete development of the human personality. In his desire for change it did not matter to him that others considered him to be utopian. He believed in utopia. His speeches "La utopía de América" (The Utopia of America, 1922) and "Patria de la justicia" (Homeland of Justice, 1925) inspired the youth, also utopian, from the Argentine University Reform, which supported democracy, liberalism, new ideas, and new methods of scholarship. He told them: "The ideal of justice comes before the ideal of culture; a man who is an ardent supporter of justice is superior to one who only aspires to his own intellectual perfection."

Henríquez Ureña died on 11 May 1946 when he was traveling from Buenos Aires to La Plata to teach a class at the university.

Translated from the Spanish by Henry Thurston

SELECTED BIBLIOGRAPHY

Editions

Ensayos críticos. Havana, 1905.
Horas de estudio. Paris, 1910.
Tablas cronológicas de la literatura española. Mexico City, 1913.
El nacimiento de Dionisos. New York, 1916.
La versificación irregular en la poesía castellana. Madrid, 1920.
En la orilla: Mi España. Mexico City, 1922.
La utopía de América. La Plata, Argentina, 1925.
El libro del idioma. In collaboration with Narciso Binayán. Buenos Aires, 1927.

Seis ensayos en busca de nuestra expresión. Buenos Aires, 1928.

"*El teatro de la América Española en la época colonial.*" *Cuadernos de cultura teatral* 3:9–50 (1936).

La cultura y las letras coloniales en Santo Domingo. Buenos Aires, 1936.

Sobre el problema del andalucismo dialectal en América. Buenos Aires, 1937.

Gramática castellana. In collaboration with Amado Alonso. Buenos Aires, 1938–1939.

Para la historia de los indigenismos. Buenos Aires, 1938.

El español en Santo Domingo. Buenos Aires, 1940.

Plenitud de España. Buenos Aires, 1940.

Literary Currents in Hispanic America. Cambridge, Mass., 1945.

Historia de la cultura en la América Hispánica. Mexico City, 1947. Posthumous.

Poesías juveniles. Bogotá, 1949. Posthumous.

Estudios de versificación española. Buenos Aires, 1961. Posthumous.

Cuentos de la Nana Lupe. Mexico City, 1966. Posthumous.

Memorias. Notas de Viaje. Diario. To be published. Alfredo A. Roggiano has published fragments in *Pedro Henríquez Ureña en los Estados Unidos*, Mexico City, 1961, and in *Revista iberoamericana* 51/130–131:321–343 (1985).

Collected Works

Epistolario íntimo. Pedro Henríquez Ureña y Alfonso Reyes (1906–1946). 3 vols. Santo Domingo, Dominican Republic, 1981.

Obras completas. Edited by Juan Jacobo de Lara. 10 vols. Santo Domingo, Dominican Republic, 1976–1980.

Anthologies

Páginas escogidas. With a prologue by Alfonso Reyes. Mexico City, 1946.

Antología. With a prologue by Max Henríquez Ureña. Ciudad Trujillo, Dominican Republic, 1950.

Ensayos en busca de nuestra expresión. Introductions by Alfonso Reyes and Ezequiel Martínez Estrada. Buenos Aires, 1952.

Plenitud de América. With an introduction by Javier Fernández. Buenos Aires, 1952.

Obra crítica. With a prologue by Jorge Luis Borges. Mexico City, 1960. Contains "Crono-bibliografía de Pedro Henríquez Ureña," by Emma Susana Speratti Piñero.

Pedro Henríquez Ureña en los Estados Unidos. Compiled by Alfredo A. Roggiano. Mexico City, 1961.

Pedro Henríquez Ureña. With a prologue by Ernesto Sábato. Buenos Aires, 1967.

Universidad y educación. Mexico City, 1969.

Ensayos. With a prologue by José Rodríguez Feo. Havana, 1973.

La utopía de América. With a prologue by Rafael Gutiérrez Girardot. Caracas, 1978.

Editions and Anthologies of the Classics

For many years, Pedro Henríquez Ureña directed the series "One Hundred Master Works" for the publisher Editorial Losada in Buenos Aires. He personally edited more than twenty classic works, for each of which he provided a prologue. Moreover, he published important authors in several anthologies:

Antología del centenario. In collaboration with Luis G. Urbina and others. Mexico City, 1910.

Cien de las mejores poesías castellanas. Buenos Aires, 1929; 2nd ed., corrected and enlarged, 1941.

Antología clásica de la literatura argentina. In collaboration with Jorge Luis Borges. Buenos Aires, 1937.

Biographical and Critical Studies

Carilla, Emilio. *Pedro Henríquez Ureña: Tres estudios.* Tucumán, Argentina, 1956.

_____ "Pedro Henríquez Ureña: Biografía comentada." *Inter-American Review of Bibliography* 27/3:227–239. (1977).

Henríquez Ureña, Max. *Hermano y maestro.* Ciudad Trujillo, Dominican Republic, 1950.

Homenaje a Pedro Henríquez Ureña. Sur 15/141:7–44 (1946).

Homenaje a Pedro Henríquez Ureña. Ciudad Trujillo, Dominican Republic, 1947.

Homenaje a Pedro Henríquez Ureña. Revista iberoamericana 21:41–42 (1956).

Lara, Juan Jacobo de. *Pedro Henríquez Ureña: Su vida y su obra.* Santo Domingo, Dominican Republic, 1976.

El libro jubilar de Pedro Henríquez Ureña. 2 vols. Santo Domingo, Dominican Republic, 1984.

Pedro Henríquez Ureña: 1884–1946. Centenario de su nacimiento. Sur 355 (July–December 1984) .

Sánchez Reulet, Aníbal. "Pensamiento y mensaje en Pedro Henríquez Ureña." *Revista iberoamericana* 21/41–42: 61–67 (1956).

Rómulo Gallegos

(1884–1969)

Jorge Ruffinelli

Rómulo Gallegos, whose complete name was Rómulo Ángel del Monte Carmelo Gallegos Freire, was born in Caracas, Venezuela, on 2 August 1884; he died in the same city on 5 April 1969. He was respected and admired for his written works, especially his widely read novel *Doña Bárbara* (1929), and for his activities as a teacher and politician.

In 1897 he experienced a strong religious calling and was on the point of entering the priesthood; later he became an agnostic with deep social preoccupations. In line with the philosophic trends of his time, above all with positivism, he became a freethinker and denounced the clerical life, calling for the removal of power and influence from the Catholic church. He advocated a collection of ideas influenced by Max Nordau, Ángel María Ganivet, Ernest Renan, and especially Jean-Jacques Rousseau. Also while young, he began to study law but gave it up during his first years at the university.

In 1909, with some friends of his generation, he founded the magazine *La alborada* (The First Dawn of Day), in which he published articles and essays that analyzed the Venezuelan social and cultural reality with a strong reformist zeal. His renown as an educator came from these essays and his later work as a teacher. Most of his numerous essays dedicated to educational questions and an examination of society

have been collected in *Una posición en la vida* (A Posture in Life, 1954).

Gallegos' ideas on politics, society, and education were products of the current predominant philosophic trends and of his country's political situation. From the nineteenth century until well into the twentieth, Venezuela was governed by authoritarian regimes. In 1899, following a short civil war, the army controlled the nation. In 1909, Juan Vincente Gómez' dictatorship began; it was to last until his death in 1935. During this period of political repression, Venezuela used its oil wealth to modernize and experienced even more rapid development in the two decades that followed Gomez' death. The country underwent an urbanization process, especially in Caracas, which became a megalopolis, losing the provincial flavor it had possessed in the nineteenth century. The country's industry and its highway network expanded during this economic boom.

On Gomez' death, other military men took his place, but in 1948, because of a coup d'état that permitted a brief period of democratic rule, Gallegos was elected president of the republic by an overwhelming majority of votes. However, popular backing was no guarantee of his tenure in the presidency; nine months after taking office, he was overthrown by the military, and the ten-year dictatorship of

Marcos Pérez Jiménez began. Gallegos lived in exile in Cuba and Mexico, making numerous visits to Central America, the United States, and Europe.

Military oppression in Venezuela and his overthrow as president increased Gallegos' political preachings and his protests against armed regimes, which he criticized as obstacles to the free and integral development of Spanish America. Gallegos' intellectual formation partook of the humanist tradition that defends spiritual values and that was given voice at the beginning of the century by José Enrique Rodó's *Ariel* (1900). The "arielist generation" of writers broke off from the modernists and from the exaggerated cult of French *parnasse* aesthetics, focusing instead on the theme of the American reality in literature and thought. Their concern was mainly with issues of a spiritual or, in some cases, political nature, but Gallegos also took the social dimension into account, especially when farmland conflicts were involved.

When Gallegos entered wholeheartedly into political life and rose to the presidency of Venezuela, he had already written and published his most important novels. Gallegos said that there had been "a loan from letters to politics, with no fixed repayment date" (*Una posición en la vida*, p. 383). The object that had been lent was himself. From 1948 on, he did not write as prolifically as before. He wrote a novel on a Cuban theme, *La brizna de paja en el viento* (Straw in the Wind, 1952) and another, on Mexico, *La tierra bajo los pies* (Land Underfoot, which appeared posthumously in 1971).

Gallegos' first two novels, *Reinaldo Solar* (first published in 1920 as *El último Solar* [The Last Solar]) and *La trepadora* (The Creeper, 1925), are the early, uncertain creations of an author who was to become a self-confident narrator with a well-defined style. In these novels Gallegos displayed several characteristics that later were developed in his major works and transformed into constant and dominant elements. For example, Gallegos often used characters and dramatic situations as symbols, extending this practice to the very titles of his novels. The original title *El último Solar* referred both to a person—the book dealt with the last of a family line—and to the family's property (*solar* means a plot of land, a rural property). In the case of the other novel, a *trepadora*

is a parasitic plant that fixes itself to a wall or a tree trunk and lives with the support of such an object while also strengthening it. Symbolically, the relationship that the plant establishes alludes to certain human behavior. The symbolic nature of both people and events becomes a weakness of Gallegos' novels when it limits the free development of his characters.

In 1949 Gallegos discussed his symbolic bent, justifying it as necessary to the creation of meaningful characters within the concrete reality of Venezuela. He said: "I am not just a plain creator of human cases, of those which may arise in my country, or any other . . . but I do point out generically characteristic aspects that as a Venezuelan hurt or please me (*Una posición en la vida*, pp. 403–404). Yet Gallegos' bent for symbols and stereotypes arises not only from a direct vision of reality and the need to find meaning in it, but also to some themes from past literature, above all, one that contrasts civilization with barbarism, an opposition that forms the dramatic and ideological basis of *Doña Bárbara* and that originated with the Argentine Domingo Faustino Sarmiento, whose book *Civilización i barbarie* (1845) carried the title in English translation *Life in the Argentine Republic in the Days of the Tyrants*. Sarmiento identified civilization with Europe and barbarism with the Spanish-American countries.

In *Reinaldo Solar*, Gallegos summarizes the experience of his generation, or at least that of the young writers closest to him who had started *La alborada*. The characters of the novel are modeled on his friends, and Gallegos sketches a living and true portrait of the psychological and intellectual atmosphere of those years. The book is the novelistic equivalent of the essays published in *La alborada*; his characters are writers and artists, and Gallegos frequently cites the names of Thomas à Kempis, Renan, Leo Tolstoy, Rousseau, Friedrich Nietzsche, Nordau, Cesare Lombroso, Lord Byron, Émile Zola, the authors he read. One of the novel's most powerful themes is the return to nature, with a strong Rousseauistic flavor. The objective is not social but individual, inspired by the romantic movement. Reinaldo Solar writes a novel and speaks the first lines aloud: "(He) was going to look there, in mother nature's bosom, for the way to reconstruct the moral being, like a plant which, deformed by culture, returns to the jungle to recover the vigor of its original savage state."

Gallegos' social optimism comes into the open in *La trepadora,* an allegorical vision of the patchwork of Venezuelan society. A rich landowner's illegitimate son, born to a humble coffee picker on the estate, feels a burning ambition for revenge; he gains social position and marries the daughter of a rich family. Their child, Victoria, bears the features of both parents, which reflect the social groups that Gallegos defines and characterizes: the "barbarism" of her illegitimate and lowborn father and the "civilization" of her wealthy mother. This novel may seem to be an example of class struggle, because it depicts an antagonism between landowners and laborers; however, that social vision is complicated by a racial ideology that sees Spanish America as a melting pot in which the genuine American is the result of a mixture of races with different and defined features and idiosyncrasies. In this racial vision, the Hispanic and Creole groups are dominant, while the natives make up the lower classes. Gallegos explained his intention: "I did not want to depict class struggle as the standpoint of *La trepadora,* rather that it should be a portrait of the formation of a people."

Beginning in 1922, Gallegos was a teacher at the secondary level. This experience led him to explore child psychology and the educational needs of Venezuela. Along with other Latin American writers after 1900, Gallegos constantly called for more education and greater support for the arts, with Europe as the model. His anti–North American stance was not so much a response to the expansionist policy of the United States as it was opposition to the pragmatism and materialism upon which, as he saw it, its culture was based. In the course of many lectures delivered in the United States, Gallegos strongly urged the development of a humanistic culture that was not to be formulated upon a quantitative or technical basis. For Gallegos, the machine (symbol of technological progress in the United States), instead of lightening the workload of the proletariat, provides more profits for the bosses and therefore becomes an enemy of the people. He also underlined the fetishism of higher education in the United States: the importance placed upon the university from which a student graduates turns a human being into merchandise in the labor market, with a higher or lower price according to the "trademark." Gallegos demanded that instruction be replaced by education, and he distinguished between humanist and technical culture, attributing to the latter and its defenders an antihumanist attitude that endangers the very existence of humanity. The antinomy of technology versus humanism is parallel and complementary to the theme of civilization versus barbarism.

As much as it is a novel of ideas, *Doña Bárbara* is a story of strong characters who personify contradictory values in a struggle that illustrates socioeconomic change throughout the Venezuelan countryside, from the wild and barren *latifundio* (a large, neglected estate) to the "civilized" small holding. It has been said that *Doña Bárbara* is the novel of the Venezuelan plains that best explains the region and its inhabitants during the time when Spanish-American cultures were concerned with their national identities and with the larger Latin American identity. Gallegos' *Canaima* (Canaima, 1935) could be called a novel of the jungle, to round out the geographical varieties in Venezuela. In both areas, until well into the twentieth century the *latifundio* dominated: the landowner played the part of a feudal lord, and the peasants were his vassals, as if they were in the Middle Ages and the era of independence were nothing more than an aborted dream. In *Doña Bárbara,* Gallegos joins the ideas of Sarmiento (civilization versus barbarism) and Juan Bautista Alberdi (to govern is to populate, to populate is to civilize) with the national stereotypes visualized through folklore. He characterizes the plainsmen as belonging to an "emphatic race" much given to speech making. He portrays the barbed-wire fence as a symbol of the division of property: it marks the beginning of the "civilization of the plains" and becomes a "civilizing innovation."

A strange element in this novel is at the same time the main feature of its originality: the feudal lord is not a man but a woman. Doña Bárbara encapsulates in her symbolic name the strength and regressive tendency that it represents. She is known as the "strong woman of Arauca," the "man eater," and "the sorceress." As if she were something to be feared by men, the Spanish-American woman was (and still is) socially and politically relegated. That a woman is the main character in the novel makes her doubly to be feared. Tension builds when Santos Luzardo arrives, determined to defend both his right to a small property he had inherited and, by implication, the right to civilization. Santos' name is his badge: he is an emissary of good (*santos*, saints) symbolically illuminated by a light that burns (*luz*, light; *ardo*, I burn). The symbolism of the names goes further: one of the accomplices of Doña Bárbara is a North American called Mister Danger.

When Doña Bárbara begins her personal war against Santos Luzardo, anything goes, even seduction. She had been raped in her adolescence, and although she has a strong desire to revenge herself and to destroy the male-dominated world, Doña Bárbara is a sensual woman, and she feels a complex attraction toward her incorruptible adversary, Santos. However, neither open violence nor witchcraft are sufficient to overcome such a powerful opponent, and because of Gallegos' faith in the progress of which Santos is the symbol, he has to be the overwhelming victor.

The novel is narrated in a compelling descriptive manner that presents a coherent design of characters and events. Its prose is rich and varied, flexible and expressive. Its main strength lies in the development of the plot and the intense changes in the condition of the characters; its meaning is not so simple and schematic as may be supposed. The characters experience real growth and form dynamic relationships. In *Don Quixote*, Sancho Panza absorbs idealism from his boss, while Don Quixote is influenced by Sancho's pragmatic character; a similar phenomenon occurs between Doña Bárbara and Santos. She shows herself capable of unexpected acts of abnegation—for example, in the end she disappears in order to resolve the struggle—and Santos, in turn, begins to feel a slight and perverse pleasure in savagery. During the rodeo, when the young bulls are castrated, Santos feels the barbaric impulse of brute force in action and thinks to himself: "After all, barbarism has its delights, and is something beautiful that is worth experiencing; it is the fullness of man rebelling against all limits." A dialogue between civilization and barbarism is established that makes more complex and interesting what was initially a Manichaean opposition.

This "impure" version of the dichotomy can be explained by the fact that European-influenced Spanish-American writers were shaken by the World War I and, ten years later, the rise of fascism, periods during which the face of barbarism showed itself where apparently civilization existed. Before this crisis of faith in Europe, Gallegos had very clearly proposed that Latin America should be inspired by Europe; America was considered "young," and Europe a "mature" continent and therefore wiser. Said Gallegos:

> Our model is Europe, which in the age of culture means maturity. America is virgin jungle, unexplored and untilled soil, empty land, desert, illiteracy, barbarism, barren and solitary instinct, lacking in principles, discipline and ideals. Europe is civilization, and civilization means tilled fields, population, roads, industry, culture, social discipline, social conscience, social ideals.
>
> (*Un posición en la vida*, pp. 85–86)

Gallegos added that his concept of Europe referred to "Europe as the cultural ideal," that is, to the idealization that Latin Americans had made of the Old World, as well as to "the inevitable spiritual penetration of culture as represented by Europe" in the coarse Spanish-American soil.

The dramatic force of *Doña Bárbara* comes from the struggle between values embedded in its characters, the unusual narrative drive that stands in contrast with the modernist and pedantic prose of the time, and its social and cultural preoccupations. The novel was rapidly and extensively disseminated throughout the continent and was quickly translated into eight different languages. At last, in *Doña Bárbara*, along with *La vorágine* (*The Vortex*, 1924) by the Colombian José Eustacio Rivera and *Don Segundo Sombra* (1926) by the Argentine Ricardo Güiraldes, Spanish America had produced novels that presented her conflicts, her goals, and her desires to leave her defeats behind.

In 1928 Gallegos delivered *Doña Bárbara* to a publishing house owned by a relative in Caracas. (The original title of the work was "La coronela" (The Colonel.) But, dissatisfied with his achievement, he destroyed what had been printed and stopped publication. He left for Europe and even tried to throw the original manuscript overboard. He finished the work in Bologna, and it was published in

1929 in Barcelona as a limited edition paid for by the author. The response to *Doña Bárbara* was immediate: the critics greeted its appearance with exhilaration, and influential intellectuals like Jorge Mañach hailed it as the great novel that America had been waiting for. A rapid succession of editions followed, and it became one of the most widely read novels in Spanish America. In 1930 it was published in Caracas and in 1931 was translated into English in New York. The doors of various countries opened for Gallegos because of *Doña Bárbara,* and he was able to live in Spain, especially during his self-imposed exile.

In 1936, with the dictator Gómez dead, Gallegos returned to Venezuela and in the Port of Guaira was met by a mass of people. Eight weeks later he was named secretary of public education, thus gaining the opportunity to put his reformist ideas into practice. However, from the moment that these reforms were announced, Gallegos met with a solid resistance from the educational sector and the press, and because of the heated debate that arose, he had to resign six weeks after taking the post.

During the period of his voluntary exile (1928–1936), Gallegos published two other novels of literary value: *Cantaclaro* (Cantaclaro, 1934) and *Canaima,* after which his work never attained the same quality. *Cantaclaro* is a polyphonic novel, and as did the earlier books, it presents life on the plains from the peculiar psychological perspective that underlies Gallegos' vision of Venezuelan man. He even proposes a theory of the plain: the extreme brightness and the monotony of the landscape form the characters, idiosyncrasies, and linguistic peculiarities of the inhabitants, as well as their characteristic imagination and even an oral literature that emerges spontaneously in the region. Since Gallegos founded his novel upon features of the local popular imagination, *Cantaclaro* has a poetic, almost lyrical, aura. The characters vary greatly in their activities and are the protagonists of diverse stories, but are united by the singer of tales, who is a kind of popular troubadour dedicated to capturing the lives of those around him with his poetry and music and who, as he crosses the plains, synthesizes and expresses their dramas. These dramas are multidimensional: Payara has a problem of conscience, believing that he maintains an incestuous relationship with Rosángela; Juan, "the

plainsman," is a peasant who, on the death of his wife and children, suddenly abandons his peaceful life and becomes a feared criminal; Juan Parao is a rebellious Negro who tries to cause a racial uprising and dreams of the country's independence. The diary of a nomadic bard who roams the plains allows Gallegos to play with legends, customs, and folkloric scenes, turning them into inspired prose. In a literary sense, *Cantaclaro* is superior to *Doña Bárbara* in the quality of the writing and its brilliant poetic tone, which place the novel, from a historic and aesthetic point of view, between fin de siècle modernism and naturalist creolism.

The tragic vision of Venezuela that permeates *Cantaclaro* recurs in *Canaima,* but this time the setting is the jungle of the Orinoco river valley. In this work Gallegos narrates the life and travels of his character, Marcos Vargas, from his childhood until he disappears to live among the Indians. Gallegos tries to make his leading character the epitome of the region: the macho, instinctive and brutal, though also capable of kindness and a strong desire for justice. Vargas is a soul searcher who carries on an almost superhuman struggle to merge with nature and to learn the "language" that man has lost because of civilization. This effort produces one of the most splendid episodes of all Gallegos' literature: the earthshattering, cosmic encounter between naked man and the jungle during a terrible storm, in the chapter titled "Tormentia" (Storm).

In *Canaima,* as in *Doña Bárbara,* justice fights against evil, embodied in a feudal family, the Ardavines, the principal tentacles of whose power are finally cut by Vargas. This novel presents Gallegos' recurring themes: the juxtaposition of civilization and barbarism, of idealism and materialism, and the search for what is firstborn and natural—all wrapped up in a story heavy with symbolism. The major symbolic event occurs at the end of *Canaima:* Vargas disappears from civilization, bent upon living with an Indian tribe, but he sends his adolescent son to the city, to his alter ego Gabriel Ureña, of whom he begs "that you educate him as you are educating your own sons." In the end, civilization overcomes instinct, and the book creates, although vaguely, the notions that culture consists of the fusion of civilization and barbarism, and that, as a nation, Venezuela should seek its future not in the destruction of one or the other of these elements, but in a balance between them.

In *Canaima*, Gallegos repeats a narrative conflict that appears in *Doña Bárbara* (that is, the rebellion of the individual against tyrannical power) but modifies the hero figure: in place of the almost totally positive Santos Luzardo appears the conflicted and passionate Vargas. This can be understood as a correction of the author's vision of Venezuelan reality and, at the same time, as a profound literary advance; Gallegos treats the basic antinomy of his novels less schematically and more richly. The central idea that runs throughout *Doña Bárbara* finds in *Canaima* a vein of deeper understanding of the reality of Venezuela and of Spanish America. In the course of his literary career, Gallegos turned away from the stereotypical, racist European point of view in favor of a more complex understanding of the autochthonous elements of the American experience, and the fine result was *Canaíma*.

While still living in Caracas, Gallegos finished another novel, *Pobre negro* (Poor Negro, 1937), which lacks the drive of his earlier books, except in its violent war scenes. Novelistic themes reappear, such as an illegitimate son fighting against his father's rich family, but essentially *Pobre negro* is a fable built around the rebellion against power, with slave uprisings that took place around 1860 as a historical backdrop.

That none of Gallegos' later novels have the quality or importance of the unplanned triptych made up of *Doña Bárbara, Cantaclaro*, and *Canaima* can be explained by the author's personal circumstances: the time devoted to politics and, later, a long exile. The meetings, speeches, and daily organizational activities of the Partido Acción Democrática (Democratic Action party) took time and effort away from Gallegos' literary creations; he wrote only some screenplays, one on Joan of Arc. It was during this period from 1935 to his death that Gallegos referred to his activities as "a loan from literature to politics."

In 1942, he published *El forastero* (The Stranger), an even weaker novel than *Pobre negro*. A rehash of a tale he had written in the 1920's, it deals with the story of a Russian immigrant who repairs a broken town-hall clock and awakens the people to rise up against the oppressive government. The details are ingenuously symbolic, as if the story were more a fable than a realistic novel. In *Sobre la misma tierra* (On the Same Land, 1943), the indomitable features of Doña Bárbara are reversed: Remota Montiel, a woman boss from the Guajira zone, is a virgin, lonely and without drive; Gallegos tries to portray her, as the critic Juan Liscano put it in 1968, as the symbol of "an untouched Venezuelan Indian and at the same time overcome by the works of the spirit."

Gallegos' last two novels were written in exile following his presidential downfall. In Havana, Gallegos wrote a story based on the political events that took place at the University of Havana after the fall of the dictator Gerardo Machado: this was *La brizna de paja en el viento*. The atmosphere of gangsterism in the university had impressed Gallegos. Politicized student groups had degenerated into delinquent mobs that seized on political circumstances as a pretext to gain advantage. This novel presents violent scenes, and the story is built on Gallegos' invariable scheme: the struggle of good against evil, personified by characters usually whittled from a single piece. Perhaps the most unreal aspect of the novel is that the student leader is portrayed with disagreeable traces of barbarism, violence, and criminality; Gallegos openly expressed the ethical disgust he felt toward his character, forgetting that a leader is usually charismatic, attracting for obscure psychological reasons the masses that follow him. Justo Rigores could never have been a leader in real life because all his followers hated him.

Gallegos was never convinced of the worth of his last novel, *La tierra bajo los pies*; for years he refused to publish it, saying it was not finished. In 1968 the Mexican poet Carlos Pellicer read the manuscript and persuaded Gallegos to complete it, but even then the author did not publish it. It finally appeared in 1971 on the approval of Gallegos' heirs. Set in the state of Michoacán, Mexico, the novel is an attempt to portray the process of social change that came as a result of reforms in the land tenure system from 1920 to 1950. The Mexican Revolution had pulverized the *latifundio*, without, however, preventing the spread of regional bossism. Together with the legal division of the large estates, the *ejidal* structure was projected as a form of communal property that was to favor the poor peasants. Once more Gallegos established opposites, even in the names of his characters: "Chano" and "Nacho" are the anagrams that represent opposed but complementary forces. Within the social symbolism so dear to Gallegos, the idea of racial and social improvement reappears in the new generations, with the sons and grandchildren.

It may seem surprising that with only a superficial knowledge of the social and historical circumstances of Cuba and Mexico, Gallegos should dedicate a novel to each of these countries, with an implied deep vision of their problems. However, it must be remembered that Gallegos was not a careful and detailed author, but rather a writer of rapid and torrential prose; for example, the original version of *Doña Bárbara* was written in twenty-eight days. Gallegos believed that the Spanish-American reality is the same no matter which country is involved. This idea weakened his last two novels; a suspicion of the flaw may have been the reason he withheld publication of *Tierra*.

In the last ten years of his life, Gallegos received a flood of homages, prizes, and acknowledgments. He was considered a central figure of Spanish-American culture, and when, after his last exile, he returned to Caracas in 1958, he won innumerable distinctions: he was named Illustrious Son of Caracas and received the Venezuelan National Literature Prize; the Order of San Martín, liberator of Argentina; the Alberdi-Sarmiento Prize in Buenos Aires; the Order of the Sun of Peru; the Order of Andrés Bello; and the Cross of the Venezuelan Air Force. In 1960 he was a candidate for the Nobel Prize in literature. He received honorary doctorates from various universities, and schools in several Spanish-American countries were named after him.

It is difficult to judge the importance of Gallegos' works in the Venezuelan, Spanish-American, and international literary context, because of the changes in the novel form in recent decades. From a historical point of view, he belongs to the realistic school, with some tendencies toward naturalism; the realists closed the modernist period for good and had nothing to do with the gallacized and gallant style that emphasized form over content. Gallegos' realism reversed the formula: he focused on content and kept to one basic form throughout his career. The structure of his novels is conventional and changes little from book to book; it is based upon the antagonism of two characters who symbolically represent opposing aspects of Venezuelan or Spanish-American life, an opposition that is usually tempered a generation later. Gallegos' novels are relatively rich in vocabulary and syntax, and emotive and emphatic expression abound. For Gallegos the novel was an excellent medium for expressing and formalizing his social preoccupations. He often pointed to his theoretical incapacity as explaining his natural bent toward narrative, which was at times no more than an illustration of the social problems that occupied him and of the ideas he could find no other way to express.

Gallegos' role was that of a writer who, in all good faith, tried to reform social, educational, and political institutions by means of intellectual works. He wished to help in the elimination of backward cultural patterns in which the majority of the people were poor, ill-fed victims of regimes based on force, and he maintained complete faith in progress.

From an aesthetic point of view, Gallegos lacked the artistic flexibility and sensibility necessary to feel the changes in the novel form and to enrich his narratives by adapting himself to those changes. The great lesson of the vanguardists passed by without changing him, as did the new Creole realistic forms (of, for example, Miguel Ángel Asturias and Alejo Carpentier) that provided an invaluable element of fantasy, giving rise to what is called "magical realism" and renewing the novel form. His novels do not awaken the same passion today as they did in the 1930's and 1940's. They belong to a period in Spanish America in which each country sought its identity and sowed the seeds of nationalism, grounding their cultures in great literary creations that illuminated their problems. Such novels as *Doña Bárbara*, *Cantaclaro*, and *Canaima* (above all, the first) were precise and effective responses to these spiritual needs. Gallegos' novels are of lasting value because they are genuine expressions of the aesthetic and social problems of his time, and they should be read in that context. As Carlos Fuentes said in 1980: "The same happens with Rómulo Gallegos as with our fathers. First we venerate them; then we detest them; finally we understand them."

SELECTED BIBLIOGRAPHY

Editions

Short Stories

Los aventureros. Caracas, 1913.
La rebelión y otros cuentos. Caracas, 1946.
Cuentos venezolanos. Buenos Aires, 1949.
La doncella y El último patriota. Mexico City, 1957.

Novels

El último Solar. Caracas, 1920. (Later published as *Reinaldo Solar.* Barcelona, 1930.)
La trepadora. Caracas, 1925.
Doña Bárbara. Barcelona, 1929.
Cantaclaro. Barcelona, 1934.
Canaima. Barcelona, 1935.
Pobre negro. Caracas, 1937.
El forastero. Caracas, 1942.
Sobre la misma tierra. Barcelona, 1943.
La brizna de paja en el viento. Havana, 1952.
La tierra bajo los pies. Estella, Spain, 1971.

Essays

Una posición en la vida. Edited by Lowell Dunham. Mexico City, 1954.

Collected Works

Novelas escogidas. Edited by Federico Sainz de Robles. Madrid, 1951.
_____. Edited by Jesús López Pacheco. 2 vols. Madrid, 1958.
Obras completas. Havana, 1949.

Translations

Doña Bárbara. Translated by Robert Malloy. New York, 1931.

Biographical and Critical Studies

Araujo, Orlando. *Lengua y creación en la obra de Rómulo Gallegos.* 2nd ed. Caracas, 1962.
Brushwood, John S. "The Year of *Doña Bárbara.*" In *The Spanish American Novel.* Austin, Tex., 1975. Pp. 68–80.
Cardon, Earl L. "Sociopolitical Aspects of the Novels of Rómulo Gallegos." Thesis, University of Miami, 1962.
Damboriena, Ángel. *Rómulo Gallegos y la problemática venezolana.* Caracas, 1960.
Díaz Seijas, Pedro. *Rómulo Gallegos, realidad y símbolo.* Caracas, 1965.
_____, ed. *Rómulo Gallegos ante la crítica.* Caracas, 1980.
Dunham, Lowell. *Rómulo Gallegos, vida y obra.* Mexico City, 1957.
_____. *Rómulo Gallegos: An Oklahoma Encounter and the Writing of the Last Novel.* Norman, Okla., 1974.
Englekirk, John E. "*Doña Bárbara,* Legend of the Llano." *Hispania* 31:259–270 (1948).
Iduarte, Andrés. *Veinte años con Rómulo Gallegos.* Mexico City, 1954.
Jones, Cyril A. *Three Spanish Novelists: A European View.* London, 1967.
Leo, Ulrich. *Rómulo Gallegos: Estudio sobre el arte de novelar.* Mexico City, 1954.
Levy, Kurt L. "*Doña Bárbara:* The Human Dimension." *International Fiction Review* 7:118–122 (1980).
Liscano, Juan. *Rómulo Gallegos.* Mexico City, 1968.
_____. *Rómulo Gallegos y su tiempo.* Caracas, 1969.
Massiani, Felipe. *El hombre y la naturaleza venezolana en Rómulo Gallegos.* Caracas, 1943.
Medina, José Ramon. *Rómulo Gallegos: Ensayo biográfico.* Caracas, 1966.
Prieto, Luis B., et al. *Relectura de Rómulo Gallegos.* Caracas, 1980.
Ramos Calles, Raúl. *Los personajes de Rómulo Gallegos a través del psicoanálisis.* Caracas, 1969.
Rodríguez Alcala, Hugo. *Nine Essays on Rómulo Gallegos.* Riverside, Calif., 1979.
Schärer-Nussberger, Maya. *Rómulo Gallegos: Un mundo inconcluso.* Caracas, 1979.
Spell, Jefferson Rea. *Contemporary Spanish American Fiction.* Chapel Hill, N.C., 1944. Pp. 205–238.
Torres-Ríoseco, Arturo. "Romulo Gallegos." In *Grandes novelistas de la América Hispana* 1. Berkeley and Los Angeles, Calif., 1949. Pp. 43–76.
Urriola, José Santos. *Rómulo Gallegos y la primera versión de "El forastero."* Caracas, 1981.
Vázquez Amaral, José. "Rómulo Gallegos and the Drama of Civilization on the South American Plains: *Doña Bárbara.*" In *The Contemporary Latin American Narrative.* New York, 1970.
Ziomek, Henryk. "Rómulo Gallegos: Some Observations on Folkloric Elements in His Novels." *Revista de estudios hispánicos* 8:23–42 (1974).

Eduardo Barrios

(1884–1963)

John Walker

Eduardo Barrios was born in Valparaiso, Chile, on 25 October 1884, the only child of his soldier-father, Eduardo Barrios Achurra, and his Peruvian mother of German descent, Isabel Hudtwalcker. He died in his seventy-ninth year in 1963, after a full life of government and private service, and an artistic career crowned by his country's highest awards.

During the eight decades of his life Barrios was to experience and reveal in his work the various changes in the Latin American literary movements, as the region struggled its way into the twentieth century. His works reflect the contrast between the romantic and realist sensibilities, and the extension of the latter into the exaggerated realism of Zolaesque naturalism, which painted the last decades of the nineteenth century as a grim and black reality. *Modernismo* (modernism), the movement heralded by the Nicaraguan poet Rubén Darío, was an attempt to escape this harsh reality through the medium of art.

In his first published work, *Del natural* (About the Natural, 1907), Barrios reflected both his naturalist and modernist models. During the first decades of the twentieth century, the traditional Latin American novel was influenced by both the twin currents of the European philosophical novel (psychological realism) and the American novel of the land, with its focus on

the issues, nature, and themes of the New World. Although Barrios' first fictional trilogy, *El niño que enloqueció de amor* (The Boy Who Went Mad with Love, 1915), *Un perdido* (A Lost Soul, 1918), and *El hermano asno* (Brother Ass, 1922), is more obviously in the philosophical or metaphysical mode, he was not averse to treating patently American themes set against the natural background, as evidenced in his later works *Tamarugal* (Tamarugo Grove, 1944) and *Gran señor y rajadiablos* (Great Lord and Hell Raiser, 1948). By the time Barrios wrote his last novel, *Los hombres del hombre* (The Men Within Man, 1950), many of the forerunners of *la nueva novela* (the new novel), writers like Agustín Yáñez, Ernesto Sábato, Miguel Ángel Asturias, and Alejo Carpentier, had already published some of their exemplary works of contemporary fiction. By the time of Barrios' death in 1963, several of the most revolutionary examples of the new novel were shocking and provoking public and critics alike. In other words, Barrios' career ran parallel to and reflected some of the most challenging and vital artistic movements in Latin American literature.

Although Barrios has been labeled by at least one critic as an autobiographical writer, this tag does a disservice to the imaginative and creative element in his work. Like all artists, Barrios used material from his own experiences in his novels, but one must not confuse psychological, analytical, even first-person narrative with autobiography. The literary detectives need not read between the lines of Barrios' novels, because the personal data are readily available. In 1923 Barrios wrote a revealing autobiographical essay, "También algo de mí" (Also Something of Me), which provides us with basic information about his life and his art. (This essay is included in *Obras completas de Eduardo Barrios,* vol. 1 [1962]; except as noted, all references to Barrios' works are to this edition.)

At the age of five, after the sudden death of his father, Barrios moved with his mother to Lima, where he attended the Jesuit College of San Pedro and various secondary schools. His maternal grandparents played a great role in his "sentimental" evolution, and are in part the models for the grandparents of Luis Bernales in *Un perdido*—especially the tender-hearted Papá Juan. In 1900, at the instigation of his paternal grandparents, he returned to Chile and entered the military college in Santiago. But, like Luis in *Un perdido,* he was painfully unsuited to the military life and obtained his discharge in 1902 so that he could return to Lima with his mother.

In "También algo di mí" and in various interviews, he relates his adventures after the death of his mother and his beloved maternal grandparents, when he wandered the continent working at various jobs. In 1903 he was part of an unsuccessful rubber-gathering mission in the eastern Andes, and he traveled to the Canal Zone of Panama. In 1904 he took a position as an administrator for a nitrate company in the north of Chile. His experiences there were to be the stuff of *Tamarugal,* published forty years later. The young Barrios, while working to earn a living (as a miner, bookkeeper, salesman, even as a weight lifter in a circus), was gaining experience and material for his future novels. In 1907 his first work, *Del natural,* appeared. On his return to Santiago in 1909 he obtained an administrative post at the university, and in the following year he married Deifiria Passe, with whom he had two children before the unhappy marriage was dissolved. (Compare the treatment of an unhappy marriage in *Los hombres del hombre.*) In 1910 his play *Mercaderes en el templo* (Merchants in the Temple) won a literary prize and premiered the

following year. Now writing for literary journals and periodicals like *Pluma y lápiz* (Pen and Pencil), *La Mañana* (The Morning), and *Zig-zag,* he staged two plays, *Por el decoro* (For the Sake of a Good Reputation, 1913) and *Lo que niega la vida* (What Life Denies, 1913). *El niño que enloqueció de amor,* his most important work to date, appeared in 1915; Barrios claimed that it was based on a personal experience. Now established as a writer, in 1916 he joined the literary group Los Diez and published his drama *Vivir* (To Live). In 1918 he consolidated his reputation as a novelist with the long work of psychological realism *Un perdido,* which contained semiautobiographical material.

In 1920 Barrios married Carmen Rivadeneira, achieving the happy marriage (including three children) that he had long desired. His literary work thrived, culminating in the triumph of his early period, *Brother Ass,* set in a Franciscan monastery. Despite unfounded accusations of plagiarism, it was and remains his most accomplished work. In 1923 his early period came to a close with the publication of *Páginas de un pobre diablo* (Pages of a Poor Devil). Although he was not to publish any new fiction for two decades, Barrios remained involved with literary and cultural matters, and with positions of responsibility in government and private business.

In 1925, ironically but fittingly, given the accusations of plagiarism, which wounded him deeply, he was appointed Guardian of Intellectual Property of the National Library, and also editor of the prestigious journal *Atenea.* In 1927 he was appointed director of libraries, archives, and museums, and also minister of education in the government of Carlos Ibáñez, whose right-wing stance corresponded to Barrios' political views. When the Ibáñez government fell in 1931, Barrios gave up his position as director of libraries and devoted himself to journalism (*El Mercurio, Las Ultimas Noticias*) and the cattle industry (in San José Maipo, where he acquired property). In 1937 he took over the management of the cattle ranch La Marquesa, an experience that was to provide him with the material, atmosphere, and character prototypes for his most popular novel, *Gran señor y rajadiablos.*

In 1944, after a twenty-year silence, he published the first novel of his later period, *Tamarugal.* Two years later he was awarded the National Prize for Literature, which seemed to give him renewed vigor. In 1948 *Gran señor y rajadiablos* appeared; this best-selling saga was awarded the Atenea Prize by the University of Concepción in 1949. In 1950 he published what was to be his last novel, *Los hombres del hombre*, a fitting conclusion, artistically and psychologically, to his literary career. Although he wrote no more fiction, Barrios continued his journalistic contributions (for example, to *La Nación* of Santiago) in 1952. The following year, he was renamed director of libraries and minister of education, and was honored with membership in the Chilean Academy of Language. By 1955 his eyesight was beginning to fail. He had corrective surgery and decided to retire from his government positions in 1959. After decades of great service to his country, the artistic community, the government, and private enterprise, Barrios died on 13 September 1963.

Barrios had a profound interest in the human condition and its metaphysical problems—hence his deserved reputation as an analytical writer and the importance of psychological values and truths in his work. Yet for Barrios psychological analysis was but a method or instrument to penetrate to the heart of man, and not just Chilean man. These important social and psychological elements are indeed subordinate to the metaphysical aspect of his works.

Barrios began his literary career with *Del natural*, a collection of three short stories and a novella in the decadent/naturalist mold. Although the work is of limited value, as Barrios confessed later, it is important as a point of departure, because it presents in embryonic form the characters, themes, and techniques to be developed in his mature novels. The three short stories, "Amistad de solteras" (The Friendship of Unmarried Girls), "Lo que ellos creen y lo que ellas son" (What Men Believe and What Women Are), and "Celos bienhechores" (Beneficent Jealousy), are mere naturalistic exercises in the portrayal of stereotyped decadent characters in luxurious settings peopled by sensuous women. The mysterious, Byronic, and satanic figures of the short stories give way to better characterization in the novella "Tirana ley" (The Tyrannical Law), which tells the story of Gastón Labarca, a young painter who finds love and inspiration in a beautiful young widow, "the angelic

Luz Avilés," who in turn sees in Gastón and his work "the synthesis of her ideal: the artist combined with the strong man" (*Obras* 1:89). The self-conscious posturing and overwriting of this early work, the result of the influence of modernism, are developed and refined in the beautiful prose of the later novels *Brother Ass* and *Los hombres del hombre*. Apart from the imagery of religion and love, the modernist concern for elegant sensuality and the role of art in life, plus Barrios' basic themes of sex, paternity, and jealousy, the reader is most struck by the all-important role of the heart and emotion vis-à-vis reason and the mind, which they displace—a key concept (rooted in romanticism) in Barrios' philosophy of life, to be developed further in future protagonists.

El niño que enloqueció de amor is the title story of a collection that also includes two lesser works. As the title suggests, it is a tragedy. This skillfully written short novel takes up the romantic theme of the tyrannical law of love, which it develops to its fatal and inevitable conclusion. It is the study of a sensitive, emotionally repressed youth, whose weakness and sentimentality have no strong counterbalancing values, like Gastón Labarca's art or his fulfilled love. The basic theme of the short novel, and the key to all of Barrios' work, is this view of emotion as a vital force, which in this case and in others leads to tragedy. For Barrios, emotion is the key to life: "Emotion is the virtual essence of things. Emotion is the soul" (*Obras* 2:625); "Emotion is *the* principle" (*Obras* 2:933). This early analysis of the emotionally disturbed nine-year-old and his relationship with his romantic ideal, suitably named Angélica, is traced through the first-person narrative of the boy's diary. The study of jealousy, the unhappiness, the illusions, the false hopes, and the final tragic disillusionment of the child, already represents one of Barrios' finest achievements. As the boy's physical illness and death wish increase, the classic symptom of hearing bells prefigures the fast approaching madness. Barrios portrays the boy's awareness of his tragedy beautifully, through the use of diminutives, simple style, and natural images, highlighting the aesthetic qualities that fuse with the metaphysical concerns. *El niño que enloqueció de amor* is nonetheless a tragedy, albeit a poetic one; it presents a harrowing view of life that will reach its peak in Barrios' next novel. The two short pieces that complete the collection, "Pobre feo" (Poor Ugly One) and "Papá y mamá," although interesting enough for Barrios' acute perception of children's minds and behavior, pale beside the tragedy of the love-mad boy.

In *Un perdido* the timid protagonist, Luis Bernales, is a more fully drawn version of the type portrayed in the love-mad boy. With the death of one set of grandparents and his beloved mother in Quillota, the sentimental Luis goes to live in the garrison town of Iquique with his equally timid alcoholic father, a colonel in the regiment there, from whom he escapes to the arms of prostitutes like La Meche. He meets Lieutenant Blanco, whose ironic philosophy of life fits Luis' deterministic view of existence. On the death of his father, Luis is obliged to live with his other grandparents in Santiago, where he reluctantly, and unsuccessfully, attends military college. After an abortive love affair with the symbolically named Blanco (compare Luz and Angélica of previous stories), Luis finds employment at a library, where he meets another rejected stray like himself, Teresa, who also rebuffs him eventually, in favor of his well-adjusted best friend, Rojitas. Now a hopeless alcoholic, Luis searches in vain for Teresa. He never recovers his emotional stability and is well on the way to a tragic death.

Un perdido is a powerful novel of philosophical insight in the European tradition; it not only paints a series of tableaux of Chilean society but also underlines the view of life that Barrios had expressed in his previous fiction. The grim mood of the novel springs from the pessimistic determinism of the German thinkers Arthur Schopenhauer and Friedrich Nietzsche, in vogue at that time. The subtle blend of literary and philosophical influences, fused with the semiautobiographical details, acute psychological analysis, and stark characterization, results in an intense, pessimistic (even exaggerated) fictional presentation that takes Luis along the painful path of life. As the novel progresses, Luis comes to the awareness that the prophetic words of his deterministic friend Blanco are clearly being realized. Inextricably bound up with his vision of the cruel absurdity of life ("How absurd, how absurd is life!" [*Obras* 1:347]) is his shrewd perception of his own character defects ("I am a type without will. But how can I help

myself?" [1:354]). Since he has no success in literature or in love, Luis' failure is complete. The double strand of self-knowledge and metaphysical awareness winds itself to a tragic close. And so it must be, Barrios implies, especially for timid, sentimental souls like Luis Bernales and the love-lost boy, in their instinctive pursuit of emotional fulfillment. Emotion is a vital and formative value in life, but in the case of abulic protagonists like Luis it will inevitably lead to tragedy.

Brother Ass is generally deemed to be Barrios' best novel because it is the culmination (in his early stage) of his aesthetic and psychological values, rooted in his metaphysical vision. *Brother Ass* is undoubtedly the most sophisticated and complex of Barrios' earlier novels, surpassing the others by means of a skillful dualism, apparent not only in the contrast between the two protagonists, Fray Lázaro and Fray Rufino, but also in the fascinating psychological makeup of Lázaro/Mario himself. The two interlinked strands of the novel, set in a Franciscan monastery in Chile, tell the story of the two monks. Fray Lázaro is an intellectual and analytical former man of the world (Mario), whose quest for spiritual peace, self-knowledge, and self-fulfillment is disturbed by the appearance at the monastery of María Mercedes, the younger sister of his former fiancée Gracia. The simple Fray Rufino, who symbolizes complete faith and the spontaneous acceptance of the mysteries of religion, has gained a reputation for holiness and asceticism. Rufino's evolving spiritual struggle, represented in terms of saintly pride and concupiscence by his temptations and Devil-inspired visions, reaches a harrowing climax in what appears to be a sexual attack on María, who is also the instrument of Fray Lázaro's carnal and spiritual troubles. Barrios' skillful weaving of both threads of the spiritual and emotional evolution (upward for Lázaro, downward for Rufino) is brought to an equally skillful climax when the tarnished reputation of the saintly Rufino is protected by Lázaro, who accepts responsibility for Rufino's crime.

Emotion, as always in Barrios' fiction, is the cause of the problems that torment both monks. The naive Rufino cannot control his newly awakened feelings, while the rational Lázaro struggles to resist the call of the flesh and the old "sin" of knowledge ("Lord, free me from analysis"; *Obras* 2:549). At the end of the novel, by means of a masterly development of character, Barrios has adeptly reversed the roles of the two monks. The innocent Rufino yields to the temptations of pride and the flesh, while the worldly, analytical Lázaro performs two acts of selfless love that reveal his charity and his humanity. By means of this self-humiliation, which appears to be out of character, Lázaro, as his name suggests, rises from the death of lust and pride to a new life of Franciscan tenderness and love. Despite these final redemptive acts, *Brother Ass* is nonetheless a tragedy, since the three protagonists are irremediably marked by the events; María is physically and emotionally damaged by the attempted violation, Fray Rufino dies grotesquely and absurdly, while Fray Lázaro has to pay for a sin that he did not commit. In this sense, then, *Brother Ass* reinforces Barrios' tragic vision of life. The novel does seem to provide a ray of hope in its open ending: despite the fate of Rufino, Lázaro is at least partly redeemed through love. Nevertheless, such a conclusion is consistent with Barrios' view that undisciplined emotion leads to tragedy.

Páginas de un pobre diablo, which marks the end of Barrios' first productive phase, is composed of two short novels, the title piece and "Canción" (Song), plus the short stories "La antipatía" (Antipathy) and "Como hermanas" (Like Sisters), a version of "Amistad de solteras" (The Friendship of Unmarried Girls) of 1907. As always, Barrios' short fiction is inferior to the novels, although it is a useful guide to themes and techniques that he developed later. The title novella, the best of the collection, is a first-person narrative about another potential lost soul, Adolfo, an orphan who takes a job in a funeral parlor owned by a heartless undertaker, Milton López. Although capable of falling into the pit like Luis and the love-mad boy, Adolfo does not meet the same fate, partly because of his writing ability, which he uses as a weapon to help him cope with the tragic business of everyday life ("I must be strong and dominate fear. . . . Be a man" [*Obras* 1:769]). Although this short novel is also open-ended, Barrios provides a conclusion that cannot be anything but optimistic: Art can be a strong force in life, especially for the sensitive and emotionally ambivalent. Adolfo's conduct reflects Barrios' subtle shift in sensibility,

which becomes even more pronounced in the second trilogy, which consists of *Tamarugal, Gran señor y rajadiablos,* and *Los hombres del hombre.*

Barrios produced no fiction for twenty years. When his next novel, *Tamarugal,* appeared in 1944, it was based on his youthful experiences as an administrator in the nitrate-mining regions of northern Chile forty years earlier. Jesús Morales, nicknamed El Hombre (The Man), is the tough administrator of a British nitrate company in Tarapacá province. He decides to marry Jenny, the sentimental daughter of one of his employees. However, before the wedding takes place, Jenny is attracted to the young seminarian Javier del Campo, who comes to visit the mine with his priest-uncle. Despite their mutual attraction and common interests, the young couple dutifully decide to honor their obligations and pursue their chosen vocations. In the epilogue we see Jenny forty years later, a rich old widow surrounded by her three successful sons and her confessor-friend, Javier del Campo, now an eminent prelate.

Despite the artistic and structural defects of the novel, and of the two accompanying short stories, "Santo remedio" (Holy Remedy) and "Camanchaca" (whose title refers to the fog peculiar to the nitrate fields), *Tamarugal* is valuable not only for its painting of natural background and regional mining customs, but also for its position in the evolution of Barrios' fiction, as he was struggling to formulate a new philosophy of life, one more balanced and less bleak than in the first trilogy. As in Barrios' previous fiction, the struggle in *Tamarugal* is between emotion and strength (compare Luis and his brother and friend), but with subtle differences. The positivist administrator, Morales, represents strength, energy, willpower, and other desirable qualities lacking in the early protagonists. But Morales is not a fully rounded character either, since he lacks the complementary good qualities of emotion and tenderness. For this reason Barrios introduces the two kindred spirits, the two sentimental young friends of the heart, Jenny and Javier, whose religious feelings and tenderness highlight Morales' godlessness and lack of sentiment. Thus one sees that at this stage in his career Barrios was still unable to fuse artistically or balance psychologically the desirable human qualities in one fictional creation.

To attain this balance, Barrios published *Gran señor y rajadiablos*. In the prologue we meet for the first time the protagonist José Pedro Valverde: "Hard and tender, serious and harum-scarum, democratic and feudal, a hell raiser . . . but a great lord" (*Obras* 2:710). This saga of Chilean rural life in the late nineteenth and early twentieth centuries is divided into five parts, or tableaux, corresponding to the various stages in Valverde's life: his childhood, youth, adolescence, maturity, and old age and death. Replete with adventure, romance, action, local color, and some fine writing, *Gran señor y rajadiablos* contrasts this strong, aggressive hero's successful relationships with both men and women to the miserable failures of Barrios' earlier protagonists, especially Luis Bernales. Barrios endows his new, well-balanced hero with the essential qualities missing in the other timid, lost souls, that is, the gifts of energy, strength, willpower, and the capacity to act—all counterbalanced by the ever-important emotion and tenderness. From childhood to death, Valverde is portrayed through various episodes (the drowning of his little friend, the murder of his father) as the strong type who meets violence with strength. Even as a child, guided by his militant priest-uncle, and without the maternal and other female comforts so important to Luis and the love-mad boy, Valverde grows up hard and brave, better equipped to face the adversities of this world. Having portrayed Valverde as sexually stable (and successful), Barrios also shows him to be a fully mature character by also providing him with the quality lacking in the strong man of Tamarugal—the vital force of emotion. This emotion, important of itself and also as the basis of religion, can, Barrios suggests, be a great moral force in life. So, too, with the gift of art, denied to Luis. By means of the civilizing influence of his beloved classical poetry, which was learned, ironically, in the seminary (compare Luis and his military college failures), Valverde is able to escape (like the mythical Pegasus, his favored winged horse) the harsh world of reality and rural barbarism. With all these advantages, Valverde is the only character Barrios presents at all stages in his life. He dies at the advanced age of eighty, still displaying his complementary qualities of tenderness and strength, showing himself to be a complete, rounded

figure that Barrios had long sought to capture in his fiction.

Los hombres del hombre, which appeared two years later, is Barrios' last novel. Clearly more analytical and psychological than *Gran señor y rajadiablos*, this final work presents again, in diary form, the anguish of the unnamed narrator, who after eleven years of marriage begins to doubt the fidelity of his wife, Beatriz, and the legitimacy of his son, Charlie. The first-person narrative records convincingly the protagonist's fears and doubts with regard to his wife and son, while he and the seven different components of his personality debate with each other. As the tormented narrator and his selfish wife drift further apart, "el hombre" finds increasing refuge and consolation in his relationship with his son, the intuitive little poet Charlie. This sensitive boy is obviously in the same line as the love-mad child, Luis, and Adolfo, just as the father is an advanced variation of the typical analytical hero (compare Gastón Labarca, Fray Lázaro). The paternity/jealousy theme harks back to "Tirana ley," with fatherhood seen as a positive value giving meaning and direction to life (compare Valverde and his son). Meaning is also created by the act of writing, which here serves a therapeutic purpose (recall Adolfo in *Páginas de un pobre diablo*). Although "el hombre," in the tradition of Barrios' earlier heroes, attains little success in the fields of everyday life, marriage, and sex, he is acutely aware of, and determined to prevent, threats to the emotional well-being of his son, whom he wants to guide along the positive paths denied to Luis, "el niño," José, and other such characters. Through the combination of his poetic instincts, controlled fantasy, self-evaluation, and disciplined emotion, Charlie—and others like him, Barrios suggests—can gain redemption from the potential tragedies of this world. The more mature Barrios, profiting from the experiences and the hard-earned knowledge of his own life, fuses all this into his last novel with one final plea ("May the wisdom of the heart guide me and goodness watch over me" [*Obras* 2:1047]). A domestic situation, which thirty years before would have produced a lost soul like Luis or the love-mad boy, is rescued from a tragic denouement by a healthy mutual relationship between father and son, thus confirming the guarded optimism implied but clumsily portrayed in *Tamarugal,* and later developed more artistically in *Gran señor y rajadiablos.*

Although Barrios described convincingly the Chilean backgrounds of his novels, much more important are the human dramas played out against the geographical settings. In this sense his novels are not only about Chilean or American life but about the human condition in general. Barrios has gained a deserved reputation as a psychological novelist and at times as a social realist whose capacity to analyze character and write social commentary has been praised in almost scientific terms by some critics. Important as these social truths and psychological values are, they become secondary to a metaphysical vision that is an essential quality in the serious novelist. There is no doubt that Barrios' view of life, although rooted in romantic pessimism, developed over the years, nurtured as it was by his own philosophical discoveries.

Although the great romantic discovery that all is not well in the world represented his metaphysical point of departure, Barrios never forgot the aesthetic lessons taught by his modernist masters. For him art and the role of the artist were sacred trusts evidenced not only in his demonstrable concern for the forms and the techniques of art in the composition of his novels but also in the roles played by art and artists in his fiction. This concern is also reflected in his view of art almost as a religion that can give meaning to life, in his own creative process, and in his definition of art, on which he agonized and pontificated long and often in interviews, essays, book reviews, and not least in the novels themselves. His search for a simple, transparent, diaphanous, musical style—"I would like to write without words," he once stated—was not a mere theory. The application of these artistic theories can be seen in all his novels, but especially in *Brother Ass,* whose perfect fusion of content and form, and unique correspondence of effect and vehicle, Barrios was never to emulate again, although parts of *Gran señor y rajadiablos* are exquisitely written poems in prose. *Los hombres del hombre,* although it cannot match *Brother Ass* for overall sustained beauty, spirituality, and simplicity of style, nevertheless displays Barrios' refinement of sensorial and poetic prose, and is in keeping with the characterization of the two cultured protagonists and

the metaphysical role of poetry, as a metaphor for all art.

Throughout his writing career, which spanned half a century, Eduardo Barrios made outstanding contributions to journalism, film and theater criticism, drama, and short fiction. He will be remembered, though, for his best novels, which capture not only the social and moral problems of his time and place but, more important, the psychological evolution of his anguished protagonists. It is a tribute to Barrios' literary skill and acute perception that he was able to raise these novels above the merely regional level to treat in a truly artistic fashion the eternal problems of the human condition.

SELECTED BIBLIOGRAPHY

Editions

Fiction

Del natural. Iquique, Chile, 1907.
El niño que enloqueció de amor. Santiago, Chile, 1915.
Un perdido. Santiago, Chile, 1918.
El hermano asno. Santiago, Chile, 1922.
Páginas de un pobre diablo. Santiago, Chile, 1923.
Tamarugal. Santiago, Chile, 1944.
Gran señor y rajadiablos. Santiago, Chile, 1948.
Los hombres del hombre. Santiago, Chile, 1950.

Drama

Lo que niega la vida. Por el decoro. Santiago, Chile, 1913.
Vivir. Santiago, Chile, 1916.

Collected Works

Obras completas de Eduardo Barrios. 2 vols. With an introduction by Milton Rossel. Santiago, Chile, 1962.
Teatro escogido: Vivir. Lo que niega la vida. Por el decoro. With a prologue by Domingo Melfi Demarco. Santiago, Chile, 1947.

Translations

Fiction

Brother Asno. Translated by Edmundo García-Girón. New York, 1969.
Brother Ass. Translated by R. Seldon Rose and Francisco

Aguilera. In *Fiesta in November*, edited by Ángel Flores and Dudley Poore. Boston, 1942.

Drama

"Papa and Mama." Translated by Willis Knapp Jones. In *Poet Lore* 33:286–290 (1922).

For the Sake of a Good Reputation. Translated by Willis Knapp Jones. In *Short Plays of the Southern Americas.* Stanford, Calif. 1944.

Biographical and Critical Studies

Brown, James W. "*El hermano asno* from *Fioretti* Through Freud." *Symposium* 25:321–332 (1971).

Davidson, Ned J. "The Dramatic Works of Eduardo Barrios." *Hispania* 41:60–63 (1958).

———. "Conflict and Identity in *El hermano asno*." *Hispania* 42:498–501 (1959).

———. "The Significance of *Del natural* in the Fiction of Eduardo Barrios." *Hispania* 44:27–33 (1961).

———. *Eduardo Barrios.* New York, 1970.

Decker, Donald M. "Eduardo Barrios Talks About His Novels." *Hispania* 45:254–258 (1962).

Fogelquist, Donald. "Eduardo Barrios, en su etapa actual." *Revista iberoamericana* 18:13–26 (1952).

Galaos, José Antonio. "Eduardo Barrios: Novelista autobiografico." *Cuadernos hispanoamericos* 56:160–174 (1963).

Hamilton, Carlos D. "La novelística de Eduardo Barrios." *Cuadernos americanos* 85:280–292 (1956).

Hancock, Joel C. "El diario como medio de estructura en *Los hombres del hombre* de Eduardo Barrios." *Hispanófila* 49:1–9 (1973).

———. "The Purification of Eduardo Barrios' Sensorial Prose." *Hispania* 56:51–59 (1973).

Lozada, Alfredo. "Humillarse y servir: El espíritu franciscano en *El hermano asno* de Eduardo Barrios." In *Estudios críticos.* Buenos Aires, 1978. Pp. 7–66.

Orlandi Araya, Julio, and Alejandro Ramírez Cid. *Eduardo Barrios: Obras—estilo—técnica.* Santiago, Chile, 1960.

Peralta, Jaime. "La novelística de Eduardo Barrios." *Cuadernos hispanoamericanos* 58:357–367 (1964).

Rossel, Milton, "El hombre y su psique en las novelas de Eduardo Barrios." *Atenea* 139:182–207 (1960).

Silva Castro, Raúl. "Eduardo Barrios (1884–1963)." *Revista iberoamericana* 30:239–260 (1964).

Spell, Jefferson Rea. "Eduardo Barrios, Psychological Novelist of Chile." In *Contemporary Spanish American Fiction.* Chapel Hill, N.C., 1944. Pp. 135–152.

Torres-Ríoseco, Arturo. *Grandes novelistas de la América Hispana 2.* Berkeley, Calif., 1943; 2d ed. 1949.

Vázquez-Bigi, Angel Manuel. "Los tres planos de la creación artística de Eduardo Barrios." *Revista iberoamericana* 29:125–137 (1963).

———. "Los conflictos psíquicos y religiosos de *El hermano asno*." *Cuadernos hispanoamericanos* 73:456–476 and 74:120–145 (1968).

Walker, John. "La evolución metafísica de Eduardo Barrios a través de sus novelas." In *Actas del Congreso VI de la Asociación Internacional de Hispanistas.* Toronto, 1980. Pp. 769–772.

———. "Anacronismo y novedad en la obra de Eduardo Barrios." *Cuadernos americanos* 236:192–207 (1981).

———. *Metaphysics and Aesthetics in the Works of Eduardo Barrios.* London, 1983.

Ricardo Güiraldes

(1886–1927)

Raúl H. Castagnino

Ricardo Guillermo Güiraldes was born in Buenos Aires on 13 February 1886, the second son of Manuel José Güiraldes and Dolores Goñi, both from families with landed interests in the pampas of the province of Buenos Aires. When Ricardo was one year old, the family moved to France, where they remained until returning to Argentina in 1890. The boy received his primary education at home from governesses and private teachers, who were also charged with continuing his French and teaching him German. He earned his high school diploma in 1904, but his university studies in architecture and law were never completed.

Güiraldes was a restless, wandering soul. He spent his formative years at his family's city residence and their *hacienda* La Porteña in San Antonio de Areco, a county in the province of Buenos Aires. Country life had a special attraction for him, and he had a deep understanding of rural customs and usages, cattle tending, and the idiosyncrasies of country dwellers. When he was twenty-five, he returned to Europe and settled in Paris. During a two-year trip, he visited Italy, Greece, India, Germany, Russia, and Japan. In 1913, he married Adelina del Carril. After returning from a trip to Brazil, his wife insisted that he put together drafts of the early prose and poetry that he had been accumulating over the years and prepare them for publication. In 1915, he published his first book, *El cencerro de cristal* (The Crystal Cowbell), which was almost immediately followed by *Cuentos de muerte y de sangre* (Stories of Death and Blood). Neither attracted the interest of the reading public or the critics.

Accompanied by Adelina and a group of friends, Güiraldes made a long voyage in the Pacific beginning in 1916. A profitable experience, the trip is reflected in *Xaimaca* (1923). In 1917, he published *Raucho*, and in 1918 *Un idilio de estación* (A Station Romance; later published in book form as *Rosaura*) appeared in a Buenos Aires weekly magazine. These works did not attract much attention either.

At the end of World War I, he again settled in France, where he began his friendship with Valéry Larbaud and other French vanguardist writers and poets. In 1920, he returned to Argentina and made a tour of the northwest of his country. He met the nativist Juan Carlos Dávalos and became acquainted with a group of young antimodernist writers. During this period, he began to sketch the first chapter of *Don Segundo Sombra*, the novel he elaborated during the last years of his life.

Until 1920, Güiraldes was, in a way, an independent writer; he had remained outside of literary bohemia and journalistic cliques. His colleagues considered his writing to be the pastime of a rich landowner who devoted his leisure to literary undertakings. Around this time, Güiraldes composed one of the poems of *Poemas solitarios* (Solitary Poems), a book published posthumously in 1928, in which he declares:

Me he acostumbrado a estar solo,
como el ombú se ha acostumbrado a la pampa.
Mi alma es una esfera mirando su centro que es vigor.
Para caminar por la vida, sé sostenerme sobre las piernas de
    mi voluntad y mi coraje.

                                        (*Obras completas*, p. 506)

I am used to being alone
as the ombu is used to the pampa.
My soul is a sphere looking at its center which is
    strength.
To walk through life, I know how to stand on my own
    two legs of will and courage.

In the early 1920's, through the poet Oliverio Girondo, he made contact with several young writers, particularly those whom literary history would call members of the Generation of 1922: Jorge Luis Borges, Alfredo Brandán Caraffa, Ernesto Palacio, Roberto Ledesma, among other self-proclaimed antimodernists and anti-Lugonians. (Leopoldo Lugones, writer and ideologist, produced both prose and poetry, and was a leading figure in the Argentine literary world. Some young writers opposed him; everyone admired him secretly.)

In 1886, when Güiraldes was born, Argentina had just entered a decisive phase of its national organization. The city of Buenos Aires, which had been made the capital in 1880, was in the process of changing from a big hamlet into a cosmopolis, its attention directed toward Europe, and Paris in particular, as a model. During the last ten years of Güiraldes' life, Argentina underwent many changes in terms of society, the intellectual world, the universities, politics, and the proletariat.

Between 1918 and 1920, residents of Buenos Aires witnessed several dramatic events: the end of World War I, workers' strikes, and the bloody, repressive episode known as the Tragic Week. In the political arena, Argentines had to choose a stance of *conservador* (conservative) or *radical* (liberal). In the social realm, the triumph of the Russian Revolution reverberated in the minds of some writers and thinkers. University reform resulted in a confrontation between the old system that favored the privileged and the new possibilities presented by universal access to higher education.

Two tendencies manifested themselves among the rising generation of writers. Two groups formed, called Boedo and Florida because of their habitual meeting places: the former, a working-class neighborhood on the outskirts of the city; the latter, in downtown Buenos Aires, an area of elegant shops and exclusive clubs.

The Boedo group counted among its members fiction writers, social essayists, and poets of popular inspiration. They turned literature into an ideological vehicle, a weapon. They sought ways to disconcert the lettered bourgeoisie with their advanced ideas. They incorporated the urban outskirts into culture and letters, and stirred up social problems. They did not disdain *lunfardo*, the marginal local jargon; instead, they exploited its literary possibilities. They energetically rejected the modernism of Rubén Darío and grew up fighting against the official figure of Leopoldo Lugones. Their most coherent organ of expression was the journal *Claridad*.

Among the Florida group, the poets who formed a subgroup known as the *martinfierristas* (named after the *gaucho* of poetic legend, Martín Fierro) prevailed. They seemed more attentive to aesthetics than to ideas, and their cohesion derived from their shared philosophical positions on art: rejection of what remained of Darío's modernism; in reaction, a foreignizing attitude toward the assimilation of novel techniques introduced by European vanguard schools. Together with the members of the Boedo group, some of the *martinfierristas* would also attack Lugones.

The Florida *martinfierrista* group included Borges, Oliverio Girondo, Leopoldo Marechal, Francisco Luis Bernárdez, Eduardo González Lanuza, Ricardo Molinari, and Conrado Nalé Roxlo. The Boedo group listed Roberto Mariani, Leónidas Barletta, Luis Emilio Soto, Enrique Raúl González Tuñón, and Nicolás Olivari.

The Florida group "invented" the mural journals *Proa* and *Prisma*. These mural journals were made up by one or more newspaper-sized sheets posted on walls for everyone to read. Güiraldes figured among the publications' editors, together with Borges, Brandán Caraffa, and Pablo Rojas Paz. The journal *Martín Fierro* was founded in 1924 and became the voice of this generation since members of both groups published in it. Güiraldes, who collaborated in it, was quite a bit older than the rest of the writers of the Generation of 1922. In his "Proyecto de carta para Guillermo de Torre" (Project of a Letter for Guillermo de Torre, 1925), found in *A modo de autobiografía* (In the Manner of an Autobiography; *Obras completas*, p. 25), he declared himself to be a reader of Lugones.

On the other hand, Güiraldes had published *El cencerro de cristal* in 1915, when Darío's influence was still operative. The poetic sense of that work moved away from Darío's modernism by using free metaphors and by practicing an antiromantic "lunar" humor—the moon, having been sentimentalized by the romantics, was now treated ironically—with antecedents in the work of Jules Laforgue and in Lugones' *Lunario sentimental* (Sentimental Lunar Book, 1909). This poetic attitude had elements in common with the "new sensibility" that would characterize the young men of 1922.

Güiraldes knew how to organize his many activities and obligations in such a way that every day he found a moment to add a few lines to whatever he was writing or to keep up with his copious correspondence. While in his lifetime he published only six books, after his death eight more were published, as well as sketches, numerous journalistic commentaries, notes, and articles. Some of his creations, such as *Don Segundo Sombra*, took him years to elaborate. There is evidence that from as early as 1917 the subject of this novel was in his mind: the book was a result of years of slow gestation, now and then interrupted by trips. In 1925, Güiraldes dedicated himself fully to this novel, which he finished in March 1926 in San Antonio de Areco.

Don Segundo Sombra, which gave Güiraldes great fame, was quickly and almost unanimously well received. Considering his less than positive experience with former books, the novelist did not expect this reception, which included the wholehearted support of Lugones. In an article published in *La Nación* on 12 September 1926, Lugones gave full praise to the work: "Above all, it inspires confidence in the national character, which seems to resonate with a genuine bronze timbre. Here man and landscape are illuminated by great brush strokes of hope and strength."

After this praise from the figure whom some young writers considered their natural enemy but whose recommendation directed many early readers to *Don Segundo Sombra*, its author was consecrated with the National Prize for Literature. Although Güiraldes knew that he had been awarded this honor, ill fate prevented him from enjoying it. His broken health caused him to go to France for medical attention. He died unexpectedly in Paris on 8 October 1927, at age forty-one.

Juan José Güiraldes and Augusto Mario Delfino, compilers of *Obras completas* (Complete Works, 1962), have divided Güiraldes' works into two groups: books published during his lifetime and after his death. The first category comprises *El cencerro de cristal, Cuentos de muerte y de sangre, Raucho, Rosaura* (or *Un idilio de estación*), *Xaimaca*, and *Don Segundo Sombra*. The second includes *Poemas místicos* (Mystical Poems, 1928), *Poemas solitarios, Seis relatos* (Six Tales, 1929), *El sendero* (The Path, 1932), *El libro bravo* (The Wild Book, 1936), and *Pampa* (1954). In addition, *Obras completas* contains "Poemas" (Poems), consisting of twenty-six unpublished compositions; "Cuentos y relatos" (Stories and Tales), with eight pieces; "Estudios y comentarios" (Studies and Commentaries), with twenty-four works of varied nature; "Notas y apuntes" (Articles and Notes), with more varied unpublished material; and "Epistolario" (Letters), made up of a selection of twenty-eight letters written to colleagues in Argentina, America, and Europe. The unpublished material allows us to have a complete profile of Güiraldes' personality, emphasizes the assiduity of his production, and demonstrates that nothing in it was improvised.

El cencerro de cristal appeared in September 1915, followed almost immediately by *Cuentos de muerte y de sangre*. In the preface to the 1952 joint edition,

Güiraldes' wife called them twin works. *El cencerro de cristal,* a lyrical volume, opens with a brief "Antedicho" (Foreword), which hints at the driving need to write that governed Güiraldes' production. As he says: "Writing is my vice. First letters, then stories, now words. Of the three habits, none is the best. It is always pleasure, whether it be writing or thinking about writing" (*Obras completas,* p. 40).

El cencerro de cristal contains forty-six compositions, in five sections: "Camperas" (Country Songs), "Plegarias astrales" (Astral Prayers), "Viaje" (Trip), "Ciudadanas" (City Songs), and "Realidades de ultramundo" (Realities of the Beyond). Descriptive prose alternates with poetic prose. The subject matter is heterogeneous, with that of the external world dominating: landscapes, impressionistic descriptions, mini tales. The collection includes satirical and humorous studies as well as reflections with a slightly skeptical slant.

Cuentos de muerte y de sangre weaves tales that provide verisimilitude through the insinuated and the implicit. A succinct "Advertencia" (Warning) informs the reader that the sketches are not solely imaginative creations of the author. They have reached him through oral traditions, and in some cases he has limited himself to simple transcription. Oral tradition is not always to be trusted; therefore he calls many of these accounts stories, since he does not aspire to historical veracity. Through insinuations and details apparently slipped in accidentally, the reader picks up references to historical figures such as Facundo Quiroga, Juan Manuel de Rosas, and Justo José de Urquiza. Indirectly, through the presence of ghosts and apparitions, *Cuentos de muerte y de sangre* aligns itself with the tradition of "relatos de fogón" (campfire stories), with such antecedents in Argentine popular literature as *Una excursión a los indios ranqueles* (An Expedition to the Ranquel Indians, 1870), by Lucio V. Mansilla, the writings of Estanislao Zeballos, and *Croquis y siluetas militares* (Military Sketches and Silhouettes, 1886), by Eduardo Gutiérrez. In the most typical of Güiraldes' twenty-six stories, "Al rescoldo" (Warmed by the Embers), the figure of Don Segundo makes an early appearance, already exhibiting the attributes of a skillful narrator. This tale shows the characteristic setting and mechanics of campfire stories. Other types of stories are included in the various sections: "Antíthesis," two contrasting vignettes; "Aventuras grotescas" (Grotesque Adventures), four sketches oscillating between the emotive and the ridiculous; and "Trilogía cristiana" (Christian Trilogy), which reveals Güiraldes' capacity to question the empty verbiage of handed-down religious beliefs.

In 1917, Güiraldes published *Raucho: Momentos de una juventud contemporánea* (Raucho: Moments in a Contemporary Young Life). In his notes for *A modo de autobiografía,* the author refers to the work: "*Raucho* was the autobiography of a diminished 'self.' It was going to be called something like *Los impulsos de Ricardito* [Young Ricardo's Impulses], the idea being that we all carry within us a character who is like us but diminished, who makes us do all kinds of foolish things. Later, the book naturally evolved toward an autonomous character" (p. 34).

A large part of *Raucho* is based on the author's experiences as a child, adolescent, and young man. He describes leaving home to go to school and his behavior at school and during holidays and summer vacations in the country. The visits to the family and neighboring *haciendas* are relived as fresh moments recovered through memory. Likewise, the accounts of obsessive traveling to Europe, of sojourns in Paris, and of nights rich in erotic adventures and pleasures are partly derived from personal experience, partly from the frivolous way in which a generation of wealthy young landowners wasted health and wealth on friends, women, and exclusive clubs. The narrative prose of *Raucho* is agile, modern, and effective. The poetic conception of the novel is to be found in the plasticity of its descriptions, in the apt, rhythmical phrasing.

Rosaura, Güiraldes' next work, was probably sketched out very early; in the dedication to his sister Lola, the writer gives the date as 1914. The 3 May 1918 issue of Horacio Quiroga's publication *El cuento ilustrado* includes the novella under the title *Un idilio de estación* adopted by its author to suit the characteristics of the weekly magazine. In later editions, Güiraldes restored the original title, *Rosaura,* the name of the heroine. In this novel, the author changed the tone and style of his narrative discourse. His prose, which in earlier stories had done away with tender adjectives and relied on manly expressions typical of the *gaucho*, now became deliberately sentimental.

The plot is simple. Only the daily train disrupts the monotony of everyday life in Lobos, a small town on the pampas. The townspeople gather on the station platform to keep up with who comes and goes. Rosaura Torres, the daughter of the owner of the livery, on several occasions notices a young, good-looking passenger watching her from the train. Rosaura's growing restlessness prompts her to walk along the platform, hoping to experience again "the unrent romance of declaratory looks." One afternoon, the young man gets off the train and stays in Lobos for a while. He is Carlos Ramallo, a landowner. He attends the Social Club ball and dances with Rosaura. Her imagination takes wing, and she dreams of a passionate love affair. Carlos finishes his business and leaves town. Rosaura returns to her routine of waiting on the platform. The next time Carlos travels, he is not alone. An elegant woman accompanies him. Rosaura becomes desperate and in a raving and frenzied state comes to an absurd and horrible death under the wheels of the train. The description of the country environment in this work is accurate, and there is great verisimilitude in the presentation of Rosaura's emotional collapse.

In the course of the trip Güiraldes made to the Pacific and to the West Indies in 1916–1917, he took notes for his novel *Xaimaca*. He finished the book in Paris in 1919, and it was published in 1923 by the press of Francisco Colombo, a friend of his from San Antonio de Areco. *Xaimaca* is structured along three lines: the first is that of a travelogue; the second records what happens to the characters on the trip; and the last weaves a novelistic plot. As regards the first aspect, Güiraldes, with watercolor strokes, reconstructs itineraries: leaving Buenos Aires by train for Mendoza and Chile, traveling by ship from Valparaiso along the Pacific coast until reaching Panama, changing ships for Jamaica, and staying there before proceeding to Cuba. The second aspect includes the presentation of some of the characters with whom Marcos Galván, the narrator, becomes acquainted. Two of them in particular will become relevant in the third aspect, the novelistic plot: Señora Clara Ordóñez and her brother Señor Peñalba. This third aspect develops the intense and

mutual attraction between Marcos and Clara, which will bloom into an exalted romance, brusquely and inexplicably interrupted by Peñalba. *Xaimaca* is a novel rich in suggestiveness, achieved through the use of an impressionistic technique. Its style and language are not the result of parodic imitation; they illustrate the classical consubstantiation of art and reality, manifested with great spontaneity.

The first edition of *Don Segundo Sombra* was published by Colombo. His son Ismael remembers: "On July 1, 1926, we finished printing *Don Segundo Sombra*, which Ricardo had finished in March of that same year" (Colombo, p. 89). Even though in his letters Güiraldes called himself "a disciple of the *gaucho*" because of the deep impression made on him in childhood by the tales and conversations he heard from country dwellers, *Don Segundo Sombra* is not an autobiographical novel. It should be approached, rather, as a novel of apprenticeship or a novel of initiation.

In his first-person discourse, the narrator presents himself as an abandoned *guachito* (an illegitimate child) who will grow up to overcome the difficulties of adolescence and accumulate vital experience and wisdom under the guidance of Don Segundo. His mentor is an expert teacher who, with discretion and without interference, will orient him until he turns him into a man, a *gaucho* in the fullest and most ennobling sense of the word. The narrator describes customs and usages, the work on the *haciendas*, the cowboys' toiling as they drive the cattle, the difficult and manly labor of horsebreaking and branding, and the way the country folk spend their free time and amuse themselves.

The external narrative continuity of the novel extends itself across twenty-seven chapters. Internally, a tripartite thematic structure first follows Fabio's growth process through childhood and adolescence, early youth, and adulthood. A second, parallel group of themes follows the progress of his initiation as a *gaucho*, as a man, and as one interested in things cultural. A third line of concerns presents him taking on responsibilities and overcoming his predicament as a *guachito*; he becomes an apprentice laborer, guided and protected by Don Segundo; finally, he is a full-fledged *gaucho* whose free, wandering life will change when he learns who his father was: on the death of his progenitor, he will become the heir to unsought and unwanted possessions that will oblige him to settle down, that will curtail his freedom.

In the narrative discourse, this tripartite thematic structure is not stated but alluded to by the presence of water. In chapter 1, the boy Fabio fishes in the river; in chapter 10, Fabio as a young man—already initiated into his tasks as a cowboy—leads a just-tamed horse to drink from the river. In chapter 27, the image of water, melancholically associated with the end of Fabio's carefree youth, suggests a future laden with responsibilities now that he must assume his position as the owner of the inherited *hacienda*. In addition, his maturity is signaled by Don Segundo Sombra leaving him because he considers his tutelary obligations to be over.

In the development of the novel's plot, Güiraldes takes advantage of Don Segundo's natural ability as a spontaneous storyteller to intercalate—by way of campfire stories—two tales in the folklore tradition, of instructive intention, mixed with circumstantial episodes related to incidents witnessed or lived by the muleteers, and details of the everyday life of the people through whose towns they travel.

In a letter dated 18 January 1927, Güiraldes wrote his friend Larbaud: "We've all written *Don Segundo*. It was in us, and we're glad to have it in print" (p. 798). This joyful expression connotes a kind of admiring identification of the author with his literary character as well as with his models of inspiration: the country workers whom he had known since his childhood. It is an identification that, starting with Segundo Ramírez, the model for Don Segundo Sombra and other countryfolk of Areco, will be projected as the totality of the national character. In the dedication, Don Segundo Ramírez, the historical man who was the model for the fictional character, is first mentioned as a real person. *Gaucho*—abstraction and generic whole—is a designation that takes on encomiastic and perfecting value.

In the literary creation, the character Don Segundo is a composite of some of the real characteristics of Segundo Ramírez combined with other features created by the novelist, who endows his *gaucho* with qualities he had observed in many other cowboys of similar merit. The character undergoes a series of stylizations, beginning with the symbolic

surname Sombra, which means "shadow." These stylizations are neither improvised nor whimsical; they are sensed in the feelings and purposes of the novelist from the very first lines and are sustained until the denouement, in the paradoxical disappearance of the old *gaucho*. Don Segundo enters the action of the novel from the shadows of nightfall; he leaves it by disappearing into the shadows. His presence in the novel is of extreme importance as guide and initiator of the protagonist, yet from a literary standpoint his condition is phantasmal. What is more, this condition has a creative role. When Fabio first notices the presence of Don Segundo, he describes him as an ethereal, unreal being: "It seemed to me that I saw a vision, a shadow, something that passes and is more an idea than an entity" (p. 352). Again, at the end of the novel, Fabio, in the mist of the night, repeats: "That which was leaving was more an idea than a man" (p. 497). The real man had been transubstantiated into a character-idea: Segundo Sombra. The reader is confronted with the paradox that, presented as an unreality, the literary character represents a real-life counterpart, idealizing all his positive aspects, as is the case with the mythical characters of the classical epics, who became symbolic personifications.

Güiraldes' personality is found in each of his posthumous publications, although part of this material was still under elaboration at the time of his death. Whether they be completed works or drafts, these publications allow us to know more fully Güiraldes' personality and his expertise in literary matters, and, to a certain extent, to reconstruct his conception of literature and the fundamentals of his poetics. The recovery of these rich sources was the work of Güiraldes' wife, Adelina del Carril, the publisher Colombo, and the author's loyal friends.

Five months after her husband's death, del Carril sent to Colombo two manuscripts, *Poemas solitarios* and *Poemas místicos*. In limited editions that appeared two days apart, they were published in 1928. *Poemas solitarios* had been written between 1921 and 1927; the volume comprises twelve poems of profound content, some of which had appeared in newspapers and anthologies. Notes of skepticism, nostalgia, and resignation filter through them. Man and things, moods, and nature are observed and enveloped by the poet's spiritualism and, above all, by his sincerity.

Poemas místicos bring together seven poems, the first three of which are usually included in another posthumous book, *El sendero*. Some of the poems are dated 1923; however, the collection expresses a giving up of the material, a progressive ascesis that corresponds to certain spiritual and physical states characteristic of the writer's last day. Borges has rightly said that this book "seems to be thought of from death or its environs . . . it is a moving book" (*Obras completas*, p. 810).

El sendero, published in Holland in 1932, consists of twenty-seven paragraphs written on cards, the last of which records a meaningful date—6 October, 1927—two days before the author's death. In the prologue to the Dutch edition, del Carril describes the book as "intimate notes." The author himself calls his poems "scattered beads of a rosary I had prayed in my poems," justifying their origin "by need of inner harmony" (*Obras completas*, p. 810). The notes of *El sendero* were not meant for publication. The writer calls them "jottings on my spiritual development in view of the future."

El libro bravo was published in 1936 in homage to his memory. It is more a project than a finished work. A table of contents enunciates nineteen topics to be developed, followed by a relatively long prologue that defines purposes. "I speak to my people," the poet says, "because I speak to my people. . . . My words are not personal, they do not aspire to express personal feelings. Among strangers I learned to distinguish what was national within me, that which is not individual but collective and common to all my people" (pp. 548–549). In fact, only two of the proposed topics are developed: "Mi orgullo" (My Pride) and "Mi hospitalidad" (My Hospitality).

Pampa, an opuscule published in 1954 with an introduction by Horacio J. Becco, contains six vignettes combining the author's impressions, moods, and experiences arising from various forms of contact with the environment, the pampas of the province of Buenos Aires.

Some of the compositions collected in *Poemas* appeared first in newspapers and magazines. Rescued and integrated into a lyrical whole, they reveal Güiraldes as an authentic poet, free from conven-

tional ties, a writer of advanced expression and experiential richness. They are the product of an artist who draws inspiration from both rustic nature and urban life, one who always bases his poetics on sincerity.

None of the eight pieces included in "Cuentos y relatos" appears in print for the first time in this volume. All had appeared separately in various publications, four of them brought out by the author. A great part of the twenty-four works collected in "Estudios y comentarios" had been separately sent by the author to different publications. Only a few appear in print in the collection for the first time. Some of the forty-two fragments of "*Notas y apuntes*" had never been published before. Others had been sent by their author to various publications or included by members of the family in occasional commemorative works. They are heterogeneous: aphorisms; notes; articles on the European war; travel impressions for a book on Majorca; witty remarks on barbarisms and euphemisms, on literature and expression; reflections on prose, poetry, criticism, and creativity.

"Epistolario" confirms Güiraldes' intellectual level and the aplomb of his judgment, along with a haughty class attitude. A mere listing of Güiraldes' correspondents reveals the caliber of his circle. They include Victoria Ocampo, distinguished Argentine writer and founder of *Sur*, a literary magazine; Valéry Larbaud, French poet; Juan Carlos Dávalos, Argentine poet and short story writer; Juana de Ibarbourou, Uruguayan poetess; Francisco Contreras, Chilean critic settled in France; Roberto Mariani, Argentine short story writer; Jules Supervielle, French poet born in Montevideo; the brothers Raúl and Enrique González Tuñón, both Argentine poets and fiction writers; Guillermo de Torre, Spanish critic; and Jorge Luis Borges, Argentine poet and essayist.

Thanks to the availability of Güiraldes' complete works, the scholar today is in the position of being able to treat Güiraldes' personality and writings as those of a total artist. This has not always been the approach of critics and experts in the field. There was a time—that of *El cencerro de cristal* and *Cuentos de muerte y de sangre*—when he was considered extravagant. There was another time—that of *Raucho*, *Rosaura*, and *Xaimaca*—when he was seen as a "daddy's little rich boy," writing for his own amusement. Then came *Don Segundo Sombra* and with it universal realization of Güiraldes' skill as a narrator and his force as a stylist. Gradually, the fidelity to one line of development and to creativity as a religion showed itself. When Güiraldes' *Obras completas* were published thirty-five years after his death, Francisco L. Bernárdez could correctly and justly affirm in his prologue: "Everything Güiraldes wrote can be reduced to poetry. His stories and tales, his great novel, his travel notes, and even his incidental production perfectly admit this description. His works have gracefully withstood the test of time and proved their literary merit" (p. 19).

Translated by Rolando Costa Picazo and Lea Fletcher

SELECTED BIBLIOGRAPHY

First Editions

Poetic Prose and Poetry

El cencerro de cristal. Buenos Aires, 1915.
Poemas místicos. San Antonio de Areco, Argentina, 1928.
Poemas solitarios. 1921–1927. San Antonio de Areco, Argentina, 1928.
El sendero: Notas sobre mi evolución espiritualista en vistas de un futuro. Maestricht, Holland, 1932.
El libro bravo. San Antonio de Areco, Argentina, 1936.
Pampa. With an introduction by Horacio J. Becco. Buenos Aires, 1954.
Poemas. Posthumously collected in *Obras completas,* below.

Narrative Prose and Novels

Cuentos de muerte y de sangre: Aventuras grotescas. Trilogía cristiana. Buenos Aires, 1915.
Raucho: Momentos de una juventud contemporánea. Buenos Aires, 1917.
Rosaura: Novela corta. San Antonio de Areco, Argentina, 1922.
Xaimaca. San Antonio de Areco, Argentina, 1923.
Don Segundo Sombra. San Antonio de Areco, Argentina, 1926.
Seis relatos. With a poem by Alfonso Reyes. San Antonio de Areco, Argentina, 1929.

Collected Works

Obras completas. Buenos Aires, 1962. Includes *Estudios y comentarios* and *Notas y apuntes.*

Translations

Don Segundo Sombra: Shadows on the Pampas. Translated by Harriet de Onís. New York, 1935.

Biographical and Critical Studies

Alegría, Fernando. *Breve historia de la novela hispanoamericana.* Mexico City, 1959.
Alonso, Amado. "Un problema estilístico en *Don Segundo Sombra.*" In *Materia y forma en poesía.* Madrid, 1955. Pp. 418–428.
Anderson Imbert, Enrique. *Historia de la literatura hispanoamericana.* Mexico City, 1954.
Ara, Guillermo. *Ricardo Güiraldes.* Buenos Aires, 1961. Includes an important bibliography.
Battistessa, Angel J. *El prosista en su prosa.* Buenos Aires, 1959.
Bazan, Robert. *Historia de la literatura americana en lengua española.* Buenos Aires, 1958.
Becco, Horacio J. "Apéndice documental y bibliografía." In Güiraldes' *Obras completas,* above. Pp. 803–862.
_____. *"Don Segundo Sombra" y su vocabulario.* Buenos Aires, 1952.
Bernárdez, Francisco L. "Prólogo" to Güiraldes' *Obras completas,* above. Pp. 9–24.
Blasi, Alberto O. *Güiraldes y Larbaud: Una amistad creadora.* Buenos Aires, 1970.
Bonet, Carmelo M. "La novela." In *Historia de la literatura argentina* 4, edited by Rafael A. Arrieta. Buenos Aires, 1959. Pp. 134–143.
Chasqui: Revista de literatura latinoamericana 6/2 (1977). Special issue dedicated to Güiraldes on the fiftieth anniversary of his death, with articles by Alberto Blasi, Raúl H. Castagnino, Hugo Rodríguez Alcalá, and Armando Zárate.
Collantes de Terán, Juan. *Las novelas de Ricardo Güiraldes.* Seville, 1959.
Colombo, Ismael. *Ricardo Güiraldes: El poeta de la pampa (1886–1927).* Buenos Aires, 1952.
Cortázar, Augusto R. *Valoración de la naturaleza en el habla del gaucho (A través de "Don Segundo Sombra").* Buenos Aires, 1941.
Díez Canedo, Enrique. *Letras de América.* Mexico City, 1944.
Etchebarne, Dora Pastoriza de. *Elementos románticos en las novelas de Ricardo Güiraldes.* Buenos Aires, 1957.

Ghiano, Juan Carlos. *Temas y aptitudes.* Buenos Aires, 1949.

_____. *Constantes de la literatura argentina.* Buenos Aires, 1953.

_____. *Testimonio de la novela argentina.* Buenos Aires, 1956.

_____. *Poesía argentina del siglo XX.* Mexico City, 1957.

_____. *Ricardo Güiraldes.* Buenos Aires, 1966. Contains a bibliography on Güiraldes.

González Lanuza, Eduardo. *Los martinfierristas.* Buenos Aires, 1961.

Güiraldes, Adelina del Carril de. "Ricardo Güiraldes: Su vida, su obra." *Revista del consejo de mujeres de la república Argentina* (Buenos Aires) 35/125:28–52(1935).

Ricardo Güiraldes. Instituto de Literatura Argentina "Ricardo Rojas." Buenos Aires, 1959. A bibliography.

Kovacci, Ofelia. *La pampa a través de Ricardo Güiraldes: Un intento de valoración de lo argentino.* Buenos Aires, 1961.

Sánchez, Luis A. *Proceso y contenido de la novela hispanoamericana.* Madrid, 1953.

Sansone, Eneida. *Ricardo Güiraldes y "Don Segundo Sombra."* Montevideo, 1951.

Soto, Luis Emilio. "El cuento." In *Historia de la literatura argentina* 4, edited by Rafael A. Arrieta. Buenos Aires, 1959. Pp. 427–428.

Spell, Jefferson R. *Contemporary Spanish-American Fiction.* Chapel Hill, N.C., 1944.

Torres Rioseco, Arturo. *Novelistas contemporáneos de América.* Santiago, Chile, 1939.

_____. *La gran literatura iberoamericana.* Buenos Aires, 1945.

Williams Álzaga, Enrique. *La pampa en la novela argentina.* Buenos Aires, 1955.

Zum Felde, Alberto. *La narrativa en hispanoamérica.* Madrid, 1964.

Manuel Bandeira

(1886–1968)

Gilberto Mendonça Teles

Manuel Carneiro de Souza Bandeira Filho was a critic, columnist, literature teacher, and undoubtedly the most popular poet of Brazilian modernism. Born in Recife on 19 April 1886, he moved with his family to Rio de Janeiro when he was ten years old and began his education at the Ginásio Nacional (National High School; now the Pedro II School), where he studied under Silva Ramos, José Veríssimo, and João Ribeiro, who greatly influenced his literary taste. In 1903, Bandeira enrolled in the Escola Politécnica (Polytechnical School) in São Paulo, planning to major in architecture, but in the following year he developed a lung condition, which forced him to quit his studies and to seek a dry, mountainous climate. He lived for some time in Teresópolis and Petrópolis, among other places, where the quietness of small-town life allowed his nostalgia, which perfectly suited his creative tendencies, to flourish. In 1913, Bandeira went to a sanatorium in Clavadel, Switzerland, where he studied German and became acquainted with Paul Éluard (pseudonym of Eugène Grindel). At the beginning of the World War I, Bandeira returned to Brazil, where in 1917 he made his literary debut with A Cinza das Horas (Ash of Hours). From 1920 on he lived in Santa Teresa (a suburb of Rio), where he met the poet Ribeiro Couto, who was to become one of his best friends. During the thirteen years that he lived there, Bandeira was in perpetual contact with the poverty and everyday struggle of life in a proletarian neighborhood, which helped him rediscover "the paths of childhood." This experience helped him to develop an acute feeling for the language of the working classes as well as a humility and a tenderness toward children that would become a strong feature of his work, both as a poet and as a columnist. At the age of fifty-two (1938), already acclaimed as a great poet, Bandeira was appointed professor of literature at the Pedro II School, and, five years later, he was nominated for the chair of Hispano-American literature at the Faculdade Nacional de Filosofia (National School of Philosophy), now the Federal University of Rio de Janeiro. He was elected to membership in the Brazilian Academy of Letters in 1946. Bandeira was compulsorily retired from the university in 1956, at the age of seventy, and he died in Rio on 13 October 1968.

Bandeira's education in literature and the main events of his intellectual life are recorded in his Itinerário de Pasárgada (Route to Pasárgada, 1954) and also in the "Cronologia" (Chronology) he wrote for the first edition of Estrela da Vida Inteira (Star of My Whole Life, 1966), in which he gathered all his poetic production with the exception of his translations of theatrical texts. He was a precocious reader. By the age of ten he had already read *Il Cuore,* by Edmondo De Amicis, as well as other children's books that helped him to shape his personal mythology. Before the age of sixteen he had begun reading the Portuguese classics (mainly Luiz Vaz de Camões) and also the works of François Coppée, Charles-Marie-René Leconte de Lisle, Charles Baudelaire, José María Heredia, António Nobre, and Hippolyte-Adolphe Taine, to name a few. Paul Éluard acquainted Bandeira with the work of Charles Vildrac, André Fontainas, and Paul Claudel, and, through Guillame Apollinaire and Leod Mac-Fiona, introduced him to free verse. Around 1913, while in Coimbra, Portugal, Bandeira tried unsuccessfully to publish a book of poems, "Poemetos Melancólicos" (Melancholy Little Poems); the text was unfortunately lost at the sanatorium. Back in Brazil, he began to read the works of Johann Wolfgang von Goethe, Nikolaus Lenau, and Heinriche Heine, some of whose poems he later translated.

Bandeira's first book, *A Cinza das Horas,* was not published until he was thirty. It was greeted with enthusiasm by João Ribeiro, a critic and grammarian, but was ignored by the poet Olavo Bilac. However, with *Carnaval* (Carnival, 1919) Bandeira aroused the sensibility of São Paulo's futurist generation.

With the publication of *Poesias* (Poems, 1924), which included his first modernist book, *O Ritmo Dissoluto* (Dissipated Rythm), Bandeira began to engage in intense intellectual activity. He wrote articles for the column "O Mês Modernista" (The Modernist Month), in the newspaper *A Noite* (The Evening), and he received his first payment for literary work. Through these years he worked as a music and film critic and traveled through northern and northeastern Brazil (1927–1928). In 1930, he published *Libertinagem* (Debauchery), and in doing so dramatically broadened the horizons of modern Brazilian poetry. In 1936, the year of his fiftieth birthday, he was honored with the publication of *Homenagem a Manuel Bandeira* (Homage to Manuel Bandeira; republished in facsimile in 1986, the year of his centennial). In 1936 he also published *Estrela da Manhã* (Morning Star), a book of poetry, and then, in 1937, *Crônicas da Província do Brasil* (Chronicles of the Province of Brazil), a collection of his

newspaper columns that had appeared in Recife, São Paulo, and Rio de Janeiro. The 1950's and 1960's brought a burst of literary activity, with the publication of new books and editions (both Brazilian and foreign) and the broadcasting of his "Crônicas" on Brazilian educational radio.

On his eightieth birthday Bandeira was honored by his publisher, Editora José Olympio, with a great celebration accompanying the publication of a collection of all his poetry, *Estrela da Vida Inteira* and a collection of his *crônicas,* entitled *Andorinha, Andorinha* (Swallow, Swallow). Bandeira was awarded the Ordem do Mérito Nacional (National Order of Merit, one of Brazil's highest decorations), the Moinho Santista Award, and several other homages. In the 1986 celebration of his centennial, many of Brazil's universities and cultural institutions devoted special programs to his life and work.

It has been said, not without a hint of irony, that from the age of eighteen on Bandeira spent his life waiting for death. This constant apprehension waned only as he gradually developed an intimacy with death: the fear of dying without having achieved anything was overcome when the poet recognized himself as an accomplished man, widely admired and loved. In the poem "Consoada" (Christmas Supper, from *Opus 10,* 1952), composed when Bandeira was nearly seventy, the poet is at last able to declare,

> Alô, iniludível!
> O meu dia foi bom, pode a noite descer.
> (A noite com os seus sortilégios.)
> Encontrará lavrado o campo, a casa limpa,
> A mesa posta,
> Com cada coisa em seu lugar.
> (*Poesias Completa e Prosa,* p. 360)

Hello, unmistakable one!
My day has been good, the night may now fall.
(The night with its enchantments.)
You will find the fields plowed, the house clean,
The table set,
With everything in its place.

These lines are the opposite of what Bandeira had written in the poem "Andorinha" (Swallow; from *Libertinagem*) more than twenty years earlier: "Passei o dia à toa, à toa!" (I've spent all my time loafing!).

The feeling of humility and modesty repeats itself throughout his work, in both poetry and prose. This feeling acts as an antiphrasis to his biography, which, although lacking in political and social significance, has a profound human meaning, so "cada vez mais cheia / De tudo" ("pregnant with everything"), as he wrote in "Canção do Vento e da Minha Vida" (Song of the Wind and of My Life), in *Lira dos Cinqüent'Anos* (The Fifty Year's Lyre, 1940).

That Bandeira's literary activity unfolded in many directions other than poetry was responsible for his great fame. His newspaper columns served as a platform for impressionistic criticism, as can be seen in his books *Crônicas da Província do Brasil, Flauta de Papel* (Paper Flute, 1957), *Andorinha, Andorinha,* and *Colóquio Unilateralmente Sentimental* (Unilaterally Sentimental Coloquium, 1968). In these books, comments about daily life in Rio, São Paulo, and Recife mesh with remarks about Brazilian and foreign writers, and particularly about his own poetic creative process, as in the essays (collected in *Poesia e Prosa*) "História de um Poema" (History of a Poem) and "Poema Desentranhado" (Disemboweled Poem). In the former essay, he explains how the poem "Oração no Saco de Mangaratiba" (Prayer of Mangaratiba Bay) was created during the crossing of that body of water:

> It was 5:30 when we arrived at Mangaratiba Beach. The train was leaving at 5:35: time enough for me to gulp down a cup of hot coffee. The rest of the trip proceeded uneventfully while I, exhausted and drowsy, transformed all that into a poem, the longest poem I've ever made. When I arrived at my apartment in Rio, where was the poem? I had only kept in my memory the few lines I've called "Oração no Saco de Mangaratiba," which are included in my book *Libertinagem.*
>
> (*Poesia e Prosa* 2, p. 445)

As a literary critic and historian (which activities are practically inseparable in Brazilian historiography), Bandeira left a great number of forewords, introductions to anthologies and to books by Brazilian poets, and critical texts among his newspaper writings: studies that are essential to understanding his poetical works as well as to the comprehension of modernist poetry in general. *Itinerário de Pasárgada* is the most important of all because in it Bandeira

recalls his learning process in poetry. His research on *Gonçalves Dias* (1952), and his *Ensaios Literários* (Literary Essays) and the texts about art criticism (*Crítica de Arte*) published in the second volume of *Poesia e Prosa* (Poetry and Prose, 1958) are also very important, for they acquaint the reader with Bandeira's own literary taste and compel a deeper perception of modernist aesthetics. His book *Noções de História das Literaturas* (Notions on the History of Literature, 1940), although figuring among the famous histories of world literature, had originally merely a didactic purpose. The same is not true of *Apresentação da Poesia Brasileira* (A Presentation of Brazilian Poetry, 1946), where Bandeira's personal taste and extensive knowledge of poetry, evident in the critical appraisal, are responsible for one of the most reliable interpretations ever made of Brazilian poetry.

Still, it is through his poetry that Bandeira's creative genius, with its refined sensibility and sophisticated style, has contributed significantly to increasing the reputation of Brazilian poetry in this century. The sum of his poetical work, though it is not very large, can be apprehended through three successive moments.

First came a period of formation, beginning at the age of fifteen and encompassing his first newspaper writings and his first two books (*A Cinza das Horas* and *Carnaval*), which were written in a Parnassian-symbolist fashion. The work of Olavo Bilac and of the French and Portuguese symbolist writers influenced Bandeira's romantic spirit, creating a conflict that later unraveled into modernity, especially after Bandeira discovered free verse and Apollinaire's compositions. Called the "Saint John the Baptist of modernism" by Mário de Andrade, Bandeira stimulated the work of the young generation of São Paulo poets. In this period he concluded his education in traditional literature and incorporated into his work the themes, forms, and techniques of the European avant-garde. At the same time he began to sense the conflict between tradition and new patterns of expression, trying to solve it by conciliation—a conciliation achieved through a playfulness with traditional forms. The poet, overwhelmed by the personal instability wrought by his tuberculosis, struggled to convert the traditional elements he loved into a carnival.

Second came a period of transformation, with *O*

Ritmo Dissoluto, Libertinagem, and *Estrela da Manhã.* These books were written between the ages of thirty-five and fifty, a period of great creative maturity, when Bandeira became a true modern poet. This was also a period of extraordinary growth for modernism in Brazil. Bandeira now chose Brazilian themes and daringly experimented with new forms, combining them with elements of colloquial language. Modern poetry increased in popularity, no longer regarded as a mere "futurist" joke. With the publication of *O Ritmo Dissoluto* in *Poesias,* Bandeira's poetic language began to overcome its symbolist resonances and acquired exquisite and suggestive images that revealed a somewhat resigned acceptance of life (or of death, always near). His poetry also developed an ironical philosophy of the small incidents that punctuated the poet's daily life. Working patiently and discreetly, in a permanent search for simplicity, Bandeira gradually adjusted the language of his poems to the ordinary reader, that is, to those familiar only with the emotions of traditional poetry. Thus, his transformation was slow and quiet. In the books of this period we find some of Bandeira's most beautiful poems, in both traditional form and free verse more in keeping with the emotion of modern poetry. Bandeira did not try to establish any dialectical relation between the old and the new, since the latter now prevailed, but concentrated rather on the relation between morality and aesthetics. At this time he also expanded his literary knowledge, experimenting with language and acquiring a higher level of precision in word selection, rhythm, and metaphor.

Finally, the third period of Bandeira's work is one of confirmation. Although it had already contained a few innovations, from *Lira dos Cinqüent'Anos* and *Belo Belo* (Beautiful Beautiful, 1948) on Bandeira's poetry became more technically refined, reaffirming an excellence of artistic expression only reached through a rigorous process of experimentation and selection. His work, however, continues to show some conventional traits. Still, in poems such as "A Estrela" (The Star), "Mozart no Céu" (Mozart in Heaven), "Canção do Vento e da Minha Vida," and "Testamento" (Testament) from *Lira dos Cinqüent'Anos;* "Neologismo" (Neologism), "O Bicho" (The Animal), and "Nova Poética" (New Poetics) from *Belo Belo;* "Consoada" from *Opus 10;* and

"Antologia" (Anthology) and "Entrevista" (Interview) from *Estrela da Tarde* (Evening Star, 1960), Bandeira achieves a perfect intertwining of the old and the new.

Poets of Bandeira's caliber continuously update artistic forms. As they renew and adjust their work, they experiment with and revive old forms that have become obsolete, and their poetic skills allow them to add new themes, forms, and techniques to poetic tradition. Although Bandeira insisted in calling himself "a minor poet" and attributed his poetical findings to a simple "intuition game" (as he wrote in *Poesia e Prosa,* "I don't write poetry when I want to, but only when *it* wants me to do it," [p. 22]), we can easily identify the albeit subtle presence of linguistic and literary expertise in his work. This knowledge assured him the freedom to carry out his experiments and endowed him with an astute perception in selecting his poetic material. His life experiences and his personal ideas about music and painting, those arts closest to poetry, led Bandeira to realize the need to control that inspiration that originates from "the highest and happiest moments of the highest and happiest spirits," as he wrote in the initial pages of *Itinerário de Pasárgada,* quoting Percy Bysshe Shelley. He reveals that "the emotional substance of my childhood recollections was exactly the same as that from a few moments of adult life: in both cases something resists intelligence and conscious memory analysis and fills me with fear and forces me to an attitude of passionate listening" (*Poesia e Prosa 2,* p. 11).

Bandeira's literary knowledge shines through many of his published essays on poets and poetry, but the skillful construction of his poems is the main sign of his literary dexterity. A contradiction, however, pervades his remarks: on one hand, he considers all his findings to be the result of intuition and the activity of the subconscious mind; on the other, he repeatedly suggests that he mastered the secrets of his art only gradually. Bandeira relates curious stories about the geneses of some of his most famous poems. About "Vou-me Embora pr'a Pasárgada" (I'm Leaving for Pasárgada; from *Libertinagem*), for instance, Bandeira writes (in *Itinerário de Pasárgada*) that, twenty years after having heard the word *Pasárgada* for the first time, the poem's first verse suddenly "jumped into my consciousness from my subconscious mind" (*ibid.*, p. 9). But not until many years later, when he found himself in a similar emotional situation, was the poet able to finish the poem. Bandeira thus suggests that there is no use in forcing inspiration. His advice follows William Wordsworth's technique of "emotion recollected in tranquillity."

Bandeira's awareness of his favorite poets' artistic proficiency can be clearly seen in his essays on Guilherme de Almeida, Mário de Andrade, Paul Valéry, Stéphane Mallarmé, Antônio Gonçalves Dias, Antero de Quental, and Antônio de Castro Alves. For Bandeira, the evolution of de Andrade's literary work represents the progress of de Andrade's "strength" and "talent" (or intuition and intelligence) from the "limbo of disconformity" to "spiritual and technical composure." As a matter of fact, the main subject in *Itinerário de Pasárgada* is the evolution from elementary creative intuition to the artistic consciousness of the poem.

The concept of "collision of words" was dear to Bandeira, as we can see in his comment about a verse by Castro Alves. Restating a sentence by Mallarmé, he writes, "The verse, understood as a poetry line, is made of words, not of ideas: poetry is like a spark that flashes from the contact of certain words" (*ibid.*, p. 22). Bandeira also reckons having learned that "poetry is made of little nothings," and he declares he writes it only "according to the wishes of God" (*ibid.*).

To understand Bandeira's thirst for knowledge, we must observe the descriptions he provides in *Itinerário de Pasárgada* concerning his learning process. It may be helpful to consider the use of the words *teach, learn,* and their synonyms. Up to the age of forty, Bandeira invariably wrote about his "ignorance," repeatedly saying that he was just learning, had recently heard about a new technique, or that a certain book or professor had just taught him something. These kinds of statements reveal how much the poet prized the concept of conscious knowledge, by which he meant an intimacy with the poetic craft and with traditional and modern poetical procedures. Only after the publication of *Libertinagem* did Bandeira's insistence on declaring himself ignorant begin to fade. Even so, Bandeira yet confessed that, as a middle-aged man, he still ignored the admirable

lyrical form of the parallelistic ballad and the English sonnets' no less admirable combination of stanzas. It is clear, however, that his concern focused on meter and free verse. In *Libertinagem* there is no philosophical analysis concerning poetry, at least not in the sense of a theory of poetical expression. But the book contains valuable information about Bandeira's approach to poetry: "The real free verse was a difficult conquest for me. The habit of metrified rhythm and fixed structures was slowly transformed through the contact with strange, desensitizing elements," such as translations, menus, recipes, formulas for skin products, and so on (p. 33).

Bandeira's literary skill led him to experiment with many possibilities of poetical production: his oeuvre is a literary patchwork, an intersection of elements from the most varied origins. Some cardinal points of Bandeira's experimentation follow.

Bandeira studied troubadour poetry, borrowing elements from it and modernizing them, as can be seen in the refrain from "Cossante" (Cossante; from *Lira dos Cinqüent'Anos*):

> Ondas da praia onde vos vi,
> Olhos verdes sem dó de mim,
> Ai Avatlântica!
> (*Poesia Completa e
> Prosa*, p. 296)

Waves from the beach where I saw thee,
Green eyes that don't pity me,
O Avalantic!

In the 1950's, Bandeira read the "concretist" poets and composed poems such as "Analianeliana" from the "subcycle" of poems called "Ponteios" (Strumming; from *Estrela da Tarde*). In *Flauta de Papel* he remarks ironically, "After reading a few essays from the concretist group I wrote a poem applying a few touches of concretism to my old-fashioned style."

In the classics, romantics, Parnassians, and symbolists, Bandeira found fixed forms and kinds of poetic license that greatly influenced his work. Bandeira wrote wonderful sonnets, and he turned traditional forms such as voltas, rondels, madrigals, ballads, and haikus into modern poetry. The poems "Balada de Santa Maria Egipcíaca" (Ballad of Saint

Mary the Egyptian; from *O Ritmo Dissoluto*) and "Balada das Três Mulheres do Sabonete Araxá" (Ballad of the Three Women on the Araxá Soap Box; from *Estrela da Manhã*) are good examples of such transformations. In the latter he comes to the point of inserting "fragments from favorite poets whose lines I had memorized in adolescence—Bilac, Castro Alves, Luís Delfino, Eugênio de Castro, Oscar Wilde. I did jokingly what Eliot does seriously" (*Poesia Completa e Prosa*, p. 105). In "Balada das Três Mulheres," lines from William Shakespeare, Arthur Rimbaud, and even Lamartine Babo, a popular Brazilian composer, also appear.

Bandeira also had enough talent and common sense to keep his work open to popular themes and forms, taking from them the substance of his modernist style. Poems such as "O Anel de Vidro" (The Glass Ring; from *A Cinza das Horas*), "Evocação do Recife" (Recollection from Recife; from *Libertinagem*), "Trem de Ferro" (Railway Train; from *Estrela da Manhã*), and the subcycle "Louvações" (Laudation; from *Estrela de Tarde*) are examples of a poetry with popular characteristics, in which theme, form, and technique either originate in oral literature or are created from popular sources by the poet. "Poetry is in everything—as much in our love affairs as in our slippers; as much in logical things as in nonsense," Bandeira writes in *Itinerário de Pasárgada* (p. 12).

Bandeira's literary experimentation extended in many directions, stretching from the most rigorous of traditional to the boldest of modern styles, from long-standing classical forms to current popular themes. He scanned and experimented with every bit of his poetical universe, but he also knew that much of it was left untouched, "sheltered from the possible arrival of a future tomb-profaner," sleeping forever (*ibid.*, p. 31).

Bandeira was a connoisseur of literary rhetoric. His use of figures of speech respected their traditional use while adapting them to the modernist idiom. In Bandeira's poetry, old patterns (meter, rhyme, fixed-form poems, metaphors) appear side by side with modern norms in a way that seems to make the new elements spring spontaneously from the old ones—almost as if asking for permission, as in the poem "Irene no Céu" (Irene in Heaven; from *Libertinagem*):

> —*Licença, meu branco!*
> *E São Pedro bonachão:*
> —*Entra, Irene. Voce não precisa pedir licenca.*
> (*Poesia Completa e Prosa*, p. 263)

> —Excuse me, whitey!
> Answers the goodhearted Saint Peter:
> —Come in, Irene. You don't need to ask for permission.

Bandeira's process of experimentation develops *inside* the language of the poem and respects its limits without breaking with syntax or making use of extralinguistic signs.

The connection between women and poetry in Bandeira's work has such suggestive power that, in his hands, a simple heptasyllabic quatrain like "Poemeto Erótico" (Little Erotic Poem; from *A Cinza das Horas*) acquires a definite touch of modernity:

> *Teu corpo claro e perfeito,*
> —*Teu corpo de maravilha,*
> *Quero possuí-lo no leito*
> *Estreito da redondilha . . .*
> (*Poesia Completa e Prosa*, p. 170)

> Your body, fair and ideal
> Your body, full of wonders,
> I want to make it whole
> On the narrow of the roundel . . .

In "Vulgívaga" (Prostitute; from *Carnaval*), Bandeira creates a rhyme for the poem's title, for which there is no rhyme in Portuguese, through the combination of two words. He also rhymes *bêbado* (drunken) with *conceba do* (to conceive) by using the technique of adjoining words. Also in *Carnaval*, in a poem called "A Dama Branca" (White Lady), he changes the syllable stress in the word *vulgívaga* without changing its grammatical accent. The reader must adapt to the poet's diction: to the eye, *vulgívaga* is a proparoxytone (a word with an acute accent on the antepenult syllable); because of the verse's structure, however, in Bandeira's poem it becomes an oxytone (a word with an acute accent or heavy stress on the last syllable):

> *Era desejo?—Credo! De tísicos?*
> *Por histeria . . . quem sabe lá?*

A Dama tinha caprichos físicos:
Era uma estranha vulgívaga. [emphasis added]
        (*Poesia Completa e Prosa*, p. 26)

Was it desire?—My goodness! For tubercular men?
Maybe she was hysterical . . . who knows?
The Lady had physical fancies:
She was a strange prostitute.

The reader should observe the simultaneously visual
and auditory element of the suspension points, which
hint at a silent expectation, only broken by the
bizarre diagnosis:

—*Respire.*
. . . . . .
—*O senhor tem uma escavação no pulmão esquerdo e o*
  pulmão direito infiltrado.
—*Então, doutor, não é possível tentar o pneumotórax?*
Não. A única coisa a fazer é tocar um tango argentino.
        (*Poesia Completa e Prosa*, pp. 246–247)

—Breathe.
. . . .
—You have a hole in the left lung and an infiltration in
  the right one.
—So, doctor, can't I try the pneumothorax?
No. The only thing to do is to play an Argentine tango.

Bandeira also wrote prose poems, such as "Poema
Tirado de uma Notícia de Jornal" (Poem Taken from
a Newspaper Headline; from *Libertinagem*). Though it
is essentially a denotative poem, further readings
reveal it can also be taken as an allegory:

João Gostoso era carregador da feira-livre e morava no morro
  da Babilônia num barracão sem número.
Uma noite êle chegou no bar Vinte de Novembro
Bebeu
Cantou
Dançou
Depois se atirou na Lagoa Rodrigo de Freitas e morreu
  afogado.
        (*Poesia Completa e Prosa*, p. 256)

Johnny Big Shot worked as a loader in the market and
  lived in the Babylon slum in a hut with no number.
One night he arrived at the Twentieth of November Bar
He drank
He sang
He danced

Then he jumped into the Rodrigo de Freitas Lagoon
  and drowned.

As in "Teresa" (Teresa; from *Libertinagem*) and the
aforementioned "Balada das Três Mulheres," Bandeira disguises the way in which he interweaves texts
into his poems. The first line of "Teresa," "A
primeira vez que vi Teresa" (The first time I saw
Teresa), is identical to a verse in the poem "Adeus"
(Farewell) by Castro Alves, except that Bandeira has
inverted the word order. Borrowing lines and metaphors from a variety of writers (actually creating
poems out of his favorite poets' verses), Bandeira was
able to transform them into something typically
Bandeirian. The following line from "Balada das
Três Mulheres" is a good example: "A mais nua é
doirada borboleta" (The most naked one is a golden
butterfly). Here Bandeira blends lines by Luis Delfino
and Castro Alves, creating a delightful dialogue. The
texts communicate with one another each time a
reader recognizes the presence of three poets in this
single line.

Bandeira often resorts to wordplay, revealing the
poet's oblique stance toward his poems. This is
especially clear in the metalinguistic neology of the
poem "Neologismo":

Beijo pouco, falo menos ainda.
Mas invento palavras
Que traduzem a ternura mais funda
E mais cotidiana.
Inventei, por exemplo, o verbo teadorar.
Intransitivo:
Teadoro, Teodora.
        (*Poesia Completa e Prosa*, p. 330)

I kiss very seldom, and speak even less.
But I make up words
That translate the deepest
And most everyday affection
I've invented, for instance, the verb *teadorar*
  [to love you]
Intransitive form:
Teadoro, Teodora [woman's name].

Further experiments in this direction led Bandeira to
attempt to write in concretist style. By the end of his
life he had produced a few visual poems of asyntactic
construction, such as "Azulejo," "Rosa Tumultuada,"

and "O nome em si" ("Ornamental Tile," "Disturbed Rose," and "The Name in Itself"; from the subcycle entitled "Composições" from *Estrela da Tarde*) and "Onda" (Wave; from the "Ponteios" subcycle of the same book). In "Onda," Bandeira takes advantage of the relationship between the sound of the word and its meaning to establish panoramic correlations that could easily be considered unjustifiable were it not that they belong to the core of poetic expression:

> a onda anda
> aonde anda
> a onda?
> a onda ainda
> ainda onda
> ainda anda
> aonde?
> aonde?
> a onda a onda
> (*Poesia Completa
> e Prosa*, p. 413)

> the wave waves
> where does the wave
> wave?
> the wave still
> waves
> where?
> where?
> the wave the wave

(Some years earlier, in his book *Claro Enigma* [Open Riddle, 1951], the poet Carlos Drummond de Andrade had published a sonnet whose first line is "Onda e amor, onde amor ando indagando" [Wave and love, where is love I keep on asking]; this beautiful decasyllabic line probably had some influence on Bandeira's concretist production.)

In Bandeira's work, such erudite techniques are balanced by the commonest of procedures. The poems "Os Sinos" and "Berimbau" (The Bells; Jews-harp; both from *O Ritmo Dissoluto*) and "Trem de Ferro," for example, are well-known instances of the use of onomatopoeia. However, the sound play in these poems is not limited to mere phonic or lexical effect: the melopoeia is present throughout, affecting their movement and visual aspect (particularly in "Trem de Ferro"). Bandeira had the ability to pass swiftly from the academic to the popular without

falling into the trap of radicalism, and he was thus able to maintain a stylistic expression of a quality theretofore unknown in Brazilian poetry.

At the same time, his talent was such that he could imprint a personal touch on classical forms. In the midst of the modernist turmoil, Bandeira's technique was one of renewal: as such, it provides a profitable lesson to good poets of all times. Bandeira's process of rescuing old models to reformulate and personalize them is clear in "Antologia," a poem written in the form of a cento, that is, made up of lines selected from other poems, either by other poets or by himself. For Bandeira, a cento could be a gathering of his most famous lines:

> A vida
> com cada coisa em seu lugar.
> Não vale a pena e a dor de ser vivida.
> Os corpos se entendem mas as almas não.
> A única coisa a fazer é tocar um tango argentino.
>
> Vou-me embora p'ra Pasárgada!
> Aqui eu não sou feliz.
> Quero esquecer tudo:
> — A dor de ser homem . . .
> Êste anseio infinito e vão
> De possuir o que me possui.
>
> Quero descansar.
> Humildemente pensando na vida e nas mulheres
> que amei . . .
> Na vida inteira que podia ter sido e que não foi.
> Quero descansar.
> Morrer.
> Morrer de corpo e alma.
> Completamente.
> (*Poesia Completa e Prosa*, p. 395)

Life
is not worth the pain of living.
Bodies can understand each other, souls cannot.
The only thing to do is to play an Argentine tango.

I'm leaving for Pasárgada!
I can't be happy here.
I want to forget everything:
— The pain of being . . .
The endless and vain anxiety
Of owning what owns me.

I want to rest.
And simply think about life and the women
   I've loved . . .
About what my whole life could have been.
I want to rest.
To die.
To die body and soul.
Completely.

Because he completely mastered his craft and constantly experimented with themes, forms, and techniques for updating his mode of expression, Bandeira was able to exert a rigorous selectivity on all levels of his work, from the creation of a single poem to the organization of his individual books of poetry and his collections. Although many of his poems are dated, Bandeira never followed "a chronological order in the publication" of his books of poetry, as he wrote in *Itinerário de Pasárgada*. Making a deliberate transition from the ancient and traditional to the modern and avant-garde, Bandeira moved from erudite language to popular expression, coordinating both in a beautiful enunciation, full of "reason and beauty." His process of selection, therefore, could never have been entirely spontaneous, despite his many claims to the contrary. His self-criticism guided him along the best and most effective poetical paths; his modesty feigned a refusal of his own work and finally called even more attention to his poetic strategies. His solutions to poetical problems often shocked his readership, causing a "strange unpleasantness" probably akin to what Bandeira said he felt on reading Mário de Andrade's first book.

This strong selectivity, which made him choose "the essential words" and the poems that "seemed to have a common intention or the same emotional tints," originated during the process of organizing his first book (*Poesia e Prosa*, p. 47). The word *selection*, as well as many of its synonyms, is present throughout *Itinerário de Pasárgada*. Through a process of selecting and refining, Bandeira declined to present "total" work, favoring only what his sensibility considered the best and most original. His oeuvre's aesthetic balance is the result of this procedure. Bandeira remained faithful to the intentions stated in "Poetica," where he asks for "[t]odos os ritmos sobretudo os inumeráveis" (every rhythm, especially the innumerable ones) and in "Nova Poética," where he

writes that "o poema deve ser como a nódoa no brim: / Fazer o leitor satisfeito de si dar o desespêro" (the poem must be as a stain on linen: / It must make the reader satisfied for having the chance to despair). Starting with common words, Bandeira arrived at new meanings; respecting language's limitations, he experimented. He never resorted to nonverbal symbols, as poets of the avant-garde often did. And even when Bandeira's poetry goes beyond the rules of grammar and rhetoric, it leaves the reader with the impression that tradition should actually be thought of as this: a coming-out that, each time, travels a little farther inside the language.

Translated from the Portuguese by Claudia Roquette-Pinto

SELECTED BIBLIOGRAPHY

Editions

Poetry

A Cinza das Horas. Rio de Janeiro, 1917.
Carnaval. Rio de Janeiro, 1919.
O Ritmo Dissoluto. In his *Poesias*. Rio de Janeiro, 1924.
Libertinagem. Rio de Janeiro, 1930.
Estrela da Manhã. Rio de Janeiro, 1936.
Lira Dos Cinqüent'Anos. In his *Poesias Completas*. Rio de Janeiro, 1940.
Belo Belo. In his *Poesias Completas*. 3rd ed. Rio de Janeiro, 1948.
Mafuá do Malungo. Barcelona, 1948. 2nd ed. Rio de Janeiro, 1954.
Opus 10. Niterói, Brazil, 1952.
Estrela da Tarde. Salvador, Brazil, 1960.

Essays, Criticism, and Chronicles

Crônicas da Província do Brasil. Rio de Janeiro, 1937.
Guia de Ouro Preto. Rio de Janeiro, 1938.
Noções de História das Literaturas. São Paulo, 1940.
Aprensentação da Poesia Brasileira. Rio de Janeiro, 1946.
Literatura Hispano-Americana. Rio de Janeiro, 1949.
Gonçalves Dias (Esboço Biográfico). Rio de Janeiro, 1952.
Itinerário de Parsárgada. Rio de Janeiro, 1954.
De Poetas e de Poesia. Rio de Janeiro, 1954.
Versifição em Língua Portuguesa. Rio de Janeiro, 1956.

Flauta de Papel. Rio de Janeiro, 1957.

Andorinha, Andorinha. Rio de Janeiro, 1966.

Os Reis Vagabundos e Mais 50 Crônicas. Rio de Janeiro, 1966.

Colóquio Unilateralmente Sentimental. Rio de Janeiro, 1968.

Collected Works

Poesias. Rio de Janeiro, 1924. Includes *A Cinza das Horas, Carnaval,* and *O Ritmo Dissoluto.*

Poesias Completas. Rio de Janeiro, 1940. 2nd ed. 1944. 3rd ed. 1948. Includes *Poesias* and *Libertinagem, Estrela da Manhã,* and *Lira Dos Cinqüent'Anos.* 3rd ed. also includes *Belo Belo.*

Poesias. Rio de Janeiro, 1954. Includes *Poesias Completas* (3rd ed.) and *Opus 10.*

Obra Poética. Lisbon, 1956. Includes same work as *Poesias,* 1954.

Estrela da Vida Inteira. Rio de Janeiro, 1966. 11th ed. 1986. Contains the following cycles: "Duas Canções do Tempo do Beco," "Louvações," "Composições," "Ponteios," and "Preparação para a Morte."

Poesia e Prosa. 2 vols. Rio de Janeiro, 1958. Contains *Poemas Traduzidos* and other translated work, including *Auto Sacramental do Divino Narciso* and *Maria Stuart,* as well as *Guia de Ouro Preto* and a selection of Bandeira's letters.

Poesias Completa e Prosa. Rio de Janeiro, 1967.

Anthologies

Alumbramentos. Salvador, 1960.

Antologia Poética. Rio de Janeiro, 1961. 7th ed. 1974.

Cinqüenta Poemas Escolhidos pelo Autor. Rio de Janeiro, 1955.

Manuel Bandeira. Paris, 1965.

Meus Poemas Preferidos. Rio de Janeiro, 1966.

Pasárgada. Rio de Janeiro, 1959.

Poesias Escolhidas. Rio de Janeiro, 1937. 2nd ed. 1948.

Preparação para a Morte. Rio de Janeiro, 1965.

Seleta em Prosa e Verso. Rio de Janeiro, 1971. Compiled by Emanuel de Moraes.

Testamento de Pasárgada. Rio de Janeiro, 1980. Compiled by Ivan Junqueira.

Vou-me Embora pra Pasárgada. Rio de Janeiro, 1986. Compiled by Emanuel de Moraes.

Translations by Manuel Bandeira

Auto Sacramental do Divino Narciso. In *Poesia e Prosa 1.* Rio de Janeiro, 1958. Pp. 731–824.

Don Juan Tenório. Rio de Janeiro, 1960.

Macbeth. In *Poesia e Prosa 1.* Rio de Janeiro, 1958. Pp. 825–946.

Maria Stuart. Rio de Janeiro, 1955.

O Advogado do Diabo. Rio de Janeiro, 1964.

Poemas Traduzidos. Rio de Janeiro, 1948.

Prometeu e Epimeteu. Rio de Janeiro, 1962.

Rubaiyat. Rio de Janeiro, 1965.

Translations

Anthology of Contemporary Latin-American Poetry. Edited by Duncan Fitts. Norfolk, Conn. 1942. Reprinted Westport, Conn. 1976. Bilingual edition, includes "Salute to Recife" and "The Cactus."

The Borzoi Anthology of Latin American Literature 2. Edited by Emir Rodriguez Monegal. New York, 1977. Pp. 640–645. Contains "Salute to Recife," "The Cactus," "Reality and Its Image," "The Sky," "Deeply," and "The Dead Ox."

A Brief History of Brazilian Literature. Edited and translated by Ralph Edward Dimmick, with additions and corrections by Bandeira. Washington, D.C., 1958. Reprinted New York 1964. This is a translation of the chapter on Brazilian literature in *Noções de História das Literaturas 2.* 4th ed. São Paulo, 1954. Pp. 50–139.

Modern Brazilian Poetry. Edited and translated by John Nist and Yolanda Leite. Bloomington, Ind., 1962. Reprinted Millwood, N.Y., 1968. Includes "Poetica," "Pneumothorax," "Moment in a Cafe," "Absolute Death," "Apple," "Profundamente," "Mozart in Heaven," "I Am Going Away to Pasagarda," and "The Morning Star."

Modern Brazilian Poetry. Edited and translated by J.C.R. Green. Breakish, Scotland, 1975. Contains "Poetica," "Apple," and "Moment in a Cafe."

Modern Poetry from Brazil. Edited and translated by J. B. Trend. Cambridge, England, 1955.

Recife. Translated by Eddie Flintoff. London, 1984. Includes "Swallow," "Recife," "Preparation for Death," "New Poetics," "Haiku," "Poetica," "Teresa," "Poem Taken from a Report in the Papers," "Irene," "The Cactus," "Profundamente," and "Pneumothorax."

Anthologies Edited by Manuel Bandeira

Antologia dos Poetas Brasileiros da Fase Romântica. Rio de Janeiro, 1937.

Antologia dos Poetas Brasileiros da Fase Parnasiana. Rio de Janeiro, 1938.

Poesias de Alphonsus de Guimarãens. Rio de Janeiro, 1938.

Sonetos Completos e Poemas Escolhidos de Antero de Quental. Rio de Janeiro, 1942.

Obras-Primas da Lírica Brasileira. São Paulo, 1943.

Obras Poéticas de Gonçalves Dias. São Paulo, 1944.

Antologia de Poetas Brasileiros Bissextos Contemporâneos. Rio de Janeiro, 1946.

Rimas de José Albano. Rio de Janeiro, 1948.

Gonçalves Dias. Rio de Janeiro, 1958.

Poesias do Brasil. In collaboration with José Guilherme Merquior. Rio de Janeiro, 1963.

O Rio de Janeiro em Prosa e Verso. Coauthored with Carlos Drummond de Andrade. Rio de Janeiro, 1965.

Biographical and Critical Studies

Aita, Giovanna. *Un poeta brasiliano di oggi; Poesia di Manuel Bandeira.* Modena, Italy, 1942.

Andrade, Carlos Drummond de. "Manuel Bandeira: Recordações Avulsas." *Correio da Manhã,* 4 April 1946.

_____. "O Poeta se Diverte." *Correio da Manhã,* 3 July 1948. Reprinted in *Passeios na Ilha.* Rio de Janeiro, 1952. Pp. 239–251. Revised as "Nota Preliminar" for *Mafuá do Malungo,* in *Poesia Completa e Prosa.* Rio de Janeiro, 1967. Pp. 417–421.

Andrade, Mário de. "Manuel Bandeira." *Revista do Brasil* 1/107:214–224 (1924).

Ataíde, Austregesilo de. "Itinerário de Pasárgada." *O Cruzeiro,* 3 July 1954.

Athayde, Tristão de. *Estudos 5.* Rio de Janeiro, 1935.

_____. "Cartas Chilenas." *O Jornal,* 22 November 1940.

_____. "Um Precursor." In *Primeiros Estudos.* Rio de Janeiro, 1948.

_____. "Poesia e Técnica." *Diário de Notícias,* 6 May 1956.

_____. "Manuel Bandeira y la poesía brasileña." *Ficcion* (Buenos Aires), January–February 1958.

_____. "Homem e Poeta de Verdade." *Jornal do Brasil,* 19 April 1966.

_____. *Manuel Bandeira: Poesia.* Rio de Janeiro, 1970.

Baciu, Stefan. *Manuel Bandeira de Corpo Inteiro.* Rio de Janeiro, 1966.

Barbosa, Francisco de Assis. "Uma Edição Crítica." *Leitura,* July 1944.

_____. "Manuel Bandeira Depõe Perante Três Testemunhas." *Flan,* April 1954.

_____. "Milagre de uma Vida." In *Poesia e Prosa 1.* Rio de Janeiro, 1958.

_____. "Cronologia da Vida e da Obra." In *Poesia Completa e Prosa.* Rio de Janeiro, 1967. Pp. 133–144.

Bastide, Roger. "A Carga Lírica." *Diario de São Paulo,* 1 March 1946.

_____. In *Poetas do Brasil.* Curitiba, Brazil, 1947. Pp. 39–48.

Bosi, Alfredo. "Bandeira, Romântico e Moderno." *O Estado de São Paulo,* 16 April 1966.

Campos, Haroldo de. "Bandeira, o Desconstalizador." In *Metalinguagem.* 2nd ed. Rio de Janeiro, 1970.

Campos, Paulo Mendes. "Homenagem." *Diário Carioca,* 21 April 1946.

_____. "Evolução da Poesia de Manuel Bandeira." *Folha de Minas* (Belo Horizonte), 19 December 1946.

_____. "Ha Setenta Anos Atrás, Nascia Manuel Bandeira." *O Semanario* 3 (1956).

_____. "Manuel Bandeira Solteirão Casado com as Musas." *Manchete,* 19 October 1957.

Cândido, Antônio. "Crítica de Arte." *Diário de São Paulo,* 7 March 1946.

Carpeaux, Oto Maria. "Última Canção—Vasto Mundo." In *Origens e Fins.* Rio de Janeiro, 1943.

_____. "Notícia Sobre Manuel Bandeira." In *Apresentação da Poesia Brasileira.* Rio de Janeiro, 1946. Pp. 7–17.

_____. "Suma de Bandeira." *Correio da Manhã,* 8 March 1958.

_____. "Estrela da Vida Inteira." *Jornal do Brasil,* 19 April 1966.

Cidade, Hernani. In *O Conceito de Poesia como Expressão de Cultura: Sua Evolução Através das Literaturas Portuguêsa e Brasileira.* São Paulo, 1946. Pp. 292–298.

Coelho, Joaquim Francisco. "Manuel Bandeira e a História dos Gosmilhos." *Estado de São Paulo,* 7 November 1970.

_____. "Uma (Re)Visão de A Cinza das Horas." *Minas Gerais, Suplemento Literário,* 3 June 1978.

_____. "No *Carnaval* de Manuel Bandeira." *Minas Gerais, Suplemento Literário,* 12 August 1978.

_____. "Sôbre *O Ritmo Dissoluto* de Manuel Bandeira." *Minas Gerais, Suplemento Literário,* 31 March and 7 April 1979.

_____. *Biopoética de Manuel Bandeira.* Recife, Brazil, 1981.

_____. *Manuel Bandeira Pré-Modernista.* Rio de Janeiro, 1982.

Dantas, Pedro. "Crônica Literária." *A Ordem,* February 1931.

_____. "A Estrela na Testa." *Diário Carioca,* 21 April 1946.

_____. "Beleza do Turf." *O Globo,* 15 December 1950.

Eneida [de Morais]. "No Aniversário do Poeta Maior." *Diário de Notícias,* 22 April 1956.

Faria, Otávio de. In *Dois Poetas.* Rio de Janeiro, 1935. Pp. 62–69.

Franco, Afonso Arinos de. "Manuel Bandeira ou o Homen Contra a Poesia." In *Homenagem a Manuel Bandeira,*

Rio de Janeiro, 1936. Reprinted in *Espelho de Três Faces.* São Paulo, 1957. Pp. 37–57.

Freyre, Gilberto. "Manuel Bandeira e o Recife." In *Homenagem a Manuel Bandeira.* Rio de Janeiro, 1936. Reprinted in *Perfil de Euclides e Outros Perfis.* Rio de Janeiro, 1944. Pp. 175–181.

———. "O Busto do Poeta." *O Jornal,* 20 April 1958.

———. "Manuel Bandeira dos Oito aos Oitenta." *Estado de São Paulo,* 16 April 1966.

Grieco, Agripino. In *Evolução da Poesia Brasileira.* 2nd ed. Rio de Janeiro, 1947. Pp. 176–185.

Guimarãens Filho, Alphonsus de. "Impossível Pureza. Inaceitável Impureza." *O Diário* (Belo Horizonte), 10 January 1945.

———. "O Menino Ainda Existe." *O Estado de São Paulo,* 11 May 1946.

Holanda, Aurélio Buarque de. "Em Torno de um Poema de Manuel Bandeira." *Correio da Manhã,* 1 January 1950.

———. *Território Lírico.* Rio de Janeiro, 1958.

Holanda, Sérgio Buarque de, and Prudente de Morais Neto. "Manuel Bandeira." *Estética* 1/2:214–224 (1925).

———. "Trajetória de uma Poesia." *Diário de Noticias,* 5, 12, and 19 September 1948. Reprinted as an introduction to *Poesia Completa e Prosa.* Rio de Janeiro, 1967. Pp. 13–30.

Homenagem a Manuel Bandeira. Rio de Janeiro, 1936. Facsimile edition Rio de Janeiro, 1986.

Ivo, Lêdo. "Manuel Bandeira Chega à Casa dos Sessenta." *O Jornal,* 14 April 1946.

———. "O Poeta da Cidade." *Correio da Manhã,* 25 April 1948.

———. "Paisagem do Leitor." *Tribuna da Imprensa,* 16 May 1956.

———. "Nota Preliminar." Preface to *Estrela da Tarde,* in *Poesia Completa e Prosa.* Rio de Janeiro, 1967. Pp. 367–369.

Jardim, Luís. "O Poeta Manuel Bandeira Apertou-me a Mão." *Diário Carioca,* 21 April 1946.

Josef, Bela. "Manuel Bandeira." In *Poetas do Modernismo 2,* edited by Leodegário A. Azevedo Filho. Rio de Janeiro, 1972.

Leão, Múcio. "Descobrimento de um Poeta." *Jornal do Brasil,* 30 October 1942.

Lima, Luís Costa. "Realismo e Temporalidade em Manuel Bandeira." In his *Lira e Antilira.* Rio de Janeiro, 1968. Pp. 23–28.

Linhares, Temístocles. "Itinerário do Poeta." *Diário de Notícias,* 8 June 1957.

Lins, Álvaro. *Jornal de Crítica* 1. Rio de Janeiro, 1941. Pp. 38–43.

Machado Filho, Aires da Mata. "Itinerário de Pasárgada." *Diário de Notícias,* 11 July 1954.

Magalhães Júnior, Raimundo. "Manuel Bandeira em Suas Encarnações." *Vamos Ler!,* 8 February 1945.

———. "Breve Notícia Sôbre um Homen sem Inveja." *Diário de Notícias,* 22 April 1956.

Martins, Luís. "Bandeira Entre os Poetas." *O Estado de São Paulo,* 26 November 1968. Literary supplement.

Martins, Wilson. "Manuel Bandeira." *Joaquim* (Curitiba), June 1946.

———. "Confissões do Poeta." *O Estado de São Paulo,* 28 September 1957.

———. "Poeta Contemporâneo." *O Estado de São Paulo,* 5 November 1966. Literary supplement.

Melo, Gladstone Chaves de. "Manuel Bandeira e o 'Estilo Brasileiro.'" *Diário de Notícias,* 17 April 1966. Literary supplement.

Melo, Tiago de. "A Estrela da Manhã." *Cultura,* 5 January 1953. Pp. 151–168.

———. "Manuel Bandeira Setentão." *Manchete,* 28 April 1956.

Mendes, Murilo. "Saudações a Manuel Bandeira." *Diário Carioca,* 3 August 1952.

Milliet, Sérgio. *Diário Crítico.* 9 vols. São Paulo, 1944–1957.

———. "Nota Preliminar." Preface to *Belo Belo,* in *Poesia Completa e Prosa.* Rio de Janeiro, 1967. Reprinted in *Diário Crítico* 6.

Monteiro, Adolfo Casais. *Manuel Bandeira.* Lisbon, 1943.

———. "Sobre Manuel Bandeira." *O Estado de São Paulo,* 8 August 1954.

———. "Bandeira e Drummond." *O Estado de São Paulo,* 29 September 1955.

Montenegro, Olívio. "Manuel Bandeira." *O Jornal,* 5 May 1955.

Moraes, Emanuel de. "Uma Vida Cada Vez Mais Cheia de Tudo." In Bandeira's *Vou-me Embora pra Pasárgada.* Rio de Janeiro, 1986.

Mota Filho, Cândido. "Manuel Bandeira." *Correio Paulistano,* 14 May 1930.

Murici, Andrade. *Panorama do Movimento Simbolista Brasileira* 3. Rio de Janeiro, 1952.

Olinto, Antônio. "Manuel Bandeira." *O Globo,* 26 April 1958.

———. "Nota Preliminar." Preface to *O Ritmo Dissoluto,* in *Poesia Completa e Prosa.* Rio de Janeiro, 1967. Pp. 215–216.

Oliveira, Franklin de. "Nota Preliminar." Preface to *Itinerário de Pasárgada,* in *Poesia Completa e Prosa.* Rio de Janeiro, 1967. Pp. 33–37.

Peregrino Júnior, João. "60 Anos." *Careta,* 18 May 1946.

Perez, Renard. "Escritores Brasileiros Contemporâneos—Manuel Bandeira." *Correio da Manhã*, 21 December 1957. Reprinted in his *Escritores Brasileiros Contemporâneos* 1. Rio de Janeiro, 1960. Pp. 261–269.

Queiroz, Dinah Silveira de. "Carta Sôbre uns Setenta." *Diário de Notícias*, 22 April 1956.

Rego, José Lins do. "O Poeta Manuel Bandeira se Confessa." *O Globo*, 20 November 1949.

Ribeiro, João. "A Poesia Nova—A Cinza das Horas." *O Imparcial*, 23 July 1917. Reprinted as "Nota Preliminar," preface to A *Cinza das Horas*, in *Poesia Completa e Prosa*. Pp. 147–151.

Sena, Homero. "Vida, Opiniões e Tendências dos Escritores—Reposta de Manuel Bandeira." In A *República das Letras*. Rio de Janeiro, 1957.

_____. "Bandeira na Casa dos Oitenta." *Correio da Manhã*, 16 April 1966.

Sousa, Gilda de Melo e. "Dois Poetas." *Revista Brasileira de Poesia*, April 1948.

Teles, Gilberto Mendonça. "Manuel Bandeira." In *La Poesia Brasileña en la Actualidad*. Montevideo, 1969.

_____. "Manuel Bandeira e Camões." In *Camões e a Poesia Brasileira*. Rio de Janeiro, 1973.

_____. "Toda a Grandeza de Bandeira, Poeta Menor." *Jornal do Brasil*, 23 May 1976.

_____. "Manuel Bandeira." In *Estudos de Poesia Brasileira*. Coimbra, Portugal, 1985.

_____. "A Experimentação Poética de Bandeira." In *Manuel Bandeira: Em Comemoração à Passagem do Centenário de Nascimento do Poeta*. Rio de Janeiro, 1986.

Viana, Hélio. "Manuel Bandeira—*Antologia dos Poetas Brasileiros da Fase Parnasiana*." In *Estudos Brasileiros*, January 1949.

Vilaça, Antônio Carlos. "Carta a um Amigo." *Diário de Notícias*, 22 April 1956.

Vítor, Nestor. "A Cinza das Horas." In *Cartas à Gente Nova*. Rio de Janeiro, 1924. Pp. 26–28.

Vitureira, Cipriano S. "A Minha Sobrevivência Até Essa Idade é um Verdadeiro Milagre." *O Globo*, 19 April 1956.

Xavier, Jairo José. *Camões e Manuel Bandeira*. Rio de Janeiro, 1973.

Pedro Prado

(1886–1952)

Fernando Alegría

Modernism, understood in Latin America and Spain as a revolt against the excesses of romanticism and as a tendency to adopt the principles of French Parnassianism and symbolism, left a peculiar imprint on the Latin America novel of the turn of the century. The subject matter of the novel was regionalistic, but its form was experimental and its mode philosophical and, often, allegorical. The Chilean novelist and poet Pedro Prado is considered by many critics as the best representative of this literary trend. His stories, long poems, and essays reveal a deep preoccupation with the social crisis affecting the modern world, a consciousness of changes taking place in an atmosphere of human anguish and desperation. Prado, however, stresses the importance of hope and the possibility of salvation in a resurrection of classical myths and philosophical idealism.

Prado was born in Santiago on 8 October 1886 and died 31 January 1952 in Viña del Mar. He completed his secondary studies at the prestigious Instituto Nacional (National Institute) of Santiago and then enrolled at the Escuela de Ingeniería (School of Engineering) of the University of Chile. He never finished his university studies, but he did practice as an architect, distinguishing himself as the designer of the building now occupied by the United States Consulate in Santiago. He is also remembered for his

oil paintings, refined and subtle in the tradition of Chilean impressionism. Prado lived the life of a retiring Chilean aristocrat on his farm, Chacra Santa Laura, surrounded by his large family—he had seven children—and by devoted friends. There was a tower on his property amidst the old trees and decayed buildings, an "ivory tower," where he received friends and admirers to discuss the new literature coming out of Europe, Mexico, Argentina, and India. His group—painters, musicians, poets, philosophers—eventually became a Tolstoyan colony. They published what is now a legendary magazine, *Los Diez* (The Ten, 1916), and they also brought out books by young authors. The colony didn't last long, but it is still remembered in Chile as a turning point in literary history. Some of the most important Chilean novelists and poets of the first half of the twentieth century published their works under Prado's tutelage.

Prado did not travel extensively; however, he did visit Peru, Colombia, and Argentina, and as a diplomat represented Chile in Bogotá (1927–1928). In 1935–1936 he journeyed to Europe for reasons of health. In 1935 he received the Academia de Roma prize, and in 1949, the Chilean National Prize of Literature.

As a poet, Prado is usually considered a postmodernist, that is, a writer moving away from the exhausted *preciosité* of Rubén Darío and his disciples, who were soberly conscious of form but more intent on expressing a philosophy of individual freedom, above dogmatism, based on love and understanding of human greatness and limitations. In his initial books he used free verse and a type of statement reminiscent of Friedrich Wilhelm Nietzsche's versicles. His most lasting poetry, however, was written in sonnet form: *Camino de las horas* (Road of the Hours, 1934) and *No más que una rosa* (Only a Rose, 1946). Raúl Silva Castro, one of his devoted critics, refers to Prado as "one of the finest sonnetists in the Spanish language." Arturo Torres-Ríoseco, in a memorable evaluation of Prado as a novelist and poet, says:

> In a cosmic harmony the poet searches for his raison d'être, the origin of his body, the infinite yearnings of his spirit; thus, upon seeing himself in a mirror, he feels great emptiness of simplicity, but on seeing his face reflected in the window that faces the garden, looking at his own shadow pierced by ribbons of sand, by flowering rose bushes, by remote stars, he thinks he understands the origin of our bodies and the yearnings that fill the human spirit. . . .
>
> Pedro Prado abundantly possesses the gift to distinguish that kind of beauty which is humble and hidden, that what is interesting in little things and what the eyes of other people haven't noticed. . . .
>
> (*Novelistas Contemporáneos de América*)

His concept of beauty is classical, yet his expression of it comes imbued with a knowledge of earthly love and the realization of human frailty. At a moment when Latin American poetry was accepting the abstractionism connected with the avant-garde, Prado emphasized the importance of meaning, the need for universality in content. Vicente Huidobro was his contemporary, yet no other two Chilean poets were farther apart: Huidobro stubborn in his search for a "new" poetic language; Prado placid and profound in seeking communication through ancient, proven words.

Of the novels he published, two seem to represent his narrative art at its best: *Alsino* (Alsino, 1920) and *Un juez rural* (Country Judge, 1924). *Alsino*, an obviously allegorical novel, can be read on several levels. It can be taken as a children's tale, the story of

a boy who breaks his back trying to fly and from his hump grows wings. It can also be considered a retelling of the Icarus myth with ideological projections alluding to the materialism of contemporary life. I prefer a different reading and interpretation.

Prado approaches classical mythology from within the social conflicts that are typical of the underdeveloped world of today. So unbelievable are the conditions in which the peasants of Latin America survive that readers of fiction by such writers as Miguel Ángel Asturias, Alejo Carpentier, Augusto Roa Bastos, Mario Vargas Llosa, or Gabriel García Márquez explain them as creations of "magical realism." Upon receiving the Nobel Prize, García Márquez was particularly careful to emphasize that there was nothing magical about his Gothic tales of the Buendías, who fly and procreate creatures with pigtails; or of dictators who sink ships loaded with children, murder thirty thousand people in one afternoon, and proclaim themselves rulers of heaven and earth. He gave statistics on infant mortality, on populations killed by pestilence, on millions of Latin American exiles wandering over the world.

The power of such a novel as *Alsino* derives from a masterful balance between the mythological significance of the story and the circumstantial conditions that tie it to present historical reality. The poetic force so evident throughout the novel has to do with man's innocence in exploring the unknown, with the sublimeness of his rebellion, and with the fire of death that becomes his punishment.

What critics have failed to notice in Prado's story is that inside this mythological framework there is another structure directly linked to problems that affect people in a more immediate sense. Alsino is a peon enslaved by the unlimited power of a rural oligarchy, and in his alienated condition he tries to break limitations that he does not understand. The parcel of land in which his family has always lived is nothing more than a barbed-wire camp where poverty, ignorance, and impotence are perennial conditions. Alsino and his people fear the presence of an undetermined enemy, a mysterious power made up of economic dominance, social prejudice, and religious bigotry. In his serfdom, the Chilean peasant must adapt to a system of rejections and coercions, he must learn the submission of a pariah and a kind of silent resistance. The landowner is a "father" for "children" who work his land, feed his family, and, when the occasion calls for it, vote for him in rigged elections. This father—who spends most of his time away from his land—will never hesitate to punish his children when they attempt to unionize.

In modern times, during Eduardo Frei's administration, armed to the teeth, the landowner will station himself at the entrance to his feudal property to kill the representative of the government's Agrarian Reform Institute, the harmless Christian Democrat militant who is supposed to inform him of the new law. Alsino would never understand the barbed wire, the use of guns, the brutal violence. He believes in another world that is beyond hatred and prejudice. In Prado's novel, he flies away toward a limitless sky where he will discover the true sense of his adolescent dreams. Caught by his enemies, he will be caged as a freak; he will escape only to be burned by a hostile sun, the same sun that burns the backs of his people.

This novel, the poetic expression of a sinister social context, written at the turn of the century by a Chilean disciple of Tolstoy, could not be conceived without the lyrical inspiration and philosophical projection of a truly romantic work of art. Prado never intended it to be a social protest; rather he wrote it as a powerful metaphor of the alienation suffered by Chilean peasants in a semicolonial society.

Both in *Alsino* and in other works, Prado avoids being obviously assertive and rejects all possible dogmatism. He has faith in the wisdom of peasant folk and he does not believe in the supremacy of any creed. He searches for the essence of a given situation through a poetic experience of reality. Prado stands for a healthy and optimistic type of skepticism: he is open to all possible enjoyment of life in spiritual communion with his fellowman. He exalts the importance of simple elegance in the use of language and the power of the poetic image.

Country Judge is the story of a common man who finds himself in the awkward position of being a judge without ever having studied law. He proceeds by instinct and intuition and he rules according to his good conscience, but he feels that by sustaining justice he only receives criticism and punishment from his fellowman. This sort of antihero appears to be an anticipation of existentialist characters in Latin American fiction. The judge is the victim of conventions and prejudices; his sense of fairness and goodness, because it is the product of a free mind, becomes anathema to society. Prado surprises the reader by reacting to this situation with gentle humor, avoiding the bitterness of later novelists.

Hernán Díaz Arrieta correctly points out the peculiar significance of the narrator's predicament:

One day, after listening to the desperate cry of a woman, the mother of a young thief who confessed and whom the judge has condemned and sentenced, the judge sends in his resignation, which becomes a legend in the archives of the town. . . . He bases his resignation on the confusion that his own conscience is experiencing. He resents having to apply penal laws that he considers unjust. He can't separate the guilty from the innocent and he refuses to chastise parents and brothers in condemning the thief. Codes speak of individuals who can be distinguished by intelligence; but the heart recognizes the link among the group and the indivisible unity of the family in the suffering of each member when one is punished by the law.

(*Los cuatro grandes de la literatura chilena*)

Chilean readers, familiar with Prado's background, tend to view this book as an autobiographical account full of personal references to individuals who played an important role in Prado's life. They mention the painter Ortiz de Zárate and the poet Manuel Magallanes Moure; they identify geographical places. To them the realistic descriptions become more significant than the narrator's poetic soliloquies and philosophical reflections. It is possible, as Díaz Arrieta suggests, that *Country Judge* is the book in which Prado reaches his maturity as a writer. Yet, it is not the one preferred by the critics, who traditionally single out *Alsino* as Prado's masterpiece.

La reina de Rapa Nui (The Queen of Rapa Nui, 1914) was Prado's first novel and obviously a tour de force. Prado never was in Easter Island (called Rapa Nui by its inhabitants), where the action takes place. He gathered geographical, historical, and anthropological information and fitted all this material into a rather loose narrative structure. The personal stories of the queen and the leaders of the island are vaguely connected to a first-person account told by a newspaperman who is supposed to be covering a devastating drought for a Valparaíso newspaper. The novel is sustained by the sheer poetic impulse of the testimonial language. Prado suggests the mysterious atmosphere of a primitive but complex civilization. The reader is aware that eventually this civilization will be wiped out by a cataclysm, and only the giant stone sculptures of Easter Island will remain. The narrator glosses over the subject, preferring instead to deal with the intimate tragedy of the queen, her ancestors, the missionaries, and M. Bornier, the outsider who provokes a civil war.

Considering the whole of his work in relation to what has transpired in the Latin American literature of the first half of the twentieth century, Pedro Prado must be considered one of the greatest prose writers of the modernist movement. *Alsino* has no equal in its masterful blending of allegory, fantasy, and regionalism. As a poet, Prado excels in the use of free verse to express a refined, subtle, nostalgic romanticism.

A book published in 1949 under the title *Viejos poemas inéditos* (Old Unpublished Poems) is a forerunner of Pablo Neruda's *Veinte poemas de amor y una canción desesperada* (*Twenty Love Poems and a Song of Despair*, 1924). Both writers seem to have been inspired by Rabindranath Tagore's *The Gardener* (1913); Prado, more in thought than imagery; Neruda, in the pure sensuality of his declarations of love. This collection comprises brief philosophical aphorisms, two sections of free-verse poems and thirty-seven sonnets, among the best he ever wrote. Prado approaches old age in a spirit of serene spiritual harmony; the poems describe moments of profound communion with the mystery of time in the experience of love and the discovery of nature. Some of these poems—"El himno" ("The Hymn"), "La estrella" ("The Star")—remain as classic examples of the best Chilean poetry to come out of the period between the death of modernism and the predominance of the avant-garde.

A man deeply attached to the roots of family, country, and tradition, Prado was eloquent in acknowledging his debt to his parents when accepting the National Prize of Literature. His speech is remembered as one of the finest pieces of testimonial oratory in Chilean literature. In simple cadence, Prado tells his memories of childhood and adolescence, growing up alone with his father—a physician, given to philosophizing in the darkness of the bedroom he shared with his only son. Prado's mother died when he was two years old. About her, he says:

> I was destined to create my own mother, a woman made of persistent irrealities. I modeled her with echoesless pleasure, with unrequited pains and impossible caresses. Thus it was that, without my knowing it, my mother became my daughter, and, myself, ended up being the child of my own youthful creation. I created her with all the grace that was unreachable to me and with all the tenderness that would always be unknown to me.
>
> (Díaz Arrieta)

In a brief poem in his book *Las copas* (1921), Prado imagines his mother as a child, resembling his own children. He caresses her, kisses her, and leading her by the hand tells her: "Go, play, my little mother. Do you hear my children? Go, play with them."

Prado's work strongly resists the passing of time. In contrast to most of the modernists, who depended heavily on formal ornamentation, Prado's bare and profound poetic discourse never ceases to appeal to the lovers of true classical beauty.

SELECTED BIBLIOGRAPHY

First Editions

Poetry

Flores de cardo. Santiago, Chile, 1908.
El llamado del mundo. Santiago, Chile, 1913.
Los pájaros errantes, poemas. Santiago, Chile, 1915.
Las copas. Buenos Aires, 1921.
Poemas en prosa. Selected by Antonio Castro Leal. Mexico City, 1923.
Camino de las horas. Santiago, Chile, 1934.
Otoño en las dunas. Santiago, Chile, 1940.
Ésta bella ciudad envenenada. Santiago, Chile, 1945.
No más que una rosa. Buenos Aires, 1946.
Antología: Las estancias del amor. Selected and with an introduction by Raúl Silva Castro. Santiago, Chile, 1949.
Viejos poemas inéditos. Santiago, Chile, 1949.
Antología. Selected and with a prologue by G. H. Enrique Pascal. Santiago, Chile, 1975.

Prose Narratives

La reina de Rapa Nui. Santiago, Chile, 1914.
Alsino. Santiago, Chile, 1920.
Un juez rural. Santiago, Chile, 1924.

Play

Androvar, poema dramático. Santiago, Chile, 1925.

Essays and Other Works

La casa abandonada: Parábolas y pequeños ensayos. Santiago, Chile, 1912.
Los Diez. Santiago, Chile, 1915.
Ensayos sobre la arquitectura y la poesía. Santiago, Chile, 1916.
Karez-I-Roshan. In collaboration with Antonio Castro Leal. Santiago, Chile, 1921.
Sus mejores poemas. An edition of the work of Manuel Magallanes Moure, selected by Pedro Prado. Santiago, Chile, 1926.

Translations

Country Judge: A Novel of Chile. Translated by Lesley Bird Simpson. With a foreword by Arturo Torres-Ríoseco. Berkeley, Calif., 1968.

Index to Anthologies of Latin American Literature in English Translation. Edited by Juan R. and Patricia M. Freudenthal. Boston, 1977. Contains a list of Prado's poems translated into English.

Biographical and Critical Studies

Alegría, Fernando. *Nueva historia de la novela hispanoamericana.* Hanover, 1986. Pp. 125–129.
Arriagada Augier, Julio, and Hugo Goldsack. *Pedro Prado, un clásico de América.* Santiago, Chile, 1952.
Concha, Jaime. *Poesía chilena, 1907–1917.* Santiago, Chile, 1971. Pp. 21–44.
Cruz A., Bernardo. *Veinte poetas chilenos (glosas críticas)* 1. San Felipe, Chile, 1948. Pp. 5–28.
Díaz Arrieta, Hernán (Published under the pseud. Alone). *Los cuatro grandes de la literatura chilena.* Santiago, Chile, 1962. Pp. 56–114.
Donoso, Armando. *La otra América.* Madrid, 1925. Pp. 133–152.
Silva Castro, Raúl. *Retratos literarios.* Santiago, Chile, 1932. Pp. 125–136.
Torres-Ríoseco, Arturo. *Novelistas contemporáneos de América.* Santiago, Chile, 1939. Pp. 379–409.

Delmira Agustini

(1886–1914)

Manuel Alvar

Delmira Agustini was born in Montevideo, Uruguay, on 24 October 1886. She was a child prodigy who wrote poetry from an early age. She married Enrique Job Reyes on 14 August 1913 but separated from him on 6 October of the same year. Despite divorce proceedings, she continued to see her husband. During one of these meetings, on 6 July 1914, Reyes murdered Agustini and committed suicide next to her.

Agustini entered the world of poetry when modernism was already established, when its scope was well known, and when Rubén Darío had spoken aesthetically for all. Darío had defined the posture of modernism according to some principles with a general application.

> You will see in my verses princesses, kings, imperial things, visions of distant or impossible countries. What do you want? I detest the life and the time into which it has been my lot to be born. I shall not be able to greet even the president of some republic in the language in which I would sing to you, Oh Halagabel, whose court—gold, silk, marble—I remember in dreams.
>
> (Rubén Darío, *Prosas profanas*. In *Obras completas*, Buenos Aires, 1952, p. 594.)

Agustini put forward her uniquely personal justification for the movement. The modernists believed that both in life and in the creator's own reality, art wields supreme power. Nevertheless, each of the movement's coryphaei furnished his own subjective evaluation within the common parameters, and Agustini succeeded in lending lyric emotion to everyday reality utilizing the irrationality of fantasy.

On the other hand, the modernists searched for lyric settings distant from the customary. An "archaeological re-creation," a poeticizing of past epochs and remote countries, created the exotic atmosphere that the modernists so abused. The Middle Ages are remembered as a fairy world of distant princesses, fantastic castles, and ruins, though at times we are allowed a glimpse of the reality behind the props. These are elements that exist in a conventional world given life by museums. One naturally thinks of the paintings of Dierik Bouts or Menlin where white swans swim, or of the elegance of Petrus Christus, Simone Martini, or Fra Filippo Lippi, and the accented profiles of their irises. This world, discovered by the French poets, is a repeated background for the modernists. The swan's legendary divine origin and history helped make the bird the ensign of lyric undertakings at the turn of the century. A large part of Agustini's lyric superficiality lies in gardens adorned with the Wagnerian bird. Hers, it must be remembered, are ornamental swans, without the symbolic complexity that they had in Darío's work.

Beside this temporal exoticism is one that the modernists looked for in distant lands. We see this in Charles Leconte de Lisle, as in Théophile Gautier. Here also, however, modernism sometimes remains very much at the surface. Agustini timidly struck this note, leaving us an Oriental reminiscence in "the Chinese vase" with its fluttering of spikenards, in Madame Butterfly in her "Capricho" (Caprice), in the "Arabesco" (Arabesque) of a dream, and in the scent and echo of Istanbul in "El hada de color de rosas" (The Rose-Colored Fairy). This poverty in exotic embellishment, the triviality in her use of symbols, and the absence of the peacock and other motifs, stems from a lack of an extensive direct contact with other modernists.

Agustini received only a reflected image of modernism, and she accepted the light that was offered her. In her distant native Uruguay, she could not partake of the entire complex field introduced by the modernists: neither the old masters, nor the mythological Renaissance, nor the dilettante delight in strange things. She needed that culture, superficial as it may have been. Her isolation explains the pallid images where her contemporaries shone brightly, the absence of many elements that would have given her literature complexity, and the great gulf between her and Darío or Julio Herrera y Reissig. Her field, where she contributed a personal note and in which she enriched the lyric nuances of modernism, was that of internal experience, the world she lived in every day and that she could analyze without the help of others.

Like the Paul Verlaine of *Sagesse* (Wisdom, 1881) and *Fêtes galantes* (Gallant Festivals, 1869), we have the Darío of "Divagación" (Wandering) and "La cartuja" (Cartusian Monastery). Opposite goodness is sin, and the antinomy results in evil. What always remains alive, however, is the conflict between these two opposing forces. Their presence produces pain in the poet's soul, inextinguishable sensual desire, and bitter sorrow.

Agustini brings the element of modernist duality into her verse by fusing personal experience with poetic judgment. The world is the arena in which two conflicting forces struggle, and man's soul, unable to resolve contradictions, surrenders to the winner.

> *. . . cayó en tus brazos mi alma herida*
> *Por todo el Mal y todo el Bien: mi alma*
> *Un fruto milagroso de la vida*
> *Forjado a sol y madurado en sombra,*
> *Acogíase a tí, como una palma*
> *¡De luz en el desierto de la Sombra!*
>
> ("A una cruz")

> *. . . my wounded soul fell into your arms*
> For all the Evil and all the Good: my soul
> A miraculous fruit of life
> Forged in the sun and ripened in the shade,
> It took refuge in you, like a palm
> Of light in the desert of Shade!
>
> (To a Cross)

And because the soul is a reflection of opposing worlds, it can be changed from a torrent of harmony into a muddy bog. In the end we find the disillusionment and disenchantment of so much modernist poetry: after the flesh's fresh clusters of fruit, death's funereal branches; after the gallant verse, the song astray; after good intentions, misfortune. We see this symbolically established in her "Nocturno" (Nocturnal), with its roses of desire and irises of purity. This conflicting duality repeatedly appears in a world where melancholy and pride lurk, where pain accompanies desire, and where, in the end, nothing remains but a fierce subjectivism by which to interpret the circumstantial world. And with this subjectivism—or because of it—there also appears an amoral skepticism.

> *Mi lecho que está en blanco, es blanco y vaporoso*
> *Como flor de inocencia.*
> *¡Como espuma de vicio!*

> My bed in white, is white and vaporous
> Like a flower of innocence.
> Like the froth of vice!

In the same way that the poet's soul vacillates in the presence of this inner hurricane, only to fall into a painful skepticism, mystery and variety become a creed representing an aesthetic laden with the remnants of past romantic feelings.

650

Y que vibre, y desmaye, y llore, y ruja, y cante
Y sea águila, tigre, paloma en un instante,
Que el Universo quepa en sus ansias divinas;

  Tenga una voz que hiele, que suspenda, que inflame,
y una frente que, erguida, ¡su corona reclame
De rosas, de diamante, de estrellas o de espinas!
                              ("La musa")

  And who quivers, and falters, and cries, and roars,
    and sings
And who is an eagle, tiger, dove in an instant,
Who can contain the Universe in her divine
    anxieties;
  Who has a voice that chills, that astounds, that
    inflames,
and a forehead that, raised high, demands its crown
Of roses, diamonds, stars, or thorns!
                              (The Muse)

Pedro Salinas has pointed out how modernism
brings, together with its sensual world, "a tone of
suffering and subjective lyricism, . . . the last metamorphosis of the elegiac in romanticism." The point
thus set forth provides a valid approach to Agustini's
poetry. Two lines from "El Cisne" (The Swan) offer
an exact definition of her verse.

      –A veces ¡toda! soy alma;
      y a veces ¡toda! soy cuerpo.–

      –Sometimes, I am soul—all of me!
      Other times, I am body—all of me!

This is a literature of intellectual paradoxes. It is
simply the elemental expression of a world of passion,
a poetry that speaks to us constantly of an almost
animal desire or of a melancholy of soft sorrows.
"Soul" represents for Agustini all one's illusions and
dreams, and "body" the dissatisfaction of each moment. The soul, beset with uncertainty and anxiety,
does not find its road to Damascus, and the body,
injured by all the anguish, is dead at twenty-eight.
These two lines contain the key to all of Agustini's
poetry: in terms of the soul, she projects romantic
sentimentality; in terms of the body, the sensual
delight of the modernists.

It is not the rhetoric of the romantics that Agustini
offers us, but unrestrained subjectivity and a lack of

cohesion between the interior world and circumstantial reality. Romanticism functions as the unifying
expression of all her periods of jubilation and despair.
The poet always places the nakedness of her spirit in
the absolute foreground, only to see this tremendous
personal sincerity succumb to the hostility around it.
Personal failure, in the face of both reality actually
experienced and reality intuited, always results in a
search for an escape through fantasy. This irrational
element serves as a kind of Saturn or Penelope in
Agustini's poetry: it fosters and engenders her world
of yearning; and when it fails out of sheer incapacity,
it devours this world and tries to create for itself
another way to flee reality or to approach it again.

  All of these motifs are aspects of the only problem
we encounter in Agustini's poetry, that of love. The
erotic theory that her verse offers reminds us repeatedly of the mystics' ideological structures, except for
the divine tribute. While the mystics try to approach
God by escaping earthly things, Agustini, who represents worldly love, converts the creature into her
god. While they try to reach the "seventh dwelling"
(in Saint Teresa of Ávila's writings, the last stage in
the spiritual journey toward union with God) by
renouncing the lures along the way, Agustini takes
no interest in her final outcome. We see in both,
however, the same "love burning bright with yearning" (as Saint John of the Cross puts it) and the same
pathway to fulfilling their longings.

  As with the mystics, the beloved reveals himself by
the emanation of his light.

      . . . tus ojos me parecen
      Dos semillas de luz entre la sombra,
        Y hay en mi alma un gran florecimiento
      Si en mí los fijas; si los bajas siento
      ¡Como si fuera a florecer la alfombra!
                        ("La noche entró . . .")

. . . your eyes seem to me
Two seeds of light in the shadow,
    And flowers bloom forth in my soul
When you fix them on me; when you lower them
    I feel
As if the carpet were going to bloom!
                        (Night Entered . . .)

Through the light that the beloved radiates, it is
possible to get a glimpse of his form—but never a

complete identification—and knowledge of the path that leads to him.

> *Amor, la noche estaba trágica y sollozante,*
> *Cuando tu llave de oro cantó en mi cerradura;*
> *Luego, la puerta abierta sobre la sombra helante,*
> *Tu forma fué una mancha de luz y de blancura.*
>
> ("El intruso")

My love, the night was tragic and filled with sobbing
When your golden key sang in my lock;
Then, the door open against the chilling darkness,
And your form was a spot of light and of whiteness.

(The Intruder)

Saint John of the Cross states that "creatures are like a footprint of God," but in the lyric emotion of his verse he has told us that the beloved "with his figure alone" beautifies the creatures, that to look for him there would not be needed:

> *. . . otra luz y guía*
> *Sino la que en el corazón ardía.*
> ("La noche oscura del alma")

. . . other light or guide
But that which was burning in the heart.
(The Dark Night of the Soul)

A reflection of this same amorous experience, carried out very similarly, appears translated into Agustini's language.

> *Mi corazón moría triste y lento . . .*
> *Hoy abre en luz como una flor febea;*
> *¡La vida brota como un mar violento*
> *Donde la mano del amor golpea!*
> ("Explosión")

My heart was dying sadly and slowly . . .
Today it is opening in the light like a shining flower;
Life gushes forth like a violent sea
Where the hand of love strikes!

(Explosion)

If love is life, then, it will share the contradiction and antinomy that life represents for the modernist poets. Thus on one occasion, in "Supremo idilio" (Supreme Idyl), Agustini exclaims "Love is all the Good and all the Evil." Love shares, therefore, the same uncertainty found in life, that emotional pull of elegiac intimacy going back to the romantics, a pain

that cannot be contained. With all the shutters closed and the light blocked, there remains only the nostalgic memory of how much was lost, and disgust for what has been gained.

> *Hoy han vuelto.*
> *Por todos los senderos de la noche han venido.*
> *A llorar en mi lecho.*
> *¡Fueron tantos, son tantos!*
> *Yo no sé cuáles viven, yo no sé cuál ha muerto.*
> *Me lloraré yo misma para llorarlos todos.*
> *La noche bebe el llanto como un pañuelo negro.*
> ("El nudo")

Today they have returned.
By all the paths of the night they have come.
To weep at my bed.
There were so many; there are so many!
I do not know which ones live, I do not know
  which have died.
I shall weep for myself to weep for all of them.
The night drinks in the weeping like a black
  handkerchief.

(The Knot)

Here there is a clear difference between Agustini's erotic intuition and the amorous scope of the mystics. A sensual progression leads the Uruguayan poet to amorous submission and surrender, but in these the body anchors itself more and more firmly to the earth that sustains it. It is the same pathway found in mysticism, but undertaken for totally different reasons. In one, we see the attempt to renounce everything in a rapture of detachment; in the other, the search for the raw clay itself from which love is formed.

Once the poet has achieved the amorous union, she is left with only two possibilities: the perpetuation of the moment or its total destruction. The former brings the fullness of love, exultant happiness, and uncontainable jubilation.

> *Si la vida es amor, ¡bendita sea!*
> *¡Quiero más vida para amar!*
> ("Explosión")

If life is love, blessed be it!
I want more life, to love!

The latter, with the previous hedonism destroyed, the fantasy vanished, the hoped-for eternity shattered, brings flight toward death as the only thing that can be truly possessed.

> *La intensa realidad de un sueño lúgubre*
> *Puso en mis manos tu cabeza muerta;*
> *Yo la apresaba como hambriento buitre . . .*
> *Y con más alma que en la vida, trémula,*
> *¡Le sonreía como nadie nunca! . . .*
> *¡Era tan mía cuando estaba muerta!*
> *Hoy la he visto en la vida, bella, impávida*
> *Como un triunfo estatuario, tu cabeza.*
> *Más frío me dió así que en el idilio*
> *Fúnebre aquel, al estrecharla muerta . . .*
> *¡Y así la lloro hasta agotar mi vida . . .*
> *Así tan viva cuanto me es ajena!*
> ("La intensa realidad . . .")

The intense reality of a dismal dream
Placed in my hands your lifeless head;
I clutched it like a hungry vulture . . .
And with more spirit than in Life, trembling,
I smiled at it like no one ever had . . .
It was so much mine in death!
  Today I have seen your head in life, beautiful,
    as dauntless
As triumph carved in stone.
It chilled me more thus than in that funereal
Episode when, grasping it, lifeless . . .
And so I weep for it until my life drains away . . .
Now as alive as it is alien to me!
  (The Intense Reality . . .)

Up to this point a clear transposition of the three paths that the mystics knew can be followed. This whole theory of love, however, was based on a two-sided world, that of the lover and the beloved. But while for the mystics, vacillation is the journey of the soul and God is the supreme love, the confident waiting, and total consolation, in Agustini's erotic poetry, there is a reversal of these elements. Love follows a steady path toward its object, which again and again escapes apprehension. Here we have, at last, a basic concept for characterizing this poetry: it is realistic with respect to certain data—the impassioned soul—and nonrealistic with respect to its end—the problematic relationship between lover and beloved. This is very important, for while the mystics embarked on their journey with the assurance of some abiding good, love in strictly human poetry begins the journey with problems clouding its success, and, to

assure its outcome, proceeds by grasping every reality it finds and getting lost at each step along the way. Two ingredients of the poetry become clearly discernible: first, the world of fantasy sought by the poet, and second, the real truth. An awareness of the relationship between these ingredients sheds light on the apparent contradiction between the realistic and nonrealistic elements in Agustini's poetry.

In Agustini's first book, written when she was twenty-one, her memory was directed to her childhood and its sweet illusions. Later, as the presence of fantasy increased, this same flight from the real world was elevated to the level of religious feeling. As with Darío, this incipient Christianity was somewhat irrational. It was based on distant poetic idealizations or on aesthetic sentimentality, although we shouldn't deny the sincerity of either of these.

In their own way, the modernists were tremendously sincere. They seem little so today, but we must remember that their world, exquisitely wrought, was, after all, too clean and too remote to immerse in the vileness and bloodshed that our age has brought. This is not a poetry tied to circumstances, yet it can become such if these circumstances are ennobled. The religious sentiments in her poetry are just as sincere as the love for France, the exoticisms, or the erotic passion. In Agustini's case we have religious lines intertwined with her romantic expressions, with her sensual desires, and with her impassioned thoughts. These lines are, perhaps, the hope and the aim of a poetry that so often proceeds only hesitatingly, but they are left unresolved. We hear only the voice, while no light is furnished for our eyes. Though blind and groping, the road still leads to Damascus.

Translated from the Spanish by Theodore Parks

SELECTED BIBLIOGRAPHY

Editions

Individual Works

El libro blanco. Montevideo, 1907.
Cantos de la mañana. Montevideo, 1910.
Los cálices vacíos. Montevideo, 1913.

El rosario de Eros. Montevideo, 1924. Posthumous.
Los astros del abismo. Montevideo, 1924. Posthumous.

Collected Works

Obras poéticas: Edición oficial. Montevideo, 1940.
Poesías completas. Edited by Alberto Zum Felde. Buenos
    Aires, 1944; 4th ed., 1971.
Poesías completas. Edited by Manuel Alvar. Barcelona,
    1971.

Biographical and Critical Studies

Alvar, Manuel. *La poesía de Delmira Agustini.* Sevilla,
    1958.
Machado, Ofelia. *Delmira Agustini.* Montevideo, 1944.
Visca, Arturo Sergio. *Delmira Agustini: Correspondencia
    íntima.* Montevideo, 1969.
Zum Felde, Alberto. *Proceso intelectual del Uruguay y crítica
    de su literatura 2.* Montevideo, 1930. Pp. 232–236.

Martín Luis Guzmán

(1887–1976)

Lanin A. Gyurko

Born in Chihuahua, Mexico, on 6 October 1887, Martín Luis Guzmán was the son of Colonel Martín Luis Guzmán y Rendón, an instructor in the Colegio Militar of Chapultepec, and Carmen Franco Terrazas. His talent for journalism was first displayed at the age of thirteen, when he started the periodical *La juventud* (Youth) in Veracruz. Guzmán later formed part of the illustrious literary group El Ateneo (Atheneum), whose members included José Vasconcelos, Pedro Henríquez Ureña, and Alfonso Reyes. In 1913 Guzmán was named to the staff of General Ramón Iturbe, then served as envoy of Venustiano Carranza in 1914, and later that same year joined the forces of the revolutionary leader Francisco ("Pancho") Villa. Imprisoned in Mexico City by Carranza, Guzmán was soon released by order of the Military Convention of Aguascalientes. From 1915 until 1920, he remained in voluntary exile, first in Spain and then in the United States. On his return to Mexico, he became chief editor of *El Heraldo de México* and was also named personal secretary to Alberto Pani, the secretary of external relations in the government of Álvaro Obregón. In 1922 Guzmán founded *El Mundo* and in 1925 left again for exile, remaining in Spain until 1936. A masterful journalist, he wrote for *El Universal* on his return to Mexico and in 1942 founded the periodical *Tiempo*. In 1958 he was awarded both the Manuel Ávila Camacho Prize and the National Prize for Literature. Guzmán died on 22 December 1976 in Mexico City.

The novelists of the Mexican Revolution, foremost among whom are Guzmán, Mariano Azuela, Agustín Yáñez, and Carlos Fuentes, have not only evoked the military phases of the conflict—the clashes between *federales* and *revolucionarios* and later, after the defeat of Victoriano Huerta, between the various factions of the Revolution, led by Carranza, Villa, and Emiliano Zapata—but have also delved extensively into the political aspects of that revolution, in particular, the incessant rivalries among the revolutionaries themselves for the presidency of Mexico. In his masterpiece, *El águila y la serpiente* (*The Eagle and the Serpent,* 1928), Guzmán gives an eyewitness account of many of the military and political leaders of the Revolution, as well as a depiction of activities off the battlefield—military conventions and speeches, banquets and dances, the conditions inside hospitals, and barracks life. Vivid, pictorial, penetrating to the soul of both leaders and followers in a crisp, dramatic, and forceful style, *The Eagle and the Serpent* defies generic classification. Perhaps because of the forthright and at times highly critical manner in which Guzmán describes powerful personalities, he himself chose to consider it a novel—a work of fiction. Others have regarded it as a collection of short stories or essays that adroitly combine biographical, autobiographical, and fantastic elements. Perhaps it can be best seen as a continuation, in the twentieth century, of one of the most important and original forms of literary expression in Mexico, from the epoch of the conquest to the present day, the chronicle—an intermingling of fiction and subjective interpretation, a combination of documentary and traditional storytelling.

Guzmán's lengthy account of the Mexican Revolution focuses on its ideologies and its aspirations, its lofty goals and the subsequent betrayal of those goals, and the initial buoyant optimism of intellectuals such as Vasconcelos and Guzmán himself, which was replaced by pessimism and even despair as the Revolution rapidly disintegrated into *personalismo* (personality cults) and factionalism, into self-aggrandizement and power-grabbing, after the defeat of Huerta. Guzmán's first-person narrative is triply fascinating: first, because of its compelling and inexhaustible theme, the revolution of 1910, which authors such as Yáñez have considered the most important event in the entire history of the nation; second, because Guzmán—like Bernal Díaz del Castillo, one of Hernán Cortés' soldiers and the author of the *Verdadera historia de la conquista de la Nueva España* (*The True History of the Conquest of New Spain*, 1632), and like Azuela, the founder of the novel of the Revolution—writes of experiences felt and lived, thus imbuing his account with immediacy and emotional conviction; and third, because of his masterful style, which is lucid, direct, eloquent, and incisive. Guzmán, who had rejected a military career on the advice of his father, repeatedly depicts the confrontations of the intellectual, the urbane and contemplative man, with the rude and crude and sometimes even barbaric forces that nonetheless were necessary to defeat the forces of *continuismo* (perpetuation of the ancien régime), those of Huerta. Guzmán also relates the many times he came close to being killed, not on the battlefield, not by the *federales*, but by the very person he supported and served, Pancho Villa, who is likened to a jaguar that has to be tamed. Guzmán records his occasional triumphs in harnessing Villa's barbaric impulse, such as when he and Enrique Llorente intervene—at the

risk of aggravating their leader's volatile temper and being shot to death themselves—and persuade an enraged and vengeful Villa not to execute 160 prisoners who had surrendered to him. Guzmán repeatedly uses psychology—the art of persuasion—to control Villa's behavior, on this occasion astutely appealing to Villa's personal sense of how a master general would treat men who had voluntarily put down their arms. Yet at other times Guzmán cannot halt "revolutionary justice," which is applied instantly, without trial or witnesses. Guzmán fails to persuade Villa's general, José Isabel Robles, and the provisional president of Mexico, Eulalio Gutiérrez, to pardon five counterfeiters whom Villa has sentenced to immediate execution, even though Villa has just given Guzmán thousands of pesos that Villa himself has just had freshly printed.

Much of the fascination and tense drama of *The Eagle and the Serpent* derives from the series of direct confrontations between Guzmán and Villa, who time and again challenges the *catrín* (dandy) to prove himself—with the pistol, with the lariat—and then, when Guzmán responds to these challenges, capriciously rewards him for his prowess. And indeed, the dominant personality of this work, which was tentatively entitled "A la hora de Pancho Villa" (The Hour of Pancho Villa), is Villa, "the centaur of the North," whom Guzmán treats with continued ambivalence—with admiration and terror, doubt and dedication—as a charismatic and deadly leader. When Guzmán encounters Villa for the first time in a darkened hovel in Ciudad Juárez, he compares him to a wild animal in his lair, despite the unrestrained enthusiasm that fellow revolutionaries like Vasconcelos had evinced for Villa's leadership. At a subsequent point in the narrative, in the episode ominously titled "La pistola de Pancho Villa" ("Pancho Villa's Pistol"), Guzmán portrays him as the very incarnation of destruction, as a man fused with his pistol. In still another episode, "El sueño del compadre Urbina" ("A Perilous Sleep"), Villa emerges as a loquacious and enigmatic raconteur, speculating on the nature of sleep and astutely enhancing his own legendary status by giving his rapt listeners an image of himself as a noble, courageous, and self-sacrificing leader. Here is the heroic Villa, whose devotion to his men is so great that he endangers his own life by pausing in his flight from the pursuing *federales* because, although he is unable to awaken an exhausted companion, Tomá Urbina, he refuses to abandon him. Villa rescues Urbina by throwing him bodily over his horse and carefully guiding him, still asleep, through the rugged and treacherous terrain.

The very title *The Eagle and the Serpent*, a reference to the emblems on the Mexican national flag, reflects Guzmán's quest not only for a just and enlightened revolutionary and national leader but also for the essence of the Mexican national identity. The young, enthusiastic, idealistic, and intrepid Guzmán plunges into the violent and chaotic military phase of the Revolution. Yet, ironically, the end of the work depicts an increasingly disillusioned and apprehensive Guzmán, seeking to flee from the clutches of Villa. Here again Guzmán uses psychology to outwit his leader. Instead of openly deserting him and thus running the risk of being fanatically pursued and perhaps killed by Villa, Guzmán boldly enters "the lion's den" to confront an increasingly desperate Villa, and requests permission to rejoin his family. At the beginning of the work, it is a heinous act of Huerta, the assassinations of Francisco and Gustavo Madero, that Guzmán condemns, but at the end it is the capricious and ignominious execution of David Berlanga—a leader whom Guzmán treats as the idealistic conscience of the Revolution—perpetrated by Rodolfo Fierro on direct orders of Villa, that causes Guzmán anguish. Indeed, the *federales* are most often only a shadowy phenomenon, such as in the chapter where Guzmán describes the city of Culiacán after the revolutionary victory, with the federal forces having fled. Time and again it is revolutionary bloodlust and despotism that Guzmán chronicles and condemns. Thus Guzmán writes of the draconian reprisals—death by the firing squad—taken by Francisco Cosío Robelo against those who defied Obregon's decree against looting. Guzmán also portrays the pathologically cruel behavior of a revolutionary commander who, in order quickly to exact from defeated *porfiristas* (supporters of the deposed dictator Porfirio Díaz) the funds to pay his troops, intimidates four of the wealthiest citizens of a town by hanging a completely innocent person who the officer knows is impoverished but whose death by hanging is certain to intimidate the others. Paralleling Azuela,

whose *Los de abajo* (*The Underdogs*, 1915) contains repeated and bitter diatribes against revolutionary excesses, Guzmán chronicles the monstrous way in which Fierro executes three hundred prisoners, by compelling them to perform a gruesome danse macabre, literally to run for their lives in an attempt to escape his bullets by reaching and scaling a wall. Time and again Guzmán, the consummate literary artist, is conscious not only of dramatic characterization and action but also of setting; here it is the blood-red and fiery sun that seems to merge with the figure of the bizarre and ruthless Fierro.

Yet one of the basic compositional principles of *The Eagle and the Serpent* is balance. At a certain point he presents Villa as a being of darkness, as a person whose body blocks out all the light and whose eyes emanate the shadow of death, but at another point, while the boisterous revolutionaries watch a documentary film at the Convention at Aguascalientes, Villa appears on the screen ringed in light. Actually this is the glaring light of the projector, but Guzmán endows it with a spiritual significance. He cannot restrain his awe and admiration for Villa, who now appears as a supernatural being, bathed in a radiant and transcendental light, with none of the irony or sarcasm found in the portrayal of Villa by Azuela or Rafael Muñoz. Indeed, Guzmán's idealization of Villa presages the heroic and mythic way in which Villa is conjured up in Fuentes' novel *Gringo viejo* (*The Old Gringo*, 1985). Countering the brutality of some of the revolutionary generals are the courage and idealism of others, such as Iturbe, the victor of Culiacán, Robles, Manuel Diéguez, and the great Felipe Ángeles, whom Guzmán portrays in an unaccustomed way, not on the battlefield but alone and meditative. Ironically, even Fierro himself, afflicted by guilt after his execution of Berlanga and confessing his act to Guzmán, is depicted as a "good general and a good revolutionary." And the continued reservations Guzmán expresses about the Villista troops—even the resplendent *dorados* (golden boys), whom he sees as menacing and cruel—are balanced by the severe misgivings he has about the leadership of Carranza, whom he unequivocally delineates not as the "new man of the Revolution" but as a continuation of the past—as a commander whose government would be a repetition of the absolutism of Porfirio Díaz. Unlike the emotional Vasconcelos or Alberto Pani, the always contemplative and measured Guzmán is hesitant to place his faith and his support in any one leader, and thus he rejects the cult of the *macho*, of the heroic leader who will redeem Mexico. Yet ironically, in *Memorias de Pancho Villa* (*Memoirs of Pancho Villa*, 1938), his mammoth biography of the revolutionary, Guzmán modifies his position and re-creates Villa as idealist and savior. Perhaps because Guzmán has failed to find the responsible and noble leader so desperately needed after the Revolution, perhaps because he himself was not willing to accept the offers repeatedly tendered to him to become a military officer, and even cabinet minister, offers which, had they been accepted, would have placed him in a position to become a national leader, Guzmán is compelled to create through his literary vision and imagination the hero whom he did not find in his youth. Unwilling to admire unstintingly any of the leaders, Guzmán is even more skeptical of the masses of revolutionary soldiers. In Azuela's *The Underdogs*, these soldiers are caricatured but are at least individualized. For Guzmán, *los de abajo* are consistently an indistinguishable mass—anonymous beings engulfed in shadows or in night, portrayed in their drunkenness as a Hydra-headed beast or as a gigantic reptile.

In his bold and fascinating narrative of the labyrinthine world of Mexican politics in the 1920's, *La sombra del caudillo* (The Shadow of the Tyrant, 1929), a novel of espionage and petropolitics, Guzmán concentrates on the somber world in an era of extreme instability and explosive conflict in Mexico. In Rodolfo Usigli's biting political satire *El gesticulador* (*The Impostor*, 1947), César Rubio, a frustrated university professor and expert on the Mexican Revolution who has assumed the role of another César Rubio, a martyred revolutionary idealist, states cynically, "In Mexico everything is politics . . . politics is our climate, the very air we breathe." *La sombra del caudillo* powerfully exemplifies this statement, as it evokes a closed-in, stifling, obsessively political and politicized atmosphere—a nebulous world of incessantly shifting allegiances and alliances that form and dissolve and coalesce again. It is a world of treacherous forces that engulf and finally destroy the protagonist, Ignacio Aguirre, identified as

a heroic victim from the very start of this highly fatalistic work. Here Guzmán captures, in a stark, classic prose, the incendiary atmosphere of revolutionary aftermath, with former generals still thirsting for battle and ready to throw their armies into the field at the slightest provocation. By writing a roman à clef instead of a historical novel, Guzmán produces a brilliant work that can apply not only to the Mexico of other eras but also to the political situation and to the struggle between tyranny and freedom in other Latin American countries. His vision is both Mexican and universal.

In *La sombra del caudillo*, Guzmán writes both a political novel and a spy thriller. Here, as in *The Eagle and the Serpent*, he is a master at creating and sustaining suspense. His narrative is carefully orchestrated, with a crescendo of intrigue, betrayal, violence, and mass murder. At the outset of the novel, the uproar and violence at the convention of the Partido Radical Progresista at Toluca, marking a rapid degeneration of the initial atmosphere of superficial cordiality and unity, adumbrate a horrendous cycle of violence begetting increased violence—the kidnapping and torturing almost to death of the innocent Axkaná by the agents of the Caudillo, the threat of the Caudillo's protégé, Hilario Jiménez, to massacre the Aguirrista supporters, the murder of the deputy Canizares, and the final bloodbath that consumes Aguirre and his followers, with only Axkaná escaping alive.

Guzmán's novel is replete with shadows—shadowy political forces, shady dealings, shadow characters with shadow loyalties, and shadow candidacies. Guzmán presents not only the world of the reclusive Caudillo but the whole of Mexico as a vast shadowland. The invisible Caudillo, who never makes public speeches and refuses to take his hat off in public because he fears assassination, constantly operates behind the scenes. His machinations are reflected everywhere—in the duplicitous behavior of the generals who earnestly and repeatedly pledge their loyalty to Aguirre but who are in fact the minions of the Caudillo; in the pusillanimous doctor who treats Axkaná after he has been forced to imbibe an immense quantity of alcohol by his mysterious captors, and yet attempts to cover up the crime of attempted murder by dismissing it as a case of mere intoxication; and in the politicians and deputies—including Jiménez, the hand-picked successor of the Caudillo—who suddenly become the recipients of lavish gifts. Not only the Caudillo but many of the other characters in *La sombra del caudillo* are mere shadows. The presidential candidacy of Aguirre, the minister of war who decides to defy the Caudillo, never really emerges from the inchoate, shadowy stage. Ironically, Aguirre, who attempts to project himself as the candidate of the people, has for his entire political career functioned as but a shadow of the Shadow—as a minister subservient to the will and whim of the Caudillo—to exploit, betray, and even eradicate the enemies of his master. Thus Aguirre, despite his naive faith in the power of public opinion to elevate his candidacy, is never really perceived by the people as a viable alternative to the Caudillo. To ensure his election as president, the historical Francisco Madero painstakingly laid the groundwork by crisscrossing Mexico, speaking to the people in state after state, and for a number of years. Madero understood what Aguirre does not, that the people will not blindly and instantaneously follow him just because of their discontent with the Caudillo, and that he must vie for that support and attempt to win it through public addresses—at which Aguirre is not adept.

Shadows—natural, political, psychological—proliferate in this work, underscoring not only the menacing power of the Caudillo, which creeps into every corner, but also the perpetual haziness, the inability in this fluctuating shadowland to distinguish between friend and foe, between loyal followers and spies. Although the insecure and extremely narcissistic Aguirre naively believes that he has many steadfast allies among the politicians and generals who pay court to him and feed his ambition for ultimate power, most of these, like Catarino Ibáñez, the sycophantic governor of the state of Mexico, and later like the ruthless general Julián Elizondo, are but shadow adherents who secretly betray him. And shadows fall over shadows. The effect is further to underscore the automaton-like nature of the characters. A fated shadow of the past falls over Aguirre as it does over the entire work of Guzmán—that of Pancho Villa. Throughout his career, the extremely malleable and indecisive Aguirre is totally distinct from the intrepid and recklessly impetuous Villa. Indifferent to the *pueblo*, making only vague promises of armed rebellion, more with the intent of keeping the Caudillo off-guard than out of any revolutionary conviction or desire to aid the oppressed, Aguirre is nonetheless equated ironically with Villa—in the manner of their brutal deaths. Both Aguirre and Villa are betrayed by their own followers, and slain on their own home ground. Aguirre has fled in panic and sought sanctuary in Toluca, the party stronghold. Villa, pursued for months by John J. Pershing, was never captured but instead died in a hail of gunfire in Parral, cut down by fellow Mexicans in his own home territory, the signal for his assassination having been given by a candy vendor whom he had known and trusted—just as Aguirre completely trusts his betrayer, Elizondo.

Like Aguirre, Jiménez is also presented as a shadow of the Shadow. Indeed, the reason the Caudillo selects Jiménez instead of the flamboyant Aguirre is that the latter is too much of a showman, too much of a Hollywood-type personality, and therefore is regarded with suspicion and even paranoia as being too independent of the Caudillo. Although the Caudillo tolerates the deals that Aguirre makes with the May-Be Petroleum Company, whose very name underscores its problematic nature, it is clear that he disapproves of making concessions to this company that will deprive the generals, who are his loyal supporters and who own the oil-rich lands, of their spoils of the Revolution. The cold, gray, bloodless Jiménez is far more amenable to control than is the sybaritic and impassioned Aguirre. Although Jiménez initially seems willing to accede to the demands for shared authority made upon him by the Partido Radical Progresista, he finally rejects compromise, on the orders of the Caudillo, who seeks total control. Aguirre is quick to perceive the essence of Jiménez as a golem of the Caudillo.

As in *The Eagle and the Serpent*, Guzmán creates a character who serves as a moral focus, a center of idealism, in contrast to the prevailing atmosphere of moral depravity and political corruption, or at best expediency. In *La sombra del caudillo*, the idealistic center is Axkaná, the alter ego of the decadent Aguirre. As Axkaná speaks to the Indian masses, the shadows that had previously fallen so thoroughly over the characters are temporarily dissipated. There is an emphasis on light—spiritual light, the contact between the lower and the upper classes, and the possibility of a genuine unity in a world relentlessly splintered by the forces of the Caudillo, who acts under a divide-and-conquer dictum. But despite the eloquence and power of Axkaná's speech, the aura of emotional and spiritual union that is generated quickly evaporates. Ibáñez, who is also temporarily moved by the speech, attempts to garner the approbation of the masses for himself, hypocritically and histrionically usurping the recognition due to Axkaná by embracing him in a false display of fraternal unity. The fatalistic words of Axkaná are brought to mind: in the tumultuous world of national politics, those who embrace as friends one day will turn against each other the next day as mortal enemies. Here, in the very moment of apparent unity, of the brief awakening of Ibáñez' political conscience, is also the shadow of future betrayal, as Ibáñez, governor of the state in which Elizondo is a division commander, will work hand in glove with him behind the scenes, in the comfortable shadows, to destroy Aguirre in order to gain the favor of the Caudillo.

There is an underlying pathetic, even tragic quality to the frantic, almost desperate hedonism of Aguirre, as he goes from one amatory encounter to another, from the house of Rosario to the bordello of La Mora and back again. It is almost as if on some level Aguirre senses that his career, and indeed his life, are on a negative, futile, and ultimately disastrous course, and is seeking to compensate. Professionally as well, there seems to be an inner drive toward self-destruction in Aguirre. In his role as minister of war, he seems to be a mere figurehead, accomplishing very little, using his powerful position as a front for his shady business transactions and capriciously exerting his authority not to assist but to thwart those who come seeking his help. The overly emotional, childish, insensitive, and even callous way in which Aguirre runs his ministry does not augur well for the way in which he would govern the nation. For all his pretensions to political power, Aguirre is characterized by a lack of willpower, by a yearning for soft, luxurious surroundings and womblike comfort. Rebuffed by the Caudillo, Aguirre, instead of planning aggressive countermeasures, immediately seeks out

the *zona sagrada* (the sacred zone)—the place of tranquillity, consolation, and comfort that is the house of Rosario, where he becomes submerged in lassitude, nurturing his emotional wounds. Here is another indication of how ill-prepared psychologically Aguirre is to launch an independent candidacy against so formidable an opponent as the Caudillo. Aguirre also fails to grasp the essentially cold-blooded and deadly nature of the game that he chooses to play. He never seems to believe that the Caudillo, to whom he responds as to a father-figure, is capable of executing him.

After he has broken with the Caudillo, a new, idealistic personality begins to emerge within Aguirre. As minister of war, he had always remained aloof from the people, but now he begins, belatedly, to develop a social consciousness that appears to be genuine. Whether consciously or not, Aguirre seeks to emulate the figure of Francisco Madero. Yet while Madero issued his call to arms to the people of Mexico from the safety of his residence in the United States, the vain and quixotic Aguirre waits for the groundswell of public acclaim for his cause while remaining in Mexico. Aguirre thus places himself and his followers in an extraordinarily dangerous position because the spontaneous uprising of the people never occurs. And Aguirre also believes that the generals will flock to his side, swayed by the moral legitimacy of his candidacy. Once again Aguirre demonstrates his lack of understanding of the Caudillo, who through a combination of bribery and intimidation stealthily and relentlessly undercuts him. Perhaps because for so long a time he has been forced to play the role of obedient surrogate son, Aguirre cannot succeed in projecting the image of the benevolent father-figure and protector of the people that is so desperately sought after. Ironically, at the very end, when he is about to be executed, the egocentric Aguirre begins to think of others, of his loyal companions who will lose their lives because they have committed themselves to his cause. For the first time in his career, Aguirre is afflicted by feelings of guilt. Only now, when it is too late, does he begin to manifest unequivocally his capacity for leadership, as he maintains his dignity and self-control. Another of the tragic flaws of Aguirre has been his self-containment, his allowing himself to be drawn along both by circumstance and by his grandiose desire for supreme power. But he is finally presented as a martyr, since Guzmán renders the heroic death of Aguirre as his way of expiating the crimes of his life.

A cyclical time process dominates *La sombra del caudillo* and underscores the fatalistic nature of Guzmán's vision. The novel both begins and ends with a description of Aguirre's Cadillac, which functions as a paradoxical symbol—both of his *machismo*, of the power and wealth he has acquired as the result of a revolution fought to benefit the poor and the oppressed, and of his betrayal of revolutionary ideals. The Cadillac is a magnet, and as he drives, or perhaps better parades, through the center of Mexico City, a bevy of prostitutes follows him in adulation. At the end of the narrative, the Cadillac again appears, now in the possession of Aguirre's slayer, Segura. Its reappearance signifies that the cycle of bloodshed brings to the top only new oppressors. Just as Aguirre fights against the *porfiristas* but after obtaining power exceeds them in conspicuous consumption—his drinking not of pulque but of expensive Hennessy Extra, his three homes—so after the destruction of Aguirre is his licentiousness perpetuated in Segura. The money Aguirre acquires through his transactions with petroleum companies is squandered in the endless rounds of orgies that he attends and hosts. Similarly, at the end, Segura spends literal blood money—the sheaf of blood-soaked bills he has stripped from Aguirre's cadaver—to buy an enormous pair of earrings for his mistress. Through emphasis on the operation of a negative cyclical time, Guzmán demonstrates how the betrayal of the ideals of the Mexican Revolution will continue, as those who seize power utilize their privileged positions to enrich themselves, heedless of the desperate needs of the people.

The last of the many shadows that haunt this narrative is the mere shadow of public opinion. The newspapers in the phantasmagorical world of *La sombra del caudillo* are mere shadows of newspapers: the press does not dare formulate an independent opinion concerning the putative "armed rebellion" of Aguirre and its rapid quelling by the Caudillo, under the pretext of protecting the national integrity and defending the principles of the Mexican Revolution. Public opinion remains a nebulous entity that never matures into what Guzmán wants it to become—a potent force that will serve as a check on political and military extremism. In *La sombre del caudillo*, Guzmán writes what the newspapers are afraid to print and what the people are fearful of discussing, as he forever dissipates the shadows of obfuscation that the Caudillo attempts to throw over the execution of Aguirre and his followers.

SELECTED BIBLIOGRAPHY

First Editions

Narrative and Dramatic Works

El águila y la serpiente. Madrid, 1928.
La sombre del caudillo. Madrid, 1929.
Kinchil. Mexico City, 1946. Subsequently entitled *Maestro rurales.*
Islas Marías, novela y drama. Mexico City, 1959.

Biographical Works

Mina el mozo: Héroe de Navarra. Madrid, 1932. Retitled *Javier Mina: Héroe de España y México,* in *Obras completas,* 1961.
Memorias de Pancho Villa. Mexico City, 1938, 1940.

Essays

La querella de México. Madrid, 1915.
A orillas del Hudson. New York, 1917.
Filadelfia, paraíso de conspiradores. Madrid, 1933.
Muertes históricas. Mexico City, 1958.
Otras páginas. Mexico City, 1958.
Pábulo para la historia. Mexico City, 1961.
Piratas y corsarios. Mexico City, 1961.
Febrero de 1913. Mexico City, 1963.
Necesidad de cumplir las leyes de reforma. Mexico City, 1963.
Crónicas de mi destierro. Mexico City, 1964.

Collected Works

Obras completas. 2 vols. Mexico City, 1961–1963.

Translations

The Eagle and the Serpent. Translated by Harriet de Onís. New York, 1965.
Memoirs of Pancho Villa. Translated by Virginia H. Taylor. Austin, Tex., 1965.

Biographical and Critical Studies

Abreu Gómez, Ermilo. *Martín Luis Guzmán.* Mexico City, 1968.

Bruce-Novoa, Juan. "Martín Luis Guzmán's Necessary Overtures." *Discurso literario* 4/1:63–83 (1986).

Carballo, Emmanuel. *Diecinueve protagonistas de la literatura mexicana del siglo veinte.* Mexico City, 1965. Pp. 61–99.

Houck, Helen Phipps. "Las obras novelescas de Martín Luis Guzmán." *Revista iberoamericana* 3/5:139–158 (1941).

Leal, Luis. "*La sombra del caudillo,* Roman à Clef." *Modern Language Journal* 36/1:16–21 (1952).

Megenney, William, ed. *Five Essays on Martin Luis Guzman.* Riverside, Calif., 1978.

Stanton, Ruth. "Martín Luis Guzmán's Place in Modern Mexican Literature." *Hispania* 26:136–138 (1943).

Ramón López Velarde

(1888–1921)

Allen W. Phillips

Modernism had by 1910 practically run its course in Mexico, that is to say, in its most superficial and exotic aspects, and the long, stifling dictatorship of Porfirio Díaz had also finally come to a close. The Mexican Revolution of 1910, led by Francisco I. Madero, had triumphed, but many years of political and social unrest were to follow the fall of Díaz. The Mexican modernist generation had produced good poets (Manuel Gutiérrez Nájera, Enrique González Martínez, Amado Nervo), and in this charged atmosphere Ramón López Velarde appeared. He brought to Mexican literature new themes and above all a unique and highly personal poetic language. He has sometimes been classified as the last of the modernists but is always considered the point of departure of contemporary Mexican poetry. As Octavio Paz has suggested in his "Introduction to the History of Mexican Poetry," "To follow after López Velarde is not easy; it demands . . . a catholicity that does not betray us and a fidelity that does not isolate or stifle us. And if it is true that we cannot return to the poetry of López Velarde, what makes this return impossible is just that his poetry marks a starting point" (Paz, 1958, p. 40).

The work of López Velarde, brief and intense, was original and authentic; he is the herald of future aesthetic development in later poets of Mexico, and few of them would deny his influence. Although López Velarde at first captured the attention of his readers by cultivating provincial themes, particularly in his early prose and poetry, he is not by any means a provincial writer. On the contrary, he is a complex and difficult poet. The mistaken myth of López Velarde as a simple, Catholic provincial writer was dispelled by Xavier Villaurrutia, one of his best critics, who correctly saw the depth of vision that led to his inner exploration of the universal themes of love and death, spirituality and the flesh. The province, in all its innocence and purity, was, however, a constant backdrop, one that was both concrete and idealized, and against which the poet expressed his inner conflicts and the dualities of human existence: carnal eroticism and religiosity; sensuality and chastity; devotion and paganism. The constant interplay between spiritual purity and temptation is fundamental to his prose and poetry.

However, the greatest attainment of López Velarde was the creation of a poetic language. In his work, literary tradition, the language of the city, and a conversational manner are fused in a new lyric voice. Words are charged with fresh meaning; his adjectives, though often unexpected, are exact, and they explore new relationships between things; and, in addressing himself directly to the reader, López Velarde probes the essence of reality. Often the subjects of his poetry are mundane objects unperceived in their true nature until revealed by the poet. However surprising his daring imagery may be, often elaborate and aggressive in nature, it corresponds to an authentic poetic vision. He searches for an exact metaphor in an expression that transcends the merely anecdotal or the descriptive. He delves deeply into his spiritual anxieties and into the very heart of Mexico itself, in spite of the deceptive repertoire of his themes (the province, lost or unrequited love and youth, Catholicism, and death). In his best poems and prose texts, López Velarde goes much deeper than the subject of the work might suggest; his expression is often arcane and baroque, but it is always exciting, if at times impenetrable. However inventive he may be in his preoccupation with language, he is never contrived, nor does he fall into the trap of sterile rhetoric. He is a genuine and sincere poet, not a mannerist, combining with irony (probably learned from the French symbolist Jules Laforgue or perhaps through the Argentine poet Leopoldo Lugones) a certain special tenderness that influences the ever-changing point of view and tonal level of his verse. This irony and detachment give his work the quality of modernity, even today.

Paradoxically, while López Velarde is generally thought of as the most truly Mexican of all Mexican poets, communicating directly with the affective and sentimental nature of his compatriots, he also reached out beyond national borders to become one of the most admired poets of Spanish America in the period of transition from modernism to the vanguard movements of the 1920's and 1930's.

There was nothing remarkable about the life of López Velarde, who was born on 15 June 1888 in Jerez, now Ciudad García, in the state of Zacatecas. He died just after his thirty-third birthday (on 19 June 1921) in Mexico City, as a result of bronchopneumonia induced by his inveterate custom of walking late at night in the high altitude of the capital. The oldest son of a family of nine children, he was brought up in the provinces and had his early education in the Seminario Conciliar de Zacatecas (1901–1902), the Seminario Conciliar de Santa María de Guadalupe de Aguascalientes (1902–1905), and the Instituto Científico y Literario de Aguasca-

lientes (1905–1907). He then entered the law school in San Luis Potosí (1908), receiving his degree by the end of 1911. He briefly occupied a judicial post in the state of San Luis Potosí before moving to Mexico City, where he lived until his death, although he did spend a year (1913) in San Luis Potosí during some of the bloodiest days of the Revolution.

His early schooling included the study of classical languages and culture. The claim that the poet was not acquainted with any language other than Spanish seems pointless. He translated Anatole France on one occasion and attended the seminars in modern French poetry given by his friend Enrique González Martínez at the university.

The religious background received in his early education was decisive as a constant source of his poetic imagery. By temperament López Velarde was orthodox and not very passionately involved in politics. However, he did strongly support Madero, whom he knew personally, and the revolutionary premises of 1910. It is often said that he collaborated in the formulation of the Plan de San Luis, the political program proclaimed by Madero, advocating effective suffrage, non-reelection, and the correction of abuses committed during the Díaz regime. Having moved to the capital, he held several modest governmental jobs and was also a professor of literature.

Two women were particularly dominant in his life and in his work: first, Fuensanta (Josefa de los Ríos), the pure and inaccessible love of his youth; then in Mexico City, Margarita Quijano, a muse of physical and sensual attraction, with whom he had an enigmatic and frustrated relationship. At one point López Velarde clearly expressed his fear of paternity, in "Meditación en la alameda" (Meditation in the Alameda). Although Margarita inspired several of his most successful poems, her name was not generally mentioned in biographical criticism about the poet until years later. At the end of his short life and in his last poems, Fuensanta again became an obsession, but by then the object of his youthful love had become a metaphysical and spectral presence, though nonetheless real.

His first verse was probably published as early as 1905, despite his father's strong objections to a literary career. While a student in Aguascalientes in 1906, he founded with other friends of literary inclination the small magazine *Bohemio,* of which only two issues were published. Soon he was a frequent contributor to reviews and to newspapers in Aguascalientes, Lagos de Moreno, and Guadalajara; particularly from 1909 on, his signature became increasingly well known in the provinces. In 1912, he published frequently in *La Nación* (The Nation), a Catholic newspaper directed by his friend Eduardo J. Correa, and during the following year, spent in San Luis Potosí, he wrote an important series of poetic prose pieces that appeared in *El Eco de San Luis* (The Echo of San Luis). Once again established in the capital, he contributed regularly to many literary reviews, among which the most significant are *Revista de revistas* (Review of Reviews), *Vida moderna* (Modern Life), *El universal illustrado* (The Illustrated World), *México moderno* (Modern Mexico), and *El maestro* (The Master). In 1917, he directed, with the poets Enrique González Martínez and Efrén Rebolledo, the important weekly *Pegaso* (Pegasus), which reached a total of some twenty issues. He was also active in the administration and creative efforts of *Cultura* (Editorial México Moderno, S.A.), an important publishing house for many intellectuals of the time.

López Velarde's publications in book form during his life were few: two small volumes of verse, *La sangre devota* (Consecrated Blood, 1916) and *Zozobra* (Anguish, 1919). The finely wrought prose texts of *El minutero* (The Minute Hand, 1923) were collected posthumously, and his last poems, including the famous "La suave patria" ("Gentle Fatherland"), formed another book, *El son del corazón* (The Sound of the Heart, 1932). In recent years, scholars have discovered and collected forgotten texts, particularly prose (*El don de febrero* [February's Gift, 1952] and *Prosa política* [Political Prose, 1953]), as well as many other chronicles and texts of both his early and late years, now incorporated into his complete works.

López Velarde not only had a good background in the ancient classics but also was familiar with Spanish and French classical writers, and he had a great affinity for the baroque poets of the seventeenth century. He knew the literature of his own country and was equally well read in both French and Spanish contemporary literature. Among the French symbolists, Charles Baudelaire and Laforgue influenced him

greatly, and much has been written about the literary relationships López Velarde had with both men. The formative influence of Rubén Darío is probably deeper than is often recognized, and López Velarde must have been impressed by the daring images of the Uruguayan poet Julio Herrera y Reissig. But above all the writer whom he most admired was Lugones, calling him "the maximum poet," whose *Lunario sentimental* (Sentimental Lunar Poems, 1909) opened new horizons for the younger poets of Spanish America. López Velarde's language and technique owe much to the acrobatic *Lunario* although one does not find either the bitter sarcastic tone or the crude and ugly elements of city life that abound in Lugones' work. Elsewhere, López Velarde shows a strong affinity for provincial poets who cultivated an idealized, nostalgic concept of the province. Also, during postmodernism (1910–1925) many poets of Spanish America turned to rural and ordinary subjects as a reaction against the exotic and decorative aspects of modernism. Although López Velarde admired some of the work of Amado Nervo and appreciated the solitary Francisco González León, it is unlikely that the latter had direct influence on him. Both poets did to some degree evolve in a common direction, perhaps by coincidence or by reading the same general sources.

Although López Velarde was always opposed to any explanation of his artistic precepts, he was a highly conscious poet and did leave materials that permit us to reconstruct his aesthetics. He rejected abstract theorizing about poetry and considered emotion as the starting point of any genuine creation. He feared that excessive intellectualization would interfere with the true expression of one's feelings and believed that poetry is never written with pure reason. López Velarde once wrote that only by feeling and intuition does the poet approach true accuracy and precision. He also stressed the importance of the senses, which contribute to genuine poetic originality ("the very sex of the poet"). He pokes fun at those who prescribe for the writer; as he affirms, his aim is to modestly capture "the magic from inside and out," eschewing doctrine or moralizing of any kind.

As his poetry and prose amply demonstrate, López Velarde was firmly convinced that national themes could be treated in literature without any sacrifice of aesthetic quality. He was not interested in trivial and merely picturesque description of types or customs. Despite his sincere desire to discover the heart and essence of Mexico and the Mexicans, López Velarde was little concerned with ancient indigenous civilizations and culture, a topic much in vogue in twentieth-century Mexican art, both literary and pictorial. It is true, however, that one can find fleeting references to Aztec rites and the fall of their empire in a few of his works.

To take one's inspiration from the past and present does not necessarily imply a lack of artistic merit, and criollismo, as espoused by López Velarde, was a true form of nationalism that surpassed any superficial concessions to the merely vernacular. He explained his approach to Mexico as an inner, subjective search for the nation, an entity neither historical nor political, but intimate. The years of suffering during the Revolution were necessary, he felt, for the creation of a country that was less artificial, more authentic and essential, one that turned inward toward an examination of its national character and its genuine being. López Velarde also believed that a great artist or thinker would be able to conceive of the formula for the new fatherland. Of course, this is exactly what López Velarde himself did in his longest and most celebrated poem, "Gentle Fatherland." Octavio Paz points out that his nationalism came from his aesthetics, not the other way around.

To measure the linguistic preoccupations of López Velarde it is necessary to turn to his essay entitled "La derrota de la palabra" (The Defeat of the Word, 1916). In it he categorically states that he wishes to excoriate and drive out any word that does not spring directly from the combustion of his bones. At the same time, he attacks what he terms verbal industrialism and believes that linguistic degeneration can be explained by the fact that the word, formerly the slave of the writer, now tyrannizes him. The grave danger is in fact that the word has become a despot. At the same time that López Velarde experimented with expanding the expressive nature of language, he reaffirmed the imperious necessity of a direct and total correspondence between word and spirit (form and content). Language then should never be divorced from life or the poet himself. López Velarde made no concessions: Poetry is a serious business.

The ideal is a complete adaptation between expression and the sentiment the poet desires to express. The purpose of poetry is to capture the nature of all things and beings; emotions and feelings are to be conveyed faithfully by the word, docile in the hands of the talented poet and recalcitrant in those of the incompetent.

The prose and poetry of López Velarde have a central point from which all themes emerge: the discovery and definition of a personality. His best poems are not descriptive in the ordinary sense but convey with dramatic intensity the spiritual conflicts within his conscience and, by extension, humanity's conscience. All lyric poetry expresses emotions and feelings, but López Velarde in his best moments strips his soul bare, with all modesty, and writes about the disillusionments, the doubts and indecisions, the joys and sorrows inherent in life itself.

Having stressed the contemplative nature of his verse, we are in a better position to examine the concrete subjects of his work. Love, both simple and complex, both ingenuous and enigmatic, is the principal theme. On one occasion, he wrote that he could not understand or feel anything expect through women. Because of women he has known, he says in "Lo soez" (Wicked), the cold dagger of atheism and even abstract questions approach him through his erotic temperament. In the early poems of *La sangre devota*, that is, prior to 1915, it is on the whole a question of a chaste and purifying, even divine, love; the presence of Fuensanta, often represented by religious images, is central to the volume, in which a pure ideal tone prevails. Their love is doomed and is impossible, as the poet reveals in "Me estás vedada tú" (You Are Forbidden), and "Y pensar que pudimos" (And To Think That We Could). However, a few of the best love poems of the book imply other less innocent and more erotic experiences, with evident carnal implications: "A Sara" (To Sara), "Boca flexible, ávida . . ." (Greedy, Docile Lips . . .), and "La tónica tibieza" (Warm Glow). In "Ser una casta pequeñez" (Chaste Tender Age), written in 1915, he wishes to be able to return to the past and to the province after his licentious and funereal experiences. His life had already been split in two: a before (the province) and an afterward (the city). In *La sangre devota*, love, as the title might in part suggest, is nevertheless platonic, despite clear allusions to a more complicated eroticism. Two or three poems of this small book deserve greater attention than can be given them here: "Mi prima Agueda" ("My Cousin Agueda"), in which a new and undefinable sensuality awakens in the young boy, and "En las tinieblas húmedas" ("In the Wet Shadows"), an enigmatic nocturne in which religious and mysterious elements are successfully fused in the chilling, dark atmosphere of the city.

In *Zozobra*, a book that disconcerted many readers of 1919, sensual love and physical passion take the place of the romantic, melancholic love associated with the province. The poet's language and his feeling are much more intense, and his sentimentality is now tinged with anxiety. The duality, hinted at in his earlier poetry, now becomes ever present. He has left the province behind, but he does not entirely forget its women, some doomed to frustration and virginity, and it is significant that the initial poem of *Zozobra* is a sincere and moving elegy inspired by the death of Fuensanta in 1917. Sexuality is undisguised in "Hormigas" ("Ants"). In "Que sea para bien" (Let It Be for the Good), the poet is aware of the profound change that has taken place. Physical passion is obvious in poems such as "Día 13" (Day 13), "La última odalisca" (The Last of the Odalisques), and many others. It is from this book that Villaurrutia aptly took the phrase "el león y la virgen" (the lion and the virgin) and used it as the title of his anthology of the best poetry of López Velarde. Another ingredient has also been added to López Velarde's complex conception of love: death, portrayed in all its macabre and horrifying attributes. In the last poem of *Zozobra*, "Humildemente" ("Humbly"), a final return to the province is envisioned, when the writer will on his knees beg forgiveness for his arrogance and transgressions. In López Velarde there is an unresolved inner struggle between the church, with its pious and traditional past, and the new world of Mexico City, at the same time liberal and sensual.

The final poems of López Velarde, published posthumously in *El son del corazón* (1932), represent in more than one sense a return to origins and constitute a more measured, less anguished meditation on the principal concerns of the poet. After having experimented with freer forms of versification, the poet returns to more traditional verse. López Velarde renews his basic themes, and any permanent reconciliation of the dualities of his spirit seems impossible. However, in the poem "Gavota" (Gavotte), he proclaims as a guiding force in his existence "la moral de la simetría" (the moral of symmetry), a phrase that describes, as does "el león y la virgen," his quest, as well as suggesting the need for total experience. Curiously enough, in several of these last poems there is a clear premonition of his own death, as well as a conscious effort at summing up his life. Again and again, the shadowy form of Fuensanta and the past are evoked. She is now at last a metaphysical being seen in cosmic visions, and she has seemingly triumphed over less authentic love. In the enigmatic and visionary poem "El sueño de los guantes negros" ("The Dream of the Black Gloves"), unfinished in the printed versions, the poet imagines an eerie meeting with Fuensanta in a cold, oceanic world of vast proportions: transfigured, she is wearing black gloves that veil the enigma of love and contribute to the funereal eroticism of the poet. Several riddles are immediately posed in the poem: Is she flesh or is she pure spirit? Though their separation has come to an end, is a true union of the lovers possible in either life or in death? The beloved one is not an active lover, bent on possession, and may be an ambiguous symbol of chastity even in this encounter in the netherworld.

It is not an exaggeration to say that the principal themes of López Velarde are subordinate to and revolve around love and woman. However, two other main sources of his work deserve further mention: death and the province. The theme of death is generally conventional and bears a close relationship to provincial life in many poems of *La sangre devota*. It reappears with renewed intensity, often morbid and macabre, in both *Zozobra* and the prose of *El minutero*. Above all, the reader is aware of a repeated fusion of death and eroticism, seemingly two sides of the same coin. As mentioned earlier, in several instances in *El son del corazón* there are premonitions of the poet's death, keenly felt despite a certain resignation to the inevitable. On the whole, death for López Velarde is both a physical and direct sensation, not a philosophic concept, and in his poetry and prose there is a marked interest in bones, skulls, skeletons, and other repugnant aspects of

death. His images are often of destruction and desolation. His fear and dread are in turn not far removed
from a popular and typically Mexican concept of
death. López Velarde, always a highly superstitious
person, fears disintegration and corruption of the
flesh; his is a vision of terror and eventual torment as
he also lives the drama of passing time and inevitable
physical impotence.

A large portion of López Velarde's work, both
prose and poetry, was indeed inspired by the province
and provincial life. Yet this does not mean that he is
a provincial poet, a classification that might be
presupposed as a limitation or imply simplicity. Nevertheless, as a theme, the province cannot be divorced from his work and person. In *La sangre devota*,
we find an entire world of religious emotion, sentimental tenderness, and observance of age-old traditions, set to the monotonous rhythm of country life.
There is also an evident hope of return to simple and
innocent pleasures in many of his last poems, although the promise of a provincial Eden has been
blurred by his life in the capital and the violence of
the Revolution. Nevertheless, the province is a point
in time and space, a longing and yearning for things
past, never to be recaptured. In this manner, the
province was a defense and a protection from his
radical loneliness and the solitude of the years he
lived in the capital. With the passing of exotic and
superficial modernism, many poets of Spanish America turned toward their own heritage in a new kind of
nativism or nationalism.

López Velarde's longest and most widely read peom
is "Gentle Fatherland." To understand the poet's
concept of Mexico, which was by this time (1921)
rebuilding from the Revolution, as well as his intentions, the prose piece collected in *El minutero* under
the title of "Novedad de la patria" (A New Fatherland) is instructive. In "Gentle Fatherland," López
Velarde, poet of intimacy, consciously turned outward to express a lyric picture of his homeland. His is
an intimate and discreet epic, not simply rhetorical
and patriotic, nor bombastic in any way; in dramatic
form he describes not the national or historical glories
of the fatherland but rather its typical flora and fauna,
its customs and traditions. It is not an easy poem but
one filled with hidden allusions, some typical and
popular in nature, as well as finely wrought baroque

metaphors. The poet has ennobled certain aspects of
his country and transformed them into memorable
images that recall Mexican mural painting of the
twentieth century. This *épica sordina* (muted epic)
ends with the exhortation that Mexico be true to
itself and to its own daily realities. It should be said
that although López Velarde was by no means a
reactionary, there is little direct reference to the
Revolution in his prose and poetry, if we discount his
Prosa política. There are, of course, exceptions: the
poems "El retorno maléfico" ("The Malefic Return"),
"Las desterradas" (The Exiled Women), and the
prose work "En el solar" (At Home).

López Velarde's prose is not inferior to his better-
known verse. It is moreover the prose of a distinguished poet, reflecting the same themes and style
that characterize his poems. His prose is fundamentally lyric in nature, and he cultivated the prose poem
with eminent success. In the early years, his chronicles generally dealt with provincial subjects, often
autobiographical ones, but after 1915, again the year
that divides his artistic trajectory into two periods, he
left romantic and sentimental themes behind, and his
prose, in part collected in *El minutero*, became—as
did his poetry—much more dense and concentrated.

His prose is noteworthy for its intrinsic merits and
also as an aid to understanding his artistic intentions
and preferences. As he moved from highly subjective
confession and autobiographical remembrances, to
the literary portrait and to the essay of ideas, he was
able to maintain in the prose of his mature years the
poetic tension found in his verse. Although López
Velarde wrote two short stories (whose theme was his
fear of matrimony and paternity) and approached
narrative form in other instances, his prose on the
whole is fragmentary and essentially poetic in form
and intent.

López Velarde is above all the creator of a personal
style, rich in metaphor, that reaches a high level of
intensity. At times he seems to search for the
disconcerting word or phrase, as did Laforgue and
Lugones, to arrive at certain poetic effects. Yet an
acute desire for the exact was foremost in López
Velarde's mind, and often his baroque and elliptical
style tends to cover up delicate situations that he does
not care to reveal fully. López Velarde also believed
in the originality of the senses in genuine poetry, and

metaphors built around sensation abound in his work. He was also fond of certain families of images and personal symbols: those of a religious or biblical nature, others implying oscillation, suspension, and flight, and still others derived from astronomy and the signs of the zodiac. López Velarde cultivated an art that utilized objects common to our daily lives, and he often fused in surprising ways the transcendent and the ordinary. His adjectives, new and fresh, contributed to the intense personal qualities of his verse and prose. López Velarde strove for a total correspondence between word and emotion, and was always wary of the conventional and never content with linguistic inertia. He daringly expressed his spiritual tension with a vocabulary that admitted the prosaic and the technical, thus departing radically from modernist diction and poetic tradition. His irony and detachment, as well as his new language, point to the future. Undeniably, Ramón López Velarde is one of the most distinguished and authentic writers of the transitional years between modernism and the advent of the movements of the vanguard. He marks the beginning of contemporary Mexican poetry.

SELECTED BIBLIOGRAPHY

Editions

La sangre devota. Mexico City, 1916.
Zozobra. Mexico City, 1919.
El minutero. Mexico City, 1923.
El son del corazón. Mexico City, 1932.

Collected Works

El don de febrero y otras prosas. Edited by Elena Molina Ortega. Mexico City, 1952.
Obras. Edited by José Luis Martínez. Mexico City, 1971. Rev. ed. Mexico City, 1979.
Obras completas. Mexico City, 1944.
Poesías completas y El minutero. Edited by Antonio Castro Leal. Mexico City, 1953.
Prosa política. Edited by Elena Molina Ortega. Mexico City, 1953.

Translations

A complete listing of translations of the poetry of López Velarde can be found in Index to Anthologies of Latin American Literature in English Translation, by Juan R. and Patricia M. Freudenthal. Boston, 1977. P. 96.

Biographical and Critical Studies

Alba, Pedro de. Ramón López Velarde: Ensayos. Mexico City, 1958.
Appendini, Guadalupe. Ramón López Velarde: Sus rostros desconocidos. Mexico City, 1971.
Berrueto Ramón, Federico. Entraña y voz de López Velarde. Saltillo, Mexico, 1958.
Calendario de Ramón López Velarde. January–December 1971. A collection of studies by different authors in twelve issues.
Canfield, Martha L. La provincia inmutable: Estudios sobre la poesía de Ramón López Velarde. Florence, Italy, 1981.
Carballo, Emmanuel. "Ramón López Velarde en Guadalajara." In Et caetera 9–10 (1952).
Cuevas, Rafael. Ramón López Velarde: Panorámica de las letras 1. Mexico City, 1956.
De la Fuente, Carmen. López Velarde: Su mundo intelectual y afectivo. Mexico City, 1971.
Del Hoyo, Eugenio. Jérez, el de López Velarde. Mexico City, 1956.
Dromundo, Baltasar. Vida y pasión de Ramón López Velardo. Mexico City, 1954.
Gálvez de Tovar, Concepción. Ramón López Velarde en tres tiempos y un apéndice sobre el ritmo velardeano. Mexico City, 1971.
González Martínez, Enrique. La apacible locura. Mexico City, 1951. Pp. 91–94.
Gorostiza, José. "Perfil humano y esencias literarias de Ramón López Velarde." México en la cultura (Novedades), 16 June 1963.
El hijo pródigo 12/39 (1946). Homage edition.
Leiva, Raúl. Imagen de la poesía mexicana contemporánea. Mexico City, 1959. Pp. 33–47.
_____, and Jorge Ruedas. La prosa de López Velarde. Mexico City, 1971.
Lozano, Rafael. "La poesía criolla de Ramón López Velarde." Prisma June: 95–105 (1922).
Martínez, José Luis, "Examen de Ramón López Velarde." In Literatura mexicana: Siglo XX 1. Mexico City, 1949. Pp. 154–177. This study is basically the same as the prologue to Obras (Mexico City, 1979), pp. 9–36,

although in *Obras* the author has included bibliographic information (pp. 37–57) and notes (pp. 791–830).

México en el arte 7 (1949). Homage edition.

México moderno 1/11–12:249–303 (1921). Homage edition.

Molina Ortega, Elena. *Ramón López Velarde: Estudio biográfico*. Mexico City, 1952.

———. *Ramón López Velarde: Poesías, cartas, documentos e iconografía*. Mexico city, 1952.

Monterde, Francisco. "La suave patria de López Velarde." In *Cultura mexicana*. Mexico City, 1946. Pp. 293–300.

Noyola Vázques, Luis. *Fuentes de Fuensanta: Tensión y oscilación de López Velarde*. Zacatecas, Mexico, 1971.

Pacheco, José Emilio. *Antología del modernismo, 1884–1921* 2. Mexico City, 1970. Pp. 127–166.

Paz, Octavio. "Introducción a la historia de la poesía mexicana." In *Las peras del olmo*. Mexico City, 1957. Pp. 3–31. Translated into English by Samuel Beckett as "Introduction to the History of Mexican Poetry." In *Anthology of Mexican Poetry*. Bloomington, Ind., 1958. Pp. 23–44.

———. "El lenguaje de López Velarde." In *Las peras del olmo*. Mexico City, 1957. Pp. 86–94.

———. "El camino de la pasión (Ramón López Velarde)." In *Cuadrivio*. Mexico City, 1965. Pp. 69–130.

Phillips, Allen W. *Ramón López Velarde: El poeta y el prosista*. Mexico City, 1962. Contains bibliography.

———. "Otra vez López Velarde." *Cuadernos de bellas artes* 4/10:25–42 (1963).

———. "González León y López Velarde." In *Francisco González León, el poeta de Lagos*. Mexico City, 1964. Pp. 58–71.

———. "Una amistad literaria: Tablada y López Velarde." In *Estudios y notas sobre literatura hispanoamericana*. Mexico City, 1965. Pp. 107–120.

———. "Ramón López Velarde en la poesía hispanoamericana del postmodernismo." In *Cinco estudios sobre literatura mexicana moderna*. Mexico City, 1974. Pp. 123–143.

———. "Novedad y lenguaje en tres poetas: Laforgue, Lugones y López Velarde. "In *El simbolismo*, edited by J. Olivio Jiménez. Madrid, 1979. Pp. 198–230.

Rivas Sáinz, Arturo. *El concepto de la zozobra*. Guadalajara, Mexico, 1944.

———. *La redondez de la creación: Ensayo sobre Ramón López Velarde*. Mexico City, 1951.

Torres Bodet, Jaime. "Cercanía de López Velarde." *Contemporáneos* 8/28–29:111–135 (1930).

Villaurrutia, Xavier. "Ramón López Velarde." In *Textos y pretextos*. Mexico City, 1940. Pp. 3–43. Also in his *Obras: Poesía, teatro, prosas varias, crítica*. 2nd ed. Mexico City, 1966. Pp. 641–659.

José Eustasio Rivera

(1888–1928)

J. David Suarez-Torres

José Eustasio Rivera, Colombia's most highly acclaimed poet and one of Latin America's greatest novelists until the recent boom in Spanish-American narrative (1960–1975), was born in Neiva, Colombia, in 1888, the first son of a family of four boys and seven girls. His father, a modest farmer, had him baptized José Eustacio, a spelling that he changed to Eustasio when he was sixteen. He later told a classmate his reason: "I changed it because I felt like it. Away with your philologies."

When he was two years old his family moved to the country, where little José Eustasio fell in love with nature, developing a relationship that would nurture his poetic vein and lay the foundation for his courageous journeys into *la selva* (the jungle). At six he entered a country school and the following year a boarding school in Neiva, the provincial capital. He did well in the year he was there, despite constant problems with teachers, classmates, and local relatives whom he regularly visited on holidays. He was a typical *chico travieso*, a mischievous lad whose lack of discipline was so pronounced that the principal refused to take him back for another year. He was thus obliged to return to the country, where at age eight he devoted all his time to the humble chores of a poor farmer's son. One of the skills he learned during this period was to ride and tame horses. He was a handsome youth, witty and charismatic; other youths admired him and followed his lead, though some disliked his arrogance. Poor as he was and working as a simple *campesino* (farmer), Rivera loved to put on airs, for example, when riding his horse through town.

Contact with nature had the effect of transforming his pure fantasy into a poetic world with firm roots in reality. To relax from the hard labors of the farm, he read voraciously. From his childhood he was intrigued by legends, fables, and the interpretation of dreams; indeed, the mysticism surrounding Rivera was enhanced by the importance he attached to having seen "his own star" in a dream. Ironically, his love for poetry is traceable to assignments given by his teachers at the boarding school as punishments for misbehavior. He learned poems by heart and would recite long series of verses from José Zorrilla, Gaspar Núñez de Arce, José de Espronceda, Juan de Dios Peza, José María Heredia, Andrés Bello, and José Joaquin de Olmedo. Sometimes he wrote. Before the age of ten he had written his first poem, which failed to satisfy him, however, for lack of "rhetoric." His satires of the city's wealthy classes were well received by his largely peasant audience. For this initiative and for his independent stance, Rivera became a leader, reaffirming his conviction of being different and called to greatness.

For twelve years Rivera was in and out of schools, back to the farm, even trying his hand at clerical jobs. His rebellious attitude can be explained as the result of an internal struggle between his talents and his milieu, the latter not sufficiently challenging for him. He dreamed of greatness and glory, but the economic limitations of meager family capital denied him the luxuries enjoyed by many of his classmates. But in spite of their poverty, Rivera's parents always sacrificed for their son, making every possible effort to provide him with the best education and to instill deep in his mind a desire for great achievements. These seeds of greatness fell on good soil. Rivera's quest for glory is evident even in his earliest poems; one includes the line "And dreaming of the caresses of glory."

Concurrently, the War of the Thousand Days (1898–1902) and the Panama disaster—the detachment of Panama from Colombia with American help (1903)—contributed to his civil and political maturity. His country as a political entity, along with the national heroes and the international problems that beset it, became the main focus of his concern and, occasionally, the inspiration for his poetry.

Rivera's eighteenth birthday coincided with an event that would change his life. Winner of a scholarship offered by the government to the most promising young pupil from each province, Rivera entered the Escuela Normal de Institutores (Teachers College) of Bogotá, directed by the Brothers of the Christian Schools, or the La Salle Brothers. The scenario changed, but not the poet's personality. Nonetheless, though his temper often set him at odds with his principal, teachers, and fellow students, a transformation was under way, owing in part to the skillful dedication of the school's headmaster. According to the memory of a classmate, Rivera was a smart student, promising, skillful, alert, naive, sincere, a wonderful companion, witty in some situations, mocking and satirical in others.

Appreciated for his poetic talents, he always participated in school celebrations and on many notable occasions served as official spokesman for the institution. During the festivities to commemorate the centennial of Colombia's declaration of independence, Rivera won a silver medal for his *Oda a España* (Ode to Spain, 1910) in a public contest. The famous Spanish critic and polyglot Miguel de Unamuno wrote to him: "I congratulate you, my dear poet, for your notable and noble *Oda a España* so well conceived, and written in the Spanish manner" (Neale-Silva, p. 99). By this time Rivera's compositions were appearing in the country's most important papers. During the political demonstrations of 1909 to protest the legalization of the separation of Panama, Rivera led the students of the Escuela Normal through the streets of Bogotá and, with several companions, was detained by the police for a number of days.

After graduation Rivera became inspector of a small school system, soon finding himself at odds with teachers' methods and administrators' inefficiency. Frustrated, he accepted a bureaucratic position in the governor's office. During his leisure time he read whatever was available, and became engrossed by the hair-raising stories of Amazon jungle adventurers. Coincidentally, by 1910 some Spanish immigrants brought the news of the Tragic Week of Barcelona, a bloody rebellion led by anarchists in 1909. This labor unrest sparked in Rivera a new concern for social problems.

With an eye to entering the sociopolitical arena of his country, Rivera enrolled in the Law School of the Universidad Nacional. At age twenty-four, he used the time left over from his studies to complete his first drama. Seven more plays, none of which was printed because of his excessive desire for perfection, form his theatrical production. After five years of study, he defended his doctoral thesis to general applause.

The year 1918 represented a milestone in Rivera's literary work. Up to that time he saw himself as a man predestined to be a lyric poet. Though he had penned a critical essay, "La emoción trágica en el teatro" (Tragical Emotion in Theater, 1911), and dreamed of becoming a playwright, he had never thought of writing a novel. Realism had attracted him but covered, as for Rubén Darío, with Queen Mab's veil. It never struck his fantasy forcefully enough for him to change the parameters of his literary dream. Nevertheless, at that moment, his expertise in inheritance law brought him back to the *llanos* (plains), this time as a lawyer. His constant encounters there with *llaneros* (cowboys) and *caucheros* (rubber collectors) provided him with a new vision of nature and of men.

In literature we often find cases of poet-novelists or novelist-poets. In Rivera, we are dealing with a poet who only by the force of circumstances became a novelist. After long scrutiny and painful sculptorial labor, he allowed the publication of his fifty-five sonnets as *Tierra de promisión* (The Promised Land, 1921). One year later, while he and his companion of adventure in the *llanos* of Casanare (in southeastern Colombia) were recounting their latest journeys, Rivera declared: "This is worth a book." To which the companion replied: "But no more poems. . . . Write a good book" (Neale-Silva, p. 222). That blunt remark and the new vision of the *llanos* did effect the miracle. In fact, on 22 April 1922, Rivera wrote: "Long before I ever fell passionately in love with any woman, I had gambled away my heart and Impetuousness had won it." The first version of the first sentence of *La vorágine* (The Vortex, 1924) had been written. A novelist had been born out of the ashes of a poet.

When Rivera wrote the first part of *The Vortex* he had been in the *llanos* but never in the jungle. In September 1922 the Colombian government appointed him secretary of the Boundary Commission to work with a similar commission from Venezuela toward solution of boundary disputes that had existed since the days of independence. After ten months in the jungle that surrounds the Orinoco River between Venezuela and Colombia, Rivera could write from personal experience and embody himself in Cova—the protagonist—not only as a daring and romantic lover but also as a victim of the *caucherías* (rubber fields). Rivera journeyed as far as Manaus, a Brazilian city in the heart of the Amazon jungle, and then returned to Bogotá to take possession of a seat in the House of Representatives offered to him by the Conservative party. He thought he was at the right place at the right time. But politics and bureaucracy do not work quickly. Three months later he gave up his seat in total frustration.

His defeat by the political machinery brought him back to his book. Now it would not be only a novel, but also a social outcry. In fact, two months later Rivera returned to the southern *llanos* of Colombia to prepare a strong and well-documented report on the invasion by Peruvians, colonists, and soldiers, even after international resolutions and bilateral treaties.

Since the end of 1923 Rivera had been working again on his novel to portray the subhuman living conditions of the *caucheros*, which were in desperate need of drastic changes. A novel, he argued, could do the job better than a private report or a lawsuit. But was the time ripe for a novel that would expose the indifference of the government toward the welfare of the inhabitants of those isolated regions? Not according to Rivera's friends. Nevertheless, he insisted that he had not conceived *The Vortex* as a diatribe, but rather as an alarm for both the government and the Colombian people about the plight of those countrymen, often victims of the system.

The book took exactly two years to complete. Haunted by his desire for perfection, seven months of corrections elapsed before it was published in November 1924. Three pictures, a fragment of a letter by Arturo Cova, a prologue and an epilogue represent efforts by the author to portray authenticity. *The Vortex* proved not only a fantastic piece of literature, but also a social document rooted in a dehumanizing reality, destined to inspire similarly concerned writers like Ricardo Güiraldes of Argentina (*Don Segundo Sombra*, 1926), Rómulo Gallegos of Venezuela (*Doña Bárbara*, 1929, and *Canaima*, 1935), and Ciro Alegría of Peru (*La serpiente de oro* [The Golden Serpent], 1935).

An advertisement paid for by Rivera in three newspapers left no doubt regarding the author's intentions: "*The Vortex* . . . deals with life in Casanare, . . . and with slavery in the rubber fields in the jungles of Colombia, Venezuela, and Brazil." The book was a sensation. The reaction to it represented a wide spectrum of admirations and rebuttals, political allegiances, professional and amature criticism. Brazil immediately appointed a commission to investigate abuses. Russian, Japanese, and Norwegian publishers asked permission for translations. And Rivera, astonished, declared in the Bogotá newspaper *El Tiempo*: "God knows that upon writing my book I had no incentive save the redemption of those unfortunates for whom the jungle is a prison."

The success of *The Vortex*, acclaimed by many

critics for its strong social content, prompted Rivera to plan another novel, to be called "La mancha de aceite" (The Oil Spot). The manuscript was supposedly well advanced at the time of the author's death, but there remains not a trace of it. In spite of his rebellion against the passivity of the government vis-à-vis the tyrannic insolence of the *enganchadores* (recruiters of rubber gatherers), Rivera never fell into the new Socialist mood nor joined the Communist flock.

In April 1928 Rivera arrived in New York to work on a revised edition of *The Vortex* and on its translation into English. There he planned to establish a book distribution center for publications from all Spanish-speaking countries, thereby giving the American people the opportunity to read Hispanic literary works. Similarly, Hispanic authors would come to know each other's publications. During numerous meetings with Hispanists, writers, and journalists, Rivera discussed the viability of a magazine for the American Hispanic community in the style of then popular American magazines. The American Association of Teachers of Spanish already had its magazine, *Hispania*, but Rivera was aiming at the general public. In the midst of all these projects, Rivera died unexpectedly on 1 December 1928.

The cause of death is still a mystery since there was no autopsy. Some, poetically, see the revenge of the *selva* against the man who uncovered its ill-fated powers. The New York Polyclinic Hospital report reads in part: "This patient had malaria in Brazil. Patient told Dr. Hurtado [his Colombian friend and physician] that he never had any other severe illness. . . . Last Saturday, patient had La Grippe. . . . Is in coma . . . breathing became labored and died. . . . "

Born to a loving family, endowed with a fabulous memory and a great faith in his own destiny, a member of the political party in power, respected as a lawyer, loved as a poet, recognized as a diplomat, selected for a seat in the House of Representatives, Rivera was never satisfied with his achievements. On the contrary, he saw his life from very early childhood to death as a series of calamities: economic shortages, mistreatment by relatives, expulsions from schools, illnesses, business failures, political and professional feuds, amorous disappointments. All of

these doubtless contributed to his isolation and frequent withdrawal from acquaintances and even from friends. Even when he succeeded, he was never content with himself. "Algo espera mi alma sin saber lo que espera" (My soul yearns for something, not knowing what it is), reads sonnet 19 (in part 3) of *Tierra de promisión*.

Rivera, like most Spanish Americans, was a Catholic by baptism. In practice he in all likelihood was more ritualistic than transcendental. Neale-Silva, his best biographer, concludes that Rivera never "produced a coherent axiological hierarchy, based on study and meditation." As a consequence, he adds, the poet never "established a direct relationship between his life and his religious beliefs," giving the impression that his righteousness, his sense of justice, and his good-hearted attitude toward mankind were more ontological than a product of religious convictions. In any case, his ethical standards were high and his conscience was adamant when truth and virtue were at stake.

Major influences in his poetic formation were romanticism and modernism. Born contemporaneously with Darío's first publication, *Azul* (1888), Rivera assimilated the metric precision of the Parnassians but not the exotic elements of the modernists. Besides, that poetry, from the pens of men sheltered by the ivory tower and aimed only at the initiated in the art of the Muses, was oblivious of the plight of the lower strata of society, particularly peasants. As for Rivera's themes, they are chiefly regional, embodying the telluric motives of farm and *llanos*. He also used political and nationalistic themes, giving his work a romantic flavor, clear legacy of his models José Joaquín de Olmedo and José María Heredia.

Rivera differs from some Spanish-American writers, particularly José Enrique Rodó, the Uruguayan essayist who admired the material culture of the North American subcontinent but who warned the youth of South America against the utilitarianism of the "time is money" culture, advising his "disciples" to prefer the more spiritual values inherited from the motherland. Rivera, though furiously nationalistic and politically enraged by the Panama affair, was enthusiastic about the American way of life and the dream of an intercontinental understanding between the two cultures.

674

SELECTED BIBLIOGRAPHY

First Editions

Oda a España. El Tropical (Ibagué, Colombia) September 1910.

"La emoción trágica en el teatro." In *El nuevo tiempo literario.* Bogotá, 1911.

Tierra de promisión. Bogotá, 1921.

La vorágine. Bogotá, 1924.

Translations

The Vortex. Translated by Earle K. James. New York, 1935.

Biographical and Critical Studies

Añez, Jorge. *De "La vorágine" a "Doña Bárbara."* Bogotá, 1944.

Herrera Molina, Luis Carlos. *Exégesis de "Tierra de promisión," a través de la "Palabra-Tema."* Caracas, 1973.

Mata, Ramiro W. *Ricardo Güiraldes, José Eustasio Rivera, Rómulo Gallegos.* Montevideo, 1961.

Neale-Silva, Eduardo. *Horizonte humano: Vida de José Eustasio Rivera.* Mexico City, 1960.

Perera Soto, Hilda. *Aspectos de "La vorágine."* Santiago, Cuba, 1956.

Gabriela Mistral

(1889–1957)

Cedomil Goic

No other contemporary Spanish-American writer has been honored in the same way as Gabriela Mistral, who has received both official and popular recognition in all the American nations. A well-known and well-loved teacher and poet, she has achieved the stature of a tribune, alongside the most prestigious voices from the worlds of politics and the spirit. She was awarded Chile's National Prize for literature, as well as the first Nobel Prize for literature given to a Spanish-American writer. Mistral's life and work were intimately linked with the life and culture of her people. Her work is widely published and read, recitals of her poems are frequently presented, and musical settings of several of her poems have been performed. In the history of Spanish-American poetry she stands as one of the most original, profound, and distinct poetical voices.

Mistral's poetry stands as a reaction to the modernism of the Nicaraguan poet Rubén Darío; it is the poetry of a passionate soul, primitive and strong, poetry of pure accent without the elegantly correct echoes of modernism. Her verse possesses a voice of its own. Its lyric motifs achieve a wide range—first within the personal, intimate experience of an anguished soul, and then in the representation of external, regional, national, as well as American subject matter. Nature and the interrelationship between man and creation are important concerns in Mistral's poetry.

Passion permeates all her work. It finds expression in tortured blessings; songs of praise, lamentation, and resentment; the tragic outcry of desperate solitude; the hopeful clamor for redemption; the most delicate descriptions of mother and child; and the ecstasy of romantic love. Time, death, and nocturnal experiences of abandonment and despair acquire a singular quality in her poetry, and this dark side of her work is one of its most recognizable characteristics. Her inimitable poetic language mixes oral qualities of rural and familiar Spanish speech, full of archaism and idiom, with a learned diction that echoes classical, biblical, medieval, and modern traditions.

Mistral's extensive essays deal mainly with Spanish-American cultural, religious, and literary matters. The condition of women, children, and the Indians was a major concern. She disliked politics, particularly as practiced in most of Latin America, but she stood forcefully for peace during the Cold War. Dreaming of a united Spanish America, and constantly seeking protection for "her" Indians, Mistral served as an educator and a diplomat, but above all as a poet.

Gabriela Mistral was born Lucila Godoy Alcayaga, in Vicuña, in the Chilean province of Coquimbo, at

759 Maipú Street, on 7 April 1889. The daughter of Jerónimo Godoy and Petronila Alcayaga, she was of Basque ancestry from her father, Indian, or *mestizo*, ancestry from her mother and maternal grandfather, and Jewish lineage from her paternal grandmother. Her father, a teacher and vagabond who played the guitar as a folksinger and wrote verse, left home in 1892 when Lucila was three years old. She was brought up and educated in the towns of Montegrande and Vicuña, under the supervision of her half sister Emelina Molina. In 1898 she entered the public school of Vicuña, where she went through a very painful experience. Mistakenly accused of stealing school materials, she was severely reprimanded by her blind teacher and stoned by her classmates. In 1901 the family moved to La Serena. By this time, Lucila had discovered her father's verse and was for the first time inspired to write poetry. She did not publish her work until 1904, when she began writing for *El Coquimbo* and *La Voz de Elqui*, newspapers of Vicuña.

She applied for admission to the normal school of La Serena but was rejected because of her allegedly socialistic ideas. In 1905 she began working as an assistant in the elementary school of La Compañía Baja, a hamlet near La Serena. There she regularly visited her paternal grandmother Isabel Villanueva, who made her read the Bible aloud on Sundays and holidays. During this period she fell in love for the first time. From 1906 to 1909 she taught in La Cantera and in the latter year worked in the secondary school of La Serena as a secretary and coordinator. In 1907 she wrote for the literary magazine *Penumbras*. During her frequent trips to pick up the mail from her sister Emelina at the Coquimbo train station, she met Romelio Ureta, a conductor for the state railway, with whom she fell in love when she was eighteen years old. For reasons apart from their relationship, Ureta committed suicide in November 1909.

In 1908 she started using the pen name Gabriela Mistral (Mystral, Mistraly). After teaching in a rural school in Barrancas, near Santiago, from 1910, she qualified formally to teach at the secondary level and received the title of teacher from the normal school of Santiago. At age twenty-one Gabriela began a new stage in her life. She met Pedro Aguirre Cerda, who

later became president of Chile and who was an important factor in the recognition of her talent. In 1911 she taught in Traiguén and then at the secondary school of Antofagasta. In that city she became involved in the Theosophic Lodge named Destellos (Sparkles). From this involvement she acquired a touch of Buddhist discipline. In 1912 she was named teacher and inspector at the secondary school of Los Andes, where she served until 1918. She fell in love for the third time, with Jorge Hubner Bezanilla, though she was later disillusioned by him. In Los Andes she wrote the series of poems "Los sonetos de la muerte" (The Sonnets of Death). In 1913, she began a friendship with the poet Manuel Magallanes Moure that lasted until 1921. In 1914, she received the Natural Flower Award, the highest distinction in the Floral Games, a poetry contest organized to stimulate interest in the form. From that time on she permanently adopted the pen name Gabriela Mistral, which she had been using hesitantly for some time.

Mistral contributed to several literary magazines: *Revista de educación* (1913–1915), *Elegancias* (1913), *Norte y sur* (1913), *Nueva luz* (1913), *Primrose* (1915–1916), *Zig-zag* (1915), *Los diez* (1917), *Cervantes* (1917–1920), *Selva lírica* (1917–1918), *Pacífico magazine* (1919), *Renacimiento* (1919), *Repertorio americano* (1921), *Chile magazine* (1921–1922), and *Lectura* (1922). She also contributed fifty-five poems and prose pieces to the reading textbook series *Libro de lectura* (1916–1917), by Manuel Guzmán Maturana. From 1918 to 1920 she served as principal and teacher of Spanish at the secondary school for girls at Punta Arenas. Around this time her friendship with Magallanes Moure suffered a crisis, ending in 1921. In 1920 she worked as the principal of the secondary school of Temuco. In this city she met the young Pablo Neruda. She taught in Santiago in 1921 and became the first principal of the recently founded Secondary School No. 6, now known as the Gabriela Mistral Secondary School.

By this point, mainly because of her publications in magazines and literary journals and her abundant correspondence with a great number of writers and intellectuals, Mistral's fame had spread throughout America. A valuable volume of letters from these relationships has been compiled by Sergio Fernández Larraín, *Cartas de amor de Gabriela Mistral* (Love

Letters, 1978). In 1922 she was invited by the president of Mexico, Álvaro Obregón, to collaborate in that country's educational reform, directed by Secretary of Education José Vasconcelos. That same year Professor Federico de Onís, of Columbia University in New York City, published *Desolación* (Desolation), her first book of poetry. Mistral was then able to end her teaching career of fifteen years in Chile and began a life of international responsibilities.

At age thirty-five, Mistral was a robust woman of 5'7", with blond hair and green eyes, serious expression, noble presence, and serene elegance; her speech was fluent, tranquil, and monotone. In Mexico she became friends with Palma Guillén, who served her as secretary and who assisted and supported her in many circumstances of her life. She became aware of the social and cultural problems of Latin American Indians. She published *Lecturas para mujeres* (A Reader for Women, 1923) and her second book of poems, *Ternura: Canciones de niños* (Tenderness: Children's Songs, 1924). In 1923 the University of Chile awarded her the title Professor of Spanish, and the following year she traveled through the United States and Europe.

Returning to Chile after three years in 1925, Mistral she was welcomed with great popular homage. As a result of her literary achievements she was awarded a special pension by the government and was named the Chilean delegate to the Institute for Intellectual Cooperation of the League of Nations and an executive member of the Institute of Educational Cinematography in Rome, serving in these capacities until 1930. In 1926, during her stay in Marseilles, she adopted her half brother's nine-month-old son, whose mother had recently died. Baptized Juan Miguel Godoy, he was nicknamed "Yin Yin." In 1928 Mistral visited Spain to attend an International Congress of University Women, and the following year she traveled to the United States to teach and lecture at Mills, Vassar, Middlebury, and Barnard colleges.

On her way back to Chile in 1931, Mistral traveled through the Central American and Caribbean nations. She gave the annual inaugural speech at the University of Puerto Rico, delivered lectures in Havana on José Martí, and received tribute from the universities of Guatemala and El Salvador. In Colón, Panama, she was awarded that nation's literary prize, the Golden Orchid. In 1932 she began a career as consul of Chile in the place of her choice (becoming Consul for Life in 1935). She served in Guatemala and Nice (1932) and also resided in Aix-en-Provence, Avignon, and Arlès. In 1933, she became an adopted daughter of Puerto Rico. In July 1933, she took charge of an honorary consulate in Madrid (1933–1935), making a living by writing for several newspapers. Her opinions in a private letter, revealed by an indiscreet addressee, forced her to leave the consulate in Madrid. She went to Lisbon as consul (1935–1937) and then to Paris (1937–1938). She worked with Marie Curie and Henri Bergson in the League of Nations. In 1938 she again served as consul in Nice. In 1937, in the Montpensier Hotel in Paris, her meeting with the Spanish writers José Bergamín, Joaquín Xirau, Carlos Rivas, and Victoria Kent reconciled her with Spain. She donated her copyrights to *Tala* (Felling, 1938) to the Residencia Infantil of Pedralbes, Catalonia, which sheltered orphans of the civil war.

The Spanish civil war and World War II deeply affected her and motivated her to leave for America. She went first to Veracruz (1938) to serve as consul, and then to Niteroi and Petropolis in Brazil (1940–1944). During these years she wrote regularly for the literary magazine *Repertorio americano* and for the newspapers *El Mercurio* of Santiago, Chile, *La Nación* of Buenos Aires, *El Tiempo* of Bogotá, and *El Universal* of Caracas. In 1937 and 1938, on her way back to Chile, she received a massive popular welcome, as well as tribute from writers and political institutions in Brazil, Uruguay, and Argentina. Victoria Ocampo, the editor of the literary magazine *Sur* and the publishing house of the same name, published Mistral's third book of poems, *Tala*. At this time, Mistral portrayed herself in this way: "I am a Christian of total democracy. I believe that Christianity, in a deep social sense, can save the nations. I have written as someone who speaks alone because I have lived alone everywhere. My inspirations in the art of guiding life are: the Bible, Dante, Tagore, and the Russian writers" ("Rasgos autobiográficos de Gabriela Mistral," *Revista de educación* 67/1:37 [1926]).

On 14 August 1943, Yin Yin died in Petropolis, at the age of seventeen. According to the police, he poisoned himself, but Mistral blamed the deed on a gang of racist youths. This tragedy was the greatest sorrow of her life. A few months earlier, her neighbor and friend, the writer Stephan Zweig had committed suicide with his wife.

In 1945 Mistral became the first Spanish-American writer to be awarded the Nobel Prize in Literature (she was the third Spanish-speaking writer, after José Echegaray and Jacinto Benavente). After her visit to Stockholm, she traveled to Paris, where she was the official guest of the French government for three days. From there she went on to Provence and Italy. She traveled to San Francisco as a delegate to the United Nations, assigned to the recently created Subcommittee on the Juridical and Social Status of Women. She became actively involved in the creation of UNICEF, for which she wrote a "Llamado por los niños" (Appeal for Children), which was distributed worldwide. She went to California to establish a consulate in Los Angeles (1945), then resided in Monrovia (1946) and Santa Barbara (1947–1950). In 1947 she received an honorary doctorate from Mills College, in Oakland, California. The next year, she went to Mexico on an invitation from the government of Miguel Alemán and his minister José Torres Bodet, who granted her 250 acres of land in Sonora on the Gulf of California.

In Mexico she resided in Veracruz, where she built a house in Miradores. The Serra Prize of the Academy of American Fransciscan History in Washington was awarded to her in 1950. Then, in New York, she boarded a ship bound for her consulate in Naples, and in 1951 she received the Chilean National Prize for Literature. She published "La palabra maldita" (The Cursed Word), a strong critique of the ideology of the Cold War, in *Repertorio americano* 47/1:2 (1951). In 1953, after residing briefly in Miami, she went to Roslyn Harbor, Long Island, as consul, as well as representing Chile at the General Assembly of the United Nations. In 1954 she received an honorary doctorate from Columbia University. That year, she returned triumphantly to Chile, where she was honored by the people and by Chilean intellectuals and where she received an honorary doctorate from the University of Chile.

She published *Lagar* (Wine Press) in 1954 and then returned to Roslyn Harbor with Doris Dana. The next year, she spoke before the Assembly of the United Nations on Human Rights Day, at the request of Secretary General Dag Hammarskjöld. The Chilean government granted her a special pension. At the end of 1956 she became seriously ill and died in Hempstead, New York, on 10 January 1957. Her body was taken to Chile, where she was given funeral services befitting a chief of state, as well as an impressive popular homage. She is buried in Montegrande. In 1957 the first volume of her collected prose was published as *Recados contando a Chile* (Messages Describing Chile). Her *Poema de Chile* (Poem of Chile), the last version of which she had not finished revising, was published posthumously in 1967.

Gabriela Mistral's poetical work is made up of five great books. The first three of these went through a number of transformations in successive editions. This is especially true of the first of the three, *Desolación*, whose contents changed significantly in the editions of 1922, 1923, and 1926. *Poemas de las madres* (Poems of the Mothers, 1950) is a separate publication of poems that belong to the "Prose" section of the first edition of *Desolación*. *Desolación* also provided the main content of her second book, *Ternura* (Tenderness, 1924), which was augmented in its second edition (Buenos Aires, 1945) with an entire section taken from *Tala* (Felling, 1938). This, her third book, also anticipated the content of *Poema de Chile* (1967), as did *Lagar* (Wine Press, 1954), with a section of its own. The definitive text of the first book, *Desolación*, is that which appears in *Poesías completas* (1958), edited by Margaret Bates under the supervision of the poet. Three out of the four sections of the book develop an existential and Christian image of life, infused with a sense of suffering and a harsh rejection of bourgeois indifference and softness. The third section, "Dolor" (Sorrow), sketches the curve of a tragic love story animated by Mistral's "poetics of blood"—her subjective lyricism of suffering. In this section there is a strong tension between desire and love, the latter considered as an extreme situation in the existential sense and as the experience of an absolute. The last section, "Naturaleza"

(Nature), projects the personal desolation of the lyrical speaker over the tragic and cold, strange and deserted landscape, carrying to an extreme the identification of woman with world. This section also shares traits with avant-garde poetry, particularly in its images, or "visions." One of the poems, "Cima" (Peak), is a version of the new poetry of Vicente Huidobro and his revolutionary concept of *creacionismo* (creationism) that was exerting its influence in those days.

This book was followed by *Ternura*, which drew in part on *Desolación*. The section "Canciones de cuna" (Cradle Songs) was transferred in its entirety. The poem "El corro luminoso" (The Luminous Ring) was transferred to the section "Rondas" (Rings around the Rosy, or Rounds), and the poem "Manitas" (Little Hands) to the section "Casi escolares" (Almost School Songs). The second edition of *Ternura*, added in 1945, is nourished in part by Mistral's third book, *Tala* (1938). The section from *Tala* called "Albricias" (Rewards) is called "Jugarretas" (Playful Tricks) in the 1945 edition of *Ternura*. Mistral defines these poems as the children's game of hide-and-seek. Their defining characteristic is the revelation or proclamation of the "finding" itself. These are compositions full of charm and verbal creation, similar to the nonsense of many children's games. The *jugarretas* are continued in her book *Lagar*, with a new section of the same name. The poetry in *Ternura* is Mistral's attempt to create a genre of children's poetry—of rounds, lullabies, children's stories, and riddles—that will constitute a true echo of the fifteenth-century *cancioneros* (songbooks) and of the poetry of the Golden Age, with its parallelistic poems and its popular stanzas (*coplas*) in linked verse. Many of these poetic strategies, brought to life once again by Mistral, have been imitated by later poets.

Her third book, *Tala*, started a new era and style in Mistralian poetry. Here she leaves behind the marked subjectivity of her first book and moves on to a poetry of objective representations and, above all, to a poetic language with a predominant accent on oxymoron and antithesis, and figures of strong contradiction. Lexical creation is abundant, with sources in the spoken language. The first section is "Muerte de mi madre" (Death of My Mother), which includes, among other poems, five *nocturnos* (nocturnes) of the

type that first appeared *Desolación*. Other notable sections are "Saudade" (Nostalgia) and "América" (America). To the latter belongs the section "Dos Himnos" (Two Hymns), which includes "Sol del trópico" (Tropical Sun) and "Cordillera" (The Andes Mountains). True hymns, they are songs of praise of the divine; the trembling and agitation of the state of mind of the lyric speakers reach the intensity of the dithyramb. One aspect that accentuates the inspired quality of the poems is the representation of a lyric speaker (made up of an American chorus and a female voice that belongs to the chorus but speaks individually). This speaker experiences the re-cognition of his religious American consciousness of the cult of the Sun and the Earth, triggering a repristination of these American myths of the Sun, of the origin of the Incas (descendants of the Sun), and of the Pachamama (Mother Earth). The speaker confesses his *extravío* (a going astray) and begs for purification and the restitution of the "sacred community" of the Native Americans.

These prodigious poems are written with the characteristic simplicity of Mistralian verse, in nine-syllable lines, with the romance rhyme scheme (*a b c b*) that pervades its metric system, organized in groups with varied numbers of lines. The poetical language is characterized by an active verbal creation (neologisms rooted in the creativity of spoken language), as well as by the use of indigenous names (Mama Ocllo, Inca Huayna, Manco Cápac, Viracocha, Quetzalcóatl) and, with a strange inconsistency within the scheme of literary *mundonovismo* (New Worldism), names from classical mythology (Atalanta, Zodíaco, Dioscuros) and romantic fiction (Byron's Mazzepa), all acting as vehicles of the imagery of the Cordillera. This textual dialogism (the convergence of disparate motifs in the same text), which strongly characterizes Mistral's New Worldism, transcends the limitations of autochthony. The figure of speech that stands out in "Cordillera" is the antithesis of strong contradiction—*concordia discors*, or the contradiction of nondisjunctive opposites—which characterizes the supernatural condition of the Cordillera. The poem develops the image of a divinity as Great Mother (tellus mater or Pachamama), unfolding in each stanza her maternal and feminine attributes (procreator, guide, nurse, beautiful lover) and her divine attributes (her awesome hugeness and energy, her mystery and fascination, her providence) in a manner unprecedented in Spanish-American poetry.

The section "Saudade" (Nostalgia) is a collection of poems that, from one perspective, represent the languid permanence of the world through the memory of what is absent, and, from another, express with unusual finesse the experience of exile, of the strangeness of the world in the perception of the "other." The poem "La extranjera" ("The Foreigner") is written in direct free style, in the voice of an unidentified speaker (*communis opinio*), who perceives the strange presence of someone different—a foreigner—amid the ordinary community. Mistral referred to such cases as "poetry between quotation marks," or "the borrowed voice":

> "Habla con dejo de sus mares bárbaros,
> con no sé qué algas y no sé qué arenas;
> reza oración a dios sin bulto y peso,
> envejecida como si muriera.
> En huerto nuestro que nos hizo extraño,
> ha puesto cactus y zarpadas hierbas.
> Alienta del resuello del desierto
> y ha amado con pasión de que blanquea,
> que nunca cuenta y que si nos contase
> sería como el mapa de otra estrella.
> Vivirá entre nosotros ochenta años,
> pero siempre será como si llega,
> hablando lengua que jadea y gime
> y que le entienden solo bestezuelas.
> Y va a morirse en medio de nosotros,
> en una noche en la que más padezca,
> con solo su destino por almohada,
> de una muerte callada y extranjera."
> (*Poesias completas*, 3rd ed., 1966)

"She speaks with the moisture of her barbarous seas
still on her tongue, with the taste
of sands and algae unknown to me.
She prays to a god without form or weight,
and is so old she is ready to die.
In our garden which has become strange to us
she grows cactus and clawing grass.
She was nourished by breath of the desert
and loved with a scorching passion
she never tells. If she told us,
it would be like the map of another star.
She will live with us eighty years,

always as if just arriving,
speaking a language that pants and moans
and that only little beasts understand.
And she will die among us
on a night when she suffers most,
only her fate for a pillow,
a death silent and *foreign*."
(Translated by Doris Dana)

Mistral's "recados" (messages) constitute an extraordinarily original poetic genre that marks, along with the novelty of the structure, a distancing from metric forms toward free verse. The poet defines it thus in the concluding notes of *Tala*:

> Letters that go to distant places and are written every three or five years usually take with them what is temporal—the week, the year, and minute—the birthday, the new year, the change of house. And when, besides, one writes them with the apprehension of a poem, still sensing in the air the fluttering of a rhythm only half broken and a few of those rhymes that I have called meddlesome, in such a case, the letter becomes this playful thing, thrown about here and there by the verse and the prose fighting over it. On the other hand, the national person with which one has lived (a country is always for me a person) steps at every turn in front of the addressee and at intervals displaces him. . . . These letters carry with them my very tone, the most recurrent, the rural lilt in which I have lived and in which I will die.

Her fourth volume of poetry, *Lagar*, was the last book published during her lifetime. The line begun with *Tala* is here developed and carried further. Among its notable poems are those of the series "Locas mujeres" (Mad Women), those of "Guerra" (War), which broaden to the European world her favorite motifs, and those of "Luto" (Mourning), poems affected by the death of her nephew.

A posthumous publication, not finally revised by the poet, *Poema de Chile* is characterized by the open format of its composition, which the author constantly expanded and modified. Some of its poems originated in *Tala*, in the sections "Tierra de Chile" (Land of Chile) and "Trozos del *Poema de Chile*" (Fragments of Poem of Chile), in which they are presented as making up part of the future book. Her description of the country, from one end to the other—landscape, flora, fauna, and minerals—is original but articulated in the old descriptive tradition begun by Andrés Bello in the poems that have come to be known as his *silvas americanas* (American odes, 1823–1826). A great part of its novelty and freshness emanates from the configuration of a wandering, ghostly group made up of an old woman who returns to the earth after her death (the speaker), and a ghostly boy and a musk deer who accompany her.

Versification in Mistral's poetry ranges from the most strict and regular metric forms (both learned and popular) through free verse to the prosaism of her "messages" and her poems in prose. Her early compositions are marked by the use of certain meters of the *arte mayor* (lines of twelve or more syllables), which modernism renewed, out of which Mistral selected the most traditional and established. Alexandrine sonnets, made up of fourteen-syllable lines (seven plus seven), make up her most artificial form, side by side with some other metric combinations, such as quartets with broken feet, that is, alexandrine lines and lines of seven syllables, as in "Amo amor" (Tyrant Love), from *Desolación*. Poems of twelve-syllable lines are infrequent, with only two examples; compositions with eleven-syllable lines are numerous, including the hendecasyllabic with no rhyme; the ten-syllable line is used in only four cases. The dominant forms are those of *arte menor*: nine- and eight-syllable-line poems are the most numerous, followed by seven-, six-, and five-syllable-line poems, especially the *canciones* (songs), the *canciones infantiles* (childrens' songs) and the rounds. Mistral has made out of the seven-syllable-line poem a unique and original form.

The ametrical versification, anisosyllabic and without rhyme, that is anticipated in some early compositions takes on a more accented character in *Tala* and *Lagar*, especially in the "messages" and in her posthumous poetry. In the early books, poems with varied metrical combinations anticipate this tendency, but they follow established stanza formations and a combination of two meters, mainly in seven- and fourteen- as well as seven- and eleven-syllable lines, but also in shorter lines, of five and seven as well as seven and three syllables. Among the metrical forms, the sonnet, regularly alexandrine or hendecasyllabic, stands out in Mistral's early work. As for the stanza, the quartet is dominant, whether it is made up of polyrhythmic alexandrine lines or plain hendecasyllabes with *a b a b* rhyme, or *a b b a* in the manner of Amado Nervo and Enrique González Martínez.

In her later works these stanza formations are replaced by stanzas in which the number of lines varies according to the content of the poem or a specific generic structure. The poems of *Desolación* and *Ternura* are especially characterized by parallel, correlative, and "disseminative-recollective" systems of juxtaposition. (In this last poetic strategy, successive parallelisms and linked verses are unified by a poetic closure at the end.) Other poems employ original systems of subordination, such as the use of the last word of one line as the first word of the following line (*anadiplosis*) in a poetic strategy of concatenation called *concatenatio*, which lends Mistral's poetry its peculiar formalization. Prominent among these last are the forms of *encadenados* or *cadenillas* (linked verses), which are found in the section called "Jugarretas" (Playful Tricks). These have precedents in the poetry of the Spanish Golden Age and in other original forms of *encadenados*, especially "La pajita" (The Straw), which has been widely imitated.

Mistralian poetics found a defined expression as early as the poet's first book. In the early editions of *Desolación* the prose sections included several pages in which the speaker's voice reflects on the meaning of her poetry and of poetry in general. She wrote a brief epilogue entitled "Voto" (Vow), in which she attempted to define the mood of her book, at the same time promising a significant change in the orientation and purpose of her future poetry: to give hope, to console mankind. This early poetics, reflected mainly in the section "Vida" (Life), has been described as a poetics of blood or of sacrifice. Its main components are Christian existentialism and the exaltation of suffering and of pain in the face of the indifference and voluptuousness of the century. From this general vision the poet goes on to the experience of the personal drama of love, disillusion, and death in the section "Dolor" (Sorrow), expressing feelings that totally suffuse the vision of the world and of the landscape in the section "Naturaleza" (Nature). The prose pieces "Colofón a modo de excusa" (Colophon as an Excuse) in *Ternura* and the "Notas" (Notes) in *Tala* shed light on her preoccupation with poetic mood and her predilection for the genres of children's poetry, as in the rounds and cradle songs of *Ternura*, and the new American themes and new forms of a poetry ignored or neglected in Spanish-American letters.

From *Tala* arise her "Dos himnos" (Two American Hymns) and her "Albricias" (Rewards, later renamed "Jugarretas"). In the same volume, her superb "Nocturnos" are refined and her "Recados" (Messages) are formulated with an originality that mixes tradition and everyday life. Her fundamental preoccupation is to move away from the lack of content and the subtlety and weakness of the poetry of her generation and to turn instead to the great themes that the Indian monumental constructions and the Andes Mountains suggest—themes that are "in need of a voice courageous enough to deal with such formidable subject matter" (notes to "Dos himnos" in *Tala*). In her abundant essayistic production, one sees evidence of her reading of the great poets, as well as her response to the innovations of the poetic avant-garde that she admired and partially accepted. Her only resistance is toward the early creationism of Vicente Huidobro, with its absolutism of the poetic image, which in the creationist poet was in truth more a battle flag than a thesis consistently maintained.

Some of Mistral's exceptional poems are characteristic of the variety and scope of her lyrical manifestations. "Amo Amor" (Tyrant Love) is a parallelistic poem with an open system that extends to the entire text, distributing the parallel elements of the poem between the hemistichs of the alexandrine lines in the first two lines of each quartet, with the last two lines making up a separate system of parallelisms. The coordination of the two systems consists of a warning followed by a consequential conclusion. In this poem are represented the emblems of *Amor Tyrannus* (love, the tyrant) and *Vis Amoris* (power of love), disclosing the attributes of absolute love throughout the text by the use of antithesis and chiasmus. These figures of speech arrange the earthly/divine:divine/earthly and the strong/weak:weak/strong in semantic schemes that uphold the depth of meaning even where the syntactic structure loses its regularity.

Love is given the attributes of omnipresence, energy, persuasion, mystery, fascination; the tremendous and the all-embracing is conceived as an absolute power in the universe. Nevertheless, the poet goes back to and makes extensive and compendious use of the traditional emblems and divine images of insurmountable love: *Amor Magus* (love, the magician), wise, cunning and astute, and bewitching, and *Amor Caecus* (love, the blind). The poem, in spite of its precisions, lacks an explicitly defined subject. Its title might be taken for the subject, if its meaning is understood. But this meaning is not easily perceived, as is seen in the differing French translations, "J'aime l'amour" and "Amour souverain," and the German version, "Amor der Herr," and even the correction of a proofreader of one of the Spanish editions, who believed he had found an error and emended the title to "Amor amor." The lack of an article contributes to the ambiguity, making it difficult to discern the noun from the adjective or the noun from the verb.

In *Desolación* the poem "Cima" (Peak) reflects the outstanding features of the new poetry of the avant-garde. In an original manner, consistent as well with her own poetic system, Mistral responds to the modality imposed on the composition of the poem and of the poetic image by Huidobro's creationism. Published for the first time in 1920 and subject later to some minor textual revisions, this poem belongs to "Naturaleza" (Nature), the section that most visibly adopts the features of the new poetry, in general by means of the new image of strong contradiction or, as Huidobro calls it, "vision." The syntactic structure of this image is a deviation from the logical structure of language through a certain semantic impertinence in the combining of subject and predicate, which Huidobro called a *situación creada*, or created situation. (For example "the hour gives its blood to the mountain.") This brief poem of eighteen lines combines eleven-syllable and seven-syllable lines, follows the assonant "romance" rhyme, typical of Mistral, and is arranged in stanzas of varying numbers of lines: 2/4/2/4/4/2.

"Cima" is made up of a series of declarative images of twilight that gradually establish by insinuation a relationship between human suffering and the bleeding splendor of the day's final hour, at first in an indeterminate way and then with a progressively more personal orientation. In one sense the song is, as an expression of the speaker's suffering, the cause of the color of the mountain illuminated by the dying sun. The relations that are established between the world and the person are suggested in terms of the Passion of Christ and the spear that wounds his side. This image is consistent with the symbolist tradition of the poet-Christ, from Rubén Darío to Huidobro.

> La hora de la tarde, la que pone
> su sangre en las montañas.
>
> Alguien en ésta hora está sufriendo;
> una pierde, angustiada,
> en éste atardecer el solo pecho
> contra el cual estrechaba.
>
> Hay algún corazón en donde moja
> la tarde aquella cima ensangrentada.
>
> El valle ya está en sombra
> y se llena de calma.
> Pero mira de lo hondo que se enciende
> de rojez la montaña.
>
> Yo me pongo a cantar siempre a ésta hora
> mi invariable canción atribulada.
> ¿Seré yo la que baño
> la cumbre de escarlata?
>
> Llevo a mi corazón la mano, y siento
> que mi costado mana.

> The time of the day: the hour that gives
> its blood to the mountains.
>
> Somebody at this time is suffering;
> someone loses in anguish
> during this evening the only one
> who used to embrace her.
>
> There is a heart in which the evening
> soaks that bloodred peak.
>
> The valley is already shaded
> and calm throughout.
> But from its depths it sees how
> the red mountain glows.

> I always sing at this hour
> my constant song of distress.
> Could I be the one who bathes
> that peak in scarlet light?
>
> I place my hand on my heart, and feel
> that my wounded side is bleeding.

Not everything in the poetry of Mistral is passion and drama. An important place is taken up by her cradle songs, some of which are of unusual transcendence, such as "Meciendo" ("Rocking"), which has a simple and brief parallelistic form, condensing meaning and charm in a few lines:

> El mar sus millares de olas
> mece, divino.
> Oyendo a los mares amantes,
> mezo a mi niño.
>
> El viento errabundo en la noche
> mece los trigos.
> Oyendo a los vientos amantes,
> mezo a mi niño.
>
> Dios padre sus miles de mundos
> mece sin ruido.
> Sintiendo su mano en la sombra
> mezo a mi niño.

> The sea rocks her thousands of waves.
> The sea is divine.
> Hearing the loving sea
> I rock my son.
>
> The wind wandering by night
> rocks the wheat.
> Hearing the loving wind
> I rock my son.
>
> God, the Father, soundlessly rocks
> His thousands of worlds.
> Feeling His hand in the shadow,
> I rock my son.
>   (Translated by Doris Dana)

Another considerable part of Mistral's poetry is dedicated to the dimension of playful enchantment;

such are the sections "Albricias" (Rewards) or "Ju-garretas" (Playful Tricks), poems which formulate a finding. The most widely known of them is "La pajita" (The Straw), a poem with an intentionally colloquial language that makes it almost impossible to translate, in spite of its rigorous hypotactic structure and its systematic play of assertion followed by negation in continuous links. An equally illustrative example is "La rata" ("The Rat"), which unfolds according to the disseminative-recollective strategy described above. This same strategy can be found in "Riqueza" ("Richness"), from the section called "Alucinación" of *Tala*:

> Tengo la dicha fiel
> y la dicha perdida:
> la una como rosa,
> la otra como espina.
> De lo que me robaron
> no fuí desposeída:
> tengo la dicha fiel
> y la dicha perdida,
> y estoy rica de púrpura
> y de melancolía.
> ¡Ay, qué amada es la rosa
> y qué amante la espina!
> Como el doble contorno
> de las frutas mellizas,
> tengo la dicha fiel
> y la dicha perdida . . .

> I have a faithful joy
> and a joy that is lost.
> One is like a rose,
> the other, a thorn.
> The one that was stolen
> I have not lost.
> I have a faithful joy
> and a joy that is lost.
> I am as rich with purple
> as with sorrow.

> Ay! How loved is the rose,
> how loving the thorn!
> Paired as twin fruit,
> I have a faithful joy
> and a joy that is lost.
> (Translated by
> Doris Dana)

A composition of exceptional value that sums up the Mistralian vision of America is "Recado terrestre" (Terrestrial Message). This work was Mistral's contribution to the Weimar Goethefeier, celebrating Johann Wolfgang von Goethe's second centennial in 1949, which, for the first time after World War II, brought together writers from all over the world. The poem develops a vision of a world in which the spirit begins to manifest itself with definite signs, rising out of the darkness of the purely natural and primeval character of life. Written in the form of a letter or "message," its *petitio* comprises an invitation to Goethe to leave the celestial place that he occupies and to descend, guided by the light of his wisdom and by love, to meet his people in the incipient world of America. As a supplication, it maintains the phraseological features of the Lord's Prayer in the first lines, and its general structure is the form of a prayer.

> Padre Goethe, que estás sobre los cielos,
> entre los Tronos y Dominaciones
> y duermes y vigilas con los ojos
> por la cascada de tu luz rasgados:
> si te liberta el abrazo del Padre,
> rompe la Ley y el cerco del Arcángel,
> y aunque te den como piedra de escándalo,
> abandona los coros de tu gozo,
> bajando en ventisqueros derretido
> o albatrós libre que llega devuelto.

> Goethe Our Father who are in Heaven
> among the Thrones and Dominations
> and sleep and wake with your eyes
> torn by the cascade
> of your heavenly light;
> if the Father frees you from his embrace,
> break with the Law and Archangel's circle,
> and regardless of their astonishment,
> leave the Chorus of your enjoyment,
> descending like a melted glacier
> or like a freed albatross coming back to us.

In one of the arguments to persuade Goethe to descend from heaven, the speaker insinuates that, in response to the prayer's request, the German poet seems to awake from his heavenly rapture, struck by memories of his earthly experience. The lyrical speaker notes the affinity between the primeval

American experience of nature and Goethe's tender nostalgia for his childhood, presenting images from the personal experience of Mistral, who when overwhelmed by abandonment and secluded in southern Chile, had found shelter in Goethe's poetry. Once the speaker identifies herself with the people of America, she confesses her consciousness of the division and hate, and of the perverse use of the wisdom inherited from Europe. Self-knowledge of the American existence takes the form of a night of antarctic half-light in which the incipient and ambiguous state of the world is not yet dispossesed of a chaos that neither the plenitude of light nor of love can reach.

This confession of *extravío* (the going astray of the human condition) is followed by a new prayer for self-knowledge, which calls upon Goethe to acknowledge her spiritual descendance at the same time that she denounces the permanence of the shapeless and the absence of purifying energy. She anticipates that, upon his return, Goethe will find everything as it has always been: a nocturnal world characterized by the evil embedded in American reality. But, in a way that is adversative and has prophetic resonance, she announces the presence of the spirit in the American world and the effective action of love, all of this perceptible through faint but definite signs. The poem is a proclamation of love as a sweet cure for the evils of the American world; its conclusion expresses the reiterated Mistralian conviction that social justice and the improvement of American life will be achieved not by means of dissension and violence but through love and compassion among men.

> Pero será por gracia de este día
> que en el percal de los aires se hace
> paro de viento, quiebro de marea.
> Como que quieres permear la Tierra,
> sajada en res, con tu río de vida,
> y desalteras al calenturiento
> y echas señales al apercibido.
> Y vuela el aire un guiño de respuesta
> un sí-es no-es de albricias, un vilano,
> y no hay en lo que llega a nuestra carne
> tacto ni sacudida que conturben,
> sino un siseo de labio amoroso
> más delgado que silbo: apenas habla.
>
> (*ibid.*)

Nevertheless it will be by grace of this day
that the fabric of the air becomes
still wind, broken tidewave.
As if you would permeate the Earth,
split as an animal, with your river of life,
soothing the feverish
and making signals to the clever.
And in the air flies a wink of an answer
an ambiguous feeling of joy, a thistle flower,
and there is nothing in what reaches our flesh
nor touch nor shaking that disturbs us,
but a hissing of loving lips,
thinner than a whistling: it barely speaks.

Mistral's vision of the primeval world of America finds its pictorial equivalent in the outstanding work of the Chilean artist Roberto Matta. His painting "Nacimiento de América" (America's Birth) is a representation of a primeval world in the midst of which is proclaimed the presence of the spirit that gives light, the discovery of love that is a sign of a coming dawn.

An important part of Mistral's work is her poetic prose. During her lifetime she published the extraordinary essays on the Cuban writer José Martí's poetry *La lengua de Martí* (1934); *Versos sencillos* (Simple Verses, 1939); *Breve descripción de Chile* (1934) and other essays; *Poemas de las madres* (Poems of the Mothers, 1950), which came from the first edition of *Desolación*; and several short works in literary magazines. Posthumously her articles or *recados* (messages) have been compiled in *Croquis mexicanos* (Mexican Sketches, 1957); the series of *motivos* (motifs) is collected in *Canto a San Francisco* (A Song to Saint Francis, 1957) and *Motivos de San Francisco* (Saint Francis' Motifs, 1965). Her articles and essays were collected under the rubric "messages" in several volumes, from *Recados contando a Chile* (Messages Describing Chile, 1957) to more recent compilations by Luis Vargas Saavedra, Roque Esteban Scarpa, and Alfonso Calderón.

Mistral is one of the most universal as well as one of the most singular and distinctive voices in Chilean and Spanish-American poetry. Her poetry has its roots in modernism but is modified with *sencillista* (simplistic) restrictions that affect versification and verbal choice and that were characteristic of the literature of her generation. The poetic language is close to spoken language, avoiding the artificial style imposed by modernism. The *sencillista* motifs (natural objects, matter, animals, flowers, trees, water, air, salt), the regionalistic motifs of familiar rural places (the house, the landscape, the village or the city, the province, the nation, the American continent in its broadest perspective), and the personal motifs (intimacy, passion, sadness and the suffering of living, sweet and loving feelings) all converge and become those of the New Worldist moment. Mistral modulates and refines these concepts and motifs, through the intensity and strangeness of her passion. On the other hand, she was familiar with the innovations of contemporary poetry, and her assumption of its forms gave her an important role in the transformation of poetic language and genres. She escaped the limitations of the poetry of her generation, which she interpreted with great lucidity and which she consciously strove to surpass. Referring to the elementarity of the poetic motifs of Spanish-American poetry, she said in her notes to "Dos himnos" in *Tala*:

> After the epic trumpet, more elephantine than metallic, of our romantics, who assumed the gesticulation of the Quintanas and the Gallegos, our generation felt an exaggerated repugnance toward the long and broad hymn, toward the major tonality. The flutes and the reeds have arrived, and not only those made out of corn, but also of rice and barley. . . . The minor tonality was now welcome, and it left us its exquisiteness, from which we can count our most intimate and perhaps our purest songs. But already we are touching the miserable bottom of the jewelry and of the creation in aconites. Upon contemplating the Indian monuments or the Cordillera, one usually longs for a total voice that will have the courage to approach those formidable materials.

In the context of Chilean poetry, her place is with the generation of Pedro Prado, Manuel Magallanes Moure, Carlos Pezoa Velis, Max Jara, and other New Worldist poets. Yet, because she was the youngest among them and had left the Chilean scene at an early age, she related more widely than her generational peers to the poetic avant-garde and the younger generations.

Mistral also occupies an outstanding place among women poets, with whom she related in reciprocal friendship and admiration. Along with Alfonsina Storni, Delmira Agustini, Juana de Ibarbourou, and Esther de Cáceres, she made a special place for women in Spanish-American poetry. The works of Mistral have varied repercussions in the work of several other Spanish-American poets. Her poetry finds echoes in Neruda as much in the Americanism of her hymns, which anticipate aspects and motifs of his *Canto General* (General Song, 1950), as in her choice of subject matter in the "Materias" poems in *Tala*, which anticipate, with their poetization of primary elements, the characteristics of Neruda's *Odas elementales* (Elemental Odes, 1954). Her "locas letanías," a series of "chaotic enumerations" that praise the human and the divine, later find significant echoes in Neruda, Octavio Paz, and other Spanish-American poets. Among the later poets of standing, Enrique Lihn masterfully imitates some Mistralian poetic strategies.

Translated from the Spanish by Irene and Nicolás Goic

SELECTED BIBLIOGRAPHY

First Editions

Poetry

Desolación. New York, 1922.
Ternura. Madrid, 1924.
Tala. Buenos Aires, 1938.
Lagar. Santiago, Chile, 1954.
Poema de Chile. Barcelona, 1967. Posthumous.

Prose

Lecturas para mujeres. Mexico City, 1923.
Breve descripción de Chile. Santiago, Chile, 1934.
La lengua de Martí. Havana, 1934.
Versos sencillos. Estudio de Gabriela Mistral. Havana, 1939.
Palabras para la Universidad de Puerto Rico: Trabajo preparado para ser leído en la Cuadragésima Cuarta Colación de Grados de la Universidad de Puerto Rico. Río Piedras, Puerto Rico, 1948.
El sentido de la profesión. Guatemala City, 1956.

Collected Works

Antología. Selected by the author. With an introduction by Ismael Edwards Matte. Santiago, Chile, 1941; 4th ed. 1955.

Antología. Selected by the author. With an introduction by Alone [Hernán Díaz Arrieta]. Santiago, Chile, 1947.

Antología. Edited and with an introduction by Emma Godoy. Mexico City, 1967.

Cartas de amor de Gabriela Mistral. Compiled and with an introduction and notes by Sergio Fernández Larraín. Santiago, Chile, 1978.

Croquis mexicanos: Gabriela Mistral en México. Mexico City, 1957.

Desolación-Ternura-Tala-Lagar. With an introduction by Palma Guillén de Nicolau. Mexico City, 1981.

Elogio de las cosas de la tierra. Selected and with an introduction by Roque Esteban Scarpa. Santiago, Chile, 1979.

Gabriela piensa en. . . . Edited and with a prologue by Roque Esteban Scarpa. Santiago, Chile, 1978.

Grandeza de los oficios. Edited and with an introduction by Roque Esteban Scarpa. Santiago, Chile, 1979.

Magisterio y niño. Selected and with an introduction by Roque Esteban Scarpa. Santiago, Chile, 1979.

Materias: Prosa inédita. Edited and with an introduction by Alfonso Calderón. Santiago, Chile, 1978.

Motivos de San Francisco. Selected and with an introduction by César Díaz-Muñoz Cormatches. Santiago, Chile, 1965. Prose poems.

Páginas en prosa. Selected and with an introduction and notes by José Pereira Rodríguez. Buenos Aires, 1962.

Pequeña antología de Gabriela Mistral. Selected by the author. Santiago, Chile, 1950.

Poesías. Edited and with a prologue by Eliseo Diego. Havana, 1967.

Poesías completas. Edited by Margaret Bates. Madrid, 1958; 3rd. ed. 1966.

Prosa religiosa. Compiled and with an introduction and notes by Luis Vargas Saavedra. Santiago, Chile, 1978.

Recados contando a Chile. Selected by Alfonso M. Escudero. Santiago, Chile, 1957.

Reino: (Poesía dispersa e inédita, en verso y prosa). Compiled and with an introduction by Gastón von dem Bussche. Valparaiso, Chile, 1983.

Translations

Selected Poems of Gabriela Mistral. Translated and with an introduction by Langston Hughes. Bloomington, Ind., 1957.

Selected Poems of Gabriela Mistral. Translated and edited by Doris Dana. Baltimore, Md., 1979.

Biographical and Critical Studies

Albanell, Norah, and Nancy Mango. "Los escritos de Gabriela Mistral y estudios sobre su obra." In *Gabriela Mistral.* Washington, D.C., 1958. Pp. 49–90.

Alegría, Ciro. *Gabriela Mistral íntima.* Lima, 1968.

Alegría, Fernando. *Genio y figura de Gabriela Mistral.* Buenos Aires, 1966.

Alone [Hernán Díaz Arrieta]. *Gabriela Mistral.* Santiago, Chile, 1946.

_____. *Los cuatro grandes de la literatura chilena durante el siglo XX.* Santiago, Chile, 1963. Pp. 119–151.

Alvarez-Borland, Isabel. "Víctor Hugo, Gabriela Mistral, y *L'interxtualité.*" *Revista de estudios hispánicos* 18/3: 371–380 (1984).

Anadón, José. "Epistolario entre Gabriela Mistral y Eduardo Barrios." *Cuadernos americanos* 36/2:228–235 (1977).

_____. "Una carta de Gabriela Mistral sobre *Desolación.*" *Hispamérica* 7/19:29–42 (1978).

Anastasía Sosa, Luis. V. *El sentido de la vida en algunas imágenes de Gabriela Mistral.* Montevideo. 1961.

Arce de Vázquez, Margot. *Gabriela Mistral: Persona y poesía.* San Juan, Puerto Rico, 1958.

_____. *Gabriela Mistral: The Poet and Her Work.* Translated by Helene Masslo Anderson. New York, 1964.

Bahamonde, Mario. *Gabriela Mistral en Antofagasta: Años de forja y valentía.* Santiago, Chile, 1980.

Bates, Margaret. "Gabriela Mistral." *The Americas* 3/21: 168–189 (1946).

_____. "A Propos an Article on Gabriela Mistral." *The Americas* 14/2: 145–151 (1957).

_____. "Gabriela Mistral's *Poema de Chile.*" *The Americas* 17/3:261–276 (1961).

_____. "The Definitive Edition of Gabriela Mistral's Poetry." *Revista interamericana de bibliografía* 16/4: 411–415 (1966).

_____. "Introduction." In *Selected Poems of Gabriela Mistral,* translated and edited by Doris Dana. Baltimore, Md., 1971. Pp. xv–xxvi.

Berchmans, Sister John, O.P. "Gabriela Mistral and the Franciscan Concept of Life." *Renascence* 5/1:40–46, 95 (1952).

Bussche, Gastón von dem. "Análisis estilístico del poema 'La copa' de Gabriela Mistral." *Anales de la Universidad de Chile* 114/101:159–163 (1956).

_____. *Visión de una poesía.* Santiago, Chile, 1957.

Cáceres, Esther de. "Alma y poesía de Gabriela Mistral." In *Poesías completas*, edited by Margaret Bates. 3rd. ed. Madrid, 1966. Pp. xv–xci.

Carrasco Muñoz, Iván. "'Intima,' de Gabriela Mistral: La escritura correctora." *Estudios filológicos* 18:35–48 (1983).

Carrión, Benjamín. *Santa Gabriela Mistral*. Quito, 1956.

Castleman, William J. *Beauty and the Mission of the Teacher: The Life of Gabriela Mistral of Chile*. Smithtown, N.Y., 1982.

Clavería, Carlos. "El americanismo de Gabriela Mistral." *Bulletin of Spanish Studies* 23:116–127 (1946).

Conde, Carmen. *Gabriela Mistral*. Madrid, 1970.

Cuneo, Ana María. "Hacia la determinación del 'arte poética' de Gabriela Mistral." *Revista chilena de literatura* 26:19–36 (1985).

Daydí-Tolson, Santiago. "El yo lírico en *Poema de Chile* de Gabriela Mistral." *Revista chilena de literatura* 19:5–20 (1982).

_____. "La locura en Gabriela Mistral." *Revista chilena de literatura* 21:47–62 (1983).

Diego, Gerardo. "La nueva poesía de Gabriela Mistral." *Revista de Indias* 6/22:811–820 (1945).

Escudero, Alfonso M. *La prosa de Gabriela Mistral: Fichas de contribución a su inventario*. Santiago, Chile, 1950; expanded ed. 1957.

Figueira, Gastón. *Gabriela Mistral: Fuerza y ternura de América*. Montevideo, 1951.

_____. *De la vida y la obra de Gabriela Mistral*. Montevideo, 1959.

_____. "La depuración estilística en Gabriela Mistral." *Cuadernos israelíes* 4:69–78 (1960).

_____. "Páginas desconocidas u olvidadas de Gabriela Mistral." *Revista interamericana de bibliografía* 20/2: 139–156 (1970).

_____. "A cincuenta años del primer libro de Gabriela Mistral." *Revista interamericana de bibliografía* 23/2: 164–178 (1973).

_____. "Las relaciones literarias y amistosas entre Gabriela Mistral y Juana de Ibarbourou. *Revista interamericana de bibliografía* 25/1:13–23 (1975).

Figueroa, Virgilio. *La divina Gabriela*. Santiago, Chile, 1933.

Finlayson, Clarence. "Spanish American Poet: The Life and Ideas of Gabriela Mistral." *The Commonweal* 35/7:160–163 (1941).

Flores, Angel. "Gabriela Mistral." In *Bibliografía de escritores hispanoamericanos, 1609–1974*. New York, 1975. Pp. 134–139.

Gazarian-Gautier, Marie-Lise. *Gabriela Mistral: La maestra de Elqui*. Buenos Aires, 1973. English version: *Gabriela Mistral, The Teacher from the Valley of Elqui*. Translated by the author. Chicago, 1975.

Godoy, Emma. "Gabriela Mistral." *Abside* 32:125–153 (1968).

Goic, Cedomil. "'Cadenillas' en la poesía de Gabriela Mistral." *Atenea* 34/374:44–50 (1957).

_____. "El emblema de 'Amor tirano' en Gabriela Mistral." *Mapocho* 24:19–26 (1977).

_____. "Himnos americanos y extravío: 'Cordillera' de Gabriela Mistral." In *Gabriela Mistral*, edited by Mirella Servodidio and Marcelo Coddou. Xalapa, Mexico, 1980. Pp. 140–148.

_____. "'Cima,' de Gabriela Mistral." *Revista iberoamericana* 48/118–119:59–72 (1982).

González Vera, José S. In *Algunos*. Santiago, Chile, 1959. Pp. 125–150.

Guillén de Nicolau, Palma. "Gabriela Mistral, 1922–1924." In *Lecturas para mujeres*. Mexico City, 1967. Pp. vii–xx.

_____. "Introducción." In *Desolación-Ternura-Tala-Lagar*, by Gabriel Mistral. Mexico City, 1981. Pp. ix–xlviii.

Guzmán, Jorge. *Diferencias latinoamericanas*. Santiago, Chile, 1984. Pp. 11–77.

Hamilton, Carlos D. "Raíces bíblicas en la poesía de Gabriela Mistral." *Cuadernos americanos* 20/5:201–210 (1961).

Iglesias, Augusto. *Gabriela Mistral y el modernismo en Chile*. Santiago, Chile, 1950.

Jiménez, Onilda A. *La crítica literaria en la obra de Gabriela Mistral*. Miami, 1982.

_____. "Dos cartas inéditas de Gabriela Mistral a Lydia Cabrera." *Hispamérica* 12/34–35:97–103 (1983).

Ladrón de Guevara, Matilde. *Gabriela Mistral, rebelde magnífica*. Santiago, Chile, 1957; Buenos Aires, 1962.

Lefebvre, Alfredo. In *Poesía española y chilena*. Santiago, Chile, 1958. Pp. 130–147.

Lida, Raimundo. "Palabras de Gabriela Mistral." *Cuadernos americanos* 16/3:234–237 (1957).

Loveluck, Juan. "Cartas de Gabriela Mistral a Amado Nervo." *Revista iberoamericana* 36/72:495–508 (1970).

Loynaz, Dulce María. "Gabriela y Lucila." In *Poesías completas*, edited by Margaret Bates. Madrid, 1958. Pp. cxvii–cxliii.

Madariaga, Salvador de. *Homenaje a Gabriela Mistral*. London, 1958.

Mañach, Jorge, et al. *Gabriela Mistral: Vida y obra. Bibliografía. Antología*. New York, 1936.

_____. In *La lírica chilena de hoy*. Santiago, Chile, 1967. Pp. 9–49.

Navarro Tomás, Tomás. "Métrica y ritmo de Gabriela

Mistral." In *Lengua-Literatura-Folklore: Estudios dedicados a Rodolfo Oroz*. Santiago, Chile, 1967. Pp.383–405.

Ocampo, Victoria. "Gabriela Mistral y el Premio Nobel." *Sur* 134:7–15 (1945).

Oelker, Dieter. "Aproximaciones a tres poemas de Gabriela Mistral." *Atenea* 43/413:159–173 (1966).

———. "La actitud mítica, poético-religiosa, en las 'Historias de loca' de Gabriela Mistral." *Atenea* 45/421–422:79–123 (1968).

Oroz, Rodolfo. "Notas al poema "Ceras eternas" de Gabriela Mistral." *Atenea* 32/358:116–121 (1955).

———. "Sobre neologismos en la poesía de Gabriela Mistral." *Boletín de la Academia Chilena* 55:29–54 (1967).

Oyarzún, Luis. "El sentimiento americano en Gabriela Mistral." *Sur* 137:48–53 (1946).

———. "Gabriela Mistral." *Atenea* 34/374:34–39 (1957).

Pinilla, Norberto. *Bibliografía crítica sobre Gabriela Mistral*. Santiago, Chile, 1940.

———. *Biografía de Gabriela Mistral*. Santiago, Chile, 1946.

Porter, Katherine Anne. "Latin America's Mystic Poet." *The Literary Digest International Book Review* 4/5:307–308 (1926).

Preston, Sister Mary Charles Ann. *A Study of Significant Variants in the Poetry of Gabriela Mistral*. Washington, D.C., 1964.

Promis, José. "Infancia y adolescencia de Gabriela Mistral (1889–1910). Años de formación y aprendizaje." *Signos* 5/1:21–47 (1971).

Rabanales, Ambrosio. "Tendencias métricas en los sonetos de Gabriela Mistral." In *Studia philologica: Homenaje ofrecido a Dámaso Alonso* 3. Madrid, 1963. Pp. 13–51.

Ríos, Rebeca. "La sintaxis en la expresión poética de Gabriela Mistral." *Boletín de filología* 9:121–176 (1956–1957).

Rosenbaum, Sidonia C. "Gabriela Mistral: Bibliografía." *Revista hispánica moderna* 3/2:135–140 (1937); reprinted in *Gabriela Mistral: Vida y obra. Bibliografía. Antología*, by Jorge Mañach et al. New York, 1936.

———. *Modern Women Poets of Spanish America*. New York, 1945. Pp. 171–203.

———. "Criollismo y casticismo en Gabriela Mistral." *Cuadernos americanos* 12/1:296–300 (1953).

Rudd, Margaret T. "The Spanish Tragedy of Gabriela Mistral." *Romance Notes* 18/1:38–48 (1977).

Saavedra Molina, Julio. *Gabriela Mistral: Su vida y su obra*. Santiago, Chile, 1947.

Sánchez, Luis Alberto. "Un ser y una voz inconfundibles." *Cuadernos* (Paris) 23:20–24 (1957).

Santandreu, Cora. *Aspectos del estilo en la poesía de Gabriela Mistral*. Santiago, Chile, 1958.

Scarpa, Roque Esteban. *Una mujer nada de tonta*. Santiago, Chile, 1976.

———. *La desterrada en su patria*. 2 vols. Santiago, Chile, 1977.

Servodidio, Mirella, and Marcelo Coddou, eds. *Gabriela Mistral*. Xalapa, Mexico, 1980.

Silva, Hernán. "La unidad poética de *Desolación*." *Estudios filológicos* 4:152–175 (1968) and 5:170–196 (1969).

Silva Castro, Raúl. *Estudios sobre Gabriela Mistral*. Santiago, Chile, 1935.

———. *Producción de Gabriela Mistral de 1912 a 1918*. Santiago, Chile, 1957.

———. "Notas sobre los 'Sonetos de la muerte' de Gabriela Mistral." *Hispanic Review* 33/1:57–62 (1965).

Subercaseaux, Bernardo. "Gabriela Mistral: Espiritualismo y canciones de cuna." *Cuadernos americanos* 35/2:208–225 (1976).

Szmulewicz, Efraín. *Gabriela Mistral: Biografía emotiva*. Santiago, Chile, 1958; expanded ed. 1974.

Taylor, Martin C. *Gabriela Mistral's Religious Sensibility*, Berkeley and Los Angeles, 1968.

———. "Parálisis y progreso en la crítica mistraliana." In *El ensayo y la crítica literaria en Iberoamérica*, edited by Kurt L. Levy and Keith Ellis. Toronto, 1970. Pp. 185–190.

Torre, Guillermo de. "Aproximaciones de *Tala*." *Sur* 45:70–75 (1938).

Torres-Rioseco, Arturo. "Gabriela Mistral." *Cosmópolis* (Madrid) 15:373–377 (1920).

———. *Gabriela Mistral*. Valencia, Spain, 1962.

Undurraga, Antonio de. "¿Fueron doce los sonetos de la muerte de Gabriela Mistral?" *Atenea* 30/336:379–385 (1953); reprinted in *La nueva democracia* 33/1:36–41 (1953).

Valéry, Paul. "Gabriela Mistral." *Atenea* 24/269–270:313–322 (1947).

Vargas Saavedra, Luis. "Hispanismo y antihispanismo en Gabriela Mistral." *Mapocho* 22:5–24 (1970).

———. "Cartas de Gabriela Mistral." *Mapocho* 23:19–29 (1970).

———. *El otro suicida de Gabriela Mistral*. Santiago, Chile, 1985.

Villegas, Juan. *Interpretación de textos poéticos chilenos*. Santiago, Chile, 1977. Pp. 49–94.

Vitier, Cintio. *La voz de Gabriela Mistral*. Santa Clara, Cuba, 1957.

Alfonso Reyes

(1889–1959)

James Willis Robb

Alfonso Reyes, Mexican essayist, poet, literary humanist, educator, and diplomat, stands out as one of Latin America's great prose stylists and cultural missionaries. In Mexican literature he represents a bridge between the Mexican concern and the aspiration of the Americas to occupy a significant place in universal culture.

Reyes was born on 17 May 1889 in Monterrey, Mexico, where his father, General Bernardo Reyes, was governor of the state of Nuevo León. General Reyes, a "man of arms and of letters," awakened the literary vocation in his son, Alfonso.

In 1906 Reyes moved to Mexico City, where he was active with a group of young poets and scholars who on the eve of the Mexican Revolution of 1910 initiated a cultural renewal and educational reform through the National Preparatory School and the National University. This group included Antonio Caso, José Vasconcelos, Jesús T. Acevedo, and the Dominican Pedro Henríquez Ureña; they came to be known as the Centennial Generation (for the centennial of Mexican independence). A lecture society was formed, focusing first on Greek and then on Hispanic-American themes, with Reyes analyzing the verse of Mexican poet Manuel José Othón. In the Preparatory School, Antonio Caso led the campaign in favor of intuitionist philosophy (Henri Bergson,

Étienne Boutroux, William James, Benedetto Croce) against the frozen positivist philosophy (Auguste Comte, Gabino Barreda) that had permeated the educational system of the Porfirio Díaz regime in Mexico. Henríquez Ureña brought his Socratic leadership to the young humanists eager to discover and rediscover the cultures of ancient Greece and Rome, the Spanish Golden Age, modern German philosophies, and French and English literatures. They formed a literary society called the Ateneo de la Juventud (Atheneum of Youth) and participated with Minister Justo Sierra in founding in 1912 the School of Higher Studies, the first humanities division of the National University, of which Reyes was secretary. There he inaugurated the chair of Spanish language and literature. In 1911 Reyes published in Paris his first volume of essays, *Cuestiones estéticas* (Aesthetic Questions), on such varied literary themes as the three Electras of Greek tragedy, Luis de Góngora, Johann Wolfgang von Goethe, Stéphane Mallarmé, and George Bernard Shaw, foreshadowing many of his interests through the years. His essay on the poetics of Góngora is a pioneer study on this Spanish mannerist-baroque poet, who was then underappreciated among Hispanists worldwide.

The tragic death of General Reyes in a counter-revolutionary coup on 9 February 1913 brought a change of destiny for his son, who chose a form of voluntary exile. He accepted appointment as second secretary of the Mexican legation in France, thus launching a diplomatic career lasting a quarter century. The German invasion of Paris in 1914, however, with the suspension of functions of the Mexican diplomatic corps, obliged Reyes to migrate with his wife and infant son to Spain, where he spent the first six difficult years earning a living with his pen in Madrid. Fortunately, he received a number of literary commissions to prepare critical editions of Spanish classics and translations of Anton Chekhov, G. K. Chesterton, Laurence Sterne, and Robert Louis Stevenson. José Ortega y Gasset entrusted him with the cultural section of his newspaper El Sol. As a scholar, Reyes became a member of the philology section of the Center for Historical Studies directed by Ramón Menéndez Pidal, together with Federico de Onís, Américo Castro, Tomás Navarro Tomás, and Antonio G. Solalinde.

With his reintegration into the Mexican diplomatic service in 1920 as second and then first secretary of the Mexican legation in Spain, he was able fruitfully to combine literary and diplomatic careers for his remaining four years in Spain and thereafter. He became a cultural bridge-builder between Spain and Mexico, and his Spanish literary friendships included most of the luminaries of his time, from Azorín and Miguel de Unamuno to Juan Ramón Jiménez, Ramón M. del Valle-Inclán, and Ramón Gómez de la Serna.

His own literary production, in creative and in critical/scholarly dimensions, was remarkable. Nostalgia for Mexico inspired his poetic essay of historical interpretation, Visión de Anáhuac (Vision of Anáhuac, 1917), which fuses poetry and erudition as it focuses on the encounter of Cortés with Montezuma and the magic world of the Aztecs, leading to a meditation on the destiny of Mexico, product of three successive civilizations. Reyes' dramatic poem Ifigenia cruel (Cruel Iphigenia, 1924), a major recreation of the Iphigenia myth, embodies a personal literary catharsis of the author's sense of exile and search for liberation, successfully performed as drama both in Spain (1958) and in Mexico (1934, 1979, 1981). His impressions of Spain crystallized in Cartones de Madrid (Sketches of Madrid, 1917) and Horas de Burgos (A Few Hours

in Burgos, 1932), both later collected in Las vísperas de España (The Twilight of Spain, 1937). While in Spain he published his first volume of verse, Huellas (Traces, 1922), and his first collected short stories, El plano oblicuo (On the Oblique Plane, 1920). Most of these lyrical fantasy tales were composed in Mexico from 1910 to 1913, including the presurrealistic "La cena" (Invitation to a Dinner) of 1912. His prolific work as an essayist took varied forms: El suicida (The Suicide, 1917), philosophical meditations; Retratos reales e imaginarios (Real and Imaginary Portraits, 1920), biographical essays; El cazador (The Hunter, 1921), artistic/literary chronicles of Paris and Madrid; and Calendario (Calendar, 1924), brief, familiar pieces of sprightly comment. His journalistic writings of a dozen years are grouped in five volumes of Simpatías y diferencias (Affinities and Differences, 1921–1926). Literary studies of Mexicans Juan Ruiz de Alarcón and Amado Nervo as well as Spanish Golden Age figures Félix Lope de Vega, Francisco de Quevedo, and Baltasar Gracián culminated in his Cuestiones gongorinas (Questions Relating to Góngora), which appeared opportunely in 1927 when the young Spanish poets gathered around Federico García Lorca and Dámaso Alonso were celebrating the Góngora tercentenary and promoting a Góngora revival. Reyes with Martín Luis Guzmán also pioneered in Spanish cinema criticism under the joint pseudonym of "Fósforo."

In late 1924 Reyes was named minister of Mexico in France, serving there until 1927. In the cosmopolitan cultural capital of Paris, he became as much a part of the literary life as in Madrid and formed congenial and lasting friendships with such writers as Jules Romains, Valery Larbaud, Paul Valéry, St. John Perse, Jules Supervielle, Jean Prévost, and Marcelle Auclair. His long-standing interest in French culture had continued since his early essay on the French symbolist poet Mallarmé, published in Paris while he was a precocious youth in Mexico, under the aegis of the Peruvian Francisco García Calderón. Calderón, along with his brother, Ventura, now joined Reyes in Paris as participants in international vanguard movements and as cultural intermediaries between France and Latin America. In his residence at 23, rue Cortambert, Reyes received French, Spanish, and Latin American friends, who included Salvadoran caricaturist Toño Salazar and Chilean poet Gabriela Mistral. It was in Paris at a family gathering with Cuban poet Mariano Brull that Reyes coined the word *jitanjáfora* for the sonorous poetic word with no semantic content, from a line of nonsense verse recited by Brull's little daughters.

Reyes was ambassador from Mexico twice alternately in Argentina and Brazil from 1927 to 1939; these countries were also the scene of his work as a cultural missionary. From the two capitals of Buenos Aires and Rio de Janeiro, South America for him was another cultural crossroads of the universe, linking North and South, East and West, Europe and the Americas. On his arrival in Buenos Aires, he was welcomed by the young vanguardist poets Ricardo Molinari, Jorge Luis Borges, and others associated with the literary reviews *Martín Fierro, Proa, Nosotros,* and *Sur. Sur's* founder, Victoria Ocampo, supreme *dame de lettres,* incorporated him into her international literary family. The young Argentine poets looked to Reyes for leadership in the absence of Ricardo Güiraldes (author of the gaucho novel *Don Segundo Sombra* [1926]), who died in Paris the year of Reyes' arrival in Buenos Aires. Reyes published an edition of six of Güiraldes' stories, prefaced by his own lyrical ode *A la memoria de Ricardo Güiraldes* (To the Memory of Ricardo Güiraldes, 1934). Reyes awoke in Borges, former *ultraísta* poet, the narrative vocation that was to lead to his worldwide celebrity as a writer of fantastic metaphysical tales. One of their many interests in common was the sophisticated detective story. The tragic assassination of Spanish poet García Lorca in 1936 inspired Reyes' poetic muse in Argentina in the *Cantata en la tumba de Federico García Lorca* (Cantata at the Tomb of Federico García Lorca, 1937), which was performed with music in Buenos Aires by Margarita Xirgu, the great dramatic interpreter of Lorca's tragic heroines. Surveying the Argentine and Brazilian scene, Reyes synthesized their respective cultures in his short essays "Palabras sobre la nación argentina" (A Few Words About the Argentine Nation), "Salutación a Brasil," and "El Brasil en una castaña" ("Brazil in a Brazil Nut," a humorous variation on the title "México en una nuez" ["Mexico in a Nutshell"] in which he evokes Mexico from South America).

Much as he had felt at home in the cosmopolitan literary world of Buenos Aires, Reyes felt a special fascination for the semitropical exuberance of the then Brazilian capital of Rio de Janeiro, which inspired a cycle of poems entitled *Romances del Río de Enero* (Songs of Rio de Janeiro, 1933) as well as a series of impressionistic prose sketches and fictions evoking Brazilian scenes, customs, folklore, plus amusing feminine characters, later to be collected in *Quince presencias* (Fifteen Presences, 1955). His cordial empathy with the Luso-Brazilian world resulted in observations on the Spanish and Portuguese sister languages, "Aduana lingüística" (On the Linguistic Frontier), as well as on the culture of Brazil. His Brazilian friendships were numerous and included poets Cecília Meireles and Manuel Bandeira, sociologist Gilberto Freyre, literary critic Alceu Amoroso Lima, and painter Cândido Portinari. Active himself on the Brazilian literary scene as a fraternal representative of the Hispanic American world, he also published a personal literary bulletin named *Monterrey,* after his native city in Mexico, to keep in touch with his literary friends throughout Europe and the Americas. Through its pages he published news notes and comments on Ruiz de Alarcón, Góngora, Marcel Proust, Paul Valéry, Graça Aranha, and recent Mexican theater, and exchanged examples of *jitanjáforas,* constantly interrelating things European with things American. From his pen came a series of brief, succinct portrait essays on great Europeans related to America: "Virgilio y América," "St.-Simon y America," "Goethe y América," "Rousseau el aduanero y México," "Paul Morand en Río," and "Garibaldi y Cuba."

Each of the fourteen numbers of *Monterrey* was "signed" with Reyes' personal emblem: a sketch of his native city dominated by the profile of its Cerro de la Silla (Saddle Mountain), with a quotation from a popular couplet referring to the all-embracing panorama to be obtained from its summit. This emblem appeared on a number of the covers of Reyes' individual published works, on his personal stationery, and finally on his tomb in the Mexican national pantheon known as the Rotonda de los Hombres Ilustres (Rotunda of Illustrious Men). It signifies Alfonso Reyes' nostalgic identification with his native land and with the mountain as a symbolic observation point from which he surveys the universe.

During his stays in Rio and Buenos Aires, Reyes the diplomat and man of letters participated as Mexican representative in international meetings such as the Seventh Interamerican Conference, held in Montevideo in December 1933; the Seventh Conference of the International Institute of Intellectual Cooperation (forerunner of UNESCO) in Buenos Aires in 1936; the Interamerican Peace Conference in Buenos Aires in December 1936; and the PEN Club Congress in Buenos Aires. In relation to these activities, Reyes made a number of addresses, among them "Posición de America" ("The Position of America"), "El sentido de América" (The Meaning of America), and "Notas sobre la inteligencia americana" ("Thoughts on the American Mind") later to be collected as essays. In them he established himself as a spokesman for Hispanic America who, having arrived late at the banquet of European civilization, ran hard to catch up, reached maturity, and was ready not only to receive but also actively to contribute to universal culture.

Strangely enough, at this time when Reyes was reaching heights of universal interamericanism, in Mexico one of his narrowly chauvinistic compatriots, Hector Pérez Martínez, accused him of "evident detachment from Mexico," reproaching him for the versatility of his universal cultural interests as manifested in *Monterrey*. Reyes felt compelled to reply in an open letter, "A vuelta de correo" (By Return Mail, 1932; in *Obras completas,* vol. 8, 1958), setting forth his position, and pointing out that he had confided to a friend in Madrid a plan to undertake a series of essays with the theme "In Search of the National Soul," beginning with his *Visión de Anáhuac;* that even his Hellenic studies were permeated with allusions to Mexico; and that, finally, as a Mexican he had a right to participate and be a spokesman for Mexico in the totality of universal culture. In sum, "the only way to be fruitfully national is to be generously universal." In spite of these famous words, he was to be the target of further such polemical attacks throughout his life and after his death from other Mexicans questioning his "Mexicanism" and censuring him for not devoting his writings exclusively to Mexican affairs. Years later, in his *Parentalia* (1959), he expressed it in these terms:

The profound root, unconscious and involuntary, is in my Mexican being: this is a fact and not a virtue. It has been a cause not only of joys, but also of bloody tears. I need not invoke it in every page to flatter the foolish, nor make concessions with patriotic fraud for the payment of my modest work. Without effort on my part and without inherent merit, it reveals itself in all my books and saturates with vegetative humidity all my thoughts. It takes care of itself. As for me, I do not wish to be weighed down with any limited tradition. The universal heritage is mine by right of love and of zeal for study and work, the only authentic rewards to which I aspire.

(ch. 2)

In February 1939 Reyes completed his last diplomatic assignment in Brazil and returned to the Mexican capital, where he devoted the final twenty years of his life almost entirely to his literary and educational pursuits. On his arrival he was able to realize his dream of housing his library in a new residence built to his specifications. It was a "library with annexes," soon thereafter baptized "La Capilla Alfonsina" (Alfonso's Chapel) by his Spanish friend Enrique Díez-Canedo, who in the wake of the Spanish civil war came to spend his last years in Mexico. The Spanish word *capilla,* having the double meaning of "chapel" and "literary circle," could be understood as signifying both a sanctuary of the muses and a place for informal literary gatherings of Reyes' friends.

The coincidence of Reyes' definitive return to Mexico in 1939 with the exodus from Spain and exile in Mexico of a number of the prominent Spanish intellectuals led to the realization of a more ambitious dream for Reyes the scholar and educator. When in 1938 President Lázaro Cárdenas sent Reyes on a final mission to Brazil, Reyes left with the president a memorandum suggesting the foundation of a cultural research center that would open its doors to exiled foreign scholars. On his return, he found that steps had been taken to found such a center, under the name of La Casa de España (The House of Spain), with Reyes himself to be director. In accepting the directorship, he insisted on certain modifications, including the change of name to El Colegio de México (1940), to signify wider functions and purposes than those of merely providing a "home" for the exiled Spanish scholars. Nevertheless, it became a Mexican equivalent of the former Centro de Estudios

Históricos of which Reyes had been a part in Madrid—a distinguished center for advanced study and research in the humanities, with emphasis in literature, philology, and history; a private institution independent of the universities and of the government. During the years of World War II, between 1942 and 1944, Reyes personally received in Mexico another distinguished exile, his friend Jules Romains from France.

Reyes was also cofounder in 1945 (with Antonio Caso, Ezequiel Chávez, painter Diego Rivera, and others) of another extra-university educational institution, El Colegio Nacional, modeled on the Collège de France in Paris. It brings together twenty of Mexico's most distinguished scholars in different specialties of the arts and sciences who, without academic formalities, offer regular series of lectures open to the general public. Reyes made himself known as the "specialist in universals," giving rise to the nickname the "Universal Mexican," and he lectured on subjects as varied as literary theory, Greek philosophy, and French medieval literature.

Reyes' contributions to the creation of these institutions of higher learning can be seen as prolongations of the educational renewal collectively brought about by the young members of the Mexican Ateneo in the years 1909–1913, and given further stimulus by José Vasconcelos as rector of the National University and secretary of education from 1920 to 1924. Reyes became a professor at the University of Morelia, Michoacán, in 1940 and at the National University in 1941. In the furthering of Franco-Mexican cultural relations, he participated in the formation of the Fédération des Alliances Françaises in Mexico (he was named its honorary president in 1954) and in that of the affiliated French Institute of Latin America.

Reyes the diplomat was not inactive during his later years. In 1945 he was Mexican delegate to the Interamerican Conference on War and Peace at Chapultepec, and in 1946–1947 he headed the Mexican delegation to the first UNESCO assembly in Paris. However, it was as a man of letters that he received greatest recognition. In 1945 he was awarded the National Prize in Literature. In the same year Gabriela Mistral received the Nobel Prize in literature, the first Latin American to receive this

honor, and she privately made overtures to the Swedish Academy to nominate Reyes for the same award. In 1955 the golden anniversary of his literary career was celebrated, through the initiative of Félix Lizaso from Cuba, joined in Mexico by the National University and the University of Nuevo León in Monterrey. At this time his publisher, Fondo de Cultura Económica, initiated publication of his complete works, of which he himself was able to prepare the first twelve volumes. A further offshoot was the definitive campaign crystallizing in 1956 for his nomination for the Nobel Prize in literature. It was launched by an Iberoamerican Writers' Society in New York; and though, like previous such attempts, it was unsuccessful, it nevertheless gave momentum to his international prestige. Reyes himself tended to discourage such efforts, smilingly remarking with an old Spanish metaphor, "No caerá esa breva" (That plum will not fall from the tree). In 1957 he was elected director of the Mexican Academy of the Language. At the age of seventy, on 27 December 1959, he died from the last of a number of heart attacks. His widow, Manuela (familiarly known as Doña Manuelita), and granddaughter, Alicia Reyes, have continued the work of the Capilla Alfonsina as a center of literary studies, under government sponsorship.

In the two final decades of Reyes' literary productivity, the fragments of his dispersed works progressively began to come together to form a diverse but coherent whole. He published a series of organic volumes centered on three themes: the theory of literature, in *La experiencia literaria* (The Literary Experience, 1942), *El deslinde* (The Demarcation, 1944), and *Al yunque* (At the Anvil, 1960); the meaning of Hispanic America in the context of universal history and culture, in *Última Tule* (Ultima Thule, 1942) and *Tentativas y orientaciones* (Experiments and Directions, 1944); and the Hellenic and Latin cultures, in *La crítica en la edad ateniense* (Criticism in the Athenean Age, 1941), *La antigua retórica* (The Ancient Rhetoricians, 1942), and *Junta de sombras* (Meeting of the Shades, 1949).

In his personal struggle to achieve unity through diversity, Reyes the creative writer kept thinking of himself in terms of the Greek myth of Isis and Osiris. As he expressed it in his "Fragmentos del arte póetica" (Fragments of Poetic Art, 1934): "Think of yourself according to the myth of Osiris; think of yourself as if you were born in pieces and diligently must put yourself together piece by piece. To conquer unity is not only your artistic task, but perhaps your essential human mission."

La experiencia literaria brings together a series of informal essays on literary theory, given a harmonious structure by the grouping of the more casually elaborated pieces in meaningful sequence after the five lead essays, each of which takes its title from a mythological, biblical, or ancient literary figure serving as a symbol of some aspect of linguistic or literary expression: "Hermes, o De la comunicación humana," "Marsyas, o Del terma popular," "Apolo, o De la literatura," "Jacob, o Idea de la poesía," and "Aristarco, o Anatomía de la crítica" ("Hermes: Of Human Communication," "Marsyas: Of the Popular Theme," "Apollo: Of Literature," "Jacob: The Concept of Poetry," "Aristarchus: Anatomy of Criticism"). These are full of artistic imagery, personal comments, and allusions; and they serve as a prelude to his more formal monographs of literary theory, notably *El deslinde,* an exhaustively systematic attempt at defining or setting the boundaries of the literary phenomenon in all its aspects, contrasting it with the other intellectual disciplines of history, mathematics, and theology. Even the formal monographs, however, participate in the personal artistic style of his familiar essays.

Reyes' works on the theme of the destiny of America and its place in universal history and culture likewise have their more and less systematic modes of approach. The volume *Última Tule* combines two such approaches. Part 1, subtitled "El presagio de América" ("Intimations of America"), is like its complement the *Visión de Anáhuac* a poetic essay of historical interpretation, offering a twenty-one-chapter panorama of the discoveries of America focused through the concept of "America as Utopia." Beginning with the Europeans' dreams of a magic world beyond, a lost Atlantis, a Plus Ultra or Ultima Thule, the concept then took form via the voyages of such explorers as Erik the Red, Christopher Columbus, and Amerigo Vespucci, arriving at the "baptism of America" in Europe and the further "destiny of America" as a site of new utopias. As in his *Visión de*

Anáhuac, historical documentation and interpretation are fused into the poetic vision of an essayist who is both an artist and a philosopher. In the second part of this volume, Reyes collects many of his addresses and miscellaneous essays on kindred themes, which can be seen as a sort of theme and variations series, with general or specific titles such as "Capricho de América," "El erasmismo en América," "Paul Valéry contempla a América," and "Valor de la literatura hispanoamericana" ("The Caprice of America," "Erasmism in America," "Paul Valéry Looks at America," "Value of Hispanic-American Literature"). Further such essays collected in *Tentativas y orientaciones* include "Position of America," "Virgil in Mexico," and "Discourse on the Language."

Reyes' Latin and Hellenic studies also range from the rigorous systematic monograph to the freer essay form. *La crítica en la edad ateniense* is a comprehensive study of ancient Greek culture through the origins and evolution of literary criticism from Socrates to Theophrastus and Menander, ending with a familiar imaginary portrait of "An Average Athenean." *Junta de sombras* is a more widely varied collection of studies overlapping with the familiar essay and includes a piece relating the Greeks to the Argentines: "The Strategy of Achilles the *Gaucho.*" His Spanish version of part 1 of Homer's *Iliad* (1951) is a free adaptation, or reelaboration by a modern poet, rather than a translation.

Not far from Reyes the Hellenist and Reyes the literary theorist is Reyes the philosopher-humanist. He synthesized his philosophy of man in "Andrenio: Perfiles del hombre" (Andrenio: Profiles of Man), a work unpublished until it was collected in the posthumous volume 20 of his *Obras completas* (Complete Works).

Reyes' numerous essays of literary criticism were collected in such volumes as the two series of *Capítulos de literatura española* (Chapters of Spanish Literature, 1939, 1945) and *Grata compañía* (Pleasant Company, 1948). Commentaries and original translations of Mallarmé are included in *Mallarmé entre nosotros* (Mallarmé Amongst Us, 1938). *Letras de la Nueva España* (Letters of New Spain, 1948) is a literary history of colonial Mexico. *Trayectoria de Goethe* (Trajectory of Goethe, 1954) is a spiritual biography of the German master much admired by Reyes.

The variety of forms of the familiar essay cultivated by Reyes constitutes one of his greatest literary achievements. A most extraordinary example is the volume *Ancorajes* (Ports of Call, 1951), which collects essays composed between 1928 and 1948. Here is a group of five essays revealing a "new Reyes" to those readers who might have identified him exclusively with the stereotype of the classical humanist imbued with the Platonic ideal of complete harmony and serenity. In contrast this is the Reyes of metaphysical anguish, with affinities to the Spanish and French existentialists Miguel de Unamuno and Albert Camus. The first of these essays, titled *La caída* (The Fall) takes off from the contemplation of an ivory carving depicting the Fall of Satan, seen by the author years before in the archeological museum of Madrid, viewed anew through the channels of memory, leading to an artistic expression of the Bergsonian theory of cosmic disintegration. This essay is followed by "La catástrofe" (The Catastrophe), "Palinodia del polvo" (Palinode of Dust), "Meditación sobre Mallarmé" (Meditation on Mallarmé), and "Metafísica de la máscara" (Meditation on the Mask), inspired by viewing some curious Mexican indigenous masks. The same volume includes "Compás poético" (Poetic Rhythm), a lyrical portrait of poets Juana de Ibarbourou, Enrique González Martínez, Ángel Aller, Eugenio Florit, and Ricardo Molinari; his fivefold "Fragmentos del arte poética" (Fragments of the Poetic Art), a most personal expression of the poet's irresistible call to be a writer; "*Quijote* en mano" (Reading *Don Quixote*), a familiar commentary on the reading and rereading of Cervantes; and *Por mayo era, por mayo* (In May It Was, in May—a quotation from an old Spanish ballad), a masterly example of the digressive familiar essay in circular form, which skips from one theme to another to return to its point of departure.

Other unusual series of familiar essays are *Los siete sobre Deva* (The Seven at Deva, 1942), a rambling series of brief meditations intertwined with anecdotes in dialogue framework; *Memorias de cocina y bodega* (Memoirs of Kitchen and Wine Cellar, 1953), culinary memoirs of a literary gourmet; and the more than two hundred miniature essays entitled *Las burlas veras* (True Jests, 1957 and 1959), which cover an infinity of subjects (including the metaphysical) in a paradoxical mode. The last of the *Burlas veras* have yet to be collected. *A campo traviesa* (Cross Country, 1960) collects eight essays composed in his last years, including the biographical essay "Alexander von Humboldt (1769–1859)."

Pedro Henríquez Ureña in 1927 had exclaimed: "At last the public is convinced that Alfonso Reyes, above all, is a poet." While observing that Reyes, who had started as a youthful budding poet, seemed to be drifting more and more toward writing in prose, he hailed the appearance of his *Ifigenia cruel* with its lyrical and dramatic depth and its authenticity in the transfusion of the poet's intimate drama into the mode of Greek tragedy. Reyes at this time had published only two other slim volumes of verse, the first of these, *Huellas*, in a poorly printed edition afflicted with numerous typographical errors, produced in Mexico while Reyes was in Spain. Caricaturist Toño Salazar later depicted him as the "Martyr of the Erratum." Nevertheless, in the prologue to this volume Reyes made a firm commitment as poet: "I began writing verse, I have continued writing verse, and I propose to continue writing verse until the end; as life goes on, in rhythm with the soul, without looking back. I go forward in haste. The night awaits me, and is anxious."

And so it was that Reyes, true to his promise, continued writing verse to the last, amid his more prolific activity through the years as an essayist. Those who wondered whether the poet had been sacrificed to the prose writer failed to note Reyes' own distinction between poetry and verse. Throughout his literary production, there is always in Reyes an essential poet: a poet in prose and a poet in verse who seeks in the poem a certain essence of lyrical expression, intimate and profound, or who writes in verse brief notes and messages to his friends that he calls verses of "courtesy" (*Cortesía* is also the title of one of his books, published in 1948), which spring as naturally from his pen as his writings in prose.

But his full stature as a poet in verse came to view finally with the collection of his *Obra poética* (1906–1952) (Poetic Work) in 1952, followed by the definitive volume 10 of his *Obras completas*, titled *Constancia poética* (Poetic Constancy), published the year he died. This volume alone would suffice to establish him as one of the important Hispanic

699

American poets of this century, of the postmodernist era. The title was chosen intentionally by Reyes to convey a double meaning. As he himself points out, the Spanish word *constancia* means both "continuity" and "documentary evidence"; it signifies his own constancy or continuity as a poet and the visible evidence of it in writing.

This final edition of Reyes' complete poetic works is carefully ordered in seven sections:

1. "Repaso poético," a poetic review of his verse production from 1906 to 1958

2. *Cortesía*, or occasional verse of 1912–1958

3. *Ifigenia cruel*, with his own introduction and final commentary

4. "Tres poemas" (Three Poems), including three major poetic works, each a complete series: *Minuta* (Menu, 1935), a playful menu in verse; *Romances del Río de Enero*; and *Homero en Cuernavaca* (Homer in Cuernavaca, 1952), a total of thirty sonnets inspired by his communing with Homer's *Iliad* during his weekend excursions to Cuernavaca to rest his heart

5. "Jornada en sonetos (1912–1956)," fifty-eight sonnets

6. "Romances sordos," six variations on the traditional Spanish ballad form

In one of his final notes he observes: "For my part, I do not distinguish between my life and my writings. Did not Goethe say, 'All my works are fragments of a general confession'?" Surely, much of Reyes' most personal work is to be found in his verse, although the autobiographical element is to be found throughout his prose and verse. Some of his most moving individual poems, soberly contained, are his later sonnets inspired by the calm acceptance of death: "Visitación" (Visitation) and "La señal funesta" (The Fatal Signal).

Nevertheless, Reyes initiated two series of systematic memoirs: the first with the titles *Parentalia* and *Albores* (Daybreak, 1960); the second entitled *Historia documental de mis libros* (Documentary History of My Books, 1955–1969), both remaining incomplete, as well as his intimate diary.

Reyes' narrative fiction is another facet of his work that for many years seemed submerged or scattered through a small number of sparse volumes (approximately seven) published during his lifetime. Like his friend Borges of Argentina, he was not drawn to the elaboration of full-length novels. In one of his stories, "La fea" (The Ugly Girl; first appeared in *Verdad y mentira*, 1950) he himself confesses his lack of vocation as a novelist: "I need constantly to interrupt my narrations with ideological developments. I would be a very poor novelist. Much more than the happenings, I am interested by the ideas for which they serve as symbols or pretexts."

Nevertheless, he is an excellent creator of characters, as we have seen in his evocation of Brazilian female personalities. As a narrator he has the virtues of his defects. The same qualities that divert him from the extensive novel make him a skillful teller of tales, a master of the brief narrative. Reyes is outstanding in imaginative short fiction sparkling with touches of poetry and humor, and in the autobiographical narrative transformed into fiction by his artistic vision. The innovative early fantasy tales of *El plano oblicuo* were followed by such masterly stories as "La mano del Comandante Aranda" (The Hand of Commander Aranda; first appeared in *Quince presencias*, 1955), a purely fantastic tale in which short story and essay are intertwined in the digressive manner suggested above by Reyes. Here a digression on the symbolism of the human hand illuminates the fantastic horror story of the Commander's severed hand, which comes alive as a monster haunting his household. At the same time, there is an implicit satire of the military character stereotype, the reverse of the benevolent, liberal governor who was Reyes' father. Two of Reyes' autobiographical tales stand out, *El testimonio de Juan Peña* (The Testimony of Juan Peña, 1930) and "Silueta del Indio Jesús" (Silhouette of the Indian Named Jesús; collected in *Vida y ficción*, 1970), both of these classifiable as Mexican indigenous tales. "Silueta del Indio Jesús" is a rapid narrative of the experience of an Indian momentarily swept up in the Mexican Revolution. These and other "Mexican" pieces offer ample refutation to those of Reyes' critics who claimed that he manifested no concern for the historico-social trials and tribulations of modern Mexico. At the same time, he leaves behind the realistic mode of the traditional "novel of the Mexican Revolution" to enter poetically into the magic of the Indian's world, as he had done in his *Visión de Anáhuac*.

Reyes carefully prepared the first twelve volumes of

his *Obras completas*, leaving the remaining volumes to be edited by his disciple Ernesto Mejía Sánchez, with the assistance of his widow, Doña Manuela de Reyes (who died in 1965). Through 1981 posthumous volumes 13 to 21 have appeared. The edition is still not complete as of this writing.

Meanwhile, there have been several posthumous surprises. "Andrenio" and several "new" Hellenic studies have found their way into the *Obras completas*. An extension to his Góngora studies took the form of a series of familiar glosses on a Góngora poem, in *El Polifemo sin lágrimas* (Reader's Guide to the *Polifemo*, 1961). In 1963 Doña Manuelita published Reyes' poignant memoir of his father, *Oración del nueve de febrero* ("Thoughts on the Ninth of February"). Her discovery of an "unfinished" manuscript for a satirical operetta, *Landrú* (Landrú, 1978) on the subject of a famous French Don Juan/Bluebeard led to its staging by Juan José Gurrola's experimental theater company, El Estudio de Investigaciones Escenicas (music by Rafael Elizondo), with its premiere in February 1964, followed by numerous successful performances. The uncollected narratives appeared with the title *Vida y ficción* (Life and Fiction, 1970). Alicia Reyes published in 1969 a portion of his diaries, *Diario (1911–1930)*, and a few volumes of Reyes' voluminous correspondence also have been published.

Even though a few last pieces of the vast mosaic constituting the literary work of Alfonso Reyes have yet to become visible, the picture is almost complete. The portrait has emerged of the man of letters who gave full artistic expression to the cultural heritage of his world in his time.

SELECTED BIBLIOGRAPHY

Editions

Poetry

Huellas. Mexico City, 1922.
Ifigenia cruel. Madrid, 1924.
Romances del Río de Enero. Maestricht, Holland, 1933.
A la memoria de Ricardo Güiraldes. Rio de Janeiro, 1934.
Minuta. Maestricht, Holland, 1935.
Cantata en la tumba de Federico García Lorca. Buenos Aires, 1937.
La crítica en la edad ateniense. Mexico City, 1941.
Pasado inmediato y otros ensayos. Mexico City, 1941.
La antigua retórica. Mexico City, 1942.
La experiencia literaria. Buenos Aires, 1942. Includes "Aduana lingüística."
Los siete sobre Deva. Mexico City, 1942.
Última Tule. Mexico City, 1942.
El deslinde. Mexico City, 1944.
Norte y sur. Mexico City, 1944.
Tentativas y orientaciones. Mexico City, 1944.
Capítulos de literatura española (II). Mexico City, 1945.
Por mayo era, por mayo . . . Mexico City, 1946.
Cortesía. Mexico City, 1948.
Grata compañía. Mexico City, 1948.
Letras de la Nueva España. Mexico City, 1948.
Junta de sombras. Mexico City, 1949.
La Ilíada 1: Aquiles agraviado. Translated by Alfonso Reyes. Mexico City, 1951.
Homero en Cuernavaca. Mexico City, 1952.
Obra poética (1906–1952). Mexico City, 1952.
Obras completas 10: Constancia poética. Mexico City, 1959.
Landrú. Monterrey, Mexico, 1978.

Prose Narratives

El plano oblicuo. Madrid, 1920.
El testimonio de Juan Peña. Rio de Janeiro, 1930.
Verdad y mentira. Madrid, 1950.
Quince presencias. Mexico City, 1955.
Vida y ficción. Edited by Ernesto Mejía Sánchez. Mexico City, 1970.

Essays

Cuestiones estéticas. Paris, 1911.
Cartones de Madrid. Mexico City, 1917.
El suicida. Madrid, 1917.
Visión de Anáhuac. San José, Costa Rica, 1917.
Retratos reales e imaginarios. Mexico City, 1920.
El cazador. Madrid, 1921.
Simpatías y diferencias. 5 vols. Madrid, 1921–1926.
Calendario. Madrid, 1924.
Cuestiones gongorinas. Madrid, 1927.
Horas de Burgos. Rio de Janeiro, 1932.
La caída. Rio de Janeiro, 1933.
Las vísperas de España. Buenos Aires, 1937.
Mallarmé entre nosotros. Buenos Aires, 1938.
Capítulos de literatura española (I). Mexico City, 1939.

Ancorajes. Mexico City, 1951. Includes "Fragmentas del arte poética."

Memorias de cocina y bodega. Mexico City, 1953.

Trayectoria de Goethe. Mexico City, 1954.

Las burlas veras (1,2). Mexico City, 1957, 1959.

A campo traviesa. Mexico City, 1960.

Al yunque. Mexico City, 1960.

El Polifemo sin lágrimas. Madrid, 1961.

Obras completas 20: Andrenio: Perfiles del hombre. Mexico City, 1979.

Monterrey (Correo literario de Alfonso Reyes). Rio de Janeiro and Buenos Aires, 1930–1937. Facsimilar edition, *Revistas Literarias Mexicanas (Antena, Monterrey, Examen, Número),* Mexico City, 1980.

Memoirs

Parentalia. Mexico City, 1959.

Albores. Mexico City, 1960.

Oración del nueve de febrero. Mexico City, 1963.

Anecdotario. With a prologue by Alicia Reyes. Mexico City, 1968.

Diario (1911–1930). With a prologue by Alicia Reyes. Guanajuato, Mexico, 1969.

Correspondence

Correspondance (1923–1952). Edited by Paulette Patout. Paris, 1972. Correspondence of Reyes and Valery Larbaud.

Epistolario Alfonso Reyes–José M. Chacón. Edited by Zenaida Gutiérrez-Vega. Madrid, 1976. Correspondence of Reyes and José M. Chacón.

Epistolario íntimo. 3 vols. Edited by Juan Jacobo de Lara. Santo Domingo, Dominican Republic, 1981–1983. Correspondence of Reyes and Pedro Henríquez Ureña.

Cartas echadas: Correspondencia 1927–1959. Edited by Héctor Perea. Mexico City, 1983. Correspondence of Reyes and Victoria Ocampo.

Collected Works

Antología. Mexico City, 1963.

Antología de Alfonso Reyes. Edited by José Luis Martínez. Mexico City, 1965.

Antología personal. Edited by E. Mejía Sánchez. Mexico City, 1983.

Obras completas. 21 vols. Mexico City, 1955–1981. Vols. 1–12 edited by Alfonso Reyes. Vols. 13–21 edited by Ernesto Mejía Sánchez. This edition not yet complete.

Prosa y poesía. Edited by James Willis Robb. Madrid, 1975. 3rd ed. Madrid, 1984.

Translations

The Position of America, and Other Essays. Translated by Harriet de Onís. With a foreword by Federico de Onís. New York, 1950. Includes "Thoughts on the American Mind."

Mexico in a Nutshell, and Other Essays. Translated by Charles Ramsdell. With a foreword by Arturo Torres-Ríoseco. Berkeley, Calif., 1964.

Biographical and Critical Studies

Alfonso Reyes: Homenaje de la facultad de filosofía y letras. Mexico City, 1981.

Alfonso Reyes: Homenaje nacional. Mexico City, 1981.

Alonso, Amado. "Alfonso Reyes." In *Materia y forma en poesía.* Madrid, 1955.

Aponte, Barbara B. *Alfonso Reyes and Spain.* Austin, Tex., 1972.

Carballo, Emmanuel. "Alfonso Reyes." In *Diecinueve protagonistas de la literatura mexicana del siglo XX.* Mexico City, 1965.

Díez-Canedo, Enrique. "Facetas de Alfonso Reyes." In *Letras de América.* 2nd ed. Mexico City, 1983.

Earle, Peter G. "Alfonso Reyes." In *Historia del ensayo hispanoamericano,* Peter G. Earle and Robert G. Mead. Mexico City, 1973.

Ellison, Fred P. "The Brazilian Friends of Alfonso Reyes." In *Papers on French-Spanish/Luso-Brazilian/Spanish-American Literary Relations.* Brockport, N.Y., 1971.

_____. "Alfonso Reyes, Brazil and the Story of a Passion." *Los Ensayistas* 18–19:55–62 (1985).

Henríquez Ureña, Pedro. "Alfonso Reyes." In *La utopía de América.* Caracas, 1978.

Homenaje de El Colegio Nacional a Alfonso Reyes. Mexico City, 1965.

Iduarte, Andrés, Eugenio Florit, and Olga Blondet. *Alfonso Reyes: Vida y obra/bibliografía/antología.* New York, 1957.

Libro jubilar de Alfonso Reyes. Edited by A. Monterroso and Ernesto Mejía Sánchez. Mexico City, 1956.

Martínez, José Luis. "Alfonso Reyes." In *El ensayo mexicano moderno 1.* 2nd ed. Mexico City, 1971.

Meléndez, Concha. "Ficciones de Alfonso Reyes." In *Figuración de Puerto Rico y otros estudios.* San Juan, 1958.

_____. *Moradas de poesía en Alfonso Reyes.* San Juan, 1973.

Morales, Jorge Luis. *España en Alfonso Reyes.* Río Piedras, Puerto Rico, 1976.

Navarro Tomás, Tomás. "Prosa y verso de Alfonso Reyes." In *Los poetas en sus versos.* Barcelona, 1973.

Olguín, Manuel. *Alfonso Reyes, ensayista: Vida y pensamiento.* Mexico City, 1956.

Patout, Paulette. *Alfonso Reyes et la France.* Paris, 1978.

Paz, Octavio. "El jinete del aire." In *Puertas al campo.* Mexico City, 1966.

Presencia de Alfonso Reyes. With an introduction by Alicia Reyes. Mexico City, 1969.

Rangel Guerra, Alfonso, and José Ángel Rendón, eds. *Páginas sobre Alfonso Reyes.* 2 vols. Monterrey, Mexico, 1955, 1957.

Reyes, Alicia. *Genio y figura de Alfonso Reyes.* Buenos Aires, 1976.

Robb, James Willis. "The Promise and Fulfillment of Alfonso Reyes." *Inter-American Review of Bibliography* 11/1:1–24 (1961).

_____. *El estilo de Alfonso Reyes.* Mexico City, 1965. 2nd ed., 1978.

_____. *Estudios sobre Alfonso Reyes.* Bogotá, 1976.

_____. *Por los caminos de Alfonso Reyes.* Mexico City, 1981.

Villaurrutia, Xavier. "Alfonso Reyes: Un hombre de caminos." In *Obras.* 2nd ed. Mexico City, 1966.

Bibliographies

Treviño González, Roberto, and Raúl Rangel Frías. *Alfonso Reyes: Datos biográficos y bibliográficos.* Monterrey, Mexico, 1955.

Robb, James Willis. *Repertorio bibliográfico de Alfonso Reyes.* Mexico City, 1974.

Victoria Ocampo

(1890–1979)

María Luisa Bastos

Writer, translator, publisher, and promoter of cultural activities, Victoria Ocampo was born in Buenos Aires on 7 April 1890, and died on 27 January 1979. She was the oldest of six sisters, the youngest of whom, Silvina, is an outstanding poet and narrator. Ocampo was a descendant of Spanish colonists, possibly of the founder of Buenos Aires, and also of a Guaraní Indian woman. She inherited a considerable fortune and many of her pages reconstruct the privileged environment in which she was born and educated. As in the majority of Argentine upper-class families, her environment was a blend of modern European, especially French, refinements and prejudices characteristic of the Hispanic tradition. Her early knowledge of French, English, and Italian and their respective literatures was a result of the family's admiration for all that was European. In Paris, where her family spent long periods of time, she took courses in literature and philosophy and, reading modern authors, augmented the knowledge imparted by her tutors in Buenos Aires, where she also seriously studied music and voice. Marguerite Moreno, a well-known French actress who had settled in Buenos Aires, taught her recitation and diction in French. In this last endeavor, Ocampo attained a professionalism recognized by two important musicians: Ernest Ansermet and Igor Stravinsky, who entrusted to her, respectively, the roles of narrator in *Le Roi David*, by Arthur Honegger, and *Perséphone*.

In her *Autobiografía 1* (1979), Ocampo speaks of her ancestors and of her family, and describes in detail household customs and the stages of her education. There she laments that, in spite of recognizing her intelligence, her father had considered it unnecessary for a woman to follow systematic studies. She also laments that her family's prejudices prevented her from dedicating herself to the theater; at the age of twenty-two, those prejudices forced her into an ill-fated marriage. But along with her spectacular beauty, which gained her notable worldly success in Buenos Aires and in Europe, Ocampo also possessed exceptional vitality, which spurred her to overcome the obstacles of convention. Not only did she separate from her husband and refuse to live as a recluse, but she also insisted on expressing herself publicly. Having discovered in childhood that writing relieved her attacks of anger and rebellion, she chose to write in order to affirm her existence.

Becoming a writer was not easy for Ocampo: her first article, which appeared in 1920 in *La Nación*, "consternated" her mother. Paradoxically, it was because of her social standing that a literary supplement dominated by the male establishment accepted this work and those that followed. Nevertheless, for a young woman to make public her own opinions was irritating to a society so intolerant of women who deviated from social norms. Two experiences that Ocampo mentions in her autobiography illustrate this point. Shortly after publishing her first article, Ocampo consulted Paul Groussac, a sort of pontiff of the literary world of Buenos Aires, about an essay on the *Divine Comedy* that she was writing; his advice was that she should discard that pedantic theme and write about some personal experience. The writer Ángel de Estrada, on the other hand, told her that her tone was so personal that nobody would doubt she was referring to herself, and she would never be forgiven for it (*Autobiografía 3*, [1981]). Ocampo ignored these contradictory opinions and finished her essay. José Ortega y Gasset, who had met her on his first visit to Buenos Aires in 1916, added an epilogue and in 1924 published the book *De Francesca a Beatrice* (From Francesca to Beatrice) through his Madrid publishing house, Revista de Occidente. The same company published the next two books by Ocampo, who very soon made public, in lectures and essays, her concern for the status of women, which in 1936 would bring her to found, along with María Rosa Oliver and Susana Larguía, the Argentine Union of Women. As Ocampo mentions many times, in those years she was often the object of men's insults in the streets of Buenos Aires for driving her own automobile.

Besides being one of the few women writers of her generation, Ocampo was host and friend to writers, artists, musicians, actors, actresses, and thinkers. Among her foreign friends were Rabindranath Tagore, Ortega y Gasset, Anna de Noailles, Le Corbusier, Count Hermann Keyserling, Leo Ferrero, Stravinsky, Paul Valéry, Pierre Drieu la Rochelle, Roger Caillois, Albert Camus, Graham Greene, and Aldous Huxley, many of whom visited Argentina at her invitation. Until the end of her life she maintained contact with intellectuals of other lands—without excluding the Argentines—and she liked to consider herself a sort of bridge between the culture of her country and that of other places in the world.

In 1931, at the request of Eduardo Mallea and Waldo Frank, she founded *Sur*, a literary review. *Sur*, which gave rise to much controversy, became a prestigious institution, fundamental to intellectual life in Argentina for forty years. On its first editorial board were, among others, Jorge Luis Borges, Pedro Henríquez Ureña, Jules Supervielle, and Ortega y Gasset. For two or three generations the expression "the *Sur* group," depending upon who used it, was synonymous with contradictory concepts: intellectual refinement; snobbery; liberalism; conservatism; sharp awareness of the present; overemphasis on the past. In the early 1940's, *Sur* was the most renowned literary magazine of the Spanish-speaking world. The Sur publishing house complemented the work begun by the review, spreading news of the international situation; many Argentines and Latin Americans recognized that the translations provided by both publisher and publication gave them their only access to writers whose language they did not know. In surroundings tragically attracted to fascism—when other Argentine publications were praising Francisco Franco and Benito Mussolini, and Adolf Hitler was a respectable name to many—*Sur* maintained an unshakably clear position against totalitarianism. Finally, the tone of *Sur* stood out for its moderation and its freedom from the oversentimentality and pompousness frequently found in many publications in Spanish.

Ocampo's energy never diminished with the years, and she traveled tirelessly, on her own or at the invitation of European or North American institutions, and by around 1950 her name was well known in international circles. When she was imprisoned in 1953 for her obvious opposition to the regime of Juan Domingo Perón (an opposition shared by the majority of Argentine intellectuals, many of whom left the country), protests appeared in many foreign newspapers. Her friends Gabriela Mistral and Jawaharlal Nehru interceded with Perón and arranged for her liberation.

By the end of the 1950's, being a writer had become an acceptable, even prestigious, activity for a woman, and Ocampo began to be openly recognized as a pioneer and a symbol. The government built on the revolution that in 1955 had overthrown Perón offered her an ambassadorship, which she declined; however, she did agree to become a member of the Directory of the National Foundation of the Arts, a post that she occupied constructively for some time.

Popular journals interviewed her and analyzed the cultural phenomenon represented by *Sur*, trying to be impartial; for their part, the more conventional publications treated her with respect. Gone were the times in which the authorities of the Catholic church would veto her nomination for participation in a benefit recital, citing her friendship with the Indian poet and thinker Rabindranath Tagore and the fact that the Indian philosopher J. Krishnamurti and the French essayist André Malraux, who had fought against Franco in the Spanish civil war, were published in *Sur*. At Ocampo's death, the list of Argentine awards she had received, in addition to her foreign honors, occupied several pages. Significantly, she made one of her last public appearances, in 1977, to be received as the first female member of the Argentine Academy of Letters, an invitation she had refused years before but accepted now because she was persuaded that her refusal might impede the entry of other women.

Ocampo published numerous translations into Spanish and twenty-six volumes of essays, nine of which carry the title *Testimonios* (Testimonies); additionally, several volumes of her autobiography have been published posthumously. Her tenacious output is apparent in a chronological review of her writings. Because of Ocampo's education, Spanish was not her literary language, and as she wrote in French, she had to have her work translated; thus the Spanish of her first books is not her own and lacks the spontaneity that came to be characteristic of her style. By around 1940 she was able to write directly in her native language and the *Testimonios* published in 1941 have all the vivacity and nuances of oral expression that is fueled by enthusiasm. In her mature style, that of about 1950, the Spanish spoken by large sectors of her generation, and possibly of the next two generations, is recognizable. At this point, the markings of her class have faded, and her writing creates the illusion of a conversational tone; it is neither affected nor regulated by taboos. As in conversation, if she judges it necessary for a connotation, she resorts to English or French, or to colloquial expressions, and her words flow smoothly.

From the start of her career, Ocampo was aware of the risks of artificial or pedantic expression: "affect and exaggeration are synonymous with abomina-

tion," she wrote in 1933 ("El cementerio marino" [The Marine Cemetery], *Testimonios*, 1935). Neither is there in her style the unpleasant aftertaste of those superfluous erudite trifles that can produce a sort of aseptic dryness, far from living language, and that tend to obscure the context. Commenting on this point in 1949, she wrote: "Erudition will serve you nothing, reader, if in your solitary dialogue with Hamlet, you do not see *ton semblable, ton frère* [your fellow man, your brother], changing and undecipherable, in that desolate prince" ("'Hamlet' y Laurence Olivier," in *Soledad sonora*, 1950).

Ocampo's essays treat extremely varied themes, but she always wrote about things that attracted her or about people whom she admired, for whatever reason; her work has a predominantly optimistic tone because, even when criticizing various aspects of Argentine reality, her purpose was to propose solutions. The series of changing topics related with current events that commanded her attention or worried her through the years constitute a rich showcase of the twentieth century. Among these topics are her interest in jazz; her admiration for functional architecture and her rejection of imitations; her enthusiasm for Stravinsky, for Pablo Picasso, for the Uruguayan painter Pedro Figari; her descriptions of fashions in clothing which capture, as in snapshots, prototypical traits of her era.

Enthusiasm for her subject nearly always brings her to connect the discontinuous images of memory in a Proustian way, linking together remote and recent experiences and connecting apparently disparate themes. These correlations—which result in a style full of nuances, never dull or monotonous—do not conceal the *I*, the person who is writing. In many essays, Ocampo describes herself subtly as she speaks of dissimilar persons who for various reasons were important at different moments of her life. She herself has pointed out the testimonial nature of her writings: "The only subject (in both meanings of the term) of which I can really speak and in whose name I have any grounds to speak is I myself" ("Malandanzas de una autodidacta" [Misfortunes of an Autodidact], *Testimonios*, 1957). This is so to the extent that, upon analyzing her essays dedicated to men and women who attracted her attention for various reasons, one almost always discovers undercurrents that in unsuspected ways identify the author with those about whom she writes.

Let suffice two examples out of many others. According to Ocampo's description, Anna de Noailles, the French poet, could not have been more different from her. Nevertheless, many pages of the *Testimonios* exude a profoundly sensual love for gardens, fruits, and fragrances, just like the one that she points out in the poetry of her friend. Ocampo "likes to breathe, to watch, to eat" the spring and summer ("Anna de Noailles y su poesia," *Testimonios*, 1935). In 1949, on the death of Eugenia Errázuriz, a woman of society whose good taste was renowned in the worldly circles of Paris, Ocampo writes: "She seemed not to know how, or not to be able, to say more than 'I like it' or 'I don't like it' about things that she knew intimately. Nevertheless, her 'I like it' or 'I don't like it' was of such persuasive intensity and clarity that we contented ourselves with that" ("A Eugenia" [To Eugenia], *Soledad sonora*). When Ocampo spoke, her assertions on subjects that interested her were characterized by an energy and conciseness equal to those of Errázuriz. It is precisely the capacity for transcending the purely anecdotal level, for charging with more than one meaning that which might have remained a merely circumstantial chronicle, that gives literary value to Ocampo's writings.

Ocampo's desire to understand herself and her eagerness to put forth, even to control, the image that the reader forms of her or of the reality that she chooses to describe, is manifest throughout her work. A rather naive expectation of being able to persuade through her personal testimony led her in 1952 to begin her autobiography, because of a "need for illumination, for a general confession" and a "wish to anticipate possible future biographies with an explicit autobiography" (*Autobiografía 1*).

Although there is no real break between the books Ocampo published while living and her posthumous work—of which she gave many partial advance views in the *Testimonios*—in the first volume of the autobiography certain characteristics of the environment that conditioned her rebellions and her loyalties are presented more deliberately. Her preferences and eccentricities, including her weaknesses, were nothing but personal responses to the stimuli of the world in which it was her fate to live. Those responses, which constituted her life and were hence the basis of her books, are, and still more will be, documents that depict a woman resolved not to accept prejudices or impositions. They function, too, as photographic slides that illustrate typical aspects of one sector of twentieth-century Argentine life. Also, like slides, they parcel reality: they do not generalize, but display; they intend to prove nothing. Given the direct exposition of many pages of the *Testimonios* and autobiography, devoid of ostentation or bigotry, one cannot help thinking of educational presentations. Their marked didactic course—which in the future will generate changing readings of the years, places, and society that Ocampo documented—puts her work near that of other Latin American masters. Like the writings of Domingo F. Sarmiento, Juan Montalvo, and José Martí, Ocampo's books are overwhelming evidence of her unshakable faith in the power of the written word.

Translated from the Spanish by Jane A. Johnson

SELECTED BIBLIOGRAPHY

Editions

De Francesca a Beatrice. Madrid, 1924.
La laguna de los nenúfares. Madrid, 1926.
Testimonios. Madrid, 1935.
Domingos en Hyde Park. Buenos Aires, 1936.
La mujer y su expresión. Buenos Aires, 1936.
Emily Brontë. Buenos Aires, 1938.
Testimonios: Segunda serie. Buenos Aires, 1941.
338171 T.E. [*Lawrence de Arabia*]. Buenos Aires, 1942.
Testimonios: Tercera serie. Buenos Aires, 1946.
Soledad sonora [Fourth volume of *Testimonios*]. Buenos Aires, 1950.
Lawrence de Arabia y otros ensayos. Madrid, 1951.
El viajero y una de sus sombras (*Keyserling en mis memorias*). Buenos Aires, 1951.
Virginia Woolf en su diario. Buenos Aires, 1954.
Testimonios: Quinta serie (1950–1957). Buenos Aires, 1957.
Habla el algarrobo. Buenos Aires, 1959.
Tagore en las barrancas de San Isidro. Buenos Aires, 1961.
Testimonios: Sexta serie (1957–1962). Buenos Aires, 1963.
Juan Sebastián Bach: El hombre. Buenos Aires, 1964.

Testimonios: Séptima serie (1962–1967). Buenos Aires, 1967.
Diálogo con Borges. Buenos Aires, 1969.
Diálogo con Mallea. Buenos Aires, 1969.
Testimonios: Octava serie (1968–1970). Buenos Aires, 1971.
Testimonios: Novena serie (1971–1974). Buenos Aires, 1975.
Testimonios: Décima serie (1975–1977). Buenos Aires, 1977.
Autobiografía 1. Buenos Aires, 1979.
Autobiografía 2. Buenos Aires, 1980.
Autobiografía 3. Buenos Aires, 1981.
Autobiografía 4. Buenos Aires, 1982.
Autobiografía 5. Buenos Aires, 1983.
Autobiografía 6. Buenos Aires, 1984.

Translations

338171 T.E. (Lawrence of Arabia). Translated by David Garnett. New York, 1963.
"Aldous Huxley." Translated by Victoria Ocampo. In *Aldous Huxley (1894–1963): A Memorial Volume,* edited by Julian Huxley. London, 1965. Pp. 73–85.
"The Lakes of the South." Translated by Harriet De Onis. In *The Green Continent,* edited by Germán Arciniegas. New York, 1944. Pp. 116–122.
"Letter to Waldo Frank." Translated by Victoria Ocampo. *Review* 11:51–52 (Spring 1974).
"Malraux's World and Ours." Translated by Victoria Ocampo. In *Malraux: Life and Work,* edited by Martine de Courcel. London, 1976. Pp. 212–221.
Tagore on the Banks of the River Plate. Translated by Victoria Ocampo. In *Rabindranath Tagore: A Centenary Volume.* New Delhi, 1961. Pp. 27–47.
"The Untranslatable Isadora." Translated by Victoria Ocampo. *Review* 17:39–41 (Spring 1976).
"Victoria Ocampo Pays Jung a Visit." Translated by Martin Nozick. In *C. G. Jung Speaking: Interviews and Encounters,* edited by William McGuire and R. F. C. Hull. Princeton, N.J., 1977. Pp. 82–84.
The Water-Lily Pond and "Misfortunes of an Autodidact." Translated by Doris Meyer. In *Contemporary Women Authors of Latin America 2,* edited by Doris Meyer and Margarite Fernández Olmos. New York, 1983. Pp. 78–106, 217–225.

Biographical and Critical Studies

Adam, Carlos. "Bio-bibliografía de Victoria Ocampo." *Sur* 346:125–179 (1980).
Anderson Imbert, Enrique. "Victoria Ocampo: *Testimonios: Tercera serie.*" *Sur* 139:72–73 (1946).
_____. "Victoria Ocampo." *Sur* 348:127–129 (1981).

Bastos, María Luisa. "Escrituras ajenas, expresión propia: *Sur* y los *Testimonios* de Victoria Ocampo." *Revista iberoamericana* 46/110–111:123–137 (1980).
_____. "Dos líneas testimoniales: *Sur,* Los escritos de Victoria Ocampo." *Sur* 348:9–23 (1981).
Bianco, José. "Victoria." *Vuelta* 53:4–6 (1981).
Christ, Ronald. "Figuring Literarily: An Interview with Victoria Ocampo." *Review* 7:5–13 (Winter 1972).
Cobo Borda, J. G. "Las memorias de Victoria Ocampo." *Eco* 38/232:433–444 (1981).
Cortázar, Julio. "Victoria Ocampo: *Soledad sonora.*" *Sur* 192–194:294–297 (1950).
Domínguez, Nora, and Adriana Rodríguez Pérsico. "La pasión del modelo: Autobiografía de Victoria Ocampo." *Lecturas críticas* 2:22–34 (1984).
Foster, David William. "Bibliography of Writings by and about Victoria Ocampo, 1890–1979." *Revista interamericana de bibliografía* 30/1:51–58 (1980).
Gigli, Adelaida. "Victoria Ocampo: V.O." *Contorno* 3:1–2 (1954).
González Lanuza, Eduardo. "La Victoria desconocida." *Sur* 348:131–135 (1981).
Henríquez Ureña, Pedro. "Victoria Ocampo: *Testimonios: Segunda serie.*" *Sur* 89:65–67 (1942).
Jurado, Alicia. "Victoria Ocampo y la condición de la mujer." *Sur* 348:137–142 (1981).
Lida, Raimundo. "Victoria Ocampo: *Testimonios: Sexta serie.*" *Sur* 291:76–79 (1964).
Magrini, César. "Victoria Ocampo: *Tagore en las Barrancas de San Isidro.*" *Sur* 272:100–102 (1961).
Marechal, Leopoldo. "Victoria Ocampo y la literatura femenina." *Sur* 52:66–70 (1939).
Martínez, Tomás Eloy. "Victoria Ocampo: Una pasión argentina." *Primera plana* 168:51–55 (1968).
Martínez Estrada, Ezequiel. "Victoria Ocampo: *338171 T.E.*" *Sur* 100:100–107 (1943).
Meyer, Doris. *Victoria Ocampo: Against the Wind and the Tide.* New York, 1979. Includes fifteen essays by Victoria Ocampo, translated by Doris Meyer.
Munro, Eleanor. "Viva Victoria." *Ms.* 3/7:76–79, 100–101 (1975).
Omil, Alba. *Frente y perfil de Victoria Ocampo.* Buenos Aires, 1980.
Pacheco, José Emilio. "Victoria Ocampo y la revista *Sur.*" *Proceso* 118, 5 February 1979.
Paz Leston, Eduardo. *El proyecto de la revista "Sur."* Buenos Aires, 1981.
Pezzoni, Enrique. "Victoria Ocampo: *Testimonios: Quinta serie.*" *Sur* 252:71–76 (1958).
_____. "Victoria Ocampo escritora." *Sur* 348:143–150 (1981).

Schultz de Mantovani, Fryda. *Victoria Ocampo.* Buenos Aires, 1963.

Sebreli, Juan José. *De Buenos Aires y su gente.* Buenos Aires, 1982.

Vázquez, María Esther. "Victoria Ocampo, una argentina universalista." *Revista iberoamericana* 46/110–111:167–175 (1980).

Victoria, Marcos. *Un coloquio sobre Victoria Ocampo.* Buenos Aires, 1934; 1963.

José Rubén Romero

(1890–1952)

Luis Leal

Although several semifictional works appeared in Mexico during the colonial period, which lasted three hundred years (1521–1821), it was not until 1816 that the first modern Latin-American novel, *El Periquillo Sarniento* (The Itching Parrot), was published in Mexico City by José Joaquín Fernández de Lizardi. That author utilized the picaresque form in order to criticize the unbearable social conditions that existed during the last years of the Spanish presence in Mexico.

The picaresque form represents the revival of a genre created in Spain during the middle of the sixteenth century and considered dead in the Spanish-speaking world one hundred years later. However, in eighteenth-century England and France, the picaresque underwent a revival, which doubtless influenced Lizardi in the selection of the form for his novel. Works such as Alain René Lesage's *Gil Blas de Santillane* (1715–1735) were well known in Mexico, and there are indications that Lizardi was acquainted with them. His example, however, was not imitated by later writers, and it was not until 1938 that another picaresque novel, *La vida inútil de Pito Pérez* (*The Futile Life of Pito Pérez*), by José Rubén Romero, was published. The novel not only made Romero famous but proved that old literary forms may remain dormant for long periods of time but cannot be considered dead.

Romero was born in Cotija, in the state of Michoacán, Mexico, on 25 September 1890, the son of Melesio Romero and Refugio González. He attended elementary school in his hometown and as an adolescent lived in Mexico City with his family for six years (1898–1904). There he attended the school of Mr. Barona, where he began to read nineteenth-century Spanish and French fiction and poetry.

When he was offered a position in the government, Romero's father went back to his native state, where he established his home in the town of Ario de Rosales. There Romero and some friends began to publish the periodical *Iris*, in which his first known verses appeared. Two years later his father was transferred to Pátzcuaro, a larger city in the state of Michoacán, and there Romero published his first prose work, "De invierno" (Of Winter). Soon after, his father was transferred once more, this time to the city of Sahuayo, where, at the age of seventeen, Romero accepted his first employment, as administrator of the revenue office. He continued to write poems, which he published in several of the state's newspapers.

Romero's first book of poems, *Fantasías* (Fantasies), appeared in 1908. The only copy in existence was for many years in the possession of the author's mother, and no critic has been able to examine it.

Although poetry was Romero's main interest during that time, he also wrote portraits of the people of the community and of rural areas. "In my town there were many fools; some roamed the streets begging; others, who were not as foolish as they appeared to be, lived at the expense of relatives" (*Obras completas* [Complete Works], p. 27).

While in Sahuayo, Romero began to court Rosa, the daughter of the richest man in town. Not approving of this relationship, Rosa's father pulled some strings and had Romero's father transferred from Sahuayo to Santa Clara del Cobre near Pátzcuaro. This maneuver put an end to Romero's first love affair.

Romero's residence in Santa Clara turned out to be of great importance in the life of the young writer, for there he met Mariana García, his future wife. There he also met a popular character, Pito Pérez, whose life was later to become the subject of his most famous novel. And there he participated in the Revolution, on the side of the rebels. While he was in Pátzcuaro, where he had been sent on a secret mission, the city fell into the hands of the rebels, and Romero had the opportunity to meet and become acquainted with several revolutionary leaders, among them Pascual Ortiz Rubio, later to be elected president of Mexico.

The young writer's revolutionary activities did not prevent him from writing poetry. In 1912 he published three books: *Rimas bohemias* (Bohemian Rhymes), *Hojas marchitas* (Withered Leaves), and *La musa heroica* (The Heroic Muse), the last a collection of patriotic verses mostly about the two best-known heroes of the Wars of Independence, Miguel Hidalgo and José María Morelos.

In the 1912 elections, the first to be held under the revolutionary government, Don Miguel Silva won the state's governorship and named Romero his private secretary, taking him to Morelia, the state's capital. The counterrevolution led by Victoriano Huerta in 1913, which resulted in the assassination of President Francisco I. Madero, affected Romero's life, because Governor Silva was forced to resign and Romero had to take refuge first in Mexico City and then in Morelia. There he escaped being executed through the intervention of his father and several friends, who assured the new governor that Romero had no intention of joining the armies of Francisco (Pancho) Villa, who had begun to fight against Huerta.

Having had his life saved, Romero settled in the city of Tacámbaro, Michoacán, where he spent the following four years managing the small store of a friend. There he had the opportunity to observe the customs of the people in a small town, but he was not yet ready to transform these observations into works of fiction. He continued to write poetry, and in 1917, the same year he married Mariana García, he published two collections, *La musa loca* (The Mad Muse) and *Alma heroica* (Heroic Soul).

Humor, the underlying characteristic of Romero's works, was evident at this early stage of his development. The author of the introduction to *La musa loca* said that the poet had written his verses while dispensing lard and beans at the store. Romero responded that the reason his book of poems had sold so well was the highly nutritious nature of the contents. Later he discovered that a woman who secretly loved him had bought most of the books. When she died, the copies were found in a box, "which for my verses was like a coffin made to order" (*Obras completas*, p. 6).

The tranquillity enjoyed by Romero in Tacámbaro came to a sudden end when the revolutionaries, under the leadership of José Inés Chávez García, devastated the town and the poet had to flee once again. This change, however, was for the good. In Morelia, where he took refuge, Ortiz Rubio, then governor, named him as his private secretary. Romero also began to teach literature in the old Colegio de San Nicolás. He held the two positions until 1919, when Ortiz Rubio sent him to Mexico City to serve as his representative. That same year he published his seventh volume of poems, *Sentimental* (Sentimental Verses), the publication costs paid for by the governor. The book was ignored by the critics.

In Mexico City from 1920 on, Romero led a rather comfortable life. That year Álvaro Obregón was elected president of Mexico, and he appointed Romero to a position in the Department of Communications. The following year Romero advanced to the foreign relations section as chief of the Department of Publicity. There he met prominent writers, among them Genaro Estrada, José Juan Tablada, and Artemio de Valle Arizpe. Tablada, who had lived in Japan for several months in 1900, had introduced the haiku into Mexican poetry. He inspired Romero to write poems in this short form, which Romero collected under the title *Tacámbaro* (Tacámbaro, 1922). The book, unlike his earlier poetic efforts, was very successful, at least among the public. In his following book, however, he went back to earlier forms, which he collected under the appropriate title *Versos viejos* (Old Verses, 1930).

In 1930, his friend Ortiz Rubio was elected president of the republic and named Romero consul general in Barcelona, Spain. There, feeling nostalgic, Romero began to write a novel, *Apuntes de un lugareño* (Notes of a Villager), which he published in 1932. Up to that time, his only prose writings had been a few sketches of popular characters and a collection of short stories, *Cuentos rurales* (Rural Stories, 1915), which apparently was destroyed by the author. The success he obtained with his first novel, however, convinced him to give up poetry and continue writing fiction. The transition was a wise one, for as a poet he could not have obtained the recognition he gained with his novels.

Returning to Mexico, in 1934 he published two more novels, *Desbandada* (Disbandment) and *El pueblo inocente* (Innocent People). In these two works, as in his first one, Romero made use of his personal experiences in the several towns in which he had lived in his native state of Michoacán. Romero was then appointed a second time to serve as consul general in Barcelona, this time by President Lázaro Cárdenas. He published there, in 1936, the novel *Mi caballo, mi perro y mi rifle* (My Horse, My Dog, and My Rifle), which is about the Mexican Revolution. In 1937, Romero was appointed ambassador to Brazil, where he wrote his most famous novel, *The Futile Life of Pito Pérez*. In 1939, he was appointed ambassador to Cuba, where he remained until 1945. During this period, he published two more novels, *Anticipación a la muerte* (Anticipating Death, 1939) and his last, *Rosenda* (Rosenda, 1946).

The recognition that Romero had received through his novels won him a chair in the Academia Mexicana de la Lengua (Mexican Academy of Language), which he occupied in July 1950. During the reception, attended by President Miguel Alemán, Romero proposed a meeting in Mexico City of all the language academies of the Spanish-speaking world. Alemán accepted the proposal, and the first meeting was held the following year, with Romero representing the Mexican Academy. He was appointed vice-president and treasurer of the permanent committee that was established, a position he held for only a short time, for he died in Mexico City on 4 July 1952.

Although Romero was a popular poet and served with distinction as a diplomat, his fame has resulted mainly from his novels. With the exception of the collection *Tacámbaro*, which has been translated into several European languages, his poetry has been almost forgotten. On the other hand, his novels, very popular and widely read, are reprinted almost yearly.

In his first novels, Romero traces the development of the Revolution as it affected the people of his state of Michoacán. Of this group of novels, the most outstanding is *Mi caballo, mi perro y mi rifle*; the author captures the essence of the struggle through the mind of a young revolutionary, as Mariano Azuela had done earlier in *Los de abajo* (The Underdogs, 1916). The protagonist, Julián Osorio, becomes disillusioned with the revolutionaries, who seem to be fighting for personal power rather than for the good of the people. The three images of the title become symbols representing the brutal force of those who hold power, the poor and unfortunate, and the violent and arbitrary nature of the Revolution. In the third and last part of the novel, the revolutionary leaders are criticized for their lack of sympathy for the poor and their greed for power.

The novel includes a surrealistic scene that seems out of place in a realistic work. Romero lacked the skill of Luis Buñuel, a master at interpolating the surrealistic into the realistic without having it appear to be an external element. In Romero's novel, the protagonist is wounded and loses consciousness; while delirious, he has a vision in which his horse, his dog, and his rifle hold a conversation regarding the nature of the Revolution; unfortunately, the scene lacks verisimilitude.

Julián wakes up to find that he has been saved by some humble *campesinos* (country people), who represent the good people of Mexico whom the revolutionaries should be helping. Julián believes that when the Revolution triumphs, the life of the common people will change for the better. The novel ends, however, with Julián completely disillusioned with the results of the Revolution, because nothing has really changed.

In *The Futile Life of Pito Pérez*, Romero was able to blend subject matter, form, and style much more skillfully than in any of his earlier novels. Although he used the traditional picaresque form, he was able to create an original *pícaro* in the person of Pito Pérez, a character taken from real life. Although Pito conforms, in general, to the concept of the *pícaro* (a rogue motivated by hunger but unwilling to work for a living, who therefore passes from master to master), Romero created a character that transcends the stereotype and becomes a real person. He accomplished this by endowing Pito with a personal philosophy, in this case disillusionment with society and with the human race in general.

Pito Pérez is an outcast who blames society for the conditions under which he and those like him have to live. His last will and testament is a strong indictment of society:

> Humanity, I know you. I have been one of your victims. As a child, you took school away from me, . . . as a young man, you took love away from me, and in my ripe age, you took faith and confidence in myself away from me. Even my name you took away to convert it into a degrading nickname.
>
> (*Obras completas*, p. 409)

The novel's pessimistic view of society is softened by the presence of a pervading humor, the main characteristic of Romero's literary works. Like the writers of the traditional picaresque novel, Romero makes use of humor to ridicule humanity's frailties. No social class, position, rank, or occupation escapes Pito's scorn; lawyers, doctors, professors, newspapermen, merchants, women, the rich, the clergy, the poor—all receive their share. Sentimentality, present in all of Romero's previous works, has disappeared, and what remains is bitterness toward humanity.

In *Rosenda*, his last novel, Romero makes use of a well-known plot, the education of an untutored woman. The story is given originality by the use of a straightforward style and structure, by the perceptive characterization of Rosenda, and by its setting, a rural area of Mexico. The result is one of Romero's best fictional efforts.

José Rubén Romero's main contribution to Mexican letters was using humor in the novel to criticize society. Equally important was his revival of the picaresque, a form perfectly suited to his purpose. Romero was fortunate, for his friendship with persons in high political office granted him a freedom of expression denied the less fortunate Fernández de Lizardi.

SELECTED BIBLIOGRAPHY

First Editions

Poetry

Fantasías. Sahuayo, Mexico, 1908.
Hojas marchitas. Pátzcuaro, Mexico, 1912.
La musa heroica. Tacámbaro, Mexico, 1912.
Rimas bohemias. Pátzcuaro, Mexico, 1912.
Alma heroíca. Tacámbaro, Mexico, 1917.
La musa loca. Morelia, Mexico, 1917.
Sentimental. Mexico City, 1919.
Tacámbaro. Mexico City, 1922.
Versos viejos. Mexico City, 1930.

Prose Narratives and Novels

Cuentos rurales. Tacámbaro, Mexico, 1915.
Apuntes de un lugareño. Barcelona, 1932.
Desbandada. Mexico City, 1934.
El pueblo inocente. Mexico City, 1934.
Mi caballo, mi perro y mi rifle. Barcelona, 1936.
La vida inútil de Pito Pérez. Mexico City, 1938.
Anticipación a la muerte. Mexico City, 1939.
Una vez fuí rico. Mexico City, 1939.
Algunas cosillas de Pito Pérez que se me quedaron en el tintero. Mexico City, 1945.
Rosenda. Mexico City, 1946.

Essays

Mis amigos, mis enemigos. Mexico City, 1921.
Breve historia de mis libros. Havana, 1942.
Rostros. Mexico City, 1942.
Viaje a Mazatlán. Mexico City, 1946.
Cómo leemos el Quijote. Mexico City, 1947.
Mis andanzas académicas. Mexico City, 1950.

Collected Works

Cuentos y poemas inéditos. Edited by William O. Cord. Mexico City, 1963.
Obras completas. Mexico City, 1957.

Later Editions

Anticipación a la muerte. Mexico City, 1976.
Apuntes de un lugareño. Mexico City, 1982.
Desbandada. Mexico City, 1946.
Mi caballo, mi perro y mi rifle. Mexico City, 1983.
Obras completas. Mexico City, 1979.
El pueblo inocente. Mexico City, 1979.
Rosenda. Mexico City, 1983.
Rostros. Mexico City, 1971.
Tacámbaro y versos viejos. Mexico City, 1939.
Una vez fui rico. Mexico City, 1975.
La vida inútil de Pito Pérez. Mexico City, 1984.

Translations

The Futile Life of Pito Pérez. Translated by William O. Cord. Englewood Cliffs, N.J., 1967.

Biographical and Critical Studies

Alba, Pedro de. *Rubén Romero y sus novelas populares.* Barcelona, 1936.
Castagnaro, R. Anthony. "Rubén Romero and the Novel of the Mexican Revolution." *Hispania* 36/3:300–304 (1953).
Cord, William Owen. "José Rubén Romero: The Writer as Seen by Himself." *Hispania* 44/3:431–437 (1961).
_____. "José Rubén Romero's Image of Mexico." *Hispania* 45/4:612–620 (1962).
Eoff, Sherman H. "Tragedy of the Unwanted Person in Three Versions: Pablo de Segovia, Pito Pérez, Pascual Duarte." *Hispania* 39/2:190–196 (1956).
González y Contreras, Gilberto. *Rubén Romero: El hombre que supo ver.* Havana, 1940.
Gulstad, Daniel E. "Antithesis in a Novel by Rubén Romero." *Hispania* 56 (special issue):237–244 (1973).
Hobart, Lois. "Wandering Rogue." *New York Times Book Review,* 29 January 1967. Pp. 4, 40.
Holzapfel, Tamara. "Soledad y rebelión en *La vida inútil de Pito Pérez.*" *Revista iberoamericana* 40/89:681–687 (1974).
Homenaje a Rubén Romero. Mexico City, 1937.
José Rubén Romero: Vida y obra. New York, 1946.
Koons, John Frederick. *Garbo y donaire de Rubén Romero.* Mexico City, 1942.
Lafarga, Gastón. *La evolución literaria de J. Rubén Romero.* Paris, 1938. Mexico City, 1939.
Larraz, José J. *Idealismo y realidad: Análisis crítico de las novelas de Rubén Romero.* Madrid, n.d.
Mackegney, James Cuthbert. "Some Non-fictional aspects of *La vida inútil de Pito Pérez.*" *Romance Notes* 6/1:26–29 (1964).
Moore, Ernest Richard. "José Rubén Romero: Bibliografía." *Revista hispánica moderna* 12/1–2:35–40 (1946).
Muñoz Domínguez, Inés. *José Rubén Romero: Novelista.* Mexico City, 1963.
Phillips, Ewart E. "The Genesis of Pito Pérez." *Hispania* 47/4:698–702 (1964).

Ana Teresa de la Parra Sanojo

(1890–1936)

Elba Mata-Kolster

Teresa de la Parra, the first major woman writer of Venezuela, was not born in Caracas, the city of white houses with red eaves that she vividly describes in her work, but in Paris on 5 October 1890 while her parents were touring Europe. She was baptized Ana Teresa Sanojo Parra, but later legally changed her name. She spent her early childhood on a sugar plantation near Caracas, years that she later referred to as "her colonial life." That time provided the most cherished recollections of her life, as well as the main theme of her literary work, for in her novels she drew an idealized picture of life in colonial Venezuela.

Parra came from an old and illustrious Spanish family. Her father died when she was only eight years old, and her mother sent her to a convent school in Spain to finish her education. There she acquired a vast European culture and developed a mystical love for nature and a strong inclination for meditation.

She returned to Venezuela between 1908 and 1911 and went to live in the old colonial family house, where she spent almost twelve years. Feeling herself a prisoner of the traditions and conservative social customs of the time, Parra devoted herself to reading and frequently visited Tazón, a plantation not far from Caracas, where she spent hours contemplating the simple life of the countryside and the colorful exuberance of the tropical foliage and immersing

herself in silent communion with nature. It was in these surroundings that Parra conceived her best-known book, *Ifigenia: Diario de una señorita que escribió porque se fastidiaba* (Iphigenia: Diary of a Young Lady Who Wrote Because She Was Bored, 1924) which she wrote between 1922 and 1924 in Macuto, a small seaside town near Caracas.

Ifigenia probes a woman's soul. It is the story of a girl, María Eugenia Alonso, who returns to Venezuela after a prolonged absence to find herself caught between the strict moral prejudices of her family and society and her young mind, which is awakening to modern ideas. María Eugenia rebels against this legacy of prejudices, but soon surrenders to the pressures and to a destiny imposed upon her by principles she does not share. Inconsistently, the heroine does not look for a way to free herself from tradition, but rather seems to wish to perpetuate such submission. The novel thus brought a message to many Latin American women who were still prisoners of traditions, and for whom there was no other foreseeable future but marriage and a subsequent total social and economic submission to man. With a refreshing sense of humor, the author criticized the romantic dreams of her heroine, but also criticized the strong colonial heritage of prejudices. *Ifigenia* is a novel about youth, written in a fluid prose full of color and descriptive power; because of its classical style and its content the book may be regarded as unique in the history not only of Venezuelan literature but of Latin American literature as well.

In 1923 Parra left Venezuela and returned to Europe. While in Paris she presided over a Hispanic literary center where she distinguished herself for her talent, her beauty, and the quality of her personality. *Ifigenia* was published in 1924 and the next year was awarded first prize in the Paris *Escritores americanos* competition. Soon she again felt the urge to isolate herself to write, and leaving behind the joys of Paris she went to Vevey, Switzerland, where in 1927 she completed *Las memorias de Mamá Blanca* (*Mama Blanca's Souvenirs*, 1929). *Mama Blanca* is the tale of an *abuela* (grandmother) narrating the recollections of her childhood, an evocation of people and places, and a simple description of life in the country. The novel describes the slow change of a Venezuelan agrarian society around 1870 to a capitalist one and reveals the author's fears of the consequences emerging from this capitalist era. The book is tinged with a mood of melancholy, resignation, and disappointment regarding time—a book in which the narrator describes the experiences of childhood with an uncommon clarity and spontaneity. In this second novel, Parra created one of the most unique characters of Venezuelan literature: Vicente Cochocho, the emancipated slave, illiterate but full of natural wisdom; the black man resigned to his destiny whatever it may be. Thus, this novel also brought a message to those who had enjoyed the simple life in the disappearing countryside.

Literary criticism has judged *Mama Blanca* to be a work superior to *Ifigenia,* with a more solid structure and a greater maturity in the descriptions of color and movement. In both *Ifigenia* and *Mama Blanca* the ghost of death is ever present, though death is seen as the end of all suffering, as a light that guides toward confidence and serenity. In both works the main characters are also the narrators; in *Ifigenia* María Eugenia Alonso writes letters to a friend far away, while in *Mama Blanca* the *abuela* narrates the experiences of her childhood. In the first book the description of the characters transcends the description of the environment and the customs, whereas in the second novel the description of the surroundings

exceeds that of the characters. Both books, however, are strongly linked to an idyllic colonial past.

The years 1929 and 1930 were full of social and literary activities for Parra. She traveled to Germany and Italy, and was invited to Colombia for a series of conferences. In her first presentation in the very conservative city of Bogotá, Parra briefly recounted her literary career and then proceeded to defend the main character of her novel *Ifigenia,* stating that she never intended to use María Eugenia Alonso to preach against moral principles, but only wanted to depict a woman's soul in a period when two quite strong and opposite influences conflicted: her right to complete independence and the weight of social tradition. The author referred to this conflict as a "contemporary sickness," the Hispanic American version of "Bovarism" (in reference to *Madame Bovary,* by Gustave Flaubert), and as the crisis of women in America, a crisis that could be overcome only when women learned to be free and economically independent. Parra continued to praise Spanish and Hispanic American women, advancing her thesis of mysticism as the feminine goal and the only way available to women to reach a state of self-realization. Parra's ideal of mysticism revealed a complex concept that seemed to include the intellectual as well as the religious world.

At a second Bogotá conference, she reminisced about the colonial past and praised the women of the period, exalting the religious life that provided the only alternative for a woman to obtain independence. She described the colonial times as an ideal life, free from political issues, wars, and other pressures, although Parra revealed a peculiar inconsistency when she indicated that she would not want to have lived during such a period, since having been born two hundred years later provided her with a magnificent opportunity to re-create and extol in her imagination the beauty and charm of colonial life.

In her third and last conference in Bogotá, after evoking the preindependence period in Venezuela, Parra painted the life in the city of white houses with red eaves with such fidelity and richness of detail that she created a close-up of life in Caracas as if she had herself truly lived there during those glorious years. Parra focused on Simón Bolívar, the hero, the man, and the lover, and on the women he loved, depicting him as a man of heroic proportions who always needed a woman at his side to encourage him in his mighty enterprises. She also drew an extraordinary picture of Manuela Sáenz, the last woman in Bolívar's life. Not surprisingly, it was during this trip to Colombia that she visited Santa Marta and San Pedro Alejandrino, where Bolívar had died one century before and where she conceived the idea of writing a biography of Bolívar. She returned to Europe in September 1931, bringing back with her a feverish fervor for Bolívar, as well as a recurrence of her mystical energy. This she interpreted as an omen of adversity to come. *Tres conferencias inéditas* (Three Unpublished Conferences, 1961) contains the texts of Parra's Bogotá addresses.

It is perhaps Parra's epistolary work that best reveals the drama of her life. Her letters are where one learns of her dreams, fears, and anxieties, and where one finds the evidence of the mystical energy that always accompanied her, especially during the last six years of her life. Written mainly between 1930 and 1935, her letters can be divided into three groups, though they exhibit an extraordinary unity of themes and ideas through the years; in them one detects the themes of books she could have written if death had not intervened.

The first group of letters were those sent to Vicente Lecuna, the official historian of Simón Bolívar; the first letter was written in 1930 (from Panama) and the last in 1932. The main theme is of course Bolívar, as Parra wanted to write a biography different from all others, depicting Bolívar's need of a woman to inspire him in his campaigns. By 1932 her projected work was just a dream, as her mystical fervor and tuberculosis sapped her energy to write.

The second group of letters, sent to the Colombian physician Dr. Luis Zea Uribe, showed her devotion to a distant friend. Zea Uribe and Parra shared many things, such as a deep love for mysticism and a metaphysical curiosity, and the two had suffered the symptoms of the "white disease," tuberculosis. Zea Uribe died in 1933, though it was not until May 1934 that Parra learned of the death of her best friend.

The third group of letters were those sent to Rafael Carías, who was in charge of her estate in Venezuela. In these letters, which began in 1924, Parra confides to Carías her fears, her depressions, her internal struggles, the progressive deterioration of her health, and the economic hardships caused mainly by her prolonged stay in the hospital at Leysing, Switzerland. But she also confides to Carías that her happiest years were those spent in Venezuela, and that she is sorry she left the country.

Seven months after returning from Colombia in 1931, Parra began experiencing deep weariness, inexplicable melancholy, and weight loss. Her physician insisted that nothing was wrong with her, but by the end of that year Parra experienced physical pains and had to be confined to the hospital for tuberculosis at Leysing. Loneliness and resignation invaded her, while at other times she would feel inexplicably happy, thinking that now she would have time to concentrate on her inner life, and would spend her days in an almost permanent contemplation of nature. This morbidity, characteristic of tuberculosis patients, oriented her mind toward another world. To her dear friend Zea Uribe she wrote that at Leysing she was extremely happy, possessed with a serene joy never felt before; she talked about a state of grace, and wondered if she had reached the state of nirvana, where even the thought of death seemed sweet and beautiful. In the midst of such happiness she had only one object of yearning: the city of white houses with red eaves, Caracas, a constant obsession.

Parra's confinement in Leysing lasted from 1932 until 1935, when at last she rebelled against the disease and decided to abandon the hospital. She traveled to Spain, but in Barcelona her physical condition deteriorated rapidly, and in desperation she went to Madrid. It was during those days in Madrid that she met Gabriela Mistral, the Chilean poet, who was deeply moved by the strange and angelic halo of grace that seemed to surround Parra during her last days. In Madrid the impatience and the quick temper peculiar to patients suffering from tuberculosis took hold of her for the first time. She wanted to go back to Leysing and its serenity, but because she was so weakened, there were days when she could hardly leave her bed, much less travel. Teresa de la Parra died on 23 April 1936, far from the city she longed to see once more. It was only in 1949 that the Venezuelan government recovered her remains and brought them back to Caracas. Parra could finally rest in the city of white houses and red eaves.

The literary work of the Venezuelan writer was completed in twelve years. From 1922 to 1931 she finished her two novels and composed the three lectures she delivered in Bogotá. In 1932, with her confinement in Leysing, began a period of close communion with nature, of strange and negative happiness, and she then started her most revealing work: her letters. It is in her epistolary work that one finds the elements of her true personality, the themes of all the books she might have written; in the letters, remarkably linked together by theme, the depth of her ideas and the power of her description reveal the true dimensions of a writer robbed by premature death from Venezuelan literature.

Although Teresa de la Parra presented herself as a feminist, she was not a revolutionary in the movement for women's rights; she only seemed revolutionary if judged within the context of the destiny of women of her time. She openly admitted fear of women's suffrage, of political life, preferring to leave the political arena to men. She praised women who studied and worked without losing their femininity, and she wrote in defense of women, of their independence and right to choose their destiny, and against the prejudices and social conventions of colonial Venezuela. Conversely, she exalted that same colonial life full of such prejudices and conventions. Suspicious and fearful of marriage and yet deeply religious, she was herself "a colonial woman"—only born centuries too late.

SELECTED BIBLIOGRAPHY

Editions

Prose Narratives

Diario de una señorita que se fastidia. Caracas, 1922.
La Mamá X. Caracas, 1923.
Ifigenia: Diario de una señorita que escribió porque se fastidiaba. Paris, 1924. 2nd ed. Paris, 1928.

Las memorias de Mamá Blanca. Paris, 1929. New York, 1932.

Nonfiction

Cartas. Caracas, 1951.
Epistolario íntimo. Caracas, 1953.
Cartas a Rafael Carías. Alcalá de Henares, Spain, 1957.
Tres conferencias inéditas. Caracas, 1961.

Later Editions

Ifigenia. Caracas, 1973.
Memorias de Mamá Blanca. Caracas, 1975, 1977.
Obra. Caracas, 1982.
Obras completas. Edited by Carlos García Prada. Caracas, 1965.

Translations

Mama Blanca's Souvenirs. Translated by Harriet de Onis. Washington, D.C., 1959.

Biographical and Critical Studies

Baralis, Marta. *"Ifigenia" de Teresa de la Parra.* Buenos Aires, 1972.
Díaz Sánchez, Ramón. *Teresa de la Parra.* Caracas, 1954.
Fuenmayor Ruíz, Victor. "Teresa de la Parra, las palabras 'sorprendidas.'" In *El inmenso llamado: Las voces en la escritura de Teresa de la Parra.* Caracas, 1974.
Llebot de Pérez, Amaya. *"Ifigenia": Caso único en la literatura nacional.* Dissertation, Biblioteca de la Universidad Central de Venezuela, 1974.
Martínez, Marco A. "Proust y Teresa de la Parra." *Imagen* 2/44:2 (1972).
Mora, Gabriela. "La otra cara de 'Ifigenia.'" *Sin nombre* 7/3:130–145 (1976).
Núñez, Enrique B. "Teresa de la Parra." In his *Teresa de la Parra: "Ifigenia" y sus criticos.* Caracas, 1927.
Tedesco, Italo. *"Memorias de Mamá Blanca,* intimismo y deleite." *Imagen* 45:16 (1972).

Bibliographies

La Casa Bello. *Teresa de la Parra: Bibliografía y otros trabajos.* Edited by C. A. de Artes Gráficas. Caracas, 1981.
Subero, Efraín, and Raquel Berlin. *Contribucion a la bibliografía de Teresa de la Parra, 1895–1936.* Caracas, 1970.

Rafael Heliodoro Valle

(1891–1959)

Georgette M. Dorn

Rafael Heliodoro Valle, Honduran poet, essayist, historian, diplomat, and one of the most influential Latin American journalists of his time, was born in Tegucigalpa on 3 July 1891. His early schooling took place in his native city, and he began publishing articles in newspapers while still in high school. Valle received a scholarship to pursue his studies in Mexico through the good offices of the Mexican consul in Tegucigalpa, the Honduran writer Rómulo E. Durón, and the president of Honduras (1903–1907), Manuel Bonilla. He studied at the Tacuba Normal School in Mexico City and quickly made the acquaintance of several prominent Central American intellectuals and politicians living in that city.

In 1911, Valle published his first book of poetry, *El rosal del ermitaño* (The Hermit's Rosebush), and in 1915, a book of essays, *Anecdotario de mi abuelo* (Grandfather's Anecdotes), which were well received. He sent his poems to the Nicaraguan poet laureate Rubén Darío, who was living in Paris. Darío acknowledged the book, urging Valle to continue writing poetry and also essays on intellectual life in Central America. By the end of 1912 Valle had returned to Honduras, where he founded, with fellow writers Alfonso Guillén Zelaya and Salatiel Rosales, El Ateneo de Honduras (The Honduras Atheneum), whose members met for scholarly conversation and to discuss each other's writings. Valle was keenly interested in improving the educational system of his country and especially in raising the literacy level. In 1912 he was named undersecretary in the Ministry of Education by President Manuel Bonilla, and for a little over a year Valle implemented theories of education he had learned in Mexico.

His endeavors were interrupted when he was named Honduran consul in Mobile, Alabama, in 1913. His first diplomatic post gave him the opportunity to learn English. In 1913 he also wrote his popular poem "Jazmines del cabo" (Cape Jasmines), extolling romantic love and the lush physical beauty of his native land. There followed three more books of poetry, *Cómo la luz del día* (Just as the Light of Day) in 1913, *El perfume de la tierra natal* (The Sweet Scent of the Fatherland) in 1917, and *Ánfora sedienta* (The Thirsty Urn) in 1922. Valle wrote musical poems that were direct and celebrated romantic love, nature, and especially nature in Honduras. They were aimed at a broad public and were meant to be recited by the masses. Written in the modernist style, his poems are often included in anthologies.

In 1919 Valle was sent to Washington, D.C., on a special mission. After it was accomplished, he visited New York City, where he befriended Luís Muñoz Marín from Puerto Rico, Salomón de la Selva from

Nicaragua, and Katherine Anne Porter, members of the Latin American literary set in that city. Valle returned to Mexico in 1921, where he plunged into journalism and began, at the same time, a series of historical and bibliographic projects, abandoning for the time being the diplomatic life. While working for the Mexican Ministry of Education under the influential educator and philosopher José Vasconcelos, he also wrote essays for the newspapers *El Universal, El Universal Ilustrado,* and *Excélsior* (he continued writing for the latter for a quarter century). In addition, Valle also found time to work as a consultant for the National Museum of Mexico City and to teach part-time at the San Jacinto Military College. He also began his most ambitious historical compilation, *La anexión de Centroamérica a México* (Central America's Annexation to Mexico). Central America was annexed to the Mexican empire under Agustín de Iturbide (1822–1823). Valle collected all the documents leading to the annexation and published them with an introduction. The first volume appeared in 1924 and the sixth in 1949. Other historical studies published during this period include *Cómo era Iturbide* (The Real Iturbide) in 1922, *La nueva poesía de América* (Spanish America's New Poetry) in 1923, *El convento de Tepotzotlán* (The Tepotzotlán Convent) in 1924, *San Bartolomé de las Casas* in 1926, and *Bibliografía de don José Cecilio del Valle* in 1934. The latter dealt with the works of the leading Honduran intellectual of the colonial era, a figure Valle particularly admired. During the 1920's, Valle's ideas were influenced by those of the Mexican writers Ramón López Velarde and Enrique González Martínez, as well as the Colombian Porfirio Barba-Jacob, whose biography he wrote. Valle also prepared a complete bibliography of Barba-Jacob's works.

After a decade devoted to journalism, bibliography, and history, Valle returned to Washington, D.C., from January to April of 1930, as a member of the Honduran delegation to the Conference on the Border Question between Honduras and Guatemala. (Poorly marked boundaries during the colonial era caused endless border disputes that remain unresolved in the 1980's.) Valle was back in Mexico during most of the 1930's and continued writing for many major newspapers throughout Spanish America, such as *La Prensa* (Buenos Aires), *La Crónica* and *El Comercio* (Lima), *Diario de la Marina* (Havana), *Diario de Yucatán* (Mérida, Mexico), *La Opinión* (Los Angeles), and *La Prensa* (New York). Valle was the most widely known Spanish-American journalist of those years. He published a bibliography on Latin American journalism entitled *La bibliografía del periodismo en la América española* (The Bibliography of Journalism in Spanish America, 1942), and also wrote *El periodismo en Honduras: Notas para su historia* (Historical Notes on Journalism in Honduras), published posthumously in 1960.

His renown as a journalist and writer prompted numerous invitations from a number of countries to deliver lectures and to participate in international congresses, presidential inaugurations, and dedications of monuments. In 1938 Valle married Laura Álvarez, a Honduran who had inspired some of his poems, and then set out with his bride for Stanford University, where he became a visiting lecturer. In 1940 Valle was awarded the Marie Moors Cabot Prize for Journalism at Columbia University, together with Eduardo Santos, former president of Colombia, and the Chilean newspaperman Agustín Edwards Bello. The three were later received in Washington by President Franklin D. Roosevelt and were honored at the Pan American Union.

In 1941, Valle, who had been widowed twelve months after his wedding, took as his second bride the Peruvian poet Emilia Romero, who shared his interest in the world of books. With his new wife, Valle undertook an extensive lecture tour through South America. In 1945 President Juan José Arévalo of Guatemala invited Valle to the inauguration of the School of Humanities at San Carlos University, where Valle was awarded an honorary doctorate. In *Excélsior* (Mexico City) and in *La Opinión* (Los Angeles), he published his famous interview with President Arévalo in which the Guatemalan president candidly enumerated his country's major obstacles to development as inadequate public health facilities, not nearly enough schools, and poor economic conditions. Valle wrote several articles about the reform-minded Arévalo in other Latin American newspapers, praising his statesmanship. Valle believed that the lack of sound political education prevented the free discussion of ideas in Central America and kept true freedom from flourishing. He held that every intellectual had an obligation to know everything about his own country and to work assiduously to further the cause of democracy. The pen was Valle's weapon in his lifelong struggle to raise the political consciousness of his countrymen and of people in Spanish America.

Although in the 1940's Valle became more active in politics, he also returned to his earlier vocation, which was teaching. He completed a doctorate in history at the National Autonomous University of Mexico in 1948. His dissertation, published in 1950, dealt with Cristóbal de Olid, conquistador of Mexico and Honduras. In 1942 Valle edited a volume of correspondence between Jeremy Bentham and José Cecilo del Valle. He wrote essays on cultural history, such as *Imaginación de México* (Mexico's Imagination, 1945), which focused on the rich legacy of pre-Columbian legends and myths, and *Semblanza de Honduras* (Honduras' Face, 1947), which analyzed the cultural history of his native land. He published works dealing with some major nineteenth-century Spanish-American figures as well as numerous bibliographies. In 1949 he completed the last volume of six on the annexation of Central America. Along with his prodigious publishing, Valle began turning to politics, a not unusual path for a Latin American intellectual.

Valle held that the Liberal and Conservative parties of Honduras differed very little, as they continued to make similar promises that they then failed to keep, and both also committed the same errors. Along with other Central American writers, Valle favored political union for the five countries of Central America, something that had been tried unsuccessfully several times over the course of a century. One of Valle's early memories was Honduran president Policarpo Bonilla's leadership in organizing a conference in 1895, for a renewed attempt at the union of Central America. Valle believed that Central American peace would come only if the countries were united. Unfortunately, politicians always thwarted these attempts. Valle was involved in efforts leading toward union in 1917, 1921, 1922, and 1951.

Turning to domestic matters, in 1947 Valle and a group of Hondurans in Mexico formed the Liberal Democratic Committee of Honduras. They urged President Tiburcio Carías Andino to step down and allow for a peaceful transition, since his long tenure in office no longer enjoyed popular support, nor had it been tested at the ballot box. Valle wanted to prevent Carías Andino from succeeding himself and supported the National party's candidate, Manuel Gálvez. In an interview with Valle on 2 May 1945, Carías Andino intimated that he might hand over his office to the president-elect, which he did on 1 January 1949.

Shortly after President Gálvez' inauguration in 1949, Valle was named ambassador to Washington, D.C. His embassy became a cultural center. He was a frequent user of the collections of the Library of Congress and recorded twenty-nine poems for the Archive of Hispanic Literature on Tape. Valle, Jorge Basadre of Peru, and Francisco Aguilera from the Library of Congress founded the [Latin] American Atheneum of Washington, which ushered in a golden age for Latin American culture in that capital during the 1950's. Symposia and lectures organized by the Atheneum were held at Georgetown University. Some of the speakers were the Spanish writers Juan Ramón Jiménez and Pedro Salinas, the Colombians Germán Pardo García and Germán Arciniégas, the Argentines Eduardo Mallea and Aníbal Sánchez Reulet, and the Nicaraguan writer Salomón de la Selva. Valle tried to acquaint North Americans with Spanish-American culture. As far back as 1929, he had published a bibliography on cooperative ventures in library science between the United States and Mexico. Valle's ambassadorship came to an abrupt halt when on 1 March 1955 he received a telegram from his Foreign Office asking for his resignation. The new president, Julio Lozano (who had replaced Gálvez in December 1954), used as an excuse an article Valle had written in February in *El Día* (Tegucigalpa) averring that the century-old border dispute between Honduras and Nicaragua remained unresolved. The opposition newspaper *El Pueblo* began a campaign to recall Valle from Washington. Meanwhile in Honduras President Lozano brought back the old ways and terminated the reform-minded measures instituted by President Gálvez.

Valle spent many months trying to defend himself from insinuations and rumors that intimated that he might have had dealings with President Anastasio

Somoza of Nicaragua, and the travail began to affect his health. In 1957 the Mexican Writers' Center organized an elaborate banquet to honor Valle's literary and journalistic achievements. The event was attended by more than one hundred important literary and political figures from many parts of the continent.

On 29 July 1959, Valle died in Mexico City. Two years before, his wife had edited a commemorative volume about his work entitled *Recuerdo a Rafael Heliodoro Valle en los cincuenta años de su vida literaria* (Honoring the Fiftieth Anniversary of Rafael Heliodoro Valle's Literary Career). More than one hundred writers and scholars from both hemispheres contributed.

Perhaps the book that best represents Valle's ideas and ideology is his *Historia de las ideas contemporáneas en Centro-América* (History of Contemporary Thought in Central America), published posthumously in 1960. In it he dealt with topics such as democracy and dictatorship, religion and the state, humanism versus materialism, philosophy, economics, culture, and literary criticism. He assessed accurately the strengths and weaknesses of Central America and analyzed in depth the work of most of its prominent writers and thinkers. Above all he castigated those thinkers who tried to blame all the ills that befell Central America on outside forces. Valle held that the citizens' own lack of willingness to work for democracy was the root of backwardness and lack of progress. The work stands as a major contribution to Central American thought.

Valle was a man for all seasons, a versatile intellectual, a poet rich in stylistic resources, a phenomenal bibliographer who saw the need to place research aids at the scholar's disposal, a historian who possessed encyclopedic knowledge and recognized the importance of preserving the past accurately, and a masterful and dedicated journalist. Valle brought his erudition, learning, and graceful poetry and prose to the service of his country as a diplomat, and to the entire hemisphere while serving in cultural and diplomatic missions for Honduras, Mexico, the United Nations, and the Organization of American States.

Valle's contributions to the field of education, whether his work in secretariats of education or his lectures in classrooms, constitute a lifetime endeavor, for which he is remembered in Honduras and in Mexico. Even though he lived the greater part of his life in Mexico, he never ceased being a real Honduran, his country's interests always with him. Through his own life, devoted to poetry, scholarship, journalism, and public service, Valle demonstrated that even while living away from one's own country, one could remain active in its civic and intellectual life.

Columbia University's dean of the graduate school of journalism Carl W. Ackerman referred to the writer in a letter to Valle's wife as one "among the distinguished journalists of this century"; when he "appears before the stacks, the books recognize him as an understanding and comprehending friend" (*Recuerdo*, p. 8). He educated and informed Spanish-speaking people of the Americas through his newspaper articles devoted to cultural, literary, and political issues, published in many capitals. Valle's numerous publications and diverse accomplishments form a solid and substantial whole, leaving behind the legacy of a tireless journalist, inspired poet, educator, and man of letters, who above all wanted to bring order and progress, and expand the cultural horizon of his fellow Spanish Americans.

SELECTED BIBLIOGRAPHY

First Editions

Poetry, Prose, Essays

El rosal del ermitaño. Tegucigalpa, 1911.
Cómo la luz del día. Tegucigalpa, 1913.
Anecdotario de mi abuelo. Tegucigalpa, 1915.
El perfume de la tierra natal. Tegucigalpa, 1917.
Ánfora sedienta: Poemas. Mexico City, 1922.
Rusticatio mexicana. Mexico City, 1924.
México imponderable. Santiago, Chile, 1936.
Tierras de pan llevar. Santiago, Chile, 1939.
Uníson amor. Mexico City, 1940.
Contigo. Mexico City, 1943.
Visión de Perú. Mexico City, 1943.
Cartas hispanoamericanas. Mexico City, 1945.
Semblanza de Honduras. Tegucigalpa, 1947.

La sandalia de fuego. Managua, 1952.
Flor de Mesoamérica. San Salvador, 1955.
Viajero feliz. San Salvador, 1959.
La rosa intemporal: Antología poética, 1908–1957. Mexico City, 1964.

Historical Works

Cómo era Iturbide. Mexico City, 1922.
La nueva poesía de América. Mexico City, 1923.
La anexión de Centroamérica a México: Documentos y escritos de 1821–1828. 6 vols. Mexico City, 1924–1949.
El convento de Tepotzotlán. Mexico City, 1924.
San Bartolomé de las Casas. Mexico City, 1926.
Policarpo Bonilla: Algunos spuntes biográficos. Mexico City, 1936.
Cronología de la cultura. Monterrey, Mexico, 1939.
Cartas de Bentham a José Cecilio del Valle. Mexico City, 1942.
Iturbide, varón de Dios. Mexico City, 1944.
Imaginación de México. Buenos Aires, 1945.
Bolívar en México. Mexico City, 1946.
Tres pensadores de América: Bolívar, Bello, Martí. Mexico City, 1946.
Animales de la América antigua. Mexico City, 1947.
Cristóbal de Olid. Mexico City, 1948, 1950.
Un diplomático mexicano en París. Edited by Rafael Heliodoro Valle. Mexico City, 1948.
Cuauhtémoc. With Salvador Toscano. Mexico City, 1953.
Jesuítas de Tepotzotlán. Bogotá, 1955.
Historia de las ideas contemporaneas en Centro-América. Mexico City, 1960.
El periodismo en Honduras: Notas para su historia. Mexico City, 1960.

Bibliographies by Valle

Índice de escritores. Mexico City, 1928.
Bibliographic Cooperation Between Mexico and the United States. Chicago, 1929.
Bibliografía mexicana. Mexico City, 1930.
Bibliografía de don José Cecilio del Valle. Mexico City, 1934.
Bibliografía maya. Mexico City, 1937–1941.
Bibliografía de historia de América. Mexico City, 1938.
Bibliografía de Manuel Ignacio Altamirano. Mexico City, 1939.
La bibliografía del periodismo en la América española. Cambridge, Mass., 1942.
La cirugía mexicana de siglo XIX. Mexico City, 1942.
Oradores americanos. Mexico City, 1946.
Bibliografía cervantina de la América española. Mexico City, 1950.
Bibliografía de Hernán Cortés. Mexico City, 1953.
Bibliografía de Porfirio Barba-Jacob. Bogotá, 1961.

Biographical and Critical Studies

Acosta, Oscar. *Rafael Heliodoro Valle: Vida y obra, biografía, estudio crítico, bibliografía y antología de un intelectual hondureño.* Tegucigalpa, 1973.
Barrientos, Alfonso Enrique. *Rafael Heliodoro Valle.* Guatemala City, 1963.
Corona a la memoria de Rafael Heliodoro Valle. Mexico City, 1963.
Murillo Soto, Céleo. *Un hondureño y una actitud política en busca de la concordancia.* Tegucigalpa, 1948.
Recuerdo a Rafael Heliodoro Valle en los cincuenta años de su vida literaria. Edited by Emilia Romero de Valle. Mexico City, 1957.

César Vallejo

(1892–1938)

Julio Ortega

The Peruvian César Vallejo is considered one of the greatest poets in the Spanish language. His reputation has grown since his death in Paris on 15 April 1938, and he is the subject of many volumes of literary criticism. Ironically, the more it has been studied, the more difficult his work has revealed itself to be: Vallejo is perhaps the most complicated poet of the Spanish language. Even more complex than that of the baroque poet Luis de Góngora y Argote, whose poetry can be translated into prose, the hermetic work of Vallejo is nearly impossible to translate.* The irony increases when one considers that this most difficult poet is also one of the most popular. His poetry always communicates an intense emotion and an active subjectivity that moves the reader, even if the complete meaning of the poem is not captured. The same phenomenon occurs with the poetry of Vallejo as happens with the painting of Pablo Picasso: we see a picture and we recognize part of a figure or a scene, but the painting does not refer to the scene in

our mind; rather, we understand that we are reading a new artistic language. The mature poetry of Vallejo corresponds to the aesthetics of cubism, to its recomposition of the figure, its representation. In his poetry, Vallejo brought into harmony a great communicative emotion and an experimental, exploratory language. His work possesses the powerful persuasion of a traditional and dramatic humanism, and the intriguing, agonizing expression of a modern and original poetic art.

César Abraham Vallejo was born on 16 March 1892 in Santiago de Chuco, a small city in the northern part of the Peruvian Andes. Set in the high altitudes, this relatively inaccessible city had preserved its rural character, although it was predominantly racially mixed and exclusively Spanish-speaking. Indians who spoke the Quechua language, however, lived throughout the spacious and rich valley of Santiago and must have exerted some influence on the rural air of the city. Vallejo was the son of Francisco de Paula Vallejo and María de los Santos Mendoza, both of mixed Spanish and Indian descent; César was their eleventh and last child. His relatives have recounted that, as a child, he would mysteriously pretend to be hungry, stealing loaves of bread from the oven in order to eat them secretly; and he once explained that the scribbles that he had

*Except where noted, translations in this essay are the work of the essay's translator, Henry Thurston. Most extracts (both Spanish and English) from Vallejo's poems that have been reproduced in this essay, however, are taken from *César Vallejo: The Complete Posthumous Poetry*, translated by Clayton Eshleman and José Rubia Barcia (Berkeley, Los Angeles, and London: University of California Press, 1978), hereafter referred to as *CPP*.

traced in the ground were a letter to his mother, telling her he was starving. In fact, his family was unpretentious but well-off, and his father had been the governor of his town.

Vallejo spent the years between 1905 and 1908 in Huamachuco, completing his secondary education. During this time his literary curiosity began to develop. Upon finishing high school he tried to begin his university studies in Trujillo, the most important coastal city in the northern part of the country, although he was not able to continue because he had to start working. His first job was in the mining zone of Quiruvilca, near Santiago. He next worked as a teacher at a nearby country estate and afterward as the cashier's helper at the sugar plantation Roma, near Trujillo. These experiences were his first serious contact with the social reality of Peru. Vallejo later took the workers of the sugar plantation as the subject of his proletarian novel *El tungsteno* (Tungsten, 1931), a simple but fierce political denunciation. In 1913, he began his formal studies at the University of Trujillo.

Trujillo was an active city, open to modern literary and political concerns, and young Vallejo quickly became one of the members of the "artistic bohemia" of the "Trujillo group." He worked as a teacher in the Centro Escolar (Student Center), and later in the Colegio Nacional de San Juan. He graduated in 1915, writing a bachelor's thesis entitled *El romanticismo en la poesía castellana* (Romanticism in Castilian Poetry), the first expression of his ideas about literature.

In Trujillo, Vallejo discovered the best literature of his time, thanks to the group of young university writers headed by the philosopher Antenor Orrego. In this group, known as the "Bohemians," Vallejo became acquainted with the work of the great poet of Latin American modernism, Rubén Darío, as well as that of Walt Whitman, Paul Verlaine, and the French symbolists. Another member of this group was Victor Raúl Haya de la Torre, the founder of the Alianza Popular Revolucionaria Americana (or, APRA); it was, therefore, a group not only of the artistic but also of the political vanguard.

When he arrived in Lima, in 1918, Vallejo had already begun to write the first poems of *Los heraldos negros* (The Black Messengers), his first book, which was published at the end of 1918. He visited Manuel González Prada, the essayist and rebel, to whom he dedicated one of the compositions in his book, and he was received by José María Eguren, the most innovative poet of that time. In Lima he also discovered two important groups of writers and intellectuals, one from the magazine *Colónida,* headed by the writer Abraham Valdelomar, a follower of Oscar Wilde and Gabriele D'Annunzio, and the other led by José Carlos Mariátegui, the brilliant essayist and social activist, founder of the Peruvian Socialist party. Vallejo worked as a teacher in a private school. The news of the death of his mother made a profound impression on him, but he was unable to travel to Santiago for her funeral. All of his experiences in Trujillo and Lima, including his tortured and dramatic romantic encounters, were revealed in his first book, which began to circulate in July 1919.

From the first poem, "Los heraldos negros," it is evident that Vallejo is a different kind of poet. While the book contained all the features of Latin American modernism, the tradition in which he had learned the poetic art, his personality prevailed over modernism's rhythmic and thematic canons. The poem begins with these verses:

> *Hay golpes en la vida tan fuertes . . . Yo no sé!*
> *Golpes como del odio de Dios; como si ante ellos,*
> *la resaca de todo lo sufrido*
> *se empozara en el alma . . . Yo no sé!*

> In life there are blows so heavy. "I don't know."
> Blows like God's hatred; as if before them
> The undertow of all that is suffered
> Should be dammed up in the soul. "I don't know."
> (*César Vallejo: Selected Poems,*
> translated by H. R. Hays, p. 11)

The opening verse contains several of the fundamental statements of this book of poetry. In the first place, we find here the notion of tragic destiny that distinguishes Vallejo: these are the "blows" of human experience, unforeseeable and irremediable, changing the individual into a suffering and agonized being. The figure of the agonized man is characteristic of Vallejo and supports his version of orphanhood as the defining key of human life. Man is an orphan in creation, not only because he has lost his faith in God, but also because he has been abandoned by his creator and because his destiny is always tragic. This orphanhood turns him into a "wretched man," without answers in the face of his own helplessness. The figure of the abandoned or lost son emerges, in this book and throughout Vallejo's work, as the prototype of the human condition. In addition, the attitude of not knowing ("I don't know") is repeated throughout the poems. An attitude of rebellious ignorance, of agonized impotence, it is also a rejection of the explanations given by society, with its commonly held ideas, religious beliefs, and Hispanic tradition, and the expression of an existential need to question the traditional ideological structure.

The point of view of the poetic analysis is, in *Los heraldos negros*, this orphan's voice, that of the confessional person who expounds and discusses his experience, his conceptions, his perceptions, values, and beliefs; he does it to free himself from those bonds and to discover his naked humanity. This is the true innovation that Vallejo brought to modernism: while the modernist poets employed names as if they were full of significance, Vallejo emptied them of content in order to question the traditional meaning of the world. In this way, the experiences of death, solitude, love, human pain, nostalgia, and the loss of faith acquire a critical, questioning element. For this reason, *Los heraldos negros* is profoundly ambiguous; it moves between poles of affirmation and negation, of knowing and not knowing, of responding and doubting, of believing and not believing. Moreover, Vallejo introduces a more everyday type of speech to modernist discourse. Compared with the affected and lyrical language of modernism, the conversational diction signals a new poetic direction.

With *Los heraldos negros*, Vallejo achieved a wide poetic reputation, although his situation in Lima was rather difficult. He lost his job as a teacher and had to find another one, again as an elementary teacher, in the Colegio Guadalupe. These were times of social and political agitation, but Vallejo lived the typical bohemian life of the semidecadent artists, frequenting the opium dens of Lima's Chinatown. He determined to set out for France, but first he decided to make a farewell visit to his hometown, arriving there in April 1920. His visit coincided with the annual town festivities in Santiago, and he found himself unintentionally involved in a popular uprising on 1 August, which led to the death of a man, the burning of a store, and assaults on public offices. A powerful family that was harmed included Vallejo in its judicial complaint. He fled, seeking refuge in Trujillo but was captured on 5 November and spent three and a half months in Trujillo's jail. Only the protests of university student associations and several prominent figures of Peruvian culture were successful in winning his release on 26 February 1921. This experience in prison marked Vallejo for the rest of his life.

In October 1922 *Trilce* appeared. One of the fundamental books of Hispanic American vanguardist poetry, it was received with indifference by the critics, who were incapable of understanding the radical intention of the poet. In 1923 Vallejo published *Escalas melografiadas* (Melographic Scales), a collection of stories, and that same year, *Fabla salvaje* (Savage Fable), a short novel. His economic situation was desperate, but with his last paycheck he purchased a boat ticket to Paris, leaving on 17 June 1923, never to return to his homeland.

The neologism *trilce* comes from the number three, and numerology is clearly important in this book. Unity, duality, and the third element of a figure are, however, not of harmony but of profound discord. Vallejo proposes, in the first place, to go beyond the aesthetic of harmony, which is based on the duality of harmonic terms, presenting himself as the champion of a new poetics, based on helplessness and the orphanhood of the uneven number. "¡Ceded al nuevo impar potente de orfandad!" (Yield the new uneven, potentate of orphanhood!), he demands in poem 36.

The attempt has been made to reconstruct the possible correlations between *Trilce* and the vanguard of its time, and there is no doubt that Vallejo was in fact acquainted with some important texts: Rafael Cansinos Assens' translation *Golpe de dados* (*Dice Thrown*) of Stéphane Mallarmé's *Un coup de dés jamais n'abolira le hasard* (*Never Will Annul Chance*, 1914) published in the literary magazine *Cervantes*, and *La poema francesca moderna* (1913), a splendid anthology of contemporary French poetry, by Enrique Diez Canedo. Any effort to describe *Trilce* must first place it within the context of the poetic changes of that time, if it is to precisely describe its great differences and peculiarities and achieve an accurate definition of what Vallejo accomplished. In a letter to Orrego, Vallejo said that he had approached a type of limit, on the edge of control, while he was writing *Trilce*—as if a kind of vertigo could almost have dragged him to a fate of incoherence—but that at the very beginning of this state of entropy he recovered his freedom. This comment tells us that in spite of the kind of unrestricted liberty taken in the text, a series of strict controls were also applied. Even when the work seems arbitrary, impenetrable, or hermetic, it possesses the need and even the logic of its system.

In *Trilce*, the analysis of temporality predominates. In the first place, time is the passing of time, but it also includes its not elapsing, something halted, as in poem 2. In addition, time is also a type of transtemporality, almost paradoxical in nature. This supposes a revertive or reversible time, which one can investigate through its insufficiency. In this way, time is seen as incomplete, as defective. Poem 2, which speculates about time in prison, ends by saying:

> *¿Qué se llama cuanto heriza nos?*
> *Se llama Lomismo que padece*
> *nombre nombre nombrE.*

What is called whatever makes us bristle? It is called
Thesame which suffers
name, name, namE.

The "It" is a tautological state, something that is a victim of its own naming, and there is no way to accept the similarity but through the name. But this knowledge is insufficient, and we rebel before the name. One side of the name, babbling, and the other side of the name, renomination, are the open paths. What we may not do, suggests the book, is to continue to call things by their names, because to do so reaffirms our defectiveness.

Another very profound experience, orphanhood, is also deduced from temporality. In poem 14 we read: "Cual mi explicación. / Esto me lacera de empranía" (Such as my explanation. / This harms me with earliness.) Since Vallejo emphasizes grammatical parody in this book, we could read instead: "This harms me with earliness as if it were my explanation," but Vallejo has transposed the syntax to call into question his own explanation. The object has disappeared; this—we do not know what "this" may be—

is whisked out of sight, and the permanent vanishing of the name is visible in the text. One of the great paths open throughout the book is precisely the notion of the "early," which is related to germination, birth, a new beginning. At the same time, there is a sort of figurative apocalypse, a world that disintegrates when faced with the series of images of the birth of a new perception.

At the end of the book, the notion of orphanhood returns us to the wretched man of the first poem, who is an orphan not only in a literal sense but also in the sense of defectiveness, which makes him an orphan of language, the worst kind of orphanhood. Confronted with language, he finds that he is not in the house of language. He instead is left to reconstruct the bleakness of language, putting the logos to the test. Thus this insufficiency of language, which is the path of the new poetics, leads to an encounter with the absurd. In the book we have different versions of what is meant by the word "absurd": "Absurdo sólo tú eres puro" (Absurd, only you are pure) he says in one poem. Vallejo establishes a way of saying without explanation, because what is pure is what has no definition. Following this logic, a dictionary would be a monument to impurity. On the other hand, there are other basic, elemental signs. In poem 73 we read: "Ha triunfado otro ay. La verdad está allí" (Another oh has triumphed. The truth is there). The purity of that immediate syllable (*ay*) summarizes the consciousness of the new poetics with the evidence of an elemental speech—new poetry is powerful in its same orphanhood.

Financial difficulties continued to trouble Vallejo upon his arrival in Paris in July 1923. He became gravely ill and required surgery. Thanks to the friendship of Max Jiménez, the Costa Rican artist, he spent a period of time sheltered in his studio. Vallejo became the friend of Juan Larrea, a Spanish writer, with whom in 1926 he would publish the magazine *Favorables, París, Poema*, although only two issues were printed. Starting in 1925, he wrote feature stories about the artistic and worldly life of Paris for the Lima magazines *Mundial* and *Variedades*. Employing the light and cosmopolitan style of the feature story, Vallejo gave an account of his aesthetic and philosophical preoccupations. His artistic consciousness began shaping itself through affinities and rejections. He felt close to those who were searching for new artistic direction but rejected the surrealists and other vanguardists, accusing them of being mechanical. He also refused to accept the similarity of American and European art. He knew that the new art should start from a vitalistic fusion with the realities of America, but he did not seem to be very clear about the formal way to achieve it. Nevertheless, he knew well that the independence of his art was proof against any creed, including political creeds. Politics attracted him, no doubt, as one answer to the modern experience of the metropolis, where he discovered that his "wretched man" and "orphan" was now a "desocupado," an unemployed worker.

In 1928, right after another illness, Vallejo traveled to the Soviet Union, where he planned to reside, but within a few weeks he was once again in Paris. After marrying Georgette Philippart, he made a long trip with her through Eastern Europe and spent another two weeks in Russia. His travel chronicles declare his new Marxist affiliation and his commitment as a militant artist. In the magazine *Bolívar* in Madrid, he published in 1930 an extensive report, which the next year was reproduced in book form as *Rusia en 1931* (Russia in 1931) and became a minor bestseller in Spain. In 1930 he joined the Spanish Communist party and at the end of that year was expelled by the French police because of his political activity. He moved to Madrid, where he eked out a living by doing translations for the publishing house Cenit. For the same firm, Vallejo wrote *El tungsteno* (Tungsten), a novel that renounces literature in the name of political commitment. He was in Madrid when the Spanish Republic was proclaimed on 14 April 1931.

During these years, Vallejo was in search of his most authentic expression, in the midst of affiliations, doubts, and rejections that forced him to balance political demands against the demands of his art. Looking for the conciliation of these demands would be his agony. Perhaps for that reason, Vallejo devoted himself more to prose than to poetry, and although during this period he wrote his mature poetic work, the series of poems that he called "human," he published only two or three compositions. He apparently did not want to publish a book

of poetry until he had resolved his own contradictions, and although he was at the point of preparing a selection of his unpublished work for printing, he never was able to finish it. Instead, he wrote plays, but even though his friend Federico García Lorca did everything possible to help him, he never saw any of them performed.

The Spanish civil war profoundly moved Vallejo, who devoted himself to the Republican cause with true passion. He increased his political activity, writing denunciatory newspaper articles and traveling twice to Republican Spain (he had by now, six years after the founding of the republic, returned to live in Paris). On his second trip to Spain, he participated in the International Congress of Anti-Fascist Intellectuals. He also wrote what would be his last work, *España, aparta de mí éste cáliz* (*Spain, Take This Cup from Me*, 1939), the most important poetic product of the Spanish civil war. Vallejo became ill in March 1938, and he died on 15 April, Good Friday, in the Aragó clinic, the victim of a fever of mysterious origins. Before dying he dictated his last words to his wife: "Whatever may be the cause that I have to defend before God, after death, I have one defender: God." Not only these words but all of his posthumous work reveals the peculiar Christian and social syncretism of this poet. In July 1939, *Poemas humanos* (*Human Poems*) was published in Paris. Edited by his widow and Raúl Porras Barrenechea, this heterogeneous collection of poems and prose written since 1923 includes the sequence *Spain, Take This Cup From Me*.

In *Human Poems*, the poet began to revise the relation between the name and the thing. In "Nómina de huesos" ("Payroll of Bones"; *CPP*, pp. 2, 3), we read:

> Se pedía a grandes voces:
> —Que muestre las dos manos a la
> vez.
> Y esto no fué posible.

> They demanded shouting:
> —Let him show both hands at the same time.
> And this was not possible.

The poem concludes with

—Que le llamen, en fin, por su nombre.
Y esto no fué posible.

—Let them call him, finally, by his name.
And this was not possible.

The dysfunction of the name when confronted with its object is postulated here, as in many of Vallejo's images, leading him to irreversible consequences in his poetry. In the process of remaking poetic discourse, it was essential that Vallejo compose his own dictionary, in which the word signified more things than the name. Figurative poets (the baroque poets, for example) also possess their own dictionaries, in which the image does not pacify the object. In Vallejo's case something more unusual occurs: Calling the thing with another name results in a dictionary that does not have the same code outside of the text itself. For this reason, the vocabularies that have been made of Vallejo's idiom fail, since the meanings of the words within the text are not limited to those words' meanings in everyday usage.

In "Altura y pelos" ("Height and Hair"), we read: "¿Quién no se llama Carlos o cualquier otra cosa?" ("Who isn't Carlos or any other thing?"; *CPP*, pp. 36, 37). Once again we have the name and its indistinct naming function. The poem continues:

¿Quién al gato no dice gato gato?
¡Ay! yo que sólo he nacido solamente
¡Ay! yo que sólo he nacido solamente!

Who to the kitty doesn't say kitty, kitty?
Aie! I alone who was solely born!
Aie! I alone who was solely born!

Vallejo perceives that his capacity for naming, or his need to name, is going in another direction. This abandonment of the name is also a sign of his agonizing work of breaking one circuit of communication in order to impose another, a project almost excessive in its radicalism.

In "Sombrero, abrigo, guantes" ("Hat, Overcoat, Gloves"), Vallejo begins with a classic use of language, the locative: "Enfrente a la Comedia Francesca está el Café / de la Regencia" ("In front of the [Comédie Française] is the Café / Regency"; *CPP*, pp.

44, 45). The words serve to say that each thing is in its place. But later, at the end of the sonnet, we read

Importa oler a loco postulando
¡qué cálida es la nieve, qué fugaz la tortuga
el cómo qué sencillo, qué fulminante el cuándo!

It is important to smell like a madman postulating
how warm the snow is, how fleeting the turtle,
the how how simple, how fulminant the when!

The nominal representative system is thus broken up, and the implication is that language is not natural. Language is natural in the sense that we have naturalized a cultural convention, but for Vallejo language is cultural in a misleading way. Vallejo seems to tell us that naming is an insufficient act and that to redeem this act we must name by contradiction, remaking the designative function of the name. Vallejo is conscious of his project and of the radical nature of his undertaking; consequently the self-irony: "It is important to smell like a madman postulating." In this poetry he postulates that language has domesticated the world and that in the situation of historicity, of modern emergency, this process of naming has no meaning. We must name by contradiction, then, precisely to restore another type of relation with living reality. A poem is, therefore, a type of linguistic apparatus that designates through contradiction and that sets forth a broken relation between the name and the thing through the bleakness of speech and from a position that lacks a pretext of historicity. In another poem, he begins, "Hoy me gusta la vida mucho menos, / pero siempre me gusta vivir: ya lo decía" ("Today I like life much less, / but I like to live anyway: I have often said it"; *CPP*, pp. 66, 67), thus revealing the reaffirming quality of natural conversation. He continues: "Casi toqué la parte de mi todo y me contuve / con un tiro en la lengua detrás de mi palabra" ("I almost the part of my whole and restrained myself / with a shot in the tongue behind my word"). This is a self-reflection on what he is doing—naming—because suddenly he was going to name the "part of his whole," he suggests, signaling that one of the possibilities of naming is synecdoche, an oft-employed recourse of the poet in this book.

Other poetic devices that Vallejo uses include

metonymy, oxymoron, and the mechanisms of antithesis, which proliferate as parts of the baroque apparatus that supports the process of renaming. But, he says, "I . . . restrained myself with a shot in the tongue behind my word," that is, he was quiet in time, he refused the name. Later in the poem we read, "Dije chaleco, dije / todo, parte, ansia, dije casi, por no llorar" (I said vest, said / whole, part, yearning, said almost, to avoid crying"). Once again, this drama of going from the part to the whole is clear, with a language that conciliates the name and the thing. The poem's consciousness of its own mechanism of production is evident: confronted with the name, the text itself shows the options of naming, of not naming, of naming the whole, the part for the whole, and the like. It is as if the process of naming were dramatized. For that reason, the opening lines of another poem propose that "después de tántas palabras, / no sobrevive la palabra!" ("after so many words / the word itself does not survive!"; *CPP*, pp. 74, 75).

It is in the exploration of speech that *Human Poems* acquires its importance. Although he worked to change the naming system, Vallejo based the change on traditional colloquial forms. These oral formulas or discursive frameworks are the salutation, the epistle, the sermon, the forensic act, and the oratorical speech, whose intonations and modulations underline the apellative quality, the demonstrative dialectic, at times of true theorem, that these poems possess. This is the landscape of the colloquy over which the text is produced.

"Salutación angélica" ("Angelic Salutation") begins with these lines: "Eslavo con respecto a la palmera, / alemán de perfil al sol" ("Slave in regard to the palm tree, / German with profile to the sun"; *CPP*, pp. 46, 47). The poem continues with a series of enumerations that create a rhythm of expectation. And then all at once: "tal el cielo / ensartado en la tierra" ("thus the sky / strung to the earth"). That is, this enumeration is a demonstrative simile built upon diction. The second verse begins with "Mas sólo tú demuestras" ("But you alone . . . demonstrate"): that is, with a "but" that cuts the previous diction with its revision. In the following verse, there is a gerund, "obrando por el hombre" ("working for man"), and then the testimony "ví" ("I saw") and also "Yo

quisiera" ("I would like"), which are the signs of a freer discursiveness. And in the last verse, he states, "Y digo bolchevique" ("And I speak, Bolshevik"), which marks the self-referentiality of the poem with a characteristic gesture of this poetry. ("Digo, es un decir" ["I mean, it's just a thought"; *CPP*, pp. 266, 267], he later wrote in *Spain, Take This Cup from Me*.) Because there is no other way to remake dialogue but within the space of colloquy, a "you" is always included, which may be the reader, the poet himself, or a friend (Georgette Vallejo tells us that two times it is she); the dialogue becomes a system of external communication, where one "I" speaks to another "I."

In this book there are a series of communication splits, including one communication within another, and that is why this colloquy has a powerful resonance, a vibrant texture, that disturbs us with its immediacy and persuasion. In "Alfonso: estás mirándome, lo veo ("Alfonso: you keep looking at me, I see"), for example, the speaker is his dead friend. Perhaps the most important function of this colloquy is that of reestablishing not only dialogue but also a certain emotionality. It is for this reason that when the language of change—oxymorons, synecdoches, antithesis, and other baroque apparatus—does not have a possible resolution, colloquy comes forth to establish an alternative through pure exclamation, the opposite of babbling, telling about an indescribable whole.

The dialogue is dissolved into pure subjectivity in these fusions of colloquy: "¡Tanta vida y jamas! ¡Y tantos años, / y siempre, mucho siempre, siempre, siempre!" ("So much life and never! And so many years, / and always, much always, always, always!"; *CPP*, pp. 66, 67); "¡Entonces! . . . ¡Claro! . . . Entonces . . . ¡ni palabra!" ("Then! . . . of course! . . . Then . . . not a word!"; *CPP*, pp. 74, 75).

The language of interrogations also belongs to this order and is very strong in this book, to such an extent that there is a way to speak by questioning. Take, for example, these lines from "Un hombre está mirando a una mujer" ("A Man Is Looking at a Woman"; *CPP*, pp. 168, 169):

> *Pregúntome entonces, oprimiéndome*
> *la enorme, blanca, acérrima costilla:*

Y éste hombre
¿no tuvo a un niño por creciente padre?
¿Y este mujer, a un niño
por constructor de su evidente sexo?

I ask myself then, pressing down
my enormous, white, most pungent rib:
And this man
hadn't he had a child as a growing father?
And this woman, a child
as a builder of her evident sex?

This diction is curiously reminiscent of colloquy from the pulpit. Vallejo is the Spanish poet who has probably best internalized such diction, that grand tradition of speech that Anglo-Saxon poetry has used magnificently, from John Donne to T. S. Eliot.

The notion of historicity in *Human Poems* is based on the disruptive forms of the modern crisis as well as the solutions attempted by leftist political forces. Vallejo himself says, in "Al revés de las aves del monte" ("Contrary to the mountain birds"; *CPP*, pp. 198, 199):

Pues de lo que hablo no es
sino de lo que pasa en esta época, y
de lo que ocurre en China y en España, y en el mundo.

For what I am talking about is
nothing other than what is taking place in our time, and
what is taking place in China and in Spain and in the
world.

He then interjects the following statement as clarification: "Walt Whitman tenía un pecho suavísimo y res- / piraba y nadie sabe lo que él hacía cuando lloraba en su comedor" ("Walt Whitman had a very soft chest and breathed and nobody knows / what he was doing when he was crying in his dining room"). A large number of critics have missed the complexity of the poet, perceiving a sorrowful and anguished Vallejo, which is a simplification of the biographical and textual Vallejo. It would seem that he himself had already foreseen that confusion. When the poet says that he does not speak but of his time, he maintains that Walt Whitman was also speaking about his time, speaking even about grass, an element very present in this poetry. The poet establishes the comparison by antithesis: Whitman speaks about history by talking about grass, but no one knew about his personal pain; when the poet speaks about history he is not speaking about himself as a suffering being. In "En suma, no poseo para expresar" ("In short, I have nothing with which to express"; *CPP*, pp. 208, 209), Vallejo says:

Ello explica, igualmente, es-
tos cansancios míos y estos despojos, mis famosos tíos. Ello
*   explica*
en fin, ésta lágrima que brindo por la dicha de los hombres.

This equally explains this weariness of mine and these
   spoils, my
famous uncles. This explains, finally, this tear that I offer
   as a toast to the
happiness of men.

We do not have to deal with "I" as a biographical protagonist but rather with "I" as a poetic protagonist, as a space of exploration that will represent in its helplessness all the other men of the present historical moment who require a new dialogue. And in case any doubt remains, in "Aniversario" ("Anniversary"), the poet explicitly states, "¡Cuánto catorce ha habido en la existencia!" ("How much 14 there has been in existence!"; *CPP*, pp. 164, 165), and continues,

¿Que te diré ahora,
quince feliz . . . ?
. . . .
que no hay nadie en mi tumba
y que me han confundido con mi llanto.

What will I say to you now,
15 happy . . . ?
. . . .
that here is no one in my tomb
and that they have taken me for my crying!

In 1937, the year before his death, Vallejo wrote *Spain, Take This Cup from Me* during the most dramatic battles of the Spanish civil war, when the fate of the Republic also appeared to have consequences for the course of modern history. (For Vallejo—as revealed in the text of his final hymn— the same notions about humanity were being decided in the apocalyptic framework of the "just war.") For

CÉSAR VALLEJO

the Republic and for the modern consciousness, the war was not simply a drama about power and its new international distribution, nor was it just an ideological and political conflict. In Vallejo's book, war is above all a subversion of human nature itself. The tragic dimension of history bursts into the poetic text, inverting the natural order. Language can give an account of this agony of consciousness only by transgressing the orders of discourse in order to, going beyond victory or defeat, construct the extreme model of a text that expresses consciousness in rebellion. In this way, this radicalism of the subverted poetic discourse corresponds to the subversion of the natural order that war imposes and demands.

The speaker (the poet who lifts up a hymn to the Republic) and the volunteers of the Republic (the heroes of the people's war) lead in the drama of a collective discourse. For this reason, the dialogue with the "voluntario de España" (Spanish volunteer) at the beginning of the first "Himno a los voluntarios de la República" ("Hymn to the Volunteers for the Republic"), starts by setting forth the same breaking of that discourse, the agony of its nascent order:

> Voluntario de España, miliciano
> de huesos fidedignos, cuando marcha a morir tu corazón,
> cuando marcha a matar con su agonía
> mundial, no sé verdaderamente
> qué hacer, dónde ponerme; corro, escribo, aplaudo,
> lloro, atisbo, destrozo, apagan, digo
> a mi pecho que acabe, al bien, que venga,
> y quiero desgraciarme . . .

> Spanish volunteer, civilian-fighter
> with veritable bones, when your heart marches to die,
> when it marches to kill with its world-wide
> agony, I don't know truly
> what to do, where to place myself: I run, write, applaud,
> cry, glimpse, tear apart, they extinguish, I tell
> my chest to end, good, to come,
> and I want to ruin myself . . .
> (CPP, pp. 222, 223)

Not knowing what to do is also a question here, like the question of how to say. It supposes the perspective of the *doing/saying* as the birth of this new discourse. This is also alluded to by the title of the book, in which history replaces religion because the

dilemmas of death and meaning now occur in consciousness. And really, the event of death as meaning in history is what begins a mythic model in the text: *Dying/killing* are the violence of history, but their meaning lies in this universal character, because this is a battle in which human nature itself is redefined. That is why Vallejo has not created a discursive epic poem but instead a fragmentary epic, whose first drama is the text itself. *I write/I tell* constitutes an incorporation of the poet and his discourse into the event, and a sort of textual action is thus established. It is a discontinuous action that confers on the text the character of an unresolved and unlimited occurring.

Another sign that joins the poet to the event is his own elemental condition. "Descúbrome la frente impersonal hasta tocar / el vaso de la sangre" ("I bare my impersonal forehead until I touch / the vessel of blood"; *CPP*, pp. 222, 223), he says, and he identifies himself as a *cuadrumano* (quadrumane). This is also what unites event and discourse in a new logic of meaning at the end of the book. If event and discourse have distinguished the tragic character, sacrifice, and rending that history demands, they have also found in it an answer, the reconstruction of history as myth and of discourse as meaning. In this way, the consciousness that history adopts from poetry is formed in the transformation of both. Both history and poetry remake themselves by constructing an extreme text, an act of faith in which social utopia is also the return of language to its original power of naming. Beyond the same history, poetry produces its own historicity, which is also an extreme freedom:

> ¡Entrelazándose hablarán los mudos, los tullidos andarán!
> ¡Verán ya de regreso, los ciegos
> y palpitando escucharán los sordos!
> ¡Sabrán los ignorantes, ignorarán los sabios!
> ¡Serán dados los besos que no pudisteis dar!
> ¡Sólo la muerte morirá!

> Entwining one another the mutes will speak, the
>   paralyzed will walk!
> The blind, upon coming back, will see
> and throbbing the deaf will hear!
> The ignorant will be wise, the wise ignorant!
> Kisses will be given that you could not give!
> Only death will die!
> (CPP, pp. 226, 227)

The same human condition will therefore be remade in that world of promise that is also the end of this upside-down world and is its fulfilled side. However, rather than being the exact design of an alternative world, this utopic zone is a presence, itself of history. In other words, the future is not merely instructive. It is rather in the demands of the present of the "sufrimiento armado" ("armed suffering"), that the inexpressible future surrenders, in the first place, as a gain, as a transformation of language. Hence, the expressible hyperbolic irony of a discourse that is capable of producing this manifestation of absent meaning. For this reason, if the others "matan al libro, tiran a sus verbos auxiliares, / a su indefensa página primera!" ("kill the book, they fire at its auxiliary verbs, / at its defenseless first page!"), the poet demands that the volunteers "matad / a la muerte, matad a los malos!" ("kill / death, kill the bad people!") for "el analfabeto a quien escribo" ("the illiterate to whom I write"; *CPP*, pp. 228, 229). The same writing acts in this cosmic drama of language that rebuilds its function.

If the universal notion of the people, of popular elements as a source, emphasizes a decisive historicity in the book, it is because several textual series—which are like the horizon of reference over which this hymn is produced—interact in it. The series of definitions, for example, is a mechanism of expansion that surpasses the analogy of lyric poetry because it seeks to present, and not resolve, the definitions as contradictions. But at the same time, these antitheses, hyperboles, and metonyms from the baroque are the primary and basic elements that are going to form part of the likewise elemental confrontation in which nature, the human order, and history will play the lead. These are symbols that, converted into a sort of exasperated and disarticulated energy, will go on to form the dramatic configuration of the text.

The protagonists of the war are at the same time more than soldiers or historical figures, because the event returns them to their elemental origin, to their paradigmatic dimension. Spain is transformed into a mythic space. In its inner sphere a more extensive battle occurs. It is of a moral order (because in its history Good and Justice are decided) and of a universal nature (because man himself transforms his condition here). It is in this way that the militiaman

becomes the universal representation of the human *criatura* (creature) and that "he sacrifices himself," like Spain itself, in this apocalypse of history formed mythically. It is this evidence that sustains the identity gained from the *doing/saying*:

> (*Todo acto o voz genial viene del pueblo*
> *y va hacia él, de frente o transmitidos*
> *por incesantes briznas, por el humo rosado*
> *de amargas contraseñas sin fortuna.*)

(Every act or brilliant voice comes from common people
and goes toward them, directly or conveyed
by incessant filaments, by the rosy smoke
of bitter watchwords which failed.)

(*CPP*, pp. 224, 225.)

The protagonists, then, have been joined together in this logic of meaning: The popular condition is the elemental cause of the meaning, the organic life of a completed dialogue, in which the deeds of history and culture look for and recognize one another. At times that encounter occurs directly, at other moments through the drama of those symbols of a fire that sends *contraseñas* (passwords) in history.

But this mythic model is also a plot about tragedy and utopia. *Spain, Take This Cup from Me* acts in at least these three directions: it responds to the event and to its heroic and agonizing dimension; it generates a polyphonic text, in which the natural order and the order of language are deconstructed; and at the same time, it produces its own space of resolutions, in which history is transmuted into myth. With the materials of the tragedy, Vallejo writes a text about the end of time that responds to itself, transforming itself into a utopic alternative.

It is the paradigmatic condition of the "just war" that elicits this prophetic intonation of discourse. The peasant's word, says the poet, is "atada a un palo" ("tied to a stick"); that is, it is like the elemental flag of a radical rearrangement, because this battle will also move to remake meaning.

> ¡*Constructores*
> *agrícolas, civiles y guerreros,*
> *de la activa hormigueante eternidad:estaba escrito*
> *que vosotros haríais la luz, entornando*
> *con la muerte vuestros ojos;*
> *que, a la caída cruel de vuestras bocas,*

vendrá en siete bandejas la abundancia, todo
en el mundo será de oro súbito
y el oro
fabulosos mendigos de vuestra propia secreción de
  sangre,
y el oro mismo será entonces de oro?

Agricultural
builders, civilian and military,
of the active, swarming eternity: it was written
that you will create the light, half-closing
your eyes in death;
that, at the cruel fall of your mouths,
abundance will come on seven trays, everything
in the world will be of sudden gold
and the gold,
fabulous beggars for your own secretion of blood,
and the gold itself will then be made of gold!
                          (CPP, pp. 224, 225)

It was written, the poet says, that the omens of the past are converted into the promises of the future from the present time of subversion. Not in vain does Vallejo write these hymns, starting from the tradition of writing itself: from the Bible and its full discourse to the epic and its legendary diction, from the chronicle and its laconic recounting to the colloquy, the epistle, and the prayer for the dead. This building of the future, then, is stripped here of its role of written language, because it occurs in that text as a rending, and the figures are not a prolongation of the names but their fracture. On the other hand, the rhetorical devices that come from the Gospels and from certain psalmodic rhythms of the Bible are used here in the service of the *parabola* (parable) and the *salmo* (psalm) of the new "suaves ofendidos" ("offended gentle ones"), the "dibiles poderoses" ("powerful weak ones"), who are now the "muertos inmortales" ("immortal dead"); that is, these mechanisms present their resonance of certainty and promise to strengthen the new order of meanings. The notion of the people and popular elements is modernized in these "defendores de Guernica" ("defenders of Guernica"). The poor of the world are included in the drama: "Los mendigos pelean por Espana / mendigando en Paris, en Roma, en Praga" ("The beggars fight for Spain, / begging in Paris, in Rome, in Prague"; CPP, pp. 242, 243). The Spanish

combatants, such as the character Pedro Rojas, are also here as "representative[s] of everyone." In this way, a complex, intertextual dialogue has been produced beneath history. The popular notions of things, with their rich texture, dynamics, and materiality, are in the book the notional substratum of a discourse that leads all those resonances to this apocalypse of popular culture. At the end, as in another myth about origin, the word is surrendered to the children when the adult world disappears and the future holds the promise of a new beginning:

si tardo,
si no veis a nadie, si os asustan
los lápices sin punta, si la Madre
Espana cae—digo, es un dicer—
salid, niños del mundo; id a buscarla! . . .

if I am late,
if you don't see anyone, if the blunt pencils
frighten you, if Mother
Spain falls—I mean, it's just a thought—
go out, children of the world, go and look for her!
                          (CPP, pp. 268, 269)

The poetic work of Cesar Vallejo is one of the most exciting creative adventures of this century, not only because of the high quality of his formal skill and expressive elaboration but also because of his passion for knowledge from poetry, which is no longer a symbolist and traditional passion but modern and critical. As of Heraclitus, it may be said of Vallejo that what we understand is magnificent, and what we do not understand is, too. Happily, to read him is always to understand the powerful persuasion of his poetic truth.

Translated from the Spanish by Henry Thurston

SELECTED BIBLIOGRAPHY

Editions

Individual Works

El romanticismo en la poesía castellana. Trujillo, Peru, 1915.
Los heraldos negros. Lima, 1918.
Trilce. With a prologue by Antenor Orrego. Lima, 1922.

2nd ed. With a prologue by José Bergamín and a salutation by Gerardo Diego. Madrid, 1930.

Escalas melografiadas. Lima, 1923.

Fabla salvaje. Lima, 1923.

El tungsteno. Madrid, 1931.

Rusia en 1931: Reflexiones al pie del Kremlin. Madrid, 1931.

España, aparta de mí éste cáliz. Barcelona, 1939.

Poemas humanos (1923–1938). Edited by Georgette Vallejo. With notes by Luis Alberto Sánchez, Jean Cassou, and Raúl Porras Barrenechea. Paris, 1939.

El arte y la revolución. Lima, 1973.

Contra el secreto profesional. Lima, 1973.

Teatro completo. With a prologue, translations, and notes by Enrique Ballón Aguirre. 2 vols. Lima, 1979.

Collected Works

Obra poética completa. With a prologue by Américo Ferrari and notes by Georgette Vallejo. Lima, 1968.

Poesía completa. Barcelona, 1978.

Translations

César Vallejo: The Complete Posthumous Poetry. Translated by Clayton Eshleman and José Rubia Barcia. Berkeley, Los Angeles, and London, 1978.

César Vallejo: Selected Poems. Translated by H. R. Hays. Old Chatham, N.Y., 1981.

Spain, Let This Cup Pass from Me. Translated by Álvaro Cardona-Hine. Los Angeles, 1968.

Spain, Take This Cup from Me. Translated by Clayton Eshleman and José Rubia Barcia. New York, 1974.

Trilce. Translated by David Smith. New York, 1973.

Biographical and Critical Studies

Abril, Xavier. *Vallejo.* Buenos Aires, 1958.

Ballón Aguirre, Enrique. *Vallejo como paradigma.* Lima, 1974.

Coyné, André. *César Vallejo y su obra poética.* Lima, 1958.

_____. *César Vallejo.* Buenos Aires, 1968.

Escobar, Alberto. *Como leer a Vallejo.* Lima, 1973.

Espejo Asturrizaga, Juan. *César Vallejo: Itinerario del hombre.* Lima, 1965.

Ferrari, Américo. *El universo poético de César Vallejo.* Caracas, 1972.

Franco, Jean. *César Vallejo: The Dialectics of Poetry and Silence.* Cambridge and New York, 1976.

Flores, Ángel. *Aproximaciones a César Vallejo.* 2 vols. Long Island City, N.Y., 1971.

Higgins, James. *Visión del hombre y de la vida en las últimas obras poéticas de César Vallejo.* Mexico City, 1970.

Larrea, Juan. *César Vallejo o Hispanoamérica en la cruz de su razón.* Córdoba, Argentina, 1958.

Meo Zilio, Giovanni. *Stile e poesia in Cesar Vallejo.* Padua, 1960.

Monguió, Luis. *César Vallejo: Vida y obra.* New York, 1952.

Ortega, Julio. *César Vallejo.* Madrid, 1974.

_____. *La teoría poética de César Vallejo.* Providence, R.I., 1986.

Paoli, Roberto. *Mapas anatómicos de César Vallejo.* Florence, Italy, 1981.

Alfonsina Storni

(1892–1938)

Marjorie Agosin

Alfonsina Storni was one of Argentina's outstanding poets for over twenty years, from 1916, when she published her first book, to 1938, the year of her death. This was a time when Buenos Aires reverberated with creative fervor in all the arts, and particularly in poetry. During this watershed period, the one-thousand-year-old Spanish poetical tradition was carefully scrutinized; the newest trends, especially those from France, were examined and remodeled; all the baggage of the new century was examined for possibilities; and a new poetical idiom was forged, one that was distinctly American.

Even in this open and innovative atmosphere, Storni was always a rebel. Today we might call her Latin America's first feminist poet. Her major themes concerned women: their subservient position in a patriarchal society; the difficulty, if not impossibility, of love between men and women when women are subjugated; the need for more personal freedom and independence. More than any other poet, her life and her lyrics were one. In both, she was daring and audacious, ironic and witty, intelligent and determined. Because she lived as she wrote and wrote as she lived, she still strikes us as very modern.

Storni was born on 29 May 1892 in Sala Capriasca, a small village in the Italian part of Switzerland. In 1896 her family emigrated to Argentina and settled in the city of San Juan. While still a child, Alfonsina helped her mother do the sewing and needlework needed to supplement the family income. In 1907, when she was fourteen years old, she joined a theatrical company and toured with the group for a year, playing a number of different roles.

In spite of hard work, Alfonsina enjoyed a great deal of personal freedom and independence during her childhood. According to her own account she grew up free as an animal, running through the streets, exploring and amusing herself. By eighteen years of age, she had obtained a certificate as a primary-school teacher from the normal school of Coronda, and the next year she began teaching in Rosario.

The year 1912 was a crucial one for Storni: her son Alejandro Alfonso was born of an illicit liaison. Her biographers say that the only concern she had for the social consequences of her situation was the negative impact it would have if her married lover's identity were discovered. Her only regret was that she was forced to abandon her lover and to live more or less anonymously in Buenos Aires. It is not easy for us today to imagine the life of a young, unmarried mother in the Buenos Aires of 1912, long before women had the right to vote or were accorded any sexual or political independence. Nevertheless,

Storni made a life for herself and moreover wrote the major part of her vast poetical work there. As time went on, she was accepted into the intellectual community of Buenos Aires. One of her close friends was the writer Horacio Quiroga, the central figure of a lively literary group called Anaconda. Quiroga's suicide in 1937 had a tragic repercussion in the suicide of Storni herself a year later.

To earn a living, Storni worked at a succession of jobs, from sales clerk to director of a children's theater. At the same time she wrote poetry, published her books, and participated fully in the literary life of the city. Beginning in 1916, her literary work proceeded with tremendous vitality. She won a number of literary prizes, among them the First Municipal Prize, awarded in 1920 for her collection of poetry called *Languidez* (Languor).

A widely read poet, loved and admired, she contributed work to the most important journals of the city. However, she suffered periods of depression that finally impelled her to withdraw into a hermetic, inner world. In 1935 Storni had a radical mastectomy that took its toll psychologically. Three years later she feared the cancer had spread to her lungs and on 25 October 1938 she committed suicide by throwing herself into the same Mar del Plata that she had written about so obsessively in her later poems. She was forty-six years old.

Storni's tumultuous life opened the way for many other women poets in Latin America. A true pioneer in presenting feminine emotion in a direct and honest way, she expressed women's deep feeling of imprisonment within the circumstances of their lives, as in the poem "Hombre pequeñito" (Little Man) from *El duce daño* (Sweet Hurt, 1918):

> Hombre pequeñito, hombre pequeñito,
> suelta a tu canario que quiere volar . . .
> Yo soy el canario, hombre pequeñito,
> déjeme saltar.

> Little man, little man
> free your canary that longs to soar . . .
> I am the canary, little man,
> let me go.

Storni began writing during the Latin American postmodernist period, which began around 1910 and signified a rupture with the earlier modernist movement dominated by the nineteenth-century Nicaraguan poet Rubén Darío. The modernists had created a cult of the image in poetry, and had adopted an exotic and artificial poetical language. In contrast, the postmodernists chose to write about everyday life in direct language that was closer to speech.

At this time poetry written by women began to enjoy tremendous popularity, with the emergence of such major figures as Gabriela Mistral of Chile, and Delmira Agustini and Juana de Ibarbourou of Uruguay. Of this group, Storni was the most daring, the most resistant to the traditional role of women, a stance she expressed in intense, fiery poems.

Storni's work can be divided into two periods. The first consists of four volumes: *La inquietud del rosal* (The Restless Rose Garden, 1916); *El dulce daño; Irremediablemente* (Without Remedy, 1919); and *Languidez*. *Ocre* (Ocher, 1925) signaled the second phase and the real beginning of Storni's mature work. It was followed by *Mundo de siete pozos* (World of Seven Wells, 1934) and *Mascarilla y trébol* (Mask and Trefoil, 1938).

In the early books, male sexuality is depicted as aggressive but necessary in the relations between the sexes. Her second phase is radically different, for she portrays man in his metaphysical circumstance, removed from personal, amorous destiny. Poems such as "Hombres de la ciudad" (Men of the City), "El hombre" (Man), and "Los aludos" (The Winged Ones) illustrate this new view.

The collection *El dulce daño* shows Storni's true poetical vocation. It is a book that comes out of her personal sentiments and amorous anxieties. The lyrical voice is personal and dramatic as it speaks of the poet's condition as woman, of her adversities and avatars. Anxiety is portrayed in direct rather than in philosophical terms. Through the inner turmoil of these poems, we hear a strong voice speaking, demanding to be heard, asking for freedom, entangled as it is with forbidden love.

In the poem that forms part of the trilogy of texts centering around the image of the she-wolf, Storni defies the hostile world that surrounds her, forcing her to passively accept society's rules and rituals. In "La loba" (The She-Wolf), from *La inquietud del rosal*, she writes:

Yo soy como la loba,
Quebré con el rebaño
y me fuí a la montaña
fatigada de llano.

I am the she-wolf
I broke with the pack
went to live in the mountain
sick of the plain.

Beginning with *El dulce daño*, Storni wrote with a defiance that would become a trademark of her poetry, along with the use of colloquial language and a poetical world modeled on everyday experience. In her early books she used traditional poetical metrics and rhyme, but abandoned them later in favor of free verse.

From 1919 on, Storni's writing as a poet and as a feminist achieved increasing prominence. In leading newspapers and magazines, such as *La Nota, Nosotros,* and *La Nación,* she wrote about women's suffrage and discussed the concept of equal salaries for equal work. During the same period, she produced an intense, almost feverish outpouring of poetical works, publishing five books in eight years.

Beginning with *Ocre,* published five years after *Languidez,* Storni appears more resigned in the face of unfulfilled love and less vehement about social conventions. She is no longer the introspective writer reflecting only her own life and circumstances; now she is a poet taking part in the larger world, writing about areas removed from her experience. This new maturity and wider view is reflected in one of her most innovative and well-received collections, *Mundo de siete pozos.* In this book, Storni experiments with different styles, using free verse and line lengths that vary from a very brief one or two syllables to a long line consisting of fourteen syllables. It is interesting that in this experimental volume Storni should use the fourteen-syllable line, one of the most traditional forms of Spanish prosody.

The title poem of the book presents the image of the human head as a world of seven wells. The poet is no longer describing her feelings about the world but her conception of it. The tone of *Mundo de siete pozos* prevails throughout the rest of her work. Here Storni is a resigned woman, tranquil in her solitude. In addition to a growing number of images of the sea as a place of repose, there is also a growing fascination with the world of poetical fantasy; the reader can observe very clearly her gradual transition to an inner world, one that she increasingly inhabited until her death.

Mascarilla y trébol, Storni's last book, prefigures her suicide. In the brief prologue, she affirms her new lyrical direction, brought about by "fundamental psychic changes." The book contains poems in free verse but also a collection of sonnets she called "antisonnets," written in fourteen-syllable lines but unrhymed, showing the two sides of her poetry: the constant need for change and the adherence to traditional forms. As in *Ocre* and *Mundo de siete pozos,* she exhibits a fascination with objects evoked in an enigmatic and mythic way that expresses a sense of loss.

Among these revealing poems are some that explore in minute detail objects such as an ear, a tooth, a hen, and a teardrop, as if the poet felt the need to anchor herself in the microcosm of inanimate objects surrounding her. It is as though naming those objects made them real and enabled the poet to maintain her place in the world by means of the magical, liberating act of naming. Images of the sea and of death surface again, particularly in the poem "Rio de la Plata en lluvia" (Rio de la Plata in Rain), in which an image of the city sinking into the water appears. Again Storni expresses the desire to be united with the cosmic forces of the sea.

Mascarilla y trébol represents a psychic journey. It is almost a plea to return to the primeval earth, as in the poem "Voy a dormir" (I Am Going to Sleep), printed posthumously in the newspaper *La Nación* of Buenos Aires.

Voy a dormir, nodriza mía, acuéstame
Ponme una lámpara a la cabecera;
una constelación; la gue te guste;
todas son buenas; bájala un poquito.

I am going to sleep, dear nurse, lay me down
Put a lamp at my head;
a constellation; whichever one you like;
they're all good; lower the flame a little.

Storni also wrote a number of works for the theater. *El amo del mundo* (Master of the World),

741

which premiered on 10 March 1927, was not well received by either the critics or the public, and ran for only three days. Today we might call *El amo del mundo* a feminist play, since it advances the notion that women do not need men in order to find personal fulfillment. Among her better-known theatrical works are *Dos farsas pirotécnicas* (Two Pyrotechnical Farces, 1932), in which the central theme is again the liberation of women. Storni's plays are not considered important, but they are interesting because they reflect the preoccupations of her poetry.

Storni also wrote some children's plays, but these are minor works, written in the midst of other duties and without any serious literary pretensions. Also included among her minor publications is a collection of experiments in poetical prose, *Poemas de amor* (Love Poems, 1926), pieces filled with lyrical images. Here the author is no longer the deceived cynic but one who yearns for an amorous union like the one she enjoyed in her youth.

Two of the most important legacies of Storni's poetry are the absolute sincerity and the great courage that she consistently exhibited in her writing. She wrote of the concerns of a modern, independent woman, and her poetry took on all the anxieties of the epoch, with valor, urgency, and impetuosity. Storni was by turns aggressive and tempestuous toward and contemptuous of the hypocrisy of Buenos Aires society. She was also at times angry and disdainful, as in "¿Qué diría?" (What Would They Say), from *El dulce daño*:

> ¡Qué diría la gente, recortada y vacía,
> Si en un día fortuito, por ultra fantasía
> me tiñera el cabello de plateado y violeta?

What would they say the empty, cookie-cutter people
if on some day or other, in an excess of fantasy
I should dye my hair silver and violet?

In her early work, Storni fought off her demons by means of fierce denunciations and fine-honed sarcasm. But in later years she opted for a more hermetic and profound poetry, removed from earthly conflicts and concerns. It was typical of her that she would exercise her free will to the end and die as she had lived, on her own terms. Ever changing, she remained the same. The fearless young girl who ran free

as an animal through the streets of San Juan in search of life finally ran to embrace the sea, to embark on the adventure of death.

Translated from the Spanish by Cola Franzen

SELECTED BIBLIOGRAPHY

First Editions

Poetry

La inquietud del rosal. Buenos Aires, 1916.
El dulce daño. Buenos Aires, 1918.
Irremediablemente. Buenos Aires, 1919.
Languidez. Buenos Aires, 1920.
Poesías. Buenos Aires, 1923.
Ocre. Buenos Aires, 1925.
Poemas de amor. Buenos Aires, 1926.
Mundo de siete pozos. Buenos Aires, 1934.
Mascarilla y trébol. Buenos Aires, 1938.

Plays

El amo del mundo. Bambalinas (Buenos Aires) 9/470, 16 April 1927.
Dos farsas pirotécnicas. Buenos Aires, 1932.

Collected Works

Alfonsina Storni: Edición conmemorativa con ocasion de cumplirse el vigesimo quinto aniversario de su muerte. Buenos Aires, 1963.
Antología poética. Buenos Aires and Mexico City, 1938. 8th ed. 1946.
Antología poética. Buenos Aires, 1956. 11th ed. 1982.
Antología poética. Buenos Aires, 1968.
Obra poética. Buenos Aires, 1946. Reprinted 1952.
Obra poética. Buenos Aires, 1948.
Obra poética completa. Buenos Aires, 1961.
Obra poética completa. Buenos Aires, 1964.
Poesías. Buenos Aires, 1961.
Poesías sueltas. Buenos Aires, 1964.

Biographical and Critical Studies

Astrada de Terzaga, Etelvina. "Figura y significación de Alfonsina Storni." *Cuadernos hispanoamericanos* 71/211:127–144 (1967).
Carrera, Julieta. *La mujer in América escribe: Semblanzas.* Mexico City, 1956.

_____. "Tres poetisas argentinas." *Revista iberoamericana* 8/15:31–47 (1944).

Diego, Rafael de. "*Ocre.*" *Nosotros* 51/196:70–77 (1925).

Etchenique, Nira. *Alfonsina Storni*. Buenos Aires, 1958.

Fernández Morano, César. "Dos épocas en la poesía de Alfonsina Storni." *Revista hispánica moderna* 24/1:27–35 (1958).

Furness, Edna Lue. "A Woman and the World." *Western Humanities Review* 9/1:96–98 (1957).

Gómez Paz, Julieta. "Los antisonetos de Alfonsina Storni." *Cuadernos americanos* 51/3:224–232 (1950).

_____. *Leyendo a Alfonsina Storni*. Buenos Aires, 1966.

Jones, Sonia. *Alfonsina Storni*. Boston, 1979.

Nalé Roxlo, Conrado. *Genio y figura de Alfonsina Storni*. Buenos Aires, 1964.

Percas, Helena. *La poesía feminina argentina (1810–1950)*. Madrid, 1958.

Phillips, Rachel. *Alfonsina Storni: From Poetess to Poet*. London, 1975.

Talamantes, Florence. "Virginia Woolf and Alfonsina Storni: Kindred Spirits." *Virginia Woolf Quarterly* 1/3:4–21 (1973).

Titiev, Janice Geasler. "Alfonsina Storni's *Mundo de siete pozos*: Form, Freedom, and Fantasy." *Kentucky Romance Quarterly* 23/2:185–197 (1976).

Ugarte, Manuel. "El drama de Alfonsina Storni." *Repertorio americano* (San José, Costa Rica) 36/21:321–322 (1939).

Von Munk Benton, Gabriele. "Recurring Themes in Alfonsina Storni's Poetry." *Hispania* 33/2:151–153 (1950).

Graciliano Ramos

(1892–1953)

Maria Isabel Abreu

Graciliano Ramos' Alagoas is a small backwater state in the northeast of Brazil, where droughts occur periodically in the backlands (*sertão*). Along the coast there are reminders of the old sugar plantation culture that marked the birth of Brazilian society. This is a troubled land, riddled with poverty and violence. Ramos has transfigured the geography, the human sufferings, the harshness of nature, and the social problems of the region into a great art. Alagoas, especially the towns of Palmeira dos Índios, Viçosa, and the state capital, Maceió, are Ramos' own territory. His family had lived in this area since the eighteenth century, experiencing periods of both prosperity and destitution. Whether good or bad, times were always rough, with constant struggling against both natural and human elements. Drawing on family history and personal experiences, Ramos wrote his stories.

Graciliano Ramos was born in Quebrângulo, Alagoas, on 27 October 1892. Two years later, his family moved to Buíque, Pernambuco, where his father, Sebastião Ramos, bought a cattle ranch. Discouraged by sudden reverses in fortune caused by drought, he resumed his former occupation of shopkeeper in Buíque. A hardworking man, Sebastião Ramos succeeded in his business, saved some money, and raised a large family. After a few years, the family returned to Alagoas, first to Viçosa and then to Palmeira dos Índios.

Ramos' grandfathers, Tertuliano Ramos and Pedro Ferreira Ferro, were both landowners. Tertuliano Ramos, a timid old man, went bankrupt. Pedro Ferro, a man of stout determination, survived the dry seasons, sometimes prospering, sometimes despairing, but always courageously pursuing a dream of fortune that did not materialize.

Ramos, as he tells us in *Infância* (*Childhood*, 1945), was a very unhappy child. Acutely sensitive, he suffered under the brutal tyranny of his stern father and neurotic and at times violent mother. He writes:

> My father and mother remained large, fearful, unknown. I see again only fragments of them, wrinkles, angry eyes, irritated mouths without lips, hands—some rough and calloused, others fine and gentle, transparent. I hear knocks, shots, curses, and jingling of spurs, the stamping of shoes on worn bricks. . . . Fear. It was fear that guided me through my first years, real terror.
> ("Clouds," in *Childhood*, 1979, pp. 24–25)

As an adult, Ramos stated that his father had taken vengeance on his children for frustrations connected with his business and political activities. The child suffered blows and shouts without knowing why; the same action could be followed either by his parents' complacent grin or the most severe punishments. He believed that he was beaten because adults were strong and therefore had the right to strike children. The result was that Ramos became increasingly timid. He tried to shrink, to nullify himself, and continued like this throughout his life. Timidity is reflected in some of Ramos' characters—they lack self-assurance, have difficulty in communicating with others, and even prefer the company of animals. Luís da Silva in *Angústia* (*Anguish*, 1936) and Fabiano in *Vidas Secas* (*Barren Lives*, 1938) are good examples.

Ramos was as unhappy in school as he was at home. Ignorant and harsh teachers treated him with the same injustice and cruelty that he received from his parents. In Ramos' adult opinion, schools in his time only made children more ignorant. Owing to the poor system of education, Ramos at the age of nine was still illiterate and had no doubt that he was an idiot.

An extraordinary event changed Ramos' life. One evening, counter to all custom, his father ordered him to bring a book and read. "Chewing the words," writes the author, "stuttering, moaning a dreadful song, indifferent to punctuation, jumping and repeating lines, I reached the bottom of the page without hearing shouts. I stopped, surprised, I turned the page, and I dragged on moaning, like a car on a road full of holes" ("The Astronomers," in *Childhood*, p. 138). So unusual was his father's behavior that the boy thought perhaps he had collected some lost debt. His father explained that the book was a novel and summarized the part they had just read. It was the story of a couple with children in a forest, chased by wolves and wild dogs. He translated "in kitchen talk several literary expressions." The child was fascinated. So there was something hidden in the despicable pages of a book after all! This scene was repeated for two more evenings and on the fourth, the father dismissed the boy, leaving him in despair. Deeply disappointed, Ramos asked his little cousin Emília for help, but she encouraged him to read alone. He objected strongly, saying that he was an animal, that everybody thought he was too stupid, and that it was impossible for him to understand the difficult words in such a complicated order. He summoned courage, however, and tried. As Ramos writes, "And the parts that were clear shed a little

light on the obscure points. The small characters grew and slowly penetrated my thick intelligence. Slowly" ("The Astronomers," p. 140).

Then the problem was acquiring books. Ramos wanted to read not dull textbooks but those about adventure, justice, love, and vengeance. However, nothing more than newspapers, almanacs, and anecdotes that appeared in the old calendars were readily available. These bits and pieces of writing only increased his desire to read, which became an obsession. His attention turned toward the library of the public notary. He often walked up the steep street, just to look through the windows at the bookcases laden with beautifully bound works in brilliant colors. Approaching that learned man was surely an impossibility. But one day he knocked at the notary's door and asked whether he could borrow one of the books. A smiling notary handed him the novel *O Guarani* (The Guarani Indian, 1857), by José de Alencar, invited him to return, and placed the whole collection at his disposal.

In a few months, Ramos read every work in the library. Devouring the books in school or at his father's store, he lived in a fantasy world. "I remained in a state of disorder, sneaking out through the corners . . ." ("Jerônimo Barreto," in *Childhood*, p. 152). His habits and language changed. Everyday life appeared alien and distorted. The only reality was that of heroes, cities, and events in the books he read. Ramos stopped considering himself an inferior being. Because of this attitude people did not annoy him any longer but looked upon him as peculiar.

At the age of twelve Ramos began writing poetry and contributing to newspapers. Abhoring schools, he dropped out of high school and must be considered a self-educated man. From a very young age, he worked in his father's store, which had prospered considerably, and eventually was promoted to manager. After moving with his family to Palmeira do Índios, he left for Rio de Janeiro when he was twenty-two, finding work there as a journalist. Either because the adventure was not successful or because the bubonic plague had killed members of his family, he returned to Palmeira do Índios after less than a year and became his father's partner.

Shortly after, he married Maria Augusta de Barros, an old friend, and purchased the store from his father.

For many years, the future writer operated his business, and, at least apparently, he was not unhappy as he had been during his childhood. Hardworking, honest, and alert, he was successful as an entrepreneur. Since there were no bookkeepers in the city, he learned accounting in spite of his dislike of numbers. All his employees praised his capacity for organization and his sense of justice.

Yet his passion was literature. Even though he worked ten hours a day in his store, Ramos still found time for intellectual endeavors. He taught himself English, French, Latin, and Italian. Local newspapers counted on his ongoing contributions. Ramos followed literary developments in Brazil and abroad through constant correspondence with leading intellectuals and by reading the most important newspapers and new books of the day. In the 1920's the modernist movements greatly attracted his attention. His store became the center of intellectual life in Palmeira dos Índios. In the afternoon, friends and acquaintances belonging to the social and political elite of the city would bring stools and chairs to chat on the wide pavement in front of the store. These conversations were stimulated by the storekeeper's knowledge. Souza Lima, in *Graciliano Ramos em Palmeira dos Índios*, remarks that Ramos was so obsessed with books that his friends would say to him, "Look, man, forget this mania; otherwise you will finish in the Tamarineira [insane asylum in Recife]!" (ch. 14).

Ramos was also a teacher. He organized a private school for children and independent courses in Portuguese, mathematics, literature, and foreign languages. He tried in vain to avoid politics and public administration. Invited to be the mayoral candidate for the government party, he refused vehemently. But he finally agreed to run and became mayor of Palmeira dos Índios in 1928.

His wife, Maria Augusta, had died in 1920 giving birth to their fourth child, leaving Ramos devastated. When he became mayor, he married for the second time. His new wife, Heloísa Medeiros, was from Maceió, and they also had four children. After serving as mayor, Ramos was consecutively director of the State Printing Office (1930–33) and director of public instruction in Alagoas (1933–36).

As mayor of Palmeira dos Índios, Ramos wrote two

reports to the governor of Alagoas, unusual for their honesty and simple precision of language. Augusto Frederico Schmidt, poet and publisher in Rio de Janeiro, read by chance one of these reports and was so impressed that he correctly guessed Ramos must have a novel in a drawer. Indeed, Ramos had finished *Caetés* (The Caeté Indians) in 1928. The novel was published in 1933 by Schmidt's publishing house, and the next year *São Bernardo* (*São Bernardo*) appeared, immediately ranking the author among the greatest Brazilian novelists. *São Bernardo* is widely considered one of the most beautiful novels in Brazilian literature.

Following these achievements, less favorable days awaited Ramos. During Getúlio Vargas' government, after an abortive leftist insurrection in 1935, a dangerous period in Brazilian political life started. For any or no reason, one could be denounced and arrested. In 1936 Ramos, without explanation, was dismissed from his job, incarcerated, and sent to Rio de Janeiro in the crowded hold of a ship; for a year he was imprisoned without trial.

It was during this period that his third novel, *Anguish*, appeared, establishing once and for all the author's fame. *Anguish* was acclaimed as the greatest novel in Brazilian literature of any period. There was, however, a sentimental reason for the enthusiasm and affection with which the book was received. The author was in prison.

After almost one year of incarceration, Ramos was released in January 1937, with no more explanation than had been given for his arrest. His health ruined, he lived a sad and uncertain life in Rio de Janeiro. However, conditions slowly improved with the help of Ramos' many friends. Besides getting an editorial position at *Correio da Manhã* (Morning Post), in 1939, to his surprise, he was appointed federal inspector of education by the same government that had imprisoned him. In Rio he wrote *Barren Lives*, his last novel, and two biographies, *Childhood* and *Memórias do Cárcere* (Memories of Prison, 1953), the latter published posthumously.

Ramos' minor accomplishments include a collection of short stories, published first as *Dois Dedos* (Two Fingers, 1945) and later, in augmented form, as *Insônia* (Insomnia, 1947); *Viagem* (Journey, 1954), a description of his travels in Eastern Europe; *Linhas*

Tortas (Crooked Lines, 1962) and *Viventes das Alagoas* (People of Alagoas, 1962), posthumous collections of his contributions to periodicals; children's books like *A Terra dos Meninos Pelados* (The Land of Hairless Children, 1939), *Histórias de Alexandre* (Stories by Alexander, 1944), and "Pequena História da República" (Short History of the Republic, 1960); and *Brandão Entre o Mar e o Amor* (Brandão Between the Sea and Love, 1942), a novel written with four other authors (Jorge Amado, José Lins do Rêgo, Aníbal Machado, and Raquel de Queiroz).

In 1945 Ramos joined the Communist party. Some scholars state that his act seems to have been one of protest against the established order rather than a statement of Marxist convictions. Elected president of the Associação Brasileira de Escritores (Brazilian Writers' Association), he made a trip in this capacity to the Soviet bloc countries in 1952 to attend a literary convention in Moscow. Upon his return, he became very ill, was operated on, and died less than a year later, on 20 March 1953.

Ramos' books have been reprinted in many editions and have been translated into English and many other languages. Versions of some of them were adapted for television and films. American and European scholars have written extensively on Ramos. He is recognized in this country, especially among Latin Americanists, as a great novelist, ranking with the most important European and American writers of this century, including Ernest Hemingway, William Faulkner, John Dos Passos, and Jean-Paul Sartre. Ramos' self-criticism, however, was usually negative. When I told him once that I had not read some of his books, he replied with a shrug of his shoulders, "Don't waste your time. They are worth nothing."

It is worthwhile to study Ramos' major works one at a time—summarize the story, sort out the theme, and indicate the method of narration. In *Caetés*, João Valério, the narrator, is writing a novel about the Caeté Indians, who lived in Alagoas at the time of Brazil's discovery by the Portuguese. João Valério is a young clerk in a store in Palmeira dos Índios, owned by the elderly Adrião Teixeira and his brother. In love with Luísa, Adrião's attractive young wife, he becomes her lover during her husband's absence. Adrião, learning about the affair, commits suicide. João Valério and Luísa then discover that they no longer have any interest in each other and they part. João Valério also abandons his novel, with the realization that he cannot understand the Indian mind. He further begins to feel that the society of Palmeira dos Índios is as cannibalistic as the Caetés. João Valério marries a young woman well placed in Palmeira dos Índios society.

The story includes a satirical chronicle of Palmeira dos Índios. Like the former inhabitants of the place, the Caeté Indians, the present residents are in a way also cannibals. The notary, the pharmacist, the priest, and others, lacking intelligence and an objective in life, just follow dull routines. To avoid the dullness of their everyday duties, they occupy themselves with gossip. As Richard Mazzara observes in *Graciliano Ramos*, "they do not seem to perceive that as they tear and are torn apart, the monster that they have created that is their culture is swallowing them up" (ch. 2).

This novel is worth reading, although it is not considered to be on the same level as Ramos' later books. It is a literary piece influenced by José Maria Eça de Queiroz and his master, Gustave Flaubert, but it represents a high achievement for a first novel. The book reveals that the author had learned a lesson from the great masters and that he was ready to start his own work. In *Caetés*, Ramos already discloses the literary processes that will characterize his art.

São Bernardo is set in Viçosa, where Ramos spent a great part of his childhood. The town and its environs had reputedly the highest rate of crime in Brazil. The small farm owners generally were eliminated by the rich landowners—either by assassination or by political and economic pressure. Only the strongest and the cruelest survived. The story, describing the life of Paulo Honório, develops in this atmosphere.

Paulo narrates his past in a state of mental turmoil. He was born to unknown parents. While still very young, he was a blind man's guide; later he was looked after by an old black woman, Margarida, who sold candies on the street. His life of hardship makes him a man of unusual drive and remarkable will, but brutal and unscrupulous. His greatest aspiration is to become the owner of São Bernardo, the plantation where he was once a laborer. Paulo Honório wants the property not out of avarice, but because, for him, humanity is divided between men of property and wretches. Through the most vicious means, including murder, he achieves his end, becoming the wealthy master of a large estate, São Bernardo.

In order to have an heir, Paulo Honório decides to marry. Although he likes his pretty young wife, he regards her as just another piece of property. A schoolteacher, intelligent, and compassionate, Madalena is quite different from her husband, and their life together is unhappy. A permanent and violent conflict develops between them, as Paulo is dominated by groundless jealousy. Life becomes so intolerable for Madalena that she commits suicide. Paulo only then realizes that he really loved his wife, and the world loses its meaning for him. In order to fill his empty days and to alleviate his restless soul, he decides to write his memoirs.

It is difficult to imagine a literary work more reduced to the essential. The paragraphs are concise, the sentences short. Ramos, through the protagonist, explains his own technique: "This is the method I have adopted. I select certain elements from a situation; what remains is waste" (Scott-Buccleuch trans., ch. 13). This technique makes the narrative more forceful.

In Anguish, considered by some Ramos' masterpiece, the narrator, Luís da Silva, tells his story and at the same time projects his paranoia, which is driving him to madness. The setting is coastal Maceió, but Luís often takes the reader to the backlands of Alagoas. Luís is a timid, frustrated young civil servant with literary ambition. He writes articles, but considers them rubbish. Luís falls in love with a neighbor, Marina. They become engaged, and Luís is reduced to destitution when he buys her a wedding ring and a trousseau. Marina then leaves him for Julião Tavares, who has everything that Luís hasn't: money, social position, arrogance, euphoria, and lack of scruples. When Julião abandons Marina because she is pregnant, Luís decides to murder his rival. The idea comes gradually and slowly develops into an obsession, until one day Luís strangles Julião. The book ends with a masterful portrayal of Luís' delirium.

Ramos employs the technique of the interior monologue. In the long, seldom-interrupted soliloquy, Luís' deranged mind confuses memories of the several phases of his life and places where he has lived. The narrative, however, is not as fluent as in Caetés and São Bernardo. It is built in fragments coming and going from present reality to memories of the past to hallucination. This gives the narrative great dramatic intensity.

In the opinion of several critics, Anguish resembles Sartres's Nausea. In both stories, we observe the constant emerging of the past, earlier events presented as if they were happening now. We also get a sense of the decay of civilization. Since Anguish was published before Nausea, there is no possibility that Ramos was influenced by Sartre. Ramos' and Sartre's work are similiar because both read Fyodor Dostoyevski and were influenced by the Russian writer.

In Barren Lives, Ramos turns to the impoverished inhabitants of the backlands. The story presents a cycle in the life of a herdsman and his family, from their arrival at a ranch as drought refugees to their flight from the same ranch. Their life is squalid, and as if to underscore their poverty and simplicity, the characters do not have full names and the boys have none. They are called only Fabiano, Sinhá (Miss) Vitória, the two boys, and the dog Baleia. It is interesting to notice that the dog has a name but the boys do not. Having very few ideas to transmit, the family is generally silent. Their rare communications are made by gestures and interjections.

While on the ranch, Fabiano is exploited by the landowner, who, besides paying very little, cheats his employee, causing the family to live in miserable conditions. In the neighboring town, Fabiano is abused by the police, specifically by the "yellow soldier," who, for no reason, insults him and throws him into jail, where he is tortured. Fabiano later encounters the soldier in the caatinga (scrub forest), where he could easily kill the trembling wretch. But in the caatinga, Fabiano is so strong and the soldier so weak that he lets him go.

In spite of all adversity, the family lives almost happily. The children have food and they all love the land and the cattle under their care. They have few desires. Sinhá Vitória's only ambition is to sleep in a real bed, but she knows that this is an impossible dream. They are happy in their misery. But another drought comes and the family departs again in search of a better life. The last sentence of the novel reads: "And to the city from the backland would come ever more and more of its sons, a never ending stream of strong, strapping brutes like Fabiano, Vitória, and the two boys" ("Flight," in *Barren Lives*).

In several ways, *Barren Lives* is similar to John Steinbeck's *Grapes of Wrath*. In both novels, the families are fleeing hunger and are treated unjustly by the authorities. In both, criticism of the social system is the basis of the narrative.

This is the only novel in which Ramos substitutes the third person for the first, as in his short stories. Yet he still writes from the point of view of one character. *Barren Lives* is Ramos' last novel; he decided to devote the major literary efforts of his last years to biography.

Childhood, although a memoir, reads like fiction because of its poetic quality. One of the most beautiful aspects of this book is the child's gradual discovery of the world enclosed in shadows and clouds. The opening paragraph reads:

> The first thing that remained in my memory was a glazed china vase, filled with pitomba fruit, hidden behind a door. I don't know where I saw it, or when, and if part of this remote event hadn't ebbed into a later time, I would have to consider it a dream.

Little by little, the child gets to know people and his surroundings. Some human figures emerge whose images would last a lifetime. There were the grandfathers, especially on the maternal side; there was José Baía, a ranch hand and the child's best friend, who sat him on his knee, sang to him, and swung him in the air; there was "the rascal José," a slave's grandson, raised by Ramos' family; the dark face of Miss Leopoldina, the faithful maid, and her large earrings; and above all, there was the memory of Ramos' parents—the father unpredictable and stern, the mother distant and angry. It was a very confusing world, full of disappointments. Ramos' first contacts with "justice" were unfavorable. Once—he was four or five years old—his father whipped him mercilessly because his broad belt was missing. A few minutes later, the father noticed that he himself had dropped the belt under the hammock. On another occasion, when his father was a substitute judge, the boy witnessed him ordering the arrest of an old beggar for the crime of asking for charity at the judge's house. "I

believe that the jailing of Venta-Romba . . ." writes Ramos, "must have contributed to the distrust that authority inspires in me" ("Venta-Romba," in *Childhood*, p. 159).

The episodes evoked by Ramos tend to confirm the pessimism that underlies his work. At home, in school, in the neighborhood, everywhere, he found brutality and injustice. *Childhood*, however, also portrays good people—Ramos' grandparents, his cousin Emília, a gentle schoolteacher, José Baía, the notary, an eccentric and kindhearted postmaster, and others—who were sympathetic and helped him to become a great writer. The book is extremely important for the interpretation of Ramos' work, since a great part of the author's fiction is based on the events and people of his childhood.

Memórias do Cárcere, published posthumously, is incomplete. Like *Childhood*, this book sheds light on Ramos' fiction. The reader notices that many of the author's personal traits and experiences found in the memoirs are infused into his novelistic characters. As the title indicates, it consists of Ramos' memories of his incarceration. In spite of his sufferings and his abhorrence of the humiliations to which his fellow inmates and he were subjected, the narrative does not reveal any self-pity or regret for the loss of freedom. It even evinces a certain gratitude for the opportunity to live in the company of types from all walks of life and to witness aspects of the human condition that he would never have encountered in his petit bourgeois life.

In *Memórias*, Ramos depicts his process of discovering man. He is constantly surprised by the kindness and solidarity displayed by officers, jailers, and other prisoners. For example, the excellent Captain Lobo, besides doing everything to diminish the hardship of prison life for him, also offers to lend him money. For the pessimist Ramos, always expecting the worst from people, this was an extraordinary occurrence. Life during his incarceration would reveal other similar peculiarities, making him aware of unexpected qualities in man. "Certainly," writes Ramos, "misfortune teaches a great deal; without it I would still judge humankind incapable of true nobility."

Social protest is the basis of Ramos' work. He is not a painter of what he finds before his eyes; he is partial to portraying man pitted against society, organized authority, and official values. Psychological analysis, regarded by some scholars as his primary interest, is, in our view, a means for him of attacking the social system. From his protagonists' interior monologues it is evident that he finds the fate of the outcasts utterly abhorrent and that he feels a deep aversion to the class of landowners, businessmen, and politicians. *Anguish*, for example, is considered his great psychological novel, and it indeed discloses the gradual deterioration of Luís da Silva's mind. However, the narrative fundamentally analyzes the inequitable social conditions in which Luís has lived. In *São Bernardo*, the same spirit of protest is found in Paulo Honório's monologues. The landowner reflects: "To be honest, I must say that I have no sympathy for these wretches. I'm sorry for the situation they find themselves in, and admit that I am partly to blame, but I don't go beyond that. There is such a gulf between us!" (ch. 37). For Ramos, this is the attitude of the rich in bourgeois society.

The author's ideals of equality were inspired by the scenes of injustice that he witnessed as a child. The feelings of contempt that dominated him since childhood are the essential element in his work. His collection of failed people live in constant dissatisfaction. Happiness is an impossibility. If the poor suffer because of destitution, the acquisition of riches does not make them less unhappy, as is clear in Paulo Honório's meditation:

> If I'd carried on scouring old mother Margarida's copper pot for her, she and I would have led a peaceful existence. . . . My ambitions would be confined within a limited circle. I should have no great worries and make an enemy of no man. And in the winter mornings . . . I'd have a nip of rum to keep out the cold and sing my way along the roads as carefree as a beggar.
>
> (ch. 36)

Paulo Honório imagines that everything would be different if he could begin his life again, but then he realizes that man is unable to defeat external forces. Indeed, Ramos believes that the environment exercises complete control over the individual. Paulo Honório's society is responsible for his crimes, for only from them could he obtain wealth and respect. Being controlled by his milieu, man is neither bad nor good; he cannot distinguish between virtue and evil. Luís da Silva, in *Anguish*, says:

> If the old man wished to suppress a neighbouring landowner, he called José Bahia, the laughing comrade who told me stories of jaguars on the veranda, settled the business with half-words, and gave him some money. And he would remain tranquil in his sandals, shirt, and cotton drawers, taking snuff, his dragging feet straddling the hammock on the varnished verandas.
>
> (L.C. Kaplan trans., pp. 157–158)

As to José Bahia, "No remorse. It was necessity. No thought. The master, who gave the order, must have had his reasons. . . . José Bahia was a good fellow" (p. 212).

The themes in Ramos' fiction reveal his bitterness toward his society, yet he depicts it with consummate art. Ramos was a master of style. Always scrupulous with respect to grammatical precision, correct terminology, economy and clarity, his language is sober and pure. Sobriety is indeed one of the key characteristics of Ramos' writings. His aim was to obtain maximum effect with minimum verbiage. His sentences and paragraphs are short, and descriptive adjectives and adverbs are used sparsely. He avoids melodramatic descriptions even for very dramatic situations. In *Barren Lives*, instead of presenting a large-scale picture of the drought, he suggests it through details, such as the vultures circling in to peck out the eyes of dying creatures. Despising flowery language but greatly concerned with high standards of literary expression, Ramos always worked to restore significance to traditional rhetoric and, after modernism, to reestablish the prestige of literary language. Consequently, he opposed the modernist notion that literature should adopt the common man's language.

In all his major works with the exception of *Barren Lives*, the writer uses the first person narrative. The perspective is thus subjective, limited to the narrator-protagonist. There are two levels of events: those which take place outside and those occurring inside the narrator's consciousness. The sequence of these two planes apparently does not follow any pattern and they alternate freely.

Ramos based his fiction upon observations and reminiscences. He used to say that he had no capacity to create. Very well acquainted with his region and with the character of its inhabitants, he uniquely portrays the spirit of the Brazilian Northeast. Several of his characters were drawn from the author's life, and some reveal striking similarities to the author himself. In *Anguish*, many of the characters are drawn from the author's life. Luís da Silva's grandfather is like Graciliano's; the henchman, José Baía, the soldier José da Luz, the Jewish revolutionary Moisés, all existed in Ramos' life. Some of the criminal and political prisoners of *Memórias do Cárcere* are characters in Ramos' short story collection *Insônia*. Also early experiences, recounted in *Childhood*, were incorporated into his fiction. João Valério, Paulo Honório, and Luís da Silva, like their creator, are writers who dislike artificial and inflated prose. Like Ramos, Paulo smokes and drinks coffee while he writes, Luís da Silva disdains his productions, and João Valério cannot write except from firsthand experience with his subject. Fabiano has Ramos' *sertanejo* (countryman) moods. He and Luís are as introspective and isolated as the writer. H. Pereira da Silva tells us that he once heard the following surprising confession from the novelist concerning his projection into his literary work: "Fabiano acts in the book pages as I would behave in life if I were in his place, as he and other characters are basically psychological fractions of myself."

Descriptions of nature are employed sparingly and usually have a purpose. His landscape in many instances projects the protagonist's inner feelings. In *Caétes* we find, for example, this passage:

Hills to the left, close and green; hills to the right, distant and blue; hills in the back, very far and white, almost invisible in the vicinity of the San Francisco River. I lit a cigarette and imagined somberly that something in that landscape inhabited me: a vast plateau encircled by mountains.

(ch. 17)

In *São Bernardo*, Paulo Honório conveys the great joy of his wedding day through São Bernardo's scenery. Information on the ceremony is limited: "Father Silvestre married us before the altar of St. Peter in the chapel at São Bernardo." However, this paragraph follows:

It was the end of January. The bignonia scattered its yellow blossom over the woods; in the morning the hilltops were hidden in mist; the little stream gurgled like a river after the recent thunderstorms, and covered itself with foam as it jumped the falls before joining the lake.

(ch. 17)

After Madalena's death, the landscape pictures grow more bleak: "The garden, the vegetable plot, the orchard are abandoned, the Peking ducks dead, the cotton and the castor beans withering away. . . ." (ch. 36).

Ramos' world is unjust and cruel. We see outcasts, beggars, impoverished workers, and abused children; we also see sordid exploitation, a corrupt press, political dishonesty. But in this pessimistic vision of life, we sense a desperate desire for liberation, an intense longing for a purified and more balanced society. Ramos seems to be making a plea for social revolution.

This is a controversial point—some of Ramos' critics do not believe that in his skepticism he has any hope for improving human conditions. For these scholars, Ramos' world is damned and cannot be made better by social reform. All concur, however, that this great master of the art of writing, through his sober and classic style, has uniquely portrayed the somber universe of evil in which man struggles. Otto Maria Carpeaux in "Visão de Graciliano Ramos" expresses well the double meaning of Ramos' writing: on one hand, there is his revolutionary socialism tending toward anarchism, which derives from his sociopolitical convictions; on the other hand, this very anarchism, sublimated, builds on the devastated earth a new world—the world of artistic creation.

SELECTED BIBLIOGRAPHY

First Editions

Novels

Caetés. Rio de Janeiro, 1933.
São Bernardo. Rio de Janeiro, 1934.
Angústia. Rio de Janeiro, 1936.
Vidas Secas. Rio de Janeiro, 1938.
Brandão Entre o Mar e o Amor. In collaboration with Jorge

Amado, José Lins do Rêgo, Aníbal Machado, and Raquel de Queiroz. Rio de Janeiro, 1942.

Short Stories

Dois Dedos. Rio de Janeiro, 1945.
Histórias Incompletas. Porto Alegre, 1946.
Insônia. Rio de Janeiro, 1947.
Histórias Agrestes. Selected and with a preface by Ricardo Ramos. São Paulo, 1960.

Memoirs

Infância. Rio de Janeiro, 1945.
Memórias do Cárcere. 4 vols. Rio de Janeiro, 1953.

Nonfiction

Viagem. Rio de Janeiro, 1954.
Linhas Tortas. São Paulo, 1962.
Viventes das Alagoas. São Paulo, 1962.
Cartas. 3rd, rev. ed. São Paulo, 1982.

Children's Books

A Terra dos Meninos Pelados. Rio de Janeiro, 1939.
Histórias de Alexandre. Rio de Janeiro, 1944.
"Pequena História da República." *Senhor* 3:64–68 and 4:63–67 (1960).

Collected Works

Obras Completas. 10 vols. São Paulo, 1961.

Translations by Ramos

Washington, Booker. *Memórias de um Negro.* Rio de Janeiro, 1940.
Camus, Albert. *A Peste.* Rio de Janeiro, 1950.

Translations

Anguish. Translated by Lewis C. Kaplan. New York, 1946. Reprinted 1972.
Barren Lives. Translated and with an introduction by Ralph Edward Dimmick. Austin, Texas, 1965, 1973.
Childhood. Translated by Celso de Oliveira, with an introduction by Ashley Brown. London, 1979.
São Bernardo. Translated by R. L. Scott-Buccleuch. London, 1975.

Biographical and Critical Studies

Abreu, Maria Isabel. "O Protesto Social na Obra de Graciliano Ramos." *Hispania* 48/4:850–855 (1965).

Bosi, Alfredo. *História Concisa da Literatura Brasileira.* 3rd ed. São Paulo, 1981.
Brasil, Assis. *Graciliano Ramos.* Rio de Janeiro, 1969.
Candido, Antonio. *Ficção e Confissão: Ensaio Sobre a Obra de Graciliano Ramos.* Rio de Janeiro, 1956.
Carpeaux, Otto Maria. "Visão de Graciliano Ramos." In *Origens e Fins.* Rio de Janeiro, 1943. Pp. 339–351.
———. "Graciliano Ramos." In *Pequena Bibliografia Crítica da Literatura Brasileira.* 3rd ed. Rio de Janeiro, 1964. Pp. 316–318.
Castello, José Aderaldo. "Aspectos da Formação e da Obra de Graciliano Ramos." In *Homens e Intenções.* São Paulo, 1960.
Chistóvão, Fernando Alves. *Graciliano Ramos: Estrutura e Valores de um Modo de Narrar.* Rio de Janeiro, 1975.
Coelho, Nelly Novaes. "Solidão e Luta em Graciliano Ramos." In *Tempo Solidão e Morte.* Sao Paulo, 1964.
Cunha, Antônio C. R. "Graciliano Ramos: An Annotated Bibliography." Master's thesis, San Diego State College, 1970.
Ellison, Fred P. "Graciliano Ramos." In *Brazil's New Novel: Four Northeastern Masters.* Berkeley and Los Angeles, 1954. Pp. 111–132.
Feldman, Helmut. *Graciliano Ramos: Reflexos de Sua Personalidade na Obra.* Fortaleza, Brazil, 1967.
Gonçalves, Floriano. "Graciliano Ramos e o Romance." Introduction to *Caetés.* 2nd ed. Rio de Janeiro, 1947.
Hamilton, Russell G. "Character and Idea in Ramos' *Vidas Secas.*" *Luzo-Brazilian Review* 5/1:86–92 (1968).
Hays, R.H. "The World's Sorrow." *New Republic* (New York), 17 June 1946.
Lima, Luís Costa. "A Reificação de Paulo Honório." In *Por que Literatura.* Petrópolis, 1966.
Lima, Valdemar de Souza. *Graciliano Ramos em Palmeira dos Índios.* 2nd ed. Rio de Janeiro, 1980.
Lucas, Fábio. "Tratavam-nos até muito bem." In *Horizontes da Crítica.* Belo Horizonte, Brazil, 1965. Pp. 60–67.
Malard, Letícia. *Ensaio de Literatura Brasileira: Ideologia e Realidade em Graciliano Ramos.* Belo Horizonte, Brazil, 1976.
Martins, Wilson. In *The Modernist Idea.* Translated by Jack E. Tomlins. New York, 1971. Pp. 300–306.
Mazzara, Richard A. *Graciliano Ramos.* New York, 1974.
———. "New Perspectives on Graciliano Ramos." *Luso-Brazilian Review* 5/1:93–100 (1968).
Mourão, Rui. *Estruturas: Ensaio sobre o Romance de Graciliano.* Belo-Horizonte, Brazil, 1969.
Pinto, Rolando Morel. *Graciliano Ramos: Autor e Ator.* Assis, São Paulo, 1962.

Pólvora, Hélio. *Graciliano, Machado, Drummond e Outros.* Rio de Janeiro, 1975.

Puccinelli, Lamberto. *Graciliano Ramos: Relações Entre Ficção e Realidade.* São Paulo, 1975.

Ramos, Clara. *Mestre Graciliano: Confirmação Humana de uma Obra.* Rio de Janiero, 1979.

Silva, H. Pereira da. *Graciliano Ramos: Ensaio Crítico Psicoanalítico.* Rio de Janeiro, 1950.

Sovereign, Marie F. "Pessimism in Graciliano Ramos." *Luzo-Brazilian Review* 7/1:57–63 (1970).

Torres-Rioseco, Arturo. "Graciliano Ramos." *Cuadernos Americanos* 12/71:281–288 (1953).

Vieira, David. "Wasteland and Backlands: John Dos Passos' *Manhattan Transfer* and Graciliano Ramos' *Angústia.*" *Hispania* 65/3:377–383 (1984).

Vicente Huidobro

(1893–1948)

Merlin H. Forster

Vicente Huidobro was one of the prime movers in the establishment of an iconoclastic avant-garde in Spanish-American literature, which in the second and third decades of the twentieth century sought to overcome the complacent conventionalities into which the preceding modernist movement had fallen. The Chilean poet and theorist is the earliest and perhaps the most international of the major Latin American figures, and his work the single oeuvre that best ties together avant-garde developments in France, Spain, and Latin America during his era.

Born in Santiago on 10 January 1893, Vicente García Huidobro Fernández grew up in a wealthy and aristocratic Chilean family, where his early inclinations toward literature and intellectual pursuits were very much encouraged. As a boy, he spent time in Europe, but he finished his secondary studies in a private Catholic school in Santiago. His first creative works were published well before he was twenty, and his essays soon began to be seen in the pages of literary journals. He was bright, well prepared, rich, and anything but humble: "Very soon in my early years," Huidobro himself observed from the vantage point of 1926,

I saw that my entire artistic life could be expressed on a scale of ambitions. When I was seventeen years old I said: I want to be the leading poet of America; after several more years I thought: I want to be the leading poet in Spanish. As time went on my ambitions grew and I said: it is necessary to be the leading poet of the century.

(*Obras completas*, vol. 1, pp. 705–706)

In 1916 Huidobro traveled to Buenos Aires, where he gave a lecture on the new theories of *creacionismo* that he was developing and arranged for the publication of a slim volume of poems entitled *El espejo de agua* (The Water Looking-Glass, 1916). He then went on to wartime Paris, where he quickly put himself in contact with such leading figures as Guillaume Apollinaire and Pierre Reverdy. He soon began to write and publish in French, in spite of what he later admitted was an insufficient command of the language, and he collaborated over the next several years in such Parisian avant-garde journals as *Sic*, *Nord-Sud*, and *L'Esprit nouveau*. Immediately following the end of the war, Huidobro traveled widely in Europe—and even returned on occasion to his native country—speaking, writing, and arguing passionately in support of his ideas on the new literature. In 1918, for example, he was in Madrid, where he served as an important nexus linking developments in France to those in Spain, connections that were apparent in both his personal life-style and the poetic works that

755

he began producing in Spanish at that time. Guillermo de Torre, one of Huidobro's earliest and most passionate critics, recalls the Chilean's stay in Madrid in the following terms: "I heard from Huidobro for the first time some of the truly significant names that would later define the dawning of a new epoch. In his home I saw the first books and journals from the schools that would thereafter give such bounteous and controversial harvests" (*Guillaume Apollinaire*, Buenos Aires, 1946, p. 20).

Huidobro's intense apostleship for *creacionismo* and a new literary expression waned somewhat after 1925. Over the next two decades he involved himself in a number of political and cultural activities, though at the same time he kept up a rapid pace of literary production and never really set aside his conviction of his own primacy. In a 1939 interview, for example, Huidobro responded to a question about illustrious past poets with this comment: "The poetry that interests me the most begins with my own generation, and speaking even more clearly, I will say that it begins with me" (quoted in René de Costa, *Vicente Huidobro y el creacionismo*, p. 84).

During World War II, Huidobro was actively involved in several of the European campaigns. According to Cedomil Goić, he held the rank of captain under the command of General de Lattre de Tassigny and was the first Spanish-speaking officer to enter Berlin with the Allied forces in 1945. Huidobro claimed to have taken as booty Hitler's private telephone, and he took great pride in exhibiting it in the months following the close of hostilities. He sustained a head wound in battle, and his death on 2 January 1948, at Llolleo, his family estate south of Cartagena, Chile, was apparently a delayed result of that injury.

For more than sixty years Vicente Huidobro has been a highly controversial literary figure, against whom Juan Jacobo Bajarlia could seriously assert that there had been a critical *leyenda negra* (black mark) and whom Julio Caillet Bois could omit without so much as a mention from his extensive 1958 anthology of Spanish-American poetry. During Huidobro's lifetime most critical commentary was impressionistic and highly emotional, taking as a central focus Huidobro's arrogant personality or his often tendentious manifestos and lectures. Examples might be the

chapters on *creacionismo* in Guillermo de Torre's 1925 book on the literary avant-garde (*Literaturas europeas de vanguardia*, Madrid, 1925, pp. 87–95), or Arturo Torres Ríoseco's terse 1942 evaluation:

> In speaking of Spanish-American poetry, one cannot avoid mentioning Vicente Huidobro, poetically a third-rate talent, but at the same time a writer who has achieved wide notoriety for his literary manifestos. . . . He gave expression to poetical theories that attracted wide attention, but his creative work was not able to maintain his reputation.
>
> (*The Epic of Latin American Literature*,
> Berkeley and Los Angeles, 1959, p. 125)

Since the 1950's, criticism has moved toward a more careful assessment of Huidobro's theories and literary production. The publication in 1964 of his *Obras completas*, in two volumes and with an insightful introductory essay by Braulio Arenas, was a boon to serious study, as was the extensive 1975 bibliography (with 1979 addendum) compiled by Nicholas Hey. A number of excellent articles and books have been published in the last twenty years or so, all of which recognize the vagaries of a very difficult personality but at the same time concentrate on careful documentation and study of someone now perceived to be a major presence in the development of twentieth-century Spanish-American literature.

Creationist Theory

Over several decades and in a number of lectures, commentaries, and manifestos, Huidobro developed coherent aesthetic principles for the new artistic expression he sought. Taken together, these materials represent, albeit at times in an overly self-centered fashion, the nature and principles of *creacionismo* as well as Huidobro's view of his own central role in its progress and mission. The earliest of these works, at least according to Huidobro himself, is "Non serviam," a lecture presented in 1914 to the Ateneo of Santiago. Huidobro takes the persona of "el joven poeta rebelde" (the young rebel poet) in announcing his independence from a conventional representation of the objective world around him:

Non serviam. I will not be your slave, Mother Nature; I will be your master. You will make use of me; of that I have no doubt. Even if I were able I would not wish it otherwise. However, I will also make use of you. I will have my trees that will not be the same as yours; I will have my rivers and my seas, my sky and my stars.

(*Obras completas*, vol. 1, pp. 653–654)

As was related above, in 1916 Huidobro spoke to the Ateneo of Buenos Aires and published in that city the first edition of *El espejo de agua.* The central point of this lecture, once again according to Huidobro himself, was to establish the creativity of the new poet: "The first condition of the poet is to create; the second, to create; and the third, to create." The collection of poems included a controversial text, "Arte poética," much cited and discussed in subsequent years, which is an early and careful statement of the creationist idea. Several individual lines are worth citing here: "Let whatever the eye sees be created"; "Invent new worlds and pay attention to your words"; "Why do you sing about the rose, oh Poets? / Make it bloom in the poem"; "The poet is a minor God."

Associated with the appearance in 1917 of *Horizon carré* (Square Horizon), Huidobro's first collection of poems in French, are two significant texts. The first is a letter written to Tomás Chazal, in which Huidobro explains the meaning of his title and provides a four-point condensation of his poetic theory:

1. All things become humanized as they pass through the consciousness of the poet; . . . 2. The vague is made precise; . . . 3. The abstract becomes concrete and the concrete abstract; . . . 4. That which is too poetic for the process of creation is transformed and created by changing its normal value.

(*Obras completas*, vol. 1, p. 680)

The second text is from the first page of the collection itself; it summarizes in three points the creationist intent:

Create a poem by taking its motifs from life and
   transforming them into new and independent life.
Nothing anecdotal or descriptive. Emotion should come
   from the unique creative virtue.
Make a POEM as nature makes a tree.

In addition, several significant theoretical texts appear in *Manifestes* (Manifestos), originally published in French in 1925. "Manifeste manifestes" (Manifesto of Manifestos) comments on dadaist and surrealist conceptions of art as compared with that of creationism. Huidobro argues against psychic spontaneity and automatic writing, and he suggests that creation is a process of the conscious mind: "Poetry is to be created by the poet, with the full strength of his awakened senses. The poet has an active rather than a passive role in the formulation of his poem." The essay "La Créationnisme," from the same volume, is an often tendentious and self-serving justification of Huidobro's primacy, but it includes this useful synthesis:

I will tell you what I understand as a created poem. It is a poem in which each part, as well as the entire structure, shows a new act or event, independent of the external world, disconnected from all reality except its own, and which takes its place in the world as a unique phenomenon, separate and distinct from all other phenomena.

In "Époque de création" (Epoch of Creation), also from *Manifestes*, Huidobro sees creation, in his own peculiar terms, as the mark of modernity: "Man no longer imitates. He invents, he adds to the realities of the natural world new realities born in his intellect: a poem, a painting, a statue, a steamship, an automobile, an airplane. . . . We must create. This is the emblem of our age."

A final example of creationist theory comes from the last years of Huidobro's life. In a short article entitled "El soneto" ("The Sonnet," published initially in 1947 in the journal *Amargo*), he takes this classic form as a pretext for yet another commentary on creation and modernity:

It is necessary to know the experiences of the past, not to repeat them, but rather to use them in the march toward new horizons. . . . Why write sonnets? Góngora, Quevedo, Lope wrote sonnets, and most beautiful ones, at an appropriate time. The old masters were great creators, in response to their own epoch. The important thing is to do as they did: create and not imitate.

(*Obras completas*, vol. 1, p. 774)

In addition to the passion for primacy that runs through all of these pronouncements, five aesthetic principles can be abstracted to serve as a résumé of creationism and as a preamble to a consideration of Huidobro's own literary work:

1. Modernity is to be esteemed above all else in the artistic expression of the modern era. Tradition can be understood, and even appreciated, but that understanding should never turn aside the search for innovation and change.

2. The "creative" poet, young and vital in his capacities, is the writer best equipped to express that modernity. As such, he has divine powers of creation and the giving of life.

3. Imitation is not creation in the modern sense envisioned by Huidobro. The creative poet should not feel obliged to imitate nature or to utilize forms taken from the recognizable external world, but should see his own creations as new, independent entities in that world. In the same sense, the great literary figures of the past should not be objects of imitation. They were sufficient to their times, and the new poet should be true to his own modern time.

4. Creation is a conscious process, controlled by the superior faculties of the new creative poet. The automatic writing of the surrealists, for instance, is a specious representation of creativity.

5. "Newness" and "creativity" are achieved by reordering conventional patterns or structures. For example, making an abstraction of something concrete, or altering accepted formal word boundaries, will result in the creation of a "new" reality.

Poetry

Huidobro's youthful verses were published in five collections, the first of which was *Ecos del alma* (Echoes of the Soul) and the last *Adán* (Adam). As might be expected, the influence of Rubén Darío's modernism is very marked in these collections, and in general neither Huidobro's themes nor his forms are strikingly novel. At times, however, there are suggestions of the formal and theoretical innovations so clearly seen in his later works. The preface to *Adán*, for example, makes the case for the freeing of poetry from established rules: "Poetry in Spanish is ill from rhetoricism," Huidobro writes. The most striking innovations, perhaps, are the "calligramistic"

(after Apollinaire's *Calligrammes*, 1913–1916) poems contained in *Canciones en la noche* (Songs in the Night) from 1913. These texts show Huidobro's command of conventional rhyme and line length while at the same time revealing an awareness of the visual effect of graphic experimentation.

The 1916 collection *El espejo de agua* was the first in a series of publications that were aggressively creationist in their imagery and structures. After arriving in Europe, Huidobro reworked a number of this volume's poems in French, and published them, together with some other poems done for the Parisian avant-garde journals, in 1917 as *Horizon carré*. As a result of his visit to Spain the following year, four separate publications appeared in Madrid in 1918, two in French and two in Spanish: *Tour Eiffel* (Eiffel Tower), *Hallali: Poème de guerre* (Hallali: War Poem), *Ecuatorial* (Equatorial), and *Poemas árticos* (Arctic Poems). Through all these collections run the insistent themes of movement, travel, and disruption, and the machines and sounds of war are a backdrop for images that convey an apocalyptic sense of impending destruction. Poetic structures are no longer conventional: lines are fragmented and separated, and the visual impact of phrases in uppercase letters and arranged on both the horizontal and diagonal planes is pronounced. This excerpt from "Alerta" (Alert; in *Arctic Poems*) is an excellent example:

> Cien aeroplanos
> Vuelan en torno a la luna

APAGA TU PIPA

Los obuses estallan como rosas maduras
Y las bombas agujerean los días
Canciones cortadas
      tiemblan entre las ramas
El viento contorsiona las calles
COMO APAGAR LA ESTRELLA DEL ESTANQUE

> A hundred airplanes
> Fly around the moon

PUT OUT YOUR PIPE

The howitzer shells explode like full-grown roses
And the bombs make holes in the days

Truncated songs
        tremble in the branches
The wind twists the streets
HOW TO PUT OUT THE STAR ON THE POND

Saisons choisies (Chosen Seasons, 1921) is an anthology of the previous works in French, with Huidobro's own introduction and translation. His production from 1918 through 1925 was gathered together in two collections in French: *Automne régulier* (Ordinary Autumn) and *Tout à coup* (Suddenly), both published in 1925. The tone of these collections is more contemplative, and the experimentation with structure and typography is much reduced. The imagery, however, is still creationist in its insistence on the reversal or transformation of conventional values or connections. These lines from section 18 of *Tout à coup* provide an indication:

> *Je reviendrai sur les eaux du ciel*
>
> *J'aime voyager comme le bateau de l'oeil*
> *Que va et vient à chaque clignottement*
> *Six fois déjà j'ai touché le seuil*
> *De l'infini qui renferme le vent*
>
> *Rien dans la vie*
> *Qu'un cri d'antichambre*
> *Nerveuses océaniques quel malheur nous poursuit*
> *Dans l'urne des fleures sans patience*
> *Se trouvent les émotions en rythme défini*

> I will return upon the waters of the heavens
>
> I like to travel like the eye ship
> Which comes and goes with each blink
> Six times already have I touched the beginning
> Of the infinite which the wind closes
>
> Nothing in this life
> But an antechamber shout
> Oceanic sinewyness what a shame it pursues us
> In the vase of impatient flowers
> The emotions are to be found in defined rhythm

Huidobro published two major works of poetry in 1931. The first of these was *Temblor de cielo* (Heavenquake), an extended prose poem that uses an idealized feminine figure to communicate the whole range of intense emotions associated with sexual love. The second was *Altazor; o, El viaje en paracaídas* (Soaring Falcon; or, A Journey by Parachute), Huidobro's longest and most complex poetic text. Written over more than a decade, the poem is organized in seven numbered cantos (plus a curious, fairy-tale-like preface) and is a complex interweaving of several thematic threads: fleeting time, life as a movement toward death, and an apocalyptic vision of the modern world. The fundamental theme shaping the poem is the impossibility of transforming poetic language into the "magnetic words" sought by the creationist poet, and, with some temporary suspensions, the direction of development is downward. The image of a fall through space implied in the full title of the poem is used constantly in the presentation of this theme: a fall from coherence to incoherence, from life to death, from verbal question to inarticulate wail. Also, the poem is constructed around a single character, Altazor, a magical figure who functions as the persona of Huidobro himself:

> *Los tormentos cambiados en inscripción de cementerio . . .*
> *aquí yace Altazor azor fulminado por la altura*
> *aquí yace Vicente antipoeta y mago*

> Storms changed into cemetery inscriptions . . .
> here lies Altazor a falcon thunderstruck by the heights
> here lies Vicente antipoet and magician
>
>   (*Obras completas*, vol. 1, p. 401)

The structure and technique of the poems show the same complexity already observed in the thematic patterning. The seven cantos, of widely differing lengths, tones, and tempi, carry along the fluctuating but constantly descending theme-line as would the movements of a major musical composition. Canto 1 is the extended theme-presentation, circuitous in structure and with considerable variation in line length and tone. Canto 2 is a contemplative *andante*, which checks for a brief moment the descending circles of the previous canto with a meditation on the grace and beauty of Woman. Canto 3 is a furious and rapid-paced denunciation of the inexpressiveness of conventional poetic language, with some samples of the brilliant skill of the "new" poet. Cantos 4 and 5 represent the unexplored segment of the journey downward, in which the poet carries out an urgent probing of the conventional limits of time, space, and verbal expression. By manipulating poetic language in several places, Huidobro blurs traditional word boundaries and creates new terms in order to demonstrate the creative powers of the poet. The best example is the well-known sequence from canto 4:

Al horitaña de la montazonte
La violondrina e el goloncelo
Descolgada ésta mañana de la lunala
Se acerca a todo galope
Y viene viene la golondrina
Ya viene viene la golonfina
Ya viene la golontrina
Ya viene la goloncima
Viene la golonchina
Viene la golonclima
Ya viene la golonrima
Ya viene la golonrisa
La golonniña
La golongira

To the horitain of the mountzon
The violo and the swallin
Disconnected this morning from the moonala
It approaches at a full gallop
The swallo comes it comes
Already the swallfo comes it comes
Already the swalltro comes
Already the swallso comes
The swallcho comes
The swallclo comes
Already the swallro comes
Already the swallstro comes
The swallkno
The swallgo

This passage can be taken as an attempt at the restructuring of language and the rebuilding of the world suggested earlier in the poem. The attempt is not entirely successful, however, and these cantos also convey a sharpened sense of anguished failure.

Canto 6 totters precariously on the edge of intelligibility and pierces with its pulsing of short, almost staccato lines the slower plateau of cantos 4 and 5. The verbal plays continue, now seeming sterile and obsessive, since meaningful expression has dissolved among the crystalline word shapes formed by the poet. Only unconnected flashes remain, conveying once again the sense of fear and anguish. Canto 7 is composed of inarticulate sound alone. Many segments bear some resemblance to recognizable words, but not enough for any degree of intelligibility. Here is the final plunge into the yawning pit of nonexpression and death, of nonbeing, toward which the poem has moved in spite of the poet's every effort to reverse its course.

Two major conclusions may be drawn from these comments on *Altazor*. First, the poem is a tour de force, a virtuoso piece whose dazzling technique makes it a prime example of the "new" poetry envisioned by Huidobro. It represents the destruction of conventional poetic forms (rhyme, line length, and stanza, among others), and its images—both in isolation and in organized patterns—make effective use of the joining of unlike qualities envisioned in creationist theory. Huidobro uses a "modern" lexicon in this poem, taking terms from science and mechanics, and displays a particularly brilliant manipulation of word boundaries in the inversion of conventional morphemic elements and the creation of neologisms.

Second, in spite of its virtuosity and conscious modernity, the direction of the poem is toward chaos and destruction (an inexorable downward fall, to use Huidobro's central image) rather than control and command. The poet does not succeed, through the images and techniques of his poem, in dominating the "magnetic words" of his "new" poetic language. For all its brilliant success, *Altazor* represents at the same time the unattainability, if not the destruction, of the creationist aesthetic.

In the years following 1931 Huidobro considerably reduced his poetic production, and he let an entire decade pass before publishing any new poetry collections. *Ver y palpar* (To See and Feel) and *El ciudadano del olvido* (Citizen of Forgetfulness), the last two works published during his lifetime, appeared in 1941. The experimentation in figurative language continues, though with less insistence, and the search for a created reality is still very much in evidence. The anguished tone, which played a major role in *Altazor*, is even more accentuated. Moments of hope punctuated *Altazor*, as did humor on occasion, but here the verbal magic has left only skeletal forms and the certainty of the end of life. The first few stanzas of "Tiempo de espera" (Waiting Time), from *El ciudadano del olvido*, communicate this sense of stagnated despair:

> Pasan los días
> La eternidad no llega ni el milagro
>
> Pasan los días
> El barco no se acerca
> El mar no se hace flor ni campanario
> No se descubre la caída
>
> Pasan los días
> Las piedras lloran con sus huesos azules
> Pero no se abre la puerta
> No se descubre la caída de la noche

> The days move on
> Eternity does not arrive nor the miracle
>
> The days move on
> The ship does not come near
> The sea does not flower nor become a belfry
> The downward fall is not to be seen
>
> The days move on
> The stones cry with their blue bones
> But the door does not open
> Nightfall is not to be seen

Prose Fiction

Huidobro came to the novel in midcareer, essentially in the late 1920's. By that time his theoretical and methodological battles were largely behind him, and such major poetic works as *Altazor* and *Temblor de cielo*, which had been in process for years, were nearing publication. In characteristic fashion Huidobro poured his energies into prose fiction as a new expressive mode and within a decade had published five novels under his own name. *Mío Cid Campeador* (My Cid Campeador, 1929; translated into English as *Portrait of a Paladin*) and *Cagliostro* (Cagliostro, 1934; translated into English as *Mirror of a Mage*) are both examples of what Huidobro called the *novela-film* (filmic novel). These

two works take historical characters (the figure of a medieval Castilian hero in the first and that of an eighteenth-century magician and necromancer in the second) as pretexts for a fanciful elaboration that, as René de Costa points out, makes effective use of the techniques of silent films (*En pos de Huidobro*, pp. 71–93). *La próxima* (The Next One, 1934) is a hauntingly accurate vision of a future war, in which the whole civilized world is destroyed and a small colony in Africa is left completely on its own. *Papá; o, El diario de Alicia Mir* (Papa; or, The Diary of Alicia Mir), also from 1934, is an examination in diary form of the difficult and changing relations between a father, mother, and daughter. *Sátiro; o, El poder de las palabras* (Satyr; or, The Power of the Word) appeared in 1939 as the last of Huidobro's novels. Bernardo Saguen, a frustrated writer, is led through his struggles with himself and the expressive written word toward dementia and destruction.

Perhaps the best example of Huidobro's capacity for invention and ironic humor is *Tres inmensas novelas* (Three Immense Novels), a work he published in 1935 in collaboration with the Alsatian poet and artist Hans Arp. Five novelettes are collected under a title that is itself ironic, three collaborative pieces with the Cervantine subtitle "Tres novelas ejemplares" (Three Exemplary Novels) and two by Huidobro himself in the playful inversion "Dos ejemplares de novela" (Two Examples of a Novel). All five novelettes are parodic (of the detective novel, for example, the historical novel, the adventure novel, or the fantasy novel) and show the effective use of exaggeration and humor. One of the two contributions by Huidobro, subtitled "Novela póstuma" (Posthumous Novel), carries a typically involved and inverted title, "El gato con botas y Simbad el marino o Badsin el marrano" (Puss in Boots and Sinbad the Sailor or Badsin the Dirty One). The narration is situated in Oratonia, a country in which everyone is an orator, and in which the persuasive—and often incorrect—spoken word dominates everything. The central figure is the Electric Orator, whose constant jaw movements are sufficient to generate enough electrical current for the entire country. The following lines, from an oration delivered at his funeral, demonstrate especially well the power and the incorrect information conveyed in the spoken word:

With what brilliance his magic words were able to paint for us the battle of Lepanto, where Shakespeare lost his arm! And the taking of Jerusalem, where Milton lost his sight; the retreat of the Ten Thousand, where Tasso did not lose a single man and Nelson met a glorious death with his heroic Sicilians. Think how much the man we mourn today had traveled, seen, and observed! As a young man he visited the famous pyramids of Rome, the same pyramids whose many centuries were commented on by Charles the Fifth before his soldiers. In Berlin he visited Napoleon's tomb.

(*Obras completas*, vol. 2, p. 1329)

Theater

During the 1930's Huidobro also wrote for the theater, though he did not bring to his theatrical writing the same intensity he brought to the novel, nor did he produce nearly as much theatrical writing. His first full-length play was *Gilles de Raíz*, a four-act surrealistic work in French, which was published in Paris in 1932; a part of the play was staged there in 1933. The central character is modeled on the historical Bluebeard figure, and, once again, Huidobro's theme serves as a pretext for a fictional creation involving mystery, violent events, and a pact with the devil. A second and better play is *En la luna* (On the Moon), which was published in Chile in 1934 but not produced there until several decades later (1965). With the subtitle "Pequeño guiñol," (Small Puppet Show), this play is a broadly presented political farce. The puppeteer, Maese López, controls the comings and goings of the numerous puppetlike actors (with such names as Fifí Fofó, Lulú Lalá, and Pipí Popó), whose actions take the play, with obvious reference to the unstable puppet governments of Latin America, through one operettalike coup after another until a court jester finally crowns himself Nadir I. The new king assembles his court to watch, of all things, a real puppet show, a play within a play, in which Nadir I can be seen in the blustering and tyrannical puppet king, North-South III, and in which offstage cries for bread from the populace are interwoven with the two-level action:

NADIR I: (*To his court*) What a poet and what a philosopher this King is. By the horns of the earth I would like to meet him!

PUPPETEER: Praised be our King.

NORTH-SOUTH III: Tatarantulas! Leave me alone—I want to meditate on my greatness. Give me a mirror.

PUPPETEER: Oh mirror of greatnesses! Contemplate your greatnesses in this mirror.

(*Hands him a mirror and exits.*

From offstage: "We want bread. Bread, bread.")

NADIR I: (*To his court*) That "Bread, bread," is it from here or from the court of that earthly King? Is it my lunar people or his earthly people who are shouting?

NORTH-SOUTH III: What is the meaning of that "Bread, bread"? Who dares to pound on my door and disturb my sleep?

NADIR I: Is it the "Bread, bread" from the moon that echoes on earth, or is it the "Bread, bread" from the earth that we can hear on the moon?

NORTH-SOUTH III: Tatarantulas! I'm the premier King of the Universe!

NADIR I: This King is getting on my nerves.

North-South III personifies yet another attempted coup, as he comes onto the full stage, establishes his own reality, and confronts Nadir I and his court. The two courts, the lunar and the earthly, are finally forced to flee by mobs representing the people, and a denunciatory and disembodied voice, through a backstage speaker, remarks on the need for a cleansing and for the sun of a new world. The puppeteer Maese López, now seeming bored with the puppet-characters and the action, asks that the play be brought to a close. One of the characters takes a pistol from his pocket, fires it, and declares that the story is finished. *En la luna* is good theater, as the pistol shot reminds us. It is a bit ahead of its time in its conscious use of absurdities of character, language, and situation, and it develops a forceful political message in its noisy and farcical slide through anarchy toward tyranny.

Vicente Huidobro was a complex and controversial figure, who constantly pushed at the limits of his world in search of a cultural and literary expression that was adequate for his vision of modernity. His theoretical writings, often arrogant and self-serving, nonetheless represent a coherent set of principles for the development of creationism and a new literary style. His own abundant creative writings—poetry, prose fiction, drama—struggle to put into practice his insistent desire for innovation, at times with brilliant success and at times with just as notable failure. When one takes into account all dimensions of his work, Huidobro is without question a major twentieth-century man of letters, whose fundamental contributions to modern Spanish-American literature are now receiving appropriate recognition.

SELECTED BIBLIOGRAPHY

Editions

Poetry

Ecos del alma. Santiago, Chile, 1911.
Canciones en la noche. Santiago, Chile, 1913.
La gruta del silencio. Santiago, Chile, 1913.
Adán. Santiago, Chile, 1914.
Las pagodas ocultas. Santiago, Chile, 1914.
El espejo de agua. Buenos Aires, 1916. 2nd ed. Madrid, 1918.
Horizon carré. Paris, 1917.
Ecuatorial. Madrid, 1918.
Hallali: Poème de guerre. Madrid, 1918.
Poemas árticos. Madrid, 1918.
Tour Eiffel. Madrid, 1918.
Saisons choisies. Paris, 1921.
Automne régulier. Paris, 1925.
Tout à coup. Paris, 1925.
Altazor; o, El viaje en paracaídas, poema en VII cantos. Madrid, 1931.
Temblor de cielo. Madrid, 1931. French ed., *Tremblement de ciel.* Paris, 1932.
Ver y palpar. Santiago, Chile, 1941.
El ciudadano del olvido. Santiago, Chile, 1941.
Ultimos poemas. Santiago, Chile, 1948.

Prose Fiction

Mío Cid Campeador, hazaña. Madrid, 1929.
Cagliostro, novela-film. Santiago, Chile, 1934.
Papá; o, El diario de Alicia Mir. Santiago, Chile, 1934.
La próxima (historia que pasó en poco tiempo más). Santiago, Chile, 1934.
Tres inmensas novelas. In collaboration with Hans Arp. Santiago, Chile, 1935.
Sátiro; o, El poder de las palabras. Santiago, Chile, 1939.

Plays

Gilles de Raíz. Paris, 1932.
En la luna. Santiago, Chile, 1934.

Essays

Pasando y pasando: Crónicas y comentarios. Santiago, Chile, 1914.
Finis Britannia! Une redoutable société secrète s'est dressée contre l'impérialisme anglais. Paris, 1923.
Manifestes. Paris, 1925. Includes "Manifeste manifestes," "Le créationnisme," "Époque de création," and others.
Vientos contrarios. Santiago, Chile, 1926.

Collected Works

Antología. Edited by Eduardo Anguita. Santiago, Chile, 1945.
Antología de verso y prosa. Edited by Hugo Montes. Santiago, Chile, 1975.
Cagliostro y poemas. Edited by Carlos Ruiz Tagle. Santiago, Chile, 1978.
Obras completas. 2 vols. Edited by Braulio Arenas. Santiago, Chile, 1964.
Obras completas. 2 vols. Edited by Hugo Montes; with a bibliography compiled by Nicholas Hey. Santiago, Chile, 1976.
Obras poéticas selectas. Edited by Hugo Montes. Santiago, Chile, 1957.
Poesía y prosa: Antología. Edited by Antonio de Undurraga. Madrid, 1957.
Poesías. Edited by Enrique Lihn. Havana, 1968.
Vicente Huidobro. Edited by Mario Céspedes. San José, 1976.

Translations

Arctic Poems. Translated by William Witherup and Serge Echeverría. Santa Fe, N. Mex., 1974.
The Selected Poetry of Vicente Huidobro. Edited by David M. Guss (various translators). New York, 1981.

Biographical and Critical Studies

Admussen, Richard L., and René de Costa. "Huidobro, Reverdy, and the *editio princeps* of *El espejo de agua.*" *Comparative Literature* 24:163–175 (1972).
Bajarlía, Juan Jacobo. *La polémica Reverdy-Huidobro: Orígen del ultraísmo.* Buenos Aires, 1964.

Bary, David. *Huidobro o la vocación poética*. Granada, Spain, 1963.

―――. *Nuevos estudios sobre Huidobro y Larrea*. Valencia, Spain, 1984.

Busto Ogden, Estrella. *El creacionismo de Vicente Huidobro en sus relaciones con la estética cubista*. Madrid, 1983.

Camurati, Mireya. *Poesía y poética de Vicente Huidobro*. Buenos Aires, 1980.

Caracciolo Trejo, Enrique. *La poesía de Vicente Huidobro y la vanguardia*. Madrid, 1974.

Concha, Jaime. "*Altazor*, de Vicente Huidobro." *Anales de la Universidad de Chile* 73:113–136 (1965).

―――. *Vicente Huidobro*. Madrid, 1980.

Costa, René de. "Del modernismo a la vanguardia: El creacionismo prepolémico." *Hispanic Review* 43:261–274 (1975).

―――. *En pos de Huidobro: Siete ensayos de interpretación*. Santiago, Chile, 1980.

―――. *Vicente Huidobro: The Careers of a Poet*. New York, 1984.

―――, ed. *Vicente Huidobro y el creacionismo*. Madrid, 1975.

―――. *Vicente Huidobro y la vanguardia*. Special number of *Revista iberoamericana* 45/106–107 (1979).

Diego, Gerardo. "Poesía y creacionismo de Vicente Huidobro." *Cuadernos hispanoamericanos* 74:528–544 (1968).

Forster, Merlin H. "Vicente Huidobro's *Altazor*: A Reevaluation." *Kentucky Romance Quarterly* 17:297–307 (1970).

―――. "Nota sobre algunos primeros poemas de Vicente Huidobro traducidos al catalán." *Revista iberoamericana* 118–119:391–396 (1982).

―――. "Elementos de innovación en la narrativa de Vicente Huidobro: *Tres inmensas novelas*." In *Prosa hispánica de vanguardia*, edited by Fernando Burgos. Madrid, 1986.

Goic, Cedomil. *La poesía de Vicente Huidobro*. Santiago, Chile, 1956. 2nd ed. 1974.

Hey, Nicholas. "Bibliografía de y sobre Vicente Huidobro." *Revista iberoamericana* 91:293–353 (1975).

―――. "Addenda a la bibliografía de y sobre Vicente Huidobro." *Revista iberoamericana* 106–107:387–398 (1979).

Holmes, Henry Alfred. *Vicente Huidobro and Creationism*. New York, 1934.

Mitre, Eduardo. *Huidobro: Hambre de espacio y sed de cielo*. Caracas, 1980.

Neghme Echeverría, Lidia. "El creacionismo político de Huidobro en *En la luna*." *Latin American Theatre Review* 18/1:75–82 (1984).

Picon Garfield, Evelyn. "Tradición y ruptura: Modernidad en *Tres novelas ejemplares* de Vicente Huidobro y Hans Arp." *Hispanic Review* 51:283–301 (1983).

Pizarro, Ana. *Vicente Huidobro, un poeta ambivalente*. Concepción, Chile, 1971.

Rutter, Frank. "La estética cubista en *Horizon Carré* de Vicente Huidobro." *Bulletin hispanique* 80/1–2:123–133 (1978).

―――. "Vicente Huidobro and Futurism: Convergences and Divergences." *Bulletin of Hispanic Studies* 58/1:55–71 (1981).

Schwartz, Jorge. "Vicente Huidobro o la cosmópolis textualizada." *Eco* 202:1009–1035 (1978).

Szmulewicz, Efraín. *Vicente Huidobro: Biografía emotiva*. Santiago, Chile, 1979.

Wood, Cecil G. *The "creacionismo" of Vicente Huidobro*. Fredricton, New Brunswick, 1978.

Yúdice, George. *Vicente Huidobro y la motivación del lenguaje*. Buenos Aires, 1978.

Jorge de Lima

(1893–1953)

Cassiano Nunes

In his youth, Joel Silveira drew a mischievous portrait of Jorge de Lima begging in the streets of Rio de Janeiro and imploring "a little praise, for God's sake. . . ." This is how Lima was caricatured by another writer. He was then in the middle of a career that was more intense than extensive. The point of the lampooning would seem to be that Lima eagerly sought the approval of his peers. Perhaps, like most of his fellows, he did enjoy praise. For what is the writing of poetry if not an attempt to find comprehension and solidarity? Yet it is probably true that Lima's desire for applause contained a good deal of innocence and simplicity.

Lima's work gives one the impression that the vastness of his talent and literary ambition go hand in hand with the distinct, incomprehensible, boyish ingenuousness of a provincial adolescent. It is pointless to try to find in Lima's work the razor-sharp acuity, the deep Jewish perceptiveness of a Fernando Pessoa (by whose messianism he was influenced). One cannot view Lima objectively, nor did he impersonally dissect himself as did his Portuguese counterpart. He flings himself impetuously into his inner vortex. He wishes to express himself, not understand himself. In Pessoa, the psychological aspect almost outshines the poetry. Lima's scrutinizing of the soul is above all a key that unlocks a poetical universe. This universe, in his mature work, is always for him a vast, dim, phantasmagoric continent. The mysterious and the terrible are his frequent visitors. Lima does not analyze himself with the detachment of a Pessoa, but plumbs his inner tumult—his artist's obsession—to distill the Christian message from this vision. His poetry has an eminently soteriological target. His objective is Salvation, Redemption.

At first glance, writing about Lima seems an uphill battle, considering the number of aesthetic movements he embraced, the variety of literary genres with which he experimented, and the diverse arts he practiced, not to mention the professions and social responsibilities he so readily took upon himself. He wrote Parnassian sonnets, picturesque modernist verse, Negro poetry, religious poems, and modern sonnets impregnated with surrealism, and crowned his career with *Invenção de Orfeu* (Invention of Orpheus, 1952), one of the most ambitious works of art ever conceived by a Brazilian, a dense, complex, and sometimes abstruse book that defies interpretation. Lima wrote poetry, novels, essays, biographies, and even a film script. As well as a writer, he was a painter, a sculptor, and a creator of photomontages. Professionally, he was a physician, a professor of literature, and a politician who rose to become president of the city council in Rio de Janeiro, then the capital. Looking at what he wrote and did, in a not particularly long life, leads one to wonder how he found time for his family and recreation. There is only one explanation: his recreation was producing his art. Like a proper surrealist, he probably made good use of his sleep, extracting material for his highly oneiric work: sleeping, the poet worked.

However, those who delve into Lima's literary universe will not be daunted when they come to summarize his work, nor will they be baffled by the multiplicity of forms in this poetic world. This is because they will encounter an existential unity in all of Lima's writings. The coalescence of art and life is readily apparent. What representation there is, in theatrical terms, will not confuse the exegete. It is genuine, without pretense. It is part of his creative process. Ralph Waldo Emerson described Henry David Thoreau as an actor of Truth. It is a label that fits Lima well. His poetry is very theatrical. "Soliloquy" is one of his favorite words; "mask," another. Steadily contemplating his masks, one is moved to discover his hidden, tragic face.

Jorge de Lima was born on Saint George's Day (hence his name) on 23 April 1893 in the town of União, in Alagoas state, Brazil. He was the son of a businessman and sugar plantation owner. In a fascinating interview with Homero Senna published in July 1945 in *Revista de o Jornal*, the poet remembers the region where he grew up, describing a walk he went on into the Barriga Hill range, where Zumbi (the most famous black slave resistance leader in seventeenth-century Brazil) founded the famous hiding place for fugitive slaves, a few miles from União:

> Without exaggerating, I can say that that was the first time I felt touched by poetry. All the immense panorama that was disclosed to me then—the river Mundaú, which is said to have sprung from the tears of Jurema, on one side the Macacos range, on the other the Jatobá plain, the green fields of Terra-Lavada, the Fundão, the Tobiba, the cane plantations and mills, the Great Western, the pottery factories and, in the distance, the church of my patron saint and the mansion where I was born—it all entered my dazzled, child's eyes and has never left me since. So much so that many years later, as an adult, these are the subjects I turned to for some of the poems

in what you might call the "northeastern" phase of my poetry.

After attending local schools, in 1903 he was sent to the Alagoas Diocesan College, run by the Marist Brotherhood, where he studied until he was fifteen. His contact with these teachers, who were specially devoted to the Virgin Mary, probably nurtured his naturally religious bent. The poet's cult of the immaculate and mysterious Muse, who frequently changes names but persists throughout his work, may have its roots in the Mariolatry of the Marist schools of the time. Lima's literary interest, which had begun early, now took firm hold. He was extraordinarily precocious.

In 1908, he moved to Salvador, where he studied medicine. The city of Salvador, a journey he made through the *sertão* (backlands) and up the São Francisco River, as well as travels in his native Alagoas, made an indelible impression on him. The absolute misery of the malaria-ridden population of the marshlands of Alagoas, who lived literally in and off the mud and ate earth for some perverse reason, moved and shocked him to the core. At the age of seventeen, Lima gained popularity with his sonnet "O Acendedor de Lampiões" (Lamplighter), written in the prevailing style. In 1914, he received a doctorate from the Rio de Janeiro Faculty of Medicine.

In 1915 Lima returned to Alagoas and set up medical offices in the capital, Maceió. Four years later he was elected state deputy. He later became director of the Alagoas Licée, general director of public education, and the representative of his state at several scientific congresses. In 1925 he was married. That same year he published a pamphlet called *O Mundo do Menino Impossível* (The Impossible Boy's World), the first poem in his truly personal, creative phase. This marked his abandonment of worn-out, academic forms. In 1927 he published *Poemas* (Poems), his first collection of modernist poems, in Maceió. The preface was written by José Lins do Rego, who was shortly to become one of the most important Brazilian novelists. Lima's first novel, *Salomão e as Mulheres* (Solomon and the Women), published the same year, was proof of his versatility. He wrote *Dois Ensaios* (Two Essays, 1929) to obtain the Brazilian literature chair at the state high school.

One essay was on Marcel Proust (of whom he was a pioneer reader and critic in Brazil) and the other on Brazilian modernist poetry. They amply demonstrate his literary understanding.

The year 1928 saw the publication of a limited edition of the immortal *Essa Negra Fulô* (This Negress Fulô). In 1929 the author published *Novos Poemas* (New Poems) in Rio de Janeiro and *Dios Ensaios* in Maceió. The 1930 revolution obliged Lima to move to Rio de Janeiro. This turned out to be a positive step for him, because in the capital he was in a much better position to express himself both as an artist and as a doctor. He set up medical offices in Cinelândia, at the heart of the city. This was where the principal artists and intellectuals of the country mixed with ordinary folk, the working class. As a doctor, Lima was idolized by the city taxi drivers, to whom he was specially devoted, caring for them and their families as part of his Christian medical mission and out of a sense of charity.

In Rio de Janeiro, Lima became one of the leading lights on the literary scene. It was a particularly important moment in the country's literary history; modernism was coming of age in a period that can confidently be called the Golden Age of Brazilian literature and art. Mário de Andrade, Oswald de Andrade, Manuel Bandeira, Carlos Drummond de Andrade, Jorge Amado, José Lins do Rego, Graciliano Ramos, Rachel de Queiroz, Marques Rebêlo, Otávio de Faria, and Lúcio Cardoso were all at their creative peaks. In music it was the age of Heitor Villa-Lobos and Francisco Mignone; in painting, of Cândido Portinari, Di Cavalcanti, and Pancetti; in architecture, of Lúcio Costa and Oscar Niemeyer. Linked to the group of writers were scientists like Edgardo Roquette-Pinto and Miguel Osório de Almeida, sociologists such as Gilberto Freyre, and historians of the stature of Sérgio Buarque de Holanda. Earlier, in Maceió, Lima had been in the company of Lins do Rego, Graciliano Ramos, Valdemar Cavalcanti, and Aurélio Buarque de Holanda.

In 1932, *Poemas Escolhidos* (Selected Poems) came out, followed by the surrealist novel *O Anjo* (The Angel, 1934). In 1935, *Tempo e Eternidade* (Time and Eternity), a collection of poems written in collaboration with another exceptional poet, Murilo Mendes, announced the establishment in Brazil of a religious

and Catholic poetry with the motto "Restauremos a poesia em Cristo" (Let us restore poetry in Christ). This poetic movement resisted the politicization of poetry. The same year, *Calunga* (Calunga), a valuable novel about the downtrodden in Alagoas, was published. In *A Túnica Inconsútil* (The Seamless Tunic, 1938), strongly inspired by the Old and New Testaments, the poet was more at ease in the line of poetry he had taken up. In 1937, Lima was appointed professor of Luso-Brazilian literature at the University of the Federal District. In 1939 his poetico-realist novel *A Mulher Obscura* (The Obscure Woman), containing some very fine passages, was published. An anthology of his verse was published in Spanish in the same year.

In 1940 the Brazilian Academy of Letters, which never admitted Lima to its ranks, awarded him its Poetry Prize. In the same year the poet began to lecture in Brazilian literature at the University of Brazil. Three years later, he published an album of photomontages entitled *A Pintura em Pânico* (Painting in a Panic). He also wrote *Mira-Celi* (Mira-Celi, 1950), a collection of fifty-nine poems that serves as a sort of prologue to the final, greatest, most sumptuous and innovative phase of his poetry. His religious scope had become broader and more complex. His focus was now less particular and limited; his message, more critical, messianic, and utopian.

In 1945, Brazil became a democracy again, and Lima entered the liberal National Democratic Union party (UDN). Two years later came his *Poemas Negros* (Negro Poems), with a preface by Gilberto Freyre and illustrations by Lazar Segall. In the same year he was elected to the Rio de Janeiro city council on a UDN ticket. The following year, he was instated as president of the city council.

Livro de Sonetos (Book of Sonnets), one of his most personal and perfect books, was published in 1949. This was followed, in 1950, by *Obra Poética* (Poetical Works) and the Argentine edition of *Mira-Celi*. In 1952, the poet published *Invenção de Orfeu*, an extensive poem in ten cantos which, despite its paraphrasing of a number of classic and modern authors, is extremely original. It is a tremendously complex work, considered abstruse in places. In the same year, Lima was elected the first president of the newly founded Society of Authors in Rio de Janeiro. This prolific and inspired writer died on 15 November

1953, after great suffering caused by illness. Shortly before his death, he tape-recorded some of his poems for the United States Library of Congress.

Lima's verse written before 1925 is of little consequence. His first book, *Quatorze Alexandrinos* (Fourteen Alexandrine Sonnets, 1914), gives no hint of a strongly personal poet in the making. Once unshackled by modernism, he did not have difficulty in making his mark. His knowledge of his native region and the experiences that had molded him became the raw material of his poetry. His personal longing to reveal his soul coincided with the nation's urge to define its identity. In Pernambuco state, under the influence of North American modernism and the Irish renaissance, Gilberto Freyre argued in favor of a genuine art, based on regional cultural values. Brazil desired a real, if crude, vision of itself that could not be culled from French books or American movies.

The great Luso-Brazilian realist tradition, which was led by José María de Eça de Queiroz and Joaquim Maria Machado de Assis and had dominated the cultural scene, was dwindling into academicism. Lima, like Bandeira and Mário de Andrade before him, rediscovered Brazil, a country of strong sunshine, which dissolved the crepuscular, gray scenarios of the literary movement known as decadence. In creating his marvelous world of poetry, the "impossible boy" simply listened to his heart as if he were putting his ear to a shell. The necessary search for what was authentic led the modernists to a Proustian submersion in childhood. They quenched their thirst in memories of their youth. Bandeira made such recollections a cornerstone of his poetry. Lima followed him closely in this typically regionalist phase, painting a picture of life in the Northeast. His verse showed his vocation for abundance; it is muralist, general, collective poetry that reminds one of the murals of Diego Rivera, José Clemente Orozco, and David Alfaro Siqueiros.

In "A Minha América" (My America), Lima states the similarities between Portuguese America (Brazil) and Spanish America. He sees the same sadness in the two:

> Marimbas da Nicaragua,
> zacapas do Peru,

> tínias, vancares, poracês,
> côcos, emboladas, xangôs de Maceió e da Bahia,
> candomblés do meu Brasil inteiro,
> tudo isso tão triste!

> Marimbas of Nicaragua,
> zacapas* of Peru,
> tínias,* vancares,* poracês,*
> coconuts, emboladas,* xangôs* of Maceió or Bahia,
> candomblés* of all my Brazil,
> all this so sad!

The poet warns Walt Whitman, Alfred Kreymborg, and North Americans in general of the difference between (mostly Anglo-Saxon) North America and South America:

> Negros,
> Selvagens,
> Amarelos,
> —o arco-íris de todas as raças canta pela boca
> de minha nova América do Sul,
> uma escala diferente da vossa escala,
> Alfred Kreymborg,
> Whitman!

> Negros,
> Savages,
> Yellow-skins,
> —the rainbow of all races sings in the mouth
> of my new South America,
> on a different scale from yours,
> Alfred Kreymborg,
> Whitman!

The Brazilian Northeast is represented in Lima's poetry in the form of a mural, a documentary film. The poems "Bahia de todos os santos" (Bahia of All Saints), "G. W. B. R." (G.[reat] W.[estern] B.[razilian] R.[ailway]), "Floriano—Padre Cícero—Lampião" (Floriano—Padre Cícero—Lampião), and "Rio de São Francisco" (São Francisco River) paint an ample and picturesque panorama of the region. The geography, customs, cults, the land and its people,

*Translator's note: *Zacapa* is an Andean Indian instrument; *tínias, vancares,* and *poracês* are Indian dances; *embolada* is a sort of music from the Brazilian Northeast; *xangôs* are voodoo saints; *candomblé* is a voodoo ceremony.

and the Northeast's social and cultural elements are magnificently portrayed in Lima's modernist poetry. It could not be more ethnographic, visual, and documentary. The poem "Xangô" (Xangô), the first with this title, precedes the Negro poems that close this phase of poetry of the land, its people, and its culture, in an anthropological sense. At the same time, Brazilian modernism was bidding farewell to regional and ethnographic themes. Brazil had been rediscovered; other tasks awaited its artists. With the exception of a handful of romantic and realist writers, the modernists were the first to provide a valuable ethnographic portrait of Brazil that was both broad in scope and true to reality. Their innovation was to be taken up by the novelists of the 1930's, who depicted Brazil with an objectivity that had been virtually unknown.

When Lima published *Tempo e Eternidade*, his religious sentiment had matured, and he felt driven to write purely religious verse. His overwhelming absorption makes for a monochord tone and a degree of monotony. Nonetheless, the poet boldly broadens his field of vision and reflection. The result is a more ecumenical, universal character, which endows the work with undeniable grandure. *Mira-Celi* takes this universality a step further, making *Tempo e Eternidade* and *A Túnica Inconsútil* seem limited to evangelical or biblical themes, despite occasional flashes of modernity. The grandiose, audacious verse in *Invenção de Orfeu* takes on ambiguous and suspect human elements, rich in poetry, that are absorbed into the religious context. An agonizing drama of high flights and falls replaces the horizontal versicles of the pious earlier works.

The critics have not yet embarked on the colossal task of interpreting *Invenção de Orfeu*. Murilo Mendes reckoned that "the exegesis of the book will have to be done slowly, over a span of years, by teams of critics who will have to tackle it with love, science and intuition and not with the cold instruments of erudition alone." The poem consists of ten cantos, like Luiz Vaz de Camões' *Os Lusíadas* (*The Lusiads*, 1572), on which it is based in parts. This heteroclite work draws its strength from Vergil, Dante, Le Comte de Lautréamont, and Arthur Rimbaud, as well, and is vaguely reminiscent of Antonio de Castro Alves and Anthero de Quental. Some critics rightly speak of its neobaroque style. The palimpsest technique and collage, employed by Ezra Pound and T. S. Eliot under the inspiration of cubist painting, are also present in this long and complicated poem whose structure has not yet been defined.

Lima's basic compositional method in this work is paraphrasing, which means that the book requires continuous intertextual reading. Lima is by no means a writer of pastiche, but an inventor or reinventor. His poetic bricolage is curiously original with strokes of genius. The metaphysical, religious, and poetic stances adopted remain the same throughout. Despite the apparent chaos, the work is contained and sustained by the artist's capacity and the poet's fundamental ideas. Each of the ten cantos is made up of several parts (180 in all). The poet is careful to alter stanza lengths, and meter is equally varied (from four to twelve feet). There are no less than sixty-six sonnets embedded in the work. Lima's sonnet writing in *Invenção de Orfeu* is as good as the finest in his excellent *Livro de Sonetos*.

SELECTED BIBLIOGRAPHY

First Editions

Poetry

Quatorze Alexandrinos. Rio de Janeiro, 1914.
O Mundo do Menino Impossível. Maceió, Brazil, 1925.
Poemas. Maceió, Brazil, 1927.
Essa Negra Fulô. Maceió, Brazil, 1928.
Novos Poemas. Rio de Janeiro, 1929.
Poemas Escolhidos. Rio de Janeiro, 1932.
Tempo e Eternidade. Porto Alegre, Brazil, 1935. Written in collaboration with Murilo Mendes.
A Túnica Inconsútil. Rio de Janeiro, 1938.
Poemas Negros. Rio de Janeiro, 1947.
Livro de Sonetos. Rio de Janeiro, 1949.
Obra Poética. Edited by Otto Maria Carpeaux. Rio de Janeiro, 1950. Contains *Anunciação e Encontro de Mira-Celi*.
Invenção de Orfeu. Rio de Janeiro, 1952.

Novels

Salomão e as Mulheres. Rio de Janeiro, 1927.
O Anjo. Rio de Janeiro, 1934.

Calunga. Porto Alegre, Brazil, 1935.
A Mulher Obscura. Rio de Janeiro, 1939.

Essays

Dois Ensaios (Proust e Todos Cantam a Sua Terra). Maceió, Brazil, 1929.

Photomontages

A Pintura em Pânico. Rio de Janeiro, 1943.

Translations

Poems. Translated by Melissa S. Hull. Rio de Janeiro, 1952.

Biographical and Critical Studies

Anselmo, Manuel. *A Poesia de Jorge de Lima: Ensaio de Interpretação Crítica.* São Paulo, 1939.

Basatto, Luiz. *Montagem em "Invenção de Orfeu."* Rio de Janeiro, 1978.

Carneiro, José Fernando. *Apresentação de Jorge de Lima.* Rio de Janeiro, 1958.

Dutra, Waltensir. *A Evolução de um Poeta: Ensaios sobre a Poesia de Jorge de Lima.* Rio de Janeiro, 1952.

Riedel, Dirce Côrtes, ed. *Leitura de "Invenção de Orfeu."* Rio de Janeiro, 1975.

Mário de Andrade

(1893–1945)

Massaud Moisés

Mário Raul de Andrade was born in São Paulo, Brazil, on 9 October 1893. After high school, he entered the Dramatic and Musical Conservatory of São Paulo. In 1917, he began his career as a writer, publishing a book of poems, Parnassian in structure, *Há Uma Gôta de Sangue em Cada Poema* (There Is a Drop of Blood in Every Poem), under the pen name of Mário Sobral. A little later, he became the leader of the avant-garde generation that promoted the Semana de Arte Moderna (Modern Art Week) in São Paulo in February 1922. In the years following the emergence of Brazilian modernism, Andrade was very active in propagating its ideas. From 1934 to 1937 he organized the Department of Culture of São Paulo. In 1938, having moved to Rio de Janeiro, he was appointed director of the Institute of Arts of the University of the Federal District. At the same time, he actively cooperated with the Ministry of Education and Culture. In 1940, he returned to São Paulo, where he died on 25 February 1945.

Andrade wrote many books, in such diverse genres and kinds as poetry, the novel, the short story, the *idílio* (idyll), the *rapsódia* (rhapsody), the essay, the chronicle, and miscellanies.

With the publication of *Paulicéia Desvairada* (Hallucinated City) in 1922 and *Macunaíma* (*Macunaíma*) in 1928, Andrade symbolically marked the frontiers of the first period of Brazilian modernism. The followers and critics of that literary movement used to call him the *Papa do modernismo* (pope of modernism). As a poet, Andrade began by cultivating the *poema piada* (joke poem), a kind of poem written by the adherents of modernism to shock the bourgeois. Guided by the old slogan *ridendo castigat mores* (laughing is the best way to reform custom), the joke poem was full of an intentional but inconsequent humor.

The poetry of circumstances, which is also part of Andrade's work in verse, follows the same pattern of immediacy. The *poema crônica* (chronicle poem), a sort of versified narrative of events and situations of everyday life, such as "Carnaval Carioca" (Carioca Carnival, in *Clã do Jabuti* [The Turtle's Clan, 1927]), is linked with that genre of poetry. The intention, in all of these poetic trends was to destroy the past, represented by Parnassianism and symbolism, and to establish modernist doctrines in its place. Paradoxically, though naturally, a strong emotivity is aroused by the poetry of commitment, inspired by the revolutionary feelings of the young generation of 1922. And with the flashes of emotion emerges the best of Andrade's poetry, especially when it is connected with the sentiment of being *paulista* (born in São Paulo). The city of São Paulo constitutes the starting point—*Hallucinated City*— and the point of arrival—*Lira Paulistana* (Lyre of São Paulo, 1946)—of his poetry. The 1922 volume opens with an exclamation full of emotivity: "São Paulo! comoção de minha vida. . . ." ("São Paulo! commotion of my life. . . ."), which suggests a lyric program or, at least, the poet's leitmotiv. Here one can find the fulcrum of Andrade's poetry, even his poetics. *Lira Paulistana* represents the climax of his technical development: it is the confluence of all his work as a poet, and his masterpiece.

"Garoa do Meu São Paulo" (Fog of My São Paulo), "O Bonde Abre A Viagem" (The Streetcar Begins Its Trip), "Eu Não Sei se Vale a Pena" (I Do Not Know if It Is Worthwhile), "Agora Eu Quero Cantar" (Now I Want to Sing), and "Quando Eu Morrer Quero Ficar" (When I Die I Want to Stay) are some of the poems of *Lira Paulistana* that exemplify Andrade's poetic skill, and are among the best poetry of early modernism. Let us take, as an example, "Garoa do Meu São Paulo":

> Garoa do meu São Paulo,
> —Timbre triste de martírios—
> Um negro vem vindo, é branco!
> Só bem perto fica negro,
> Passa e torna a ficar branco.
>
> Meu São Paulo da garoa,
> —Londres das neblinas finas—
> Um pobre vem vindo, é rico!
> Só bem perto fica pobre,
> Passa e torna a ficar rico.
>
> Garoa do meu São Paulo,
> —Costureira de malditos—
> Vem um rico, vem um branco,
> São sempre brancos e ricos . . .
>
> Garoa, sai dos meus olhos.
> (*Poesias Completas*, p. 353)

Fog of my São Paulo,
—Sad timbre of tortures—
One black man is coming, he is white!
Only closer is he black,
He passes, and becomes white.

My foggy São Paulo,
—You London of fine mists—
One poor man is coming, he is rich!
Only closer is he poor,
He passes, and becomes rich.

Fog of my São Paulo,
—Dressmaker of damned people—
A rich man comes, a poor man comes,
They are always white and rich . . .

Fog, go out from my eyes.

As a prose writer, Andrade started in 1926 with *Primeiro Andar* (The First Floor), a collection of stories written from 1914 to 1923. In the second edition of this book (1943), he added stories written between 1929 and 1939, eliminated others, and transferred one, "O Besouro e a Rosa" (The Bug and the Rose), to *Histórias de Belazarte* (Belazarte's Stories, 1944, the title of the second edition of *Belazarte* [Belazarte, 1934]). In the edition of the author's collected works, from 1944 on, the volume was included in *Obra Imatura* (Immature Work).

Mário de Andrade, in the early stages, was a short story writer typical of the *belle époque*, searching for his themes either in the realm of the fantastic or in regionalism, thus following the example of Afonso Arinos, Valdomiro Silveira, and several others. He was also interested in the golden times of bohemian life. *Primeiro Andar* also includes two small dramatic plays and a fragment of the novel *Café* (Coffee, 1930), later converted into the homonymous "melodramatic work." In 1942, Andrade wrote a play entitled *Café* and subtitled "Concepção Melodramática" (melodramatic conception) or "Tragédia Secular" (centennial tragedy).

In *Belazarte*, Andrade imagines himself a storyteller named Belazarte, and portrays a gallery of human types taken from the daily life of São Paulo during the 1920's. Most of the characters are Italian immigrants living sad love stories. The dramatic scheme varies from story to story, but its ingredients are the same. And the vision of reality, showing the persistence of melodramatic situations among that people, remains immutable. Hence Andrade gives us a kind of moving realism, grounded in a poetic outlook and in an empathy with those humble people and their sorrows that stems not from the author's ideological convictions but from his religious beliefs.

Although "Piá não Sofre? Sofre" (Doesn't the Boy Suffer? He Suffers) can be detached as one of the masterpieces among Andrade's short stories, the book is quite homogeneous due to its obsession with the deeply human. Giving up on the iconoclastic tendency of 1922, he could reach the highest level in his career as an author of short stories.

The posthumous publication of *Contos Novos* (New Short Stories, 1946, previously entitled *Contos Piores* [Worst Short Stories]) offers the opportunity to make a safer judgment of all of Andrade's literary achievement. The book contains nine short stories, one of them, "Nelson" (Nelson), without the final corrections that the author certainly would have made before the story was printed. As a rule, the texts were recast many times; the oldest, "Frederico Paciência" (Frederick Patience), was written in 1924. Others were outlined in 1927—"Atrás da Catedral de Ruão" (Behind Rouen Cathedral)—or had their earlier versions in 1930—"O Ladrão" (The Thief)—or 1934—"Primeiro de Maio" (Labor Day).

From the linguistic point of view, the narratives included in the book differ from the models praised by the modernists of 1922. Either the short stories were shaped in a style less bold than was usual at the time, or the author, during their recasting, stamped them with the diction of a mature prose writer, free from the juvenile rebellion of Modern Art Week and aware of the fact that the perpetuation of a literary work depends, first of all, on its form. Struggling for a concise style, he moved in the direction of a Machadian (after Machado de Assis, 1839–1908) tone, as in "Primeiro de Maio." Obviously, one can find some peculiar devices typical of colloquial speech, but one must say that the prose rhythm is that of Assis, open to certain uses and abuses of Brazilian Portuguese. Rejecting the support of his narrator (Belazarte), the author takes over the command of the stories, and the first-person narration unchains a process of autobiographic reminiscences. The flashes of insight into the remote personal past seem to indicate an inclination for memorializing, an inclination that has been prevented by the iconoclastic circumstances of modernism. Andrade's voluminous and sustained correspondence with people all around the country confirms a narcissistic bent for autobiography, and simultaneously arouses our suspicion that the author must have at least once contemplated writing a book of memoirs.

The reminiscent atmosphere explains why *Contos Novos* shows a weakness that does not exist in *Histórias de Belazarte*: the stories contain numerous details that are not directly relevant to the plot. Concentrating attention on the mysteries of language, even of metalanguage, and on Andrade's autobiographical recollections, "Frederico Paciência" reminds us of *O Ateneu* (The Atenaeum, 1888), the well-known novel by Raul Pompéia, who also lengthened his narratives with extraneous details. The andante movement of the stories is underlined by the fact that they sometimes revolve around a joke whose effects are obviously slackened by the delay in unveiling the privileged moment on which the joke is based. "O Peru de Natal" ("The Christmas Turkey"), thanks to its concision, rhythm, originality, and fitness, is Andrade's masterpiece in the field of the short story. Not even good stories, such as "Atrás da Catedral de Ruão" and "Frederico Paciência," are exempt from the defects of general lengthening—defects that stress by contrast the Machadian luminosity of "The Christmas Turkey."

Analyzed in their totality, Andrade's short stories give us a panorama of his literary career. First of all, let us consider the texts before 1930. From 1922 to 1928, he was entirely absorbed by his literary activities. Years later, when he took up those narratives again or wrote new ones, he seemed to recapture his juvenile period of intense literary activity in spite of the peculiar cadence of a mature man.

Second, when recasting his stories in 1942–1945, Andrade was consistent with his past ideas and feelings but did not yet foreshadow the author of *Macunaíma*, nor had he been touched by the impact of the new fiction of the 1930's, mainly that of the social novel, as might have been expected in view of the evolution of his vision of reality.

After 1930, as he increased his interest in politics, ethnography, anthropology, and the like, he lost part of his old passion for literary studies. That is why *Contos Novos* does not fully reflect the author as he was in 1943 but as he had been in 1922–1928 or even before, as evidenced by the *belle époque* flavor of

"Atrás da Catedral de Ruão" and "Nelson." In short, Andrade in 1942–1943 was still the "modernist" of 1922. He carefully tuned up his instrument but looked for the subject of his stories in his memories or experiences of youth instead of observing the reality of his contemporary life.

Like many other writers, Andrade began his career by practicing those genres—for example, the short story—that are usually thought to provide a kind of literary training, before venturing on more tortuous paths. *Amar, Verbo Intransitivo* (To Love, Intransitive Verb), published in 1927, was subtitled "Idyll," which immediately suggests the ambiguity of the narrative. This work was translated into English as *Fräulein* in 1933 and was also made into the film "Lição de Amor" (A Lesson of Love), with relative success. The story centers on Elza, a fräulein hired by a rich man, Sousa Costa, to initiate his son, Carlos Alberto, in the mysteries of love. Indeed, the term "idyll," taken in its common conception, may well suit the plot of the novel, but not its structure. The story of the sexual initiation of a fifteen-year-old adolescent, involving the payment of a good amount of money, flows linearly and ends without surprise. It raises some questions, however, not because of the unusual theme but because of the way the author chose to face it.

First of all, it is evident that the author had a sociological aim when he picked such a theme: certainly his purpose was not to offer an "idyll" to entertain the middle classes but to shock them. In developing his project in the frontier region between literature and sociology, however, he fell into a duality that perhaps was not intentional.

Is it not paradoxical that Andrade chose a young German lady as the novel's main character? It is obvious that the choice was not aleatory: the situation focused on by the novel would be quite different if a Japanese woman had been chosen instead of a fräulein (one should remember that Sousa's servant is from Japan), or a mulatta, a choice which would have been more natural in a novel placed in a tropical country like Brazil.

I think it would not be impertinent to conclude that a kind of anti-Aryanism pervades the pages of *Amar, Verbo Intransitivo.* A reaction against Oliveira Viana's Aryan thesis? Viana, an essayist of the first

decades of this century, defended the idea that white blood is "purer" than black blood. But in this case, is it not a kind of inverted racism? One can be persuaded of this possibility—no matter if it lies outside the author's intentions—by simply taking into account some of the opinions of the German woman:

> Take a look at the example of Germany. Is there any stronger race? None. That is so because the concept of family is stronger and indestructible among the Germans. Their children are robust. Their women are big and white. They are fecund. The noble man's destiny is to keep himself healthful and look for a prodigiously healthful wife. A wife of a superior race, as herself, Fräulein. The blacks are of an inferior race. So are the Indians. And the Portuguese.

How to admit, without perplexity, that such ideas could occur to someone who works as a "teacher of love"? One must add that throughout the narrative other surprising thoughts cross the fräulein's mind: she held the opinion, for example, that her job was as worthy as any other. That was not, however, Sousa Costa's or the narrator/author's point of view.

On the other hand, the narrator/author, who often interrupts the narration in order to insert pieces of dissertation, frequently analyzes the Germans as he would in a sociological essay:

> There are two persons in the native of Germany: the typical German, the man-of-dreams; and the man-of-life, a practical specimen of the man-of-the-world, as Socrates called himself.
>
> The first kind of German is the one who dreams, is clumsy, obscure, nostalgically philosophic, religious, incorrigibly idealistic, extremely serious, closely linked with his country and his family, sincere, and weighs 230 pounds.

Or, without entirely disguising his xenophobia, he describes the slow social rise of the immigrants:

> And little by little Brazil is going to belong to the Brazilians, for God's sake! Mrs. Maria Wright Blavatsky, Mrs. Carlotinha I-do-not-know-what Manolo. When there is illness at home, Dr. Serapião de Lucca comes. The engineer of the neocolonial bungalow (Asia and two Americas! All right: Chandernagor, Bay Shore, and Tabatinguera) is Mr. Peri Sternheim.

Obviously forgetting his antibourgeois ideology, the author puts before those exclamation marks the following observations: "With what horrible company Sousa Costa's people have been involved! But in Brazil it is always like that; and nothing better could be done!"

Of course, the narrator was trying to give an ironic treatment of the novel's main theme. It seems that he wanted to transfer to Sousa Costa's world the tone of the joke poem that was fashionable in the 1920's. It is in a tone between seriousness and jocosity that he refers to Carlos Alberto's initiation in love, since his anti-Aryanism did not allow him to eulogize the bourgeois class.

On the contrary, the condemnation of the wealthy middle classes—which bought love with money— was perhaps his main intention, disguised, involuntarily, by the attack on Aryanism or even on the ascendant flux of immigration. The narrator's frequent interpolations, including those referring to his theory of the novel, are an evidence of his purpose. He says: "What a lie, my God! that one could say that Fräulein is my invention and my construction! I did not construct anything. One day, it was Wednesday, Elza appeared to me, while I had no intention of seeking her." He says so smiling, and also insinuating that he was only relating the facts. At another moment, still making use of the same gestures, he says: "Ah! . . . I almost forget to warn you that this idyll is an imitation of Bernardin de Saint-Pierre's French. Of the French language. Bernardin de Saint-Pierre's French language."

The digressions, more characteristic of an essayist than of a novelist, are well suited to the novel's structure and subject. They are also unexpectedly more modern—modern in the sense of making a metanovel, in which the writer thinks about the art of the novel at the same time as he writes one—than the book's audacious dramatic situation. On the other hand, they explain the progression of the plot too much, removing all the mystery that could exist in the idyll between an experienced fräulein and the young Carlos Alberto. And they prolong unnecessarily the story, giving the impression that the narrator/ author was not sure of the novel's effectiveness without those comments and interruptions.

It is easy to suspect, one may add, that the

narrative, after the evening dates between the main characters had become a routine, would have slipped little by little into other situations of Sousa Costa's familiar context. Besides, when the lesson of love is over, and both the idyll and Elza's job in that middle-class family have come to an end, the narrator/ author decides to show us, without a plausible justification, the fräulein engaged with another adolescent ignorant of sex.

From these facts one may infer that, except for the psychological and chronological aspects of the dramatic situation, the narrative could well be classified as a short story deliberately inflated. In classifying it as an idyll, the author reveals that he certainly was aware that the love story between Elza and Carlos Alberto structurally wavers between the short story and the novel. He probably believed that any other label would dissipate its purposive experimental and eclectic atmosphere, as he confesses in a letter dated 10 October 1924 to Manuel Bandeira:

> I believe that Fräulein [that is, Amar, Verbo Intransitivo,] will go together [with this letter]. I have just copied it. It is a research work. Is it madness? I like very much my Fräulein. If I were a humorist, the book would represent the best I could do in this matter of humor with comments. But I am afraid that I am wrong. The book is an incredible mixture. There is everything in it. Criticism, theory, psychology, and even fiction: it is I. And I am a researcher.

Macunaíma, published one year after Amar, Verbo Intransitivo, goes in the same direction, under the same sign of experimentation, but with specific differences, which probably make this book the author's masterpiece. The hero, who gives the novel its title, is "pitch black, a son of night fear," born of a tapanhumas Indian (of the state of Mato Grosso) in the middle of the jungle. He later learns to speak. Very early he shapes his motto: "Ah, what laziness!" He is fond of women; he likes to "play" (make love) with young girls, even with those who are engaged to his brothers, Jiguê and Maanape. One day, he and his brothers "left home without any destination." Macunaíma receives a muiraquitã (a green stone of the Amazon, with the power of an amulet) from Ci, a woman with whom he had made love, who is called "Mãe do Mato" (Mother of the Jungle). He loses the magic stone in one of his many adventures but is told that the stone is in São Paulo with a giant, Venceslau Pietro Pietra.

After leaving his conscience in the island of Marapatá, he goes to São Paulo in order to recover the amulet. There, he becomes the protagonist of more adventures. Later, in Rio de Janeiro, he attends a *macumba* (voodoo) session, and then returns to São Paulo. He writes a letter to his subjects, the *Icamiabas*, in a classic style. He becomes ill, recovers, and kills the giant. He and his brothers return to the jungle. He brings the *muiraquitã* in his lips. He also brings artifacts of civilization: a gun, a watch, and a cage with a cock and hen.

He returns to Marapatá to reclaim his conscience. Not finding it, he takes one belonging to a South American. His brothers die. Diving in a lagoon where Iara (the goddess of the waters) lives, the hero loses his amulet and one leg. "Then Macunaíma did not find any more fun in this earth," and decided to go to heaven, where he is transformed into the Great Bear: "He is the same lame hero who, after suffering in an unhealthy land full of saúva ants [a leaf-cutting ant common in Brazil], became bored with everything, went away, and meditates in solitude in the vast field of heaven."

With the subtitle "O Herói Sem Nenhum Caráter" (A Hero Without Any Character), *Macunaíma* is classified by its author as a rhapsody. By rejecting the usual literary denominations in favor of a word borrowed from music, Andrade intended above all to point out the miscellaneous structure of his book, or its indeterminate position in the group of literary genres. In doing so, he was indeed right. The narration of Macunaíma's pilgrimage from birth to death shares aspects of the epic and of the novel, and simultaneously takes advantage of the rich Luso-Afro-Indian folklore: the mosaic of the historic, geographic, and social realities of Brazil is indelibly represented in the rhapsodic tissue of the narrative and its hero.

Thanks to its supernatural character, *Macunaíma* is linked with the epic genre, as far as it is also devoted to the glorification of the central myth of a people. It differs, however, from the traditional epic poem, for its mythology is not Hellenic or Christian but Amerindian and black, with the impregnation of a surrealistic absurdity. A mythology conceived as a perennial make-believe and performed by a naive people, based on the legends and candid beliefs taken from the main races that constitute the Brazilian people—this is the substratum of *Macunaíma*.

Just as Guesa, Joaquim de Sousandrade's (1833–1902) romantic hero, wanders through the immense land of the Americas, the hero of *Macunaíma*, a kind of Brazilindian, travels all over the country, facing and embodying, practically in every adventure, its rich and varied universe of fables. The supernatural, as if emerging from the reality of the land and its people, is the space of his wanderings, which come to an end only when he passes away.

Macunaíma resembles a novel in the linear sequence of its episodes and adventures, with heroes that, in the manner of knights of the Middle Ages, crossed the Brazilian continent in quest of the *muiraquitã*. But one knight "without any character" abandoned himself to an inconsequent availability typical of one who is half man, half Indian boy, subject to his instincts and full of stratagems to survive the dangers of the jungle and the big city. And as in medieval romances and narrative poems, the rhapsody transcends the boundaries of time and space: like "The Quest of the Holy Grail" or *Amadis of Gaul*, it is achronological and unspacial. Its time and space are the time and space of the fantastic, without any respect for the law of probability.

Deliberately conceived as a kind of divertissement *Macunaíma* centers its action on a hero akin to François Rabelais' characters, a true antihero since he is "without any character," showing the racial melting pot of the Brazilian people, and the lack of solid values, from the author's point of view, of the typical Brazilian. A Dionysiac hero, Macunaíma lives exclusively for fun, for the gratification of his senses, without the high aims that historically marked those natural demigods, the heroes of tradition. He is a "satyromaniac," fond of feasting, a vagabond, a rogue without malice, innocent in practice of good and evil because he is beyond them, as if he had been shaped under the influence of Friedrich Nietzsche's philosophy. Macunaíma tries all the human emotions, including fear, hatred, despair, envy, and anger; he escapes from perils, cries, and even dies; and his conversion into the Great Bear represents the climax of the abandonment of his heroic condition.

Macunaíma was published in the same year as *Retrato do Brasil* (*Portrait of Brazil,* 1928) by Paulo Prado, and it seems that Andrade's intention was to show its mythic or folkloric counterpart: both books have identical theses, centered on the idea that lust is a Brazilian obsession and the origin of all of the country's evils. The rhapsody seems to work as an illustration of Prado's essay, for Macunaíma's wanderings are those of a primitive man, Adamic, without restrictions of any order, immoderately devoted to erotic games, from whence result all the troubles and evils he suffers in his lifetime. The hero is weak when in the presence of perils; he saves himself by cheating and lying, or by using the mythical licenses that allow him to perform magic tricks through which he can overcome the difficulties interposed by other people and by nature. His mythic "works" are those of an anti-Heracles, relapsing and amoral, always aiming at the satisfaction of his fleshly appetites, deprived of a higher purpose in life.

A "hero without any character," lacking the mythical quality of the demigods, Macunaíma liberates himself from his (bad) human condition and embarks on aimless adventures, the symbolic import of which either is evident—the adventures point up his lack of character—or resists interpretation. It is difficult, for instance, to see what is symbolized, from the mythical standpoint, by the episode in which Macunaíma falls ill with leprosy, afterward transmitting the illness "to seven other persons, who suddenly became cured." This recording of a popular belief in miraculous cures reveals something about the historical Brazilian collective psyche, but it does not suggest larger symbolic meanings.

Written in a few days, yet incorporating a vast amount of material that the author had been collecting throughout his life, as shown by the solid erudition on which it is based, *Macunaíma* is undoubtedly a prodigious victory over chronology. Nonetheless, either because of the feverish speed with which the rhapsody was plotted, or in consequence of its fictional and mythical material, the book shows a structural unevenness that has to be pointed out if we want to make reliable judgments about it.

The rhapsody is composed of seventeen chapters and an epilogue. In chapter 9 the letter that the hero sent to his subjects is inserted, written in pedantically correct Portuguese; its intention is to satirize the purists of the Brazilian *belle époque* and the writers subservient to diction used in Portugal, as, for example, Ruy Barbosa and Coelho Neto.

Symbolically set in the middle of the story, if we consider the epilogue also as a chapter, the letter divides the narrative into two parts. In the first, there is a succession of supernatural episodes, giving the impression that we are reading a story of enchantment. After Macunaíma's speech to his subjects, telling of his adventures in São Paulo, the pilgrimage of the hero "without any character" seems to conform to logic in the sequence of the scenes, presented in a sort of linear organization. The element of surprise is very strong in the first episodes:

The other day, the brothers went fishing and hunting; the old woman went to the cleared land, and Macunaíma remained behind with Jiguê's girlfriend. Then, he was transformed into an ant, and bit Iriqui for fun. But the girl threw the ant away. Then Macunaíma became an annatto [bush]. The beautiful Iriqui smiled, took the seeds, and with coquetry made up her face and badges. She became extremely beautiful. Then Macunaíma, just to play the cocky one, turned into a person again, and lived with Jiguê's girlfriend.

(chapter 2)

In the same portion of the narrative, the element of surprise visibly decreases, either because of the repetition of the same magic tricks or because the atmosphere of absurdity is attenuated:

He was passing by when he heard the "hist!" of a woman. He stopped, full of fear. Then, a tall and ugly old lady, with braids falling to her feet, came out from among the crooked trees. And, whispering, she asked the hero:
—Have they already gone away?
—Of course, who?
—The Dutchmen!
—You're getting crazy, no matter the Dutchmen. There is not a single Dutchman, lady!

(chapter 11)

Apart from the fact that the chronological climate of nonsense does not cause any impact on the reader, one should observe that the expository rhythm of the fragment sounds quite banal. Neither does it matter that all the chapters of *Macunaíma* were composed in a different order from that in which they finally appear in the book. Giving them such a sequence, the author created, perhaps undeliberately, a difference in dramatic temperature, as though the regularity of Macunaíma's letter to his subjects should have contaminated all the development of the last chapters. So much so that the purism of the letter is obviously present in one of the hero's dialogues: "—Patience, brothers! no! I won't go to Europe, no. I am American, and my place is in America. The European civilization certainly destroys the integrity of our character" (chapter 12).

Mário de Andrade wrote *Macunaíma* as if he were playing; it seems he wrote it for fun. He made a book of humor—perhaps to redeem himself of the sociological gravity of *Amar, Verbo Intransitivo*—as if he were telling a series of jokes about the *homo brasilicus*, according to his outlook and to his generation. One could say that Macunaíma's temperament might have influenced the author himself, compelling him to draw the hero's portrait and that of his people in a spirit of great fun, without any obligation. Andrade's work was probably a healthful catharsis, since he included himself in the laughing provoked by the hero's erotic feats.

Obviously, as an objective portrait of Brazilian reality, and as a warning, *Macunaíma* was more successful than Prado's *Portrait of Brazil*, which was too pessimistic to lead the reader to a full realization of his social and historical background. On the other hand, the emphasis upon one element of the Brazilian anthropological constitution (lust) reduces the scope of its diagnosis. In any case, *Macunaíma* has all the conditions to be considered one of the masterpieces of the period that started in 1922, and of Brazilian literature as a whole. It is a mirror that reflects all the complexity of a people created in the likeness of Macunaíma, "the hero without any character," the "hero of our people."

Besides being a poet, a novelist, a short story writer, a "rhapsode," and a literary critic, Mário de Andrade wrote hundreds of letters to a great variety of people, dealing with problems of literature and aesthetics. His collected letters are indispensable material for the interpretation of his own work and that of his contemporaries. He used his letters to offer help and guidance to younger writers, and to enlighten and stimulate those of his own generation, as one can see in *Cartas a Manuel Bandeira* (Letters to Manuel Bandeira, 1958), *Setenta e Uma Cartas de Mário de Andrade* (Seventy-One Letters of Mário de Andrade, 1963), and *Mário de Andrade Escreve a Alceu, Meyer e Outros* (Mário de Andrade Writes to Alceu [Amoroso Lima], Meyer [Augusto] and Others, 1968).

Less modern, or less modernist, than many companions of his generation, Mário de Andrade is, despite this fact, or perhaps because of it, the most representative writer of the first period of Brazilian modernism. He did not orthodoxly accept the bolder gestures of 1922, which were a tribute to the anarchical; nor did he accept the necessarily ephemeral "modern," which had been inspired by futurism and other "isms" of the first decades of this century. As a matter of fact, he rejected everything of the past that could bring immobility or the repetition of wasteful aesthetic solutions. In doing so, he was able to reach the equilibrium characteristic of the "classics" who sustain and enlarge the literary activity of a country.

SELECTED BIBLIOGRAPHY

First Editions

Poetry

Paulicéia Desvairada. São Paulo, 1922.
Losango Cáqui. São Paulo, 1926.
Clã do Jabuti. São Paulo, 1927. Includes "Carnaval Carioca."
Remate de Males. São Paulo, 1930.
Lira Paulistana. São Paulo, 1946. Includes "Garoa do Meu São Paulo."

Prose Narratives

Primeiro Andar. São Paulo, 1926.
Amar, Verbo Intransitivo. São Paulo, 1927.
Macunaíma. São Paulo, 1928.
Belazarte. São Paulo, 1934.

Contos Novos. São Paulo, 1947. Includes "Nelson," "Frederico Paciência," "Atrás da Catedral de Ruão," "O Ladrão," "Primeiro de Maio," and "O Peru de Natal."

Essays

A Escrava que não é Isaura. São Paulo, 1925.
O Aleijadinho e Álvares de Azevedo. Rio de Janeiro, 1935.
O Movimento Modernista. Rio de Janeiro, 1942.
Aspectos da Literatura Brasileira. Rio de Janeiro, 1943.
O Baile das Quatro Artes. São Paulo, 1943.
Os Filhos da Candinha. São Paulo, 1943.
O Empalhador de Passarinho. São Paulo, 1944(?).
Táxi e Crônicas no Diário Nacional. São Paulo, 1976.

Nonfiction

Compêndio de História da Música. São Paulo, 1929. Rev. ed., with the title of *Pequena História da Música*, São Paulo, 1942.
Modinhas Imperiais. São Paulo, 1930.
Música, Doce Música. São Paulo, 1933.
A Música e a Canção Populares no Brasil. São Paulo, 1936.
Namoros com a Medicina. Pôrto Alegre, Brazil, 1939.
A Expressão Musical dos Estados Unidos. Rio de Janeiro, 1940.
Música do Brasil. Curitiba, Brazil, 1941.
Danças Dramáticas do Brasil. 3 vols. São Paulo, 1959. Posthumous.
Música de Feitiçaria no Brasil. São Paulo, 1963. Posthumous.
Aspectos das Artes Plásticas no Brasil. São Paulo, 1965. Posthumous.

Letters

Cartas de Mário Andrade a Manuel Bandeira. Rio de Janeiro, 1958.
Setenta e Uma Cartas de Mário de Andrade. Edited by Lygia Fernandes. Rio de Janeiro, 1963.
Mário de Andrade Escreve a Alceu, Meyer e Outros. Edited by Lygia Fernandes. Rio de Janeiro, 1968.

Diary

O Turista Aprendiz. São Paulo, 1977.

Collected Works

Obras Completas de Mário de Andrade. 20 vols. São Paulo, 1944——.

Modern Editions

Amar, Verbo Intransitivo. Edited by Telê Porto Ancona Lopez. São Paulo, 1982.
Macunaíma. Edited by Telê Porto Ancona Lopez. São Paulo, 1978.
Poesias Completas. Edited by Diléa Zanotto Manfio. Belo Horizonte and São Paulo, 1987.

Translations

"The Christmas Turkey." Translation of "O Peru de Natal" by Richard B. Brenneman. *Latin-American Literary Review* 7/14:96–102 (1979).
Fräulein. Translation of *Amar, Verbo Intransitivo* by Margaret Richardson Hollingsworth. New York, 1933.
Hallucinated City [Paulicéia Desvairada]. Translated and with an introduction by Jack E. Tomlins. Nashville, Tenn., 1968. Bilingual edition.
Macunaíma. Translated by Edward Arthur Goodland. New York, 1984.

Biographical and Critical Studies

Almeida, Fernando Mendes de. *Mário de Andrade.* São Paulo, 1962.
Athayde, Tristão de. In *Estudos 1.* Rio de Janeiro, 1927. "Actualidades," pp. 58–66; "Sinais," pp. 67–76.
———. In *Estudos 2.* Rio de Janeiro, 1934. "Romancistas do Sul," pp. 26–29.
———. In *Estudos 5.* Rio de Janeiro, 1935. "Mais Vozes de Perto," pp. 125–134.
Bandeira, Antônio Rangel. *Espírito e Forma.* São Paulo, 1957.
Bandeira, Manuel. *Apresentação da Poesia Brasileira.* Rio de Janeiro, 1946.
Bastide, Roger. *Poetas do Brasil.* Curitiba, Brazil, 1947.
Campos, Haroldo de. *Morfología do Macunaíma.* São Paulo, 1973.
Dassin, Joan. *Política e Poesia em Mário de Andrade.* São Paulo, 1978.
Grieco, Agrippino. "Mário de Andrade—Belazarte." In *Gente Nova do Brasil.* Rio de Janeiro, 1935. Pp. 120–129.
Ivo, Lêdo. *Lição de Mário de Andrade.* Rio de Janeiro, 1952.
Lins, Álvaro. "Poesia e Forma." In *Jornal de Crítica 2.* Rio de Janeiro, 1943. Pp. 22–32.
———. "A Crítica de Mário de Andrade." In *Jornal de Crítica 5.* Rio de Janeiro, 1947. Pp. 75–82.
Lopez, Telê Porto Ancona. "Cronología Geral da Obra de

Mário de Andrade." *Revista de Estudos Brasileiros* (São Paulo) 7:139–172 (1969).

———. *Mário de Andrade: Ramais e Caminho.* São Paulo, 1972.

Lucas, Fábio. "Em Torno de Mário de Andrade." In *Horizontes da Crítica.* Belo Horizonte, Brazil, 1965. Pp. 30–60.

Machado Filho, Aires da Mata. "Mário de Andrade e Seu Estilo." In *Crítica de Estilos.* Rio de Janeiro, 1956. Pp. 229–236.

Martins, Wilson. "Inventário de Mário de Andrade." In *Interpretações.* Rio de Janeiro, 1946. Pp. 153–185.

Mello e Sousa, Gilda de. *O Tupi e o Alaúde.* Uma Interpretação de Macunaíma, 1979. São Paulo, 1981.

Milliet, Sérgio. In *Diário Crítico* 1. São Paulo, 1944. Pp. 166–174.

———. In *Diário Crítico* 5. São Paulo, 1948. Pp. 86–93.

Nist, John. In *The Modernist Movement in Brazil: A Literary Study.* Austin, Tex., 1967. Pp. 59–70.

Proença, M. Cavalcanti. *Roteiro de Macunaíma.* São Paulo, 1955.

Revista do Arquivo Municipal de São Paulo. Homenagem a Mário de Andrade. 6 (January 1946).

Ribeiro, João. *"Macunaíma."* In *Crítica: Os Modernos.* Rio de Janeiro, 1952. Pp. 81–84.

Schwartz, Roberto. "O Piscologismo na Poética de Mário de Andrade." In *A Sereia e o Desconfiado.* Rio de Janeiro, 1965. Pp. 1–11.

Alceu Amoroso Lima

(1893–1983)

Vera Regina Teixeira

"Alceu Amoroso Lima, nearly ninety years old, dies of a heart attack after a prolonged illness" read the morning headlines of Rio de Janeiro newspapers on 15 August 1983. At dusk a crowd of mourners joined the family, friends, students, intellectuals, politicians, cardinals of the Catholic church, and fellow members of the Brazilian Academy of Letters who had gathered to pay their last respects to Dr. Alceu, as the philosopher and professor was affectionately called. The scholar and Catholic leader was laid to rest beside Maria Teresa, his wife of sixty-seven years, on the Feast of the Assumption, a date that marked the fifty-fifth anniversary of his conversion to Catholicism, on 15 August 1928.

Amoroso Lima, a champion of social justice and an unrelenting fighter for political and intellectual freedom, attained national recognition as a literary critic and essayist in 1935 when he was elected to the Brazilian Academy of Letters, the first of innumerable honors he received for his contributions to the twentieth-century history of ideas and to the advancement of moral and social thought in Brazil. Tristão de Athayde, the pseudonym Amoroso Lima adopted at the beginning of his literary career, became synonymous with erudition and discerning critical judgment. His influence was a determining factor in the country's intellectual life during the twentieth century. In addition, Amoroso Lima was a prominent intellectual who dared to lead an ideological war against the revolution of 1964 from the forum of his weekly newspaper column (writing as Tristão de Athayde) in *Jornal do Brasil.* Unrelentingly, he denounced the reign of fear and tyranny the military regime had installed in Brazil in an attempt to silence and oppress the young and the old, the poor and the middle class, the illiterate masses and, most particularly, the intellectual elite. As a prominent university professor for nearly forty years, Amoroso Lima inspired generations of students by his scholarship, vigor, and perseverance.

As the author of approximately eighty books over a period of some sixty years, the Brazilian humanist developed a praxis that dealt with a wide range of subjects—from economics and religion to sociology, politics, and literature—and was predicated upon a general philosophy of existence. In "A Morte de Alceu" (The Death of Alceu), a special section of the *Jornal do Brasil* of 15 August 1983, Gilberto Mendonça Teles, a poet and critic, remembers Amoroso Lima's existential preoccupation with the political, social, and religious destiny of the Brazilian man, as well as his pleasure in literature, a "joy that characterizes the Thomistic concept of art." Mendonça Teles' article "Alceu na Palavra dos Amigos e

781

Discipulos" (Alceu in the Words of Friends and Disciples) stresses that "only in literature, the art of arts because it is the art of the word, does man reach the highest domain of his creative freedom."

Writing as Tristão de Athayde, Amoroso Lima also promoted the revival of literary discourse and theory, departing from the premise that "it is impossible to judge a work without having understood it." He sustained this posture by establishing a coherence between a theoretical conceptualization firmly based on the Catholic ideology and the aesthetic postulate formulated in the preface to his first book, *Affonso Arinos* (Affonso Arinos, 1922)—"art is a form of life." An individual judging a work of art must also recognize that "there is no true criticism without a philosophy of life or a value judgment based upon the internal law that governs the critic's intellectual activity."

Amoroso Lima lived his long, productive life in Rio de Janeiro, the capital of Brazil from 1763 to 1960. He was born on the shores of the Carioca River in Laranjeiras (Orange Grove), one of the city's aristocratic neighborhoods, on 11 December 1893, at the height of a political crisis. The four-year-old republic, which had replaced the monarchy, was crumbling, and the country stood divided. The navy had staged a blockade of Rio in an ill-fated coup d'etat intended to force President Floriano Peixoto, the "Iron Marshal," to yield to the constitutional law of succession. Manuel José Amoroso Lima, a successful businessman, a positivist, and a fervent republican, wished to name his son after the strong man Peixoto, but the mother prevailed and the boy was called Alceu, after Alcaeus, the Greek lyric poet of the sixth century B.C. who was in love with freedom.

From an early age, Amoroso Lima enjoyed a climate of learning, sophistication, and refinement in the family residence, known as "A Casa Azul" (the Blue House), which he always remembered fondly. Rainer Maria Rilke once said, "There is no other homeland besides childhood; if the homeland is small, large is the dream." In an interview titled "Arquiros Impláveis" (Unforgiving Archives) for *O Cruzeiro* (2 January 1954), the sixty-year-old Amoroso Lima confessed to José Condé that "of all things I have written, I have only reread with pleasure the evocation of the house where I was born." Many

years later, in 1973, while working with Claudio Medeiros Lima on the *Memórias Improvisadas* (Improvised Memoirs), Amoroso Lima once again recalled the fundamental role the Blue House had played in his formative years, when his father and João Kopke, a schoolteacher, were the dominant influences in his life. However, his family's considerable intellectual resources and brilliant circle of friends must also have been of marked importance. They knew such prominent individuals as Joaquim Maria Machado de Assis, the greatest Brazilian writer, South America's finest nineteenth-century novelist, and the founder of the Brazilian Academy of Letters; Ruy Barbosa, the minister of finance in the first cabinet of the new regime, a master of rhetoric and oratory, and the principal author of the Brazilian constitution of 1890; and the elder Affonso Arinos, a writer from Minas Gerais with broad European experience and a long commitment to the study of Brazilian legends and folklore. This last writer's personality, rather than his regionalistic prose, so fascinated Amoroso Lima that he became the subject of his first book, *Affonso Arinos.*

Between the years in Laranjeiras and his literary debut, Amoroso Lima took courses in the humanities and studied Brazilian literature with Coelho Neto, a premodernist author and perhaps the most respected literary figure between the sunset of naturalism and the dawn of Brazilian modernism. In 1909 Amoroso Lima began to study law at the Faculdade de Direito e Ciências Juridicas e Sociais in Rio de Janeiro, where one of his contemporaries was Ronald de Carvalho, future poet, critic, and member of the "carioca" modernist movement.

There is little doubt about the intellectual environment of the law school in Rio, where Silvio Romero—a disciple of Auguste Comte, Hippolyte Taine, and Gustave Flaubert—taught the philosophical and aesthetic canons in vogue at the time. Radically opposing all forms of romantic subjectivity, Romero espoused the narrowest possible sociological criticism prevalent in the second half of the nineteenth century. Upon graduating, Amoroso Lima traveled to Europe, mainly to Italy and France, where he studied with Henri Bergson at the Collège de France. There the young Brazilian heard the anti-intellectual, antirationalist French philosopher lecture on the ability of the mind to collect and recollect past experiences, a theory in accord with the teachings of Immanuel Kant, the father of modern critical philosophy. Bergson's lessons, during those formative years, left an indelible mark on Amoroso Lima's philosophical posture.

In "Alceu e as Duas Encarnações do Mefistófeles Fascista" (Alceu and the Two Incarnations of the Fascist Mephistopheles), published in the satiric weekly review *Pasquim* in November 1983, the novelist Antônio Callado confirms Amoroso Lima's admiration for his French mentor with a list of the most powerful intellectual influences on Amoroso Lima's life. In a series of dialogues between Amoroso Lima and Medeiros Lima for *Memórias Improvisadas*, Callado counted sixteen mentions of Bergson and as many mentions of Georges Bernanos, one of the foremost twentieth-century French Catholic authors, whose writing Amoroso Lima admired greatly and whom he had met personally. Machado de Assis, the intellectual paramount and family friend of his childhood, appears just as many times, followed by Silvio Romero with fourteen entries. Only two names appear more often. There are twenty-seven references to Jackson de Figueiredo, a close friend whose powerful spiritual influence endured beyond his death. The French philosopher Jacques Maritain, an inspiration and role model, mentioned on thirty-two occasions, heads the list.

While in Paris in 1913, Amoroso Lima met Graça Aranha, a respected member of the cultural elite of Rio de Janeiro and São Paulo, a novelist, and a theoretician fascinated with the experiments of the early European avant-garde. Graça Aranha alerted the young liberal that the times called for substantial change. Amoroso Lima's familiarity with the expressionism of the Italian philosopher Benedetto Croce as well as with Bergson's intuitive philosophy, predicated on a conscience liberated from the idea of space and time, made it easier for him to grasp the need for philosophical and aesthetic renewal. It was not, however, until a year later, after a stay in Venice marred by discouragement and disillusion with himself and the world, that Amoroso Lima felt ready to assume the mission of his generation. The chaos of World War I had helped to drive

home the realization that it was imperative to break away from the established molds and to invent new solutions.

By 1919 the young lawyer had settled in Rio, where he joined his father's business in an administrative capacity and married Maria Teresa Faria. His intellectual preoccupations led him to found the Grupo Goethe, a group dedicated to the propagation of the humanistic ideals of Johann Wolfgang von Goethe. That same year, Renato Toledo Lopes invited Amoroso Lima to join his staff as a literary critic for *O Jornal*, a publication founded for the dissemination of "new" ideas. Afraid that such a task might not be compatible with his image of entrepreneur, Amoroso Lima accepted the invitation with the condition that his writings appear under a pseudonym.

The first issue of *O Jornal*, published on 17 June 1919, marked the birth of Tristão de Athayde, the pen name the writer used exclusively until 1928. From that year on, both names appeared in most books, but Amoroso Lima signed all the contributions to *O Jornal*, the *Diário de Notícias* and the *Jornal do Brasil* with his pen name. His columns were published to the end of his life and even posthumously. Tristão de Athayde also sent occasional articles to the *Jornal do Comércio*, the *Revista do Brasil* as well as to *O Estado de Minas* and other papers of the time, including the Argentine *La Prensa* of Buenos Aires. His collaboration in *O Jornal* with a column entitled "Vida Literaria" (Literary Life), which regularly ended with a request for books to be reviewed, lasted until 1945.

Put in a broader perspective, it appears that the adoption of a pen name was as much a need to express critical opinions without social constraints as a symptom of the spiritual crisis Amoroso Lima was undergoing. Those troubled times culminated in 1928 with his conversion to Catholicism, followed two months later by the news of Jackson de Figueiredo's drowning. That untimely death, and Amoroso Lima's sense of loyalty, led him to chart for himself a new course in life in order to carry on Jackson's interrupted mission as an influential Christian leader. In a letter to Sérgio Buarque de Holanda, "Adeus à Disponibilidade" (A Farewell to Availability), Amoroso Lima wrote in 1929:

The new generations love the potentiality of what may come to be, while I believe that there must be a necessary option to be. They love temporal things, while I maintain it is our duty not to allow time to defeat us. They choose the subordination of the individual to the masses, while I see the necessity of saving the individual.

The phase of literary and aesthetic militancy was over. Amoroso Lima's writings became from that moment increasing ideological, totally committed to the defense and propagation of Catholic doctrine and human rights. For that purpose he took off the mask Tristão de Athayde and took full charge of his mission as an educator and writer.

A move away from the realm of literature toward social thought initiated Amoroso Lima's third intellectual phase. The liberal humanist published a series of books on the subject of social justice: *Revolução, Reação ou Reforma?* (Revolution, Reaction, or Reform?, 1964), *Pelo Humanismo Ameaçado* (In Defense of Threatened Humanism, 1965), and *A Experiência Reacionária* (The Reactionary Experience, 1968). All three confirmed Amoroso Lima's self-imposed mission to denounce the military regime. Amoroso Lima's protest against tyrants continued in the form of several articles and two books: *Os Direitos do Homem e o Homem sem Direitos* (The Rights of Man and the Man Without Rights, 1974) and *Em Busca da Liberdade* (In Search of Freedom, 1975).

It is, however, Tristão de Athayde who signs *Meio Século de Presença Literária* (Half a Century of Literary Presence), a book that appeared in 1969 in commemoration of the golden jubilee of his adoption of this pen name. The work, a collection of representative essays published over the years, marks the beginning of yet another phase in the life of Amoroso Lima. The nom de plume of the troubled years now has come to stand for persisting illusions and memories of things past: the volume opens with a letter from Alceu to Tristão as a public gesture of reconciliation, an admission of an inescapable symbiotic relationship between the two literary personalities.

In the letter, dated 31 January 1969, Alceu confesses that he had thought of abandoning Tristão at the time of his conversion and Jackson's death. After 1928, Alceu and Tristão coexisted. While Amoroso Lima's name appeared on the book covers, Tristão de Athayde signed the weekly newspaper columns. The

symbiosis was such that the readers and critics would not differentiate between the two personalities. Carlos Drummond de Andrade wrote in the introduction to *Meio Século de Presença Literária*: "Alceu and Tristão: the name and the pseudonym show a unity of soul in the unity of love."

In *Estudos* (Studies), a series of literary essays collected in five volumes and published between 1927 and 1933, Amoroso Lima appears as the author, but the pseudonym is given in parenthesis as well. Tristão de Athayde is the coauthor of *Problema da Burguesia* (A Problem of the Bourgeoisie), a philosophical and socioeconomic study of class structures from medieval to contemporary societies, published in 1932. By 1935 it was Amoroso Lima who published *No Limiar da Idade Nova* (At the Threshold of the New Age), which was followed in 1938 by *Idade, Sexo e Tempo* (Age, Sex, and Time). This, in the writer's own estimation his most important book, deals with the contemporary revolution against sexual taboos, and contrasts the extreme positions of puritanism and libertinism. In it he defends sexuality as a fundamental human instinct, but condemns all unruly sexual activity.

Inspired by Thomas More's *Utopia* (1516), Amoroso Lima published in 1943 *A Igreja e o Novo Mundo* (The Church and the New World), a philosophical analysis of man and religion since the discovery of America. *O Crítico Literário* (The Literary Critic) and *A Estética Literária* (Literary Aesthetics), two landmarks in Amoroso Lima's career as a literary critic and essayist, appeared in 1945. In 1956 Amoroso Lima brought out *Introdução à Literatura Brasileira* (Introduction to Brazilian Literature) and *Quadro Sintético da Literatura Brasileira* (A Schematic View of Brazilian Literature), excellent tools for understanding and classifying Brazilian letters.

In twentieth-century Brazilian letters, Amoroso Lima, Afrânio Coutinho, and Antônio Cândido share a position analogous to that held by José Veríssimo, Araripe Junior, and Silvio Romero, the powerful late-nineteenth-century triad of naturalist literary critics. While Veríssimo and Araripe Junior professed an eclectic literary criticism, it was Romero, a rather dogmatic figure and a distinguished professor of law, who at first exerted a more direct influence on Amoroso Lima's intellectual construct.

Later in life, when he became an established scholar, Amoroso Lima challenged Romero's perception of literature as "a direct expression of natural and social factors or as biosociological determinism," which sustained the point of view that the best literary criticism was "genetic rather than formalist." Amoroso Lima further questioned Romero's tenet that the merit of a literary work increased in direct proportion to the measure of accuracy with which it "mirrored society," rather than in its demonstrable formal or stylistic qualities. Romero's philosophical position reflected, and was consistent with, the wide influence of European thought on Brazilian intellectuals since 1868, especially Taine's reformulations of the evolutionist theories of Charles Darwin and Herbert Spencer. Amoroso Lima's mature work also disputed Romero's view of history as the reflection of deterministic factors and aspired to promote the progress of humanity.

Amoroso Lima's legacy to modern philosophical, ethical, and aesthetic thought is considerable and demonstrates a trajectory that culminated in the author's choice of French humanistic philosophy as the most adequate vehicle for his own expression, with Jacques Maritain as his model. Maritain's *Philosophy of Bergson* (1914) and *Art and Scholasticism* (1920) revised Bergson's aesthetics and admitted Bergson's "creative intuition" only in the context of several faculties that the whole man comprises. In a series of important works Maritain posited the possibility of a neo-Thomism that would harmonize the concepts of art and religion, in keeping with the religious, political, and ethical values set forth by Thomas Aquinas. During 1980 Tristão de Athayde published a series of articles, such as "Romero e Becket" (*Jornal do Brasil*, 25 April), specifically questioning matters related to social justice in Latin America.

In "Meditação Sobre a Palavra" (Meditation About the Word), published in *Jornal do Brasil* in August 1980, a review of Aires da Mata Machado Filho's philological study *A Palavra é de Ouro* (The Word Is Made of Gold, 1980), Amoroso Lima recognizes that "the word is, in reality, the macrocosm of this microcosm that is man. A macrocosm, because it translates our whole being in its plenitude, for good or for evil." He further develops the theme by establishing that "the word, as a tool for the noblest of all animals, is its maximum form of expression." In conclusion, the critic says that "the poet is the sole creator of the word for the sake of the word. . . . Freedom in itself, however, is a mere tool, which can only reach utter freedom as an instrument in the service of a cause." Several articles published in 1980 attest to Amoroso Lima's commitment to the fight for freedom: "O Pensamento Distributista" (The Distributist Thought), "O Distributivo e o Brasil" (The Distributive and Brazil), "Terra Minada" (Mined Field), and "Santo Orgulho e Santa Ira" (Holy Pride and Holy Wrath) appeared in the *Jornal do Brasil* on 17 and 18 April and 1 and 30 May, respectively.

At the beginning of the 1980's, his advanced age also accentuated Amoroso Lima's philosophical and aesthetic conviction that life is a continuous development, a rediscovery, a reaching back into the past. There is never enough time for such a review process, a verification that another disciple of Bergson, Marcel Proust, had also agonized over in À *la recherche du temps perdu* (*Remembrance of Things Past*, 1913–1928). In "Transcendência e Imanência" (Transcendence and Immanence), in *Jornal do Brasil* (February 1980), Amoroso Lima placed the work of the Anglo-Austrian philosopher Karl R. Popper in a broad perspective by comparing *The Self and Its Brain* (1977) to Bergson's *L'evolution créatrice* (*Creative Evolution*, 1907): "Popper, a product of the Vienna School of thought, now considered one of the greatest, if not the greatest philosopher alive . . . might be considered as the Bergson of this half of the century." Popper conceives a "creative emergence" and proposes an ascendent evolution of beings organized into twelve categories. Human beings, the most perfect of all organisms, occupy the higher tier of the pyramid, at the level of the "ecosystems." Bergson conceptualized the passage of human culture through three ascendent phases, the vegetative, the intellectual, and the sapient. Inspired by Bergson and Popper, the Brazilian thinker searched for a formula to enhance humanist values in his own society. While the play on words in Portuguese is difficult to render precisely in English, a rough approximation of his formula would be "cultivation, culture, and cult. To till the soil, to nurture intelligence, and to worship Wisdom."

On the subject of man's evolution to a higher state,

Amoroso Lima published "Graus de Cultura" (Degrees of Culture) on 27 June 1980, during Pope John Paul II's first visit to Brazil. The article appeared in Tristão de Athayde's regular column of the *Jornal do Brasil* and compared the semantic value of the words *cultivo* (cultivation) and *cultura* (culture), two very different concepts—"the passage from a precivilized state to a state of culture . . . from a primitive, purely instinctive culture to a culture based on instruction and education . . . a positive and even imperative progress for the individual destiny of each human being and, consequently, for the collective destiny of all peoples."

"Esquecer e Lembrar" (To Forget and to Remember; *Jornal do Brasil*, 6 June 1980) once more echoes Bergsonian metaphysics as well as the psychoanalytical studies of Sigmund Freud and Carl Gustav Jung. Affirming that "to forget is good, but to remember is better," Amoroso Lima invites the reader to "this somewhat exotic, brief excursion through the secret paths of our inner forest." A television newscast that showed Iranian students preparing to go to war against the United States brought to mind "that tragic summer in 1914, those weeks in August when the *belle époque* was dying and with it a civilization," a memory of a time Amoroso Lima wished to forget. He then pondered the semantic as well as the philosophical connotations of "forgetting and obliterating" and "remembering and recalling." He wrote, "To forget is to transfer memory from the conscious to the subconscious. To obliterate is to transfer it to the unconscious. It is the suppression of memory instead of its mere passage into a latent existence, ready to resurface." On the national scene, there were reports of the Brazilian economic boom and images of Rio's volatile stock exchange where fortunes melted away as fast as new millionaires looked for fresh tricks to dodge the runaway inflation. For Amoroso Lima, the sight of the frenetic speculation triggered thoughts of the crash of 1891, and the similarity of the two situations was cause for alarm. He remembered the monetary fever of nearly a century earlier, "which took hold of a people deluded by the euphoria of the death of the Empire and already disillusioned by the dawn of a republic that did not quite measure up to their dreams."

Amoroso Lima proceeded to explain that it is precisely such historical circumstances that constitute the stuff to be stored in the national subconscious as a lesson to be remembered and as a warning to be heeded by future generations of individuals and governments. The article concluded with the exhortation that forgetting is an appropriate selective mechanism that leads to wisdom, whereas obliteration is an intellectual impoverishment that may even lead to insanity, the pathological condition that deprives the individual of normal mental functions, including the capacity to exercise judgment or to enjoy freedom. To remember is to relive one's life experience in an intelligent and creative fashion in order to advance on the road to perfection. This ambition is the supreme law of the evolution of the species on the way to that "angelitude from which poets and mystics beckon to us."

The editor's note to *Meio Século de Presença Literária* meticulously compiles the dates of all of Amoroso Lima's first editions and accurately reviews the author's intellectual trajectory and evolution. This important volume also includes a complete chronology of the various official functions and public services the distinguished Catholic social leader carried out during his lifetime: president of the Centro Dom Vital in Rio de Janeiro, a center for the propagation of Catholic thought; editor of the journal *A Ordem* (The Order) from 1928 to 1968; founder of the Brazilian Catholic Coalition (1932); president of the national committee of Brazilian Catholic Action (1934); and cofounder of the Christian Democratic Movement of Latin America in Montevideo (1947). Amoroso Lima's commitment to the teachings and the propagation of the Roman Catholic faith resulted in his appointment to Pope Paul VI's pontifical commission on justice and peace in 1967.

Amoroso Lima participated in several international conferences as a Brazilian and a Latin American delegate. Among many prizes and honors, he received honorary doctoral degrees from Catholic University in Washington, D.C., and from New York University. In 1969 he shared with three other distinguished journalists the Mary Moors Cabot prize for contribution to continental understanding in international journalism. *Meio Século de Presença Literária* closes with a bibliography listing Amoroso Lima's original titles in Portuguese and his translations of foreign works, especially those by Maritain and by the American writer and Trappist monk Thomas Merton. A reference to Amoroso Lima's work translated into French and Spanish completes the bibliography, which is up to date as of November 1969.

On the occasion of Amoroso Lima's death, Antônio Cândido, an internationally recognized Brazilian scholar, recalled *Affonso Arinos* as a well-balanced biographical analysis, a general view of the literary trends of the time, and an exercise in methodology. In "Mestre Alceu em Estado Nascente" (The Incipient Master Alceu), an article published on 28 August 1983 in *O Estado de São Paulo* Cândido praised the critical and linguistic craftsmanship of that early work as the product of a superb intellect projecting daring ideas.

In the preface to *Affonso Arinos*, Amoroso Lima had introduced himself as an "expressionist." Cândido noted that this "expressionism" probably should be understood in the sense of Croce's conceptualization of "expression," and that the term, as defined by Amoroso Lima, synthesized a critical system that presupposed the critic's affectionate immersion in the work in order to capture its spirit. Such a process, triggered by an affective, rather than a reflective intelligence, would result in an emotional bond between the critic and the author. Antônio Cândido further pointed out Amoroso Lima's familiarity with Freud and Jung, as demonstrated by his use of a psychoanalytic approach to literary criticism—a novelty in the intellectual circles of Rio de Janeiro shortly after World War I.

In *Affonso Arinos*, Amoroso Lima had contrasted the provincial and metropolitan realities of his country and reflected on the opposing nature of thought and society in Brazil and Europe, two worlds he knew well. In 1955 he published *Pela América do Norte* (Passing Through North America), a collection of weekly articles written while he lived in the United States from 1951 to 1953. In two small volumes he recorded his new experiences and contrasted the American way of life with the more familiar Brazilian and European patterns. The year before, he had published the first edition of *A Realidade Americana* (The American Reality), which appeared in a second edition in 1955. The long interpretative essay begins

with his first impression of a "cubist" Manhattan: "cubist in deep winter . . . a new Adamastor [Luiz Vaz de Camões' metaphorical sea monster in *Os Lusíadas* (*The Lusiads*), 1572] in the waters of the Hudson . . . the cold wind bares our bones. And it was a shivering skeleton that immediately sensed the struggle between the mainland and the island, power and liberty, on each side of the Hudson."

In *Quadro Sintético da Literatura Brasileira*, Amoroso Lima credited Afrânio Coutinho, the leading neomodernist critic, with the introduction of the postulates of postmodernist criticism in Brazil. Coutinho's 1955 and 1956 prefaces to *A Literatura no Brazil* (Literature in Brazil) endorsed the school of "new criticism," which emphasized the text itself, style, form, and language, and presupposed the treatment of the creative work with analytic and scientific rigor.

In a later article, "O Globalismo Crítico" (Critical Globalism) from *Jornal do Brasil*, November 1970, Amoroso Lima explained that "it is this neoobjectivity that is leading a generation of younger critics to elaborate a new systematization that I called globalist, because it presents a most important preoccupation with the aesthetic and philosophical totality." Amoroso Lima closes the article with high praise for Eduardo Portela, the youngest of the postmodernist generation, whose *Teoria da Comunicação Literária* (Theory of Literary Communication, 1970) constitutes a complete departure from the amateur critic's impressionistic judgments and represents a turning point in the history of literary criticism in Brazil. Taking exception to Portela's structuralist bent, which the seasoned transcendentalist critic had difficulty in accepting, Amoroso Lima compliments the novice for "the richest methodology, which he proposes, and his integral vision of criticism as creative plenitude."

Amoroso Lima also singled out Gilberto Mendonça Teles, another member of the younger generation, for his concern with aesthetic fact, for his profound analytical mind, and for his comprehension of what is meant by "creative criticism." In an interview recorded with students at the Catholic university of Rio de Janeiro in 1974, Amoroso Lima said that in Mendonça Teles he perceived the coexistence of the poet and the critic, a combination that might well make him the embodiment of an ideal critic.

In 1980 Mendonça Teles published *Tristão de Athayde: Teoria, crítica e história literária* (Tristão de Athayde: Theory, Criticism, and Literary History). This collection gathers the most representative segments of Amoroso Lima's works on the theory of literary art, the theory of literary criticism, and the critic's mission, selected and edited by Amoroso Lima as well as by Mendonça Teles. Since it is also accompanied by a lucid study of Tristão de Athayde's aesthetic coordinates, it constitutes an invaluable research source for understanding the complex personality of Alceu Amoroso Lima, one of twentieth-century Brazil's finest analytical and theoretical minds.

SELECTED BIBLIOGRAPHY

Editions

Literature

Affonso Arinos. Rio de Janeiro, 1922.
Estudos. 5 vols. Rio de Janeiro, 1927–1933.
O Espírito e o Mundo. Rio de Janeiro, 1936.
Contribuição à História do Modernismo 1: O Premodernismo. Rio de Janeiro, 1939.
Poesia Brasileira Contemporânea. Belo Horizonte, Brazil, 1941.
Três Ensaios Sobre Machado de Assis. Belo Horizonte, Brazil, 1941.
O Crítico Literário. Rio de Janeiro, 1945.
A Estética Literária y o Crítico. Rio de Janeiro, 1945. 2nd ed. 1954.
Primeiros Estudos. Contribuição à História do Modernismo Literário. Rio de Janeiro, 1948.
Manhãs de S. Lourenço. Rio de Janeiro, 1950.
Introdução à Literatura Brasileira. Rio de Janeiro, 1956. 4th ed. 1968.
Quadro Sintético da Literatura Brasileira. Rio de Janeiro, 1956. 2nd ed. 1959.
A Crítica Literária no Brasil. Rio de Janeiro, 1959.
O Teatro Claudeliano. Rio de Janeiro, 1959.
O Jornalismo como Gênero Literário. Rio de Janeiro, 1960. 2nd ed. 1969.
Problemas de estética. Rio de Janeiro, 1960.

Da Inteligência à Palavra. Rio de Janeiro, 1962.
Adeus à Disponibilidade e Outros Adeuses. Rio de Janeiro, 1969.
Meio Século de Presença Literária. Rio de Janeiro, 1969.
Companheiros de Viagem. Rio de Janeiro, 1971.

Philosophy

Freud. Rio de Janeiro, 1929.
Debates Pedagógicos. Rio de Janeiro, 1931.
Idade, Sexo e Tempo: Três Aspéctos da Psicologia Humana. Rio de Janeiro, 1938.
Humanismo Pedagógico. Estudos de Filosofia da Educação. Rio de Janeiro, 1944.
O Existencialismo. Rio de Janeiro, 1951.
Meditação Sobre o Mundo Interior. Rio de Janeiro, 1954.
O Existencialismo e Outros Mitos do Nosso Tempo. Rio de Janeiro, 1956.
O Espírito Universitário. Rio de Janeiro, 1959. 2nd ed. 1962.
Pelo Humanismo Ameaçado. Rio de Janeiro, 1965.

Religion

Tentativa de Itinerário. Rio de Janeiro, 1928.
De Pio VI a Pio XI. Rio de Janeiro, 1929.
Contra-revolução Espiritual. Cataguases, Brazil, 1933.
Pela Ação Católica. Rio de Janeiro, 1935.
Elementos da Ação Católica. Rio de Janeiro, 1938.
O Cardeal Leme. Rio de Janeiro, 1943.
A Igreja e o Novo Mundo. Rio de Janeiro, 1943.
Pela Cristianização da Idade Nova. 2 vols. Rio de Janeiro, 1946.
Mensagem de Roma. Rio de Janeiro, 1950.
A Vida Sobrenatural e o Mundo Moderno. Rio de Janeiro, 1956.
A Missão de São Paulo. Rio de Janeiro, 1962.
João XXIII. Rio de Janeiro, 1966.
Comentários à Populorum Progressio. Rio de Janeiro, 1969.
Violência ou Não. Petrópolis, Brazil, 1969.
Tudo é Mistério 1: Pecado. 2: Dons do Espírito Santo. 3: Virtudes. Petrópolis, Brazil, 1983.

Sociology

Preparação à Sociologia. Rio de Janeiro, 1931.
Problema da Burguesia. Rio de Janeiro, 1932.
Pela Reforma Social. Cataguases, Brazil, 1933.
Da Tribuna e da Imprensa. Rio de Janeiro, 1935.
Meditação Sobre o Mundo Moderno. Rio de Janeiro, 1942.
Mitos do Nosso Tempo. Rio de Janeiro, 1943.

Voz de Minas. Rio de Janeiro, 1945. 2nd ed. 1946.

A Realidade Americana: Ensaio de Interpretação dos Estados Unidos. Rio de Janeiro, 1954. 2nd ed. 1955.

A Família no Mundo Moderno. Rio de Janeiro, 1960. 2nd ed. 1967.

Visão do Nordeste. Rio de Janeiro, 1960.

Europa e América: Duas Culturas. Rio de Janeiro, 1962.

Economy

Esboço de Uma Introdução à Economia Moderna. Rio de Janeiro, 1930. 2nd ed. *Introdução à Economia Moderna.* Rio de Janeiro, 1933.

Economia Pré-política. Rio de Janeiro, 1932.

O Problema do Trabalho. Rio de Janeiro, 1947.

A Segunda Revolução Industrial. São Paulo, 1958. 2nd ed. 1960.

O Trabalho no Mundo Moderno. Rio de Janeiro, 1959.

O Gigantismo Econômico. Rio de Janeiro, 1962.

Politics

Política. Rio de Janeiro, 1932. 4th ed. 1956.

Introdução ao Direito Moderno. Rio de Janeiro, 1933.

A Materialismo Jurídico e Suas Fontes. Rio de Janeiro, 1933.

No Limiar da Idade Nova. Rio de Janeiro, 1935.

Indicações Políticas. Rio de Janeiro, 1936.

Pela União Nacional. Rio de Janeiro, 1942.

Europa de Hoje. Rio de Janeiro, 1951.

O Sentido da União Pan Americana. Rio de Janeiro, 1953.

Pela América do Norte. 2 vols. Rio de Janeiro, 1955–1956.

Cultura Interamericana. Rio de Janeiro, 1962.

Revolução, Reação ou Reforma? Rio de Janeiro, 1964.

A Experiência Reacionária. Rio de Janeiro, 1968.

Collected Works

Alceu Amoroso Lima: Biografia. Edited by Antônio Carlos Villaça. Rio de Janeiro, 1985.

Diálogos: Tristão de Athayde e Lourenço Dantas Mota. Edited by Lourenço Dantas Mota. São Paulo, 1983.

Estudos Literários. Edited by Afrânio Coutinho. Rio de Janeiro, 1966.

A Evolução Intelectual do Brasil. 2 vols. Rio de Janeiro, 1971.

O Golpe de 64: A Imprensa Disse Não. Edited by Thereza Cesário Alvim. Rio de Janeiro, 1979.

Memorando dos 90: Entrevistas e Depoimentos. Edited by Francisco de Assis Barbosa. Rio de Janeiro, 1984.

Memórias Improvisadas. Edited by Claudio Medeiros Lima. Petrópolis, Brazil, 1973.

Obras Completas de Alceu Amoroso Lima. 35 vols. Rio de Janeiro, 1948–1955.

Tristão de Athayde: Teoria, crítica e história literária. Edited and with an introduction by Gilberto Mendonça Teles. Rio de Janeiro, 1980. Contains a complete bibliography.

Biographical and Critical Studies

Andrade, Mário de. *Aspéctos da Literatura Brasileira.* Rio de Janeiro, 1943.

Bosi, Alfredo. *História Concisa da Literatura Brasileira.* São Paulo, 1970.

Carpeaux, Otto Maria. *Origens e fins.* Rio de Janeiro, 1943.

———. *Pequena Bibliografia Crítica da Literatura Brasileira.* Rio de Janeiro, 1951.

———. *Alceu Amoroso Lima.* Rio de Janeiro, 1978.

Carvalho, Ronald. *Estudos Brasileiros 2.* Rio de Janeiro, 1931.

Duriau, Jean. *Fragments de sociologie chrétienne.* Paris, 1934.

Figueiredo, Jackson de. *Literatura Reacionária.* Rio de Janeiro, 1924.

———. *Correspondência.* 3rd ed. Rio de Janeiro, 1946.

Fusco, Rosário. *Política e Letras.* Rio de Janeiro, 1940.

———. *Vida Literária.* São Paulo, 1940.

Grieco, Agrippino. *Evolução da Prosa Brasileira.* Rio de Janeiro, 1933.

Houaiss, Antônio. "Alceu Amoroso Lima: Pensamento e Pregação." *Tempo Brasileiro* 33/34 (April–June 1973).

Lafetá, João Luiz. *A Crítica e o Modernismo.* 2nd ed. São Paulo, 1974.

Linhares, Temístocles. "O Crítico do Modernismo Brasileiro." *Journal of Inter-American Studies* 7/1 (1965).

Lins, Alvaro. *Jornal de Crítica 5.* Rio de Janeiro, 1947.

Lustosa, E. J., and Eduardo Magalhães. *Las Edades del Hombre: Edad, Sexo y Tiempo.* Buenos Aires, 1943.

Martins, Wilson. *Interpretações.* São Paulo, 1946.

Milliet, Sérgio. *Diário Crítico 6.* São Paulo, 1950.

Moisés, Massaud, and José Paulo Paes. *Pequeno Dicionário de Literatura Brasileira.* 2nd ed. São Paulo, 1980.

Montello, Josué. "Mestre Alceu." *Tempo Brasileiro* 33/34 (April–June 1973).

O'Neill, M. A. M. Ancilla. *Tristão de Athayde and the Catholic Social Movement in Brazil.* Washington, D.C., 1939.

Portella, Eduardo. "A Posição de Alceu Amoroso Lima." In appendix to *A Crítica Literária no Brasil.* Rio de Janeiro, 1959.

Putnam, Samuel. "Alceu Amoroso Lima." In *Books Abroad* 21/4. Norman, Okla., 1947.

Senna, Homero. *República das Letras.* Rio de Janeiro, 1957.

Silveira, Enio. "Alceu-85: Monumento à Dignidade Humana." In *Encontros com a Civilização Brasileira*. Rio de Janeiro, December 1978. This commemorative issue on Alceu Amoroso Lima's eighty-fifth birthday contains thirteen other articles and interviews.

Tavares, J. Neiva Moreira. *A Mensagem Cristã de Tristão de Athayde*. Turin, Italy, 1962.

Villaça, Antônio Carlos. "Quarenta Anos de Crítica." *A Ordem* (April 1959).

_____. "Quarenta Anos de Pensamento Católico." *Jornal do Brasil* (14 June 1959).

_____. "Tristão de Athayde." *Jornal do Brasil* (June and September 1959).

José Carlos Mariátegui

(1894–1930)

Eugenio Chang-Rodríguez

One of the most important Peruvian essayists and political thinkers of the twentieth century, José Carlos Mariátegui was self-taught. He was born on 14 June 1894 in Moquegua. Abandonment of the family by his father, sickness, and a chronic frail condition affected his entire life. Lean economic circumstances permitted him to finish only primary school and, at the age of fifteen, forced him to find a job to help support his family. He began as copyboy at the daily *La Prensa* of Lima, where four years later he had become a respected journalist. In 1918 he began to work for the daily *El Tiempo* and did so until his departure for Europe the following year. By then he had published thirty-seven articles on literary criticism and art, thirty-seven poems, and fifteen short stories, and had collaborated in writing two plays and in publishing two short-lived dailies and *Nuestra época,* a magazine. Mariátegui later was to refer to this early period of his life as his "stone age." With a government assignment as agent of news, propaganda, and publicity in Italy, the young newspaperman departed for Europe at the close of 1919. Criticism of his decision was not long in coming.

During his four years in Europe, Mariátegui met several outstanding intellectuals, such as Henri Barbusse, Benedetto Croce, and probably the Communist leaders Antonio Gramsci and Palmiro Togliatti.

He married Anna Chiappe, an Italian woman, and had his first child, Sandro, who would become senator and president of the cabinet of Peru from 1980 to 1985. During two and a half years in Italy, six months in Berlin, and several months in Paris, Vienna, Prague, and Budapest, the young Peruvian, with unrelenting curiosity, witnessed the intellectual and political development of the postwar years. He read many volumes of revolutionary material, and more important, he became aware of the tragedy of his own country. Apparently thoroughly won over by Marxism and other new ideas, he returned to Peru on 20 March 1923.

Once settled in Lima, Mariátegui was invited by his friend Víctor Raúl Haya de la Torre to lecture at the González Prada People's Universities. In October 1923, before being sent into exile, Haya designated Mariátegui as his successor to the general editorship of *Claridad,* a publication of those universities. Mariátegui slowly became the outstanding leftist personality in the country, fraternizing with artists and writers of different ideologies and artistic orientations. In the lectures he addressed to the student association and the People's Universities, he expounded on the international situation and disseminated socialist ideas. Some of the less conservative followers of Augusto B. Leguía, then president of the

791

country, also sought his friendship. *Variedades* (Variations), a weekly journal published between 1908 and 1932 and edited by Clemente Palma, son of the writer Ricardo Palma, continued to feature Mariátegui's short essays, many of which were to be collected in his future books. His articles also appeared in another important journal in Lima, *Mundial*. This publication was active from 1920 to 1931, and many of Mariátegui's articles were printed in the column entitled "Peruanicemos al Perú" (Let's Make Peru Peruvian). Notwithstanding his connections with journals of the right, Mariátegui continued advocating socialist ideas and solidifying his contacts with labor leaders such as Adalberto Fonkén, a Chinese-Peruvian anarchist who had been Haya's syndicalist teacher and comrade in arms. Like Manuel González Prada and Haya de la Torre before him, Mariátegui believed in the necessity and viability of a united front of manual workers and intellectuals.

The end of 1923 and the beginning of 1924 were filled with hectic activity for the young writer. Partly because he was overworked, the illness that had begun in his youth worsened to the point that his right leg had to be amputated. After recovering from the operation, Mariátegui dedicated himself once again to writing for national and foreign journals. His house again became a meeting place for avant-garde intellectuals and artists, university students, and labor leaders. In 1925, in a cooperative venture with his brother, Julio César, he established a publishing house, where two of his books were printed.

Mariátegui had returned from Europe with the thought of founding a leftist publication that would serve as a clarion for new ideas applicable to Peru and for the promulgation of socialist ideals. With the aid of avant-garde intellectuals and artists and future leaders of the Alianza Popular Revolucionaria Americana (American Popular Revolutionary Alliance), or APRA, and of the Socialist and Communist parties, Mariátegui turned out the first issue of *Amauta* in September 1926. The journal soon won solid international acclaim. The first nine issues were published with no government interference. Although in the eighth issue, its editor had very clearly come out against subordinating the individual to deterministic materialism and imperative dogmatism, and for the free exercise of will, the journal was

interdicted on 8 June 1927. In a public letter addressed to the publisher of the daily *El Comercio*, Mariátegui admitted to being "a tried and true Marxist," but emphatically denied any association with the Russian Communist movement or any other Communist movement in the Americas or Europe. Outstanding personalities in the world intellectual community raised their voices in protest and expressed their support for Mariátegui and for the reappearance of *Amauta*.

Six months later the interdiction was lifted, and the tenth issue of the journal was permitted to appear. A year after that, in November 1928, Mariátegui published the first issue of *Labor*, planned as a bimonthly newspaper and designed to defend the interests of the working class, as an extension of *Amauta*. *Labor* was closed down after its tenth issue, of 7 September 1929. *Amauta* continued to be printed under the editorship of its founder until the twenty-ninth issue, of February–March 1930, the last he edited before dying on 16 April 1930. Ricardo Martínez de la Torre, *Amauta*'s administrator, managed to publish three more, spurious issues, keeping Mariátegui's name as director to cover up the abandonment of his ideals and the adoption of a doctrinaire Marxism of rabid anti-APRA vein.

Although Mariátegui's progressive radicalization is evident, as noted by his editorial in issue 17 (September 1928), he continued to embrace an open-minded socialism to such an extent that, several decades later, orthodox Marxist scholars pointed to a "slight inconsistency between his theoretical and methodological positions" in his *Siete ensayos de interpretación de la realidad peruana* (*Seven Interpretative Essays on Peruvian Reality*, 1928) as well as in *Amauta*.

On the outskirts of Lima, on 16 September 1928, six persons decided "to create a socialist, not a Communist party." This small group and Mariátegui founded in Lima the Partido Socialista del Perú (Peruvian Socialist Party), or PSP, on 7 October 1928, as a "broad-based" organization, open to workers, peasants, middle-class elements, and intellectuals. Early in 1929, Mariátegui assisted some labor leaders in the establishment of a May First Committee to serve as the organizing group of the Confederación General de Trabajadores del Perú (Peruvian

General Federation of Workers), or CGTP, which was founded on 17 May 1929. For these pioneering and decisive actions, Mariátegui is rightly acknowledged as founder of both the PSP and CGTP.

Traditionally, more emphasis has been placed on Mariátegui's contributions to politics than on his literary achievements. The latter can be divided into two periods: the writings of his early youth, between 1914 and 1919, and his more mature publications, dating from 1920 to 1930. Neither period has been the subject of exhaustive study. Mariátegui made his entrance into the world of letters at the age of nineteen, with articles on art criticism and modernist chronicles. During the following years, his short stories, poems, and plays were published by the newspapers and journals for which he worked. Like other romantics of his generation, Mariátegui began to develop in the direction of Spanish-American modernism, which dated from 1876 to 1916. Later, influenced by Abraham Valdelomar, Mariátegui attempted to transcend that literary movement with a new kind of aesthetics. He collaborated in Valdelomar's *Colónida*, the first important Peruvian literary journal of the twentieth century, and together they wrote *La mariscala* (The Wife of the Army Marshal), a drama in verse, part of which was published posthumously.

Mariátegui's articles and chronicles about writers, literary works, and artistic tendencies should be considered as part of his literary creativity. At the beginning, he paid little attention to the technical skills of the writers, focusing more on their historical significance. It is evident that in his early works he was interested more in context than in text. He singled out the most manifest and exotic biographical details, and added anecdotes that often had little to do with the material he was attempting to analyze.

On the other hand, his interest in poetry and his familiarity with the rules of versification that he learned from his poet friends enabled him to sort out sonority, cadence, strength of imagery, and sensual dimension, as well as to recognize vigor of expression and power in a writer's imagination. And his experience in writing poetry prepared him to search for the apt disposition of sentences and harmony in the selection of words, in order to exploit the unique qualities of language. Without any formal literary training but with tremendous intuition and an innate aesthetic sense, Mariátegui in his own way was able to develop a style during his youth that provided the basis for his literary criticism. However, at that time, he was not in the habit of considering discourse as an aesthetic unit in and of itself, divorced from time and space. The tendency to link an author's work with his biography and environment continued in his mature years, even after he developed his own eclectic Marxist-analytic approach. Nonetheless, it is surprising to note that the young Mariátegui turned intuitively to those who hypothesized that literary writing expresses the emotions of the author and that it represents an instrument conducive to action. Perhaps he was led along this path by his newspaper career, his copious literary production, and his reading and conversations with other writers. At that time he seemed to embrace the tenet: I feel, therefore I am.

The urgent demands of journalism, the gaps in his intellectual background, and his desire to popularize knowledge imposed both technical and aesthetic limitations on his early efforts. He was generally given to writing short pieces. His thirty-seven poems, almost all sonnets, are short. So are his fifteen short stories, each consisting of fewer than two thousand words. More representative of this period are his 840 chronicles and articles, plus his thirty-seven essays of criticism, which contain an average of a thousand words. It is evident that he lacked a definitive theoretical background, a well-established basis for criticism, and an adherence to a clear-cut literary school. As varied and multifaceted, contradictory and paradoxical as is his early work, it nevertheless provides clues about his later, eclectic efforts. After his so-called stone-age period, certain constants, elements from this epoch, remained for the rest of his life: his profound religiosity, his romantic antipositivism, his philosophical irrationalism, his antagonism toward traditional academic postures, his exaltation of heroism, and his heterodoxy. His strength was such that, when he was exposed to new ideological and aesthetic influences in Europe, he molded them to conform to his own preferences. This is the key to the full understanding of his originality.

Mariátegui's religious dimension is extremely important, yet this fact has been neglected by most of his critics. Even after his political radicalization in Europe, he never divested himself of the religious convictions of his youth. On the contrary, his studies in Europe made him more determined than ever to link Peruvian reality to the religious component. His boldest ideas on the subject are found in the fifth essay of *Seven Interpretative Essays.* They are by any standard quite unorthodox for a convinced Marxist and explain a statement he includes in the section on González Prada in the seventh essay: "The slogans the Soviets display on their propaganda posters, like 'Religion is the opium of the people,' have no meaning. Communism is essentially religious. . . ." In other articles, included later in his complete works, Mariátegui writes of religion as an intuitive dynamic force in men, which compels them to act and support their actions. For him, religion is an inborn instinct, an inherited creativity, with traditions and customs, subject to crises and revisions, always bound to a particular vision of the world. Since man is a metaphysical creature, he requires a metaphysical vision of the world, which myth provides. This reasoning leads him to state, in the second section of *El alma matinal* (The Morning Soul, 1950), that the myth of the social revolution is a religious, mystical, and spiritual force that replaces the moribund myths of the bourgeoisie.

Just as Mariátegui's perception of Marxism exerted influence on his religious ideas, his religiosity in turn modified his political outlook. This Peruvian thinker added a mystical dimension to his interpretation of socialism. The word *religion* acquired a new meaning and value for him. It became a belief in the supreme good, translated into revolutionary action. In short, it might be argued that Mariátegui anticipated the theoreticians of the theology of liberation, like Father Gustavo Gutiérrez, classmate-to-be of Javier, Mariátegui's son. Mariátegui was one of the first Latin Americans to break with the prejudice that confines religion to the intimacy of the conscience, which leaves the history of institutions to pursue its own independent course, divorced from traditional religious salvation. We deduce from his writings that he saw his political options endorsed by the Gospel, which he considered to be consubstantial with the manifestation of God in the world. He saw himself as a devoted son of the people, respectfully loyal to the faith on which he was nurtured, a faith transformed by his European experience into one that was militant and revolutionary. His philosophical premises and ideological conclusions were useful to those who subsequently forged the theology of liberation.

Mariátegui's political choices were bound up with his allegiance to God. His revolutionary involvement was derived in large measure from his religious development, his recognition of the commitment Jesus made to the poor, the working class, and the exploited. His powerful faith in a living God and in the love of his neighbor was consonant with his support of the proletariat. In his judgment, Christianity and Marxism were not only compatible, they converged. Perhaps that is why he attributed a messianic mission to Peru's industrial proletariat and the peasantry. Their salvation meant liberation, and liberation meant revolution. The salvation of Calvary would culminate with the advent of the socialist paradise. For Mariátegui, man's final revolution had to be waged on all fronts, on the spiritual as well as the economic. He foresaw the necessity of a synthesis of politics and faith, of belief and practice.

In his more mature years, when he was writing at his best, Mariátegui continued to limit himself to the average length of the works written in his youth. The only two books published during his lifetime, *La escena contemporánea* (The Contemporary Scene, 1925) and *Seven Interpretative Essays,* are collections of short works that were written with no thought that they would be published in book form, according to what he states in the foreword to the latter. Fourteen of the twenty volumes of his posthumously published complete works are composed of articles collected from the magazines and dailies of his time. Undoubtedly journalism rendered dynamism to his writings, and provided him with fluidity of syntax and precision in the use of the parts of speech. Mariátegui's originality lies precisely in his creation of a distinct critical approach—one superior to that of the historicist, or to the schematic and simplistic analysis practiced by Marxist critics and advocated by other movements of the period. His writings indicate he was well informed about Marx's economic view of man, which incorporates aesthetics as an important dimension, and also about Marx's awareness of man's capacity for artistic creation and the enjoyment of aesthetic pleasures. Mariátegui was alert to the variety of Marxist interpretations of thought. He clearly opted for artistic freedom, with its unrestricted expression, and for that reason his sympathy was with the avant-garde.

Mariátegui's refracted Marxism shaped a vision for him that was conditioned by the analytical methodological eclecticism he evolved before 1923. To interpret the artistic spectrum, he made use of cultural anthropology, Freudian psychoanalysis, history, Georges Sorel's theory of myth, and other disciplines—all secondary to his basic concepts. His methodological flexibility, however, did not neglect the central principle of Marxist monism, based on the uniqueness of literature vis-à-vis the rest of human endeavor. His eclectic Marxist approach to the literary question led him beyond a strict analysis of a work. He felt the need for a global perspective that would incorporate previously utilized points of view and would at the same time include the Marxist position on art. He was Marxist when he viewed art as an economic superstructure, conditioned by class struggle and subject to the market price of surplus goods. He was an eclectic when, compelled by his basic precepts, he adopted heterodox ideas in contradiction to dogmatism, arbitrary authority, and the presumed infallibility of the high priests of intelligence, art, and politics. His open-ended ideology and his eclectic methodology of analysis revealed to him an intellectual and artistic crisis of capitalism. For him, this crisis presaged the advent of a new art, consonant with the socialist society about to be created.

Translated from the Spanish by Sylvia Ehrlich Lipp

SELECTED BIBLIOGRAPHY

First Editions

Individual Works

La escena contemporánea. Lima, 1925.
Siete ensayos de interpretación de la realidad peruana. Lima, 1928.

Defensa del marxismo. Santiago, Chile, 1934.
El alma matinal y otras estaciones del hombre de hoy. Lima, 1950.
La novela y la vida: Siegfried y el profesor Canella. Lima, 1955.
El artista y la época. Lima, 1959.
Historia de la crisis mundial: Conferencias (años 1923 y 1924). Lima, 1959.
Signos y obras. Lima, 1959.
Temas de nuestra América. Lima, 1960.
La organización del proletariado. Lima, 1967.
Cartas de Italia. Lima, 1969.
Crítica literaria. Buenos Aires, 1969.
Ideología y política. Lima, 1969.
Figuras y aspectos de la vida mundial. Lima, 1970.
Peruanicemos al Perú. Lima, 1970.
El proletariado y su organización. Mexico City, 1970.
Temas de educación. Lima, 1970.
Fascismo sudamericano: Los intelectuales y la revolución y otros artículos inéditos (1923–1924). Lima, 1975.
Las tapadas. In collaboration with Julio Baudoin. Lima, 1976.

Collected Works

Ediciones populares de las obras completas de José Carlos Mariátegui. 20 vols. Lima, 1959–1970. This collection of paperback volumes, published by Editorial Amauta, excludes works written prior to 1919 and a few articles written subsequently. It includes four volumes by other writers: one of poems dedicated to Mariátegui (vol. 9), two biographies (vols. 10 and 20), and an incomplete index of *Amauta*, poorly prepared (vol. 19). The second biography (vol. 20) includes two of Mariátegui's pieces written in 1916: an interview with Manuel González Prada and an article on a lecture by José de la Riva Agüero.

Translations

Seven Interpretative Essays on Peruvian Reality. Translated by Marjory Urquidi and with an introduction by Jorge Basadre. Austin, Tex., 1971.

Biographical and Critical Studies

Aricó, José, ed. *Mariátegui y los orígenes del marxismo latinoamericano.* Mexico City, 1978.
Baines, John M. *Revolution in Peru: Mariátegui and the Myth.* University, Ala., 1972.
Banning, Beverly. "*Amauta* (1926–1930)." Ph.D. diss., Tulane University, 1972.

Barrenechea, Ana María. "El intento novelístico de José Carlos Mariátegui." In *Textos hispanoamericanos*. Caracas, 1978. Pp. 263–287.

Belaúnde, Víctor Andrés. "En torno a los *Siete ensayos* de José Carlos Mariátegui." In *La realidad nacional*. Lima, 1980. Pp. 1–152.

Carnero Checa, Génaro. *La acción escrita: José Carlos Mariátegui, periodista (ensayo)*. Lima, 1980.

Chang-Rodríguez, Eugenio. *La literatura política de González Prada, Mariátegui y Haya de la Torre*. Mexico City, 1957.

———. *Poética e ideología en José Carlos Mariátegui*. Madrid, 1983.

Chavarría, Jesús. *José Carlos Mariátegui and the Rise of Modern Peru, 1890–1930*. Albuquerque, N.Mex., 1979.

Cornejo Polar, Antonio. "Apuntes sobre la literatura nacional en el pensamiento crítico de Mariátegui." In *Mariátegui y la literatura*, by Xavier Abril et al. Lima, 1980. Pp. 49–60.

Crawford, William Rex. "José Carlos Mariátegui (1895–1930) [*sic*]." In *A Century of Latin American Thought*. Rev. ed. New York, 1966. Pp. 182–189.

Earle, Peter G. "Ortega y Gasset y Mariátegui frente al 'arte nuevo'." In *Homenaje a Luis Leal: Estudios sobre literatura hispanoamericana*, edited by Donald W. Bleznick and Juan O. Valencia. Madrid, 1978. Pp. 115–127.

Flores Galindo, Alberto. *La agonía de Mariátegui*. Lima, 1980.

García Salvattecci, Hugo. *Sorel y Mariátegui*. Lima, [1979].

Garrels, Elizabeth Jane. "The Young Mariátegui and His World (1894–1919)." Ph.D. diss., Harvard University, 1974.

Germaná, César. "La polémica Haya-Mariátegui." *Análisis* 2–3:143–181 (1977). Also as *La polémica Haya de la Torre–Mariátegui*. Lima, 1977.

Klaiber, Jeffrey. "Eulogy to an Ascetic Cell." In *Religion and Revolution in Peru, 1824–1976*. Notre Dame, Ind., 1977. Pp. 92–114.

Kossok, Manfred, et al. *Mariátegui y las ciencias sociales*. Lima, 1982.

Mead, Robert G., Jr. "Recordación de Mariátegui." *La nueva democracia* 36/4:62–63 (1956).

Melis, Antonio, Adalberto Dessau, and Manfred Kossok. *Mariátegui: Tres estudios*. Lima, 1971.

Meseguer Illán, Diego. *José Carlos Mariátegui y su pensamiento revolucionario*. Lima, 1974.

Moretic, Yerko. *José Carlos Mariátegui: Su vida e idearios, su concepción del realismo*. Santiago, Chile, 1970.

Núñez, Estuardo. *La experiencia europea de José Carlos Mariátegui y otros ensayos*. Lima, 1978.

Orrillo, Winston. "Primeras huellas de Mariátegui en Cuba." *Casa de las Américas* 17/100:178–181 (1977).

Posada, Francisco. *Los orígenes del pensamiento marxista en Latinoamérica: Política y cultura en José Carlos Mariátegui*. Madrid, 1968; Havana, 1968; Bogotá, 1977.

Prado, Jorge del. *En los años cumbres de Mariátegui*. Lima, 1983.

Quijano, Aníbal. *Reencuentro y debate: Una introducción a Mariátegui*. Lima, 1981.

Reedy, Daniel. "The Cohesive Influence of José Carlos Mariátegui on Peruvian Art and Politics." In *Artists and Writers in the Evolution of Latin America*, edited by Edward D. Terry. University, Ala., 1969. Pp. 137–149.

Rouillón, Guillermo. *La creación heroica de José Carlos Mariátegui*. 2 vols. Lima, 1975, 1984.

Salazar Bondy, Augusto. "El pensamiento de Mariátegui y la filosofía marxista." In *Historia de las ideas en el Perú contemporáneo*. Lima, 1965. Pp. 311–342.

Stabb, Martin S. "The New Humanism and the Left." In *In Quest of Identity: Patterns in the Spanish American Essay of Ideas, 1890–1960*. Chapel Hill, N.C., 1967. Pp. 102–145.

Valcárcel, Luis E., et al. *El problema del indio . . .* Lima, 1976.

Vanden, Harry E. *National Marxism in Latin America: José Carlos Mariátegui's Thought and Politics*. Boulder, Colo., 1986.

Wise, David O. "'Amauta,' 1926–1930: A Critical Examination." Ph.D. diss., University of Illinois at Urbana-Champaign, 1978.

———. "*Labor* (Lima, 1928–1929), José Carlos Mariátegui's Working Counterpart to *Amauta*." *Revista de estudios hispánicos* 14/3:117–128 (1980).

Samuel Eichelbaum

(1894–1967)

L. Howard Quackenbush

Samuel Eichelbaum was born 14 November 1894, the son of Russian Jewish immigrants who, under the patronage of the wealthy French banker Baron de Hirsch, settled in the Jewish colonies of the province of Entre Ríos, in the township of Domínguez, Argentina. Eichelbaum wrote his first three-scene *sainete* (a short, burlesque Argentine comedy of manners), "El lobo manso" (The Tame Wolf), at the age of seven. It was not until 1919 and the presentation of the one-act play *La quietud del pueblo* (The Stillness of the Town) by the Muiño-Alippi players, however, that his career as a dramatist really began. In his early years Eichelbaum was known for his short stories as well as for his plays, and he eventually published three volumes of stories—*Un monstruo en libertad* (A Monster Running Free, 1925), *Tormenta de Dios* (The Tempest of God, 1929), and *El viajero inmóvil* (The Stationary Traveler, 1933). On another occasion, he tried his hand at novel writing, but the resultant work, entitled "El casamentero" (The Matchmaker), was never published.

Most likely due to the unfamiliar ring of his surname in a Spanish-speaking country, Eichelbaum had to contend with repeated allusions to possible foreign influences in his writing. The controversy surrounding his creative inspiration became a troublesome matter for this writer who prided himself on his participation in establishing an Argentine national theater.

In his mind and according to some Argentine critics, Eichelbaum broke ranks with the folkloric *gaucho* (cowboy) tradition that was an important element of the Argentine theater until the early twentieth century. His themes, settings, and characterization, however, scarcely can be termed cosmopolitan. The influence of *costumbrista* authors (those who treat local color and customs) of the River Plate theater—writers who depicted the *gaucho* and his decline, like Florencio Sánchez, Eduardo Gutiérrez, Ernesto Herrera, and Fernán Silva Valdés—had a continuing impact on audiences and on the younger generation of authors, including Eichelbaum. His intentions were not to break with his cultural roots, but to establish an intermediate zone thematically situated between local legend and universality. True to his goal of establishing a national theater, Eichelbaum criticized the nature of Argentine motivation but never the norms or underlying values of that society. He disregarded the external trappings of his country's folk tradition in order to concentrate on the spirit and the internal strength of his people.

Eichelbaum's works contribute to the transformation and coming of age of the Argentine theater. Without the dramatic example of his more realistic topics and settings, the swing to greater objectivity and to standard Western theater conventions undoubtedly would have taken much longer. It is likely that, without Eichelbaum, the transition would have been more radical and perhaps more destructive to the future of his nation's stage. The Argentine public always has loyally and liberally supported theater groups and dramatists, but for many years that public's taste in theater seemed to prefer the flavor of the unrefined, picturesque life of the pampa. Eichelbaum's theater explores other directions, without losing sight of the popular theatrical past, but without overemphasizing it.

Eichelbaum's most successful plays capitalize on the national cohesiveness and the sense of pride and honor of his characters and his audience, and his theater retains a strong provincial and nationalistic foundation in both thought and action. Critics who credit him with achieving universality in the Argentine theater misclassify his work and misunderstand his contribution. The rural flavor of rustic language, the proud independence of the people, the obstinate illogic of their reasoning, the earthiness of the expressions of their humanity—these are the ingredients of Eichelbaum's declaration of a maturing Argentine national consciousness. He should be viewed as an author of transition between romantic *gaucho costumbrismo* and cosmopolitan realism. He and his colleagues provided the subsequent generation of writers with the tools and the stimulus to break cleanly with the folkloric past during the period following World War II.

Eichelbaum's writing style has been compared to the powerful, biting realism and psychological penetration of such contemporaries as Henrik Ibsen, August Strindberg, and Eugene O'Neill. Eichelbaum's characters, however, are neither as psychologically profound nor as convincingly human as those developed by these writers. In their own right, nevertheless, Eichelbaum's creations become mirrors for his introspective desire to shake off childish, outdated *gaucho* fantasies. Through them, he attempted to aid in his countrymen's process of maturation, both individual and collective, but always within the confines of a common, beloved heritage.

Speaking of his theatrical preferences, Eichelbaum stated: "I am a maniac for introspection. Any action,

however insignificant, causes me to dive obstinately inside myself." To select but one commentary on the popularity of what has been termed "Eichelbaum's psychological melodrama," Theodore Apstein said that *Cuando tengas un hijo* (When You Have a Child, premiered in 1931) is "one of the most moving, heartbreaking, simple, unassuming, real plays ever written."

Notwithstanding the truth in that critical hyperbole, Eichelbaum's theater has been criticized in certain areas, particularly that of characterization. Some of his characters become so engrossed in their own circumstances and individual peculiarities that they lose their capacity to serve as symbols of human behavior. Others hide behind impassive dramatic masks and become separated from the natural flow of the action; the withdrawal from external dramatic circumstance causes them to appear aloof and detached. And the author, instead of limiting these tendencies or attempting to clarify his characters' motivations, sometimes heightens their perplexing nature by preferring enigmatic conclusions to his works. His principal characters have been known to make unexpected decisions, to change substantially, and even to die between acts. These artificial manipulations are particularly apparent in cases where the human ego and its idiosyncrasies overpower and frustrate the logical sequence of events, as in *Las aguas del mundo* (The Waters of the World, premiered in 1957), *Pájaro de barro* (Bird of Clay, premiered in 1940), and *Un guapo del 900* (A Gallant for 900, premiered in 1940).

The attitude of self-sufficiency and the emotional distance established by his most popular protagonists tends to deprive those characters of a communicative proximity to the audience and of the spontaneity that might be expected in a psychological drama. Equally disconcerting for some action-oriented spectators is Eichelbaum's preference for static discourse over kinetic staging and physical vitality. The author's penchant to analyze behavior favors a style of characterization that separates his creations from energetic physical activity. Characters are formed whose mental machinations may alienate them from the sympathies of audiences, while at the same time they gain the public's respect and admiration for their emotional fortitude. Some critics, therefore, agree that Eichelbaum does not write a theater based on action that leads to character definition, but rather a theater founded on the power of reason and persuasion. These characteristics, which some call peculiar or defective, have become the standard methods of characterization and staging in the contemporary Argentine theater of manners.

Because of his characters' manic, psychological preoccupation with morality and values, Eichelbaum's works have been linked to the writings of Sigmund Freud; however, Eichelbaum's theater could never accurately be considered psychoanalytic. His protagonists are far too headstrong, determined, and free from self-doubt to be categorized as Freudian. It is enough to say that Eichelbaum's central characters tend to be lonely, solitary individuals, locked in a struggle for identity and self-fulfillment, expressing to some degree the encumbrances of their social and ethnic realities.

Argentine literary history has long coupled Eichelbaum's name with those of two contemporaries, Francisco Defilippis Novoa and Armando Discépolo. They shared Eichelbaum's quest to improve the dramatic quality, the artistry, the themes, and the discipline of the Argentine theater between 1920 and 1940. All three dedicated their efforts to capturing a more varied national identity through situational pieces that describe the struggles of character types from the lower classes of rural migrants, tradesmen, and foreign immigrants. They charted the course of the painfully slow struggle of these groups to break through the maze of class and ethnic differences in order to gain acceptance and equal status in a modern Argentine society where achievement and industry govern one's progression and social position.

Eichelbaum enjoyed developing *criollo* (creole) types who retain the vestiges of a Spanish-*gaucho*, mixed-blood past. In a very popular play, *Un guapo del 900*, the author depends on the symbols of rustic Argentine manhood and *gaucho* honor that hardly correspond to those of culturally more mature peoples. Eichelbaum's desire to champion Argentine national pride often challenges logic and civilized behavior, while liberating his characters from the fetters of narrow social biases. Many objective and experienced spectators would have difficulty sympathizing with a folk hero who is the bodyguard of a

political kingpin and the assassin of the boss's rival, regardless of the young tough's very Latin and noble intention to avenge the honor of his political chief and punish the infidelity of the latter's wife. Ecuménico's words, "I have to kill or let others kill me," hardly seem convincing and perhaps are more revealing as a commentary on corrupt Latin American politics than they are an explanation of a code of honor. Ecuménico tries to justify his brutal knifing of a local politico, even though he knows his conscience will force him to pay the price of his action. Regardless of the cultural prejudices that spectators may struggle with as they view this play, Ecuménico's moral dilemma, coupled with the irony caused by the juxtaposition of rural *gaucho* and urban Argentine ethical codes, makes *Un guapo del 900* one of Eichelbaum's most intriguing and popular plays.

Reflecting the harsh country environment from which they are carved, many of Eichelbaum's women resemble men more than they do some of their frail, feminine, North American and European counterparts from the same period. His female characters are solitary, stoic individuals, quite independent and headstrong, especially within the context of the traditional male-female roles of his time.

Eichelbaum has long been considered a master in the delineation of stark, rough-hewn, and altogether noble female characters. They almost always steal the show, even where there is a strong male lead role. In *Un guapo del 900*, the wine-guzzling Natividad López, a woman of humble origins, shows the determination and will to confront the politician who controls the destiny of everyone in his district. In an attempt to save her gangster son, Ecuménico, she shames the political leader for not coming to his aid. She fears that, after being released on insufficient evidence, Ecuménico will not be permitted by his conscience to live a lie and that he will confess his crime and hang for it. Natividad's pride in her son's strength of character is paradoxically counterpoised by her maternal love and her need to save him from the gallows. Both Natividad and Ecuménico exemplify Eichelbaum's search for virtue in the shabbiness and tainted loyalties of simple people caught up in the maelstrom of political opportunism, common people who somehow find the inner strength to rise above common expectations.

Eichelbaum's female characters are more spontaneous, more liberated from society's restraint, and more decisive than his men. They demonstrate a rebelliousness and dignity that puts them at odds with parents, as in *Señorita* (Young Lady, premiered in 1930). Defiant of peer pressure, Goya in *Vergüenza de querer* (The Shame of Love, premiered in 1941) abandons her loveless marriage when true passion presents itself. Just as steadfast and courageous in her own human error, and contemptuous of wagging tongues, Amancia, of *Los aguas del mundo*, calmly accepts her disgrace and the responsibility of her illegitimate child.

Although love is a motivating force for the women in Eichelbaum's plays, and although love is inexorably connected to feelings of responsibility, oddly enough it seldom relates to husband and wife. Marriage, when it appears at all in Eichelbaum's work, represents a sad, contentious, and unfulfilling experience. If his characters find happiness in marriage, it is only through enormous pain and sacrifice.

Eichelbaum's plays have received recognition and won awards both within Argentina and abroad. Perhaps the most popular works for Argentines have been *Un guapo del 900*, which won the Municipal and National Drama Prizes for 1940, *Cuando tengas un hijo*, *Señorita*, and *Soledad es tu nombre* (Solitude Is Your Name, premiered in 1932). In domestic as well as foreign theaters, *Un tal Servando Gómez* (A Guy Named Servando Gómez, premiered in 1942) and *Pájaro de barro* have been extremely popular and have traveled well.

Eichelbaum's dramatic sensibilities tend to parallel those of his audience. Even when he depicts an urban milieu, his most distinctive characters retain the mannerisms, language, and cultural habits of the common people of the rural interior. This aspect of his writing unites the Buenos Aires playwright with his small-town beginnings. The folk elements in his works, to some degree, must be attributed to a basic Argentine self-perception. Most cultured, cosmopolitan urbanites of Buenos Aires like to believe that they retain linguistic and social customs that link them to their rural *gaucho* heritage.

Statements such as Apstein's that call Eichelbaum "the only true playwright in Argentina" and "the most important living playwright whose language is Spanish" can only be termed hyperbolic. Even so, his impact on the Argentine contemporary theater, his dramatic soundings of the human consciousness, and his combination of feelings of alienation with antisocial behavior and intense human conviction, although seemingly distorted and extreme, must be recognized as the same tendencies that ten or twenty years later traced new dramatic trajectories throughout the world. These elements are ingredients of theatrical expressionism, existentialism, and absurdism, to say nothing of the Argentine theater's own antecedent of the absurd, the *grotesco criollo* (creole grotesque).

Eichelbaum sensed the changing climate both in his own national theater and in world theater, but he was either unwilling or unable to make the extreme shifts in perception necessary to adopt or create totally new, avant-garde theatrical methods. Yet he must be credited with beginning the process of looking beyond the quaint and typical Argentine microcosm. He broadened the vistas of those dramatists who later found greater universality in their portrayals of the life and values of a modern Argentina whose international and human concerns made it a leader in both the Latin American and the world communities.

Samuel Eichelbaum died 4 May 1967 in Buenos Aires.

SELECTED BIBLIOGRAPHY

First Editions

Plays

La quietud del pueblo. Buenos Aires, 1919.
La mala sed. Buenos Aires, 1920.
Un romance turco. Written with Pedro E. Pico. N. p., 1920.
La cáscara de nuez. Written with Pedro E. Pico. Buenos Aires, 1921.
El dogma. In *Bambalinas 236.* Buenos Aires, 1922.
Un hogar. In *Bambalinas 361.* Buenos Aires, 1922.
El camino del fuego. In *Bambalinas 236.* Buenos Aires, 1922.
El ruedo de las almas. In *La Escena 259.* Buenos Aires, 1923.
La hermana terca. Buenos Aires, 1924.
N. N. homicida. Buenos Aires, 1928.
Señorita. Buenos Aires, 1931.

Cuando tengas un hijo. Buenos Aires, 1931.

Soledad es tu nombre. Buenos Aires, 1932.

Ricardo de Gales, príncipe criollo. Buenos Aires, 1933.

En tu vida estoy yo. Buenos Aires, 1934.

Pájaro de barro. Buenos Aires, 1940.

Un guapo del 900. Buenos Aires, 1940.

Un tal Servando Gómez. Vergüenza de querer. Divorcio nupcial. Buenos Aires, 1942.

El gato y su selva. Un guapo del 900. Pájaro de barro. Dos brasas. Buenos Aires, 1952.

Tejido de madre. Nadie la conoció nunca. Buenos Aires, 1956.

El judío Aarón. Buenos Aires, 1956.

Las aguas del mundo. Buenos Aires, 1959.

Un cuervo sobre el imperio. Buenos Aires, 1966.

Rostro perdido. Un cuervo sobre el Imperio. Gabriel, el olvidado. Subsuelo. Buenos Aires, 1966.

Un patricio del 80. Written with Ulises Petit de Murat. Buenos Aires, 1969.

Short Story Collections

Un monstruo en libertad. Buenos Aires, 1925.

Tormenta de Dios. Buenos Aires, 1929.

El viajero inmóvil. Buenos Aires and Montevideo, 1933.

Biographical and Critical Studies

Apstein, Theodore. "Samuel Eichelbaum, Argentine Playwright." *Books Abroad* 18–19 (1944–1945).

Berenguer Carisomo, Arturo. "Introduction." In *Teatro argentino contemporáneo.* Madrid, 1960. Pp. xi–xliv.

Berrutti, Alejandro E. "Influencia del teatro gauchesco en la evolución del teatro argentino." *Lyra* 17:174–176 (1959).

Blanco Amores de Pagella, Angela. *Nuevas temas en el teatro argentino: La influencia europea.* Buenos Aires, 1965. Pp. 60–65.

Canal Feijóo, Bernardo. "Cuatro piezas de Eichelbaum." In *El gato y su selva. Un guapo del 900. Pájaro de barro. Dos brasas,* by Samuel Eichelbaum. Buenos Aires, 1952. Pp. 7–20.

Cerretani, Arturo. "El teatro de Samuel Eichelbaum." *Síntesis* 3/36:213–229 (1930).

Cruz, Jorge. *Samuel Eichelbaum.* Buenos Aires, 1962.

Foppa, Tito Livio. *Diccionario teatral del Río de la Plata.* Buenos Aires, 1961–1962. Pp. 270–271.

Gerchunoff, Alberto. "Samuel Eichelbaum." In *Un tal Servando Gómez. Vergüenza de querer. Divorcio nupcial,* by Samuel Eichelbaum. Buenos Aires, 1942.

Giusti, Roberto F. *Historia de la literatura argentina 4: El teatro.* Buenos Aires, 1959.

Godoy Froy, Marta Lía. *Introducción al teatro de Samuel Eichelbaum.* Buenos Aires, 1982.

Goldstein, R. "Sobre *En tu vida estoy yo.*" *Claridad* 13:4–6 (1934).

González, Roura O., Jr. "Dramáticas: *La mala sed.*" *La Nota* 4:2399–2401 (1920).

Guardia, Alfredo de la. "Raíz y espíritu del teatro de Eichelbaum." In *Imagen del drama.* Buenos Aires, 1954. Pp. 131–144.

_____. "Samuel Eichelbaum, dos estudios psicológicos." *Nosotros* (Second period) 14/64:84–86 (1941).

Guibourg, Edmundo. "Una semblanza de Samuel Eichelbaum." Prologue to *El viajero inmóvil,* by Samuel Eichelbaum. Buenos Aires and Montevideo, 1933. Pp. 9–12.

_____. "La forma de *En tu vida estoy yo.*" *Crítica* (August 1934).

Jones, Willis Knapp. "Three Great Latin American Dramatists: Eichelbaum, Usigli and Marqués." *Specialia* 1:43–49 (1969).

Mastronardi, Carlos. "Un nuevo drama de Eichelbaum." *Sur* 12/93:67–69 (1942).

Monner Sans, José María. *Desde la platea.* Buenos Aires, 1930.

Morán, Julio César. "Conducta humana y coherencia existencial en *Un guapo del 900* de Samuel Eichelbaum." In *Estudios literarios e interdisciplinarios.* La Plata, Argentina, 1968. Pp. 71–96.

Ordaz, Luis. *Breve historia del teatro argentino 7.* Buenos Aires, 1965.

_____. *El teatro en el Río de la Plata: Desde sus orígenes hasta nuestros días.* 2nd ed. Buenos Aires, 1957. Pp. 162–165.

Pagano, José León. "Prologo." In *La mala sed,* by Samuel Eichelbaum. Buenos Aires, 1920. Pp. i–iv.

Palant, Pablo T. "Samuel Eichelbaum." In *Pájaro de barro, Vergüenza de querer,* by Samuel Eichelbaum. Buenos Aires, 1965. Pp. 5–11.

_____. "El joven Samuel Eichelbaum." *Davar* 72:89–92 (1957).

Plá, Roger. "El teatro de Eichelbaum." *Contrapunto* 1/1:8–9, 15 (1944).

Sáenz y Quesada, Héctor. "Ubicación social del compadre." In *El compadrito.* Buenos Aires, 1945.

Soto, Luis Emilio. "Ensayo sobre el teatro de Eichelbaum." In *Cuando tengas un hijo,* by Samuel Eichelbaum. Buenos Aires, 1931.

Juana de Ibarbourou

(1895–1979)

Marjorie Agosin

Juana de Ibarbourou occupies a special place in the literary history of Uruguay and of Latin America. She is one of Uruguay's most celebrated and best-loved poets and one of the last feminine voices of the postmodernist period in Latin America, the years between 1910 and 1920. The postmodernist movement represented a reaction to the highly elaborate lyrical style of the earlier modernist period. The younger generation sought a simpler poetic language and was concerned with capturing daily life and natural speech in poetry.

Ibarbourou, born Juana Fernández on 8 March 1895 in the small village of Melo in the interior of Uruguay, enjoyed a happy childhood in the country. It is said that as a child she was given to daydreaming, to flights of the imagination, and to identifying very closely with nature, characteristics that would persist throughout her career as a poet. In 1914, she married Captain Lucas Ibarbourou and after living in various locations in Uruguay, the family settled down in Montevideo in 1918.

Her literary career began that same year when a well-known literary critic of the periodical *La Razón* dedicated an article to her that made her famous. From that date until her death, her fame never wavered. A veritable myth grew up about her. She was venerated, praised, even "crowned" in 1929 with the title Juana de América in a public ceremony in Montevideo. Her honors included the Gold Medal of Francisco Pizarro, given in 1935 by the government of Peru; the Order of the Condor of the Andes, conferred in 1937 by Bolivia; special homage offered by UNESCO in 1954; and, in 1959, the highest literary honor of her native country, the National Prize for Literature. The enduring success of Ibarbourou is due to the freshness, spontaneity, and charm of her lyrics. Not experimental or profound in a philosophical sense, her poetry is sensual and erotic and possesses an original lyricism that uses striking images of nature. From the beginning, she was a unique voice within the Latin American poetry of her time.

Las lenguas de diamante (The Diamond Tongues), Ibarbourou's first book, published in 1919, served as the base on which all her subsequent lyrical work would rest. For more than fifty years, she continued to perfect and refine the ideas presented in her first book.

Las lenguas de diamante presents poems of audacious sensuality and eroticism. The poet celebrates love as an essential element of life, as an exuberant activity that is as natural as breathing, akin to breezes, water, flowers, and fragrances of the earth. She displays a fervent pantheism that sees the poet as an integral part of the natural world, a point of view illustrated as well in Ibarbourou's second book of prose poems, *El cántaro fresco* (The Cool Water Jar, 1920). In "Presentimientos" (Presentiments), she writes:

Hace ya miles de años, yo tuve raíces y gajos, dí flores, sentí pendientes de mis ramas, que eran como brazos; . . . fuí un arbusto humilde y alegre, enraizado a la orilla montuosa de un río.

(Obras completas, p. 421)

Thousands of years ago, I had roots and shoots, I flowered, I felt them hanging from my branches, which were like arms; . . . I was a simple bush rooted in the steep bank of a river.

The central image of the poet as part of the cosmos, surrendering to the forces of nature, is one of the most distinctive traits of Ibarbourou. As Jorge Arbeleche notes in *Juana de Ibarbourou: Antología* (*poesía y prosa 1919–1971*),* her eros is one of flora and fauna. Nature is a backdrop offering its assortment of aromas, forests, animals, and enchantments. The poems are inhabited by sorceresses, spirits, fireflies, elements that make Ibarbourou's verses as appealing and magical as fairy tales.

The poems of *Las lenguas de diamante* express a feeling of urgency to enjoy the present moment and the abundance of nature and of love. In "La hora" (The Hour), addressed, like many others, to a lover, she says:

Tómame ahora que aún es temprano
Y que llevo dalias nuevas en la mano.
. . . .
Ahora, que tengo la carne olorosa,
Y los ojos limpios y la piel de rosa.

(p. 7)

Take me now while it's still early
And while I have new dahlias in my hands.
. . . .
Now while my flesh is fragrant
My eyes clear and my skin like a rose.

Love in all its aspects is presented in a totally open and natural manner, with no tinge of the sadness, tragedy, or reserve so typical of feminine poetry of

*All page numbers in text refer to this volume of collected works, unless otherwise noted.

years ago. In "El fuerte lazo" (The Strong Tie), the poet speaks in clear and direct language, wanting to be understood, wanting to tell of the ardor of a primeval love.

Florí
Para ti.
Córtame. Mi lirio
Al nacer dudaba ser flor o ser cirio.

Fluí
Para ti.
Bébeme. El cristal
Envidia lo claro de mi manantial.

(p. 12)

I flowered
For you.
Cut me. My new-born
Lily wavered between being flower or candle.

I flowed
For you.
Drink me. Crystal
Envies the clearness of my fountain.

El cántaro fresco retains certain similarities to *Las lenguas de diamante* in the celebration of things of the earth, grain, moss, crickets, but it shows a more mature Ibarbourou, more reflective. *El cántaro fresco* was published in 1920, and that same year Ibarbourou gave birth to her first and only child, which may account for the changing tone of her poetry, now more subtle and restrained. But the book still sings of the joy of the sun, the damp woods, the mystery of butterflies. Her next book, *Raíz salvaje* (Wild Root, 1922), continues the themes begun in *Las lenguas de diamante*. In "Noche de lluvia" (Rainy Night), the woman, enamored of her body and of youth, speaks.

Espera, no te duermas. Ésta noche
Somos acaso la raíz suprema
De donde debe germinar mañana
El tronco bello de una raza nueva.

(p. 88)

Wait, don't go to sleep. Tonight
We are perhaps the supreme root
From which will spring tomorrow
The beautiful trunk of a new race.

The primitive element and lyric force of *Las lenguas de diamante* has been moderated in *Raíz salvaje*, but the lyrical speaker seeks to return to the freedom of youthful days, as in the poem that is the epigraph for the collection:

> ¡Si estoy harta de ésta vida civilizada!
> ¡Si tengo ansias sin nombre de ser libre y feliz!
> ¡Si aunque florezca en rosas, nadie podrá cambiarme
> > La salvaje raíz!
> > > (p. 83)

If I am fed up with this civilized life
If I yearn ceaselessly to be free and happy
Even if I blossom into roses, nobody will be able to
change
> My wild root.

Indeed she never lost her wild root. That was how she remembered herself and her young years.

Yet in *Raíz salvaje* she becomes aware of another reality that begins to haunt her verses: death. In "Carne inmortal" (Immortal Flesh) she writes:

> Yo le tengo horror a la muerte.
> . . . a veces cuando pienso
> Que bajo de la tierra he de volverme
> Abono de raíces.
> > (p. 102)

I have a horror of death
. . . at times when I think
That beneath the earth I will have to become
Nourishment for roots.

Note the change of imagery, of becoming food for roots, in contrast to the earlier feeling of being integrated with the earth.

La rosa de los vientos (The Wind Rose, 1930) marks a change of direction in Ibarbourou's lyrics. The tone here is melancholy, at times elegiac. There is no evocation of a prodigal past; the poet speaks from the perspective of a desolate and listless present. Before, life was expressed as light, nature, and the wild root of her being. Now it is represented as pain, loss, and sadness. The images have become more elaborate; the symbolism is no longer transparent. Faced with the necessity of exploring new themes, Ibarbourou

must also invent a new language. She exhibits in "Timonel de mi sueño" (Helmsman of My Dreams) a persistent obsession with dreams, with the idea that only they can provide the tranquillity and rest so longed for.

> Toma la dirección de mi navío
> Tú, que noche a noche recorres
> Las rutas fieles de mi sueño.
> > (p. 133)

Take the helm of my ship,
You, who night after night traverse
The exact roads of my dreams.

The metaphor of the voyage also appears in this book. The second section is called "Claros caminos de América" (The Bright Roads of America); it is not a book of praise for the South American continent but a series of vignettes of voyages, in which the figure of the seafarer and the desire to depart are the predominant images. In "Atlántico" (Atlantic), she writes:

> Océano que te abres lo mismo que una mano
> A todos los viajeros y a todos los marinos:
> Tan sólo para mí eres puño cerrado;
> Para mí solamente tú no tienes caminos.
> > (p. 159)

Ocean so you open like a hand
To all voyagers and sailors:
Only to me are you a closed fist,
For me alone you have no roads.

Loores de Nuestra Señora (Songs of Praise to Our Lady, 1934) and *Estampas de la Biblia* (Bible Sketches, 1934) are written in poetic prose and are again a new direction for Ibarbourou. A strong religious feeling vibrates through these verses; a mystical spirit already glimpsed in *La rosa de los vientos* is more prominent here as Ibarbourou tries to break her ties to worldly pleasures. However, there is no exaggerated religious fervor; the poet balances the religious and the everyday. She re-creates the world of the Bible with delicacy, with attention to detail, seeing it as rooted in nature in the same way that ours is. In *Estampas de la Biblia*, her Rebecca speaks this way:

Tardecita de mi país, cargada de aromas. Un olor a salvia corría en el viento y la planta de la artemisa, alegre y áspera, florecía en menudas corolas amarillas alrededor de la fuente.

(p. 534)

Late afternoon in my land, laden with aromas. There was a smell of sap in the air and yarrow bushes, gay and rough, full of flowers with tiny yellow corollas, were blooming all around the fountain.

Perdida (Lost, 1950), *Azor* (Falcon, 1953), *Mensajes del escriba* (Messages of the Scribe, 1953), *Dualismo* (Dualism, 1953), *Oro y tormenta* (Gold and Storm, 1956), and *Elegía* (Elegy, 1967) are the works of Ibarbourou's mature years. The bright and vivid imagery of earlier books has given way to the opaque, to grays, to passivity, immobility, to solitude, melancholy, and death. Ibarbourou has become the poet alone, uprooted from Nature, dissatisfied with life. Closed spaces abound in these poems. Even nature is closing in. In "Elegía por una casa" (Elegy for a House), she refers to the fog that veils her face and finds the earth has turned metallic and unrecognizable.

> *Aquí la tierra ni siquiera es tierra;*
> . . . .
> *Se han vuelto acero hasta las golondrinas,*
> *Y de hierro y estaño son las hojas.*
>
> (p. 175)

> Here the earth is not even earth;
> . . . .
> Even the seagulls have turned into steel,
> And the leaves are made of iron and tin.

In this last phase, nothingness and the hovering presence of death seem palpable: in "Ahora" (Now), she writes, "Ya son mis ojos grandes cementerios" (Now my eyes have become immense graveyards; p. 192). There is one exception among the later poems, *Las canciones de Natacha* (Natacha's Songs), included in *Dualismo*. These lullabies return for a moment to childhood joys.

Ibarbourou wrote some books of prose, including *Chico Carlo* (Boy Carlo, 1944), a group of sketches of people from her childhood, and *Juan Soldado* (Soldier Juan, 1971), a book of short stories or vignettes. With these works, the literary production of Ibarbourou came to an end. She died in seclusion at her home in Montevideo in 1979 at the age of eighty-four.

She was indeed a singular phenomenon in Latin-American poetry. Already a poet at a very early age, she displayed a natural talent for a lyricism based on spontaneity, love of nature, and an ardent desire to live in harmony with the simple things of the earth. Her joy in nature and sensual pleasure was transformed into a poetry with language and images of great clarity, blazing with emotional fire.

Her first book was published when she was twenty-four years old, and her last one appeared when she was seventy-six. She was so direct, so without guile, that it is easy to see why she appealed to so many, was so beloved and so honored. Her poetry remains alive and green to this day.

Translated from the Spanish by Cola Franzen

SELECTED BIBLIOGRAPHY

Editions

Poetry

Las lenguas de diamante. Buenos Aires, 1919.
Poesías escogidas. Montevideo, 1920.
Raíz salvaje. Montevideo, 1922.
La rosa de los vientos. Montevideo, 1930.
Perdida. Buenos Aires, 1950.
Azor. Buenos Aires, 1953.
Dualismo. First appeared in *Obras completas.* Madrid, 1953.
Romances del destino. Madrid, 1955.
Elegía. Puerto Rico, 1967.
La pasajera. Buenos Aires, 1967.

Prose

El cántaro fresco. Montevideo, 1920.
Ejemplario. Montevideo, 1928.
Páginas de literatura contemporánea. Montevideo, 1928.
Estampas de la Biblia. Buenos Aires, 1934.
Loores de Nuestra Señora. Montevideo, 1934.
Chico Carlo. Buenos Aires, 1944.
Mensajes del escriba. First appeared in *Obras completas.* Madrid, 1953.
Canto rodado. Buenos Aires, 1956.
Juan Soldado. Buenos Aires, 1971.

806

Theater

Los sueños de Natacha. Montevideo, 1945.

Later Editions

Las lenguas de diamante. Montevideo, 1963; Buenos Aires, 1969.

Collected Works

Antología poética. Santiago, Chile, 1940.
Antología poética. Montevideo, 1967.
Antología poética. Edited by Dora Isella Russell. Madrid, 1970.
El dulce milagro. Buenos Aires, 1964.
Juana de Ibarbourou: Antología (poesía y prosa 1919–1971). Edited by Jorge Arbeleche. Buenos Aires, 1972. 2nd ed. 1977.
Juana de Ibarbourou: Sus mejores poesías. Madrid, 1930.
Los más bellos versos. Los Angeles, 1936.
Los mejores poemas. Edited by Jorge Arbaleche. Montevideo, 1968.
Las mejores poesías. Barcelona, 1929.
Sus mejores poesías. Santiago, Chile, 1930.
Obras completas. Edited by Dora Isella Russell. Madrid, 1953. 2nd ed. 1960; 3rd ed. 1967.
Oro y tormenta. Santiago, Chile, 1956.
Poemas. Buenos Aires, 1942.
Tiempo. Barcelona, 1962.

Biographical and Critical Studies

Andrade Coello, Alejandro. *Cultura feminina uruguaya: Juana de Ibarbourou.* Quito, 1943.
Athayade, Tristán de. "Las tres poetisas del sur." *Atenea* 2/3:225–239 (1925).
Babigian, Consuelo. "Juana de Ibarbourou." *Modern Language Forum* 25:9–17 (1940).
Barbero, Teresa. "Juana de Ibarbourou, Juana de América." *La estafeta literaria* 540:16–17 (1974).
Barrios, Eduardo. "¿Juana de Ibarbourou se entristece?" *Repertorio americano* 8:76 (1924).

Basave, A. "La condesa de Noailles y Juana de Ibarbourou." *Revista de revistas* 6:49–52 (1928).
Blanco-Fombona, Rufino. *El espejo de tres fases.* Santiago, Chile, 1937.
Bollo, Sarah. "La poesía de Juana de Ibarbourou." *Revista nacional* 2/34:111–118 (1940).
Carrera, Julieta. *La mujer in América escribe: Semblanzas.* Mexico City, 1956.
Córdoba, Diego. *Presencia y poemas de Juana de Ibarbourou.* Mexico City, 1964.
Delgado, J. M. "Juana de Ibarbourou." *Conferencia* 7/22: 491–509 (1935).
Díez-Canedo, Enrique. "Dos poetisas de Uruguay." *Nosotros* 43:418–420 (1923).
Fernández Fraga, Germán. "Ese noble pueblo uruguayo donde nació Juana de Ibarbourou." *Abside* 25:110–114 (1961).
Figueira, Gastón. "Perfil lírico de Juana de Ibarbourou." *Revista interamericana* 3/1:3–6 (1941).
_____. "El cinquecentenario de *Las lenguas de diamante.*" *Asomante* 26:68–74 (1970).
_____. "Páginas olvidadas de Juana de Ibarbourou." *Revista interamericana de bibliografía* 13:311–324 (1963).
_____. "Las relaciones literarias y amistosas entre Gabriela Mistral y Juana de Ibarbourou." *Revista interamericana de bibliografía* 25/1:13–23 (1975).
Filartigas, J. M. *Artistas del Uruguay: Impresiones literarias.* Montevideo, 1923. Pp. 59–65.
Gonzales Ruano, César. *Literatura americana: Ensayos de madrigal y de cántica.* Madrid, 1924.
Henriquez Ureña, Max. "En torno a Juana de Ibarbourou." *Lyceum* 10/36:23–29 (1953).
Jiménez Borja, José. "Juana de Ibarbourou, Juana de América." *Mercurio peruano* 19:407–410 (1929).
Luisi, Luisa. "Ibarbourou, Juana de." *Repertorio americano* 8:57–58, 61–62 (1924).
Rosenbaum, Sidonia C. *Modern Women Poets of Spanish America.* New York, 1945. Pp. 229–256.
Salaverry, Vicente. "La poetisa Ibarbourou." *Nosotros* 31/117:186–196 (1919).
Tudela, Ricardo. "*Estampas de la Biblia* de Juana de Ibarbourou." *Atenea* 30:390–393 (1935).

Ezequiel Martínez Estrada

(1895–1964)

Delfín Leocadio Garasa

Ezequiel Martínez Estrada, original and polemical writer and thinker, was born on 14 September 1895 in the province of Santa Fe, Argentina. Although his literary career started early (in 1917, he was already publishing in the Buenos Aires review *Nosotros*), he did not become well known until 1933, with the appearance of his *Radiografía de la pampa* (*X-Ray of the Pampa*), a pitiless analysis of Argentine reality in terms of its historical development and essential character. He was an eager reader and took in many ideas from important artists and philosophers, but his own thought was much more that of a romantic and passionate poet than that of a systematic intellectual. He was a self-taught and lonely man, although he had friendly links with important figures of his time, including Leopoldo Lugones, Horacio Quiroga, and Victoria Ocampo. He was never totally adapted to his country, where he worked for thirty years, mainly as a simple post-office employee and sometimes as a teacher. He suffered an extended, painful illness and many sorrows, often produced by his difficult personality.

Martínez Estrada became a bitter man in response to his personal misfortunes, Argentina's situation from 1929 onward, the incompetence shown by the honorable but old president, Hipólito Irigoyen, and the military coup of 1930, which set up an endemic constitutional instability. He became an apocalyptic prophet and a prosecutor of the congenital and acquired flaws of a country he went on loving, in spite of everything. His bitterness grew during World War II and the rise to power of Juan Domingo Perón. Perón's fall in 1955 did not mean the end of the author's sorrows, for he saw the persistence of corruption in certain sections of society. This perception led him to abandon Buenos Aires and settle in Bahía Blanca, where he devoted himself to agriculture. His books *¿Qué es esto?* (What's This?, 1956), *Exhortaciones* (Exhortations, 1957), and *Cuadrante del pampero* (Quadrant of the Pampa Wind, 1956) belong to this period. He then went to Mexico and later to Cuba, where he edited some publications for the publishing house Casa de las Américas.

As a result of his revolutionary enthusiasm and his stand against American capitalism, Martínez Estrada wrote *Martí, revolucionario* (Marti, the Revolutionary, 1967) and *El verdadero cuento del tío Sam* (Uncle Sam's True Story, 1963). But not even in Cuba did he find peace, for he felt "old, feeble and foreign, an expatriate and an unknown person" (*Mi experiencia cubana* [My Cuban Experience], 1965). In 1962, he went back to Argentina and settled in Bahía Blanca, where he died on 3 November 1964. Some time before his death, he wrote, in the prologue to his

Antología (Anthology, 1964), "I hope that someday my work will be read with impartiality, as the creation of an artist and a thinker."

Martínez Estrada's poetry stood out during his lifetime, and while it is not easy to place his work within a defined movement, many critics have highly praised it. His first poems coincide with the end of Rubén Darío's modernist movement and the reactions against its prevalence by Lugones, Enrique Banchs, and Baldomero Fernández Moreno. *Oro y piedra* (Gold and Stone, 1918) demonstrates a renewed emphasis on themes and images as opposed to story. Four years later, in Buenos Aires, a magazine called *Martín Fierro* became the symbolic center and practical means of communication of the avant-garde generation, but Martínez Estrada did not belong to that group, which included Ricardo Güiraldes, Jorge Luis Borges, Oliverio Girondo, and Leopoldo Marechal. In *Nefelibal* (1922), he exhibited his preference for verbal exoticism and his admiration for Victor Hugo, Charles Baudelaire, Paul Verlaine, and Walt Whitman. *Motivos del cielo* (Sky Motives, 1924) is a baroque book that points to the infinite through images of smoke and wind.

In 1927, Martínez Estrada published *Argentina,* an optimistic view of Argentina's land, nature, history, and destiny. The atmosphere of this book is very far from the bitter tone of his later essays. It describes city of Buenos Aires and the landscapes of the countryside with admiration and affection, and the sometimes hermetic lines contain romantic echoes. His *Títeres de pies ligeros* (Light-Footed Puppets, 1929), in which Pierrot, Columbine, and Harlequin carry on a tragicomical game, is clearly inspired by the commedia del l'arte.

Humoresca (1929) was his last poetic work, a book that contains intimate references to his hometown, his friends, and his preferences. The last poems clearly reveal his disillusionment about life's boredom and briefness. Martínez Estrada's poetry was a filter through which he distilled his talent for expression.

Martínez Estrada wrote some pieces for the theater. In 1941, he presented *Lo que no vemos morir* (What We Do Not See Dying, 1957), about which the critics were not very enthusiastic. According to Juan Carlos Ghiano, this play—and two others: *Sombras* (Shades, 1957) and *Cazadores* (Hunters, 1957)—

possess a dramatic sense in terms of their conflicts and characters.

The author wrote short stories all his life. The themes and topics that he dealt with reflect his personal view of man and the world, which can be traced in terms of plot as well as at the level of general meaning, in terms of structure as well as language. In his stories, man is the victim of inexorable forces that condemn him to failure or loneliness. Some of the short stories are studies of manners, written with an obvious satirical intention, for example, "Por favor, doctor, sálve me usted" (Please, Doctor, Save Me). Others are aimed at creating a hallucinatory atmosphere, such as "Un crimen sin recompensa" (A Crime Without Reward), in which the action takes place in a somewhat ghostly bus that travels between two imaginary cities. "Florisel y Rudolf" is written with the marvelous naïveté of the medieval fable and describes the pure and deep passion of two lovers. In Martínez Estrada's stories, the disposition of different elements of narrative (plot, narrator, character, time, physical setting) determines the relative amounts of realism, fantasy, and absurdity. As in much modern fiction (compare Juan Rulfo, Carlos Fuentes, Julio Cortázar), these stories require that the reader take part in the act of communication.

Marta Riquelme (first published in 1949) is a story in which Martínez Estrada acts as fictitious narrator, using his own name. The plot is a puzzle in which an enigmatic woman's history is reconstructed through a game of successive revelations and concealments, suppositions and false hints. Some critics have pointed out the story's debt to Franz Kafka, to whom Martínez Estrada later devoted an essay and whose nightmare vision he shared in many of his stories. Another Kafkaesque story is "Sábado de gloria" (Easter Saturday; first published in 1944). The story describes the ironic tribulations of a bureaucrat who tries in vain to enjoy his holidays, which are constantly and indefinitely postponed by a series of events in his private life that appear fated to occur. An oppressive and overwhelming climate seems to lurk in the dark, and everyone feels caught up in a nonsensical vortex. "Abel Cainus" (1957) is a tragic echo of the war. "La inundación" (The Flood; first published in 1943) is a terrifyingly realistic picture made up of personal recollections and transcendental and symbolic suggestions. Its action takes place in a church in which a whole town has sought protection from the coming waters. In the church's aisle, the town is formed again, with all the hierarchies, hatreds, and systems of living together that had existed before the population had to hurry away. "La inundación" is an excellent story that describes different human types in brief, strong portraits, drawn without oversentimentality. The story traces a symbol of human destiny: man is an unhappy being, abandoned to his own means by a God who has forgotten him.

The persistent cough that overcomes the main character in a short story with that name ("La tos," 1957) is a symbol of the essential lack of communication among human beings; even among close friends or relatives, each person is shut up in his own egotism. Though Kafka's influence is obvious, the hero does not need to be turned into an insect, as was Gregor Samsa, to build an impenetrable wall around himself. It is enough for him to catch a cold and get a constant cough, a situation that is both tragic and grotesque. In all of Martínez Estrada's short stories, we can trace the presence of a skillful narrator, whose worlds carry the unavoidable mark of bitterness and sarcasm that prevails even more strongly in his more intellectual essays.

As in the case of other analysts of Argentine reality, in his essays Martínez Estrada wanted to base his characterization on an intuition that could illuminate his country's history and nature. His consideration of the Argentine man was influenced by his knowledge of Friedrich Nietzsche, Georg Simmel, Arthur Schopenhauer, Oswald Spengler, and Sigmund Freud—thinkers who shared an antirationalist attitude and therefore an exaltation of the instincts, the unconscious, myths, and the dark forces of blood and earth. X-Ray of the Pampa reflects these influences. Its somber concepts, controversial but undeniably influential for later generations, are rooted in Martínez Estrada's historical times, his readings, and a certain temperamental tendency toward bitterness.

His analysis starts with a consideration of the discovery and conquest of the extreme south of the South American continent. The protagonists in that adventure felt they were the victims of a mirage. They had been let down by a Nature that destroyed their illusions, for they had come not to settle down but to take immediate riches back to Europe. For those sons of Spanish hidalgos (noblemen), the idea of having to work was nearly a defeat. There was neither gold nor silver in the pampas. Only the land was there, the land that with time would be divided into estates, signs of noble lineage. It is understandable that the few early inhabitants would feel the insecurity and fear that would later characterize the ways of life of their offspring: the gaucho, the compadre, the guarango, the caudillo.

Independence was not an idea borrowed from foreign liberalism, but a chaotic and instinctive force. Martínez Estrada did not agree with Domingo F. Sarmiento regarding the concept and dilemma of "civilization versus barbarism," in spite of the fact that he greatly admired Sarmiento and devoted a number of studies to him, including Sarmiento (1946), "Sarmiento, escritor" (Sarmiento, the Writer, 1950), and Los invariantes históricos en el Facundo (Historical Invariables in Facundo, 1947). For Sarmiento, civilization was light and progress and barbarism nefarious darkness; for Martínez Estrada, barbarism was the repressed energy, the uprootedness, the ferocity visible in so many literary works. He wrote poetic paragraphs on the animism of the knife (el cuchillo). After the "desert conquest," as cruel as that of the North American West, the rulers of the pampas felt part of a higher society, and the state took on a false prestige. It was then that the Argentine man looked toward Europe, and, being a nomad, like his cattle, he left farming to the despicable immigrant. When the railroads were built, they became more an isolating factor than an integrating one, and national independence consolidated this isolation instead of overcoming it. According to Martínez Estrada, these factors caused Argentina's lack of relationship with the other countries of the continent and the easiness with which the nation was economically and culturally dominated and turned into a mere producer of raw materials, a "suburban farm" of Europe.

Martínez Estrada was a determinist. Argentine fatalism was a consequence of the boundless space where towns without distinguishing features sprang up, to be inhabited by lonely men who clung to ideas of patriotic Utopias, to empty laws, superstitions with religious trappings, and anachronistic ways of life, which led to the worship of courage and which molded the effectiveness, the culture, and the politics of the country. *X-Ray of the Pampa* is not history, though it makes constant references to the past; nor is it sociology, though it deals with the individual and society, and the psychology of the masses (under the influence of José Ortega y Gasset). It is, in truth, a personal reaction to a reality that deeply hurt the writer—a book that is interesting, courageous, genuine, exaggerated, irritating, and aggressive.

In *X-Ray of the Pampa*, Martínez Estrada dealt, for the first time, with the subject of the city of Buenos Aires, which he describes as having a case of urban hypertrophy or macrocephaly, which he discusses in detail in another essay, *La cabeza de Goliat* (Goliath's Head, 1940). Buenos Aires is the center from which the forms of politics, education, and financial activity spread toward the "interior," which accepts them with reverence and perhaps some resentment. Several levels of cultural development coexist in Buenos Aires. It is like a temporary beehive, a city that resists being taught: it can only be *seen*, as a collection of rapidly aging photographs. Martínez Estrada illustrates his deeply poetic, though pessimistic, view of the city with a gallery of human types. He deplores the absence of birds, and this nostalgia leads him to the evocation of William Henry Hudson, the Anglo-Argentine writer who lived in great intimacy with nature and to whom he devoted a book, *El mundo maravilloso de Guillermo Enrique Hudson* (William Henry Hudson's Marvelous World, 1951). Nothing can escape his observation. He is interested in everything, from the tango to the bureaucracy, from the passion for soccer and the horse races to the people's ingratitude to their poet Lugones, to the depressing view of the hospital where he visited his good friend Quiroga.

In 1948, in Mexico City, Martínez Estrada published *Muerte y transfiguración de Martín Fierro* (The Death and Transfiguration of Martín Fierro), an interpretation of José Hernández' poem *El gaucho Martín Fierro* (1872), its political climate, its idiosyncrasy, and its language. The influence of psychoanalysis is evident in this stimulating and controversial study. The author shows us that Hernández, overshadowed and displaced by his hero, did not feel love but resentment toward the *gaucho*; at best, he was ambivalent. The *gaucho* represented a cruel world, from which Hernández could be freed only if he objectified it in a work of art. *Martín Fierro* is a symbolic transposition of its narrator-protagonist's frustrations. Martínez Estrada does not agree with those who see Martín Fierro as a historical character, but neither does he believe that he is a personification of the Argentine man.

For the *gaucho*, to become part of a family or a society is a surrender. He prefers what he believes to be freedom, but what is, in truth, a form of fear. His biography not only represents a people and a time but is a protest and a challenge. He is unfolded in several characters: Cruz, the friend, is the dark side of his personality, because, for the *gaucho*, who despises women, friendship is stronger than love; the old Vizcacha represents the adaptation to an unscrupulous world; the elder son is the scapegoat, while the younger son and Picardía, the son of Cruz, embody the roguish tradition. To be a *gaucho* means to break with all that is culturally established. That is why his figure was rejected by cultured readers, who saw themselves reflected in a not very flattering mirror. They preferred *Anastasio el pollo* (1866), the parody of the *gaucho* created by Estanislao del Campo, and the melodramatic serial stories of Eduardo Gutiérrez and his *Juan Moreira* (1879–1880), in which corrupt officials and merchants were blamed for all the flaws of Argentina. This rejected man was also turned into a mythic hero, without roots or future, a victim of fate. For Martínez Estrada, Martín Fierro is the quintessential *gaucho*. He is the historical clue to America, nature's voice, the expression of dissatisfaction, and the symbol of hostility toward order and the forms of "civilized" life.

There is no doubt that Martínez Estrada's view is based on a polarization. Argentina was never a pleasant Utopia or a gloomy hell. It is better to see the country as a place for struggle, for different attempts, for conflict between light and dark forces. New nations never present a definite physiognomy; they are always building themselves. It is naive to think that culture will completely remove barbarism, because the two forces endure in constant tension, in unstable balance, within man and his work. To read Martínez Estrada is always rewarding, because the reading puts us face-to-face with a fighter and a sharp observer and critic, who shouts his truth without expecting gratitude but, on the contrary, attacks and sorrow. Martínez Estrada deserves our respect, which is not to say that we must always accept his conclusions without discussion.

SELECTED BIBLIOGRAPHY

First Editions

Poetry

Oro y piedra. Buenos Aires, 1918.
Nefelibal. Buenos Aires, 1922.
Motivos del cielo. Buenos Aires, 1924.
Argentina. Buenos Aires, 1927.
Títeres de pies ligeros. Buenos Aires, 1929.
Humoresca. Buenos Aires, 1929.

Short Stories

Tres cuentos sin amor. Buenos Aires, 1956. Includes "La inundación."
Sábado de gloria, Juan Florido, padre e hijo, minervistas. Buenos Aires, 1956.
Marta Riquelme: Examen sin conciencia. Buenos Aires, 1956.
La tos y otros entretenimientos. Buenos Aires, 1957.

Essays

Radiografía de la pampa. Buenos Aires, 1933.
La cabeza de Goliat. Buenos Aires, 1940.
Sarmiento. Buenos Aires, 1946.
Panorama de las literaturas. Buenos Aires, 1946.
Los invariantes históricos en el "Facundo." Buenos Aires, 1947.
Muerte y transfiguración de Martín Fierro. Mexico City, 1948.
El mundo maravilloso de Guillermo Enrique Hudson. Mexico City, 1951.
Cuadrante del pampero. Buenos Aires, 1956.
¿Qué es esto? Buenos Aires, 1956.
Exhortaciones. Buenos Aires, 1957.
El hermano Quiroga. Montevideo, 1957.
Las 40. Buenos Aires, 1957.
Heraldos de la verdad: Montaigne—Balzac—Nietzsche. Buenos Aires, 1958.
Diferencias y semejanzas entre los países de América Latina. Mexico City, 1962.
El verdadero cuento del tío Sam. Havana, 1963.
Realidad y fantasía en Balzac. Bahía Blanca, Argentina, 1964.

Mi experiencia cubana. Montevideo, 1965. Posthumous edition.
Martí, revolucionario. Havana, 1967. Posthumous edition.
El torno a Kafka y otros ensayos. Barcelona, 1967. Posthumous edition.
Para una revisión de las letras argentinas. Buenos Aires, 1967. Posthumous edition.

Collected Works

Antología. Mexico City, 1964.
Cuentos completos. Madrid, 1975.
Poesía. Buenos Aires, 1947.
Tres dramas: Lo que no vemos morir. Sombras. Cazadores. Buenos Aires, 1957.

Translations

X-Ray of the Pampa. Translated by Alain Swietlicki. London and Austin, Tex., 1971.

Biographical and Critical Studies

Adam, Carlos. *Bibliografía y documentos de Ezequiel Martínez Estrada.* La Plata, Argentina, 1968.
Contorno 4 (1954). Special issue dedicated to Martínez Estrada.
Diccionario de la literatura argentina 4. Washington, D.C., 1960. Contains biographical, bibliographical, and critical notes by Alfredo A. Roggiano.
Earle, Peter G. *Prophet in the Wilderness.* Austin, Tex., 1971.
Ghiano, Juan Carlos. *Poesía argentina del siglo XX.* Mexico City, 1957.
Homenaje a Ezequiel Martínez Estrada. Casa de las Américas 5/33 (1965).
Homenaje a Ezequiel Martínez Estrada. Bahía Blanca, Argentina, 1968.
Mafud, Julio. *El desarraigo argentino.* Buenos Aires, 1959.
Murena, H. A. *El pecado original de América.* Buenos Aires, 1954.
Orgambide, Pedro. *Genio y figura de Martínez Estrada.* Buenos Aires, 1985.
Sebrelli, Juan José. *Martínez Estrada: Una rebelión inútil.* Buenos Aires, 1960.
Soto, Luis Emilio. *Crítica y estimación.* Buenos Aires, 1938.
Stabb, Martín S. "Ezequiel Martínez Estrada: The Formative Writings." *Hispania* 49/1:54–60 (1966).
Torchia Estrada, Juan C. *La filosofía en la Argentina.* Washington, D.C., 1961.
Zum Felde, A. *Índice crítico de la literatura hispanoamericana.* Mexico City, 1954.

Manuel Rojas

(1896–1973)

Cedomil Goic

Manuel Rojas was born on 8 January 1896 in the Boedo district of Buenos Aires, Argentina. He was the only child of Manuel Rojas Córdoba and Dorotea Sepúlveda, impoverished Chilean immigrants. In 1899, the family moved to Santiago, Chile. Their neighborhood in Santiago left the child with a vision of so-called ex-men, a lumpenproletariat that survives in the pages of his *Imágenes de infancia* (Images of Childhood, 1955). When Manuel's father died in 1903, he and his mother returned to Buenos Aires. They lived in various locations, staying for a while in a housing project with a Spanish family with whom they had lived in Boedo years before. This family served as the real-life model for the family of Aniceto Hevia, the protagonist of Rojas' novel *Hijo de ladrón* (Born Guilty, 1951). Manuel received his primary education in several schools in the Boedo, Caballito, and Flores districts. A family economic crisis forced the young Rojas to take a series of jobs, first as a tailor's apprentice, then as a porter, and finally as an employee of a messenger service. This last job permitted him his greatest pleasure, which was to wander from one end of Buenos Aires to the other. He also served as a saddler's apprentice.

In 1908, Manuel and his mother moved to the city of Rosario, Argentina, where they lived in the house of an Argentine family. In Rosario, at the age of fourteen, Rojas abandoned his high school studies in order to work exclusively. It was at this time that he discovered literature in the form of the novels of Emilio Salgari. At his third place of residence in Rosario, he read for the owner of the house, an elderly woman. During this same period, Rojas found employment as a mechanical carpenter for the Central Railroad of Argentina.

In the winter of 1910, Rojas moved again with his mother, this time to Mendoza, Argentina, where he worked as an electrician's assistant, a house painter, a circus guard, and a worker in a vineyard. In 1911, he separated from his mother in order to take a job at Las Cuevas as a laborer on the stretch of the Trans-Andean railroad going from Mendoza to Los Andes. In Mendoza, he was initiated into literature by an anarchist teacher, and he came into contact with exiled Chilean anarchists. He traveled around the interior of the province of Cuyo to Palmira, San Martín, and Gutiérrez. On 29 April 1912, he returned to Chile. At the age of sixteen, he worked as a boat guard, or watchman, on the bay of Valparaiso and as a stevedore in the port. In 1915, he began to write for the anarchist newspapers *La Batalla* (The Battle) and *La Protesta* in Buenos Aires. Stimulated by the Chilean poet José Domingo Gómez Rojas, he composed his first poems, under the influence of *modernismo*, and an essay in defense of a companion who had been unjustly accused. During this time, he wrote indefatigably and spent long hours reading in the National Library. He had grown into a tall man—he was over six feet two, solidly built, with wide shoulders—whose physique contrasted with his mild manners and kindly expression.

Rojas' first published sonnet, "Lo mismo que un gusano que hilara su capullo . . ." (Like a worm spinning its cocoon . . .), appeared in 1917 in the literary review *Los diez*. In 1919, he traveled as a prompter with the theatrical company of the actor Alejandro Flores to Chiloé, in the southern part of Chile. During the winter of 1920, he worked as a linotype operator for Imprenta Numen in Santiago, where *Verba Roja*, an anarchist organ, was printed. He experienced the political repression of those years and traveled again as a prompter to Punta Arenas. Among the young intellectuals of the Federation of Students, he made friends with José Santos González Vera, Alberto Rojas Jiménez, and Domingo Gómez Rojas ("Daniel Vásquez"), a poet who was tragically condemned. In 1921, he went on tour in Argentina and Uruguay with the Mario-Padín theatrical company. That same year, while in Mendoza, he published his first group of poems, *Poéticas* (Poetics), in the magazine *Ideas y figuras*. In 1922, he abandoned the tour and looked for employment in Buenos Aires, but without success.

Rojas remained in Buenos Aires from 1922 to 1924. He entered a literary contest sponsored by the daily newspaper *La Montaña*, and won second prize with his short story "Laguna" (Laguna), his first prose publication, inspired by experiences in the mountains. In 1923, he won a prize from the review *Caras y caretas* for his story "El hombre de los ojos azules" (The Man with the Blue Eyes). He also wrote "El cachorro" (The Cub) and "Un espíritu inquieto" (An Uneasy Spirit). In 1924, he completed "El bonete Maulino" (The Maulino Hat), based on a story that his mother had told him. In 1926, Rojas published his first collection of short stories, *Hombres del sur* (Men of the South), which included those mentioned above. The following year, he published *Tonada del transeúnte* (Transient's Song). In this volume of poetry he followed the tendencies of

Vicente Huidobro and Pablo Neruda, rejecting punctuation.

In Chile, in 1927, Rojas went on his last tour as a prompter for theatrical companies. Leaving behind the marginal world of the itinerant worker, he gradually became a convert to the intellectual world of literature, journalism, and publishing. He worked for the daily newspaper *La Nación* in Santiago, Chile, as a linotype operator. In 1928, he was given a position as a third-class librarian at the National Library. The same year he married the poet and teacher María Baeza, with whom he had three children. In 1929 his mother, an important influence in his life, died. That year he received the Marcial Martínez and *Atenea* prizes for his book of short stories *El delincuente* (The Delinquent). In 1931, he was appointed director of the press at the University of Chile. Rojas received an award given by the newspaper *La Nación* for his novel *Lanchas en la bahía* (Barges in the Bay) in 1932. That same year he began his involvement with the newspaper *Las Últimas Noticias*, for which he worked for the next nine years. His wife died in 1936. In 1937, he was elected president of the Society of Chilean Writers. The following year, he became an employee of the Hipódromo Chile racetrack, where he worked for sixteen years. In 1941, Rojas married Valeria López Edwards.

In his maturity, Rojas brought forth the most abundant and significant production of his life as a writer. In 1951, he became director of the *Anales de la Universidad de Chile* (Annals of the University of Chile). In that year, he published his most famous novel, *Born Guilty*, the first in a cycle that includes *Mejor que el vino* (Sweeter than Wine, 1958), *Sombras contra el muro* (Shadows on the Wall, 1964), and *La oscura vida radiante* (The Dark Shining Life, 1971). All of these novels, based on the life of their author, place in sharp relief the formative years, the amorous exploits, the ideological formation, and the permanent wandering of the protagonist, Aniceto Hevia. In 1957, Rojas received the National Award for Literature. He visited the United States for the first time, invited by the State Department. In the summer of 1959, he taught at Middlebury College in Vermont. On his return trip to Chile, he traveled to Puerto Rico and Venezuela. *Población esperanza* (Hopetown), his only dramatic work of interest, written in collaboration with Isidora Aguirre, premiered in 1959.

Following the Cuban Revolution, Rojas' newspaper activity became more militant. He collaborated on the review *Punto final* (Full Stop). In 1960, he lived for several months in Buenos Aires. In the same year, he published *Punta de rieles* (Tip of the Tracks), a novel. Not part of the aforementioned cycle, it was partially based on a story given to him by the dramatist Julio Asmussen in 1927. Twenty years later, the other part came to him in the form of a personal confession. In a manner similar to that of William Faulkner in *Wild Palms* (1939), Rojas combines these two stories in an original montage: while the first is told by one character, the second is evoked by his listener.

In the final stage in Rojas' career, he was the most important narrative writer in Chile and one of the most prominent in Latin America. In 1961 and 1962, he was invited to teach at the University of Washington in Seattle and the University of California at Los Angeles. During part of 1962, he resided in Mexico. He and Valeria López Edwards separated that year. He was invited in 1963 to teach at the University of Oregon. After divorcing his second wife, Rojas married Hortensia Dittborn.

In 1965, Rojas traveled to Europe, visiting France and Czechoslovakia. In 1966, he went to Cuba as a member of the jury for the Casa de las Américas Literary Award and was invited to attend the Tricontinental Conference in Havana as an observer. He traveled in Spain, Portugal, France, Italy, the Soviet Union, and Czechoslovakia. He then returned to Chile. In 1967, he went to Cuba and Mexico. He also traveled to Israel in response to an official invitation. The death of Che Guevara in 1967 caused him to be critical of the party line of the left. In 1970, he finished writing his last novel, *La oscura vida radiante*. He maintained lively contact with Cuba in 1971 and served once again as a member of the jury for the Casa de las Américas Award. He died of cancer at the age of seventy-seven in Santiago, Chile, on 11 March 1973. Rojas left behind various unpublished manuscripts and a novel he had recently begun.

Rojas is the most important Chilean narrative writer of his generation, which includes Luis Durand,

Alberto Romero, José Santos González Vera, Juan Marín, Rubén Azócar, Marta Brunet, and Benjamín Subercaseaux. His strongest literary and moral links were to the works and personalities of González Vera and Enrique Espinoza, the Argentine writer who was a longtime resident of Chile and director of the review *Babel*. Along with these writers, he represents a reaction against the *criollismo*—the nationalist literary trend—of the previous generation, with whom they established a dialogue that was respectful and at the same time dissident. There is an undeniable collectivist *mondonoviste* influence in his literature, especially in his short narratives, but at the same time there is a modification of that literature by means of internalization and sparseness. The fundamental themes in his narrative are related to the varied and sensitive tensions caused by human bonding, brotherhood, and desire, to the crisis of the bonding with the "other."

In Rojas' early work, it is possible to see clear indications of the vanguardist tendencies that would later become dominant. Initially, there is a certain exultant admiration for energy, the animation of work, and mechanical forces, with clear futurist overtones. But the spectacle of activity of muscle and machine was later significantly displaced by unanimism, or feeling. Some of these elements were absorbed by a central aspect of Rojas' ideology: the anarchist vision of the world, a critique of a society that deforms natural bonds, that is bureaucratic and alienating, forgetful and scornful of contact that is spontaneous, direct, and existential, alive with the truth of reality. Rojas' narrative voice and certain of his characters develop the novelistic paradoxes characteristic of this deformation. The world of the worker, starting with the anarchist and union movements of the early twentieth century, is a central setting for Rojas' characteristic themes.

Rojas' writing is particularly distinguished from that of other contemporary Latin American novelists by its sphere of animated reality. Avoiding the idealizing symmetries and the propagandistic and ideological deformations of socialist realism, his narrative works concern a human appraisal of workingmen, and, in the sense of the works of Maxim Gorki (widely read by that generation, along with those of Leonid Andreyev, Mikhail Artzybashev, Knut Hamsun, Panait Istrati, and Isaac Babel), of so-called ex-men. These ex-men are portrayed as wasted by society and ignored by their peers. Nevertheless, the narrator discovers in them, under their almost petrified and inexpressive exteriors, the persistent necessity of the "other." The sympathetic face, the understanding smile or glance; the silence in which two existences communicate wordlessly in true companionship; unsolicited help generously offered—these things (along with the cancerous outward appearance that surrounds the existence and the expression of ex-men) erupt in an ordinary way in scenes that are delicately motivated by the desire to return men to the kingdom of humanity.

The life values of laborers and outcasts are recreated in the works of Rojas in terms that are difficult to find in any other writer of our time. With the same strong energy with which they lift up the fallen existence of men frozen in their dumbness, silent loneliness, and reserved aloofness, the works of Rojas punish different forms of degradation such as vice, shame, and lost dignity, the contemplation of which always arouses in the narrator repugnance and fierce rejection. The context of the 1920's—the awakening of labor movements and the political and social reforms that recognized the rights of workers and instituted social security—dominates his works. Street struggle and police repression achieve their first significant representation in the twentieth-century novel in Rojas' works.

Rojas shows a clear consciousness of the characteristics of twentieth-century literature in the essays *De la poesía a la revolución* (From Poetry to Revolution, 1938) and *El árbol siempre verde* (The Evergreen Tree, 1960), which define the autonomy of the literary work. However, his novels also show traits notably close to the autobiography and to his personal experience, in terms of both plot and ideological content. Rojas sets in high relief the priority of what is human over what is nature—this is one of the outstanding elements in his vision of the world, his reaction against the fundamental prominence granted to nature by the *mondonoviste* generation (that of the great Venezuelan writer Rómulo Gallegos and of Mariano Latorre in Chile). In this regard, Rojas belongs to a group of writers that includes, in Latin America, Miguel Ángel Asturias, Alejo Car-

pentier, Eduardo Mallea, Enrique Amorim, and Agustín Yáñez.

Rojas' first novel, *Lanchas en la bahía*, is a small masterpiece that describes the initiation into life of an adolescent who enters adulthood by means of true rites of passage. The protagonist, Eugene, emerges renewed, but only after descending into experiences of fear, exhaustion, and wounded pride. The assistance he receives from generous helpers and sensitive guides permits him to survive with success the hard challenges of an adolescent thrown into the world completely on his own and without the support of parents. The work, reprinted many times, underwent in its first three editions significant textual modifications. The novel was stripped of its initial excessive imagistic ornamentation, which was an obvious echo of the poetic vanguard. The character of Eugene anticipates the figure of Aniceto Hevia, who provides the constant autobiographical element for the cycle of Rojas' principal novels. The initiation into life, the solidarity between ordinary men, the erotic and maternal meaning of women, and the perpetual *Bildungsroman* are clearly foreshadowed in *Lanchas en la bahía*. Also anticipated are the perceptions of nature as a symbol of that which is unconditioned, as opposed to the harshness of social conditioning.

Born Guilty is Rojas' most important novel, the best composed and most perfectly written, a masterwork of Latin American literature. Apart from the ideological and human elements previously referred to, *Born Guilty* is remarkable for its structure, and for the expressive value it acquires by the juxtaposition of the violent *découpage* of its first parts with the linearity of its final part. The first parts correspond strictly to the anguished and difficult experiences of the adolescent; the final part corresponds to the serenity, the satisfied and fulfilled character, that his existence achieves. The initial *découpage* is ordered in a series of flashbacks between the present situation and the remote past, in an attempt to present what underlies the current difficulties. In essence, what is portrayed is the prominently exposed character of an illegal immigrant who wants to integrate himself into society but who, because of his origin, encounters constant problems. He is functioning without the support of his family—without parents and with his brothers and sisters dispersed throughout the world—and he is in an unfamiliar setting, unable to make the kinds of contacts that could help lessen the difficulties of his situation. He is without legal documents but must make his way in a society that is controlled by consulates, customs officials, port authorities, and employers. He suffers the ultimate experiences that society imposes on the individual over and above the natural and human certainties.

The recounting of these experiences produces different levels of narration. The novel relates the story of the sixteen early years of the adolescent Aniceto Hevia, but the narrator is a mature man who narrates autobiographically the youthful segment of his life. From his adult perspective, he inevitably submits his remembrances to certain considerations that only maturity makes possible and that the child and adolescent cannot comprehend while living through the experience. This scheme gives rise to clearly distinguished planes of narration and commentary. New planes develop from the stories that the characters introduce in narrating their lives. To recount one's own life is to express trust and to create a stimulus for human communication. To receive a confidential narration or to offer one becomes a communicative act par excellence. Some commentaries in *Born Guilty* develop existential themes in which critics have seen parallels with Thomas Mann's *Der Zauberberg* (*The Magic Mountain*, 1924).

In its aspects that are most critical of human society, Rojas' novel postulates a vision of the absurd and of the gratuitousness of social demands in opposition to natural and existential certainties for the individual. He presents the deformation of the functionary, whose position prevents him from recognizing, in the "other," his sincere and true fellow man. The functionary sees instead only a number or a bearer of legitimizing documents, which are ultimately doubtful or false. As ingenuous as this vision might appear, it includes that part of anarchism that places a high value on the ideal form of natural life. In Rojas' narratives, wind and sky, sun and sea, symbolize what is not conditioned. They represent the continual free play of nature, its dynamic energy and its unlimited extension, a spectacle that is a joy to contemplate, that calms the soul and balances man's aspirations, one that the unfortunate perceive

and experience only as a compensation for their instability and frustrated hopes.

Rojas' short stories have given him a distinguished place alongside the short story writers of his generation. His literary affinities are closer to those of Horacio Quiroga than to the subtle intelligence of the more contemporary stories of Jorge Luis Borges, even when the great Argentine storyteller selects his topics from the slums. The universal projection that Borges achieves by postulating the archetypical situation is pursued and attained by Rojas in a tempered comprehension of elemental human ties, within the limits of painful awareness of the fall from human dignity and of defeat.

Translated from the Spanish by David Wolfe

SELECTED BIBLIOGRAPHY

First Editions

Novels and Short Stories

Hombres del sur. Santiago, Chile, 1926.
El delincuente. Santiago, Chile, 1929.
Lanchas en la bahía. Santiago, Chile, 1932.
Travesía: Novelas breves. Santiago, Chile, 1934.
La ciudad de los Césares. Santiago, Chile, 1936.
Hijo de ladrón. Santiago, Chile, 1951.
Mejor que el vino. Santiago, Chile, 1958.
Punta de rieles. Santiago, Chile, 1960.
Sombras contra el muro. Santiago, Chile, 1964.
La oscura vida radiante. Buenos Aires, 1971.

Poetry

Poéticas. Ideas y figuras (Mendoza, Argentina) 13:7–11 (1921).
Tonada del transeúnte. Santiago, Chile, 1927.
Deshecha rosa. Santiago, Chile, 1954.

Essays, Travel, and Autobiography

De la poesía a la revolución. Santiago, Chile, 1938.
Imágenes de infancia. Santiago, Chile, 1955.
Apuntes sobre la expresión escrita. Caracas, 1960.
El árbol siempre verde. Santiago, Chile, 1960.
Historia breve de la literatura chilena. Santiago, Chile, 1965.
Pasé por México un día. Santiago, Chile, 1965.
A pie por Chile. Santiago, Chile, 1967.
Viaje al país de los profetas. Buenos Aires, 1969.

Collected Works

Antología de cuentos. Santiago, Chile, 1957.
Cuentos. Buenos Aires, 1970.
Imágenes de infancia y adolescencia. Santiago, Chile, 1983.
Obras. Madrid, 1973.
Obras completas. Santiago, Chile, 1961.
Obras escogidas. 2 vols. Santiago, Chile, 1969.

Translations

Born Guilty. Translated by Frank Gaynor. New York, 1955.

Biographical and Critical Studies

Alegría, Fernando. "Manuel Rojas: Trascendentalismo en la novela chilena." *Cuadernos americanos* 103/2: 244–258 (1959). Also in *Fronteras del realismo.* Santiago, Chile, 1962. Pp. 83–112.

Boorman, Joan Rea. In *La estructura del narrador en la novela hispanoamericana contemporánea.* Madrid, 1976. Pp. 130–133.

Cannizo, Mary. "Manuel Rojas, Chilean Novelist and Author." *Hispania* 41/1:200–201 (1958).

Cortés, Darío A. "Bibliografía del cuento y ensayo de Manuel Rojas Sepúlveda." *Chasqui* 10/1:43–70 (1980).

Cortés Larrieu, Norman. "*Hijo de ladrón* de Manuel Rojas: Tres formas de inconexión en el relato." *Anales de la Universidad de Chile* 120:193–202 (1960).

_____. "*Hijo de ladrón,* una novela existencial." *Revista del Pacífico* 1/1:33–50 (1964).

Díaz Arrieta, Hernán. *Historia personal de la literatura chilena.* Santiago, Chile, 1962.

Espinoza, Enrique. *Tres epístolas.* Santiago, Chile, 1969.

_____. "Notas sobre Manuel Rojas." *Atenea* 31/346–347:108–121 (1954).

Fuenzalida, Héctor. "Recuerdos de la universidad: Manuel Rojas." *Mapocho* 4/11:203–210 (1965).

Gertel, Zunilda. "Función estructural del 'leitmotiv' en *Hijo de ladrón.*" *Revista hispánica moderna* 35/4: 363–369 (1969).

Goic, Cedomil. "*Hijo de ladrón:* Libertad y lágrimas." *Atenea* 398:103–113 (1960). Also in *Cien años de novela chilena.* Santiago, Chile, 1961. Pp. 103–113.

_____. *La novela chilena: Los mitos degradados.* Santiago, Chile, 1968. Pp. 124–143, 204–208.

_____. "Introducción." In *Lanchas en la bahía,* by Manuel Rojas. 9th ed. Santiago, Chile, 1974. Pp. 7–23.

González Vera, José Santos. "Manuel Rojas." In *Algunos.* Santiago, Chile, 1959. Pp. 175–205.

Huasi, Julio. "Manuel Rojas." *Crisis* (Buenos Aires) 1:3–10 (1973).

Hunneus, Cristián. "El caso de Manuel Rojas." *Mundo nuevo* 4:83–85 (1966).

Jensen, Alfred W. "The Changing Face of Humor in the Novels of Manuel Rojas." *Proceedings of the Pacific Northwest Conference on Foreign Languages* 21/1: 170–172 (1976).

Lichtblau, Myron I. "Ironic Devices in Manuel Rojas' *Hijo de ladrón.*" *Symposium* 19/3:214–225 (1965).

_____. "Elementos estilísticos de *Hijo de ladrón.*" *Humanitas* 5:323–339 (1964).

_____. "Los últimos capítulos de *Hijo de ladrón.*" *Revista hispánica moderna* 34/3–4:707–713 (1968).

_____. "El tono irónico en *Sombras contra el muro,* de Manuel Rojas." *Hispamérica* 8:45–53 (1974).

_____. "La ironía en *Mejor que el vino* de Manuel Rojas." *Revista de estudios hispánicos* 9/2:163–179 (1975).

_____. "Narrative Voice and Irony in Manuel Rojas' *La oscura vida radiante.*" *Symposium* 36/3:220–236 (1982).

Param, Charles. "Horacio Quiroga and Manuel Rojas." *Proceedings of the Pacific Northwest Conference on Foreign Languages* 22:144–152 (1971).

_____. "Humor and Manuel Rojas." *Proceedings of the Pacific Northwest Conference on Foreign Languages* 25/ 1:177–183 (1974).

Pontiero, Giovanni. "The Two Versions of *Lanchas en la bahía:* Some Observations on Rojas' Approach to Style." *Bulletin of Hispanic Studies* 45/2:123–132 (1968).

Robles, Mercedes M. "Thomas Mann's *The Magic Mountain* and Manuel Rojas' *Born Guilty.*" *Latin American Literary Review* 12/23:15–24 (1983).

Rodríguez Monegal, Emir. In *Narradores de esta América.* Montevideo, 1962. Pp. 57–63.

Rodríguez Reeves, Rosa. "Bibliografía de y sobre Manuel Rojas." *Revista iberoamericana* 42/95: 285–313 (1976).

Rojas Rivera, J. A. "Manuel Rojas y Aniceto Hevia: Simbiosis literaria." In *La novela iberoamericanas contemporánea.* Caracas, 1968. Pp. 261–269.

Schwartz, Kessel. *A New History of Spanish American Fiction* 1. Coral Gables, Fla., 1972. Pp. 245–248.

Silva Castro, Raúl. "Manuel Rojas." In *Historia crítica de la novela chilena.* Madrid, 1960. Pp. 319–330.

_____. "Manuel Rojas, novelista." *Cuadernos hispanoamericanos* 44/130:5–19 (1960).

_____. "Manuel Rojas y sus cuentos." *Revista hispánica moderna* 27/3–4:325–328 (1961).

_____. "Manuel Rojas: Chilean Novelist and Essayist." *Books Abroad* 37/4:400–402 (1963).

Viñas, David. "Manuel Rojas de perfil (y sin retoques)." *Casa de las Américas* 21/121:88–92 (1980).

Luis Palés Matos

(1898–1959)

Aníbal González-Pérez

The work of Luis Palés Matos, one of the founders of modern Puerto Rican poetry, the initiator of the literary movement known as *negrismo*, and a major twentieth-century Latin American poet in his own right, has been a subject of critical interest and scrutiny for over forty years, ever since the publication of his first important book of poems, *Tuntún de pasa y grifería* (Drumbeats of Kink and Blackness, 1937). Palés' work has been studied and commented on by such eminent Hispanists as Federico de Onís and Margot Arce de Vázquez, as well as by writers like Fernando Ortiz, Tomás Blanco, and Juan Antonio Corretjer. Today, Palés' poems, like many other Latin American classics, continue to be read and reinterpreted by younger generations of critics and writers, from José Luis González and Arcadio Díaz Quiñones to Luis Rafael Sánchez and Ana Lydia Vega.

Palés' poetry has, however, had less influence on Puerto Rican poets than on Puerto Rican essayists and novelists. This is particularly true of Palés' "Afroantillean" (that is, Afro-Caribbean), or *negrista*, poetry, most of which is collected in *Tuntún*. For many readers in Puerto Rico and throughout Latin America, Palés is chiefly remembered as the founder, along with the Cuban Nicolás Guillén, of *negrismo*, a poetic mode that sought to emphasize and exalt the black contribution to Latin American history and culture. Although Palés' *negrista* poems in *Tuntún* are his most original poetic achievement, an understanding of these poems, as well as of Palés' influential views on literature and culture, would not be complete without consideration of his abundant poetic production outside the *negrista* vein, collected in his books *Azaleas* (Azaleas, 1915) and *Poesía 1915–1956* (Poetry 1915–1956, 1957). Before discussing Palés' writings and their influence in more detail, however, a brief examination of some aspects of his life is required: the poetry of Palés, like that of many post-*modernista* writers, contains an evident autobiographical or confessional component, and this makes the story of his life particularly relevant to any discussion of his poetry.

Luis Palés Matos was born in the town of Guayama, on the southeastern coast of Puerto Rico, on 20 March 1898. Both the place and the date are significant in terms of his work. Guayama was a small, provincial town surrounded by sugarcane plantations; it had a sizable black population. Even today, Guayama is popularly known as the "witches' town" because of the supposed prevalence of Afro-Caribbean witchcraft in the area. And 1898 was the year of the Spanish-American War, when Cuba, Puerto Rico, and the Philippines, Spain's last major overseas possessions, fell into the hands of the United States. The United States' invasion of Puerto Rico cut short the first halting steps of the Puerto Rican creole elite toward political autonomy under the Spanish regime and ushered in a thirty-year period of political confusion and sociocultural trauma that engendered a deep-seated pessimism in the generation of intellectuals that arose after the American takeover. According to Corretjer, this pessimism about Puerto Rico's future is reflected in Palés' poetry, which is permeated by themes of futility, boredom, and self-doubt. Palés himself tended to attribute his pessimism (following the "geographic determinism" in vogue during the 1920's and 1930's in Western intellectual circles) to the physical and moral environment of Guayama: a backwater town in a backwater country, surrounded by the arid, sunbaked terrain typical of the Puerto Rican southeast—a landscape tellingly evoked by Palés in his poem "Topografía" (Topography, 1925), discussed below.

However the social, political, or even the geographic conditions of his early life may have affected Palés, his family background was extremely favorable to his development as a poet. Both of his parents, Don Vicente Palés Anés and Doña Consuelo Matos Vicil, were poets, and the Palés household, though poor (Don Vicente was a schoolteacher), was the site of frequent literary *tertulias* (gatherings) among local men and women of letters. Palés' father was a liberal, a freethinker and a freemason in the nineteenth-century mold, who taught French and read the works of Ernest Renan, Victor Hugo, the Comte de Volney, and Charles Darwin. His death in 1913 must have had a profound impact on the young Palés, not only because it left the household in an even more precarious economic situation but also because of the manner in which Don Vicente died: he collapsed after reciting his poem "El cementerio" (The Cemetery) during an homage to the visiting Peruvian poet José Santos Chocano. For Palés, the peculiar circumstances of his father's death served to underscore his family's utter devotion to poetry and letters. Everyone, including his brothers, Vicente and Gustavo, and his sister, Consuelo, wrote verse. Palés himself was precocious: he wrote his first poems in 1911, when he was thirteen, and published his first volume of poetry, *Azaleas*, when he was seventeen. The

poems in *Azaleas*, written very much in the mold of the *modernista* poetry of Rubén Darío, Leopoldo Lugones, and Julio Herrera y Reissig, already show a surprising maturity and the same careful poetic diction and attention to detail that would characterize all of Palés' later work.

After the death of his father, Palés, unable to continue his studies, worked at odd jobs in journalism and as a secretary and bookkeeper. In 1918 he married his childhood sweetheart, Natividad Suliveres, who bore a son, Edgardo (named after Edgar Allan Poe, one of Palés' favorite writers). She died of tuberculosis a year later. During this period (1919–1921) Palés wrote but left unpublished what would have been his second book of poems, "El palacio en sombras" (The Darkened Palace). In 1921, Palés, who had been living in the northern town of Fajardo, moved to the capital, San Juan.

For Palés, who had never traveled outside Puerto Rico (and who, save for trips to New York and the Lesser Antilles undertaken late in his life, would never leave the island), San Juan was a cosmopolitan city. There he came into contact with many of the distinguished Puerto Rican writers of his day, including the *modernista* poet Luis Lloréns Torres (who held court at a *tertulia* at the restaurant La Mallorquina) and the essayist Nemesio Canales. He also met, or rejoined, there several of the young writers of his own generation, like José I. de Diego Padró, Evaristo Ribera Chevremont, Antonio Coll y Vidal, Bolívar Pagán, and Luis Muñoz Marín. Through the poet Ribera Chevremont, who returned in 1924 from a four-year stay in Spain, Palés and his colleagues learned a great deal about the new avant-garde movements in literature and the arts, particularly their Spanish manifestation, the poetic movement known as *ultraísmo* (of which, incidentally, Jorge Luis Borges was a propagandist in Argentina). Ribera Chevremont was among those who began to disseminate in Puerto Rico the work of the Spanish thinker José Ortega y Gasset and who introduced Ortega's journal, the *Revista de Occidente* (Western Review). Ortega's essays, as well as those by various German authors (Max Scheler, Oswald Spengler, Leo Frobenius, and Hermann Alexander Keyserling, among others) that appeared in Spanish translation in the pages of the *Revista de Occidente*, are of key importance to Spanish-American intellectual life in the 1920's and 1930's, and their relevance to the work of Palés is direct and profound.

Before Ribera Chevremont's return from Spain, however, Palés, along with de Diego Padró, already, in 1921, had launched the first avant-garde movement in Puerto Rican literary history. The movement, known as *diepalismo* (a compound derived from the two poets' surnames), was extremely short-lived, and produced only one manifesto and one poem, collaboratively written, called "Orquestación diepálica" (Diepalic Orchestration), whose main novelty was the abundant use of onomatopoeia. Palés was to return to onomatopoeia in his Afroantillean poems, but his rather tentative incursion into avant-garde verse forms left few traces in most of the poetry he wrote between 1922 and 1925, which Palés collected in a manuscript entitled "Canciones de la vida media" (Songs at Mid-Life). In fact, at the time he compiled the "Canciones," Palés was only twenty-seven years old. Again, he did not publish the manuscript.

Palés' first Afroantillean poem, "Pueblo negro" (Black Town), was published in the newspaper *La Democracia* under the title "Africa" in March 1926; later that year he published another *negrista* poem, "Danza negra" (Black Dance). As Federico de Onís has rightly pointed out in his introduction to *Poesía*, Palés' "first black poetry is prior to that of the Cubans, and independent from it." The first Cuban poem with an Afro-Cuban theme is José Manuel Poveda's "Grito abuelo" (Grandfather Cry, 1927). Palés may thus legitimately be seen as an independent precursor of *negrista* poetry. Later, of course, as the Cuban version of *negrismo* became better known through the works of Guillén, Emilio Ballagas, and Alejo Carpentier, among others, Palés' poetry was often evaluated along with that of the Cubans. Nevertheless, as critics from Onís to Arcadio Díaz Quiñones have stressed, Palés' *negrista* poetry, while it cannot be divorced from the literary-historical background of the period, must also be understood in terms of Palés' own poetic project. From 1925 to 1937, Palés continued writing the Afroantillean poems that he would later collect in *Tuntún de pasa y grifería*. By 1937, Palés' Afroantillean poems already had been widely disseminated throughout the

Spanish-speaking world through their publication in newspapers and journals and by means of the poetry recitals of such well-known *declamadores* (orators) as the Spaniard José González Marín, the Cuban Eusebia Cosme, and the Puerto Rican Leopoldo Santiago Lavandero.

In 1927, José Robles Pazos published the first critical appraisal of Palés' poetry in the Madrid journal *La gaceta literaria* (Literary Gazette). He was followed in 1929 by Ángel Valbuena Prat, who wrote a favorable review of Palés' work for the Puerto Rican journal *Hostos* (Hostos), which he would later rework into the prologue to the first edition of *Tuntún*. The following year (1930), the Puerto Rican writer Tomás Blanco published the first critical piece about Palés in English in *The American Mercury* (21:72–75). That Palés was able to capture the attention of serious Iberian critics and writers was no mean achievement at a time when Spain itself was producing the so-called Generation of 1927, its most remarkable group of poets since the *siglo de oro* (golden age): Federico García Lorca, Jorge Guillén, Vicente Aleixandre, Rafael Alberti, Gerardo Diego, and others. Indeed, as several of these poets later testified, they saw in Palés a kindred spirit because of his desire— fueled by the avant-garde's neoprimitivism and irrationalism—to create a radically new Caribbean poetry by going back to the basics, as it were, of Hispano-Caribbean language and culture.

The fact that Palés' Afroantillean poems were widely read and commented on before their publication in a single volume gave rise to a persistent tendency among critics to read them out of context, and this in turn caused numerous misunderstandings about *Tuntún* and about the nature of Palés' poetic enterprise. In Puerto Rico itself, Palés' *negrista* poems, though universally admired for their technical virtuosity, provoked a lively and frequently acrimonious debate about the nature of Puerto Rican and Hispano-Caribbean society and culture. The debate specifically began in 1932, after the publication in *El Mundo* of an interview in which Palés set forth his views about Hispano-Caribbean culture as the product of the fusion of the Spanish and African cultures on Caribbean soil. His remarks scandalized many Puerto Rican intellectuals, who in reaction to the North American domination of their country had retreated into a nostalgic Hispanophilia. Even de Diego Padró, Palés' comrade of his avant-gardist days, attempted to refute him in two essays published in 1932. The next year another poet, Graciany Miranda Archilla, published an article in *Alma latino* (Latin Soul) significantly titled "La broma de una poesía prieta en Puerto Rico" (The Joke About a Black Poetry in Puerto Rico). Palés brilliantly defended his ideas in an important article, "Hacia una poesía antillana" (Toward an Antillean Poetry, 1932), published shortly after his controversial interview. Other writers were to rally to Palés' side in the debate, including some of his most distinguished critics, like Arce de Vázquez and Blanco. Nevertheless, echoes of the scandal provoked by the appearance of Palés' Afroantillean poems could still be heard in Puerto Rican intellectual circles as late as the 1970's in a debate centering around the work of the Puerto Rican essayist and short story writer José Luis González.

In the two decades following the publication of *Tuntún*, Palés' reputation continued to grow, even though he wrote little and published even less. It is significant that after *Tuntún*, he did not write any more *negrista* poems, save for a second version of the translated final poem in *Tuntún*, "Mulata-Antilla" (Antillean Mulatto Woman, 1949; translated as "Mulata-Antilla"), and "Plena del menéalo" (Shake-It-Up Song, 1953), Palés instead began to write poems that were recognizably "Antillean," though without emphasizing the black cultural element, such as "Menú" (Menu, 1942) and "Canción de mar" (Song of the Sea) and "Aires bucaneros" (Buccaneer Songs), both from 1943. In 1949 he began to write a remarkable cycle of love poems devoted to a woman he would name only as "Filí-Melé" (that name and some of the images used in the poems are reminiscent of the Afroantilleanism in "Mulata-Antilla"). These poems are widely regarded as some of the most beautiful and graceful love lyrics in Puerto Rican literature.

Outside of his writings, Palés' life was relatively uneventful. He had married again in 1930, to María Valdés Tous, with whom he had two children, Ana Mercedes and Guido. In 1942 his son Edgardo died, and in 1946 Palés' mother also passed away. All this while, Palés held various obscure bureaucratic posts in the island's government, until in 1944 he was named poet-in-residence at the University of Puerto Rico. In 1948 Palés suffered his first heart attack, a symptom of the illness that was to cause his death. In 1950 he traveled to the United States for the first and only time in his life to attend a series of activities held in his honor by the Hispanic Institute of Columbia University. Among the important critics and writers participating were Onís, Eugenio Florit, Andrés Iduarte, José A. Portuondo, and Max Henríquez Ureña. That same year, the second revised and augmented edition of *Tuntún de pasa y grifería* was published by the Biblioteca de Autores Puertorriqueños, with a prologue by Jaime Benítez. The first edition of Palés' book *Poesia 1915–1956*, with a prologue by Onís, appeared in 1957. Palés also wrote several chapters of an autobiographical novel, "Litoral: Reseña de una vida inútil" (Littoral: Account of a Useless Life), which he published in Puerto Rican newspapers in 1949 and 1951. He never completed the book.

Meanwhile, Palés' health continued to deteriorate. Since his youth, Palés had lived a bohemian life: long nights spent "philosophizing" in a cloud of cigar smoke around a table at a café, drinking bouts that lasted until early morning, long afternoon excursions to eat fried fish at obscure seaside eateries. His married life and his various bureaucratic jobs had little interfered with these habits. Palés, as he frequently said of himself, was of a melancholy disposition, and in his later years events helped to make him even sadder. The death of his granddaughter, Verónica Méndez Palés, in 1958, was a particularly heavy blow. To cheer him up, his old friend Luis Muñoz Marín, who had become Puerto Rico's first elected governor, took him on a trip to the Windward Islands (Saint Martin, Saba, Dominica, Guadeloupe, Martinique, Les Saintes), of which Palés had sung in "Canción festiva para ser llorada" (Festive Song to Be Cried) in *Tuntún*, but which he had never seen. Already aware of the condition of his health, Palés had written in his poem "El llamado" ("The Call," 1953):

> Me llaman desde allá . . .
> larga voz de hoja seca,
> mano fugaz de nube
> que en el aire de otoño se dispersa.
> Por arriba el llamado

tira de mí con tenue hilo de estrella,
abajo, el agua en tránsito,
con sollozo de espuma entre la niebla.
Ha tiempo oigo las voces
y descubro las señas.

(*Obras* 1, p. 576)

They call me from over there . . .
long voice of dead leaves,
fleeting hand of cloud
that vanishes in the autumn air.
From above, the call
tugs at me with a tenuous thread of starlight,
below, the water passes,
with a sobbing of froth amid the fog.
For a long time I have been hearing the voices
and discovering the signals.

Luis Palés Matos died at his home in Santurce of a heart attack on 23 February 1959 at age sixty-one.

Palés' first book of poems, *Azaleas*, owes much to the *modernista* and post-*modernista* poetic traditions. The book is composed mainly of sonnets written in various styles: there are "decadent" sonnets like "Neurosis," "Media noche" (Midnight), and "Fantasía" (Fantasy); metaphysical sonnets like "El reloj" (The Clock); sonnets in the *criollista* (nativist) mold, which evoke the Puerto Rican flora, like "La guajana" (The Sugarcane Flower) and "La ceiba" (The Cottonwood Tree); and even a few political and patriotic sonnets, such as "Compasión" (Compassion; with a dedication to the turn-of-the-century Puerto Rican politican Luis Muñoz Rivera) and "Sacra ira" (Sacred Wrath). As a whole, the book shows the young Palés' technical ability as well as his familiarity with the themes of Spanish-American *modernismo*. Indeed, for critics who are fond of looking for influences in a writers' works, a book like *Azaleas* is at the same time encouraging and confusing: encouraging because one can see in it the traces of Palés' readings of *modernista* poets (such as Darío, Lugones, and Herrera y Reissig, as well as of Puerto Rican poets like Lloréns Torres and Antonio Pérez Pierret), but also confusing because Palés' poems cannot be neatly identified with a specific type or period of *modernista* poetry. Some poems in *Azaleas* resemble the early "decadent" poems of Darío's *Prosas*

profanas (1892), while others fall into the more prosaic language of Darío's later poems in *Cantos de vida y esperanza* (Songs of Life and Hope, 1905) and of Lugones in his *Lunario sentimental* (Sentimental Lunar Poems, 1909) and *Romances de Río Seco* (Ballads of Río Seco, 1938). Still others contain language reminiscent of the bizarre metaphors favored by Herrera y Reissig (a style that makes Herrera a transitional figure between late *modernismo* and the early Hispanic avant-garde). If one goes beyond the simplistic search for "influences," however, the reason for this heterogeneity in *Azaleas* is not difficult to grasp; it is a consequence of Palés' poetic belatedness and of his lifelong penchant for experimentation. In *Azaleas*, Palés displays a catalog, as it were, of his readings and engages in critical dialogue with the various different modalities of *modernista* verse without showing that he favors one over the others. Palés, however, absorbed some general *modernista* traits that remained with him throughout his poetic career in spite of his avant-garde experiments: particularly the belief in poetry as an expression of cosmic order and a superior harmony, and as a reconciliation of opposites.

In his next two books of poetry after *Azaleas*, "El palacio en sombras" and "Canciones de la vida media" (which, though he had published neither at the time, Palés selected from in compiling his anthology *Poesía 1915–1956*), Palés opts for a more prosaic, though still harmonious, poetic style. Although he still writes decorative poems full of typical *modernista* allusions to Louis XIV, the mad king Ludwig II of Bavaria, religion, Greek myths, and the Orient, the most striking poems in both books are those in which he evokes the environment of the tropics through the use of powerful sensory images. Palés is one of the most sensory poets in the Spanish language since Luis de Góngora and Francisco de Quevedo; few Hispanic poets have been as adept as Palés at suggesting a particular ambience through the use of synesthesia, or the mixing of visual imagery with other types of metaphor (auditory, olfactory, gustatory, or tactile). A good example may be seen in some lines from the poem "Topografía" from "Canciones de la vida media":

Ésta es la tierra estéril y madrastra.
Cunde un tufo malsano

de cosa descompuesta en la marisma
por el fuego que baja de lo alto;
fermento tenebroso que en la noche
arroja el fuego fatuo,
y da esas largas formas fantasmales
que se arrastran sin ruido sobre el páramo.

(*Obras* 1, p. 400)

This is the barren stepmother-land.
An evil stink grows
from things being rotted in the shallows
by the fire from on high;
a gloomy ferment which by night
gives off the will-o'-the-wisp,
and those long ghostly shapes
that crawl noiselessly over the wasteland.

Palés also gives memorable expression to the *modernista* theme of the poet's alienation from society, which leads the poet to live in solitary reverie. Thus, in "El pozo" ("The Well"), Palés compares his soul with "un pozo de agua sorda y profunda" ("a well of still, deep waters") in the depths of which "una rana misántropa y agazapada sueña" ("a hidden, misanthropic frog dreams"). In Palés' writings, as in those of many other authors from Quevedo to Borges, dreams stand for literature and for writing itself.

A good deal of continuity connects the dreamy, sensuous writing of Palés' two early books of poems, *Azaleas* and "El palacio," and that of his first major work, *Tuntún de pasa y grifería. Tuntún* may be seen as the retelling of a utopian dream about Caribbean culture, and in it Palés makes full use of all the rhetorical devices he learned from *modernista* as well as avant-garde writing. Many misunderstandings about Palés' Afroantillean poetry have arisen because of the fact that, with few exceptions, *Tuntún* has rarely been read as a book, but rather as a handful of isolated poems. However, *Tuntún* is without a doubt Palés' most successful attempt to produce a unified, coherent poetic discourse about the Caribbean in a mold similar to the great narrative poems in Western literature (such as the classical and Renaissance epics, Dante's *Divine Comedy,* or the nineteenth-century Argentine poetry about the *gaucho*, or cowboy). More precisely, Palés' book aims to become the poetic equivalent of the essays about Spanish-American cultural identity that were being written at the same time, such as the Mexican José Vásconcelos' *La raza cósmica* (The Cosmic Race, 1925), the Argentine Ezequiel Martínez Estrada's *Radiografía de la pampa* (X-Ray of the Pampas, 1933), and the Puerto Rican Antonio S. Pedreira's *Insularismo* (Insularism, 1934). *Tuntún*'s poetic discourse about Caribbean identity is supplemented by various later prose texts by Palés, including his aforementioned essay "Hacia una poesía antillana."

A direct relationship also obtains between Palés' focus on the black component of Caribbean culture in *Tuntún* and the newfound interest in black culture that was being awakened in so many different ways throughout Europe and the United States in the 1920's and 1930's, an awakening represented by such diverse phenomena as the Harlem renaissance; jazz; the "primitivist" paintings of Pablo Picasso and Henri Matisse; the poetry of Blaise Cendrars, Langston Hughes, and Nicolás Guillén, and the ethnological research of Frobenius and of Fernando Ortiz. This renewed interest in things African arose from the feeling—common among intellectuals at the time—that Western, that is, European, culture was in a period of decline and that new sources of vitality could be found in the so-called younger or primitive cultures. Such an idea was given intellectual legitimacy by the German thinker Oswald Spengler's book *The Decline of the West* (1917). This extremely influential book (more so among artists and writers than among professional historians, anthropologists, or sociologists) was translated into Spanish in 1923 by Manuel García Morente, with a prologue by Ortega y Gasset. In Spengler's attempt at divining the morphology, or structure, of the movement of history, he followed the usual practice of the so-called scientific racism of the nineteenth century, dividing humankind into "races," "cultures," or "nations" (these terms were interchangeable for him). For Spengler, the history of each individual "race" followed a circular path akin to the cycle of birth, development, maturity, and old age followed by individual living beings. Though a racist, Spengler was not ethnocentric, since he believed that no culture was intrinsically superior to another and that each, in following its predetermined historical cycle, was like a wheel in a larger and more mysterious "cycle of cycles," which made up universal history. Spengler believed that while some cultures—such as that of Europe—might be in their decline, others might be at the beginnings of their cycle; among these, he specifically referred to African culture.

The reasons for Spengler's popularity among intellectuals in what would now be called the Third World are not difficult to see: during the 1920's and 1930's, intellectuals from Africa to Latin America found in Spengler's ideas powerful arguments for their burgeoning anticolonialism. Palés was an avid reader of Spengler, and he quoted from Spengler's work frequently in his essays and interviews. Although *The Decline of the West* is by no means the main source for *Tuntún*, it does provide much of the book's underlying ideology and even its structure. Palés' thesis in *Tuntún* is that the Hispanic Caribbean is the birthplace of a new culture that arises from the fusion of the European and African cultures on Antillean soil. This new *mulato* culture would be, in Palés' view, a synthesis in which the disparate cycles of white and black history and society would mesh in a harmonious cycle of cycles. Following the Cuban historian Ramiro Guerra y Sánchez' observations in *Azúcar y población en las Antillas* (*Sugar and Society in the Caribbean*, 1927), Palés sees the sugar mill and the process of sugar production as the meeting ground for this melding of cultures. The sugar mill transforms the white man's secularized notion of temporality as linear progression into a cyclical one, bound to the rhythms of sugar production, thus bringing it closer to the black's sense of time, which Palés, following Spengler, considers to be inherently circular, as befits a so-called primitive culture with a religious sense of life. As can be expected, the privileged cultural expression of such a synthesis, of such a meshing of cycles and rhythms, lies in music and the dance: music marks the beat of the liturgical, sacred time of the Negro, while the dance mimics in its gestures the movements of the body at work in the process of sugar production. Some lines from "Majestad negra" (Black Majesty), written in 1934, give a good idea of the way Palés tried to represent the fusion of dance with production, of ritual with work, of music's tempo with the tempo of the sugar mills in his Afroantillean poems (Palés' rhythmic effects get lost in translation, unfortunately):

Culipandeando la Reina avanza,
y de su inmensa grupa resbalan
meneos cachondos que el gongo cuaja
en ríos de azúcar y de melaza.
Prieto trapiche de sensual zafra,
el caderamen, masa con masa,
exprime ritmos, suda que sangra,
y la molienda culmina en danza.
(*Obras* 1, p. 485)

Swaying her hips the Queen advances,
and from her immense buttocks flow
salacious movements the drums curdle
into rivers of sugar and molasses.
Dark sugar mill of a sensuous harvest,
her thighs, mass against mass,
squeeze out rhythms, sweat till they bleed,
and the milling culminates in dance.

Palés' Spenglerianism in *Tuntún* is not confined to the ideological level; it also affects the very structure of the book. The poems in *Tuntún* are grouped in four sections and correspond closely to Spengler's description of the "life cycle" of a culture: "Tronco" (Trunk/Stock), "Rama" (Branch), "Flor" (Flower), and "Otros poemas" (Other Poems). The poems in "Tronco" have to do mostly with the African origins of the Caribbean blacks. "Jungla africana—Tembandumba / Manigua haitiana—Macandal" (African jungle—Tembandumba / Haitian forest—Macandal) goes the refrain in "Numen" (Spirit), alluding to two famous black historical figures, one from Africa, the other from Haiti. The poems in "Rama" all carry the dominating motif of travel, of extension: "Pueblo negro" (Black Town) and "Kalahari" ("Kalahari") are imaginary voyages to Africa; "Canción festiva para ser llorada" tells of a long trip through the Antilles; "Majestad negra" describes Queen Tembandumba's walk down "la encendida calle antillana" (the burning Antillean street); and, lastly, "Ñáñigo al cielo" ("Ñáñigo to Heaven") and "Falsa canción de baquiné" (False Song of Mourning for a Child's Death) represent, respectively, the syncretic voyage of a *ñáñigo*—a member of an Afro-Cuban cult—to a caricatural Christian heaven, and the return to Guinea of the soul of a dead black child. The poems in "Flor," on the other hand, find their unity in the theme of cultural synthesis or fusion, particularly in

"Ten con ten" (Making Both Ends Meet) and in the book's culminating poem, "Mulata-Antilla," in which Palés symbolizes the future harmony of a racially mixed Caribbean in the lyrical figure of the mulatto woman.

The fourth section of *Tuntún*, "Otros poemas," contains poems from "Canciones de la vida media," such as "Topografía" and "Pueblo" (The Town; translated as "Pueblo"), which, although they are not in the Afroantillean mode, do deal with the question of "cultural decadence," mainly the white creole culture that is portrayed as being in decline. "Piedad, Señor, piedad para mi pobre pueblo / donde mi pobre gente se morirá de nada!" (Have mercy, oh Lord, have mercy on my poor town / where my poor people will die of nothing!) goes the refrain in "Pueblo." Palés aims to produce in *Tuntún* a utopian vision of a harmonious future for Hispano-Caribbean culture, a harmony to be achieved through the reconciliation of opposite races and cultures in the "racial type" (as Palés would say) of the mulatto. Read as a book, *Tuntún* produces the impression of a vast fresco of the Caribbean, not unlike the pictorial representations of Mexican culture being painted at about the same time by such artists as Diego Rivera.

If Palés' Afroantillean poems and their emphasis on the Hispanic Caribbean's black heritage bothered some Hispanophilic Puerto Rican intellectuals, Palés' treatment of his black subjects has elicited negative comments from other critics, who feel that Palés, being a white man, was hardly in a position to understand what it means to be a black person and that Palés frequently caricatured blacks, portraying them through the use of demeaning stereotypes; even Palés' symbolic elevation of the *mulata-antilla* has been seen as a male-oriented racist stereotyping of the Caribbean woman. There is a good deal of truth in this, and literary critics should always be sensitive to the social implications of the works they study, but, as Borges has warned on occasion, literary criticism should not be confused with police work. Also, it is well to remember that caricature is a feature common to a good deal of avant-garde writing; even Guillén, with whom Palés is frequently contrasted and who is himself a mulatto, resorted to similar racial stereotyping in his early poems in *Motivos de son* (Son Motifs, 1930). Palés was in fact rather impartial in his use of

caricature. If he referred to some blacks (particularly those who wished to imitate Western culture too closely, thus denying their blackness) as "apes," he also spoke of the United States as "a dark bulldog" chewing on the bones of the islands, of Puerto Rican politicians as "a cageful of tropical parrots politicking among the trees," and of himself (in different poems) as a "frog" and as a "tired old horse."

As Corretjer and Díaz Quiñones have pointed out, rather than blaming Palés for merely being in many ways a (white) man of his time and place, the positive elements in his Afroantillean poems should be stressed. For many critics, these include their anticolonialism, their occasionally overt tone of social protest, their artistic vindication of the Hispanic Caribbean's black heritage, and their utopian vision of pan-Caribbean unity. This does not mean that Palés' Afroantillean poems, like those of other *negrista* writers, are not without serious contradictions; the main problem that is left unsolved in *Tuntún* (as in other *negrista* works) is the difficulty in reconciling the serious social and cultural issues that motivate the poems with the frivolity and spontaneity required by avant-garde writing. Traces of this contradiction may be found in the titles of some of the poems, such as "Canción festiva para ser llorada," and in the book's very title: "Tuntún," aside from its sound suggestive of the beating of drums, is used in Spanish in such expressions as *al buen tuntún* and *al tuntún*, which mean "something done without thought or planning, without any knowledge of the matter."

Although the sincerity with which he presented his views on Hispano-Caribbean culture cannot be doubted, we should remember that Palés was, after all, not a sociologist but a poet. In view of his partial abandonment of Afroantilleanism in his later poems, it seems clear that *Tuntún* was one episode in Palés' literary exploration of the power and the limits of poetry. In several of his later poems—particularly "Asteriscos para lo intacto" (Asterisks for What Is Untouched), "Puerta al tiempo en tres voces" ("Doorway to Time in Three Voices"), and "La Búsqueda asesina" (The Murderous Search)—Palés seems more concerned with an inquiry into the value and the mechanisms of literary representation itself. Seeking to escape the contradictions of his earlier works, Palés focuses his attention on language, on words themselves, but only to discover in them a similar ambivalence: language is at the same time material and immaterial, rooted and rootless, frivolous and transcendent. For Palés, the writing of poetry is fated to be a celebration of melancholy, as in "Canción festiva para ser llorada," or better yet, a "murderous search" for an impossible harmony. This lesson has been learned well by many of the writers who came after him. The debt of today's young Puerto Rican novelists and short story writers to Palés is particularly strong and is visible in such outstanding works as Luis Rafael Sánchez' *La guaracha del Macho Camacho* (*Macho Camacho's Beat,* 1976), Ana Lydia Vega's *Encancaranublado* (Gray Skies, 1982), and Edgardo Rodríguez Juliá's *El entierro de Cortijo* (Cortijo's Burial, 1983). Though they often disagree with his views, all of these writers agree in regarding Palés as a founding figure in modern Puerto Rican letters.

SELECTED BIBLIOGRAPHY

First Editions

Poetry

Azaleas. Guayama, Puerto Rico, 1915.
Tuntún de pasa y grifería (*Poemas afroantillanos*) *Otros poemas.* With a prologue by Ángel Valbuena Prat. San Juan, 1937.
Poesía 1915–1956. With an introduction by Federico de Onís. San Juan, 1957.

Novels

"Litoral: Reseña de una vida inútil." *El Diario de Puerto Rico* (*San Juan*), 5 February–25 April, 1949.

Essays

"El dadaísmo." *La semana* 1/5:21,30 (1922).
"El arte y la raza blanca." *Poliedro* 1/16:5 (1927).
"Hacia una poesía antillana." *El Mundo* (San Juan), 26 November 1932.
"Presencia de Jorge Artel: Palabras de presentación." *Alma latina* (San Juan), 8 April 1950. Pp. 6–7, 50.

Later Editions

Tuntún de pasa y grifería. With a prologue by Jaime Benítez; includes a glossary of black, Afroantillean, and regional terms. San Juan, 1950.

Collected Works

Obras 1914–1959. 2 vols. Edited, with prologue, chronology, notes, and variants by Margot Arce de Vázquez; with an introduction by Federico de Onís. San Juan, 1984. Contains all of Palés' poems (including all the previously unpublished ones), as well as a substantial selection of his prose.
Poesía completa y prosa selecta. Edited, with a prologue and chronology, by Margot Arce de Vázquez. Caracas, 1978. Contains all of Palés' published poetry and most of his unpublished verse, as well as the full text of *Litoral* and several essays and interviews.

Translations

Few of Palés' poems or prose works have been translated into English. A few individual poems have, however, been translated and can be found in the following anthologies and journals.
Anthology of Contemporary Latin American Poetry. Edited by Dudley Fitts. Norfolk, Conn., 1942. Contains "Clair de Lune," "Elegy of the Duke of Marmalade," "Look Out for the Snake," "Ñáñigo to Heaven," and "The Well."
Borinquen: An Anthology of Puerto Rican Literature. Edited by María Teresa Babín and Stan Steiner. New York, 1974. Contains "Black Dance," "Pueblo," and "The Call."
Doors and Mirrors: Fiction and Poetry from Spanish America, 1920–1970. Edited by Hortense Carpentier and Janet Brof. New York, 1972. Contains "From 'The Animals Within'" and "Spurious Song for a Baquiné."
Inventing a Word: An Anthology of Twentieth–Century Puerto Rican Poetry. Edited by Julio Marzan. New York, 1980. Contains "Doorway to Time in Three Voices," "Elegy for the Duke of Marmalade," "Kalahari," and "Neither This Nor That."
The Penguin Book of Latin American Verse. Edited by Enrique Caracciolo-Trejo. Middlesex, England, 1971. Contains "Mulata-Antilla" and "The Unknown Pain" in prose translations.
Poetry 26:144–146 (1925). Contains "San Sabas." Translated by Muna Lee.

Poetry 62:79 (1943). Contains "Lament." Translated by H. R. Hays.

Spanish American Literature in Translation: A Selection of Poetry, Fiction, and Drama Since 1888. Edited and translated by Willis Knapp Jones. New York, 1963–1966. Contains "The Wall" and "Green Lizard."

Biographical And Critical Studies

Agrait, Gustavo. Luis Palés Matos: Un poeta puertorriqueño. San Juan, 1973.

Aleixandre, Vicente. "Encuentro con Luis Palés Matos." La torre 8/29–30:147–150 (1960).

Anderson Imbert, Enrique. "Luis Palés Matos desde la Argentina." Asomante 15/3:39–40 (1959).

Arce de Vázquez, Margot. Impresiones. San Juan, 1950. Contains the following essays on Palés: "Los poemas negros de Luis Palés Matos," "Los adjetivos en la 'Danza negra' de Luis Palés Matos," "Luis Palés Matos, mago de la palabra," and "Rectificaciones."

_____. "Unidad de la obra poética de Luis Palés Matos." Asomante 15/3:32–38 (1959).

_____. "Tres pueblos negros: Algunas observaciones sobre el estilo de Luis Palés Matos." La torre 8/29–30: 163–187 (1960).

_____. "Puerta al tiempo en tres voces' de Luis Palés Matos." Río Piedras 1/1:9–30 (1972).

Babín, María Teresa. "Edgar Allan Poe y Luis Palés Matos." In Journadas literarias. San Juan, 1967. Pp. 91–95.

Bellini, Giuseppe. "Luis Palés Matos, intérprete del alma antillana." Asomante 15/3:20–31 (1959).

Blanco, Tomás. Sobre Palés Matos. San Juan, 1950.

Cartey, Wilfred George Onslow. "Three Antillian Poets." Ph.D. diss., Columbia University, 1965.

Corretjer, Juan Antonio. "Spengler: Una proyección criolla" and "Lo que no fué Palés." In Laurel negro 1: Poesía y revolución, edited by Joserramón Meléndez. Río Piedras, Puerto Rico, 1981. Pp. 184–187 and 191–193, respectively.

Coulthard, G. R. Race and Colour in Caribbean Literature. London, 1962.

De Diego Padró, José I. Luis Palés Matos y su trasmundo poético. Río Piedras, Puerto Rico, 1973.

Díaz Quiñones, Arcadio. In El almuerzo en la hierba: Lloréns Torres, Palés Matos, René Marqués. Río Piedras, Puerto Rico, 1982. Pp. 73–129.

Diego, Gerardo. "La palabra poética de Luis Palés Matos." La torre 8/29–30:81–94 (1960).

Enguídanos, Miguel. La poesía de Luis Palés Matos. Río Piedras, Puerto Rico, 1961.

González, Josemilio. "La individualidad poética de Luis Palés Matos." La torre 8/29–30:291–329 (1960).

González, José Luis. "Literatura e identidad nacional en Puerto Rico." In his El país de los cuatros pisos y otros ensayos. Río Piedras, Puerto Rico, 1979. Pp. 45–90.

Jackson, Richard. The Black Image in Latin American Literature. Albuquerque, N. Mex., 1976.

Medina, José Ramón. "Luis Palés Matos en la poesía hispanoamericana." La torre 8/29–30:259–265 (1960).

Onís, Federico de. Luis Palés Matos (1898–1959): Vida y obra. San Juan, 1960.

Ortiz, Fernando. "Más acerca de la poesía mulata: Escorzos para su estudio." Revista bimestre cubana 37:23–39 (1936).

_____. "Luis Palés Matos, poemas afroantillanos." Estudios africanos (Havana) 1/7:156–159 (1937).

Rivera de Alvarez, Josefina. "Luis Palés Matos (1898–1959)." In Diccionario de literatura puertorriqueña 2, part 2. 2nd ed. San Juan, 1970–1974. Pp. 1142–1149.

Ward, James H. "Bibliografía de Luis Palés Matos." La torre 21/79–80:221–230 (1973).

Jorge Mañach Robato

(1898–1961)

Nicolás Álvarez

Jorge Mañach Robato, one of the best essayists in contemporary Spanish literature, was born in the province of Las Villas in Cuba on 14 February 1898. His father, Eugenio Mañach Couceiro, was a Spaniard from Galicia who had settled in Cuba in the 1880's; his mother, a Cuban, was Consuelo Robato Turró. In 1907, the family moved to Spain, where Jorge lived until 1912, when the Mañachs returned to Cuba. There Jorge continued his studies until 1915, when his father sent him to study at the Cambridge High and Latin School, in Cambridge, Massachusetts.

After finishing high school in 1917, Jorge received a scholarship from Harvard University. He graduated from Harvard cum laude in only three years, with a Bachelor of Science degree. In 1921, Harvard awarded him the Sheldon Travelling fellowship to study romance philology at the Sorbonne. Mañach instead registered at the School of Law of the University of Paris. During his one-year stay in France, he traveled throughout Europe, writing a series of articles on his impressions of European cities and traditions that he sent to the Cuban newspaper *Diario de la marina.* He returned to Cuba in 1922 and two years later graduated from the University of Havana with a doctorate in civil law. He immediately registered at the School of Philosophy and Letters of the same university; in 1928 he received a doctorate in philosophy and letters.

In 1923 Mañach had joined a group of young Cuban intellectuals, the so-called Grupo Minorista (Minority Group), whose members were discontented with the political and cultural situation of their country. From 1926 to 1928, Mañach worked as a deputy district attorney for the district attorney's office in Havana. He resigned his post when he objected to political interference in a case he was trying in court. His first book was published in 1924 with the title *Glosario* (Glossary). In 1925, he lectured on "La crisis de la alta cultura en Cuba" (The Crisis of Intellectual Life in Cuba). In 1926, he also published his first short story, "O.P. No. 4," and his second book, *Estampas de San Cristóbal* (Vignettes of Saint Christopher). The same year, he married Margot Baños y Fernández Villamil. They had one son, Jorge, born in 1927.

Along with four other young Cuban intellectuals, Mañach founded *Revista de avance* in 1927. This magazine was devoted to the Cuban expression of the Latin-American vanguardist movement. An array of famous writers from both Spain and Latin America (Miguel de Unamuno, Américo Castro, Eugenio D'Ors, Jaime Torres Bodet, César Vallejo, Miguel Ángel Asturias) contributed articles of value.

Mañach was the central theoretician of the Cuban vanguardist movement. In 1928, he published *Indagación del choteo* (Analysis of Teasing), *Tiempo muerto* (Dead Time), and *Goya*. By the time that *Revista de avance* stopped publication in 1930, Mañach had become widely known both in Spain and throughout Latin America.

The political situation in Cuba became critical during the second presidential term of General Gerardo Machado Morales, since the 1901 constitution proscribed reelection. ABC, a clandestine organization, was created to overthrow the government. Mañach wrote most of the *Manifiesto Programa del Partido ABC* (ABC's Manifesto and Political Platform). Machado's dictatorship crumbled in 1933. Mañach's political writings published between 1930 and 1933 are collected in *Pasado vigente* (Present Past, 1939). In 1932, Mañach founded *La universidad del aire* (The University of the Airwaves), a cultural radio broadcast intended to fill the vacuum created by the closing of the University of Havana by the Machado dictatorship. In 1933, Mañach published *Martí, el apóstol (Martí, Apostle of Freedom)*, which is considered to date the best biography of José Martí, the Cuban founding father and world-renowned writer. The new Cuban government of Carlos Mendieta appointed Mañach secretary of education in 1934. He resigned the post shortly after because of continuing political upheavals and left the country for his first exile.

During the next four years (1935–1939), Mañach taught courses on Spanish- and Latin American literatures at Columbia University in New York City. He devoted himself to strictly academic activities: he was appointed director of Hispanic studies of the Instituto de las Españas (Institute of the Spains) and member of the editorial board of *Revista hispánica moderna*, in which he published many articles and reviews. At Columbia he taught courses on Spanish Golden Age literature, Latin American thinkers (Andrés Bello, Domingo Faustino Sarmiento, Juan Bautista Alberdi, Juan Montalvo, Bonilla Eugenio María de Hostos, Justo Sierra, José Martí, Enrique José Varona, José Enrique Rodó, Alfonso Reyes), gauchesque poetry, and Spanish-American postmodernism. The City University of New York offered him the chairmanship of the Department of Romance Languages, but he declined the invitation and returned to his homeland in 1939.

Back in Cuba, Mañach was elected to the Constituent Assembly of 1940. After undergoing the required examinations, he was awarded a full professorship at the University of Havana, in charge of the newly created chair of history of philosophy. From then on, both political and intellectual pursuits became essential to his life and writings. From 1940 to 1944, he served in the Cuban Congress as senator, and he was appointed secretary of state in 1944. He was elected to the Cuban Academy of History in 1943, and a year later to the Academy of Arts and Letters. He published *Historia y estilo* (History and Style) in 1944.

During the 1940's, Mañach reached the pinnacle of his intellectual and public career. His name was internationally recognized when he was elected corresponding member of the Real Academia de la Lengua Española (The Royal Academy of the Spanish Language) as well as of the Ateneo de Buenos Aires (Athenaeum of Buenos Aires). France awarded him the rosette of Commandant of the Legion of Honor, and he received similar honors from the governments of Chile, Cuba, Haiti, Mexico, Panama, Peru, and Venezuela. The Mexican Congress made him an honorary member. He founded the Cuban chapter of the P.E.N. Club, presided over the Asociación Cubana del Congreso por la Libertad de la Cultura (the Cuban Association of the Congress for the Freedom of Culture), and became a member of the editorial board of *Cuadernos*, a journal published in Paris. In 1950, Mañach published a monograph on Miguel de Cervantes' famous novel, entitled *Examen del quijotismo* (Analysis of Quixoticism). In 1951, he published a sui generis study of José Martí, *El espíritu de Martí* (The Inner Soul of José Martí), and a collection of his most important philosophical essays, *Para una filosofía de la vida* (Toward a Philosophy of Life). In 1959, he published *Dewey y el pensamiento americano* (Dewey and American Thought).

On 10 March 1952, when General Fulgencio Batista effected a coup d'etat that took power away from the constitutional government of Carlos Prío Socarrás, Mañach immediately condemned the de facto regime in numerous speeches and publications. He joined with other public figures in founding an emergency political party to oppose the institutional crisis created by the coup, but he finally decided to leave the country in 1957. For his second exile, Mañach went to Milan to attend a meeting of the Congress for the Freedom of Culture. From Italy, he went on to Spain, taking the opportunity to visit some of his relatives in Galicia. After settling in Madrid, Mañach joined the intellectual circles of the Spanish capital. In 1958, his health took a turn for the worse; a surgery revealed that he had terminal cancer. During his stay in Spain, he wrote articles for the newspaper *ABC* and sent contributions to *Cuadernos hispanoamericanos* (Madrid) and *Cuadernos* (Paris). *Visitas españolas* (Spanish Sojourns) was published in Madrid in 1960. Batista's dictatorship had been overthrown a year before by the revolutionary movement led by Fidel Castro. From Spain, Mañach welcomed the revolutionary government and defended it against its European critics. He sent many articles for publication to *Bohemia*, the popular Cuban weekly, praising the new political order. He returned to Cuba at the end of 1959. Resuming his teaching at the University of Havana, he once again became involved in Cuban politics, writing numerous articles on current political events. These articles reveal a gradual change in his support for the new regime, which he thought had departed from the democratic path that its leaders had originally advocated.

In November 1960, Mañach left Cuba for his third and final exile. At the invitation of his good friend, the university president Jaime Benítez, he went to Puerto Rico to teach at the Río Piedras campus of the University of Puerto Rico. Shortly after his arrival his health deteriorated further. He died on 25 June 1961 and is buried next to the tomb of the Spanish writer Pedro Salinas in the cemetery of Porta Coeli, Bayamón, Puerto Rico. Despite his physical condition, Mañach devoted the last months of his life to the writing of several lectures that he intended to deliver to his students. These lectures were left unfinished. After his death, his beloved friend Concha Meléndez compiled them, following guidelines prepared by Mañach. *Teoría de la frontera* (*Frontiers in the Americas*) was published posthumously in 1970 in Puerto Rico.

Martí, Apostle of Freedom is perhaps Mañach's most outstanding contribution to Spanish-language prose

and historiography. The life of José Martí was rigorously documented, but most important, Mañach displayed his mastery of Spanish prose in a superb novelistic narration. He not only portrayed the main events in Martí's life, but also re-created, with an array of literary devices, Martí's personality as well as the general historical background. Mañach altered his writing style to best portray the tone of each situation and introduced symbols for specific narrative effects. The biography went through three editions. In each case, Mañach took extraordinary care to revise and update its documentation and to perfect the style. Mañach considered the 1961 edition to be definitive. *Martí, Apostle of Freedom* has been critically acclaimed as the best biography of Martí and one of the best biographies ever written in Spanish, because of its skillful combination of painstaking historical accuracy and narrative mastery.

Mañach devoted another book to the study of Martí, *El espíritu de Martí*. The methodology used was both unorthodox and intricate, based on reflections made from historical, psychological, sociopolitical, and literary perspectives. Mañach asserted that Martí's inner self consisted of the "genial integration" of three essential qualities: his sensitivity regarding ethics and art, his intellectual capacity, and his will. What was unique about Martí was that these qualities acquired the highest degree of integration. Moreover, this integration was in the "key" of love. Mañach based his assertions on biographical data and his own theoretical interpretations derived from various fields of knowledge. This valuable study has been little known except to specialists on Mañach. Mañach wrote many other studies of Martí, which later scholarship suggests were highly authoritative.

Although in his *Indagación del choteo* Mañach focused his study on this Cuban-style humor, his arguments and conclusions have made this book a classic reference work for the study of Hispanic humor in general. By using a phenomenological approach, Mañach was able to characterize the peculiarities of Hispanic humor. His elucidation of this aspect of Hispanic culture is unsurpassed. In the two academic speeches that are included in *Historia y estilo*, Mañach offered his most encompassing views on Cuban culture. "La nación y su formación histórica" (The Nation and Its Historical Development) presents a sociohistorical synthesis of Cuban culture. Mañach named, defined, and extrapolated different historical phases. The fundamental thesis of his study is that literary style is a product of the history of a country while history is a dynamic force moving toward the achievement of freedom. Noticeable are the influences of Georg Hegel, Joseph-Ernest Renan, Benedetto Croce, and José Ortega y Gasset. This theory was put to the test in a second speech, "El estilo en Cuba y su sentido histórico" (Style in Cuba and its Historical Sense), which has great value in its explication of many Cuban writers.

Examen del quijotismo is Mañach's best piece of literary criticism. In it he argued against those critics who thought that Cervantes was defending idealism, as portrayed by Don Quixote, and was opposed to the naturalism incarnated in Sancho. How, he argued, could those critics justify the ridicule cast on both characters if such an apology was intended? After an astonishing display of erudition, Mañach concluded that Sancho incarnated a naturalistic view of life, not realism, and that Cervantes' immortal novel was not intended to favor either idealism or naturalism, but was rather an integration of the two philosophical stances. What Cervantes proposed in his novel was the "necessary coexistence of the ideal with experience." Sancho is as important a character as Don Quixote.

During his third exile, Mañach prepared a series of lectures to be delivered to his students at the University of Puerto Rico. The posthumous *Frontiers in the Americas* presents Mañach's most elaborate integration of his thinking on history and culture. The Anglo-Saxon culture and the Hispanic culture were the objects of a special theory. Mañach examined different types of frontiers: Greece and Asia Minor, the Roman Empire and the Germanic invasions, Spain and the Arabic culture, as well as the most recent frontiers in the Americas, such as the western frontier in the United States, the *bandeirantes* in Brazil, the Chilean frontier with the Araucanian Indians, and Mexico and its struggle with the United States. Insularism was also another type of frontier, as in the case of Puerto Rico, in which both Hispanic and Anglo-Saxon cultures were present.

Mañach pointed out that Western civilization had accentuated the predominance of rationalism, but

that it would be a mistake to discriminate in favor of neglected spiritual values. The integration of Anglo-Saxon rationalism and Hispanic sensitivity was the ideal proposed by the continental frontiers in the Americas. History did not present inexorable dilemmas since history is ruled by material as well as spiritual forces. Moreover, these antagonistic forces would eventually become integrated. The world was progressing toward new horizons of understanding and enjoyment: the forces of freedom would not succumb nor would those of communism, which, when it discarded some of its most ferocious doctrines, would be of value to humankind. The book is an intellectual and stylistic masterpiece.

According to some critics, Jorge Mañach is the best Cuban essayist and one of the best in the Hispanic world.

SELECTED BIBLIOGRAPHY

First Editions

Books

Glosario. Havana, 1924.
Estampas de San Cristóbal. Havana, 1926.
Tiempo muerto. Havana, 1928.
Indagación del choteo. Havana, 1928.
Martí, el apóstol. Madrid, 1933.
Pasado vigente. Havana, 1939.
Historia y estilo. Havana, 1944.
Examen del quijotismo. Buenos Aires, 1950.
El espíritu de Martí. Havana, 1951.
Para una filosofía de la vida. Havana, 1951.
Dewey y el pensamiento americano. Madrid, 1959.
José Martí: Sus mejores páginas. Selected and with a preface by Jorge Mañach Robato. Lima, 1959.
Visitas españolas: Lugares, personas. Madrid, 1960.
Teoría de la frontera. With an introduction by Concha Meléndez. Río Piedras, Puerto Rico, 1970.

Short Works

La crisis de la alta cultura en Cuba. Havana, 1925.
La pintura en Cuba. Havana, 1925.
Belén, el Ashanti. Havana, 1925.

Goya. Havana, 1928.

El pensamiento político y social de Martí. Havana, 1941.

La universidad nueva. Havana, 1942.

La nación y la formación histórica. Havana, 1943.

Miguel Figueroa (1851–1893). Havana, 1943.

Lo histórico en la obra de Chacón y Calvo. Havana, 1945.

Filosofía del quijotismo. Havana, 1947.

Semblante histórico de Varona. Havana, 1949.

Discurso en el homenaje en memoria de José Martí y Zayas Bazán. Havana, 1953.

El pensamiento de Dewey y su sentido americano. Havana, 1953.

Imagen de Ortega y Gasset. Havana, 1956.

Universalidad de Alfonso Reyes. Mexico City, 1957.

Luz y "El Salvador." Havana, 1958.

El sentido trágico de la "Numancia." Havana, 1959.

Paisaje y pintura en Cuba. Madrid, 1959.

José Martí. Havana, 1960.

Articles by Jorge Mañach

"Una conversación con Varona." Revista de avance 1: 288–291 (1927).

"El hombre que amaba el mar." Revista de avance 2/15:72–75 (1927). Story.

"Tántalo." Revista de avance 1:258–261 (1927).

"Tres estampas de Castilla." Revista de avance 1/8:183–185 (1927).

"O.P. No. 4." In Evolución de la cultura cubana 13, edited by José Manuel Carbonell. Havana, 1928. Pp. 341–348. Story.

"Utilitarismo y cultura." In Evolución de la cultura cubana 11, edited by José Manuel Carbonell. Havana, 1928. Pp. 223–233.

"El arte de José de Creeft." Revista hispánica moderna 4/1:81–85 (1937).

"Gabriela: Alma y tierra." Revista hispánica moderna 3:106–110 (1937).

"Carlos Reyles." Revista hispánica moderna 5:18–20 (1939).

"Perfil de Martí." Archivo José Martí 2/1:22–34 (1941).

"Picasso." Revista de la Universidad de La Habana 34:52–64 (1941).

"Martí, ala y raíz." Archivo José Martí 5/2:163 (1945).

"La ausente presencia de Sanín Cano." Revista iberoamericana 13/26:291–295 (1948).

"El arcano de cierta poesía nueva." Bohemia, 25 September 1949. Pp. 78, 90.

"José Martí." Revista cubana 24:399–423 (1949).

"Perfil de nuestras letras." Boletín de la Academia Cubana de la Lengua 1/1:348–369 (1952).

"Las direcciones del pensamiento de Martí." Boletín de la Academia Cubana de la Lengua 3/3–4:168–185 (1954).

"Santayana y D'Ors." Cuadernos americanos 14/83:77–101 (1955).

"Dualidad y síntesis en Ortega." Papeles de son armadans 5/13:13–32 (1957).

"Heredia y el romanticismo." Cuadernos hispanoamericanos 30:195–220 (1957).

"Dos cartas del exilio." Bohemia, 4 October 1959. P. 69.

"La revolución cubana y sus perspectivas" Cuadernos del Congreso por la Libertad de la Cultura 35:3–9 (1959).

"Obra y gracia de Alfonso Reyes." Boletín de la Academia Cubana de la Lengua 9:34–47 (1960).

"Carta a Agustín Acosta." Boletín de la Academia Cubana de la Lengua 10/3–4:6–13 (1961).

"Habla para 'Bohemia libre' el Dr. Jorge Mañach." Bohemia libre, 18 June 1961. Pp. 26–27, 67, 82.

"José Martí: Rompeolas de América." Bohemia libre, 23 July 1961. Pp. 7, 95.

Translations

Frontiers in the Americas: A Global Perspective. Translated by Philip H. Phenix. With an introduction by Lambros Comitas. Appendix, "Jorge Mañach on His Last Frontier," by Concha Meléndez. New York, 1975.

Martí, Apostle of Freedom. Translated by Coley Taylor. With a preface by Gabriela Mistral. New York, 1950.

Biographical and Critical Studies

Acosta, Agustín. "Al Dr. Jorge Mañach, en La Habana." Boletín de la Academia Cubana de la Lengua 10/3–4:14–18 (1961).

Álvarez, Nicolás E. La obra literaria de Jorge Mañach. Potomac, Md., 1979.

Arredondo, Alberto. "Veinticuatro horas de la vida de Jorge Mañach." Bohemia, 26 May 1946. Pp. 42–47, 49, 56–58, 64–66.

Baquero, Gastón. "Jorge Mañach, o la tragedia de la inteligencia en la América Hispana." Cuba nueva 1/12:18–30 (1962).

Boletín de la Academia Cubana de la Lengua 10/3–4:5–45 (1961). "En recuerdo de Jorge Mañach."

Chacón y Calvo, José María. "Historia y estilo, por Jorge Mañach." Revista cubana 18:183–186 (1944).

Jorge Mañach (1898–1961): Homenaje de la nación cubana. San Juan, Puerto Rico, 1972.

Martí, Jorge L. El periodismo literario de Jorge Mañach. Río Piedras, Puerto Rico, 1977.

Meléndez, Concha. "Jorge Mañach y la inquietud cubana." In her *Signos de Iberoamérica.* Mexico City, 1936. Pp. 153–167.

Mistral, Gabriela. "Algo sobre Jorge Mañach." *Repertorio americano* 15:33–36 (1948).

Souvirón, José María. "Conversaciones con Jorge Mañach." *Cuadernos hispanoamericanos* 47/139:79–83 (1961).

Torre, Amalia de la. *Jorge Mañach, Maestro del ensayo.* Miami, 1978.

Valdespino, Andrés. *Jorge Mañach y su generación en las letras cubanas.* Miami, 1971.

Vitier, Medardo. "Carta abierta a Jorge Mañach." *Bohemia,* 26 May 1946. Pp. 20, 63.

Ricardo E. Molinari

(1898–   )

Alfredo A. Roggiano

The Argentine poet Ricardo E. Molinari did not attend a college or a university, but is of a refined cultural background, and it can be seen in his work, which is exclusively poetry, that he had read the medieval and Renaissance poets of Spain, Italy, and France, the English and German romantics, the symbolists and vanguardist writers.

Born in Buenos Aires 20 March 1898, Molinari almost lacks biography. He was married but had no children. He worked as an obscure employee of the Argentine senate library. Upon retirement he occupied with his wife, Amelia, an apartment on Paraguay Street, in Palermo, a residential suburb of Buenos Aires.

It may be said that his life is in his poetry. He lived during the years of the greatest influence of the vanguardists in Argentina and the rest of Hispanic America. In 1933 he traveled to Spain and Portugal, where he formed friendships with the great poets of that time: Federico García Lorca, Gerardo Diego, Rafael Alberti, Manuel Altolaguirre, José Moreno Villa, all of whom later illustrated beautifully decorated editions of Molinari's *plaquettes* (pamphlets, brochures) and notebooks, which were financed by an admirer of his poetry who was wealthy and had good taste. These luxurious works were numbered, limited-distribution editions for select private libraries.

Molinari began publishing poems in the journals *Inicial* (1923–1925) and *Proa* (Prow, 1924–1925) and was one of the group of vanguardist poets gathered around the journals *Prisma, Proa,* and *Martín Fierro* from 1921 to 1927, the year in which he published his first book, *El imaginero* (painter or sculptor of religious images), with the editorial seal of *Proa.* That same year some of his poems were included in one of the first anthologies of Argentine vanguardist poetry, *Exposición de la actual poesía argentina* (published by Pedro Juan Vignale and César Tiempo, Buenos Aires, 1927). In Spain he was praised by Rafael Cansinos-Assens, mentor of ultraism, in *La nueva literatura* (Madrid, 1927, p. 449), "for his refined contrite grace in a form so avidly seeking clarity." In 1928 he was selected as one of the "twelve new poets" that Evar Méndez published in the journal *Síntesis,* and Jorge Luis Borges publicly extolled him that year in the eighth issue of the same journal. In 1929 he published a book of poems, *El pez y la manzana* (The Fish and the Apple), and in 1930 the long work *Panegírico de Nuestra Señora de Luján* (Panegyric for Our Lady of Luján), which received the Third Poetry Prize of the Municipality of Bueno Aires. Néstor Ibarra spoke highly of him in *La nueva poesía argentina* (Buenos Aires, 1930), and his work began to be considered what it became shortly afterward: "the highest poetic value in Argentina" and "one of the fundamental expressive achievements in the Spanish-speaking world," as testimonials appeared on the dust jacket of·*Un día, el tiempo, las nubes* (Day, Time, Shadows, 1964), a selection from his works made by Molinari himself.

In 1933, he obtained the First Municipal Prize in Poetry, a highly prestigious award in Argentina. In 1947 he was given the Second National Prize and in 1969 the Sash of Honor of the Argentine Society of Writers. The Argentine Academy of Letters selected him as *miembro de número* (associate member) in 1968. In his inauguration speech before this body—for him a rare, perhaps unique composition in prose—he defined himself as a man and as a poet in these words: "Poetry is my constant musing, that portion of time that consumes itself in nothingness and issues forth unchangeable from the fog and flavor of the soul. In it I have hidden from harm the freedom and desires of a man serene and by himself."

In an interview of Molinari by Juan Carlos Ghiano, published in *La Nación* (Buenos Aires, 6 December 1970) with the title "Ricardo E. Molinari, un solitario," we find assertions which, taken together, can constitute his poetic theory, a poetic theory that has as thematic ingredients solitude and separation from the world, evocation, remembrance, and the desire to see himself in the pure lyric act. In that manner, he creates himself, in an imaginary, elegiac space, where he exists only as a poetic voice, although the references may be his beloved, his place or country of birth, a literary reminiscence, a historical act or personage, inscriptions, a flower, a bird, the wind, clouds, or, more intimately or metaphysically, the soul, time, eternity, and, above all, poetry. The pampa, the south, Barranca Yaco, Facundo, "una camelia cortada" (a cut camellia), a Spanish poet, a popular song, or *dezir*, of the Middle Ages, are motifs that act only as signs or signals—concrete, intuited, or proposed—for a linguistic construction of images, metaphors, symbols, and emblems, which Molinari controls and fixes in preceptive traditional forms: sonnet, ode, romance, elegy, Hispanic popular verse forms and meters. Examples may be found in *Cancionero del Príncipe de Vergara* (Anthology of Canzonets of the Prince of Vergara, 1933), "Liras" (Lyres), "Homenaje a Lope de Vega" (Homage to

Lope de Vega), the sonnets to Garcilaso and others, "Cinco casidas donde la tarde es un pájaro" (Five Love Songs Where the Afternoon Is a Bird), his odes, possibly the densest part of his work, and the *canciones*, the most delicate and transparent. Thus, this poet who expresses so well the immensity, desolation, and "the emptiness of an endless territory . . . of broad horizons," as stated by the English critic J. M. Cohen (*Visión, Revista internacional*, 15 January 1960, p. 85), can also be the reflection of *un vacío espiritual* (a spiritual void).

But Molinari is, above all, the poet who hides from the world, in an inventiveness between hermetic and luminous, to be sustained lyrically, he says, in a *voz desnuda y sola* (naked and solitary voice). Because "writing is company for thought, so as not to be alone, it is the same as remembering," he told Ghiano. And in the same interview he insisted: "What I have written has been for my own pleasure, my joy and my entertainment. . . . Poetry is sacred, not massive. I have dedicated my life to a very beautiful and delicate thing. . . . To say what one's own self is about, even though it may not matter to anyone."

Whether employing romanticism, symbolism or creationism, by which he was nourished, Molinari, like some mystics and certain poets of the Renaissance, is a poet of unique and singular voice, one that becomes insistent, introspective, and implacable in shunning what is different and odd, what is not shared. Take, for example, lines such as the following from *Un día, el tiempo, las nubes*:

Diferente y quieto, y ya en mí, siento mi sangre voltear con alegría
la soledad y mi juventud perdida.
¡Unicamente mi cabeza, la alcorza de mi cuerpo, respira y juega
con el tiempo!

("Oda Terceva a la Pampa")

Different and calm, and all to myself, I feel my blood turn with joy
my solitude and my lost youth.
Only my head, my body's adornment, breathes and plays with time!

(Third Ode to the Pampa)

This solitude and creation within one's self is repeated when he evokes his beloved:

te desearía inmersa en mi cabello;
atmósfera sedienta, comenzando
la aurora, el otro mundo. ¡ay!, perdido
("Cuaderno de la madrugada")

I desire you immersed in my hair:
thirsting atmosphere, beginning
the dawn, the other world, ¡ah!, lost.

All of the themes are repeated or concentrated: absence, melancholy, desire, the contemplation of *mundos de madrugada* (dawn worlds), the evocation of *noches detenidas* (slumbering nights), a *flor dura sin delirio* (hard flower without ecstasy), or the astonishment with which he questions, without answering:

Quién me verá desnudo, sin alma,
semilla de río solo, por el atardecer!
("Cuaderno de la madrugada")

Who will see me naked, soulless
river seed alone, at nightfall!.

From 1940 on, Molinari—as well as Borges—was the foremost poetic figure among those published in Argentina. Three prestigious editorial houses (Losada, Emecé, and Sur) have brought together, in volumes easily and widely distributed, numerous texts before accessible to only the poet's personal friends and admirers. However, in spite of many titles and short and luxurious folios in exquisite print, Molinari's work is neither extensive nor varied.

The same level of sustained intimate tone and conscientiously baroque expression gives unity to Molinari's entire production, which is a single, continuous poem about states of the soul reiterated to the point of self-absorption and sublimation. The themes can vary, and we find them forming groups (Ghiano points out three in *Ficción* 15:83 [1958]), but what is most important is the nucleus of his life experiences, which determines his very personal vision of reality, be it of his physical surroundings, immediate resonances, or national motifs, or be it of a transcendent idealization of certain metaphysical instances such as time, the essence of being, death, nothingness, or God. And this nucleus occurs from Molinari's first book, *El imaginero*, with its formal title but with its roots bound to tender circumstance, thus placing it within Borgian principles and within the "Martín Fierro" group. There is an essential difference, however, even though stylistically this work meets what Borges had said about ultraism: "It tends toward the primary goal of all poetry, that is, the transmutation of the world's palpable reality into a reality that is interior and emotional." And the essence of Molinari's verse does not appear to be, as suggested by the quotation from Mallarmé that appears at the end of *El imaginero*, "une sonore, vaine et monotone ligne" (a sonorous, vain, and monotonous line)—but to the contrary this verse is the quintessence of the poet's soul and his habitual environment. Thus Molinari meets the demands of ultraism and French symbolism. In that first book we find, sketched in categories, the unmistakable outlines of what will be the definitive and permanent constants of all of Molinari's poetry. In "Poema del almacén" (Poem of the Warehouse), the title, the development of the theme, and the expressive mode are Borgian. But Molinari has insinuated, as a distinctive note, an evocative-sentimental nuance with its own principles of lyric intent, as might be expected from one who feels himself to be a poet. This sentimental, evocative note, with extreme personal delicateness and a hazily romantic base, of content in shadow, will never fail to appear in his work. It is a condition of his lyricism, its very quality, the "quid" of his poetic being, composed of the confluence of what appears to be the two opposed poles of his human and aesthetic attitude: separation from the reality of the world and aspiration to an ineffable ideal. In the words of "Poema de la niña velazqueña" in *El imaginero*:

Yo deseo tener una ventana
que sea el centro del mundo,
y una pena
como la flor de la magnolia
que si la tocan se oscurece

I desire a window
that is the center of the world,
and a sorrow
like the magnolia flower
which if touched darkens.

The reason for this desire to escape toward the ineffable and intangible can be found in a later book:

Cuando pienses lo inútil que es todo,
qué infinita tristeza es la de vivir en la tierra,
la de estar huyendo de la pestilencia como de un largo día
  sofocante.

("El ansioso," in Las sombras, 1974)

When you think how useless it all is,
what infinite sadness it is to live on this earth,
to be fleeing pestilence like a long suffocating day.
(The Anxious One)

In El imaginero, too, there appears another of his most clearly persistent notes in "Elegía para un recuerdo presente" (Elegy for the Present Souvenir), the sensation of solitude and abandonment, the absence of love and a condition of anxiety:

Si tu vivieras,
tu sombra, qué dulzura
no tendría para mis ojos;
ya que todo lo hemos compartido
en padre y madre
y en ausencia.

If you lived
your shadow, what sweetness
would it not have for my eyes;
since we have shared everything
in father and mother
and in absence.

From the need to remember, to escape toward a gravitating age comes these lines from "El poema del año nuevo" (Poem of the New Year):

La tarde está para rememorar,
mientras se siente cómo llora el mar.
Allá en tierras de adentro, fui un niño,
que no gustó el cariño! . . .
Libros de santos y juguetes rotos,
oraciones y cánticos devotos.
Por eso, cuando llora el mar,
siento ansias de llorar! . . .

The evening is for remembering, while one hears how
  the sea cries.
There, further inland, I was a child,
who didn't like affection! . . .
Books, saints, and broken toys, prayers and pious
songs.
Because of that, when the sea cries,
I want to weep.

This confession is confirmed in Un día, el tiempo, las nubes:

El lamento de toda mi existencia,
lo que a mí solo me interesa.
("Hostería de la
rosa y del clavel")

The lament of my whole existence,
what only interests me.

This note of essential abandonment may well be the cause of other themes just as characteristic and clearly evident: the conditionality of all knowledge or fully vital realization, the peremptory and imprecise nature of things, which he expresses in the conditional forms of the verb —si tuviera, si pudiera, si fuera, and so on (if I had, I could, I were)— and the desiring attitude, either declarative (yo deseo, I desire) or subjective (yo quisiera, I would like), always as an unattainable aspiration.

Alone, introspective, obsessive, the objects of the immediate world, beings or facts toward which one turns in search of a place to cling, on contact lose their natural condition and are transformed into entities symbolic of the poet's own existence. And thus there arise montes de acero (steel hills), blusa de piedra (stone blouse), sed polvorienta (dusty thirst), ciegas riberas (blind shores), and so forth. Rivers, plains, the sea, the ocean, birds, trees, flowers, historical personages (Quiroga, Lavalle), a city that has disappeared (Esteco) are, to repeat, like the emblems of an internal time, without specification of period or place, the underpinnings for a construction of a metaphysical sort, with its basis in ontological doubt. Thus the constant questions at the beginning of verses, de qué, por qué, en qué (of what, why, in which), and finally, the exclamative state of his confessed impossibility and his indetermination in the face of permanent uncertainty (ah, oh, ay) to which he opposes—romantic contrast—the beginnings of verses with an "I" that pretends to be categorical: Yo sé que su bondad . . . (I know that his goodness . . .); *Yo en mi niñez tuve* . . . (I in my childhood had . . .).

All of this lends Molinari's poetry an air of melancholic ode or existential elegy, compositions in which, certainly, he attains the highest degrees of lyric intensity and poetic quality. His language in the odes and elegies originates from his baroque phrasing, consisting in general of brilliant rhetorical figures, ludic creations with medieval and pre-Renaissance forms, and he thus devises a quite original style based on the most common words, but with the most unpredictable relationships. His attitude of separation and desire, of nothing and never, of what he is and what he might want, do not allow him to say things directly (he approaches them, but does not achieve a concrete communion with them); he must apprehend them by way of their accidents, attributes, or qualities that do not belong to them but which his seeing and feeling gives them. And when he cannot adjust that seeing and feeling to an expression which captures them, he makes use of suggestions, half tones, correspondences, figurative relations of labyrinthine inventiveness.

Nevertheless, what is least important in Molinari is what comes through to us with clear and precise meanings. What is important, however, is his creation of an atmosphere of delicateness and enchanting elegance, subtle intricacy, like a Gothic miniature or Oriental arabesque, with luminous darkness and transparency in mystery, awakening insistent attempts at a kind of Orphic communication, with an indecipherable common magic between the poet and the reader. Molinari is not hermetic, because there is no need to explain him. His world is there, clear and distinct, if we know how to comprehend that the poet must create the circumstance of the motif which he surrounds in such a way, with confluent details, that the motif seems to disappear—or to have never existed. His poetry thus becomes a manner that the poet acts out in his manner of creating; but it is never the objective result, the soul's conformity to that action. From there proceeds the dissolution of his life (much more than its definition, although this is also a way of defining it) in surprising expressive modes, disconcerting but compelling, which give his style that captivating richness of strange contacts and the most uncommon and unexpected joinings of acts and objects, which Borges once called "Molinari's pleasant disorderings."

What happens is that for Molinari image and metaphor constitute reality itself. One's hair must be *venturosos* (fortunate), hands *de fuego* (of fire), or, to cite another example, "y las estrellas funden sus lucientes trenzas dentros del agua" (and the stars merge their shining braids within the water). There is added to this a natural predisposition for poetic creationism ("tu dedal me ha de servir de mausoleo" [your thimble will be my mausoleum]), with ultraist forms ("Teléfonos de olvido, en vuestros postes yo pongo el oído" [Telephones of forgetfulness, I press my ear to your posts]), and the special manner of a unique rhetoric with personal symbolism, at times difficult, sometimes incoherent, that makes it necessary to penetrate as if it were an encoded space, in order to grasp the essence of his poetry, hidden, one could say, using his own image, "en la tiniebla de la manzana" (in the apple's darkness).

In "Oda descalza," from *El imaginero*, it is a footstep in the air, in "sepultura del agua" (grave of water), a presence that weeps over the dryness of a rose but wants to remember the sea. In the "Pórtico" of *Panegírico* (1930) Molinari has created the very symbol of the poet, an unsubstitutable image of his song, transferred to the thrush, "volador oscuro" (dark flyer), a beautiful image of something real and at the same time of its symbolic transcendence in meaningful intentionality: the poet, like the thrush, is *volador oscuro*. The same occurs in "Delta" (1932; in *Un día, el tiempo, las nubes*) with the symbol of the rose,

> *flor rigurosa;*
> *tan alta en la luz del día*
> *que nadie puede tocarla*
> *Transparente maravilla*

> rigorous flower;
> so tall in daylight
> that none can touch her.
> Transparent marvel.

This motif is found even in one of his later books, *Ésta rosa oscura del aire* (1949), for example, with the same

atmósfera distraída
pura, sobre un campo oscuro
donde un rio de ceniza
quema los jardines

> distracted atmosphere
> pure, on a dark field
> where an ashen river
> burns the gardens.

To conclude, and as proof that Molinari never departs from an attitude and a reiterative expression that can be trying, monotonous, and almost sterile, even in its perfection, like everything that is closed and finished, let us look at some examples from his notebook, *Poemas a un ramo de la tierra purpúrea* (Montevideo, 1959):

En el aire limpio y rosado de la tarde campea una luna fría
y menuda, seca y clara,
en la luminosidad perdida del cielo.
La sierra como una inmensa nave quemada se cubre de
*   pronto con la noche,*
y las últimas luces caen hacia el oeste, verdes y
anaranjadas —sobre nuestro país— debajo del horizonte del
*   campo . . .*
¡La sierra, obscura, con su alteza y sombra se corona!

In the clean, pink evening air hangs a moon cold
and small, dry and clear,
in the lost luminosity of the heavens.
The mountains like an immense burnt ship are suddenly
    covered by the night,
and the last light falls toward the west, green and
orange—over our country—under the field's horizon . . .
The mountains, dark, with their majesty and shadow
    crown themselves!

There persist until today the two forms of cultured poetry and traditional Spanish popular poetry that also appeared in *El imaginero:*

> *Llama el aire por la noche;*
> *llama y solo corre*
> *sin llenar la obscuridad.*
> *El aire, el viento, la memoria!*

> The air calls through the night;
> it calls and runs alone
> without filling the darkness.
> Air, wind, memory!

And:

> *Qué flor es el sueño,*
> *vida,*
> *que con las hojas se mueve,*
> *sin conocer*
> *que la balancea!*
> *¡Trigo parece sobre el agua!*

> What a flower is dreaming,
> life,
> that moves with the leaves,
> without knowing
> that it rocks it!
> Wheat it seems on the water!

Another duality is the long verse, without internal or external rhyme, as opposed to classical forms like the *lira*, the romance, or the sonnet. His sonnets (for example, those dedicated to "una camelia cortada" [a cut camellia]) and his re-creations of themes and forms from the ancient *cancioneros* (poetry collections) are among the most artificial of Molinari's work, *ejercicios poéticos* (poetic exercises), exhibits of formal skill and another manner of escape by way of pure technique.

Molinari may then be considered a very important Argentinian poet who is most representative of the Latin American avant-garde movement of the 1930's. His poems have a postromantic symbolist texture and a pure lyricism that sustain his verse by means of creationist images.

Translated from the Spanish by Bruce Stiehm

SELECTED BIBLIOGRAPHY

First Editions

El imaginero (with drawings by Norah Borges). Buenos Aires, 1927.
El pez y la manzana (with drawings by Norah Borges). Buenos Aires, 1929.
Panegírico de Nuestra Señora de [del] Luján. Buenos Aires, 1930. Third Municipal Prize.
Delta. Buenos Aires, 1932.
Cancionero del Principe de Vergara. Buenos Aires, 1933.
Elegía. Buenos Aires, 1933.
Hostería de la rosa y del clavel (with a portrait of the author

by José Moreno Villa). Buenos Aires, 1933. First Municipal Prize.

Nunca. Madrid, 1933.

El desdichado. Buenos Aires, 1934.

Una rosa para Stefan George (with a drawing by Federico García Lorca). Buenos Aires, 1934.

El tabernáculo (with drawings by Federico García Lorca). Buenos Aires, 1934.

Epístola satisfactoria (with a drawing by Norah Borges). Buenos Aires, 1935.

La tierra y el héroe. Buenos Aires, 1936.

Casida de la bailarina (with a drawing by Federico García Lorca). Buenos Aires, 1937.

Elegías de las altas torres (with six drawings by Alberto Morera). Buenos Aires, 1937.

Libro de la paloma. Buenos Aires, 1937.

La muerte en la llanura (with a watercolor by Rodolfo Castagna). Buenos Aires, 1937.

Nada. Buenos Aires, 1937.

Cinco canciones de amigo. Buenos Aires, 1939.

La corona (with an etching by Alberto Morera). Buenos Aires, 1939.

Dos sonetos. Buenos Aires, 1939.

Elegía a Garcilaso. Buenos Aires, 1939.

Libro de las soledades del poniente (with an etching by Alberto Morera). Buenos Aires, 1939.

Oda de amor (with a drawing by Fafael Alberti). Buenos Aires, 1940.

Odas a orillas de un viejo río (with a colored etching by Mane Bernardo). Buenos Aires, 1940.

Seis cantares de la memoria. Buenos Aires, 1941.

El alejado. Buenos Aires, 1943; 2nd ed. 1957. Second National Prize.

El huésped y la melancolía. Buenos Aires, 1946.

Ésta rosa oscura del aire (with a colored etching by Alberto Morera). Buenos Aires, 1949.

Sonetos a una camelia cortada. Buenos Aires, 1949.

Sonetos portugueses (with three watercolors by Alberto Morera). Buenos Aires, 1953.

Días donde la tarde es un pájaro. Buenos Aires, 1954.

Inscripciones y sonetos. San Miguel de Tucuman, Argentina, 1954.

Oda (with a tempera by Raúl Russo). Buenos Aires, 1954.

Cinco canciones a una paloma que es el alma (with a tempera by Santiago Cogorno). Buenos Aires, 1955.

Romances de las palmas y los laureles (with a drypoint by Raúl Russo). Buenos Aires, 1955.

Oda a la pampa (with an etching by Rafael Onetto). Buenos Aires, 1956.

Unida noche. Buenos Aires, 1957. First National Prize.

Poemas para un ramo de la tierra purpúrea. Montevideo, 1959.

Alfonso Reyes, Elegía. Buenos Aires, 1960.

Árboles muertos (with fourteen etchings by Rodolfo Castagna). Buenos Aires, 1960.

Un río de amor muere. Buenos Aires, 1960.

Homenaje a Georges Braque. Buenos Aires, 1963.

Oda a un soldado. Buenos Aires, 1963.

Cuatro vidalas para una dama. Buenos Aires, 1965.

Una sombra antigua canta. Buenos Aires, 1966.

El desentendido. Buenos Aires, 1967.

La hoguera transparente. Buenos Aires, 1970.

La cornisa. Buenos Aires, 1977.

La escudilla. Buenos Aires, 1977.

El desierto viento delante. Buenos Aires, 1982.

Collected Works

El cielo de las alondras y las gaviotas. Buenos Aires, 1963. John F. Kennedy Prize.

Un día, el tiempo, las nubes. Buenos Aires, 1964.

Mundos de la madrugada. Buenos Aires, 1943. Anthology containing plaquettes, notebooks, and former books.

Páginas de Ricardo Molinari. Selection by the author and with a study by Antonio Pagés Larraya. Buenos Aires, 1983.

Las sombras de [sic] pájaro tostado: Obra poetica, 1923–1973. Buenos Aires, 1974.

Biographical and Critical Studies

Alonso Gammo, José Maria. *Tres poetas argentinas, Marechal, Molinari, Bernárdez.* Madrid, 1951.

Anderson Imbert, Enrique. *Spanish-American Literature: A History.* Translated by John V. Falconier. Detroit, 1963.

Arístides, Julio. *Ricardo E. Molinari o la agonía del ser en el tiempo.* Buenos Aires, 1965.

Borges, Jorge Luis. "Ricardo E. Molinari, El imaginero." *Síntesis* 50:242 (1928). Included in *El idioma de los argentinos.* Buenos Aires, 1928.

Calamaro, Eduardo S. "La lucha por la poesía: Ricardo E. Molinari." *Correo literario* 2/9:3 (1944).

Cansinos-Assens, Rafael. "La poesía folklórica de Ricardo E. Molinari." In *Verde y dorado en las letras americanas.* Madrid, 1947. Pp. 45–57.

Cohen, John M. "Un nuevo continente poético. Cuatro latinoamericanos, vanguardia de la lírica mundial." *Visión. Revista internacional,* 15 January 1960. Pp. 84–87.

_____. *Poetry of This Age.* London, 1960. Pp. 221–223.

Curry, Richard K. "La fundión poética en dos sonetos de

Ricardo E. Molinari." *Hispanic Journal* 512:17–28 (1984).

Chapman, Arnold G. "Molinari, Ricardo: Días donde la tarde es un pájaro." In *Handbook of Latin American Studies* 20, edited by Francisco Aguilera. New York, 1968. P. 252.

Chouhy Aguirre, Ana Maria. "Seis cantares de la memoria Ricardo E. Molinari." *Verde memoria* 1:22 (1942).

Diego, Gerardo. "Los poetas angélicos." *La Nación* (Buenos Aires) 13 April 1960.

Dondo, Oswaldo Horacio. "Anotaciones." *Criterio* 60:535 (1929).

Gallo, Ugo, and Giuseppe Bellini. In *Storia della letteratura ispano-americana*. Milan, 1958. Pp. 284–286.

Ghiano, Juan Carlos. "Las *Odas* de Ricardo E. Molinari." In *Cuadernos de la Costa* 1 (1950).

——. In *Poesia argentina del siglo XX*. Buenos Aires and Mexico City, 1957. Pp. 148–155

——. "Dos poetas fieles: Molinari y Ledesma." *Ficción* (Buenos Aires) 15:79–84 (1958).

González Gandiaga, Nora. *Poesía y estila de las odas de Ricardo E. Molinari*. Santa Fe, Argentina, 1983.

Grieben, Carlos F. "La poesía de Ricardo E. Molinari a los veinticinco años de *El imaginero*." *Sur* 221:129–134 (1953).

Guillen, H. E. "Ricardo E. Molinari: Duración y produccion." *Nordeste* 8:173–223 (1986).

Hernández, J[uan] J[osé]. "Ricardo E. Molinari: *Unida noche*." *Sur* 252:87–89 (1958).

Ibarra, Néstor. In *La nueva poesía argentina*. Buenos Aires, 1930. Pp. 78–82.

Lacan, María Hortensia. "La lengua poética de Ricardo E. Molinari." *Buenos Aires literaria* 5:6–16 (1953).

Larralde, Pedro. "*Mundos de la madrugada*, por Ricardo E. Molinari." *Correo literario* 2/6:6 (1944).

Leonardo, Sergio. "Diálogo con un poeta." *La Nación* (Buenos Aires) 26 November 1967.

López Palmero, M[anuel]. "*El imaginero*: Ricardo E. Molinari." *Nosotros* 61/280 (1928).

Mazzei, Angel. "Un perenne modo de cantar." *La Nación* (Buenos Aires), 14 May 1967.

Méndez, Evar. "Doce poetas nuevos." *Síntesis* 2/4:15–34 (1927).

Mijica Lainez, Manual. "Discurso en la recepción de Ricardo E. Molinari." *Boletín* (Academia Argentina de Letra) 34/3:131–132 (1969).

Pérez Pollán. Felipe L. "La ausencia y la soledad en la poesía de Ricardo E. Molinari." *Cuadernos hispanoamericanos* 151:140–153 (1962).

Pinto, Juan. In *Panorama de la literatura argentina contemporánea*. Buenos Aires, 1941. Pp. 257–259.

——. In *Breviario de la literatura argentina*. Buenos Aires, 1958. Pp. 167–168.

Pousa, Narciso. *Ricardo E. Molinari*. Buenos Aires, 1961.

Roggiano, Alfredo A. "El primer libro de Ricardo E. Molinari." *Panorama* (Tucumán, Argentina) 2:8–26 (1952).

Running, Thorpe. "The Outer Edges of Ultra: Molinari and Girondo." In *Borges' Ultraist Movement and Its Poets*. Lathrup Village, Mich., 1981. Pp. 123–146.

Solana, Rafael. "Ricardo E. Molinari." *Taller* 10:46 (1940).

Varela, A[lfredo] (?). "Molinari, poeta del viento." *Correo literario* 5/87:14 (1954).

Varela, L[orenzo]. "El alejado." *Correo literario* 2/14:7 (1944).

Jorge Luis Borges

(1899–1986)

Jaime Alazraki

In the period from the early 1960's, when Jorge Luis Borges' first collections of fiction were published in the United States (both *Ficciones* and *Labyrinths* appeared in 1962), to the late 1970's, Borges became a driving and dominant force in contemporary world letters. By 1967, John Barth had defined him as "one of the old masters of twentieth-century fiction." Two years earlier, John Updike in *The New Yorker* magazine saw in Borges' work a possible "clue to the dead-end and downright trashiness of present American fiction." In 1970, a critic writing for the *New York Times Book Review* described an important segment of American fiction written in the last three years as "the Borgesian phase," and a book published the next year—Tony Tanner's *City of Words*, 1971—viewed Borges and Vladimir Nabokov as "two writers whose work has exerted a strong influence on the American fiction of the last two decades (1950–1970)." George Steiner best summarized Borges' pervasive presence in American letters when he wrote in 1970: "There is a sense in which Borges is now the most original of Anglo-American writers." On the Latin American side, Carlos Fuentes went as far as writing in 1969 that "without Borges' prose there simply would not be a modern Spanish-American novel." With the Formentor International Publishers' Prize, shared with Samuel Beckett in 1961, Borges established himself as a powerful presence in twentieth-century literature. Poet, essayist, fiction writer, he is an innovator and a leading figure in the three genres. He has been translated into most European and many non-European languages, and received most of the international literary awards, the Nobel Prize being the exception.

The reader of Borges' metaphysical stories cannot but be perplexed by his poems dedicated to colonels and generals, to battles and violent deaths. This seeming paradox has two explanations. First, those names of heroic men and war actions are part of Borges' biography. His great grandfather, Colonel Suárez, led a Peruvian cavalry charge in one of the last great battles against Spain at Junín in 1820. His grandfather, Colonel Borges, fought in Argentine civil wars and was killed in 1874 in the battle of La Verde. Of his maternal grandfather, Isidoro Acevedo, he has written, "He fought when Buenos Aires asked him in Cepeda, in Pavón, and on the beach of Corrales." Miguel E. Soler, a general who led the vanguard of San Martín's army and became governor of Buenos Aires in 1820, is another of Borges' ancestors. So is Francisco Narciso de Laprida, president of the pivotal Congress of Tucumán that in 1816 declared Argentine independence. Ironically, one of his great-great grandmother's brothers was Juan Manuel de Rosas, the dictator who dominated the country from 1829 to 1852. Someone has even managed to establish that Borges' family tree goes as far back as Juan de Garay, the founder of the city of Buenos Aires in 1580. Thus, the saga of his family encapsulates the official history of Argentina.

The second explanation follows from the first. It lies in Borges' preference for epic literature or, rather, for the epic character of certain literature. In justifying his admiration for George Bernard Shaw's work, he explained:

There is in Shaw an epic significance. He is the only writer of our time who has imagined and presented heroes to his reader. On the whole, modern writers tend to reveal men's weaknesses, and seem to delight in their unhappiness; in Shaw's case, however, we have characters like Major Barbara or Caesar, who are heroic and whom one can admire. In Shaw's work the greatest human virtues are extolled. For example that a man can forget his own fate, that a man may not value his own happiness, that he may say like our Almafuerte: "I am not interested in my own life," because he is interested in something beyond personal circumstances.

(In Guibert, pp. 97–98)

This preference partly explains his numerous stories devoted to knife-fighters or *compadres* whose bravado he has described as a kind of "low epic." It could also explain Borges' enthusiasm for Western films: "I think nowadays," he commented, "while literary men seem to have neglected their epic duties, the epic has been saved for us, strangely enough, by the Westerns."

Fanny Haslam, Borges' paternal grandmother, on the other hand, was British, from Staffordshire. She was a great reader and spoke mostly English at home. She met Colonel Francisco Borges in Paraná and married him. Borges' father, Jorge Guillermo, was the younger of two sons born in Entre Ríos. He was a lawyer and eventually became a psychology teacher at a normal school where he conducted his classes in English. Leonor Acevedo, Borges' mother, came from old Argentine and Uruguayan families. She learned English through her husband, became a proficient and assiduous reader in that language, and eventually translated William Saroyan, Nathaniel Hawthorne, and an art book by Herbert Read.

Borges, the older of two children, was born in Buenos Aires on 24 August 1899. He grew up in a home where both English and Spanish were commonly used, and until nine he was educated by an English governess. Most of his early reading was of works in English: *Huckleberry Finn, Roughing It, Flush Days in California, First Men in the Moon, Treasure Island, Don Quixote* (first read in English), *Tom Brown's School Days*, Edgar Allan Poe, Henry Wadsworth Longfellow, Charles Dickens, Lewis Carroll, Grimm's *Fairy Tales*, and Sir Richard Burton's *The Thousand Nights and a Night*. So much was English Borges' reading language that when years later he read *Don Quixote* in the original, it sounded to him—as he remarked in his autobiography—like a bad translation. At nine he translated Oscar Wilde's "The Happy Prince" into Spanish, and it was published in one of the Buenos Aires dailies. At thirteen, his first original story was published, a dramatic sketch about tigers, "El rey de la selva" (The King of the Jungle). His first poem, written about the same time under the influence of the Argentine poet Hilario Ascasubi, was about the native cowboys, or *gauchos*.

In 1914, his father's eyesight had begun to fail. He took an early retirement and moved with his family to Europe. After several weeks in Paris, they settled in Geneva. Borges and his sister, Norah, attended the Collège de Calvin where Borges found his two bosom friends, Simon Jichlinsky and Maurice Abramowicz. In addition to learning the languages taught at school—French and Latin—Borges undertook the study of German with a German-English dictionary and a copy of Heinrich Heine's *Lyrisches Intermezzo*. Soon he was able to read Gustav Meyrink's novel *Der Golem* and made his first attempts at reading Arthur Schopenhauer. It was also in Geneva where Borges first read Walt Whitman through a German translation and where he wrote his first sonnets in English, imitating William Wordsworth, and in French, after the symbolist manner.

The family remained in Switzerland until 1919. Before returning to Argentina, they spent more than a year in Spain, first in Majorca and then in Seville, where Borges made his first contacts with a group of poets who published the literary journal *Grecia* and defined themselves as ultraists, the Spanish version of the European avant-garde. It was in that journal that Borges saw his first poem, "Hymn to the Sea," into print. "I tried my hardest to be Walt Whitman," he said of it years later ("An Autobiographical Essay"), and it was indeed an imitation of the master in his own language. But it was in Madrid where Borges met Rafael Cansinos-Asséns, the animator of *ultraísmo*. A converted Jew, a polyglot, and a committed man of letters, he has been described by Borges as "a tall man with the Andalusian contempt for all things Castilian." More important, Borges thought of Cansinos as his master. In his autobiographical essay he wrote: "I still like to think of myself as his disciple." During his stay in Madrid, Borges became an habitué of the ultraist group gatherings in the Café Colonial. There and under the aegis of Cansinos, subjects such as metaphor, free verse, and poetry were discussed until daybreak. When Borges and his family returned to Buenos Aires toward the end of March 1921, he became the emissary and instigator of *ultraísmo* in the New World. With a group of friends and fellow poets, he, published the magazines *Prisma* and *Proa*, which together with articles and manifestos that appeared in other journals (primarily *Nosotros* and *Martín Fierro*) defined and propagated the new poetic credo.

Poetry

Borges' encounter with his native town after six long and nostalgic years in Europe resulted in a series of poems devoted to the city and collected in his first published book, *Fervor de Buenos Aires* (Passion for Buenos Aires, 1923). Within short spans two more collections of poems would follow: *Luna de enfrente* (Moon Across the Way, 1925) and *Cuaderno San Martín* (San Martín Copybook, 1929). The sense of rediscovery of Buenos Aires and wistful overtones resonate throughout this early poetry:

> La ciudad está en mi como un poema
> que no he logrado detener en palabras

> The city is inside me like a poem
> I have not been able to arrest with words

he writes in "Vanilocuencia," one of the earliest poems from his first collection. In "Un patio" the city

is captured through intimate corners, familiar spaces, and personal emblems:

> Grato es vivir en la amistad oscura
> de un zaguán, de una parra y de un aljibe.

> It is lovely to live in the dark friendliness
> of covered entrance way, arbor, and wellhead.
> (in *Selected Poems*)

The country as a whole is perceived and defined in terms of a few personal and family icons: "Mi patria es un latido de guitarra, unos retratos y una vieja espada" (My country is a guitar beat, a few portraits, and an old sword).

From these early poems of the 1920's to his last collections—*El oro de los tigres* (The Gold of the Tigers, 1972), *La rosa profunda* (The Unending Rose, 1975), *La moneda de hierro* (The Iron Coin, 1976), *Historia de la noche* (A History of the Night, 1977), and *La cifra* (The Cipher, 1981)—Borges' poetry traveled a long way. It moved from that rediscovery of his birthplace to a cult of his ancestors and a very personal history of his country: heroes, antiheroes, counterheroes. He then found that metaphysical subjects, literary artifacts, and religious beliefs were not unworthy material for poetry: "La noche ciclica" ("The Cyclical Night," 1949), "Composición escrita en un ejemplar de la gesta de Beowulf" ("Poem Written in a Copy of Beowulf," 1964), and "El Golem" ("The Golem," 1958) are samples that illustrate this later period. His perception of poetry in those years could be defined, in T. S. Eliot's dictum, "not as a turning loose of emotions, but as an escape from emotion; not as the expression of personality, but as an escape from personality"—a reflective and ruminative poetry. His ruminations are not about the fortunes or misfortune of the heart, or existential angst, or the conundrum of life, but about the monuments of imagination, and particularly those of literature: intellect as passion, culture as the true adventure, knowledge as invention. A rather selfless poetry, a poetry in which the most powerful presence of the self is its absence.

A grandson and great-grandson of military heroes, Borges turned his poetry into an epic exploration by conjuring everything poetry can possibly conjure other than his own personal drama. In his late poetry this drama is defined as a lack of personal drama.

Borges muses relentlessly and painfully about his life devoid of heroic violence: "Soy . . . él que no fue una espada en la guerra" (I am that who did not wield a sword in battle) he writes in "Soy" ("I am") from *La rosa profunda*. In the same collection he iterates more explicitly this denial in a poem titled "1972":

> Estoy ciego. He cumplido los setenta;
> No soy el oriental Francisco Borges
> Que murió con dos balas en el pecho,
> Entre las agonías de los hombres,
> En el hedor de un hospital de sangre.

> I am blind, and I have lived out seventy years.
> I am not Francisco Borges the Uruguayan
> Who died with a brace of bullets in his breast
> Among the final agonies of men
> In the dead-stench of hospital blood.

The motif reappears once more in the same collection in a poem entitled "Yo" ("I"): "Soy también la memoria de una espada" (I am also the memory of a sword). Since he was denied a sword, that is, the military destiny of his ancestors, he turned poetry into a sword; since epic action has been ruled out of his life, he converted poetry into an epic exercise. In the poem "Espadas" (Swords) from *La rosa profunda*, he writes:

> Déjame, espada, usar contigo el arte;
> Yo, que no he merecido manejarte.

> Let me, sword, render you in art;
> I, who did not deserve to wield you.

How was this accomplished? By effacing himself from his own poetry, by speaking of everybody but himself. Yet what Borges defends is not impersonality but an epic sense of life. The poet disregards his own tribulations to become the singer of virtues, values, people, and literary works dear to him. Haunted by the memory of his ancestors' "romantic death," Borges celebrates the courage of heroes and knife-fighters ready to die in defense of a cause or belief more precious to them than life. Since he was denied an epic destiny on the battlefield, he would turn literature into his own battlefield by refusing to speak about himself, by lending his voice to others. This epic attitude has been deliberate, and it stems from

his family background as well as from the fact that his father's library was, as he put it, "the chief event" in his life. For Borges, books are events, intellection stands for life, the past is lived as present, literature is experienced as passion.

Until 1964. That year, Borges published a sonnet entitled "1964" with which he inaugurates a new theme in his poetry. To what he has called his "habits"—Buenos Aires, the cult of his ancestors, the study of old Germanic languages, the contradiction of time—he now adds his broodings over what can be referred to as a vocation for unhappiness. The sonnet opens with the line: "Ya no seré feliz. Tal vez no importa" (I shall no longer be happy. Perhaps it doesn't matter), a motif that appears and reappears in his five collections between 1969 and 1976, and culminates in the 1976 sonnet "Remordimiento" (Remorse), included in *La moneda de hierro*. It opens with two strong, fateful, and resigned lines:

> He cometido el peor de los pecados
> Que un hombre puede cometer. No he sido
> Feliz . . .

> I have committed the worst sin of all
> That a man can commit. I have not been
> Happy . . .

Borges' treatment of this intimate side of his life has little to do with romantic confessionalism, or with yielding to the same weakness he earlier condemned in modern literature. If he now breaks the silence about himself and tells us about his unhappiness, he does so without self-pity, without tears or pathos, but simply by acknowledging it as fact, or rather, as a sin. The poem represents the acceptance of that sin as guilt, and throughout the poem he assumes this sin of unhappiness with the same poise and endurance with which epic heroes accept defeat. He breaks the diffidence of his previous poetry without outcries, almost restating his early selflessness, since his misfortune, his having been unhappy, is not a torment one mourns over but a sin one must accept quietly or even expiate, or perhaps sublimate in the silence of a verse. "One destiny," he wrote in his short story "Biografía de Tadeo Isidoro Cruz (1829–1874)" ("The Life of Tadeo Isidoro Cruz," 1940), "is no better than another, but . . . every man must obey the one he carries within him." Such is the spirit of his own acceptance: a heroic stamina that welcomes triumph and adversity with equal courage.

In a later collection—*Historia de la noche*—new paths into the elusive territory of his intimacy are added. The accomplished writer, the celebrated poet, the man who welcomes love and death with equal resignation and exultation, feels now that decorum could also be a display of vanity, that modesty in the face of death is but another form of pettiness blocking total reconciliation. The circle of life closes in, unhappiness no longer matters, and a mundane virtue matters even less. Borges seeks oblivion, but since this is a privilege denied to his memory, in "El grabado" (The Picture) he backtracks and delves into memory's meanders and deep chambers:

> *A veces me da miedo la memoria.*
> *En sus cóncavas grutas y palacios*
> *(Dijo San Agustín) hay tantas cosas*
> *El infierno y el cielo están en ellas.*

Sometimes I fear memory.
In its concave grottoes and palaces
(Said Saint Augustine) there are so many things.
Hell and Heaven lie there.

(in *The Gold of the Tigers: Selected Later Poems*)

And in "The Thing I Am" there is no way out of memory but death:

> *Soy el que sabe que no es más que un eco,*
> *El que quiere morir enteramente.*

I am he who knows he is but an echo,
The one who wants to die completely.

(*ibid.*)

Two elements set *Historia de la noche* apart from his previous collections: a restrained celebration of love, and a serene acceptance of everything life brings, for better or for worse, including the imminence of death. Not that the old motifs or "habits" are missing here. They are present, but in a different way. They are part of his indefatigable memory, and as such they inevitably reappear: tigers, mirrors, books, dreams, time, ancestors, friends, authors, knives, cities, and countries. The manner in which these motifs enter into the poem has changed. "El tigre" (The Tiger), for example, is an evocation of the animal that fascinates Borges as an obsession of his childhood, for

its beauty, and because it brings reverberations of William Blake, Victor Hugo, and Shere Khan. Yet the last line reads: "We thought it was bloody and beautiful. Norah, a girl, said: It is made for love." This last line makes the difference, and gives the poem an unexpected twist. The reminisced anecdote—a visit to the Palermo Zoo—was an old strand in his memory, but only now has its true momentum been recaptured, only now does the tiger's face of love surface and overshadow all previous faces to mirror the author's own. In no other book of poems has Borges allowed himself to deal with love with such freedom and with a distance that ultimately is the condition of love's magic. Two examples at hand are "El enamorado" (The Lover) and "La espera" (The Waiting). They are love poems in which Borges tersely reviews some of his old literary tics—moons, roses, numbers, seas, time, tigers, swords—but they are now shadows that vanish to yield to the only presence that truly counts:

> *Debo fingir que hay otros. Es mentira.*
> *Sólo tú eres. Tú, mi desventura*
> *Y mi ventura, inagotable y pura.*

I should feign that there are others. It's a lie.
Only you exist. You, my misfortune
And my fortune, inexhaustible and pure.

The poetry of Borges' last decade went through several changes. His earliest poems strive to convey a conversational tone. They are a dialogue with the familiar city, its myths and favorite corners, sometimes bearing Whitmanesque overtones. To emphasize that intimate and nostalgic accent, he often uses free verse, local words, and Argentine slang. Then, when he "went from myths of the outlying slums of the city to games with time and infinity (*Dreamtigers*, p. 51), he opted for more traditional meters and stanzaic forms. This alone conferred a certain stilted inflection on his poetic voice. Rhymes were strong and at times even hammering ("Golem" was made to rhyme with "Scholem," the Yiddish for Shalom). He brought the hendecasyllable and the sonnet to new heights, stimulated undoubtedly by his advanced blindness. In spite of this sculptural perfection, there was still a declamatory falsetto in his voice that was particularly apparent when he read aloud his own poetry. This stiffness, however slight, disappeared in his best poems. In 1969, five years after his previous collection *El otro, el mismo* (The Self and the Other, 1964), he published *Elogio de la sombra* (In Praise of Darkness). With this volume, Borges freed his verse from any linguistic slag. The sonnet, the most frequent form he used thereafter, bordered on perfection: these sonnets are masterfully carved, with chiseled smoothness and a quiet flow that turns them into verbal music.

Poetry as music has always been to Borges a crystallizing point at which language succeeds in bringing forth its rhythmic core. This is not a music produced by sound; the poem turns words into a transparent surface that reveals a certain cadence, a harmony buried under the opacities of language, much in the same manner as music rescues a privileged order of sound and silence from a chaotic mass of sounds. In the prologue to the collection *El otro, el mismo,* he has explained this understanding of poetry:

> On occasion, I have been tempted into trying to adapt to Spanish the music of English or of German; had I been able to carry out that perhaps impossible adventure, I would be a great poet, like Garcilaso, who gave us the music of Italy, or like the anonymous Sevilian poet who gave us the music of Rome, or like Darío, who gave us that of Verlaine and Hugo. I never went beyond rough drafts, woven of words of few syllables, which very wisely I destroyed.
>
> (in *Selected Poems*)

Borges, whose "destiny"—as he put it—"is in the Spanish language" ("Mi destino es la lengua castellana"), found in his latest poetry not the music of English or German or of any other poet, but his own voice, and through it a music the Spanish language did not know before him. Not that Spanish did not produce great poets. It certainly did, and each of them represents an effort to strike a different chord of that musical instrument language becomes at the best moments of its poetry.

In *Historia de la noche* there is hardly a subject or motif that has not been dealt with in his previous collections, love being the exception. But precisely because he returns to his old subjects, theme matters less than the voice. Furthermore, the voice is the subject. Borges further refines a device first developed in "Another Poem of Gifts": the poem as a long list,

and listing as a poetic exercise. The device accentuates the magic character of poetry as a voice speaking in the dark, as words reaching out for meanings that are beyond words. What prevails is a music that speaks from its innumerable variations. These variations, far from being repetitons, are, as in the art of the fugue, new versions of the same tune to further explore, condense, and simplify a given theme. It is as if Borges had put behind him his old habits as themes to focus on the tones and inflections of his own voice. In the poem "Las causas" (The Causes) from *Historia de la noche,* he goes through an inventory of mementoes from history, literature, and life. The list encompasses some of the most memorable components of his own poetry and becomes a sort of miniature of his poetic *oeuvre.* The poem closes with two equally compressed lines: "Se precisaron todas esas cosas / Para que nuestros manos encontraran" (All those things were needed / so that our hands could meet), a masterful coda that renders his tight survey of motifs into a love poem. This is the surface, however impeccable, of the text, its outer meaning. But what the text also says is that this laconic eloquence, terse to the point of diaphaneity, is sustained by sixty long years of poetic creation, the understated notion being: all those earlier poems were needed so that this one could be written. The idea appears at the end of one of his most relaxed and subtly personal short stories, "La busca de Averroes" ("Averroes' Search," 1949): "I felt, on the last page, that my narration was a symbol of the man I was as I wrote it and that, in order to compose that narration, I had to be that man and, in order to be that man, I had to compose that narration, and so on to infinity." But this last poem does not form a circle with the others; it is rather the answer to the others, a sort of prism that reintegrates the dispersed shades of his poetry into one text, and this text gleams like a single beam of white light with a radiant simplicity that none of the individual texts has. With *Historia de la noche* Borges' poetry finds an equilibrium that undoubtedly conveys his own inner serenity. But this serenity, being a linguistic externalization, is also a song through which the Spanish language elicits a music unheard before: an austere, poised, dignified, and quiet music. The young poet who once delighted in the exhilaration of his own performance has been left far behind. The voice we hear now is that of a consummate musician who has achieved total mastery over his medium. The music we hear now is that of the Spanish language attuned to its own registers, and that of a poet skillfully true to his own perceptions.

Fiction

Between 1937 and 1946, Borges worked at the Buenos Aires Municipal Library, in one of its modest branches located in a drab neighborhood in the southwest part of town. Borges turned this unexciting and rather depressing job into an intellectual adventure. Riding back and forth on the tram, a couple of hours each day, he read *The Divine Comedy* in its original Tuscan with the help of John Aitken Carlyle's prose translation. At work, he would do all his library cataloging in the first hour and then steal away to the basement and pass the next five hours reading or writing. "I remember"—he tells in his autobiography—"rereading, in this way, the six volumes of Gibbon's *Decline and Fall* and the many volumes of Vicente Fidel López' *History of the Argentine Republic*. I read Léon Bloy, Claudel, Groussac, and Bernard Shaw. On holidays, I translated Faulkner and Virginia Woolf."

Borges enjoyed thinking that his beginning as a short story writer was a serendipitous event. In 1938, the same year his father died, he had an accident running up a stairway. He hurt his scalp hitting a freshly painted open casement window. The wound became poisoned and when he was rushed to the hospital after he lost his power of speech septicemia was diagnosed. For a month he was on the verge of dying, and even when recovery began, he feared for his mental integrity. He first tested his intellectual capability by agreeing to let his mother read to him aloud from C. S. Lewis' *Out of the Silent Planet*. Understanding brought tears but also additional fears: could he ever write again? He had previously written poetry and essays. He decided to answer that question by trying something he had never done before, fiction, so that—the reasoning went—"if I failed at that it wouldn't be so bad and might even prepare me for the final revelation." "Pierre Menard, autor del *Quixote*" ("Pierre Menard, Author of the *Quixote*,"

1939) was written with this concern in mind. As much as the ruse worked for him, the truth is that Borges had already written fiction before the accident. In 1935, he wrote "El acercamiento a Almotásim" ("The Approach to al-Mu'tasim") as a pseudoessay purporting "to be a review of a book published originally in Bombay three years earlier." It was included in a collection of essays—*Historia de la eternidad* (A History of Eternity)—published a year later, in 1936. But even before that he had written "Hombre de la esquina rosada" (Streetcorner Man), which originally appeared in a collection of stories and sketches entitled *Historia universal de la infamia* (A Universal History of Infamy) published in 1935. It is this collection of stories of infamy adapted from stories written by others and whose sources Borges indicates on the last page of the book that truly marks his beginning as a fiction writer. Writing as rewriting (of stories written by other authors) would remain his major narrative strategy. He formulated it years later in his essay "For Bernard Shaw," where he writes: "One literature differs from another, either before or after it, not so much because of the text as for the manner in which it is read." And if in the preface of the 1954 edition of this volume he warns that those stories "are the irresponsible game of a shy young man who dared not write stories and so amused himself by falsifying and distorting the tales of others," this shy approach of fabricating his writings from other writings nevertheless remained his narrative technique par excellence. The method for writing adopted in this first collection was to become a permanent feature of his poetics for fiction found in the next collections. When he wrote the 1954 preface he already knew that he was going to remain shy for the rest of his literary career, but he turned this shyness into his most daring weapon. What he said about his tales of infamy applies also to his entire narrative work. After *Ficciones* (Fictions, 1944) and *El Aleph* (The Aleph, 1949), he repeated, in the same apologetic tone of the 1954 preface, that he was rewriting what others had already written: "Everything I have written"—he said in a 1962 interview—"could be found in Poe, Stevenson, Wells, Chesterton, and some others." The statement is neither literally accurate nor completely false; it is rather a casual formulation, with modesty as its dress, of what can be regarded as the cornerstone of his narrative poetics. Throughout prologues and comments, he would tirelessly restate this central notion, anticipating his critics and commentators by revealing his sources and intertexts. Those acknowledgments, found in all his books as "debts to the original tellers," are of one piece with his proposition of literature as "the diverse intonations of a few metaphors" stated in an informal yet unequivocal way in a short note of 1933—"La metáfora" included in *Historia de la eternidad*. Unknowingly, Borges was placing himself at the very center of one of the most modern approaches to literary theory. The Russian formalists strove to define literature in terms similar to those enunciated by Borges. They believed that texts are not born in a vacuum, but evolve from other texts: what changes is less the ideas elicited by them than the new syntax that governs the rewriting of the old text. They concluded that Alexander Blok canonized the themes and rhythms of the "Gypsy Song," that Anton Chekhov bestowed literary status to the *Budilnik*, a comic newspaper in nineteenth-century Russia, and that Fyodor Dostoyevsky brought the devices of the dime novel to a level of literary form. Their overall conclusion was that new forms come about not in order to express new contents but in order to replace old forms. Borges was not acquainted with the ideas of the Russian formalists. He was working on his own, and he arrived independently at conclusions similar to theirs. Yet he did what the formalists did not: he incorporated some of his ideas about literature into his creative writing, thus amalgamating theory and craft.

The stories of infamy are important in Borges' development as a writer less as theme than as form. His keen interest in infamy is present in the later stories but without the tongue-in-cheek characteristic of the first collection. The letter is present, but the spirit has changed. Infamy is no longer a show of sheer burlesque, but one more character in a much broader fictional drama. It is in the form that *A Universal History* represents a real breakthrough. When Borges wrote the stories of infamy, he definitely left behind the contorted baroque style of his ultraist years. In an essay of 1927 that appeared a year later in his book *El idioma de los argentinos* (The Language of Argentines,), he harshly criticized "the

ornaments, lavishness and pretended wealth" of the Spanish language as forms of fraud, and he saw in "its perfect synonymity and its profuse verbal parade" a dead language, a display of ghosts and mummies. In that same essay, he proposed a goal that was the very opposite of that showy, expressionless, and affected style: "Total invisibility and total effectiveness." In the 1954 preface to the stories of infamy, he renewed that attack, now free of the controversial circumstances of 1927 and also free of his own earlier insecurities: "I should define as baroque that style which borders on its own caricature. . . . Baroque is the final stage of any given art, when it parades and squanders its own means of expression." And regarding his own tales of infamy, he added: "The very title of these pages flaunts their baroque character." The prose of *A Universal History*, however, is far from suffering from that baroque ill of his youth. In those "falsified and distorted" stories, as he calls them, Borges found his voice, the ripe style of the mature writer. Several features of this prose—its precision and conciseness, its careful perfection and exactness—would become the attributes of Borges' later prose.

"Pierre Menard, Author of *Quixote*" constitutes, thus, not so much a point of departure of his fiction writing, as Borges would have wanted us to believe, but a point of arrival, the culmination of a search for a voice and a narrative method. "Tlön, Uqbar, Orbis Tertius" and "Las ruinas circulares" ("The Circular Ruins") appeared in 1940 in *Sur*, the same journal that published "Pierre Menard." The following year, "La lotería en Babilonia" ("The Lottery in Babylonia") and "Examen de la obra de Herbert Quain" were printed in the same magazine. So were "La muerte y la brújula" ("Death and the Compass"), "La biblioteca de Babel" ("The Library of Babel"), and "El jardín de senderos que se bifurcan" ("The Garden of Forking Paths"), in 1941. "Funes el memorioso" ("Funes the Memorious") and "La forma de la espada" ("The Shape of the Sword") appeared in *La Nación* the same year. Borges collected eight of these mature stories and published them in 1941 in a volume entitled *The Garden of Forking Paths*, which later was incorporated into *Ficciones* in the editions of 1944 and 1956. *El Aleph* was published in 1949 and in an augmented edition in 1952. *El hacedor* (*Dreamti-*

gers) appeared in 1960. These three collections of fiction include the work of the Borges internationally known and admired. The next two collections—*El informe de Brodie* (*Doctor Brodie's Report*) and *El Libro de Arena* (*The Book of Sand*) of 1970 and 1975, respectively—correspond to his later input, when he became blind and was forced to dictate his writing. His style and conception of the short story changed. They became more straightforward and less encased in labyrinthine sequences of Chinese boxes. The old thematic obsessions reappeared, but devoid of the machinery of allusions and the chiseled prose of his earlier fiction. The epilogue closing his best collection of essays, *Otras inquisiciones* (*1937–1952*) (*Other Inquisitions* [*1937–1952*], 1952), provides a suitable starting point for a discussion of his fiction: "As I corrected the proofs of this volume, I discovered two tendencies in these miscellaneous essays. The first tendency is to evaluate religious or philosophical ideas on the basis of their aesthetic worth and even for what is singular and marvelous about them. . . . The other tendency is to presuppose (and to verify) that the number of fables or metaphors of which men's imagination is capable is limited" (p. 201).

These two tendencies constitute, by odd coincidence, the ordinate and the abscissa on which he has woven his narrative world. Borges believes, as do the inhabitants of his planet Tlön, that metaphysics is a branch of fantastic literature. Referring to an anthology of fantastic fiction he compiled with two fellow writers (*Antología de la literatura fantástica*, 1940), he admits "the embarrassing omission of the unsuspected and greatest masters of the genre: Parmenides, Plato, John Scotus Erigena, Albertus Magnus, Spinoza, Leibnitz, Kant, Francis Bradley." He further ponders: "In fact, what are H. G. Wells' or Poe's wonders—a flower that comes to us from the future, a dead man under hypnosis—compared with the inventions of God, with the laborious theory of a being that in some way is three and that solitarily endures beyond time" (*Discusión*, p. 172).

The implication is clear: philosophical theories and theological speculations are by far more fictional, and even more fantastic, than any piece of fantastic fiction. Bertrand Russell provides an explanation for this paradox. In *Our Knowledge of the External World* he writes: "In the classical tradition of philosophy, since the Greeks, the world has been constructed by means of logic, with little or no appeal to concrete experience . . . , and while it liberates imagination as to what the world may be, it refuses to legislate as to what the world is" (p.15).

If this is indeed the case, if theology and philosophy are the true repositories of human imagination, why bother forging new (and imperfect) stories? Why not use the fabrications of metaphysics and the beliefs of religions as the raw material for fiction? This is what Borges has done. His story "Tlön, Uqbar, Orbis Tertius" is a disguised metaphor for our own planet as conceived by philosophical idealism:

> Who are the inventors of Tlön? . . . this brave new world is the work of a secret society of astronomers, biologists, engineers, metaphysicians, poets, chemists, algebraists, moralists, painters, geometers . . . directed by an obscure man of genius. . . . The nations of this planet are congenitally idealist. Their language and the derivations of their language—religion, letters, metaphysics—all presuppose idealism. . . . the classic culture of Tlön comprises only one dicipline: psychology. . . . there are no sciences on Tlön. . . . The paradoxical truth is that they do exist, and in almost uncountable number.
>
> (*Labyrinths*, pp. 7–10)

As fantastic as Tlön may seem, it is our planet in disguise, our planet as a creation of human culture, from the houses we inhabit up to the ways we die. Claude Lévi-Strauss confirms this conclusion when he defines human culture as "that artifical universe in which we live as members of a given society." Borges conceives the universe as a labyrinth constructed by gods, and since only angels can penetrate a divine mind, he reasons, man is condemned forever to wander on its fringes (a reverberation of K's quest in Franz Kafka's *The Castle*). Confronted with this insoluble labyrinth (the original universe), man has created by means of culture his own labyrinth, his own planet, Tlön. "How could one do other than submit to Tlön, to the minute and vast evidence of an orderly planet?" asks Borges, to reply: "It is useless to answer that reality is also orderly. Perhaps it is, but in accordance with divine laws—I translate: inhuman laws—which we never quite grasp. Tlön is surely a labyrinth, but it is a labyrinth devised by men, a labyrinth destined to be deciphered by men" (*Labyrinths*, pp. 17–18).

"The First Encyclopedia of Tlön" stands for any encyclopedia, as its parody in the sense that encyclopedias store the sum of information about the world created (or invented) by human culture. The fantastic in Tlön stems from a strategic ruse: the idealist theory, its epistemological premises and figuration, are assumed and presented literally, as if Bishop Berkeley's idea of reality were indeed reality.

Borges is, of course, far from believing that reality can be at all grasped, let alone described. He has given it up long ago, at least as a human possibility. As early as 1932 he wrote in the preface to his second most important volume of essays, *Discusión* (1932), this lapidary statement: "My life is devoid of life and death. From this poverty stems my laborious love for these minutiae" Many years later, in his "Autobiographical Essay" of 1970, he iterated his loyalty to the planet Tlön, that is, to the world of books: "If I were asked to name the chief event of my life, I should say my father's library. In fact, I sometimes think I have never strayed outside that library."

His story "La casa de Asterion" ("The House of Asterion," 1947) can be read as Borges' own metaphor. In it, the Minotaur chooses to stay in the labyrinth where he has been imprisoned: "One afternoon"—he confesses—"I did step into the street; if I returned before night, I did so because of the fear that the faces of the common people inspired in me" *(Labyrinths)*. Confronted with the chaos of the world, Asterion the Minotaur chooses the orderly space he has found in a human construction, Daedalus' labyrinth. Borges has made a similar choice: confronted with the chaos of the world, he has chosen the order of the library, the safety of a decipherable labyrinth. His books grew out of other books. He wrote fiction based on theologies and philosophies, literature founded in literature. He knew that the hard face of reality lingers on every corner of life, but he renounced it, he said, because of its impenetrable nature. Instead, he anchored his writings in the order of the intellect, in the chartable waters of the library. What he wrote about Paul Valéry is applicable to himself: "In a century that adores the chaotic idols of blood, earth, and passion, [he] always preferred the lucid pleasures of thought and the secret adventures of order" ("Valéry as a Symbol," in *Other Inquisitions*).

In an early essay of 1939, before he even wrote his first short stories, Borges laid the foundations of what was to become the edifice of his narrative world: "Let us admit what all idealists admit: the hallucinatory nature of the world. Let us do what no idealist has done: seek unrealities which confirm that nature. We shall find them, I believe, in the antinomies of Kant and in the dialectic of Zeno" ("Avatars of the Tortoise," in *Labyrinths*). Many of his short stories do precisely that: they present unrealities (a man who dreams a man and inserts him into reality, a library of unreadable books, a year contained in one minute) in which the reader recognizes the conceptualization of metaphysics and the hypostases of theology. Yet they are stories, plots in whose sets of events and interplays of characters a resemblance of life as we know it has been conveyed. But it is only a resemblance, since the story aims not so much—like conventional fiction—at capturing a "slice of life" as at advancing an "argumentum theologicum or philosophus."

This strategy evolved from the conviction that "the inventions of philosophy are no less fantastic than those of art," and from a definitive abhorrence of literary realism often equated with the trite, predictable, and fastidious sides of life. It also evolved, as we have seen, from Borges' perception of his own life as lacking any drama worth recording or commenting on, at least as far as fiction is concerned. Any form of knowledge that challenged his skeptical understanding of the world met with his strong disapproval and even condemnation: "The meritorious mission that Valéry performed (and continues to perform) is that he proposed lucidity to men in a basely romantic age, in the melancholy age of . . . dialectical materialism, the age of the augurs of Freud's doctrine and the traffickers in *surréalisme*." Borges indicts and harshly condemmns literary movements (romanticism and surrealism) and forms of thought (Marxism and psychoanalysis) that deal not so much with sheer abstract reasoning (although in a highly abstract fashion), but with questions concerning life: distrust of and revolt against rational order, class order, and ego order. Life as adventure and chance, as struggle and desire, seems to horrify him, and any human effort addressed to exploring or charting the depths of those waters has been met with resistance and frowns. Borges is an intellectual animals, a solipsist locked—like the Minotaur of his story—in a labyrinth of his own construction.

If everyday life was thought of as a swarm of miseries, the fantastic was seen by him as the embodiment of art. The question he faced in attempting to write fiction with "the inventions of philosophy" was how to flesh out those abstractions, how to render them into literature. Since for Borges literature meant "fantastic" or, more precisely, antirealist fiction, it was only natural—given his strong bent for metaphysics—that religious and philosophic ideas would lend him those marvelous and singular elements he considered worthy of becoming literature. But how to go about this process of regeneration? How to turn one system into another?

Pantheism constitutes the axial notion around which his story "El immortal" ("The Immortal," 1949) is built. Borges is not seeking to prove either the merits or the demerits of this doctrine. He knows that the time of this theological relic has past, and that much ink, as well as blood, has been spilt over it. But what if one were to assume its tenets as the true laws governing reality? What if one were to describe life as if pantheism were its underlying principle? The result is a character who through the narrative becomes several characters, an individual who, having been given immortality, can become any individual, born or unborn, dead or alive—Homer, for example, or even the same writer telling the very story that is recording the phenomenon. Borges was repeating the feat accomplished by Leopoldo Lugones, his predecessor in Argentina, who wrote fiction with bits and pieces of theosophical doctrine. Lugones felt strongly that theosophy, in its various creeds, was fantastic enough to become fiction by means of his simply quoting or paraphrasing some of those ideas. Borges expanded on this idea. He probed the fantastic appeal of other religions, and he ventured into the more variegated territory of philosophy. Science becomes fiction when the yet unfulfilled potentials of the former are rendered factual by the writer's imagination. The accomplishments of science have been so magnified, so hyperbolically aggrandized—in the same way that the edge of a used razor blade becomes a mountain range when seen under the microscope—that they generate a new space whose scale is popularly referred to as "sci-fi."

The reality of scientific accomplishment has been turned into the unreality of fiction. The narrative process followed by Borges, although not quite the same, is similar: by transferring the dogmas of religion and the "proven truths" of philosophy from their respective systems to the realm of fiction, he has made those dogmas and truths become fictional. Semiotics has shown that each human endeavor, each discipline seeking to establish and organize human knowledge constitutes a system of signs that can operate and "make sense" only within the bounds of its own framework. Transfer those same signs that are part of a given system to a different one and the "sense" becomes non-sense, their relevance loses ground, their "reality" turns into unreality or, what amounts to the same, into fiction.

But then, Ernst Cassirer has already warned us that all forms of human knowledge are but "arbitrary schemes, airy fabrics of the mind, a kind of fiction." "A fiction," he adds, "that recommends itself by its usefulness, but must not be measured by any strict standard of truth, if it is not to melt away into nothingness" (*Language and Myth*, pp. 7–8).

Borges seems to have understood and accepted this conclusion, hence his insistence on defining himself as "a skeptic who turns that respected system of perplexities we call philosophy into the forms of literature." Transferring the signs of one system to another—doctrines from theology to the plots of literature—defines an operation rhetoricians call *hypallage*. The figure designates "a change in the relation of words whereby a word, instead of agreeing with the word it logically qualifies, is made to agree grammatically with another word ('Kindred strife of men' for 'Strife of kindred men')." Borges has made frequent use of this stylistic device in his own prose, but the rhetorical figure also defines a narrative strategy by means of which the relation of two systems, philosophy and fiction, has been changed, and one idea, instead of agreeing with the system it logically qualifies, has been made to agree grammatically with another system.

In religion, pantheism is in a logical as well as a grammatical relation with its system. Switch pantheism to a different system, that of literature, and it becomes fiction (grammatical relation), but fiction, in turn, acquires a new urgency borrowed from religion. This new relation establishes a link that, if it is not logical in the conventional sense, elicits nevertheless a different kind of logic contained in the notion that religious ideas are more inventive, and even more fantastic than the inventions of fiction. By exploring the philosophical possibilities of fiction, Borges has also dramatized the fictive nature of philosophy, and vice versa—by positing the fantastic nature of philosophy, he was able to discover the philosophical possibilities of fantastic literature.

But since literature is not philosophy, and since the laws controlling one system are different from those governing the other, Borges had to acclimatize his borrowings from philosophy and religion to the requirements of fiction. He had to bestow on those ideas and beliefs a fictive reality appealing to his reader. Sometimes this was achieved through a strong and well-developed plot; at other times, through the beauty of his prose and the pleasures of his style; at still other times, by means of exact and symmetrical structures and labyrinthine patterns (mirrors, Chinese boxes, Russian dolls); and on occasion, by resorting to architecture. In most instances, the architecture tends to emphasize the abnormal. The deliberate intention is to underline the monstrous nature of those narrative environments where a fantastic event is occurring or is about to occur.

Architecture participates in this effort to envelop a given notion or belief—immortality, for example—in weird clothes. Immortality is an idea as old as mankind, yet one thinks of it as realistically untenable. To make it believable, not as a theory or doctrine but as an event, Borges followed the advice given in the classic Shakespearean formula:

. . . one fire burns out another's burning;
   One pain is less'ned by another's anguish;
Turn giddy, and be holp by backward turning;
   One desperate grief cures with another's languish.
Take thou some new infection to thy eye,
And the rank poison of the old will die.
                              (*Romeo and Juliet*, I, 2)

Likewise, Borges seems to be saying that a fantastic environment lends credibility to an otherwise incredible event; the unreality of a singular architecture induces the reader to accept as more real the other-

wise uncanny or too intellectual nature of the story. Borges is fully aware of this principle of compensation. When he sought to explain the magic produced by the confrontation of two events, one real and one unreal, and its effect on the reader, he asked at the close of his essay "Magias parciales del *Quixote*" ("Partial Enchantments of the *Quixote*, 1949):

> Why does it make us uneasy to know that the map is within the map and the thousand and one nights are within the book of *A Thousand and One Nights*? Why does it disquiet us to know that Don Quixote is a reader of the *Quixote* and Hamlet is a spectator of *Hamlet*? I believe I have found the answer: those inversions suggest that if the characters in a story can be readers or spectators, then we, their readers or spectators, can be fictitious.
>
> (in *Other Inquisitions*)

Early in the essay he noted that Miguel de Cervantes "delights in fusing the objective and the subjective, the world of the reader and the world of the book." Borges shares this delight and this play of reversibility. He mixes, in his fiction, apocryphal books with authentic ones, fictive characters with real ones, bogus authors with true ones, historic events with invented ones. The effect is similar to the one noted regarding Cervantes: the reader loses his grip as to what is and what is not real. Pantheism, or for that matter any other reputed doctrine or theory, is presented as fantastic and, vice versa, the fantastic situation narrated in the story takes on a transcendental aura elicited by the doctrine.

Architecture plays a similar role in his stories: it reinforces the fantastic intent to compensate for the intellectual indulgence of the story. Immortality and pantheism are abstract categories, but in the story "El immortal" they resolve themselves in narrative terms. To undergo this change, a literary machinery—of which architecture is only a piece—has been put together. If immortality is no longer an intellectualization but a "living experience," how do immortals live? What kind of emotions and feelings do they have? In what type of dwellings do they live? How are their cities?

With the exception of the palace, the city goes undescribed. Yet, what the reader has been told is enough to allow him to picture it as a structure befitting Immortals, a city where nothing needs to be functional or even beautiful since these are human, and therefore mortal concepts. A city of Immortals, on the other hand, forgoes all finality and purpose, all meaning and order, since—as Borges explains—"in an infinite period of time, all things happen to all men." From which it follows that "all our acts are just, but they are also indifferent. There are no moral or intellectual merits."

Borges' City is a flight from human reality. It is an exploration of what an architectural space for Immortals is like, and, as such, it only induces us to accept our own world, if not as the best of all possible worlds, at least as the one where human life has been carved to conform to its hard reality. The dehumanized architecture of the City is a direct consequence of its inhuman dwellers:

> Death . . . makes men precious and pathetic. . . . every act they execute may be their last. . . . Everything among the mortals has the value of the irretrievable and the perilous. Among the Immortals, on the other hand, every act (and every thought) is the echo of others. . . . There is nothing that is not as if lost in a maze of indefatigable mirrors. Nothing can happen only once, nothing is preciously precarious. The elegiacal, the serious, the ceremonial, do not hold for the Immortals.
> (*Labyrinths*, pp. 115–116)

The implication is clear: the City of Immortals is a negation of human life. Its monstrous architecture is but a reflection of immortality as an inhuman condition. "La biblioteca de Babel" ("The Library of Babel," 1941) offers another example of this type of dehumanized architecture. The "Infinite Library" is not, cannot be, a human creation. How could it be if its books are unreadable, at least by human beings? Since the story opens with the phrase "The universe (which others call the Library)," we know from the beginning that the library is a metaphor for the universe: its stairways are abysmal, its distances remote, its books impenetrable, its hexagons infinite. The conclusion advanced in "Tlön, Uqbar, Orbis Tertius" is iterated here: the Library is a divine creation and, as such, it is inaccessible to a human mind. If it has an order, its order is in accordance with inhuman laws no human can decipher.

These instances illustrate that for Borges there are two basic types of architecture: one, the product of God, and one that is built by humans. Both have their laws and embody a certain order, but while the former is a space created by a superbeing and therefore meant to accommodate the mind and the presence of this superior creature, the latter is a human space tailored and suited to human beings. The story "La casa de Asterion," as anticipated, best dramatizes this duality. It recreates the legend of the Minotaur as told by Apollodorus. Borges hides the identity of the monster until the very last line of the narrative, but throughout it there are clear indications and hints that the narrator of the story is the mythological Minotaur. To justify the rewriting of this ancient myth, Borges patterns his story after the riddle as a literary form. This approach alone would have been insufficient to warrant the retelling of an old story if it were not for the fact that the myth has been infused with new meaning. Pierre Menard, Borges' character from the story of the same name, did the same: he rewrote Cervantes' *Don Quixote* in the twentieth century, and while his text was identical to Cervantes', Menard's, Borges adds, was infinitely richer.

Borges has no qualms in rewriting old stories. Furthermore, he believes that since the storehouse of stories has long ago been emptied, a writer's task is to retell old ones. Retelling, of course, is not repeating them. The operation has been accurately described by modern semiotics: literature is a process by means of which "the content of a former expression becomes the expression of a further or new content." (U. Eco, *A Theory of Semiotics*, 1976, p. 55). In Borges' version of Apollodorus' legend, the new content lies in the confrontation between a divine labyrinth (the world) and a human one (Daedalus' construction). What this confrontation tells us is that Daedalus' labyrinth is a human architecture, a product of culture and, as such, an environment where the Minotaur—a metaphor for man—can find his habitat and one that he can understand and accept as his way of living in the world. Beyond this human construction, there are the fourteen seas and the fourteen temples—Nature, the cosmic labyrinth created by gods, which terrifies Asterion and forces him to return to his own labyrinth where he can live and even enjoy some moments of happiness. In that human labyrinth, he has found an alternative to the other one, an alternative to infinity and chaos, a human alternative.

Borges' fiction seems to pivot round these two poles: men and gods, the human and the inhuman, culture and Nature. But culture, being an artificial product of humankind, stands not so much for what man or woman is, as for what he or she should be. What Russell has pointed out about idealism could be said of Borges' world: "It has been constructed by means of logic with little or no appeal to concrete experience." His stories deal with the adventure of human knowledge, with people entangled in a net of philosophical theories and religious doctrines, with the world of culture, but they teach us very little or nothing about the human condition as a flesh and blood experience. Since his narrative world stems from the confines of his personal library, from books (and books are for Borges a great part of his deeper personal experience), he has tempered this intellectual and bookish side of his fiction by means of beautifully crafted plots, elegant symmetries, and dazzling mirror images; also, by means of inversions, he has promoted fiction to the rank of philosophical fantasies, and he has demoted metaphysics and theology to the rank of fiction. He has enacted a similar inversion with respect to architectural spaces. If the world appears in his fiction as an unresolvable labyrinth, as a construction too abstruse and complex to be grasped by humans, as an incomprehensible and uninhabitable architecture (the City of Immortals), the space designed and built by people, the products of human culture, tend to be presented as fantastic or even as phantasmagorical: the house of Asterion (not in relation to the Minotaur but to the man for whom the monster stands), the mysterious tower where a fleeing student meets a despoiler of corpses in "The Approach to al-Mu'tasim," the destroyed temple in "The Circular Ruins," the chaotic book in "The Garden of Forking Paths," the symmetrical and "infinite" house in "Death and the Compass," the strange prison in "La escritura del Dios" ("The Handwriting of God," 1949), the basement in Carlos Argentino's house with its iridescent Aleph, and the labyrinth in "Abenjacán el Bojarí, muerto en su Laberito" ("Ibn Hakkan al-Bokhari, Dead in His Labyrinth," 1952)—all these structures can be included in a catalog of eerie architecture with captions provided by Borges' stories. Under the labyrinth built by Daedalus one would read: "All parts of the house are repeated many times, any place is another place. There is no one pool, courtyard, drinking trough, manger; the mangers, drinking troughs, courtyards, pools are fourteen (infinite) in number. The house is the same size as the world; or rather it is the world" ("The House of Asterion," in *Labyrinths*).

The tower presented in "The Approach to al-Mu'tasim" is none other than a dakhma or "Tower of Silence" where the Parsees in Bombay dispose of their dead. Although Borges chose not to identify this construction, he has given enough information to warn the alert reader: the student "seeks refuge in the [circular] tower. He climbs an iron ladder . . . and on the flat roof, which has a blackish pit in the middle, comes upon a squalid man in a squatting position, urinating vigorously by the light of the moon. The man confides to him that his profession is stealing gold teeth from the white-shrouded corpses that the Parsis leave on the roof of the tower."

Of the ruined temple where a magician arrives to dream a man, Borges writes: "The circular opening [was] watched over by a stone tiger, or horse, which once was the color of fire and is now the color of ash. This opening is a temple which was destroyed ages ago by flames, which the swampy wilderness later desecrated, and whose god no longer receives the reverence of men" ("The Circular Ruins").

Of the infinite "Garden of Forking Paths" one character says: "After more than a hundred years . . . Ts'ui Pên must have said once: *I am withdrawing to write a book*. And another time: *I am withdrawing to construct a labyrinth*. Every one imagined two works; to no one did it occur that the book and the maze were one and the same thing" (*Labyrinths*). And so on with other buildings mentioned in other stories.

These are all products of human manufacture, spaces and structures made to accommodate human life, but in order to compete with divine spaces and construction they have to be dehumanized and made to look inhuman. Why compete with gods? Because for Borges, life in its everyday flow, in its struggles and passions, in its daily pains and joys, miseries and accomplishments, failures and successes, is too trite, too poor, too uninteresting to merit literary attention. For him, the intellect is the true adventure, the mind is the true passion, the world is a library, and life is but a dream (at least in literary terms). He has, consequently, avoided human experience in favor of intellectual knowledge. He has maintained an aloof attitude toward things too human and he has denounced "the tendency of modern literature to reveal men's weaknesses and to delight in their unhappiness and guilt." Instead he has sought a more heroic side of human nature, one that brings people closer to gods, in deeds as well as in intelligence. Hence his preference for the epic. Hence his exaltation of human knowledge. As the builders of the Tower of Babel sought to reach for their god in order to become his equal, human labyrinths too are the counterpart to divine ones because, as Borges says in his poem "The Golem," man too "yearns to know that which God knows." Architecture is, therefore, one more pawn in this game with Heaven, an additional stretch in this race with the unattainable. Human spaces are like scientific pursuits in relation to science fiction: too much part of the pragmatic world and, consequently, undeserving of any attention. The challenge lies in the purely intellectual, in that sphere of the imagination uncontaminated yet by the imprint of human hands.

Because he saw writing as rewriting, and because he showed—in theory as well as in practice—that "one literature differs from another . . . not so much because of the text as for the manner in which it is read," he fascinated structuralists as well as semioticians. Because he concluded in "Pierre Menard" that "Cervantes' text and Menard's are verbally identical, but the second is almost infinitely richer," he dazzled the followers of intertextuality. When he wrote in 1953 that since Homer all metaphors have been recorded, to further add: "This does not mean, of course, that the number of metaphors has been exhausted; the ways of stating or hinting at the terms of a given metaphor are, in fact, endless" (*Historia de la eternidad*, p. 74), he advanced a central tenet in the theory of the Russian formalists, and prompted John Barth to write his now famous essay "Literature of Exhaustion." Finally, because of his invisible and rigorous style, he became—as Carlos Fuentes put it—a sort of father figure of the contemporary Spanish-American novel.

Paradoxically, his literary work is the recasting of

previous texts. In 1945, in a speech he made to thank the Argentine Society of Writers for the honorary prize he was awarded as an apology for his not having received the National Prize for Literature upon the publication of *Ficciones*, he described the core of his creative laboratory. He said:

> For many years I believed I had been raised in a suburb of Buenos Aires. The truth is that I was raised in a garden, behind a long iron fence, and in a library of endless English books. The Palermo of the knife-fights and of the guitar was roaming about the street corners, but those who peopled my mornings and brought enjoyable horror to my evenings were R. L. Stevenson's blind buccaneer, agonizing under the hoofs of the horses, and the traitor who abandoned his friend in the moon, and the time traveler who brought from the future a withered flower, and the genie locked up in Solomon's jug for many centuries, and the Veiled Prophet from Khurasan who concealed his leprosy with a veil of white silk embossed with precious stones. Thirty years have gone by, the house where those fictions have been revealed to me was demolished, I have traveled through a number of European cities, I have forgotten thousands of pages and thousands of irreplaceable human faces, but I am inclined to think that, essentially, I have never stepped out from that library and from that garden. What I did since then, and what I'll continue to do, is simply to weave and unweave stories derived from those early ones.
>
> (*Sur*, July 1945)

In the poetry volume *The Gold of the Tigers* of 1972, he wrote an updated version of that early poetics. In the brief prose entitled "Los cuatro ciclos" ("The Four Cycles"), he reviews four stories. One is about a city under siege and defended by courageous men (the Troy of the Homeric poems); a second is about a return (Ulysses comes back to Ithaca); the third, a variation of the latter, is about a search (Jason and the Golden Fleece, the thirty birds and the Simurg, Ahab and the whale, the heroes of Henry James or Kafka); and the last one is about a sacrifice of a god (Attis, Odin, Christ). Borges then concludes: "Four are the stories. During the time left to us we will continue telling them, transformed" (p. 129). This fictional modus operandi is verifiable throughout most of his stories. The narration becomes a mirror that either inverts or reverts a previous text. Borges was not jesting when he posited the task of literature as that of rewriting old metaphors. In *The New Yorker* magazine (30 October 1965) John Updike said of Borges' essays that "they have a quality I can only call *sealed.*" To further explain: "They are structured likes mazes and, like mirrors, they reflect back and forth on one another. . . . From his immense reading he has distilled a fervent narrowness. The same parables, the same quotations recur." Where then does Borges' originality lie? Does it amount—as John Barth has suggested—to his having written "original works of literature, the implicit theme of which is the difficulty, perhaps the necessity, of writing original works of literature?" (*The Atlantic,* August 1967). It was Paul de Man who, perhaps, came closer to an answer. De Man dismisses the philosophical nature of his fiction as the possible explanation for his originality. "Borges"—he writes—"should be read with expectations closer to those one brings to Voltaire's *conte philosophique* than to the nineteenth-century novel." And then he adds: "He differs, however, from his eighteenth-century antecedents in that the subject of the stories is the creation of style itself. . . . *His stories are about the style in which they are written*" ("A Modern Master," *New York Review of Books,* 19 November 1964). Even Borges' technique par excellence, that of fabricating his writings from other writings, is an appropriation from Thomas de Quincey.

Other critics have attested Borges' marriage not with the world of actual experience but with that of intellectual propositions. In the 2 May 1971 *New York Times Book Review,* Alfred Kazin underscores the solipsistic bent of his writings. "Borges"—he says—"has built his work, and I suspect his life itself, out of the same effort to make a home in his own mind. . . . He certainly does not put us in close touch with his own country. His Argentina remains a place of dreams. Borges's mind is the realest thing in it" ("Meeting Borges"). George Steiner in *The New Yorker,* 20 June 1970, reminds us that "Borges is a curator at heart." To explain: "He has built an *anti-world,* a perfect, coherent space in which his mind can conjure at will. . . . His inventions move away from the active disarray of life." Patricia Marivale, who has compared Borges' work with Nabokov's, concludes with the following distinction:

"While Nabokov usually dismisses his actors 'into thin air' and returns us to the real world, Borges takes the argument to its conclusion, and perpetually reminds us that both author and reader 'are such stuff / As dreams are made on'" ("The Flaunting of Artifice in V. Nabokov and J. L. Borges." *Wisconsin Studies in Contemporary Literature* 8/1 [1967]). The overall conclusion is inescapable: Borges is a magician with words and a master of artifice. Such is Updike's stance: "Ironic and blasphemous as Borges' hidden message may seem"—he writes—"the texture and method of his creations, though strictly inimitable, answer to a deep need in contemporary fiction—the need to confess the fact of artifice."

Latin American writers such as Gabriel García Marquez, Carlos Fuentes, Ernesto Sabato, Mario Vargas Llosa, and others have acknowledged their debt to Borges in terms of a language Spanish literature did not have before him. Julio Cortázar best summarized the extent of that debt: "The great lesson Borges taught us was neither a lesson in themes nor in contents or techniques. It was a lesson in writing, an attitude. The attitude of a man who, when writing a sentence, has very carefully thought not which adjective to add, but which one to suppress. His attitude towards the written page was the attitude of a Mallarmé, of extreme rigor and precision" (Ernesto González Bermejo, *Conversaciones con Cortázar*).

Did Borges know that his legacy would be exactness and rigor in language, that is, a code rather than a message, a style rather than substance, aesthetic artifacts cut off from the real world? He not only knew it, he was inflexible in defending that view. In a 1968 interview, he put it squarely:

The "Parable of the Palace" is . . . about art existing in its own plane but not being given to deal with reality. As far as I can recall it, if the poem is perfect then there's no need for the palace. I mean if art is perfect, then the world is superfluous. . . . And besides, I think that the poet never can cope with reality. So I think of art and nature, well, nature as the world, as being two different worlds.

(R. Burgin, *Conversations with Jorge Luis Borges,* p. 80)

Alfred Kazin was right: the most real thing in Borges' work *is* his mind. Borges knew it and wanted it to be that way. In 1960, he closed his miscellaneous volume *Dreamtigers* with an epilogue in which he confessed: "Few things have happened to me, and I have read many. Or rather, few things have happened to me more worth remembering than Schopenhauer's thought or the music of England's words."

On 14 June 1986, Jorge Luis Borges died in Geneva, Switzerland, where he had been living for three months.

SELECTED BIBLIOGRAPHY

Editions

Poetry

Fervor de Buenos Aires. Buenos Aires, 1923.
Luna de enfrente. Buenos Aires, 1925.
Cuaderno San Martín. Buenos Aires, 1929.
Poemas (1922–1943). Buenos Aires, 1943.
Poemas (1923–1953). Buenos Aires, 1954.
Poemas (1923–1958). Buenos Aires, 1958.
Obra poética (1923–1964). Buenos Aires, 1964.
Para las seis cuerdas. Buenos Aires, 1965.
Obra poética (1923–1966). Buenos Aires, 1966.
Obra poética (1923–1967). Buenos Aires, 1967.
El otro, el mismo. Buenos Aires, 1969.
Elogio de la sombra. Buenos Aires, 1969.
El oro de los tigres. Buenos Aires, 1972.
La rosa profunda. Buenos Aires, 1975.
La moneda de hierro. Buenos Aires, 1976.
Historia de la noche. Buenos Aires, 1977.
La cifra. Buenos Aires, 1981.
Los conjurados. Madrid, 1985.

Fiction

Historia universal de la infamia. Buenos Aires, 1935, 1954.
El jardín de senderos que se bifurcan. Buenos Aires, 1942.
Ficciones (1935–1944). Buenos Aires, 1944; 2nd, augmented ed. 1956.
El Aleph. Buenos Aires, 1949; 2nd, augmented ed. 1952.
El hacedor. Buenos Aires, 1960.
El informe de Brodie. Buenos Aires, 1970.
El Congreso. Buenos Aires, 1971.
El Libro de Arena. Buenos Aires, 1975.
Veinticinco Agosto 1983 y otros cuentos. Madrid, 1983.

Essays

Inquisiciones. Buenos Aires, 1925.
El tamaño de mi esperanza. Buenos Aires, 1926.
El idioma de los argentinos. Buenos Aires, 1928.
Evaristo Carriego. Buenos Aires, 1930; 2nd, augmented ed. 1955.
Discusión. Buenos Aires, 1932; 2nd, augmented ed. 1957.
Historia de la eternidad. Buenos Aires, 1936; 2nd, augmented ed. 1953.
Otras inquisiciones (1937–1952). Buenos Aires, 1952; 2nd, augmented ed. 1960.
Textos cautivos; ensayos y reseñas en "El Hogar" (1936–1939). Buenos Aires, 1952; 2nd, augmented ed. 1960; 1986.
Prólogos; con un prólogo de prólogos. Buenos Aires, 1975.
Borges oral. Buenos Aires, 1979.
Siete noches. Buenos Aires, 1980.

Anthologies

Antología personal. Buenos Aires, 1961.
Nueva antología personal. Buenos Aires, 1968.

Collected Works

Obras completas. Buenos Aires, 1974.

Works In Collaboration

With Adolfo Bioy Casares
Seis problemas para don Isidro Parodi. Published under pseudonym H. Bustos Domecq. Buenos Aires, 1942.
Un modelo para la muerte. Published under pseudonym B. Suárez Lynch. Buenos Aires, 1946.
Dos fantasías memorables. Published under pseudonym Bustos Domecq. Buenos Aires, 1946.
Los orilleros. El paraíso de los creyentes. Buenos Aires, 1955. Film scripts.
Crónicas de Bustos Domecq. Buenos Aires, 1967.

With Betina Edelberg
Leopoldo Lugones. Buenos Aires, 1955.

With Margarita Guerrero
El Martín Fierro. Buenos Aires, 1953.
Manual de zoología fantástica. Buenos Aires and Mexico City, 1957.
El libro de los seres imaginarios. Buenos Aires, 1967. Augmented ed. of *Manual de zoología fantástica*.

With Delia Ingenieros
Antiguas literaturas germánicas. Buenos Aires and Mexico City, 1951.

With Luisa Mercedes Levinson
La hermana de Eloísa. Buenos Aires, 1955.

With María Esther Vázquez

Introducción a la literatura inglesa. Buenos Aires, 1965.

Literaturas germánicas medievales. Buenos Aires, 1966. Augmented ed. of *Antiguas literaturas germánicas.*

With Esther Zemborain de Torres

Introducción a la literatura norteamericana. Buenos Aires, 1967.

Anthologies in Collaboration

With Adolfo Bioy Casares

Los mejores cuentos policiales. Buenos Aires, 1943; 2nd, augmented ed. 1951.

Prosa y verso de Francisco de Quevedo. Buenos Aires, 1948.

Cuentos breves y extraordinarios. Buenos Aires, 1955.

Poesía gauchesca. 2 vols. Mexico City, 1955.

Libro del cielo y del infierno. Buenos Aires, 1960.

With Silvina Bullrich Palenque

El compadrito. Su destino, sus barrios, su música. Buenos Aires, 1945; 2nd, augmented ed. 1968.

With Pedro Henríquez Ureña:

Antología clásica de la literatura argentina. Buenos Aires, 1937.

With Adolfo Bioy Casares and Silvina Ocampo:

Antología de la literatura fantástica. Buenos Aires, 1940; 2nd, augmented ed. 1965.

Translations

The Aleph and Other Stories (1933–1969). Edited and translated by Norman Thomas de Giovanni in collaboration with the author. New York, 1970; London, 1971. Contains "Autobiographical Essay."

The Book of the Imaginary Beings (in collaboration with Margarita Guerrero). Revised, enlarged, and translated by Norman Thomas di Giovanni in collaboration with the author. New York, 1969.

The Book of Sand. Translated by Norman Thomas di Giovanni. New York, 1977.

Chronicles of Bustos Domecq (in collaboration with A. Bioy Casares). Translated by Norman Thomas di Giovanni. New York, 1976.

Doctor Brodie's Report. Translated by Norman Thomas di Giovanni. New York, 1972; London, 1974.

Dreamtigers [*El hacedor*]. Translated by Mildred Boyer and Harold Morland. Austin, Tex., 1964.

Evaristo Carriego: A Book About Old-Time Buenos Aires. Translated by Norman Thomas di Giovanni. New York, 1983.

Extraordinary Tales. Edited and translated by Anthony Kerrigan. New York, 1971.

Ficciones. Translated by Anthony Kerrigan et al. New York, 1962. Includes *The Garden of Forking Paths.*

Fictions. Edited by Anthony Kerrigan. London, 1965.

The Gold of the Tigers: Selected Later Poems. Translated by Alastair Reid. New York, 1977. Bilingual edition.

An Introduction to American Literature (in collaboration with Esther Zemborain de Torres). Translated and edited by L. Clark Keating and Robert O. Evans. Lexington, Ky., 1971.

Labyrinths: Selected Stories and Other Writings. Edited by Donald A. Yates and James E. Irby. New York, 1962.

Other Inquisitions 1937–1952. Translated by Ruth L. C. Simms. Austin, Tex., 1964.

A Personal Anthology. Edited by Anthony Kerrigan. New York, 1967.

In Praise of Darkness. Translated by Norman Thomas di Giovanni. New York, 1974. Bilingual edition.

Selected Poems 1923–1967. Translated by Norman Thomas di Giovanni et al. New York and Boston, 1972; 2nd ed. New York, 1973. Bilingual edition.

Six Problems for Don Isidro Parodi. Translated by Norman Thomas di Giovanni. New York, 1981.

A Universal History of Infamy. Translated by Norman Thomas de Giovanni. New York, 1972; London, 1973.

Biographical and Critical Studies

Books

Agheana, Ion T. *The Prose of Jorge Luis Borges; Existentialism and the Dynamics of Surprise.* New York, 1984.

Aizenberg, Edna. *El tejedor del Aleph; Biblia, Kábala y judaísmo en Borges.* Madrid, 1986.

Alazraki, Jaime. *Jorges Luis Borges.* New York and London, 1971. Columbia Essays on Modern Writers, 57.

——. *La prosa narrativa de Jorge Luis Borges.* Madrid, 1968; 3rd, enlarged ed. 1983.

——. *Versiones. Inversiones. Reversiones: El espejo como modelo estructural del relato en los cuentos de Borges.* Madrid, 1977.

——, ed. *El escritor y la crítica: Borges.* Madrid, 1976; 3rd reprint 1986.

——, ed. *Critical Essays on Jorge Luis Borges.* Boston, 1987.

——, ed. *Borges and the Kabbalah and Other Essays on His Fiction and Poetry.* New York, 1988.

Balderston, Daniel. *El precursor velado: R.L. Stevenson en la obra de Borges.* Buenos Aires, 1985.

Barrenechea, Ana María. *Borges the Labyrinth Maker*. New York, 1965.

Barrientos, Juan José. *Borges y la imaginación*. Mexico City, 1986.

Bastos, María Luisa. *Borges ante la crítica argentina 1923–1960*. Buenos Aires, 1974.

Bell-Villada, Gene H. *Borges and His Fiction: A Guide to His Mind and Art*. Chapel Hill, N.C., 1981.

Berveiller, Michel. *Le cosmopolitisme de Jorge Luis Borges*. Paris, 1973.

Bosco, María Angélica. *Borges y los otros*. Buenos Aires, 1967.

Cédola, Estela. *Borges o la coincidencia de los opuestos*. Buenos Aires, 1987.

Cheselka, Paul. *The Poetry and Poetics of Jorges Luis Borges*. New York, 1987.

Christ, Ronald J. *The Narrow Act: Borges' Art of Allusion*. New York, 1969.

Cohen, J.M. *Jorge Luis Borges*. Edinburgh, 1973.

Cortínez, Carlos, ed. *Simply a Man of Letters: Papers of a Symposium on Jorge Luis Borges*. Orono, Me., 1982.

————, ed. *Borges the Poet*. Fayetteville, Ark., 1986.

Covizzi, Lenira Marques. *O insólito em Gimarães Rosa e Borges*. São Paulo, 1978.

Cozarinsky, Edgardo. *Borges y el cine*. Buenos Aires, 1974.

Crossan, John Dominic. *Raid on the Articulate: Comic Eschatology in Jesus and Borges*. New York, 1976.

Dunham, Lowell, and Ivar Ivask, eds. *The Cardinal Points of Borges*. Norman, Okla., 1971.

Echavarría, Arturo. *Lengua y literatura de Borges*. Barcelona, 1983.

Ferrer, Manuel. *Borges y la nada*. London, 1971.

Flores, Ángel, ed. *Expliquémonos a Borges como poeta*. Mexico City, 1984.

Friedman, Mary Lusky. *The Emperor's Kites; A Morphology of Borges' Tales*. Durham, N.C., 1987.

Gertel, Zunilda. *Borges y su retorno a la poesía*. New York, 1967.

Goloboff, Mario G. *Leer Borges*. Buenos Aires, 1978.

Gutiérrez Girardot, Rafael. *Jorge Luis Borges: Ensayo de interpretación*. Madrid, 1959.

Ibarra, Néstor. *Borges et Borges*. Paris, 1969.

Lagos, Ramona. *Jorge Luis Borges 1923–1980; laberintos del espíritu, interjecciones del cuerpo*. Barcelona, 1986.

McMurray, George R. *Jorge Luis Borges*. New York, 1980.

Madrid, Lelia. *Cervantes y Borges: La inversión de los signos*. Madrid, 1987.

Marco, Joaquín, ed. *Asedio a Jorge Luis Borges*. Madrid, 1982.

Massuh, Gabriela. *Borges: Una estética del silencio*. Buenos Aires, 1980.

Matamoro, Blas. *Jorge Luis Borges o el juego trascendente*. Buenos Aires, 1971.

Molloy, Sylvia. *Las letras de Borges*. Buenos Aires, 1979.

Murillo, Luis A. *The Cyclical Night: Irony in James Joyce and Jorge Luis Borges*. Cambridge, Mass., 1968.

Newman, Charles, and Mary Kinzie, eds. *Prose for Borges*. Evanston, Ill., 1974.

Orgambide, Pedro. *Borges y su pensamiento político*. Mexico City, 1978.

Paoli, Roberto. *Borges: Percorsi di significato*. Messina and Florence, Italy, 1977.

Pellicer, Rosa. *Borges: el estilo de la eternidad*. Zaragoza, 1987.

Pérez, Alberto Julián. *Poética de la prosa de Jorge Luis Borges. Hacia una crítica bakhtiana de la literatura*. Madrid, 1986.

Pickenhayn, Jorge Oscar. *Borges: Álgebra y fuego*. Buenos Aires, 1982.

Prieto, Adolfo. *Borges y la nueva generacíon*. Buenos Aires, 1954.

Rest, Jaime. *El laberinto del universo: Borges y el pensamiento nominalista*. Buenos Aires, 1976.

Rivas, José Andrés. *Alrededor de la obra de Jorge Luis Borges*. Buenos Aires, 1984.

Rodríguez Monegal, Emir. *Jorge Luis Borges: A Literary Biography*. New York, 1978.

Running, Thorpe. *Borges' Ultraist Movement and Its Poets*. Lathrup Village, Mich., 1981.

Shaw, D. L. *Critical Guides to Spanish Texts: Borges' Ficciones*. London, 1976.

Sosnowski, Saúl. *Borges y la Cábala*. Buenos Aires, 1976.

Stabb, Martin S. *Jorge Luis Borges*. New York, 1970.

Stark, John. *The Literature of Exhaustion: Borges, Nabokov, and Barth*. Durham, N.C., 1974.

Sturrock, John. *Paper Tigers: The Ideal Fiction of Jorge Luis Borges*. London, 1977.

Sucre, Guillermo. *Borges, el poeta*. Mexico City, 1967; Caracas and Monte Avila, 1968.

Vázquez, María Esther. *Borges: Imágenes, memorias, diálogos*. Caracas, 1977.

Wheelock, Carter. *The Mythmaker: A Study of Motif and Symbol in the Short Stories of Jorge Luis Borges*. Austin, Tex., 1969.

Yates, Donald A. *Jorge Luis Borges: Life, Work, and Criticism*. Fredericton, Canada, 1985.

Special Issues Of Academic Journals

L'Herne. Jorge Luis Borges (Paris; 1964).

Iberoromania. 3 (Erlangen, West Germany; May 1975).

Modern Fiction Studies 19/3. (West Lafayette, Ind.; Autumn 1973).

Revista Iberoamericana 43/100–101 (Pittsburgh, Pa.; July–December 1977). "40 Inquisiciones sobre Borges."

Review 73 (Center for Inter-American Relations) (Spring, 1973).

Interviews

Alifano, Roberto. *Twenty-four Conversations with Borges.* Various translators. Housatonic, Me., 1984

Barnstone, Willis, ed. *Borges at Eighty: Conversations.* Bloomington, Ind., 1982.

Barone, Orlando. *Borges-Sábato: Diálogos.* Buenos Aires, 1976.

Burgin, Richard. *Conversations with Jorge Luis Borges.* New York, 1969.

Carrizo, Antonio. *Borges el memorioso: Conversaciones de Jorge Luis Borges con Antonio Carrizo.* Mexico City and Buenos Aires, 1982.

Charbonnier, Georges. *Entretiens avec Jorge Luis Borges.* Paris, 1967.

Ferrari, Osvaldo. *Borges en diálogo. Conversaciones.* Buenos Aires, 1985.

Giovanni, Norman Thomas di, Daniel Halpern, and Frank MacShane, eds. *Borges on Writing.* New York, 1973.

Guibert, Rita. *Seven Voices.* New York, 1973.

Milleret, Jean de. *Entrevistas con Jorge Luis Borges.* Caracas, 1970.

Sorrentino, Fernando. *Seven Conversations with Jorge Luis Borges.* Translated by Clark M. Zlotchew. Troy, N.Y., 1982.

Vázquez, María Esther. *Borges: Imágenes, memorias, diálogos.* Caracas, 1977.

Bibliographies

Becco, Horacio Jorge. *Jorge Luis Borges: Bibliografía total 1923–1973.* Buenos Aires, 1973.

Foster, David William. *Jorge Luis Borges: An Annotated Primary and Secondary Bibliography.* New York, 1984.

Dictionaries

Matamoro, Blas. *Diccionario privado de Jorge Luis Borges.* Madrid, 1979.

Stortini, Carlos R. *El diccionario de Borges.* Buenos Aires, 1986.

Miguel Ángel Asturias

(1899–1974)

Jean Franco

Miguel Ángel Asturias was the first Latin American novelist to win the Nobel Prize. When the award was announced in 1967, few people outside the Hispanic world had read any of his writing, and even today his novels are not as widely read as those of Gabriel García Márquez or Manuel Puig. This is not only because his novels are written in a highly complex language that employs all the linguistic resources of poetry as well as the narrative form, but also because they are based on indigenous mythic structures.

Critic have held very diverse opinions of Asturias' writing, some of them, like the novelist Mario Vargas Llosa, describing it as "primitive" (although he would later modify this opinion) and others, like Ariel Dorfman and the British critic Gerald Martin, seeing Asturias' narrative as the paradigm of modern Latin American fiction.

Asturias was born on 19 October 1899, a significant period for his native Guatemala; in 1898, Manuel Estrada Cabrera had instituted a bizarre form of personal dictatorship that lasted until 1920. The dictatorship made a deep impression on Asturias. His father, a lawyer, and his mother, a schoolteacher, left the capital in 1903 for fear of persecution, settling in the remote town of Salamá. Until 1907, Asturias lived in the provinces, where he became familiar with the indigenous peoples who formed the bulk of the peasantry. However, to complete his schooling, he returned to the capital, Guatemala City. His childhood among the rural peasantry and his adolescence, spent largely in an environment permeated by an atmosphere of oppressive fear, provided the material from which nearly all his novels are drawn.

Asturias began writing when he was a student. The first draft of a story that he would later expand into the novel *El señor presidente* (1946; originally translated as *The President* in England, the book carried the original Spanish title in the U.S. edition of the translation) dates from 1922, two years after Estrada Cabrera's downfall. Critics have been acutely aware of the importance of biographical data for the study of Asturias' work, and many have been tempted to decipher his works in relation to key biographical and historical events of his formative years. Such biographical criticism has been encouraged by the fact that well-known Guatemalan and Latin American personalities can be recognized in the characters of *El Señor Presidente*. Furthermore, the events mythically presented in the novel *Hombres de maíz* (*Men of Maize*, 1949) have been shown to be closely related to the crucial historical periods through which Asturias lived as a young man. The earthquake of 1917, which destroyed most of Guatemala City, figures prominently in his prose poem *Tres de cuatro soles* (Three Out of Four Suns, 1977) and is also mentioned in *Mulata de tal* (*Mulata* [Mulatto], 1963) and *El alhajadito* (*The Bejeweled Boy*, 1961). His novel *Viernes de dolores* (Good Friday, 1972) takes place in 1920 and describes the student movement in which Asturias participated and which finally helped to bring an end to the dictatorship of Estrada Cabrera. Yet these biographical data do not provide the only, or even an adequate, reading of the novels, which challenge in a profound way the ethnocentrism that has marginalized Latin American cultures, whether indigenous or nonindigenous.

It is important to stress that Asturias' literary and political formation occurred at an important period in Latin America. The Mexican Revolution gave rise to major social reforms in that country in the 1920's, and a strong student movement that began in Córdoba, Argentina, and rapidly spread to other parts of Latin America, including Guatemala, inspired young intellectuals like Asturias to try to break down centuries-old class stratifications. To that end, Asturias helped to found the People's University of Guatemala in 1922. During this period, he was at work on his dissertation, "El problema social del indio" (The Social Problem of the Indian), which was completed in 1923. The dissertation, rooted in the positivism that still predominated in the social sciences, described the degeneration of the indigenous peoples, focusing on the alcoholism and venereal disease that afflicted the communities, and advocated measures to incorporate the Indians, as citizens, into modern society.

Like many of the young intellectuals of the period, Asturias believed that the backwardness of the nation stemmed from the marginalization of the illiterate rural peasantry and the domination of the country by a comparatively small, literate population made up of members of the urban professional classes and absentee landowners. Class stratification was aggravated by racial difference, since the peasant population was composed largely of the descendants of the once-powerful Mayas, now fragmented into linguistically diverse groups. For these people, the family was an economic, cultural, and social unit whose traditions were passed from generation to generation through oral transmission and ritual. Influenced by the nine-

teenth-century idea of progress, the young Asturias believed that the indigenous populations should be "modernized" and incorporated into national life, although his interest in indigenous culture would later lead him to recognize autochthonous values and to perceive that their survival was threatened by modernization.

Asturias' interest in indigenous societies led him, in 1924, to study in Paris with the anthropologist Georges Raynaud; during this period, his positivist theories on the indigenous peasantry underwent radical revision. During his stay in the French capital, where he remained until 1933, he translated the Mayan "bible," the *Popol Vuh* (Book of Counsel) and the *Annals of the Xahil* (the Cakchiquels) into Spanish, not from the original indigenous languages (which he did not speak), but from Raynaud's French translations. These studies provided him with the knowledge of indigenous myth that would later be incorporated into his novels.

Asturias studied ethnography in Paris at a particularly crucial period, one in which poets such as Michel Leiris and writers like Georges Bataille and Henri Michaux were actively challenging the hierarchies on which the dichotomized concepts of civilized and savage were based. In Paris, Asturias also came to know many of the leading figures of the literary vanguard, including Paul Eluard and James Joyce. He experimented with surrealist texts and wrote his *Leyendas de Guatemala* (Legends of Guatemala, 1930) for which Paul Valéry wrote an introduction. Though he declared that these legends were handed down to him by his grandmother, they have little in common with the sketches of popular life and customs that filled the pages of newspapers and journals in Latin America. They are not collections of existing legends but re-creations of mythic beings that foreshadow the techniques he would use in *Men of Maize* and *Mulata*.

Asturias returned to Guatemala in 1933, having written not only *Leyendas de Guatemala* but also a novella, *The Bejeweled Boy*, and a novel, *El Señor Presidente*, although these would not be published until much later. Guatemala was once again living under a dictatorship, that of Jorge Ubico. Until the overthrow of the dictatorship in 1944, Asturias worked as a journalist and in 1937 founded a radio news program, the "Diario del aire" (The Radio

Newspaper). Although he did not participate in the movement that brought President Juan José Arévalo to power in 1944, he was appointed cultural attaché in Mexico during Arévalo's presidency. Indeed, he lived abroad during much of the next decade. Although Asturias, unlike other intellectuals, lived on the margins of this revolution, the political events affected his work. He wrote novels of social protest— the so-called banana trilogy—and after the overthrow of President Jacobo Arbenz, a denunciatory novel, *Weekend en Guatemala* (Weekend in Guatemala, 1956).

After the fall of Arbenz, Asturias spent several years in Buenos Aires. His later years, however, were not without controversy, partly because he accepted the position of ambassador to Paris in the government of Julio C. Méndez Montenegro; a fierce war against the guerrilla opposition led to serious human-rights abuses on the part of the government. He was awarded the Nobel Prize in literature in 1967 when still serving as ambassador. His final years were spent in Madrid, where he died on 9 June 1974.

Though much of his fiction is inspired by political themes, Asturias believed the writer to be "above the combat," answering to longer-term commitments than those of the state. He liked to think of himself as the prophet, or "great tongue," of his nation, a man whose power with words gave him a special place in society. Even his most politically committed writing is tinged with poetry, just as his most mythic writing responds to political and social questions.

Asturias' contribution to Latin American literature is twofold. He pioneered "myth creation" as a narrative device, a procedure that would be adopted by many later writers, notably Carlos Fuentes. And having lived in Paris at the height of the surrealist movement, he was one of the first Latin American writers to grasp the significance of surrealism not as a style but as a perception of reality. Nevertheless, in an interview with Manuel M. Azaña and Claude Mie, he made a distinction between his French surrealist experiments—for instance, a text called "la barba provisional" (the provisional beard), which he published in *Les temps modernes*—and his novels, in which "surrealism acquires a completely magical and very different character. It is not an intellectual attitude but a vital attitude of the Indian, whose primitive, childlike mentality mingles the real and the imaginary, the real and dream." As his reference to the "childlike mentality" of the Indian shows, Asturias had not completely emancipated himself from positivism. Nor can his novels be read as mere reflections of the indigenous world. Rather, they represent mythic constructions of his own that employ his personal interpretations of indigenous lore.

The novel on which Asturias' reputation stands is *El Señor Presidente,* which many critics hold to be a coded novel of the Estrada Cabrera dictatorship. The seed of the book is found in a very early story, "Los mendigos políticos" (The Political Beggars), written in 1922, after the overthrow of Estrada Cabrera. When he began serious work on the novel, Asturias first gave it the title "Tohil," the name of a Mayan deity of fire and destruction, a deity who, like the main character, demanded human sacrifice. Though he had substantially completed the novel in 1932, Asturias made other significant modifications and additions before its final publication in 1946. Asturias gave the dates of the novel at the end of the first edition as "Guatemala, December 1922, Paris, November 1925, and 8 of December 1932," which suggests that, though started in his positivist period, the text underwent considerable modifications after his stay in Paris. In an important essay included in the introduction to the Spanish 1978 edition of *El Señor Presidente,* Gerald Martin discusses some additions made after 1932 that not only flesh out the most sympathetic person in the novel, Camila, but also offer significant clues to Asturias' view of writing.

While the novel relies on historical figures and personalities from the period of Estrada Cabrera, its innovative language owes much to the influence of cinema and of surrealism. For this reason, it is rightly considered a prototype of the "new" Latin American novel. It is also the first "new novel" to go beyond realism and attempt to produce "from the inside," as it were, the effects of the "culture of fear" created by totalitarian dictatorships. Though later novelists such as García Márquez in *El otoño del patriarca* (The Autumn of the Patriarch,* 1975) and Augusto Roa Bastos in *Yo, el supremo* (I, the Supreme, 1974) found solutions to the problem of depicting a state that is inseparable from the person of the dictator, Asturias can be said to have inaugurated the modern treatment of the theme.

Though the novel is structured chronologically, Asturias uses a poetic language, with semantic patternings and associations that cannot be reduced to narrative causality. The opening sentence, which begins with the words "Alumbra, lumbre de alumbre, Luzbel de piedralumbre!"—roughly translated as "Light up, light of fire, Lucifer of flintstone fire"—cannot be easily rendered into English, since the Spanish words suggest in their sound the tolling of heavy cathedral bells and make punning allusions to fire, light, the theft of fire, sacrifice, birth, and Satanic rebellion—all of which are themes interwoven in the novel. The novel also presents a total universe, one in which the rules of good and evil have been created by the supreme power, the President. This universe allows for the subversion of power, which occurs beyond the control of the "rationality" of the totalitarian state.

The events recounted in the novel center on an elaborate plan devised by the President's favorite, Miguel Ángel (known as "Angel Face") to save Camila, a general's daughter, from the vengeance that has fallen on her family. However, all personal acts of freedom or initiative eventually become manipulated in the master plot, which is always organized and controlled by the President. Angel Face is a Lucifer rebelling against the god of the state, and like Lucifer, he falls swiftly as soon as his will differs from that of the all-powerful being, the President. The state machine converts the entire city into one vast, all-seeing eye; inhabitants spy on one another, forming a web of communication that always leads back to the President. Even Angel Face's brief idyllic marriage to Camila and their honeymoon, spent in an Edenic countryside, can only take place under the eye of the President.

From being a member of a privileged elite, Angel Face becomes an anonymous prisoner, whose will is eventually broken by devious means. Critics have seen Angel Face as a surrogate for the Latin American intellectual in his relationship with the state, which though technologically advanced can be socially bonded only through primitive human sacrifice of the "other." But the novel is more than the story of Angel Face. It is also that of the entire population:

a doctor who had dared criticize; a student, Fedina Rodas, whose crime is only the fact that Camila is her child's godmother and who suffers terrible punishment when her child dies of starvation and she is sold to a brothel; the beggars; a sexton; prostitutes. A virtuoso use of wordplay, onomatopoeia, alliteration, personification, and the grotesque makes the novel one of the most important attempts to represent the culture of fear; at the same time, it introduces a Utopian element, represented by Camila and her child, the only characters in the novel who escape the dictator's vengeance.

Men of Maize was Asturias' first attempt to create a wholly mythic novel. Using many devices drawn from pre-Columbian narratives, the novel depicts the dispossession of the Indians from their land by the *ladinos* and the subsequent transformation of their culture. Unlike most novels about the Indian, Asturias' does not assume that Indian culture is unchanging or primitive but rather that it is a dynamic force that, though beaten and suppressed, constantly generates new myths and legends. By the time he came to write the novel, extensive research had been done on the *Popol Vuh*. This unique document had been compiled after the conquest (probably in the mid-sixteenth century) by an indigenous scribe who had mastered phonetic script but wrote down the tribal history in the Quiche language. Its existence was unknown to those outside the Quiche community before the beginning of the eighteenth century, when it was shown to the Dominican priest Father Ximénez; he copied out the text from the Quiche original, which must then have been returned to its Indian guardians, since it has never been examined by anyone else outside the Indian community.

Asturias' translation from the French of Raynaud made him familiar with this impressive "history of the Quiche," which tells the story of creation and of various attempts by the gods to make people who would adore them. As commentators have pointed out, the story of the four stages of creation can be read historically as the story of a people of hunters and gatherers who made the transition to an agrarian, patriarchal society. The *Popol Vuh* does not have to be read as a myth, as defined by Claude Lévi-Strauss; rather it can be seen as a history in which the creator of the world and his hypostatized attributes create the true society, that of the "men of maize." The transition from an earlier matriarchal stage to this new stage is the work of a pair of heavenly twins, Hunahpú and Ixbalanqué.

For Asturias, the *Popol Vuh* was the great American text. There was no need, he wrote, "to go begging at other doors for beauty, truth, and wisdom, because it holds these in its heart, locked by the keys of symbolism" (*America, fábula de fábulas*, p. 286). These words first appeared in an article published in San Salvador in 1954 and have since been reprinted in a collection of essays published in 1972. They emphasize the importance Asturias attached to this expression of native American civilization. "The Maya-Quiche reaches, in his own authentic conceptions, the heights reached by men of other cultures. . . . The privilege of American man from the very beginning is that brute force is never celebrated in its pages. The beginning of humanity is deified in flute players, in the magic painters, in the ball players, in those who play with words. There are no warriors, no armed triumphs" (*ibid.*).

In drawing on this "bible," Asturias departed from some of his contemporaries or near contemporaries (for instance, Fuentes) who viewed myth and ritual as essentially timeless. Asturias also valued the Mayan sacred text for its truly American spirit, which he tried to instill in his novel and which he described as a "closed world for those who do not want to see, hear, or feel America." His novel *Men of Maize* indeed can be considered the continuation into the near present of the story of the Quiche peoples begun in the *Popol Vuh*. Because of its poetic language and unfamiliar style, *Men of Maize* frequently has been dismissed or criticized for a lack of unity and for tediousness. Many critics have found it incomprehensible, and Asturias himself admitted that he had not written it to be understood: "I believed that it was not a novel that would be understood, and I think that we have not understood it."

It is only since the late 1960's and particularly with the in-depth studies of Gerald Martin that *Men of Maize* has come to be recognized as one of the great contemporary Latin American texts. Martin was the first critic to point out that the vast historical range of the novel, which deals with the confrontation between the indigenous peoples and the industrialized world, encloses another history—that of the writer's own life, since the chronology of events coincides with several important life crises—the death of his mother, his divorce, and his remarriage. However, the novel is neither an allegory of the self nor an allegory of a race or nation; rather it is a narrative that reinvents mythic thought—it *simulates* myth rather than drawing on existing myths—in order to show the constitution of "colonized subjectivity." Asturias' mythic writing is not a visit to the pre-Columbian past but rather a recasting of recent history in autochthonous terms.

Men of Maize has six major episodes, which are linked narratively and symbolically. A culture hero, Gaspar Ilom, one of the men of maize, for whom the cultivation of maize with the help of fire and water is a sacred ritual, is pitted against the *ladinos* who move in to work the land for profit. Ilom is treacherously poisoned and throws himself into the river; he is symbolically absorbed into the water, the element most opposed to the fire that had been used to clear the forest for the *ladinos*. His wife, "la Piojosa Grande" (the Great Filthy One), disappears, and supernatural beings, "the firefly wizards," begin to bring about the death or sterility of all who have betrayed Ilom. The first to die are members of the family who had supplied the poison. Young Machojón, riding to meet his bride, Candelaria Reinosa, is swallowed up in a cloud of fireflies and disappears. His father, Tomás, and his wife, the *ladina* Vaca Manuela, are also consumed by fire, as is Coronel Chalo Godoy, Ilom's main opponent. But in addition to being an agent of vengeance, fire—along with water and maize—is one of the positive symbolic components of the novel, as it is of the *Popol Vuh*.

As a consequence of the treachery against Ilom, sterility and loss repeatedly affect the male characters, several of whom are deserted by their wives. The first of the characters to sustain this loss is Goyo Yic, a blind man whose wife, Maria Tecún, disappears with their children, giving rise to folk legends of *tecunas*, or runaway women. Goyo Yic, whose fate is representative of the destruction of the indigenous community, becomes an itinerant beggar and vendor whose one aim is to recover his wife and the lost security of hearth and home. To this end, he undergoes an operation that restores his sight; but Maria

Tecún does not come back. Accused of selling contraband alcohol, Goyo Yic is sent to a penal settlement off the coast.

Another symbolic character is Nicho Aquino, a postman whose *nahual*, or shamanistic spirit, is the coyote. Nicho, like Goyo Yic, has been abandoned by his wife. Lured by a legendary magician, he burns the mail, in symbolic rejection of his role in the modern state, and descends for nine days into an underworld, where he learns of the death of his wife. Emerging from this experience, he too leaves for the coast, where he is instrumental in bringing about the reunion of Goyo Yic and Maria Tecún. The novel ends with a brief Utopian epilogue, which foresees the rebirth of the men of maize as descendants of Goyo Yic and Maria Tecún.

This schematic summary can give only the bare idea of the originality and richness of this novel, which draws continually on Mayan symbolism and mythic narrative—for example, colors, numbers, animal helpers, and magical transformations—and which also uses sacrifice as a transformative device. The operation that cures Goyo Yic's blindness is a form of sacrifice, as is Nicho Aquino's burning of the mail. The very structure of the novel, which early critics found to be loose and episodic, has been shown to be highly organized, although understanding this organization presupposes not only a careful reading but also some knowledge of the great indigenous texts of America. Just as many Western European texts presuppose a knowledge of the Bible or the Greek classics, *Men of Maize* makes no concessions to those not prepared to familiarize themselves with the pre-Columbian classical texts.

The novel, however, can be read on many different levels, for example, as an allegory of authorship that relates the story of the appropriation of writing by the *ladino* state and the recovery of indigenous (in the widest sense) consciousness. The language in which the novel is written is extremely inventive and corresponds to the shifts in subjectivity that occur in the course of the narrative. The novel's early chapters, for example, use many of the devices found in pre-Columbian poetry. Elsewhere, the novelist incorporates the mode of discourse of the state. He also parodies various types of demotic Spanish, such as *ladino* dialects spiced with local variants and the idiosyncratic Spanish of the indigenous peoples, for whom Spanish is the language of the conqueror.

Having reached this virtuoso level of invention, Asturias wrote a "banana trilogy" of social protest novels that are less interesting from a formal and a linguistic point of view. In an interview with Günter W. Lorenz, he described the novels as having originated in 1949 from a visit to the regions of Guatemala in which the United Fruit Company was operating. "My visits to those plantations, my conversations with the poor workers and their families, who had to live in those miserable camps as if they were convicts—all this provided me with the basic elements of *Strong Wind*." Asturias saw the writing of *Viento fuerte* (*Strong Wind*, 1949) and the other two novels of the trilogy, *El papa verde* (*The Green Pope*, 1954) and *Los ojos de los enterrados* (*The Eyes of the Interred*, 1960), as expressions of his political transformation. Nevertheless, as he points out in the interview, he did not altogether abandon mythical elements, for the strong wind of the title is also Huracán, one of the Mayan deities. In *The Green Pope*, the central character is a North American adventurer who becomes head of the corporation that owns vast lands in eastern Guatemala and that forms a state within a state. The final novel in the trilogy, *The Eyes of the Interred*, ends on a Utopian note with the triumph of the people over the banana company. Another social protest novel is Asturias' *Weekend en Guatemala*, which tells the story of the North American–inspired coup that overthrew the government of President Arbenz.

Most critics would agree that the social protest novels form a parenthesis in Asturias' work and that they are less innovative than the novels that precede and follow them. His idiosyncratic form of myth-narrative again reached virtuoso level in *Mulata*, in which characters shrink to the size of dwarfs or become gigantic. As in *Men of Maize*, the text is generated by an unholy act—a pact that Celestino Yumi makes with the devil in order to obtain wealth—which leads to his love affair and struggle against the supernatural *mulata*. The use of the pact with the devil is particularly interesting since, as the anthropologist Michael Taussig (*The Devil and Commodity Fetishism*, 1980) has shown, such pacts are part of folk culture in many parts of Latin America, where they provide a rationale for the peasantry, for whom working for money does not appear natural. The novel ends with the death of Yumi, the destruction of his land by earthquake, and the arrival of the Christian priest into a devastated, silent, and depopulated land.

Asturias again uses a mythic structure in *Viernes de dolores,* in which Lenten carnival celebrations replace indigenous myth as the narrative device for presenting metamorphosis and transformation. *The Bejeweled Boy* also illustrates this tendency of his later work to bring narrative closer to poetry; within its tripartite structure, the first part corresponds to the imaginary, the second to the symbolic, and the third to the real.

In addition to these major narratives, Asturias has published a collection of short stories, *El espejo de Lida Sal* (Lida Sal's Mirror, 1967), and before his death, he wrote a remarkable prose poem, *Tres de cuatro soles,* which underwent many revisions. This prose poem is of particular interest since it represents a statement of his poetic creed. The title comes from Aztec mythology, according to which the world went through different stages; a new sun came into being with the destruction of each stage. Asturias chose three out of the four suns of Aztec mythology because he wished to represent the Spanish element, the indigenous, and the *mestizo.* However, one cannot read the text as simple allegory, for the aspect of greatest interest is Asturias' extraordinary invention of language, which draws on all the devices of poetry and wordplay. It is in this prose poem that Asturias can most clearly be seen as founding a new American language. On the level of the "real," *Tres de cuatro soles* evokes the earthquake that destroyed Guatemala City in 1917. But the earthquake is also a metaphor for creation, which, according to indigenous myth, is always a recomposition of elements already in existence rather than a creation out of nothingness.

During the first sun, "the sun of four tigers" in Aztec mythology, the poem is generated by the "devouring tiger," and central importance is given to the mouth. The second sun, which in Aztec belief was a period dominated by the monkeys, is a journey through night, which is also a body and earth. It seems to be the maternal counterpart of the destructive "masculine" imagery of the first sun. In the third sun, all is in motion, "fixed and yet in motion." This

is the sun of fire, of poetic creation, which is analogous to sexuality.

Though Asturias' major work explores this relationship of poetry and narrative, he published plays and several collections of poems. His poetry is extremely diverse, ranging from variations on Horatian themes to sonnets. The collection that comes closest to the spirit of his prose writing is *Clarivigilia primaveral* (Clearvigil of Spring, 1965), in which he re-creates the "house of song" of Mayan belief, in which

Mágicos-Hombres-Mágicos
Se manifiestan en la Casa de las Cinco Rosas,
Donde el tiempo no es fecha,
    sino flecha.

(p. 60)

Magicians-Men-Magicians
come to life in the House of the Five Roses,
where time is not date but arrow.

In this collection, Asturias sets out a poetics that corresponds to "the alchemy of the word" set firmly in native American tradition.

Asturias was a regular contributor to newspapers in Mexico, Venezuela, Argentina, and other Latin American countries. Many of his newspaper articles have been reprinted in the collection *América, fábula de fábulas.* In these articles, he comments on fellow writers—Rafael Alberti, Gabriela Mistral, Heinrich Heine, Antonio Machado—on technology and modernization, on science fiction, on political figures such as Gandhi, on the Mayas and Guatemala, on his own novels, and, above all, on literature and creativity.

Asturias' essays add another dimension to his preoccupation with an American aesthetic: his insistence on literature as a humanistic activity, and his concern with the dilution of indigenous culture because of the influence of the tourist industry. Written over a period that covers thirty years of literary activity, they monitor the achievements of Western progress, the conquest of space, and the heavy price paid in environmental deterioration and the dehumanization of the planet. Though his observations are not particularly original, they place his aesthetic in an all-embracing concern for the future of humanity and a technological progress that might bring about an end to the dance of civilization.

A prolific writer, Asturias began to attract serious critical attention only after the award of the Nobel Prize. However, he is not a writer who can be easily read or classified, since the language of his novels requires a level of intense reading normally reserved for poetry. His narrative represents one of the most serious attempts in contemporary literature to reconstruct literature as autochthonous myth.

SELECTED BIBLIOGRAPHY

Editions

Collected Works

The first edition of selected works was published in two volumes by Aguilar in Madrid in 1964. The same publishing house also issued a three-volume complete works, with a prologue by José María Souviron, in 1969. These editions have been superseded by critical editions published by Klincksieck Editions, Paris, and Fondo de Cultura Económica, of Mexico City, Madrid, and Buenos Aires. Twenty-four volumes have been planned, each of which contains critical essays by well-known authorities, as well as an established text. Since 1977, four volumes have been published. Available volumes are annotated below as *EC* (Edición crítica).

Fiction

Leyendas de Guatemala. Madrid, 1930.
El señor presidente. Mexico, 1946. Buenos Aires, 1948; 2nd ed. 1955.
———. *EC*, vol. 3, 1978. Edited by Ricardo Navas Ruiz and Jean-Marie Saint-Lu. With introductory studies by Navas Ruiz, Saint-Lu, Gerald Martin, Charles Minguet, and Iber H. Verdugo.
Hombres de maíz. Buenos Aires, 1949.
———. *EC*, vol. 4, 1981. Edited by Gerald Martin. With introductory essays by Mario Vargas Llosa, Gerald Martin, and Giovanni Meo Zilio.
Viento fuerte. Guatemala City, 1949. Buenos Aires, 1950.
El papa verde. Buenos Aires, 1954.
Weekend en Guatemala. Buenos Aires, 1956.
Los ojos de los enterrados. Buenos Aires, 1960.
El alhajadito. Buenos Aires, 1961.
Mulata de tal. Buenos Aires, 1963.

El espejo de Lida Sal. Mexico, 1967.
Maladrón. Buenos Aires, 1969.
Viernes de dolores. Buenos Aires, 1972.
———. *EC*, vol. 13, 1978. Edited by Iber H. Verdugo. With introductory essays by Claude Couffon and Iber H. Verdugo.
Tres de cuatro soles. EC, vol. 19, 1977. With an introduction and notes by Dorita Nouhaud. Posthumous edition.

Poetry

Poesía: Sien de alondra. With a preface by Alfonso Reyes. Buenos Aires, 1949. First completed in 1932, additions were included in 1942 and 1948, and the complete edition was finally published in 1954.
Ejercicios poéticos en forma de sonetos sobre temas de Horacio. Buenos Aires, 1951.
Obras escogidas. 3 vols. Madrid, 1955.
Clarivigilia primaveral. Buenos Aires, 1965.
Sonetos de Italia. Milano, 1965.

Plays

Teatro. Buenos Aires, 1964. Includes *Chantaje, Digue Seco, Soluna, La audiencia de los confines.*

Essays

America, fábula de fábulas y otros ensayos. Edited and with an introduction by Richard J. Callan. Caracas, 1972.
Guatemalan Sociology: The Social Problem of the Indian / Sociología guatemalteca: El problema social del indio. In English and Spanish. English translation by Maureen Ahern. With an introduction by Richard J. Callan. Tempe, Ariz., 1977.

Interviews

Azaña, Manuel M., and Claude Mie. "Entrevista con Miguel Ángel Asturias: Premio Nóbel." *Bulletin hispanique* (Bordeaux) 70/1–2: 134–139 (1968).
López Álvarez, Luis. *Conversaciones con Miguel Ángel Asturias.* Madrid, 1974.
Lorenz, Günter W. "An Interview with Miguel Ángel Asturias." Translated by Tom J. Lewis. *Review 75* (Center for Inter-American Relations) 15:5–11 (1975).

Translations

The Bejeweled Boy. Translated by Martin Shuttleworth. Garden City, N.Y., 1971.
The Cyclone [Viento fuerte]. Translated by Darwin Flakoll and Claribel Alegría. London, 1967.

The Eyes of the Interred. Translated by Gregory Rabassa. New York, 1973.

The Green Pope. Translated by Gregory Rabassa. New York, 1971.

Men of Maize. Translated by Gerald Martin. New York, 1975.

Mulata. Translated by Gregory Rabassa. New York, 1967.

The President. Translated by Frances Partridge. London, 1963. Reprinted Harmondsworth, 1972. American edition, under the title *El Señor Presidente,* New York, 1964.

Strong Wind [*Viento fuerte*]. Translated by Gregory Rabassa. New York, 1968.

Biographical and Critical Studies

There are a vast number of critical articles and books on Asturias, as well as special issues of periodicals dedicated to his work. Of these the most substantial are found in *Revista iberoamericana* 67:135–267 (1969) and *Escritura* (Caracas) 3/5 and 6 (1978). A collection of essays edited by Helmy F. Giacoman was published in *Homenaje a Miguel Ángel Asturias,* Long Island City, N.Y., 1972.

Leading scholars who have concentrated on Asturias' writing include Giuseppe Bellini, Gerald Martin, Iber Verdugo, and Claude Couffon. Essays by these and other critics, based on detailed analysis of Asturias'

works and written in Spanish, are included in the Fondo de Cultura editions mentioned above.

A complete bibliography would include several hundred works. A partial bibliography that concentrates on works in Spanish is to be found in Edna Coll's *Índice informativo de la novela hispanoaméricana* 2 (Puerto Rico, 1977), pp. 129–143. Within the series of critical editions mentioned above, a projected volume of bibliographical data (vol. 24) has not yet appeared, but bibliographical data are included for the specific works included in each volume. The following selection concentrates on pioneer studies in Spanish and on works in English.

Bellini, Giuseppe. *La narrativa de Miguel Ángel Asturias.* Buenos Aires, 1969.

Brotherston, Gordon. "The Presence of Mayan Literature in *Hombres de maíz* and Other Works by Miguel Ángel Asturias." *Hispania* 58:68–74 (1975).

Callan, Richard J. *Miguel Ángel Asturias.* New York, 1970.

Dorfman, Ariel. "Myth as Time and Word." Translated by Paula Speck. *Review* 15:12–22 (1975).

Harss, Luis, and Barbara Dohmann. "Miguel Ángel Asturias." In *Into the Mainstream: Conversations with Latin American Writers.* New York, 1967, Pp. 68–101.

Prieto, Rene. "The Unifying Principle of *Hombres de maíz.*" *Modern Language Notes* (Spring 1986).

Willis, Susan. "Nobody's Mulata." *Ideologies and Literature* 17:146–162 (1983).

Salvador (Salarrué) Salazar Arrué

(1899–1975)

Ramón L. Acevedo

Novelist, short story writer, and painter, Salvador Salazar Arrué, better known as Salarrué, was an artist of powerful originality and El Salvador's main literary figure. He was a prolific writer, and his *Cuentos de barro* (Stories Made of Clay, 1933) is considered a classic in Latin America, although he wrote much more that is little known outside his native country.

Salarrué was born in Sonsonate, El Salvador, on 22 October 1899. His mother, María Teresa Arrué, was the educated daughter of a schoolteacher; before Salarrué's birth she divorced, and was thus forced to support herself and, later, her only son. Salarrué's father, Joaquín Salazar, a customhouse officer, visited him occasionally.

Salarrué went to primary school in El Salvador and began his secondary school studies at the Instituto Nacional. At first, he studied commerce but early on felt strongly attracted to the arts. A Russian painter who lived in El Salvador gave him his first formal painting classes; Salarrué's family, noting his talent, decided to send him to the United States to continue his education as an artist. The Salvadoran government gave him a small grant, and in 1917 he became a student at the Corcoran Academy in Washington, D.C., where he held his first exhibition.

When Salarrué was a child, he had heard and told tales, and when he was twelve years old, he published his first writings in the *Diario del Salvador* (Salvador Daily), an important newspaper. Later, as an art student in the United States, he came across *El libro del trópico* (The Book of the Tropics, 1907), by Arturo Ambrogi, in a New York bookstore. This older Salvadoran writer awakened in Salarrué the desire to capture his country's landscape, its people, and its customs. Because his grant was too small to cover living and studying expenses in the United States, he returned to El Salvador in 1919. He then began working as a writer and illustrator for two literary journals, *Espiral* (Spiral) and *Germinal,* in which he published his first regional short stories; he illustrated them himself.

In 1922 he married Zelié Lardé, a primitivist painter who came from a prominent family of well-known writers and intellectuals. (The couple's three daughters also became painters.) During his first years of marriage, because of financial difficulties, Salarrué lived in a covered wagon that belonged to the Red Cross and worked for that organization. Before that, he had established a small studio in San Marcos, where the poets Claudia Lars, Serafín Quiteño, and Alberto Guerra Trigueros visited him. They believed in theosophy and read esoteric literature. According to Salarrué, shortly after his marriage he experienced strange phenomena. He sometimes felt that he escaped from his own body to travel at incredible speed, and he had strange poetic and sometimes terrible visions. The scientific responses of medical doctors did not satisfy him. He did find convincing explanations in the theosophical and esoteric books that his friends advised him to read. To the end, he remained a firm believer in these doctrines.

In 1926, Salarrué published his first book, *El Cristo negro* (The Black Christ), a short novel surprising for its beauty and profound ethical content. From that time on, he produced books regularly until his death. Salarrué's friend, the essayist Alberto Masferrer, began in 1928 to publish the newspaper *Patria* (Native Land). Salarrué became one of its main collaborators and for some time also served as its director and chief editor. In *Patria* he published essays and articles, some of the tales later collected in *Cuentos de barro* and stories that appeared in the first edition of *Cuentos de cipotes* (Stories Children Tell, 1945; definitive edition, 1961). He also wrote for the newspaper *Queremos*, in which he published urban and provincial sketches, and for *Cactus*, a literary journal. His work as a painter and illustrator continued, and he occasionally created sculptures.

Two of Salarrué's strangest books, *O'Yarkandal* (O'Yarkandal) and *Remotando el Uluán* (Going Back to the Remote Uluán), appeared in 1929 and 1932, respectively. The year 1932 was a violent one in El Salvador; more than 30,000 people died as a result of the brutal suppression of a peasant revolt ordered by the president, General Maximiliano Hernández Martínez. This same year Salarrué published his most renowned book, *Cuentos de barro*. In this work, which brought him international fame, he presented with deep sympathy the hard, simple life of the Salvadoran peasants.

Following the publication of *Cuentos de barro*, Salarrué traveled throughout Central America and met the Chilean poet Gabriela Mistral, later a Noble Prize winner, who praised him as a short story writer and made possible a Chilean edition of *Cuentos de barro*. During these years he wrote some lyric poetry and experimented with drama, but he realized that his talent was much better suited to the short story. In 1940 he published *Eso y más* (That and More), a collection of strange and sometimes fantastic stories,

very different from *Cuentos de barro*. Five years later, he came back to his familiar regional world with *Cuentos de cipotes*.

By this time, Salarrué's fame as a writer had attracted government authorities. They recognized his talent by designating him, in 1946, officer in charge of cultural affairs in the United States. He was paid six hundred dollars a month, the highest salary he ever earned. He lived in New York for approximately three years, but in 1951, after touring a good part of the United States, he returned to El Salvador. He continued painting and writing, and published new works: *Trasmallo* (Net, 1954), *La espada y otras narraciones* (The Sword and Other Stories, 1960), and *Obras escogidas* (Selected Works, 1969–1970). The latter included some previously unpublished works, such as *El libro desnudo* (The Naked Book), *Íngrimo* (Alone), and *La sombra y otros motivos literarios* (The Shadow and Other Literary Themes).

From 1962 to 1964, Salarrué served as general director of fine arts, but he resigned from this position in protest over the government's lack of cooperation. In 1967 he traveled to Panama to act as a member of the jury for the Ricardo Miró National Literary Prize, and in 1969 he received, along with the Salvadoran poet Claudia Lars, the highest honors from the Salvadoran Academy of Language.

During the 1970's Salarrué's last books appeared: *La sed de Sling Bader* (Sling Bader's Thirst, 1971), an adventure novel for children; *Mundo nomasito* (Just the World, 1975), his only book of poetry; and *Catleya Luna* (Catleya Luna, 1974), his last novel. Salarrué died in El Salvador in November 1975.

The most recent critical appraisal of Salarrué's oeuvre distinguishes two main currents: stories that are deeply rooted in his vernacular Salvadoran world, realistic and popular in style; and imaginative, fantastic, cosmopolitan stories—quite different from his vernacular themes—that are written in a rich, elegant, poetic style and in which he presents his ethical and metaphysical beliefs and obsessions. These two currents, exemplified by *Cuentos de barro* and *O'Yarkandal*, flow independently, although in *El Cristo negro* and a few other stories, they tend to merge.

El Cristo negro, Salarrué's first book, was one of his best. A short novel, it recreates early colonial times in Central America. The protagonist is a strange *mestizo* (person of mixed European and Indian ancestry) saint, San Uraco de la Selva. His father, a Spanish soldier, and his mother, an Indian, are executed by order of the Captain General. Uraco finds refuge in a monastery, where he becomes a friar. But he develops and practices a paradoxical moral theory: He feels that his mission is to sacrifice himself by doing evil so that others may not sin; he feels he has to condemn himself in order to save his fellow men. Throughout his short, intense life, he steals, kills, and commits horrible sacrileges and sins, but with pure heart and good intentions, for love of God and his brothers in Christ. He is misunderstood and persecuted and finally dies, crucified like Jesus, for having committed a horrible sacrilege that a group of Indians was planning to commit. Only the other *mestizos* can understand him and one of them, Quirio Cataño, makes a black wooden Christ where his soul, going to neither heaven nor hell, seeks refuge after death. This Black Christ is El Cristo Negro de Esquipulas, still venerated all over Central America.

This strange tale is built on paradox, contradiction, and irony, qualities that also characterize the strange saint and the colonial world in which he lives and dies. It is a world where the supposed criminals and heretics—*mestizos* and Indians—are really innocent and pure, while the Spanish Christians are really criminals and heretics with evil intentions. This makes San Uraco's final crucifixion both a grotesque parody and an authentic repetition of Christ's sufferings and death. This short novel is, in this sense, a subtle condemnation of the Spanish conquest and the colonial regime that came after it. That regime, in many ways, explains Central America's present situation.

From the beginning of *El Cristo negro*, Salarrué is a mature writer. His light, flexible, even humorous tone is designed to give the story an oral quality. The style—highly suggestive, metaphorical, and lyrical at times—contributes to the strange beauty of the book, which, because of its effective and fluid combination of natural and supernatural elements, is a clear and early manifestation of magical realism.

Salarrué was less successful in his effort to integrate the various elements of his second novel, *El señor de la burbuja* (The Man from the Bubble, 1927), set in contemporary El Salvador. The author's main pur-

pose was to explain and dramatize his philosophical ideas about life through his narration of the protagonist's painful quest for spiritual perfection, with the negation of self, love, and goodness as the final outcome.

In the short story collections *O'Yarkandal* and *Remotando el Uluán*, Salarrué abandoned nativism and set loose his powerful poetic imagination to create marvelous worlds essentially verbal in nature. In the first of these books, the author disappears and a narrator, Saga, steps forward to tell strange stories, translated from an unknown language, about a remote world, impossible to locate in time and space, where marvelous things happen. Some of Salarrué's obsessions are presented through the poetic-symbolic modality of these short stories. In "La isla del ser y del no ser" (The Island of Being and Not Being), for example, the problem of personal identity is dramatized. In "Yansidara y Hianasidri" (Yansidara and Hianasidri), vital communion through art is the main theme. In *Remotando el Uluán* the exploration of the mysterious and marvelous takes the form of a fragmented tale by a traveler who is fascinated by a world of strange beauty where he finds gigantic illuminated serpents, subterranean stars, waterfalls of fire, and other extraordinary visions. The sensuous, metaphorical, and dazzling poetic style, the tendency to make the abstract concrete, the powerful imagination, and the oneiric atmosphere of these two books bring Salarrué, possibly unintentionally, very close to surrealism and creationism, creationism being an antirealist tendency that tends to create new imaginary realities and opposes mere reproduction of the world as it is.

His *criollista* (nativist) short stories, later published in *Cuentos de barro*, date from these same years. Some of the elements that unify these two extremes of his literary production are his poetic vision, his linguistic creativity, and his authentic human concerns, which infuse everything he wrote with deep tenderness for his fellow men.

In *Cuentos de barro* Salarrué presents the lives of peasants from the western region of El Salvador, dominated by the impressive Izalco volcano. But these short stories go beyond typical regionalism. Salarrué creates an original and intensely poetic style based on popular language. Besides, his stories are not merely picturesque recreations. His characters are desolate human beings—peasants who do not own the land, smugglers, farmhands, prostitutes, laborers who try to escape from poverty by illegally crossing the border to Honduras, hungry children, and criminals who cry when they realize they have done something wrong. Violence and death preside over this world, although humor, tenderness, and poetic style modify their crude impact.

More than twenty years after *Cuentos de barro* was published, Salarrué returned to this world and its characters in *Trasmallo*. He did not add anything substantially new, although some of these later short stories are as good as the earlier ones. There are also some surprises, as in "El espantapájaro"(The Scarecrow), in which the violent repression against the peasants in 1932 forms part of the story.

The definitive edition of *Cuentos de cipotes* was published in 1961. These are very short, witty, and innocent stories for adults told by child narrators, in the popular language of Salvadoran street children. The same technique is used in the work *Íngrimo*, a poetic recreation of preadolescence. The young protagonist, who has a lively imagination and a fondness for wordplay and linguistic creation, fabricates for himself an imaginary identity through the notes that he writes and that the reader reads. Reality and imagination are confused until the surprise ending.

In the collection *Eso y más* Salarrué develops yet another type of narrative: the tale in which fantastic, strange, or supernatural elements erupt into everyday reality, generally in urban settings. The style, sober and elegant, with no trace of popular regional language, is yet charged with lyrical poetic qualities that are also reflected in the stories' themes. Salarrué's esoteric, mystical beliefs, his paradoxical vision of man and of good and evil find here a suitable vehicle of expression. Reincarnations, voyages through time, objects with magical powers, the doubling, or division, of self into two or more beings, and extraordinary scientific experiments and discoveries are some of his favorite themes in this book and in *La espada y otras narraciones*. In some of the tales, such as "La momia" (The Mummy), he comes close to science fiction; in others, such as "La escultura invisible" (The Invisible Sculpture), poetic fantasy predominates. In "El doble del dictador" (The Dictator's

Double), he anticipates a well-known episode in Gabriel García Márquez' novel *El otoño del patriarca* (The Autumn of the Patriarch, 1975), and in "El muerto" (The Dead Man), he reminds us of Juan Rulfo's magical realism. In other stories, such as "Angel 140" (Angel 140), fantasy grows from within the character's obsessions and the narrator's internal perspective. His novel *Catleya Luna* also makes use of this combination of philosophical, poetic, strange, and subjective elements.

Salarrué was an author of powerful originality who made an important contribution to regionalist literature but also went beyond it by focusing on the profound humanity of Salvadoran characters and situations. He was also successful in his flexible use of popular language, which led him to carry out some interesting literary experiments. His poetic imagination and his creative use of language resulted in a very personal kind of fiction akin to surrealism and magical realism. He should be considered one of the founders of contemporary Latin American narrative literature.

SELECTED BIBLIOGRAPHY

Editions

Poetry

Mundo nomasito. San Salvador, 1975.

Novels

El Cristo negro. San Salvador, 1926.
El señor de la burbuja. San Salvador, 1927.
La sed de Sling Bader. San Salvador, 1971.
Catleya Luna. San Salvador, 1974.

Short Stories

O'Yarkandal. San Salvador, 1929.
Remotando el Uluán. San Salvador, 1932.
Cuentos de barro. San Salvador, 1933.
Eso y más. Santa Ana, El Salvador, 1940.
Cuentos de cipotes. 2 vols. San Salvador, 1945. Augmented, definitive ed. 1961.
Trasmallo. San Salvador, 1954.
La espada y otras narraciones. San Salvador, 1960.

Collected Works

Obras escogidas. 2 vols. San Salvador, 1969–1970.

Biographical and Critical Studies

Acevedo, Ramón L. "Salarrué, novelista o la esencial paradoja de la existencia." In *La novela centroamericana.* Río Piedras, Puerto Rico, 1982. Pp. 153–181.

Alegría, Fernando. "Salarrué: El mago de Ilobasco." In *La venganza del General.* Caracas, 1969. Pp. 73–78.

Escalante Dimas, Mireille. "Salarrué." *Cultura* (San Salvador) 51:157–172 (1969).

Lindo, Hugo. "Prólogo." In *Obras escogidas* 1, by Salvador Salazar Arrué. San Salvador, 1969. Pp. vii–cxviii.

Ramírez, Sergio. "Prólogo." In *Salarrué: El ángel del espejo y otros relatos.* Caracas, 1977. Pp. ix–xxv.

Roberto Arlt

(1900–1942)

Aden W. Hayes

In the nearly half-century since his death, Roberto Arlt has come to be acknowledged as one of Argentina's most important and most innovative writers of prose fiction. His influence, particularly in matters of prose style, vocabulary, and dialogue, has been as great as that of any twentieth-century writer from the region of the River Plate. This reputation was several decades in the making. During his lifetime (Arlt died of a heart attack on 26 July 1942), his works were accused of being crudely made and poorly written, and of containing scenes and terms too unseemly to bring before the reading public. Arlt himself was vilified for his supposed lack of good taste, his sensationalism, and his untutored approach to the Argentine world of letters, which was then largely the province of a moneyed leisure class for whom literature was often a hobby rather than a calling.

In his day Arlt was a popular writer, but his works were ephemeral. Published in inexpensive editions by mass-market houses, they were, with one exception, not reprinted during the author's lifetime. The resurrection of his literature, and with it his literary reputation, began only some years after his death. The growing interest in him among a wide range of readers, including some of Argentina's most important writers, is due to a combination of changes in political and social circumstances, and in literary tastes and techniques.

Arlt's literary opus consists of three novels (the second was published in two parts, with two separate titles), two collections of short stories, several plays, and more than two hundred topical newspaper pieces collected under several titles. By far the most important and influential part of this legacy are his three novels: *El juguete rabioso* (The Angry Toy, 1926); *Los siete locos* (*The Seven Madmen*, 1929) and *Los lanzallamas* (The Flamethrowers, 1931); and *El amor brujo* (Love, the Sorcerer, 1932).

The world of Arlt's fiction is almost invariably that of working-class Buenos Aires, the world from which the author himself came. Arlt was born on 2 April 1900, the only son of two immigrants who had arrived in Argentina as adults. Arlt's father was Prussian, and his mother came from the South Tyrol region of the Austro-Hungarian Empire. Both spoke Spanish imperfectly and preferred to speak German at home. Thus German, rather than Spanish, was the young Arlt's first language. Since his formal education ended when he was expelled from school in the third grade, Arlt was almost completely an autodidact, and the Spanish language, which was to be his master tool as a writer, was learned on the Buenos Aires streets and from his eclectic reading: the usual

881

boy's adventure books, thriller and crime novelists like Ponson du Terrail and Emilio Salgari, Jules Verne, and later Cervantes, and most of all the nineteenth-century Russians, Leo Tolstoy, Fyodor Dostoyevski, Nikolay Gogol, and Leonid Andreyev. Arlt claimed to find little value in most of the Argentine writers of his own day, calling many of them "useless."

Several of his contemporaries, including his editor, claimed that Arlt could not distinguish the differences among styles and levels of the Spanish language, and it is true that Arlt often paid little attention to these distinctions, particularly in analytic or descriptive passages. A character's musings on his own estate might include, by turns, Buenos Aires underworld argot, Genoese dialect and the French of Marseilles, scientific terminology, and the poetic vocabulary of Spanish-American *modernismo*. But Arlt proved, even in his first novel, that in dialogue he could use different vocabularies and even different forms of address to indicate the social classes and orientations of his characters. Similarly, Arlt was careful not to put working-class or criminal slang into the mouth of an engineer, or into the speech of his respectful young protagonist when he is talking to a professional man. Nevertheless it is true that Arlt's own spoken language and his literary language coincide at many points, so that his characters often reflect Arlt's own foibles and deficiencies.

Arlt left home when he was barely a teenager, and from then on he earned his living as a docker, a factory worker, a day laborer on a construction crew, a traveling salesman, and, later, as a newspaperman. He started his journalistic career covering the crime beat and ended it as the most popular columnist in Buenos Aires. Arlt's "Aguafuertes porteñas" (Buenos Aires Etchings) depicted aspects of everyday life in the Argentine capital from an ironic, and sometimes almost cynical, point of view. His audience loved it. On the days Arlt's column appeared, *El Mundo* doubled its normal circulation.

When he was in his early twenties, Arlt met and married Carmen Antinucci, of the provincial city of Córdoba. Six months after the wedding his wife revealed that she was a victim of tuberculosis, a fact she had hidden from Arlt during their courtship. The marriage soured, and Arlt moved out of their house.

From then until a second marriage to Elizabeth Mary Shine, in the last year of his life, Arlt lived in modest circumstances, mostly in boardinghouses in Buenos Aires.

In his mid-thirties Arlt forsook writing fiction and sought to reach wider audiences and, through them, to earn more money with his work. His first endeavor was in drama. He wrote seven plays, most of which were eventually produced. At about this time he turned seriously to inventing (it had long been a hobby) and actually received a patent for a rubber-reinforced lady's stocking that resisted running. But Arlt realized little financial gain from his plays, and none from his inventions.

In the 1920's, when Arlt was beginning to write, the Buenos Aires literary world was commonly perceived to be divided into two opposed, and sometimes feuding, camps—the groups of Florida and Boedo. Florida, named for the fashionable downtown shopping street where the group met and where many lived, was in touch with the European avant-garde movements of Dada, surrealism, futurism, and expressionism in literature, and cubism and fauvism in plastic art. They published their work in the magazines *Proa*, *Prisma*, and especially *Martín Fierro*. Boedo was and still is a small street in an outlying neighborhood of Buenos Aires. Boedo's writers came mostly from working-class backgrounds and, to some extent, espoused leftist social causes. Their magazine, first called *Los pensadores*, later became *Claridad*, in conjunction with the international socialist Clarté movement.

Arlt actually bridged the two groups. He served for a time as secretary to one of Florida's best-known and most successful writers, Ricardo Güiraldes, and published two sections of his first novel in *Martín Fierro*. But he also counted among his best friends members of the Boedo group, and his personal background would have seemed to ally him more with them. He published a story and a section of his second novel in *Claridad*. Arlt himself played down the notion of an ideological rivalry between the two groups and simply distinguished the Florida writers as Francophiles and those of Boedo as Russophiles. Within this division, Arlt clearly belonged to Boedo.

In 1926 two landmark works appeared in Argentine fiction: Roberto Arlt's first novel, *El juguete rabioso,* and Güiraldes' last, *Don Segundo Sombra.* The former is the story of a working-class adolescent struggling against confusion and overpowering forces in the city. Beaten down again and again, exploited and ostracized, he ends up a failure. The latter is the story of a boy discovering adventure and adult values on the pampas through his alliance with the old gaucho Don Segundo Sombra. The boy learns much from his idol and mentor and, in an O. Henry–like ending, inherits the enormous ranch on which he has been working.

Each novel is, in its own way, unmistakably Argentine in its ambience, its language, its characters, and its substance. Güiraldes' last effort (he died the following year) was received with applause and enthusiasm as the apotheosis of gaucho literature, a genre with a long tradition in Argentina. Arlt's more difficult and contentious novel passed almost unremarked, save for a very few messages of solidarity from Boedo writers.

Before Arlt there had been other Argentine novels set in the city—among their authors were Eugenio Cambaceres, Julián Martel, and Manuel Gálvez—but none was as graphic, as forceful, or as successful in rendering the nature of city life as was Arlt's. It is with *El juguete rabioso* that Argentine fiction begins the definitive break with its nineteenth-century identity, with the idealization of life in the countryside and on the frontier. With more than one third of the nation's populace residing in the capital alone, it was in the urban novel that Argentine national identity would be written in the twentieth century. Many did not recognize this enormous change for some years, but the evidence was there, in Arlt's first novel, for all to consult.

Arlt's three novels appeared in the six-year period from 1926 to 1932. Each develops around a central character (we cannot call him a hero) who, just beneath the superficial uniqueness imparted by his immediate circumstances, bears unmistakable likenesses to the other two. Arlt's protagonist is always a male, and that man is a misfit. Arlt's few female characters exist mainly as the protagonists' idealizations; but Arlt's men are really misogynists who brutalize women physically, verbally, and psychologically. Always threatened by his surroundings, his perilous circumstances, and by the city of Buenos

Aires itself, Arlt's central character seeks security but is driven to the borders of insanity. Frustrated by failure to achieve either economic well-being or social acceptance, he makes himself, as Silvio Astier of *El juguete rabioso* declares, "a hero of failure." He commits a seemingly gratuitous evil act, betraying and punishing the one person who is close to him. His subsequent castigation is self-inflicted: rupture from the society that would not have him, and exile, estrangement, or death.

The loose plots of the three novels develop these patterns, patterns that are also traced in Arlt's short stories "Ester Primavera" (Esther Spring), "Noche terrible" (Terrible Night), "El jorobadito" (The Little Hunchback), and "Las fieras" (The Wild Beasts), which were collected in an edition titled *El jorobadito* (1933).

Silvio Astier, the young narrator of *El juguete rabioso,* finds himself turned out of his house and then dismissed from one menial job after another, for reasons that are outside his control. He daydreams of finding love, prosperity, and even fame, after the manner of the heroes of the adventure novels he reads. But this fiction is a poor guide for urban existence. Sentenced to a perpetual "struggle for life," in the words of his friend Lucio, Silvio commits the first in a series of gratuitous acts of evil that Arlt's later protagonists will continue. Silvio informs on his friend and benefactor, El Rengo. He orchestrates El Rengo's capture by the police, then flees in shame to the wastes of Tierra del Fuego, in the extreme south of Argentina.

Remo Erdosain of *Los siete locos* and *Los lanzallamas* is an impoverished bill collector for a sugar company. He swindles his employers and is caught at it. After he is fired, his wife leaves him. He takes up with a prostitute, then joins a band of pseudorevolutionaries who plan to take over the country and finance their "revolution" with a chain of bordellos. Erdosain obviously is not in full control of his life or of his own mind, but he is surrounded by characters even more demented than he: the Astrologer, a eunuch who is the nominal head of the revolutionaries; Haffner, a former mathematics professor now turned pimp; Bromberg, released from an insane asylum into the Astrologer's care and now the latter's "slave," who will commit even murder on his master's orders; and several others. Much of their preparation for the revolution is playacting, but neither the characters nor the reader can quite distinguish the real from the melodrama.

Throughout the novel Erdosain grows ever more desperate as he finds himself confused and manipulated by the revolutionaries. He lives in a cheap boardinghouse where he seduces the landlady's daughter. One night, in an act that dwarfs Silvio's betrayal of El Rengo, Erdosain coldly shoots his lover while she sleeps. She looks at him, horrified, just before she dies, and cries, "What harm did I ever do you?" It is the question that might be asked by the victims of all of Arlt's protagonists, and the answer is as simple as it is distressing—that evil is the only mode of self-affirmation available to these deprived and corrupt characters.

Eugenio Balder of *El amor brujo* is perhaps outwardly more civilized than Silvio or Erdosain, but just beneath his veneer of charm and ingenuousness lies an antisocial vein of deceit and debasement. He is almost neurasthenically inactive. Although trained as an architect, he contents himself with earning a meager living as a draftsman. Balder takes up with Irene, an attractive teenager from a middle-class family fallen on hard times, and comes to enjoy his manipulation and humiliation at the hands of Irene and her calculating mother. His own act of betrayal takes the form of a lie, as he publicly accuses his young lover of having lost her virginity before she met him. He then abandons her on these grounds. The novel ends with Balder's irrational rantings about Irene's past, even as a demonic voice rings in his brain, predicting his return to the degrading relationship.

By now it should be obvious that Arlt's singular characters are Argentine originals. They are not the gauchos of the vast and sunny pampas, but urban proletarians tortured by the rigorous geometry of their city. Rather than Don Segundo's sense of liberation at riding off toward the horizon, they feel quite physically overpowered by the concrete cubes of buildings and by the oppressive heat reflected from the asphalt streets. Like Franz Kafka's Josef K., they are trapped in endless pursuit of what they will never have. Like Ernest Hemingway's Nick Adams, they discover that behind the thin veil of bourgeois

language and its myths lie only deceit and disappointment. It is not an exaggeration to assert that it is Arlt—not Güiraldes with all his years of residence in Paris—who guides the vessel of Argentine literature into the mainstream of European modernism.

In spite of their spiritual impoverishment, Arlt's protagonists all achieve one triumph, and it is a significant one: the transformation of their failed lives into art, into the texts we read. Silvio Astier is the narrator of his own story; Erdosain recounts his adventures in painstaking detail to an amanuensis shortly before his own death by suicide; and Balder takes pride in his ability to invent fictions that other characters will accept as fact. Each is supremely conscious of the power of the art of narration, and each carefully employs the fiction-making processes of selection, ordering, plotting, and embellishment. Silvio, especially, is careful to distinguish between his persona as character in his narration and his identity as narrator. He recognizes that the world takes note of him not for his social and economic failures but for his artistic triumph called *El juguete rabioso*.

Thus narration and language itself are principal components of Arlt's novels. The language used by Silvio, Erdosain, and Balder is powerful and evocative precisely because of the unlikely and arresting combinations of phrases, mixtures of vocabulary, and varieties of style they employ. One of Arlt's valuable contributions to Argentine literary language was to show that a writer could make use of the full range of the Spanish language as spoken in Argentina, including slang, terms from Italian, French, and English, and even ungrammatical constructions. Arlt was among the first writers in his country to allow his characters to use the *voseo*, the standard River Plate second-person form of address among friends—the *porteño* (Buenos Aires) substitute for *tú*. Although in almost universal oral usage, its employment in literature was, in Arlt's time, considered substandard.

When they appeared, Arlt's novels came under heavy critical fire because these linguistic novelties had no place in the contemporary notion of belles lettres. But Arlt argued that, with his newspaper column, his fiction, and his inventions, he did not have time to create art in a high style, and rather than evoke the pleasing aura of beautiful prose, he wanted his books to pack the force of "a cross to the jaw." (That Arlt looked to the boxing world for the image and used the English noun "cross" gives some idea of the reception range of his linguistic antennae.) Ironically, but not surprisingly, it is precisely this range of language, along with Arlt's fecund imagination and his unmistakably *porteño* settings and characters, that later generations found most original and most worthy of imitation.

The rediscovery of Arlt in Argentina began in the late 1940's, more than fifteen years after the publication of his last novel. Literary critics undertook to study Arlt's works and his characters (and sometimes Arlt himself, through his characters), as cases of abnormal psychology, as autobiography of the author, and, most frequently, from a Marxist standpoint as fictional representations of the proletariat oppressed by the international capitalist order.

Writers of fiction—the testimony of Julio Cortázar and Juan Carlos Onetti is particularly strong on this—began to admire Arlt's powerful scenes, his original characters, and the authenticity of his representations of the city of Buenos Aires. During the wave of nationalist sentiment that swept Argentina in the late 1940's and early 1950's, many writers thought it necessary to decry Argentine literature's traditional orientation toward Europe in general and France in particular. Against this history they raised the standard of Arlt's unmistakably Argentine fiction. In 1954 the literary magazine *Contorno* dedicated a special number to Arlt and his work, with contributions by several of Argentina's most promising young writers. New editions of Arlt's prose works were published in 1950, 1958, and 1963.

By the mid-1960's Arlt's eclectic approach to fiction—precisely what had earned him the enmity of many writers and critics of his own time—had been vindicated. Arlt's works stand as testimony to the idea, voiced by Cortázar, that the novel is "an ostrich that can devour anything." In Arlt's novels disparate elements do not simply fit, they fit together. Crime, love, gas laboratories, chemical factories, sneak thieves, confidence artists, maniacs, schizophrenics, sexual deviates, slang, epithets, Spanish pig latin, translations of Baudelaire, dreams, drunkenness, and nightmares—all belong in Arlt's work because he knew them all and saw that they, in the rich combinations he provided, could evoke the phantasmagoric world of Buenos Aires.

Arlt's triumph was his courage, his daring to use his own material rather than that willed to him, as it was to others, in the national literary legacy. As Onetti wrote nearly three decades after Arlt's death: "I'm still deeply and completely convinced that, if any resident of these humble shores [of the River Plate] ever approached literary genius, his name was Roberto Arlt."

SELECTED BIBLIOGRAPHY

First Editions

Fiction

El juguete rabioso. Buenos Aires, 1926.
Los siete locos. Buenos Aires, 1929.
Los lanzallamas. Buenos Aires, 1931.
El amor brujo. Buenos Aires, 1932.
El jorobadito. Buenos Aires, 1933.
El criador de gorilas. Buenos Aires, 1951.

Plays

Trescientos millones. Buenos Aires, 1932.
El fabricante de fantasmas. Buenos Aires, 1951.
La isla desierta. Buenos Aires, 1951.
Saverio el cruel. Buenos Aires, 1951.
El desierto entra en la ciudad. Buenos Aires, 1952.

Collected Newspaper Columns

Aguafuertes porteñas. Buenos Aires, 1933.
Aguafuertes españolas. Buenos Aires, 1936.
Nuevas aguafuertes porteñas. Buenos Aires, 1950.
Cronicón de sí mismo: El idioma de los argentinos. Buenos Aires, 1969.
Entre crotos y sabihondos. Buenos Aires, 1969.
Las muchachas de Buenos Aires. Buenos Aires, 1969.

Collected Works

Novelas completas y cuentos. 3 vols. Buenos Aires, 1963.
Obra completa. 2 vols. Buenos Aires, 1981.
Obras de Roberto Arlt. 9 vols. Buenos Aires, 1950–1951.
Obras de Roberto Arlt. 4 vols. Buenos Aires, 1958.
Teatro completo. 2 vols. Buenos Aires, 1968.

ROBERTO ARLT

Translations

The Seven Madmen. Translated by Naomi Lindstrom. Boston, 1984.

Biographical and Critical Studies

Bianco, José. "En torno a Roberto Arlt." *Casa de las Américas* 1/5:45–57 (1961).

Castagnino, Raúl. *El teatro de Roberto Arlt.* La Plata, Argentina, 1964.

Flint, J. M. "The Prose Style of Roberto Arlt: Towards a Reappraisal." *Ibero-amerikanisches Archiv* 5 n.s.2:161–177 (1979).

Ghiano, Juan Carlos. "Mito y realidad de Roberto Arlt." *Ficción* 17:96–100 (1959).

Giordano, Jaime. "Roberto Arlt o la metafísica del siervo." *Atenea* 166/419:73–104 (1968).

Gnutzmann, Rita. *Roberto Arlt: o, El arte del calidoscopio.* Bilbao, Spain, 1984.

Goloboff, Gerardo Mario. "La primera novela de Roberto Arlt: El asalto a la literatura." *Revista de crítica literaria latinoamericana* 2:35–49 (1975).

Hayes, Aden W. *Roberto Arlt: La estrategia de su ficción.* London, 1981.

Larra, Raúl. *Roberto Arlt; El torturado.* Buenos Aires, 1951.

Maldavsky, David. *Las crisis en la narrativa de Roberto Arlt.* Buenos Aires, 1968.

Masotta, Oscar. *Sexo y traición en Roberto Arlt.* Buenos Aires, 1965.

Norton, Robert Lee. "The Novels of Roberto Arlt: A New Direction in Spanish American Fiction." Ph.D. diss., University of Missouri, 1974.

Núñez, Angel. *La obra narrativa de Roberto Arlt.* Buenos Aires, 1968.

Onetti, Juan Carlos. "Semblanza de un genio rioplatense." In *Nueva novela latinoamericana 2*, edited by Jorge Lafforgue. Buenos Aires, 1972. Pp. 363–377.

Piglia, Ricardo. "Roberto Arlt: La ficción del dinero." *Hispamérica* 7:25–28 (1974).

Prieto, Adolfo. "La fantasía y lo fantástico en Roberto Arlt." In *Estudios de literatura argentina.* Buenos Aires, 1969. Pp. 83–103.

Scroggins, Daniel. *Las aguafuertes de Roberto Arlt.* Buenos Aires, 1981.

Sebreli, Juan José. "Inocencia y culpabilidad de Roberto Arlt." *Sur* 223:109–119 (1953).

Viñas, David. "Prólogo." In *Antología Roberto Arlt.* Havana, 1967. Pp. i–xix.

Leopoldo Marechal

(1900–1970)

Graciela Maturo

Leopoldo Marechal is one of the most prominent figures in Argentine literature. He made significant contributions in several literary genres; a great poet and an esteemed playwright, he is also considered one of the initiators of the so-called new Latin American novel. In addition, he wrote other narrative pieces, as well as essays and epistles. His work—remarkably coherent philosophically, aesthetically, and in religious terms—rests in a unique way at the crossroads between the classical Hispanic tradition and contemporary avant-garde movements. Marechal, who possessed a clear and reflective attitude toward his writings, opened the way to a new literary conception, one of a spiritual and New Worldly character.

Marechal is often included in the so-called Generation of 1922, as a result of his belonging—particularly from his second book onward—to the group that published the magazines *Proa* and *Martín Fierro*. In spite of this group's overall reforming and vanguardist trend, it did not attain the uniformity of a true literary generation. Among its members were writers who after some time diverged considerably: Jorge Luis Borges, Ricardo E. Molinari, Oliverio Girondo, Alfredo Brandán Caraffa, and Francisco Luis Bernárdez. The so-called Florida group, which included Marechal, developed a *criollo* spirit and a decided preference for creative language. For a short time, they opposed the Boedo group of poets and narrative writers, whose orientation was socialist and reflected an interest in the common people.

Marechal is also linked to the Argentine avant-garde movements, to which he contributed not only with his poetry, but with his outstanding innovations in all genres, particularly the novel. He is associated as well with the most representative figures of the Argentine national tradition, such as José Hernandez, Leopoldo Lugones, Ricardo Rojas, and Arturo Jauretche, sharing with them an undeniable devotion to his country and a great esteem for popular works. Marechal was forward-looking; he had in common with the younger generation audacious ideas, new social designs, and forms of expression that went beyond those of his contemporaries.

Marechal's life was that of an honest, faultless man. Evangelic in spirit, he was kind and most firm in his loyalty to his beliefs. Born in Buenos Aires on 11 June 1900, he belonged to a modest middle-class family, with immigrant ancestors of Spanish, Italian, and French heritage. Occasional visits to the countryside in the province of Buenos Aires impressed Marechal as a child, and he later used these memories and settings in his literary works. When he was twenty years old, he started working as a schoolteacher, a task he carried out with sincere devotion until the 1940's. In 1922, he began his lifelong participation in literary and artistic groups, started working as a journalist, and traveled to Europe, where he associated with avant-garde artists. By this time, Marechal had already experienced a great event: a religious conversion that included a clear embracing of Catholicism. His spiritual position became richer and philosophically more flexible in his later years, but he never betrayed his faith.

In 1941, Marechal was awarded the Premio Nacional de Poesía (National Poetry Award). Starting in 1943, he took part in politics, first as a follower of the Nationalists and later as a supporter of the Peronist movement. He was president of the education council in the Province of Santa Fe, the nation's general director of culture, and the director of artistic teaching. After the death of his first wife, María Zoraida Barreiro, who bore him two daughters, María de los Angeles and María Magdalena, Marechal married Elbia Rosbaco in 1950. His second wife, a writer, inspired many of his works and shared his life until his death.

Marechal's political commitment to *peronismo* and the intense changes in Argentine life were the cause of the ostracism he suffered from 1955 to 1965; he put up with the situation stoically. From 1965 on, with the publication of new works—his second novel, *El banquete de Severo Arcángelo* (Severo Arcángelo's Banquet, 1966), and the volume of poetry *El heptamerón* (The Heptameron, 1966)—Argentine and foreign critics renewed their interest in his unique teachings, rich aesthetics, and wide knowledge. He died on 26 June 1970, some time before his third novel, *Megafón, o la guerra* (Megafón, or War, 1970), was published.

Personally disposed and spiritually committed to mysticism, Marechal was a metaphysician of a traditional—especially Christian—philosophic background, and he was also receptive to modern science. His understanding of the world had a religious basis, as did his conceptions of literature and language. Literature was not a mere artifice for him, but a "living metaphor," in Paul Ricoeur's words, a symbol that emerged from reality and expressed it profoundly. He praised more the "vivifying spirit" of words than their "letter," which he condemned when

it lacked profound meaning. His conception of history was religious as well, for he considered it a human and superhuman process endowed with transcendence.

Marechal's work contains philosophical, existential, religious, and political messages. He warns about the excesses of modern individualism and the dangers of collectivism, and stresses the Christian idea of a community based on respect for the human person. He believed that an authentic construction of the Christian community depended on individuals experiencing personal conversions, awakenings to an ethical ideal and historical responsibility.

Marechal's poetic conception, which appeared in his novels and poems, found complete expression in his work *Descenso y ascenso del alma por la belleza* (Descent and Ascent of the Soul Through Beauty, 1939), a veritable treatise on aesthetics based on a Plotinian view. Conceived in Paris during a period of intense spiritual crisis and thought out for many years, this meditation on the meaning of art moves from a formal to a religious level, from the effect to its transcendent cause. Beginning with a quotation from Saint Isidore of Seville, Marechal arrives at the following conclusions: Beauty is not a component of created forms but is placed above them; between the particularity of created forms and the universality of the creative principle, Beauty acts as a bridge that links the creature with its origin; therefore, Beauty possesses an anagogic power: it conduces toward the higher spheres; from this power is inferred its initiatory virtue, a characteristic recognized by the Ancients; and in consequence, Beauty is one of the transcendentals. Thus beautiful forms that can send the soul astray can in turn become the way that leads back to God. This is a concept of Greek Orphism, preserved by various poetic schools: the medieval troubadours, the Compagnia dei Fedeli di Amore and their Renaissance, baroque, romantic, and symbolist descendants.

As Marechal clearly presented it, art is a spiritual way; it is the mediator between ideal essences and the material world. Knowledge of the forms, far from being a mere technique, becomes in the "artist's science" a mystic wisdom that can be sensitively communicated to everyone. Intuitive vision reveals its capacity for understanding and the possibility of transformation: To love is to become what is loved. Marechal plays with the image of Hermes' lyre of reason made like a tortoiseshell. The lyre, considered as an expression of the intellect of love, is a stairway to God. This is a Christian aesthetic conception that estimates the value of incarnation and the unity of spirit and matter, that is to say, the possibility of finding traces of the Creator in worldly forms: such were the ways of Saint Francis, Dante, and Saint John of the Cross, as opposed to a negative mysticism. In Marechal's opinion, man should assume his role as pontiff of Nature and its principal.

Thus his conception of Beauty is bound to a conception of Love, which is the impulse of the soul toward Unity. The symbol of thirst is always present in Marechal's heroes: the water offered to the lover—the mystic pursuer of Unity—is always scarce. Descent to the created world precedes the ascent toward Unity.

Poetry

Marechal's poetry, which appeared throughout successive aesthetic movements, maintains a great unity of style and a remarkable continuity in its lyricism and its philosophical attitude. His symbolic inclination is introduced progressively in his work, together with a didactic condensation that turns many of his poems into veritable lessons of a classic tenor.

When he was twenty-two, Marechal published his first book, *Los aguiluchos* (The Eaglets, 1922), which he later left aside because of its easy forms. This book appears to be linked to romantic and modernist symbolism rather than to the avant-garde movements of those days. It is a work that strongly reveals Marechal's classic and romantic temperament and his constant intuitions, as they anticipate his cosmic vision that produced epic and dramatic pictures of the world and of history.

His next two books, *Días como flechas* (Days as Arrows, 1926) and *Odas para el hombre y la mujer* (Odes for Man and Woman, 1929), are products of his period of ultraism, an aesthetic tributary of the Spanish-American and European vanguards. In these pages, Marechal poetized his beloved days and places,

his relationships with pupils and friends, and through them his discovery of the meaningful essentiality of everyday life. He enjoyed the power and the fruition of words and so was driven to a playful creation of metaphors. His poetry does not tend to an absurd imagism, as does the work of other poets of his generation, but instead tends to a figurative shaping that reveals the archetypal matrix so strongly engraved in him.

Odas para el hombre y la mujer is, in this sense, a clear step forward toward the symbolic order that distinguished his next period. Marechal called it "a concentration movement following an expansion movement." The poem titled "Niña de encabritado corazón" (The Girl with a Runaway Heart), which opens *Odas*, collects in a symbolic synthesis the image of the Woman-Guide, the first sketch of the Earthly Solveig later transmuted into the Heavenly Solveig, and the representation of the Girl-Homeland.

The second period starts with *Laberinto de amor* (The Labyrinth of Love, 1935) and includes *Cinco poemas australes* (Five Austral Poems, 1937), *El centauro* (The Centaur, 1940), and *Sonetos a Sophía y otros poemas* (Sonnets to Sophia and Other Poems, 1940). His conscious use of symbols placed Marechal at a distance from avant-garde artists who featured personal elements in their work and showed the way to a philosophic and didactic sphere that reflects his commitment to Christian dogma. This period runs parallel with his return to classicism and his reading of Dante and Saint John of the Cross.

Marechal's adopting an openly spiritual and religious attitude does not contradict his vanguardism; in the European and American vanguards there existed the hope of uniting science and metaphysics. In this period, Marechal's artistic boldness was adapted to the Spanish classicist precept. In any case, Marechal did not diminish his originality and reforming spirit, which would be remarkably evident later in his novelistic and dramatic work.

Laberinto de amor marks the voluntary impoverishment of Marechal's style, an act of religious humility on the part of a poet who had begun to feel guided and interpreted by a doctrine: the Gospel. His poems echo those of Gonzalo de Berceo and Saint John of the Cross. They recall the soul's pilgrimage through the worldly creatures and the exit from the labyrinth made possible by the divine call: "Every Labyrinth has an upward exit." In this work and the following one, the submission of the Dionysiac impulse to aesthetic forms and the subordination of the artistic to the religious are evident.

> My song, whether lost, whether in bliss
> Shall be an idiom on an even balance.

Cinco poemas australes shows a similar eagerness for an architectonic order and strictness. The theme of the homeland is developed through a series of symbolic images: the wind, the land, the sky, the horses, and the south. The tamer, seen in his childhood in the countryside of Maipo, appears as a paradigm of Argentine man. The homeland is again embodied in the adolescent figure, free and wild.

In 1940, Marechal was awarded the Premio Nacional de Literatura (National Literature Award) and published *El centauro* and *Sonetos a Sophía*. Composed as an allegorical and philosophic dialogue, *El centauro* belongs to the best Hispanic lyrical tradition, depicting the victory of the new age, personified by Christ, over the ancient times, symbolized by the Centaur.

In the twelve masterly poems of *Sonetos a Sophía* the poet sings to the figure of Woman in her archetypal dimension as Guide and Intelligence, the silver bridge that leads to God. Sophía, as Mary, is the world's axis in Marechal's Catholic vision. Poetry goes together with theology in his search for definitions, for assertions and symbols. Marechal adapts his work to a Renaissance and baroque precept—European as well as American—not as a formal imitator, but as a result of an innermost spiritual kinship that leads his poetic act from an experimental to a cosmic level, from a descriptive to an axiomatic dimension. His celebration of Sophía becomes a treatise on the soul and a far-reaching vision of the Universe.

Heptamerón is the synthesis of Marechal's earlier work. All the themes have been developed previously, and the poet treats them now in a mature way and with evident self-reference. In his *Sonetos a Sophía*, the past appeared as an itinerary seen from the destination. In *Heptamerón*, he lays out this attitude and goes more deeply into it, looking at the past with a critical view. After carrying out his search

with the aid of different wisdoms, the poet relies on the support of the Science acquired through Sophía. His most evident addressee is Elbiamor—this is how he names his wife Elbia—seen as a pilgrim; thus the didactic, classic tenor of these chants. The model of the week serves as a structural pattern for the poems, which go beyond a rigid formality and employ amply rhythmed versicles. The fourth of the seven chants reserves a central place for Christ. Once again we see the pilgrimage through life, with the sacred horizon as the poet's north, in this account that includes a poetic treatise, a lesson on history, and an autobiography.

The poem "Didáctica de la alegría" (Didactics of Joy) presents the joy of the one who has reached salvation and spares us the "tired monsters of literature." *Heptamerón* includes a vision of history, of the homeland, of the soul, of love, and of death. In this spiritual compendium, the poet's person is sketched as a teacher and a seeker of light.

El poema de Robot (Robot Poem, 1966) belongs to Marechal's later works and has a philosophic and didactic attitude. It adopts a parabolic form: the character Robot's original sin is that it was generated by the Technocrat who, pretending to be God, wishes to create a being that resembles man. The Technocrat and the Robot are two specific figures of the Iron Age. Only a Robot, not a man, can create another Robot. The poem is the story of Robot, killed finally by the Poet. The philosophical substance of the poem is very rich and very applicable to our times; lacking mystery and a superior intellect, the Robot possesses a mechanic honesty. He must be destroyed in order for true science to be recovered.

Marechal's poems "De la física" (On Physics) and "De psiquis" (On Psyche)—published after the poet's death with the title *Poemas de la creación* (Poems on Creation) in 1979—are also philosophic-didactic poems of great richness. The poem "De la física" displays a cosmology and a religious anthropology that shows the universe as a continuity of kingdoms: the outer one of Physics, the middle one of Psyche, and the central one of the spiritual world, to which we belong and are bound to accede in a centripetal movement opposite to the wearing out and entropy of things. Marechal's poetry here reaches prophetic and admonitory keys typical of his later period. The work reflects Marechal's knowledge of modern science and its connection to ancient philosophy. He leaves us a legacy: the need to restore the Book, the Temple that has been destroyed. The poem "De psiquis," although personal and autobiographical, reaches a universal projection as it refers to the wandering of the soul in its journey through life. Psyche is identified with woman and with poetry, which guides the pilgrim.

Christian symbols are always present in Marechal's poetry. Christ is called "Pescador Admirable" (Wonderful Fisherman), "Tañedor Celeste" (Heavenly Musician) and "Arquero" (Archer); he is the center of life and history. The Virgin is the feminine archetype, the only possibility of uniting opposites through charity and love. Too didactic for some, of a rich and inexhaustible substance for others, Marechal's poetic work has not yet been studied with the dedication and depth it deserves, although it has been worked upon partially and some eminent essays have been produced.

Novels

Marechal published three novels, which form a veritable trilogy. Although he repeated themes in a symphonic way, each book is an autonomous world with its own structures and laws. *Adán Buenosayres* (Adán Buenosayres, 1948), the first novel, is centered on the awakening of the inner self, a decisive moment that unites man with his Creator and thus renders sense to the individual life and the flow of history. *El banquete de Severo Arcángelo*, of a strongly allegoric and symbolic conception, is an interpretation of history as a battle that has a subliminal applicability to Argentine history. Prophetic in tone, *Megafón, o la guerra* constitutes a philosophic and poetic treatise.

Written over several years, *Adán Buenosayres* was received by the critics with great reserve. As an exception, Julio Cortázar pointed out its originality, calling it "a drizzle of seven hundred looking glasses." Some years later, many critics saw in this work one of the first expressions of the new Latin American novel. It is divided into three parts, a structure that combines an autobiographical sketch, a poetic and religious treatise, and a satiric Dantesque vision of Argentine life. It is clearly influenced by Dante's *Vita nuova* (*The New Life*) and the *Commedia* (*The Divine Comedy*).

This novel is one of a series of works that deals with the awakening of the inner self. The novels of Juan Rulfo, Carlos Fuentes, and Augustín Yáñez also present thorough statements on the awakening of consciousness and its linking to a transcendent level, a moment when the understanding of the world expands, along with the vision of the past and the future. This inner commotion produces a new attitude toward the conception of time that results in the overlapping of events, a shifting of the narrative perspective, and overall, pervasive innovation and originality in form and technique. The narrator returns to his all-knowing view. Inclined to an ample recapitulation, he links different moments and events and looks for their articulations. He places his story during the decisive day and a half in Adán's life when his "death" and his later "new birth" take place. The meaning of his journey is expanded by Marechal's use of poetic symbols and comments. The symbols act in a paradigmatic way and guide the reader: the fish on the hook, the ship, the Virgin as guide.

The poet Marechal, evident hero of the novel, is an existential example as well as a universal human model. Many of Adán's friends during his youthful adventures are renowned characters of the Argentine literary world: Jorge Luis Borges; the poet Jacobo Fijman, who was converted to Catholicism and lived in a mystic delirium; the esoteric artist Xul Solar; Norah Lange; Oliverio Girondo; and Raúl Scalabrini Ortiz, who years later wrote the famous essay *El hombre que está solo y espera* (*The Man Who Is Alone and Waits*, 1931). The work expands concentrically in order to contain individuals, the group, and the national life, and to open the way to a religious interpretation of the story. The second part of the book, "Cuaderno de tapas azules" (The Blue-covered Copybook), includes a doctrinary body, an aesthetic and religious consideration that sheds light on the book and constitutes its key. The Sophía of the poetry is here called Solveig, the woman who has to ascend from her worldly condition to Heaven, away from the transformations of time: she will be the Girl That Shall Happen No More. As the Woman-

Guide, she is an incarnation of poetry; like Dante's Beatrice and Petrarch's Laura, she incarnates the archetypal figure of the Virgin.

The "Cuaderno," which reconstructs in a novelistic way the aesthetic treatise *Descenso y ascenso del alma por la belleza*, belongs to a Plotinian philosophic tradition and has a mystic origin, well known by Marechal. Poetry is the memory of a previous, deeper state, of an ineffable essence: the search for the uncreated form, the Origin, through the forms of the world. Works of art are produced with the intention of saving the things and beings of this world from their wearing out and unavoidable death. Nevertheless, it is possible to distinguish an order of creation and another of salvation, which will be dealt with in Marechal's following works.

In the third part, "Viaje a la oscura ciudad de Cacodelphia" (Voyage to the Dark City of Cacodelphia), Marechal created a work, which resembles Dante's *Divine Comedy*, that shows various infernal circles in which he placed characters who typify a decadent world. Some of them were his own contemporaries, who became enraged when they found themselves portrayed in such a way. This section of the novel introduces a theme that will be developed in later works: the old, stereotyped Argentina, in need of a profound renovation. Marechal possesses a sense of humor, which is expressed sometimes in a kindly manner and at other times in a sarcastic way that contains political and social criticism.

Marechal reinterprets the ancient myth of Adam in a Christian way, as the fifteen-century Italian humanists had done. His Adam is Odysseus tied to the mast in order to avoid the Mermaid's temptation; he is also Christ tied to the Cross. Marechal's purpose is to resist the erosion of time and to start a heroic adventure, the return to spiritual sources. The liveliness and variety of his style are remarkable. His prose his highly communicative, as he alternates lyricism and humor, sharp dialogue and profound doctrine. His expressive range encompasses the theologic treatise and the *sainete* (burlesque), and includes the farce, the poem, and the philosophic dialogue.

Marechal's second novel, *El banquete de Severo Arcángelo*, is more uniform from a formal point of view, narratively better structured than the previous book, and more hermetic and full of symbolism. Its

prologue proclaims that it is "an adventure or mystery novel" addressed not to children but to men "in transit to the child," with a clear evangelic intention. Marechal masks his story through the presentation of an author-editor, offering us Lisandro Farías' "story," written in the first person and told as an allegoric account that includes symbolic figures of a theologic lineage. In *Adán Buenosayres*, he had already talked about Hesiod's theory of the historic ages, in which modern times would be the last step of a descending staircase. From the Golden Age—cried for since the Greek rhapsodies—to the Iron Age, there is, in Marechal's view, a descending movement; Christians are commanded to reverse the Fall with a heroic effort, and so the mythic incentive is placed at the end of History. It is the Man of Blood who permits, with his sacrifice, such a reversion of the Ages. Lisandro Farías, Marechal's autobiographical figure, delivers the account of his adventure to the author, who has connected him with a theological and historical mission: the preparing of the Banquet. Severo Arcángelo, a character of a fiendish nature—he is a blacksmith and has a terrible temper—is redeemed by his convocation of a group of initiates to carry out this grand task. (That group brings to mind a previous novel, Roberto Arlt's *Los siete locos* [The Seven Madmen, 1929], which moves in a different direction.) The author includes in this work the representation of successive calls that lead us from Severo Arcángelo to Pablo Inaudi, Brother Jonah, and the Window Psalmodist, and after them, in an implicit way, to Christ, the Great One Who Summons. The author assumes the role of a spokesman of his own historic age.

The condition needed to participate in this enterprise is the breaking with ordinary life, through various situations. Lisandro Farías, Doctor Frobenius, who is a mad scientist, Professor Bermúdez, and others have to go through successive purifying stages before the fulfillment of the eternally postponed Banquet. The novel, as History itself, has an open ending. Among the complex allegories intermingled in the text are the transformation of the Iron Man into the Man of Gold by means of the sacrifice of the Man of Blood, the experience of the Synthesis Funnel, the Councils, and the Water Hill, placed in a remote and unspecified province. "The Theorem must remain whole and open to the Soul's Inquisitions," says the author in the prologue. The work is developed upon a biblical correlation that sees History as a Providential project, achieved with both the assistance and the opposition of men. This mythic background coexists with the contemporary historic moment. The author has situated the beginning of the novel on a precise date: 14 April 1963; his participation in recent events and his own political commitment are connected to the confirmation of his faith that had been expressed in his previous work.

In discussing Marechal's novelistic production, we have emphasized the playful level that adds a humorous dimension to the theological and mysterious adventure; the narrative direction that is unfolded as a succession of enigmas: the ingenious dialogues in which Marechal acts as a schoolteacher; the satiric vein that contains an overt criticism of society; a metaphorical and hyperbolic trend; and the concrete realism, in which transcendent statements incarnate. All these characteristics coincide in an aesthetics of incarnation, justified by Marechal in his poetics.

Megafón is incorporated into Marechal's novelistic trilogy as the symphony's highest and boldest note. This novel surpasses the previous ones in its unity and its atypical language, but it continues the social epic and the inner voyage, with an important addition: an urgency that emerges from the prophetic quality of this chronicle of modern times. Marechal again follows his teacher Homer in the symbolism of war, which is expressed in two battles: the heavenly and the worldly. He considers human history as the reflection of a greater duel between good and evil forces. The worldly battle aims at a new Argentina, "open to what may happen," stripped—as the serpent—of its old skin and standing firmly on its own cultural identity. Marechal declares the death of an old life-style and foresees another one that will bring a greater social balance. He is cruelly satiric in his treatment of the military bureaucrat, the powerful executive, and the *homo economicus,* who are typical of modern, commercial society. Like other Latin American writers, Marechal assumes the role of a postmodern man, although not a reactionary one. He emphasizes the importance of a return to sources as a necessary step before facing the future. The search for the verticality of the heavenly battle is for him the

way to reverse the course of this somber age. His attitude toward modern technical discoveries is not one of rejection; instead he warns of the metaphysical void in a world lacking a sacred direction.

Megafón, as his name suggests, is the prophet of social and spiritual change. This character can be seen on two levels: in a way, he is an autobiographical character who repeats many aspects of Marechal's own life and work; on the other hand, he stands for the political leader in a rather obvious way, thus opening the cycle of the *novela del caudillo* (novel of the popular leader). He is not a pilgrim hero but a triumphant one who, after overcoming his mistakes and adventures, is able to lead his people in the skirmishes of the national adventure, resembling in this the old, wise Oedipus. In the skirmishes of a police and an adventurer's raid, the characters are induced to chase tirelessly the Interceding Woman—Isis, Venus, the Virgin—a symbol of the ascent to Unity.

The chapters of this novel are called rhapsodies, and they are informed by tones that are alternately theatrical, farcical, satiric, and doctrinaire. Buenos Aires is again the setting for a national epic, where characters already known to Marechal's readers—such as Samuel Tesler—relate their adventures and opinions. His wife, Patricia Bell, is his confidante, a disciple who follows the teacher's lessons and direction. The raid consists of episodes that compose a large comic event that yet retains its interest as doctrine. There is an adventure that tends to restore the harmony broken by an unfair situation that keeps Samuel Tesler locked in a lunatic asylum. As in his first novel, Marechal refers to his friend the poet Jacobo Fijman, in real life secluded in a madhouse, who is considered by Marechal as "a born militant of the Heavenly Battle." The author presents typical situations, relates theology to the circumstances of everyday life, and includes characters that can be recognized from past and present Argentine history.

The recreation of the classic myth of Dionysus is evident, along with the Christian myth and the political aim of the book. Megafón, as Orpheus, carries out his greatest task when he engages in the rescue of the infernal prisoner—once again the descent to Hell praised by the esoteric tradition and often reproduced in Marechal's work. The meaning of the collective sacrifice is also revealed: Death is seen as a triumph and Christic body is distributed between the members of the community.

This work, hard to include in any of the genres, synthesizes in a bold way multiple elements that constitute a veritable theological, philosophic, and political summa: a Christian anthropological treatise that contains an individual ethic and a common salvation. In a more emphatic way than in other works, this novel offers a compound of sublime and ridiculous tones, doctrine and everyday reality, vital aspects and great symbolic statements.

Theater

Marechal's dramatic vision informed many of his works: some of his poems have a dramatic structure, and in his novels there are chapters of a pure scenic style. Marechal's theatrical conception is similar to that of the classic and medieval liturgic drama, the Hispanic *auto sacramental* (allegorical or religious play), and the farce or the *sainete*.

His dramatic production includes the poetic oratory *Canto de San Martín* (San Martín's Chant), an homage to General San Martín in the first centennial of his death (1950), performed in Mendoza in 1950 and sung by the choir of the Universidad Nacional de Cuyo (Mendoza), with Julio Perceval's music. In this work, Marechal succeeded in the difficult task of realizing a play, in an epic operatic style, that combines a historical theme with some very modern, humorous strokes.

Antígona Vélez (Antígona Vélez, premiered in 1951) is a recreation of the myth of Antigone with an Argentine variation. Sophocles' conception is impregnated with an apocalyptical sense and a Jewish and Christian finality. The myth contains a symbolic projection of the historic conflict. The topic of destiny, so classic and always present in the Hispanic theater, has a great force in this play. Its prose has rich poetic and even rhetorical hues; the character's speech does not become artificial, although it is a little archaic. The lyric monologue illuminates Antígona's personal consciousness, and the dialogue is fluid and has a good dramatic structure, expressed by the scenic changes, the movements, and the overall

scenic display. Premiered in 1951, the play has been performed very few times.

Marechal's second play, *La batalla de José Luna* (José Luna's Battle), premiered in 1967. The author called it an "angelic sainete" or a "sainete divine style," because of its farcical humor and its theological inspiration, which produces the eternal battle between the Light and the Shadows. The five acts of the play are preceded by a prologue that classifies angelic and devilish spirits and are followed by an epilogue. The play is set in the city, in a room in the Gato Rabón (The Bobtailed Cat), a tenement in the quarter of Villa Crespo. José Luna, a former boxer and Bible seller, will perform an evangelic mission there. His "battle" has been introduced by an angel who appears in the prologue. Our understanding of the meaning of this play is intensified if we compare it with the novel *El banquete de Severo Arcángelo*, which was conceived at the same time. In both works, political action is based upon theological and metaphysical grounds.

Don Juan was not performed or published while the author was alive; the first edition appeared in 1978. It is another example of Marechal's theological and salvational concern. He chose as the protagonist the Spanish Don Juan, a figure with a long history in both the Western and Eastern traditions, who combined in his person the traits of Dionysus and Satan, with their positive and negative aspects: knowledge, vitality, love of the earth and progress, but also excess and infringement of the laws. Marechal's Don Juan is of a Christian lineage, nearer to Juan Zorrilla de San Martín's character than to Tirso de Molino's: he is redeemed through love and grace. Marechal has preserved interesting folkloric motives in an audacious, surrealist scenic conception.

The comedy *Las tres caras de Venus* (The Three Faces of Venus, premiered in 1952) presents the themes of love and salvation translated to a farcical level, and adds a satiric stroke that attacks social dehumanization. Marechal considered another short play, *Athanor*, an "alchemic sainete"; it presents the confrontation between traditional wisdom and modern science.

Marechal also left sketches of incomplete plays, stories, essays, epistles, and lectures. In his *Cuaderno de navegación* (Logbook, 1966), he put together various philosophic and critical papers that shed light on his literary production. This work, which has attracted the attention of Argentine and foreign critics, is a lesson in Christian humanism, and a motivation to work toward a new era amid the ruins of our suicidal civilization.

Translated from the Spanish by Silvia Pellarolo

SELECTED BIBLIOGRAPHY

Editions

Poetry

Los aguiluchos. Buenos Aires, 1922.
Días como flechas. Buenos Aires, 1926.
Odas para el hombre y la mujer. Buenos Aires, 1929.
Laberinto de amor. Buenos Aires, 1935.
Cinco poemas australes. Buenos Aires, 1937.
El centauro. Buenos Aires, 1940.
Sonetos a Sophía y otros poemas. Buenos Aires, 1940.
La rosa en la balanza. Buenos Aires, 1944. Anthology.
El viaje de la primavera. Buenos Aires, 1945.
Antología poética. With a preface by Juan Carlos Ghiano. Buenos Aires, 1950.
Leopoldo Marechal. With a preface by Rafael Squirru. Buenos Aires, 1961. Anthology.
El heptamerón. Buenos Aires, 1966.
El poema de Robot. Buenos Aires, 1966.
Poemas de Marechal. Buenos Aires, 1966. Anthology.
"Tres poemas sobre la Pasión." In *La poesía religiosa argentina,* by Roque Raúl Aragón. Buenos Aires, 1967.
Antología poética. With a preface by Oscar Grandov. Buenos Aires, 1969.
Antología poética. With a preface by Alfredo Andrés. Buenos Aires, 1969.
Canto de San Martín. Buenos Aires, 1979.
Poemas de la creación. Buenos Aires, 1979.
Poesía (1924–1950) por Leopoldo Marechal. With a preface by Pedro Luis Barcia. Buenos Aires, 1984.

Novels

Adán Buenosayres. Buenos Aires, 1948. Havana, 1969. Reprinted 1973.
El banquete de Severo Arcángelo. Buenos Aires, 1966.
Megafón, o la guerra. Buenos Aires, 1970. Posthumous edition.

Plays

Antígona Vélez. Buenos Aires, 1965. Reprinted 1970.
Las tres caras de Venus. Buenos Aires, 1966. Reprinted 1970.
La batalla de José Luna. Santiago, Chile, 1970.
Athanor (Sainete Alquímico). In *Megafón.*
Don Juan. With a preface by Juan O. Ponferrada. Buenos Aires, 1978.

Essays and Other Prose

Historia de la calle Corrientes. Buenos Aires, 1937.
Descenso y ascenso del alma por la belleza. Buenos Aires, 1939. Reprinted 1965. Definitive version.
Vida de Santa Rosa de Lima. Buenos Aires, 1943. Reprinted 1977.
"Prólogo." In *Cántico espiritual,* by San Juan de la Cruz. Buenos Aires, 1944.
"Proyecciones culturales del momento argentino." In *Argentina en marcha.* Buenos Aires, 1947.
Cuaderno de navegación. Buenos Aires, 1966.
Palabras con Leopoldo Marechal. Interview and anthology by Alfredo Andrés. Buenos Aires, 1968.
La nueva literatura argentina. Buenos Aires, 1970. Dialogue with Horacio Armani and Miguel Bustos.
"*El beatle final*" *y otras páginas.* With a preface by Ángel Núñez. Buenos Aires, 1981.

Biographical and Critical Studies

Alonso Gamo, José M. "Marechal." In *Tres poetas argentinos: Marechal, Molinari, Bernárdez.* Madrid, 1951. Pp. 7–56.
Ara, Guillermo. In *Los argentinos y la literatura nacional.* Buenos Aires, 1966. Pp. 77–84, 128–129.
Blanco Amor, José. "Un gran 'banquete' de Leopoldo Marechal." *Cuadernos hispanoamericanos* 65/195: 565–567 (1966).
Borges, Jorge Luis. "Diás como flechas." *Martín Fierro* 36:8 (1926). Reprinted in *Martín Fierro (1924–1927),* by B. Sarlo Sabajanés. Buenos Aires, 1969. Pp. 160–161.
Camozzi, Rolando. "Dos obras de Leopoldo Marechal." *Cuadernos hispanoamericanos* 74/221:448–455 (1968).
Cavallari, Hector. "Leopoldo Marechal: De la metafísica a la revolución nacional [sobre *Megafón, o la guerra*]." *Ideologies and Literature* 2/9:3–33 (1979).
_____. "Adán Buenosayres: Discurso, texto, significación." *Texto crítico* 16–17:149–168 (1980).
_____. "Discurso metafísico/discurso humanista: Ideología

y proceso estético." *Revista de crítica literaria latinoamericana* 7/13:23–28 (1981).

Centro de Investigaciones Literarias Buenosayres. "Pruebas y hazañas de *Adán Buenosayres.*" In *Nueva novela latinoamericana* 2. Buenos Aires, 1972. Pp. 89–139.

Chiesi, Bernardo. *La espiritualización del eros en la obra de Leopoldo Marechal.* Buenos Aires, 1982.

Cortázar, Julio. "Leopoldo Marechal: *Adán Buenosayres.*" *Realidad* 14:232–238 (1949).

Coulson, Graciela. *Marechal: La pasión metafísica.* Buenos Aires, 1974.

Cricco, Valentin, et al. *Marechal, el otro.* Buenos Aires, 1985.

Del Corro, Gaspar Pío. "Leopoldo Marechal: La visión metagónica." In *La mujer: Símbolo del mundo nuevo,* by Vicente Cicchitti et al. Buenos Aires, 1976. Pp. 53–82.

––––––. "Los primeros libros de Marechal: Un proceso hacia el símbolo." *Megafón* 1/2:121–134 (1975).

––––––. "Leopoldo Marechal o la lucidez combatiente." *Megafón* 2/3:5–20 (1976).

Dumitrescu, Domnita. "*Adán Buenosayres:* Metáfora y novela." *Texto crítico* 16–17:169–181 (1980).

Foti, Jorge. *Aproximación al "Banquete" de Leopoldo Marechal.* Buenos Aires, 1983.

Ghiano, Juan C. "Leopoldo Marechal." In *Poesía argentina del siglo XX.* Mexico City and Buenos Aires, 1957. Pp. 141–148.

Gil, Nilda Noemí. "Crecimiento simbólico en la narrativa de Leopoldo Marechal." *Megafón* 5/9–10:209–236 (1979).

González, Manuel Pedro. "Leopoldo Marechal y la novela fantástica." *Cuadernos americanos* 151/2:200–211 (1967).

Hardy, William. "Life and Works of Leopoldo Marechal." Ph.D. diss., University of Missouri, 1973.

Jitrik, Noé. "*Adán Buenosayres:* La novela de Leopoldo Marechal." *Contorno* 5–6:38–45 (1955).

Jofré, Manuel. "El motivo del viaje en *Adán Buenosayres.*" *Revista chilena de literatura* 5–6:73–109 (1972).

Kant, Cleres. "Lectura simbólica de *El poema de Robot.*" *Megafón* 1/2:159–169 (1975).

Marechal, Elbia Rosbaco de. *Mi vida con Leopoldo Marechal.* Buenos Aires, 1973.

Martin Crosa, Ricardo. "El nacimiento del enigma." *Universitas* 44:61–72 (1977).

Maturo, Graciela. "La novela de Leopoldo Marechal: *Adán Buenosayres.*" *Revista de literaturas modernas* 2. Pp. 45–65 (1960).

––––––et al. "Jornadas de homenaje a Leopoldo Marechal." *Cuadernos de la dirección de cultura* 3 (1980).

––––––. "El tema del mal en el 'Don Juan' de Leopoldo Marechal." *Megafón* 14 (1984).

––––––. "La historia y la novela: *El banquete de Severo Arcángelo* de Leopoldo Marechal." *Letras* 14 (1985).

Montero Díaz, Santiago. *La poesía de Leopoldo Marechal.* Madrid, 1943.

Nuñez, Angel. "La novela experimental: Marechal." *Capítulo* 47 (1968).

––––––. "Leopoldo Marechal." *Capítulo* 97 (1981).

Pagano, Ana. "Alrededor de la voz, en el *Don Juan* de Leopoldo Marechal." *Megafón* 5/9–10:253–258 (1979).

Palermo, Zulma. "*Megafón* o la conciencia del símbolo." *Megafón* 1/2:135–157 (1975).

Sábato, Ernesto. "Homenaje a Leopoldo Marechal." *Megafón* 4/7:193–196 (1978).

Stabb, Martín. "Argentine Letters and the Peronato: An Overview." *Journal of Inter-American Studies and World Affairs* 13/3–4:434–455 (1971).

Torres Roggero, Jorge. "Historicidad y trascendencia en el *Adán Buenosayres* de Leopoldo Marechal." *Lugones* 1:119–126 (1968).

Zum Felde, Alberto. *Indice crítico de la literatura hispanoamericana* 2: *La narrativa.* Mexico City, 1959. Pp. 469–474.

Germán Arciniegas

(1900–   )

J. David Suarez-Torres

On 6 December 1900, Germán Arciniegas was born in Bogotá, Colombia. The son of a Colombian father and a Cuban mother, he has been a rebellious man whose life has reflected the vicissitudes of the twentieth century. His activities throughout the continent have made him a Spanish American, a Latin American, in short, an American, rather than simply a Colombian.

The influences on Arciniegas' life have been numerous. They include the Mexican Revolution, the university reforms in Córdoba, Bogotá, and Lima, the ensuing politicization of the universities, the Spanish Civil War, the two world wars, the Yankee-Go-Home Movement, the strengthening of the working class, the incipient proletarianism in Latin America, the change from a predominantly rural to a predominantly urban society, the increasing political power of the man on the street, the birth of Christian political organizations, and the decision of many Latin American countries to assume control of their material resources and political destinies.

From Bogotá, Arciniegas participated in and led some of the movements that shaped his country during the twentieth century. Committed to traditional Colombian liberalism, Arciniegas has been active in the political life of his country since his university years, when he was a delegate to the first National Student Conference. He has often played a leadership role. At age nineteen, he founded and directed the magazine *La voz de la juventud* (The Voice of Youth, 1919–1920). As a student he was also instrumental in the first steps taken toward the unionization of university students in Colombia. After completing his law degree in 1924, he founded and directed another magazine, *Universidad* (University, 1925–1929), a publication whose contributing editors emerged as prominent figures in Colombian journalism, and he established a publishing house, Ediciones Colombia, which between 1926 and 1928 printed some thirty titles in inexpensive editions.

Arciniegas' whole life has been one of service to his country and its people, and to Spanish-American letters. He has served as ambassador to Italy, congressman, member of the Colombian Academy of Letters, president of the Colombian Academy of History, honorary member of the Institute of Arts and Letters of the United States, vice-president of the American Committee for Freedom of Culture, and corresponding member of the academies of history of Argentina, Mexico, Cuba, Venezuela, Ecuador, and Chile. In addition, he has been visiting professor at the University of California, the University of Chicago, and Mills College, and he was a full member of the faculty of Columbia University from 1947 to 1959.

When the occasion calls for it, Arciniegas rises as the spokesman for America, making no distinctions between North and South, Hispanic, Anglo-Saxon, or Portuguese. For example, during a meeting in Berlin, he rebuffed a speaker who was portraying democracy as a European invention. Arciniegas reminded the speaker and the audience that in 1723, before Jean Jacques Rousseau's *Contrat Social* (*Social Contract*) of 1762, the Indians of Paraguay, led by some creoles, had proclaimed the right of *el comun* (the common people) to reject the orders of the king when those orders were not in the best interest of the people. He also reminded them that in 1780, before the French Revolution, the *comuneros* (common people) of Colombia had revolted, and that before the French Republic was created, Philadelphia had been proclaimed capital of a new republic in the Americas. He noted further that all American republics are older than all European ones—except France—and to complete the list, that the Mexican Revolution predated the Bolshevik uprising.

Yet Arciniegas is not blind to Latin American shortcomings. His pen can be as sharp as that of Juan Montalvo, the Ecuadorian writer known for his political virulence. He concedes that Latin America lags behind other parts of the world in many respects and is degraded by skepticism, cynicism, and lack of unity. He finds that Latin America has yielded its birthright as a "new world" to more aggressive and industrious regions of the globe, such as the new Soviet empire, post–World War II Africa, and Israel.

When criticizing, Arciniegas knows how to be diplomatic. In alluding to the territorial losses of Colombia and Mexico at the hands of the United States, he calls this result of Manifest Destiny "a reflection not of the philosophy formulated in Philadelphia, but of the imperial impulse that finds its origin in the history of the West, cradle and crown of the great European states" (*Cosas del pueblo* [Concerns of the People, 1962], p. 15).

A born writer, Arciniegas has written about history, culture, art, and travel in sociopolitical and critical essays, biographies, and hundreds of articles in magazines and newspapers all over America. The majority of his works represent a delightful blend of

fact, insight into the philosophy of history, and playful fantasy. He has served as director of the literary supplement of *El Tiempo,* one of Colombia's leading newspapers, and as editor in chief of that daily. Arciniegas explains his peripatetic career by saying that "in South America, we all have to be a little bit of everything; thus, if at the bullfight there is no matador, we shall be one, and if there is no bull, we play the bull" (Federico Córdova, *Vida y obras de Germán Arciniegas* [Life and Works of Germán Arciniegas, 1950], p. 22).

If we accept Hippolyte Taine's contention concerning the importance of psychology in a national literature and of the literature itself in the unfolding of the national character, we can take Arciniegas' literary legacy as an excellent point of departure from which to penetrate into the Colombian and, perhaps, the Latin American psyche. For years, historians of literature from both sides of the Atlantic have debated whether or not Spanish-American literature does, in fact, exist and if so, when it began. Arciniegas does not discuss or argue this point. Referring to Columbus' diary, he simply states that the first page of Spanish-American literature was written on 13 October 1492: "This is the only case in history in which the exact date, almost the hour, of the birth of a literature can be pinpointed," he explains. And, to support his assertion, he adds, "On that day, a European tongue—a Romance language—was used for the first time to describe the American landscape and to paint a picture of its people."

Arciniegas is a skillful observer of society. When reading his works, one has the impression of entering a bazaar where everything is small and colorful and where there are many sounds and noises, low prices, bargains, and a constant movement of people—in other words, action at low cost. This is not to imply that Arciniegas' works are meaningless, disorganized, or without a sense of direction. He is a truly gifted raconteur with his own technique and method, and in general, he is faithful to his own system. He composes many independent essays, some long, profound in scope, rich in information, and dense in style. Others are short, anecdotal, and humorous. *Entre la libertad y el miedo* (Between Liberty and Fear, 1952; published in English as *The State of Latin America*), a series of sociopolitical essays, is a good example of the first type. *Transparencias de Colombia* (Transparencies of Colombia, 1973), two small books containing sixty-seven narratives—halfway between Ramón Gómez de la Serna's *greguerías* (very personal impressions in prose of aspects of reality) and Ricardo Palma's *Tradiciones peruanas* (Peruvian Traditions, 1872)—epitomize his second type. *Jiménez de Quesada* (*The Knight of Eldorado*, 1938) is a tale of the discovery and conquest of what is today Colombia. The reader who may expect only dry facts and rigorous analysis will be pleasantly surprised by chapters such as "El barro, las niguas y la india" ("Mud, Chiggers and the Indian Woman"). Another case in point is his *Nueva imagen del Caribe* (New Face of the Caribbean, 1970), a sequel to his *Biografía del Caribe* (1945, published in English as *Caribbean: Sea of the New World*). In that work one finds chapter titles such as "Panamá, pollera y tamborito" (Panama, Skirt and a Little Drum) and "La gran ratonera" (The Big Mousehole).

Colombia (1969) and *Los comuneros* (The Common People, 1938) are similar in content but very different in approach. The revolution for independence from Spain is the central theme in both—expressed in the first as "Itinerario y espíritu de la independencia" (Itinerary and Spirit of the Independence Movement) and as "revolución de los comuneros" (the revolution of the common people) in the second. The similarity ends there. While the first is a series of official documents of the war for independence, the other has all the excitement of a romantic novel in a delightful blend that defies all efforts to separate fact from fantasy.

Arciniegas' contribution to the cause of the common people is outstanding, as can be noted in his writings on José Antonio Galán, the insurgent *mestizo* (person of mixed European and American Indian ancestry) who led the revolt of the *comuneros* in 1780 and who is presented by Arciniegas as the first actor in the declaration of independence from Spain. Arciniegas' book *Los comuneros* has inspired painters, sculptors, poets, and playwrights, who in the last five decades have re-created the heroic exploits of the great *caudillo* (popular leader) Galán in murals, statues, poems, and plays.

Arciniegas did not join the boom of the 1960's and 1970's with the great Spanish-American novelists in

either sales, production, or style. He remained more traditional. But his tireless efforts have contributed to move Colombia, a country known for its conservative attitudes, into a more contemporary and liberal mood. Arciniegas' publications have both the virtues and defects of journalism. The journalistic community has recognized his merits by awarding him the Cabot Prize, the Premio Alberdi-Sarmiento of *La Prensa* of Buenos Aires, the Hammarskjöld International Prize for Journalism and Diplomacy, and the international Premio de la Madonnina of Milan.

As a historian, Arciniegas complains that the textbooks of history are limited to political history, "what government officials and warriors did." He takes pride in writing "la pequeña historia" (the little history), or what Miguel de Unamuno has called "intrahistoria" (inner history). He has written a book about students, *El estudiante de la mesa redonda* (The Student of the Round Table, 1932), several on the man on the street, among them *Diario de un peatón* (Diary of a Pedestrian, 1936) and *Cosas del pueblo*, and one on the peasants, *Los comuneros*. He has written thousands of pages devoted to narratives of common people, common events, and common things. As minister of education, he founded the People's Library, which published some 110 titles by Colombian authors.

Arciniegas' populist tendency is evident in his emphasis on the importance of the *comuneros*. These are the people who, for Arciniegas as for Ernesto Sábato, existed in early communities with a profound feeling for love and death, for compassion and heroism. They were the people who comprised a group known as the *hijos de nada*, the have-nots of the nation. To help redeem them, Arciniegas wrote *Cosas del pueblo*, which focuses on common people from both Spain and Latin America. As a historian, he asks in the last chapter if "the twentieth century will be the century of the people and for the people."

Arciniegas is also a revolutionary, but his revolution is a student revolution, a university revolution. He applauds the 1767 expulsion of the Jesuits that permitted, particularly in Bogotá, the birth of the new universities, which brought together the students and the people. So, 151 years later, when the students of the University of Córdoba in Argentina rose up against the academic establishment, Arciniegas declared that those young men of Córdoba were expressing the will of all the students of America, and that "the revolution was proclaimed not as a political, but as a university revolution." All of this is because "the student is the conscience of America." That uprising in 1918 and the ensuing academic changes are known as the University Reform. Since then, Spanish-American universities have never been the same. They have been politicized. As a university student, Arciniegas resisted the government of his country in the same way Rómulo Gallegos did in Venezuela and Alejo Carpentier did in Cuba. The governments reacted, but "everything was and still is useless," declared Arciniegas, adding that "we have always been the seeds of revolution. . . . We students have been traditional conspirators at all times. . . . We carry revolution in our souls" (*El estudiante de la mesa redonda*, p. 9).

The most controversial aspect of Arciniegas' writings is his treatment of Spain. He still belongs to the core of romantic Americanists who, during the nineteenth century, fought for what they called "spiritual independence from Spain." Arciniegas never misses an opportunity to criticize the *conquistadores* (Spanish conquerors), the crown, and the colonial system in general. He puts the brunt of the blame on the Catholic church, pointing out, by way of contrast, the development of the Netherlands, England, and the United States, all largely Protestant countries. He is a firm believer in the *Leyenda negra*, or Black Legend, which holds that the *conquistadores* killed the Indians, the colonists exhausted the mines, and the officials of the Spanish crown did nothing but justify the abuses that they themselves often perpetrated.

However, sixty years after his first scolding of the *conquistadores*, Arciniegas acknowledged that "what there is of cruelty in the conquest belongs to systems that were universally accepted in Europe." This brings Arciniegas a little closer to Charles F. Lummis, a non-Hispanic and a staunch defender of the Spanish conquest. Moreover, Arciniegas emphasizes that it took only thirty years to conquer America, change the map of the world, give a new direction to the history of Europe, and uncover civilizations that could compete with those of Egypt, Babylon, Rome, and Carthage, and that all this was accomplished by ordinary people, some from the lowest strata of

Hispanic society. His description of the exploratory expeditions cannot but enhance the heroic status of many of these Castilians whose anonymity is an injustice to their bravery.

As far as influence is concerned, though he is well known in Colombia and in Latin American intellectual circles, two factors appear not to work in Arciniegas' favor: his audience and his style. In fact, he intends to reach the common reader, and he succeeds. Unfortunately, the common reader is not the one who makes history nor the one who changes history already written. On the other hand, Arciniegas' style, flowery here, frisky there, has been judged by some members of the intellectual elite as entertaining but banal. In spite of this, he continues his work with devotion and pride. The celebration of his eighty-sixth birthday in 1986 found him mentally alert, intellectually vigorous, professionally productive, and devoted to the principles for which he fought during his university years.

SELECTED BIBLIOGRAPHY

First Editions

Individual Works

El estudiante de la mesa redonda. Madrid, 1932.
La universidad colombiana. Bogotá, 1933.
Memorias de un congresista. Bogotá, 1934.
Diario de un peatón. Bogotá, 1936.
América, tierra firme. Santiago, Chile, 1937.
Los comuneros. Bogotá, 1938.
Jiménez de Quesada. Bogotá, 1938.
Los alemanes en la conquista de América. Buenos Aires, 1941.
Biografía del Caribe. Buenos Aires, 1945.
En el país de los rascacielos y las zanahorias. 2 vols. Bogotá, 1945.
Este pueblo de América. Mexico City, 1945. Expanded later and published as Cosas del pueblo.
El pensamiento vivo de Andrés Bello. Buenos Aires, 1946.
En medio del camino de la vida. Buenos Aires, 1949.
Entre la libertad y el miedo. Mexico City, 1952.
Amerigo y el Nuevo Mundo. Mexico City, 1955.
Italia, guía para vagabundos. Buenos Aires, 1957.

América mágica: Los hombres y los meses. Buenos Aires, 1959.

América mágica: Las mujeres y las horas. Buenos Aires, 1961.

Cosas del pueblo: Crónica de la historia vulgar. Mexico City, 1962. An expanded edition of *Este pueblo de América.*

El mundo de la bella Simonetta. Buenos Aires, 1962.

Entre el Mar Rojo y el Mar Muerto. Barcelona, 1964.

El continente de siete colores. Buenos Aires, 1965.

Genio y figura de Jorge Isaacs. Buenos Aires, 1967.

Nuevo diario de Noé. Caracas, 1968.

Colombia: Itinerario y espíritu de la independencia. Cali, Colombia, 1969.

Medio mundo entre un zapato. Buenos Aires, 1969.

Nueva imagen del Caribe. Buenos Aires, 1970.

Roma secretissima. Salamanca, Spain, 1972.

Transparencias de Colombia. 2 vols. Bogotá, 1973.

Estancia en Rumania. Bucharest, 1974.

América en Europa. Buenos Aires, 1975.

El zancudo: Introducción a la historia de la caricatura en Colombia. Bogotá, 1975.

Antología de León de Greiff. Bogotá, 1976.

Fernando Lorenzana. Bogotá, 1978.

Fernando Botero. Paris, 1979.

El revés de la historia. Bogotá, 1980.

Simón Bolívar. Rome, 1980.

20,000 comuneros hacia Santa Fe. Bogotá, 1981.

Los pinos nuevos. Tunja, Colombia, 1982.

Bolívar y la revolución. Bogotá, 1984.

Collected Works

Páginas escogidas (1932–1973). Madrid, 1975.

Translations

Amerigo and the New World. Translated by Harriet de Onís. New York, 1955.

Caribbean: Sea of the New World [*Biografía del Caribe*]. Translated by Harriet de Onís. New York, 1946.

Germans in the Conquest of America. Translated by Ángel Flores. New York, 1943.

The Knight of Eldorado [*Jiménez de Quesada*]. Translated by Mildred Adams. New York, 1942.

Latin America: A Cultural History [*Cosas del pueblo*]. Translated by Joan MacLean. New York, 1966.

The State of Latin America [*Entre la libertad y el miedo*]. Translated by Harriet de Onís. New York, 1952.

Biographical and Critical Studies

Córdova, Federico. *Vida y obras de Germán Arciniegas.* Havana, 1950.

González Blanco, Pedro. *Against Arciniegas.* Ciudad Trujillo, Dominican Republic, 1956.

Mariano Picón Salas

(1901–1965)

Guillermo Sucre

Mariano Picón Salas was born on 26 January 1901, in Mérida, a city in the Venezuelan Andes known for its magnificent landscapes and cultural tradition. His family's heroic past and intellectual tradition lent a rich and lively setting to his childhood and adolescence. With his French tutor, Picón Salas studied languages and science, and even took on a touch of ideological rebellion. One of his first readings with the tutor was François Fénelon's *Télémaque* (1699). When he entered the university in 1917 he was precocious; he delivered a lecture that fall entitled "Las nuevas corrientes del arte" (The New Currents in Art). When Picón Salas arrived in Caracas to study law in 1920, he published his first book, *Buscando el camino* (Searching for the Road). These essays are concerned with the constant spiritual search that characterizes Picón Salas' work. He remained in Caracas for only two years. He felt little desire to study law (there were too many lawyers in Venezuela, he contended), and the spectacle of Juan Vicente Gómez' long tyranny, which had begun in 1908, oppressed him.

Upon his return to Mérida in 1923, Picón Salas was met with the financial collapse of his family. In order to make his living he decided to travel to Chile—"the cheapest country in South America, as well as the freest," he would write in 1959. "My last

Paradise was vanishing. . . . the weariness of yet another peregrination had begun." *Peregrination* is a key word in Picón Salas' destiny. The years that he spent abroad amounted to almost half of his life. He became acquainted with many countries and wrote about them from the point of view not of the professional traveler but of the pilgrim who had undertaken the adventure in search of experience and knowledge.

The thirteen years spent in Santiago, Chile, were years of spiritual growth. The young man confronted and overcame vicissitudes and hardships to which he was unaccustomed. He studied history and obtained his doctorate in philosophy and literature in 1928; later he worked as a librarian and professor. He published the first of his narrative works and essays, which are a search for what he called "a Latin American historic conscience," that is, a will to transform the unrelenting pathos of life in Latin America into a lucid collective enterprise. During these years, his political conception was already keenly perceptive. Within the rather sterile controversy of his exiled fellow countrymen about ideologies and tactics to be applied in Venezuela, Picón Salas let his own response be heard: "The idea of nation exists before the idea of classes." The mind at work in such a realistic analysis was also a sensibility shaped by literature and art, fields in which he taught at the University of Chile.

Picón Salas returned to Caracas in 1936, shortly after the death of the dictator Gómez and in time to experience the opening up of the possibility of democracy in his country. He was more valuable than a mere specialist; he possessed an intelligence apt to confront, with moderation as well as efficiency, the problems of a nation that seemed only then to be entering the twentieth century. Although he left his mark in the little he was given to do (especially in education), the circumstances were not in his favor. In the summer of 1936, he was appointed chargé d'affaires to Prague. From Prague he visited various countries in the Europe he so admired; their dramatic image is reflected in his first great book of essays, *Preguntas a Europa* (Questions for Europe), which first appeared in Santiago, Chile, in 1937, where Picón Salas had returned and lived until 1938, again as a professor.

The following four years, spent in Caracas, were more propitious for his work. He founded and directed the *Revista nacional de cultura*; he taught and wrote new books. In 1940, three of these were published; among them was the first modern study of Venezuelan literature. The period from 1942 to 1944 was one of his most creative and productive. He traveled to the United States and taught at Smith College, Middlebury College, and Columbia University. Two of his books were published in Mexico, revealing the richness of his personality. *Viaje al amanecer* (Journey to Dawn, 1943) is a subtle fictional evocation of his childhood. *De la conquista a la independencia: Tres siglos de historia cultural hispanoamericana* (1944; published in English as *A Cultural History of Spanish America: From Conquest to Independence*) earned him international prestige as a scholar. Picón Salas had achieved a mastery that allowed him to reconcile public life with the intimate life of the writer. In 1946 he founded the Faculty of Philosophy and Letters of the Central University at Caracas, initiating modern humanistic studies in Venezuela.

Again Picón Salas chose, at times as a self-exile, to be an itinerant professor in Puerto Rico, Mexico, and the United States. He also filled various diplomatic posts, as ambassador to Colombia from 1947 to 1948, to Brazil from 1958 to 1959, to UNESCO in Paris from 1959 to 1962, and to Mexico in 1962. His work did not suffer and remained as rich and varied as ever. In 1947, he expanded his original work on the old continent in *Europa-América* (Europe-America). Within the next six years, Picón Salas published three biographies that are also reconstructions of different periods: of Francisco de Miranda and independence; of Pedro Claver and the colonial years; and of the dictator Cipriano Castro and the Venezuela of 1900. To his travel literature, he added books and essays about Mexico and Brazil. Picón Salas' last books gained intensity: they are the dramatic though serene vision of an essayist who returns to tackle the dilemmas of modern man with a more radical perspective. This new vision appeared for the first time in 1959 with *Regreso de tres mundos* (Return from Three Worlds), an autobiography and spiritual testament. In 1962, he continued the new vein with *Los malos salvajes* (The Ignoble Savages).

During the whole of 1964, Picón Salas had worked to organize one of the cultural enterprises that had always moved him, a National Institute of Culture and Fine Arts. He died in Caracas on 1 January 1965, and the institute became official in the same month; for the first time in Venezuela the state had established an extensive cultural policy. Picón Salas died pursuing his lifelong desire to reconcile the aesthetic man and the man of action. The speech he had prepared for the inauguration of the institute is a model of tolerant and perceptive humanism. He also left a volume of essays that, with the title *Suma de Venezuela* (A Summary of Venezuela, 1966), was a new version that broadens and enriches the earlier book *Comprensión de Venezuela* (Understanding Venezuela, 1949). In the brief prologue, dated "at the end of 1964," he concludes: "Fortunately, living is more problematic or more poetic than certain simplistic entrepreneurs of myths, who are also usually candidates for the position of hangman, would presume."

Picón Salas' work includes various genres: the essay, the narrative, studies on literature and art, autobiography, history, and biography. It would not be difficult to point to what defines the author in each one. However, we would then run the risk of missing the more subtle qualities, sometimes complex and even unorthodox, that characterize the whole and the best of his work.

He was often a magnificent narrator, but not, paradoxically, in his fictional works. Even in his most ambitious novels—*Odisea de tierra firme* (Mainland Odyssey, 1931) and *Los tratos de la noche* (Night Deals, 1955), the narrative interest is lost in the badly wrought plot and in the intrusive intellectual digressions. Furthermore, the time periods that each novel evokes, the Venezuela of the provincial *caudillos* and the modern Venezuela of the oil boom, are poorly drawn, more alluded to than re-created. The contrast is striking when we turn to other works in which the narrative is vivid and elegant, the delineation of characters strong, the reconstruction of the settings suggestive, and the interplay among these elements dynamic. These traits are well adapted to the autobiography and biography; they are even inherent aspects of both genres. Within them, Picón Salas wrote some of his most perfect books—perfect, however, in a peculiar way. His autobiographies are far from being records of his life: the first is a fusion of fiction and reality; the second is more a testimony, but it is also more introspective. This second autobiography is one of Picón Salas' greatest books of essays—essays that originate in his own experience.

In Picón Salas' biographies, the imaginative counts as much as the documental evidence, and the imaginative is found not in inventions, but in the tone of a style that captures the spirit of an age. In *Miranda* (1946), Picón Salas makes use of the dynamic setting in the historical epic and drama to highlight the victorious yet tragic destiny of the character. In *Pedro Claver, el santo de los esclavos* (Pedro Claver, The Saint of Slaves, 1950), the narrator is a craftsman-painter who painstakingly reproduces a woeful and mystic time, the colonial years. In *Los días de Cipriano Castro* (The Days of Cipriano Castro, 1953), the biographer is a chronicler with a modern, sarcastic mind: the facts he stores and then confronts give shape to the comedy, sometimes grotesque as well as naive, of the Venezuela of 1900.

These traits, so characteristic of Picón Salas, would seem incompatible with the erudite historical studies and essays to which he owes a great part of his renown. Should not a historian describe and analyze the facts he is studying objectively? Should not an

essayist, as he reveals ideas or impressions, follow a logical train of thought? Picón Salas did not disregard these demands, but neither did he follow the norms submissively. He succeeded in transforming these norms by referring them back to their original context. Picón Salas, that is, wrote like a man of letters, in the humanistic sense of the word.

A Cultural History of Spanish America is an example. In it, three centuries of Latin American culture, somewhat ignored until then, are analyzed and clearly ordered. Furthermore, the major currents that continue to give form to Latin American thought and that constitute its collective memory are underscored: the writings of the *cronistas* (chroniclers), the aesthetic of the baroque, and the influence of the Enlightenment. The book is written as an agile and brilliant synthesis that orders its material in a novel way: it presents not a mere summary for the reader but rather the intimate rhythm of the facts and of the imagination that re-creates them. Picón Salas succeeded in creating not so much another norm as a new perspective in historical studies. For Picón Salas, history was more an art than a science, not only in its analysis, but also in its insights and comparisons. History must be rescued from the negligence of specialists and given back its reputation "as one of the most exemplary disciplines in the humanities." "To write history," he argued, "is much more than a technique for bringing together documents and marking off time periods; it is a way of casting light upon life's unfolding plot" (*Viejos y nuevos mundos* [Old and New Worlds], pp. 507–508). Picón Salas possessed an essential gift, one that was linked to his verbal imagination and to his talent for synthesis. It is this gift that truly makes *A Cultural History of Spanish America* a valuable book, as it does his best research work, whether in history, literature, or art.

When, in 1953, Picón Salas wrote a preface to his *Obras selectas* (Selected Works), he spoke of his work as a work of literature. It is literature that truly connects him to everything, and which, in turn, makes everything connect to him. The essay—a genre that for its very broadness and preciseness creates a space where thought and imagination come together—is the genre that most faithfully defines Picón Salas. He was essentially an essayist, and he had what distinguishes the most genuine among those writers—the ability to give ideas a concrete form. From the writings of Michel Eyquem de Montaigne ("patron of essayists," he called him), Picón Salas learned that the essay originates in the questioning of absolute truths, and that, therefore, its language should free itself of any claim to infallibility. Thus, Picón Salas' style is characterized by tentative, doubting, and interrogative forms. His writing shows an aesthetic and ethical courtesy toward the reader and persuades, as it were, by establishing a dialogue in which the reader hears his own voice, his own doubts and expectations.

Ángel Rosenblat, a wise and learned philologist, considered Picón Salas to be the greatest prose writer in Venezuela and one of the greatest in the Spanish language. Picón Salas' prose has the warm lucidity of one who cultivates the concurrence of ideas. Meditation upon language underlies Picón Salas' thought. In the presence of a verbalistic or dogmatic Spanish tradition, Picón Salas longs for an ideal of moderation and simplicity capable of grasping the concrete. Above all, he is opposed to the perversion of language into a form of power. He continuously denounces the dizzying manipulation of ideologies. Picón Salas claimed that never more than in our time "has lying, a monstrous public business, had so much pull" (*Viejos y nuevos mundos,* pp. 490–491). He strove, then, to restore the integrity of words and to strengthen the primary freedom of man: his conscience. No form of justice, no dazzling utopia could be set above this freedom.

These ideas inform the major theme in *Regreso de tres mundos*: the struggle of a conscience to deliberate justly among the false myths that oppress modern life and that create the deluded obligation of a brotherhood by decree. This, however, is not the sole value of the book. There is also the narrative voice that evokes a life and its daily wanderings, not in order to educate or preach but simply for the pleasure of retelling the adventure. For Picón Salas, it is the journey that is most interesting as a metaphor for life. This metaphor works to restore freedom to everything: one lives, Homer says, so that everything can later be turned into a story, a song, a memory. Once again, aesthetic and history, life and form come together in Picón Salas' work. He states in the first chapter: "Only for a story that is also called history do we narrate what has happened to us. Telling stories is more than a practical lesson; it is a liberating force within the weariness of men."

The worldwide recognition of Latin American literature and culture is due in part to writers such as Picón Salas. He did more than help Latin Americans to see themselves as a whole, a unity within a pluralism, and to become, at the same time, more intelligible to others. He also tried to make Latin Americans, in turn, understand the world in a more problematic light so that they would not fall prey to the myths that, far from stimulating a creative spirit, isolated them in a confused, obstinate, and endless search for an identity. Therein lies Picón Salas' desire to oppose the myth of the "New World" that seemed to condemn Latin Americans to historical abeyance. Seemingly in possession of a privileged, original, and almost paradisiacal reality, Latin Americans have not acted in the face of their destiny, but rather have waited for the myth to come true, as if by the grace of God. More than in the search for an identity, though he never put this aside, and more than in the cult of illusory myths, Picón Salas was interested in the creative will. From this interest came his challenge to small nations: the fact that they are kept at the margin of international political and economic power—a position that frequently leads to self-sufficiency—should make these nations more inventive in the field of culture. "Art and culture are the only forms of salvation to which small nations can aspire," he wrote in *Viejos y nuevos mundos* (p. 397). This does not imply a resignation, but rather a form of wisdom, the meditation of a Latin American on the world. His work attempted to make Latin America a subject and not merely an object of its own history and of history as a whole; he simultaneously explored the human condition and the adventure of a freedom opposed to determinism.

Picón Salas' work reveals a struggle of the spirit against all forms of power. He believed that education should teach us not to possess but to exist, and that culture, in turn, is knowing how to live together, not how to dominate each other. This is Picón Salas' greatest achievement: he created a universal dialogue that originated in his Latin American experience.

SELECTED BIBLIOGRAPHY

First Editions

Essays

Buscando el camino. Caracas, 1920.

Intuición de Chile y otros ensayos en busca de una conciencia histórica. Santiago, Chile, 1935.

Preguntas a Europa. Santiago, Chile, 1937.

Un viaje y seis retratos. Caracas, 1940.

1941: Cinco discursos sobre pasado y presente de la nación venezolana. Caracas, 1940.

Europa-América: Preguntas a la esfinge de la cultura. Mexico City, 1947. Includes Preguntas a Europa.

Comprensión de Venezuela. Caracas, 1949.

Dependencia e independencia en la historia hispanoamericana. Caracas, 1952.

Gusto de México. Mexico City, 1952.

Suramérica: Período colonial. Mexico City, 1953.

Crisis, cambio, tradición. Caracas and Madrid, 1955.

Las nieves de antaño: Pequeña añoranza de Mérida. Maracaibo, Venezuela, 1958.

Los malos salvajes: Civilización y política contemporáneas. Buenos Aires, 1962.

Hora y deshora. Caracas, 1963.

Suma de Venezuela. Caracas, 1966. A collection of his writings on Venezuela, prepared by Picón Salas.

Prose Narratives and Novels

Mundo imaginario. Santiago, Chile, 1927.

Odisea de tierra firme. Madrid, 1931.

Registro de huéspedes. Santiago, Chile, 1934.

Los tratos de la noche. Barquisimeto, Venezuela, 1955.

Cultural Histories

Problemas y métodos de la historia del arte. Santiago, Chile, 1934.

Formación y proceso de la literatura venezolana. Caracas, 1940.

De la conquista a la independencia: Tres siglos de historia cultural hispanoamericana. Mexico City, 1944.

Perspectiva de la pintura venezolana. Caracas, 1954.

Estudios de literatura venezolana. Caracas and Madrid, 1961. Revised and enlarged edition of Formación y proceso de la literatura venezolana.

Autobiographies

Viaje al amanecer. Mexico City, 1943.

Regreso de tres mundos: Un hombre en su generación. Mexico City, 1959.

Biographies

Miranda. Buenos Aires, 1946.

Pedro Claver, el santo de los esclavos. Mexico City, 1950.

Los días de Cipriano Castro (Historia venezolana del 1900). Caracas, 1953.

Collected Works

Ensayos escogidos. Edited by Juan Loveluck and with a prologue by Ricardo A. Latcham. Santiago, Chile, 1958.

Obras selectas. Caracas and Madrid, 1953; 2nd ed. 1962. Prepared by Picón Salas, these are selected pieces written after 1933. The author's preface provides valuable insight.

Later Editions

Comprensión de Venezuela. Edited and with a preface by Guillermo Sucre. Caracas, 1976.

Dependencia e independencia en la historia latinoamericana. With an introduction by Roberto Esquenazi Mayo. Caracas, 1977. Selections from Intuición de Chile, Europa-América, and the book with the same title.

Formación y proceso de la literatura venezolana. With an introduction by María Fernanda Palacios and an updated bibliography by Rafael A. Rivas. Caracas, 1984. This volume reproduces the 1961 edition of Estudios de literatura venezolana.

Las formas y las visiones. Edited and with a preface by Juan C. Palenzuela. Caracas, 1984. This volume collects almost all of the author's writings on art, including those not previously published in book form.

"Viaje al amanecer" y "Pedro Claver, el santo de los esclavos." Barcelona, 1980.

Viejos y nuevos mundos. Edited and with an introductory study and chronology by Guillermo Sucre and a bibliography by Rafael A. Rivas. Caracas, 1983. Selected essays.

Translations

A Cultural History of Spanish America: From Conquest to Independence. Translated by Irving A. Leonard. Berkeley, Calif., 1962.

The Ignoble Savages. Translated by Herbert Weinstock. New York, 1965.

Biographical and Critical Studies

Arcila Farías, Eduardo. "Mariano Picón Salas; Su obra histórica." Revista de historia 4/22:51–56 (1965).

Azzario, Esther. La prosa autobiográfica de Mariano Picón Salas. Caracas, 1980.

Bente, Thomas Otey. "Man and Circumstance: A Study of Mariano Picón Salas' Works." Ph.D. diss., University of California, Los Angeles, 1969.

Earle, Peter G., and Robert G. Mead. "Mariano Picón Salas." In *Historia del ensayo hispanoamericano.* Mexico City, 1973.

Feliú Cruz, Guillermo. *Para un retrato psicológico de Mariano Picón Salas.* Santiago, Chile, 1970.

Freyre, Gilberto. "Mariano Picón Salas y su imagen de Brasil." *Política* 4/39:27–33 (1965).

Grases, Pedro. *Mariano Picón Salas, o la Inquietud hispanoamericana.* Caracas, 1966.

Henríquez Ureña, Pedro. "Mariano Picón Salas." In *Carnet crítico.* Montevideo, 1962.

Liscano, Juan. "Mariano Picón Salas." In *Panorama de la literatura venezolana actual.* Caracas, 1973. Pp. 319–328.

Morin, Thomas D. *Mariano Picón Salas.* Twayne's World Authors Series no. 545. Boston, 1979. The most complete study in English.

Rosenblat, Ángel. "Mariano Picón Salas." In *La primera visión de América y otros estudios.* 2nd ed. Caracas, 1969. Pp. 223, 248.

Siso Martínez, J. M. *Mariano Picón Salas: Ensayo inacabado.* Caracas, 1970.

Uslar Pietri, Arturo. "El regreso de los mundos de Mariano Picón Salas." In *En busca del nuevo mundo.* Mexico City, 1969. Pp. 161–167.

José Lins do Rego

(1901–1957)

Bobby J. Chamberlain

Of the major Brazilian novelists of the 1930's and 1940's, José Lins do Rego is probably the one whose fiction was most intimately connected with the experiences of his childhood and early adolescence. He was born on 3 June 1901, on the sugar plantation of his maternal grandfather in rural Paraíba state, and was raised by maiden aunts, after losing his mother at the age of eight months. He grew up amid the field hands, mill workers, domestics, storytellers, and other former slaves and their children who still served the members of the decadent landed aristocracy of the coastal northeastern cane region. The events and characters of this crumbling patriarchal society would later yield much of the raw material for his early, quasi-autobiographical fiction. When he was ten, José was sent to boarding school in the town of Itabaiana, a woeful experience that served as the subject of one of his first novels. He later continued his studies in the state capital of João Pessoa (then called Paraíba), before enrolling in the law school at Recife in 1919.

There he came into contact with Gilberto Freyre, José Américo de Almeida, Olívio Montenegro, and others who were to help shape his career as a writer and with whom he joined in 1926 to form the Regionalist Movement. While proclaiming allegiance to northeastern values and themes and at the same time avowing its independence from the modernists of São Paulo and Rio de Janeiro, that movement served to blend the new aesthetic innovations of Europe and the urban South with the regionalist, rural, and more sociologically oriented concerns of the Brazilian Northeast. By this time, Zé Lins, as he came to be called, had already begun writing literary reviews and political articles for newspapers and journals in Paraíba and Recife. This journalistic activity was to continue throughout his life. In 1932, he published his first work of fiction, *Menino de Engenho* (*Plantation Boy*), which was widely acclaimed. It was soon followed by a string of other novels (which eventually totaled twelve), as well as volumes of children's stories, essays, and memoirs. In 1935, he moved to Rio de Janeiro. He was elected to the Brazilian Academy of Letters in 1955, and he died on 12 September 1957 in Rio de Janeiro.

Lins do Rego is best known for his creation of what he termed the Sugar Cane Cycle, a series of novels, beginning with *Plantation Boy*, that also includes *Doidinho* (literally Daffy Boy, 1933; translated into English as *Doidinho*), *Bangüê* (literally The Old Plantation, 1934; translated into English as *Bangüê*), *O Moleque Ricardo* (Black Boy Richard, 1935), *Usina* (The Sugar Refinery, 1936), and his masterpiece, *Fogo Morto* (Dead Fires, 1943). In *Fogo*

909

Morto, he chronicles the progressive economic and social decay of the once-prosperous sugar plantations as they are forced to give way to the larger, mechanized, and more financially viable sugar mills owned by absentee corporations. Whatever the social and economic injustices fostered by the former, he seems to argue, the latter were in some ways no improvement, replacing an oppressive, patriarchal, but personalistic system with one that was just as exploitative but that, for the most part, lacked the human element. Such novels, however, were not merely documentaries of the painful socioeconomic transition from late feudalism to early capitalism. Lins do Rego's style and tone have often been characterized as *memorialista* (autobiographical), nostalgic, folkloric, or as imitative of those of the traditional northeastern storyteller. Indeed, all of these elements are present, particularly in his early works. The wistful, bittersweet, and at times somber first-person reminiscences of the protagonist's childhood have been likened to the sentimental vision expressed by the Brazilian novelist Raul Pompéia in *O Ateneu* (The Atheneum, 1888), which recounts the author's agonizing experiences as a young student at an authoritarian boarding school.

That novels such as *Plantation Boy* and *Doidinho* rely heavily on details from Lins do Rego's childhood is confirmed by his later volume of memoirs, *Meus Verdes Anos* (My Tender Years, 1956). While unquestionably nostalgic in their evocation of times past, the novels are fraught with the protagonist's unquenched longing for maternal love, his pessimism and sadness, and his ever-present fear of death and disease amid the debris of a vanishing order. But it would be a mistake to regard such works as mere autobiographical accounts of the author's formative years, for the imprint of his creative imagination is ever present, and it is never easy to determine where real life ends and fiction begins, so skillfully intertwined are the two elements.

The linearity of the narration, the seemingly episodic plot structure, and the author's frequent description of picturesque local customs, superstitions, and character types have led critics to compare the style of the early works with that of traditional storytellers. While there are valid points of similarity, many elements distinguish Lins do Rego's fiction from the popular formulaic narrative: the adult narrator's constant juxtapositions of past and present, of his former naïveté with his current sophistication, and of his erstwhile unquestioning acceptance of the societal status quo with his later critical attitude. At times, he seems, in fact, to be obsessed with placing the two attitudes in confrontation, as if by doing so he could better explain the one with the other. Thus, to the more obvious sentimentalization of childhood is added a second, ironic dimension; while with one hand the narrator paints a nostalgic picture, with the other he strives vigorously to undercut this vision.

Still, the novelist's preference for the portrayal of local customs and character types—religious festivals, sexual initiation rites, superstitions, bandits, storytellers, mystics, and the like—cannot but suggest the popular flavor of the northeastern folktales. Some critics have also seen in his creation of such types as the severe but merciful patriarch, the weak-willed, profligate son, and assorted shrinking, sanctimonious female characters an attempt to transport to the realm of fiction the findings of Freyre's sociohistorical treatises on traditional northeastern patriarchal society. Others have alleged the presence of racial stereotyping in the novelist's depiction of such types as the black mammy and the lustful *mulata* (woman of mixed black and white ancestry). Whatever the validity of these claims, it is certain that, like the storytellers of the region, Lins do Rego draws freely not only on character typing but also on caricature, hyperbole, and repetition to convey meaning. Hence the larger-than-life, sometimes almost cartoonlike quality of many of his finest characters; unidimensional though they may be, like some of the characters of Charles Dickens, they somehow escape the woodenness that ought by rights to doom them.

This is not to say, however, that the novelist neglects the psychological dimension of his characters. In fact, the opposite is true; Lins do Rego generally downplays the obvious social concerns of his fiction in order to devote greater attention to the thoughts, feelings, behavior, and motivations of his characters, for he sees individuals, rather than abstract classes and institutions, as embodying the social forces of a particular historical period. If a society possesses deficiencies and inequities, they will be displayed in the character flaws of its citizens. So too should the societal imperfections of a particular fictional universe be reflected in the psychological and moral fabric of its dramatis personae. Like William Faulkner, who sought to depict the decadent economic, social, and moral conditions of the traditional American rural South through psychological portraiture of its inhabitants, Lins do Rego approaches a similar situation first and foremost from the standpoint of the inner workings and development of characters. Less audacious than the Mississippian in his use of such experimental narrative techniques as direct interior monologue and stream of consciousness, he is much more inclined to exploit traditional, even folkloric modes of narration and characterization, which some critics have regarded not as an indication of his lesser literary skill, but rather as a kind of deceptive simplicity expressly designed to draw attention away from the "literariness" of his work. More inclined to the "unsophisticated" overstatement of Jorge Amado than to the subtle and often ironic understatement of Graciliano Ramos or Joaquim Maria Machado de Assis, he has not always been as appreciated as he should have been from a strictly aesthetic point of view.

Central to the Sugar Cane Cycle is its continuing, sagalike story, which the author weaves together with the aid of ongoing characters. In *Plantation Boy*, we witness the childhood of Carlos de Melo on the Santa Rosa plantation owned by his grandfather, Coronel José Paulino. The novel ends with Carlos' departure for boarding school. *Doidinho* is the story of his school days and is followed by *Bangüê*, set ten years later, which tells of his return to Santa Rosa to take control of its operation and of the failure with which he meets. *O Molegue Ricardo* is a spin-off from the central story line. It recounts the adventures of one of Carlos' poor childhood playmates, who has gone to live in the slums of Recife and whose political agitation eventually leads to his imprisonment on the island of Fernando de Noronha. Despite its change of setting and theme, the author considered the novel as part of the cycle. Indeed, Ricardo appears in several other novels of the cycle and in *Usina* returns to the sugarcane region, only to die a miserable death. Chronologically, *Usina* concludes the process of modernization as Santa Rosa, now under the direction of Dr. Juca, is mechanized and loses much of its human character; and thematically, this novel deals more extensively with the presence of migrants from the drought-plagued interior (the *sertão*), a topic that Lins do Rego takes up and explores in greater depth and from other angles in later novels.

Although written and published after *Usina*, *Fogo Morto* deals with an earlier period in the decline of the old plantations. It is divided into three parts, the first of which narrates the story of Mestre José Amaro, a poor but proud independent craftsman, who, after a long, silent agony, is driven to suicide by a host of adversities, among them his daughter's insanity, his abandonment by his wife, and his public humiliation. The second part is about Coronel Lula de Hollanda Chacon, owner of the bankrupt Santa Fé plantation. An impoverished aristocrat, obsessed with the trappings of wealth and power connected to his once exalted position, he is unable to face his hostile circumstances and attempts to conceal them from the world through ever more ludicrous displays of refinement. The third part of the triptych centers on Capitão Vitorino Carneiro da Cunha, a quixotic figure who is perhaps the author's most memorable character. Trailed by gangs of jeering ragamuffins, he rides from plantation to plantation perched atop an aging jenny, for the purpose of righting wrongs and defending the underdog.

What distinguishes *Fogo Morto* from the earlier novels, besides the characters themselves, is, on the one hand, its tripartite division (the sections serve to complement each other well, both stylistically and thematically) and, on the other, its greater reliance on dialogue (alongside interior monologue and the narrator's external description) to convey the inner workings of the three principal characters. More than in the author's previous works, the characters are seen not only through their thoughts, or subjectively, through the eyes of first-person narrator-agents, but from various angles, such as the thoughts of other characters about them and their conversations with other characters. Disparities often emerge between a character's ego and his public persona or between his feelings and his actions, thus giving rise to irony. Furthermore, the novelist's use of the regional vernacular, while endowing the narrative with greater authenticity and local color, tends to belie its increased universality.

Pedra Bonita (Wondrous Rock, 1938) and *Cangaceiros* (The Bandits, 1953) are set in the dry *sertão*. The first deals with the problem of religious fanaticism, which has plagued the region since the earliest days of the Portuguese colony. The second, in some respects a continuation of the first, revolves around the organized banditry that was rife in the *sertão* through the first third of the twentieth century. *Pureza* (Purity, 1937; published in English as *Pureza*), which takes place in the bucolic setting of a small railway stop, celebrates the regenerative powers of nature, while in *Riacho Doce* (Freshwater Creek, 1939), *Água-Mãe* (The Water Mother, 1941), and *Eurídice* (Eurydice, 1947), Lins do Rego seeks to escape the regionalist mold by turning to other locales and setting his plots in the present day. In each of the last four works, moreover, he consciously attempts to address the universal human condition, stripped of its parochial trappings.

During his lifetime, Lins do Rego was regarded by much of the Brazilian critical establishment as one of the finest novelists ever to come out of the Northeast. In recent years, however, critical assessment of his works has been mixed. Some critics hold the view that his fiction has been overrated, resting primarily on a popular preference during the 1930's and 1940's for works that were first and foremost social documents; in their opinion, his literary standing can only diminish. Others regard his works as overly sentimental, unsophisticated, or simplistic in construction. And some have contended that, even from an ideological standpoint, much of Zé Lins' fiction leaves a great deal to be desired, appearing at times to express as much sympathy for the oppressor as for the oppressed. Yet still others have begun to reassess the novels of the Sugar Cane Cycle, as well as the author's other works, finding in both ample reason for predicting that in the future he will be held in even greater esteem than he was by his contemporaries.

Whether one admires the Paraíban novelist or dismisses him as possessing only historical importance, it seems clear that he was probably the most representative northeastern novelist of his generation and that his true literary value can best be gauged within the aesthetic context of his times. For the most part, even his most ardent detractors find it difficult to deny the status of *Fogo Morto* as a literary masterpiece or to consign characters such as Vitorino Carneiro da Cunha or Mestre José Amaro to oblivion. Lins do Rego's reputation as a writer will in all likelihood continue to fluctuate according to the prevailing literary tastes and aesthetic values of the moment.

SELECTED BIBLIOGRAPHY

Editions

Novels

Menino de Engenho. Rio de Janeiro, 1932.
Doidinho. Rio de Janeiro, 1933.
Bangüê. Rio de Janeiro, 1934.
O Moleque Ricardo. Rio de Janeiro, 1935.
Usina. Rio de Janeiro, 1936.
Pureza. Rio de Janeiro, 1937.
Pedra Bonita. Rio de Janeiro, 1938.
Riacho Doce. Rio de Janeiro, 1939.
Água-Mãe. Rio de Janeiro, 1941.
Brandão entre o Mar e o Amor. São Paulo, 1942. With Jorge Amado, Graciliano Ramos, Aníbal Machado, and Rachel de Queiroz. Lins do Rego contributed the second part, "Mistério de Brandão (Glória)."
Fogo Morto. Rio de Janeiro, 1943.
Eurídice. Rio de Janeiro, 1947.
Cangaceiros. Rio de Janeiro, 1953.

Memoirs

Meus Verdes Anos. Rio de Janeiro, 1956.

Children's Literature

Histórias da Velha Totônia. Rio de Janeiro, 1936. In some more recent editions, called *Estórias da Velha Totônia.*

Collections of Essays and Articles

Gordos e Magros. Rio de Janeiro, 1942.
Poesia e Vida. Rio de Janeiro, 1945.
Homens, Seres e Coisas. Rio de Janeiro, 1952.
A Casa e o Homem. Rio de Janeiro, 1954.
Presença do Nordeste na Literatura Brasileira. Rio de Janeiro, 1957.
O Vulcão e a Fonte. Rio de Janeiro, 1958. Posthumous edition.
Dias Idos e Vividos: Antologia. Rio de Janeiro, 1981. Posthumous edition.

Lectures, Speeches

Pedro Américo. Rio de Janeiro, 1943.
Conferências no Prata (Tendências do Romance Brasileiro, Raul Pompéia, Machado de Assis). Rio de Janeiro, 1946.
Discursos de Posse e Recepção na Academia Brasileira de Letras. Rio de Janeiro, 1957.

Travel Descriptions

Bota de Sete Léguas. Rio de Janeiro, 1951.
Roteiro de Israel. Rio de Janeiro, 1955.
Gregos e Troianos. Rio de Janeiro, 1957.

Collected Works

Ficção Completa. 2 vols. Rio de Janeiro, 1976.
Obras. 11 vols. Rio de Janeiro, 1947.
Romance de José Lins do Rego. 12 vols. Rio de Janeiro, 1956. Includes introductory studies. New ed. 1968.
Romances Reunidos e Ilustrados de José Lins do Rego. 5 vols. Rio de Janeiro, 1960–1961.
Romances Reunidos e Ilustrados de José Lins do Rego. 12 vols. Rio de Janeiro and Brasília, 1980.

Translations

"Dead Fires" (ten-page excerpt). Translated by Susan Hertelendy. In *The Borzoi Anthology of Latin American Literature* 1, edited by Emir Rodríguez Monegal. New York, 1977. Pp. 446–458.
Plantation Boy. Translated by Emmi Baum. New York, 1966. Includes translations of *Menino de Engenho* (*Plantation Boy*), *Doidinho*, and *Bangüê*.
Pureza: A Brazilian Novel. Translated by Lucie Marion. London, 1948.

Biographical and Critical Studies

Castello, José Aderaldo. *José Lins do Rego: Modernismo e Regionalismo.* São Paulo, 1961.
_____. "Introdução aos Romances de José Lins do Rego."

In *Menino de Engenho*, by José Li[ns] Rio de Janeiro, 1969. Pp. xvii–
Coutinho, Edilberto. *José Lins do Re[go]* Brasília, 1971.
_____. *O Romance do Açúcar: J[osé]* *Obra.* Rio de Janeiro and Br[
Dacanal, José Hildebrando. "Fo[go] pretação Genética Estrutur[
Porto Alegre, Brazil, 197[0
Ellison, Fred P. *Brazil's Ne[w]* *Masters.* Berkeley, Calif.
Gomes, Heloísa Toller. *O Po[* 1981. Compares *Fogo [* *Absalom!*
Hulet, Claude L. *Brazilian[* 1975. Pp. 271–282.
Laws, David Paul. "From[do Rego's 'Ciclo d[University of Illin[
Lima, Luiz Costa. In[Afrânio Coutinh[283–304.
Lins, Álvaro, Otto[son. *José Lins[
Martins, Wilson.[Rego." Prefa[Rio de Jane[
Pacheco, João.[de Janeiro[
Rose, Theod[Develop[Brazil a[Rego.'[
Seniff, De[teriz[(19[
Silveira[R[([
Sobr[

Sov[

Cecília Meireles

(1901–1964)

Regina Igel

Cecília Benevides Meirelles, who signed her name Meireles, was born on 7 November 1901 in Rio de Janeiro, Brazil, and there she died on 9 November 1964. She has been recognized by literary critics and historians, and praised by the public, as one of the most prolific authors of her country in modern times. The diversity of her activities as fictionist, chronicler, playwright, journalist, folklorist, and educator was transcended by her poetic endeavors, and poetry became Meireles' enduring and most memorable literary legacy.

Literary scholars have recognized three main recurrent themes in Meireles' poetry: life's brevity, the transience of things, and death. They are expressed with imagery enriched by metaphors mostly related to nature's mutations, such as the revolving of days and nights and the growth and decay of flora, and by allusions to living beings and their ultimate disappearance from the world. The recurrence of these and other related images tend to unify the three main subjects of Meireles' poetry.

Following Darcy Damasceno, the poet's main biographer and principal editor, who first cited both the dramatic experiences of Meireles' childhood and her fondness for Oriental philosophy as the author's primary poetic sources, Meireles' critics have tended to search in the poet's early years and in her intellectual pursuits for the roots of her themes and metaphors.

Meireles' career as an author and a scholar invites comparison to the life cycles of a plant. As in the development of a healthy flower, which obeys an invisible logic, Meireles' poetic and intellectual course can be divided into four phases. The proposed nomenclature for each of them borrows from the already established botanical appellation. Obviously, in the vegetal realm, differentiating phases are clearly separated; this does not occur in the passages of one's life, where they tend to overlap one another. Meireles' literary career is no exception. In this respect, she advanced by retaining some of the characteristics of the previous period, while transforming and enriching the next one by new creative endeavors. All of her poetic phases are linked by a respect for literary tradition, a search for musical effects of words, and a commitment to aesthetic perfection.

First there was a period of germination (1919–1939), when the poet pursued her poetic inclinations, showing an acute interest in the techniques of the Parnassian and symbolist movements and incorporating some of them in her poems. This phase was followed by emergence (1939–1944), when two books of poetry revealed strong signs of a definite poetic talent, and one of them was awarded the Brazilian

Academy of Letters Poetry Prize for 1939, the first official recognition of her poetry. The third period, the most prolific of all, was one of constant growth (1945–1960), in which she published many books of poetry and prose, and her other intellectual activities were in full bloom. Finally came the period of maturity (1960–1963), which summed up a life dedicated to existential inquiry within the framework of poetic creativity. Poems posthumously published may be considered, for the most part, to belong to the phase of growth.

The poet never knew her father, Carlos Alberto de Carvalho Meirelles, an employee at the Central Bank of Brazil who died at age twenty-six, three months before Cecília was born. Her mother, Matilde Benevides Meirelles, an elementary-school teacher, died when the poet was three years old. Both parents had suffered from incurable—but fortunately not hereditary—diseases. They had three children who had died before Cecília was born. The author was raised by her maternal grandmother, Jacinta Garcia Benevides, her only relative.

The poet spent her childhood in Rio de Janeiro, having as companions for most of the time her grandmother and a live-in nanny named Pedrina. Their house was surrounded by luxurious vegetation, where the young girl had her first contact with nature—with the flowers, birds, butterflies, morning dew and fog, clouds and tropical rains that would be recalled by her poetic memory often in later life, and would populate her works of poetry and prose.

Meireles always remembered those years as true relics, as she said in an interview published in *Manchete* (Headline), a Brazilian magazine (3 October 1953), eventually reprinted in collections of her poetic work edited by Darcy Damasceno: "I recall starry skies, storms, rain on the flowers, ripe fruits, shuttered houses . . . night in the trees, the sound of an echo, the morning song of the *sabiás* [birds], lizards on walls, butterflies . . . the howling of dogs . . ." (*Obra Poética*, 1967, p. 78).* At different times in her literary career, these elements appear amalgamated into lyrical compositions enhanced by conciseness and poetic elegance.

*English rendition of Meireles' statements and verses in this article are the author's unless otherwise noted. No attempt is made to capture the original poetic value; translations are semantic.

Naturally, the two women in the house could not entirely fulfill the girl's needs for companionship. She felt lonely from a tender age, as she recalled in that same interview:

My lonely childhood gave me two things that seem to be negative, but have always been positive for me: silence and solitude. This has always been the area of my life. A magical area in which kaleidoscopes invented fabulous geometrical worlds, where watches revealed the secret of their mechanisms, and dolls the secret of their look.

(p. 78)

Solitude nurtured her creative imagination and was reflected in her poetic work as a constant search for the meaning of human destiny and for a reason for our being in this world. The deaths in her family were also reflected in her literary production: she transformed her experience of missing the loved ones into a philosophical approach to life, and the lyrical vein of her poetry became entwined with a probing of death as life's ultimate mystery. Thus her poetry balances an array of motifs, stemming from her closeness to the fragility of life, her awareness of arbitrary changes brought by the passing of time, and her perception of the ultimate reality of death.

She grew up in an atmosphere of constructive entertainment provided by her grandmother's stories about events that took place in the Azores, her homeland, and by Brazilian folk songs and games taught by the nanny. In interviews she relates that as a child she was attracted and amused by large books, such as the ones bound with paper covers that imitate the designs of a marble slab, trimmed with golden ribbons. During the years of elementary school, she was allured and mesmerized by the broad contents of illustrated dictionaries, which ranged from world history to plastic arts to Oriental culture. As she grew into adulthood, she pursued these topics in scholarly research, and taught and lectured on some of them, such as the folk sculpture of Brazil and Indian poetry.

Meireles graduated from elementary school with honors. She was then awarded a Gold Medal of Merit, bestowed upon her by Olavo Bilac, a renowned poet recognized by Brazilian literary historians as the most important representative of the Parnassian movement and highly praised in his lifetime for his poetic works; he was a school superintendent at the occasion of Meireles' graduation. Parnassianism was a literary movement that prevailed in Brazil from the late nineteenth century well into the second decade of the twentieth century. Reacting against the subjective emotionalism of the romantic movement, the Parnassians centered on an objective poetry, characterized by such classical formalities as precision of poetic technique, in which the personality of the poet is reduced to a minimum or entirely eliminated.

The germination period of Meireles' career saw the publication of *Espectros* (Specters, 1919), *Nunca Mais . . . e Poema dos Poemas* (Never More . . . and Poem of Poems, 1923), *Baladas para El-Rei* (Ballads for the King, 1925), and *Viagem* (Journey, 1939). Her earliest poems reflected Parnassianism, which she soon abandoned. She then leaned toward the symbolist course of freeing poetry from the restrictions of conventional versification by the use of delicate lyricism and by the combination of concrete images that represent an ideal world of which this one is a mere reflection. During this phase, she made use of the sonnet and practiced a kind of "objective poetry," in which the poet's personal feelings were neglected in favor of a descriptive tone of aloofness. *Espectros*, her first book of poems, was clearly influenced by this goal of objectivity. It gathered together seventeen sonnets concerning personalities of world history and mythology. The poems are devoid of any particular feature that might indicate the paths the poet would take in her future development. Eventually, she chose to eliminate this title from her bibliography, dismissing the work as "mere verses."

In the books *Nunca Mais . . . e Poema dos Poemas* (published as one volume) and in *Baladas para El-Rei*, Meireles emphasized the mystical aspects of symbolism, showing a strong bent toward the supernatural and an atmosphere of languor, lethargy, and slowness. The poet's mood is one of melancholic and mystical awe when describing her feelings about, say, a deserted landscape bathed by the moonlight, as in the following verses of "A Minha Princesa Branca" (To My Pale Princess):

> Por sôbre as almas vagueia:
> Almas santas . . . Almas bôas . . .

> E' um pallor de lua cheia,
> Na agua morta das lagôas . . .
>
> . . .
>
> E vou, soffrendo degredos,
> A dominar os espaços . . .
> Só quero beijar-lhe os dedos
> E adormecer-lhe nos braços!
>   ("A Minha Princesa Branca,"
>   in *Nunca Mais . . .*
>   *e Poema dos Poemas*)

> Over souls they float:
> Holy souls . . . Good souls . . .
> It is a whiteness of a full moon,
> in the lake's dead waters . . .
>
> . . .
>
> And there I am, in command of the spaces,
> suffering exiles . . .
> I only want to kiss her fingers
> and have her sleeping in my arms!

A symbolist tone of sadness; feelings of abandonment, depression, and disillusionment; and a search for a divine or a superior entity's answer predominate.

The technique employed in these three books is characterized by an abundance of suspension punctuations (. . .), a deliberate choice of vocabulary related to feelings of pain and suffering, and a respect for traditional poetics. Though these traits were attenuated later in Meireles' career, the elevation of mind and spirit already perceptible in these early poetic efforts was sustained in her future works. Her mental and spiritual inquiry resulted in philosophical quests into such esoteric sectors as human destiny, life's mutations and purposes, the existence of experiences after death, and reincarnation.

In the early 1920's, when Meireles was involved in these pursuits, an important cultural change was taking place in Brazil. It dealt with reform of the concept and practice of Brazilian plastic arts, literature, and music, and proposed a rupture with the past and the cultivation of Brazilian roots in all realms of creativity. The movement became known in Brazilian artistic history as modernism. Its followers engaged in a separation from tradition, mostly of Portuguese origin, and pursued a nationalistic character in all literary and artistic expressions. Meireles opposed this exaggerated nationalism because it rejected universal and traditional symbols. Hers was a poetry of respect for past literary trends, revitalizing some of their traits and giving expression to spiritual concerns. These tendencies led her to join with other like-minded poets and authors, who became known as the "spiritualists" or the "Catholic writers." In 1927, Meireles collaborated in the founding of *Festa* (Celebration), one of their literary journals, to which she contributed poems.

However, her independent mind soon guided her toward her own measurement of spirituality and her own concern for tradition and universalism. As a result, it became a difficult task for literary critics to classify her as belonging to any of the literary trends of her time. She represented rather a combination of individualism and universalism, searching for the sources of her poetry in personal remembrances and in the evolution of past artistic movements, while at the same time focusing on perennial concerns of mankind.

Brazil also became involved in many educational reforms during the germinative phase of Meireles' career. Meireles' contribution to this aspect of her country's life was obvious in her founding in 1934 of a pilot library for children, designed and operated according to the latest models of functional education. The painter Fernando Correia Dias, her husband since 1921, helped her in this endeavor; he also was her companion in the visit she made to Portugal in 1935, where she lectured on Brazilian literature at several Portuguese universities. Upon their return to Brazil, her husband commited suicide in their house, apparently victimized by depression. His death compounded the loss of her grandmother, who had died of natural causes in 1933. The poet was left with the couple's three young daughters: Maria Elvira, Maria Matilde, and Maria Fernanda. At the time of their father's death, the oldest was ten years old, the youngest eight.

Fourteen years elapsed between the publication of *Baladas para El-Rei* and of *Viagem*, the book that marked the author's emergence and impact on the literary scene of Brazil at the beginning of the 1940's. The poems of *Viagem*, which relied on disciplined metrics, conveyed universal concerns about human destiny and other philosophical questions. *Viagem* was awarded the Brazilian Academy of Letters Prize for 1939, in the midst of opposition from some modernists who objected to Meireles' conservative style. This book can be viewed as the transition between the poet's past allegiance to Parnassianism and symbolism and the emergence of a more individual style. Meireles' worldview, as shown in most of the poems of *Viagem*, involves adherence to the idea that impersonal circumstances mold the destinies of human beings. The poem "Destino" (Destiny) reflects such a perception:

> Pastora de nuvens, fui posta a serviço
> por uma campina tão desamparada
> que não principia nem também termina,
> e onde nunca é noite e nunca madrugada.
>
> · · · ·
>
> Pastora de nuvens, por muito que espere,
> não há quem me explique meu vário rebanho.
> Perdida atrás dele na planície aérea,
> não sei se o conduzo, não sei se o acompanho.
> ("Destino," in *Obra Poética,* 1967)

Shepherdess of clouds, I was put to work
along a field so forsaken
that it does not begin or end,
and where it is never night nor dawn.

· · ·

Shepherdess of clouds, for as long as I await,
there is nobody who can explain to me my diversified
    herd.
Lost behind it in the aerial prairie,
I don't know whether I lead or I follow it.

In essence, the poems in *Viagem* convey the attempt to bridge the gap between us and everything that lies beyond our intellectual reach. The awareness that time has wings, that life is fragile, that death is painful and mysterious, and that all of this cannot be explained by our senses, became the core of Meireles' anguish as expressed in her poetry. Her manipulation of metrics in this volume ranged from the well-measured syllabic meter to free verse, imbuing her images with meaning and pictorial suggestions, as in "Herança" (Legacy):

> Eu vim de infinitos caminhos,
> e os meus sonhos choveram lúcido pranto
> pelo chão.

Quando é que frutifica, nos caminhos infinitos,
essa vida, que era tão viva, tão fecunda,
porque vinha de um coração?

I came from infinite ways,
and my dreams rained a lucid cry
along the ground.

When does it become fruitful, in the infinite ways,
this life, which was so lively, so prolific,
because it came from a heart?
(*Obra Poética*, 1967)

The period of emergence (1939–1944) slightly overlapped the previous one of germination, for the publication of the aforementioned *Viagem* was a revelation in contemporary Brazilian letters. The poet then conveyed her personal view on the making of poetry, melding tradition and self-expression with universal themes. In *Vaga Música* (Vague Music, 1942), Meireles' philosophical quests were formulated in a poetic manner, through which the poet's senses and imagination tried to capture the inner and invisible essence of the unknown, as in these lines from "Recordação" (Memory): "Agora, o cheiro áspero das flôres / leva-me os olhos por dentro de suas pétalas" (Now, the rustic smell of the flowers / guides my eyes to the inner part of their petals).

Starting with such earthly subjects as a dancer's movements, a bird, or even the remains of a shipwreck, she gave them spiritual connotations through associative meanings. "Canção Mínima" (Minimal Song) reveals this association of ideas and images:

No mistério do Sem-Fim,
equilibra-se um planêta.

E, no planeta, um jardim,
e, no jardim, um canteiro;
no canteiro, uma violeta,
e, sobre ela, o dia inteiro,

entre o planeta e o Sem-Fim,
a asa de uma borboleta.
(*Obra Poética*, 1967)

In the mystery of the Endless,
a planet balances itself.

And, in the planet, a garden,
and, in the garden, a bed of flowers;
in the bed of flowers, a violet,
and, on it, the whole day,

between the planet and the Endless,
the wing of a butterfly.

The poems of *Vaga Música* describe a metaphoric world that is more dynamic, lyrical, and colorful than that of her previous period, yet remains highly spiritualized. The poet became conscious, through the years, of her own limitations in dealing with transcendental topics, as she implies in "Explicação" (Explanation): "O pensamento é triste; o amor, insuficiente; / e eu quero sempre mais do que vem nos milagres" (Thoughts are sad; love is not enough; / and I always want more than what comes through miracles). Such a perception influenced her poetic directions until the end of her life and gave a somber cast to most of her later poetry.

In her growth period (1945–1960), Meireles accomplished a wide variety of tasks as poet, educator, folklorist, and lecturer. In 1940, she had met and married Heitor Grillo, who remained her companion for the rest of her life. Following this event, the poet became immersed in the most prolific period of her life. In this fifteen-year span, she published about twelve books; participated in cultural radio programs; translated plays and fictional works from English, French, and Spanish into Portuguese; and maintained a busy schedule of visits abroad, mostly as a guest of honor and lecturer. In these capacities, she visited the Azores, Western Europe, India, Israel, Spanish America, and the United States. She deepened her interest in folklore—researching, writing, and organizing symposia on the topic—and became recognized as a leading figure in the field.

During that period of her life, her poetry became open to a multiplicity of inspirations: human beings (from unassuming people to historic figures), the countries she visited, Brazilian historical episodes, lives of saints, and natural phenomena. A yearning for the mother she barely knew surfaced in many poems of that period. Still troubled by the great mysteries of life—that is, the purpose of our existence and the meaning of death—she wrote about these themes as well. Her choice of metaphors reflected her interest in life's mutations. Her favorite imagery included oceans, rivers, lakes, mirror reflections, the life cycles of flowers and plants, sudden transformations in the weather, the silence of the night, the cries of children, the chirping of crickets and singing of birds, and landscapes.

Each book published during her phase of growth showed greater mastery of techniques and more refined feelings than the previous one: from *Mar Absoluto e Outros Poemas* (Absolute Sea and Other Poems, 1945), to *Doze Noturnos da Holanda* (Twelve Nocturnes of Holland, 1952), to *Metal Rosicler* (Pyrite Rock, 1960), the poet's works are permeated with expressiveness, lyricism, metaphoric originality, and care in the selection of words. In prose, the author was also a conscientious artist. From nostalgic chronicles of travels, such as *Evocação Lírica de Lisboa* (Lyrical Remembrances of Lisbon, 1948), to chronicles (later gathered in anthologies), to lectures for international audiences, such as *Rabindranath Tagore and the East-West Unity* (1961), delivered in India, Meireles imbued her works with her lyrical gift, mingling the real with the ideal, describing concrete circumstances along with poetic abstractions. Her talent for wit and tact was matched by a deep knowledge of her subject, which ranged from daily life in a big city to recollections of her own childhood to contemporary events of national and social importance.

During the last period of her career, maturity, Meireles was able to finish and review, shortly before her death, the book *Solombra* (Sun and Shade, 1963). A premonition of the ending of her life seems to reverberate in these poems, which gather together memory and being, and a worldview sublimated throughout her career. The poems of *Solombra* represent, in relation to the poet's past work, an intensification of her questioning of life's complexities, mainly the passing of time and death. All of the twenty-eight poems are untitled, a technique that may indicate the author's desire not to disturb the solemn atmosphere flowing from them. A certain sense of conformity appears to flow from the solemn verses, which appeals to a feeling of introspection. Her words are serene, and their connotations fit with grace and sensitivity in the conciseness of the poetic limits. The perennial questions of her life are also present:

Quem fostes vós? Quem sois? Quem vimos, nos lugares
da vossa antiga sombra? E por quem procuramos?
Que pretendem concluir impossíveis diálogos?

Longe passamos. Todos sozinhos.
(*Obra Poética*, 1967, p. 794)

Who were you? Who are you? Who did we see, in those places
of your old shade? And whom do we search for?
What conclusion is sought in impossible dialogues?

Far away we go by. All of us lonely.

Meireles died of cancer in 1964, at a time when her career reflected accomplishments only achievable by a disciplined mind and a refined spirit. Having gone through several stages of creative development, she reached in her last writings a high degree of maturity and sublimity. Had this final phase continued, the author undoubtedly would have produced works of the highest technical and artistic merit. She had and still has an important influence on Brazilian literature that is attributed to her purified technique, her keen sensitivity to the Portuguese language, and her exhortation to readers to embark on quests of universal appeal. The poet's examination of both life and death, which occupied most of her years of poetic productivity, seems to point to a double message of mankind's search since the beginning of intelligent life: life can be seen as a preamble, bathed in light, to death, an ultimate path to a darkened resort; paradoxically, the poems also convey exactly the contrary, as if life were a dark, obscure condition that we all have to go through in order to reach the road to a bright place. In the variety of her contribution to Brazilian letters, Meireles was unique and innovative, yet sensitive to her literary heritage.

SELECTED BIBLIOGRAPHY

Editions

Poetry

Espectros. Rio de Janeiro, 1919.
Nunca Mais . . . e Poema dos Poemas. Rio de Janeiro, 1923.

Baladas para El-Rei. Rio de Janeiro, 1925.

Viagem. Lisbon, 1939.

Vaga Música. Rio de Janeiro, 1942.

Mar Absoluto e Outros Poemas. Porto Alegre, Brazil, 1945.

Retrato Natural. Rio de Janeiro, 1949.

Amor em Leonoreta. Rio de Janeiro, 1951.

Doze Noturnos da Holanda e O Aeronauta. Rio de Janeiro, 1952.

Romanceiro da Inconfidência. Rio de Janeiro, 1953.

Pequeno Oratório de Santa Clara. Rio de Janeiro, 1955.

Pistóia, Cemitério Militar Brasileiro. Rio de Janeiro, 1955.

Canções. Rio de Janeiro, 1956.

Romance de Santa Cecília. Rio de Janeiro, 1957.

A Rosa. Salvador (Bahia), Brazil, 1957.

Metal Rosicler. Rio de Janeiro, 1960.

Poemas Escritos na Índia. Rio de Janeiro, 1962.

Solombra. Rio de Janeiro, 1963.

Ou Isto ou Aquilo. São Paulo, 1964.

Crônica Trovada da Cidade de Sam Sebastiam no Quarto Centenário da sua Fundação pelo Capitão-Mor Estácio de Saá. Rio de Janeiro, 1965.

Poemas Italianos. São Paulo, 1968. Portuguese-Italian edition.

Fiction

Olhinhos de Gato. Lisbon, 1939–1940. 2nd ed. São Paulo, 1980.

Evocação Lírica de Lisboa. Lisbon, 1948.

Giroflê, Giroflá. Rio de Janeiro, 1956.

Eternidade de Israel. Rio de Janeiro, 1959.

Escolha o Seu Sonho (Crônicas). Rio de Janeiro, 1964.

Inéditos (Crônicas). Rio de Janeiro, 1967.

Ilusões do Mundo (Crônicas). Rio de Janeiro, 1976.

O Que Se Diz e o Que Se Entende (Crônicas). Rio de Janeiro, 1980.

Essays

O Espírito Vitorioso. Rio de Janeiro, 1929.

Saudação à Menina de Portugal. Rio de Janeiro, 1930.

Batuque, Samba e Macumba. Lisbon, 1935.

Notícia da Poesia Brasileira. Coimbra, Portugal, 1935.

Introdução ao Estudo da Literatura. Rio de Janeiro, 1943.

Poetas Novos de Portugal. Rio de Janeiro, 1944.

Problemas da Literatura Infantil. Belo Horizonte, Brazil, 1951. 2nd ed. São Paulo, 1979.

Panorama Folclórico dos Açores, Especialmente da Ilha de S. Miguel. Ponta Delgada, Azores, 1955.

Artes Populares. Rio de Janeiro, 1958.

"Expressão Feminina da Poesia na América." In *Três Con-ferências Sôbre Cultura Hispano-Americana.* Rio de Janeiro, 1959.

Rabindranath Tagore and the East-West Unity. Rio de Janeiro, 1961.

Notas de Folclore Gaúcho-Açoriano. Rio de Janeiro, 1968.

Textbooks

Criança, Meu Amor. Rio de Janeiro, 1924. 2nd ed. 1977.

Rute e Alberto Resolveram Ser Turistas. Porto Alegre, Brazil, 1938.

Rute e Alberto. Edited by Virginia Joiner. Boston, 1945.

Rui: Pequena História de Uma Grande Vida. Rio de Janeiro, 1948. 2nd ed. 1949.

Plays

O Menino Atrasado. Rio de Janeiro, 1966.

Collected Works

Antologia Poética. Lisbon, 1968.

Cecília Meireles, Poesia. Rio de Janeiro, 1974.

Flor de Poemas. Rio de Janeiro, 1972.

Flores e Canções. Rio de Janeiro, 1979.

Obra Poética. Critical study by Darcy Damasceno. Rio de Janeiro, 1958. 2nd ed., expanded, Rio de Janeiro, 1967. 3rd ed., rev., Rio de Janeiro, 1972.

Poesias Completas. Vols. 1–9. Rio de Janeiro, 1973–1974.

Seleta em Prosa e Verso de Cecília Merieles. Selected by Darcy Damasceno. Rio de Janeiro, 1973.

Translations

Cecilia Meireles. Poemas em Traduçao/Poems in Translation. Translated by Henry Keith and Raymond Sayers. Washington, D.C., 1977.

"The Dead Horse." Translated by Jack Tomlins. "Bird." Translated by Alexis Levitin. *The Literary Review* 21:205–207 (1978).

Poesia Brasileira Moderna: A Bilingual Anthology. Edited by José M. Neistein. Translations by Manoel Cardozo. Washington, D.C., 1972.

Biographical and Critical Studies

Andrade, Mário de. "Cecília e a Poesia." In *O Empalhador de Passarinho* 20. 2nd ed. São Paulo, 1955. Pp. 71–75.

Azevedo Filho, Leodegário A. de. *Poesia e Estilo de Cecília Meireles.* Rio de Janeiro, 1970.

Bonapace, Adolphina Portella. *O Romanceiro da Inconfidência: Meditação Sôbre o Destino do Homen.* Rio de Janeiro, 1974.

Cavalieri, Ruth Villela. *Cecília Meireles, o Ser e o Tempo na Imagem Refletida.* Rio de Janeiro, 1984.

Coelho, Nelly Novaes. "O Eterno Instante na Poesia de Cecília Meireles." In *Tempo, Solidão e Morte.* São Paulo, 1964. Pp. 7–26.

Damasceno, Darcy. *Cecília Meireles, o Mundo Contemplado.* Rio de Janeiro, 1967.

———. "A Poesia do Sensível e do Imaginário" and "Notícia Biográfica." In *Cecília Meireles, Obra Poetica* (all editions).

Dantas, José Maria de Souza. *A Consciência Poética de Uma Viagem Sem Fim: A Poética de Cecília Meireles.* Rio de Janeiro, 1984.

García, Ruben. "Symbolism in the Early Works of Cecilia Meireles." *Romance Notes* 21/1:16–22 (1980).

Grossman, Judith. "Painel de Cecília Meireles." *Cadernos Brasileiros* 37:7–20 (1966).

Igel, Regina. "Cecília Meireles." In *Letras Femininas* 1:61–69 (1975).

———. "Despedida da Vida e Acercamento à Morte." *Minas Gerais, Suplemento Literario,* 28 June 1975. Pp. 6–7.

Kerr, John A., Jr. "Notes on Cecilia Meireles' Reflections on the Indian Reality." *Language Quarterly* 16/1–2: 47–50 (1977); 16/3–4:36–38 (1978); and 17/1–2: 51–54 (1978).

Nist, John. "The Poetry of Cecilia Meireles." *Hispania* 46:252–258 (1963).

———. "Cecilia Meireles." In *The Modernist Movement in Brazil.* Austin, Tex., 1967. Pp. 190–204.

Rónai, Paulo. "The Character of a Poet: Cecilia Meireles and Her Work." *The Literary Review* 21:193–207 (1978).

Sadlier, Darlene J. "Metaphor and Metamorphosis: A Study of the Sea Imagery in Cecilia Meireles' 'Mar Absoluto.'" *Kentucky Romance Quarterly* 27:361–370 (1980).

———. *Imagery and Theme in the Poetry of Cecilia Meireles: A Study of "Mar Absoluto."* Potomac, Md., 1983.

———. *Cecília Meireles and João Alphonsus.* Brasília, Brazil, 1984.

Sayers, Raymond. "O Universo Poético de Cecília Meireles." In *Onze Estudos de Literatura Brasileira.* Rio de Janeiro, 1983. Pp. 9–31.

Stackhouse, Kenneth A. "The Sea in the Poetry of Cecilia Meireles." *Luso-Brazilian Review* 18/1:183–195 (1981).

Zagury, Eliane. *Cecília Meireles.* Petrópolis, Brazil, 1973.

José Gorostiza

(1901–1979)

J. E. Pacheco

José Gorostiza's epic-length poem *Muerte sin fin* was published on 28 September 1939, three weeks after the start of World War II and at the close of an era. It is one of the great poems of the Spanish language and has been compared to Paul Valéry's *Le cimetière marin* (*The Graveyard by the Sea*, 1922) and to T. S. Eliot's *Four Quartets*. Nevertheless, to this date only one complete translation into English exists, Laura Villaseñor's *Death Without End*.

It can be said that the poets who were born between 1892 and 1906 on the Iberian Peninsula and in Latin America and shared the same language form a single literary generation. These poets include Jorge Luis Borges, Vicente Huidobro, Pablo Neruda, and César Vallejo, as well as members of the Spanish "Group of 1927"—Rafael Alberti, Vicente Aleixandre, Dámaso Alonso, Manual Altolaguirre, Luis Cernuda, Gerardo Diego, Federico García Lorca, Jorge Guillén, and Pedro Salinas. Also belonging to this generation are the Mexican writers in Gorostiza's circle who contributed to the magazine *Contemporáneos* between 1928 and 1931. They are Jorge Cueste, Enrique González Rojo, Elías Nandino, Salvador Novo, Gilberto Owen, Bernardo Ortiz de Montellano, Carlos Pellicer, Jaime Torres Bodet, and Xavier Villaurrutia; these writers became known as the Contemporáneos.

If one accepts the hypothesis of a single generation, the poets who were born during these years and who wrote in Spanish constitute one of the most important groups of poets in any language. Although Gorostiza may not have the reputation of Borges, Guillén, Neruda, or Vallejo, and he did not win a Nobel Prize, as Aleixandre did, his writing shows great affinity with theirs, and because of *Death Without End* he deserves to be ranked alongside them as one of the major poets of his generation.

Like Lorca and Alberti, Gorostiza bridges the gap between the popular and the more sophisticated literatures and rediscovers—through the perspective of the avant-garde movement—the Spanish medieval and renaissance tradition. His poetry does not show the absolute formal novelty of Vallejo's *Trilce* (1922), Huidobro's *Altazor* (1919), or Neruda's *Residencia en la tierra* (1933), but *Death Without End* would not have been written had it not been for the radical experiences of the 1920's.

Gorostiza was a poet and critic like his Spanish contemporary Jorge Guillén. Their admiration for Valéry is evident from the fact that they believed that poetry is not an external object completely free of the constraints of space and time. They felt it was necessary to adapt poetry to the moment, but at the same time to liberate it from the worship of the

923

dislocated and fragmentary, which was prevalent during the era. Without ever renouncing the aspect of play, which was essential for the avant-garde, both poets sought to extract as much from their common tradition as would enable them to write in an authentic and rigorous form. As Guillén said, true artistic labor does not operate in the realm of formlessness and incoherence. It requires technique, and therefore effort, and it exists only as it "traverses and illuminates different kinds of raw material."

Although he was a citizen of a poor and technologically backward country, Gorostiza wrote a poem that equaled the artistic and intellectual stature of the best poetry of Europe and the United States of America. Analyzing the similarities and differences between *Death Without End* and the great works of Eliot and Valéry, Mordecai S. Rubín wrote in 1964 that "from the standpoint of perfection, *The Waste Land* and *Four Quartets*, alongside *Death Without End*, almost appear to have been written in a hurry."

Eliot did not read Spanish, nor was he interested in Spanish culture. Nevertheless, Eliot's magazine *Criterion* had high praise for the Contemporáneos. In his 1985 book, *Los Contemporáneos ayer*, Guillermo Sheridan reports that in 1931 the magazine described the Mexican poets as "a fine example of a Revolution which has freed not only a country, but its own intellectual resources." The *Criterion* was not mistaken: in its own way *Death Without End* is also a product of the Mexican Revolution as well as the result of a local tradition that had evolved for centuries.

Unmistakably, death is an eternal theme of poetry. Indeed it can be claimed that poetry is born as a response to our mortality. Universal elements reappear in Gorostiza with Hispanic—and in particular Mexican—characteristics. The Aztec culture, in contrast with those cultures that preceded it, was conscious of its end and lived awaiting it. All its art is a memento mori, a reminder that we are going to die. Mexico was conquered by a medieval Spain that was still obsessed with the massive death caused by the plague. Diseases against which they had no defense, the slavery to which they were subjected, and the physical and spiritual violence with which they saw their world destroyed and their gods transformed into devils impressed upon the Indian mind a

torturous sense of death. It has been pointed out that death and deception are touchstones of the baroque poetry that predominated in New Spain during its three centuries of existence. The popular culture of Mexico expresses this sentiment in thousands of forms. Commonplace are the confected sugar skeletons and the engravings of the popular artist José Guadalupe Posada, whose illustrations deal with crimes and executions. Aside from deaths in his family during his youth, there were three events involving death that would have profoundly affected Gorostiza: the slaughter of millions of soldiers during World War I, the million deaths caused by the Mexican Revolution, and the epidemic of Spanish influenza that devastated the population of the world in 1918–1919. Moreover, *Death Without End* was written during the Spanish civil war years, 1936–1939, and it appears in the shadows of that catastrophe as a somber and unintended presentiment of Auschwitz, Hiroshima, and the Gulag.

Biography

José Gorostiza was born in the riverport city of Villahermosa on 10 November 1901. Villahermosa was the capital of the state of Tabasco in the Mexican tropical zone. Carlos Pellicer, the other great poet of the Contemporáneos, was also from Villahermosa. Pellicer, who was born in 1897 and died in 1977, was completely different from Gorostiza, yet was his closest friend. Gorostiza was a descendant of Manuel Eduardo de Gorostiza (1789–1851), a playwright who made his career in Spain with such works as *Indulgencia para todos* (Indulgence for Everyone) and *Contigo, pan y cebolla* (Bread and Onions with You); later, before serving as foreign minister, he represented the Mexican government in European capitals and, on the brink of the Mexican war, in Washington, D.C. He subsequently fought in the war himself. José Gorostiza's brother, Celestino (1904–1967), a playwright and critic, was also a participant in *Contemporáneos*. He wrote such works as *El color de nuestra piel* (The Color of Our Skin) and *La leña está verde* (The Wood Is Green).

José and Celestino Gorostiza were sons of a retired soldier who had a business in Villahermosa. When their father later accepted employment at a bank, he was transferred with his family to Guanajuato and then to Aguascalientes in central Mexico. José Gorostiza studied at the Instituto Científico y Literario in Aguascalientes, the same institute Ramón López Velarde had attended. Gorostiza published a student magazine there and served as president of the student body. In 1915 the victorious armies of the Mexican Revolution convened in Aguascalientes in an unsuccessful effort to resolve their differences. During the same year and in the same city, General Álvaro Obregón completed the defeat of Francisco Villa in the last great battle of the series initiated at Celaya. The fighting drove the Gorostizas and many other families out of the city, forcing them to seek refuge in the capital of the country.

By this time, nearly all the fin de siècle poets and the great essayists of the Generation of 1910 had been chased into exile; the revolution had isolated Mexico from its French cultural models. During the civil war, intellectual life in Mexico revolved around the poet Enrique González Martínez and the philosopher Antonio Caso. The works of authors present and absent alike left their imprint on Gorostiza's literary and intellectual development. During these years he must also have read the Spanish poets who lived before the Golden Age, and Luis de Góngora, who had been rescued from oblivion and scorn by new researchers, including the Mexican Alfonso Reyes. These writers awakened Gorostiza's interest in the pre-Socratic philosophers of ancient Greece and in Oriental thought, which he studied in the writings of José Vasconcelos.

At the Escuela Nacional Preparatoria (National Preparatory School), Gorostiza met Pellicer, who introduced his first poems in the magazine *San-Ev-Ank* in 1918 with the following comment: "Though a mere adolescent, he captures emotions that reveal a temperament out of which will soon spring a great poet." López Velarde also gave him his support in 1919 in *El universo ilustrado:* "I never cease to be surprised at the lyrical magnificence of America. These two young men, José Gorostiza Alcalá and Bernardo Ortiz de Montellano, barely more than boys, are the latest example of the inborn talents that animate youth."

After editing *Revista nueva* with Enrique González

Rojo, in 1920 Gorostiza had the privilege—an extraordinary one for a young man of nineteen—of directing the Cultura collection for the publisher México Moderno. When Vasconcelos began working at the Ministry of Education, he invited many of the new writers to the ministry to help him with his great cultural campaign. His program included bringing literacy to the Mexican people, promoting mural painting, elevating the stature of indigenous arts and crafts, and producing massive printings of classic works. Gorostiza participated in this project as editor of the magazine *El maestro* (The Teacher), which was distributed free of charge to schools throughout Latin America. He also edited *Lecturas clásicas para niños* (Readings in the Classics for Children).

During these years of genuine cultural revolution, the *estridentismo* (stridentism) movement, which was a local variant of Italian futurism, blossomed. Gorostiza did not join the ranks of the militant avant-garde, and he felt that *estridentismo* was a "school of blunder." In contrast with his friends, he published very little and revised what he had already published. In fact, his only essay of this period was about López Velarde (1924). He was interested in "synthetic" drama—short one-act pieces along the lines drawn by the Italian futurists in Marinetti's manifesto *Teatro sintetico futurista* (1916)—and he wrote some sketches for theater revues, the Mexican equivalent of music hall theater.

He began his first book, *Canciones para cantar en las barcas* (Songs to be Sung Aboard Ships) in 1918. It was published in 1925 and contains mostly poems about the sea, the fruit of trips to Veracruz and Havana. In the same year Gorostiza and his literary colleagues were formally recognized as a group in a lecture given by Xavier Villaurrutia. In this lecture, which was titled "La poesía de los jóvenes de México" (The Poetry of the Young Men of Mexico), Villaurrutia called Gorostiza the most intelligent and critical of the new poets.

The group was already so visible, active, and brilliant that it had aroused the hostility of other writers who criticized its departure from all that was Mexican, its passion for foreign, especially French, literature, and its avant-garde style that rendered its work incomprehensible to the common reader. Among the group's enemies were, on the one hand, the *estridentistas* (strident ones), who included Manuel Maples Arce, and, on the other, the writers of the early part of the century such as Federico Gamboa. This literary war was initiated in 1924, when Julio Jiménez Rueda published an article in *El universal ilustrado* calling for a "virile literature," a literature that would reflect the new country born of the Revolution. During 1927 and 1928, while his friends were producing avant-garde plays, publishing the magazine *Ulises*, editing the controversial *Antología de la poesía mexicana moderna* (1928), and starting the publication that gave them their name, *Contemporáneos*, a title that had been suggested by Gorostiza (according to Ermilo Abreu Gómez), Gorostiza worked in the Mexican consulate in London. While he was there, he probably read Eliot, who was experiencing his climb to fame. When Gorostiza returned to Mexico City, he taught Mexican literature at the UNAM (Universidad Nacional Autónoma de México) and modern history at the Escuela Nacional de Maestros (National Teacher's College). For several months he wrote the critical column "Torre de señales" (Signal Tower), which covered music, theater, and film as well as literature, for *El universal ilustrado*.

In 1932 he was head of the Department of Fine Arts in the Ministry of Education. He also sponsored the experimental theater group Teatro de Orientación and participated in the final phase of the debate over nationalism and literature, which had begun seven years earlier. Furthermore, he translated from French both *La conversation* by André Maurois and *Maya* by Simón Gantillón. That same year, Rubén Salazar Mallén's novel, *Cariátide* (Caryatid), was published in the magazine *Examen* by Jorge Cuesta, the Contemporáneo whose ideas had perhaps influenced Gorostiza most heavily. The publication of this work provoked the great offensive against the Contemporáneos. Cuesta and Salazar Mallén were arrested for obscenity and all of the Contemporáneos had to abandon their positions at the Ministry of Education.

In a country with few publishers and few readers, poets could survive only by working for the government. The leaders of the Revolution had arrived at a tacit agreement with them: their task would be to modernize poetry and literature; political justification and propaganda were to be left in the hands of the muralists. However, with the fall of General Plutarco Elías Calles and Lázaro Cárdenas' assumption of power in 1934, writers opposed to the Contemporáneos reached the Chamber of Deputies. These writers insisted that the Contemporáneos be expelled from their public posts, even in ministries other than the Ministry of Education, and that they be relieved of classes that they were teaching in government schools, judging their internationalism adverse to the interests of the Mexican people. A few of the Contemporáneos, Gorostiza included, were able to find minor diplomatic posts. Nevertheless, the literary war wounded him deeply. He came to believe that writers were superfluous in a country committed to material reconstruction. Writing could contribute nothing to the well-being of society and much to personal malaise. Now that it had become an activity that did not pay for itself and was disdained, "there was nothing more natural for the writer than to make his vocation into a refined and secret pastime and not to worry whether others understand him."

Whereas *Canciones para cantar en las barcas* had been written in the Mexico of Vasconcelos, which sought to enlarge the reading public, *Death Without End* is a hermetic poem that renounces all easy accessibility and concedes that it will have few readers. (In fact only 550 copies of the first edition were printed; the poem wasn't reprinted until 1952.) The wide diffusion of *Death Without End* was due to the publication in 1944 of *Laurel: Antología de la poesía española e hispanoamericana*, edited by Villaurrutia, Emilio Prados, Octavio Paz, and Juan Gil-Albert. Nevertheless, to this date only one complete translation into English exists, Laura Villaseñor's *Death Without End*.

Gorostiza was third secretary to the Mexican legation in Copenhagen and private secretary to the foreign minister, General Eduardo Hay, from 1937 to 1939. Because of his position at the Foreign Ministry, he was able to observe from up close (but also from outside) the great events of the time, the consolidation of fascism and nazism, the invasion of Ethiopia (Abyssinia), the Spanish civil war, the Munich Pact, and the liquidation of the old Bolsheviks by Joseph Stalin. Mexican president Lázaro Cárdenas was opposed to Benito Mussolini because of his attack on

Abyssinia; he also supported the Republic against Franco and, above all, he thrust himself into international conflict through the expropriation of United States and British petroleum interests in Mexico. It was under these circumstances that Gorostiza wrote the texts he would later call "Del poema frustrado" (From the Frustrated Poem). These texts are, in reality, tentative outlines and initial approaches to his masterwork, *Death Without End*, which he claims to have written during a few weeks in 1939 in his office at the ministry. When the poem first appeared, he was already in Rome serving as secretary to the Mexican legation. He went from Rome to Guatemala and Cuba. He was director of political affairs and adviser to the Mexican delegations at several events: the Conference of Chapultepec, the founding of the United Nations in San Francisco, and the establishment of UNESCO in London. As delegate to the ninth Interamerican Conference in Bogotá in 1948, he was witness to the days of violence that passed into history as the *bogotazo* (the rage of Bogotá). While there he wrote his last poem, "Declaración de Bogotá" (Bogotá Declaration), which is a poem of love, not a political text.

In later years he was the ambassador to Holland and Greece, Mexican representative to the United Nations, subsecretary of the Foreign Ministry (1953–1963), and head of the ministry between April and November of 1964. That year he published *Poesía*, his collected works in verse. In 1968 he received the National Literature Prize. Miguel Capistrán published his prose in the volume *Prosa* the following year. Gorostiza's last post was head of the National Commission on Nuclear Energy from 1965 to 1970. He died in Mexico City on 16 March 1979.

Poetics

Gorostiza formulated his poetics fifteen years after *Death Without End* in a speech given on the occasion of his initiation into the Mexican Academy. In his comments, which were later to form the basis of the prologue to *Poesía*, he called poetry a "network of luminous, exact, and palpitating words, an investigation into certain essences—love, life, death, and God." It is an effort to shatter language in order to make it more transparent, to make language a window onto the interior of these essences. It is speculation: a set of mirrors where words are reflected in one another endlessly until they recombine into a world of pure images. It is there that the poet establishes mastery over the hidden human powers and makes contact with what lies in the beyond.

Poetry, Gorostiza continues, has always been written and read by people educated to enjoy its pleasures. It is music and song. And it no longer requires the support of music, for poets have, through their work with language, fitted poetry to the regularity and conciseness of music. They have submitted it to measure, accentuation, periodicity, and relationship. Unrestricted freedom does not exist. But the rules do not oppress; they simply outline a territory in which the genius of the poet can develop without limit. In contrast with prose, poetry (like song) asks the reader for his eyes and his voice.

A poem grows like a painting in the sense that it has to fill a surface. Its development is dynamic, and once put into motion, it advances or climbs in continuous progress until it explodes in climax and then plummets to its ending. It has to grow and take form imperceptibly, like a living being, like a fruit or flower, until it effortlessly achieves the size and proportion determined by its own vital spirit. It is an architectonic unity: its name itself implies intelligent organization of the poetic material. For the whole to turn out to be truly a poem, all its parts must be poetic.

Gorostiza laments the loss, by 1954, of the large-scale poetic structures that existed in the vast poems of earlier eras. Lyrical autobiography is in vogue: but poetry has abandoned to drama and to the novel a large part of the role it had played as a vehicle for telling stories and presenting dialogue and discussion. He asks himself whether at the dawn of the nuclear age humanity isn't entering a world inhabited only by technical experts, a world from which poetry can be expelled for being a scandalous manifestation of primitive thought.

Poetry, concludes Gorostiza, is a revelation of beauty, a beauty that is not natural, but rather artificial and poetic. It is like a secret tunnel that allows us to escape from our passions, from the ugliness and horror that surrounds us, to infinite spaces illuminated by the splendor of beauty. In today's urbanized and polluted world, we humans need poetry to beautify our lives and to make them worthy of being endured.

This is a communal task, one which presupposes the combined efforts of many. Poetry is not eternal: the same instruments that give it form cause its demise. If it doesn't seep into the foundation of popular wisdom, it will be no more than an object of archaeological curiosity and a source of inspiration for other poets. They have no reason to know these things, since historical consciousness will not allow them to continue writing. The poet "must feel like the only inhabitant of a abandoned world who, for the first time, has been granted the pleasure of giving names to things. . . . In poetry, as with miracles, what matters is intensity."

Themes

Gorostiza always was opposed to his poetry being read like a philosophical treatise. In a 1965 interview with Emmanuel Carballo, in *Protagonistas de la literatura mexicana*, he said: "I don't know what *Death Without End* is, nor what it means. The speculations of the learned, who have tried to uncover this point . . . leave me dumbfounded. It simply occurred to me (and this was nothing new) that life and death constitute a single, unitary process and that each one, life and death, could be admired in its full splendor from the opposite shore."

In other words, Gorostiza has formulated with admirable verbal tools the same questions asked by all philosophers and poets: What is the meaning of existence? Why do we live if we have to die? And in a way he finds the same answers: the fact that we are transitory and unrepeatable gives value to our actions; for each person the idea of immortality is more terrifying than the idea of death.

There is no fixed symbology in Gorostiza. Broadly speaking, we can say that the duality of water and vessel represents not only poetry and the form in which it is embodied, but also life and the individual in which it is made concrete. When the vessel breaks, never to be made whole again, the water it held is free to seek other vessels and to repose in them

until they too are destroyed. The triumph of death is a tragedy for the individual and a victory for the plurality of existence, which in this way affirms its renewal and continuation. There is no escape from this drama: we are here thanks to the fact that others died and we ourselves die so that others may live. Our life is possible only because of universal death: the death of our ancestors and of all living beings, all animals and plants that give us food, clothing, a place to stay, tools for our work, and sources of energy.

In the first part of *Death Without End,* yo (I), the narrative voice of the poem, says he is situated inside his body, suffocated by a god he cannot touch. His aspiration to rise above the clay that is the earth and of which the earth is made has been extinguished. He identifies with water, that volatile and ungraspable material that can as readily be sea as river, cloud, foam, or steam, but that is "molded by the rigor of the clarifying glass," that "strangling crystal net," which makes it at the same time into a flower, a transparent image, an eye, a mirror. Perhaps God, that great absence, that great silence, is also a vessel that gives beauty to the world through its transparency, in the same way the wound and the fever do. We cannot see him because he is in all things. He distributes worlds inside the chaos and articulates rhythmically, symphonically, the cycle of birth-death-birth ("plant-seed-plant"). He creates the human flesh that collapses when it tries to elevate itself, tortured by passion, weeping, hatred, rancor, anguish, tumor, ulcer, chancre, and decrepitude.

And so, the process of life demands a "death without end." Intelligence is "flaming solitude" because it can conceive all, but cannot create anything. Like blood and love, flowers, trees, and fruits can be sweet or bitter. On the other hand, water neither smells nor tastes like anything, but without it the cycle life-death-life would not exist. Water is thirsty and wants to reflect itself. The vessel possesses it and gives it a countenance. Since desire cannot fertilize water, it is left unsatisfied: lucidity and rigor are clarity in the dark, a form that is not realized in and of itself.

Poetry is an illusion, a "gentle narcotic peopling of the senses with phantoms." No sooner has matter reached the fullness of its form than death intrudes and that splendor returns to ashes. Matter becomes shapeless once again. Water abandons itself to its death. Everything returns to the original sopor to create the scene of Nothingness. "The sleepless dart [returns] into the perfect night of its quiver." Poetry, eulogy for the world, ends up as dust and silence. The return to origins is the return to the primeval Nothing. All lovely beings of the earth give in to a frenzy of death. Whatever has sprung from roots becomes petrified. All beings devour their fellow beings. In this grim festival, form finds death a liberating pleasure. Form returns to the great waters of the beginning, above which the Spirit floats alone.

This time of intense reflection is interrupted by the parody of a child's game: The devil bursts in and with him comes the bitter joy of consuming everything before it is snatched away by death. Perhaps God himself has died and the thing we call by his name is only the light of an extinguished star that has taken centuries to reach us. The poem ends with a "dance." In this dance, the ever-lurking death that courts the "I" of the poem is considered a "little wench" and sent to the devil; that is, into flight and oblivion.

Who did Gorostiza send to the devil in 1939, death or poetry? Why did he resume writing poems only once again, and afterward dwell in a silence that, like E. M. Forster's, made his prestige grow with every new book that he did *not* publish? Valéry has said that the "true sense" of a text does not exist, for every generation and every reader reads it in his own way. We can cite here only a few of the thousands of different interpretations of Gorostiza's poem. For the Roman Catholic critic, he is saying that in the absence of God, the world gives in to a "frenzy of death" where only Nothingness, that "sinister bird of smoke," rules. A materialist interpretation of the poem denies the immortality of the soul, the promised paradise, and the chastisements of hell: we have only this world, this life, and afterward we return to absolute Nothing.

In a brilliant essay he wrote in 1951 entitled "Muerte sin fin," Octavio Paz portrays the work as the end of a cycle: another poem like Gorostiza's is "impossible and unthinkable" and his work "is the monument that form has erected to its own death." For other critics, the artistic triumph of *Death Without End* is its denial of that which it expresses conceptually: the poem speaks of the impossibility of poetry at the same time it incarnates poetry in all its powers and infinite variety.

In his book dedicated exclusively to Gorostiza, Andrew P. Debicki regards the great poem as an epic work, the epopee of the mind in its struggle to discover the meaning of the world and a yearning to give permanence to at least part of what is human: the products of one's imagination and of one's intelligence. Debicki shares with the reader what the author confided to him: it wasn't disenchantment with poetry that prevented him from continuing to write, but rather his work for the Mexican government. Nevertheless, *Death Without End* continues and will continue to generate a variety of interpretations. For Salvador Elizondo, for instance, the poem is an example of apocatastasis, or the return of things to their origins, such as occurs in Alejo Carpentier's story, "Viaje a la semilla" (Journey Back to the Seed, 1944). A new generation of critics has taken up Gorostiza's challenge. In 1984 Juan Gelpí saw in the poem a rebellion against the divine, and also Valérian, rigor that constrains poetic expression. In *Death Without End* Latin American poetry affirms itself, both in the face of its European models and against the narrowness of literary nationalism. In so doing, it produces a new and dynamic text.

Prose

The Contemporáneos—all of whom were outstanding and, in some cases, great poets—were also outstanding critics and essayists. Gorostiza did not work in these genres in a systematic way, despite having earned a reputation as a critic in his youth for the brief notes and reviews he wrote for magazines of the era. In 1969 Capistrán collected these writings into the single volume, *Prosa*.

There are articles in this book on theater, painting, music, and film, though the majority of them discuss poetry and narrative. Many of the articles are intelligent readings of friends like Ortiz de Montellano, Torres Bodet, Pellicer, and Salvador Novo. From 1938 until 1954, when he delivered his speech before the academy, Gorostiza published only one prose piece. This was a sketch entitled "Metamorfosis del amigo" (Metamorphosis of the Friend), which some writers believe was the start of a novel. The only author to whom he referred in two very different moments of his life—1924 and 1963—was López Velarde. His final published page, an homage to Pellicer, saw public light in 1968. In this homage he writes, "Gorostiza the poet is the result of Pellicer the poet. He is my master in the true sense of the word." Though this collection of his prose is short, it displays excellent literary journalism and shows the great importance of the Contemporáneos' work in this field. Their efforts helped create a new audience for avant-garde art and a tradition for Mexican literature of the twentieth century.

Language and Style

In 1919 Pedro Henríquez Ureña's *Antología de la versificación rítmica* (Anthology of Rhythmic Versification) was published in the series Cultura. This book must have been extremely important for the young poet. With folk songs, ballads, and poems it showed that not all verse in Spanish is syllabic. Rhythmic forms exist in which verses lack a fixed number of syllables but still have marked accentuation. Just as pre-Columbian and African art inspired much of the painting and sculpture of the avant-garde, Gorostiza took inspiration from *sequidillas* (stanzas of four or seven five- and seven-syllable verses) and *cantarcillos* (short folk songs) that were linked to popular ballads and dances. Hence the title of his first book, *Canciones* (Songs). In this book, as many beginning poets do, Gorostiza successfully imitates the prevailing styles, adds something original and, using them as a base, finds his own voice. Some of the poems in *Canciones* were awakened by the moral reflections of González Martínez; others show affinity with López Velarde. In "Dibujos sobre un puerto" (Sketches of a Port) one notices an assimilation of the haiku that José Juan Tablada had recently adapted to verse in Spanish. At the same time, one can see the influence of the colloquialism of the North American "new verse."

The anthology *Poesía*, which was published in 1964, contains a set of texts under the heading "Del poema frustrado" (From the Frustrated Poem). Rather than being fragments of a possible whole, these texts are notes and exercises for *Death Without End*. They include four sonnets—the only ones he ever wrote, and among the best in the language. Through rupturing forms, decomposing syntax, and through the presence of the most obvious manifestations of the new age—the cinema, the airplane, the automobile—his generation had rediscovered classic verse, and in the 1930's almost all poets began to write sonnets again. Gorostiza's sonnets represent a very personal reversion to the baroque style of seventeenth-century Spain that was called "conceptism." Its themes of death, love, form, insomnia, thirst, movement, and, once again, water, point very directly to his great poem. This set of texts ends with the poem on Bogotá that is a sort of epilogue to *Death Without End* and a farewell, forever, to poetry.

The basic rhythmic pattern of *Death Without End* is hendecasyllabic (eleven syllables), which corresponds to the iambic pentameter of English poetry. Although imported from Italy in the sixteenth century, the hendecasyllabic has been the meter par excellence of sophisticated poetry in Spanish because of its flexibility and similarity to the rhythm of natural speech. Like so many other poets of the twentieth century who combined long and short verses, Gorostiza found a verbal fluidity that was as natural as that of the best prose. His distant historic model is the *silva* of the Golden Age, although he doesn't use its rhyme. *Death Without End* derives part of its intensity from the collision between sophisticated meter and vocabulary on the one hand, and on the other, its octasyllabic verses, which are characteristic of popular poetry in the Spanish-speaking world. The octosyllables interrupt his philosophical discourse with the rhythm of a dance and are equivalent to the "minuets" or rhymed passages that Eliot includes in each of the *Four Quartets*. No translation can do justice to the musicality of Gorostiza nor to the precision of his vocabulary. *Death Without End* was written with all the resources of the language. In this great poem, Spanish finds a supreme example of its own infinite poetic possibilities, possibilities that broadened and enriched José Gorostiza so much.

Translated from the Spanish by S. G. Stauss

SELECTED BIBLIOGRAPHY

Editions

Poetry

Canciones para cantar en las barcas. Mexico City, 1925.
Muerte sin fin. Mexico City, 1939. 2nd ed., with a commentary by Octavio Paz, Mexico City, 1952.

Collections

Poesía. Mexico City, 1964.
Prosa. Edited by Miguel Capistrán. With an epilogue by Alfonso Reyes. Guanajuato, Mexico, 1969.

Translations by Gorostiza

Gantillón, Simón. *Maya.* Mexico City, 1930.
Maurois, André. *La conversación.* Mexico City, 1931.

Translations

Death Without End. Translated by Laura Villaseñor. With an introduction by Salvador Novo. Austin, Tex., 1969.
Poems translated into English are listed in *Index to Anthologies of Latin American Literature in English Translation.* Edited by Juan R. and Patricia M. Freudenthal. Boston, 1977. Pp. 72–73.

Biographical and Critical Studies

Blanco, José Joaquín. "La crítica de Gorostiza." In *La paja en el ojo.* Mexico City, 1980. Pp. 71–81.
Carballo, Emmanuel. *Protagonistas de la literatura mexicana.* Mexico City, 1986.
Dauster, Frank. *Ensayos sobre poesía mexicana. Asedio a los Contemporáneos.* Mexico City, 1963.
Debicki, Andrew P. *La poesía de José Gorostiza.* Mexico City, 1962.
Dehennin, Elsa. *Antithèse, oxymore et paradoxisme: Approches rhétoriques de la poésie de José Gorostiza.* Paris, 1973.
Durán, Manuel. *Antología de la revista Contemporáneos.* Mexico City, 1973.
Fernández, Sergio. *Homenajes: A Sor Juana, a Lopez Velarde, a José Gorostiza.* Mexico City, 1972.

Forster, Merlin H. *Los Contemporáneos, 1920–1932. Perfil de un experimento vanguardista mexicano.* Mexico City, 1964.
Garza Cuarón, Beatriz. "Simetrías y correspondencias en *Muerte sin fin* de José Gorostiza." In *Deslindes literarios.* Mexico City, 1977. Pp. 83–94.
Gelpí, Juan. *Enunciación y dependencia en José Gorostiza. Estudio de una máscara poética.* Mexico City, 1984.
Godoy, Emma. "*Muerta sin fin* de Gorostiza." In *Sombras de Magia.* Mexico City, 1968. Pp. 9–70.
Gómez, Ocampo de, Aurora Maura, and Ernesto Prado Velásquez. "Gorostiza, José." In *Diccionario de escritores mexicanos.* Mexico City, 1967. Pp. 156–158. Contains lengthy bibliography.
Labastida, Jaime. *El amor, el sueño y la muerte en la poesía mexicana.* Mexico City, 1969.
Mejía Valera, Manuel. "El pensamiento de Gorostiza." *Sábado,* supplement of *Unomásuno* (Mexico City) 219:12–13 (2 January 1982).
Mullen, Edward J. *Contemporáneos, revista mexicana de cultura.* Salamanca, Spain, 1972.
Paz, Octavio. *El arco y la lira.* Mexico City, 1956.
——. "Muerte sin fin." In *Las peras del olmo.* Mexico City, 1957. Pp. 105–114.
——. *Los hijos del limo.* Barcelona, 1974.
——. *Xavier Villaurrutia en persona y en obra.* Mexico City, 1978.
——. *Sombras de obras.* Barcelona, 1983.
Rubín, Mordecai S. *Una poética moderna. "Muerte sin fin" de José Gorostiza. Análisis y comentario.* With a prologue by Eugenio Florit. Mexico City, 1966.
Schneider, Luis Mario. *Ruptura y continuidad. La literatura mexicana en polémica.* Mexico City, 1968.
——. "Los primeros poemas de José Gorostiza." *Hojas de crítica,* supplement to *Revista de la Universidad de Mexico* (Mexico City) 22/11:2–4 (1968).
Sheridan, Guillermo. *Los Contemporáneos ayer.* Mexico City, 1985.
Villaurrutia, Xavier. "José Gorostiza" and "La poesía de los jóvenes de Mexico." In his *Obras.* Mexico City, 1966. Pp. 680–683; 819–835.
Xirau, Ramón. *Tres poetas de la soledad: Villaurrutia, Gorostiza, Paz.* Mexico City, 1955.
——. "Muerte sin fin o del poema objeto." In *Poesía iberoamericana contemporánea.* Mexico City, 1972. Pp. 61–70.

Jaime Torres Bodet

(1902–1974)

Sonja P. Karsen

Jaime Torres Bodet began his literary career at a time when Enrique González Martínez—the last Mexican modernist and the first postmodernist—was considered Mexico's major poet. Ramón López Velarde exerted a strong influence on the younger poets of Torres Bodet's generation. Torres Bodet and his contemporaries learned the love of pure form, precise language, and intellectual modesty from González Martínez; López Velarde gave them a more plastic and original metaphor, a sense of color, and a curiosity about new sensations. It was their poetry that largely served as the starting point for a number of Mexican poets who came to be known as the Contemporáneos.

Torres Bodet was born in Mexico City on 17 April 1902. His father, Alejandro Torres Girbent, was a theatrical producer and a businessman. His mother, Emilia Bodet, was of French descent, and at an early age he listened to her recite French texts and fragments from Alphonse de Lamartine and Victor Hugo as well as read poems by José de Espronceda y Delgado and Gustavo Adolfo Bécquer. In this way he became equally proficient in French and Spanish. He was devoted to his mother, to whom he owed his love of literature.

The writer began his secondary education at the National Preparatory School in Mexico City. Span-ish literature, taught by the poet Enrique Fernández Granados, was the class that inspired him to write his first verse at the age of twelve. By the time he graduated from secondary school, he had collected a number of poems that he published as *Fervor* (Fervor, 1918).

Between 1918 and 1921, he studied law and attended the lectures of the philosopher Antonio Caso at the National University. In 1921 the philosopher José Vasconcelos, then chancellor of the National University, named Torres Bodet as his private secretary. Shortly thereafter Vasconcelos became minister of education and asked Torres Bodet to head the Department of Libraries. This position marked the beginning of the poet's long career in the service of his country as educator and diplomat.

From 1924 to 1928 Torres Bodet taught French literature at the National University. Between 1922 and 1928 he published seven books of verse and an anthology. During that period his first novel, *Margarita de niebla* (Margaret Enveloped by Fog, 1927), and a book of essays, *Contemporáneos* (Contemporaries, 1928), appeared. In addition, from 1922 to 1923 he edited the review *La Falange* (The Phalanx) together with Bernardo Ortiz de Montellano. Contrary to the belief of many writers, Torres Bodet felt that it was good for a writer to be engaged in regular work and thus participate in everyday life. As a representative of his country he traveled to Cuba, Canada, and the United States in 1928. It was during this journey that he first thought of starting a new literary review whose aim was to acquaint Mexican literati with contemporary literary movements. The magazine, *Contemporáneos*, appeared from 1928 to 1931. Because of its well-known contributors the review was seen as representing a clearly defined period in Mexican literature.

In 1929 Torres Bodet joined the diplomatic service and was assigned as third secretary to the Mexican legation in Madrid. Before he went to Europe, he married Josefina Juárez. His wife's devotion and constant support were important factors in the success of his professional career. In Madrid he made the acquaintance of poets and writers of the Generation of 1936: Pedro Salinas y Serrano, Benjamín Jarnés, Federico García Lorca, and Rafael Albertí. In the Spanish capital he wrote the poetry published in *Destierro* (Exile, 1930) and the works of fiction *La educación sentimental* (The Education of the Heart, 1929) and *Proserpina rescatada* (Proserpina Redeemed, 1931). More than six years later, he was called back to Mexico to serve as head of the diplomatic section of the Ministry of Foreign Affairs. In 1937 he went to Europe as chargé d'affaires of the Mexican embassy in Brussels. When he returned to Mexico in 1940 he was appointed undersecretary of foreign affairs by President Manuel Ávila Camacho.

The president then named him minister of education in 1943, requesting that he find a solution to one of Mexico's gravest problems: illiteracy. Torres Bodet saw the problem not merely as one of teaching Mexicans to read and write; rather he felt that "it was part of a world battle for peace, for democracy and justice." He saw as the most important challenges to be undertaken by his office "the coordination of school programs and textbooks, the improvement and the modernization of teaching techniques, the strengthening of the teaching profession on a nationwide basis, and increased school construction throughout the Republic" (*Discursos [1941–1964]*, p. 761).

The campaign against illiteracy began after a bill was passed by Congress on 21 August 1944. All Mexicans joined in this concerted action, which was inspired by the slogan Each One Teach One. Within two years more than a million Mexicans had learned to read and write. In 1945 Torres Bodet represented Mexico as minister of education on the UNESCO Preparatory Commission, which was instrumental in formulating the constitution of the United Nations Educational, Scientific, and Cultural Organization (UNESCO).

After Miguel Alemán became president in 1946, he appointed Torres Bodet minister of foreign affairs, a position he occupied until 1948, when he replaced Julian Huxley as director general of UNESCO. He left a definite mark on the organization's program. He envisioned the establishment of a global network of fundamental education centers over a period of twelve years. The project was actually a worldwide campaign against illiteracy. Since statistics showed that more than half the world's population was illiterate, Torres Bodet was convinced that as long as such inequality existed world security would be an illusion.

On 22 November 1952 he resigned the director-generalship in protest over a large budget cut made by the UNESCO Conference. He felt that the organization's program could not be carried out under such stringent financial restrictions. After an absence of many years he returned to Mexico, where he devoted himself to his literary calling, publishing *Fronteras* (Frontiers, 1954), his first book of verse in five years. The hiatus was not to last very long; in 1954 President Ruiz Cortines appointed him ambassador to France. Official duties during the four years he spent in Paris left him enough time to publish an autobiography, a collection of essays, and two books of verse.

In 1958 Torres Bodet was appointed to a second term as minister of education in the government of President Adolfo López Mateos. Six years later he left the ministry of education, having accomplished his goals of making it possible for every Mexican to get an elementary education, of training thousands of teachers to make this promise a reality, and finally of providing the necessary schools.

Torres Bodet again returned to his literary career and devoted the last ten years of his life to writing his memoirs. Suffering from an incurable disease, he shot and killed himself at home in Mexico City on 13 May

1974. His suicide note deserves to be remembered for its courage: "Being under the threat of death from day to day," he wrote, "I think it better to summon death myself, at the right time" (*Excelsior* [Mexico City] 14 May 1974).

His poetry may be divided into three distinct cycles. The first consists of his earliest poems contained in *Fervor, El corazón delirante* (The Impassioned Heart, 1922), *Canciones* (Songs, 1922), *La casa* (The House, 1923), *Los días* (The Days, 1923), *Nuevas canciones* (New Songs, 1923), *Poemas* (Poems, 1924), and *Biombo* (Folding Screen, 1925). The second cycle includes the poetry of maturity represented by *Destierro* and *Cripta* (Crypt, 1937). To the third phase of his work, which shows an even greater mastery of substance and form, belong the poems written beginning in the late 1940's: *Sonetos* (Sonnets, 1949), and his later collections of verse *Fronteras* (Frontiers, 1954), *Sin tregua* (No Truce, 1957), and *Trébol de cuatro hojas* (Four-Leaf Clover, 1958). Certain themes recur; among these are the search for his identity and the attempt to establish an identity with his fellow man. Another theme is that of loneliness, of being and not being. There is the constant awareness of fleeting time, which leads to the ever-present theme of death. In later years the subconscious world of dreams appears in his poetry.

Torres Bodet saw *Fervor*, which he published at age sixteen, as the result of "youthful fervor, not a genuine achievement." Just the same, the themes that characterize his mature poetry are already contained in that early work.

The themes in *El corazón delirante* are indicated by the title—poetic renderings of various kinds of love. In *Canciones* we find the expression of a moment in which the emotion of the poet and the voice of the man strive for unity. Love, the major theme of the collection, follows different moods. It can be light-hearted or passionate, yet the poet realizes that time and beauty are evanescent and that in every beginning there is present an end. In "Canción de las voces serenas" ("Song of Serene Voices"), he wrote:

> y se nos irá la vida
> sin sentir otro rumor
> que el del agua de las horas
> que se lleva el corazón . . .

and life will be spent
with hardly a sound
but the stream of hours
bearing the heart away. . ."*

La casa and *Los días* show a more direct and simple poetry distinguished by clarity. *Los días* chronicles a year in the poet's life, in which he tried to find a point of contact with the poor—their joys and sorrows, their simplicity and fervor. From that immersion in poverty and humility arose the poem "Mediodía" (Noon). The composition expresses the poet's pleasure in the simple things in life, because he is "finally mature enough to see in things, / nothing more than what they are: bread, sun, honey . . ."

In *Poemas*, the unity of *La casa* and *Los días* is broken. Here the main theme is not clearly indicated, and throughout the volume Torres Bodet searches for the identity that would make him part of life. He fully understands, however, that the ideal cannot be reached and that a sound relationship cannot endure, a theme that is developed in one of his most stirring poems, "Ruptura" ("Rupture").

Biombo was an answer to those who claimed to find a subjectivity that was perhaps too abstract in Torres Bodet's verse. This volume constitutes a transition to greater complexity and symbolism in his interpretation of reality. He has also become more analytical of his own feelings; here the musical quality of his poetry and the use of color in his imagery assume greater importance as well.

Torres Bodet himself stated that the year 1926 marked a sudden move away from his previous poetry. During the years 1927, 1928, and 1929 he wrote very little verse. Prose interested him more, and in those years he produced two brief novels, *Margarita de niebla* and *La educación sentimental*. In 1930 he returned to poetry with *Destierro*. In this collection the graceful compositions of his early works are replaced by surrealism and the nebulous world of dreams, as in the poem "Buzo" ("Diver"):

> Lento
> y con ruedas de espuma en el insomnio,
> giró el acuario rápido del sueño.

*All translations of Jaime Torres Bodet's poetry are from *Selected Poems of Jaime Torres Bodet*, translated by Sonja P. Karsen.

935

Slowly
with wheels of foam in sleeplessness
revolves the rapid aquarium of our dreams.

Destierro was followed by *Cripta*, which contains perhaps his most striking poetry. It was also, as he said, the first of the volumes of verse "in which I now recognize myself." The strongest emotional impact is produced by "Dédalo" ("Labyrinth"), which conveys a feeling of tremendous loneliness:

> *Enterrado vivo*
> *en un infinito*
> *dédalo de espejos*
> *me oigo, me sigo,*
> *me busco en el liso*
> *muro del silencio.*
>
> *Pero no me encuentro.*

Buried alive
in an infinite
labyrinth of mirrors
I hear myself, follow myself,
look for myself
in this smooth wall of silence.

But I do not find myself.

In *Cripta* the poet is also preoccupied with time. Time is frequently represented by the *peldaños* (steps) of a staircase that inexorably leads us down to the last step, which symbolizes death.

Sonetos, which appeared after a hiatus of twelve years, was written between trips and diplomatic assignments, speeches and treaty ratifications. During those active years in government service the only possible way for Torres Bodet to express these profound callings of the inner voice was through poetry. In this collection the poet meditates on the secret forces of life and death. And yet in "Círculo" ("Circle") he encounters a new soul in the death that is lived with each heartbeat, which he describes as "muriendo y renaciendo a cada instante" ("dying and being born again with each moment"). In *Destierro*, *Cripta*, and *Sonetos* he was particularly interested in looking for truth within himself, whereas the poet of *Fronteras* sees in his self-centered concern a symbol of suffering humanity. The poet is felt to play a major

role in the search for universal brotherhood, "because any poem / is a pact of peace among men," as he states in "Porque todo poema . . ." (Because Any Poem . . .).

Sin tregua develops further the themes already encountered in *Fronteras*. As the title indicates, there is no truce until we reach the top—that is, the end of our anguished existence—because life is a constant struggle and all our dignity lies in facing it with fortitude.

Trébol de cuatro hojas pays tribute to four members of the Contemporáneos group: Bernardo Ortiz de Montellano, Carlos Pellicer, José Gorostiza, and Xavier Villaurrutia. Each of the four cantos bears the title of a book written by one of the poets whose life and work Torres Bodet describes. The individual poems try to capture the spirit and the style of the poet he honors. In order to be more convincing Torres Bodet uses the highly original stylistic device of incorporating some of their verses into his own.

The poet's selection of his fifty most significant poems is found in *Poesía de Jaime Torres Bodet* (Poems by Jaime Torres Bodet, 1965). The compositions included exemplify his concept of "poesía vivida," poetry that finds its inspiration in the experiences of daily life.

In addition to being one of Mexico's most famous poets, Torres Bodet occupies an important place in the history of the contemporary Mexican novel. His six novels and lone volume of short stories belong to an early stage in his literary career. After 1941 he no longer wrote narrative prose because he regarded himself as primarily a poet and an essayist.

He and his literary group, the Contemporáneos, created a type of prose that drew on new techniques introduced by European writers of the time. Most admired by the Contemporáneos were the writings of Jean Giraudoux, Benjamín Jarnés, D. H. Lawrence, Marcel Proust, James Joyce, and Franz Kafka. Torres Bodet's first novel, *Margarita de niebla*, shows the influence of the new psychology and methods of analysis first developed by Proust and Giraudoux. He was the first to apply these techniques in Mexican literature. *La educación sentimental* continues many of these influences. Since the story of the novel was in some respect like Gustave Flaubert's well-known prose narrative, Torres Bodet gave it the same title.

The novel analyzes in great detail the friendship of two young men.

Proserpina rescatada is based on mythology. The novel is constructed on two levels: antiquity and the present are related and ultimately fused in a duality that is found not only in the main character's personality but also in the composition of the story. *Estrella de día* (Movie Star, 1933) is very much like *Proserpina* in style. Here, too, the author highlights a duality in theme: the world of the imagination as opposed to the everyday reality in which we live. The theme of *Primero de enero* (January First, 1935) is indicated by its title—New Year's Day marks a new beginning in many people's lives, and the protagonist here takes full advantage of this tradition, leaving the past behind. The hero of the novel is a solitary tycoon bored with the empty life he leads. He decides to change his identity and as a result meets people from different walks of life, including a poverty stricken unwed mother and her son. Moved by their plight, he decides to take care of them. By working for the good of those less fortunate, he is able to forge the happiness of his new friends as well as his own. *Primero de enero* is the only one of Torres Bodet's novels that contains an explicit social message.

Perhaps the most successful of all the novels from the point of view of technique is his last, *Sombras* (Shades, 1937). It is the story of an elderly woman, the sole survivor of a once wealthy aristocratic family now plunged into economic ruin. *Nacimiento de Venus y otros relatos* (The Birth of Venus and Other Short Stories, 1944), composed between 1928 and 1937, belongs to the same time period as his novels. In his fiction he strove for an absolute that is hidden beneath the fleeting world of appearances, from which it must be detached and given form as an artistic creation.

Once he had achieved mastery in the writing of novels and short stories, Torres Bodet turned again to the essay, which he had favored as a genre at the beginning of his literary career. The first literary criticism he published was an analysis of André Gide's work in the form of an introduction to the French novelist's *Les limites de l'art* (1901), which Torres Bodet translated into Spanish as *Los límites del arte y algunas reflexiones de moral y de literatura* (The Limits of Art and Some Thoughts on Morality and Literature, 1920). This was followed by *Contemporáneos: Notas de crítica* (Contemporaries: Notes on Literary Criticism, 1928) and *Perspectiva de la literatura mexicana actual 1915–1928* (View of Present-Day Mexican Literature 1915–1928, 1928), volumes essential to an understanding of Mexican literature of that era. *Tres inventores de realidad* (Three Inventors of Reality, 1955) speaks of the difficulties of literary creation and the predicament that life and art presented for Stendhal, Fyodor Dostoyevsky, and Benito Pérez Galdós. He continued writing literary criticism with the study *Balzac* (1959), a careful analysis of the writer's work. The Mexican writer's great admiration for the author of *War and Peace* led him to write *León Tolstoi: Su vida y su obra* (Leo Tolstoy: His life and Work, 1965). A year later he published *Rubén Darío*, a critical analysis of the work of one of Spanish America's greatest poets. The year 1967 saw the publication of *Tiempo y memoria en la obra de Proust* (Time and Memory in the Work of Proust), a particularly penetrating study of the French novelist's literary technique.

Representative of Torres Bodet's best prose are his memoirs, which he began to publish in 1955. *Tiempo de arena* (Time of Sand) chronicles the first twenty-seven years of the writer's life. There is no better explanation of the literary influences on the young poets of his time. He continues the story of his life in five subsequent volumes: *Años contra el tiempo* (Years Against Time, 1969), *La victoria sin alas* (Wingless Victory, 1970), *El desierto internacional* (The International Desert, 1971), *La tierra prometida* (The Promised Land, 1972), and *Equinoccio* (Equinox, 1974).

Even though a large number of Torres Bodet's speeches had appeared, beginning with *Educación mexicana* (Mexican Education, 1944), it was only with the publication of *Discursos (1941–1964)* (Speeches [1941–1964], 1965), a volume of two hundred of his most significant discourses, that the magnitude of his contributions as educator and diplomat could be fully understood.

Torres Bodet's endeavor was always to avoid divorcing art from life. His main concern was with the higher moral values of man and the problems man faces in the present-day world. He always separated his life as a civil servant from his life as a writer, yet it would hardly be possible to speak of one without the other. We would not know what inspired the actions of the educator or diplomat without considering his work as poet, novelist, essayist, and orator. His outstanding contribution to Mexican letters was recognized when he was awarded the National Prize for Literature by President Gustavo Díaz Ordaz in 1966. For his exemplary service to the nation the Mexican Senate honored Torres Bodet in 1971 with the Belisario Domínguez Medal.

SELECTED BIBLIOGRAPHY

Editions

Poetry

Fervor. Mexico City, 1918.
Canciones. Mexico City, 1922.
El corazón delirante. Mexico City, 1922.
La casa. Mexico City, 1923.
Los días. Mexico City, 1923.
Nuevas canciones. Mexico City, 1923.
Poemas. Mexico City, 1924.
Biombo. Mexico City, 1925.
Destierro. Madrid, 1930.
Cripta. Mexico City, 1937.
Sonetos. Mexico City, 1949.
Fronteras. Mexico City, 1954.
Sin tregua. Mexico City, 1957.
Trébol de cuatro hojas. Paris, 1958. Private edition. 2nd ed. Jalapa, Mexico, 1960.
Poesía de Jaime Torres Bodet. Mexico City, 1965.

Prose Narratives

Margarita de niebla. Mexico City, 1927.
La educación sentimental. Madrid, 1929.
Proserpina rescatada. Madrid, 1931.
Estrella de día. Madrid, 1933.
Primero de enero. Madrid, 1935.
Sombras. Mexico City, 1937.
Nacimiento de Venus y otros relatos. Mexico City, 1941.

Criticism

Contemporáneos: Notas de crítica. Mexico City, 1928.
Perspectiva de la literatura méxicana actual 1915–1928. Mexico City, 1928.
Tres inventores de realidad. Mexico City, 1955.

Balzac. Mexico City, 1959.
Maestros venecianos. Mexico City, 1961.
León Tolstoi: Su vida y su obra. Mexico City, 1965.
Rubén Darío: Abismo y cima. Mexico City, 1966.
Tiempo y memoria en la obra de Proust. Mexico City, 1967.

Memoirs

Tiempo de arena. Mexico City, 1955.
Años contra el tiempo. Mexico City, 1969.
La victoria sin alas. Mexico City, 1970.
El desierto internacional. Mexico City, 1971.
La tierra prometida. Mexico City, 1972.
Equinoccio. Mexico City, 1974.

Speeches

Educación méxicana. Mexico City, 1944.
Educación y concordia internacional. Mexico City, 1948.
Discursos (1941–1964). Mexico City, 1965.

Translations by Torres Bodet

Los límites del arte y algunas reflexiones de moral y de literatura. (By André Gide.) Mexico City, 1920.

Collected Works

Obra poética. 2 vols. With an introduction by Rafael Solana. Mexico City, 1967.
Obras escogidas. Mexico City, 1961.
Poesías escogidas. Buenos Aires, 1954.
Versos y prosas. With an introduction by Sonja P. Karsen. Madrid, 1966.

Translations

The Modern Mexican Essay. Translated by H. W. Hilborn. Edited by José Luis Martínez. Toronto, 1965. Pp. 280–299.
Selected Poems of Jaime Torres Bodet. Translated and with an introduction by Sonja P. Karsen. Bloomington, Ind., 1964.

Biographical and Critical Studies

Brushwood, John S. In *Mexico in Its Novel.* Austin, Tex., and London, 1966. Pp. 195–199, 213–214.
Burgos, Fernando. "*Proserpina rescatada*: Metáforas de una metamorfosis." In *De la crónica a la nueva narrativa mexicana: Coloquio sobre literatura mexicana,* edited by Merlin H. Forster and Julio Ortega. Oaxaca, Mexico, 1986. Pp. 139–149.

Carballo, Emmanuel. In *Diecinueve protagonistas de la literatura mexicana del siglo XX*. Mexico City, 1965. Pp. 211–227.

_____. *Jaime Torres Bodet*. Mexico City, 1968.

Colín, Eduardo. In *Rasgos*. Mexico City, 1934. Pp. 47–65.

Cowart, Billy. *La obra educativa de Torres Bodet en lo nacional y lo internacional*. Mexico City, 1966.

Dauster, Frank. "La poesía de Jaime Torres Bodet." *Revista iberoamericana* 25/49:73–94 (1960).

Forster, Merlin H. In *Los contemporáneos 1920–1932*. Mexico City, 1964. Pp. 24–55.

_____. "Three Versions of a Poem by Jaime Torres Bodet." *Romance Notes* 10/1:32–36 (1968).

González de Mendoza, José María. In *Ensayos selectos*. Mexico City, 1970. Pp. 306–329.

Jaime Torres Bodet en quince semblanzas. With an introduction by Marte R. Gómez. Mexico City, 1965.

Jarnés, Benjamín. In *Ariel disperso*. Mexico City, 1946. Pp. 46–49, 167–170, 200–206, 208–213.

Karsen, Sonja P. *A Poet in a Changing World*. Saratoga Springs, N.Y., 1963.

_____. *Jaime Torres Bodet*. New York, 1971.

Leal, Luis. "Torres Bodet y los 'Contemporáneos.'" *Hispania* 40:290–296 (1957).

Leiva, Raúl. *Imagen de la poesía méxicana contemporánea*. Mexico City, 1959. Pp. 123–136.

Miller, Beth K. *La poesía constructiva de Jaime Torres Bodet*. Mexico City, 1974.

_____. *Ensayos contemporáneos sobre Jaime Torres Bodet*. Mexico City, 1976.

Mullen, E. J. "Poetic Revision in Jaime Torres Bodet's 'Canción de cuna.'" *Papers on Language and Literature* 6:180–187 (1970).

_____. "*Destierro* y la visión superrealista de Jaime Torres Bodet." *Hispanófila* 17/50:85–98 (1974).

Peden, Margaret S. "Una nota sobre la muerte del modernismo: 'Nacimiento de Venus,' de don Jaime Torres Bodet." *Cuadernos hispanoamericanos* (Madrid) 284:431–436 (1974).

Pérez Firmat, Gustavo. In *Idle Fictions*. Durham, N.C., 1982. Pp. 3–7, 16–18, 81–99.

Reyes, Alfonso. "Jaime Torres Bodet." *Memoria de El Colegio Nacional* 2:87–91 (1953).

Solana, Rafael. "Jaime Torres Bodet." *Estaciones* 2/6:105–109 (1957).

Toussaint, Manuel. "La obra literaria y educativa de Jaime Torres Bodet." *Memoria de El Colegio Nacional* 2/8:119–132 (1953).

Rogelio Sinán

(1902–   )

Ismael García

Rogelio Sinán, pseudonym of Bernardo Domínguez Alba, uses this name exclusively, even within his own family; most people are unaware that it is a pen name and have no idea what his birth name is. Sinán was born on 25 April 1902, on Taboga, a small island in the Gulf of Panama. He attended secondary school in the city of Panama, graduating in 1924. In his senior year, he won first prize in a short story contest. It was this prize that stimulated his desire to be a writer. In 1924 he enrolled in the School of Education in Santiago, Chile. It was there that Gabriela Mistral said to him, "If you want to be a writer, what are you doing in Santiago? Go to Rome, learn Italian, read *The Divine Comedy.*" That is exactly what he did. In Rome he wrote his first book of poetry, *Onda* (Wave, 1929), and created his pseudonym. He had read that there were at least one hundred writers with the name Domínguez. So he chose his father's first name, added the name of a hill on Taboga (Sinai), and called himself Rogelio Sinán.

As with most aspiring authors, Sinán was not able to support himself by writing, so he worked at established positions off and on for most of his life. Returning to Panama in 1930, he taught high-school Spanish, but in 1932 went to Paris for a year. He then returned to Panama, where he again taught Spanish. In 1938 he was appointed consul in Calcutta, India.

After a year, during which he traveled all over India, he resigned to visit most of the countries of the South Pacific. Back in Panama in 1939, he held various government positions, at the same time continuing to write and publish. In 1953 he went to Mexico, where he remained until 1959, serving as secretary of the embassy of Panama during part of that time and studying at the University of Mexico, where he obtained his diploma. Returning to Panama, he taught theater history and directed plays at the University of Panama until 1968. In 1968 he became cultural adviser to the Department of Education. Since 1964 he has been a member of the Academia Panameña de la Lengua (Panamanian Academy of Language).

Sinán entered the literary field with *Onda,* a volume that consisted of forty-five short poems. In this work he ignored *modernismo* in favor of free verse, already in use in Europe. When the book appeared in Panama, it was not at first well received. With its free form, titles without capitals, unfamiliar images and visions, and implications of sensuous pleasures, it was offensive to some, while others viewed the book as the harmless caprice of a young writer. But the ultimate consensus of the intellectuals of Panama was that the book had great merit. They not only wrote articles in its favor but defended it against conservatives who considered it childish and of little value. Younger writers were intrigued, and in a few years the controversy more or less ended in a victory for Sinán. He is considered to have brought the avant-garde movement to Panama. Love and nature are the principle themes of the poems, and although some of them might be considered erotic, others are delicate and tender: the sensuality evaporates and only a perfume of the soul is breathed.

El viejo sol está borracho de luz
y tiene sustos
de niño que por travieso
duerme con el sueño inquieto.

Se le derrama la luz
goteándole de la boca . . .
   ¡Mira . . . ! Mira, como
   caen
al agua del río
las gotas! . . .

      ("Sol")

The ancient sun is drunk with light
and has fears
like a restless child
who sleeps with disturbing dreams.

And so the light is spilled
drooling from the mouth . . .
Look . . . ! O look, how the drops
fall
to the river water below! . . .

      (Sun)

—*¡Mangos! . . . ¡Mira! . . . ¡Tantos!*
Oh! . . . ¡Uno maduro . . . !
(Dio un salto . . . ¡y salióse
su seno, desnudo!)

   ("Balada del seno desnudo")

—Mangos! . . . Look! . . . So many!
Oh! . . . A ripe one . . . !
(She jumps . . . and out pops
her naked breast!)

   (Ballad of the Naked Breast)

Traje a tí
mi soledad
para que
le dieras alma.
Pero la dejaste sola
en el camino;
¡qué sola
dejaste mi soledad . . . !

   ("Soledad")

I brought you
my loneliness
that you would give soul to it.
but you left it
on the road;
how alone
you left my solitude . . . !

   (Loneliness)

In 1944 *Incendio* (The Fire) was published. This poem was inspired by a tragic fire that Sinán witnessed. The horror of the flames, the ruins, and the victims so affected the poet's emotions that he was unable to sleep. His catharsis came after writing the poem in one sitting. In three parts (the voice of panic, the voice of agony, and the voice of supplication), the poem is suggestive of Dante's *Divine Comedy*.

Semana santa en la niebla (Foggy Holy Week) won first prize in the 1949 Ricardo Miró poetry contest. This book of twenty-five stanzas of eight lines each is a kind of surrealistic creation in which Sinán took twenty-five themes from the Bible and related them to the tropics and the island of Taboga. Sinán, moved by the beauty of throbbing nature, adapts incidents from the Gospels to elements in nature. Throughout the book he depicts a visionary world in which nature is exalted by reflecting biblical themes.

Lamiendo tierra, arena, raíces y bazofias,
tumbo a tumbo al origen precipítase el río.
Los oros del poniente despilfarró en cabriolas
de ondulante premura por liquidar su opimo
caudal de margaritas y alas de mariposa.
Vuelve enjuto, lodoso, pordiosero de estío,
y, añorando caricias de paternales olas,
arrójase en el seno del Mar, arrepentido.

   ("El hijo pródigo")

first prize in the Concurso Interamericano del Cuento (inter-American short story contest) sponsored by *El Nacional* of Mexico. It is the only one of Sinán's stories translated into English. This fascinating story of two abnormal people uses surrealism, a pseudo-scientific prose style, and flashback to create an ambiguous drama. Dr. Paul Ecker, an eminent ichthyologist, and his assistant, Linda Olsen, come to a tropical island to study the spawning of fish. The story is unfolded through Ecker's answers to the judge who interrogates him about Linda's death and his memories of everything from his first meeting with Linda to their life on the island.

Also to be explained is the reason for Ecker's disposal of Linda's baby, who died almost immediately after its birth. Four possibilities are presented: the baby had been fathered by Ecker and was deformed; it had been fathered by Joe Ward, a Negro from the navy base, and was black; it had been fathered by Ben Parker, a sailor from the base, and was blond; it was a mermaid and slipped from Ecker's hands into the sea. This enigma is presented to the reader, but no solution is given. The reader, just as the viewer of Akiva Kurosawa's classic film *Rashomon*, must choose the possibility that is the most credible.

Many writers have said that metaphor, magic, myth, and ambiguity are essential to good literature. If so, Sinán's work meets the requirements. All his literature is tropical, with his characters almost always Panamanian. His protests are usually directed at the injustices practiced in the Canal Zone, but he never becomes a provincial writer. He never repeats his subject matter, continually creating something new. Although Sinán sprinkles Panamanian expressions throughout his prose, he never gives up conventional syntax or a superior command of Spanish. And throughout there is evidence of a keen sense of humor. Oneiric themes, surrealism, visions, magical realism, symbols, and the subconscious are all found in Sinán's work.

On his eightieth birthday, Sinán remarked, "I am not eighty years old. These years are the years that I have not yet had." Never too busy to encourage and help young writers, this prodigious poet, novelist, short story writer, essayist, and dramatist remains Panama's outstanding man of letters.

SELECTED BIBLIOGRAPHY

First Editions

Poetry

Onda. Rome, 1929.
Incendio. Panama City, 1944.
Semana santa en la niebla. Panama City, 1949.
Saloma sin salomar. Panama City, 1969. Includes *Incendio*.

Novels

Plenilunio. Panama City, 1947.
La isla mágica. Panama City, 1979.

Short Stories

A la orilla de las estatuas maduras. Panama City, 1946.
Todo un conflicto de sangre. Panama City, 1946.
Dos adventuras en el Tejano. Panama City, 1947.
Los pájaros del sueño. Panama City, 1954.
La boina roja y cinco cuentos. Panama City, 1954.
Cuna común. Panama City, 1963.
Cuentos de Rogelio Sinán. San José, Costa Rica, 1971.
El candelabro de los malos ofidios y otros cuentos. Panama City, 1982.

Essays

"Rutas de la novela panameña." *Lotería* 2/23:103 (1957).
"Significado de Juárez y Maximilian en dos tragedias modernas." *Letras de Panama* 3:2 (1959).
"Poesía en Panamá." *Lotería* 5/60:53 (1960).
"Doña Perfecta, Doña Bárbara y la Negra Augustias." *Revista Tareas* 3:3 (1961).
"Un modernista panameño: Darío Herrera." *Boletín Primer Congreso Regional de Academias de la Lengua de Centroamerica y Panama.* Managua, Nicaragua, 1967.
"Mi poesía: Una retrospetiva." *Letras de Panamá.* Supplement no. 1, February 1970.

Plays

Chiquilinga. Panama City, 1961. Farce for children.

Translations

"The Red Beret." Translated by Dennis Seager. In *The Spanish American Short Story: A Critical Anthology*, edited by Seymour Menton. Los Angeles, 1980. Pp. 294–317.

Biographical and Critical Studies

Bermúdez, Ricardo J. "El mago de la isla." *Boletín de la Academia Panameña de la Lengua* 5/1:42 (1980).

_____. *Sinán: Cuarenta años después de "Onda."* *Lotería* 14/164:23 (1969).

García, Ismael. In *Historia de la literatura panameña.* Mexico City, 1964. Pp. 113–117, 141–144.

_____. "La isla mágica, novela panameña e hispanoamericana." *Boletín de la Academia Panameña de la Lengua* 5/1:38 (1980).

_____. *Medio siglo de poesía panameña.* Mexico City, 1956.

Guardia, Gloria. "Cuentos de Rogelio Sinán: Una revisión de la vanguardia de Panamá." *Boletín de la Academia Panameña de la Lengua* 4/2:58 (1974).

Isaza Calderon, Baltasar. "Rogelio Sinán y su *Plenilunio.*" *Epocas* 2:17 (1947).

Jaramillo Levi, Enrique. *Homenaje a Rogelio Sinán.* Mexico City, 1982.

_____, ed. *Homenaje a Rogelio Sinán.* *Maga* 5–6:66–188 (1985).

Martínez Ortega, Aristedes. *La modalidad vanguardista en la poesía panameña.* Panama City, 1973. Pp. 31–35, 113–122.

Mejía Dutary, Miguel. *"La isla mágica."* *Boletín de la Academia Panameña de la Lengua* 5/1:48 (1980).

Miró, Rodrigo. "Los cuarenta años de *Onda.*" *Lotería* 14/164:3 (1969).

Ricord, Elsie Alvarado de. "Homenaje a Rogelio Sinán." *Boletín de la Academia Panameña de la Lengua* 5/1:31 (1980).

Roy Arosemena, Milantia. *"Semana santa en la niebla."* *Lotería* 18/208:50 (1973).

Nicolás Guillén

(1902–   )

Vera M. Kutzinski

Nicolás Guillén, born in the Cuban province of Camagüey on 10 July 1902, has been called the greatest poet in the Hispanic world since Rubén Darío. His work has been widely acclaimed and anthologized, and translations of his poetry have appeared in more than thirty languages. Cuba's national poet and president of the National Union of Cuban Writers and Artists (UNEAC) since 1961, Guillén has always been identified with the ideological movement that prepared the path for the Cuban Revolution in 1959. As a result of his political allegiances, many of his prerevolutionary poems are considered sociopolitical prophecies. Similarly, his later works are generally perceived as praise songs celebrating the accomplishments of the Fidel Castro regime against the backdrop of United States imperialism. Guillén is frequently labeled an avowed Marxist poet, and most critical studies of his poetry concentrate on ideological, rather than literary, matters. However, while there is no doubt that Guillén's commitment to Marxism and to the objectives of the Cuban Revolution lends a certain thematic coherence both to his journalistic writings and his poetry, this coherence is as superficial as it is obvious. One need not question the sincerity of Guillén's ideological stance to acknowledge that there is also another side to his poetry. Almost all of Guillén's poetry is rooted in the cross-cultural imagination of

the Caribbean—*mestizaje,* as he himself has called it—and the resistance to any kind of dogmatism is an important part of that historical legacy.

Little attention has been paid to this side of Guillén's poetry and to his assertion of true artistic and ideological freedom above and beyond communist doctrines. Guillén's poetry is permeated by a keen sense of history, though history understood as more than a chronology of dates and events: as a process to be reinvented by the poet's imagination. Moreover, Guillén's idea of Cuban (and Caribbean) history cannot be separated from his embrace of Afro-Hispanic culture. As he insists in his prologue to *Sóngoro cosongo* (1931): "The African injection [in Cuba] is so profound, and in our well-irrigated social hydrography so many bloodlines crisscross that one would have to be a miniaturist to unravel that hieroglyph." In the same vein, the poem "Llegada" ("Arrival"), which opens *Sóngoro cosongo,* proclaims that "We [the African slaves and their descendants] bring / our features to the final profile of America."

Although Guillén has publicly distanced himself from the radicalism of the Negritude movement, launched by a group of Francophone-Caribbean students in Paris in the 1930's, his poetry has always been dedicated to asserting the influential role Afro-Americans played in the formation of New World

947

cultures. Unlike Negritude poets, such as Senegal's Léopold Sédar Senghor, Guillén is not interested in proclaiming black superiority; nor does his work exhibit any nostalgia for Africa as a lost origin.

A mulatto by birth and raised in a family that belonged to Cuba's black middle class, Guillén literally stands at the crossroads of at least two cultures: the African and the Hispanic. His poetry is very much concerned with the literary potential of that mixed cultural heritage. This is especially true of the early *poesía negra* (black poetry) or *poesía mulata* (mulatto poetry) of *Motivos de son* (Son Motifs, 1930), *Sóngoro cosongo*, and *West Indies, Ltd.* (1934).

The first two volumes in particular are generally considered part of the Afro-Antillean movement that began to flourish in Cuba during the mid to late 1920's under the reflected impact of modern Europe's "rediscovery" of African and Afro-American cultures. Perhaps the most influential book of that period was Oswald Spengler's *The Decline of the West* (1918–1922), which kindled the interest of European intellectuals—ethnographers such as Leo Frobenius and artists such as Pablo Picasso and Henri Matisse—in non-Western cultures. In Cuba, where Spenglerian ideas were disseminated mainly through the *Revista de Occidente* the anthropologists Fernando Ortiz and Lydia Cabrera were instrumental in laying the foundations for the Afro-Antillean movement. The impact of their research on Guillén's poetry was tremendous. Among the group that constituted the Afro-Antillean movement, which roughly coincided both with the Harlem Renaissance in the United States and Indigenism in Haiti, were the novelist-to-be Alejo Carpentier, the Puerto Rican poet Luis Palés Matos, and the Cuban poets Emilio Ballagas, Ramón Güirao, and José Zacarías Tallet. Guillén was the only black member of the movement, unless one were to include the Cuban painter Wifredo Lam, who was also part Chinese.

Motivos, a collection of eight short poems written in black Cuban vernacular, first appeared on 20 April 1930 in the section of the *Diario de la Marina* entitled "Ideales de una raza" (Ideals of a Race), where the year before Guillén had published an article that inaugurated his brilliant career as a journalist, "El camino de Harlem" (The Way of Harlem, 1929), which contained a warning against racial segregation

and Negrophobia and also indirectly prepared the path for *Motivos*. The stir these poems provoked remains unparalleled in Cuban literary history. For the most part, their reception was enthusiastic, but some critics were disturbed by the aesthetic and social implications of Guillén's use of the *son*, a popular musical form, as the basis for his poems.

Guillén's *poemas-son* (son-poems) were indeed a daring literary experiment. Not only did they call attention to racial prejudice, as in "Negro bembón" ("Thick-Lipped Cullud Boy"), "Mulata" (Mulatto), and "Tú no sabe inglé" ("Don' Know No English"), and to economic injustice as in "Si tú supiera" (If You Knew) and "Búcate plata" ("No Sirrie! [Git Some Cash]"); they also disregarded conventional poetic forms in favor of the *son*, a bold gesture that in itself constituted a powerful symbolic statement about Cuban culture and literature. The *son* is a formal synthesis of the Spanish, African, and Taino (Arawak) cultures that make up the Caribbean. It combines fifteenth- and sixteenth-century Spanish *romance* (ballad) lines with a responsorial structure that is not only African but also derived from the *areito*, a Taino celebration whose name means "dancing to remember." The earliest known *son* is the legendary "Son de la Ma' Teodora" (Son of Ma' Teodoro), presumed to have been composed and performed by the black Dominican Teodora Ginés around 1580. Accompanied by the rhythmic beating of a staff (*palo*) and the *bandola*, a three-stringed guitar, Teodora's performance kept alive the memory of the three cultural traditions that contribute to her *son*.

Popularized in the twenties and thirties by the Trio Matamoros and the Sexteto Habanero from the western province of Oriente, the *son* poses the question of Cuba's national identity, which is central to all of Guillén's poetry. It is not surprising, then, that his insistence on Afro-Cuban culture as a vital factor in that search for a national identity was upsetting to some of his contemporaries. The *Motivos* also recalled the nineteenth-century antislavery novel in Cuba. The black characters who raise their voices in Guillén's poems are quite reminiscent of those portrayed, for instance, in Cirilo Villaverde's *Cecilia Valdés* (1888).

Motivos appeared as a booklet soon after its initial publication, and in October 1931 an unexpected lottery prize enabled Guillén to put into print *Sóngoro cosongo*. Composed of fifteen poems written over almost two years, *Sóngoro* lacks the tight unity of *Motivos*, but that lack of unity effectively dramatizes the absence of social, political, and cultural harmony in Cuba, a theme that appears in condensed form in "Caña" ("Cane"). Guillén continues in this collection his critical examination of racial topics. The above-mentioned "Arrival," an antecedent of Guillén's family elegy "El apellido" ("My Last Name," 1951), addresses the African influence on Cuba's cultural identity, while "La canción del bongó" ("Song of the Bongó") appeals to Afro-Cuban mythology. "Bongó," as well as "Canto negro" (Black Song), "Rumba," "Velorio de Papá Montero" ("Wake for Papa Montero"), "Quirino," and "Secuestro de la mujer de Antonio" ("Abduction of Antonio's Woman") also continue to explore the lyric potential of popular musical forms. The most emphatic treatment of economic strife is the short "Pregón" (Street Cry), which closes the collection. In addition to these familiar topics, another theme begins to emerge in *Sóngoro*: that of cultural and political imperialism, particularly on the part of the United States, the "yanqui." The struggle against United States imperialism was to become the main motivating force behind Guillén's poems. It rises to prominence as early as *West Indies, Ltd.* and culminates in *El diario que a diario* (The Daily Daily, 1972).

To understand the development of Guillén's anti-imperialistic sentiments and the impact they had on his poetry, it is helpful to return to his birth date. The year 1902 in which Guillén was born was also the year when the Republic of Cuba was established on the basis of a constitution, whose most telling feature was the Platt Amendment. This amendment allowed the United States, whose military involvement in the Spanish-American War helped free Cuba from Spain only four years earlier, to intervene in Cuban foreign and fiscal policies to protect its strategic and financial interests in the island. Born on that highly symbolic date, the young Guillén was no stranger to Cuban politics. His father, Nicolás Guillén y Urra, had fought in the Second War of Independence (1895–1898). He was a leader of the National Liberal Party in Camagüey and a senator, as well as editor of *Las dos repúblicas* and *La Libertad*. As

a result of joining an armed protest against Mario García Menocal and his schemes to hold on to the presidency after his term had expired, Nicolás' father was assassinated in 1917, leaving the fourteen-year-old as the main supporter of his family.

Having been trained in typography in his father's printing office, Guillén began to work for the journal *El nacional* while attending night classes to finish his secondary education. He graduated in 1920 and went to Havana to study law. But his interest in legal matters waned quickly, and after his first year he abandoned his studies to return to Camagüey, where he had already gained a reputation as a poet and journalist. Some of his poems had appeared in *Camagüey Gráfico* in 1919, and he had also collaborated in several journals, among them *Orto* and *Las dos repúblicas*.

In 1922, the journal *Alma mater* published a series of three sonnets entitled "Al margen de mis libros de estudio" (In the Margin of My Textbooks), which chronicle the personal conflict that led Guillén to abandon his legal studies. In the same year, he also collected the fifty-four poems of *Cerebro y corazón* (Brain and Heart), several of which had appeared in *Lis*, a short-lived magazine of which Guillén was cofounder and editor. However, *Cerebro* remained unpublished until 1962, when Ángel Augier included it as an appendix in the first volume of his seminal study of Guillén. In these early poems Guillén demonstrated, above all, his mastery of traditional poetic forms, particularly the sonnet and the *romance*. There are definitive signs of the influence of Rubén Darío in "Madrigal trirrimo" (Triple-Rhymed Madrigal), "Hoja de álbum" (Page from an Album), and "Mariposa de cristal" (Glass Butterfly); the Colombian modernist poet José Asunción Silva in "Rima triste" (Sad Rhyme); as well as the Italian futurists in "El aeroplano" ("The Airplane").

But with *Motivos* and *Sóngoro*, Guillén had already made the transition from modernism to vanguardism and begun to develop a form of poetry distinctly his own. His abundant use of African and African-derived words, which some regard as *jitanjáfora* (presumably nonsensical words employed for rhythmic purposes, as for instance the very title itself of *Sóngoro cosongo*), distinguished his poems from those of Darío, Silva, and later their Cuban heirs José Lezama

Lima and the *Orígenes* group (1944–1956). In addition, his poetic lines frequently ended on a stressed syllable, which, to a Spanish ear, was cacophonous rather than pleasing. The peculiar poetic line, which went very much against the grain of Spanish literary convention, distinguished Guillén's early Afro-Cuban poems from those of Ballagas, Güirao, and Tallet and has since become the trademark of a Guillén poem. But Guillén's development as a poet took time. Caught up in journalistic activities, he wrote no poetry at all between 1922 and 1927. The poems written between 1927 and 1930 (with the exception of *Motivos*) are published in the section "Poemas de transición" (Transitional Poems) in his *Obra poética* (1972–1973).

It was not until 1934 that another major collection of Guillén's poems appeared: *West Indies, Ltd.*, which occupies a central position in the context of Guillén's canon because it contains, in embryo, all the principal forms and themes elaborated in his later poems. The long title poem, "West Indies, Ltd.," brings into focus the economic plight of the Caribbean countries while at the same time emphasizing a shared cultural heritage as a potential basis for counteracting the encroachment of United States imperialism. "West Indies, Ltd." also marks an important step in Guillén's practice of creating the long poem as a collage of many different poetic forms. This development can be traced through the *Elegías* (Elegies, 1958), all the way to *El diario*.

Afro-Hispanic culture in particular, with its long history of resistance to white hegemony, supplies important models and strategies for Guillén's literary battle against neocolonialism. He frequently compares the tensions between the Antilles and the "colossus of the North" to the historical relationship between black slaves and white masters. The poem "Sensemayá: Canto para matar una culebra" ("Sensemayá: Chant for Killing a Snake") thrives on that analogy. Put to music in 1937 by the Mexican composer Silvestre Revueltas, "Sensemayá" uses the traditional Afro-Cuban festival of the Día de Reyes (Day of Kings, which was celebrated on the Epiphany) as a model for resistance through subversion. The Día de Reyes carnival brought about a symbolic suspension of existing power structures. The black slaves were freed for the day and were allowed to perform their own rituals and worship their own gods. For Guillén, the Día de Reyes, like the synchretic *son*, is a metaphor for Cuban culture, with which he rhetorically undermines North American influences. He strikes a similar note in the "Balada del güije" ("Ballad of the Water-Demon"), where the Afro-Cuban legend of the èvil water spirit, who is also a trickster figure, is evoked for the same subversive purpose. Other important poems in this collection are devoted to the complementarity of black and white cultural elements in Cuba. Among them are the "Balada de los dos abuelos" ("Ballad of the Two Grandfathers"), "El abuelo" ("The Grandfather"), "Dos niños" ("Two Kids"), and "Canción de los hombres perdidos" (Song of the Lost Men). On the whole, *West Indies, Ltd.*, like *Motivos* and *Sóngoro*, is a concerted effort to raise to the level of consciousness "the fleeting tender dark shadow of the [African] grandfather, / who put an indelible curl into your yellow hair."

Two books of poems that appeared in 1937, *Cantos para soldados y sones para turistas* (Songs for Soldiers and Sones for Tourists), published in Mexico on Guillén's first trip outside of Cuba, and *España: Poema en cuatro angustias y una esperanza* (Spain: Poem in Four Anguishes and One Hope) both find their immediate source in *West Indies, Ltd.*, particularly in those poems marked by an overtly militant posture. That more pronounced political aggressiveness may well have been the result of the changing intellectual climate in Cuba after the demise of the Gerardo Machado dictatorship in 1933, an event that Guillén regarded as one of the most important in his life. A period of resolute political activity and one of the most productive in Guillén's career as a journalist and editor, those years brought to fruition in his poetry an extended desire for solidarity both across racial and national boundaries. *Cantos para soldados*, which Guillén dedicated to his father "muerto por soldados" (killed by soldiers), is a forceful plea to soldiers all over the world to join the oppressed rather than being mere instruments of the ruling classes. In keeping with Guillén's increasing interest in communism at that time, he portrayed the soldier as a potential revolutionary and a political ally of the *sonero*, the singer who confronts American tourists in "José Ramón Cantaliso" and "Cantaliso en un bar" (Cantaliso in a Bar). The best-known of these soldier poems is "No sé por qué piensas tú" ("I Don't Know Why [You Should Think]"), which again uses *son* rhythms.

"Soldados en Abisinia" ("Soldiers in Abyssinia") even more explicitly internationalizes Guillén's revolutionary concerns by drawing connections between Latin America and Africa. That link will be reconfirmed in a later poem, "Son de Angola" (Angola's Son, 1977), which recounts South Africa's aggression against Angola and Castro's military intervention. The Spanish civil war enters the scene in *España*, written shortly before Guillén's visit to the Second International Writers' Congress for the Defense of Culture in Valencia, Barcelona, and Madrid. Guillén's declaration of solidarity with Spain is not exclusively political; it is also a literary statement particularly evident in his homage to the Andalusian poet Federico García Lorca in the "Angustia cuarta" ("The Fourth Anguish"). Despite his ties with Spain, however, Guillén remains adamant about his identity as an American poet, as in "La voz esperanzada" (The Hopeful Voice), which concludes *España*.

Upon his return to Cuba in 1938, Guillén worked in several editorial capacities with *Hoy*, the mouthpiece of the Communist party, whose ranks he had formally joined in Valencia the year before. He also ran for mayor in his native Camagüey in 1940, as well as campaigned with the union leader Jesús Menéndez, who was assassinated on 22 January 1948 in Manzanillo, Oriente, and to whose memory Guillén later dedicated his "Elegía a Jesús Menéndez" ("Elegy for Jesús Menéndez," 1951). In 1942 Guillén visited Haiti at the invitation of Jacques Roumain, whom he had met in Paris in 1937. Roumain, who died at a young age in 1944, was also to become the subject of one of Guillén's elegies, the "Elegía a Jacques Roumain" ("Elegy for Jacques Roumain"), written in 1948 during his stay in Brazil. These and four other Antillean elegies were collected in the 1958 edition of *Elegías*: "El apellido" ("My Last Name"), written in Paris in 1951; "Elegía cubana" ("Cuban Elegy"), written in Havana probably in 1952; "Elegía a Emmett Till" ("Elegy for Emmett Till"), written in Paris in 1956; and "Elegía camagüeyana" ("Elegy for Camagüey"), begun in Havana in 1952 and completed in Paris in 1958.

As is evident from the different places where these elegies were written over a period of roughly ten years, Guillén spent most of his time in the 1950's outside of Cuba. His extensive travels, in fact, began in 1945 when he went to Caracas at the request of the Venzuelan poet Miguel Otero Silva. This journey was the beginning of a three-year tour of Latin America, including Colombia, Peru, Chile, Argentina, Uruguay, and Brazil. During Guillén's stay in Buenos Aires in 1947, the publishing house Pleamar issued *El son entero; suma poética 1929–1946* (The Entire Son; Complete Poetry 1929–1946). This edition contained selections from Guillén's previously published poetry as well as some more recent poems that had appeared in the 1942 edition of *Sóngoro cosongo y otros poemas* (Sóngoro Consongo and Other Poems), such as "Guitarra" ("Guitar"), "Ébano real" (Royal Ebony), and the famous "Son número 6" ("*Son* Number 6"), another precursor of "My Last Name." In this poem Guillén celebrates his multicultural heritage: "Yoruba I am, am Lucumi, / Mandinga, Congo, Carabali." *Sóngoro* also included Guillén's only play, *Poema con niños* (Poem with Children), which had been staged in 1943 by the Teatro Principal de la Comedia in Havana.

Alarmed at the murder of Jesús Menéndez, Guillén returned to Cuba in 1948 to resume his work with *Hoy*. He wrote numerous articles as well as a series of satires attacking the Socarrás administration. In 1949 he left again to attend peace conferences in New York and Paris. A visit to Moscow followed in 1951, as did trips to the German Democratic Republic, Romania, Bulgaria, Austria, and China. After several brief returns to Cuba, during which he was arrested twice because of his anti-Batista activities, he finally departed for Chile in 1953, a journey that was the beginning of a six-year exile. Two months later, Fidel Castro led the attack on the Moncada barracks, and the regime officially outlawed the Communist party. From 1955 to 1958, Guillén lived in Paris, until he went to Buenos Aires.

His literary production during those years of exile led to *La paloma de vuelo popular* (The Dove of Popular Flight), published in December 1958 together with the *Elegías*. The book's title, in fact, refers to a line from the final part of the "Elegy for Jesús Menéndez." With the publication of this collection ended a dramatic episode in the life of

Guillén, who had been traveling almost incessantly to peace conferences all over the world—in 1954, he even received the Lenin Peace Prize.

La paloma reflects those travels by combining a painful sense of exile with the desire to reach out to these different countries and races in an all-encompassing gesture of peace, symbolized by the image of the flying dove. Following the lament of "Exilio" ("Exile") are the "Canción puertorriqueña" ("Puerto Rican Song"), reminiscent of "West Indies, Ltd.," as well as "Mau-Maus," "Ciudades" ("Cities"), "Hacia el Paraguay lejano" (Toward the Far Paraguay), "Tres canciones chilenas" (Three Chilean Songs), "A Guatemala" (To Guatemala), "Balada guatemalteca" (Guatemalan Ballad), and the love poem, "La pequeña balada de Plóvdiv" ("Little Ballad of Plovdiv"), to name only the most important ones.

United States imperialism and racism continue to be major targets for Guillén, but his language, particularly in "Pequeña letanía grotesca en la muerte del senador McCarthy" ("Short Grotesque Litany on the Death of Senator McCarthy") and "Little Rock" (about the failure of school desegregation in Little Rock, Arkansas), is much more biting and impatient than in previous poems. On the other hand, "Ríos" ("Rivers") is characterized by a meditative tenderness that recalls the poem "The Negro Speaks of Rivers" by Langston Hughes. Guillén and Hughes had been friends since the latter's visit to Cuba in 1930, and Hughes also translated a number of Guillén's early poems, which appeared in 1948 under the title *Cuba Libre*. Yet another category of poems in *La paloma* pays tribute to the postrevolutionary regimes of China ("Tres canciones chinas" ["Three Chinese Songs"], which also alludes to Cuba's Chinese population) and the Soviet Union ("Sputnik 57").

Guillén's enforced exile came to an end barely a month after the publication of *La paloma* and only three weeks after the triumph of Castro's rebel army on 1 January 1959. Upon his return to his native land, Guillén undertook a variety of tasks on behalf of the revolution. He again gave public poetry readings and helped establish the National Union of Cuban Writers and Artists. He also resumed his journalistic and literary activities. In 1964 he published *Tengo* (I Have; published in English as *Tengo*),

a collection of sixty-four poems divided into an initial section of nineteen poems and three other sections, whose titles testify to his literary versatility: "Sones, sonetos, baladas y canciones" (Sones, Sonnets, Ballads, and Songs); "Romancero" (Collection of Ballads); and "Sátira" (Satire). As a careful consideration of the book's title suggests, *Tengo* is not simply a propagandistic celebration of revolutionary achievements, but a call for a firm cultural basis that would nurture the spirit of those initial accomplishments. This sense of responsibility leads Guillén to renew his emphasis on Cuba's fundamental *mestizaje* in "Vine en un barco negrero" ("I Came on a Slave Ship") together with attacks against United States racism (in "Está bien" [It Is All Very Well"] and "¡Ay, qué tristeza que tengo" ["How Sad I Feel and Sorry"]). Most remarkable about *Tengo* is Guillén's relentless search for new poetic forms to match new historical realities. *Tengo* is not a wholesale rejection of Cuba's past; rather, it is an attempt to reassess that past and bring to the forefront those aspects of the country's history that had been neglected or ignored. Guillén continues this monumental task in *La rueda dentada* (The Gear, 1972) and especially in *El diario*.

The bold formal experiments of the latter poem are anticipated in *El gran zoo* (The Great Zoo) of 1967, one of Guillén's most biting satires as well as an exquisitely humorous book. As is typical of Guillén's poetry, it combines with ease several different literary traditions. On the one hand, it is a bestiary in the long tradition of writers such as Aesop, Jean de La Fontaine, Guillaume Apollinaire, Jorge Luis Borges, and Pablo Neruda. On the other hand, it recalls the chronicles of the Indies, those first accounts of the New World filled with all kinds of fabulous creatures embodying the confrontation of the European literary imagination with those new and unfamiliar surroundings. The chronicles are not only sources for modern Latin American novels by such writers as Gabriel García Márquez and Carlos Fuentes, as is frequently argued; they are also important foundations for much of Latin America's poetry. *El diario* will confirm this even more. Antecedents of *The Great Zoo* in Guillén's own work can be traced back as far as "The Airplane" and "Sol de lluvia" (Sunny Rain), both written in 1927, as well as "Reloj" ("The Clock") of 1929. More recent precursors are "Un largo lagarto

952

verde" (A Long Green Lizard) and the "Short Gro-tesque Litany on the Death of Senator McCarthy" from *La paloma*. Yet another set of references alludes to *Cerebro* (in "Luna" [Moon]), *Motivos* and *Sóngoro cosongo* (in "El chulo" [The Pimp]), *West Indies, Ltd.* (in "Guitar" and "Policía" [Police]), and the "Elegy for Jesús Menéndez" (in "Lynch" and "Las águilas" [The Eagles]).

The Great Zoo is not just a collection of separate poems but a single long poem, as the "Aviso" ("Announcement") in the beginning already sug-gests: "By resolution of the Municipality / this great zoo was created / for natives as well as foreigners / and for the pride of our nation." While the phrase "for the pride of our nation" certainly has its ironic dimensions, especially when we consider some of the "animals" in Guillén's "zoo," it also, on another level, firmly establishes the fabulous or "marvelous American reality" (in Alejo Carpentier's phrase) as the foundation of Cuban culture and literature. This may well be *The Great Zoo*'s most significant poetic achievement.

La rueda dentada, one of the two books of poetry published in 1972, has more in common with *Tengo* than with *The Great Zoo*, both thematically and formally. Like the former collection, it is subdivided into several parts. The opening section consists of eighteen poems on a wide variety of topics: "Prólogo" (Prologue) introduces the gear wheel not only as a metaphor for the reconstruction of Cuba in the spirit of the revolution, but also as a figure lending coher-ence to the book as a whole. "¿Qué color?" ("What Color?"), commemorating the death of Martin Lu-ther King, Jr., and "Ángela Davis" proclaim solidar-ity with the political struggle of North American blacks, while "Noche de negros junto a la catedral" (Night of Blacks next to the Cathedral) and "Ances-tros" ("Ancestry") recall the injustices and violence of nineteenth-century Cuban slavery. Other poems, such as "Pequeña oda a Viet Nam" (Little Ode to Vietnam) and "En el museo de Pyongyang" (In the Pyongyang Museum), imply the decline of United States imperialism, which is more openly heralded in "Papel de tapizar" (Wallpaper), "Poetas" (Poets), and "A las ruinas de Nueva York" (To the Ruins of New York City). Those initial pieces are followed by a set of five poems about five Cuban painters dedi-cated to René Portocarrero. Of the remaining six parts of *La rueda dentada*, two are of particular interest: the first one is "Ex corde" (From the Heart), which includes a lovely tribute to the young black Cuban poet Nancy Morejón ("Nancy"). "Ex corde" recalls the earlier love poems of *Poemas de amor* (Love Poems, 1964), most of which were reprinted in 1975 as *El corazón con que vivo* (The Heart with Which I Live). The second one is "Tránsitos" (Transitions), with three poems for Che Guevara, who had died in Bolivia in 1967: "Che comandante," "Guitarra en duelo mayor" (Guitar in Grief Major), and "Lectura de domingo" (Sunday Reading). One is reminded here of Neruda's poetic homage to Simón Bolívar as well as of Guillén's own *Cantos para soldados* and his elegies. The poems for Che Guevara, which had been published separately in 1967, 1968, and 1969, stress Guillén's preoccupation in *La rueda dentada* with mechanisms of defense and resistance to external ideological threats, a concern that extends to *El diario*, though in a different way.

El diario, a sixty-four page collage, is Guillén's most radical poetic experiment. Posing both as a newspa-per and as an historical chronicle, *El diario* assembles a multitude of fragments—newspaper clippings, edi-torials, advertisements, public ordinances—from all areas and periods of Cuban life. The poem, in which Guillén's journalistic and poetic activities join forces, is divided into five sections, which roughly corre-spond to different stages in Cuban history: the Spanish conquest and colonial rule up to 1762; the English occupation of Havana (1762–1763); the period of French influence, due to the Bourbon dynasty's accession to the Spanish throne and mas-sive immigration from Haiti at the time of the Haitian Revolution (1791–1805); the Ten Years' War (1868–1878); and the final years of struggle for independence from Spain and the period of United States intervention (1898–1959). Although this structural division creates the semblance of chronol-ogy, the poem is more of a play on history than a strictly linear historical portrait.

El diario is also a play on language, literary conven-tions, and traditional genre boundaries. As history is liberated from the constraints of chronology, multi-ple, sometimes seemingly impenetrable layers of lan-guage and meaning accumulate in this boisterous, satirical anti-epic. This dense linguistic layering, like the intermingling of different historical periods, is an aspect of the kind of "stylelessness" that Guillén, much like Carpentier, regards as the most salient feature of Latin American culture. By grounding that baroque "stylelessness" in Afro-Cuban carnival, specifically the Día de Reyes, Guillén revises and reinvents the Carpenterian concept of the "marvelous American reality." This use of carnival as a model for resistance to cultural and political oppression and imperialism appears in Guillén's poetry as early as "Sensemayá," where it subverts the "official" image of Cuba as a culturally "white" society. By situating itself squarely in the controversial carnivalesque space between freedom and oppression, *El diario* turns this process of subversion into a poetics of "Cubanness."

A careful reading of this poem, in conjunction with *Sol de domingo* (Sunday's Sun, 1982), reveals that Guillén, even in his latest works, is no less preoccupied with the contribution of Afro-Cuban culture to his country's national identity than he was at the outset of his poetic career. *Sol de domingo*, a collection of previously unpublished prose and poetry with which Guillén celebrated his eightieth birthday, joins *El diario* in confirming the poet's refusal to submit to any one ideological doctrine. This posture appears due not to a lack of political commitment, but to Guillén's realization that the Cuban Revolution may well turn into an oppressive system unless it nurtures its historical legacies. Though it seems rather contradictory to his official image as Cuba's poet laureate, such implicitly critical poetic posturing is precisely what lends distinction to Guillén's poetic voice. It is also what has enabled him with perhaps surprising consistency to explore to their fullest the possibilities of poetic language without ultimately submitting his work to the perilous demands of partisan politics.

SELECTED BIBLIOGRAPHY

Editions

Poetry

Motivos de son. Havana, 1930.
Sóngoro cosongo: Poemas mulatos. Havana, 1931.
West Indies, Ltd.: Poemas. Havana, 1934.
Cantos para soldados y sones para turistas. Mexico City, 1937.

España: Poema en cuatro angustias y una esperanza. Mexico City and Valencia, 1937.
Elegía a Jacques Roumain en el cielo de Haití. Havana, 1948.
Elegía a Jesús Menéndez. Havana, 1951. Reprinted 1962.
Elegía cubana. Havana, 1952.
La paloma de vuelo popular. Elegías. Buenos Aires, 1958. Reprinted 1959. 2nd ed. 1965.
Buenos días, Fidel. Mexico City, 1959.
Poemas de amor. Havana, 1964.
Tengo. Santa Clara, Cuba, 1964.
Che comandante. Mexico City and Havana, 1967.
Cuatro canciones para el Che. Havana, 1969.
El gran zoo. Havana, 1967. Reprinted Madrid, 1971.
El diario que a diario. Havana, 1972. 2nd ed. 1979.
La rueda dentada. Havana, 1972.
El corazón con que vivo. Havana, 1975.
Poemas manuables. Havana, 1975.
Por el mar de las Antillas anda un barco de papel. Havana, 1977.
Música de cámara. Havana, 1979.
Sol de domingo. Havana, 1982.

Collected Works

Antología mayor; el son entero y otros poemas. Havana, 1964. 2nd ed. 1969. Expanded to include *El gran zoo, Poemas para el Che,* and *La rueda dentada.*
Cantos para soldados y sones para turistas. El son entero. Buenos Aires, 1952. 2nd ed. 1957.
Sus mejores poemas. Havana, 1959. Contains selections from *Motivos de son, Sóngoro cosongo, West Indies, Ltd., Cantos para soldados y sones para turistas, España, El son entero,* and *La paloma de vuelo popular.*
Los mejores versos. Buenos Aires, 1961.
Poesías. Havana, 1962.
El son entero; suma poética 1929–1946. Buenos Aires, 1947. Contains *Motivos de son, Sóngoro cosongo, West Indies, Ltd., Cantos para soldados y sones para turistas, España,* and *El son entero* [unpublished].
Sóngoro cosongo y otros poemas de Nicolás Guillén. Havana, 1942. 2nd ed. 1943.
Sóngoro cosongo. Motivos de son. West Indies, Ltd. España: Poema en cuatro angustias y una esperanza. Buenos Aires, 1952. Reprinted 1957, 1967, 1971.
Versos negros. Selected by José Luis Varela. Madrid, 1950. Contains *Motivos de son, Sóngoro cosongo,* and selections from *West Indies, Ltd.* and *El son entero.*

Later Editions

Antología clave. Santiago, Chile, 1971.
Antología mayor: El son entero y otros poemas. Havana, 1964. Reprinted Mexico City, 1972.

Elegía a Jesús Menéndez. Havana, 1951. Reprinted 1982.
Obra poética, 1920–1972. Edited by Ángel Augier. 2 vols. Havana, 1972–1973. 2nd ed. 1974.
El libro de las décimas. Edited by Nancy Morejón. Havana, 1980.

Prose

Prosa de prisa; crónicas. Santa Clara, Cuba, 1962.
Prosa de prisa. 1929–1972. Edited by Ángel Augier. 3 vols. Havana, 1975–1976.
Páginas vueltas. Memorias. Havana, 1982.

Translations

Cuba Libre: Poems by Nicolás Guillén. Translated by Langston Hughes and Ben Frederic Carruthers. Los Angeles, 1948.
Man-Making Words: Selected Poems of Nicolás Guillén. Translated, annotated, and with an introduction by Robert Márquez and David Arthur McMurray. Amherst, Mass., 1972.
¡Patria o muerte! The Great Zoo and Other Poems by Nicolás Guillén. Translated and edited by Robert Márquez. New York, 1972.
Tengo. Translated by Richard J. Carr. Detroit, 1974.

Biographical and Critical Studies

Aguirre, Mirta. "En torno a la 'Elegia a Jesús Menéndez.'" *Revista de literatura cubana* 1:25–33 (1982).
Augier, Ángel. *Nicolás Guillén: Notas para un estudio biográfico-crítico.* 2 vols. Santa Clara, Cuba, 1962. 2nd ed. Havana, 1964–1965.
———. *Nicolás Guillén.* Havana, 1971.
Bottiglieri, Nicola. "Consideraciones y apuntes sobre 'El gran zoo' de Nicolás Guillén." *Casa de las Américas* 22/132:108–116 (1982).
Boulware-Miller, Kay. "La 'Balada del güije' de Nicolás Guillén: Un experimento en el folclor." *Casa de las Américas* 22/132:99–107 (1982).
Brathwaite, Edward Kamau. "The African Presence in Caribbean Literature." In *Slavery, Colonialism, and Racism,* edited by Sidney W. Mintz. New York, 1974.
Cartey, Wilfred G. *Black Images.* New York, 1970. Includes a chapter on Guillén.
Cobb, Martha K. *Harlem, Haiti, and Havana: A Comparative Critical Study of Langston Hughes, Jacques Roumain, and Nicolás Guillén.* Washington, D.C., 1979.
Coulthard, Gabriel R. *Race and Colour in Caribbean Literature.* London, 1962.

Davis-Lett, Stephanie. "Literary Games in the Works of Nicolás Guillén." *Perspectives on Contemporary Literature* 6:135–142 (1980).
Ellis, Keith. *Cuba's Nicolás Guillén: Poetry and Ideology.* Toronto, 1983.
Fernández Retamar, Roberto. *El son de vuelo popular.* Havana, 1972.
González Echevarría, Roberto. "Literature of the Hispanic Caribbean." *Latin American Literary Review* 8/16:1–20 (1978). Special issue on Hispanic Caribbean literature.
Hernández Novás, Raúl. "La más reciente poesia de Nicolás Guillén." *Casa de las Américas* 13/75:159–162 (1972).
Jackson, Richard. *Black Writers in Latin America.* Albuquerque, N. Mex., 1979.
Kutzinski, Vera M. *Against the American Grain: Myth and History in William Carlos Williams, Jay Wright, and Nicolás Guillén.* Baltimore, 1987.
———, ed. *Callaloo 31* 10/2 (1987). Special issue on Guillén.
McMurray, David Arthur. "Dos negros en el Nuevo Mundo: Notas sobre el 'americanismo' de Langston Hughes y la cubanía de Nicolás Guillén." *Casa de las Américas* 14/82:122–128 (1974).
Mansour, Mónica. "Transformaciones en la poesia de Nicolás Guillén." *Plural* 11/139:4–11 (1982).
Martínez Estrada, Ezequiel. *La poesía afrocubana de Nicholás Guillén.* Montevideo, 1966.
———. *La poesia de Nicolás Guillén.* Buenos Aires, 1977.
Morejón, Nancy. *Nación y mestizaje en Nicolás Guillén.* Havana, 1982.
———, ed. *Recopilación de textos sobre Nicolás Guillén.* Havana, 1974.
Piedra, José. "From Monkey Tales to Cuban Songs: On Signification." *MLN* Hispanic Issue 100/2:361–390 (1985). On "Ballad of the Water-Demon."
Rivera-Rodas, Oscar. "La imagen de los Estados Unidos en la poesía de Nicolás Guillén." *Casa de las Américas* 20/120:154–160 (1980).
Ruscalleda Bercedóniz, Jorge M. *La poesía de Nicolás Guillén.* Río Piedras, Puerto Rico, 1975.
Sabourín Fornaris, Jesús. "De 'Negro bembón' a 'El apellido' (lectura de un poema de Nicolás Guillén)." *Casa de las Américas* 22/132:91–98 (1982).
Sardinha, Dennis. *The Poetry of Nicolás Guillén.* London, 1976.
Williams, Lorna V. *Self and Society in the Poetry of Nicolás Guillén.* Baltimore, 1982.

Carlos Drummond de Andrade

(1902–1987)

Luiz Costa Lima

Brazilian poet, columnist, translator, and short story writer Carlos Drummond de Andrade was born on 31 October 1902 in Itabira do Mato Dentro, a small town in the state of Minas Gerais. Although he graduated as a pharmacist in 1925, he never followed this profession, earning his living instead as a journalist and civil servant. In 1920 his parents moved to Belo Horizonte, the capital of Minas Gerais. It was there that Drummond first came into contact with São Paulo's modernists. In 1924 he met the movement's leading exponents, Mário de Andrade, Oswald de Andrade, and Tarsila do Amaral. Four years later his controversial poem "No Meio do Caminho" ("In the Middle of the Road") was published in the São Paulo modernists' magazine, *Revista de Antropofagia*. Drummond's first book appeared in 1930, a five-hundred-copy edition of *Alguma Poesia* (Some Poetry).

In 1934 Drummond moved to Rio de Janeiro to serve as the cabinet chief of the minister of education and public health, Gustavo Campanema. That same year he published his second volume of verse, *Brejo das Almas* (Morass of Souls), in an edition of two hundred copies. For the next few years Drummond remained a poet with a very narrow readership. His third book, *Sentimento do Mundo* (Sense of the World), was released in 1940. Its small printing of 150 copies showed the continuation of his limited audience. In fact, until 1942 the poet had to finance the publication of his works. However, with the introduction that year of his collection *Poesias* (Poetry), his work finally became available to the reading public at large, and he was soon to become a public figure. The year 1945 turned out to be an important one for Drummond personally as well as for his country. Soon after the end of World War II, the Brazilian dictator Getúlio Vargas was ousted. Drummond recorded his feelings about this period in the most politically committed of all his books, *A Rosa do Povo* (The People's Rose). It was at this time that he also renounced his position in the office of Capanema to become coeditor of the newly founded Communist paper, *Tribuna Popular*. Some months later, however, he broke with the party and left the paper's editorship. Reentering public service, he became director of the National Historical and Artistic Heritage Service of Brazil.

In 1951 Drummond's first collection of poems was published in Madrid. Three years later the publication of his collected works in *Fazendeiro do Ar e Poesia Até Agora* (Farmer of the Clouds and Poetry Until Now) brought him recognition as a great poet of Brazilian modernism. By then he had already brought out in 1943 and 1947, respectively, his translations of

François Mauriac's *Thérèse Desqueyroux* (1927) and Choderlos de Laclos' *Les liaisons dangereuses* (1782); his first short-story book, *Contos de Aprendiz* (Stories by an Apprentice Story Writer, 1951); the first volume of poems he had written after his phase of political commitment, *Claro Enigma* (Clear Enigma, 1951); the collection of his occasional poems, *Viola de Bolso* (Pocket Viola, 1952); and *Passeios na Ilha* (Strolls on the Island, 1952), a selection of articles and short literary essays he had originally written for his column in the Rio de Janeiro newspaper *Correio da Manhã* (The Morning Courier).

Although Drummond retired from government service in 1962, it was not until 1984 that he discontinued his work as a columnist. He nevertheless continued to publish. His poems have been translated into Spanish, English, German, French, Swedish, and Czech. In 1984 he released a volume of prose entitled *Boca de Luar* (Moonlight Mouth) as well as a work in verse called *Corpo* (Body). The next year he published another book of poems, *Amar Se Aprende Amando* (Loving Is Learned by Loving), and a personal diary, *O Observador no Escritório* (The Observer in His Study). Drummond died on 17 August 1987.

Because the Portuguese language ranks among the least propagated of the neo-Latin languages, from the viewpoint of international diffusion, writing in Portuguese implies, at best, a sparse and tardy reception. This rule holds true even in Hispanic America, where it might be expected that the proximity of Brazil to its Spanish-speaking neighbors must have contributed to the dissemination of works written in Portuguese. Since this did not occur, the non-Portuguese-speaking reading public remains unaware of some of the best examples of twentieth-century poetic production. Works that have not received their proper recognition include those of the Portuguese Mário de Sá-Carneiro, Fernando Pessoa, and Sofia de Mello Brayner, and the Brazilians Manuel Bandeira, Murilo Mendes, João Cabral de Melo Neto, and, more recently, the concrete poets Augusto de Campos, Haroldo de Campos, and Décio Pignatari. Of these, Pessoa is the most outstanding writer, with Drummond ranking alongside him in excellence. Drummond's *Alguma Poesia* had just been published when Mário de Andrade, the pundit of Brazilian modernism, reviewed some of the then recent books of poetry and wrote that Drummond's volume was "the richest in rhythms." Mário de Andrade himself would not be able to realize the whole scope of his remark. For as Drummond's subsequent work would demonstrate, his plurality of rhythms encompassed a great variety of dictions rather than mere technical variability.

When *Alguma Poesia*—a sheaf of poems written between 1925 and 1930—came out, Brazilian modernism, which was an outgrowth of São Paulo's Modern Art Week of 1922, sounded like an awfully daring proposition. Unlike its Hispanic American counterpart, Brazilian modernism owed nothing to fin de siècle symbolism; instead of the exploration of uncommon rhythms or the insistence on precious words, Brazilian modernism had as its primary tenet, as propagated by Emilio Filippo Tommaso Marinetti's futurism, the ideal of liberating the word from convention. Instead of adhering to preestablished stanzaic systems or to rhymes in obligatory positions, the earlier phase of Brazilian modernism was anarchic—as the European avant-garde movements at the beginning of the twentieth century had been. This ideal of libertarian anarchism, a product of the disintegration of values brought about by World War I, collided with the syncretic tradition prevalent in Brazil beginning with the last decades of the nineteenth century. As a result, for such older poets as Manuel Bandeira, modernism represented the necessity of a new apprenticeship.

One must be careful not to distort the significance of the modernist movement in Brazil by focusing on its identification with the course of the avant-garde movement in Europe. In Brazil, from the very outset, modernism aroused an interest in a better knowledge of the country, of its popular culture, of the rhythms and colors neglected by an art immoderately guided by European models. Rather than being a product of the new European currents, modernism was the stimulus to a new way of seeing Brazil. Hence the contemporariness of modernism blended with an effort toward the reinterpretation of Brazilian history as represented by Gilberto Freyre's *Casa Grande e Senzala* (The Masters and the Slaves, 1933) and Sérgio Buarque de Holanda's *Raízes do Brasil* (Roots of Brazil, 1936). Its influence was felt as well on the musical work of Heitor Villa-Lobos, who would try to combine erudite mastery with the vein of popular and regional rhythms, and on the pictorial work of Tarsila do Amaral. The movement stood for much more than the propagation of irrationalism and hatred for the hypocrisy of the civilization that had caused the genocide of 1914–1918. Brazilian modernism, as critic Antonio Candido stated, was connatural with the country's roots. It was, therefore, a sort of cultured neoprimitivism that blended the latest lessons from European poetry and arts with forms of knowledge and culture that had remained unnoticed and despised by the local intelligentsia.

Hence there was a preference among Brazilian modernist authors for plain, unadorned, colloquial language with no subordination to grammatical patterns that were appropriate only to Portugal. Yet this did not make the modernist momentum less radical. Since the introduction of romanticism, sadness, melancholy, and the sense of exile had become part of Brazilian literature. The topos of the poet as a displaced man had lodged in European literature beginning in the late eighteenth century with the German *Sturm und Drang*. This topos had also spread throughout Brazil and Hispanic America, though for very different sociological reasons. In Europe, the romantic sensibility emerged as a response to a feeling of disintegration raised by the advance of a bourgeois and capitalist way of life. That response became increasingly complex, first in reaction to the hope that was created by the libertarian ideals of 1789 and then in the face of the almost immediate frustration that resulted from the development of the French Revolution. William Wordsworth and Samuel Taylor Coleridge recorded the diverse reactions, as did Friedrich Hölderlin in his *Hyperion* (1797, 1799).

In South America, which had just emerged from the colonial domination of Spain and Portugal, social conditions favoring romanticism were extremely diverse. On the one hand, the intellectuals, who were limited in number, could survive and flourish only if they actively participated in the establishment of the emerging states; on the other hand, they felt that they belonged to a society that was still too rustic and shapeless to be able to understand or encourage them or to back them up. For this reason, although Latin American romanticism was characterized by an emphasis on local folkways, it was also a product of the contradictory feeling that a wide gulf divided the cultured elite from the rest of the populace. It was no wonder then that exile songs became the pièce de résistance of the national poets. Moreover, since recognition of their works could only be given in terms of European models, Latin American intellectuals were reluctant to remove themselves from imported values and for that very reason they contented themselves with internalizing them.

These conflicting currents are dramatically demonstrated in Drummond's first book. There is a pronounced clash between the modernist libertarian message of the book and the cautious, institutionalized diction in which it is written. The voice dominating these poems is sentimental and gloomy. The young author, however, realized that this approach would contradict the anarchic joy that had been described by his friend Mário de Andrade. Drummond tried to check the book's melancholy mood through the systematic use of irony. It is the tension between that sentimental voice and the antidote of irony that characterizes his first book. Drummond devised a precise technique, which may be called the technique of fragmentation, to resolve the tension. The technique consists of avoiding a continuous narrative and opting instead for varied and scattered shifts in narrative direction and the superimposition of multiple elements, which prevent the dominance of the melancholy-sentimental voice. This can be seen in the first two stanzas of the opening poem:

> *Quando nasci, um anjo torto*
> *desses que vivem na sombra*
> *disse: Vai, Carlos! ser gauche na vida.*
>
> *As casas espiam os homens*
> *que correm atrás de mulheres*
> *A tarde talvez fosse azul,*
> *não houvesse tantos desejos.*
> ("Poema de Sete Faces")

When I was born, a crooked angel
one of those living in shadow
said, Go Carlos, and be *gauche* in life.

The houses peep at the men
who are running after women.
The afternoon might be blue,
were it not for so many desires.
(Poem with Seven Faces)

As if the author had taken hold of a movie camera and abruptly cut from scene to scene, he presents disparate images that follow one after the other. The personal perspective, governed by romantic nostalgia, gives way to an attentive observation of the bustling town. The self loses its privilege and disperses amid what it sees, selects, and keeps in. Ruled then by outward, "objective" phenomena, the poem is made up of this constellation of fragments. The same technique is applied in "Casamento do Céu e do Inferno" (Marriage of Heaven and Hell) with the addition of a variation that aims at assuring the dissolution of the old lyrical ideal through the use of common words associated with illness and pharmaceutics, such as "metileno" (methylene) and "diurética" (diuretic):

> No azul do céu de metileno
> a lua irônica
> diurética
> é uma gravura de sala de jantar.

> In the methylene blue of the sky
> the moon, ironic
> diuretic
> is a print in a dining room.

In this way, the fragmentation of the narrative is more than a mere technical process. It is intended to assail institutionalized diction and to offer an alternative to it, namely, to substitute, in the poem, a sense of time and its changes for the primacy of the self and its sorrows.

The changes that Drummond recorded were not negligible. While the pieces of *Alguma Poesia* were being composed, Brazil ceased to be the farming and raw material exporting nation that it had been during the first four centuries of its existence, and the poet captured in seemingly trivial verses the simultaneity of overlapping times:

> Os meninos seguem para a escola,
> Os homens olham para o chão.
> Os ingleses compram a mina.

> Só, na porta da venda, Tutu Caramujo cisma na derrota
> incomparável.
>
> ("Itabira, Lanterna Mágica")

The boys are going to school.
The men look down at the ground.
The Englishmen buy up the mine.

> Alone, at the grocer's doorway, Tutu Caramujo broods
> over the incomparable defeat.
>
> (Itabira, Magic Lantern)

Or in "Explicação" (Explanation):

> Estou no cinema vendo fita de Hoot Gibson,
> de repente ouço a voz de uma viola . . .

> I'm in a flick watching a Hoot Gibson movie,
> suddenly I hear the voice of a viola

Tutu Caramujo and the twang of the viola tell of the slow rural world defined by farms and horses and the scions of well-to-do families. Into this existence new habits were creeping, in the wake of the influence of foreign investors who had taken over iron ore mines and promoted the Americanization of urban life. It is important, then, to stress that Drummond's rejection of established lyricism was not an act in favor of either the rural tradition or the values of the new, rapidly expanding cities. Had Drummond chosen a defense of the traditional way of life, he would have become mired in the past, and his brand of modernism would have been equivocal. Had he advocated only the modern notions of speed, development, and shock, he would have been no more than the equivalent of the Argentine Oliverio Girondo, author of *Veinte Poemas para Ser Leídos en el Tranvía* (*Twenty Poems to Be Read in the Tramway*, 1922). Drummond instead rejected both partialities and turned his poems into a stage on which the signs of antagonistic and contradictory times are presented and condensed. It was the very tension of contemporary life in Brazil of the late 1920's that became his subject matter.

Drummond's contempt for the primacy of private feelings did not result in the production of an impersonal poetry attached only to events and objects. He did not employ irony to clear the poem of his experiences and their traces, but rather to show them from a distance, like anyone's traits. From this perspective, two poems are especially important because they concern sexual initiation and religious experience. In "Iniciação Amorosa" (Amorous Initiation) feelings created by the evocation of the heat of the day and its accompanying erotic fervor are ironically dissipated by the reminiscence of the fever that was to affect the beginner. In "Igreja" (Church) the sense of distance that moves God away from the unbeliever becomes evident. The importance of these two poems will be more evident when the poet's memorialistic phase is explained.

Just as Drummond's rejection of a confidential voice did not result in depersonalized poetry, so did his distancing posture not convey a disdain for the traditional themes in Latin America that resulted from the influence of the Enlightenment and the romantic movement. The most common theme of all has been the conflict between the longed-for civilization and the prevalent barbarism. It was this theme that became the subtitle of Domingo Faustino Sarmiento's *Facundo* (1845). Drummond borrowed the theme, but gave it a parodistic treatment. The usual way of dealing with this theme had been to deplore the barbarism that persisted in the tropics and either to dream of a redeeming travel to Europe or to fight for a quick entry into the realm of the civilized. This is precisely the view that is parodied in "Fuga" (Escape):

> Vou perder-me nas mil orgias
> do pensamento greco-latino.
> Museus! estátuas! catedrais!
> O Brasil só tem canibais.

> I'll give myself up to a thousand orgies
> of Greco-Latin thought.
> Museums! statues! cathedrals!
> Brazil has only cannibals.

A similar irreverence will turn Father Christmas into a paltry burglar:

> Papai Noel entrou pela porta dos fundos
> (no Brasil as chaminés não são praticáveis)
> entrou cauteloso que nem marido depois da farra.
>   ("Papai Noel às Avessas")

> Father Christmas came in through the back door
> (in Brazil chimneys are not negotiable)
> came in cautiously just like a husband after a spree.
>   ("Santa Claus in Reverse," Nist trans.)

In short, the passage of time has shown that in his first book Drummond was much more than a talented beginner or someone who knew how to fertilize the new aesthetics of modernism. A rural man whose life experience would go no farther than the route from Itabira to Belo Horizonte, he had elected as his raw material the changes that were putting a new face on the country, the meaning of which only now is fully recognized. A descendant of a family of plantation owners, Drummond adopted the severe ethos of the traditional society in which he was raised. This, however, did not prevent him from participating in and witnessing the changes that were altering both the world and his own country. Anticipating a feeling that was to become widespread some decades later with the disclosure of the horrors of Auschwitz, the Mineiro poet realized that poetry would only be possible if its texture were reinvented. In fact, since his youth he had never shown any special zeal for the new. He simply recognized its presence and mixed his life with it, without knowing where it would lead:

> Um novo, claro Brasil
> surge, indeciso, da pólvora.
> Meu Deus, tomai conta de nós.
>   ("Outubro 1930")

> A new, clear-cut Brazil
> looms hesitantly up from the gunpowder.
> My God, take care of us all.
>   (October 1930)

Drummond continued to use the technique of fragmentation and to employ irony to formulate the problematic nature of the world in his work *Sentimento do Mundo*. But he also introduced a new element, the sense of participation. This addition led to an increase in the tension and conflictive quality of his world vision. The ironic-fragmentary technique was in fact deepened into what could be labeled the corrosion principle. The closing stanza of "Confidência do Itabirano" ("The Itabiran's Confession") reveals some of the basic characteristics of the principle:

> Tive ouro, tive gado, tive fazendas.
> Hoje sou funcionário público.
> Itabira é apenas uma fotografia na parede.
> Mas como dói!

961

I've had gold, cattle, plantations.
Today I'm a civil servant.
Itabira is only a photograph on the wall.
But it aches, and how!

                              (Nist trans.)

At first reading, especially if taken out of context, the lines appear to be simply confessional. But within Drummondian poetics this is a false impression. In this work Drummond went beyond the detachment of *Alguma Poesia* and was successful in broadening the references to his past and converting his experiences into a vision that transcended the merely individual. This is what corrosion, raised to the level of a principle, made possible.

An examination of another stanza will further demonstrate the point:

A soma da vida é nula.
Mas a vida tem tal poder:
na escuridão absoluta,
como líquido, circula.
                    ("Noturno à Janela
                      do Apartamento")

The sum of life is null.
But life has so much power;
in absolute darkness,
it, like a liquid,
circulates.
                    ("Nocturne at My Apart-
                     ment Window," Nist trans.)

These four lines presuppose an opposition between two appraisals of existence. Seen from outside, from an "arithmetical" viewpoint, its sum is null—its result, none. But seen from inside, the result becomes transformed and reversed. The terms used—"outside" and "inside"—are quite provisional, but the use of them permits a clearer analysis. For what might such an existence, endowed with such a power, be but one that is regarded from a collective, or historical, perspective, rather than from a strictly personal one? The result of life is null if we think of it from the point of view of the individual self. But, if we view existence from a historical perspective, then the result is reversed, and existence is seen as being produced in absolute darkness. And like an underground river, what circulates and is summed up occurs beyond our eyes, beyond our particularized vision. The clash between the two points of view

results in the perception of not only another border of life but also a secondary place of personalized hopes and ambitions. Thus, life moves in "absolute darkness," whereas for the individual it is simply null.

This contradiction is fundamental to an understanding of the working of what may be called corrosion. Without taking into account the failure to which old age and ultimately death condemn the individual, the assertion of the motion of history would be only a poor repetition of the Enlightenment idea of the progress of mankind. On the other hand, without asserting that motion, the emphasis on the individual's irreparable disaster would be only a variation of the Heideggerian contention that man is a being projected for death. The corrosion principle supposes the amalgam of these opposing aspects. From the contradiction that keeps it alive it ensues that history moves blindly, that is, with losses, and that only the remnants persist. Facing the individual, history is corrosion. But, as history does not mingle with an individual project, this corrosion is not only a loss but also a change. Thus, the corrosion principle offers the prism for expressing the personalized that was absent from *Alguma Poesia*.

In summary, the corrosion principle is a way of formulating the historical, of speaking of individual participation in the flow of history. In this sense, it opens out for both the outside—the world of events—and the inside—the naming of family remnants. In opening for the outside, it makes it possible for the poet to name the dawn without falling into a pamphleteering tone:

Havemos de amanhecer. O mundo
se tinge com as tintas da antemanhã
e o sangue que escorre é doce, de tão necessário
para colorir tuas pálidas faces, aurora.
                    ("A Noite Dissolve os Homens")

We'll sure see daylight. The world
gets tinged with foremorn tints
and the blood that flows off is sweet, being so necessary
to color your face, dawn.

                    (The Night Dissolves Men)

In opening for the inside, it makes it no less possible for him to carry out the first of his countless family portraits:

Havia a um canto de sala um álbum de fotografias
    intoleráveis
alto de muitos metros e velho de infinitos minutos,
em que todos se debruçavam
na alegria de zombar dos mortos de sobrecasaca.

Um verme principiava a roer as sobrecasacas indiferentes
e roeu as páginas, as dedicatórias e mesmo a poeira dos
    retratos.
Só não roeu o imortal soluço de vida que rebentava
que rebentava daquelas páginas.

             ("Os Mortos de Sobrecasaca")

In a corner of the parlor was an album of intolerable
    photographs,
many meters high and infinite minutes old
over which everybody used to lean
for the pleasure of laughing at the dead men in their
    frock coats.
A worm began to gnaw the unconcerned frock coats
and gnawed the pages, the dedications and even the dust
    of the portraits.
It only did not gnaw the immortal sob of life that was
    gushing
gushing out of those pages.

             ("The Dead in Frock Coats," Nist trans.)

It cannot be denied that there is a certain imbalance between one and the other face; the address to dawn—belonging to the beginning of the author's political commitment—is not so well resolved as the face turned to the family past. But what is basically important is the broadening of the field of experience for the word, a field that was merely being prepared in *Alguma Poesia*, that is, the range of a generative principle. Yet so that a generative principle may not be a straitjacket, so that it may really make for a creative process, it should not be mistaken for a conscious motto, for a sort of superegoistic model that was to be followed to the letter. Actually, Drummond benefited by having never attempted to turn what we call corrosion into a conceptual formulation.

In Drummond's subsequent work, *José* (published in the collection *Poesias*), the peculiar dialectics are explicit in "O boi" ("The Ox"). Men and oxen are portrayed as equivalent as long as they are surrounded by one and the same loneliness. They are under the sway of an identical fate, which can only be interrupted by a flash of hope in a redeeming catastrophe,

or be dispelled by the recognition of something more powerful:

Se uma tempestade de amor caísse!
As mãos unidas, a vida salva . . .
Mas o tempo é firme. O boi é só
No campo imenso a tôrre de petróleo.

If a love storm broke loose!
Hands united, life saved . . .
But the weather is steady. The ox is alone.
In the vast open country: the oil derrick.

             (Nist trans.)

The superposition of this passage on those quoted from *Sentimento do Mundo* leads us to understand that the weather is not only steady; materializing its presence through the visualization of the oil derrick, the weather shares the stage with the loneliness of animals and men and indicates the permanence under the change to which the territory of our existence is subjected. The reference to oil exploration is not gratuitous. The first serious attempts at searching for oil in Brazil were carried out about the year *José* was published. Since the process of industrialization had been launched only in the 1930's, so the discussion about how to undertake oil exploration had just recently begun. An indicator of the structural change taking place all over the country, the derrick could not by itself annul the solitude of living creatures. Nor could solitude annul the sign of what was changing. Two worlds—that of the farmlands and that of industrial prospecting—appear to be contiguous, but without contaminating each other. Historic changes do not affect the isolation of living beings, nor does the isolation make those changes derisible. For it is indeed an extra-individual vision that commands the tensions of Drummond poetics. Without reducing each other, history and the individual interfere with each other, and what remains lasts under losses. Corrosion supposes therefore the nontransitivity, the nontransparency of the faces that make up existence. Life is then made of indissoluble clots. The "universal mediation" dreamed of by the Enlightenment philosophers no longer fascinated this poet of a time and a country in process of accelerated changes.

As was said above, Drummondian poetics has benefited from the fact that its constituent principle did not turn into a principle of a superegoistic order. But it is necessary to consider the reverse of the medal. Because it has no conceptual support, Drummondian corrosion has always been in danger of tilting toward one or the other side of its basic tension. In other words, it has run the risk of stressing the hope that a new order could improve the individual condition itself or of concentrating only on the lack that eats away at human beings. This risk is not yet actualized in *José*. Here, poems or portions of poems about the family stand out. The opening of "No País dos Andrades" (In the Andrades' Land) is an example:

> No país dos Andrades, onde o chão
> é forrado pelo cobertor vermolho de meu pai,
> indago um objeto desaparecido há trinta anos,
> que não sei se furtaram mas só acho formigas.

In the Andrades' land, where the ground
is covered with my father's red blanket,
I inquire for an object disappeared thirty years ago,
which I don't know if it was stolen, but I find only ants.

In the travel mentioned in the closing couplet— "Adeus, vermelho / (viajarei) cobertar de meu pai" (Good-bye, red / (I'll travel) blanket of my father)— the tense relationship between the individual and history, which guides Drummond's poetics, is condensed. The red not only indicates the color of the object that once existed but also shows the symbol of that which, to the poet of that time, represented the possibility of social redemption. In both of them the thing that circulates has the connotation of blood, that is, of that which is lost and at the same time transformed. Thus, the reference to "travel" makes the full meaning of corrosion explicit, as testified to by the body of the poet himself. For to the son of plantation owners, now reduced to the condition of a civil servant, and a poet, traveling implies a loss and at the same time the appearance of another scene.

If corrosion is a means of articulating history and a particular individual, it cannot be either only exultant and dazzling or only depressive and gloomy. The solidarity the poet then imposes on himself requires a grave restraint. That which lasts in the past alone belongs to a decrepit world. But to sing of the future would not be less destructive of so sensitive a dialectic:

> Não serei o poeta de um mundo caduco.
> Também não cantarei o mundo futuro.
> Estou prêso à vida e olho meus companheiros.
> ("Mãos Dadas")

I won't be the poet of a doting world.
Nor shall I sing of the future world.
I'm tied to life and I look at my fellowmen.
("Hand in Hand," Nist trans.)

Corrosion is present in both scenes, without privileges or restrictions.

In *José*, beside the memory-digging poems, there are noteworthy poems about poetry itself. In "O Lutador" ("The Wrestler"), the poet's struggle with words is written in the manner of hand-to-hand fighting, or rather as an erotic and amorous combat:

> Palavra, palavra
> (digo exasperado),
> se me desafias,
> aceito o combate
> Quisera possuir-te
> neste descampado,
> sem roteiro de unha
> ou marca de dente
> nessa pele clara.

Word, word
(I say infuriatedly),
if you challenge me,
I accept the fight.
I wish I possessed you
on this barren ground,
without a nail scratch
or a tooth mark
on your fair skin.
(Nist trans.)

Like love and like the family portraits, poetry, too, does not count on an open country ahead. All of them are adjustable to the poem only on the condition that it declares its mixing of contraries. The refusal of this rule would imply, as Drummond himself was to show later on, thematizing the world one-sidedly and proposing either the complete subversion of its order or the mistaking of it for an empty shell. *José* is still safe from such risks. Instead, the entire book is dominated by a feeling of fear. To understand this better, it is necessary to remember the year of its publication. In 1942 World War II was at its peak, and the Nazi defeat was not yet assured. Though he was writing in a country that, from the viewpoint of the planet's history, continued to be marginal, Drummond combined the agony of the times with his own. And the fear before the threat of a common ghastly fate converged on a feeling of loneliness, which was aggravated by the understanding that life is unconcerned about men; that there is no sense save in searching for a meaning to life; that, moreover, behind it all, irrespective of meanings or lack of meanings, individual history goes on pointing inexorably to old guilts and no less old remorses. The guilts seem to be rooted to the relationship with the father, with whom contact becomes possible only when a live relationship is no longer feasible:

> Só hoje nos conhecermos!
> Óculos, memórias, retratos
> fluem no rio do sangue.
> As águas já não permitem
> distinguir seu rosto longe,
> para lá de setenta anos . . .
> ("Viagem na Família")

> Only now to know each other!
> Spectacles, memories, portraits
> flow in the river of blood.
> The waters no longer permit
> to discern his face far off,
> over seventy years . . .
> (Travelling as a Family)

The remorse seems no less to refer to the notion of sin or, more precisely, to the area of sexuality:

> Minha mão está suja.
> Preciso cortá-la.
> Não adianta lavar.
> A água está podre.
> Nem ensaboar.
> O sabão é ruim.
> A mão está suja,
> suja há muitos anos.
> (A Mão Suja")

> My hand is dirty.
> I've got to cut it off.

> It's no use washing.
> The water is rotten.
> No use lathering too.
> The soap is shoddy.
> The hand is dirty,
> dirty for many years.
> ("The Dirty Hand,"
> Nist trans.)

Time, therefore, does not only gnaw the dead, as a line of "Travelling as a Family" says; it also, or especially, gnaws the survivor.

If the corrosion principle allowed the poet a form of selection that was not epigonic either of the established melancholy or of the anarchic dynamism of the contemporary avant-garde, it also implied, however, a limitation on the speakable. In the grip of corrosion, the poet's word enlarged, ranging from a reflection on the solitary act through the remembrance of father and family to a vision of the present time. For that reason, few twentieth-century books are as dense as *José*, or as regrettably ignored. But Drummond's early production was not limited to *José*. In 1945, after the end of both World War II and the Vargas dictatorship in Brazil, Drummond published *A Rosa do Povo*. Perhaps because of a greater freedom of expression granted to writers or because this freedom coincided with the author's political evolution, *A Rosa do Povo* contains a large number of politico-participative poems, including "Notícias" (News), "América," "Carta a Stalingrado" (Letter to Stalingrad), "Telegrama de Moscou" (Telegram from Moscow), "Com o Russo em Berlim" (With the Russians in Berlin), and "Canto ao Homem do Povo Charlie Chaplin" ("Song to the Man of the People: Charlie Chaplin").

Although the corrosion principle maintains a precarious balance, within it there is a strong tendency to emphasize the side of hope, of resistance, of the expectation that the world not only changes but changes for the better. Had that aspect dominated, *A Rosa do Povo* would represent the amalgam of the seven earlier and scattered faces. But the participative poems offset that potential dominance and provided another perspective. The opening poem itself, "Consideração do Poema" (Consideration of the Poem) carries on an already noted line of reflection on poetic creation. The quintessence of Drummondian poetics until this point, the poem retrospectively offers to modernism the practical manifesto it had been in need of:

> *Não rimarei a palavra sono*
> *Com a incorrespondente palavra outono.*
> *Rimarei com a palavra carne*
> *ou qualquer outra, que todas me convêm.*
> *As palavras não nascem amarradas,*
> *elas saltam, se beijam, se dissolvem,*
> *no céu livre por vezes um desenho,*
> *são puras, largas, autênticas, indevassáveis.*

> I won't rhyme the word *sono* [sleep]
> with the noncorresponding word *outono* [autumn].
> I'll rhyme it with the word *carne* [flesh]
> or any other, since all of them suit me.
> Words are not born tied up,
> they jump, kiss one another, fade out,
> In the free sky sometimes a drawing,
> they are pure, broad, genuine, impenetrable.

As is often the case in Drummond, the reflection on the poem does not follow a merely aesthetic motivation. And the formulation of the ideal of the words existing in complete freedom, as in the first stanza, is completed by the closing lines: " . . . *Tal uma lâmina, / o povo, meu poema, te atravessa*" (. . . Like a blade, / the people pierce through you, my poem).

There is furthermore an excited tone in the poem that elicits from itself fragments that are seen only in other poems. This poetics scrutinizes time, or rather, notices that time is made of remnants. These remnants, eroded images of what lingers on, are the poet's raw material:

> *(É um antigo piano, foi*
> *de alguma dona, hoje*
> *sem dedos, semqueixo, sem*
> *música na fria mansão.*
> *Um pedaço de velha, um resto*
> *de cova, meu Deus, nesta sala*
> *onde ainda há pouco falávamos.)*
> ("Onde Há Pouco Falávamos")

> (It is an old piano, belonging
> to some old lady, today
> with no fingers, no chin, no
> music in the cold mansion.
> A piece of an old lady, a wreck
> of a grave, my God, in this room

where a short while ago we were talking.)
(Where a Short While Ago We Were Talking)

In other words, the fragment changes from a technical device into the very source from which the word flowers.

Even at the height of the participative phase, Drummond was still guided by the prenotion that the meaning of the world lies in the manner in which one lives it—or better yet, one reads it:

> *Todos os homens voltam para casa.*
> *Estão menos livres mas levam jornais*
> *e soletram o mundo sabendo que o perdem.*
> ("A Flor e a Náusea")

> All the men are return home.
> They're less free but they take along newspapers
> and spell out the world, knowing they lose it.
> (Nausea and the Flower)

For that very reason, his time is one of disintegration. In "Nosso Tempo" (Our Time) it is a "tempo de divisas, / tempo de gente cortada" (time of boundaries / time of chopped up people) and of outer and inner partitions. And since there is no unity, either within or without, the umbilical cord tying the poet to the world is made of leftovers, shards, fragments:

> *Fragmentos de borracha*
> *e*
> *cheiro de rolha queimada!*
> *eis quanto me liga ao mundo.*
> ("Rola Mundo")

> Scraps of rubber
> and
> smell of burned cork—
> here is all that binds me to the world.
> (Roll, World)

Therefore, time closes in on itself and expels us—the uncertain passersby of its impassibility. To open it up, to be in tune with it, one must simply see and hear its sea of debris. In "Desfile" (Parade) this is our single and risky gift: "Tudo foi prêmio do tempo / e no tempo se converte" (All has been a prize of time / and in time converts itself). But the interpreter must be careful not to make the objects he is analyzing uniform.

If it seems that there is a dominant line in *A Rosa do Povo*, the interpreter must not forget the presence of pieces that oppose that line. Such a break of unity exists in the balladlike poems "Morte no Avião" (Death in the Airplane) and "Morte do Leiteiro" (The Milkman's Death). In an effort to keep the poems near the collective experience, Drummond moved away from the technique of the fragment. The internalization of the fragmentary vision, however, appeared in the narrative poems themselves. Through them we perceive that the precarious balance of the corrosion principle was beginning to be destroyed. In fact, infiltrations were already visible in *Alguma Poesia*, that is, when the structuring principle was being prepared. In opting for narrative poems, the poet seemed to declare that something did not any longer hark back to the remnants of lived experiences, that another form was being imposed upon him as a means of ensuring communication with the reader.

Novos Poemas (New Poems, 1948) was the author's first book after his political disillusion. Symptomatically, the lofty diction changed from a dominated and rarefied tone to a dominant one, as in "Jardim" (Garden), "Canto Esponjoso" ("Spongy Song"), and "Estâncias" ("Stanzas"). In a still more symptomatic way, the poet's visualization of the world was modified, as conveyed in the line "O enigma tende a paralisar o mundo" (The riddle tends to paralyze the world"), from "O Enigma" (The Riddle). The poet was tired of pointing to feeble signs of communion with the world and instead of using leftovers, the spoils with which he had composed his sense of things, he decided to accept the world as subject matter only for verbal arabesque. And in "Jardim" he refused to speak of the lake with its fish, "matéria putrescível" (putrescible matter), preferring the image of "pálidas contas de colares / que alguém vai desatando" (the pale beads of necklaces / which somebody is undoing).

Drummondian poetics came into a new phase. Its major monuments would be *Claro Enigma, Fazendeiro do Ar, A Vida Passada a Limpo* (Life Revised, 1959), and *Lição de Coisas* (Lesson of Things, 1962). From the viewpoint of language, Drummond from now on would be the poet of a lofty diction, isosyllabic lines, and sonnets and elegies. A grave composure is all that

is left of the old ironic mood. Instead of being a poetry about facts and scenes—*Claro Enigma* has as its epigraph a quotation from Paul Valéry, "les événéments m'ennuient" (events bore me)—it has become a poetry of a thoughtful tenor. If things are seen or remembered, it is with a view to form an empty circle that the world converts into a cell ("A Ingaia Ciência" [The Ungay Science]). Where previously the remnants were mixed up in order to actualize the dialectics of corrosion, now there prevails the effort to see them from an absolute distance, almost through a prism of what is beyond matter:

> Do que restou, como compor um homem
> e tudo que ele implica de suave,
> de concordâncias vegetais, mumúrios
> de riso, entrega, amor e piedade?
> ("Confissão")

Out of what has been left how to compose a man
and all that he implies of gentle,
of vegetal consonances, whispers
of laughter, surrender, love, and compassion?
("Confession," Nist trans.)

Corrosion turns into occlusion. What is the use of knowing that history is fed on remnants, that personal or even collective ideas and plans are converted by it into results that their authors would not recognize? The world precedes human principles; it is closed and void. The arabesque proclaims it is no longer a product of any attempt to conjoin the multiple and dispersed into one form; it is only an ornament of nothingness. One might even think that the poet's maturity made him find forces to assert things he had previously repressed or derided, or that his political disenchantment stimulated the retaking of the religious belief he had abandoned. But this is not true. Minas Gerais is mentally revisited through poems about its churches, museums, and cheap hotels. The churches trod through reminiscence do not welcome a prodigal son. On the contrary, in "Evocação Mariana" ("Evocation: Mary's Month) the former child who had attended them now feels that the nave of the temples and his own body are freed from the land that had once contained them: "De seu peso terrestre a nave libertada, / Como do tempo atroz imunes nossas almas" ("From its earthly weight the nave [is] liberated / as from a wicked time our immune souls").

It is not that corrosion has suddenly disappeared; it only has lost its privilege as an articulating principle. It is reduced to its position in nature as an eroder of matter:

> Lá vão, enxurrada abaixo,
> as velhas casas honradas
> em que se amou e pariu,
> em que se guardou moeda
> e no frio se bebeu.
> ("Morte das Casas de Ouro Preto")

> There they go, washed downhill,
> the honest old houses
> where love was made and child born,
> where coins were hoarded,
> and in cold days a drink was taken in.
> (Death of Ouro Preto's Houses)

What the eyes see or the mind recalls is no longer subject to any transcendence, even that of simple human history. If the possibility of a crisis and religious conversion was false, the attraction now exerted by a merely aesthetic link with life is not false. Yet Drummond remains too vital to be satisfied with the submission of life to beauty. The lofty tone of his language and his search for a poetry of the sublime have led to a production that is oriented by that which would go beyond matter—that which is not in a certain place but which is reached only in the verse that names it. If all tried ways of participation and of summoning up hope have failed, there at least remains the attention to what surrounds the poet, an attention resulting from the "contentamento de escrever," or enjoyment of writing ("Remissão" [Remission]). It is the very act of composing, not of composing on behalf of this or that, that now guides him and keeps him interested in poetry. Poetry is the small door that shelters him from the manifest occlusion of the world.

We have called attention to the fact that one of his metapoems, "The Wrestler," took the fight with words as an equivalent of an erotic encounter. Coincidentally, this form of disenchantment with transcendence corresponds to the emergence of his great love poems. Passionate love upholds contact with the world, but not so as to idealize a new meaning pinned to existence. What is sung of love is the push that brings it about, which does not efface the recognition of the discordance that ends dissolving it:

> Êste o nosso destino: amor sem conta,
> distribuído pelas coisas pérfidas ou nulas,
> doação ilimitada a uma completa ingratidão,
> e na concha vazia do amor a procura medrosa,
> paciente, de mais e mais amor.
> ("Amar")

> This is our destiny: limitless love,
> scattered among deceitful or useless things,
> unbounded donation to absolute ingratitude,
> and in the empty shell of love the search, in fear
> and patience, of more and more love.
> ("To Love," Nist trans.)

Everything had been desecrated and disenchanted, except libido itself, which, nevertheless, had been removed from any human compensation.

Drummond will never take the step we find in Samuel Beckett, for whom love itself is a companion of squalor and decrepitude. If religion had not offered him meaning, if the meaning summoned up by history had proved too feeble to be kept, something sacred would be held by the Brazilian poet so that the pleasure of writing would have a justifying reason. That is why he has said in one of his greatest love poems, "Compo de Flores" ("Field of Flowers") "Amanhecem de novo as antigas manhãs / que não vivi jamais, pois jamais me sorriram" ("Bygone mornings are dawning again, / those I never lived, as to me they never smiled"). Thus the matter of the world stops being thematized as a remnant, a disjunction of old units that would prepare unexpected units, in order to become an evocation of what exists only in the pure presence of the word. Former life has been washed away by rain and time; its figurants are dead; word is the only thing left with which to reconstruct, on another plane, the drawing of a desolate land:

> Onde estás, capitão, onde estás João Francisco,
> do alto de tua serra en te sinto sozinho
> e sem filhos e netos interrompes a linha
> que veio dar a mim neste chão esgotado.
> ("Os Bens e o Sangue")

Where are you, Captain, where are you, João Francisco,
from the top of your sierra I feel you are lonely,
and with no sons and grandsons you've broken the line
that ended up in me on this worn-out ground.
("The Property and the Blood," Nist trans.)

In the postcorrosion phase the poet revealed that which has been deposited in the memory. And he, a disinherited descendant, regards himself as one who has been put in charge of tilling a strange and diverse farm; he becomes a farmer of the clouds. The concreteness with which he sees again his dead can no longer be mixed up with that through which, a short time ago, he revisited them while he thought of the time they had not known. If one takes separately the pieces written after *Novos Poemas*, they seem barely distinct from those that bore witness of the corrosion principle. One must read them as a whole to understand that they evince the contemplation of all that has been dissolved:

O meu pai arquiteto e fazendeiro!
Faz casas de silêncio, e suas roças
de cinza estão maduras, orvalhadas
por um rio que corre o tempo inteiro,
e corre além do tempo, enquanto as nossas
murcham num sôpro fontes represadas.
("Encontro")

Oh my father architect and farmer!
He builds houses of silence, and his crops
of ashes are ripe, bedewed
by a river that runs all the time,
and runs beyond the time, while ours
wilt in a breath, dammed up fountains.
("Encounter," Nist trans.)

Thus, if the evocation of love is a means of keeping contact with the sensible world, it is still through a form of love that the family is revisited by this glance indifferent to history:

. . . palavras
que ditas naquele tempo
teriam mudado a vida
(não convém mudar agora),
vem tudo à mesa e se espalha
qual inédita vitualha.
("A Mesa")

. . . words
that if they had been said at that time
they would have changed our lives
(it is not fit to change now),
all is put on the table and spread over it
like an unheard-of victual.
("The Table," Nist trans.)

In this way, the last lines of the poem that closes *Claro Enigma* could be taken as an epigraph for this phase:

. . . O columbário
já cinza se concentra, pó de tumbas,
já se permite azul, risco de pombas.
("Relógio do Rosário")

. . . The columbarium
now gray, concentrates itself, dust of tombs,
then it allows itself to be blue, a flit of doves.
(Rosário Clock)

Love hangs over so that the poem "Nudez" ("Nakedness") thematizes death and its neighborhood:

Que sentimento vive, e já prospera
cavando em nós a terra necessária
para se sepultar à moda austera
de quem vive sua morte?

What feeling lives, and even thrives
by digging in us enough ground
to bury itself in the austere fashion
of one who lives one's own death?
(Nist trans.)

A poet whose sensibility is motivated by tension, Drummond does not now become the kind of man who would sing of death as if it were a last refuge. Nothing would be more alien to him. Death is searched for not as an appeasement but as something inscribed in all living things. Combining what had been said about the previous phase with what is said about this one, it may be concluded that for Drummond, existence supposes two faces. With the first one, the outstanding conflicts are those from which all remnants, all rags of projects, fragments of bodies and of constructions eroded by the passage of time are derived. With the second one, or rather, its reverse, what is taken into account is the never visualized instant of the end of this process, the beyond of matter. With both faces, poetry finds its raw material in things. With the first one they are seen in their duration, that is, in their impairment and metamorphosis; with the second, they are seen in the immobility of an afterward beyond all human vision. If it is reasonable to speak of impairment of the beyond-matter, it is only so in the sense that the poet, in order to name things, has at his disposal nothing but word itself.

Poetry about the past is as much evocative as it is revealing of what it comes to be in word. And what a farm, one among others, had been and what personages only locally famous had been exist again as unique scenes and beings ("Fazenda" [Farm], "O Muladeiro" [The Muleteer], "O Sátiro" [The Satyr], "A Santa" [The Saintly Woman]). For that reason the poetic of disillusionment is also capable of humor, laughter, and even joy—a joy that certainly cannot be complete. The word, existing beyond life's circuit, incorporates and also prolongs the pain of the existent. And love itself, the importance of which has been stressed as something that justifies the act of writing, is no backwater. Lovers are the nourishment of love, which makes use of them and then destroys them:

> Os amantes se amam cruelmente
> e com se amarem tanto não se vêem.
> Um se beija no outro, refletido.
> Dois amantes que são? Dois inimigos.
> ("Destruição")

Lovers love one another cruelly
and by loving so much they don't see one another.
One kisses oneself reflected in the other.
Two lovers, what are they? Two enemies.
(Destruction)

If divinity departed from the unbeliever's mind, it was not in order that he should pantheistically sing the union with nature. As a passage from "A Mão" (The Hand) in Lição de Coisas says, what exists is not designed "aplacar a sede dos companheiros" (to slake the buddies' thirst), but "principalmente para aguçá-la" (mainly to whet it). In the last analysis, the giving up of the corrosion principle has meant Drummond's absorption in the sheer stoicism of knowing that the

life cycle includes man, as it includes everything else, without privilege or solace:

> Algumas folhas de amendoeira expiram em
>   degradado vermelho.
> Outras estão apenas nascendo,
> verde polido onde a luz estala.
> O tronco é o mesmo
> e todas as folhas são a mesma antiga
> folha
> a brotar de seu fim
> enquanto vorazmente
> a vida, sem contraste, me destrói.
> ("Janela")

Some leaves of the almond trees expire in defiled red.
Others are just budding,
a polished green where the light cracks.
The trunk is the same
and all leaves are the same old
leaf
shooting out of its own end
while gnawingly
life, without contrasting, destroys me.
("Window," Nist trans.)

To make the creative act into a pure manifestation of joy would be a naïveté or a nonsense. To be sure, joy and pleasure will never be forced out of the world; nevertheless, they are nothing but the other side of pain and disharmony. Neither of the two faces has any transcendence. The tension between them is what matters. In this way, the disillusion that presides over Drummond's subsequent phase does not avert the tense and problematic character that is the starting point of his whole work and its expression. The renunciation of any comforting and justifying center, whether political or religious or aesthetic, does not diminish, therefore, the problematicizing root from whence the poet had started. This is undoubtedly the founding principle of Carlos Drummond de Andrade.

Immediately after the publication of Lição de Coisas, Drummond came out with Boitempo (Oxtime, 1968), Menino Antigo (Onetime Boy, 1973), and Esquecer para Lembrar (Forgetting in Order to Remember, 1979), in which he presents in the form of poems the autobiography of his boyhood. This framework is misleading, yet explainable. It is explainable in that the author, admittedly a diffident person who abhors publicity, by giving a poematic treatment of his childhood memories, began to count on an instrument capable of guarding him against saying what he did not want to say. We would like to assert that the series starting with *Boitempo* adopted the versified form as a strategy of self-restraint. If we accept that, we will be able to verify what the memoirs add to the comprehension of the author's poetics. The scenes that stand out do not aim at composing an autobiography in the usual sense of the word. Thus, there is in them not even a chronological sequence or a coincidence of the pieces, that is to say, the "poems," with new situations temporally pinpointed. There are special memories that do not speak of the onetime boy except insofar as the experiences are those that will mark the adult.

A view of the family house appears immediately and profusely. The building up of the fatherly manor is recalled in "Casa" (Home). Its topographic placement is given—near the centers of power, the town hall and the mother church. Its internal partition is described and includes not a few rooms to shelter relatives, friends, and protégés, with doors "sempre abertas do olho e pisar do chefe" (always open to the master's glance and tread); an alcove; "um pátio quase espanhol" (an almost Spanish patio); and a kitchen as large as those of the plantation houses of colonial times. The henhouse and backyard are also mentioned, and the memorialist does not forget the stable, since riding horseback is a dignity that no rural chieftain could dispense with. The whole description would have only a documentary weight if the mysterious chemistry of the "onetime boy" were not being elaborated in the space and in the interstices of the house. And because it is reviewed by what results from that chemistry, the construction of the house is soon accompanied by a vision of its decadence, or rather the decadence of the power that had engendered it.

In "Recinto Defeso" (Forbidden Precinct) what is in question is not yet the decadence but the prohibition (for the boy?) to pass to the noble part of the mansion, the drawing room, which is reserved for adults of high rank. The "porta hermetica" (hermetic door) barring the entrance will work for the future poet as an index of the enigma of beings and things,

an index of what will appear to him to be characteristic of man, as though the door hindered the access to secrets that, if communicated, would give meaning to the "máquina do mundo" (machine of the world). A little further on, without an explanation that the reader would like to have, the liquidation of the house is announced:

> A casa foi vendida com todas as lembranças
> todos os móveis todos os pesadelos
> todos os pecados cometidos ou em via de cometer.
> ("Liquidaçao")

> The house was sold out with all memories
> all furniture all nightmares
> all sins committed or about to be committed.
> (Sellout)

What was he trying so hard to find there? Certainly not the explanatory key to his own self. More accurately he aimed at seeing again the space and context where he had been transfused into what he became. Among the objects that furnished this space-context is the clock that will always accompany him—"este relógio vai comigo" (this clock goes with me). It is not the clock from his own home but the one that used to strike on the top of the mother church: "A hora do relógio da matriz é grave / como a consciência" (The hour on the church clock sounds grave / like the conscience).

The reason for this gravity is clarified in "Cemitério do Cruzeiro" (Cemetery of the Cross):

> Ouvimos o galo do cruzeiro
> nitidamente
> cantar a ressurreição.
> Não atendemos à chamada.

> We hear the cock on the cross
> distinctly
> hail the resurrection.
> We don't answer the call.

It does not matter whether the weathercock on the cross is quite different from the clock on the mother church. In the reconstitution of the past both represent the unanswered call. Given the importance of religious values in the rural Brazil of the beginning of the twentieth century, we can understand that the disobedience to the call meant more than a mere withdrawal from the congregation of believers. It was, indeed, the icon of all of Drummond's coming rebellions and the source of his future remorse. The rebellion was above all against paternal authority. "Gesto e Palavra" (Gesture and Word) seems to reconstruct one of the capital scenes:

> Tomar banho, pentear-se
> calçar botina apertada
> ir à missa, que preguiça.

> To take a bath, comb the hair
> put on tight high shoes
> go to the Mass, what a laziness.

To all obligations the boy prefers to spend the morning in the midst of the countless attractions of the day. He enumerates, among others, the tasty touch of "secretas sereias" (secret sirens). Before the defiance to the ritual, the father threatens to beat him, and the boy's "mão se ergue em defesa" (hand rises in defense). The clamor goes on resounding along the years:

> —Parricida! Parricida!
> alguém exclama entre os dois.
> Abaixa-se a mão erguida
> e fica o nome no ar.

> —Parricide! Parricide!
> Someone cries between them.
> The raised hand lowers
> and the name remains in the air.

The ominous word protracts and connects the disobedience to the clock stroke. The word contains more than the dictionaries tell us of its meaning. The revolt against the father merges with the erotic attraction, secretly hinted at, and both point out the place of somebody who refuses the religious space of obedience to divine and human paternity. This place is less that of plain rebelliousness than that of remorse. An outsider ("Go, Carlos, and be *gauche* in life," said the opening poem of his first book) comes into being.

The feeling of remorse will not prevent him from going ahead in his detour. The very option for poetry will be later lived as guilt, a guilt that is added to the one caused by the disobedience to the call of the clock of the mother church. In the psychical chemistry that goes into work, this disobedience is converted into an impulse to rebel against different masters and into a no less intense sensation of remorse and guilt. Remorse will be present whenever the father is remembered, and it will be extended in the antagonistic comparison the poet makes of his life as a man of letters to the kind of life he had cut short, that is, that of the landowners. The comparison will be made explicit, for example, in the following passage:

> Bois longínquos, éguas enevoadas
> no cinza além da serra, estrume de fazenda,
> a colheita de milho, o enramado feijão
> e . . .
> Fim.
> A raça que já não caça.
> ela em ti é caçada.
>
>   ("A Consciência Suja")

> Far off oxen, hazy mares
> in the gray beyond the sierra, farm dung,
> the maize crop, the entangled bean
> and . . .
> the end.
> The race that hunts no more
> is hunted in you.
>
>   (The Dirty Conscience)

Guilt will take on yet another road in the memories associated with sex. These crystallize into an obsession with sin, with dirt (of which there is no way of cleaning his hand), and with suffering. The beginning and the end of "Amor, Sinal Estranho" (Love, a Strange Sign) in *Esquecer para Lembrar* attest to it:

> Amo demais, sem saber que estou amando,
> as moças a caminho da reza
> . . . .
> Estou me preparando para sofrer
> assim como os rapazes estudam para médico ou advogado.

> I love too much, without knowing I'm loving,
> the girls who are on their way to church.
> . . . .
> I'm preparing to suffer
> as the lads study to be a doctor or lawyer.

From a strictly poetic standpoint, of Drummond's most recent books only *As Impurezas do Branco* (Impurities of White, 1973) has the qualities that match his previous works. In this volume there are three poems that are worthy of the most selected anthology of Drummond's production, "Amor e Seu Tempo" (Love and Its Time), "Beethoven," and the best of his metapoems, "Paisagem: Como se Faz" (Landscape: How to Do It). Through these poems the poet reiterates that his conception of poetry is not so much identified with the recovery of time as with the effort to reconstruct it in a distinct space. Occupied with what is left of that which has passed or is passing, or still with the echo of remnants, without prejudice to their character of document or evidence, poetry is not only a record of what there has been or there is. It is not even only a record of who has written it. It is indeed the form that lodges the problematics of what lives.

Translated from the Portuguese by José Laurênio de Mello

SELECTED BIBLIOGRAPHY

First Editions

Poetry

Alguma Poesia. Belo Horizonte, Brazil, 1930.
Brejo das Almas. Belo Horizonte, Brazil, 1934.
Sentimento do Mundo. Rio de Janeiro, 1940.
A Rosa do Povo. Rio de Janeiro, 1945.
Claro Enigma. Rio de Janeiro, 1951.
Viola de Bolso. Rio de Janeiro, 1952.
Lição de Coisas. Rio de Janeiro, 1962.
Boitempo. Rio de Janeiro, 1968.
As Impurezas do Branco. Rio de Janeiro, 1973.
Menino Antigo. Rio de Janeiro, 1973.
Discurso de Primavera. Rio de Janeiro, 1977.
Esquecer para Lembrar. Rio de Janeiro, 1979.
A Paixão Medida. Rio de Janeiro, 1980.
Corpo. Rio de Janeiro, 1984.
Amar se Aprende Amando. Rio de Janeiro, 1985.

Prose Narratives

Confissões de Minas. Rio de Janeiro, 1944.
Contos de Aprendiz. Rio de Janeiro, 1951.

Passeios na Ilha. Rio de Janeiro, 1952.
Fala, Amendoeira. Rio de Janeiro, 1957.
Contos Plausíveis. Rio de Janeiro, 1981.
Boca de Luar. Rio de Janeiro, 1984.
O Observador no Escritório. Rio de Janeiro, 1985.

Translations by Carlos Drummond de Andrade

Uma Gota de Veneno [*Thérèse Desqueyroux*, by François Mauriac]. Rio de Janeiro, 1943.
As Relações Perigosas [*Les liaisons dangereuses*, by Choderlos de Laclos]. Porte Alegre, Brazil, 1947.
A Fugitiva [*Albertine disparue*, by Marcel Proust]. Porto Alegre, Brazil, 1956.
Artimanhas de Scapino [*Les fourberies de Scapin*, by Molière]. Rio de Janeiro, 1962.

Collected Works

Antologia Poética. Rio de Janeiro, 1962.
Fazendeiro do Ar e Poesia Até Agora. Rio de Janeiro, 1954.
Nova Reunião. 2 vols. Rio de Janeiro, 1983.
Obra Completa. Rio de Janeiro, 1967.
Poesias. Rio de Janeiro, 1942.
Poesia Até Agora. Rio de Janeiro, 1948. (Includes *Novos Poemas.*)
Reunião. Rio de Janeiro, 1969.

Translations

In the Middle of the Road: Selected Poems. Translated by John Nist. Tucson, Ariz., 1965.
The Minus Sign. Translated by Virginia de Araújo. Redding Ridge, Conn., 1980.
Souvenir of the Ancient World. Translated by Mark Strand. New York, 1976.
Travelling in the Family. Translated by Thomas Colchie, Mark Strand, Elizabeth Bishop, and Gregory Rabassa. New York, 1987.

Biographical and Critical Studies

Brasil, Assis. *Carlos Drummond de Andrade.* Rio de Janeiro, 1971.
Candido, Antonio. "Inquietudes na Poesia de Drummond." In *Vários Escritos.* São Paulo, 1970. Pp. 93–122.
Coelho, Joaquim Francisco. *Terra e Família na Poesia de Carlos Drummond de Andrade.* Belém, Brazil, 1973.

Costa Lima, Luiz. *Lira e Antilira.* Rio de Janeiro, 1968.

Houaiss, Antônio. "Introdução." In *Reunião.* Rio de Janeiro, 1969. Pp. 15–39.

Martins, Hélcio. *A Rima na Poesia de Carlos Drummond de Andrade.* Rio de Janeiro, 1968.

Mendonça Teles, Gilberto. *Drummond: A Estilística da Repetição.* Rio de Janeiro, 1970.

Merquior, José Guilherme. *Verso Universo em Drummond.* Rio de Janeiro, 1975.

Nist, John. "Conscience of Brazil: Carlos Drummond de Andrade." *Américas* 15/1:32–35 (1963).

Romano de Sant'Ans. Affonso. *Drummond o 'Gauche' no Tempo.* Rio de Janeiro, 1972.

Sternberg, Ricardo da Silveira Lobo. "The Precarious Self: Carlos Drummond de Andrade's *Brejo das Almas.* *Hispania* 65/1:45–50 (1982).

_____. *The Unquiet Self: Self and Society in the Poetry of Carlos Drummond de Andrade.* Valencia, Spain, 1986.